ninth edition

Fundamental Managerial Accounting Concepts

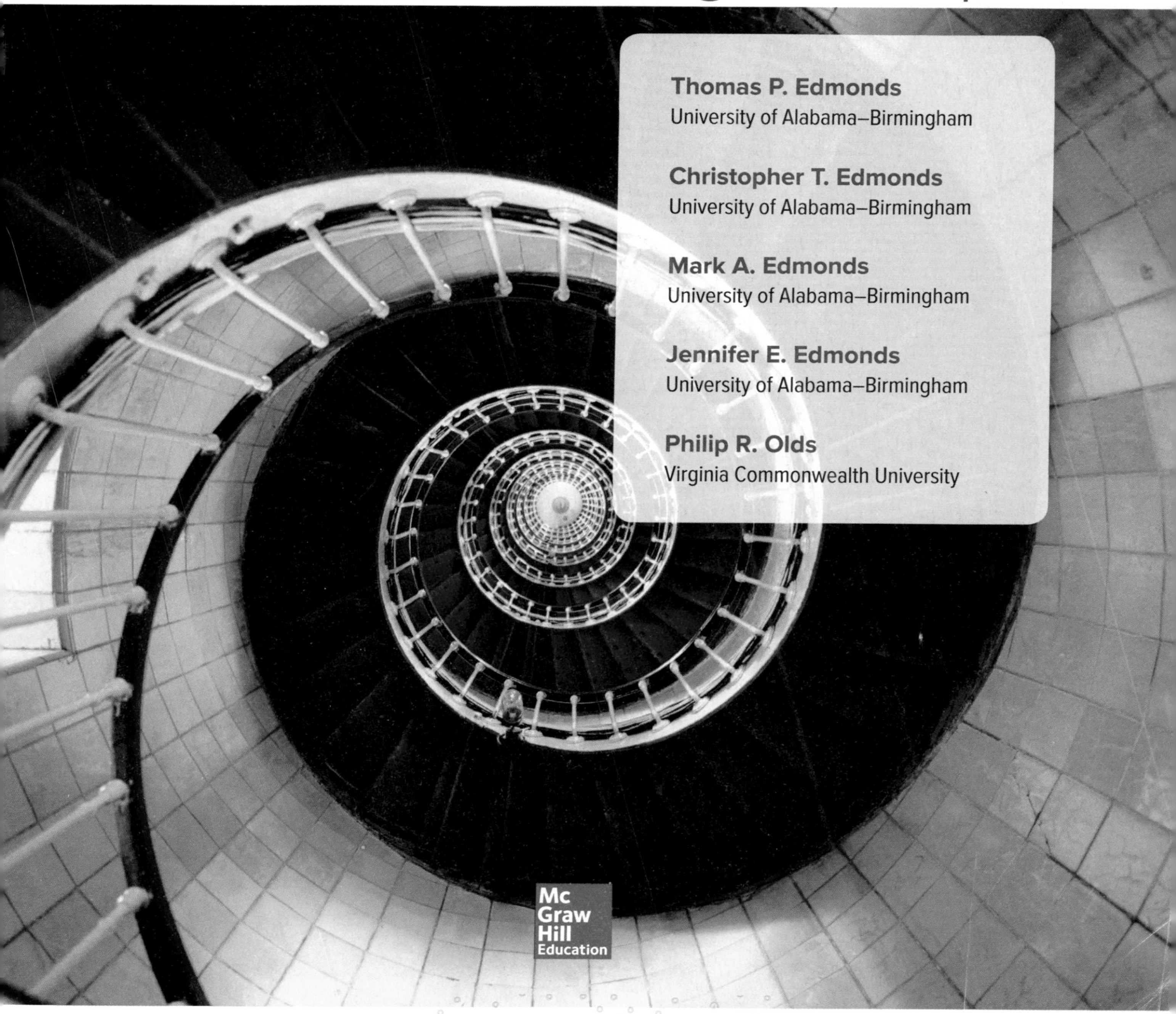

Thomas P. Edmonds
University of Alabama–Birmingham

Christopher T. Edmonds
University of Alabama–Birmingham

Mark A. Edmonds
University of Alabama–Birmingham

Jennifer E. Edmonds
University of Alabama–Birmingham

Philip R. Olds
Virginia Commonwealth University

Mc Graw Hill Education

FUNDAMENTAL MANAGERIAL ACCOUNTING CONCEPTS

Published by McGraw-Hill Education, 2 Penn Plaza, New York, NY 10121.

This book is printed on acid-free paper.

1 2 3 4 5 6 7 8 9 LWI 21 20 19

ISBN 978-1-260-56548-5
MHID 1-260-56548-3

Cover Image: © *Westend61/Getty Images*

mheducation.com/highered

This book is dedicated to our students, whose questions have so frequently caused us to reevaluate our method of presentation that they have, in fact, become major contributors to the development of this text.

NOTE FROM THE AUTHORS

UNIQUE USER PERSPECTIVE

This text focuses on the development of decision-making skills. The decision-making emphasis is evident from a review of the table of contents. You will notice that topics related to decision making are placed first while procedural topics like manufacturing cost flow, job order, and process costing are placed at the end of our text. In addition, we have made an effort to reduce coverage of recording procedures. Indeed, you will notice that the text does not require the use of debits and credits. Accordingly, the text is a natural fit for schools that have decided to take a user-oriented approach for their introductory financial accounting course.

The text places an unusually heavy emphasis on service companies. For example, the budgeting chapter uses a merchandising business while most traditional texts use a manufacturing company. Using a service company is not only more relevant but also simplifies the learning environment, thereby making it easier for students to focus on budgeting concepts rather than procedural details. For a more detailed description of the unique features of this text, see the "How Does Edmonds Help Students See the Big Picture?" section on page x.

INNOVATIVE INSTRUCTIONAL METHODOLOGY

This text is accompanied by the most comprehensive set of ***instructional videos*** on the market today. These instructional videos explain the content associated with every learning objective introduced throughout the text. ***The videos have been developed by a member of the author team.*** They have the touch and feel of a live lecture as opposed to a canned PowerPoint presentation. The benefits are enormous. Videos allow students to pause for contemplation and note-taking. They permit students to repeat difficult concepts or fast forward through content they have mastered. In other words, videos enable self-paced learning. No longer is the lecture too fast for some and too slow for others. Now the lecture satisfies the needs of each individual student.

Many accounting educators have taught in professional exam prep courses that make extensive use of video lectures. Now you can bring that prep course learning approach into your everyday classroom. Here are some examples of how you can use instructional videos to improve the classroom environment.

Traditional Courses

You do not have to change the way you teach your class to reap many of the benefits available from video instruction. Students who have to miss class or who have trouble comprehending certain concepts can benefit from watching video lectures. Also, many students who attend class will be able to build confidence by watching videos that reinforce the concepts presented in class. Since the videos are tied directly to the learning objectives, you can develop a specific plan for students who are struggling with specific topics. Alternatively, you may offer video instruction to enable advanced students to cover additional topics.

Distance Learning Courses

One of the fastest growing markets in higher education today is Internet-based courses. Many students struggle with these courses. Generally, they would prefer to learn from a lecture but due to timing or location are unable to attend class.

Prerecorded video lectures solve this problem by allowing students to access lectures on demand. Until now the only way to provide video coverage was for the instructor to make personal recordings. Anyone who has tried this knows it is a time-consuming activity. We offer a standardized turn-key course that is composed of prerecorded instructional videos, student directed self-assessment quizzes, and instructor-generated evaluative exams. The instructor simply selects the learning objectives to be covered. There is no simpler way to develop a distance learning course.

Flip Courses

Instructional videos enable instructors to flip the traditional teaching model. Specifically, instead of providing a lecture in class and then assigning homework, ***flip courses*** deliver the lecture at home and use the classroom as a place for students to work problems and ask questions. The teacher's function moves from lecturer to coach and tutor. Without a requirement to deliver a lecture, the instructor is free to tutor students in small groups or individually. Instruction becomes more focused and individualized. Indeed, when coupled with Connect technology, instructors can obtain real-time feedback that allows them to identify and approach specific students who are having difficulty without disturbing those students who are able to digest the material independently.

Hybrid Courses

Many instructors are developing hybrid classes where some classes involve face-to-face time with the instructor and other class time is devoted to group work, individualized instruction, case study, or other activities. This means there is less time for traditional lectures. Instructional videos are ideal for filling the lecture gap. Instructors can cover the key concepts in their lectures and leave the detailed presentation to the video lectures.

Mass Section Courses

Many schools deliver live lectures to mass section classes. Students then break into small groups that are led by teaching assistants or adjunct faculty. While this approach is cost-effective, it frequently results in dissatisfaction. Students often find it difficult to see and hear in large lecture halls. Also, the lecture must be set at an average pace that, by its nature, is too fast for many students and too slow for others. Prerecorded video lectures resolve these issues. They enable students to study the lecture before class. They can then bring questions about the lecture to the breakout sessions. Since videos eliminate the need for mass lectures, there is more time for students to meet in small groups where they are able to receive more individualized attention.

Competency-Based Learning Courses

Video instruction enables the implementation of a competency-based grading system. Since learning is self-paced, grades can be assigned on the basis of how far students go into the content as opposed to an averaging approach. For example, content could be divided into modules. Grades could be assigned based on the number of modules completed successfully. Weaker students could repeat lower-level modules while stronger students move on to more advanced topics. When you are no longer forced to move students through your class in a lock-step fashion, the potential for improving the learning environment is virtually limitless.

There are many different competency-based models that can be applied to introductory accounting. At this point, our objective is to introduce the general possibilities for improving learning. If you are interested in developing a specific competency-based approach for your classroom, you can speak directly with a member of the author team who has used videos in a variety of settings (contact information is provided below). Standardized lesson plans that can be adapted for use in your individual classroom are available upon request. These are only a few opportunities made possible by video lectures. If you would like to discuss these or other possible applications please contact Chris Edmonds at **cedmonds@gmail.com.**

INSTRUCTORS' RESOURCE KIT (IRK)

As many students choose to adopt the electronic version of textbooks, instructors are beginning to face a situation where students do not have textbooks available in the classroom. Accordingly, working a particular exercise or problem in class is frustrated by the fact that students do not have access to the exercise and problems being worked. To resolve this issue we now offer an ***Instructors' Resource Kit (IRK)***.

The IRK includes a general set of instructions for how to conduct flipped, online, and hybrid classes. It has a chapter-by-chapter Microsoft Word document that contains an ***instructor version*** of all B set exercises and problems. The corresponding solution is shown directly below each exercise and problem. The matching of exercises and problems with solutions makes it easy for instructors to toggle between the items and the solution when making classroom presentations. An example of Exercise 2-7B instructor version appears as follows.

Exercise 2-7B Fixed versus variable cost behavior (LO 2-1)

Shawn Corder needs extra money quickly to help cover some unexpected school expenses. Mr. Corder has learned fortune-telling skills through his long friendship with Fred Molloy, who tells fortunes during the day at the city market. Mr. Molloy has agreed to let Mr. Corder use his booth to tell fortunes during the evening for a rent of $90 per night.

Required

a. What is the total and per customer booth rental cost if the number of customers is 5, 10, 15, 20, or 25? Round your figures to 2 decimal points.

Number of Customers (a)	5	10	15	20	25
Total rental cost (b)	**$90**	**$90**	**$90**	**$90**	**$90**
Cost per customer (b) ÷ (a)	**$18.00**	**$9.00**	**$6.00**	**$4.50**	**$3.60**

b. Is the cost of renting the fortune-telling booth fixed or variable relative to the number of customers?

Since the cost of renting the booth is $90 regardless of the number of customers, it is a fixed cost.

The IRK also includes a separate chapter-by-chapter Word document that contains a ***student version*** of the B set of exercises and problems. These documents show each exercise and problem with a corresponding working paper directly below it. For example, Exercise 2-7B student version appears as follows.

Exercise 2-7B Fixed versus variable cost behavior (LO 2-1)

Shawn Corder needs extra money quickly to help cover some unexpected school expenses. Mr. Corder has learned fortune-telling skills through his long friendship with Fred Molloy, who tells fortunes during the day at the city market. Mr. Molloy has agreed to let Mr. Corder use his booth to tell fortunes during the evening for a rent of $90 per night.

Required

a. What is the total and per customer booth rental cost if the number of customers is 5, 10, 15, 20, or 25? Round your figures to 2 decimal points.

Number of Customers	5	10	15	20	25
Total rental cost					
Cost per customer					

b. Is the cost of renting the fortune-telling booth fixed or variable relative to the number of customers?

Since the IRK is composed in Microsoft Word, instructors can easily "cut and paste" the materials to customize content for their particular classes. Materials can be delivered to students through electronic files or printouts. Also, the Word format enables the development of customized electronic overhead slides with pop-up solutions, thereby eliminating the need for chalkboard presentations. Not only will you avoid the annoying chalk dust, but your students will appreciate a presentation that perfectly matches their working paper forms. The IRK contains a video that shows you how to implement this very attractive feature.

ABOUT THE AUTHORS

Courtesy of Thomas Edmonds.

Thomas P. Edmonds

Thomas P. Edmonds, Ph.D., is Professor Emeritus in the Department of Accounting at the University of Alabama at Birmingham (UAB). He has been actively involved in teaching accounting principles throughout his academic career. Dr. Edmonds has coordinated the accounting principles courses at the University of Houston and UAB. He has taught introductory accounting in mass sections and in distance learning programs. He has received five prestigious teaching awards, including the Alabama Society of CPAs' Outstanding Educator Award, the UAB President's Excellence in Teaching Award, and the distinguished Ellen Gregg Ingalls Award for excellence in classroom teaching. He has written numerous articles that have appeared in many publications, including *Issues in Accounting,* the *Journal of Accounting Education, Advances in Accounting Education, Accounting Education: A Journal of Theory, Practice and Research,* the *Accounting Review, Advances in Accounting,* the *Journal of Accountancy, Management Accounting,* the *Journal of Commercial Bank Lending,* the *Banker's Magazine,* and the *Journal of Accounting, Auditing, and Finance.* Dr. Edmonds has served as a member of the editorial board for *Advances in Accounting: Teaching and Curriculum Innovations* and *Issues in Accounting Education.* He has published five textbooks, five practice problems (including two computerized problems), and a variety of supplemental materials, including study guides, work papers, and solutions manuals. Dr. Edmonds's writing is influenced by a wide range of business experience. He is a successful entrepreneur. He has worked as a management accountant for Refrigerated Transport, a trucking company. Dr. Edmonds also worked in the not-for-profit sector as a commercial lending officer for the Federal Home Loan Bank. In addition, he has acted as a consultant to major corporations, including First City Bank of Houston (now Citi Bank), AmSouth Bank in Birmingham (now Regions Bank), Texaco, and Cortland Chemicals. Dr. Edmonds began his academic training at Young Harris Community College in Young Harris, Georgia. He received a B.B.A. degree with a major in finance from Georgia State University in Atlanta, Georgia. He obtained an M.B.A. degree with a concentration in finance from St. Mary's University in San Antonio, Texas. His Ph.D. degree with a major in accounting was awarded by Georgia State University. Dr. Edmonds's work experience and academic training have enabled him to bring a unique user perspective to this textbook.

Christopher T. Edmonds

Christopher T. Edmonds, PhD, is an Associate Professor in the Department of Accounting and Finance at the UAB Collat School of Business. He is the course coordinator for the face-to-face and online principles of accounting courses. Dr. Edmonds specializes in teaching and developing engaging face-to-face and online introductory accounting courses. He is a frequent speaker at conferences and universities on best teaching practices and has delivered over 20 professional teaching workshops. His passion for helping students learn inspired him to create hundreds of short videos teaching the fundamental concepts of accounting. This work led to the publication of the first interactive video textbook for introductory accounting. Dr. Edmonds has received seven prestigious teaching awards, including the UAB President's Outstanding Teaching Award, UAB Faculty Student Success Award, UAB Transformative Online Course Award, UAB Loudell Ellis Robinson Classroom Teaching Award, UAB Disability Support Recognition Award, and the Virginia Tech Favorite Faculty Award. He has published four textbooks and has written numerous articles that have appeared in publications, including *The Accounting Review, Journal of Accounting and Public Policy, Issues in Accounting Education, Advances in Accounting Education, Advances in Accounting,* and *Review of Quantitative Finance and Accounting.* He currently serves on several editorial boards. Dr. Edmonds started his career as a web application developer creating software solutions to put newspapers online. He began his academic training at Colorado State University. He obtained an M.B.A. from UAB. His Ph.D. with a major in accounting was awarded by Virginia Polytechnic Institute and State University. Check out his blog at **www.accountingstepbystep.com.**

Mark A. Edmonds

Mark A. Edmonds, Ph.D., CPA, is an Assistant Professor in the Department of Accounting and Finance at the University of Alabama at Birmingham. He has taught principles and advanced accounting classes in face-to-face, flipped, and online formats. Dr. Edmonds began his career providing assurance services for the internationally recognized accounting firm Ernst & Young. At the conclusion of his professional service, he obtained his Ph.D. from Southern Illinois University–Carbondale. He serves as the education adviser on the board of the Institute of Internal Auditors, Birmingham Chapter. Dr. Edmonds's research focuses on alternative learning strategies and auditor decision making.

Courtesy of Mark Edmonds.

Jennifer E. Edmonds

Jennifer Echols Edmonds, Ph.D., is an Associate Professor at the University of Alabama at Birmingham (UAB) Collat School of Business. Her primary teaching areas are financial and managerial accounting. She has experience teaching in the undergraduate, MAC, and MBA programs and currently serves as the course coordinator for the managerial accounting sequence at UAB. She has received the UAB Loudell Ellis Robinson Classroom Teaching Award, as well as teaching grants from Deloitte, UAB, and Virginia Tech. She created teaching resources for incorporating International Financial Reporting Standards into intermediate accounting. The teaching resources were published online at the American Accounting Association. Dr. Edmonds is also active in the research community. She has published articles in prominent journals such as *Journal of Accounting and Public Policy, Advances in Accounting, Research in Accounting Regulation,* and *The CPA Journal*. Dr. Edmonds received a bachelor's degree in accounting from Birmingham-Southern College and completed her master's and Ph.D. degrees in accounting at Virginia Polytechnic Institute and State University.

Courtesy of Jennifer Edmonds.

Philip R. Olds

Professor Olds is Associate Professor of Accounting at Virginia Commonwealth University (VCU). He serves as the coordinator of the introduction to accounting courses at VCU. Professor Olds received his A.S. degree from Brunswick Junior College in Brunswick, Georgia (now Costal Georgia College). He received a B.B.A. in accounting from Georgia Southern College (now Georgia Southern University) and his M.P.A. and Ph.D. degrees are from Georgia State University. After graduating from Georgia Southern, he worked as an auditor with the U.S. Department of Labor in Atlanta, Georgia. A former CPA in Virginia, Professor Olds has published articles in various professional journals and presented papers at national and regional conferences. He also served as the faculty adviser to the VCU chapter of Beta Alpha Psi for five years. In 1989, he was recognized with an Outstanding Faculty Vice-President Award by the national Beta Alpha Psi organization. Professor Olds has received both the Distinguished Teaching Award and the Distinguished Service Award from the VCU School of Business. Most recently, he received the university's award for maintaining High Ethical and Academic Standards While Advocating for Student-Athletes and Their Quest Towards a Degree.

Courtesy of Philip Olds.

HOW DOES EDMONDS HELP

"This text is the 'gold standard' for managerial accounting courses both in undergraduate business programs and MBA programs. I appreciate that it's scalable in that I can teach a variety of groups of students from the same text by altering the exercises, problems, cases, Connect exercises, and supplemental materials I provide the students."

ROBERT CORNELL, UNIVERSITY OF NEVADA, LAS VEGAS

"I believe this text is a bit easier and more interesting to read than many other Managerial texts. Plus, it has a heavy focus on real business decision making."

SCOTT PAXTON, VALENCIA COLLEGE

PRINCIPAL FEATURES

Our goal in writing this text is to teach students managerial accounting concepts that will improve their ability to make sound business decisions. The text differs from traditional managerial accounting books in the following ways.

Decision-Making Skills Emphasized

Notice that the table of contents places decision making first. Procedural topics like manufacturing cost flow, job order, and process costing are placed at the end of our text, while traditional books discuss these topics early. We put decision making front and center because we believe it is important. Beyond placement, we introduce topics within a decision-making context. For example, in Chapter 2 we introduce "cost behavior" within the context of operating leverage. We focus on how cost behavior affects decisions such as "Am I sure enough that volume will be high that I want to employ a fixed cost structure, or do I want to reduce operating leverage risk by building a variable cost structure?" Further, notice that Chapter 3 is written around a realistic business scenario where a management team is using CVP data to evaluate decision alternatives. Indeed, all chapters are written in a narrative style with content focused on decision-making scenarios. This makes the text easy to read and interesting as well as informative.

Service Companies Emphasized

For example, our budgeting chapter uses a merchandising business while most traditional texts use a manufacturing company. Using a service company is not only more relevant but also simplifies the learning environment, thereby making it easier for students to focus on budgeting concepts rather than procedural details. This is only one example of our efforts to place greater emphasis on service companies.

Isolating Concepts

How do you promote student understanding of concepts? We believe new concepts should be isolated and introduced individually in decision-making contexts. For example, we do not include a chapter covering cost terminology (usually Chapter 2 in traditional approaches). We believe introducing a plethora of detached cost terms in a single chapter is ineffective, as students have no conceptual framework for the new vocabulary.

Interrelationships between Concepts

Although introducing concepts in isolation enhances student comprehension of them, students must ultimately understand how business concepts interrelate. The text is designed to build knowledge progressively, leading students to integrate the concepts they have learned independently. For example, see how the concept of relevance is compared on page 255 of Chapter 6 to the concept of cost behavior (which is explained in Chapter 2) and how the definitions of direct costs are contrasted on page 154 of Chapter 4 with the earlier introduced concepts of cost behavior. Also, Chapters 1 through 12 include a comprehensive problem designed to integrate concepts across chapters. The problem builds in each successive chapter with the same company experiencing new conditions that require the application of concepts across chapters.

Context-Sensitive Nature of Terminology

Students can be confused when they discover the exact same cost can be classified as fixed, variable, direct, indirect, relevant, or not relevant. For example, the cost of a store manager's salary is fixed regardless of the number of customers that shop in the store. The cost of store manager salaries, however, is variable relative to the number of stores a company operates. The salary costs are directly traceable to particular stores but not to particular sales made in a store. The salary cost is relevant when deciding whether to eliminate a given store but not relevant when deciding whether to eliminate a department within a store. Students must learn to identify the circumstances that determine the classification of costs. The chapter material,

"This book is excellent for the non-accounting major because it is user-oriented. This book actually interests non-accounting majors. I have seen many students actually get excited about what they are learning because they can relate the information to the real world."

JACQUELINE BURKE, HOFSTRA UNIVERSITY

"I think Edmonds' approach to introducing concepts, and his flow of topics, is the best of any accounting textbook I have used. His approach allows me to emphasize a piece of the puzzle at a time [while] building to the whole picture."

GARY REYNOLDS, OZARK TECHNICAL COMMUNITY COLLEGE

"One of the reasons I chose the Edmonds textbooks is because I have always enjoyed the 'horizontal statements model' used by Edmonds in his financial accounting textbooks. In my opinion, it gives the students a much better picture of how each business transaction affects the financial statements."

JEROLD K. BRAUN, DAYTONA STATE COLLEGE

exercises, and problems in this text are designed to encourage students to analyze the decision-making context rather than to memorize definitions. ATC 4-1 in Chapter 4 illustrates how the text teaches students to interpret different decision-making environments.

ANALYZE, THINK, COMMUNICATE

ATC 4-1 Business Applications Case ***Allocating fixed costs at HealthSouth Corporation***

HealthSouth Corporation claims to be "the nation's leading owner and operator of inpatient rehabilitation hospitals and a leader in home-based care (home health and hospice), offering services in 36 states and Puerto Rico." As of December 31, 2017, the company derived 96.7 percent of its hospital revenues from inpatient services. During 2017 it treated and discharged 171,922 patients, and the average length of a patient's stay was 12.7 days. If one patient occupying one bed for one day represents a "patient-day," then HealthSouth produced 2,183,409 patient-days of output during 2017 (171,922 × 12.7 = 2,183,409). During this period, HealthSouth incurred depreciation and amortization costs of $183,800,000. For the purpose of this problem, assume that all of this is depreciation that is related to the property, plant, and equipment of inpatient hospitals.

Required

a. Indicate whether the depreciation cost is a:

(1) Product (i.e., patient) cost or a general, selling, and administrative cost.

(2) Fixed or variable cost relative to the volume of production.

(3) Direct or indirect cost if the cost object is the cost of patient services provided in 2017.

b. Assume that HealthSouth incurred depreciation of $15,320,000 during each month of the 2017 fiscal year, but that it produced 196,000 patient-days of service during February and 166,000 patient-days of service during March. Based on monthly costs and service levels, what was the average amount of depreciation cost per patient-day of service provided during each of these two months, assuming each patient-day of service was charged the same amount of depreciation?

"Given the current economic environment, [Edmonds'] extensive coverage of corporate governance is critical to accounting."

PATRICK STEGMAN, COLLEGE OF LAKE COUNTY

Corporate Governance

Accountants have always recognized the importance of ethical conduct. However, the enactment of Sarbanes–Oxley (SOX) has signaled the need for educators to expand the subject of ethics to a broader concept of corporate governance. We focus our expanded coverage on four specific areas, including:

- Quality of Earnings—We explain how financial statements can be manipulated.
- The *Statement of Ethical Professional Practice* for Management Accountants—Our coverage focuses on the policies and practices promulgated by the Institute of Management Accountants.
- The Fraud Triangle—We discuss the three common features of criminal and ethical misconduct, including opportunity, pressure, and rationalization.
- Specified Features of Sarbanes–Oxley (SOX)—We cover four key provisions of SOX that are applicable to managerial accountants.

Corporate governance is introduced in Chapter 1. This chapter includes four exercises, two problems, and one case that relate to the subject. Thereafter, a corporate governance case is included in every chapter, thereby enabling continuing coverage of this critically important topic.

Excel Spreadsheets

Spreadsheet applications are essential to contemporary accounting practice. Students must recognize the power of spreadsheet software and know how accounting data are presented in spreadsheets. We discuss Microsoft Excel spreadsheet applications where appropriate throughout the text. In most instances, the text illustrates actual spreadsheets. End-of-chapter materials include problems students can complete using spreadsheet software. A sample of the logo used to identify problems suitable for Excel spreadsheet solutions is shown here.

"[The text is] easy to read and it is innovative for including Excel spreadsheets and the accounting template."

WEDE ELLIOTT-BROWNELL, SOUTHERN UNIVERSITY/A&M COLLEGE

Problem 1-24A ***Service versus manufacturing companies*** LO 1-4

Wang Company began operations on January 1, Year 1, by issuing common stock for $70,000 cash. During Year 1, Wang received $88,000 cash from revenue and incurred costs that required $65,000 of cash payments.

Required

Prepare a GAAP-based income statement and balance sheet for Wang Company for Year 1, under each of the following independent scenarios.

a. Wang is a promoter of rock concerts. The $65,000 was paid to provide a rock concert that produced the revenue.

b. Wang is in the car rental business. The $65,000 was paid to purchase automobiles. The automobiles were purchased on January 1, Year 1, and have five-year useful lives, with no expected salvage value. Wang uses straight-line depreciation. The revenue was generated by leasing the automobiles.

c. Wang is a manufacturing company. The $65,000 was paid to purchase the following items:

(1) Paid $10,000 cash to purchase materials that were used to make products during the year.

(2) Paid $20,000 cash for wages of factory workers who made products during the year.

(3) Paid $5,000 cash for salaries of sales and administrative employees.

(4) Paid $30,000 cash to purchase manufacturing equipment. The equipment was used solely to make products. It had a three-year life and a $6,000 salvage value. The company uses straight-line depreciation.

CHECK FIGURES

a. Net income: $23,000
b. Total assets: $145,000
c. Net income: $54,500

HOW DOES EDMONDS

The Curious Accountant

©mike davies/Alamy

In the first course of accounting, you learned how retailers, such as Target, account for the cost of equipment that lasts more than one year. Recall that the equipment was recorded as an asset when purchased, and then it was depreciated over its expected useful life. The depreciation charge reduced the company's assets and increased its expenses. This approach was justified under the matching principle, which seeks to recognize costs as expenses in the same period that the cost (resource) is used to generate revenue.

Is depreciation always shown as an expense on the income statement? The answer may surprise you. Consider the following scenario. Skyrocket, LLC., manufactures the Sky Viper Streaming FPV Video Drone that it sells to Target. Assume that in order to produce the video drone, Skyrocket had to purchase a robotic machine that it expects can be used to produce 1,000,000 drones.

Do you think Skyrocket should account for depreciation on its manufacturing equipment the same way Target accounts for depreciation on its registers at the checkout counters? If not, how should Skyrocket account for its depreciation? Remember the matching principle when thinking of your answer. (Answer on

Answers to The Curious Accountant

As you have seen, accounting for depreciation related to manufacturing assets is different from accounting for depreciation for nonmanufacturing assets. Depreciation on the checkout equipment at Target is recorded as depreciation expense. Depreciation on manufacturing equipment at Skyrocket is considered a product cost. It is included first as part of the cost of inventory and eventually as part of the expense, cost of goods sold. Recording depreciation on manufacturing equipment as an inventory cost is simply another example of the matching principle, because the cost does not become an expense until revenue from the product sale is recognized.

FOCUS ON INTERNATIONAL ISSUES

FINANCIAL ACCOUNTING VERSUS MANAGERIAL ACCOUNTING—AN INTERNATIONAL PERSPECTIVE

©Adam Roundtree/Bloomberg/Getty Images

This chapter has already explained some of the conceptual differences between financial and managerial accounting, but these differences have implications for international businesses as well. With respect to financial accounting, publicly traded companies in most countries must follow the generally accepted accounting principles (GAAP) for their country, but these rules can vary from country to country. Generally, companies that are audited under the auditing standards of the United States follow the standards established by the Financial Accounting Standards Board (FASB). Most companies located outside the United States follow the standards established by the International Accounting Standards Board (IASB). For example, the United States is one of very few countries whose GAAP allow the use of the LIFO inventory cost flow assumption.

Conversely, most of the managerial accounting concepts introduced in this course can be used by businesses in any country. For example, *activity-based costing (ABC)* is a topic addressed in Chapter 5 and is used by many companies in the United States. Additionally, while accrual-based earnings can differ depending on whether a company uses U.S. GAAP or IFRS, cash flow will not. As you will learn in this course, managerial accounting decisions often focus on cash flow versus accrual-based income. Therefore, managerial accounting concepts are more univer

☑ CHECK YOURSELF 1.5

A strike at a General Motors brake plant caused an almost immediate shutdown of many of the company's assembly plants. What could have caused such a rapid and widespread shutdown?

Answer A rapid and widespread shutdown could have occurred because General Motors uses a just-in-time inventory system. With a JIT inventory system, there is no stockpile of inventory to draw on when strikes or other forces disrupt inventory deliveries. This illustrates a potential negative effect of using a just-in-time inventory system.

Real-World Examples

This text provides a variety of thought-provoking, real-world examples of managerial accounting as an essential part of the management process.

The Curious Accountant

Each chapter opens with a short vignette that sets the stage and helps pique student interest. These vignettes pose a question about a real-world accounting issue related to the topic of the chapter. The answer to the question appears in a separate sidebar a few pages further into the chapter.

Focus on International Issues

These boxed inserts expose students to international issues in accounting.

Check Yourself

These short question/answer features occur at the end of each main topic and ask students to stop and think about the material just covered. The answer is then given to provide immediate feedback before students go on to a new topic.

"I especially like the Check Yourself and A Look Back/A Look Forward features because they help students to review and refresh topics as they progress through the chapter."

ANNA L. LUSHER, SLIPPERY ROCK UNIVERSITY

"The Curious Accountant, the real-world examples, and the Check Yourself boxes are unique features."

RONALD REED, UNIVERSITY OF NORTHERN COLORADO

MOTIVATE STUDENTS?

Reality Bytes

Real-world applications related to specific chapter topics are introduced through this feature. *Reality Bytes* may offer survey results, graphics, quotations from business leaders, and other supplemental topics that enhance opportunities for students to connect the text material to actual accounting practice.

REALITY BYTES

Unethical behavior occurs in most large organizations, but some organizations seem to have fewer ethics problems than others. In its 2015 report, ***The State of Ethics in Large Companies,*** the Ethics Resource Center reported its findings of the occurrences and reporting of unethical behavior in large American corporations, based on a survey it conducts every two years.

Forty-five percent of those surveyed reported having observed unethical conduct during the past year. This was the lowest level reported in the 17 years the survey has been conducted. Sixty-five percent of those who said they had observed misconduct went on to report it to their employer. However, fear of retaliation for reporting misconduct was a concern. Of respondents who said they had reported misconduct at their companies, 22 percent said they had experienced some form of retaliation, such as being excluded from decision making.

© Purestock/SuperStock

Overall, 51 percent of individuals surveyed reported having observed unethical conduct at their company. However, in companies that had an effective ethics program, only 33 percent reported seeing misconduct, while 61 percent of those in companies without such programs reported seeing misconduct. Employees in companies with effective programs were also much more likely to report what they saw than those in other companies, 87 percent versus 32 percent. Additionally, when misconduct was reported, only 4 percent of employees in companies with effective programs reported retaliation, compared to 59 percent of those in other companies.

The definition of ethical misconduct used in the study was quite broad, and included misuse of company time, abusive behavior, abusing company resources, lying to employees, and violating the company's policies for using the Internet.

For more information go to www.ethics.org.

Chapter Focus Company

Each chapter introduces important managerial accounting topics within the context of a realistic company. Students see the impact of managerial accounting decisions on the company as they work through the chapter. When the Focus Company is presented in the chapter, its logo is shown so the students see its application to the text topics.

"By following one company through several situations as the chapter progresses, more of a 'real world' decision-making process is obtained."

ALEECIA HIBBETS, UNIVERSITY OF LOUISIANA AT MONROE

"I like the different approaches to have real-world examples and the problems within the chapter that show how to do things."

CHRISTINA WILLIAMS, NORTHEASTERN UNIVERSITY

A Look Back/A Look Forward

Students need a roadmap to make sense of where the chapter topics fit into the "whole" picture. *A Look Back* reviews the chapter material and *A Look Forward* introduces students to what is to come.

<< A Look Back

The essential topics of this chapter are the master budget, flexible budgets, and variance analysis. The *master budget* is determined by multiplying the standard sales price and per unit variable costs by the planned volume of activity. The master budget is prepared at the beginning of the accounting period for planning purposes. It is not adjusted to reflect differences between the planned and actual volume of activity. Since this budget remains unchanged regardless of actual volume, it is also called a *static budget. Flexible budgets* differ from static budgets in that they show the estimated amount of revenue and costs expected at different levels of volume. Both static and flexible budgets are based on the same per unit standard amounts and the same fixed costs. The total amounts of revenue

>> A Look Forward

In addition to distinguishing costs by product versus SG&A classification, other classifications can be used to facilitate managerial decision making. In the next chapter, costs are classified according to the *behavior* they exhibit when the number of units of product increases or decreases (volume of activity changes). You will learn to distinguish between costs that vary with activity volume changes versus costs that remain fixed with activity volume changes. You will learn not only to recognize *cost behavior* but also how to use such recognition to evaluate

HOW ARE CHAPTER CONCEPTS

Regardless of the instructional approach, there is no shortcut to learning accounting. Students must practice to master basic accounting concepts. The text includes an ample supply of practice materials, exercises, and problems.

Video lectures and accompanying self-assessment quizzes are available in *Connect* for all learning objectives.

SELF-STUDY REVIEW PROBLEM

Tuscan Manufacturing Company makes a unique headset for use with mobile phones. During Year 1 Tuscan experienced the following accounting events. Other than the adjusting entries for depreciation, assume that all transactions are cash transactions.

1. Acquired $850,000 cash from the issue of common stock.
2. Paid $50,000 of research and development costs to develop the headset.
3. Paid $140,000 for the materials used to make headsets, all of which were started and completed during the year.
4. Paid salaries of $82,200 to selling and administrative employees.
5. Paid wages of $224,000 to production workers.
6. Paid $48,000 to purchase furniture used in selling and administrative offices.
7. Recognized depreciation on the office furniture. The furniture, acquired January 1, had an $8,000 estimated salvage value and a four-year useful life. The amount of depreciation is computed as [(Cost − Salvage) ÷ Useful life]. Specifically, [($48,000 − $8,000) ÷ 4 = $10,000].
8. Paid $65,000 to purchase manufacturing equipment.
9. Recognized depreciation on the manufacturing equipment. The equipment, acquired January 1 had a $5,000 estimated salvage value and a three-year useful life. The amount of depreciation is computed as [(Cost − Salvage) ÷ Useful life]. Specifically, [($65,000 − $5,000) ÷ 3 = $20,000].
10. Paid $136,000 for rent and utility costs on the manufacturing facility.
11. Paid $41,000 for inventory holding expenses for completed headsets (rental of warehouse space, salaries of warehouse personnel, and other general storage costs).
12. Tuscan started and completed 20,000 headset units during Year 1. The company sold 18,400 headsets at a price of $38 per unit.
13. Compute the average product cost per unit and recognize the appropriate amount of cost of goods sold.

Self-Study Review Problem

These representative example problems include a detailed, worked-out solution and provide another level of support for students before they work problems on their own. These review problems are included as animated audio presentations available in the *Connect Library*.

"End-of-chapter exercise and problem materials are varied and first rate."

DARLENE COARTS, UNIVERSITY OF NORTHERN IOWA

PROBLEMS—SERIES A

connect **All applicable Problems in Series A are available in *Connect*.**

LO 8-1

excel

CHECK FIGURES
a. NI = $124,000
c. NI = $130,000

Problem 8-18A ***Flexible budget planning***

Howard Cooper, the president of Glacier Computer Services, needs your help. He wonders about the potential effects on the firm's net income if he changes the service rate that the firm charges its customers. The following basic data pertain to fiscal Year 3.

Standard rate and variable costs	
Service rate per hour	$60.00
Labor cost	32.00
Overhead cost	5.76
Selling, general, and administrative cost	3.44
Expected fixed costs	
Facility maintenance	$320,000
Selling, general, and administrative	120,000

Required

a. Prepare the pro forma income statement that would appear in the master budget if the firm expects to provide 30,000 hours of services in Year 3.

b. A marketing consultant suggests to Mr. Cooper that the service rate may affect the number of service hours that the firm can achieve. According to the consultant's analysis, if Glacier charges customers $56 per hour, the firm can achieve 38,000 hours of services. Prepare a flexible budget using the consultant's assumption.

Exercise Series A & B and Problem Series A & B

There are two sets of problems and exercises, Series A and B. Instructors can assign one set for homework and use the other set for in-class work.

Check Figures

The figures provide a quick reference for students to check their progress in solving the problem. These are included for all problems in Series A.

Excel

Many exercises and problems can be solved using the Excel spreadsheet templates located in the *Connect Library*. A logo appears in the margins next to these exercises and problems for easy identification.

REINFORCED?

Analyze, Think, Communicate (ATC)

Each chapter includes an innovative section called Analyze, Think, Communicate (ATC). This section contains:

- **Writing Assignments**
- **Group Exercises**
- **Ethics Cases**
- **Internet Assignments**
- **Real Company Examples**

"The students also seem to like the ATC group assignments. These work very well as an in-class activity."

CASSIE BRADLEY, DALTON STATE COLLEGE

Mastering Excel and Using Excel

The Excel applications are used to make students comfortable with this analytical tool and to show its use in accounting.

"The innovative end-of-chapter materials are especially on target as an aid to improving student critical thinking and writing skills. The Excel spreadsheet applications are also excellent real-world activities."

DAN R. WARD, UNIVERSITY OF LOUISIANA, LAFAYETTE

ANALYZE, THINK, COMMUNICATE

ATC 1-1 Business Applications Case ***Financial versus managerial accounting***

The following information was taken from Starbucks Corporation's SEC filings.

	Fiscal Year Ended	
	October 1, 2017	October 2, 2016
Number of employees	277,000	254,000
Revenues (in millions)	$ 22,387	$ 21,316
Properties (in thousands)	6,322 square feet	6,277 square feet
Total assets (in millions)	$ 14,366	$ 14,313
Company-owned stores	13,275	12,711
Net earnings (in millions)	$ 2,885	$ 2,818

Required

a. Explain whether each line of information in the preceding table would best be described as being primarily financial accounting or managerial accounting in nature.
b. Provide some additional examples of managerial and financial accounting information that could apply to Starbucks.
c. If you analyze only the data you identified as financial in nature, does it appear that Starbucks' 2017 fiscal year was better or worse than its 2016 fiscal year? Explain.
d. If you analyze only the data you identified as managerial in nature, does it appear that Starbucks' 2017 fiscal year was better or worse than its 2016 fiscal year? Explain.
e. Did Starbucks appear to be using its facilities more efficiently or less efficiently in 2017 than in 2016?

ATC 1-2 Group Assignment ***Product versus upstream and downstream costs***

Victor Holt, the accounting manager of Sexton, Inc., gathered the following information for Year 4. Some of it can be used to construct an income statement for Year 4. Ignore items that do not appear on an income statement. Some computation may be required. For example, the cost of manufacturing equipment would not appear on the income statement. However, the cost of manufacturing equipment is needed to compute the amount of depreciation. All units of product were started and completed in Year 4.

1. Issued $864,000 of common stock.
2. Paid engineers in the product design department $10,000 for salaries that were accrued at the end of the previous year.
3. Incurred advertising expenses of $70,000.
4. Paid $720,000 for materials used to manufacture the company's product.
5. Incurred utility costs of $160,000. These costs were allocated to different departments on the basis of square footage of floor space. Mr. Holt identified three departments and determined the square footage of floor space for each department to be as shown in the following table.

Department	Square Footage
Research and development	10,000
Manufacturing	60,000
Selling and administrative	30,000

eXcel

ATC 3-6 Spreadsheet Assignment ***Using Excel***

Bishop Company has provided the estimated data that appear in rows 4 to 8 of the following spreadsheet.

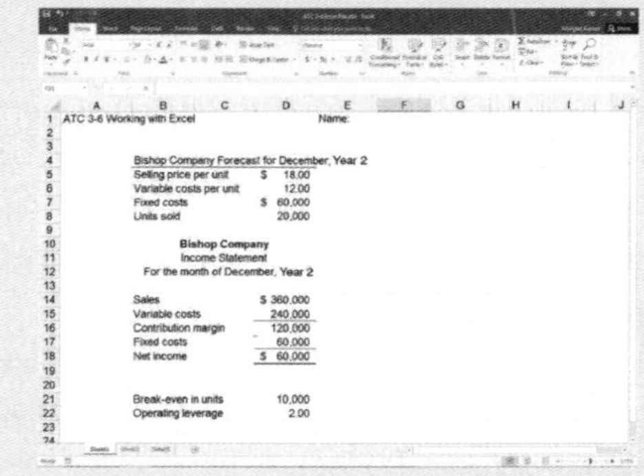

Source: Microsoft Excel 2010

Required

Using the spreadsheet tips that follow, construct a spreadsheet that allows you to determine net income, break-even in units, and operating leverage for the estimates at the top of the spreadsheet and see the effects of changes to the estimates. Set up this spreadsheet so that any change in the estimates will automatically be reflected in the calculation of net income, break-even, and operating leverage.

Spreadsheet Tip

To center a heading across several columns, such as the Income Statement title, highlight the area to be centered (columns B, C, and D), choose Format, then choose Cells, and click on the tab titled Alignment. Near the bottom of the alignment window, place a check mark in the box titled Merge cells.

WHAT WE DID TO MAKE IT BETTER!

WHAT'S NEW IN THIS EDITION?

We thank our reviewers and focus group participants for their suggestions for the ninth edition. Many of these suggestions motivated the changes described as follows.

Chapter 1 Management Accounting and Corporate Governance

- Revised learning objective seven.
- Updated *Curious Accountant* feature.
- Revised horizontal financial statement model format to include statement titles for greater clarity.
- Added algorithmic questions to self-assessment quizzes associated with video lectures for all learning objectives.
- Updated exercises, problems, and ATC cases.

Chapter 2 Cost Behavior, Operating Leverage, and Profitability Analysis

- Reorganized chapter content to improve readability.
- New *Curious Accountant* feature.
- Updated two *Reality Bytes* features.
- New *Focus on International Issues* feature.
- Added algorithmic questions to self-assessment quizzes associated with video lectures for all learning objectives.
- Updated exercises, problems, and ATC cases.

Chapter 3 Analysis of Cost, Volume, and Pricing to Increase Profitability

- New *Curious Accountant* feature.
- New *Focus on International Issues* feature.
- Updated *Reality Bytes* feature.
- Added algorithmic questions to self-assessment quizzes associated with video lectures for all learning objectives.
- Updated exercises, problems, and ATC cases.

Chapter 4 Cost Accumulation, Tracing, and Allocation

- Updated *Reality Bytes* feature.
- Added algorithmic questions to self-assessment quizzes associated with video lectures for all learning objectives.
- Updated exercises, problems, and ATC cases.

Chapter 5 Cost Management in an Automated Environment: ABC, ABM, and TQM

- Updated *Curious Accountant* feature.
- Updated *Reality Bytes* feature.
- New *Focus on International Issues* feature.
- Added algorithmic questions to self-assessment quizzes associated with video lectures for all learning objectives.
- Updated exercises, problems, and ATC cases.

Chapter 6 Relevant Information for Special Decisions

- Updated *Curious Accountant* feature.
- Updated *Reality Bytes* feature.
- Added New *Reality Bytes* feature.
- Added algorithmic questions to self-assessment quizzes associated with video lectures for all learning objectives.
- Updated exercises, problems, and ATC cases.

Chapter 7 Planning for Profit and Cost Control

- Updated *Focus on International Issues* feature.
- Updated *Reality Bytes* feature.
- Added algorithmic questions to self-assessment quizzes associated with video lectures for all learning objectives.
- Updated exercises, problems, and ATC cases.

Chapter 8 Performance Evaluation

- New *Curious Accountant* feature.
- Updated *Reality Bytes* feature.
- Added algorithmic questions to self-assessment quizzes associated with video lectures for all learning objectives.
- Updated exercises, problems, and ATC cases.

Chapter 9 Responsibility Accounting

- Updated *Curious Accountant* feature.
- Updated *Reality Bytes* feature.
- Revised *Focus on International Issues* feature.
- Added algorithmic questions to self-assessment quizzes associated with video lectures for all learning objectives.
- Updated exercises, problems, and ATC cases.

Chapter 10 Planning for Capital Investments

- Updated *Curious Accountant* feature.
- Added algorithmic questions to self-assessment quizzes associated with video lectures for all learning objectives.
- Updated exercises, problems, and ATC cases.

Chapter 11 Product Costing in Service and Manufacturing Entities

- Updated *Reality Bytes* feature.
- Added algorithmic questions to self-assessment quizzes associated with video lectures for all learning objectives.
- Updated exercises, problems, and ATC cases.

Chapter 12 Job-Order, Process, and Hybrid Costing Systems

- New *Curious Accountant* feature.
- New *Focus on International Issues* feature.
- Added algorithmic questions to self-assessment quizzes associated with video lectures for all learning objectives.
- Updated exercises, problems, and ATC cases.

Chapter 13 Financial Statement Analysis

- New *Curious Accountant* feature.
- New *Reality Bytes* feature.
- Added algorithmic questions to self-assessment quizzes associated with video lectures for all learning objectives.
- Updated exercises, problems, and ATC cases.

Chapter 14 Statement of Cash Flows

- New *Curious Accountant* feature.
- New *Reality Bytes* feature.
- Updated Exhibit 14.4.
- Added algorithmic questions to self-assessment quizzes associated with video lectures for all learning objectives.
- Updated exercises, problems, and ATC cases.

Assurance of Learning Ready

Many educational institutions today are focused on the notion of assurance of learning, an important element of some accreditation standards. *Fundamental Managerial Accounting Concepts,* 9e, is designed specifically to support your assurance of learning initiatives with a simple, yet powerful, solution. Each test bank question for *Fundamental Managerial Accounting Concepts,* 9e, maps to a specific chapter learning outcome/objective listed in the text. You can use *Connect* to easily query for learning outcomes/objectives that directly relate to the learning objectives for your course. You can then use the *Connect* reporting features to aggregate student results in similar fashion, making the collection and presentation of assurance of learning data simple and easy.

AACSB Statement

McGraw-Hill Education is a proud corporate member of AACSB International. Recognizing the importance and value of AACSB accreditation, we have sought to recognize the curricula guidelines detailed in AACSB standards for business accreditation by connecting selected questions in Edmonds 9e with the general knowledge and skill guidelines found in the AACSB standards. The statements contained in Edmonds 9e are provided only as a guide for the users of this text. The AACSB leaves content coverage and assessment clearly within the realm and control of individual schools, the mission of the school, and the faculty. The AACSB does also charge schools with the obligation of doing assessment against their own content and learning goals. While Edmonds 9e and its teaching package make no claim of any specific AACSB qualification or evaluation, we have labeled selected questions according to the six general knowledge and skills areas. The labels or tags within Edmonds 9e are as indicated. There are, of course, many more within the test bank, the text, and the teaching package which might be used as a "standard" for your course. However, the labeled questions are suggested for your consideration.

McGraw Hill Education **connect**®

Students—study more efficiently, retain more and achieve better outcomes. Instructors—focus on what you love—teaching.

SUCCESSFUL SEMESTERS INCLUDE CONNECT

FOR INSTRUCTORS

You're in the driver's seat.

Want to build your own course? No problem. Prefer to use our turnkey, prebuilt course? Easy. Want to make changes throughout the semester? Sure. And you'll save time with Connect's auto-grading too.

65%
Less Time Grading

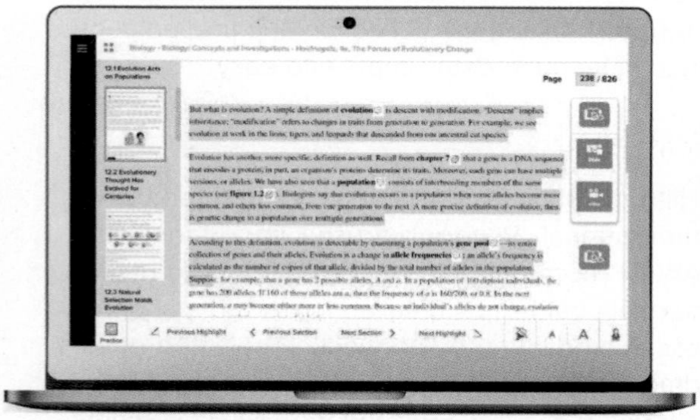

They'll thank you for it.

Adaptive study resources like SmartBook® help your students be better prepared in less time. You can transform your class time from dull definitions to dynamic debates. Hear from your peers about the benefits of Connect at **www.mheducation.com/highered/connect**

Make it simple, make it affordable.

Connect makes it easy with seamless integration using any of the major Learning Management Systems—Blackboard®, Canvas, and D2L, among others—to let you organize your course in one convenient location. Give your students access to digital materials at a discount with our inclusive access program. Ask your McGraw-Hill representative for more information.

©Hill Street Studios/Tobin Rogers/Blend Images LLC

Solutions for your challenges.

A product isn't a solution. Real solutions are affordable, reliable, and come with training and ongoing support when you need it and how you want it. Our Customer Experience Group can also help you troubleshoot tech problems—although Connect's 99% uptime means you might not need to call them. See for yourself at **status.mheducation.com**

FOR STUDENTS

©Shutterstock/wavebreakmedia

Effective, efficient studying.

Connect helps you be more productive with your study time and get better grades using tools like SmartBook, which highlights key concepts and creates a personalized study plan. Connect sets you up for success, so you walk into class with confidence and walk out with better grades.

> "I really liked this app—it made it easy to study when you don't have your textbook in front of you."
>
> —Jordan Cunningham, Eastern Washington University

Study anytime, anywhere.

Download the free ReadAnywhere app and access your online eBook when it's convenient, even if you're offline. And since the app automatically syncs with your eBook in Connect, all of your notes are available every time you open it. Find out more at **www.mheducation.com/readanywhere**

No surprises.

The Connect Calendar and Reports tools keep you on track with the work you need to get done and your assignment scores. Life gets busy; Connect tools help you keep learning through it all.

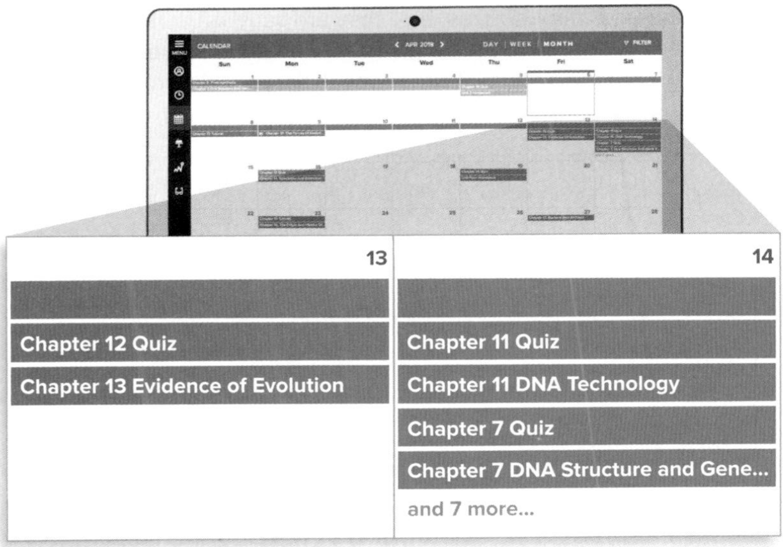

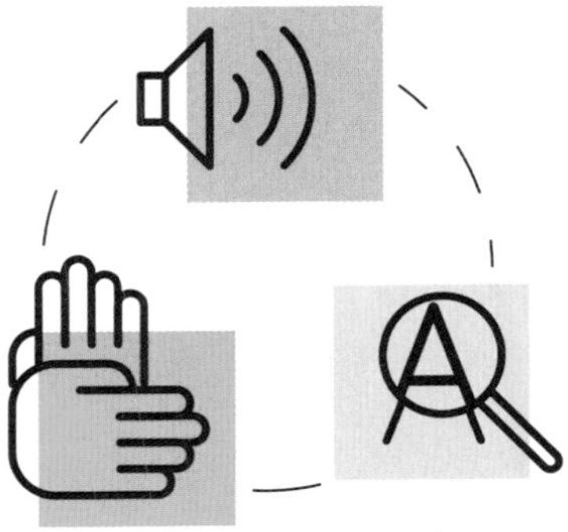

Learning for everyone.

McGraw-Hill works directly with Accessibility Services Departments and faculty to meet the learning needs of all students. Please contact your Accessibility Services office and ask them to email accessibility@mheducation.com, or visit **www.mheducation.com/about/accessibility.html** for more information.

HOW CAN TECHNOLOGY HELP

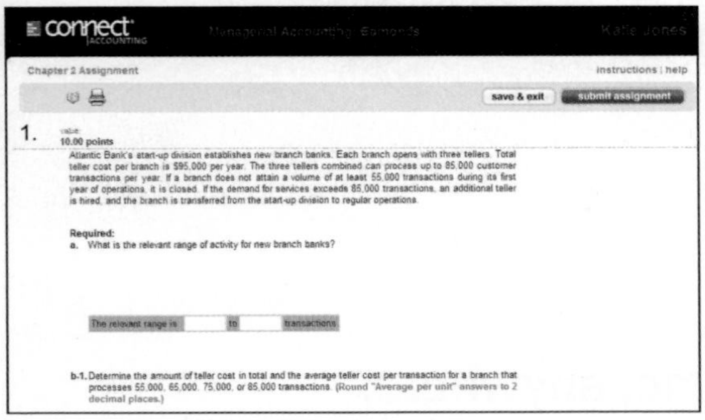

Online Assignments

Connect helps students learn more efficiently by providing feedback and practice material when and where they need it. *Connect* grades homework automatically and students benefit from the immediate feedback that they receive, particularly on any questions they may have missed. Also, select questions have been redesigned to test students' knowledge more fully. They now include tables for students to work through rather than requiring that all calculations be done offline.

Lecture Videos

One or more lecture videos are available for every learning objective introduced throughout the text. The videos have been developed by a member of the author team and have the touch and feel of a live lecture. The videos are accompanied by a set of self-assessment quizzes. Students can watch the videos and then test themselves to determine if they understand the material presented in the video. Students can repeat the process, switching back and forth between the video and self-assessment quizzes, until they are satisfied that they understand the material. Incorporating lecture videos as a resource for students to learn the material is great way to flip your classroom.

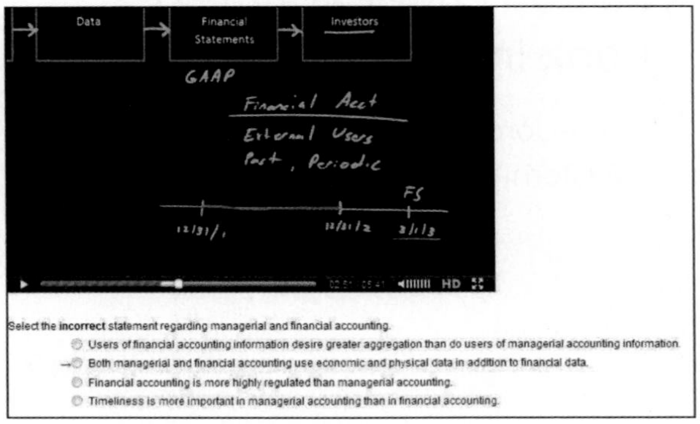

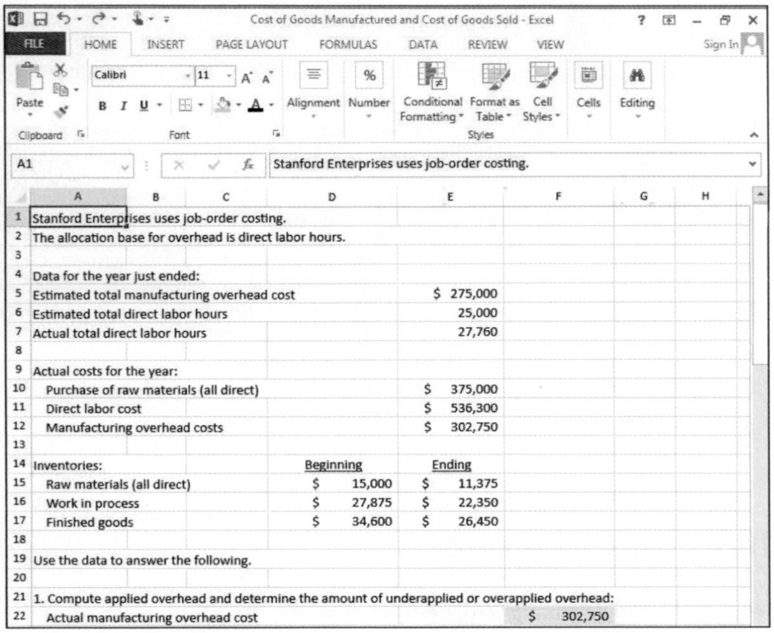

Excel Simulations

Simulated Excel Questions, assignable within *Connect*, allow students to practice their Excel skills—such as basic formulas and formatting—within the content of managerial accounting. These questions feature animated, narrated Help and Show Me tutorials (when enabled), as well as automatic feedback and grading for both students and professors.

IMPROVE STUDENT SUCCESS?

Guided Examples

The Guided Examples in *Connect* provide a narrated, animated, step-by-step walk-through of select exercises similar to those assigned. These short presentations can be turned on or off by instructors and provide reinforcement when students need it most.

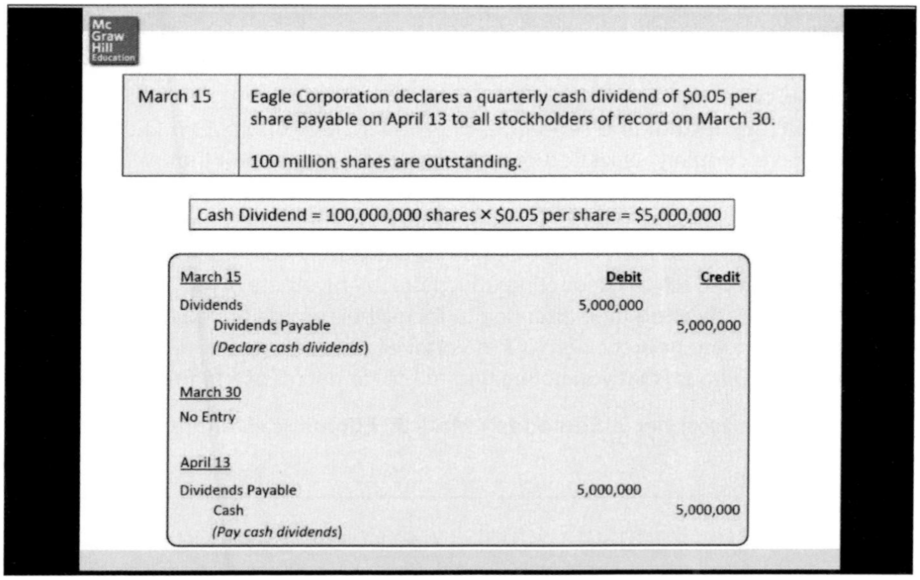

McGraw-Hill Customer Experience

At McGraw-Hill, we understand that getting the most from new technology can be challenging. That's why our services don't stop after you purchase our products. You can e-mail our Product Specialists 24 hours a day to get product training online. Or search our knowledge bank of Frequently Asked Questions on our support website. For Customer Support, call **800-331-5094** or visit www.mhhe.com/support. One of our Technical Support Analysts will be able to assist you in a timely fashion.

ACKNOWLEDGMENTS

Special thanks to the talented people who prepared the supplements. These take a great deal of time and effort to write, and we appreciate their efforts. Thank you to Debby Bloom, CMA, CFM, CSCA with Queens University of Charlotte for her revision work on the Instructor Manuals and PowerPoint presentations for the 9th edition; Dr. Helen Roybark, Radford University, for her accuracy checking of the text, solution manuals, Instructor Manuals and PowerPoint presentations; Beth Kobylarz for her accuracy checking of the text, solution manuals, and test bank; Jack Terry of Jack E. Terry & Associates for preparing the Excel Templates; Patti Lopez with Valencia College and Beth Kobylarz for their accuracy check work on Connect. A special thank you to Jean Bissel for all of her expertise on the Connect updates and reviews. Thank you also to Molly G. Brown, CPA, CMA with James Madison University for her keen eye in accuracy checking the Lecture Videos. Thank you also to Helena Hunt and Kristina Dehlin of Agate and Katherine Ward for their work on this project.

Our Portfolio Manager, Elizabeth Eisenhart, and Product Developers, Erin Quinones and Danielle McLimore, have certainly facilitated our efforts to prepare a book that will promote a meaningful understanding of accounting. Even so, their contributions are to no avail unless the text reaches its intended audience. We are most grateful to Katherine Wheeler and the sales staff for providing the informative marketing that has so accurately communicated the unique features of the concepts approach to accounting educators. Many others at McGraw-Hill Education at a moment's notice redirected their attention to focus their efforts on the development of this text. We extend our sincere appreciation to Tim Vertovec, Dana Pauley, and Brian Nacik. We deeply appreciate the long hours that you committed to the formation of a high-quality text.

Thomas P. Edmonds • Christopher T. Edmonds • Mark A. Edmonds • Jennifer E. Edmonds • Philip R. Olds

---

We express our sincere thanks to the following individuals who provided extensive reviews for the ninth edition:

Reviewers

Solochidi Ahiarah, *Buffalo State College*
Jennifer Brown, *University of Massachusetts*
Scott Cazadd, *Jefferson College*
Amy Conley, *Genesee Community College*
Cheryl Corke, *Genesee Community College*
Doris Donovan, *Dodge City Community College*
Mary Ellen Fletcher, *Mount Mary University*
Andy Garcia, *Bowling Green State University*
Kimberly Hansen, *Riverland Community College*
Trent Henke, *Virginia Tech–Blacksburg*
Susan Little, *Saint Leo University*
Rebecca Martin, *Virginia Tech–Blacksburg*
Michael Miceli, *Champlain College*
Bruce Neumann, *University of Colorado–Denver*
Cynthia Phipps, *Lake Land College*
Nathan Slavin, *Hofstra University*
Steven Sossei, *Siena College*
Sean Stein-Smith, *Fairleigh Dickinson University Teane*
Emily Vera, *University of Colorado Denver*
Jennifer Williams, *Virginia Tech–Blacksburg*

Our appreciation to those who reviewed previous editions:

Jed Ashley, *Grossmont College*
Walter Austin, *Mercer University*
Anthony B. Ross, Sr, *Concordia University, Texas*
Kristen Ball, *Dodge City Community College*
Lisa Banks, *Mott Community College*
Rebecca Barta, *Blinn College*
James Bates, *Mountain Empire Community College*
Frank Beigbeder, *Rancho Santiago College*

Daniel Benco, *Southeastern Oklahoma University*
Dorcas Berg, *Wingate College*
Ashton Bishop, *James Madison University*
Amy Bourne, *Tarrant County College*
Cassie Bradley, *Dalton State College*
Jerold K. Braun, *Daytona State College*
Kenneth Bronstein, *Western Washington University*
Amy Browning, *Ivy Tech Community College*
Steve Buchheit, *Texas Tech University*
Georgia Buckles, *Manchester Community College*
Jacqueline Burke, *Hofstra University*
Alan Campbell, *Troy University–Montgomery Campus*
Dennis Caplan, *Iowa State University*
Eric Carlsen, *Kean University*
Chiaho Chang, *Montclair State University*
Chak-Tong Chau, *University of Houston–Downtown*
Julie Chenier, *Louisiana State University*
Darlene Coarts, *University of Northern Iowa*
Ron Collins, *Miami University*
Cheryl Corke, *Genesee Community College*
Robert M. Cornell, *University of Nevada, Las Vegas*
Sue Counte, *Jefferson College*
Rich Criscione, *Morehead State University*
Jill D'Aquila, *Iona College*
David Deeds, *University of Northern Iowa*
Naman Desai, *Florida State University–Tallahassee*
Walt Doehring, *Genesee Community College*
Burak Dolar, *Western Washington University*
Patricia Douglas, *Loyola Marymount University*
Jan Duffy, *Iowa State University*
Dean Edmiston, *Emporia State University*
Terry Elliot, *Morehead State University*
Wede Elliott-Brownell, *Southern University and A&M College*
Robert Elmore, *Tennessee Technological University*
James Emig, *Villanova University*
Diane Eure, *Texas State University, San Marcos*
Robert Fahnestock, *University of West Florida*
Alana Ferguson, *Mott Community College*
Jeffrey Galbreath, *Greenfield Community College*
William Geary, *College of William and Mary*
Nashwa George, *Montclair State University*
John Goetz, *University of Texas Arlington*
Dinah Gottschalk, *James Madison University*
Donald Gribbin, *Southern Illinois University*
Richard Griffin, *The University of Tennessee at Marin*
Deborah L. Habel, *Wayne State University*
Judith Harris, *Nova Southeastern University*
Larry Hegstad, *Pacific Lutheran University*
Aleecia Hibbets, *University of Louisiana at Monroe*
Lyle Hicks, *Danville Area Community College*
Jay Holmen, *University of Wisconsin at Eau Claire*
Robyn Jarnagin, *Montana State University–Bozeman*
Fred Jex, *Macomb Community College*
Shondra Johnson, *Bradley University*
Sheila Johnston, *University of Louisville, Louisville*
Marrk Kaiser, *SUNY at Plattsburg*
Thomas Klammer, *University of North Texas*
Lawrence Klein, *Bentley College*
Mehmet Kocakulah, *University of Southern Indiana*
Lynn Krausse, *Bakersfield College*
Robert Landry, *Massassoit Community College*
Chor Lau, *California State University at Los Angeles*
Mark Lawrence, *University of Alabama at Birmingham*
Chuo-Hsuan Lee, *SUNY Plattsburgh*
Deborah Lee, *Northeastern State University*
Minwoo Lee, *Western Kentucky University*
Elliott Levy, *Bentley College*
Bruce Lindsey, *Genesee Community College*
Bob Linn, *Western Washington University*
Philip Little, *Western Carolina University*
Julie Lockhart, *Western Washington University*
Cathy Lumbattis, *Southern Illinois University*
Anna L. Lusher, *Slippery Rock University*
Nancy Lynch, *West Virginia University–Morgantown*
Suneel Maheshwari, *Marshall University*
Lois Mahoney, *University of Central Florida*
Jeanette Maier-Lytle, *University of Southern Indiana*
Mary Malina, *University of Colorado Denver*
Florence McGovern, *Bergen Community College*
Brian McGuire, *University of Southern Indiana*
David McIntyre, *Clemson University*
Pat McMahon, *Palm Beach Community College*
Michael Meyer, *Ohio University*

Pam Meyer, *University of Louisiana at Lafayette*
John Moore, *Virginia State University*
Arabian Morgan, *Orange Coast College*
Michelle Moshier, *SUNY at Albany*
Lisa Murawa, *Mott Community College*
Irvin Nelson, *Utah State University*
Bruce Neumann, *University of Colorado–Denver*
Hossein Nouri, *College of New Jersey*
Connie O'Brien, *Minnesota State University Mankato*
Ashton Oravetz, *Tyler Junior College*
Chei Paik, *George Washington University*
Scott Paxton, *Valencia College*
Thomas Phillips, Louisiana Tech University
Marjorie Platt, *Northeastern University*
Letitia Pleis, *Metropolitan State College of Denver*
Wendy K. Potratz, *University of Wisconsin, Oshkosh*
Emil Radosevich, *Albuquerque TVI Community College*
Ronald Reed, *University of Northern Colorado*
Roy Regel, *University of Montana at Missoula*
Jane Reimers, *Florida State University*
Celia Renner, *Boise State University*
Gary Reynolds, *Ozark Technical Community College*
Diane Riordan, *James Madison University*
Tom Robinson, *University of Alaska*
Luther Ross, *Central Piedmont Community College*
T. Brian Routh, *University of Southern Indiana*
Harold Royer, *Miami-Dade College*
Nancy Ruhe, *West Virginia University, Morgantown*
Charles Russo, *Bloomsburg University of Pennsylvania*
Marilyn Salter, *University of Central Florida*
Angela Sandberg, *Jacksonville State University*
Kathryn Savage, *Northern Arizona University*
John Shaver, *Louisiana Tech University*
Bob Smith, *Florida State University*
Walter Smith, *Siena College*
John Sneed, *Jacksonville State University*
John Stancil, *Florida Southern College*
Patrick Stegman, *College of Lake County*
Scott Steinkamp, *College of Lake County*
Scott Stroher, *Glendale Community College*
Holly Sudano, *Florida State University*
Bill Talbot, *Montgomery College*
Pavani Tallapally, *Slippery Rock University*
Suneel Udpa, *St. Mary's College*
Michael VanBreda, *Southern Methodist University*
Sharon T. Walters, *Morehead State University*
Scott Wandler, *University of New Orleans*
Dan Ward, *University of Louisiana, Lafayette*
Anne Williams, *Gateway Community College*
Christina Williams, *Northeastern University*
Sean Wright, *DeVry Institute of Technology, Phoenix*
Allan Young, *DeVry Institute of Technology, Atlanta*
James F. Zeigler (CPA), *Bowling Green State University*
Ronald Zhao, *Monmouth University*
Nan Zhou, *Binghamton University*

Many others have contributed directly or indirectly to the development of the text. Participants in workshops and focus groups have provided useful feedback. Colleagues and friends have extended encouragement and support. Among these individuals our sincere appreciation is extended to Lowell Broom, Samford University; Bill Schwartz, Home School of Technology Management; Ed Spede, Virginia Commonwealth University; Doug Cloud, Pepperdine University–Malibu; Charles Bailey, University of Memphis; Bob Holtfreter, Central Washington University; Kimberly Temme, Maryville University; Beth Vogel, Mount Mary College; Robert Minnear, Emory University; Shirish Seth, California State University at Fullerton; Richard Emery, Linfield College; Gail Hoover, Rockhurst; Bruce Robertson, Lock Haven University; Jeannie Folk, College of DuPage; Marvelyn Burnette, Wichita State University; Ron Mannino, University of Massachusetts; John Reisch, Florida Atlantic University; Rosalie Hallbauer, Florida International University; Lynne H. Shoaf, Belmont Abbey College; Jayne Maas, Towson University; Ahmed Goma, Manhattan College; John Rude, Bloomsburg University; Jack Paul, Lehigh University; Terri Gutierrez, University of Northern Colorado; Khondkar Karim, Monmouth University; Carol Lawrence, University of Richmond; Jeffrey Power, Saint Mary's University; Joanne Sheridan, Montana State University; and George Dow and Steve Muller, Valencia College.

BRIEF CONTENTS

CONTENTS

P&G

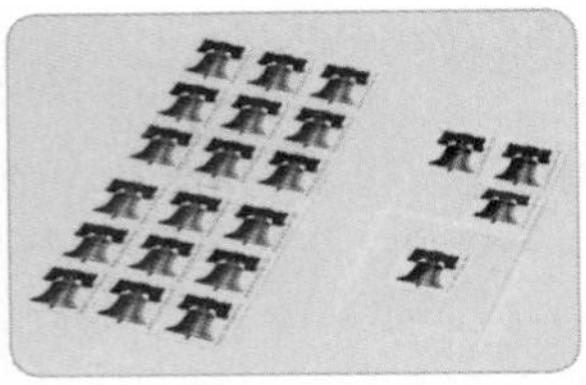

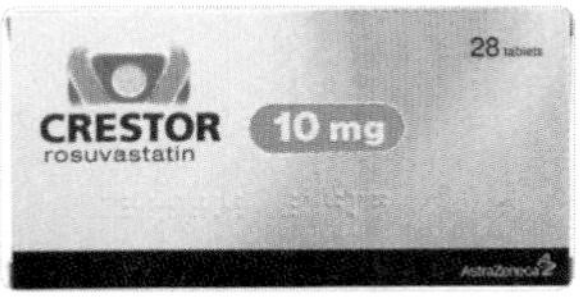

Chapter 6 Relevant Information for Special Decisions 254

Chapter 7 Planning for Profit and Cost Control 306

Chapter 8 Performance Evaluation 350

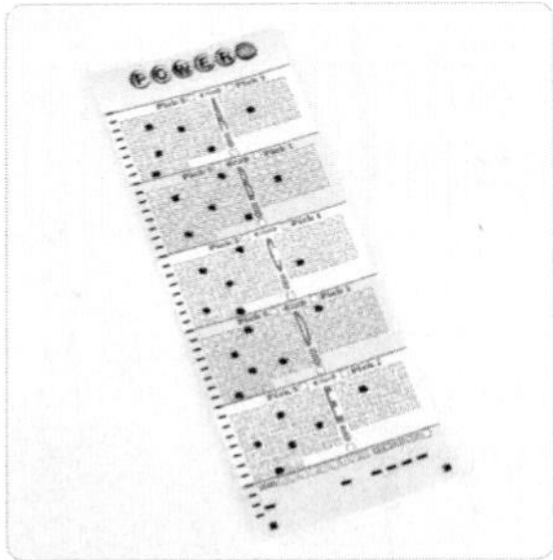

Chapter 12 Job-Order, Process, and Hybrid Costing Systems 536

Chapter 13 Financial Statement Analysis 588

Chapter 14 Statement of Cash Flows 638

ninth edition

Fundamental Managerial Accounting Concepts

CHAPTER 1

Management Accounting and Corporate Governance

LEARNING OBJECTIVES

After you have mastered the material in this chapter, you will be able to:

LO 1-1 Distinguish between managerial and financial accounting.

LO 1-2 Identify the cost of manufacturing a product.

LO 1-3 Show how manufacturing product costs affect financial statements.

LO 1-4 Compare the treatment of upstream, midstream, and downstream costs in manufacturing, service, and merchandising companies.

LO 1-5 Show how just-in-time inventory can increase profitability.

LO 1-6 Identify the key components of corporate governance.

LO 1-7 Identify the key features of total quality management (TQM) and activity-based management (ABM). (Appendix).

Video lectures and accompanying self-assessment quizzes are available in Connect® for all learning objectives.

CHAPTER OPENING

Andy Grove, former CEO of Intel Corporation, is credited with the motto "Only the paranoid survive." Mr. Grove described a wide variety of concerns that made him paranoid. Specifically, he stated:

> I worry about products getting screwed up, and I worry about products getting introduced prematurely. I worry about factories not performing well, and I worry about having too many factories. I worry about hiring the right people, and I worry about morale slacking off. And, of course, I worry about competitors. I worry about other people figuring out how to do what we do better or cheaper, and displacing us with our customers.

Do Intel's historically based financial statements contain the information Mr. Grove needs? No. **Financial accounting** is not designed to satisfy all the information needs of business managers. Its scope is limited to the needs of external users such as investors and creditors. The field of accounting designed to meet the needs of internal users is called **managerial accounting.**

The Curious Accountant

©mike davies/Alamy

In the first course of accounting, you learned how retailers, such as **Target**, account for the cost of equipment that lasts more than one year. Recall that the equipment was recorded as an asset when purchased, and then it was depreciated over its expected useful life. The depreciation charge reduced the company's assets and increased its expenses. This approach was justified under the matching principle, which seeks to recognize costs as expenses in the same period that the cost (resource) is used to generate revenue.

Is depreciation always shown as an expense on the income statement? The answer may surprise you. Consider the following scenario. **Skyrocket, LLC.**, manufactures the Sky Viper Streaming FPV Video Drone that it sells to Target. Assume that in order to produce the video drone, Skyrocket had to purchase a robotic machine that it expects can be used to produce 1,000,000 drones.

Do you think Skyrocket should account for depreciation on its manufacturing equipment the same way Target accounts for depreciation on its registers at the checkout counters? If not, how should Skyrocket account for its depreciation? Remember the matching principle when thinking of your answer. (Answer on page 12.)

DIFFERENCES BETWEEN MANAGERIAL AND FINANCIAL ACCOUNTING

LO 1-1

Distinguish between managerial and financial accounting.

While the information needs of internal and external users overlap, the needs of managers generally differ from those of investors or creditors. Some distinguishing characteristics are discussed in the following section.

Users and Types of Information

Financial accounting provides information used primarily by investors, creditors, and others *outside* a business. In contrast, managerial accounting focuses on information used by executives, managers, and employees who work *inside* the business. These two user groups need different types of information.

Internal users need information to *plan, direct,* and *control* business operations. The nature of information needed is related to an employee's job level. Lower-level employees use nonfinancial information such as work schedules, store hours, and customer service policies. Moving up the organizational ladder, financial information becomes increasingly important. Middle managers use a blend of financial and nonfinancial information, while senior executives concentrate on financial data. To a lesser degree, senior executives also use general economic data and nonfinancial operating information. For example, an executive may consider the growth rate of the economy before deciding to expand the company's workforce.

External users (investors and creditors) have greater needs for general economic information than do internal users. For example, an investor debating whether to purchase stock versus bond securities might be more interested in government tax policy than financial statement data. Exhibit 1.1 summarizes the information needs of different user groups.

Level of Aggregation

External users generally desire *global information* that reflects the performance of a company as a whole. For example, an investor is not so much interested in the performance of a particular Sears store as she is in the performance of Sears Roebuck Company versus that of JCPenney Company. In contrast, internal users focus on detailed information about specific subunits of the company. To meet the needs of the different user groups, financial accounting data are more aggregated than managerial accounting data.

EXHIBIT 1.1

Relationship between Type of User and Type of Information

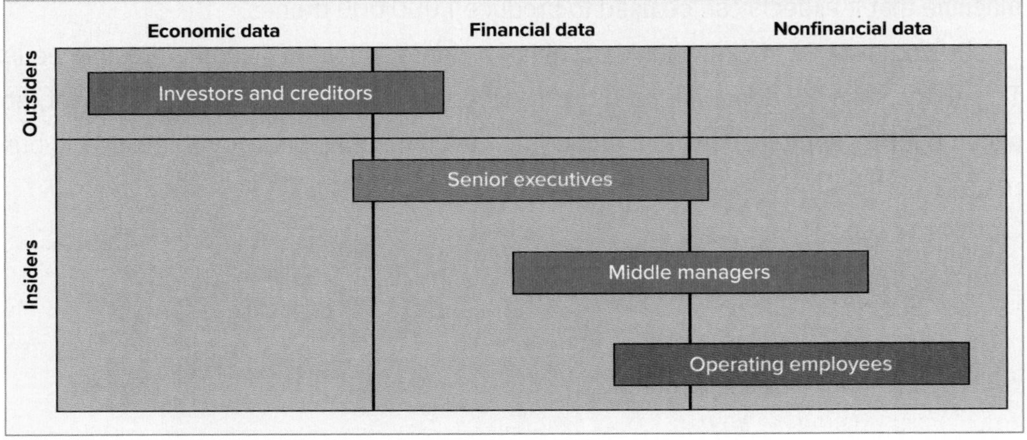

Regulation

©Scott J. Ferrell/Getty Images

Financial accounting is designed to generate information for the general public. In an effort to protect the public interest, Congress established the **Securities and Exchange Commission (SEC)** and gave it authority to regulate public financial reporting practices. The SEC has delegated much of its authority for developing accounting rules to the private-sector **Financial Accounting Standards Board (FASB),** thereby allowing the accounting profession considerable influence over financial accounting reports. The FASB supports a broad base of pronouncements and practices known as **generally accepted accounting principles (GAAP).** GAAP severely restrict the accounting procedures and practices permitted in published financial statements.

Beyond financial statement data, much of the information generated by management accounting systems is proprietary information not available to the public. Since this information is not distributed to the public, it need not be regulated to protect the public interest. Management accounting is restricted only by the **value-added principle.** Management accountants are free to engage in any information gathering and reporting activity so long as the activity adds value in excess of its cost. For example, management accountants are free to provide forecasted information to internal users. In contrast, financial accounting as prescribed by GAAP does not permit forecasting.

Information Characteristics

While financial accounting is characterized by its objectivity, reliability, consistency, and historical nature, managerial accounting is more concerned with relevance and timeliness. Managerial accounting uses more estimates and fewer facts than financial accounting. Financial accounting reports what happened yesterday; managerial accounting reports what is expected to happen tomorrow.

Time Horizon and Reporting Frequency

Financial accounting information is reported periodically, normally at the end of a year. Management cannot wait until the end of the year to discover problems. Planning, controlling, and directing require immediate attention. Managerial accounting information is delivered on a continuous basis.

Exhibit 1.2 summarizes significant differences between financial and managerial accounting.

PRODUCT COSTING IN MANUFACTURING COMPANIES

LO 1-2

Identify the cost of manufacturing a product.

A major focus for managerial accountants is determining **product cost.**[1] Managers need to know the cost of their products for a variety of reasons. For example, **cost-plus pricing** is a common business practice.[2] **Product costing** is also used to control business operations. It is useful in answering questions such as: Are costs higher or lower than expected? Who is responsible for the variances between expected and actual costs? What actions can be taken to control the variances?

Components of Product Cost

Generally accepted accounting principles (GAAP) recognize three types of cost that are incurred in the process of making products. Specifically, the company must pay for (1) the

[1]This text uses the term *product* in a generic sense to mean both goods and services.

[2]Other pricing strategies will be introduced in subsequent chapters.

EXHIBIT 1.2

Comparative Features of Managerial versus Financial Accounting Information

Features	Managerial Accounting	Financial Accounting
Users	Insiders, including executives, managers, and operators	Outsiders, including investors, creditors, government agencies, analysts, and reporters
Information type	Economic and physical data as well as financial data	Financial data
Level of aggregation	Local information on subunits of the organization	Global information on the company as a whole
Regulation	No regulation, limited only by the value-added principle	Regulation by SEC, FASB, and other determiners of GAAP
Information characteristics	Estimates that promote relevance and enable timeliness	Factual information that is characterized by objectivity, reliability, consistency, and accuracy
Time horizon	Past, present, and future	Past only, historically based
Reporting frequency	Continuous reporting	Delayed, with emphasis on annual reports

materials used to make the products, (2) the *labor* used to transform the materials into products, and (3) the **overhead** (other resources such as utilities and equipment consumed in the process of making the products). If the company stores its products, the costs of the materials, labor, and overhead used in making the products are maintained in an inventory account until the products are sold. For a detailed explanation of how product costs flow through the financial statements, refer to the following example of Tabor Manufacturing Company.

Tabor Manufacturing Company

Tabor Manufacturing Company makes wooden tables. The company spent \$1,000 cash to build four tables: \$390 for materials, \$470 for a carpenter's labor, and \$140 for tools used in making the tables. How much is Tabor's expense? The answer is zero. The \$1,000 cash has been converted into products (four tables). The cash payments for materials, labor, and tools (overhead) were *asset exchange* transactions. One asset (cash) decreased while another asset (tables) increased. Tabor will not recognize any expense until the tables are sold; in the meantime, the cost of the tables is held in an asset account called **Finished Goods Inventory.** Exhibit 1.3 illustrates how cash is transformed into inventory.

Average Cost per Unit

How much did each table made by Tabor cost? The *actual* cost of each of the four tables likely differs. The carpenter probably spent a little more time on some of the tables than others. Material and tool usage probably varied from table to table. Determining the exact cost of each table is virtually impossible. Minute details such as a second of labor time cannot be effectively measured. Even if Tabor could determine the exact cost of each table, the information would be of little use. Minor differences in the cost per table would make no difference in pricing or other decisions management needs to make. Accountants therefore normally calculate cost per unit as an *average*. In the case of Tabor Manufacturing, the **average cost** per table is \$250 (\$1,000 ÷ 4 units). Unless otherwise stated, assume *cost per unit* means *average cost per unit*.

EXHIBIT 1.3

Transforming the Asset Cash into the Asset Finished Goods Inventory

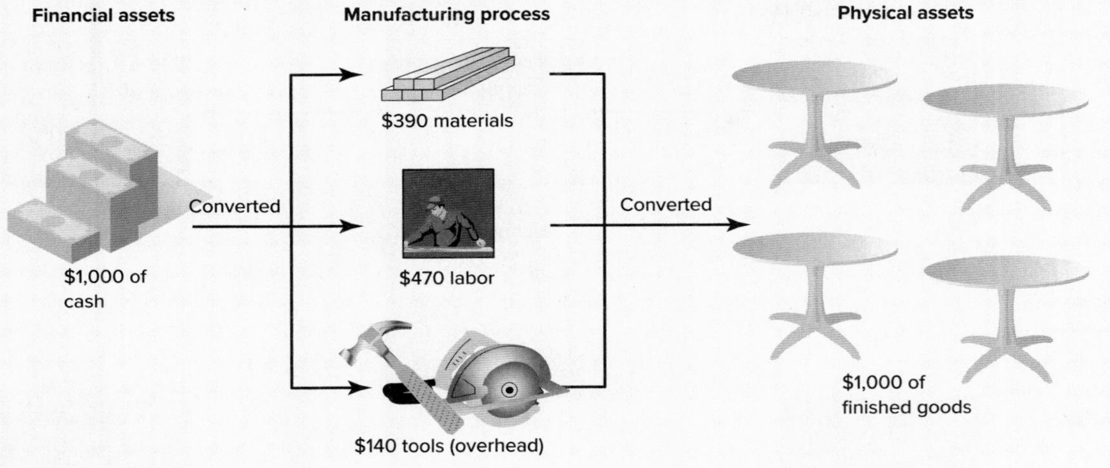

CHECK YOURSELF 1.1

All boxes of General Mills' Total Raisin Bran cereal are priced at exactly the same amount in your local grocery store. Does this mean that the actual cost of making each box of cereal was exactly the same?

Answer No, making each box would not cost exactly the same amount. For example, some boxes contain slightly more or less cereal than other boxes. Accordingly, some boxes cost slightly more or less to make than others do. General Mills uses average cost rather than actual cost to develop its pricing strategy.

Costs Can Be Assets or Expenses

It might seem odd that wages paid to production workers are recorded as inventory instead of being expensed. Remember, however, that expenses are assets used in the process of *earning revenue*. The cash paid to production workers is not used to produce revenue. Instead, the cash is used to produce inventory. Revenue will be earned when the inventory is used (sold). So long as the inventory remains on hand, all product costs (materials, labor, and overhead) remain in an inventory account.

When a table is sold, the average cost of the table is transferred from the Inventory account to the Cost of Goods Sold (expense) account. If some tables remain unsold at the end of the accounting period, part of the *product cost* is reported as an asset (inventory) on the balance sheet while the other part is reported as an expense (cost of goods sold) on the income statement.

Costs that are not classified as product costs are normally expensed in the period in which they are incurred. These costs include *general operating costs, selling and administrative costs, interest costs,* and the *cost of income taxes.*

To illustrate, return to the Tabor Manufacturing example. Recall that Tabor made four tables at an average cost per unit of $250. Assume Tabor pays an employee who sells three of the tables a $200 sales commission. The sales commission is expensed immediately. The total product cost for the three tables (3 tables × $250 each = $750) is expensed on the income statement as cost of goods sold. The portion of the total product cost remaining in inventory

EXHIBIT 1.4

Cost Classification for Tabor Manufacturing Company

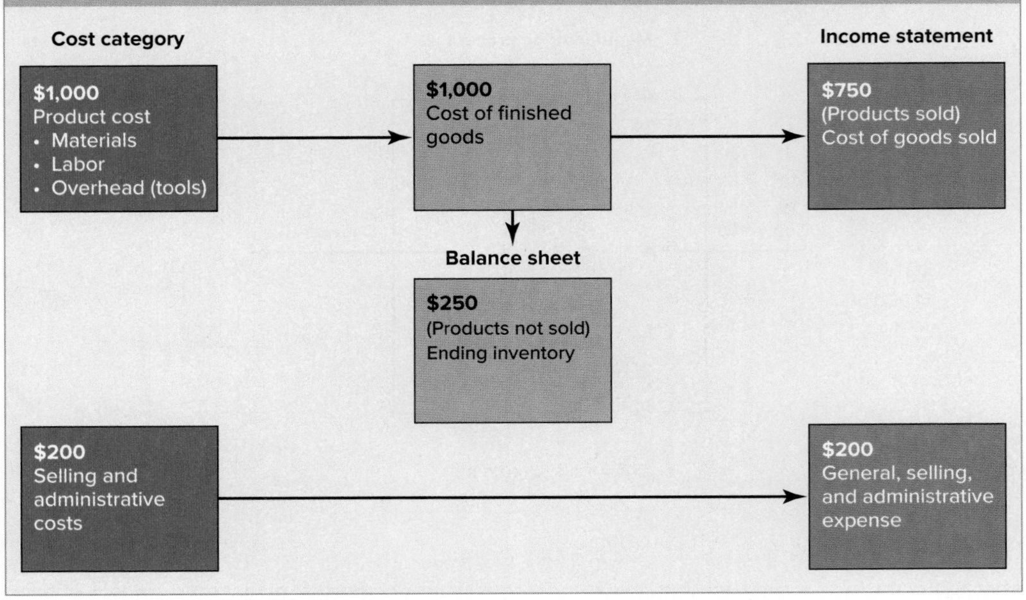

is $250 (1 table × $250). Exhibit 1.4 shows the relationship between the costs incurred and the expenses recognized for Tabor Manufacturing Company.

PRODUCT COSTS ON FINANCIAL STATEMENTS

LO 1-3

Show how manufacturing product costs affect financial statements.

We illustrate accounting for product costs in manufacturing companies with Patillo Manufacturing Company, a producer of ceramic pottery. Patillo, started on January 1, Year 1, experienced the following accounting events during its first year of operations.[3] *Assume that all transactions except 6, 8, and 10 are cash transactions.*

1. Acquired $15,000 cash by issuing common stock.
2. Paid $2,000 for materials that were used to make products. All products started were completed during the period.
3. Paid $1,200 for salaries of selling and administrative employees.
4. Paid $3,000 for wages of production workers.
5. Paid $2,800 for furniture used in selling and administrative offices.
6. Recognized depreciation on the office furniture purchased in Event 5. The furniture was acquired on January 1, had a $400 estimated salvage value, and a four-year useful life. The annual depreciation charge is $600 [($2,800 − $400) ÷ 4].
7. Paid $4,500 for manufacturing equipment.
8. Recognized depreciation on the equipment purchased in Event 7. The equipment was acquired on January 1, had a $1,500 estimated salvage value, and a three-year useful life. The annual depreciation charge is $1,000 [($4,500 − $1,500) ÷ 3].
9. Sold inventory to customers for $7,500 cash.
10. The inventory sold in Event 9 cost $4,000 to make.

[3]This illustration assumes that all inventory started during the period was completed during the period. Patillo therefore uses only one inventory account, Finished Goods Inventory. Many manufacturing companies normally have three categories of inventory on hand at the end of an accounting period: Raw Materials Inventory, Work in Process Inventory (inventory of partially completed units), and Finished Goods Inventory. Chapter 11 discusses these inventories in greater detail.

EXHIBIT 1.5

Effect of Product versus Selling and Administrative Costs on Financial Statements

	Balance Sheet											Income Statement				
	Assets								Equity							
Event No.	Cash	+	Inventory	+	Office Furn.*	+	Manuf. Equip.*	=	Com. Stk.	+	Ret. Earn.	Rev.	−	Exp.	=	Net Inc.
1	15,000	+	NA	+	NA	+	NA	=	15,000	+	NA	NA	−	NA	=	NA
2	(2,000)	+	2,000	+	NA	+	NA	=	NA	+	NA	NA	−	NA	=	NA
3	(1,200)	+	NA	+	NA	+	NA	=	NA	+	(1,200)	NA	−	1,200	=	(1,200)
4	(3,000)	+	3,000	+	NA	+	NA	=	NA	+	NA	NA	−	NA	=	NA
5	(2,800)	+	NA	+	2,800	+	NA	=	NA	+	NA	NA	−	NA	=	NA
6	NA	+	NA	+	(600)	+	NA	=	NA	+	(600)	NA	−	600	=	(600)
7	(4,500)	+	NA	+	NA	+	4,500	=	NA	+	NA	NA	−	NA	=	NA
8	NA	+	1,000	+	NA	+	(1,000)	=	NA	+	NA	NA	−	NA	=	NA
9	7,500	+	NA	+	NA	+	NA	=	NA	+	7,500	7,500	−	NA	=	7,500
10	NA	+	(4,000)	+	NA	+	NA	=	NA	+	(4,000)	NA	−	4,000	=	(4,000)
Totals	9,000	+	2,000	+	2,200	+	3,500	=	15,000	+	1,700	7,500	−	5,800	=	1,700

*Negative amounts in these columns represent accumulated depreciation.

The effects of these transactions on the balance sheet and income statement are shown in Exhibit 1.5. Study each row in this exhibit, paying particular attention to how similar costs such as salaries for selling and administrative personnel and wages for production workers have radically different effects on the financial statements. The example illustrates the three elements of product costs–materials (Event 2), labor (Event 4), and overhead (Event 8). These events are discussed in more detail as follows.

Materials Costs (Event 2)

Materials used to make products are usually called **raw materials.** The cost of raw materials is first recorded in an asset account (Inventory). The cost is then transferred from the Inventory account to the Cost of Goods Sold account at the time the goods are sold. Remember that materials cost is only one component of total manufacturing costs. When inventory is sold, the combined cost of materials, labor, and overhead is expensed as *cost of goods sold*. The costs of materials that can be easily and conveniently traced to products are called **direct raw materials** costs.

Labor Costs (Event 4)

The salaries paid to selling and administrative employees (Event 3) and the wages paid to production workers (Event 4) are accounted for differently. Salaries paid to selling and administrative employees are expensed immediately, but the cost of production wages is added to inventory. Production wages are expensed as part of cost of goods sold at the time the inventory is sold. Labor costs that can be easily and conveniently traced to products are called **direct labor** costs. The cost flow of wages for production employees versus salaries for selling and administrative personnel is shown in Exhibit 1.6.

Overhead Costs (Event 8)

Although depreciation cost totaled $1,600 ($600 on office furniture and $1,000 on manufacturing equipment), only the $600 of depreciation on the office furniture is expensed directly on the income statement. The depreciation on the manufacturing equipment is split between the income statement (cost of goods sold) and the balance sheet (inventory). The depreciation cost flow for the manufacturing equipment versus the office furniture is shown in Exhibit 1.7.

EXHIBIT 1.6

Flow of Labor Costs

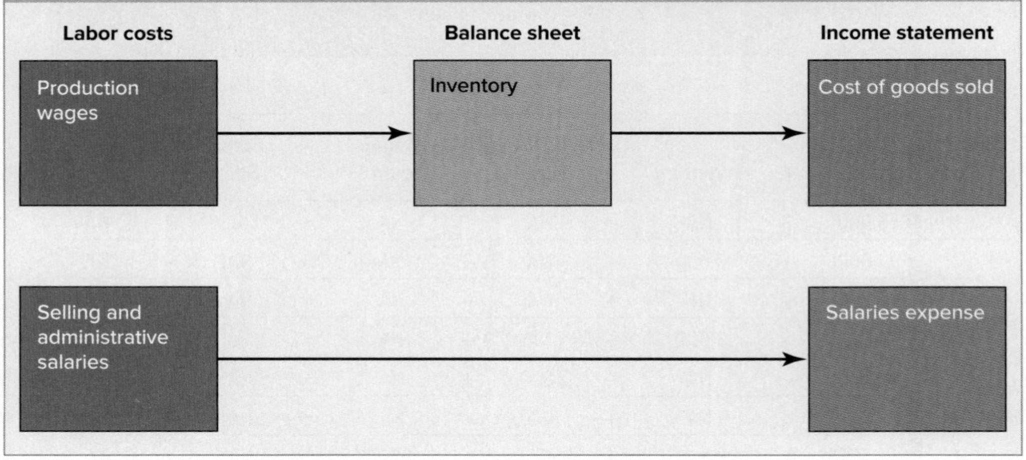

EXHIBIT 1.7

Flow of Depreciation Costs

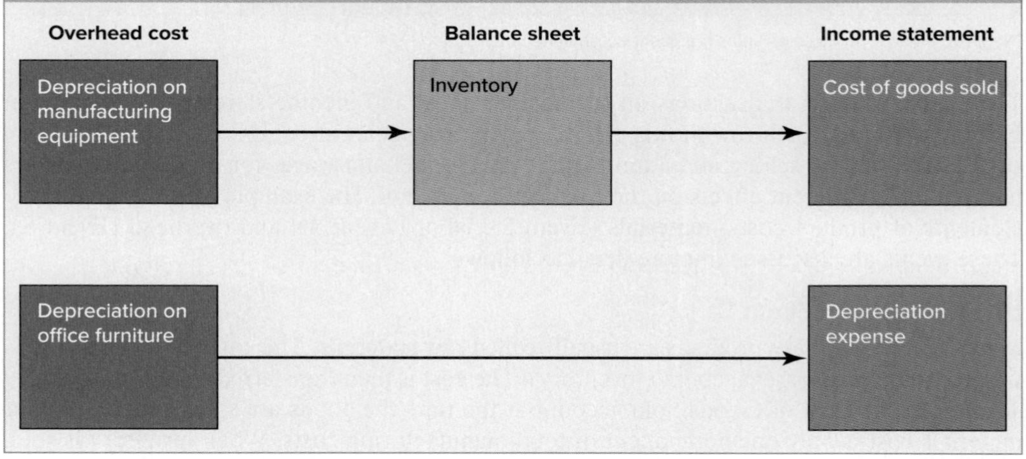

Total Product Cost. A summary of Patillo Manufacturing's total product cost is shown in Exhibit 1.8.

Financial Statements

The GAAP-based income statement and balance sheet for Patillo Manufacturing are displayed in Exhibit 1.9.

Product Costs. The $4,000 cost of goods sold reported on the income statement includes a portion of the materials, labor, and overhead costs incurred by Patillo during the year. Similarly, the $2,000 of finished goods inventory on the balance sheet includes materials, labor, and overhead costs. These product costs will be recognized as an expense in the next accounting period when the goods are sold. Initially classifying a cost as a product cost delays, but does not eliminate, its recognition as an expense. All product costs are ultimately recognized as an expense (cost of goods sold).

Selling, General, and Administrative Costs. Selling, general, and administrative costs (SG&A) are normally expensed *in the period* in which they are incurred. Because of this recognition

EXHIBIT 1.8

Schedule of Inventory Costs

Materials	$ 2,000
Labor	3,000
Manufacturing overhead*	1,000
Total product costs	6,000
Less: Cost of goods sold	(4,000)
Ending inventory balance	$ 2,000

*Depreciation [($4,500 − $1,500) ÷ 3]

EXHIBIT 1.9

PATILLO MANUFACTURING COMPANY

Financial Statements

Income Statement for Year 1

Sales revenue		$ 7,500
Cost of goods sold		(4,000)
Gross margin		3,500
SG&A expenses		
Salaries expense		(1,200)
Depreciation expense—office furniture		(600)
Net income		$ 1,700

Balance Sheet as of December 31, Year 1

Cash		$ 9,000
Finished goods inventory		2,000
Office furniture	$ 2,800	
Accumulated depreciation	(600)	
Book value		2,200
Manufacturing equipment	4,500	
Accumulated depreciation	(1,000)	
Book value		3,500
Total assets		$16,700
Stockholders' equity		
Common stock		$15,000
Retained earnings		1,700
Total stockholders' equity		$16,700

pattern, nonproduct expenses are sometimes called **period costs.** In Patillo's case, the salaries expense for selling and administrative employees and the depreciation on office furniture are period costs reported directly on the income statement.

Overhead Costs: A Closer Look

Costs such as depreciation on manufacturing equipment cannot be easily traced to products. Suppose that Patillo Manufacturing makes both tables and chairs. What part of the depreciation is caused by manufacturing tables versus manufacturing chairs? Similarly, suppose a production supervisor oversees employees who work on both tables and chairs. How much of the supervisor's salary relates to tables and how much to chairs? Likewise, the cost of glue used in the production department would be difficult to trace to tables versus chairs. You could count the drops of glue used on each product, but the information would not be useful enough to merit the time and money spent collecting the data.

Costs that cannot be traced to products and services in a *cost-effective* manner are called **indirect costs.** The indirect costs incurred to make products are called **manufacturing overhead.** Some of the items commonly included in manufacturing overhead are indirect materials, indirect labor, factory utilities, rent of manufacturing facilities, and depreciation on manufacturing assets.

☑ CHECK YOURSELF 1.2

Lawson Manufacturing Company paid production workers wages of $100,000. It incurred materials costs of $120,000 and manufacturing overhead costs of $160,000. Selling and administrative salaries were $80,000. Lawson started and completed 1,000 units of product and sold 800 of these units. The company sets sales prices at $220 above the average per-unit production cost. Based on this information alone, determine the amount of gross margin and net income. What is Lawson's pricing strategy called?

Answer Total product cost is $380,000 ($100,000 labor + $120,000 materials + $160,000 overhead). Cost per unit is $380 ($380,000 ÷ 1,000 units). The sales price per unit is $600 ($380 + $220). Cost of goods sold is $304,000 ($380 × 800 units). Sales revenue is $480,000 ($600 × 800 units). Gross margin is $176,000 ($480,000 revenue − $304,000 cost of goods sold). Net income is $96,000 ($176,000 gross margin − $80,000 selling and administrative salaries). Lawson's pricing strategy is called *cost-plus* pricing.

EXHIBIT 1.10

Cost Allocation

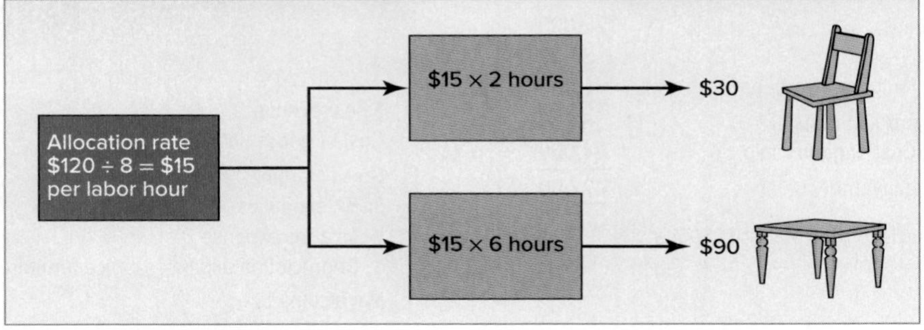

Since indirect costs cannot be effectively traced to products, they are normally assigned to products using **cost allocation,** a process of dividing a total cost into parts and assigning the parts to relevant cost objects. To illustrate, suppose that production workers spend an eight-hour day making a chair and a table. The chair requires two hours to complete and the table requires six hours. Now suppose that $120 of utilities cost is consumed during the day. How much of the $120 should be assigned to each piece of furniture? The utility cost cannot be directly traced to each specific piece of furniture, but the piece of furniture that required more labor also likely consumed more of the utility cost. Using this line of reasoning, it is rational to allocate the utility cost to the two pieces of furniture based on *direct labor hours* at a rate of $15 per hour ($120 ÷ 8 hours). The chair would be assigned $30 ($15 per hour × 2 hours) of the utility cost and the table would be assigned the remaining $90 ($15 × 6 hours) of utility cost. The allocation of the utility cost is shown in Exhibit 1.10.

We discuss the details of cost allocation in a later chapter. For now, recognize that overhead costs are normally allocated to products rather than traced directly to them.

Manufacturing Product Cost Summary

As explained, the cost of a product made by a manufacturing company is normally composed of three categories: direct materials, direct labor, and manufacturing overhead. Relevant information about these three cost components is summarized in Exhibit 1.11.

Answers to The Curious Accountant

As you have seen, accounting for depreciation related to manufacturing assets is different from accounting for depreciation for nonmanufacturing assets. Depreciation on the checkout equipment at Target is recorded as depreciation expense. Depreciation on manufacturing equipment at Skyrocket is considered a product cost. It is included first as part of the cost of inventory and eventually as part of the expense, cost of goods sold. Recording depreciation on manufacturing equipment as an inventory cost is simply another example of the matching principle, because the cost does not become an expense until revenue from the product sale is recognized.

EXHIBIT 1.11

Components of Manufacturing Product Cost

Component 1—Direct Raw Materials
Sometimes called *raw materials*. In addition to basic resources such as wood or metals, it can include manufactured parts. For example, engines, glass, and car tires can be considered as raw materials for an automotive manufacturer. If the amount of a material in a product is known, it can usually be classified as a direct material. The cost of direct materials can be easily traced to specific products.

Component 2—Direct Labor
The cost of wages paid to factory workers involved in hands-on contact with the products being manufactured. If the amount of time employees worked on a product can be determined, this cost can usually be classified as direct labor. Like direct materials, labor costs must be easily traced to a specific product in order to be classified as a direct cost.

Component 3—Manufacturing Overhead
Costs that cannot be easily traced to specific products. Accordingly, these costs are called *indirect costs*. They can include but are not limited to the following:

1. Indirect materials such as glue, nails, paper, and oil. Indeed, note that indirect materials used in the production process may not appear in the finished product. An example is a chemical solvent used to clean products during the production process but not a component material found in the final product.
2. Indirect labor such as the cost of salaries paid to production supervisors, inspectors, and maintenance personnel.
3. Rental cost for manufacturing facilities and equipment.
4. Utility costs.
5. Depreciation.
6. Security.
7. The cost of preparing equipment for the manufacturing process (i.e., setup costs).
8. Maintenance cost for the manufacturing facility and equipment.

UPSTREAM, MIDSTREAM, AND DOWNSTREAM COSTS

LO 1-4

Compare the treatment of upstream, midstream, and downstream costs in manufacturing, service, and merchandising companies.

Accountants frequently classify cost into three categories including (1) upstream, (2) midstream, and (3) downstream costs. The following section explains the treatment of these costs in manufacturing, service, and merchandising companies.

Cost Classification in Manufacturing Companies

For manufacturing companies, **midstream costs** are composed of the costs incurred in the process of making products including direct materials, direct labor, and manufacturing overhead. **Upstream costs** are costs that are incurred prior to manufacturing process including research and development costs and product design costs. **Downstream costs** are costs incurred after the manufacturing process including marketing, distribution, and customer services. A summary of this cost classification scheme as it relates to an automobile manufacturing company is shown in Exhibit 1.12.

Note that the upstream, midstream, and downstream costs of one company can become the midstream costs of another company. For example, the upstream, midstream, and downstream costs of a steel manufacturing company are passed on as a midstream cost (direct materials) to an auto parts manufacturing company when it purchases steel. Likewise, the upstream, midstream, and downstream costs of the auto parts company are passed on to an automobile manufacturing company as part of its midstream (direct materials) costs when it

EXHIBIT 1.12

Upstream Costs:

- Research and development
- Product design

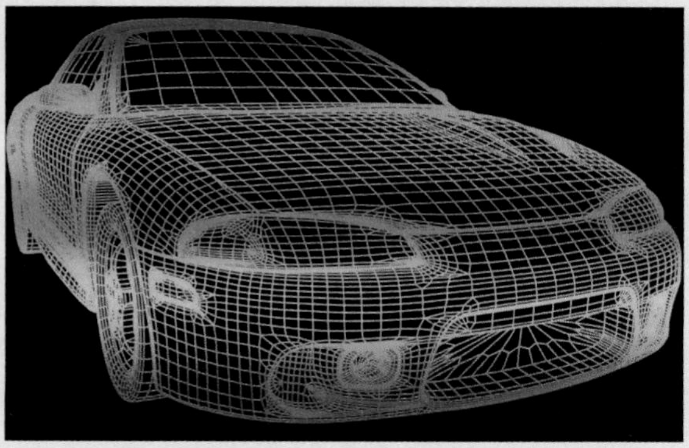

©Science Photo Library/Getty Images

Midstream Costs:

- Direct materials
- Direct labor
- Manufacturing overhead

©Monty Rakusen/Getty Images

Downstream Costs:

- Marketing
- Distribution
- Customer service

©John Lund/Marc Romanelli/Blend Images LLC

purchases auto parts. Also, note that the same type of cost can be classified as an upstream, midstream, or downstream cost. For example, salaries of a researcher may be classified as an upstream cost, while salaries of a production worker are classified as midstream costs, and salaries of a salesperson are classified as a downstream cost.

Generally accepted accounting principles (GAAP) require midstream costs to be reported separately from upstream and downstream costs on public financial statements. More specifically, the midstream costs (direct materials, direct labor, and manufacturing overhead) are classified as product costs and are expensed as cost of goods sold at the time goods are sold. In contrast, upstream and downstream cost are classified as general, selling, and administrative expenses and are expensed in the period they are incurred. In general, cost of goods sold is subtracted from sales revenue to determine the amount of gross margin and then upstream and downstream costs are subtracted from gross margin to determine the amount of net income. The format of a typical GAAP-based income statement is shown in Exhibit 1.13.

EXHIBIT 1.13

Sales revenue
– Cost of goods sold (midstream costs)
= Gross margin
– General, selling, and administrative costs (upstream and downstream costs)
= Net income

Cost Classification in Service and Merchandising Companies

Companies are frequently classified as being service, merchandising, or manufacturing businesses. As the name implies, service organizations provide services, rather than physical products, to consumers. For example, St. Jude Children's Hospital provides treatment programs aimed at healing patient diseases. Other common service providers include public accountants, lawyers, restaurants, dry cleaning establishments, and lawn care companies. Merchandising businesses are sometimes called retail or wholesale companies; they sell goods to other companies. The Home Depot Inc.; Costco Wholesale Corporation, and Best Buy Co. Inc., are merchandising companies. Manufacturing companies make the goods they sell to their customers. Toyota Motor Corporation; Texaco Inc., and American Standard Companies Inc., are manufacturing businesses.

Do service and merchandising companies incur materials, labor, and overhead costs? Yes; for example, Wendy's has materials costs (meat, potatoes, etc.), labor costs (cooks, packaging staff), and overhead (depreciation on equipment). Can the costs incurred by service and merchandising companies be classified as being upstream, midstream, and downstream? Yes. Continuing the Wendy's example, the company incurs research and development costs to produce its recipes and to find new locations (upstream costs); meat, labor, and overhead costs to make its food products (midstream costs); and sales staff and janitorial salaries and costs incurred to provide space for customers to consume their food (downstream costs).

So how do manufacturing companies differ from service and merchandising businesses? ***The primary difference between manufacturing entities and service companies is that the finished products provided by service companies are consumed immediately.*** For example, advice from a doctor is being consumed as it is being delivered to the patient. In contrast, products made by manufacturing companies can be held in the form of inventory until they are sold to consumers.

While merchandising companies frequently hold inventory, they differ from manufacturing companies in that they do not make the products they sell. Rather, they buy finished goods from suppliers and simply hold those products until they are delivered to customers. Indeed, most labor and overhead costs incurred by merchandising companies result from providing assistance to customers. These costs are normally treated as selling, general, and administrative expenses rather than accumulated in inventory accounts. This is why merchandising companies are often viewed as service companies rather than considered a separate business category.

The important point to remember is that all business managers are expected to control costs, improve quality, and increase productivity. Like managers of manufacturing companies, managers of service and merchandising businesses can benefit from the analysis of the cost of satisfying their customers. For example, Wendy's, a service company, can benefit from knowing how much a hamburger costs in the same manner that Bayer Corporation, a manufacturing company, benefits from knowing the cost of a bottle of aspirin.

CHECK YOURSELF 1.3

The cost of making a Burger King hamburger includes the cost of materials, labor, and overhead. Does this mean that Burger King is a manufacturing company?

Answer No, Burger King is not a manufacturing company. It is a service company because its products are consumed immediately. In contrast, there may be a considerable delay between the time the product of a manufacturing company is made and the time it is consumed. For example, it could be several months between the time Ford Motor Company makes an Explorer and the time the Explorer is ultimately sold to a customer. The primary difference between service and manufacturing companies is that manufacturing companies have inventories of products and service companies do not.

Managerial versus Financial Treatment of Upstream, Midstream, and Downstream Costs in Manufacturing Companies

To avoid having one system for external reporting and a different system for internal reporting, many companies use generally accepted accounting principles (GAAP) for internal as well as external reports. Unfortunately, the effort to maintain consistency between internal and external reporting systems can lead to mistakes in decision making. Specifically, managers may fail to include upstream and downstream costs when establishing sales prices and/or measuring product profitability. If upstream or downstream costs are not included in determining the cost of products, those products will be undercosted. This may lead managers to set prices that are below the total cost of producing and selling products, thereby leading to long-term losses rather than profitability.

CHECK YOURSELF 1.4

To illustrate, Warm Zero, Inc., makes down jackets. The manufacturing costs per unit include $30 direct materials, $35 direct labor, and $15 manufacturing overhead. These costs are based on a production and sales volume of 4,000 units. Advertising costs amounted to $50,000. Research and development cost for the cloth materials used in the jackets amounted to $60,000. Companywide administrative costs amounted to $90,000. Fashion design costs amounted to $40,000. To be competitive Warm Zero's management team used industry standards to establish the sales price at 160 percent of GAAP-defined product cost.

Required

a. Determine the total amount of upstream costs.

b. Determine the total amount of downstream costs.

c. Determine the total amount of midstream costs.

d. Determine the sales price per unit.

e. Prepare a GAAP-based income statement.

f. Provide a plausible explanation as to why the company incurred the loss shown on the income statement prepared to satisfy requirement *e*. (*Hint:* Calculate the full cost of making and selling the jackets.)

Answer

a. Upstream costs = $60,000 research and development + $40,000 fashion design = $100,000

b. Downstream costs = $50,000 advertising + $90,000 administrative costs = $140,000

c. Midstream costs = ($30 direct materials + $35 direct labor + $15 manufacturing overhead) × 4,000 units = $320,000

d. Sales price = GAAP-defined product cost × 160% = [($30 direct materials + $35 direct labor + $15 manufacturing overhead) × 1.6] = $128

e.

Sales revenue ($128 price × 4,000 jackets)	$ 512,000
Cost of goods sold ($80 cost × 4,000)	(320,000)
Gross margin	192,000
General, selling, and administrative costs	
Upstream costs (R&D and design)	(100,000)
Downstream costs (administrative and advertising)	(140,000)
Net loss	(48,000)

f. It appears that management failed to give appropriate consideration to upstream and downstream costs when pricing the product. Only the GAAP-based product cost was used to determine the price. The total cost of making a down jacket is upstream cost + midstream cost + downstream cost. In this case, total cost per unit includes:

Midstream cost = ($30 direct materials + $35 direct labor + $15 manufacturing overhead) = $80

Upstream cost = ($100,000 R&D and design) ÷ 4,000 units = $25

Downstream cost = ($140,000 administrative and advertising) ÷ 4,000 units = $35

Total cost = $80 midstream + $25 upstream + $35 downstream = $140

Note that the selling price of $128 is below the total cost per unit of $140. This explains the loss incurred by the company.

JUST-IN-TIME INVENTORY

LO 1-5

Show how just-in-time inventory can increase profitability.

Companies attempt to minimize the amount of inventory they maintain because of the high cost of holding it. Many **inventory holding costs** are obvious: financing, warehouse space, supervision, theft, damage, and obsolescence. Other costs are hidden: diminished motivation, sloppy work, inattentive attitudes, and increased production time.

Many businesses have been able to simultaneously reduce their inventory holding costs and increase customer satisfaction by making products available **just in time (JIT)** for customer consumption. For example, hamburgers that are cooked to order are fresher and more individualized than those that are prepared in advance and stored until a customer places an order. Many fast-food restaurants have discovered that JIT systems lead not only to greater customer satisfaction but also to lower costs through reduced waste.

Just-in-Time Illustration

To illustrate the benefits of a JIT system, consider Paula Elliot, a student at a large urban university. She helps support herself by selling flowers. Three days each week, Paula drives to a florist, purchases 25 single-stem roses, returns to the school, and sells the flowers to individuals from a location on a local street corner. She pays $2 per rose and sells each one for $3. Some days she does not have enough flowers to meet customer demand. Other days, she must discard one or two unsold flowers; she believes quality is important and refuses to sell flowers that are not fresh. During May, she purchased 300 roses and sold 280. She calculated her driving cost to be $45. Exhibit 1.14 displays Paula's May income statement.

EXHIBIT 1.14

Income Statement for May

Sales revenue (280 units × $3 per unit)	$ 840
Cost of goods sold (280 units × $2 per unit)	(560)
Gross margin	280
Driving expense	(45)
Excess inventory waste (20 units × 2)	(40)
Net income	$ 195

After studying just-in-time inventory systems in her managerial accounting class, Paula decided to apply the concepts to her small business. She *reengineered* her distribution system by

EXHIBIT 1.15

Income Statement for June

Sales revenue (310 units × $3 per unit)	$ 930
Cost of goods sold (310 units × $2 per unit)	(620)
Gross margin	310
Driving expense	0
Net income	$ 310

purchasing her flowers from a florist within walking distance of her sales location. She had considered purchasing from this florist earlier but had rejected the idea because the florist's regular selling price of $2.25 per rose was too high. After learning about *most-favored customer status,* she developed a strategy to get a price reduction. By guaranteeing that she would buy at least 30 roses per week, she was able to convince the local florist to match her current cost of $2.00 per rose. The local florist agreed that she could make purchases in batches of any size so long as the total amounted to at least 30 per week. Under this arrangement, Paula was able to buy roses *just in time* to meet customer demand. Each day she purchased a small number of flowers. When she ran out, she simply returned to the florist for additional ones.

The JIT system also enabled Paula to eliminate the cost of the *nonvalue-added activity* of driving to her former florist. Customer satisfaction actually improved because no one was ever turned away because of the lack of inventory. In June, Paula was able to buy and sell 310 roses with no waste and no driving expense. The June income statement is shown in Exhibit 1.15.

Paula was ecstatic about her $115 increase in profitability ($310 in June − $195 in May = $115 increase), but she was puzzled about the exact reasons for the change. She had saved $40 (20 flowers × $2 each) by avoiding waste and eliminated $45 of driving expenses. These two factors explained only $85 ($40 waste + $45 driving expense) of the $115 increase. What had caused the remaining $30 ($115 − $85) increase in profitability? Paula asked her accounting professor to help her identify the remaining $30 difference.

The professor explained that May sales had suffered from *lost opportunities*. Recall that under the earlier inventory system, Paula had to turn away some prospective customers because she sold out of flowers before all customers were served. Sales increased from 280 roses in May to 310 roses in June. A likely explanation for the 30 unit difference (310 − 280) is that customers who would have purchased flowers in May were unable to do so because of a lack of availability. May's sales suffered from the lost opportunity to earn a gross margin of $1 per flower on 30 roses, a $30 **opportunity cost.** This opportunity cost is the missing link in explaining the profitability difference between May and June. The total $115 difference consists of (1) $40 savings from waste elimination, (2) $45 savings from eliminating driving expense, and (3) opportunity cost of $30. The subject of opportunity cost has widespread application and is discussed in more depth in subsequent chapters of the text.

CHECK YOURSELF 1.5

A strike at a General Motors brake plant caused an almost immediate shutdown of many of the company's assembly plants. What could have caused such a rapid and widespread shutdown?

Answer A rapid and widespread shutdown could have occurred because General Motors uses a just-in-time inventory system. With a JIT inventory system, there is no stockpile of inventory to draw on when strikes or other forces disrupt inventory deliveries. This illustrates a potential negative effect of using a just-in-time inventory system.

CORPORATE GOVERNANCE

LO 1-6

Identify the key components of corporate governance.

Corporate governance is the set of relationships between the board of directors, management, shareholders, auditors, and other stakeholders that determines how a company is operated. Until recently, corporations were generally free to govern themselves. However, several high-profile scandals have motivated governmental authorities to enact legislation designed to influence corporate governance. This section of the chapter examines the factors affecting corporate governance. We examine the motives and means of management corruption. Further, we introduce the mechanisms for self-control, including codes of ethics and internal controls. Finally, we discuss recent legislation designed to influence managerial responsibility for financial reporting.

Management accountants are at the forefront of corporate governance. They are the guardians of the information used to report on the financial condition of their companies. The information they prepare and analyze is used by the board of directors and company executives to formulate the company's operating strategy. Indeed, management accountants constitute the intelligence function of corporate governance. Scandals usually begin with schemes to manipulate a company's financial reports and end when the falsification is so great it becomes obvious the reports no longer represent reality. The appropriate management of the information function is a highly effective force against corrupt governance. It is little wonder why recent legislation requires the chief financial officer along with the chief executive officer to personally certify that the company's annual report does not contain false statements or omit significant facts.

The Motive to Manipulate

Many managers are judged on their company's financial statements or the company's stock price–which is determined, in part, by the financial statements. Managers are rewarded for strong financial statements with promotions, pay raises, bonuses, and stock options. Weak financials can result in a manager being passed over for promotions, demoted, or even fired. It is little wonder that some executives are tempted to manipulate financial statements.

To illustrate implications of statement manipulation, consider the events experienced by Marion Manufacturing Company (MMC) during its first year of operations. All transactions are cash transactions.

1. MMC was started when it acquired $12,000 from issuing common stock.
2. MMC incurred $4,000 of costs to design its product and plan the manufacturing process.
3. MMC incurred specifically identifiable product costs (materials, labor, and overhead) of $8,000 to make 1,000 units of product, resulting in a cost per unit of $8 ($8,000 ÷ 1,000 units).
4. MMC sold 700 units of inventory for $18 each.

Exhibit 1.16 displays a balance sheet and income statement prepared under the following two scenarios.

Scenario 1: The $4,000 of design and planning costs are classified as selling and administrative expenses.

Scenario 2: The $4,000 of design and planning costs are classified as product costs, meaning they are first accumulated in the Inventory account and then expensed when the goods are sold. Given that MMC made 1,000 units and sold 700 units of inventory, 70% (700 ÷ 1,000) of the design cost has passed through the Inventory account into the Cost of Goods Sold account, leaving 30 percent (300 ÷ 1,000) remaining in the Inventory account.

EXHIBIT 1.16

Financial Statements under Alternative Cost Classification Scenarios

Income Statements	Scenario 1	Scenario 2
Sales revenue (700 × $18)	$12,600	$12,600
Cost of goods sold	(5,600)[1]	(8,400)[3]
Gross margin	7,000	4,200
Selling and administrative expense	(4,000)	0
Net income	$ 3,000	$ 4,200
Balance Sheets		
Assets		
Cash	$12,600	$12,600
Inventory	2,400[2]	3,600[4]
Total assets	$15,000	$16,200
Stockholders' equity		
Common stock	$12,000	$12,000
Retained earnings	3,000	4,200
Total stockholders' equity	$15,000	$16,200

[1] 700 units × $8 per unit = $5,600
[2] 300 units × $8 per unit = $2,400
[3] [$5,600 + ($4,000 × 0.70)] = $8,400
[4] [$2,400 + ($4,000 × 0.30)] = $3,600

Statement Differences

Comparing the financial statements prepared under Scenario 1 with those prepared under Scenario 2 reveals the following:

1. There are no selling and administrative expenses under Scenario 2. The design cost was treated as a product cost and placed into the Inventory account rather than being expensed.
2. Cost of goods sold is $2,800 ($4,000 design cost × 0.70) higher under Scenario 2.
3. Net income is $1,200 higher under Scenario 2 ($4,000 understated expense − $2,800 overstated cost of goods sold).
4. Ending inventory is $1,200 ($4,000 design cost × 0.30) higher under Scenario 2.

Practical Implications

The financial statement differences shown in Exhibit 1.16 are *timing differences*. When MMC sells the remaining 300 units of inventory, the $1,200 of design and planning costs included in inventory under Scenario 2 will be expensed through cost of goods sold. In other words, once the entire inventory is sold, total expenses and retained earnings will be the same under both scenarios. Initially recording cost in an inventory account only delays eventual expense recognition. However, the temporary effects on the financial statements can influence the (1) availability of financing, (2) motivations of management, and (3) timing of income tax payments.

Availability of Financing. The willingness of creditors and investors to provide capital to a business is influenced by their expectations of the business's future financial performance. In general, more favorable financial statements enhance a company's ability to obtain financing from creditors or investors.

Management Motivation. Financial statement results might affect executive compensation. For example, assume that Marion Manufacturing adopted a management incentive plan that provides a bonus pool equal to 10 percent of net income. In Scenario 1, managers would receive \$300 (\$3,000 × 0.10). In Scenario 2, however, managers would receive \$420 (\$4,200 × 0.10). Do not be deceived by the small numbers used for convenience in the example. We could illustrate with millions of dollars just as well as with hundreds of dollars. Managers would clearly favor Scenario 2. In fact, managers might be tempted to misclassify costs to manipulate the content of financial statements.

Income Tax Considerations. Since income tax expense is calculated as a designated percentage of taxable income, managers seek to minimize taxes by reporting the minimum amount of taxable income. Scenario 1 in Exhibit 1.16 depicts the most favorable tax condition. In other words, with respect to taxes, managers prefer to classify costs as expenses rather than assets. The Internal Revenue Service is responsible for enforcing the proper classification of costs. Disagreements between the Internal Revenue Service and taxpayers are ultimately settled in federal courts.

Statement of Ethical Professional Practice

The preceding discussion provides some insight into conflicts of interest management accountants might face. It is tempting to misclassify a cost if doing so will significantly increase a manager's bonus. Management accountants must be prepared not only to make difficult choices between legitimate alternatives but also to face conflicts of a more troubling nature, such as pressure to:

1. Undertake duties they have not been trained to perform competently.
2. Disclose confidential information.
3. Compromise their integrity through falsification, embezzlement, bribery, and so on.
4. Issue biased, misleading, or incomplete reports.

To provide management accountants with guidance for ethical conduct, the Institute of Management Accountants (IMA) issued the *Statement of Ethical Professional Practice,* which is shown in Exhibit 1.17. Management accountants are also frequently required to abide by organizational codes of ethics. Failure to adhere to professional and organizational ethical standards can lead to personal disgrace, loss of employment, or imprisonment.

The Fraud Triangle

Unfortunately, it takes more than a code of conduct to stop fraud. People frequently engage in activities that they know are unethical or even criminal. The auditing profession has determined that the following three elements are typically present when fraud occurs:

1. The availability of an *opportunity.*
2. The existence of some form of *pressure* leading to an incentive.
3. The capacity to *rationalize.*

The three elements are frequently arranged in the shape of a triangle as shown in Exhibit 1.18.

Opportunity is shown at the head of the triangle because without opportunity, fraud could not exist. The most effective way to reduce opportunities for ethical or criminal misconduct is to implement an effective set of internal controls. *Internal controls* are policies and procedures that a business implements to reduce opportunities for fraud and to ensure that its objectives will be accomplished. Specific controls are tailored to meet the individual needs of particular businesses. For example, banks use elaborate vaults to protect cash and safety deposit boxes, but universities have little use for this type of equipment. Even so, many of the same procedures are used by a wide variety of businesses.

EXHIBIT 1.17

Statement of Ethical Professional Practice

Members of IMA shall behave ethically. A commitment to ethical professional practice includes overarching principles that express our values, and standards that guide our conduct. IMA's overarching ethical principles include: Honesty, Fairness, Objectivity, and Responsibility. Members shall act in accordance with these principles and shall encourage others within their organizations to adhere to them. A member's failure to comply with the following standards may result in disciplinary action.

Competence Each member has a responsibility to

- Maintain an appropriate level of professional expertise by continually developing knowledge and skills.
- Perform professional duties in accordance with relevant laws, regulations, and technical standards.
- Provide decision support information and recommendations that are accurate, clear, concise, and timely.
- Recognize and communicate professional limitations or other constraints that would preclude responsible judgment or successful performance of an activity.

Confidentiality Each member has a responsibility to

- Keep information confidential except when disclosure is authorized or legally required.
- Inform all relevant parties regarding appropriate use of confidential information. Monitor subordinates' activities to ensure compliance.
- Refrain from using confidential information for unethical or illegal advantage.

Integrity Each member has a responsibility to

- Mitigate actual conflicts of interest and avoid apparent conflicts of interest. Advise all parties of any potential conflicts.
- Refrain from engaging in any conduct that would prejudice carrying out duties ethically.
- Abstain from engaging in or supporting any activity that might discredit the profession.

Credibility Each member has a responsibility to

- Communicate information fairly and objectively.
- Disclose all relevant information that could reasonably be expected to influence an intended user's understanding of the reports, analyses, or recommendations.
- Disclose delays or deficiencies in information, timeliness, processing, or internal controls in conformance with organization policy and/or applicable law.

Resolution of Ethical Conflict In applying these standards, you may encounter problems identifying unethical behavior or resolving an ethical conflict. When faced with ethical issues, follow your organization's established policies on the resolution of such conflict. If these policies do not resolve the ethical conflict, consider the following courses of action:

- Discuss the issue with your immediate supervisor except when it appears that the supervisor is involved. In that case, present the issue to the next level. If you cannot achieve a satisfactory resolution, submit the issue to the next management level. Communication of such problems to authorities or individuals not employed or engaged by the organization is not considered appropriate, unless you believe there is a clear violation of the law.
- Clarify relevant ethical issues by initiating a confidential discussion with an IMA Ethics Counselor or other impartial advisor to obtain a better understanding of possible courses of action.
- Consult your own attorney as to legal obligations and rights concerning the ethical conflict.

Source: Institute of Management Accountants, Inc.

EXHIBIT 1.18

The Fraud Triangle

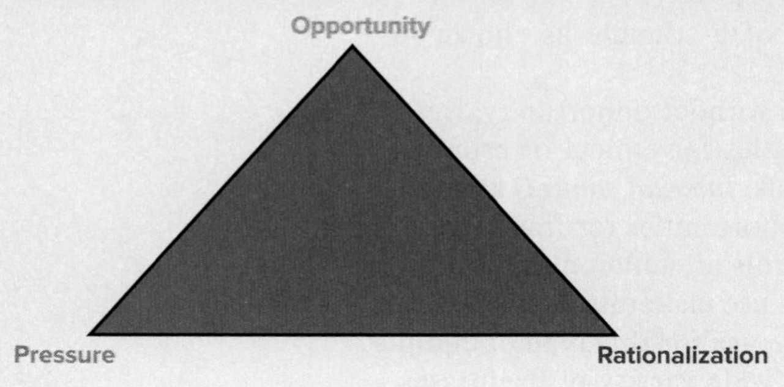

Exhibit 1.19 contains a summary of many of the internal control policies and procedures that have gained widespread acceptance.

Only a few employees turn to the dark side even when internal control is weak and opportunities abound. So, what causes one person to commit fraud and another to remain honest? The second element of the fraud triangle recognizes *pressure* as a key ingredient of misconduct. A manager who is told to either make the numbers or be fired is more likely to cheat than one who is told to tell it like it is. Pressure can come from a variety of sources, including:

- Personal vices such as drug addiction, gambling, and promiscuity.
- Intimidation from superiors.

EXHIBIT 1.19

Common Internal Control Practices

Internal Control Practice	Explanation
Separating duties	Separating the duties necessary to complete a task and assigning the separated duties to two or more employees reduces the opportunity for either employee to defraud the company. It would require collusion between the two employees.
Hiring competent personnel	Cheap labor is not a bargain if the employees are incompetent. Employees should be properly trained and have a record that attests to personal integrity.
Bonding employees	Employees in positions of trust should be bonded through insurance policies that protect a company from losses caused by employee dishonesty.
Requiring extended absences	Forcing extended absences (such as vacations) creates an opportunity for the temporary replacement employee to check the work of the absent employee. Fraud is difficult to cover up if you are not present to do so.
Establishing clear lines of authority and responsibility	Employees tend to be more zealous in supporting company policies when they have clear authority to exercise enforcement. Further, they take their work more seriously when they realize that they cannot shirk responsibility.
Using prenumbered documents	Missing documents become apparent when there are gaps in a recorded sequence of numbers. For example, a stolen check would become apparent if a check register omits a check number.
Establishing physical controls	Keeping money in a safe; holding inventory in locked warehouses; and bolting computers to a desk are examples of using physical controls designed to protect assets.
Performing evaluations at regular intervals	Knowing that inventory will be counted on a regular basis encourages the inventory control manager to maintain documents that support the actual balance of inventory on hand. Similarly, verifying the mileage on a car will encourage employees to use company-owned vehicles for legitimate business purposes. Regular evaluations and examinations are strong deterrents to the inappropriate utilization of company-owned assets.

- Personal debt from credit cards, consumer loans, mortgage loans, or poor investments.
- Family expectations to provide a standard of living that is beyond one's capabilities.
- Business failure caused by poor decision making or temporary factors such as a poor economy.
- Loyalty or trying to be agreeable.

The third and final element of the fraud triangle is *rationalization*. Few individuals think of themselves as evil. They develop rationalizations to justify their misconduct. Common rationalizations include the following:

- Everybody does it.
- They are not paying me enough. I'm taking only what I deserve.
- I'm only borrowing the money. I'll pay it back.
- The company can afford it. Look what it is paying the officers.
- I'm taking what my family needs to live like everyone else.

Most people are able to resist pressure and the temptation to rationalize ethical or legal misconduct. However, some people will yield to temptation. What can companies do to

REALITY BYTES

©Purestock/SuperStock

Unethical behavior occurs in most large organizations, but some organizations seem to have fewer ethics problems than others. In its 2015 report, ***The State of Ethics in Large Companies,*** the Ethics Resource Center reported its findings of the occurrences and reporting of unethical behavior in large American corporations, based on a survey it conducts every two years.

Forty-five percent of those surveyed reported having observed unethical conduct during the past year. This was the lowest level reported in the 17 years the survey has been conducted. Sixty-five percent of those who said they had observed misconduct went on to report it to their employer. However, fear of retaliation for reporting misconduct was a concern. Of respondents who said they had reported misconduct at their companies, 22 percent said they had experienced some form of retaliation, such as being excluded from decision making.

Overall, 51 percent of individuals surveyed reported having observed unethical conduct at their company. However, in companies that had an effective ethics program, only 33 percent reported seeing misconduct, while 61 percent of those in companies without such programs reported seeing misconduct. Employees in companies with effective programs were also much more likely to report what they saw than those in other companies, 87 percent versus 32 percent. Additionally, when misconduct was reported, only 4 percent of employees in companies with effective programs reported retaliation, compared to 59 percent of those in other companies.

The definition of ethical misconduct used in the study was quite broad, and included misuse of company time, abusive behavior, abusing company resources, lying to employees, and violating the company's policies for using the Internet.

For more information go to www.ethics.org.

protect themselves from unscrupulous characters? The answer lies in personal integrity. The best indicator of personal integrity is past performance. Accordingly, companies must exercise due care in performing appropriate background investigations before hiring people to fill positions of trust.

Sarbanes–Oxley Act

In spite of ethics training and accounting controls, fraud and its devastating consequences persist. Enron, WorldCom, and HealthSouth are examples of massive scandals that destroyed or crippled major U.S. corporations in recent years. These high-profile cases led government officials to conclude that the force of law would be necessary to restore and maintain confidence in the capital markets. The **Sarbanes-Oxley (SOX) Act,** which became effective July 30, 2002, provides the muscle that Congress hopes will deter future fiascos. SOX affects four groups including management, boards of directors, external auditors, and the Public Company Accounting Oversight Board (PCAOB). In this text, we focus on how SOX affects corporate management. While extensive coverage of SOX is beyond the scope of this text, all management accountants should be aware of the following:

- SOX holds the chief executive officer (CEO) and the chief financial officer (CFO) responsible for the establishment and enforcement of a strong set of internal controls. Along with its annual report, companies are required to report on the effectiveness of their internal controls. Also, the company's external auditors are required to attest to the accuracy of the internal controls report.
- SOX charges the CEO and the CFO with the ultimate responsibility for the accuracy of the company's financial statements and the accompanying notes. Even though lower-level managers will likely prepare the annual report, the CEO and CFO are required to certify that they have reviewed the report and that, to their knowledge, the report does not contain false statements or significant omissions. An intentional misrepresentation is punishable by a fine of up to $5 million and imprisonment of up to 20 years.

FOCUS ON INTERNATIONAL ISSUES

FINANCIAL ACCOUNTING VERSUS MANAGERIAL ACCOUNTING—AN INTERNATIONAL PERSPECTIVE

©Adam Roundtree/Bloomberg/Getty Images

This chapter has already explained some of the conceptual differences between financial and managerial accounting, but these differences have implications for international businesses as well. With respect to financial accounting, publicly traded companies in most countries must follow the generally accepted accounting principles (GAAP) for their country, but these rules can vary from country to country. Generally, companies that are audited under the auditing standards of the United States follow the standards established by the Financial Accounting Standards Board (FASB). Most companies located outside the United States follow the standards established by the International Accounting Standards Board (IASB). For example, the United States is one of very few countries whose GAAP allow the use of the LIFO inventory cost flow assumption.

Conversely, most of the managerial accounting concepts introduced in this course can be used by businesses in any country. For example, *activity-based costing (ABC)* is a topic addressed in Chapter 5 and is used by many companies in the United States. Additionally, while accrual-based earnings can differ depending on whether a company uses U.S. GAAP or IFRS, cash flow will not. As you will learn in this course, managerial accounting decisions often focus on cash flow versus accrual-based income. Therefore, managerial accounting concepts are more universal than financial accounting rules.

- SOX requires management to establish a code of ethics and to file reports on the code in the company's annual 10-K report filed with the Securities and Exchange Commission.
- SOX demands that management establish a hotline and other mechanisms for the anonymous reporting of fraudulent activities. Further, SOX prohibits companies from punishing whistleblowers, employees who legally report corporate misconduct.

The accounting profession and government authorities are becoming increasingly intolerant of unethical conduct and illegal activity. A single mistake can jeopardize an accountant's career. A person guilty of white-collar crime loses the opportunity for white-collar employment. Second chances are rarely granted.

A Look Back <<

Managerial accounting focuses on the information needs of *internal* users, while *financial accounting* focuses on the information needs of *external* users. Managerial accounting uses economic, operating, and nonfinancial, as well as financial, data. Managerial accounting information is local (pertains to the company's subunits), is limited by cost/benefit considerations, is more concerned with relevance and timeliness, and is future-oriented. Financial accounting information, on the other hand, is more global than managerial accounting information. It supplies information that applies to the whole company. Financial accounting is regulated by numerous authorities, is characterized by objectivity, is focused on reliability and accuracy, and is historical in nature.

Both managerial and financial accounting are concerned with product costing. Financial accountants need product cost information to determine the amount of inventory reported on the balance sheet and the amount of cost of goods sold reported on the income statement. Managerial accountants need to know the cost of products for pricing decisions and for control and evaluation purposes. When determining unit product costs, managers use the average cost per unit. Determining the actual cost of each product requires an unreasonable amount of time and record keeping and it makes no difference in product pricing and product cost control decisions.

Product costs are the costs incurred to make products: the costs of direct materials, direct labor, and overhead. *Overhead costs* are product costs that cannot be cost effectively traced to a product; therefore, they are assigned to products using *cost allocation*. Overhead costs include indirect materials, indirect labor, depreciation, rent, and utilities for manufacturing facilities. Product costs are first accumulated in an asset account (Inventory). They are expensed as cost of goods sold in the period the inventory is sold. The difference between sales revenue and cost of goods sold is called *gross margin*.

Selling, general, and administrative costs are classified separately from product costs. They are subtracted from gross margin to determine net income. Selling, general, and administrative costs can be divided into two categories. Costs incurred before the manufacturing process begins (research and development costs) are *upstream costs*. Costs incurred after manufacturing is complete (transportation) are *downstream costs*.

Service companies, like manufacturing companies, incur materials, labor, and overhead costs, but the products provided by service companies are consumed immediately. Therefore, service company product costs are not accumulated in an Inventory account.

A *code of ethical conduct* is needed in the accounting profession because accountants hold positions of trust and face conflicts of interest. In recognition of the temptations that accountants face, the IMA has issued the *Statement of Ethical Professional Practice,* which provides accountants guidance in resisting temptations and in making difficult decisions.

The Appendix discusses emerging trends such as *just-in-time inventory* and *activity-based management,* methods that many companies have used to reengineer their production and delivery systems to eliminate waste, reduce errors, and minimize costs. Activity-based management seeks to eliminate or reduce *nonvalue-added activities* and to create new *value-added activities*. Just-in-time inventory seeks to reduce inventory holding costs and to lower prices for customers by making inventory available just in time for customer consumption.

>> A Look Forward

In addition to distinguishing costs by product versus SG&A classification, other classifications can be used to facilitate managerial decision making. In the next chapter, costs are classified according to the *behavior* they exhibit when the number of units of product increases or decreases (volume of activity changes). You will learn to distinguish between costs that vary with activity volume changes versus costs that remain fixed with activity volume changes. You will learn not only to recognize *cost behavior* but also how to use such recognition to evaluate business risk and opportunity.

APPENDIX

Using Total Quality Management (TQM) and Activity-Based Management (ABM) to Reengineer Production and Delivery Systems

LO 1-7

Identify the key features of total quality management (TQM) and activity-based management (ABM).

Global competition has forced many companies to reengineer their production and delivery systems to eliminate waste, reduce errors, and minimize costs. A key ingredient of successful **reengineering** is benchmarking. **Benchmarking** involves identifying the **best practices** used by world-class competitors. By studying and mimicking these practices, a company uses benchmarking to implement highly effective and efficient operating methods. Best practices employed by world-class companies include total quality management (TQM), activity-based management (ABM), and value-added assessment.

Total Quality Management

To promote effective and efficient operations, many companies practice **total quality management (TQM).** TQM is a two-dimensional management philosophy using (1) a systematic problem-solving philosophy that encourages frontline workers to achieve *zero defects* and (2) an organizational commitment to achieving *customer satisfaction*. A key component of TQM is **continuous improvement,** an ongoing process through which employees strive to eliminate waste, reduce response time, minimize defects, and simplify the design and delivery of products and services to customers.

Activity-Based Management

Simple changes in perspective can have dramatic results. For example, imagine how realizing the world is round instead of flat changed the nature of travel. A recent change in perspective developing in management accounting is the realization that an organization cannot manage *costs*. Instead, it manages the *activities* that cause costs to be incurred. **Activities** represent the measures an organization takes to accomplish its goals.

The primary goal of all organizations is to provide products (goods and services) that their customers *value*. The sequence of activities used to provide products is called a **value chain. Activity-based management (ABM)** assesses the value chain to create new or refine existing **value-added activities** and to eliminate or reduce *nonvalue-added activities*. A value-added activity is any unit of work that contributes to a product's ability to satisfy customer needs. For example, cooking is an activity that adds value to food served to a hungry customer. **Nonvalue-added activities** are tasks undertaken that do not contribute to a product's ability to satisfy customer needs. Waiting for the oven to preheat so that food can be cooked does not add value. Most customers value cooked food, but they do not value waiting for it.

To illustrate, consider the value-added activities undertaken by a pizza restaurant. Begin with a customer who is hungry for pizza; certain activities must occur to satisfy that hunger. These activities are pictured in Exhibit 1.20. At a minimum, the restaurant must conduct research and development (devise a recipe), obtain raw materials (acquire the ingredients), manufacture the product (combine and bake the ingredients), market the product (advertise its availability), and deliver the product (transfer the pizza to the customer).

Businesses gain competitive advantages by adding activities that satisfy customer needs. For example, Domino's Pizza grew briskly by recognizing the value customers placed on the convenience of home pizza delivery. Alternatively, Little Caesar's has been highly successful by satisfying customers who value low prices. Other restaurants capitalize on customer values pertaining to taste, ambience, or location. Businesses can also gain competitive advantages by identifying and eliminating nonvalue-added activities, providing products of comparable quality at lower cost than competitors.

Value Chain Analysis across Companies

Comprehensive value chain analysis extends from obtaining raw materials to the ultimate disposition of finished products. It encompasses the activities performed not only by a particular organization but also by that organization's suppliers and those who service its

EXHIBIT 1.20

Value Chain

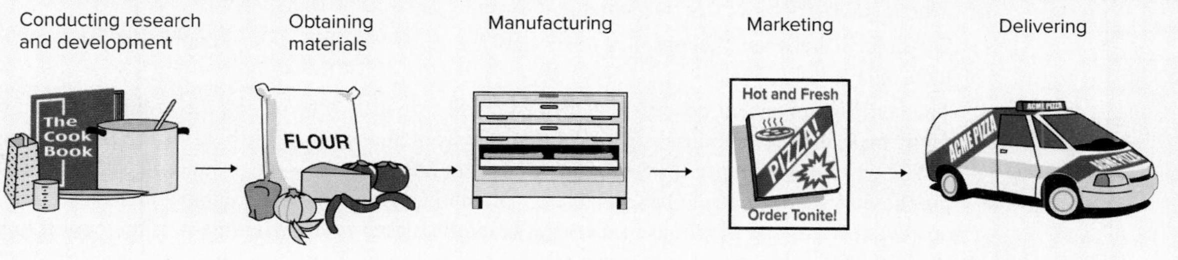

finished products. For example, PepsiCo must be concerned with the activities of the company that supplies the containers for its soft drinks as well as the retail companies that sell its products. If cans of Pepsi fail to open properly, the customer is more likely to blame PepsiCo than the supplier of the cans. Comprehensive value chain analysis can lead to identifying and eliminating nonvalue-added activities that occur between companies. For example, container producers could be encouraged to build manufacturing facilities near Pepsi's bottling factories, eliminating the nonvalue-added activity of transporting empty containers from the manufacturer to the bottling facility. The resulting cost savings benefits customers by reducing costs without affecting quality.

Video lectures and accompanying self-assessment quizzes are available in *Connect* for all learning objectives.

SELF-STUDY REVIEW PROBLEM

Tuscan Manufacturing Company makes a unique headset for use with mobile phones. During Year 1 Tuscan experienced the following accounting events. Other than the adjusting entries for depreciation, assume that all transactions are cash transactions.

1. Acquired $850,000 cash from the issue of common stock.
2. Paid $50,000 of research and development costs to develop the headset.
3. Paid $140,000 for the materials used to make headsets, all of which were started and completed during the year.
4. Paid salaries of $82,200 to selling and administrative employees.
5. Paid wages of $224,000 to production workers.
6. Paid $48,000 to purchase furniture used in selling and administrative offices.
7. Recognized depreciation on the office furniture. The furniture, acquired January 1, had an $8,000 estimated salvage value and a four-year useful life. The amount of depreciation is computed as [(Cost − Salvage) ÷ Useful life]. Specifically, [($48,000 − $8,000) ÷ 4 = $10,000].
8. Paid $65,000 to purchase manufacturing equipment.
9. Recognized depreciation on the manufacturing equipment. The equipment, acquired January 1 had a $5,000 estimated salvage value and a three-year useful life. The amount of depreciation is computed as [(Cost − Salvage) ÷ Useful life]. Specifically, [($65,000 − $5,000) ÷ 3 = $20,000].
10. Paid $136,000 for rent and utility costs on the manufacturing facility.
11. Paid $41,000 for inventory holding expenses for completed headsets (rental of warehouse space, salaries of warehouse personnel, and other general storage costs).
12. Tuscan started and completed 20,000 headset units during Year 1. The company sold 18,400 headsets at a price of $38 per unit.
13. Compute the average product cost per unit and recognize the appropriate amount of cost of goods sold.

Required

a. Show how these events affect the balance sheet and income statement by recording them in a horizontal financial statements model.

b. Prepare a GAAP-based income statement for the year.

c. Distinguish between the product costs and the upstream and downstream costs that Tuscan incurred.

d. The company president believes that Tuscan could save money by buying the inventory that it currently makes. The warehouse supervisor said that would not be possible because the purchase price of $27 per unit was above the $26 average cost per unit of making the product. Assuming that the purchased inventory would be available on demand, explain how the company president could be correct and why the warehouse supervisor could be biased in his assessment of the option to buy the inventory.

Solution to Requirement *a*

	Balance Sheet														Income Statement				
	Assets							=	Equity										
Event No.	Cash	+	Inventory	+	Office Furn.*	+	Manuf. Equip.*	=	Com. Stk.	+	Ret. Earn.		Rev.	—	Exp.	=	Net Inc.		
1	850,000	+	NA	+	NA	+	NA	=	850,000	+	NA		NA	—	NA	=	NA		
2	(50,000)	+	NA	+	NA	+	NA	=	NA	+	(50,000)		NA	—	50,000	=	(50,000)		
3	(140,000)	+	140,000	+	NA	+	NA	=	NA	+	NA		NA	—	NA	=	NA		
4	(82,200)	+	NA	+	NA	+	NA	=	NA	+	(82,200)		NA	—	82,200	=	(82,200)		
5	(224,000)	+	224,000	+	NA	+	NA	=	NA	+	NA		NA	—	NA	=	NA		
6	(48,000)	+	NA	+	48,000	+	NA	=	NA	+	NA		NA	—	NA	=	NA		
7	NA	+	NA	+	(10,000)	+	NA	=	NA	+	(10,000)		NA	—	10,000	=	(10,000)		
8	(65,000)	+	NA	+	NA	+	65,000	=	NA	+	NA		NA	—	NA	=	NA		
9	NA	+	20,000	+	NA	+	(20,000)	=	NA	+	NA		NA	—	NA	=	NA		
10	(136,000)	+	136,000	+	NA	+	NA	=	NA	+	NA		NA	—	NA	=	NA		
11	(41,000)	+	NA	+	NA	+	NA	=	NA	+	(41,000)		NA	—	41,000	=	(41,000)		
12	699,200	+	NA	+	NA	+	NA	=	NA	+	699,200		699,200	—	NA	=	699,200		
13	NA	+	(478,400)	+	NA	+	NA	=	NA	+	(478,400)		NA	—	478,400	=	(478,400)		
Totals	763,000	+	41,600	+	38,000	+	45,000	=	850,000	+	37,600		699,200	—	661,600	=	37,600		

*Negative amounts in these columns represent accumulated depreciation.

The average cost per unit of product is determined by dividing the total product cost by the number of headsets produced. Specifically, ($140,000 + $224,000 + $20,000 + $136,000) ÷ 20,000 = $26. Cost of goods sold is $478,400 ($26 × 18,400).

Solution to Requirement *b*

TUSCAN MANUFACTURING COMPANY Income Statement For the Year Ended December 31, Year 1	
Sales revenue (18,400 units × $38)	$ 699,200
Cost of goods sold (18,400 × $26)	(478,400)
Gross margin	220,800
R&D expenses	(50,000)
Selling and admin. salaries expense	(82,200)
Admin. depreciation expense	(10,000)
Inventory holding expense	(41,000)
Net income	$ 37,600

Solution to Requirement *c*

Inventory product costs (midstream costs) for manufacturing companies focus on the costs necessary to make the product. The cost of research and development (**Event 2**) occurs before the inventory is made and is therefore an upstream cost, not an inventory (product) cost. The inventory holding costs (**Event 11**) are incurred after the inventory has been made and are therefore downstream costs, not product costs. Selling costs (included in **Events 4 and 7**) are normally incurred after products have been made and are therefore usually classified as downstream costs. Administrative costs (also included in **Events 4 and 7**) are not related to making products and are therefore not classified as product costs. Administrative costs may be incurred before, during, or after products are made, so they may be classified as either upstream or downstream costs. Only the costs of materials, labor, and overhead that are actually incurred for the purpose of making goods (**Events 3, 5, 9, and 10**) are classified as product costs.

Solution to Requirement *d*

Since the merchandise would be available on demand, Tuscan could operate a just-in-time inventory system thereby eliminating the inventory holding expense. Since the additional cost to purchase is \$1 per unit (\$27 − \$26), it would cost Tuscan an additional \$20,000 (\$1 × 20,000 units) to purchase its product. However, the company would save \$41,000 of inventory holding expense. The warehouse supervisor could be biased by the fact that his job would be lost if the company purchased its products and thereby could eliminate the need for warehousing inventory. If Tuscan does not maintain inventory, it would not need a warehouse supervisor.

KEY TERMS

Activities 27
Activity-based management (ABM) 27
Average cost 6
Benchmarking 26
Best practices 26
Continuous improvement 27
Cost allocation 12
Cost-plus pricing 5
Direct labor 9
Direct raw materials 9
Downstream costs 13
Financial accounting 3
Financial Accounting Standards Board (FASB) 5
Finished Goods Inventory 6
Generally accepted accounting principles (GAAP) 5
Indirect costs 11
Inventory holding costs 17
Just in time (JIT) 17
Managerial accounting 3
Manufacturing overhead 11
Midstream costs 13
Nonvalue-added activities 27
Opportunity cost 18
Overhead 6
Period costs 11
Product cost 5
Product costing 5
Raw materials 9
Reengineering 26
Sarbanes–Oxley (SOX) Act 24
Securities and Exchange Commission (SEC) 5
Selling, general, and administrative costs (SG&A) 10
Total quality management (TQM) 26
Upstream costs 13
Value-added activity 27
Value-added principle 5
Value chain 27

QUESTIONS

1. What are some differences between financial and managerial accounting?
2. What does the value-added principle mean as it applies to managerial accounting information? Give an example of value-added information that may be included in managerial accounting reports but is not shown in publicly reported financial statements.
3. What are the two dimensions of a total quality management (TQM) program? Why is TQM being used in business practice? (Appendix)
4. How does product costing used in financial accounting differ from product costing used in managerial accounting?
5. What does the statement "costs can be assets or expenses" mean?
6. Why are the salaries of production workers accumulated in an inventory account instead of being expensed on the income statement?
7. How do product costs affect the financial statements? How does the classification of product cost (as an asset vs. an expense) affect net income?
8. What is an indirect cost? Provide examples of product costs that would be classified as indirect.
9. How does a product cost differ from a selling, general, and administrative cost? Give examples of each.
10. Why is cost classification important to managers?
11. What is cost allocation? Give an example of a cost that needs to be allocated.
12. How has the Institute of Management Accountants responded to the need for high standards of ethical conduct in the accounting profession?
13. What are some of the common ethical conflicts that accountants encounter?
14. What costs should be considered in determining the sales price of a product?
15. What is a just-in-time (JIT) inventory system? Name some inventory costs that can be eliminated or reduced by its use.
16. What does the term *reengineering* mean? Name some reengineering practices. (Appendix)
17. What does the term *activity-based management* mean? (Appendix)
18. What is a value chain? (Appendix)
19. What do the terms *value-added activity* and *nonvalue-added activity* mean? Provide an example of each type of activity. (Appendix)

MULTIPLE-CHOICE QUESTIONS

Multiple-choice questions are available in *Connect*.

EXERCISES—SERIES A

connect **All applicable Exercises in Series A are available in *Connect*.**

LO 1-1

Exercise 1-1A *Identifying financial versus managerial accounting items*

Required

Indicate whether each of the following items is representative of managerial or of financial accounting.

a. Information is factual and is characterized by objectivity, reliability, consistency, and accuracy.
b. Information is reported continuously and has a current or future orientation.
c. Information is provided to outsiders, including investors, creditors, government agencies, analysts, and reporters.
d. Information is regulated by the SEC, FASB, and other sources of GAAP.
e. Information is based on estimates that are bounded by relevance and timeliness.
f. Information is historically based and usually reported annually.
g. Information is local and pertains to subunits of the organization.
h. Information includes economic and nonfinancial data as well as financial data.
i. Information is global and pertains to the company as a whole.
j. Information is provided to insiders, including executives, managers, and employees.

Exercise 1-2A *Identifying product versus selling, general, and administrative (SG&A) costs* LO 1-2

Required

Indicate whether each of the following costs should be classified as a product cost or as an SG&A cost in accordance with GAAP:

a. Direct materials used in a manufacturing company.
b. Indirect materials used in a manufacturing company.
c. Salaries of employees working in the accounting department.
d. Commissions paid to sales staff.
e. Interest on the mortgage for the company's corporate headquarters.
f. Indirect labor used to manufacture inventory.
g. Attorney's fees paid to protect the company from frivolous lawsuits.
h. Research and development costs incurred to create new drugs for a pharmaceutical company.
i. The cost of secretarial supplies used in a doctor's office.
j. Depreciation on the office furniture of the company president.

Exercise 1-3A *Classifying costs: Product or SG&A cost; asset or expense* LO 1-2

Required

Use the following table to classify each cost as a product cost or an SG&A cost. Also indicate whether the cost would be recorded as an asset or an expense. Assume product cost is defined by generally accepted accounting principles. The first item is shown as an example.

Cost Category	Product/SG&A	Asset/Expense
Wages of production workers	Product	Asset
Advertising costs		
Promotion costs		
Production supplies		
Depreciation on administration building		
Depreciation on manufacturing equipment		
Research and development costs		
Cost to set up manufacturing equipment		
Utilities used in manufacturing facility		
Cars for sales staff		
Real estate tax levied on a factory		
General office supplies		
Raw materials used in the manufacturing process		
Cost to rent office equipment		

LO 1-3

Exercise 1-4A *Identifying effect of product versus SG&A costs on financial statements*

Required

Finch Corporation recognized accrued compensation cost. Use the following model to show how this event would affect the company's financial statements under the following two assumptions: (1) the compensation is for office personnel and (2) the compensation is for production workers. Use the letter *I* for increase or the letter *D* for decrease to show the effect on each element. If an element is not affected, indicate so by placing the letters *NA* under the appropriate heading.

	Balance Sheet					Income Statement				
	Assets	**=**	**Liab.**	**+**	**Equity**	**Rev.**	**−**	**Exp.**	**=**	**Net Inc.**
1.	NA	=	NA	+	NA	NA	−	NA	=	NA
2.	NA	=	NA	+	NA	NA	−	NA	=	NA

LO 1-3

Exercise 1-5A *Identifying effect of product versus SG&A costs on financial statements*

Required

Driscoll Industries recognized the annual cost of depreciation on its December 31, Year 2, financial statements. Using the following horizontal financial statements model, indicate how this event affected the company's GAAP-based financial statements under the following two assumptions: (1) the depreciation was on office furniture and (2) the depreciation was on manufacturing equipment. Indicate whether the event increases (*I*), decreases (*D*), or has no effect (*NA*) on each element of the financial statements. Show accumulated depreciation as a decrease in the book value of the appropriate asset account.

	Balance Sheet											Income Statement				
	Assets								Equity							
Event No.	**Cash**	**+**	**Inventory**	**+**	**Manuf. Equip.**	**+**	**Office Furn.**	**=**	**Com. Stk.**	**+**	**Ret. Ear.**	**Rev.**	**−**	**Exp.**	**=**	**Net Inc.**
1.	NA	+	NA	+	NA	+	NA	=	NA	+	NA	NA	−	NA	=	NA
2.	NA	+	NA	+	NA	+	NA	=	NA	+	NA	NA	−	NA	=	NA

LO 1-2, 1-3

Exercise 1-6A *Identifying product versus SG&A costs*

A review of the accounting records of Baird Manufacturing indicated that the company incurred the following payroll costs during the month of March. Assume the company's financial statements are prepared in accordance with GAAP.

1. Salary of the company president–$75,000.
2. Salary of the vice president of manufacturing–$50,000.
3. Salary of the chief financial officer–$42,000.
4. Salary of the vice president of marketing–$40,000.
5. Salaries of middle managers (department heads, production supervisors) in manufacturing plant–$147,000.
6. Wages of production workers–$703,500.
7. Salaries of administrative secretaries–$60,000.
8. Salaries of engineers and other personnel responsible for maintaining production equipment–$133,500.
9. Commissions paid to sales staff–$146,000.

Required

a. What amount of payroll cost would be classified as SG&A expense?

b. Assuming that Baird made 5,000 units of product and sold 4,000 of them during the month of March, determine the amount of payroll cost that would be included in cost of goods sold.

Exercise 1-7A *Recording product versus SG&A costs in a financial statements model* LO 1-3

Weib Manufacturing experienced the following events during its first accounting period:

1. Recognized revenue from cash sale of products.
2. Recognized cost of goods sold from sale referenced in **Event 1.**
3. Acquired cash by issuing common stock.
4. Paid cash to purchase raw materials that were used to make products.
5. Paid wages to production workers.
6. Paid salaries to administrative staff.
7. Recognized depreciation on manufacturing equipment.
8. Recognized depreciation on office furniture.

Required

Use the following horizontal financial statements model to show how each event affects the GAAP-based balance sheet and income statement. Indicate whether the event increases (*I*), decreases (*D*), or has no effect (*NA*) on each element of the financial statements. The first transaction has been recorded as an example. Show accumulated depreciation as a decrease in the book value of the appropriate asset account.

	Balance Sheet									Income Statement				
	Assets							Equity						
Event No.	Cash	+	Inventory	+	Manuf. Equip.	+	Office Furn.	=	Com. Stk.	+	Ret. Ear.	Rev.	−	Exp.	=	Net Inc.
1.	I	+	NA	+	NA	+	NA	=	NA	+	I	I	−	NA	=	I

Exercise 1-8A *Allocating product costs between ending inventory and cost of goods sold* LO 1-3

Mustafa Manufacturing Company began operations on January 1. During the year, it started and completed 3,000 units of product. The financial statements are prepared in accordance with GAAP. The company incurred the following costs:

1. Raw materials purchased and used–$6,200.
2. Wages of production workers–$7,400.
3. Salaries of administrative and sales personnel–$3,000.
4. Depreciation on manufacturing equipment–$4,400.
5. Depreciation on administrative equipment–$2,200.

Mustafa sold 2,400 units of product.

Required

a. Determine the total product cost for the year.

b. Determine the total cost of the ending inventory.

c. Determine the total of cost of goods sold.

Exercise 1-9A *Upstream, midstream, and downstream costs* LO 1-4

Required

Identify each of the items shown in the left column of the following table as being an upstream, a midstream, or a downstream cost by placing an *X* in the one of the columns to the right of the items column. The first item is shown as an example.

Item	Upstream	Midstream	Downstream
Direct materials		X	
Research and development			
Product design			
Manufacturing overhead			
Sales salaries			
Cost of delivering merchandise to customers			
Cost to create a copyright			
Salaries of product engineers			
Salaries of production line workers			
Direct labor			
Cost of heating the manufacturing plant			
Advertising expenses			
Patent filing fees			
Salary of company president			
Depreciation on manufacturing equipment			
Depreciation on office equipment			

LO 1-4

Exercise 1-10A *Identifying upstream and downstream costs*

During Year 1, Rooney Manufacturing Company incurred $8,000,000 of research and development (R&D) costs to create a long-life battery to use in computers. In accordance with FASB standards, the entire R&D cost was recognized as an expense in Year 1. Manufacturing costs (direct materials, direct labor, and overhead) are expected to be $45 per unit. Packaging, shipping, and sales commissions are expected to be $8 per unit. Rooney expects to sell 2,000,000 batteries before new research renders the battery design technologically obsolete. During Year 1, Rooney made 440,000 batteries and sold 400,000 of them.

Required

a. Identify the upstream and downstream costs.

b. Determine the Year 1 amount of cost of goods sold and the ending inventory balance that would appear on the financial statements that are prepared in accordance with GAAP.

c. Determine the sales price assuming that Rooney desires to earn a profit margin that is equal to 25 percent of the *total cost* of developing, making, and distributing the batteries.

d. Prepare a GAAP-based income statement for Year 1. Use the sales price developed in Requirement *c*.

e. Given that the price was properly established using total cost (upstream, midstream, and downstream costs), why does the GAAP-based income statement prepared in Requirement *d* show a loss?

LO 1-2, 1-4

Exercise 1-11A *Identifying product costs in a manufacturing company*

Anne Wood was talking to another accounting student, Don Kirby. Upon discovering that the accounting department offered an upper-level course in cost measurement, Anne remarked to Don, "How difficult can it be? My parents own a toy store. All you have to do to figure out how much something costs is look at the invoice. Surely you don't need an entire course to teach you how to read an invoice."

Required

a. Identify the three main components of product cost as defined by GAAP for a manufacturing entity.

b. Explain why measuring product cost for a manufacturing entity is more complex than measuring product cost for a retail toy store.

Exercise 1-12A *Financial statement effects for manufacturing versus service organizations*

LO 1-3, 1-4

The following financial statements model shows the effects of recognizing depreciation in two different circumstances. One circumstance represents recognizing depreciation on equipment used in a factory. The other circumstance recognizes depreciation on computers used in a consulting firm. The effects of each event have been recorded using the letter *I* for increase, *D* for decrease, and *NA* for no effect.

	Balance Sheet									Income Statement				
	Assets						Equity							
Event No.	Cash	+	Inventory	+	Equip.	=	Com. Stk.	+	Ret. Ear.	Rev.	−	Exp.	=	Net Inc.
1.	NA	+	NA	+	D	=	NA	+	D	NA	−	I	=	D
2.	NA	+	I	+	D	=	NA	+	NA	NA	−	NA	=	NA

Required

a. Identify the event that represents depreciation on the computers.

b. Explain why recognizing depreciation on equipment used in a manufacturing company affects financial statements differently than recognizing depreciation on computers used in a service organization.

Exercise 1-13A *Identifying the effect of a just-in-time inventory system on financial statements*

LO 1-5

After reviewing the financial statements of Perez Company, Lou Brewer concluded that the company was a service company. Mr. Brewer based his conclusion on the fact that Perez's financial statements displayed no inventory accounts.

Required

Explain how Perez's implementation of a 100 percent effective just-in-time inventory system could have led Mr. Brewer to a false conclusion regarding the nature of Perez's business.

Exercise 1-14A *Using JIT to minimize waste and lost opportunity*

LO 1-5

Becky Shelton, a teacher at Kemp Middle School, is in charge of ordering the T-shirts to be sold for the school's annual fund-raising project. The T-shirts are printed with a special Kemp School logo. In some years, the supply of T-shirts has been insufficient to satisfy the number of sales orders. In other years, T-shirts have been left over. Excess T-shirts are normally donated to some charitable organization. T-shirts cost the school $5 each and are normally sold for $12 each. Ms. Shelton has decided to order 700 shirts.

Required

a. If the school receives actual sales orders for 600 shirts, what amount of profit will the school earn? What is the cost of waste due to excess inventory?

b. If the school receives actual sales orders for 800 shirts, what amount of profit will the school earn? What amount of opportunity cost will the school incur?

c. Explain how a JIT inventory system could maximize profitability by eliminating waste and opportunity cost.

Exercise 1-15A *Using JIT to minimize holding costs*

LO 1-5

Gwen Pet Supplies purchases its inventory from a variety of suppliers, some of which require a six-week lead time before delivering the goods. To ensure that she has a sufficient supply of goods on hand, Ms. Leblanc, the owner, must maintain a large supply of inventory. The cost of this inventory averages $67,000. She usually finances the purchase of inventory and pays a 5 percent annual finance charge. Ms. Leblanc's accountant has suggested that she establish a relationship with a single large distributor who can satisfy all of her orders within a two-week time period. Given this quick turnaround time, she will be able to reduce her average inventory balance to $17,000. Ms. Leblanc also believes that she could save $9,000 per year by reducing phone bills, insurance, and warehouse rental space costs associated with ordering and maintaining the larger level of inventory.

Required

a. Is the new inventory system available to Ms. Leblanc a pure or approximate just-in-time system?

b. Based on the information provided, how much of Ms. Leblanc's inventory holding cost could be eliminated by taking the accountant's advice?

LO 1-6

Exercise 1-16A *Applications of the Sarbanes-Oxley Act*

The CFO of the Jordan Microscope Corporation intentionally misclassified a downstream transportation expense in the amount of $575,000 as a product cost in an accounting period when the company made 5,000 microscopes and sold 4,000 microscopes. Jordan rewards its officers with bonuses that are based on net earnings.

Required

a. Indicate whether the elements on the financial statements (i.e., assets, liabilities, equity, revenue, expense, and net income) would be overstated or understated as a result of the misclassification of the downstream transportation expense. Determine the amount of the overstatement or understatement for each element.

b. Based on the provisions of the Sarbanes-Oxley Act, what is the maximum penalty that the CFO could face for deliberately missrepresenting the financial statements?

LO 1-6

Exercise 1-17A *Professional conduct and code of ethics*

In February 2006, former senator Warren Rudman of New Hampshire completed a 17-month investigation of an $11 billion accounting scandal at Fannie Mae (a major enterprise involved in home mortgage financing). The Rudman investigation concluded that Fannie Mae's CFO and controller used an accounting gimmick to manipulate financial statements in order to meet earnings-per-share (EPS) targets. Meeting the EPS targets triggered bonus payments for the executives. Fannie Mae's problems continued after 2006, and on September 8, 2008, it went into conservatorship under the control of the Federal Housing Financing Agency. The primary executives at the time of the Rudman investigation were replaced, and the enterprise reported a $59.8 billion loss in 2008. By June 2012, the federal government had spent $170 million to assist Fannie Mae as a result of mismanagement.

Required

Review the statement of ethical professional practice shown in Exhibit 1.17. Identify and comment on which of the ethical principles the CFO and controller violated.

LO 1-7

Exercise 1-18A *Value chain analysis (Appendix)*

Soundwave Company manufactures and sells high-quality audio speakers. The speakers are encased in solid walnut cabinets supplied by Walton Cabinet, Inc. Walton packages the speakers in durable moisture-proof boxes and ships them by truck to Soundwave's manufacturing facility, which is located 40 miles from the cabinet factory.

Required

Identify the nonvalue-added activities that occur between the companies described in the above scenario. Provide a logical explanation as to how these nonvalue-added activities could be eliminated.

PROBLEMS—SERIES A

connect **All applicable Problems in Series A are available in *Connect.***

LO 1-1

Problem 1-19A *Characteristics of financial versus managerial accounting*

Required

Use the following table to indicate whether the information is more representative of managerial versus financial accounting. The first item is shown as an example.

Information Item	Financial Accounting	Managerial Accounting
Estimates of future revenue		X
GAAP-based product cost		
Salary of the manager of a particular branch of a bank		
Salary expense for all company employees shown in the income statement		
Historical-based information included in financial statements		
Reporting rules established by government authorities		
Reports designed for the company president		
Daily time clock reports		
A company's annual report to stockholders		
Budgets		
Information provided to investors and creditors		
Vacation schedules for key employees		
Customer satisfaction survey results		
Amount of total assets shown on the balance sheet		

Problem 1-20A *Product versus selling, general, and administrative (SG&A) costs*

LO 1-2, 1-3

CHECK FIGURES
a. Average cost per unit: $5.30
f. $102,600

Stuart Manufacturing Company was started on January 1, Year 1, when it acquired $89,000 cash by issuing common stock. Stuart immediately purchased office furniture and manufacturing equipment costing $32,000 and $40,000, respectively. The office furniture had an eight-year useful life and a zero salvage value. The manufacturing equipment had a $4,000 salvage value and an expected useful life of six years. The company paid $12,000 for salaries of administrative personnel and $21,000 for wages to production personnel. Finally, the company paid $26,000 for raw materials that were used to make inventory. All inventory was started and completed during the year. Stuart completed production on 10,000 units of product and sold 8,000 units at a price of $9 each in Year 1. (Assume that all transactions are cash transactions and that product costs are computed in accordance with GAAP.)

Required

a. Determine the total product cost and the average cost per unit of the inventory produced in Year 1.

b. Determine the amount of cost of goods sold that would appear on the Year 1 income statement.

c. Determine the amount of the ending inventory balance that would appear on the December 31, Year 1, balance sheet.

d. Determine the amount of net income that would appear on the Year 1 income statement.

e. Determine the amount of retained earnings that would appear on the December 31, Year 1, balance sheet.

f. Determine the amount of total assets that would appear on the December 31, Year 1, balance sheet.

Problem 1-21A *Effect of product versus period costs on financial statements*

LO 1-3

excel

CHECK FIGURES
Cash balance: $54,200
Net income: $14,500

Sinclair Manufacturing Company experienced the following accounting events during its first year of operation. With the exception of the adjusting entries for depreciation, assume that all transactions are cash transactions and that financial statement data are prepared in accordance with GAAP.

1. Acquired $68,000 cash by issuing common stock.
2. Paid $8,700 for the materials used to make its products, all of which were started and completed during the year.
3. Paid salaries of $4,500 to selling and administrative employees.
4. Paid wages of $10,000 to production workers.

5. Paid $9,600 for furniture used in selling and administrative offices. The furniture was acquired on January 1. It had a $1,600 estimated salvage value and a four-year useful life.
6. Paid $16,000 for manufacturing equipment. The equipment was acquired on January 1. It had a $1,000 estimated salvage value and a five-year useful life.
7. Sold inventory to customers for $35,000 that had cost $14,000 to make.

Required

Explain how these events would affect the balance sheet and income statement by recording them in a horizontal financial statements model as indicated here. The first event is recorded as an example.

	Balance Sheet											Income Statement				
	Assets								Equity							
Event No.	Cash	+	Inventory	+	Manuf. Equip.*	+	Office Furn.*	=	Com. Stk.	+	Ret. Ear.	Rev.	−	Exp.	=	Net Inc.
1.	68,000	+	NA	+	NA	+	NA	=	68,000	+	NA	NA	−	NA	=	NA

*Record accumulated depreciation as negative amounts in these columns.

LO 1-3

CHECK FIGURES
Net income: $1,050
Total assets: $13,050

Problem 1-22A *Product versus SG&A costs*

The following transactions pertain to Year 1, the first-year operations of Gibson Company. All inventory was started and completed during Year 1. Assume that all transactions are cash transactions.

1. Acquired $12,000 cash by issuing common stock.
2. Paid $4,700 for materials used to produce inventory.
3. Paid $2,400 to production workers.
4. Paid $900 rental fee for production equipment.
5. Paid $350 to administrative employees.
6. Paid $400 rental fee for administrative office equipment.
7. Produced 400 units of inventory of which 360 units were sold at a price of $25 each.

Required

Prepare an income statement and a balance sheet in accordance with GAAP.

LO 1-4

CHECK FIGURES
b. $70,000
e. Net loss: $40,000

Problem 1-23A *Upstream, midstream, and downstream costs*

Power-To-Spare, Inc., makes a smartphone case that includes a battery that extends the operating life of an iPhone. The manufacturing costs per unit include $15 direct materials, $17 direct labor and $8 manufacturing overhead. These costs are based on a production and sales volume of 4,000 units. Advertising costs amounted to $25,000. Research and development cost for the materials used in the phone cases amounted to $30,000. Companywide administrative costs amounted to $45,000. Fashion design costs amounted to $20,000. Power-To-Spare's management team established the sales price at 150 percent of GAAP-defined product cost.

Required

a. Determine the total amount of upstream costs.
b. Determine the total amount of downstream cost.
c. Determine the total amount of midstream cost.
d. Determine the sales price per unit.
e. Prepare a GAAP-based income statement.
f. Provide a plausible explanation as to why the company incurred the loss shown on the income statement prepared to satisfy Requirement *e.* (*Hint:* Calculate the full cost of making and selling the cases.)

Problem 1-24A *Service versus manufacturing companies*

LO 1-4

Wang Company began operations on January 1, Year 1, by issuing common stock for $70,000 cash. During Year 1, Wang received $88,000 cash from revenue and incurred costs that required $65,000 of cash payments.

Required

Prepare a GAAP-based income statement and balance sheet for Wang Company for Year 1, under each of the following independent scenarios.

a. Wang is a promoter of rock concerts. The $65,000 was paid to provide a rock concert that produced the revenue.

b. Wang is in the car rental business. The $65,000 was paid to purchase automobiles. The automobiles were purchased on January 1, Year 1, and have five-year useful lives, with no expected salvage value. Wang uses straight-line depreciation. The revenue was generated by leasing the automobiles.

c. Wang is a manufacturing company. The $65,000 was paid to purchase the following items:

(1) Paid $10,000 cash to purchase materials that were used to make products during the year.

(2) Paid $20,000 cash for wages of factory workers who made products during the year.

(3) Paid $5,000 cash for salaries of sales and administrative employees.

(4) Paid $30,000 cash to purchase manufacturing equipment. The equipment was used solely to make products. It had a three-year life and a $6,000 salvage value. The company uses straight-line depreciation.

(5) During Year 1, Wang started and completed 2,000 units of product. The revenue was earned when Wang sold 1,500 units of product to its customers.

d. Refer to Requirement *c*. Could Wang determine the actual cost of making the 500th unit of product? How likely is it that the actual cost of the 500th unit of product was exactly the same as the cost of producing the 501st unit of product? Explain why management may be more interested in average cost than in actual cost.

CHECK FIGURES
a. Net income: $23,000
b. Total assets: $145,000
c. Net income: $54,500

Problem 1-25A *Using JIT to reduce inventory holding costs*

LO 1-5

Kenta Manufacturing Company obtains its raw materials from a variety of suppliers. Kenta's strategy is to obtain the best price by letting the suppliers know that it buys from the lowest bidder. Approximately four years ago, unexpected increases in demand resulted in materials shortages. Kenta was unable to find the materials it needed even though it was willing to pay premium prices. Because of the lack of raw materials, Kenta was forced to close its manufacturing facility for two weeks. Its president vowed that her company would never again be at the mercy of its suppliers. She immediately ordered her purchasing agent to perpetually maintain a one-month supply of raw materials. Compliance with the president's orders resulted in a raw materials inventory amounting to approximately $1,200,000. Warehouse rental and personnel costs to maintain the inventory amounted to $8,000 per month. Kenta has a line of credit with a local bank that calls for a 10 percent annual rate of interest. Assume that Kenta finances the raw materials inventory with the line of credit.

CHECK FIGURES
a. $216,000

Required

a. Based on the information provided, determine the annual holding cost of the raw materials inventory.

b. Explain how a JIT system could reduce Kenta's inventory holding cost.

c. Explain how most-favored-customer status could enable Kenta to establish a JIT inventory system without risking the raw materials shortages experienced in the past.

Problem 1-26A *Using JIT to minimize waste and lost opportunity*

LO 1-5

CIA Review, Inc., provides review courses twice each year for students studying to take the CIA exam. The cost of textbooks is included in the registration fee. Text material requires constant updating and is useful for only one course. To minimize printing costs and ensure availability of books on the first day of class, CIA Review has books printed and delivered to its offices two weeks in advance of the first class. To ensure that enough books are available, CIA Review normally orders 10 percent more than expected enrollment. Usually there is an oversupply and books are thrown away. However, demand occasionally exceeds expectations by more than 10 percent and there are too few books available for student use. CIA Review has been forced to turn away students because of a lack of textbooks. CIA Review expects to enroll approximately 200 students per course. The tuition fee is $2,000 per student. The cost of teachers

CHECK FIGURES
a. $3,000
b. $37,000

is $50,000 per course, textbooks cost $150 each, and other operating expenses are estimated to be $75,000 per course. Assume all financial statements data are prepared in accordance with GAAP.

Required

a. Prepare an income statement, assuming that 200 students enroll in a course. Determine the cost of waste associated with unused books.

b. Prepare an income statement, assuming that 240 students attempt to enroll in the course. Note that twenty students are turned away because of too few textbooks. Determine the amount of lost profit resulting from the inability to serve the twenty additional students.

c. Suppose that textbooks can be produced through a high-speed copying process that permits delivery *just in time* for class to start. The cost of books made using this process, however, is $160 each. Assume that all books must be made using the same production process. In other words, CIA Review cannot order some of the books using the regular copy process and the rest using the high-speed process. Prepare an income statement under the JIT system assuming that 200 students enroll in a course. Compare the income statement under JIT with the income statement prepared in Requirement *a*. Comment on how the JIT system would affect profitability.

d. Assume the same facts as in Requirement *c* with respect to a JIT system that enables immediate delivery of books at a cost of $160 each. Prepare an income statement under the JIT system, assuming that 240 students enroll in a course. Compare the income statement under JIT with the income statement prepared in Requirement *b*. Comment on how the JIT system would affect profitability.

e. Discuss the possible effect of the JIT system on the level of customer satisfaction.

LO 1-3, 1-6

CHECK FIGURES

a. Option 1: NI = $20,000
Option 2: Total assets = $112,000

Problem 1-27A *Importance of cost classification*

Campbell Manufacturing Company (CMC) was started when it acquired $80,000 by issuing common stock. During the first year of operations, the company incurred specifically identifiable product costs (materials, labor, and overhead) amounting to $75,000. CMC also incurred $60,000 of engineering design and planning costs. There was a debate regarding how the design and planning costs should be classified. Advocates of Option 1 believe that the costs should be classified as general, selling, and administrative costs. Advocates of Option 2 believe it is more appropriate to classify the design and planning costs as product costs. During the year, CMC made 5,000 units of product and sold 4,000 units at a price of $35 each. All transactions were cash transactions.

Required

a. Prepare a GAAP-based income statement and balance sheet under each of the two options.

b. Identify the option that results in financial statements that are more likely to leave a favorable impression on investors and creditors.

c. Assume that CMC provides an incentive bonus to the company president equal to 20 percent of net income. Compute the amount of the bonus under each of the two options. Identify the option that provides the president with the higher bonus.

d. Assume a 30 percent income tax rate. Determine the amount of income tax expense under each of the two options. Identify the option that minimizes the amount of the company's income tax expense.

e. Comment on the conflict of interest between the company president as determined in Requirement *c* and the owners of the company as indicated in Requirement *d*. Describe an incentive compensation plan that would avoid a conflict of interest between the president and the owners.

LO 1-6

Problem 1-28A *Internal control procedures*

Ted Cowan is a model employee. He has not missed a day of work in the last five years. He even forfeits his vacation time to make sure that things run smoothly. Ted literally does the work of two people. He started out working as the purchasing agent in charge of buying raw materials for a small manufacturing company. Approximately five years ago the inventory control agent in the receiving department resigned. Ted agreed to assume the duties of the control agent until a replacement could be hired. After all, Ted said that he knew what was supposed to be delivered to the company because as the purchasing agent he had been the person who placed orders for the inventory purchases. Ted did such a good job that the company never got around to hiring a replacement. Ted received the employee of the year award five out of the last six years. Ted is also very active in his community. He works with underprivileged children. His weekends are always filled with community service. Indeed, his commitment to social consciousness is described by some people as bordering on fanatical.

Ted recently had a serious heart attack. People said that he had overworked himself. His hospital room was filled with flowers and a steady stream of friends visited him. So, people were in shock when Ted was charged with embezzlement. Ultimately, it was revealed that while Ted was in the hospital his replacement discovered that Ted had been purchasing excess quantities of raw materials. He then sold the extra materials and kept the money for himself. This became apparent when the companies to whom Ted had been selling the excess materials called to place new orders. It was difficult to determine the extent of the embezzlement. After the accounting department paid for Ted's excess purchases, he would remove the paid voucher forms from the accounting files and destroy them. Since the forms were not numbered, it was impossible to determine how many of the paid forms were missing. At his trial, Ted's only explanation was: "I did it for the children. They needed the money far more than the company needed it."

Required

a. If the internal control procedures shown in Exhibit 1.19 had been followed, this embezzlement could have been avoided. Name the internal control procedures that were violated in this case.

b. Identify the specific components of the fraud triangle that were present in this case.

Problem 1-29A *Value chain analysis (Appendix)* LO 1-7

Vernon Company invented a new process for manufacturing ice cream. The ingredients are mixed in high-tech machinery that forms the product into small round beads. Like a bag of balls, the ice cream beads are surrounded by air pockets in packages. This design has numerous advantages. First, each bite of ice cream melts rapidly when placed in a person's mouth, creating a more flavorful sensation when compared to ordinary ice cream. Also, the air pockets mean that a typical serving includes a smaller amount of ice cream. This not only reduces materials cost but also provides the consumer with a low-calorie snack. A cup appears full of ice cream, but it is really half full of air. The consumer eats only half the ingredients that are contained in a typical cup of blended ice cream. Finally, the texture of the ice cream makes scooping it out of a large container a very easy task. The frustration of trying to get a spoon into a rock-solid package of blended ice cream has been eliminated. Vernon Company named the new product Sonic Cream.

Like many other ice cream producers, Vernon Company purchases its raw materials from a food wholesaler. The ingredients are mixed in Vernon's manufacturing plant. The packages of finished product are distributed to privately owned franchise ice cream shops that sell Sonic Cream directly to the public.

Vernon provides national advertising and is responsible for all research and development costs associated with making new flavors of Sonic Cream.

Required

a. Based on the information provided, draw a comprehensive value chain for Vernon Company that includes its suppliers and customers.

b. Identify the place in the chain where Vernon Company is exercising its opportunity to create added value beyond that currently being provided by its competitors.

EXERCISES—SERIES B

Exercise 1-1B *Financial versus managerial accounting items* LO 1-1

Required

Indicate whether each of the following items is representative of financial or managerial accounting.

a. Financial results used by stockbrokers to evaluate a company's profitability.

b. Quarterly budgets used by management to determine future borrowing needs.

c. Financial statements prepared in accordance with GAAP.

d. Annual financial reports submitted to the SEC in compliance with federal securities laws.

e. Projected budget information used to make logistical decisions.

f. Condensed financial information sent to current investors at the end of each quarter.

g. Audited financial statements submitted to bankers when applying for a line of credit.

h. A weekly cash budget used by the treasurer to determine whether cash on hand is excessive.

i. Monthly sales reports used by the vice president of marketing to help allocate funds.

j. Divisional profit reports used by the company president to determine bonuses for divisional vice presidents.

LO 1-2

Exercise 1-2B *Identifying product versus selling, general, and administrative (SG&A) costs*

Required

Indicate whether each of the following costs should be classified as a product cost or as an SG&A cost in accordance with GAAP.

a. Wages paid to workers in a manufacturing plant.
b. The salary of the receptionist working in the sales department.
c. Supplies used in the sales department.
d. Wages of janitors who clean the factory floor.
e. The salary of the company president.
f. The salary of the cell phone manufacturing plant manager.
g. The depreciation on administrative buildings.
h. The depreciation on the company treasurer's computer.
i. The fabric used in making a customized sofa for a customer.
j. The salary of an engineer who maintains all manufacturing plant equipment.

LO 1-2

Exercise 1-3B *Classifying costs: product or SG&A cost; asset or expense*

Required

Use the following table to classify each cost as a product cost or as an SG&A cost. Also indicate whether the cost would be recorded as an asset or an expense. Assume that product costs are defined in accordance with GAAP. The first cost item is shown as an example.

Cost Category	Product/SG&A	Asset/Expense
Cost of merchandise shipped to customers	SG&A	Expense
Depreciation on vehicles used by salespeople		
Wages of administrative building security guards		
Supplies used in the plant manager's office		
Purchase of computers for the accounting department		
Depreciation on computers used in factory		
Natural gas used in the factory		
Cost of television commercials		
Wages of factory workers		
Paper and ink cartridges used in the cashier's office		
Raw material used to make products		
Lubricant used to maintain factory equipment		
Cost of a delivery truck		
Cash dividend to stockholders		

LO 1-3

Exercise 1-4B *Effect of product versus SG&A costs on financial statements*

Required

Ocean Plastics Company accrued a tax liability for $7,000. Use the following horizontal financial statements model to show the effect of this accrual under the following two assumptions: (1) the tax is on administrative buildings, or (2) the tax is on production equipment. Use letter *I* for increase or letter *D* for decrease to show the effect on each element. If an element is not affected, indicate so by placing the letters *NA* under the appropriate heading. Assume the financial statements are prepared in accordance with GAAP.

	Balance Sheet					Income Statement				
	Assets	=	Liab.	+	Equity	Rev.	−	Exp.	=	Net Inc.
1.	NA	=	NA	+	NA	NA	−	NA	=	NA
2.	NA	=	NA	+	NA	NA	−	NA	=	NA

Exercise 1-5B *Effect of product versus SG&A costs on financial statements*

LO 1-3

Required

Gilchrist Corporation recognized the annual expiration of insurance on December 31, Year 2. Using the following horizontal financial statements model, indicate how this event affected the company's GAAP-based financial statements under the following two assumptions: (1) the insurance was for office equipment, or (2) the insurance was for manufacturing equipment. Indicate whether the event increases (*I*), decreases (*D*), or does not affect (*NA*) each element of the financial statements.

	Balance Sheet									Income Statement				
	Assets					=	Equity							
Event No.	Cash	+	Prepaid Insurance	+	Inventory	=	Com. Stk.	+	Ret. Ear.	Rev.	−	Exp.	=	Net Inc.
1.	NA	+	NA	+	NA	=	NA	+	NA	NA	−	NA	=	NA
2.	NA	+	NA	+	NA	=	NA	+	NA	NA	−	NA	=	NA

Exercise 1-6B *Product versus SG&A costs*

LO 1-2, 1-3

In reviewing Larson Company's September accounting records, Andy Miranda, the chief accountant, noted the following depreciation costs. Assume product costs are defined by GAAP.

1. Factory buildings–$75,000.
2. Computers used in manufacturing–$12,000.
3. A building used to display finished products–$24,000.
4. Trucks used to deliver merchandise to customers–$18,000.
5. Forklifts used in the factory–$30,000.
6. Furniture used in the president's office–$15,000.
7. Elevators in administrative buildings–$20,000.
8. Factory machinery–$36,000.

Required

a. What amount of depreciation cost would be classified as selling, general, and administrative expense?

b. Assume that Larson manufactured 3,000 units of product and sold 2,000 units of product during the month of September. Determine the amount of depreciation cost that would be included in cost of goods sold.

Exercise 1-7B *Recording product versus SG&A costs in a financial statements model*

LO 1-3

Mueller Electronics Company experienced the following events during its first accounting period.

1. Received $87,000 cash by issuing common stock.
2. Paid $30,000 cash for wages to production workers.
3. Paid $15,000 for salaries to administrative staff.
4. Purchased for cash and used $16,000 of raw materials.
5. Recognized $1,000 of depreciation on administrative offices.
6. Recognized $1,500 of depreciation on manufacturing equipment.
7. Recognized $48,000 of sales revenue from cash sales of products.
8. Recognized $30,000 of cost of goods sold from the sale referenced in **Event 7.**

Required

Use a horizontal financial statements model to show how each event affects the balance sheet and income statement. Assume the financial statements are prepared in accordance with GAAP. Indicate whether the event increases (*I*), decreases (*D*), or does not affect (*NA*) each element of the financial statements. The first transaction is shown as an example. (*Note:* Show accumulated depreciation as a decrease in the book value of the appropriate asset account.)

	Balance Sheet											Income Statement				
	Assets								Equity							
Event No.	Cash	+	Inventory	+	Manuf. Equip.	+	Adm. Offices	=	Com. Stk.	+	Ret. Ear.	Rev.	−	Exp.	=	Net Inc.
1.	I	+	NA	+	NA	+	NA	=	I	+	NA	NA	−	NA	=	NA

LO 1-3

Exercise 1-8B *Allocating product costs between ending inventory and cost of goods sold*

Fuji Manufacturing Company began operations on January 1. During January, it started and completed 6,000 units of product. Assume all financial statement data are prepared in accordance with GAAP. The company incurred the following costs.

1. Raw materials purchased and used–$8,100.
2. Wages of production workers–$6,500.
3. Salaries of administrative and sales personnel–$3,200.
4. Depreciation on manufacturing equipment–$3,400.
5. Depreciation on administrative equipment–$3,000.

Fuji sold 4,800 units of product.

Required

a. Determine the total product cost.
b. Determine the total cost of the ending inventory.
c. Determine the total of cost of goods sold.

LO 1-4

Exercise 1-9B *Identify upstream, midstream, and downstream costs*

Required

Identify each of the items shown in the left column of the following table as being an upstream, a midstream, or a downstream cost by placing an *X* in the one of the columns to the right of the items column. The first item is shown as an example.

Item	Upstream	Midstream	Downstream
Telephone cost of a manufacturing plant		X	
Steering wheel used to assemble a car			
Wages of a manufacturing plant			
Cost of product warranty			
Cost of researching a cancer treatment drug			
Plant manager's salary			
Sales commissions			
Cost of pursuing FDA's approval on a new drug			
Cost of product advertisement			
Cost of providing Internet service in a plant			
Year-end bonus paid to factory forepersons			
Shipping manager's salary			
Cost of research and development			
Depreciation on vehicles used by salespersons			
Depreciation on vehicles used in a plant			

Exercise 1-10B *Upstream and downstream costs*

LO 1-4

During Year 1, Hutton Pharmaceutical Company incurred $35,000,000 of research and development (R&D) costs to develop a new hay fever drug called Allergone. In accordance with FASB standards, the entire R&D cost was recognized as expense in Year 1. Manufacturing costs (direct materials, direct labor, and overhead) to produce Allergone are expected to be $20 per unit. Packaging, shipping, and sales commissions are expected to be $3 per unit. Hutton expects to sell 5,000,000 units of Allergone before developing a new drug to replace it in the market. During Year 1, Hutton produced 800,000 units of Allergone and sold 600,000 of them. Assume all financial statement data are prepared in accordance with GAAP.

Required

a. Identify the upstream and downstream costs.

b. Determine the Year 1 amount of cost of goods sold and the December 31, Year 1, ending inventory balance.

c. Determine the unit sales price Hutton should establish assuming it desires to earn a profit margin equal to 40 percent of the *total cost* of developing, manufacturing, and distributing Allergone.

d. Prepare an income statement for Year 1 using the sales price from Requirement *c*.

e. Given that the price was properly established using total costs (upstream, midstream and downstream costs), why does the GAAP-based income statement prepared in Requirement *d* show a loss?

Exercise 1-11B *Product costs in a manufacturing company*

LO 1-2, 1-4

Because friends and neighbors frequently praise her baking skills, Susan Nazari plans to start a new business baking cakes for customers. She wonders how to determine the cost of her cakes. Assume financial statement data are prepared in accordance with GAAP.

Required

a. Identify and give examples of the three components of product cost incurred in producing cakes.

b. Explain why measuring product cost for a bakery is more complex than measuring product cost for a retail store.

Exercise 1-12B *Financial statement effects for manufacturing versus service organizations*

LO 1-3, 1-4

The following horizontal financial statements model shows the effects of recording the expiration of insurance in two different circumstances. Assume all financial statement data are prepared in accordance with GAAP. One circumstance represents the expiration of insurance on a factory building. The other circumstance represents the expiration of insurance on an administrative building. The effects of each event have been recorded using the letters *I* for increase, *D* for decrease, and *NA* for no effect.

	Balance Sheet									Income Statement				
	Assets						Equity							
Event No.	Cash	+	Prepaid Insurance	+	Inventory	=	Com. Stk.	+	Ret. Ear.	Rev.	−	Exp.	=	Net Inc.
1.	NA	+	D	+	I	=	NA	+	NA	NA	−	NA	=	NA
2.	NA	+	D	+	NA	=	NA	+	D	NA	−	I	=	D

Required

a. Identify the event that represents the expiration of insurance on the factory building.

b. Explain why recognizing the expiration of insurance on a factory building affects financial statements differently than recognizing the expiration of insurance on an administrative building.

LO 1-5

Exercise 1-13B *Effect of a just-in-time inventory system on financial statements*

In reviewing Fargo Company's financial statements for the past two years, Lilian Stone, a bank loan officer, noticed that the company's inventory level had increased significantly while sales revenue had remained constant. Such a trend typically indicates increasing inventory carrying costs and slowing cash inflows. Ms. Stone concluded that the bank should deny Fargo's credit line application.

Required

Explain how implementing an effective just-in-time inventory system would affect Fargo's financial statements and possibly reverse Ms. Stone's decision about its credit line application.

LO 1-5

Exercise 1-14B *Using JIT to minimize waste and lost opportunity*

Denise Jensen is the editor-in-chief of her school's yearbook. The school has 1,200 students and 40 faculty and staff members. The firm engaged to print copies of the yearbook charges the school $20 per book and requires a 10-day lead time for delivery. Denise and her editors plan to order 1,000 copies to sell at the school fair for $30 each.

Required

a. If the school sells 900 yearbooks, what amount of profit will it earn? What is the cost of waste due to excess inventory?

b. If 100 buyers are turned away after all yearbooks have been sold, what amount of profit will the school earn? What amount of opportunity cost will the school incur?

c. How could Denise use a JIT inventory system to maximize profits by eliminating waste and opportunity cost?

LO 1-5

Exercise 1-15B *Using JIT to minimize holding costs*

Melinda's Beauty Salon purchases inventory supplies from a variety of vendors, some of which require a four-week lead time before delivering inventory purchases. To ensure that she will not run out of supplies, Melinda Lowe, the owner, maintains a large inventory. The average cost of inventory on hand is $12,000. Ms. Lowe usually finances inventory purchases with a line of credit that has a 9 percent annual interest charge. Her accountant has suggested that she purchase all inventory from a single large distributor that can satisfy all of her orders within a three-day period. With such prompt delivery, Ms. Lowe would be able to reduce her average inventory balance to $2,000. She also believes that she could save $5,000 per year through reduced phone bills, insurance costs, and warehouse rental costs associated with ordering and maintaining the higher level of inventory.

Required

a. Is the inventory system the accountant suggested to Ms. Lowe a pure or approximate just-in-time system?

b. Based on the information provided, how much inventory holding cost could Ms. Lowe eliminate by taking the accountant's advice?

LO 1-6

Exercise 1-16B *The fraud triangle*

The accounting records of Abbott Manufacturing Company (AMC) revealed that the company incurred $3 million of materials, $5 million of production labor, $4 million of manufacturing overhead, and $6 million of selling, general, and administrative expense during Year 1. It was discovered that AMC's chief financial officer (CFO) included $1.5 million of upstream research and development expense in the manufacturing overhead account when it should have been classified as selling, general, and administrative expense. AMC made 5,000 units of product and sold 4,000 units of product in Year 1.

Required

a. Indicate whether the elements on the Year 1 financial statements (i.e., assets, liabilities, equity, revenue, expense, and net income) would be overstated or understated as a result of the misclassification of the upstream research and development expense. Determine the amount of the overstatement or understatement for each element.

b. Speculate as to what would cause the CFO to intentionally misclassify the research and development expense. (*Hint:* Review the chapter material regarding the fraud triangle.)

Exercise 1-17B *Applications of the Sarbanes–Oxley Act*

LO 1-6

Greg Madrid, a HealthSouth billing clerk, filed a suit under the False Claims Act charging that HealthSouth purchased computer equipment from a company owned by Richard Scrushy's parents at prices two and three times the normal price. At the time, Richard Scrushy was the CEO of HealthSouth. The overcharges inflated HealthSouth's expense ratios that the government used when calculating a Medicare reimbursement rate. As a result, the government was overcharged for services provided by HealthSouth. While refusing to recognize any wrongdoing, HealthSouth agreed to pay an $8 million settlement related to the lawsuit brought by the whistleblower.

Required

Explain how the provisions of Sarbanes–Oxley would provide protection to a whistleblower such as Greg Madrid.

Exercise 1-18B *Value chain analysis (Appendix)*

LO 1-7

Fastidious Vincent washed his hair at home and then went to a barbershop for a haircut. The barber explained that shop policy is to shampoo each customer's hair before cutting, regardless of how recently it had been washed. Somewhat annoyed, Vincent submitted to the shampoo, after which the barber cut his hair with great skill. After the haircut, the barber dried his hair and complimented Vincent on his appearance. He added, "That will be $18; $3 for the shampoo and $15 for the cut and dry." Vincent did not tip the barber.

Required

Identify the nonvalue-added activity described. How could the barber modify this nonvalue-added activity?

PROBLEMS—SERIES B

Problem 1-19B *Characteristics of financial versus managerial accounting*

LO 1-1

Required

Use the following table to indicate whether the information is more representative of managerial versus financial accounting. The first item is shown as an example.

Information Item	Financial Accounting	Managerial Accounting
Cost per unit of individual products		X
Profit margin of individual products		
Annual report filed with SEC		
Cash flow of the company as a whole		
Income statement prepared according to GAAP		
Balance sheet prepared according to market-value estimates		
Estimated profit of a new product ready to be launched		
Footnote disclosures required by FASB		
Cost analysis provided to production manager		
Facility utilization report provided to company president		
Financial figures released to press		
Financial statements provided to creditors		
Report on employee turnover		
Cost of goods sold as reported according to GAAP		

LO 1-2, 1-3

Problem 1-20B *Product versus selling, general, and administrative (SG&A) costs*

Zell Manufacturing Company was started on January 1, Year 1, when it acquired $98,000 cash by issuing common stock. Zell immediately purchased office furniture and manufacturing equipment costing $28,000 and $58,000, respectively. The office furniture had a four-year useful life and a zero salvage value. The manufacturing equipment had a $4,000 salvage value and an expected useful life of six years. The company paid $20,000 for salaries of administrative personnel and $27,000 for wages of production personnel. Finally, the company paid $39,000 for raw materials that were used to make inventory. All inventory was started and completed during the year. Zell completed production on 12,000 units of product and sold 10,000 units at a price of $15 each in Year 1. (Assume that all transactions are cash transactions and that all financial statement data are prepared in accordance with GAAP.)

Required

a. Determine the total product cost and the average cost per unit of the inventory produced in Year 1.

b. Determine the amount of cost of goods sold that would appear on the Year 1 income statement.

c. Determine the amount of the ending inventory balance that would appear on the December 31, Year 1, balance sheet.

d. Determine the amount of net income that would appear on the Year 1 income statement.

e. Determine the amount of retained earnings that would appear on the December 31, Year 1, balance sheet.

f. Determine the amount of total assets that would appear on the December 31, Year 1, balance sheet.

LO 1-3

Problem 1-21B *Effect of product versus SG&A costs on financial statements*

Ito Company experienced the following accounting events during its first year of operation. With the exception of the adjusting entries for depreciation, all transactions were cash transactions. Also, assume that all financial statement data are prepared in accordance with GAAP.

1. Acquired $87,000 cash by issuing common stock.
2. Paid $17,000 for the materials used to make its products. All products started were completed during the period.
3. Paid salaries of $7,000 to selling and administrative employees.
4. Paid wages of $10,000 to production workers.
5. Paid $12,000 for furniture used in selling and administrative offices. The furniture was acquired on January 1. It had a $1,500 estimated salvage value and a seven-year useful life.
6. Paid $18,000 for manufacturing equipment. The equipment was acquired on January 1. It had a $3,000 estimated salvage value and a five-year useful life.
7. Sold inventory to customers for $58,000 that had cost $26,000 to make.

Required

Explain how these events would affect the balance sheet and income statement by recording them in a horizontal financial statements model as indicated here. The first event is recorded as an example.

	Balance Sheet						Income Statement		
	Assets				Equity				
Event No.	Cash +	Inventory +	Manuf. Equip.* +	Office Furn.* =	Com. Stk. +	Ret. Ear.	Rev. −	Exp. =	Net Inc.
1.	87,000 +	NA +	NA +	NA =	87,000 +	NA	NA −	NA =	NA

*Record accumulated depreciation as negative amounts in these columns.

LO 1-3

Problem 1-22B *Product versus SG&A costs*

The following transactions pertain to Year 1, the first year of operations of Fuzhou Company. All inventory was started and completed during the accounting period. All transactions were cash transactions.

1. Acquired $50,000 of contributed capital from its owners.
2. Paid $10,500 for materials used to produce inventory.
3. Paid $8,600 to production workers.
4. Paid $4,900 rental fee for production equipment.
5. Paid $2,100 to administrative employees.
6. Paid $2,900 rental fee for administrative office equipment.
7. Produced 1,200 units of inventory of which 1,100 units were sold at a price of $27 each.

Required

Prepare an income statement and a balance sheet. Assume the statements are prepared in accordance with GAAP.

Problem 1-23B *Upstream, midstream, and downstream costs*

LO 1-4

Distant Ride, Inc., develops and makes a battery for electrical cars. The manufacturing costs per unit include $450 direct materials, $180 direct labor, and $300 manufacturing overhead. These costs are based on a production and sales volume of 5,000 units per year. Advertising costs amounted to $400,000. Product design cost for the battery amounted to $520,000. Companywide administrative costs amounted to $250,000. Research and development on battery technology amount to $1,800,000. Distant Ride's management team established the sales price at 160 percent of GAAP-defined product cost.

Required

a. Determine the total amount of upstream costs.
b. Determine the total amount of downstream costs.
c. Determine the total amount of midstream costs.
d. Determine the sales price per unit.
e. Prepare a GAAP-based income statement.
f. Provide a plausible explanation as to why the company incurred the loss shown on the income statement prepared to satisfy Requirement *e*. (*Hint:* Calculate the full cost of making and selling the units.)

Problem 1-24B *Service versus manufacturing companies*

LO 1-4

Packer Company began operations on January 1, Year 1, by issuing common stock for $120,000 cash. During Year 1, Packer received $98,000 cash from revenue and incurred costs that required $90,000 of cash payments.

Required

Prepare a GAAP-based income statement and balance sheet for Packer Company for Year 1, under each of the following independent scenarios.

a. Packer is an employment agency. The $90,000 was paid for employee salaries and advertising.
b. Packer is a trucking company. The $90,000 was paid to purchase two trucks. The trucks were purchased on January 1, Year 1, and had five-year useful lives and no expected salvage value. Packer uses straight-line depreciation.
c. Packer is a manufacturing company. The $90,000 was paid to purchase the following items:
   (1) Paid $18,000 cash to purchase materials used to make products during the year.
   (2) Paid $22,000 cash for wages to production workers who make products during the year.
   (3) Paid $2,000 cash for salaries of sales and administrative employees.
   (4) Paid $48,000 cash to purchase manufacturing equipment. The equipment was used solely for the purpose of making products. It had a four-year life and a $8,000 salvage value. The company uses straight-line depreciation.
   (5) During Year 1, Packer started and completed 2,500 units of product. The revenue was earned when Packer sold 2,000 units of product to its customers.
d. Refer to Requirement *c*. Could Packer determine the actual cost of making the 960th unit of product? How likely is it that the actual cost of the 960th unit of product was exactly the same as the cost of producing the 961st unit of product? Explain why management may be more interested in average cost than in actual cost.

LO 1-5

Problem 1-25B *Using JIT to reduce inventory holding costs*

Garza Automobile Dealership, Inc. (GAD), buys and sells a variety of cars made by Perez Motor Corporation. GAD maintains about 30 new cars in its parking lot for customers' selection; the cost of this inventory is approximately $750,000. Additionally, GAD hires security guards to protect the inventory from theft and a maintenance crew to keep the facilities attractive. The total payroll cost for the guards and maintenance crew amounts to $80,000 per year. GAD has a line of credit with a local bank that calls for a 12 percent annual rate of interest. Recently, Tom Randall, the president of GAD, learned that a competitor in town, Hanna Dealership, has been attracting some of GAD's usual customers because Hanna could offer them lower prices. Mr. Randall also discovered that Hanna carries no inventory at all but shows customers a catalog of cars as well as pertinent information from online computer databases. Hanna promises to deliver any car that a customer identifies within three working days.

Required

a. Based on the information provided, determine GAD's annual inventory holding cost.

b. Name the inventory system that Hanna uses and explain how the system enables Hanna to sell at reduced prices.

LO 1-5

Problem 1-26B *Using JIT to minimize waste and lost opportunity*

Mark's Hamburger is a small fast-food shop in a busy shopping center that operates only during lunch hours. Mark Thorpe, the owner and manager of the shop, is confused. On some days, he does not have enough hamburgers to satisfy customer demand. On other days, he has more hamburgers than he can sell. When he has excess hamburgers, he has no choice but to dump them. Usually, Mr. Thorpe prepares about 300 hamburgers before the busy lunch hour. The product cost per hamburger is approximately $1.50 and the sales price is $4.50 each. Mr. Thorpe pays general, selling, and administrative expenses that include daily rent of $80.00 and daily wages of $50.00.

Required

a. Prepare an income statement based on sales of 240 hamburgers per day. Determine the cost of wasted hamburgers if 300 hamburgers were prepared in advance.

b. Prepare an income statement assuming that 360 customers attempt to buy a hamburger. Since Mr. Thorpe has prepared only 300 hamburgers, he must reject 60 customer orders because of insufficient supply. Determine the amount of lost profit.

c. Suppose that hamburgers can be prepared quickly after each customer orders. However, Mr. Thorpe must hire an additional part-time employee at a cost of approximately $30.00 per day. The per-unit cost of each hamburger remains at $1.50. Prepare an income statement under the JIT system assuming that 240 hamburgers are sold. Compare the income statement under JIT with the income statement prepared in Requirement *a.* Comment on how the JIT system would affect profitability.

d. Assume the same facts as in Requirement *c* with respect to a JIT system that requires additional labor costing $30.00 per day. Prepare an income statement under the JIT system, assuming that 360 hamburgers are sold. Compare the income statement under JIT with the income statement prepared in Requirement *b.* Comment on how the JIT system would affect profitability.

e. Explain how the JIT system might be able to improve customer satisfaction as well as profitability.

LO 1-3, 1-6

Problem 1-27B *Importance of cost classification*

Briggs Company was started when it acquired $150,000 by issuing common stock. During the first year of operations, the company incurred specifically identifiable product costs (materials, labor, and overhead) amounting to $120,000. Briggs also incurred $20,000 of product development costs. There was a debate regarding how the product development costs should be classified. Advocates of Option 1 believed that the costs should be included in the selling, general, and administrative cost category. Advocates of Option 2 believed it would be more appropriate to classify the product development costs as product costs. During the first year, Briggs made 10,000 units of product and sold 8,000 units at a price of $20 each. All transactions were cash transactions.

Required

a. Prepare a GAAP-based income statement and balance sheet under each of the two options.

b. Identify the option that results in financial statements that are more likely to leave a favorable impression on investors and creditors.

c. Assume that Briggs provides an incentive bonus to the company president that is equal to 10 percent of net income. Compute the amount of the bonus under each of the two options. Identify the option that provides the president with the higher bonus.

d. Assume a 35 percent income tax rate. Determine the amount of income tax expense under each of the two options. Identify the option that minimizes the amount of the company's income tax expense.

e. Comment on the conflict of interest between the company president as determined in Requirement *c* and the stockholders of the company as indicated in Requirement *d.* Describe an incentive compensation plan that would avoid conflicts of interest between the president and the owners.

Problem 1-28B *The fraud triangle, ethics, and the Sarbanes-Oxley Act*

LO 1-6

The CEO and the CFO of Automation Company were both aware that the company's controller was reporting fraudulent revenues. Upper-level executives are paid very large bonuses when the company meets the earnings goals established in the company's budgets. While the CEO had pushed the CFO and controller to "make the numbers," he had not told him to "make up the numbers." Besides, he could plead ignorance if the fraud was ever discovered. The CFO knew he should prohibit the fraudulent reporting but also knew the importance of making the numbers established in the budget. He told himself that it wasn't just for his bonus but for the stockholders as well. If the actual earnings were below the budgeted target numbers, the stock price would drop and the shareholders would suffer. Besides, he believed that the actual revenues would increase dramatically in the near future and they could cover for the fraudulent revenue by underreporting these future revenues. He concluded that no one would get hurt and everything would be straightened out in the near future.

Required

a. Explain why the internal control practice of separation of duties failed to prevent the fraudulent reporting.

b. Identify and discuss the elements of the fraud triangle that motivated the fraud.

c. Explain how the provisions of the Sarbanes-Oxley Act would serve to deter this type of fraudulent reporting.

d. Review the statement of ethical professional practice shown in Exhibit 1.17. Identify and comment on which of the ethical principles were violated by the CFO.

Problem 1-29B *Value chain analysis (Appendix)*

LO 1-7

Nancy Watson visited her personal physician for treatment of flu symptoms. She was greeted by the receptionist, who gave her personal history and insurance forms to complete. She needed no instructions; she completed these same forms every time she visited the doctor. After completing the forms, Ms. Watson waited for 30 minutes before being ushered into the patient room. After waiting there for an additional 15 minutes, Dr. Holt entered the room. The doctor ushered Ms. Watson into the hallway where he weighed her and called her weight out to the nurse for recording. Ms. Watson had gained 10 pounds since her last visit, and the doctor suggested that she consider going on a diet. Dr. Holt then took her temperature and asked her to return to the patient room. Ten minutes later, he returned to take a throat culture and draw blood. She waited another 15 minutes for the test results. Finally, the doctor returned and told Ms. Watson that she had strep throat and bronchitis. Dr. Holt prescribed an antibiotic and told her to get at least two days of bed rest. Ms. Watson was then ushered to the accounting department to settle her bill. The accounting clerk asked her several questions; the answers to most of them were on the forms that she had completed when she first arrived at the office. Finally, Ms. Watson paid her required co-payment and left the office. Three weeks later, she received a bill indicating that she had not paid the co-payment. She called the accounting department and after a search of the records, the clerk verified that the bill had in fact been paid. The clerk apologized for the inconvenience and inquired as to whether Ms. Watson's health had improved.

Required

a. Identify at least three value-added and three nonvalue-added activities suggested in this scenario.

b. Provide logical suggestions for how to eliminate the nonvalue-added activities.

ANALYZE, THINK, COMMUNICATE

ATC 1-1 Business Applications Case *Financial versus managerial accounting*

The following information was taken from Starbucks Corporation's SEC filings.

	Fiscal Year Ended	
	October 1, 2017	October 2, 2016
Number of employees	277,000	254,000
Revenues (in millions)	$ 22,387	$ 21,316
Properties (in thousands)	6,322 square feet	6,277 square feet
Total assets (in millions)	$ 14,366	$ 14,313
Company-owned stores	13,275	12,711
Net earnings (in millions)	$ 2,885	$ 2,818

Required

a. Explain whether each line of information in the preceding table would best be described as being primarily financial accounting or managerial accounting in nature.

b. Provide some additional examples of managerial and financial accounting information that could apply to Starbucks.

c. If you analyze only the data you identified as financial in nature, does it appear that Starbucks' 2017 fiscal year was better or worse than its 2016 fiscal year? Explain.

d. If you analyze only the data you identified as managerial in nature, does it appear that Starbucks' 2017 fiscal year was better or worse than its 2016 fiscal year? Explain.

e. Did Starbucks appear to be using its facilities more efficiently or less efficiently in 2017 than in 2016?

ATC 1-2 Group Assignment *Product versus upstream and downstream costs*

Victor Holt, the accounting manager of Sexton, Inc., gathered the following information for Year 4. Some of it can be used to construct an income statement for Year 4. Ignore items that do not appear on an income statement. Some computation may be required. For example, the cost of manufacturing equipment would not appear on the income statement. However, the cost of manufacturing equipment is needed to compute the amount of depreciation. All units of product were started and completed in Year 4.

1. Issued $864,000 of common stock.
2. Paid engineers in the product design department $10,000 for salaries that were accrued at the end of the previous year.
3. Incurred advertising expenses of $70,000.
4. Paid $720,000 for materials used to manufacture the company's product.
5. Incurred utility costs of $160,000. These costs were allocated to different departments on the basis of square footage of floor space. Mr. Holt identified three departments and determined the square footage of floor space for each department to be as shown in the following table.

Department	Square Footage
Research and development	10,000
Manufacturing	60,000
Selling and administrative	30,000
Total	100,000

6. Paid $880,000 for wages of production workers.
7. Paid cash of $658,000 for salaries of administrative personnel. There was $16,000 of accrued salaries owed to administrative personnel at the end of Year 4. There was no beginning balance in the Salaries Payable account for administrative personnel.
8. Purchased manufacturing equipment two years ago at a cost of $10,000,000. The equipment had an eight-year useful life and a $2,000,000 salvage value.
9. Paid $390,000 cash to engineers in the product design department.

10. Paid a $258,000 cash dividend to owners.
11. Paid $80,000 to set up manufacturing equipment for production.
12. Paid a one-time $186,000 restructuring cost to redesign the production process to implement a just-in-time inventory system.
13. Prepaid the premium on an insurance policy covering non-manufacturing employees. The policy cost $72,000 and had a one-year term with an effective starting date of May 1. Four employees work in the research and development department and eight employees work in the selling and administrative department. Assume a December 31 closing date.
14. Made 69,400 units of product and sold 60,000 units at a price of $70 each.

Required

a. Divide the class into groups of four or five students per group, and then organize the groups into three sections. Assign Task 1 to the first section of groups, Task 2 to the second section of groups, and Task 3 to the third section of groups.

Group Tasks

(1) Identify the items that are classified as product costs and determine the amount of cost of goods sold reported on the Year 4 income statement.

(2) Identify the items that are classified as upstream costs and determine the amount of upstream cost expensed on the Year 4 income statement.

(3) Identify the items that are classified as downstream costs and determine the amount of downstream cost expensed on the Year 4 income statement.

b. Have the class construct an income statement in the following manner. Select a member of one of the groups assigned Group Task (1), identifying the product costs. Have that person go to the board and list the costs included in the determination of cost of goods sold. Anyone in the other groups who disagrees with one of the classifications provided by the person at the board should voice an objection and explain why the item should be classified differently. The instructor should lead the class to a consensus on the disputed items. After the amount of cost of goods sold is determined, the student at the board constructs the part of the income statement showing the determination of gross margin. The exercise continues in a similar fashion with representatives from the other sections explaining the composition of the upstream and downstream costs. These items are added to the income statement started by the first group representative. The final result is a completed income statement.

ATC 1-3 Research Assignment *Identifying product costs at Snap-on, Inc.*

Use the December 31, 2017, Form 10-K for Snap-on, Inc., to complete the following requirements. To obtain the Form 10-K, you can use the EDGAR system following the instructions in Appendix A, or it can be found under "Corporate Information" on the company's corporate website at www.snapon.com. Read carefully the following portions of the document:

- "Products and services" on page 6.
- "Consolidated Statement of Earnings" on page 68.
- The following parts of Note 1 on page 74 and 75:
  - "Shipping and handling"
  - "Advertising and promotion"
- "Note 4: Inventories" on page 85.
- "Note 5: Property and equipment" on page 86.

Required

a. Does the level of detail that Snap-on provides regarding costs incurred to manufacture its products suggest the company's financial statements are designed primarily to meet the needs of external or internal users?

b. Does Snap-on treat shipping and handling costs as product or nonproduct costs?

c. Does Snap-on treat advertising and promotion costs as product or nonproduct costs?

d. In the first accounting course, you learned about a class of inventory called merchandise inventory. What categories of inventory does Snap-on report in its annual report?

e. What is the cost of the land owned by Snap-on? What is the cost of its machinery, equipment, and software?

ATC 1-4 Writing Assignment *Emerging practices in managerial accounting*

On January 4, 2017, Macy's, Inc., faced with declining revenues and profits announced a series of actions it planned to implement to try to improve its operations. In its press release the company reported:

> *Macy's, Inc. today announced a series of actions to streamline its store portfolio, intensify cost efficiency efforts, and execute its real estate strategy. These actions bolster the company's strategy to further invest in omnichannel capabilities, improve customer experience and create shareholder value. The actions include:*
>
> - *The closure of 68 stores and the reorganization of the field structure that supports the remaining stores, reinforcing the strategy of fewer stores with better customer experience. These store closures are part of the approximately 100 closings announced in August 2016.*
> - *The significant restructuring of the Macy's, Inc. operations to focus resources on strategic priorities, improve organizational agility and reduce expense.*
> - *The sale of properties consistent with the previously announced real estate strategy.*
>
> *The actions announced today are estimated to generate annual expense savings of approximately $550 million, beginning in 2017, enabling the company to invest an additional $250 million in growing the digital business, store-related growth strategies, Bluemercury, Macy's Backstage and China. These savings, combined with savings from initiatives implemented in early 2016, exceed the $500 million goal communicated in fall of 2015, one year earlier than expected.*

Required

Assume that you are Macy's vice president of human relations. Write a letter to the employees who are affected by the restructuring. The letter should explain why it was necessary for the company to undertake the restructuring. Your explanation should refer to the ideas discussed in the section "Using Total Quality Management (TQM) and Activity-Based Management (ABM) to Reengineer Production and Delivery Systems" of this chapter (Appendix).

ATC 1-5 Ethical Dilemma *Product cost versus selling and administrative expense*

Emma Emerson is a proud woman with a problem. Her daughter has been accepted into a prestigious law school. While Ms. Emerson beams with pride, she is worried sick about how to pay for the school; she is a single parent who has worked hard to support herself and her three children. She had to go heavily into debt to finance her own education. Even though she now has a good job, family needs have continued to outpace her income and her debt burden is staggering. She knows she will be unable to borrow the money needed for her daughter's law school.

Ms. Emerson is the chief financial officer (CFO) of a small manufacturing company. She has just accepted a new job offer. Indeed, she has not yet told her employer that she will be leaving in a month. She is concerned that her year-end incentive bonus may be affected if her boss learns of her plans to leave. She plans to inform the company immediately after receiving the bonus. She knows her behavior is less than honorable, but she believes that she has been underpaid for a long time. Her boss, a relative of the company's owner, makes twice what she makes and does half the work. Why should she care about leaving with a little extra cash? Indeed, she is considering an opportunity to boost the bonus.

Ms. Emerson's bonus is based on a percentage of net income. Her company recently introduced a new product line that required substantial production start-up costs. Ms. Emerson is fully aware that GAAP requires these costs to be expensed in the current accounting period, but no one else in the company has the technical expertise to know exactly how the costs should be treated. She is considering misclassifying the start-up costs as product costs. If the costs are misclassified, net income will be significantly higher, resulting in a nice boost in her incentive bonus. By the time the auditors discover the misclassification, Ms. Emerson will have moved on to her new job. If the matter is brought to the attention of her new employer, she will simply plead ignorance. Considering her daughter's needs, Ms. Emerson decides to classify the start-up costs as product costs.

Required

a. Based on this information, indicate whether Ms. Emerson believes the number of units of product sold will be equal to, less than, or greater than the number of units made. Write a brief paragraph explaining the logic that supports your answer.

b. Explain how the misclassification could mislead an investor or creditor regarding the company's financial condition.

c. Explain how the misclassification could affect income taxes.

d. Identify the specific components of the fraud triangle that were present in this case.

e. Review the *Statement of Ethical Professional Practice* shown in Exhibit 1.17 and identify at least two ethical principles that Ms. Emerson's misclassification of the start-up costs violated.

f. Describe the maximum penalty that could be imposed under the Sarbanes-Oxley Act for the actions Ms. Emerson has taken.

g. Comment on how proper internal controls could have prevented fraudulent reporting in this case.

ATC 1-6 Spreadsheet Assignment *Using Excel*

The following transactions pertain to Year 1, the first year of operations of the Barlett Company. All inventory was started and completed during Year 1. Assume that all transactions are cash transactions.

1. Acquired $2,000 cash by issuing common stock.
2. Paid $400 for materials used to produce inventory.
3. Paid $600 to production workers.
4. Paid $200 rental fee for production equipment.
5. Paid $160 to administrative employees.
6. Paid $80 rental fee for administrative office equipment.
7. Produced 300 units of inventory of which 200 units were sold at a price of $7.00 each.

Required

Construct a spreadsheet that includes the income statement and balance sheet.

ATC 1-7 Spreadsheet Assignment *Mastering Excel*

Mantooth Manufacturing Company experienced the following accounting events during its first year of operation. With the exception of the adjusting entries for depreciation, assume that all transactions are cash transactions.

1. Acquired $50,000 by issuing common stock.
2. Paid $8,000 for the materials used to make its products, all of which were started and completed during the year.
3. Paid salaries of $4,400 to selling and administrative employees.
4. Paid wages of $7,000 to production workers.
5. Paid $9,600 for furniture used in selling and administrative offices. The furniture was acquired on January 1. It had a $1,600 estimated salvage value and a four-year useful life.
6. Paid $13,000 for manufacturing equipment. The equipment was acquired on January 1. It had a $1,000 estimated salvage value and a three-year useful life.
7. Sold inventory to customers for $25,000 that had cost $14,000 to make.

Construct a spreadsheet of the financial statements model as shown here.

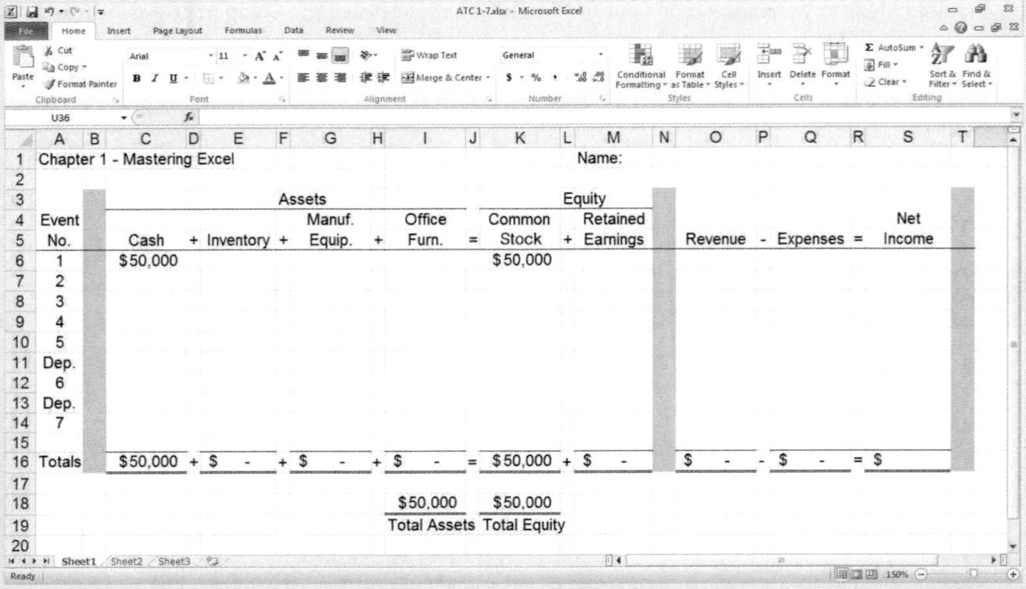

Source: Microsoft Excel 2010

Required

Place formulas in row 16 to automatically add the columns. Also add formulas in column S to calculate net income after each event, and add formulas in row 18 to compute total assets and equity. Notice that you must enter the events since only the first one is shown as an example.

Spreadsheet Tips

1. The column widths are set by choosing Format, then Column, and then Width.
2. The shading in columns B, N, and T is added by highlighting a column and choosing Format, then Cells, and then clicking on the tab titled Patterns and choosing a color.
3. The sum function is an easy way to add a column or row. For example, the formula in cell C16 is = SUM(C6:C15).
4. As an example of the formulas in column S (net income), the formula in cell S7 is =O7−Q7.
5. If you find that some of the columns are too far to the right to appear on your screen, you can set the zoom level to show the entire spreadsheet. The zoom is set by choosing View, then Zoom, and then clicking on Custom and typing "100 percent" in the box. The shortcut method to set the zoom is to click in the box on the right side of the top tool bar that appears immediately below the menu.

COMPREHENSIVE PROBLEM

Magnificent Modems, Inc., makes modem cards that are used in notebook computers. The company completed the following transactions during Year 1. All purchases and sales were made with cash.

1. Acquired $750,000 of cash from the owners.
2. Purchased $270,000 of manufacturing equipment. The equipment has a $30,000 salvage value and a four-year useful life. Label the purchase of the equipment as **Event 2a** and the recognition of depreciation as **Event 2b.**
3. The company started and completed 5,000 modems. Direct materials purchased and used amounted to $40 per unit.
4. Direct labor costs amounted to $25 per unit.
5. The cost of raw materials used in manufacturing amounted to $4 per unit.
6. The company paid $50,000 to rent the manufacturing facility.
7. Magnificent sold all 5,000 units at a cash price of $120 per unit. Label the recognition of the sale as **Event 7a** and the cost of goods sold as **Event 7b.** (*Hint:* It will be necessary to determine the manufacturing costs in order to record the cost of goods sold.)
8. The sales staff was paid a $6 per unit sales commission.
9. Paid $39,000 to purchase equipment for administrative offices. The equipment was expected to have a $3,000 salvage value and a three-year useful life. Label the purchase of the equipment as **Event 9a** and the recognition of depreciation as **Event 9b.**
10. Administrative expenses consisting of office rental and salaries amounted to $71,950.

Required

a. Record the transaction data for Magnificent Modems, Inc. in the financial statements like the one shown as follows. The first transaction is recorded as an example.

	Balance Sheet														Income Statement				
	Assets							=	Equity								
Event No.	Cash	+	Inventory	+	Manuf. Equip.*	+	Office Equip.*	=	Com. Sock.	+	Ret. Ear.	Rev.	−	Exp.	=	Net Inc.
1.	750,000	+	NA	+	NA	+	NA	=	750,000	+	NA	NA	−	NA	=	NA
End Bal.	544,050	+	0	+	210,000	+	27,000	=	750,000	+	31,050	600,000	−	568,950	=	31,050

*Negative amounts in these columns represent accumulated depreciation.

b. Use the following forms to prepare an income statement and balance sheet.

MAGNIFICENT MODEMS, INC. Income Statement For the Period Ended December 31, Year 1	
Sales	
Cost of goods sold	
Gross margin	
Sales commission	
Depreciation expense	
Administrative expense	
Net income	$31,050

MAGNIFICENT MODEMS, INC. Balance Sheet As of December 31, Year 1	
Assets:	
Cash	
Manufacturing equipment, net of acc. depreciation	
Office equipment, net of acc. depreciation	
Finished goods inventory	
Total assets	$781,050
Equity	
Common stock	
Retained earnings	
Total stockholders' equity	$781,050

CHAPTER 2

Cost Behavior, Operating Leverage, and Profitability Analysis

LEARNING OBJECTIVES

After you have mastered the material in this chapter, you will be able to:

LO 2-1 Identify and describe fixed, variable, and mixed cost behavior.

LO 2-2 Demonstrate the effects of operating leverage on profitability.

LO 2-3 Prepare an income statement using the contribution margin approach.

LO 2-4 Calculate the magnitude of operating leverage.

LO 2-5 Select an appropriate time period for calculating the average cost per unit.

LO 2-6 Use the high-low method, scattergraphs, and regression analysis to estimate fixed and variable costs.

Video lectures and accompanying self-assessment quizzes are available in Connect® for all learning objectives.

CHAPTER OPENING

Three college students are planning a vacation. One of them suggests inviting a fourth person along, remarking that four can travel for the same cost as three. Certainly, some costs will be the same whether three or four people go on the trip. For example, the hotel room costs $800 per week, regardless of whether three or four people stay in the room. In accounting terms, the cost of the hotel room is a **fixed cost.** The total amount of a fixed cost does not change when volume changes. The total hotel room cost is $800 whether one, two, three, or four people use the room. In contrast, some costs vary in direct proportion with changes in volume. When volume increases, total variable cost increases; when volume decreases, total variable cost decreases. For example, the cost of tickets to a theme park is a **variable cost.** The total cost of tickets increases proportionately with each vacationer who goes to the theme park. Cost behavior (fixed versus variable) can significantly impact profitability. This chapter explains cost behavior and ways it can be used to increase profitability.

©chrisdorney/Shutterstock

The Curious Accountant

News flash! For the third quarter of 2017, **Best Buy, Inc.**'s revenues increased 4.2 percent compared to those of the same quarter of 2016; however its operating earnings increased by 12.2 percent. For the third quarter of 2017, **Conagra Brands, Inc.**, reported that its revenues for 2017 were 4.1 percent higher than revenues for 2016, but its earnings increased 78.3 percent. During third quarter of 2017, **The Walt Disney Co.** saw its revenues decrease 0.3 percent compared to the third quarter of 2016. Unfortunately, during this period its operating earnings fell 13.5 percent.

Can you explain why such relatively small changes in these companies' revenues resulted in such relatively large changes in their earnings or losses? In other words, if a company's sales increase 10 percent, why do its earnings not also increase 10 percent? (Answer on page 67.)

COST BEHAVIOR

LO 2-1

Identify and describe fixed, variable, and mixed cost behavior.

How much more will it cost to send one additional employee to a sales meeting? If more people buy our products, can we charge less? If sales increase by 10 percent, how will profits be affected? Managers seeking answers to such questions must consider **cost behavior.** Knowing how costs behave relative to the level of business activity enables managers to more effectively plan and control costs. To illustrate, consider the entertainment company Star Productions, Inc. (SPI).

Fixed Cost Behavior

SPI specializes in promoting rock concerts. It is considering paying a band $48,000 to play a concert. Obviously, SPI must sell enough tickets to cover this cost. In this example, the relevant activity base is the number of tickets sold. The cost of the band is a fixed cost because it does not change regardless of the number of tickets sold. Exhibit 2.1 illustrates the fixed cost behavior pattern, showing the *total cost* and the *cost per unit* at three different levels of activity.

Total versus *per-unit* fixed costs behave differently. The total cost for the band remains constant (fixed) at $48,000. In contrast, fixed cost per unit decreases as volume (number of tickets sold) increases. The term *fixed cost* is consistent with the behavior of *total cost.* Total fixed cost remains constant (fixed) when activity changes. However, there is a contradiction between the term *fixed cost per unit* and the *per-unit behavior pattern of a fixed cost.* Fixed cost per unit is *not* fixed. It changes with the number of tickets sold. This contradiction in terminology can cause untold confusion. Study carefully the fixed cost behavior patterns in Exhibit 2.2.

The fixed cost data in Exhibit 2.1 help SPI's management decide whether to sponsor the concert. For example, the information influences potential pricing choices. The per-unit costs represent the minimum ticket prices required to cover the fixed cost at various levels of activity. SPI could compare these per-unit costs to the prices of competing entertainment events (such as the prices of movies, sporting events, or theater tickets). If the price is not competitive, tickets will not sell and the concert will lose money. Management must also consider the number of tickets to be sold. The volume data in Exhibit 2.1 can be compared to the band's track record of ticket sales at previous concerts. A proper analysis of these data can reduce the risk of undertaking an unprofitable venture.

EXHIBIT 2.1

Fixed Cost Behavior

Number of tickets sold (a)	2,700	3,000	3,300
Total cost of band (b)	$48,000	$48,000	$48,000
Cost per ticket sold (b ÷ a)	$ 17.78	$ 16.00	$ 14.55

EXHIBIT 2.2

Fixed Cost Behavior

	When Activity Increases	When Activity Decreases
Total fixed cost	Remains constant	Remains constant
Fixed cost **per unit**	Decreases	Increases

Variable Cost Behavior

To illustrate variable cost behavior, assume SPI arranges to pay the band $16 per ticket sold instead of a fixed $48,000. Exhibit 2.3 shows the total cost of the band and the cost per ticket sold at three different levels of activity.

Since SPI will pay the band $16 for each ticket sold, the *total* variable cost increases in direct proportion to the number of tickets sold. If SPI sells one ticket, total band cost will be $16 (1 × $16); if SPI sells two tickets, total band cost will be $32 (2 × $16); and so on. The total cost of the band increases proportionately as ticket sales move from 2,700 to 3,000 to 3,300. The variable cost *per ticket* remains $16, however, regardless of whether the number of tickets sold is 1, 2, 3, or 3,000. The behavior of variable cost *per unit* is contradictory to the word *variable.* Variable cost per unit remains *constant* regardless of how many tickets are sold. Study carefully the variable cost behavior patterns in Exhibit 2.4.

EXHIBIT 2.3

Variable Cost Behavior

Number of tickets sold (a)	2,700	3,000	3,300
Total cost of band (b)	$43,200	$48,000	$52,800
Cost per ticket sold (b ÷ a)	$ 16	$ 16	$ 16

EXHIBIT 2.4

Variable Cost Behavior

	When Activity Increases	When Activity Decreases
Total variable cost	Increases proportionately	Decreases proportionately
Variable cost **per unit**	Remains constant	Remains constant

Cost Behavior Graphs

Exhibit 2.5 provides a visual depiction of fixed cost behavior. *Total* fixed cost stays constant (remains fixed) regardless of changes in volume. However, the cost per unit *varies inversely* with changes in the level of activity. As activity increases, fixed cost per unit decreases. As activity decreases, fixed cost per unit increases.

Exhibit 2.6 provides a visual depiction of variable cost behavior. *Total* variable increases or decreases (varies) proportionately with changes in the volume of activity. In contrast, variable cost *per unit* remains *fixed* at all levels of activity.

EXHIBIT 2.5

Graphical Presentation of Fixed Cost Behavior

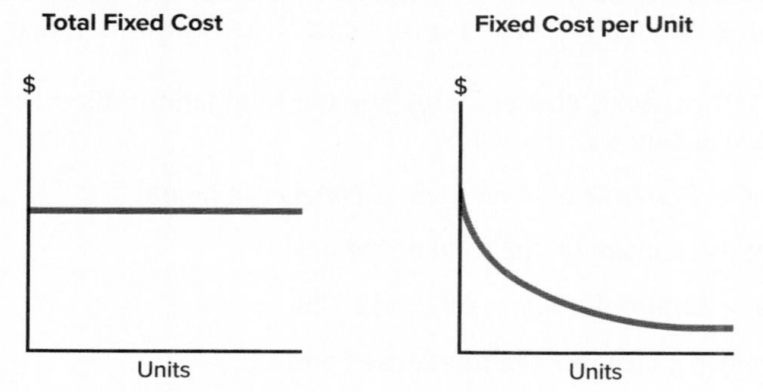

EXHIBIT 2.6

Graphical Presentation of Variable Cost Behavior

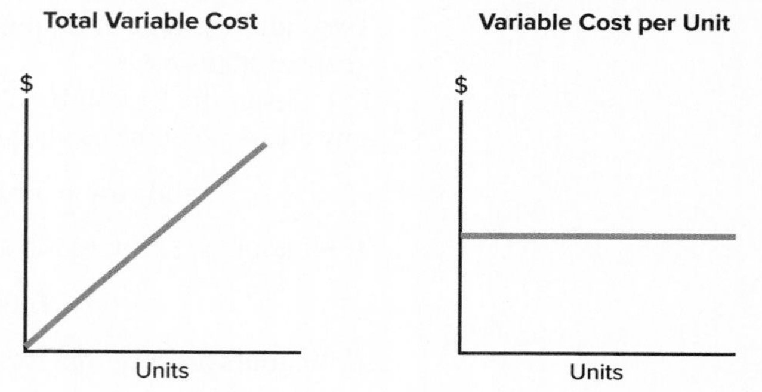

The relationships between fixed and variable costs are summarized in the chart in Exhibit 2.7. Study these relationships thoroughly.

EXHIBIT 2.7

Fixed and Variable Cost Behavior

When Activity Level Changes	Total Cost	Cost per Unit
Fixed costs	Remains constant	Changes *inversely*
Variable costs	Changes in direct proportion	Remains constant

Mixed Costs (Semivariable Costs)

Mixed costs (semivariable costs) include both fixed and variable components. For example, suppose Star Productions, Inc., has to pay for janitorial services. The charge for these services includes a base fee of $1,000 plus $20 per hour required to do a cleanup. The $1,000 base fee is fixed. It is the same no matter how many hours it takes to accomplish the cleanup. In contrast, the $20 hourly cost is a variable cost because the total cost increases with each

EXHIBIT 2.8

Examples of Mixed Costs

Type of Cost	Fixed Cost Component(s)	Variable Cost Component(s)
Cost of sales staff	Monthly salary	Bonus based on sales volume
Truck rental	Monthly rental fee	Cost of gas, tires, and maintenance
Legal fees	Monthly retainer	Reimbursements to attorney for out-of-pocket costs (copying, postage, travel, filing fees)
Outpatient service cost	Salaries of doctors and nurses, depreciation of facility, utilities	Medical supplies such as bandages, sterilization solution, and paper products
Phone services	Monthly connection fee	Per-minute usage fee
LP gas utility cost	Container rental fee	Cost of gas consumed
Cable TV services	Monthly fee	Pay-per-view charges
Training cost	Instructor salary, facility cost	Textbooks, supplies
Shipping and handling	Salaries of employees who process packages	Boxes, packing supplies, tape, and other shipping supplies, postage
Inventory holding cost	Depreciation on inventory warehouse, salaries of employees managing inventory	Delivery costs, interest on funds borrowed to finance inventory, cost of supplies

additional hour it takes to complete the cleanup. Since the total janitorial cost is composed of fixed and variable components, it is frequently called a mixed cost. It may also be called a semivariable cost.

Given the $1,000 base plus $20 per hour cost components, the total janitorial cost for any cleanup can be easily computed as follows:

$$\text{Total cost} = \text{Fixed cost} + (\text{Variable cost per hour} \times \text{Number of hours})$$

If 60 hours are required to accomplish a cleanup, the total mixed cost is:

$$\text{Total cost} = \$1{,}000 + (\$20 \times 60) = \$2{,}200$$

If 90 hours are required to accomplish a cleanup, the total mixed cost is:

$$\text{Total cost} = \$1{,}000 + (\$20 \times 90) = \$2{,}800$$

Exhibit 2.8 illustrates a variety of mixed costs businesses commonly encounter.

The Relevant Range

Suppose SPI must pay $5,000 to rent a concert hall with a seating capacity of 4,000 people. Is the cost of the concert hall fixed or variable? Since total cost remains unchanged regardless of whether one ticket, 4,000 tickets, or any number in between is sold, the cost is fixed relative to ticket sales. However, what if demand for tickets is significantly more than 4,000? In that case, SPI might rent a larger concert hall at a higher cost. In other words, *the cost is fixed only for a designated range of activity (1 to 4,000).*

A similar circumstance affects many variable costs. For example, a supplier may offer a volume discount to buyers who purchase more than a specified number of products. The point is that descriptions of cost behavior pertain to a specified range of activity. The range of activity over which the definitions of fixed and variable costs are valid is commonly called the **relevant range.**

Context-Sensitive Definitions of Fixed and Variable

The behavior pattern of a particular cost may be either fixed or variable, depending on the context. For example, the cost of the band was fixed at $48,000 when SPI was considering

EXHIBIT 2.9

Cost Behavior Relative to Number of Concerts

Number of concerts (a)	1	2	3	4	5
Cost per concert (b)	$48,000	$48,000	$ 48,000	$ 48,000	$ 48,000
Total cost (a × b)	$48,000	$96,000	$144,000	$192,000	$240,000

hiring it to play a single concert. Regardless of how many tickets SPI sold, the total band cost was $48,000. However, the band cost becomes variable if SPI decides to hire it to perform at a series of concerts. The total cost and the cost per concert for one, two, three, four, or five concerts are shown in Exhibit 2.9.

In this context, the total cost of hiring the band increases proportionately with the number of concerts while cost per concert remains constant. The band cost is therefore variable. The same cost can behave as either a fixed cost or a variable cost, depending on the **activity base.** When identifying a cost as fixed or variable, first ask, fixed or variable *relative to what activity base?* The cost of the band is fixed relative to the *number of tickets sold for a specific concert; it is variable relative to the number of concerts produced.*

☑ CHECK YOURSELF 2.1

Is the compensation cost for managers of Pizza Hut Restaurants a fixed cost or a variable cost?

Answer The answer depends on the context. For example, since a store manager's salary remains unchanged regardless of how many customers enter a particular restaurant, it can be classified as a fixed cost relative to the number of customers at a particular restaurant. However, the more restaurants that Pizza Hut operates, the higher the total managers' compensation cost will be. Accordingly, managers' salary cost would be classified as a variable cost relative to the number of restaurants opened.

OPERATING LEVERAGE

LO 2-2

Demonstrate the effects of operating leverage on profitability.

Heavy objects can be moved with little effort using *physical* leverage. Business managers apply **operating leverage** to magnify small changes in revenue into dramatic changes in profitability. The *lever* managers use to achieve disproportionate changes between revenue and profitability is fixed costs. The leverage relationships between revenue, fixed costs, and profitability are displayed in Exhibit 2.10.

When all costs are fixed, every sales dollar contributes one dollar toward the potential profitability of a project. Once sales dollars cover fixed costs, each additional sales dollar represents pure profit. As a result, a small change in sales volume can significantly affect profitability. To illustrate, assume SPI estimates it will sell 3,000 tickets for $18 each. A 10 percent difference in actual sales volume will produce a 90 percent difference in profitability. Examine the data in Exhibit 2.11 to verify this result.[1]

EXHIBIT 2.10

Operating Leverage

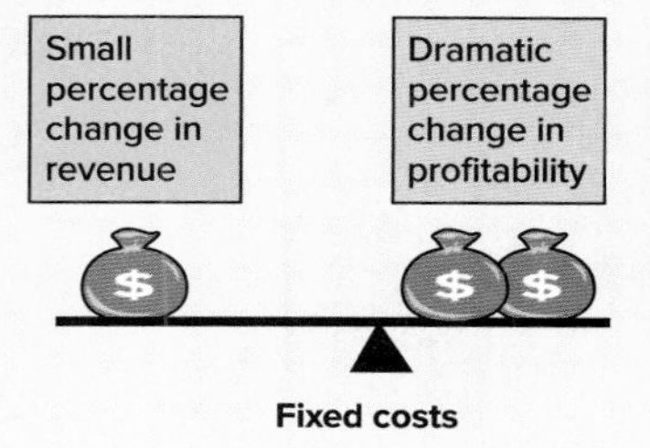

Calculating Percentage Change

The percentages in Exhibit 2.11 are computed as follows:

(Alternative measure − Base measure) ÷ Base measure = % change

[1]Do not confuse operating leverage with financial leverage. Companies employ *financial leverage* when they use debt to profit from investing money at a higher rate of return than the rate they pay on borrowed money. Companies employ *operating leverage* when they use proportionately more fixed costs than variable costs to magnify the effect on earnings of changes in revenues.

EXHIBIT 2.11

Effect of Operating Leverage on Profitability

Number of tickets sold	2,700	⇐ −10% ⇐	3,000	⇒ +10% ⇒	3,300
Sales revenue ($18 per ticket)	$ 48,600		$ 54,000		$ 59,400
Cost of band (fixed cost)	(48,000)		(48,000)		(48,000)
Gross margin	$ 600	⇐ −90% ⇐	$ 6,000	⇒ +90% ⇒	$ 11,400

The base measure is the starting point. To illustrate, compute the percentage change in gross margin when moving from 3,000 units (base measure) to 3,300 units (the alternative measure).

(Alternative measure − Base measure) ÷ Base measure = % change

($11,400 − $6,000) ÷ $6,000 = 90%

The percentage *decline* in profitability is similarly computed:

(Alternative measure − Base measure) ÷ Base measure = % change

($600 − $6,000) ÷ $6,000 = (90%)

Fixed Cost Risk and Reward Assessment

Risk refers to the possibility that sacrifices may exceed benefits. A fixed cost represents a commitment to an economic sacrifice. It represents the ultimate risk of undertaking a particular business project. If SPI pays the band but nobody buys a ticket, the company will lose $48,000. SPI can avoid this risk by substituting *variable costs* for the *fixed cost.*

Variable Cost Risk and Reward Assessment

Shifting the cost structure from fixed to variable enables SPI to avoid the fixed cost risk. Recall that under the fixed cost structure, SPI was locked into a $48,000 cost for the band regardless of how many tickets are sold. If no tickets are sold, SPI will have to report a $48,000 loss on its income statement. The risk of incurring this loss is eliminated by the variable cost structure that requires SPI to pay the band only $16 per ticket sold. If SPI sells zero tickets, then the cost of the band is zero. For each ticket sold, SPI earns a $2 profit ($18 ticket sales price − $16 fee paid to band).

Shifting the cost structure from fixed to variable reduces not only the level of risk but also the potential for profits. Managers cannot avoid the risk of fixed costs without also sacrificing the benefits. Variable costs do not offer operating leverage. Exhibit 2.12 shows that a variable cost structure produces a proportional relationship between sales and profitability. A 10 percent increase or decrease in sales results in a corresponding 10 percent increase or decrease in profitability. While the variable cost structure reduces risk, Exhibit 2.12 demonstrates that it also limits the opportunity to benefit from operating leverage.

The risk versus reward trade-off of cost structure is widespread in business practice. For example, borrowing money to buy an office building may require a company to commit to a fixed monthly principal and interest payment. If the company's revenue stream unexpectedly declines, the company still has to make its monthly payment. Indeed, many companies are

EXHIBIT 2.12

Variable Cost Eliminates Operating Leverage

Number of tickets sold	2,700	⇐ −10% ⇐	3,000	⇒ +10% ⇒	3,300
Sales revenue ($18 per ticket)	$ 48,600		$ 54,000		$ 59,400
Cost of band ($16 variable cost)	(43,200)		(48,000)		(52,800)
Gross margin	$ 5,400	⇐ −10% ⇐	$ 6,000	⇒ +10% ⇒	$ 6,600

forced into bankruptcy because they cannot satisfy their fixed debt commitments. Many companies avoid these fixed cost risks by renting their office space instead of purchasing buildings. If revenue dips, the company simply reduces the amount of office space it rents, thereby reducing its rental cost. Other real-world examples of fixed cost risk avoidance include using temporary employees instead of hiring for permanent positions and paying a variable retainer fee to an independent law firm instead of creating a legal department within the company. These examples demonstrate the widespread applicability of the trade-offs associated with cost structure. Managers continually apply professional judgment to assess the risks of locking in costs with the opportunities provided by operating leverage.

CHECK YOURSELF 2.2

Suppose that you are sponsoring concert featuring a local band. You estimate that approximately 2,000 people will buy tickets to attend the concert. The tickets are expected to be priced at $12 each. Would you prefer a contract that agrees to pay the band $10,000 or one that agrees to pay $5 per ticket purchased?

Answer Your answer would depend on how certain you are that 2,000 people will purchase tickets. If it were likely that many more than 2,000 tickets would be sold, you would be better off with a fixed cost structure, agreeing to pay the band a flat fee of $10,000. If attendance numbers are highly uncertain, you would be better off with a variable cost structure, thereby guaranteeing a lower cost if fewer people buy tickets.

Effect of Cost Structure on Profit Stability

The preceding discussion suggests that companies with higher levels of fixed costs are more likely to experience earnings volatility. To illustrate, suppose three companies produce and sell the same product. Each company sells 10 units for $10 each. Furthermore, each company incurs costs of $60 in the process of making and selling its products. However, the companies operate under radically different **cost structures.** The entire $60 of cost incurred by Company A is fixed. Company B incurs $30 of fixed cost and $30 of variable cost ($3 per unit). All $60 of cost incurred by Company C is variable ($6 per unit). Exhibit 2.13 displays income statements for the three companies.

When sales change, the amount of the corresponding change in net income is directly influenced by the company's cost structure. The more fixed cost, the greater the fluctuation in net income. To illustrate, assume sales increase by one unit; the resulting income statements are displayed in Exhibit 2.14.

Company A, with the highest level of fixed costs, experienced a $10 ($50 − $40) increase in profitability; Company C, with the lowest level of fixed cost (zero), had only a $4 ($44 − $40) increase in profitability. Company B, with a 50/50 mix of fixed and variable

EXHIBIT 2.13

Income Statements with Sales of 10 Units

	Company Name		
	A	B	C
Variable cost per unit (a)	$ 0	$ 3	$ 6
Sales revenue (10 units × $10)	$100	$100	$100
Variable cost (10 units × a)	0	(30)	(60)
Fixed cost	(60)	(30)	0
Net income	$ 40	$ 40	$ 40

EXHIBIT 2.14

Income Statements with Sales of 11 Units

	Company Name		
	A	B	C
Variable cost per unit (a)	$ 0	$ 3	$ 6
Sales revenue (11 units × $10)	$110	$110	$110
Variable cost (11 units × a)	0	(33)	(66)
Fixed cost	(60)	(30)	0
Net income	$ 50	$ 47	$ 44

EXHIBIT 2.15

Income Statements with Sales of 9 Units

	Company Name		
	A	B	C
Variable cost per unit (a)	$ 0	$ 3	$ 6
Sales revenue (9 units × $10)	$ 90	$ 90	$ 90
Variable cost (9 units × a)	0	(27)	(54)
Fixed cost	(60)	(30)	0
Net income	$ 30	$ 33	$ 36

cost, had a midrange $7 ($47 – $40) increase in net income. The effect of fixed cost on volatility applies to decreases as well as increases in sales volume. To illustrate, assume sales decrease by one unit (from 10 to 9 units). The resulting income statements are displayed in Exhibit 2.15.

Company A again experiences the largest variance in earnings ($10 decrease). Company B had a moderate decline of $7, and Company C had the least volatility with only a $4 decline.

What cost structure is the best? Should a manager use fixed or variable costs? The answer depends on sales volume expectations. A manager who expects revenues to increase should use a fixed cost structure. On the other hand, if future sales growth is uncertain or if the manager believes revenue is likely to decline, a variable cost structure makes more sense.

CHECK YOURSELF 2.3

If both Kroger Food Stores and Delta Airlines were to experience a 5 percent increase in revenues, which company would be more likely to experience a higher percentage increase in net income?

Answer Delta would be more likely to experience a higher percentage increase in net income because a large portion of its cost (e.g., employee salaries and depreciation) is fixed, while a large portion of Kroger's cost is variable (e.g., cost of goods sold).

REALITY BYTES

Most of the time when a company's revenue increases or decreases we assume it occurred because the company sold greater or fewer units of goods or services. But, revenue can also change because the price per unit changes. This is especially an issue in industries where prices are very volatile, such as petroleum products.

During the third quarter of 2015 the average spot price of Brent crude oil was $48.77 per barrel. A year later, in the third quarter of 2016, the average price had dropped to $44.68 per barrel, and two years later, in the third quarter of 2017 it was back up to $50.10. As the price of crude oil changes, the price of other petroleum products, such as gasoline, also change. Obviously this means that revenues at large oil companies will change due to the changing price of oil, but, much of their expenses, such as labor, rent, and depreciation, are relatively fixed. This situation suggests their profits should change by a bigger percentage than the change in their revenues.

Presented as follows are data for Chevron Corporation and Exxon Mobil Corporation for the quarters ending on September 30, 2015, 2016, and 2017. Dollar amounts are in millions.

Chevron	Revenues	Earnings
Third quarter 2015	$34,315	$2,057
Third quarter 2016	30,140	1,301
Third quarter 2017	36,205	1,986
Percentage change from 2015 to 2016	(12.2%)	(36.8%)
Percentage change from 2016 to 2017	20.1%	52.7%
Exxon Mobil	**Revenues**	**Earnings**
Third quarter 2015	$67,344	$4,384
Third quarter 2016	58,677	2,889
Third quarter 2017	66,165	4,085
Percentage change from 2015 to 2016	(12.9%)	(34.1%)
Percentage change from 2016 to 2017	12.8%	41.4%

© Francis Dean/123RF

As the data reveal, both companies' earnings changed by a larger percentage than the change in their revenues. As noted, this is because their fixed costs did not change proportionally to the change in revenues.

Answers to The Curious Accountant

The primary explanation for how a company's earnings can rise faster, as a percentage, than its revenue is operating leverage, and operating leverage is due entirely to fixed costs. As the chapter explains, when a company's output increases, its fixed cost per unit decreases. As long as it can keep prices about the same, this lower unit cost will result in higher profit per unit sold. In real-world companies, the relationship between changing sales levels and changing earnings levels can be very complex, but the existence of fixed costs helps to explain why a 4.2 percent rise in revenue can cause a 12.2 percent rise in net earnings. Chapter 3 will investigate the relationships among an entity's cost structure, output level, pricing strategy, and profits earned in more depth.

AN INCOME STATEMENT UNDER THE CONTRIBUTION MARGIN APPROACH

LO 2-3

Prepare an income statement using the contribution margin approach.

The impact of cost structure on profitability is so significant that managerial accountants frequently construct income statements that classify costs according to their behavior patterns. Such income statements first subtract variable costs from revenue; the resulting subtotal is called the **contribution margin.** The contribution margin represents the amount available to cover fixed expenses and thereafter to provide company profits. Net income is computed by subtracting the fixed costs from the contribution margin. A contribution margin style income statement cannot be used for public reporting (GAAP prohibits its use in external financial reports), but it is widely used for internal reporting purposes. Exhibit 2.16 illustrates income statements prepared using the contribution margin approach.

EXHIBIT 2.16

Income Statements

	Company Name	
	Bragg	Biltmore
Variable cost per unit (a)	$ 6	$ 12
Sales revenue (10 units × $20)	$ 200	$ 200
Variable cost (10 units × a)	(60)	(120)
Contribution margin	140	80
Fixed cost	(120)	(60)
Net income	$ 20	$ 20

Using Fixed Cost to Provide a Competitive Operating Advantage

Mary MaHall and John Strike have established tutoring companies to support themselves while they attend college. Both Ms. MaHall and Mr. Strike function as owner/managers; they each hire other students to actually provide the tutoring services. Ms. MaHall pays her tutors salaries; her labor costs are fixed at $16,000 per year regardless of the number of hours of tutoring performed. Mr. Strike pays his employees $8 per hour; his labor is therefore a variable cost. Both businesses currently provide 2,000 hours of tutoring services at a price of $11 per hour. As shown in Exhibit 2.17, both companies currently produce the same profit.

EXHIBIT 2.17

Comparative Profitability at 2,000 Hours of Tutoring

		MaHall		Strike
Number of hours of tutoring provided		2,000		2,000
Service revenue ($11 per hour)		$ 22,000		$ 22,000
Cost of tutors	Fixed	(16,000)	Variable ($8 × 2,000)	(16,000)
Net income		$ 6,000		$ 6,000

Suppose Ms. MaHall adopts a strategy to win over Mr. Strike's customers by reducing the price of tutoring services from $11 per hour to $7 per hour. If Ms. MaHall succeeds, her company's income will double as shown in Exhibit 2.18. Mr. Strike is in a vulnerable position because if he matches Ms. MaHall's price cut he will lose $1 ($7 new per-hour price − $8 cost per hour for tutor) for each hour of tutoring service that his company provides.

EXHIBIT 2.18

MaHall's Profitability at 4,000 Hours of Tutoring

		MaHall
Number of hours of tutoring provided		4,000
Service revenue ($7 per hour)		$ 28,000
Cost of tutors	Fixed	(16,000)
Net income (loss)		$ 12,000

Is Mr. Strike's business doomed? Not necessarily; Ms. MaHall's operating leverage strategy only works if volume increases. If Mr. Strike matches Ms. MaHall's price, thereby maintaining the existing sales volume levels between the two companies, both companies incur losses. Exhibit 2.19 verifies this conclusion. Under these circumstances, Ms. MaHall would be forced to raise her price or to face the same negative consequences that she is attempting to force on Mr. Strike.

EXHIBIT 2.19

Comparative Profitability at 2,000 Hours of Tutoring

		MaHall		Strike
Number of hours of tutoring provided		2,000		2,000
Service revenue ($7 per hour)		$ 14,000		$ 14,000
Cost of tutors	Fixed	(16,000)	Variable ($8 × 2,000)	(16,000)
Net income (loss)		$ (2,000)		$ (2,000)

MEASURING OPERATING LEVERAGE USING CONTRIBUTION MARGIN

LO 2-4

Calculate the magnitude of operating leverage.

A contribution margin income statement allows managers to easily measure operating leverage. The magnitude of operating leverage can be determined as follows:

$$\text{Magnitude of operating leverage} = \frac{\text{Contribution margin}}{\text{Net income}}$$

Applying this formula to the income statement data reported for Bragg Company and Biltmore Company in Exhibit 2.16 produces the following measures:

Bragg Company:

$$\text{Magnitude of operating leverage} = \frac{\$140}{\$20} = 7$$

Biltmore Company:

$$\text{Magnitude of operating leverage} = \frac{\$80}{\$20} = 4$$

The computations show that Bragg is more highly leveraged than Biltmore. Bragg's change in profitability will be seven times greater than a given percentage change in revenue. In contrast, Biltmore's profits change by only four times the percentage change in revenue. For example, a 10 percent increase in revenue produces a 70 percent increase (10 percent × 7) in profitability for Bragg Company and a 40 percent increase (10 percent × 4) in profitability for Biltmore Company. The income statements in Exhibits 2.20 and 2.21 confirm these expectations.

EXHIBIT 2.20

Comparative Income Statements for Bragg Company

Units (a)	10		11
Sales revenue ($20 × a)	$ 200	⇒ +10% ⇒	$ 220
Variable cost ($6 × a)	(60)		(66)
Contribution margin	140		154
Fixed cost	(120)		(120)
Net income	$ 20	⇒ +70% ⇒	$ 34

EXHIBIT 2.21

Comparative Income Statements for Biltmore Company

Units (a)	10		11
Sales revenue ($20 × a)	$ 200	⇒ +10% ⇒	$ 220
Variable cost ($12 × a)	(120)		(132)
Contribution margin	80		88
Fixed cost	(60)		(60)
Net income	$ 20	⇒ +40% ⇒	$ 28

Operating leverage itself is neither good nor bad; it represents a strategy that can work to a company's advantage or disadvantage, depending on how it is used. The next section explains how managers can use operating leverage to create a competitive business advantage.

CHECK YOURSELF 2.4

Boeing Company's 10-K annual report filed with the Securities and Exchange Commission refers to "operating margins in our Commercial Airplanes business." Is Boeing referring to gross margins or contribution margins?

Answer Since the data come from the company's external annual report, the reference must be to gross margins (revenue − cost of goods sold), a product cost measure. The contribution margin (revenue − variable cost) is a measure used in internal reporting.

COST AVERAGING

LO 2-5

Select an appropriate time period for calculating the average cost per unit.

Lake Resorts, Inc. (LRI), offers water skiing lessons for guests. Since the demand for lessons is seasonal (guests buy more lessons in July than in December), LRI has chosen to rent (rather than own) the necessary equipment (boats, skis, ropes, life jackets) only when it is needed. LRI's accountant has collected the following data pertaining to providing ski lessons:

1. The daily fee to rent equipment is $80.
2. Instructors are paid $15 per lesson hour.

EXHIBIT 2.22

Analysis of Total and Unit Cost

	Fri.	Sat.	Sun.
Number of lessons (a)	2	10	20
Cost of equipment rental	$ 80	$ 80	$ 80
Cost of instruction (a × $15)	30	150	300
Cost of fuel (a × $2)	4	20	40
Total cost (b)	$114	$250	$420
Cost per lesson (b ÷ a)	$ 57	$ 25	$ 21

3. Fuel costs are $2 per lesson hour.
4. Lessons take one hour each.
5. LRI can provide up to 20 lessons in one day.

During a recent weekend, LRI provided 2 lessons on Friday, 10 on Saturday, and 20 on Sunday. Exhibit 2.22 shows the total cost per day and the average cost per lesson for each of the three days. Since equipment rental cost is fixed relative to the number of lessons provided, the cost per lesson declines as the number of lessons increases. This explains why the cost per lesson is significantly lower on Sunday than Friday.

Assume LRI uses a cost-plus pricing strategy. The cost per lesson figures shown in Exhibit 2.22 are not useful in determining the price to charge customers. For example, it makes no sense to charge more for lessons on days like Friday when demand is low. Indeed, many businesses lower prices on days when demand is low in order to stimulate business.

The pricing problem can be solved by using a **cost averaging** approach, which averages the costs over a longer span of time.

REALITY BYTES

Alice is a business student who works part time at Costco Wholesale Corporation to help pay for her college expenses. She is currently taking a managerial accounting course and has heard her instructor refer to depreciation as a fixed cost. However, as a requirement for her first accounting course, Alice reviewed Costco's financial statements for 2013, 2015, and 2017. The depreciation expense increased about 45 percent over these five years. She is not sure why depreciation expense would be considered a fixed cost.

©niloo138/123RF

Alice's accounting instructor reminded her that when an accountant says a cost is fixed, he or she means the cost is fixed in relation to one particular factor. A cost that is fixed in relation to one factor can be variable when compared to some other factor. For example, the depreciation for a retailer may be fixed relative to the number of customers who visit a particular store, but variable relative to the number of stores the company opens. In fact, Costco's depreciation increased from 2013 to 2017 mainly because the company built and opened additional stores.

Alice's instructor suggested that Costco's depreciation expense would be more stable if analyzed on a per-store basis, rather than in total. Being curious, Alice prepared the following table, where costs are in millions. Over the five years, she noted that total depreciation expense increased 44.8 percent, while depreciation per store increased only 23.9 percent. Although the costs on a per-store basis were more stable than the total depreciation costs, they still were not fixed, so she asked her instructor for further explanation.

Fiscal Year	Number of Costco Stores	Total Depreciation Expense (millions)	Average Depreciation Expense per Store
2013	634	$ 946	$1,492,114
2015	688	1,127	1,638,081
2017	741	1,370	1,848,853

The instructor suggested Costco's average per-store depreciation costs were increasing because the equipment and buildings purchased for the new stores (opened from 2013 to 2017) probably cost more than those purchased for the older stores and Costco's new stores are often bigger than its older stores. Additionally, when old equipment in existing stores is replaced, the new equipment probably cost more than the old equipment did, which would also cause the per-store depreciation expense to increase. This would raise the average depreciation expense per store. The instructor also reminded her that in the real world very few costs are perfectly fixed or perfectly variable.

To illustrate, assume LRI uses the weekly average instead of a daily average. Further, assume that the costs for the week include the following:

Equipment rental (7 days × $80 per day)	$ 560
Cost of instruction ($15 × 50 lessons)	750
Cost of fuel ($2 × 50 lessons)	100
Total	$1,410
Average cost per lesson	$1,410/50 lessons = $28.20

If LRI desires to earn a profit of $10 per lesson, the company will set the price at $38.20 ($28.20 weekly average cost per lesson + $10.00 profit) per lesson regardless of the day of the week that a lesson is administered. On slow days, the daily profit margin is less than $10 per lesson. Indeed, on Friday, when only two lessons are provided, LRI incurs a loss of $18.80 per lesson ($38.20 price per lesson − $57 daily average cost per lesson). This loss is offset on busy days when the daily profit margin exceeds the $10 weekly average. For example, on Sunday, when 20 lessons are administered, the profit margin is $17.20 per lesson ($38.20 price per lesson − $21 daily average cost per lesson). The differences in the daily profit margins average out over the course of the week. As a result, LRI is able to charge the same price per lesson regardless of the daily demand and still attain an average profit margin of $10 per lesson for the week.

The need for a weekly average occurs because the number of lessons per day fluctuates radically, thereby causing significant differences in the cost per lesson when calculated on a daily basis. A similar problem occurs if the number of lessons per week fluctuates radically from week to week. For example, the demand for skiing lessons may increase significantly during the week of July 4th or other holidays. Similarly, the demand for lessons may taper off toward the end of the summer. In this case, it will be necessary to expand the time frame for which the average is calculated, perhaps over the summer months or even several seasons.

Distortions can occur when the time period is too long as well as too short. For example, the price of fuel and equipment rental changes over time. If older costs are mixed with newer costs, the average does not represent current conditions. Choosing the best time frame for calculating the average cost of a product or service requires thoughtful analysis and judgment.

USE OF ESTIMATES IN REAL-WORLD PROBLEMS

LO 2-6

Use the high-low method, scattergraphs, and regression analysis to estimate fixed and variable costs.

Imagine trying to classify as fixed or variable all the different costs incurred by a large company such as Delta Air Lines. Record keeping would be horrendous. Further complications would arise because some costs are mixed costs. Consider the cost Delta incurs to use airport facilities. An airport may charge Delta a flat annual rental fee for terminal space plus a charge each time a plane takes off or lands. The flat rental fee is a fixed cost while the charge per flight is variable. The total facilities cost is mixed.

To minimize the record-keeping difficulties involved in identifying actual fixed and variable costs, many companies make decisions using estimated rather than actual costs. Several techniques exist to divide total cost into estimated fixed and variable components.

High-Low Method of Estimating Fixed and Variable Costs

The management of Rainy Day Books (RDB) wants to expand operations. To help evaluate the risks involved in opening an additional store, the company president wants to know the amount of fixed cost a new store will likely incur. Suppose RDB's accountant decides to use the **high-low method** to supply the president with the requested information. The estimated amount of fixed cost for the new store would be developed in the following four steps.

Step 1 ***Assemble sales volume and cost history for an existing store.*** Assuming the new store will operate with roughly the same cost structure, the accountant can use the

EXHIBIT 2.23

Cost Data

Month	Units Sold	Total Cost
January	30,000	$450,000
February	14,000	300,000
March	12,000	150,000
April	25,000	440,000
May	10,000	180,000
June	11,000	240,000
July	20,000	350,000
August	18,000	400,000
September	17,000	360,000
October	16,000	320,000
November	27,000	490,000
December	34,000	540,000

historical data to estimate the fixed cost likely to be incurred by the new store. To illustrate, assume the accounting data set for the existing store is displayed in Exhibit 2.23.

Step 2 ***Select the high and low points in the data set.*** In this example, the month with the lowest number of units sold does not correspond to the month with the lowest total cost. The lowest point in units sold occurred in May; the lowest total cost occurred in March. Because the total cost depends on the *number of units sold,* May should be classified as the low point. The high point in sales volume occurred in December. The units sold and cost data for the December and May high and low points follow.

	Units Sold	Total Cost
High (December)	34,000	$540,000
Low (May)	10,000	$180,000

Step 3 ***Determine the estimated variable cost per unit.*** The variable cost per unit is determined by dividing the difference in the total cost by the difference in the number of units sold. In this case, the variable cost per unit is as follows:

$$\frac{\text{Variable}}{\text{cost per unit}} = \frac{\text{Difference in total cost}}{\text{Difference in volume}} = \frac{(\$540{,}000 - \$180{,}000)}{(34{,}000 - 10{,}000)} = \frac{\$360{,}000}{24{,}000} = \$15$$

Step 4 ***Determine the estimated total fixed cost.*** The total fixed cost can now be determined by subtracting the variable cost from the total cost using either the high point or the low point. Either point yields the same result. Computations using the high point follow:

$$\text{Fixed cost} + \text{Variable cost} = \text{Total cost}$$

$$\text{Fixed cost} = \text{Total cost} - \text{Variable cost}$$

$$\text{Fixed cost} = \$540{,}000 - (\$15 \times 34{,}000 \text{ units})$$

$$\text{Fixed cost} = \$30{,}000$$

Once determined, the *total* fixed cost and variable cost *per unit* estimates can be used to predict expected total cost at any volume of activity as follows:

$$\text{Total cost} = \text{Fixed cost} + (\text{Variable cost per unit} \times \text{Number of units})$$

If 22,000 books are sold, the total estimated cost is:

$$\text{Total cost} = \$30{,}000 + (\$15 \times 22{,}000) = \$360{,}000$$

If 32,000 books are sold, the total estimated cost is:

$$\text{Total cost} = \$30{,}000 + (\$15 \times 32{,}000) = \$510{,}000$$

Although 12 data points are available, the high-low method uses only 2 of them to estimate the amounts of fixed and variable costs. If either or both of these points is not representative of the true relationship between fixed and variable costs, the estimates produced by the high-low method will be inaccurate. *The chief advantage of the high-low method is its simplicity; the chief disadvantage is its vulnerability to inaccuracy.* RDB's accountant decides to test the accuracy of the high-low method results.

Scattergraph Method of Estimating Fixed and Variable Costs

Scattergraphs are sometimes used as an estimation technique for dividing total cost into fixed and variable cost components. To assess the accuracy of the high-low estimate of fixed cost, RDB's accountant constructs a **scattergraph.** The horizontal axis is labeled with the number of books sold and the vertical axis with total costs. The 12 data points are plotted on the graph, and a line is drawn through the high and low points in the data set. The result is shown in Exhibit 2.24.

After studying the scattergraph in Exhibit 2.24, the accountant is certain that the high and low points are not representative of the data set. Most of the data points are above the high-low line. As shown in the second scattergraph in Exhibit 2.25, the line should be shifted upward to reflect the influence of the other data points.

EXHIBIT 2.24

Scattergraph Depicting High-Low Estimate

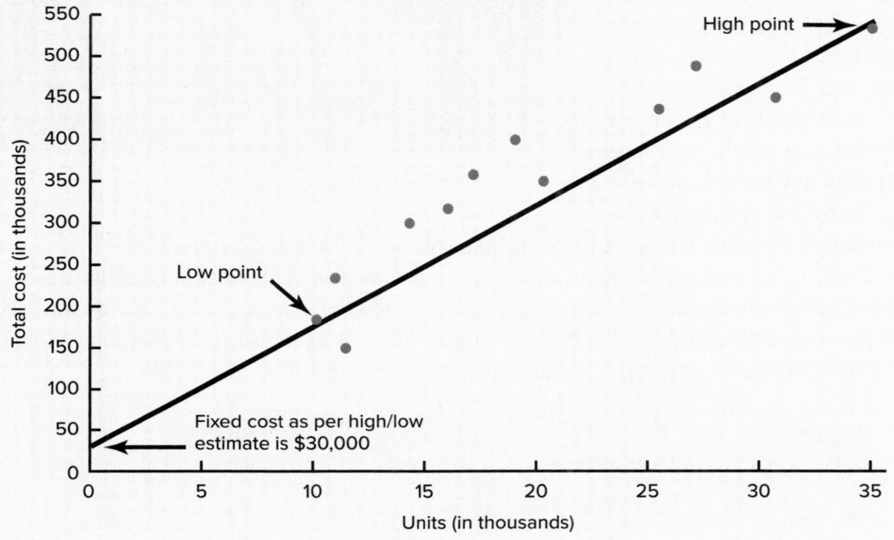

EXHIBIT 2.25

Scattergraph Depicting Line Drawn by Visual Inspection

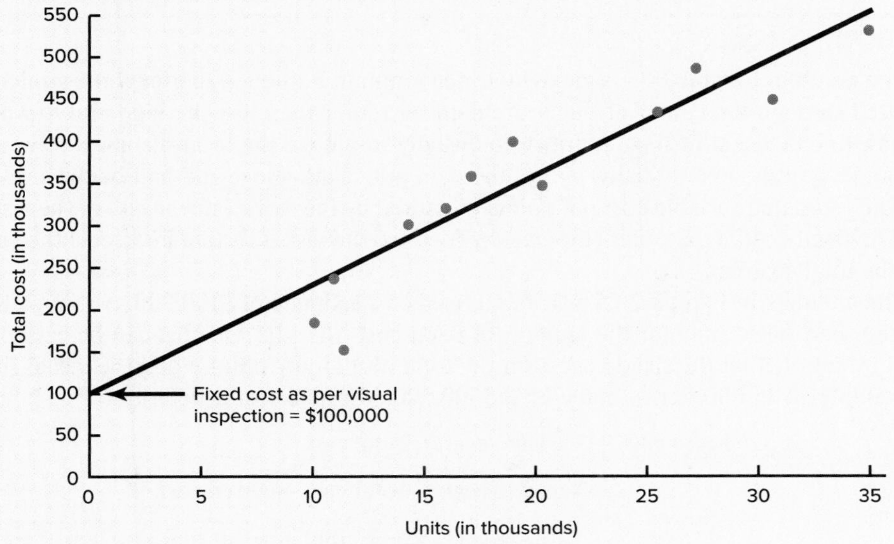

FOCUS ON INTERNATIONAL ISSUES

ANOTHER REASON FIXED COSTS AREN'T ALWAYS FIXED

© Lestertair/Shutterstock

Suppose that a company is renting a facility at an annual rental rate that does not change for the next five years *no matter what.* Is this a fixed cost? By now, you are aware that the proper response is to ask fixed in relation to what? Is the rental cost of this facility fixed in relation to the activity at this facility? The answer seems to be yes, but it might be "not necessarily."

Consider the large multinational company **Samsung Electronics Company**, which has its headquarters in Suwon, South Korea. Although Samsung does a lot of business in Korea where the currency is the Korean won, it does 90 percent of its business in other countries. Suppose Samsung rents facilities in Japan. The annual rental fee is usually stated and paid in the currency of the local country, which in Japan is the yen. Even though Samsung may be paying the same number of yen in rent each year, Samsung's rental cost in won could vary greatly over time due to fluctuation in the exchange rate between the won and the yen. Such potential foreign currency exchange fluctuations cause companies to enter very complex hedging arrangements to add stability to transactions that must be paid in foreign currencies.

The following information, taken from Samsung's 2016 financial statements, gives a perspective of the international dimensions of the company. Before a multinational company can answer the question, "Is a cost fixed?" it must determine what currency the person asking the question has in mind. Even though Samsung measures its activities using the Korean won, its financial transactions take place using dozens of different currencies, which have exchange rates that are constantly changing. The symbol for the Korean won is "₩."

Geographic Area	Segment Earnings*	Percentage of Total	Total Assets*	Percentage of Total
American	₩ 68,728,575	34%	₩ 7,041,731	7%
Asia and Africa	39,099,991	19	9,626,711	10
Europe	38,253,185	19	730,490	1
China	35,583,166	18	11,132,720	11
Korea	20,201,828	10	68,978,040	71
Totals	₩201,866,745	100%	₩97,509,692	100%

*Amounts in millions of won.

The graph in Exhibit 2.25 is identical to the graph in Exhibit 2.24 except the straight line is plotted through the center of the entire data set rather than just the high and low points. The new line, a **visual fit line,** is drawn to visually minimize the total distance between the data points and the line. Usually, half of the data points are above and half below a visual fit line. The estimated variable cost per unit is measured by the slope (steepness) of the visual fit line. The fixed cost is the point (the *intercept*) where the visual fit line intersects the vertical axis (the total cost line).

The intercept in Exhibit 2.25 provides a fixed cost estimate of $100,000. Although RDB's president had asked only for the amount of fixed cost, the variable cost can be easily determined by subtracting the fixed cost from the total cost at any point along the visual fit line. For example, at 15,000 units, total cost is $300,000. Variable cost is determined as follows:

$$\text{Fixed cost} + \text{Variable cost} = \text{Total cost}$$
$$\text{Variable cost} = \text{Total cost} - \text{Fixed cost}$$
$$\text{Variable cost} = \$300{,}000 - \$100{,}000$$
$$\text{Variable cost} = \$200{,}000$$

Variable cost per unit is \$13.3333, calculated by dividing the total variable cost by the number of units (\$200,000 ÷ 15,000 units = \$13.3333 per unit).

As with the high-low method, these *total* fixed cost and variable cost *per unit* estimates can be used to predict expected total cost at any volume of activity as follows:

Total cost = Fixed cost + (Variable cost per unit × Number of units)

If 22,000 books are sold, the total estimated cost is:

Total cost = \$100,000 + (\$13.3333 × 22,000) = \$393,333

If 32,000 books are sold, the total estimated cost is:

Total cost = \$100,000 + (\$13.3333 × 32,000) = \$526,666

Clearly, the visual fit scattergraph approach produces different estimates of total cost than the high-low method provides. Remember, both approaches produce estimates about anticipated future costs. Accuracy cannot be determined until actual costs are incurred. Accountants must exercise judgment in deciding which method is the best approach for the particular circumstances under consideration.

Regression Method of Cost Estimation

Since the scattergraph is drawn by simple visual inspection, it is subject to human error. A better fit can be obtained using a statistical procedure known as **least-squares regression.**[2] Many of today's spreadsheet programs include a regression procedure. For example, the regression estimates shown in Exhibit 2.26 were generated in an Excel spreadsheet by performing the following functions:

1. Enter the data in spreadsheet columns[3] (see columns B and C, rows 3 through 14 in Exhibit 2.26).
2. Click the *Data* tab.
3. Click *Data Analysis*.[4]
4. Click *Regression* and then *OK.*
5. Define data ranges and click *Line Fit Plot.*
5. Click *OK.*

Cost Estimates

The regression function returns a fixed cost estimate of \$72,848 and a variable cost estimate of \$14.30 per unit. These estimates are highlighted in blue in the spreadsheet shown in Exhibit 2.26. As with the high-low and visual fit scattergraph methods, the *total* fixed cost and variable cost *per unit* estimates computed using regression can be used to predict expected total cost at any volume of activity as follows:

Total cost = Fixed cost + (Variable cost per unit × Number of units)

[2]Although the least-squares regression is a more accurate method than the high-low method and the visual scattergraph method, the three methods follow the same logical reasoning. Basically, the procedure locates a straight line on a coordinate with the Y axis representing the cost in dollars and the X axis representing the cost driver. In the examples shown in this chapter, the measurement of production in units is used as the cost driver and appears on the X axis. The basic regression model can be explained in the following equation:

$$Y = a + bX$$

Where

a = Total fixed cost, or the Y intercept of the regression line

b = Variable cost per unit of X, or the slope of the regression line

X = Independent variable

Y = Dependent variable

[3]Statistical reliability requires an information set that includes more than 30 data points. The illustration shown here has been limited in size to simplify the demonstration.

[4]If the data tab does not contain a data analysis option, it is likely that the statistical functions have not been activated in your program. You will need to consult the Excel user manual or help routine for instructions to activate the statistical functions.

EXHIBIT 2.26

Excel Spreadsheet Showing the Results of Least-Squares Regression

Month	Units Sold	Total Cost
January	30,000	$450,000
February	14,000	300,000
March	12,000	150,000
April	25,000	440,000
May	10,000	180,000
June	11,000	240,000
July	20,000	350,000
August	18,000	400,000
September	17,000	360,000
October	16,000	320,000
November	27,000	490,000
December	34,000	540,000

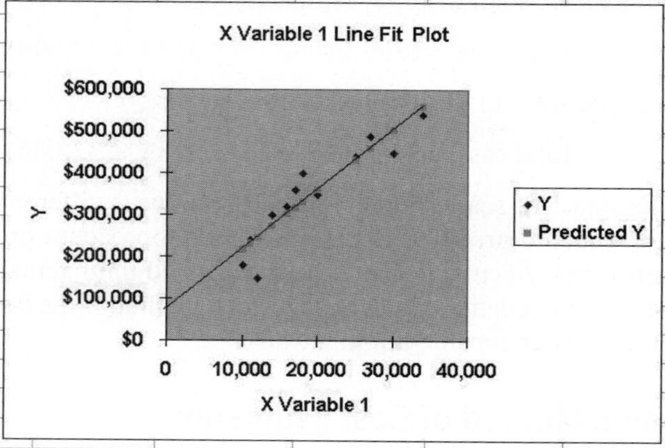

Regression Statistics	
Multiple R	0.9278612
R Square	0.8609264
Adj R Squar	0.8470191
Std Error	47284.664
Observatior	12

	Coefficient	*Standard Erro*	*t Stat*	*P-value*	*Lower 95%*	*Upper 95%*	*Lower 95.0%*	*Jpper 95.0%*
Intercept	72848.35	37975.2811	1.91831	0.084043	-11765.863	157462.56	-11765.863	157462.56
X Variable	14.29838	1.81729728	7.86793	1.36E-05	10.249184	18.347567	10.249184	18.347567

Sheet4 Sheet5 Sheet1 Sheet2 Sheet3

Source: Microsoft Excel 2010

If 22,000 books are sold, the total estimated cost is:

$$\text{Total cost} = \$72,848 + (\$14.30 \times 22,000) = \$387,448$$

If 32,000 books are sold, the total estimated cost is:

$$\text{Total cost} = \$72,848 + (\$14.30 \times 32,000) = \$530,448$$

As with the high-low method, **regression analysis** can be skewed by data points that are not representative of the complete data set. Here also, such outliers can be identified using visual fit scattergraphs. Again, management accountants must use common sense when interpreting the cost estimates. Choosing among the high-low method, visual fit scattergraphs, or regression analysis requires judgment. All three methods may be used to evaluate the consistency of the results.

Regression Statistics

An advantage of the regression method is that it provides statistics that give insight as to the reliability of the cost estimates. The R Square (R^2), highlighted in red in Exhibit 2.26, is the most commonly used measure of reliability. The **R^2 statistic** represents the percentage of change in the dependent variable (total cost) that is explained by a change in the independent variable (units sold). In the case of Rainy Day Books, the R^2 suggests that 86 percent of the change in the total monthly cost of operating a new store is caused by a change in the number of books sold. In other words, some factors other than the number of books sold also affect total costs. For example, the weight and size of the books, as well as the number sold, may affect shipping costs.

The R^2 values vary between zero and 100 percent. Higher R^2 values suggest that the independent variable more strongly influences the dependent variable. For Rainy Day Books, the relatively high R^2 of 86 percent suggests that the number of books sold will significantly affect the total cost of operating a new store.

Multiple Regression Analysis

As discussed earlier, Rainy Day Books' dependent variable (total cost) is influenced by more factors than the single independent variable (units sold). **Multiple regression analysis** is a statistical tool that permits analysis of how a number of independent variables simultaneously affect a dependent variable. Multiple regression analysis can improve the accuracy of fixed and variable cost estimates. A trial and error process using multiple regression analysis is frequently used to assess the relative importance of a variety of independent variables. The regression analysis is performed repeatedly, dropping and adding independent variables, until an acceptable level of accuracy is achieved.

A Look Back <<

To plan and control business operations effectively, managers need to understand how different costs behave in relation to changes in the volume of activity. Total *fixed cost* remains constant when activity changes. Fixed cost per unit decreases with increases in activity and increases with decreases in activity. In contrast, total *variable cost* increases proportionately with increases in activity and decreases proportionately with decreases in activity. Variable cost per unit remains constant regardless of activity levels. The definitions of fixed and variable costs have meaning only within the context of a specified range of activity (the relevant range) for a defined period of time. In addition, cost behavior depends on the relevant volume measure (a store manager's salary is fixed relative to the number of customers visiting a particular store but is variable relative to the number of stores operated). A mixed cost has both fixed and variable cost components.

Fixed costs allow companies to take advantage of *operating leverage.* With operating leverage, each additional sale decreases the cost per unit. This principle allows a small percentage change in volume of revenue to cause a significantly larger percentage change in profits. The *magnitude of operating leverage* can be determined by dividing the contribution margin by net income. When all costs are fixed and revenues have covered fixed costs, each additional dollar of revenue represents pure profit. Having a fixed cost structure (employing operating leverage) offers a company both risks and rewards. If sales volume increases, costs do not increase, allowing profits to soar. Alternatively, if sales volume decreases, costs do not decrease and profits decline significantly more than revenues. Companies with high variable costs in relation to fixed costs do not experience as great a level of operating leverage. Their costs increase or decrease in proportion to changes in revenue. These companies face less risk but fail to reap disproportionately higher profits when volume soars.

Under the contribution margin approach, variable costs are subtracted from revenue to determine the *contribution margin*. Fixed costs are then subtracted from the contribution margin to determine net income. The contribution margin represents the amount available to pay fixed costs and provide a profit. Although not permitted by GAAP for external reporting, many companies use the contribution margin format for internal reporting purposes.

Cost per unit is an average cost that is easier to compute than the actual cost of each unit and is more relevant to decision making than actual cost. Accountants must use judgment when choosing the time span from which to draw data for computing the average cost per unit. Distortions can result from using either too long or too short a time span.

Fixed and variable costs can be estimated using such tools as the *high-low method, scattergraphs*, and *regression analysis*. The high-low method and scattergraphs are easy to use. Regression analysis is more accurate.

>> A Look Forward

The next chapter will show you how changes in cost, volume, and pricing affect profitability. You will learn to determine the number of units of product that must be produced and sold in order to break even (the number of units that will produce an amount of revenue that is exactly equal to total cost). You will learn to establish the price of a product using a cost-plus pricing approach and to establish the cost of a product using a target-pricing approach. Finally, the chapter will show you how to use a break-even chart to examine potential profitability over a range of operating activity and how to use a technique known as *sensitivity analysis* to examine how simultaneous changes in sales price, volume, fixed costs, and variable costs affect profitability.

Video lectures and accompanying self-assessment quizzes are available in *Connect* for all learning objectives.

SELF-STUDY REVIEW PROBLEM

Mensa Mountaineering Company (MMC) provides guided mountain climbing expeditions in the Rocky Mountains. Its only major expense is guide salaries; it pays each guide $4,800 per climbing expedition. MMC charges its customers $1,500 per expedition and expects to take five climbers on each expedition.

Part 1

Base your answers on the preceding information.

Required

a. Determine the total cost of guide salaries and the cost of guide salaries per climber assuming that four, five, or six climbers are included in a trip. Relative to the number of climbers in a single expedition, is the cost of guides a fixed or a variable cost?

b. Relative to the number of expeditions, is the cost of guides a fixed or a variable cost?

c. Determine the profit of an expedition assuming that five climbers are included in the trip.

d. Determine the profit assuming a 20 percent increase (six climbers total) in expedition revenue. What is the percentage change in profitability?

e. Determine the profit assuming a 20 percent decrease (four climbers total) in expedition revenue. What is the percentage change in profitability?

f. Explain why a 20 percent shift in revenue produces more than a 20 percent shift in profitability. What term describes this phenomenon?

Part 2

Assume that the guides offer to make the climbs for a percentage of expedition fees. Specifically, MMC will pay guides $960 per climber on the expedition. Assume also that the expedition fee charged to climbers remains at $1,500 per climber.

Required

g. Determine the total cost of guide salaries and the cost of guide salaries per climber assuming that four, five, or six climbers are included in a trip. Relative to the number of climbers in a single expedition, is the cost of guides a fixed or a variable cost?

h. Relative to the number of expeditions, is the cost of guides a fixed or a variable cost?

i. Determine the profit of an expedition assuming that five climbers are included in the trip.

j. Determine the profit assuming a 20 percent increase (six climbers total) in expedition revenue. What is the percentage change in profitability?

k. Determine the profit assuming a 20 percent decrease (four climbers total) in expedition revenue. What is the percentage change in profitability?

l. Explain why a 20 percent shift in revenue does not produce more than a 20 percent shift in profitability.

Solution to Part 1, Requirement *a*

Number of climbers (a)	4	5	6
Total cost of guide salaries (b)	$4,800	$4,800	$4,800
Cost per climber (b ÷ a)	1,200	960	800

Since the total cost remains constant (fixed) regardless of the number of climbers on a particular expedition, the cost is classified as fixed. Note that the cost per climber decreases as the number of climbers increases. This is the *per-unit* behavior pattern of a fixed cost.

Solution to Part 1, Requirement *b*

Since the total cost of guide salaries changes proportionately each time the number of expeditions increases or decreases, the cost of salaries is variable relative to the number of expeditions.

Solution to Part 1, Requirements *c, d,* and *e*

Number of Climbers	4	Percentage Change	5	Percentage Change	6
Revenue ($1,500 per climber)	$6,000	⇐ −20% ⇐	$7,500	⇒ +20% ⇒	$9,000
Cost of guide salaries (fixed)	4,800		4,800		4,800
Net income	$1,200	⇐ −55.6% ⇐	$2,700	⇒ +55.6% ⇒	$4,200

Percentage change in revenue: ±$1,500 ÷ $7,500 = ±20%

Percentage change in profit: ±$1,500 ÷ $2,700 = ±55.6%

Solution to Part 1, Requirement *f*

Since the cost of guide salaries remains fixed while volume (number of climbers) changes, the change in net income, measured in absolute dollars, exactly matches the change in revenue. More specifically, each time MMC increases the number of climbers by one, revenue and net income increase by $1,500. Since the base figure for net income ($2,700) is lower than the base figure for revenue ($7,500), the percentage change in net income ($1,500 ÷ $2,700 = 55.6 percent) is higher than the percentage change in revenue ($1,500 ÷ $7,500). This phenomenon is called *operating leverage.*

Solution to Part 2, Requirement *g*

Number of climbers (a)	4	5	6
Per climber cost of guide salaries (b)	$ 960	$ 960	$ 960
Cost per climber (b × a)	3,840	4,800	5,760

Since the total cost changes in proportion to changes in the number of climbers, the cost is classified as variable. Note that the cost per climber remains constant (stays the same) as the number of climbers increases or decreases. This is the *per-unit* behavior pattern of a variable cost.

Solution to Part 2, Requirement *h*

Since the total cost of guide salaries changes proportionately with changes in the number of expeditions, the cost of salaries is also variable relative to the number of expeditions.

Solution to Part 2, Requirements *i, j,* and *k*

Number of Climbers	4	Percentage Change	5	Percentage Change	6
Revenue ($1,500 per climber)	$6,000	⇐ −20% ⇐	$7,500	⇒ +20% ⇒	$9,000
Cost of guide salaries (variable)	3,840		4,800		5,760
Net income	$2,160	⇐ −20% ⇐	$2,700	⇒ +20% ⇒	$3,240

Percentage change in revenue: ±$1,500 ÷ $7,500 = ±20%

Percentage change in profit: ±$540 ÷ $2,700 = ±20%

Solution to Part 2, Requirement *l*

Since the cost of guide salaries changes when volume (number of climbers) changes, the change in net income is proportionate to the change in revenue. More specifically, each time the number of climbers increases by one, revenue increases by $1,500 and net income increases by $540 ($1,500 − $960). Accordingly, the percentage change in net income will always equal the percentage change in revenue. This means that there is no operating leverage when all costs are variable.

KEY TERMS

Activity base 63
Contribution margin 67
Cost averaging 70
Cost behavior 60
Cost structure 65
Fixed cost 58
High-low method 71
Least-squares regression 72
Mixed costs (semivariable costs) 61
Multiple regression analysis 77
Operating leverage 63
R^2 statistic 76
Regression analysis 76
Relevant range 62
Scattergraph 72
Variable cost 59
Visual fit line 74

QUESTIONS

1. Define *fixed cost* and *variable cost* and give an example of each.
2. How can knowing cost behavior relative to volume fluctuations affect decision making?
3. Define the term *operating leverage* and explain how it affects profits.
4. How is operating leverage calculated?
5. Explain the limitations of using operating leverage to predict profitability.
6. If volume is increasing, would a company benefit more from a pure variable or a pure fixed cost structure? Which cost structure would be advantageous if volume is decreasing?
7. Would a fixed or variable cost structure be more advantageous if volume is decreasing?
8. Explain the risk and rewards to a company that result from having fixed costs.
9. Are companies with predominately fixed cost structures likely to be more profitable?
10. How is the relevant range of activity related to fixed and variable cost? Give an example of how the definitions of these costs become invalid when volume is outside the relevant range.
11. Sam's Garage is trying to determine the cost of providing an oil change. Why would the average cost of this service be more relevant information than the actual cost for each customer?
12. When would the high-low method be appropriate for estimating variable and fixed costs? When would least-squares regression be the most desirable?
13. Between the variable cost structure and the fixed cost structure, which has the greater risk? Explain.
14. The president of Bright Corporation tells you that he sees a dim future for his company. He feels that his hands are tied because fixed costs are too high. He says that fixed costs do not change and therefore the situation is hopeless. Do you agree? Explain.
15. All costs are variable because if a business ceases operations, its costs fall to zero. Do you agree with this statement? Explain.
16. Because of seasonal fluctuations, Norel Corporation has a problem determining the unit cost of the products it produces. For example, high heating costs during the winter months causes per-unit cost to be higher than per-unit cost in the summer months even when the same number of units of product is produced. Suggest several ways that Norel can improve the computation of per-unit costs.
17. Verna Salsbury tells you that she thinks the terms *fixed cost* and *variable cost* are confusing. She notes that fixed cost per unit changes when the number of units changes. Furthermore, variable cost per unit remains fixed regardless of how many units are produced. She concludes that the terminology seems to be backward. Explain why the terminology appears to be contradictory.

MULTIPLE-CHOICE QUESTIONS

Multiple-choice questions are available in *Connect*.

EXERCISES—SERIES A

connect **All applicable Exercises in Series A are available in *Connect*.**

LO 2-1

Exercise 2-1A *Identifying cost behavior*

Rachael's Restaurant, a fast-food restaurant company, operates a chain of restaurants across the nation. Each restaurant employs eight people; one is a manager paid a salary plus a bonus equal to 4 percent of sales. Other employees, two cooks, one dishwasher, and four servers, are paid salaries. Each manager is budgeted $3,000 per month for advertising costs.

Required

Classify each of the following costs incurred by Rachael's Restaurant as fixed, variable, or mixed.

a. Advertising costs relative to the number of customers for a particular restaurant.
b. Rental costs relative to the number of restaurants.
c. Cooks' salaries at a particular location relative to the number of customers.
d. Cost of supplies (cups, plates, spoons, etc.) relative to the number of customers.
e. Manager's compensation relative to the number of customers.
f. Servers' salaries relative to the number of restaurants.

Exercise 2-2A *Identifying cost behavior*

LO 2-1

At the various activity levels shown, Harper Company incurred the following costs.

	Units Sold	20	40	60	80	100
a.	Rental cost per unit of merchandise sold	$ 36.00	$ 18.00	$ 12.00	$ 9.00	$ 7.20
b.	Total phone expense	80.00	100.00	120.00	140.00	160.00
c.	Cost per unit of supplies	1.00	1.00	1.00	1.00	1.00
d.	Total insurance cost	480.00	480.00	480.00	480.00	480.00
e.	Total salary cost	1,200.00	1,600.00	2,000.00	2,400.00	2,800.00
f.	Total cost of goods sold	1,800.00	3,600.00	5,400.00	7,200.00	9,000.00
g.	Depreciation cost per unit	240.00	120.00	80.00	60.00	48.00
h.	Total rent cost	3,200.00	3,200.00	3,200.00	3,200.00	3,200.00
i.	Total cost of shopping bags	2.00	4.00	6.00	8.00	10.00
j.	Cost per unit of merchandise sold	90.00	90.00	90.00	90.00	90.00

Required

Identify each of these costs as fixed, variable, or mixed.

Exercise 2-3A *Determining fixed cost per unit*

LO 2-1

Fanning Corporation incurs the following annual fixed costs.

Item	Cost
Depreciation	$ 80,000
Officers' salaries	190,000
Long-term lease	42,000
Property taxes	48,000

Required

Determine the total fixed cost per unit of production, assuming that Fanning produces 4,000, 4,500, or 5,000 units.

Exercise 2-4A *Determining total variable cost*

LO 2-1

The following variable production costs apply to goods made by O'Brien Manufacturing Corporation.

Item	Cost per Unit
Materials	$ 6.00
Labor	3.00
Variable overhead	3.50
Total	$12.50

Required

Determine the total variable production cost, assuming that O'Brien makes 4,000, 8,000, or 12,000 units.

LO 2-1

Exercise 2-5A *Fixed versus variable cost behavior*

Tanaka Company's cost and production data for two recent months included the following.

	March	April
Production (units)	300	600
Rent	$1,800	$1,800
Utilities	$ 600	$1,200

Required

a. Separately calculate the rental cost per unit and the utilities cost per unit for both March and April.

b. Identify which cost is variable and which is fixed. Explain your answer.

LO 2-1

Exercise 2-6A *Fixed versus variable cost behavior*

Leach Trophies makes and sells trophies it distributes to little league ballplayers. The company normally produces and sells between 6,000 and 12,000 trophies per year. The following cost data apply to various activity levels.

Number of Trophies	6,000	8,000	10,000	12,000
Total costs incurred				
Fixed	$ 60,000			
Variable	60,000			
Total costs	$120,000			
Cost per unit				
Fixed	$ 10.00			
Variable	10.00			
Total cost per trophy	$ 20.00			

Required

a. Complete the preceding table by filling in the missing amounts for the levels of activity shown in the first row of the table. Round all cost-per-unit figures to the nearest whole penny.

b. Explain why the total cost per trophy decreases as the number of trophies increases.

LO 2-1

Exercise 2-7A *Fixed versus variable cost behavior*

Bell Entertainment sponsors rock concerts. The company is considering a contract to hire a band at a cost of $84,000 per concert.

Required

a. What are the total band cost and the cost per person if concert attendance is 2,000, 2,500, 3,000, 3,500, or 4,000?

b. Is the cost of hiring the band a fixed or a variable cost?

c. Draw a graph and plot total cost and cost per unit if attendance is 2,000, 2,500, 3,000, 3,500, or 4,000.

d. Identify Bell's major business risks and explain how they can be minimized.

LO 2-1

Exercise 2-8A *Fixed versus variable cost behavior*

Bell Entertainment sells souvenir T-shirts at each rock concert that it sponsors. The shirts cost $7 each. Any excess shirts can be returned to the manufacturer for a full refund of the purchase price. The sales price is $16 per shirt.

Required

a. What are the total cost of shirts and cost per shirt if sales amount to 2,000, 2,500, 3,000, 3,500, or 4,000?

b. Is the cost of T-shirts a fixed or a variable cost?

c. Draw a graph and plot total cost and cost per shirt if sales amount to 2,000, 2,500, 3,000, 3,500, or 4,000.

d. Comment on Bell's likelihood of incurring a loss due to its operating activities.

Exercise 2-9A *Graphing fixed cost behavior*

LO 2-1

The following graph setups depict the dollar amount of fixed cost on the vertical axes and the level of activity on the horizontal axes.

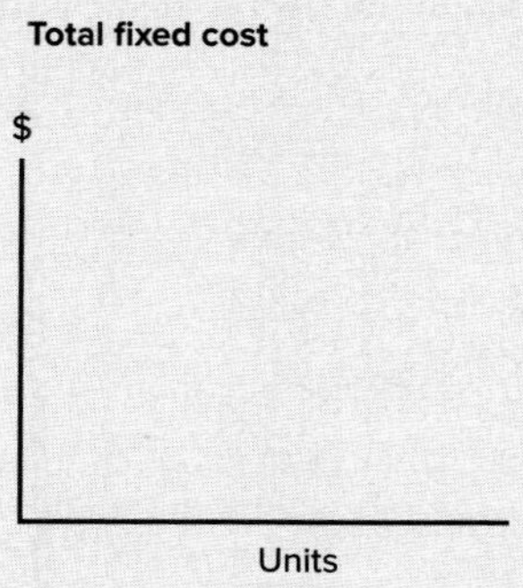

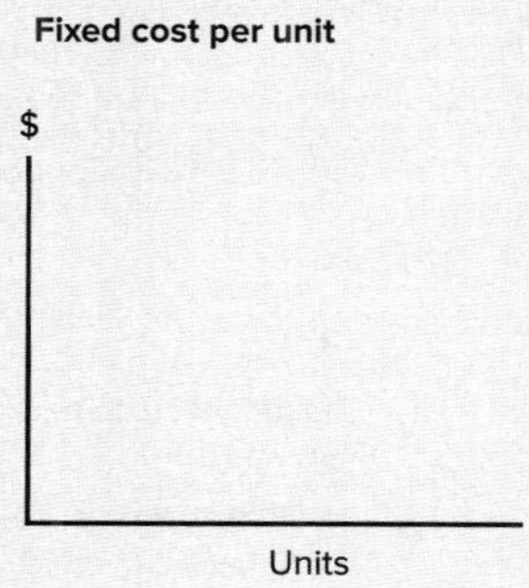

Required

a. Draw a line that depicts the relationship between total fixed cost and the level of activity.

b. Draw a line that depicts the relationship between fixed cost per unit and the level of activity.

Exercise 2-10A *Graphing variable cost behavior*

LO 2-1

The following graph setups depict the dollar amount of variable cost on the vertical axes and the level of activity on the horizontal axes.

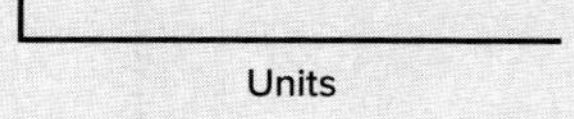

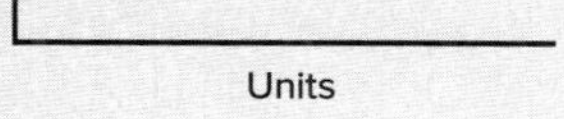

Required

a. Draw a line that depicts the relationship between total variable cost and the level of activity.

b. Draw a line that depicts the relationship between variable cost per unit and the level of activity.

Exercise 2-11A *Mixed cost at different levels of activity*

LO 2-1

Solomon Corporation paid one of its sales representatives $4,000 during the month of March. The rep is paid a base salary plus $10 per unit of product sold. During March, the rep sold 300 units.

Required

Calculate the total monthly cost of the sales representative's salary for each of the following months.

Month	April	May	June	July
Number of units sold	320	180	360	200
Total variable cost				
Total fixed cost				
Total salary cost				

LO 2-1, 2-2

Exercise 2-12A *Using fixed cost as a competitive business strategy*

The following income statements illustrate different cost structures for two competing companies.

Income Statements		
	Company Name	
	Hill	Creek
Number of customers (a)	200	200
Sales revenue (a × $200)	$ 40,000	$ 40,000
Variable cost (a × $140)	N/A	(28,000)
Variable cost (a × $0)	0	N/A
Contribution margin	40,000	12,000
Fixed cost	(28,000)	0
Net income	$ 12,000	$ 12,000

Required

a. Reconstruct Hill's income statement, assuming that it serves 400 customers when it lures 200 customers away from Creek by lowering the sales price to $120 per customer.

b. Reconstruct Creek's income statement, assuming that it serves 400 customers when it lures 200 customers away from Hill by lowering the sales price to $120 per customer.

c. Explain why the price-cutting strategy increased Hill Company's profits but caused a net loss for Creek Company.

LO 2-3, 2-4

Exercise 2-13A *Using contribution margin format income statement to measure the magnitude of operating leverage*

The following income statement was drawn from the records of Joel Company, a merchandising firm.

JOEL COMPANY Income Statement For the Year Ended December 31, Year 1	
Sales revenue (2,000 units × $125)	$ 250,000
Cost of goods sold (2,000 units × $65)	(130,000)
Gross margin	120,000
Sales commissions (10% of sales)	(25,000)
Administrative salaries expense	(30,000)
Advertising expense	(20,000)
Depreciation expense	(24,000)
Shipping and handling expenses (2,000 units × $1.00)	(2,000)
Net income	$ 19,000

Required

a. Reconstruct the income statement using the contribution margin format.

b. Calculate the magnitude of operating leverage.

c. Use the measure of operating leverage to determine the amount of net income Joel will earn if sales increase by 10 percent.

Exercise 2-14A *Assessing the magnitude of operating leverage* LO 2-4

The following income statement applies to Kawai Company for the current year.

Income Statement	
Sales revenue (200 units × $60)	$12,000
Variable cost (200 units × $36)	(7,200)
Contribution margin	4,800
Fixed costs	(1,600)
Net income	$ 3,200

Required

a. Use the contribution margin approach to calculate the magnitude of operating leverage.

b. Use the operating leverage measure computed in Requirement *a* to determine the amount of net income that Kawai Company will earn if it experiences a 10 percent increase in revenue. The sales price per unit is not affected.

c. Verify your answer to Requirement *b* by constructing an income statement based on a 10 percent increase in sales revenue. The sales price is not affected. Calculate the percentage change in net income for the two income statements.

Exercise 2-15A *Averaging costs* LO 2-5

Mountain Camps, Inc., leases the land on which it builds camp sites. Mountain is considering opening a new site on land that requires $2,500 of rental payment per month. The variable cost of providing service is expected to be $6 per camper. The following chart shows the number of campers Mountain expects for the first year of operation of the new site.

Jan.	Feb.	Mar.	Apr.	May	June	July	Aug.	Sept.	Oct.	Nov.	Dec.	Total
120	250	200	200	300	500	650	650	350	380	100	300	4,000

Required

Assuming that Mountain wants to earn $5.50 per camper, determine the price it should charge for a camp site in February and August.

Exercise 2-16A *Estimating fixed and variable costs using the high-low method* LO 2-6

Sterling Boat Company makes inexpensive aluminum fishing boats. Production is seasonal, with considerable activity occurring in the spring and summer. Sales and production tend to decline in the fall and winter months. During Year 2, the high point in activity occurred in June when it produced 200 boats at a total cost of $720,000. The low point in production occurred in January when it produced 100 boats at a total cost of $450,000.

Required

a. Use the high-low method to estimate the amount of fixed cost incurred each month by Sterling Boat Company.

b. Determine the total estimated cost if 150 boats are made.

c. Comment on the strengths and weaknesses of the high-low method.

d. Explain how a visual fit scattergraph could be used to improve accuracy.

PROBLEMS—SERIES A

connect All applicable Problems in Series A are available in *Connect*.

LO 2-1

Problem 2-17A *Identifying cost behavior*

Required

Identify the following costs as fixed or variable.

Costs related to plane trips between Boston, Massachusetts, and San Diego, California, follow. Pilots are paid on a per-trip basis.

a. Pilots' salaries relative to the number of trips flown.
b. Depreciation relative to the number of planes in service.
c. Cost of refreshments relative to the number of passengers.
d. Pilots' salaries relative to the number of passengers on a particular trip.
e. Cost of a maintenance check relative to the number of passengers on a particular trip.
f. Fuel costs relative to the number of trips.

Metro National Bank operates several branch offices in grocery stores. Each branch employs a supervisor and two tellers. Costs related to Metro's branch operations follow.

g. Tellers' salaries relative to the number of tellers in a particular district, which is composed of branches.
h. Supplies cost relative to the number of transactions processed in a particular branch.
i. Tellers' salaries relative to the number of customers served at a particular branch.
j. Supervisors' salaries relative to the number of branches operated.
k. Supervisors' salaries relative to the number of customers served in a particular branch.
l. Facility rental costs relative to the size of customer deposits.

Costs related to operating a fast-food restaurant follow.

m. Depreciation of equipment relative to the number of restaurants.
n. Building rental cost relative to the number of customers served in a particular restaurant.
o. Manager's salary of a particular store relative to the number of employees.
p. Food cost relative to the number of customers.
q. Utility cost relative to the number of restaurants in operation.
r. Company president's salary relative to the number of restaurants in operation.
s. Land costs relative to the number of hamburgers sold at a particular restaurant.
t. Depreciation of equipment relative to the number of customers served at a particular restaurant.

LO 2-1

eXcel

CHECK FIGURES
c. Total supplies cost for cleaning 30 houses: $210
d. Total cost for 20 houses: $1,740

Problem 2-18A *Cost behavior and averaging*

Janice Huffman has decided to start Janice Cleaning, a residential housecleaning service company. She is able to rent cleaning equipment at a cost of $600 per month. Labor costs are expected to be $50 per house cleaned and supplies are expected to cost $7 per house.

Required

a. Determine the total expected cost of equipment rental and the average expected cost of equipment rental per house cleaned, assuming that Janice Cleaning cleans 10, 20, or 30 houses during one month. Is the cost of equipment a fixed or a variable cost?
b. Determine the total expected cost of labor and the average expected cost of labor per house cleaned, assuming that Janice Cleaning cleans 10, 20, or 30 houses during one month. Is the cost of labor a fixed or a variable cost?
c. Determine the total expected cost of supplies and the average expected cost of supplies per house cleaned, assuming that Janice Cleaning cleans 10, 20, or 30 houses during one month. Is the cost of supplies a fixed or a variable cost?
d. Determine the total expected cost of cleaning houses, assuming that Janice Cleaning cleans 10, 20, or 30 houses during one month.

e. Determine the average expected cost per house, assuming that Janice Cleaning cleans 10, 20, or 30 houses during one month. Why does the cost per unit decrease as the number of houses increases?

f. If Ms. Huffman tells you that she prices her services at 30 percent above cost, would you assume that she means average or actual cost? Why?

Problem 2-19A *Context-sensitive nature of cost behavior classifications*

LO 2-1

Seattle Bank's start-up division establishes new branch banks. Each branch opens with three tellers. Total teller cost per branch is $96,000 per year. The three tellers combined can process up to 90,000 customer transactions per year. If a branch does not attain a volume of at least 60,000 transactions during its first year of operations, it is closed. If the demand for services exceeds 90,000 transactions, an additional teller is hired and the branch is transferred from the start-up division to regular operations.

CHECK FIGURE

b. Average teller cost for 60,000 transactions: $1.60

Required

a. What is the relevant range of activity for new branch banks?

b. Determine the amount of teller cost in total and the average teller cost per transaction for a branch that processes 60,000, 70,000, 80,000, or 90,000 transactions. In this case (the activity base is the number of transactions for a specific branch), is the teller cost a fixed or a variable cost? Round your figures to two decimal points.

c. Determine the amount of teller cost in total and the average teller cost per branch for Seattle Bank, assuming that the start-up division operates 10, 15, 20, or 25 branches. In this case (the activity base is the number of branches), is the teller cost a fixed or a variable cost?

Problem 2-20A *Context-sensitive nature of cost behavior classifications*

LO 2-1

excel

Rita Jekyll operates a sales booth in computer software trade shows, selling an accounting software package, *Abacus.* She purchases the package from a software company for $210 each. Booth space at the convention hall costs $8,400 per show.

CHECK FIGURES

a. Average cost at 400 units: $231

b. Average price at 250 units: $293.60

Required

a. Sales at past trade shows have ranged between 200 and 400 software packages per show. Determine the average cost of sales per unit if Ms. Jekyll sells 200, 250, 300, 350, or 400 units of *Abacus* at a trade show. Use the following chart to organize your answer. Is the cost of booth space fixed or variable? Round your computation to two decimal points.

	Sales Volume in Units (a)				
	200	250	300	350	400
Total cost of software (a × $210)	$42,000				
Total cost of booth rental	8,400				
Total cost of sales (b)	$50,400				
Average cost per unit (b ÷ a)	$ 252				

b. If Ms. Jekyll wants to earn a $50 profit on each package of software she sells at a trade show, what price must she charge at sales volumes of 200, 250, 300, 350, or 400 units?

c. Record the total cost of booth space if Ms. Jekyll attends one, two, three, four, or five trade shows. Record your answers in the following chart. Is the cost of booth space fixed or variable relative to the number of shows attended?

	Number of Trade Shows Attended				
	1	2	3	4	5
Total cost of booth rental	$8,400				

d. Ms. Jekyll provides decorative shopping bags to customers who purchase software packages. Some customers take the bags; others do not. Some customers stuff more than one software package into a single bag. The number of bags varies in relation to the number of units sold, but the relationship is not proportional. Assume that Ms. Jekyll uses $30 of bags for every 50 software packages sold. What is the additional cost per unit sold? Is the cost fixed or variable?

LO 2-2, 2-3

CHECK FIGURES

Part 1, b: $8,000

Part 2, h: $8,800 & 10 percent

Part 3, k: cost per student for 22 (estimated) students: $30

Problem 2-21A *Effects of operating leverage on profitability*

Franklin Training Services (FTS) provides instruction on the use of computer software for the employees of its corporate clients. It offers courses in the clients' offices on the clients' equipment. The only major expense FTS incurs is instructor salaries; it pays instructors $6,000 per course taught. FTS recently agreed to offer a course of instruction to the employees of Novak Incorporated at a price of $700 per student. Novak estimated that 20 students would attend the course.

Base your answers on the preceding information.

Part 1:

Required

a. Relative to the number of students in a single course, is the cost of instruction a fixed or a variable cost?

b. Determine the profit, assuming that 20 students attend the course.

c. Determine the profit, assuming a 10 percent increase in enrollment (i.e., enrollment increases to 22 students). What is the percentage change in profitability?

d. Determine the profit, assuming a 10 percent decrease in enrollment (i.e., enrollment decreases to 18 students). What is the percentage change in profitability?

e. Explain why a 10 percent shift in enrollment produces more than a 10 percent shift in profitability. Use the term that identifies this phenomenon.

Part 2:

The instructor has offered to teach the course for a percentage of tuition fees. Specifically, she wants $300 per person attending the class. Assume that the tuition fee remains at $700 per student.

Required

f. Is the cost of instruction a fixed or a variable cost?

g. Determine the profit, assuming that 20 students take the course.

h. Determine the profit, assuming a 10 percent increase in enrollment (i.e., enrollment increases to 22 students). What is the percentage change in profitability?

i. Determine the profit, assuming a 10 percent decrease in enrollment (i.e., enrollment decreases to 18 students). What is the percentage change in profitability?

j. Explain why a 10 percent change in enrollment produces a proportional 10 percent change in profitability.

Part 3:

FTS sells a workbook with printed material unique to each course to each student who attends the course. Any workbooks that are not sold must be destroyed. Prior to the first class, FTS printed 20 copies of the books based on the client's estimate of the number of people who would attend the course. Each workbook costs $30 and is sold to course participants for $50. This cost includes a royalty fee paid to the author and the cost of duplication.

Required

k. Calculate the workbook cost in total and per student, assuming that 18, 20, or 22 students attempt to attend the course. Round your computation to two decimal points.

l. Classify the cost of workbooks as fixed or variable relative to the number of students attending the course.

m. Discuss the risk of holding inventory as it applies to the workbooks.

n. Explain how a just-in-time inventory system can reduce the cost and risk of holding inventory.

Problem 2-22A *Effects of fixed and variable cost behavior on the risk and rewards of business opportunities*

LO 2-2

Kenton and Denton Universities offer executive training courses to corporate clients. Kenton pays its instructors $5,000 per course taught. Denton pays its instructors $250 per student enrolled in the class. Both universities charge executives a $450 tuition fee per course attended.

CHECK FIGURES
a. Kenton NI: $4,000
b. NI: $4,600

Required

a. Prepare income statements for Kenton and Denton, assuming that 20 students attend a course.
b. Kenton University embarks on a strategy to entice students from Denton by lowering its tuition to $240 per course. Prepare an income statement for Kenton, assuming that the university is successful and enrolls 40 students in its course.
c. Denton University embarks on a strategy to entice students from Kenton University by lowering its tuition to $240 per course. Prepare an income statement for Denton, assuming that the university is successful and enrolls 40 students in its course.
d. Explain why the strategy described in Requirement *b* produced a profit but the same strategy described in Requirement *c* produced a loss.
e. Prepare income statements for Kenton and Denton Universities, assuming that 10 students attend a course, and assuming that both universities charge executives a $450 tuition fee per course attended.
f. It is always better to have fixed rather than variable cost. Explain why this statement is false.
g. It is always better to have variable rather than fixed cost. Explain why this statement is false.

Problem 2-23A *Analyzing operating leverage*

LO 2-4

excel

Arnold Vimka is a venture capitalist facing two alternative investment opportunities. He intends to invest $800,000 in a start-up firm. He is nervous, however, about future economic volatility. He asks you to analyze the following financial data for the past year's operations of the two firms he is considering and give him some business advice.

	Company Name	
	Larson	Benson
Variable cost per unit (a)	$ 16.00	$ 7.00
Sales revenue (8,000 units × $25)	$200,000	$200,000
Variable cost (8,000 units × a)	(128,000)	(56,000)
Contribution margin	$ 72,000	$144,000
Fixed cost	(24,000)	(96,000)
Net income	$ 48,000	$ 48,000

Required

CHECK FIGURES
b. % of change for Larson: 15%
c. % of change for Benson: 30%

Round your figures to two decimal points in all required computation.

a. Use the contribution margin approach to compute the operating leverage for each firm.
b. If the economy expands in coming years, Larson and Benson will both enjoy a 10 percent per year increase in sales, assuming that the selling price remains unchanged. Compute the change in net income for each firm in *dollar amount* and in *percentage*. (*Note:* Since the number of units increases, both revenue and variable cost will increase.)
c. If the economy contracts in coming years, Larson and Benson will both suffer a 10 percent decrease in sales volume, assuming that the selling price remains unchanged. Compute the change in net income for each firm in *dollar amount* and in *percentage*. (*Note:* Since the number of units decreases, both total revenue and total variable cost will decrease.)
d. Write a memo to Arnold Vimka with your analyses and advice.

Problem 2-24A *Selecting the appropriate time period for cost averaging*

LO 2-5

Lakeshore Cinemas is considering a contract to rent a movie for $1,980 per day. The contract requires a minimum one-week rental period. Estimated attendance is as follows.

Monday	Tuesday	Wednesday	Thursday	Friday	Saturday	Sunday
450	300	200	550	1,000	1,000	500

CHECK FIGURES
a. Monday: $4.40
b. Friday: $4.98

Required

a. Determine the average cost per person of the movie rental contract separately for each day.

b. Suppose that Lakeshore chooses to price movie tickets at cost as computed in Requirement *a* plus $3. What price would it charge per ticket on each day of the week?

c. Use weekly averaging to determine a reasonable price to charge for movie tickets. Round your figures to two decimal points.

d. Comment on why weekly averaging may be more useful to business managers than daily averaging.

LO 2-5

Problem 2-25A *Identifying relevant issues for cost averaging*

Nepal Corporation offers mountain-climbing expeditions for its customers, providing food, equipment, and guides. Climbs normally require one week to complete. The company's accountant is reviewing historical cost data to establish a pricing strategy for the coming year. The accountant has prepared the following table showing cost data for the most recent climb, the company's average cost per year, and the five-year average cost.

	Span of Time		
	Recent Climb	One Year	Five Years
Total cost of climbs (a)	$6,000	$324,800	$1,350,000
Number of climbers (b)	10	560	2,500
Cost per climber (a ÷ b)	$ 600	$ 580	$ 540

Required

Write a memo that explains the potential advantages and disadvantages of using each of the per-unit cost figures as a basis for establishing a price to charge climbers during the coming year. What other factors must be considered in developing a pricing strategy?

LO 2-6

CHECK FIGURE
b. FC = $1,540

Problem 2-26A *Estimating fixed and variable cost*

Thornton Computer Services, Inc., has been in business for six months. The following are basic operating data for that period.

	Month					
	July	Aug.	Sept.	Oct.	Nov.	Dec.
Service hours	120	136	260	420	320	330
Revenue	$6,000	$6,800	$13,000	$21,000	$16,000	$16,500
Operating costs	$4,300	$5,300	$ 7,100	$11,200	$ 9,100	$10,600

Required

a. What is the average service revenue per hour in each month and the overall average for the six-month period?

b. Use the high-low method to estimate the total monthly fixed cost and the variable cost per hour.

c. Determine the average contribution margin per hour.

d. Use the scattergraph method to estimate the total monthly fixed cost and the variable cost per hour.

e. Compare the results of the two methods and comment on the difference.

LO 2-6

Problem 2-27A *Estimating fixed and variable cost*

Myrick Woodcraft Company (MWC) manufactures "antique" wooden cabinets to house modern televisions. MWC began operations in January of last year. Sidney Myrick, the owner, asks for your assistance. He believes that he needs to better understand the cost of the cabinets for pricing purposes. You have collected the following data concerning actual production over the past year.

Month	Number of Cabinets Produced	Total Cost
January	800	$21,000
February	3,600	32,500
March	1,960	29,500
April	600	18,600
May	1,600	29,000
June	1,300	27,000
July	1,100	25,600
August	1,800	31,000
September	2,280	32,000
October	2,940	31,500
November	3,280	32,000
December	400	16,500

CHECK FIGURE
b(1). VC/unit: $5

Required

a. To understand the department's cost behavior, you decide to plot the points on graph paper and sketch a total cost line.

(1) Enter the number of units and their costs in increasing order.

(2) Plot the points on the graph.

(3) Sketch a graph so the line "splits" all of the points (half of the points appear above and half below the line).

(4) Using the line you just sketched, visually estimate the total cost to produce 2,000 units.

b. Using the high-low method, compute the total cost equation for the preceding data.

(1) Compute the variable cost per unit.

(2) Compute total fixed costs.

(3) Sketch a line between the high and low points on your graph.

(4) Calculate the total cost assuming 2,000 cabinets are made.

c. Comment on which method you believe is better.

Problem 2-28A *Estimating fixed and variable cost using the regression method*

LO 2-6

Dean and Powell Tax Services Company has 31 branch offices in the nation. Each office has about three to six professional accountants and one to two secretaries. In a busy season, the office manager, who is also a professional accountant, can hire temporary employees for support work such as document filing and typing. Norman Dean, the president, is wondering whether he should expand his business by opening more offices. One of the factors that he is considering is how to estimate office support costs. Andrea Jones, the accountant, collected the following cost data for all 31 offices.

CHECK FIGURES
b. VC/hr: $15.19
FC: $1,142

Branch	Professional Hours	Support Costs	Branch	Professional Hours	Support Costs
A1	225	$4,241	F2	165	$3,856
A2	113	3,435	G1	358	5,936
A3	387	6,398	G2	471	8,615
A4	412	6,502	G3	492	9,639
B1	258	4,140	G4	328	5,968
B2	146	3,368	G5	359	7,115
B3	275	3,820	G6	174	3,287
D1	364	6,396	H1	394	7,515
D2	190	3,946	H2	386	7,374
D3	484	8,189	I2	279	5,376
D4	251	4,506	I5	314	5,784
D5	377	6,744	J2	283	5,426
E1	264	4,645	J3	198	4,418
E2	169	6,073	J4	226	4,506
E3	338	6,290	J5	341	6,488
F1	437	9,113			

Required

a. The company uses the number of professional hours as the cost driver for office support costs. Use an algebraic equation to describe how total office support costs can be estimated.

b. Use a spreadsheet program to perform a regression analysis. Use office support costs as the dependent variable (Y) and the professional hours as the independent variable (X). Determine the total fixed cost per office and variable cost per professional hour.

c. Identify the R^2 statistic provided by the Excel program and explain what it means.

d. Mr. Dean plans to open a new branch office in a Dallas suburb. He expects that the monthly professional hours will be 3,000. Estimate the total office support cost for Mr. Dean. What portion of the total cost is fixed and what portion is variable?

e. Explain how multiple regression analysis could be used to improve the accuracy of the cost estimates.

EXERCISES—SERIES B

LO 2-1

Exercise 2-1B *Identifying cost behavior*

Borris Copies Company provides professional copying services to customers through the 35 copy stores it operates in the southwestern United States. Each store employs a manager and four assistants. The manager earns $4,000 per month plus a bonus of 3 percent of sales. The assistants earn hourly wages. Each copy store costs $3,000 per month to lease. The company spends $5,000 per month on corporate-level advertising and promotion.

Required

Classify each of the following costs incurred by Borris Copies as fixed, variable, or mixed.

a. Lease cost relative to the number of copies made for customers.

b. Assistants' wages relative to the number of copies made for customers.

c. Store manager's salary relative to the number of copies made for customers.

d. Cost of paper relative to the number of copies made for customers.

e. Lease cost relative to the number of stores.

f. Advertising and promotion costs relative to the number of copies a particular store makes.

LO 2-1

Exercise 2-2B *Identifying cost behavior*

At the various sales levels shown, Parsons Company incurred the following costs.

	Units Sold	50	100	150	200	250
a.	Depreciation cost per unit	$ 30.00	$ 15.00	$ 10.00	$ 7.50	$ 6.00
b.	Total rent cost	600.00	600.00	600.00	600.00	600.00
c.	Total shipping cost	40.00	80.00	120.00	160.00	200.00
d.	Rent cost per unit of merchandise sold	12.00	6.00	4.00	3.00	2.40
e.	Total utility cost	200.00	300.00	400.00	500.00	600.00
f.	Supplies cost per unit	4.00	4.00	4.00	4.00	4.00
g.	Total insurance cost	500.00	500.00	500.00	500.00	500.00
h.	Total salary cost	1,500.00	2,000.00	2,500.00	3,000.00	3,500.00
i.	Cost per unit of merchandise sold	8.00	8.00	8.00	8.00	8.00
j.	Total cost of goods sold	4,000.00	8,000.00	12,000.00	16,000.00	20,000.00

Required

Identify each of these costs as fixed, variable, or mixed.

Exercise 2-3B *Determining fixed cost per unit*

LO 2-1

Tameron Corporation incurs the following annual fixed production costs.

Item	Cost
Insurance cost	$ 26,000
Patent amortization cost	400,000
Depreciation cost	160,000
Property tax cost	14,000

Required

Determine the total fixed production cost per unit if Tameron produces 10,000, 20,000, or 50,000 units.

Exercise 2-4B *Determining total variable cost*

LO 2-1

The following variable manufacturing costs apply to goods produced by Bure Manufacturing Corporation.

Item	Cost per Unit
Materials	$4.20
Labor	3.40
Variable overhead	1.40
Total	$9.00

Required

Determine the total variable manufacturing cost if Bure produces 4,000, 6,000, or 8,000 units.

Exercise 2-5B *Fixed versus variable cost behavior*

LO 2-1

Russell Company's production and total cost data for two recent months follow.

	January	February
Units produced	1,000	500
Total depreciation cost	$6,000	$6,000
Total factory supplies cost	$2,000	$1,000

Required

a. Separately calculate the depreciation cost per unit and the factory supplies cost per unit for both January and February.

b. Identify which cost is variable and which is fixed. Explain your answer.

Exercise 2-6B *Fixed versus variable cost behavior*

LO 2-1

Nielsen Chairs Corporation produces ergonomically designed chairs favored by architects. The company normally produces and sells from 2,000 to 5,000 chairs per year. The following cost data apply to various production activity levels.

Number of Chairs	2,000	3,000	4,000	5,000
Total costs incurred				
Fixed	$ 80,000			
Variable	20,000			
Total costs	$100,000			
Per-unit chair cost				
Fixed	$ 40.00			
Variable	10.00			
Total cost per chair	$ 50.00			

Required

a. Complete the preceding table by filling in the missing amounts for the levels of activity shown in the first row of the table.

b. Explain why the total cost per chair decreases as the number of chairs increases.

LO 2-1

Exercise 2-7B *Fixed versus variable cost behavior*

Shawn Corder needs extra money quickly to help cover some unexpected school expenses. Mr. Corder has learned fortune-telling skills through his long friendship with Fred Molloy, who tells fortunes during the day at the city market. Mr. Molloy has agreed to let Mr. Corder use his booth to tell fortunes during the evening for a rent of $90 per night.

Required

a. What is the booth rental cost both in total and per customer if the number of customers is 5, 10, 15, 20, or 25? Round your figures to two decimal points.

b. Is the cost of renting the fortune-telling booth fixed or variable relative to the number of customers?

c. Draw two graphs. On one, plot total booth rental cost for 5, 10, 15, 20, and 25 customers; on the other, plot booth rental cost per customer for 5, 10, 15, 20, or 25 customers.

d. Mr. Corder has little money. What major business risks would he take by renting the fortune-telling booth? How could he minimize those risks?

LO 2-1

Exercise 2-8B *Fixed versus variable cost behavior*

In the evenings, Shawn Corder works telling fortunes using his friend Fred Molloy's booth at the city market. Mr. Molloy pays the booth rental, so Mr. Corder has no rental cost. As a courtesy, Mr. Corder provides each customer a soft drink. The drinks cost him $0.50 per customer.

Required

a. What is the soft drink cost both in total and per customer if the number of customers is 5, 10, 15, 20, or 25?

b. Is the soft drink cost fixed or variable?

c. Draw two graphs. On one, plot total soft drink cost for 5, 10, 15, 20, and 25 customers; on the other, plot soft drink cost per customer for 5, 10, 15, 20, and 25 customers.

d. Comment on the likelihood that Mr. Corder will incur a loss on this business venture.

LO 2-1

Exercise 2-9B *Graphing fixed cost behavior*

Parry Computers leases space in a mall at a monthly rental cost of $3,000. The following graph setups depict rental cost on the vertical axes and activity level on the horizontal axes.

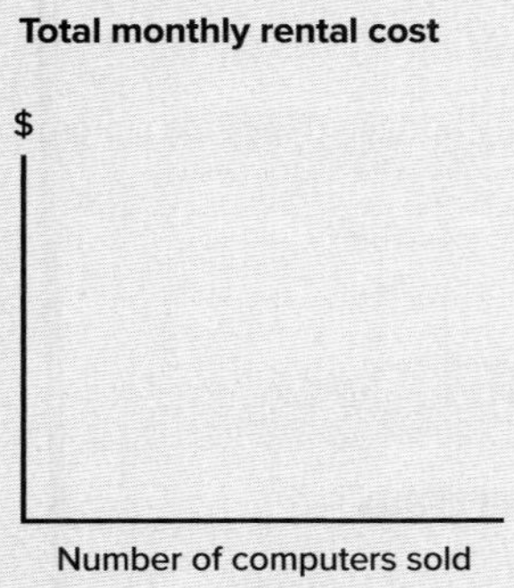

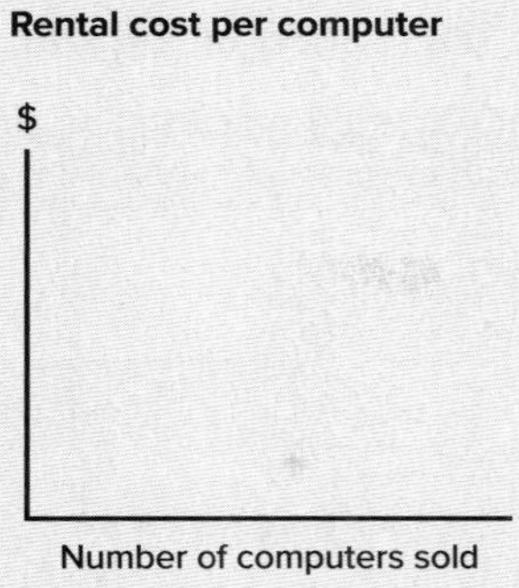

Required

a. Draw a line that depicts the relationship between the total monthly rental cost and the number of computers sold.

b. Draw a line that depicts the relationship between rental cost per computer and the number of computers sold.

Exercise 2-10B *Graphing variable cost behavior* LO 2-1

Dillon Computers purchases computers from a manufacturer for $500 per computer. The following graph setups depict product cost on the vertical axes and activity level on the horizontal axes.

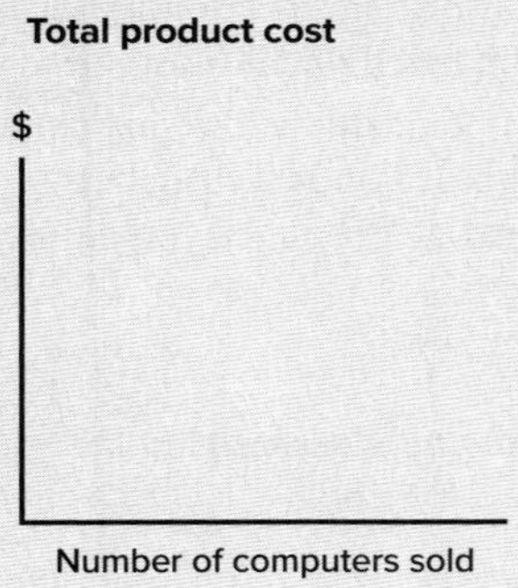

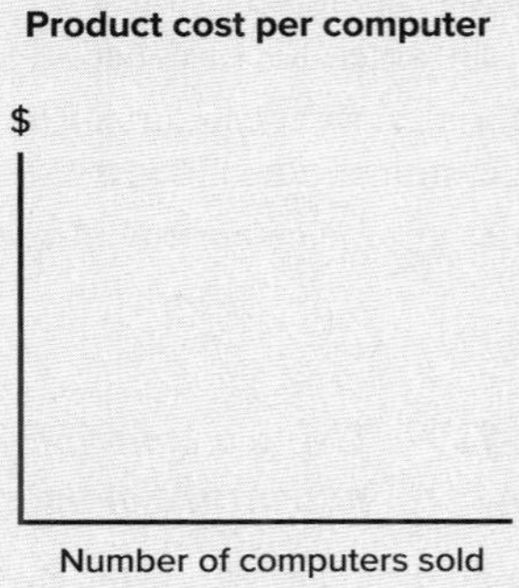

Required

a. Draw a line that depicts the relationship between total product cost and the number of computers sold.

b. Draw a line that depicts the relationship between product cost per computer and the number of computers sold.

Exercise 2-11B *Mixed cost at different levels of activity* LO 2-1

Top Hats Corporation uses workers in Indonesia to manually weave straw hats. The company pays the workers a daily base wage plus $0.50 per completed hat. On Monday, workers produced 100 hats for which the company paid wages of $95.

Required

Calculate the total cost of the workers' wages for each of the following days.

Day	Monday	Tuesday	Wednesday	Thursday
Number of hats woven	100	120	160	80
Total variable cost				
Total fixed cost				
Total wages cost				

LO 2-1, 2-2

Exercise 2-12B *Effect of cost structure on projected profits*

Standard and Variant compete in the same market. The following budgeted income statements illustrate their cost structures.

Income Statements		
	Company	
	Standard	**Variant**
Number of customers (a)	150	150
Sales revenue (a × $160)	$24,000	$24,000
Variable cost (a × $90)	N/A	(13,500)
Contribution margin	24,000	10,500
Fixed costs	(13,500)	N/A
Net income	$10,500	$10,500

Required

a. Assume that Standard can lure all 150 customers away from Variant by lowering its sales price to $85 per customer. Reconstruct Standard's income statement based on 300 customers.

b. Assume that Variant can lure all 150 customers away from Standard by lowering its sales price to $85 per customer. Reconstruct Variant's income statement based on 300 customers.

c. Why does the price-cutting strategy increase Standard's profits but result in a net loss for Variant?

LO 2-3, 2-4

Exercise 2-13B *Using a contribution margin format income statement to measure the magnitude of operating leverage*

Nagano Company, a merchandising firm, reported the following operating results.

Income Statements	
Sales revenue (2,400 units × $100)	$ 240,000
Cost of goods sold (2,400 units × $65)	(156,000)
Gross margin	84,000
Sales commissions (10% of sales revenue)	(24,000)
Administrative salaries expense	(15,000)
Advertising expense	(20,000)
Depreciation expense	(10,600)
Shipping and handling expense (2,400 units × $1)	(2,400)
Net income	$ 12,000

Required

a. Reconstruct the income statement using the contribution margin format.

b. Calculate the magnitude of operating leverage.

c. Use the measure of operating leverage to determine the amount of net income that Nagano will earn if sales revenue increases by 10 percent.

Exercise 2-14B *Assessing the magnitude of operating leverage* LO 2-4

The following budgeted income statement applies to Johnson Company.

Income Statement	
Sales revenue (1,000 units × $89)	$ 89,000
Variable cost (1,000 units × $50)	(50,000)
Contribution margin	39,000
Fixed costs	(26,000)
Net income	$ 13,000

Required

a. Use the contribution margin approach to calculate the magnitude of operating leverage.

b. Use the operating leverage measure computed in Requirement *a* to determine the amount of net income that Johnson Company will earn if sales volume increases by 10 percent. Assume the sales price per unit remains unchanged at $89.

c. Verify your answer to Requirement *b* by constructing an alternative income statement based on a 10 percent increase in sales volume. The sales price per unit remains unchanged at $89. Calculate the percentage change in net income for the two income statements.

Exercise 2-15B *Averaging costs* LO 2-5

Century Entertainment Company operates a movie theater that has monthly fixed expenses of $4,000. In addition, the company pays film distributors $1.00 per ticket sold. The following chart shows the number of tickets Century expects to sell in the coming year.

Jan.	Feb.	Mar.	Apr.	May	June	July	Aug.	Sept.	Oct.	Nov.	Dec.	Total
2,000	1,600	3,200	3,400	3,200	4,200	4,700	4,000	5,000	3,100	3,000	2,600	40,000

Required

Assume that Century wants to earn $3.00 per movie patron. What price should it charge for a ticket in January and in September?

Exercise 2-16B *Estimating fixed and variable costs using the high-low method* LO 2-6

Pettit Ice Cream Company produces various ice cream products for which demand is highly seasonal. The company sells more ice cream in warmer months and less in colder ones. Last year, the high point in production activity occurred in August when Pettit produced 50,000 gallons of ice cream at a total cost of $82,000. The low point in production activity occurred in February when the company produced 20,000 gallons of ice cream at a total cost of $46,000.

Required

a. Use the high-low method to estimate the amount of fixed cost per month incurred by Pettit Ice Cream Company.

b. Determine the total estimated monthly cost when 40,000 gallons of ice cream are produced.

c. What factors could cause the estimate determined in Requirement *b* to be inaccurate?

d. Explain how regression analysis could be used to improve accuracy. Your explanation should include a discussion of the R^2 statistic as well as the potential impact of multiple regression analysis.

PROBLEMS—SERIES B

LO 2-1

Problem 2-17B *Identifying cost behavior*

Required

Identify the following costs as fixed or variable.

Costs related to operating a retail gasoline company follow.

a. Depreciation of equipment relative to the number of customers served at a station.
b. Property and real estate taxes relative to the amount of gasoline sold at a particular station.
c. Depreciation of equipment relative to the number of stations.
d. Cashiers' wages relative to the number of customers served in a station.
e. Salary of a manager of a particular station relative to the number of employees.
f. Gasoline cost relative to the number of customers.
g. Utility cost relative to the number of stations in operation.
h. The company's cost of national TV commercials relative to the number of stations in operation.

Costs related to shuttle bus trips between JFK International Airport and downtown New York follow. Each bus driver receives a specific salary per trip. A manager schedules bus trips and supervises drivers, and a secretary receives phone calls.

i. A driver's salary relative to the number of passengers on a particular trip.
j. Fuel costs relative to the number of trips.
k. Fuel costs relative to the number of passengers on a particular trip.
l. Drivers' salaries relative to the number of trips driven.
m. Office staff salaries relative to the number of passengers on a particular trip.
n. Depreciation relative to the number of buses in service.

Sussie's Barbershop operates several stores in shopping centers. Each store employs a supervisor and three barbers. The supervisor is paid a specific salary per month. Each barber receives a specific salary per month plus a 10 percent commission based on the service revenues he or she has generated. Costs related to Sussie's Barbershop follow.

o. Store rental costs relative to the number of customers.
p. Barbers' commissions relative to the number of customers.
q. Supervisory salaries relative to the number of customers served in a particular store.
r. Barbers' salaries relative to the number of barbers in a particular district.
s. Supplies cost relative to the number of hair services provided in a particular store.
t. Barbers' salaries relative to the number of customers served at a particular store.

LO 2-1

Problem 2-18B *Cost behavior and averaging*

Chris Quill asks you to analyze the operating cost of his lawn services business. He has purchased the needed equipment with a cash payment of $90,000. Upon your recommendation, he agrees to adopt straight-line depreciation. The equipment has an expected life of four years and no salvage value. Mr. Quill pays his workers $20 per lawn service. Material costs, including fertilizer, pesticide, and supplies, are expected to be $10 per lawn service.

Required

a. Determine the total cost of equipment depreciation and the average cost of equipment depreciation per lawn service, assuming that Mr. Quill provides 40, 50, or 60 lawn services during one month. Is the cost of equipment a fixed or a variable cost?
b. Determine the total expected cost of labor and the average expected cost of labor per lawn service, assuming that Mr. Quill provides 40, 50, or 60 lawn services during one month. Is the cost of labor a fixed or a variable cost?
c. Determine the total expected cost of materials and the average expected cost of materials per lawn service, assuming that Mr. Quill provides 40, 50, or 60 lawn services during one month. Is the cost of fertilizer, pesticide, and supplies a fixed or a variable cost?

d. Determine the total expected cost per lawn service, assuming that Mr. Quill provides 40, 50, or 60 lawn services during one month.

e. Determine the average expected cost per lawn service, assuming that Mr. Quill provides 40, 50, or 60 lawn services during one month. Why does the cost per unit decrease as the number of lawn services increases?

f. If Mr. Quill tells you that he prices his services at 30 percent above cost, would you assume that he means average or actual cost? Why?

Problem 2-19B *Context-sensitive nature of cost behavior classifications* LO 2-1

Kelly and Valdez Tax Services' Development Department is responsible for establishing new community branches. Each branch opens with four tax accountants. Total cost of payroll per branch is $240,000 per year. Together the four accountants can process up to 5,000 simple tax returns per year. The firm's policy requires closing branches that do not reach the quota of 3,000 tax returns per year. On the other hand, the firm hires an additional accountant for a branch and elevates it to the status of a regular operation if the customer demand for services exceeds 5,000 tax returns.

Required

a. What is the relevant range of activity for a new branch established by the Development Department?

b. Determine the amount of payroll cost in total and the average payroll cost per transaction for a branch that processes 3,000, 4,000, or 5,000 tax returns. In this case (the activity base is the number of tax returns for a specific branch), is the payroll cost a fixed or a variable cost?

c. Determine the amount of payroll cost in total and the average payroll cost per branch for Kelly and Valdez Tax Services assuming that the Development Department operates 20, 30, or 40 branches. In this case (the activity base is the number of branches), is the payroll cost a fixed or a variable cost?

Problem 2-20B *Context-sensitive nature of cost behavior classifications* LO 2-1

Sean Franklin sells a newly developed camera, Panorama Vision. He purchases the cameras from the manufacturer for $150 each and rents a store in a shopping mall for $6,000 per month.

Required

a. Determine the average cost of sales per unit if Mr. Franklin sells 100, 200, 300, 400, or 500 units of Panorama Vision per month. Use the following chart to organize your answer.

	Sales Volume in Units (a)				
	100	200	300	400	500
Total cost of cameras (a × $150)	$15,000				
Total cost of store rental	6,000				
Total cost of sales (b)	$21,000				
Average cost per unit (b ÷ a)	$210.00				

b. If Mr. Franklin wants to make a gross profit of $30 on each camera he sells, what price should he charge at sales volumes of 100, 200, 300, 400, or 500 units?

c. Record the total cost of store rental if Mr. Franklin opens a camera store at one, two, three, four, or five shopping malls. Record your answers in the following chart. Is the cost of store rental fixed or variable relative to the number of stores opened?

	Shopping Malls				
	1	2	3	4	5
Total cost of store rental	$6,000				

d. Mr. Franklin provides decorative ornaments to customers who purchase cameras. Some customers take the ornaments, others do not, and some take more than one. The number of ornaments varies in relation to the number of cameras sold, but the relationship is not proportional. Assume that, on average, Mr. Franklin gives away $150 worth of ornaments for every 100 cameras sold. What is the additional cost per camera sold? Is the cost fixed or variable?

LO 2-2, 2-3

Problem 2-21B *Effects of operating leverage on profitability*

CFEs R Us conducts CFE review courses. Public universities that permit free use of a classroom support the classes. The only major expense incurred by CFEs R Us is the salary of instructors, which is $5,000 per course taught. The company recently planned to offer a review course in Boston for $400 per candidate; it estimated that 50 candidates would attend the course.

Complete these requirements based on the preceding information.

Part 1:

Required

a. Relative to the number of CFE candidates in a single course, is the cost of instruction a fixed or a variable cost?

b. Determine the profit, assuming that 50 candidates attend the course.

c. Determine the profit, assuming a 10 percent increase in enrollment (i.e., enrollment increases to 55 students). What is the percentage change in profitability?

d. Determine the profit, assuming a 10 percent decrease in enrollment (i.e., enrollment decreases to 45 students). What is the percentage change in profitability?

e. Explain why a 10 percent shift in enrollment produces more than a 10 percent shift in profitability. Use the term that identifies this phenomenon.

Part 2:

The instructor has offered to teach the course for a percentage of tuition fees. Specifically, he wants $100 per candidate attending the class. Assume that the tuition fee remains at $400 per candidate.

Required

f. Is the cost of instruction a fixed or a variable cost?

g. Determine the profit, assuming that 50 candidates take the course.

h. Determine the profit, assuming a 10 percent increase in enrollment (i.e., enrollment increases to 55 students). What is the percentage change in profitability?

i. Determine the profit, assuming a 10 percent decrease in enrollment (i.e., enrollment decreases to 45 students). What is the percentage change in profitability?

j. Explain why a 10 percent shift in enrollment produces a proportional 10 percent shift in profitability.

Part 3:

CFEs R Us sells a workbook to each student who attends the course. The workbook contains printed material unique to each course. Workbooks that are not sold must be destroyed. Prior to the first class, CFEs R Us printed 50 copies of the books based on the estimated number of people who would attend the course. Each workbook costs $32 and is sold for $50. This cost includes a royalty fee paid to the author and the cost of duplication.

Required

k. Calculate the total cost and the cost per candidate of the workbooks, assuming that 45, 50, or 55 candidates attempt to attend the course. Round your figures to two decimal points.

l. Classify the cost of workbooks as fixed or variable relative to the number of candidates attending the course.

m. Discuss the risk of holding inventory as it applies to the workbooks.

n. Explain how a just-in-time inventory system can reduce the cost and risk of holding inventory.

Problem 2-22B *Effects of fixed and variable cost behavior on the risk and rewards of business opportunities*

LO 2-2

Canton Club and Tobin Club are competing health and recreation clubs in Orlando. They both offer tennis training clinics to adults. Canton pays its coaches $4,800 per season. Tobin pays its coaches $120 per student enrolled in the clinic per season. Both clubs charge a tuition fee of $200 per season.

Required

a. Prepare income statements for Canton and Tobin, assuming that 40 students per season attend each clinic.

b. The ambitious new director of Canton Club tries to increase his market share by reducing the club's tuition per student to $112 per clinic. Prepare an income statement for Canton, assuming that the club attracts all of Tobin's customers and therefore is able to enroll 80 students in its clinics.

c. Independent of Requirement *b*, Tobin Club tries to lure Canton's students by lowering its price to $112 per student. Prepare an income statement for Tobin, assuming that the club succeeds in enrolling 80 students in its clinics.

d. Explain why the strategy described in Requirement *b* produced a profit while the same strategy described in Requirement *c* produced a loss.

e. Prepare an income statement for Canton Club and Tobin Club, assuming that 20 students attend a clinic at the original $200 tuition price.

f. It is always better to have fixed rather than variable cost. Explain why this statement is false.

g. It is always better to have variable rather than fixed cost. Explain why this statement is false.

Problem 2-23B *Analysis of operating leverage*

LO 2-4

June Wade has invested in two start-up companies. At the end of the first year, she asks you to evaluate their operating performance. The following operating data apply to the first year.

	Company Name	
	Cook	Penn
Variable cost per unit (a)	$ 16	$ 8
Sales revenue (8,000 units × $25)	$ 200,000	$200,000
Variable cost (8,000 units × a)	(128,000)	(64,000)
Contribution margin	72,000	136,000
Fixed cost	(40,000)	(104,000)
Net income	$ 32,000	$ 32,000

Required

a. Use the contribution margin approach to compute the operating leverage for each firm.

b. If the economy expands in the coming year, Cook and Penn will both enjoy a 10 percent per year increase in sales volume, assuming that the selling price remains unchanged. (*Note:* Since the number of units increases, both revenue and variable cost will increase.) Compute the change in net income for each firm in dollar amount and in percentage.

c. If the economy contracts in the following year, Cook and Penn will both suffer a 10 percent decrease in sales volume, assuming that the selling price remains unchanged. (*Note:* Since the number of units decreases, both revenue and variable cost decrease.) Compute the change in net income for each firm in both dollar amount and percentage.

d. Write a memo to June Wade with your evaluation and recommendations.

LO 2-5

Problem 2-24B *Selecting the appropriate time period for cost averaging*

The Magic Amusement Park is considering signing a contract to hire a circus at a cost of $3,000 per day. The contract requires a minimum performance period of one week. Estimated circus attendance is as follows.

Monday	Tuesday	Wednesday	Thursday	Friday	Saturday	Sunday
400	350	300	500	800	1,250	1,400

Required

a. For each day, determine the average cost of the circus contract per person attending. Round your figures to two decimal points.

b. Suppose that the park prices circus tickets at cost as computed in Requirement *a* plus $2.00. What would be the price per ticket charged on each day of the week?

c. Use weekly averaging to determine a reasonable price to charge for the circus tickets.

d. Comment on why weekly averaging may be more useful to business managers than daily averaging.

LO 2-5

Problem 2-25B *Identifying relevant issues for cost averaging*

West Tours, Inc., organizes adventure tours for people interested in visiting a desert environment. A desert tour generally lasts three days. West provides food, equipment, and guides. Dan Silva, the president of West Tours, needs to set prices for the coming year. He has available the company's past cost data in the following table.

	Span of Time		
	Recent Tour	One Year	Ten Years
Total cost of tours (a)	$4,800	$234,000	$1,620,000
Number of tourists (b)	32	1,500	12,000
Cost per tourist (a ÷ b)	$ 150	$ 156	$ 135

Required

Write a memo to Mr. Silva explaining the potential advantages and disadvantages of using each of the different per-tourist cost figures as a basis for establishing a price to charge tourists during the coming year. What other factors must Mr. Silva consider in developing a pricing strategy?

LO 2-6

Problem 2-26B *Estimating fixed and variable costs*

Kane Legal Services provides legal advice to clients. The following data apply to the first six months of operation.

	Month					
	Jan.	Feb.	Mar.	Apr.	May	June
Service hours	80	100	140	180	200	220
Revenue	$8,000	$10,000	$14,000	$18,000	$20,000	$22,000
Operating costs	7,400	8,200	9,660	10,600	10,900	11,600

Required

a. What is the average service revenue per hour for the six-month time period?

b. Use the high-low method to estimate the total monthly fixed cost and the variable cost per hour.

c. Determine the average contribution margin per hour.

d. Use the scattergraph method to estimate the total monthly fixed cost and the variable cost per hour.

e. Compare the results of the two methods and comment on any differences.

Problem 2-27B *Estimating fixed and variable cost*

LO 2-6

Jenkins Frames Company, which manufactures ornate frames for original art work, began operations in January, Year 1. Bruce Preston, the owner, asks for your assistance. He believes that he needs to better understand the cost of the frames for pricing purposes. You have collected the following data concerning actual production over the past year.

Month	Number of Frames Produced	Total Cost
January	1,600	$42,000
February	7,200	65,000
March	3,920	59,000
April	1,200	37,200
May	3,200	58,000
June	2,600	54,000
July	2,200	51,200
August	3,600	62,000
September	4,560	64,000
October	5,880	63,000
November	6,560	64,000
December	800	33,000

Required

a. To understand the department's cost behavior, you decide to plot the points on graph paper and sketch a total cost line.

(1) Enter the number of units and their costs in increasing order.

(2) Plot the points on the graph.

(3) Sketch a graph so the line "splits" all of the points (half of the points appear above and half appear below the line).

(4) Using the line you just sketched, visually estimate the total cost to produce 4,000 units.

b. Using the high-low method, compute the total cost equation for the preceding data.

(1) Compute the variable cost per unit.

(2) Compute total fixed costs.

(3) Sketch a line between the high and low points on your graph.

(4) Using the high-low method, estimate the total cost to produce 4,000 units.

c. Name a third method that could be used to determine the fixed and variable cost estimate and comment on the advantages of your suggested approach.

Problem 2-28B *Estimating fixed and variable cost using the regression method*

LO 2-6

Stan Fox, the production manager of Hollis Construction Components, is trying to figure out the cost behavior of his factory supplies cost. The company uses machine hours as the cost driver. Joe Parrish, the assistant manager, collected the following cost data for the last 32 weeks.

Week No.	Machine Hours	Supplies Costs	Week No.	Machine Hours	Supplies Costs
1	86	$3,819	17	64	$3,856
2	72	3,610	18	88	4,279
3	79	3,916	19	129	5,633
4	62	2,915	20	137	5,298
5	91	4,327	21	144	6,721
6	42	2,214	22	37	2,448
7	37	2,106	23	56	3,528
8	33	2,390	24	49	2,837
9	23	2,107	25	12	1,359
10	96	4,868	26	57	3,296
11	94	5,021	27	54	3,472
12	91	4,811	28	65	3,264
13	72	3,580	29	77	3,925
14	60	2,800	30	85	4,002
15	48	2,269	31	92	4,583
16	53	2,748	32	82	3,523

Required

a. The company uses the number of machine hours as the cost driver for factory supplies costs. Use an algebraic equation to describe how total factory supplies costs can be estimated.

b. Use a spreadsheet program to perform a regression analysis. Use factory supplies costs as the dependent variable (Y) and the machine hours as the independent variable (X). Determine the total fixed cost per week and variable cost per machine hour.

c. Identify the R^2 statistic provided by the Excel program and explain what it means.

d. Identify a potential weakness of regression analysis and explain what can be done to minimize it.

e. Determine the estimated total cost of factory supplies if machine-hour usage amounts to 100 hours for the next week. What portion of the total cost is fixed and what portion is variable?

ANALYZE, THINK, COMMUNICATE

ATC 2-1 Business Applications *Operating leverage*

Description of business for Facebook, Inc.

Our mission is to give people the power to share and make the world more open and connected. Our top priority is to build useful and engaging products that enable people to connect and share through mobile devices, personal computers, and other surfaces. We also help people discover and learn about what is going on in the world around them, enable people to share their opinions, ideas, photos and videos, and other activities with audiences ranging from their closest friends to the public at large, and stay connected everywhere by accessing our products . . .

Facebook, Inc.	2016	2015
Revenue	$27,638	$17,928
Operating earnings	12,427	6,225

Description of business for Lowe's Companies, Inc.

Lowe's Companies, Inc. and subsidiaries (the Company or Lowe's) is a Fortune® 50 company and the world's second largest home improvement retailer. As of February 3, 2017, Lowe's operated 2,129 home improvement and hardware stores, representing approximately 213 million square feet of retail selling space.

These operations were comprised of 1,820 stores located across 50 U.S. states, including 87 Orchard Supply Hardware (Orchard) stores, as well as 299 stores in Canada, and 10 stores in Mexico.

Lowe's, Inc.	2016	2015
Revenue	$65,017	$59,074
Operating earnings	5,846	4,971

Required

a. Determine which company appears to have the higher operating leverage.

b. Write a paragraph or two explaining why the company you identified in Requirement *a* might be expected to have the higher operating leverage.

c. If revenues for both companies increased by 5 percent, which company do you think would likely experience the greater percentage increase in operating earnings? Explain your answer.

ATC 2-2 Group Assignment *Operating leverage*

The Parent Teacher Association (PTA) of Meadow High School is planning a fund-raising campaign. The PTA is considering the possibility of hiring Eric Logan, a world-renowned investment counselor, to address the public. Tickets would sell for $28 each. The school has agreed to let the PTA use Harville Auditorium at no cost. Mr. Logan is willing to accept one of two compensation arrangements. He will sign an agreement to receive a fixed fee of $10,000 regardless of the number of tickets sold. Alternatively, he will accept payment of $20 per ticket sold. In communities similar to that in which Meadow is located, Mr. Logan has drawn an audience of approximately 500 people.

Required

a. In front of the class, present a statement showing the expected net income assuming 500 people buy tickets.

b. The instructor will divide the class into groups and then organize the groups into four sections. The instructor will assign one of the following tasks to each section of groups.

Group Tasks

(1) Assume the PTA pays Mr. Logan a fixed fee of $10,000. Determine the amount of net income that the PTA will earn if ticket sales are 10 percent higher than expected. Calculate the percentage change in net income.

(2) Assume that the PTA pays Mr. Logan a fixed fee of $10,000. Determine the amount of net income that the PTA will earn if ticket sales are 10 percent lower than expected. Calculate the percentage change in net income.

(3) Assume that the PTA pays Mr. Logan $20 per ticket sold. Determine the amount of net income that the PTA will earn if ticket sales are 10 percent higher than expected. Calculate the percentage change in net income.

(4) Assume that the PTA pays Mr. Logan $20 per ticket sold. Determine the amount of net income that the PTA will earn if ticket sales are 10 percent lower than expected. Calculate the percentage change in net income.

c. Have each group select a spokesperson. Have one of the spokespersons in each section of groups go to the board and present the results of the analysis conducted in Requirement *b*. Resolve any discrepancies between the computations presented at the board and those developed by the other groups.

d. Draw conclusions regarding the risks and rewards associated with operating leverage. At a minimum, answer the following questions:

(1) Which type of cost structure (fixed or variable) produces the higher growth potential in profitability for a company?

(2) Which type of cost structure (fixed or variable) faces the higher risk of declining profitability for a company?

(3) Under what circumstances should a company seek to establish a fixed cost structure?

(4) Under what circumstances should a company seek to establish a variable cost structure?

ATC 2-3 Research Assignment *Fixed versus variable cost*

Use the 2017 Form 10-K for Stanley Black & Decker, Inc., to complete the following requirements. To obtain the Form 10-K, you can use the EDGAR system (see Appendix A at the back of this text for instructions), or it can be found under "Corporate" and "Investor Information"on the company's corporate website at www.stanleyblackanddecker.com. Be sure to read carefully the following portions of the document:

- "Item 1. Business" on pages 3–4.
- "Consolidated Statement of Operations" on page 57.

Required

a. Calculate the percentage increase in Stanley's sales and its "earnings from continuing operations" from 2016 to 2017.

b. Would fixed costs or variable costs be more likely to explain why Stanley's operating earnings increased by a bigger percentage than its sales?

c. On page 99, Stanley reported that it incurred research and development costs of $252.3 million in 2017. If this cost is thought of in the context of the number of units of products sold, should it be considered as primarily fixed or variable in nature?

d. If the research and development costs are thought of in the context of the number of new products developed, should they be considered as primarily fixed or variable in nature?

ATC 2-4 Writing Assignment *Cost averaging*

Candice Sterling is a veterinarian. She has always been concerned for the pets of low-income families. These families love their pets but frequently do not have the means to provide them proper veterinary care. Dr. Sterling decides to open a part-time veterinary practice in a low-income neighborhood. She plans to volunteer her services free of charge two days per week. Clients will be charged only for the actual costs of materials and overhead. Dr. Sterling leases a small space for $300 per month. Utilities and other miscellaneous costs are expected to be approximately $180 per month. She estimates the variable cost of materials to be approximately $10 per pet served. A friend of Dr. Sterling who runs a similar type of clinic in another area of town indicates that she should expect to treat the following number of pets during her first year of operation.

Jan.	Feb.	Mar.	Apr.	May	June	July	Aug.	Sept.	Oct.	Nov.	Dec.
18	26	28	36	42	54	63	82	42	24	20	15

Dr. Sterling's friend has noticed that visits increase significantly in the summer because children who are out of school tend to bring their pets to the vet more often. Business tapers off during the winter and reaches a low point in December when people spend what little money they have on Christmas presents for their children. After looking at the data, Dr. Sterling becomes concerned that the people in the neighborhood will not be able to afford pet care during some months of operation even if it is offered at cost. For example, the cost of providing services in December would be approximately $42 per pet treated ($480 overhead ÷ 15 pets = $32 per pet, plus $10 materials cost). She is willing to provide her services free of charge, but she realizes that she cannot afford to subsidize the practice further by personally paying for the costs of materials and overhead in the months of low activity. She decides to discuss the matter with her accountant to find a way to cut costs even more. Her accountant tells her that her problem is cost *measurement* rather than cost *cutting*.

Required

Assume that you are Dr. Sterling's accountant. Write a memo describing a pricing strategy that resolves the apparent problem of high costs during months of low volume. Recommend in your memo the price to charge per pet treated during the month of December.

ATC 2-5 Ethical Dilemma *Profitability versus social conscience (effects of cost behavior)*

Advances in biological technology have enabled two research companies, Bio Labs, Inc., and Scientific Associates, to develop an insect-resistant corn seed. Neither company is financially strong enough to develop the distribution channels necessary to bring the product to world markets. World Agra Distributors, Inc., has negotiated contracts with both companies for the exclusive right to market their seed. Bio Labs signed an agreement to receive an annual royalty of $1,000,000. In contrast, Scientific Associates chose an agreement that provides for a royalty of $0.50 per pound of seed sold. Both agreements have a 10-year term. During Year 1, World Agra sold approximately 1,600,000 pounds of the Bio Labs, Inc., seed and 2,400,000 pounds of the Scientific Associates seed. Both types of seed were sold for $1.25 per pound. By the end of the Year 1, it was apparent that the seed developed by Scientific Associates was superior. Although insect infestation was virtually nonexistent for both types of seed, the seed developed by Scientific Associates produced corn that was sweeter and had consistently higher yields.

World Agra Distributors' chief financial officer, Roger Weatherstone, recently retired. To the astonishment of the annual planning committee, Mr. Weatherstone's replacement, Ray Borrough, adamantly recommended that the marketing department develop a major advertising campaign to promote the seed developed by Bio Labs, Inc. The planning committee reluctantly approved the recommendation. A $100,000 ad campaign was launched; the ads emphasized the ability of the Bio Labs seed to avoid insect infestation. The campaign was silent with respect to taste or crop yield. It did not mention the seed developed by Scientific Associates. World Agra's sales staff was instructed to push the Bio Labs seed and to sell the Scientific Associates seed only on customer demand. Although total sales remained relatively constant during Year 2, sales of the Scientific Associates seed fell to approximately 1,300,000 pounds while sales of the Bio Labs, Inc., seed rose to 2,700,000 pounds.

Required

a. Determine the amount of increase or decrease in profitability experienced by World Agra in Year 2 as a result of promoting the Bio Labs seed. Support your answer with appropriate commentary.

b. Did World Agra's customers in particular and society in general benefit or suffer from the decision to promote the Bio Labs seed?

c. Review the statement of ethical professional practice in Exhibit 1.17 of Chapter 1 and comment on whether Mr. Borrough's recommendation violated any of the standards in the code of ethical conduct.

d. Comment on your belief regarding the adequacy of the statement of ethical professional practice in terms of directing the conduct of management accountants.

e. Are the actions of Ray Borrough in violation of the provisions of Sarbanes-Oxley that were described in Chapter 1? Explain your answer.

ATC 2-6 Spreadsheet Assignment *Using Excel*

Charlie Stork rented a truck for his business on two previous occasions. Since he will soon be renting a truck again, he would like to analyze his bills and determine how the rental fee is calculated. His two bills for truck rental show that on September 1, he drove 1,000 miles and the bill was $1,500, and on December 5, he drove 600 miles and the bill was $1,380.

Required

Construct a spreadsheet to calculate the variable and fixed costs of this mixed cost that will allow Mr. Stork to predict his cost if he drives the truck 700 miles. The cells that show as numbers should all be formulas except C5, C6, E5, E6, and C18. Constructing the spreadsheet in this manner will allow you to change numbers in these five cells to recalculate variable cost, fixed cost, or predicted total cost.

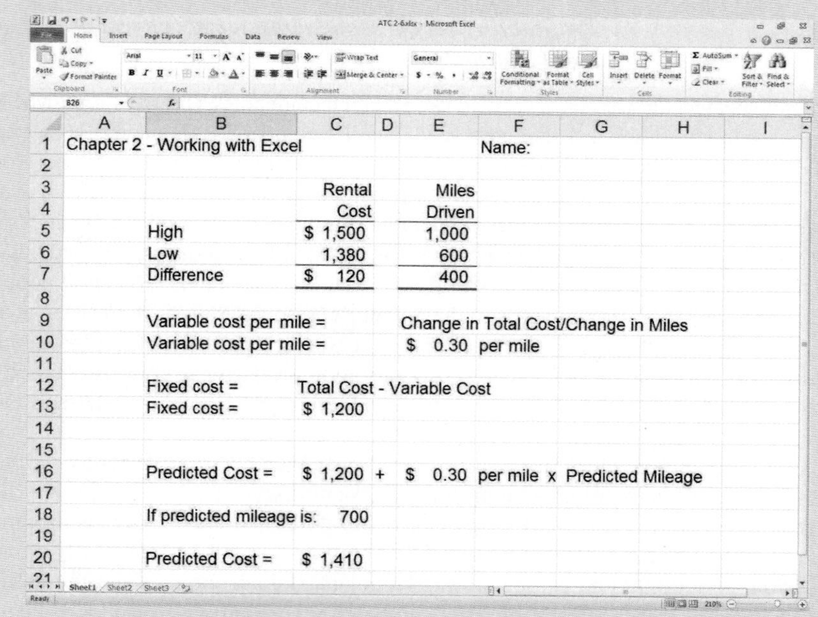

	A	B	C	D	E	F	G	H
1	Chapter 2 - Working with Excel					Name:		
2								
3			Rental		Miles			
4			Cost		Driven			
5		High	$ 1,500		1,000			
6		Low	1,380		600			
7		Difference	$ 120		400			
8								
9		Variable cost per mile =			Change in Total Cost/Change in Miles			
10		Variable cost per mile =			$ 0.30 per mile			
11								
12		Fixed cost =	Total Cost - Variable Cost					
13		Fixed cost =	$ 1,200					
14								
15								
16		Predicted Cost =	$ 1,200 +		$ 0.30 per mile x Predicted Mileage			
17								
18		If predicted mileage is:	700					
19								
20		Predicted Cost =	$ 1,410					

Source: Microsoft Excel 2010

Spreadsheet Tip

1. To format cells to show dollar signs, commas, or both, choose Format, Cells, then click on the tab titled Numbers, and choose Accounting.

ATC 2-7 Spreadsheet Assignment *Mastering Excel*

Siwa Company makes and sells a decorative ceramic statue. Each statue costs $50 to manufacture and sells for $75. Siwa spends $3 to ship the statue to customers and pays salespersons a $2 commission for each statue sold. The remaining annual expenses of operation are administrative salaries, $70,000; advertising, $20,000; and rent, $30,000. Siwa plans to sell 9,000 statues in the coming year.

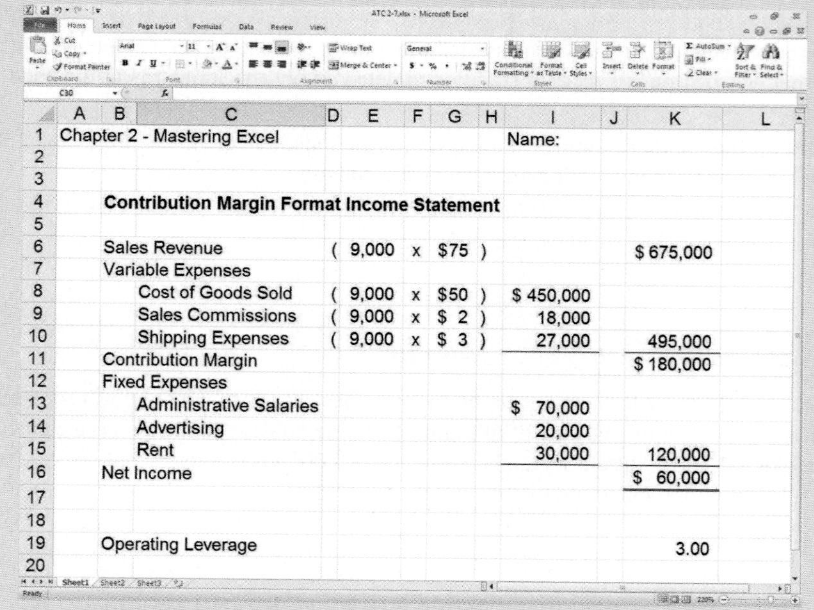

1	Chapter 2 - Mastering Excel		Name:		
4	**Contribution Margin Format Income Statement**				
6	Sales Revenue	(9,000 x $75)		$ 675,000	
7	Variable Expenses				
8	Cost of Goods Sold	(9,000 x $50)	$ 450,000		
9	Sales Commissions	(9,000 x $ 2)	18,000		
10	Shipping Expenses	(9,000 x $ 3)	27,000	495,000	
11	Contribution Margin			$ 180,000	
12	Fixed Expenses				
13	Administrative Salaries		$ 70,000		
14	Advertising		20,000		
15	Rent		30,000	120,000	
16	Net Income			$ 60,000	
19	Operating Leverage			3.00	

Source: Microsoft Excel 2010

Required

Construct a spreadsheet that shows a contribution margin format income statement and that calculates operating leverage. Place formulas in the spreadsheet to allow changes to any of the preceding information to be automatically reflected in the income statement and operating leverage.

COMPREHENSIVE PROBLEM

Use the same transaction data for Magnificent Modems, Inc., as was used in Chapter 1.

Required

a. Based on these data, identify each cost incurred by the company as (1) fixed versus variable relative to the number of units produced and sold; and (2) product versus selling, general, and administrative (SG&A). The solution for the first item is shown as an example.

Cost Item	Fixed	Variable	Product	SG&A
Depreciation on manufacturing equipment	X		X	
Direct materials				
Direct labor				
Manufacturing supplies				
Rent on manufacturing facility				
Sales commissions				
Depreciation on administrative equipment				
Administrative costs (rent and salaries)				

b. Replace the question marks in the following table to indicate the product cost per unit assuming levels of production of 5,000, 6,000, 7,000, and 8,000.

Cost of goods sold	$455,000	?	?	?
Divided by number of units	5,000	6,000	7,000	8,000
Cost per unit	$ 91	?	?	?

CHAPTER 3

Analysis of Cost, Volume, and Pricing to Increase Profitability

LEARNING OBJECTIVES

After you have mastered the material in this chapter, you will be able to:

LO 3-1 Determine the sales volume necessary to break even or to earn a desired profit.

LO 3-2 Explain how a change in sales price, sales volume, variable cost, or fixed cost affects profitability.

LO 3-3 Draw and interpret a cost-volume-profit graph.

LO 3-4 Calculate and interpret the margin of safety measure.

LO 3-5 Conduct sensitivity analysis using spreadsheet software and the equation method.

LO 3-6 Perform multiproduct cost-volume-profit analysis.

Video lectures and accompanying self-assessment quizzes are available in Connect® for all learning objectives.

CHAPTER OPENING BRIGHT DAY

The president of Bright Day Distributors recently completed a managerial accounting course. He was particularly struck by the operating leverage concept. His instructor had demonstrated how a small percentage increase in sales volume could produce a significantly higher percentage increase in profitability. Unfortunately, the discussion had been limited to the effects of changes in sales volume. In practice, changes in sales volume are often related to changes in sales price. For example, reducing selling prices often leads to increases in sales volume. Sales volume may also change in response to cost changes such as increasing the advertising budget. Furthermore, significant changes in sales volume could redefine the relevant range, changing the fixed and variable costs. Bright Day's president realized that understanding operating leverage was only one piece of understanding how to manage a business. He also needed to understand how changes in prices, costs, and volume affect profitability. Bright Day's president is interested in **cost-volume-profit (CVP) analysis.**

The Curious Accountant

©Jonathan Weiss/Shutterstock

Procter & Gamble (P&G) is a large consumer products company that produces hundreds of products ranging from *Head & Shoulders* shampoo, to *Oral B* toothbrushes, to *Pampers* diapers. The company was founded in 1905 and grew continuously. However, in 2012 the company announced a major restructuring of its business strategy designed to reduce its cost of operations by $10 billion by the end of 2016. One of the ways P&G hoped to achieve these savings was to focus on its 40 largest and most profitable businesses, its 20 largest innovations, and its 10 most important developing markets. In practical terms, this meant the company was going to reduce the number of brands it sold and the size of its work force. In 2017 P&G announced that it had "divested, discontinued, or consolidated 105 brands."

Obviously, a company's profits will increase if it can decrease its costs without decreasing its sales, but P&G's actions were certainly going to reduce sales as well as costs. Why would a company that had spent over 100 years expanding its product offerings suddenly decide to reduce them significantly? Do you believe such a strategy will be successful? (Answers on page 119.)

DETERMINING THE BREAK-EVEN POINT

LO 3-1

Determine the sales volume necessary to break even or to earn a desired profit.

Bright Day Distributors sells nonprescription health food supplements including vitamins, herbs, and natural hormones in the northwestern United States. Bright Day recently obtained the rights to distribute the new herb mixture Delatine. Recent scientific research found that Delatine delayed aging in laboratory animals. The researchers hypothesized that the substance would have a similar effect on humans. Their theory could not be confirmed because of the relatively long human life span. The news media reported the research findings; as stories turned up on television and radio news, talk shows, and in magazines, demand for Delatine increased.

Bright Day plans to sell the Delatine product at a price of $36 per bottle. Delatine costs $24 per bottle. Bright Day's management team suspects that enthusiasm for Delatine will abate quickly as the news media shift to other subjects. To attract customers immediately, the product managers consider television advertising. The marketing manager suggests running a campaign of several hundred cable channel ads at an estimated cost of $60,000.

Bright Day's first concern is whether it can sell enough units to cover its costs. The president made this position clear when he said, "We don't want to lose money on this product. We have to sell at least enough units to break even." In accounting terms, the **break-even point** is where profit (income) equals zero. So how many bottles of Delatine must be sold to produce a profit of zero? The break-even point is commonly computed using either the *equation method,* the *contribution margin per unit method,* or the *contribution margin ratio method.* All three of these approaches produce the same result. They are merely different ways to arrive at the same conclusion.

Equation Method

The **equation method** begins by expressing the income statement as follows:

$$\text{Sales} - \text{Variable costs} - \text{Fixed costs} = \text{Profit (Net income)}$$

As previously stated, profit at the break-even point is zero. Therefore, the break-even point for Delatine is computed as follows:

$$\text{Sales} - \text{Variable costs} - \text{Fixed costs} = \text{Profit}$$
$$\$36N - \$24N - \$60{,}000 = \$0$$
$$\$12N = \$60{,}000$$
$$N = \$60{,}000 \div \$12$$
$$N = 5{,}000 \text{ units}$$

Where:

N = Number of units
$36 = Sales price per unit
$24 = Variable cost per unit
$60,000 = Fixed costs

CHECK YOURSELF 3.1

B-Shoc is an independent musician who is considering whether to independently produce and sell a CD. B-Shoc estimates fixed costs of $5,400 and variable costs of $2 per unit. The expected selling price is $8 per CD. Use the equation method to determine B-Shoc's break-even point.

Answer

$$\text{Sales} - \text{Variable costs} - \text{Fixed costs} = \text{Profit}$$

$$\$8N - \$2N - \$5{,}400 = \$0$$

$$\$6N = \$5{,}400$$

$$N = \$5{,}400 \div \$6$$

$$N = 900 \text{ Units (CDs)}$$

Where:

N = Number of units

$8 = Sales price per unit

$2 = Variable cost per unit

$5,400 = Fixed costs

Contribution Margin per Unit Method

Recall that the *total contribution margin* is the amount of sales minus total variable cost. The **contribution margin per unit** is the sales price per unit minus the variable cost per unit. Therefore, the contribution margin per unit for Delatine is:

Sales price per unit	$ 36
Less: Variable cost per unit	(24)
Contribution margin per unit	$ 12

For every bottle of Delatine it sells, Bright Day earns a $12 contribution margin. In other words, every time Bright Day sells a bottle of Delatine, it receives enough money ($24) to cover the variable cost of the bottle of Delatine and still has $12 left to go toward paying the fixed cost. Bright Day will reach the break-even point when it sells enough bottles of Delatine to cover its fixed costs. Therefore the break-even point can be determined as follows:

$$\text{Break-even point in units} = \frac{\text{Fixed costs}}{\text{Contribution margin per unit}}$$

$$\text{Break-even point in units} = \frac{\$60{,}000}{\$12}$$

$$\text{Break-even point in units} = 5{,}000 \text{ units}$$

This result is the same as that determined under the equation method. Indeed, the contribution margin per unit method formula is an abbreviated version of the income statement formula used in the equation method. In other words, both methods are simply different derivations of the same formula.[1]

[1]The formula for the *contribution margin per unit method* is (where N is the number of units at the break-even point):

N = Fixed costs ÷ Contribution margin per unit

The income statement formula for the *equation method* produces the same result as shown below (where N is the number of units at the break-even point):

Sales − Variable costs − Fixed costs = Profit
Sales price per unit (N) − Variable cost per unit (N) − Fixed costs = Profit
Contribution margin per unit (N) − Fixed costs = Profit
Contribution margin per unit (N) − Fixed costs = 0
Contribution margin per unit (N) = Fixed costs

N = Fixed costs ÷ Contribution margin per unit

Both the *equation method* and the *contribution margin per unit method* yield the amount of break-even sales measured *in units.* To determine the amount of break-even sales measured *in dollars,* multiply the number of units times the sales price per unit. For Delatine, the break-even point measured in dollars is \$180,000 (5,000 units × \$36 per unit). The following income statement confirms this result.

Sales revenue (5,000 units × \$36)	\$ 180,000
Total variable expenses (5,000 units × \$24)	(120,000)
Total contribution margin (5,000 units × \$12)	60,000
Fixed expenses	(60,000)
Net income	\$ 0

Contribution Margin Ratio Method

The equation method and the contribution margin per unit method produce a break-even point measured *in units*. The break-even point expressed *in dollars* can be determined using the contribution margin ratio method. We begin by determining the **contribution margin ratio,** which is defined as follows:

$$\text{Contribution margin ratio} = \text{Contribution margin} \div \text{Sales}$$

The ratio can be computed using the total amount of the contribution margin and sales or by using per unit amounts. Either approach will yield the same result, as shown here.

Using total dollar values:

$$\text{Contribution margin ratio} = \text{Contribution margin in dollars} \div \text{Sales in dollars}$$

$$\text{Contribution margin ratio} = \$60{,}000 \div \$180{,}000 = 0.3333333$$

Using per unit values:

$$\text{Contribution margin ratio} = \text{Contribution margin per unit} \div \text{Sales price per unit}$$

$$\text{Contribution margin ratio} = \$12 \div \$36 = 0.3333333$$

Using the *contribution margin ratio method* the break-even point in dollars is computed by dividing the fixed cost by the contribution margin ratio. The computations for Bright Day follow:

$$\text{Break-even point in dollars} = \frac{\text{Fixed costs}}{\text{Contribution margin ratio}}$$

$$\text{Break-even point in dollars} = \frac{\$60{,}000}{0.333333}$$

$$\text{Break-even point in dollars} = \$180{,}000 \text{ sales revenue}$$

The break-even volume measured in units can be determined by dividing the total sales revenue by the sales price per unit as follows:

$$\text{Break-even point} = \$180{,}000 \text{ Sales revenue} \div \$36 = 5{,}000 \text{ units}$$

The *contribution margin ratio method* yields the same results as the *contribution margin per unit method* and the *equation method.* The results are the same because all three methods are merely different derivations of the income statement formula.

Determining the Sales Volume Necessary to Reach a Desired Profit

Bright Day's president decides the ad campaign should produce a $40,000 profit. He asks the accountant to determine the sales volume that is required to achieve this level of profitability. Using the *equation method,* the sales volume in units required to attain the desired profit is computed as follows:

$$\text{Sales} - \text{Variable costs} - \text{Fixed costs} = \text{Profit}$$

$$\$36\text{N} - \$24\text{N} - \$60{,}000 = \$40{,}000$$

$$\$12\text{N} = \$60{,}000 + 40{,}000$$

$$\text{N} = \$100{,}000 \div \$12$$

$$\text{N} = 8{,}333 \text{ units}$$

Where:

N = Number of units

$36 = Sales price per unit

$24 = Variable cost per unit

$60,000 = Fixed costs

$40,000 = Desired profit

The accountant used the *contribution margin per unit method* to confirm these computations as follows:

$$\text{Sales volume in units} = \frac{\text{Fixed costs} + \text{Desired profit}}{\text{Contribution margin per unit}}$$

$$= \frac{\$60{,}000 + \$40{,}000}{\$12} = 8{,}333.33 \text{ units}$$

The required volume in sales dollars is this number of units multiplied by the sales price per unit (8,333.33 units × $36 = $300,000). The following income statement confirms this result; all amounts are rounded to the nearest whole dollar.

Sales revenue (8,333.33 units × $36)	$ 300,000
Total variable expenses (8,333.33 units × $24)	(200,000)
Total contribution margin (8,333.33 units × $12)	100,000
Fixed expenses	(60,000)
Net income	$ 40,000

In practice, the company will not sell partial bottles of Delatine, so the accountant rounds 8,333.33 bottles to 8,334 whole units. For planning and decision making, managers frequently make decisions using approximate data. Accuracy is desirable, but it is not as important as relevance. Do not be concerned when computations do not produce whole numbers. Rounding and approximation are common characteristics of managerial accounting data.

☑ CHECK YOURSELF 3.2

VolTech Company manufactures small engines that it sells for $130 each. Variable costs are $70 per unit. Fixed costs are expected to be $100,000. The management team has established a target profit of $188,000. Use the contribution margin per unit method to determine how many engines VolTech must sell to attain the target profit. Use the contribution margin ratio method to determine the amount of sales volume in dollars required to attain the desired profit.

Answer

Contribution margin per unit approach:

$$\text{Sales volume in units} = \frac{\text{Fixed costs} + \text{Desired profit}}{\text{Contribution margin per unit}} = \frac{\$100{,}000 + \$188{,}000}{\$130 - \$70} = 4{,}800 \text{ units}$$

Contribution margin ratio approach:

$$\text{Sales volume in \$} = \frac{\text{Fixed costs} + \text{Desired profit}}{\text{Contribution margin ratio}} = \frac{\$100{,}000 + \$188{,}000}{(\$60 \div \$130)} = \$624{,}000$$

Proof that the two approaches produce the same result:

$$\text{Sales price} \times \text{No. units} = \text{Sales in dollars}$$

$$\$130 \times 4{,}800 \text{ units} = \$624{,}000$$

COST-VOLUME-PROFIT VARIABLES: HOW INDEPENDENT CHANGES IMPACT PROFITABILITY

LO 3-2

Explain how a change in sales price, sales volume, variable cost, or fixed cost affects profitability.

The mix of sales price, sales volume, variable cost, and fixed cost has a significant impact on profitability. Bright Day's president called a management team meeting to examine how each of these variables could be controlled to maximize profitability.

Assessing the Effects of Changes in Sales Price or Volume

After reviewing the accountant's computations, the president asked the marketing manager, "What are our chances of reaching a sales volume of 8,334 units?" The manager replied, "Slim to none." She observed that no Bright Day product has ever sold more than 4,000 bottles when initially offered. Further, she feels the $36 price is too high. She asked who set the $36 price and how it was established.

The accountant explained that the price was established using a **cost-plus pricing** strategy. The normal policy is to price products at variable cost plus 50 percent of the variable cost. In this case, the variable cost was $24, resulting in a price of $36 [$24 + ($24 × 0.5)]. The accountant knew the price was high but expected Delatine to sell anyway. Indeed, he supported his position by referencing a strategy known as **prestige pricing.** Many people will pay a premium to be the first to use a new product. Similarly, people will pay more for a product with a prestigious brand name. The accountant noted that the widespread news coverage coupled with Bright Day's brand identity makes Delatine a prime product for prestige pricing.

The marketing manager recognized the accountant's arguments, but contended that news coverage will fade rapidly, competitors will enter the market, and therefore Delatine cannot support a $36 price for an extended period of time. As an alternative, she suggested they use a strategy known as target costing. **Target costing** begins by determining the market price at which a product will sell. This becomes the target price. The focus then shifts to developing the product at a cost that will enable the company to be profitable while selling the product at the target price.

Market research indicates that Delatine could sustain long-term sales at a price of $28 per bottle. At this price, the new contribution margin becomes a mere $4 ($28 Sales price − $24 Variable cost per unit). Lowering the contribution margin per unit will dramatically increase the sales volume necessary to attain the desired profit. Using the *equation method,* the sales volume in units required to attain the desired profit when the sales price per unit is reduced to $28 is as follows:

$$\text{Sales} - \text{Variable costs} - \text{Fixed costs} = \text{Profit}$$
$$\$28N - \$24N - \$60{,}000 = \$40{,}000$$
$$\$4N = \$60{,}000 + \$40{,}000$$
$$N = \$100{,}000 \div \$4$$
$$N = 25{,}000 \text{ units}$$

Where:

N = Number of units
$28 = Sales price per unit
$24 = Variable cost per unit
$60,000 = Fixed costs
$40,000 = Desired profit

The accountant used the *contribution margin per unit method* to confirm these computations as follows:

$$\text{Sales volume in units} = \frac{\text{Fixed costs} + \text{Desired profit}}{\text{Contribution margin per unit}}$$
$$= \frac{\$60{,}000 + \$40{,}000}{\$4} = 25{,}000 \text{ units}$$

The required sales volume *in dollars* is $700,000 (25,000 units × $28 per bottle). The following income statement confirms these results.

Sales revenue (25,000 units × $28)	$ 700,000
Total variable expenses (25,000 units × $24)	(600,000)
Total contribution margin (25,000 units × $4)	100,000
Fixed expenses	(60,000)
Net income	$ 40,000

The marketing manager recognized that it would be impossible to sell 25,000 bottles of Delatine. She noted that this is where target costing enters the picture. Delatine must be made at a cost that will enable the company to earn the desired profit of $40,000 while selling at a price of $28 per bottle. Clearly, the cost structure must change, and the marketing manager has some suggestions for making the necessary changes.

Assessing the Effects of Changes in Variable Costs

The previously discussed $24 cost is for a bottle of 100 capsules, each containing 90 milligrams (mg) of pure Delatine. The manufacturer is willing to provide Delatine to Bright Day in two alternative package sizes: (1) a bottle costing $12 that contains 100 capsules of 30-mg strength pure Delatine and (2) a bottle costing $3 that contains 100 capsules containing 5 mg of Delatine mixed with a vitamin C compound. The 5-mg dosage is the minimum required to permit a package label to indicate the product contains Delatine. The marketing manager observes that either option would enable Bright Day to sell Delatine at a price customers would be willing to pay.

The president vehemently rejected the second option, calling it a blatant attempt to deceive customers by suggesting they were buying Delatine when in fact they were getting vitamin C. *He considered the idea unethical and dangerous.* He vowed that he would not be seen on the six o'clock news trying to defend a fast-buck scheme while his company's reputation went up in smoke. After calming down, he agreed that the first option had merit.

FOCUS ON INTERNATIONAL ISSUES

COST-VOLUME-PROFIT ANALYSIS AT A GERMAN COMPANY

The greater the percentage of a company's total costs that are fixed, the more sensitive the company's earnings are to changes in revenue or volume. Operating leverage, the relationship between the changes in revenue and changes in earnings, introduced earlier, applies to companies throughout the world, large or small.

©Denis Linine/Shutterstock

Manufacturing and software companies have significant fixed costs. It takes a lot of plant and equipment to manufacture the machinery that is used in power plants and transportation, Siemens AG is a large, conglomerate company headquartered in Munich, Germany. Its businesses range from those that provide solutions and services for generating electricity, to those that supply technology for healthcare organizations. From 2013 through 2017 Siemens' revenues increased only 9.4 percent, but its earnings increased 42.2 percent. In other words, its profit grew over four times as fast as its revenue (volume). This is a classic example of the effects of fixed costs, whether measured in dollars, yen, or euros.

Studying Siemens offers insight into a true global enterprise. Though headquartered in Germany, it does business in almost every county in the world. Only 129 of its 1,031 subsidiary companies are in Germany; 165 are in the Americas. Its financial statements are presented in euros and prepared in accordance with international financial accounting standards. Its stock is currently traded on the Frankfurt Stock Exchange, but it was also traded on the New York Stock Exchange until 2014, and it can still be purchased in the over-the-counter market in the United States.

The appropriate dosage for Delatine was uncertain; customers who wanted 90 mg per day could take three capsules instead of one. He asked the accountant, "What's the effect on the bottom line?"

The variable cost changes from \$24 to \$12 per bottle. The contribution margin per unit increases from \$4 per bottle (\$28 sales price − \$24 variable cost per bottle) to \$16 per bottle (\$28 sales price − \$12 variable cost per bottle). The significant increase in contribution margin per unit dramatically decreases the sales volume necessary to attain the target profit.

Using the *equation method,* the sales volume in units required to attain the desired profit when the variable cost per unit is reduced to \$12 per bottle is as follows:

$$\text{Sales} - \text{Variable costs} - \text{Fixed costs} = \text{Profit}$$
$$\$28N - \$12N - \$60{,}000 = \$40{,}000$$
$$\$16N = \$60{,}000 + \$40{,}000$$
$$N = \$100{,}000 \div \$16$$
$$N = 6{,}250 \text{ units}$$

Where:

N = Number of units

\$28 = Sales price per unit

\$12 = Variable cost per unit

\$60,000 = Fixed costs

\$40,000 = Desired profit

Answers to The Curious Accountant

The management of Procter & Gamble (P&G) believed that, while its actions might reduce sales, they would increase profits and shareholders' value. Specifically, in 2012 management stated that its restructuring efforts should reduce the company's cost of goods sold by:

- Improving quality and reliability.
- Reducing capital cost per unit of volume.
- Simplifying and standardizing manufacturing.

Did the strategy work? The following table compares selected operating results for 2017 with 2012. Dollar amounts are in millions.

	2017	2012	Percentage Change
Net sales	$65,058	$83,680	(22.3%)
Operating income	13,955	13,292	5.0%
Net earnings	15,411	10,904	41.3%
Gross margin percentage	50.0%	49.3%	1.4%
Operating income as a percentage of sales	12.8%	8.3%	55.2%

Source: Procter & Gamble's SEC filings.

The accountant used the *contribution margin per unit method* to confirm these computations as follows:

$$\text{Sales volume in units} = \frac{\text{Fixed costs} + \text{Desired profit}}{\text{Contribution margin per unit}}$$

$$= \frac{\$60{,}000 + \$40{,}000}{\$16} = 6{,}250 \text{ units}$$

The required sales volume in sales dollars is $175,000 (6,250 units × $28 per bottle). The following income statement confirms these amounts.

Sales revenue (6,250 units × $28)	$175,000
Total variable expenses (6,250 units × $12)	(75,000)
Total contribution margin (6,250 units × $16)	100,000
Fixed expenses	(60,000)
Net income	$ 40,000

Although the drop in required sales from 25,000 units to 6,250 was significant, the marketing manager was still uneasy about the company's ability to sell 6,250 bottles of Delatine. She observed again that no other Bright Day product had produced sales of that magnitude. The accountant suggested reducing projected fixed costs by advertising on radio rather than television. While gathering cost data for the potential television ad campaign, the accountant had consulted radio ad executives who had assured him radio ads could equal the TV audience exposure at about half the cost. Even though the TV ads would likely be more effective, he argued that since radio advertising costs would be half those of TV, the desired profit could be attained at a significantly lower volume of sales. The company president was impressed with the possibilities. He asked the accountant to determine the required sales volume if advertising costs were $30,000 instead of $60,000.

Assessing the Effects of Changes in Fixed Costs

Changing the fixed costs from \$60,000 to \$30,000 will dramatically reduce the sales level required to earn the target profit. Using the *equation method,* the sales volume in units required to attain the desired profit when fixed costs are reduced to \$30,000 is as follows:

$$\text{Sales} - \text{Variable costs} - \text{Fixed costs} = \text{Profit}$$
$$\$28N - \$12N - \$30{,}000 = \$40{,}000$$
$$\$16N = \$30{,}000 + \$40{,}000$$
$$N = \$70{,}000 \div \$16$$
$$N = 4{,}375 \text{ units}$$

Where:

N = Number of units
\$28 = Sales price per unit
\$12 = Variable cost per unit
\$30,000 = Fixed costs
\$40,000 = Desired profit

The accountant used the *contribution margin per unit method* to confirm these computations as follows:

$$\text{Sales volume in units} = \frac{\text{Fixed costs} + \text{Desired profit}}{\text{Contribution margin per unit}}$$
$$= \frac{\$30{,}000 + \$40{,}000}{\$16} = 4{,}375 \text{ units}$$

The required sales volume in sales dollars is \$122,500 (4,375 units × \$28). The following income statement confirms these amounts.

Sales revenue (4,375 units × \$28)	\$122,500
Total variable expenses (4,375 units × \$12)	(52,500)
Total contribution margin (4,375 units × \$16)	70,000
Fixed expenses	(30,000)
Net income	\$ 40,000

The marketing manager supported using radio instead of television ads. Obviously, she could not guarantee any specific sales volume, but she felt confident that sales projections within a range of 4,000 to 5,000 units were reasonable.

The Effect of Cost Structure on the Break-Even Point

Reducing fixed cost from \$60,000 to \$30,000 also significantly reduces the break-even point. This conclusion is confirmed by computing the break-even point before and after the reduction of the fixed cost as follows:

$$\text{Break-even point} = \text{Fixed costs} \div \text{Contribution margin per unit}$$
$$\text{Break-even point before fixed cost reduction} = \$60{,}000 \div \$16 = 3{,}750 \text{ units}$$
$$\text{Break-even point after fixed cost reduction} = \$30{,}000 \div \$16 = 1{,}875 \text{ units}$$

The lower break-even point is consistent with the conclusion reached in Chapter 2 regarding operating leverage. Recall that higher risk exists for companies with high fixed cost structures while variable cost structures limit risk. It follows that companies with high fixed cost structures will have higher break-even points than companies with low fixed cost structures. A high break-even point suggests that a company must attain a high sales volume or face operating losses. Indeed, failure to attain the required sales volume will result in leveraged losses. In other words, operating leverage will cause any change in sales revenue to have a disproportionately larger impact on net income.

USING THE COST-VOLUME-PROFIT GRAPH

LO 3-3

Draw and interpret a cost-volume-profit graph.

To visually analyze the revised projections, Bright Day's accountant prepared a cost-volume-profit (CVP) graph that pictured CVP relationships over a range of sales activity from zero to 6,000 units. The accountant followed the steps below to produce the CVP graph (sometimes called a *break-even chart*) shown in Exhibit 3.1. The graph is drawn under the following assumptions:

- The contribution margin is $16 (Sales price $28 − Variable cost $12 per bottle).
- The fixed cost is $30,000.
- The desired profit is $40,000.

Procedures for Drawing the CVP Graph

1. *Draw and label the axes:* The horizontal axis represents activity (expressed in units) and the vertical axis represents dollars.
2. *Draw the fixed cost line:* Total fixed costs are constant for all levels of activity. Draw a horizontal line representing the amount of fixed costs across the graph at $30,000, the fixed cost level.
3. *Draw the total cost line:* The total cost line representing the combination of fixed and variable costs is a diagonal line that rises as it moves from left to right. To draw the line, plot one point of the total cost line at the intersection of the fixed cost line and the vertical axis. In this case, plot the first point at the zero level of activity and $30,000 (fixed cost). Next, select an arbitrary activity level. In this case, we assume 6,000 units. At this volume, the total cost is $102,000 [(6,000 units × $12) + $30,000 fixed cost]. Plot a point at the coordinates of 6,000 units and $102,000. Draw a straight line through these two points.
4. *Draw the sales line:* Draw the revenue line using a procedure similar to that described for drawing the total cost line. Select some arbitrary level of activity and multiply that volume by the sales price per unit. Plot the result on the graph and draw a line from the origin (zero units, zero revenue) through this point. For example, at a volume of 6,000 units, the revenue is $168,000 (6,000 units × $28). Plot a point at the coordinates of 6,000 units and $168,000. Draw a line from the origin through the plotted point.

EXHIBIT 3.1

Cost-Volume-Profit Graph

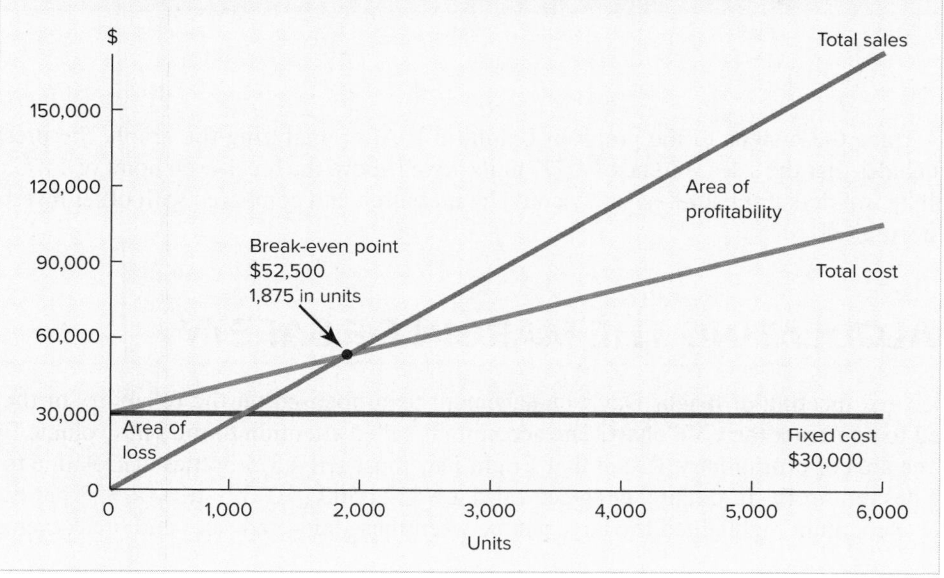

REALITY BYTES

As this chapter notes, CVP analysis for a particular set of data is only valid within the "relevant range" of the variables, such as fixed costs and variable costs. One important relevant range consideration is the maximum capacity at which a business can operate without having to add fixed costs. In academic settings, such as this course, theoretical examples are often presented showing a business doubling or tripling output with no change in fixed costs. Is this true in the real world?

A few years ago one of the coauthor's students asked him what the average operating capacity percentage for most businesses is. Though this seems like an obvious question, of the more than ten thousand students the instructor has taught, this was the only student to have asked the question. So, what is the answer? Some companies disclose operating capacity in their annual reports; examples from hotels and airlines are shown in the following table.

©Christopher Robbins/Image Source

	2017	2016
Marriott Hotels occupancy rate	73.2%	72.5%
Hilton Hotels occupancy rate	75.5	75.0
Delta Air Lines passenger load factor	85.6	84.6
Southwest Airlines passenger load factor	83.9	84.0

Although the annual reports of most companies do not report the percentage of plant capacity that is being used, the United States Census Bureau publishes these results for manufacturers, in great detail, in its *Quarterly Survey of Plant Capacity Utilization.** The average percentage of plant capacity utilized by all manufacturing entities surveyed for the third quarter of 2017 was 72.1 percent. Of course some specific industries were much higher and some much lower. Periodical publications reported a utilization rate of 99.4 percent while ready-mix concrete manufacturers reported a rate of 44.6 percent.

What does this mean for CVP analysis? Consider that if a company is operating at 80 percent of capacity, it can increase its output by only 25 percent before reaching full capacity (0.25 × 80% = 20%; 80% + 20% = 100%). Furthermore, a company cannot operate at 100 percent of capacity for very long without systems breaking down. Therefore, many businesses in the real world will need to add capacity, and thus fixed costs, if their output increases by more than 10 to 15 percent.

When doing real-world analysis, relevant range must be considered.

*www.census.gov/manufacturing/capacity/.

Trace these steps to the graph in Exhibit 3.1. After analyzing the graph, the president concludes that the sales volume of 4,375 units is well above the break-even point of 1,875 units. Still he wonders if the level of safety could be measured and compared with other investment opportunities.

CALCULATING THE MARGIN OF SAFETY

LO 3-4

Calculate and interpret the margin of safety measure.

The final meeting of Bright Day's management team focused on the reliability of the data used to construct the CVP chart. The accountant called attention to the sales volume figures in the area of profitability. Recall that Bright Day must sell 4,375 bottles of Delatine to earn the desired profit. In dollars, budgeted sales are $122,500 (4,375 bottles × $28 per bottle). The accountant highlighted the large gap between these budgeted sales and break-even sales.

The amount of this gap, called the *margin of safety,* can be measured in units or in sales dollars as shown here:

	In Units	In Dollars
Budgeted sales	4,375	$122,500
Break-even sales	(1,875)	(52,500)
Margin of safety	2,500	$ 70,000

The **margin of safety** measures the cushion between budgeted sales and the break-even point. It quantifies the amount by which actual sales can fall short of expectations before the company will begin to incur losses.

To help compare diverse products or companies of different sizes, the margin of safety can be expressed as a percentage. Divide the margin of safety by the budgeted sales volume[2] as shown here:

$$\text{Margin of safety} = \frac{\text{Budgeted sales} - \text{Break-even sales}}{\text{Budgeted sales}}$$

$$\text{Margin of safety} = \frac{\$122{,}500 - \$52{,}500}{\$122{,}500} = 57.14\%$$

This analysis suggests actual sales would have to fall short of expected sales by more than 57 percent before Bright Day would experience a loss on Delatine. The large margin of safety suggests the proposed radio advertising program to market bottles of 30-mg Delatine capsules has minimal risk. As a result, the project team recommends that Delatine be added to the company's line of products. The steps Bright Day's project team experienced to arrive at this decision are summarized in Exhibit 3.2.

CHECK YOURSELF 3.3

Suppose that Bright Day is considering the possibility of selling a protein supplement that will cost the company $5 per bottle. Bright Day believes that it can sell 4,000 bottles of the supplement for $25 per bottle. Fixed costs associated with selling the supplement are expected to be $42,000. Does the supplement have a wider margin of safety than Delatine?

Answer Calculate the break-even point for the protein supplement.

$$\text{Break-even volume in units} = \frac{\text{Fixed costs}}{\text{Contribution margin per unit}} = \frac{\$42{,}000}{\$25 - \$5} = 2{,}100 \text{ units}$$

Calculate the margin of safety. Note that the margin of safety expressed as a percentage can be calculated using the number of units or sales dollars. Using either units or dollars yields the same percentage.

$$\text{Margin of safety} = \frac{\text{Budgeted sales} - \text{Break-even sales}}{\text{Budgeted sales}} = \frac{4{,}000 - 2{,}100}{4{,}000} = 47.5\%$$

The margin of safety for Delatine (57.14 percent) exceeds that for the protein supplement (47.5 percent). This suggests that Bright Day is less likely to incur losses selling Delatine than selling the supplement.

[2]The margin of safety percentage can be based on actual as well as budgeted sales. For example, an analyst could compare the margins of safety of two companies under current operating conditions by substituting actual sales for budgeted sales in the computation, as follows: [(Actual sales − Break-even sales) ÷ Actual sales].

EXHIBIT 3.2

Recap of Delatine Decision Process

Management considers a new product named Delatine. Delatine has a projected sales price of $36 and variable cost of $24 per bottle. Fixed cost is projected to be $60,000. The break-even point is 5,000 units [$60,000 ÷ ($36 – $24) = 5,000].

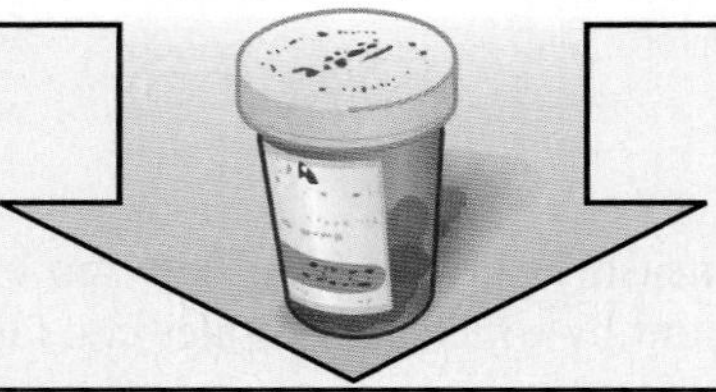

Management desires to earn a $40,000 profit on Delatine. The sales volume required to earn the desired profit is 8,334 units [($60,000 + $40,000) ÷ ($36 – $24) = 8,334].

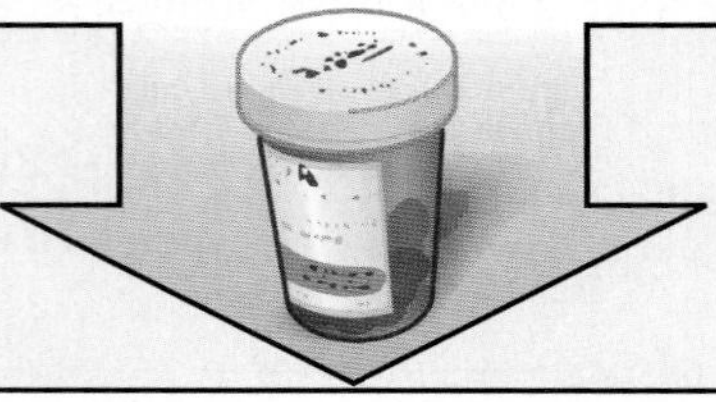

The marketing manager advocates a target pricing approach that lowers the proposed selling price to $28 per bottle. The sales volume required to earn a $40,000 profit increases to 25,000 units [($60,000 + $40,000) ÷ ($28 – $24) = 25,000].

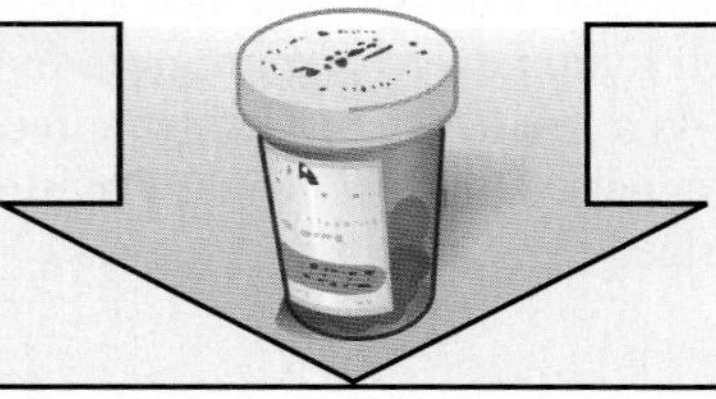

Target costing is employed to reengineer the product, thereby reducing variable cost to $12 per bottle. The sales volume required to earn a $40,000 profit decreases to 6,250 units [($60,000 + $40,000) ÷ ($28 – $12) = 6,250].

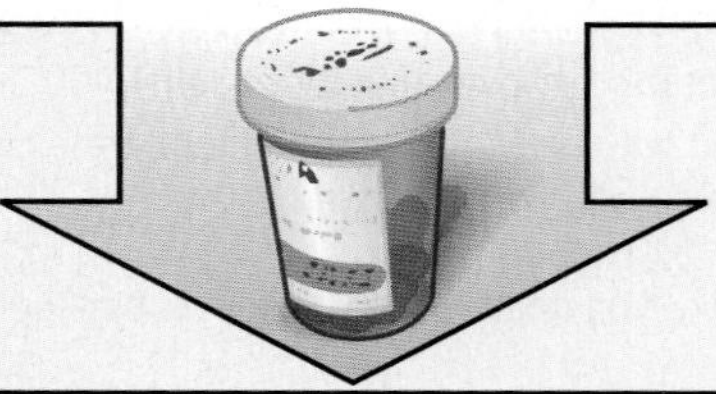

Target costing is applied further to reduce fixed cost to $30,000. The sales volume required to earn a $40,000 profit decreases to 4,375 units [($30,000 + $40,000) ÷ ($28 – $12) = 4,375]. The new break-even point is 1,875 units [$30,000 ÷ ($28 – $12) = 1,875].

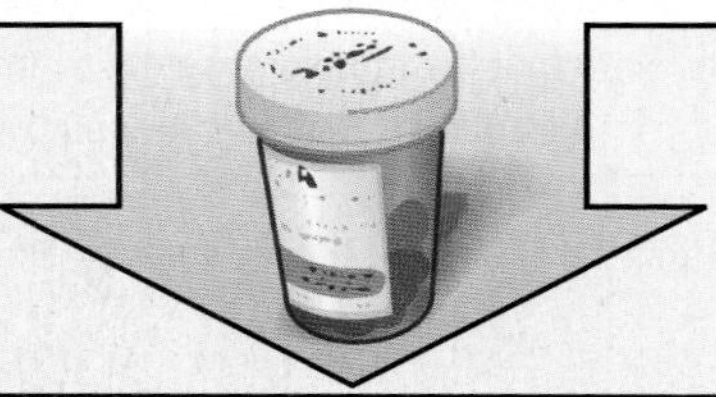

In view of a 57.14% margin of safety [(4,375 – 1,875) ÷ 4,375 = 0.5714], management decides to add Delatine to its product line.

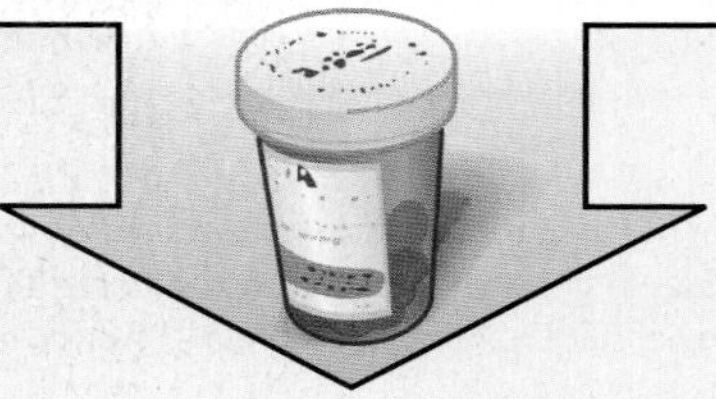

USING SENSITIVITY ANALYSIS TO EXAMINE HOW SIMULTANEOUS CHANGES AMONG COST-VOLUME-PROFIT VARIABLES IMPACT PROFITABILITY

LO 3-5

Conduct sensitivity analysis using spreadsheet software and the equation method.

While the margin of safety is easy to calculate and understand, it delivers a limited view of risk. It provides no insight as to how simultaneous changes in sales price, sales volume, variable cost, or fixed cost could impact profitability. To provide a broader assessment of risk, the management team decides to use sensitivity analysis to examine several possible simultaneous changes.

Perform Sensitivity Analysis Using Spreadsheet Software

While useful, the margin of safety offers only a one-dimensional measure of risk—change in sales volume. Profitability is affected by multidimensional forces. Fixed or variable costs, as well as sales volume, could differ from expectations. Exhibit 3.3 uses data pertaining to Bright Day's proposed project for marketing Delatine to illustrate an Excel spreadsheet showing the sensitivity of profits to simultaneous changes in fixed cost, variable cost, and sales volume. Recall the accountant estimated the radio ad campaign would cost $30,000. The spreadsheet projects profitability if advertising costs are as low as $20,000 or as high as $40,000. The effects of potential simultaneous changes in variable cost and sales volume are similarly projected.

The range of scenarios illustrated in the spreadsheet represents only a few of the many alternatives management can analyze with a few quick keystrokes. The spreadsheet program recalculates profitability figures instantly when one of the variables changes. If the president asks what would happen if Bright Day sold 10,000 units, the accountant merely substitutes the new number for one of the existing sales volume figures, and revised profitability numbers are instantly available. By changing the variables, management can get a real feel for the sensitivity of profits to changes in cost and volume. Investigating a multitude of what-if possibilities involving simultaneous changes in fixed cost, variable cost, and volume is called **sensitivity analysis.**

EXHIBIT 3.3

Spreadsheet Report to Facilitate "What-If" Analysis

Selling Price = $ 28.00

If Fixed Cost is	While Variable Cost is	And Sales Volume is 2,000	3,000	4,000	5,000	6,000
		Then Profitability Will Be				
$ 20,000	11	$14,000	$31,000	$48,000	$65,000	$82,000
20,000	12	12,000	28,000	44,000	60,000	76,000
20,000	13	10,000	25,000	40,000	55,000	70,000
30,000	11	4,000	21,000	38,000	55,000	72,000
30,000	12	2,000	18,000	34,000	50,000	66,000
30,000	13	-	15,000	30,000	45,000	60,000
40,000	11	(6,000)	11,000	28,000	45,000	62,000
40,000	12	(8,000)	8,000	24,000	40,000	56,000
40,000	13	(10,000)	5,000	20,000	35,000	50,000

Source: Microsoft Excel 2010

After reviewing the spreadsheet analysis, Bright Day's management team is convinced it should undertake radio advertising for Delatine. Only under the most dire circumstances (if actual sales are significantly below expectations while costs are well above expectations) will the company incur a loss.

Perform Sensitivity Analysis Using the Equation Method

When spreadsheet software is not available, the effects of simultaneous changes in CVP variables can be examined using the equation method. To illustrate several possible scenarios, assume Bright Day has developed the budgeted income statement in Exhibit 3.4.

EXHIBIT 3.4

Budgeted Income Statement

Sales revenue (4,375 units × \$28 sale price)	\$122,500
Total variable exp. (4,375 units × \$12 cost per bottle)	(52,500)
Total contribution margin (4,375 units × \$16)	70,000
Fixed expenses	(30,000)
Net income	\$ 40,000

A Decrease in Sales Price Accompanied by an Increase in Sales Volume

The marketing manager believes reducing the sales price per bottle to \$25 will increase sales volume by 625 units. The expected sales volume would become 5,000 (4,375 + 625). Variable cost per unit is expected to remain at \$12. Should Bright Day reduce the price? Compare the projected profit without these changes (\$40,000) with the projected profit if the sales price is \$25 and volume increases to 5,000 units.

$$\text{Sales} - \text{Variable costs} - \text{Fixed costs} = \text{Profit}$$

$$(\$25 \times 5{,}000 \text{ units}) - (\$12 \times 5{,}000) - \$30{,}000 = \text{Profit}$$

$$\$35{,}000 = \text{Profit}$$

Since budgeted income falls from \$40,000 to \$35,000, Bright Day should not reduce the sales price.

An Increase in Fixed Cost Accompanied by an Increase in Sales Volume

Return to the budgeted income statement in Exhibit 3.4. If the company buys an additional \$12,000 of advertising, management believes sales can increase to 6,000 units. The sales price remains at \$28 and variable cost per unit at \$12. Should Bright Day incur the additional advertising cost, increasing fixed costs to \$42,000 and sales volume to 6,000 units? The expected profit would be:

$$\text{Sales} - \text{Variable costs} - \text{Fixed costs} = \text{Profit}$$

$$(\$28 \times 6{,}000 \text{ units}) - (\$12 \times 6{,}000) - \$42{,}000 = \text{Profit}$$

$$\$54{,}000 = \text{Profit}$$

Since budgeted income increases from \$40,000 to \$54,000, Bright Day should seek to increase sales through additional advertising.

A Simultaneous Reduction in Sales Price, Fixed Costs, Variable Costs, and Sales Volume

Return again to the budgeted income statement in Exhibit 3.4. Suppose Bright Day negotiates a \$4 reduction in the cost of a bottle of Delatine. The management team considers passing some of the savings on to customers by reducing the sales price to \$25 per bottle. Furthermore, the team believes it could reduce advertising costs by \$8,000 and still achieve sales of 4,200 units. Should Bright Day adopt this plan to reduce prices and advertising costs?

The contribution margin would increase to $17 per bottle ($25 revised selling price − $8 revised variable cost per bottle) and fixed cost would fall to $22,000 ($30,000 − $8,000). Based on a sales volume of 4,200 units, the expected profit is:

Sales − Variable costs − Fixed costs = Profit

($25 × 4,200 units) − ($8 × 4,200) − $22,000 = Profit

$49,400 = Profit

Because budgeted income increases from $40,000 to $49,400, Bright Day should proceed with the revised operating strategy.

Many other possible scenarios could be considered. The contribution approach can be used to analyze independent or simultaneous changes in the CVP variables.

MULTIPRODUCT COST-VOLUME-PROFIT ANALYSIS

LO 3-6

Perform multiproduct cost-volume-profit analysis.

To this point we have simplified our discussion of CVP by assuming a company sells only one product. In the real world, most companies sell many products. Each product has an independent impact on the profitability of the company. Calculating the break-even point requires an analyst to consider the simultaneous impact of the contribution margins of all products. This impact can be easily measured by computing the weighted average contribution margin.

To illustrate, we assume that Bright Day's management team is examining its annual Vitamin C Sales Days event. The sales event focuses on two products. One product is labeled Synthetic C; the other is called Organic C. The sales price, variable cost, and contribution margin for each bottle of each product are shown here:

	Synthetic C	Organic C
Sales price	$7	$9
Variable cost	5	6
Contribution margin	$2	$3

Due to its lower cost, Synthetic C has consistently outsold Organic C. Indeed, Synthetic C historically accounts for approximately 80 percent of the total sales, with Organic C making up the remaining 20 percent. The fixed costs for the annual sales event are expected to be $2,112. These fixed costs are largely composed of advertising and training expenses. Based on this information, the management team begins its examination by determining the break-even point.

Determining the Break-Even Point

The first step in determining the break-even point is to compute the *weighted average contribution margin per unit.* The weighted average depends on each product's proportionate share of the total sales. In accounting terms, the relative proportions in which a company's products are sold is called the **sales mix.** The expected sales mix for the annual sales event is 80 percent for Synthetic C and 20 percent for Organic C. In other words, the two products in the event have an 80/20 sales mix. Based on this sales mix, the weighted average contribution margin per bottle is computed as follows.

	Contribution Margin	Times Proportionate Share	Weighted Average
Synthetic C	$2	× 0.8	$1.60
Organic C	3	× 0.2	0.60
Weighted average contribution margin			$2.20

Using the per unit contribution margin approach, the break-even point in total units can be determined by dividing the fixed cost by the weighted average contribution margin as follows:

$$\text{Break-even point} = \text{Fixed costs} \div \text{Weighted average contribution margin per unit}$$

$$\text{Break-even point} = \$2{,}112 \div \$2.20 = 960 \text{ total units}$$

The 960 units represent the total number of bottles of both products combined. To determine the number of bottles of each product, multiply the total number of bottles times the proportionate share of the sales mix as follows:

$$\text{Break-even point} = \text{Total units} \times \text{Proportionate share of sales mix}$$

$$\text{Break-even point for Synthetic C} = 960 \text{ bottles} \times 0.8 \text{ share of sales mix} = 768 \text{ bottles}$$

$$\text{Break-even point for Organic C} = 960 \text{ bottles} \times 0.2 \text{ share of sales mix} = 192 \text{ bottles}$$

The following income statement confirms that these sales volume figures constitute the break-even point.

Sales of Synthetic C (768 bottles × $7)	$ 5,376
Sales of Organic C (192 bottles × $9)	1,728
Total sales	7,104
Variable cost of Synthetic C (768 bottles × $5)	(3,840)
Variable cost of Organic C (192 bottles × $6)	(1,152)
Contribution margin	2,112
Fixed cost	(2,112)
Net income	$ 0

Determining the Sales Volume Necessary to Reach a Desired Profit

Suppose Bright Day's president wants to know the number of bottles of each product that must be sold to earn a profit of $264 from the sales event. This information can be easily determined by adding the amount of the desired profit to the amount of fixed cost and then dividing the total by the weighted average contribution margin per unit. The computations are as follows:

$$\text{Sales volume in units} = \frac{\text{Fixed cost} + \text{Desired profit}}{\text{Weighted average contribution margin per unit}}$$

$$= \frac{\$2{,}112 + \$264}{\$2.20} = 1{,}080 \text{ total units}$$

The 1,080 units represent the total number of bottles of both products combined. To determine the number of bottles of each product, multiply the total number of bottles times the proportionate share of the sales mix as follows:

$$\text{Break-even point} = \text{Total units} \times \text{Proportionate share of sales mix}$$

$$\text{Break-even point for Synthetic C} = 1{,}080 \text{ bottles} \times 0.8 \text{ share of sales mix} = 864 \text{ bottles}$$

$$\text{Break-even point for Organic C} = 1{,}080 \text{ bottles} \times 0.2 \text{ share of sales mix} = 216 \text{ bottles}$$

The following income statement confirms that these sales volume figures constitute the sales volumes necessary to earn a desired profit of $264.

Sales of Synthetic C (864 bottles × $7)	$ 6,048
Sales of Organic C (216 bottles × $9)	1,944
Total sales	7,992
Variable cost of Synthetic C (864 bottles × $5)	(4,320)
Variable cost of Organic C (216 bottles × $6)	(1,296)
Contribution margin	2,376
Fixed cost	(2,112)
Net income	$ 264

Managing the Sales Mix

Bright Day's president asks the management team to consider possibilities for increasing profitability. The team first considers the possibility of increasing the total number of bottles of vitamins sold. The marketing manager is pessimistic about this possibility. She notes that there are only so many people buying vitamin C. Trying to convince the same number of customers to purchase more bottles of the vitamin is not likely. The accountant notes that it is not necessary to sell more bottles of vitamins. Indeed, he argues that profitability can be increased even if sales volume remains flat. His solution is to change the sales mix.

Since Organic C has a higher contribution margin, shifting customers from Synthetic C to Organic C will increase profitability. The accountant demonstrates his point by computing the level of profitability assuming the sales mix shifts from an 80/20 split to a 60/40 mix. The income statement for a total sales volume of 1,080 bottles under a 60/40 sales mix is developed as follows.

The 1,080 units represent the total number of bottles of both products combined. To determine the number of bottles of each product using the 60/40 sales mix, multiply the total number of bottles times the proportionate share of the sales mix:

Break-even point = Total units × Proportionate share of sales mix

Break-even point for Synthetic C = 1,080 bottles × 0.6 share of sales mix = 648 bottles

Break-even point for Organic C = 1,080 bottles × 0.4 share of sales mix = 432 bottles

The following income statement confirms that the revised sales mix produces a higher net income. Indeed, in this case net income increases from $264 to $480 given the same total sales volume of 1,080 total bottles of vitamin C.

Sales of Synthetic C (648 bottles × $7)	$ 4,536
Sales of Organic C (432 bottles × $9)	3,888
Total sales	8,424
Variable cost of Synthetic C (648 bottles × $5)	(3,240)
Variable cost of Organic C (432 bottles × $6)	(2,592)
Contribution margin	2,592
Fixed cost	(2,112)
Net income	$ 480

The president is very impressed with this potential increase in profitability. His immediate response is to ask, how do we change the sales mix? A number of possibilities are examined, including slanting the advertising to emphasize Organic C and training the sales staff to promote the product. After careful consideration, the team implements the most promising ideas. Ultimately, the team would compare the expected income statement with actual results to evaluate and fine-tune the strategy. Variance analysis and performance evaluation are important subjects that will be covered in coming chapters.

It is important to note that the sales mix affects all aspects of CVP analysis. For example, the new break-even point for a sales mix of 60/40 is computed as discussed here. The first step is to compute the weighted average contribution margin per unit as follows.

	Contribution Margin	Times Proportionate Share	Weighted Average
Synthetic C	$2	× 0.6	$1.20
Organic C	3	× 0.4	1.20
Weighted average contribution margin			$2.40

Using the per unit contribution margin approach, the break-even point in total units can be determined by dividing the fixed cost by the weighted average contribution margin as follows:

Break-even point = Fixed costs ÷ Weighted average contribution margin per unit

Break-even point = $2,112 ÷ $2.40 = 880 total units

Note that the break-even point is 80 units less (960 units − 880 units) than when the sales mix was 80/20. This demonstrates that shifting the sales mix not only increases net income but also reduces the break-even point. The 880 units represent the total number of bottles of both products combined that must be sold under a 60/40 sales mix for the company to break even. To determine the number of bottles of each product, multiply the total number of bottles times the proportionate share of the sales mix as follows:

Break-even point = Total units × Proportionate share of sales mix

Break-even point for Synthetic C = 880 bottles × 0.6 share of sales mix = 528 bottles

Break-even point for Organic C = 880 bottles × 0.4 share of sales mix = 352 bottles

The following income statement confirms that these sales volume figures constitute the break-even point.

Sales of Synthetic C (528 bottles × $7)	$ 3,696
Sales of Organic C (352 bottles × $9)	3,168
Total sales	6,864
Variable cost of Synthetic C (528 bottles × $5)	(2,640)
Variable cost of Organic C (352 bottles × $6)	(2,112)
Contribution margin	2,112
Fixed cost	(2,112)
Net income	$ 0

The contribution margin per unit formula can be used to determine the number of units required to attain a target profit. Simply add the desired profit to the fixed costs and then divide by the weighted average contribution margin per unit. The resulting formula is:

$$\text{Sales volume in units} = \frac{\text{Fixed costs} + \text{Desired profit}}{\text{Weighted average contribution margin per unit}}$$

COST-VOLUME-PROFIT LIMITATIONS

©Ryan McVay/Getty Images

CVP is limited by a number of underlying assumptions. These assumptions include:

1. The selling price is constant. It does not increase or decrease regardless of changes in sales volume.
2. Costs are linear.
   a. The variable cost per unit is constant and moves in direct proportion with changes in sales volume.
   b. Total fixed costs do not change with changes in sales volume.
   c. Efficiency and productivity are constant.
3. The sales mix in multiproduct companies is constant.
4. Inventory levels in manufacturing companies are constant.
5. All CVP variables are within the relevant range.

Violating these assumptions will produce inaccuracies in CVP analysis. Unfortunately, some violations are unavoidable in practice. For example, some companies may offer a discounted sales price for large orders, thereby violating the first assumption. Similarly, managers may desire to analyze operations at levels of sales volume that are outside the relevant range. Fortunately, many violations are insignificant. Further, accountants can make appropriate adjustments if serious violations are unavoidable. The widespread use of CVP in the real world suggests that the benefits of the analysis exceed the minor inaccuracies that inevitably occur. Even so, accountants must remain vigilant to avoid inaccuracies in the advice they render.

A Look Back <<

Profitability is affected by changes in sales price, costs, and the volume of activity. The relationship among these variables is examined using *cost-volume-profit (CVP) analysis*. The *contribution margin,* determined by subtracting variable costs from the sales price, is a useful variable in CVP analysis. The *contribution margin per unit* is the amount each unit sold provides to cover fixed costs. Once fixed costs have been covered, each additional unit sold increases net income by the amount of the per-unit contribution margin.

The *break-even point* (the point where total revenue equals total cost) can be determined by the equation method, the contribution margin method, or the contribution margin ratio method. All three methods produce the same result because all three methods are derivations of the income statement formula:

Sales − Variable costs − Fixed costs = Profit

Beyond determining the break-even point, all three methods can also be used to assess the effects in other CVP relationships.

Many methods are available to determine the prices at which products should sell. In *cost-plus pricing,* the sales price per unit is determined by adding a percentage markup to the cost per unit. In contrast, *target costing* begins with an estimated market price customers would be willing to pay for the product and then develops the product at a cost that will enable the company to earn its desired profit.

A *break-even graph* can depict cost-volume-profit relationships for a product over a range of sales activity. The horizontal axis represents volume of activity and the vertical axis represents dollars. Lines for fixed costs, total costs, and sales are drawn based on the sales price per unit, variable cost per unit, and fixed costs. The graph can be used to determine the break-even point in units and sales dollars.

The *margin of safety* is the number of units or the amount of sales dollars by which actual sales can fall below expected sales before a loss is incurred. The margin of safety can also be expressed as a percentage to permit comparing different size companies. The margin of safety can be computed as a percentage by dividing the difference between budgeted sales and break-even sales by the amount of budgeted sales.

Spreadsheet software as well as the contribution margin approach can be used to conduct sensitivity analysis of cost-volume-profit relationships. *Sensitivity analysis* predicts the effect on profitability of different scenarios of fixed costs, variable costs, and sales volumes. The effects of simultaneous changes in all three variables also can be assessed.

Cost-volume-profit analysis is built on certain simplifying assumptions. The analysis assumes true linearity among the CVP variables and a constant level of inventory. Although these assumptions are not literally valid in actual practice, CVP analysis nevertheless provides managers with helpful insights for decision making.

>> A Look Forward

The next chapter introduces a new cost classification scheme. Specifically, you will learn how to classify costs as being either direct or indirect costs. Direct costs are directly traceable to cost objects. Cost objects are items for which management needs to determine their cost. For example, a manager may need to determine the cost of making a product, providing a service, or operating a department. In these cases, the cost object is the product, the service, or the department. Indirect costs are those costs that cannot be directly traced to a cost object. The chapter will discuss techniques such as cost tracing and cost allocation, which are used to assign indirect costs to various objects.

Video lectures and accompanying self-assessment quizzes are available in *Connect* for all learning objectives.

SELF-STUDY REVIEW PROBLEM

Sharp Company makes and sells pencil sharpeners. The variable cost of each sharpener is $20. The sharpeners are sold for $30 each. Fixed operating expenses amount to $40,000.

Required

a. Determine the break-even point in units and sales dollars.

b. Determine the sales volume in units and dollars that is required to attain a profit of $12,000. Verify your answer by preparing an income statement using the contribution margin format.

c. Determine the margin of safety between sales required to attain a profit of $12,000 and break-even sales.

d. Prepare a break-even graph using the cost and price assumptions outlined above.

Solution to Requirement *a*

Formula for Computing Break-Even Point in Units
Sales − Variable costs − Fixed costs = Profit
Sales price per unit (N) − Variable cost per unit (N) − Fixed costs = Profit
Contribution margin per unit (N) − Fixed costs = Profit
N = (Fixed costs + Profit) ÷ Contribution margin per unit
N = ($40,000 + 0) ÷ ($30 − $20) = 4,000 units

Break-Even Point in Sales Dollars	
Sales price	$ 30
× Number of units	4,000
Sales volume in dollars	$120,000

Solution to Requirement *b*

Formula for Computing Unit Sales Required to Attain Desired Profit

Sales − Variable costs − Fixed costs = Profit
Sales price per unit (N) − Variable cost per unit (N) − Fixed costs = Profit
Contribution margin per unit (N) − Fixed costs = Profit
N = (Fixed costs + Profit) ÷ Contribution margin per unit
N = ($40,000 + $12,000) ÷ ($30 − $20) = 5,200 units

Sales Dollars Required to Attain Desired Profit	
Sales price	$ 30
× Number of units	5,200
Sales volume in dollars	$156,000

Income Statement	
Sales volume in units (a)	5,200
Sales revenue (a × $30)	$ 156,000
Variable costs (a × $20)	(104,000)
Contribution margin	52,000
Fixed costs	(40,000)
Net income	$ 12,000

Solution to Requirement *c*

Margin of Safety Computations	Units	Dollars
Budgeted sales	5,200	$ 156,000
Break-even sales	(4,000)	(120,000)
Margin of safety	1,200	$ 36,000

Percentage Computation

$$\frac{\text{Margin of safety in \$}}{\text{Budgeted sales}} = \frac{\$36,000}{\$156,000} = 23.08\%$$

Solution to Requirement *d*

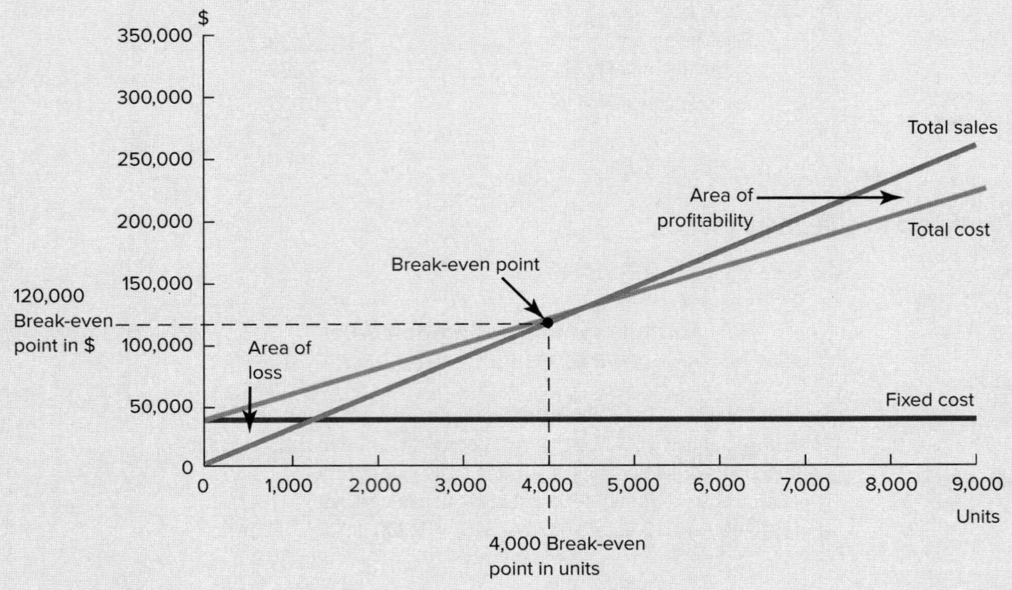

KEY TERMS

Break-even point 112
Contribution margin per unit 113
Contribution margin ratio 114
Cost-plus pricing 116
Cost-volume-profit (CVP) analysis 111
Equation method 112
Margin of safety 123
Prestige pricing 116
Sales mix 127
Sensitivity analysis 123
Target costing 116

QUESTIONS

1. What does the term *break-even point* mean? Name the two ways it can be measured.
2. How does a contribution margin income statement differ from the income statement used in financial reporting?
3. In what three ways can the contribution margin be useful in cost-volume-profit analysis?
4. If Company A has a projected margin of safety of 22 percent while Company B has a margin of safety of 52 percent, which company is at greater risk when actual sales are less than budgeted?
5. What variables affect profitability? Name two methods for determining profitability when simultaneous changes occur in these variables.
6. When would the customer be willing to pay a premium price for a product or service? What pricing strategy would be appropriate under these circumstances?
7. What are three alternative approaches to determine the break-even point? What do the results of these approaches show?
8. What is the equation method for determining the break-even point? Explain how the results of this method differ from those of the contribution margin approach.
9. If a company is trying to find the break-even point for multiple products that sell simultaneously, what consideration must be taken into account?
10. What assumptions are inherent in cost-volume-profit analysis? Since these assumptions are usually not wholly valid, why do managers still use the analysis in decision making?
11. Mary Hartwell and Jane Jamail, college roommates, are considering the joint purchase of a computer that they can share to prepare class assignments. Ms. Hartwell wants a particular model that costs $2,000; Ms. Jamail prefers a more economical model that costs $1,500. In fact, Ms. Jamail is adamant about her position, refusing to contribute more than $750 toward the purchase. If Ms. Hartwell is also adamant about her position, should she accept Ms. Jamail's $750 offer and apply that amount toward the purchase of the more expensive computer?
12. How would the algebraic formula used to compute the break-even point under the equation method be changed to solve for a desired target profit?
13. Setting the sales price is easy: Enter cost information and desired profit data into one of the cost-volume-profit formulas, and the appropriate sales price can be computed mathematically. Do you agree with this line of reasoning? Explain.
14. What is the relationship between cost-volume-profit analysis and the relevant range?

MULTIPLE-CHOICE QUESTIONS

Multiple-choice questions are available in *Connect*.

EXERCISES—SERIES A

connect **All applicable Exercises in Series A are available in *Connect*.**

Exercise 3-1A *Equation method* LO 3-1

Dannica Corporation produces products that it sells for $40 each. Variable costs per unit are $25, and annual fixed costs are $360,000. Dannica desires to earn a profit of $150,000.

Required

a. Use the equation method to determine the break-even point in units and dollars.
b. Determine the sales volume in units and dollars required to earn the desired profit.

Exercise 3-2A *Per-unit contribution margin approach* LO 3-1

Chang Corporation sells products for $120 each that have variable costs of $80 per unit. Chang's annual fixed cost is $720,000.

Required

Use the per-unit contribution margin approach to determine the break-even point in units and dollars.

Exercise 3-3A *Contribution margin ratio* LO 3-1

Santiago Company incurs annual fixed costs of $66,000. Variable costs for Santiago's product are $34 per unit, and the sales price is $50 per unit. Santiago desires to earn an annual profit of $34,000.

Required

Use the contribution margin ratio approach to determine the sales volume in dollars and units required to earn the desired profit.

Exercise 3-4A *Determining variable cost from incomplete cost data* LO 3-1

Barclay Corporation produced 250,000 watches that it sold for $32 each during Year 2. The company determined that fixed manufacturing cost per unit was $16 per watch. The company reported a $2,400,000 gross margin on its Year 2 financial statements.

Required

Determine the variable cost per unit, the total variable cost, and the total contribution margin.

Exercise 3-5A *Contribution margin per unit approach for break-even and desired profit* LO 3-1

Information concerning a product produced by Hansen Company appears as follows.

Sales price per unit	$ 180
Variable cost per unit	$ 100
Total annual fixed manufacturing and operating costs	$720,000

Required

Determine the following:

a. Contribution margin per unit.
b. Number of units that Hansen must sell to break even.
c. Sales level in units that Hansen must reach to earn a profit of $240,000.

Exercise 3-6A *Cost structure, risk, and the break-even point* LO 3-2

Fowler Company produces a product that sells for $200 per unit and has a variable cost of $125 per unit. Fowler incurs annual fixed costs of $450,000.

Required

a. Determine the sales volume in units and dollars required to break even.

b. Calculate the break-even point assuming fixed costs increase to $600,000.

c. Explain how a fixed cost structure affects risk and the break-even point.

LO 3-2

Exercise 3-7A *Cost-volume-profit relationship*

Stone Corporation is a manufacturing company that makes small electric motors it sells for $45 per unit. The variable costs of production are $25 per motor, and annual fixed costs of production are $800,000.

Required

a. How many units of product must Stone make and sell to break even?

b. How many units of product must Stone make and sell to earn a $120,000 profit?

c. The marketing manager believes that sales would increase dramatically if the price were reduced to $40 per unit. How many units of product must Stone make and sell to earn a $160,000 profit, if the sales price is set at $40 per unit?

LO 3-2

Exercise 3-8A *Target costing*

The marketing manager of Griffin Corporation has determined that a market exists for a telephone with a sales price of $36 per unit. The production manager estimates the annual fixed costs of producing between 40,000 and 80,000 telephones would be $450,000.

Required

Assume that Griffin desires to earn a $150,000 profit from the phone sales. How much can Griffin afford to spend on variable cost per unit if production and sales equal 50,000 phones?

LO 3-2

Exercise 3-9A *Target costing*

Askew Enterprises produces a product with fixed costs of $200,000 and variable cost of $9 per unit. The company desires to earn a $100,000 profit and believes it can sell 20,000 units of the product.

Required

a. Based on this information, determine the target sales price.

b. Assume a competitor is currently selling a similar product for $20 per unit. Explain how Askew can use target costing to maintain its desired profitability.

LO 3-3

Exercise 3-10A *Components of break-even graph*

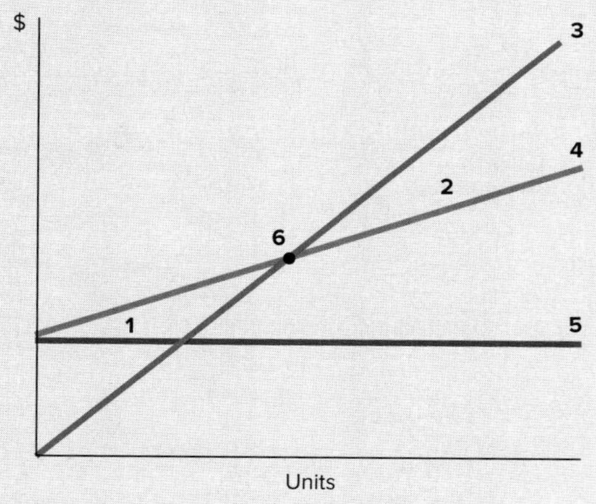

Required

Match the numbers shown in the graph with the following items:

a. Fixed cost line

b. Total cost line

c. Break-even point

d. Area of profit

e. Revenue line

f. Area of loss

Exercise 3-11A *Margin of safety* LO 3-4

Owen Company makes a product that sells for $61 per unit. The company pays $37 per unit for the variable costs of the product and incurs annual fixed costs of $360,000. Owen expects to sell 20,000 units of product.

Required

Determine Owen's margin of safety expressed as a percentage.

Exercise 3-12A *Conducting sensitivity analysis using a spreadsheet* LO 3-5

Use Exhibit 3.3 in this chapter to answer the following questions.

Required

a. Determine the sales volume, fixed cost, and variable cost per unit at the break-even point.

b. Determine the expected profit if Bright Day projects the following data for Delatine: sales, 4,000 bottles; fixed cost, $20,000; and variable cost per unit, $13.

c. Bright Day is considering new circumstances that would change the conditions described in Requirement *b*. Specifically, the company has an opportunity to decrease variable cost per unit to $11 if it agrees to conditions that will increase fixed cost to $30,000. Volume is expected to remain constant at 4,000 bottles. Determine the effects on the company's profitability if this opportunity is accepted.

Exercise 3-13A *Conducting sensitivity analysis using the equation method* LO 3-5

Cobb Company currently produces and sells 9,000 units annually of a product that has a variable cost of $20 per unit and annual fixed costs of $195,000. The company currently earns a $228,000 annual profit. Assume that Cobb has the opportunity to invest in new labor-saving production equipment that will enable the company to reduce variable costs to $16 per unit. The investment would cause fixed costs to increase by $25,000 because of additional depreciation cost.

Required

a. Use the equation method to determine the sales price per unit under existing conditions (current equipment is used).

b. Prepare a contribution margin income statement, assuming that Cobb invests in the new production equipment. Recommend whether Cobb should invest in the new equipment.

Exercise 3-14A *Conducting sensitivity analysis using the equation method* LO 3-5

Malone Company produces a product that has a variable cost of $54 per unit and a sales price of $79 per unit. The company's annual fixed costs total $750,000. It had net income of $250,000 in the previous year. In an effort to increase the company's market share, management is considering lowering the selling price to $74 per unit.

Required

a. If Malone desires to maintain net income of $250,000, how many additional units must it sell to justify the price decline?

b. Assume that in addition to lowering its selling price to $74, Malone also desires to increase its net income by $50,000. Determine the number of units the company must sell to earn the desired income.

Exercise 3-15A *Multiple product break-even analysis* LO 3-6

Riku Company manufactures two products. The budgeted per-unit contribution margin for each product follows.

	Super	Supreme
Sales price	$ 68	$ 94
Variable cost per unit	(38)	(44)
Contributon margin per unit	$ 30	$ 50

Riku expects to incur annual fixed costs of $540,000. The relative sales mix of the products is 70 percent for Super and 30 percent for Supreme.

Required

a. Determine the total number of products (units of Super and Supreme combined) Riku must sell to break even.

b. How many units each of Super and Supreme must Riku sell to break even?

LO 3-6

Exercise 3-16A *Multiple product sales mix to achieve a desired profit*

The Blanket Company (TBC) manufactures two types of blankets. One is made of nylon. The other is made of wool. The budgeted per-unit contribution margin for each product follows.

	Nylon	Wool
Sales price	$136	$188
Variable cost per unit	(76)	(88)
Contribution margin per unit	$ 60	$100

TBC expects to incur annual fixed costs of $716,000. The relative sales mix of the products is 80 percent for Nylon and 20 percent for Wool.

Required

a. Determine the total number of products (units of Nylon and Wool combined) TBC must sell to earn a $100,000 profit.

b. How many units each of Nylon and Wool blankets must TBC sell to earn a $100,000 profit?

c. Confirm the answer computed in Requirement *b* by preparing an income statement using the contribution margin format.

PROBLEMS—SERIES A

connect All applicable Problems in Series A are available in *Connect*.

LO 3-1

Problem 3-17A *Determining the break-even point and preparing a contribution margin income statement*

excel

CHECK FIGURE
a. 10,000 units

Ritchie Manufacturing Company makes a product that it sells for $150 per unit. The company incurs variable manufacturing costs of $60 per unit. Variable selling expenses are $18 per unit, annual fixed manufacturing costs are $480,000, and fixed selling and administrative costs are $240,000 per year.

Required

Determine the break-even point in units and dollars using each of the following approaches:

a. Use the equation method.

b. Use the contribution margin per unit approach.

c. Use the contribution margin ratio approach.

d. Confirm your results by preparing a contribution margin income statement for the break-even sales volume.

LO 3-1, 3-2

Problem 3-18A *Analyzing change in sales price using the contribution margin ratio*

CHECK FIGURE
c. 54,000 units

Massey Company reported the following data regarding the product it sells.

Sales price	$ 25
Contribution margin ratio	40%
Fixed costs	$810,000

Required

Use the contribution margin ratio approach and consider each requirement separately.

a. What is the break-even point in dollars? In units?

b. To obtain a profit of $270,000, what must the sales be in dollars? In units?

c. If the sales price increases to $30 and variable costs do not change, what is the new break-even point in dollars? In units?

Problem 3-19A *Effect of converting variable to fixed costs*

LO 3-1, 3-2

Bauer Manufacturing Company reported the following data regarding a product it manufactures and sells. The sales price is $100.

CHECK FIGURE
b. 13,000 units

Variable costs	
Manufacturing	$30 per unit
Selling	12 per unit
Fixed costs	
Manufacturing	$360,000 per year
Selling and administrative	$162,000 per year

Required

a. Use the per-unit contribution margin approach to determine the break-even point in units and dollars.

b. Use the per-unit contribution margin approach to determine the level of sales in units and dollars required to obtain a profit of $232,000.

c. Suppose that variable selling costs could be eliminated by employing a salaried sales force. If the company could sell 12,000 units, how much could it pay in salaries for salespeople and still have a profit of $232,000? (*Hint:* Use the equation method.)

Problem 3-20A *Determining the break-even point and preparing a break-even graph*

LO 3-1, 3-3

Reid Company is considering the production of a new product. The expected variable cost is $27 per unit. Annual fixed costs are expected to be $810,000. The anticipated sales price is $72 each.

CHECK FIGURE
a. $1,296,000

Required

Determine the break-even point in units and dollars using each of the following:

a. Use the equation method.

b. Use the contribution margin per unit approach.

c. Use the contribution margin ratio approach.

d. Prepare a break-even graph to illustrate the cost-volume-profit relationships.

Problem 3-21A *Margin of safety and operating leverage*

LO 3-4, 3-5

Hampton Company is considering the addition of a new product to its cosmetics line. The company has three distinctly different options: a skin cream, a bath oil, or a hair coloring gel. Relevant information and budgeted annual income statements for each of the products follow.

CHECK FIGURE
b. NI:

Skin Cream	$270,000
Bath Oil	$270,000
Color Gel	$240,000

Relevant Information

	Skin Cream	Bath Oil	Color Gel
Budgeted sales in units (a)	120,000	216,000	72,000
Expected sales price (b)	$7.00	$4.00	$10.00
Variable costs per unit (c)	$2.00	$1.00	$6.00
Income statements			
Sales revenue (a × b)	$ 840,000	$ 864,000	$ 720,000
Variable costs (a × c)	(240,000)	(216,000)	(432,000)
Contribution margin	600,000	648,000	288,000
Fixed costs	(480,000)	(540,000)	(120,000)
Net income	$ 120,000	$ 108,000	$ 168,000

Required

a. Determine the margin of safety as a percentage for each product. Round your figures to two decimal points.

b. Prepare revised income statements for each product, assuming a 25 percent increase in the budgeted sales volume.

c. For each product, determine the percentage change in net income that results from the 25 percent increase in sales. Which product has the highest operating leverage? Round your figures to two decimal points.

d. Assuming that management is pessimistic and risk averse, which product should the company add to its cosmetics line? Explain your answer.

e. Assuming that management is optimistic and risk aggressive, which product should the company add to its cosmetics line? Explain your answer.

LO 3-1, 3-2, 3-5

eXcel

CHECK FIGURE

a. 6,400 units

Problem 3-22A *Analyzing sales price and fixed cost using the equation method*

Cahill Company is considering adding a new product. The cost accountant has provided the following data.

Expected variable cost of manufacturing	$57 per unit
Expected annual fixed manufacturing costs	$216,000

The administrative vice president has provided the following estimates.

Expected sales commission	$3 per unit
Expected annual fixed administrative costs	$104,000

The manager has decided that any new product must at least break even in the first year.

Required

Use the equation method and consider each requirement separately.

a. If the sales price is set at $110, how many units must Cahill sell to break even?

b. Cahill estimates that sales will probably be 8,000 units. What sales price per unit will allow the company to break even?

c. Cahill has decided to advertise the product heavily and has set the sales price at $115. If sales are 7,200 units, how much can the company spend on advertising and still break even?

LO 3-1, 3-2, 3-3, 3-4, 3-5

CHECK FIGURES

b. 5,000 units

c. 9,000 units

e. 9,500 units

Problem 3-23A *Comprehensive CVP analysis*

Trevino Company makes and sells products with variable costs of $24 each. Trevino incurs annual fixed costs of $315,000. The current sales price is $87.

Required

The following requirements are interdependent. For example, the $252,000 desired profit introduced in Requirement *c* also applies to subsequent requirements. Likewise, the $80 sales price introduced in Requirement *d* applies to the subsequent requirements.

a. Determine the contribution margin per unit.

b. Determine the break-even point in units and in dollars. Confirm your answer by preparing an income statement using the contribution margin format.

c. Suppose that Trevino desires to earn a $252,000 profit. Determine the sales volume in units and dollars required to earn the desired profit. Confirm your answer by preparing an income statement using the contribution margin format.

d. If the sales price drops to $80 per unit, what level of sales is required to earn the desired profit? Express your answer in units and dollars. Confirm your answer by preparing an income statement using the contribution margin format.

e. If fixed costs drop to $280,000, what level of sales is required to earn the desired profit? Express your answer in units and dollars. Confirm your answer by preparing an income statement using the contribution margin format.

f. If variable cost rises to $30 per unit, what level of sales is required to earn the desired profit? Express your answer in units and dollars. Confirm your answer by preparing an income statement using the contribution margin format.

g. Assume that Trevino concludes that it can sell 10,000 units of product for $80 each. Recall that variable costs are $30 each and fixed costs are $280,000. Compute the margin of safety in units and dollars and as a percentage.

h. Draw a break-even graph using the cost and price assumptions described in Requirement *g.*

Problem 3-24A *Assessing simultaneous changes in CVP relationships using the equation method*

LO 3-1, 3-2, 3-3, 3-4, 3-5

CHECK FIGURES
a. $750,000
c. 6,250 units

Vaughn Corporation sells hammocks; variable costs are $75 each, and the hammocks are sold for $125 each. Vaughn incurs $240,000 of fixed operating expenses annually.

Required

a. Determine the sales volume in units and dollars required to attain a $60,000 profit. Verify your answer by preparing an income statement using the contribution margin format.

b. Vaughn is considering implementing a quality improvement program. The program will require a $10 increase in the variable cost per unit. To inform its customers of the quality improvements, the company plans to spend an additional $10,000 for advertising. Assuming that the improvement program will increase sales to a level that is 4,000 units above the amount computed in Requirement *a,* should Vaughn proceed with plans to improve product quality? Support your answer by preparing a budgeted income statement.

c. Determine the new break-even point in units and sales dollars as well as the margin of safety percentage, assuming that the quality improvement program is implemented.

d. Prepare a break-even graph using the cost and price assumptions outlined in Requirement *c.*

Problem 3-25A *Determining the break-even point and margin of safety for a company with multiple products*

LO 3-6

eXcel

Kidd Company produces two products. Budgeted annual income statements for the two products are provided as follows.

	Power				Lite				Total	
	Budgeted Number	Per Unit		Budgeted Amount	Budgeted Number	Per Unit		Budgeted Amount	Budgeted Number	Budgeted Amount
Sales	160	@ $500	=	$ 80,000	640	@ $450	=	$ 288,000	800	$ 368,000
Variable cost	160	@ 320	=	(51,200)	640	@ 330	=	(211,200)	800	(262,400)
Contribution margin	160	@ 180	=	28,800	640	@ 120	=	76,800	800	105,600
Fixed cost				(12,000)				(54,000)		(66,000)
Net income				$ 16,800				$ 22,800		$ 39,600

Required

CHECK FIGURE
d. Power: 100 units
Lite: 400 units

a. Based on budgeted sales, determine the relative sales mix between the two products.

b. Determine the weighted-average contribution margin per unit.

c. Calculate the break-even point in total number of units.

d. Determine the number of units of each product Kidd must sell to break even.

e. Verify the break-even point by preparing an income statement for each product as well as an income statement for the combined products.

f. Determine the margin of safety based on the combined sales of the two products.

EXERCISES—SERIES B

LO 3-1

Exercise 3-1B *Equation method*

Ziegler Corporation manufactures products that it sells for $32 each. Variable costs are $18 per unit, and annual fixed costs are $840,000. Ziegler desires to earn a profit of $140,000.

Required

a. Use the equation method to determine the break-even point in units and dollars.

b. Determine the sales volume in units and dollars required to earn the desired profit.

LO 3-1

Exercise 3-2B *Per-unit contribution margin approach*

Halsey Corporation manufactures products that have variable costs of $60 per unit. Its fixed cost amounts to $360,000. It sells the products for $90 each.

Required

Use the per-unit contribution margin approach to determine the break-even point in units and dollars.

LO 3-1

Exercise 3-3B *Contribution margin ratio*

Martinez Company incurs annual fixed costs of $300,000. Variable costs for Martinez's product are $42 per unit, and the sales price is $70 per unit. Martinez desires to earn a profit of $120,000.

Required

Use the contribution margin ratio approach to determine the sales volume in dollars and units required to earn the desired profit.

LO 3-1

Exercise 3-4B *Determining variable cost from incomplete data*

Clifford Corporation produced 60,000 tires and sold them for $100 each during Year 1. The company determined that fixed manufacturing cost per unit was $25 per tire. The company reported gross profit of $2,400,000 on its Year 1 financial statements.

Required

Determine the variable cost per unit, the total variable cost, and the total contribution margin.

LO 3-1

Exercise 3-5B *Contribution margin per unit approach for break-even and desired profit*

Information concerning a product produced by Finn Company appears as follows.

Sales price per unit	$ 180
Variable cost per unit	$ 100
Total fixed manufacturing and operating costs	$780,000

Required

Determine the following:

a. Contribution margin per unit.

b. Number of units Finn must sell to break even.

c. Sales level in units that Finn must reach in order to earn a profit of $240,000.

LO 3-2

Exercise 3-6B *Cost structure, risk, and the break-even point*

Morse Company manufactures a product that sells for $200 per unit. It incurs fixed costs of $840,000. Variable cost for its product is $80 per unit.

Required

a. Determine the sales volume in units and dollars required to break even.

b. Calculate the break-even point assuming fixed costs increase to $960,000.

c. Explain how a fixed cost structure affects risk and the break-even point.

Exercise 3-7B *Cost-volume-profit relationship* LO 3-2

Delaney Corporation manufactures faucets. The variable costs of production are $30 per faucet. Fixed costs of production are $900,000. Delaney sells the faucets for a price of $75 per unit.

Required

a. How many faucets must Delaney make and sell to break even?

b. How many faucets must Delaney make and sell to earn a $270,000 profit?

c. The marketing manager believes that sales would increase dramatically if the price were reduced to $66 per unit. How many faucets must Delaney make and sell to earn a $270,000 profit, assuming the sales price is set at $66 per unit?

Exercise 3-8B *Target costing* LO 3-2

After substantial marketing research, Yilan Corporation management believes that it can make and sell a new battery with a prolonged life for laptop computers. Management expects the market demand for its new battery to be 100,000 units per year if the battery is priced at $64 per unit. A team of engineers and accountants determines that the fixed costs of producing 60,000 units to 130,000 units is $2,400,000.

Required

Assume that Yilan desires to earn a $1,200,000 profit from the battery sales. How much can it afford to spend on the variable cost per unit if production and sales equal 100,000 batteries?

Exercise 3-9B *Prestige pricing* LO 3-2

Leon Company is considering the production and sale of a new product with fixed costs of $32,000 and variable cost of $7 per unit. Based on its normal profit margins, Leon desires to earn a $40,000 profit and believes it can sell 8,000 units of the product.

Required

a. Based on this information, determine the target sales price.

b. Explain how prestige pricing could be used to increase profitability.

Exercise 3-10B *Components of break-even graph* LO 3-3

Trent, a 10-year-old boy, wants to sell lemonade on a hot summer day. He hopes to make enough money to buy a new iPad. Joe, his older brother, tries to help him compute his prospect of doing so. The following is the relevant information.

Variable costs	
Lemonade	$0.30 per cup
Paper cups	$0.10 per cup
Fixed costs	
Table and chair	$36.00
Price	$1.00 per cup

The following graph depicts the dollar amount of cost or revenue on the vertical axis and the number of lemonade cups sold on the horizontal axis.

Required

a. Draw a line that depicts the total cost.

b. Draw a line that depicts the total revenue.

c. Identify the break-even point.

d. Identify the area representing profit.

e. Identify the area representing loss.

LO 3-4

Exercise 3-11B *Margin of safety*

Vogel Company manufactures scanners that sell for $150 each. The company pays $60 per unit for the variable costs of the product and incurs fixed costs of $1,800,000. Vogel expects to sell 60,000 scanners.

Required

Determine Vogel's margin of safety expressed as a percentage. Round the computation to two decimal points.

LO 3-5

Exercise 3-12B *Conducting sensitivity analysis using a spreadsheet*

Use Exhibit 3.3 in this chapter to answer the following questions.

Required

a. Determine the mix of sales volume, fixed cost, and variable cost per unit required to produce a desired profit of $82,000.

b. Determine the expected profit if Bright Day projects the following data for Delatine: sales, 5,000 bottles; fixed cost, $30,000; and variable cost per unit, $12.

c. Bright Day is considering new circumstances that would change the conditions described in Requirement *b*. Specifically the company has an opportunity to decrease fixed cost to $20,000 if it agrees to conditions that will increase variable cost to $13. Volume is expected to remain constant at 5,000 bottles. Determine the effects on the company's profitability if this opportunity is accepted.

LO 3-5

Exercise 3-13B *Conducting sensitivity analysis using the equation method*

Arnold Company currently produces and sells 10,000 units of a telephone per year that has a variable cost of $10 per unit and a fixed cost of $500,000. The company currently earns a $200,000 annual profit. Assume that Arnold has the opportunity to invest in a new machine that will enable the company to reduce variable costs to $8 per unit. The investment would cause fixed costs to increase by $50,000.

Required

a. Use the equation method to determine the sales price per unit under existing conditions (current machine is used).

b. Prepare a contribution margin income statement assuming Arnold invests in the new technology. Recommend whether Arnold should invest in the new technology.

LO 3-5

Exercise 3-14B *Conducting sensitivity analysis using the equation method*

Tobin Company manufactures a product that has a variable cost of $38 per unit and a sales price of $78 per unit. The company's annual fixed costs total $720,000. It had net income of $360,000 in the previous year. In an effort to increase the company's market share, management is considering lowering the selling price to $74 per unit.

Required

a. If Tobin desires to maintain net income of $360,000, how many additional units must it sell to justify the price decline?

b. Assume that in addition to lowering its selling price to $72, Tobin also desires to increase its net income by $54,000. Determine the number of units the company must sell to earn the desired income.

Exercise 3-15B *Multiple product break-even analysis*

LO 3-6

Oxford Company makes two products. The budgeted per-unit contribution margin for each product follows.

	Deluxe	Luxury
Sales price	$40	$80
Variable cost per unit	24	50
Contribution margin per unit	$16	$30

Oxford expects to incur fixed costs of $390,000. The relative sales mix of the products is 75 percent for Deluxe and 25 percent for Luxury.

Required

a. Determine the total number of products (units of Deluxe and Luxury combined) Oxford must sell to break even.

b. How many units each of Deluxe and Luxury must Oxford sell to break even?

Exercise 3-16B *Multiple product sales mix to achieve a desired profit*

LO 3-6

Colorado Sports (CS) manufactures two types of tents. One is made of plastic. The other is made of gortex. The budgeted per-unit contribution margin for each product follows:

	Plastic	Gortex
Sales price	$ 550	$ 820
Variable cost per unit	(400)	(720)
Contribution margin per unit	$ 150	$ 100

CS expects to incur annual fixed costs of $450,000. The relative sales mix of the products is 60 percent for plastic and 40 percent for gortex.

Required

a. Determine the total number of products (units of plastic and gortex combined) CS must sell to earn a $200,000 profit.

b. How many units each of plastic and gortex tents must CS sell to earn a $200,000 profit?

c. Confirm the answer computed in Requirement *b* by preparing an income statement using the contribution margin format.

PROBLEMS—SERIES B

Problem 3-17B *Determining the break-even point and preparing a contribution margin income statement*

LO 3-1

Vezinov Company manufactures portable heaters and sells them for $200 each. According to the company's records, the variable costs, including direct labor and direct materials, are $80. Factory depreciation and other fixed manufacturing costs are $960,000 per year. Vezinov pays its salespeople a commission of $20 per unit. Annual fixed selling and administrative costs are $240,000.

Required

Determine the break-even point in units and dollars, using each of the following:

a. Use the equation method.

b. Use the contribution margin per unit approach.

c. Use the contribution margin ratio approach.

d. Confirm your results by preparing a contribution margin income statement for the break-even point sales volume.

LO 3-1, 3-2

Problem 3-18B *Analyzing change in sales price using the contribution margin ratio*

Kilner Company reported the following data regarding the one product it sells.

Sales price	$40
Contribution margin ratio	30%
Fixed costs	$540,000 per year

Required

Use the contribution margin ratio approach and consider each requirement separately.

a. What is the break-even point in dollars? In units?

b. To obtain a $90,000 profit, what must the sales be in dollars? In units?

c. If the sales price increases to $50 and variable costs do not change, what is the new break-even point in units? In dollars?

LO 3-1, 3-2

Problem 3-19B *Effect of converting variable to fixed costs*

Stackhouse Company manufactures and sells its own brand of digital cameras. It sells each camera for $250. The company's accountant prepared the following data.

Manufacturing costs	
Variable	$90 per unit
Fixed	$300,000 per year
Selling and administrative expenses	
Variable	$10 per unit
Fixed	$60,000 per year

Required

a. Use the per-unit contribution margin approach to determine the break-even point in units and dollars.

b. Use the per-unit contribution margin approach to determine the level of sales in units and dollars required to obtain a $120,000 profit.

c. Suppose that variable selling and administrative costs could be eliminated by employing a salaried sales force. If the company could sell 4,200 units, how much could it pay in salaries for the salespeople and still have a profit of $120,000? (*Hint:* Use the equation method.)

LO 3-1, 3-3

Problem 3-20B *Determining the break-even point and preparing a break-even graph*

Executive officers of Norman Company are assessing the profitability of a potential new product. They expect that the variable cost of making the product will be $60 per unit and fixed manufacturing cost will be $720,000. The executive officers plan to sell the product for $80 per unit.

Required

Determine the break-even point in units and dollars using each of the following approaches:

a. Use the contribution margin per unit approach.

b. Use the equation method.

c. Use the contribution margin ratio approach.

d. Prepare a break-even graph to illustrate the cost-volume-profit relationships.

Problem 3-21B *Margin of safety and operating leverage*

LO 3-4, 3-5

Jerome Company has three distinctly different options available as it considers adding a new product to its automotive division: engine oil, coolant, or windshield washer. Relevant information and budgeted annual income statements for each product follow.

Relevant Information

	Engine Oil	Coolant	Windshield Washer
Budgeted sales in units (a)	25,000	40,000	200,000
Expected sales price (b)	$2.40	$2.85	$1.15
Variable costs per unit (c)	$1.00	$1.25	$0.35
Income Statements			
Sales revenue (a × b)	$ 60,000	$114,000	$230,000
Variable costs (a × c)	(25,000)	(50,000)	(70,000)
Contribution margin	35,000	64,000	160,000
Fixed costs	(24,500)	(32,000)	(60,000)
Net income	$ 10,500	$ 32,000	$100,000

Required

a. Determine the margin of safety as a percentage for each product.

b. Prepare revised income statements for each product, assuming 20 percent growth in the budgeted sales volume.

c. For each product, determine the percentage change in net income that results from the 20 percent increase in sales. Which product has the highest operating leverage? Round computation to the nearest whole percent.

d. Assuming that management is pessimistic and risk averse, which product should the company add? Explain your answer.

e. Assuming that management is optimistic and risk aggressive, which product should the company add? Explain your answer.

Problem 3-22B *Analyzing sales price and fixed cost using the equation method*

LO 3-1, 3-2, 3-5

Egan Company is analyzing whether its new product will be profitable. The following data are provided for analysis.

Expected variable cost of manufacturing	$24 per unit
Expected fixed manufacturing costs	$65,000 per year
Expected sales commission	$6 per unit
Expected fixed administrative costs	$10,000 per year

The company has decided that any new product must at least break even in the first year.

Required

Use the equation method and consider each requirement separately.

a. If the sales price is set at $45, how many units must Egan sell to break even?

b. Egan estimates that sales will probably be 7,500 units. What sales price per unit will allow the company to break even?

c. Egan has decided to advertise the product heavily and has set the sales price at $48. If sales are 9,000 units, how much can the company spend on advertising and still break even?

LO 3-1, 3-2, 3-3

Problem 3-23B *Comprehensive CVP analysis*

O'Hara Company makes a product that it sells for $200. O'Hara incurs annual fixed costs of $250,000 and variable costs of $160 per unit.

Required

The following requirements are interdependent. For example, the $50,000 desired profit introduced in Requirement *c* also applies to subsequent requirements. Likewise, the $180 sales price introduced in Requirement *d* applies to the subsequent requirements.

a. Determine the contribution margin per unit.

b. Determine the break-even point in units and in dollars. Confirm your answer by preparing an income statement using the contribution margin format.

c. Suppose that O'Hara desires to earn a $50,000 profit. Determine the sales volume in units and dollars required to earn the desired profit. Confirm your answer by preparing an income statement using the contribution margin format.

d. If the sales price drops to $180 per unit, what level of sales is required to earn the desired profit? Express your answer in units and dollars. Confirm your answer by preparing an income statement using the contribution margin format.

e. If fixed costs drop to $200,000, what level of sales is required to earn the desired profit? Express your answer in units and dollars. Confirm your answer by preparing an income statement using the contribution margin format.

f. If variable costs drop to $130 per unit, what level of sales is required to earn the desired profit? Express your answer in units and dollars. Confirm your answer by preparing an income statement using the contribution margin format.

g. Assume that O'Hara concludes that it can sell 5,000 units of product for $180 each. Recall that variable costs are $130 each and fixed costs are $200,000. Compute the margin of safety in units and dollars and as a percentage.

h. Draw a break-even graph using the cost and price assumptions described in Requirement *g*.

LO 3-1, 3-2, 3-3, 3-4, 3-5

Problem 3-24B *Assessing simultaneous changes in CVP relationships using the equation method*

Milton Company sells tennis racquets; variable costs for each are $45, and each is sold for $135. Milton incurs $540,000 of fixed operating expenses annually.

Required

a. Determine the sales volume in units and dollars required to attain a $270,000 profit. Verify your answer by preparing an income statement using the contribution margin format.

b. Milton is considering establishing a quality improvement program that will require a $15 increase in the variable cost per unit. To inform its customers of the quality improvements, the company plans to spend an additional $150,000 for advertising. Assuming that the improvement program will increase sales to a level that is 5,000 units above the amount computed in Requirement *a*, should Milton proceed with plans to improve product quality? Support your answer by preparing a budgeted income statement.

c. Determine the new break-even point and the margin of safety percentage, assuming Milton adopts the quality improvement program. Round your figures to two decimal points.

d. Prepare a break-even graph using the cost and price assumptions outlined in Requirement *c*.

LO 3-6

Problem 3-25B *Determining the break-even point and margin of safety for a company with multiple products*

Executive officers of Roth Company have prepared the annual budgets for its two products, Washer and Dryer, as follows.

	Washer			Dryer			Total	
	Budgeted Quantity	Per Unit	Budgeted Amount	Budgeted Quantity	Per Unit	Budgeted Amount	Budgeted Quantity	Budgeted Amount
Sales	500	@ $540 =	$ 270,000	2,000	@ $300 =	$ 600,000	2,500	$ 870,000
Variable cost	500	@ 300 =	(150,000)	2,000	@ 180 =	(360,000)	2,500	(510,000)
Contribution margin	500	@ 240 =	120,000	2,000	@ 120 =	240,000	2,500	360,000
Fixed costs			(50,000)			(94,000)		(144,000)
Net income			$ 70,000			$ 146,000		$ 216,000

Required

a. Based on the number of units budgeted to be sold, determine the relative sales mix between the two products.

b. Determine the weighted-average contribution margin per unit.

c. Calculate the break-even point in total number of units.

d. Determine the number of units of each product Roth must sell to break even.

e. Verify the break-even point by preparing an income statement for each product as well as an income statement for the combined products.

f. Determine the margin of safety based on the combined sales of the two products.

ANALYZE, THINK, COMMUNICATE

ATC 3-1 Business Applications *Cost-volume-profit behavior at Netflix, Inc.*

As the data on the partial income statements shown as follows reveal, Netflix, Inc. increased its revenues by 72 percent from 2015 to 2017, while its operating income during this period increased by 174 percent.

Netflix, Inc.
Partial Statement of Operations
(amounts in thousands)

	Year Ended December 31		
	2017	2016	2015
Revenues	$11,692,713	$8,830,669	$6,779,511
Cost of revenues	7,659,666	6,029,901	4,591,476
Marketing	1,278,022	991,078	824,092
Technology and development	1,052,778	852,098	650,788
General and administrative	863,568	577,799	407,329
Operating income	$ 838,679	$ 379,793	$ 305,826

Required

a. What concept explains, at least in part, how Netflix's net income could rise by 174 percent when its revenue rose only 72 percent?

b. Does the concept identified in Requirement *a* result from fixed costs or variable costs?

c. Analyze the data for the four expense categories presented. Which one seems the most responsible for the causing percentage increase in operating income to be so much greater than the percentage increase in revenues? Explain your answer with computations. *Note:* You will need to use some creative thought for this, as the material in the chapter does not show an exact demonstration, but the concepts involved should be familiar.

ATC 3-2 Group Assignment *Effect of changes in fixed and variable cost on profitability*

In a month when it sold 200 units of product, Queen Manufacturing Company (QMC) produced the following internal income statement.

Revenue	$8,000
Variable costs	(4,800)
Contribution margin	3,200
Fixed costs	(2,400)
Net income	$ 800

QMC has the opportunity to alter its operations in one of the following ways:

1. Increasing fixed advertising costs by $1,600, thereby increasing sales by 120 units.
2. Lowering commissions paid to the sales staff by $8 per unit, thereby reducing sales by 10 units.
3. Decreasing fixed inventory holding cost by $800, thereby decreasing sales by 20 units.

Required

a. The instructor will divide the class into groups and then organize the groups into two sections. For a large class (12 or more groups), four sections may be necessary. At least three groups in each section are needed. Having more groups in one section than another section is acceptable because offsetting advantages and disadvantages exist. Having more groups is advantageous because more people will work on the task, but it is also disadvantageous because the greater number of people involved complicates communication.

Group Task

The sections are to compete with each other to see which section can identify the most profitable alternative in the shortest period of time. No instruction is provided regarding how the sections are to proceed with the task. In other words, each section is required to organize itself with respect to how to accomplish the task of selecting the best alternative. A total quality management (TQM) constraint is imposed that requires zero defects. A section that turns in a wrong answer is disqualified. Once an answer has been submitted to the instructor, it cannot be changed. Sections continue to turn in answers until all sections have submitted a response. The first section to submit the correct answer wins the competition.

b. If any section submits a wrong answer, the instructor or a spokesperson from the winning group should explain how the right answer was determined.

c. Discuss the dynamics of group interaction. How was the work organized? How was leadership established?

ATC 3-3 Research Assignment *Using real-world data from Southwest Airlines*

Use the 2017 Form 10-K for Southwest Airlines to complete the requirements below. To obtain the Form 10-K you can use either the EDGAR system (see instructions in Appendix A at the back of this text), or it can be found under "Investor Relations," which is under the "About Southwest" link on the company's corporate website, www.southwest.com. The company includes its Form 10-K as a part of its 2017 Annual Report. Be sure to read carefully the "Item 6. Selected Financial Data" section of the document.

Required

a. "Item 6. Selected Financial Data" lists data for several measures of activity. List the items from this table that might be used by Southwest as an activity base for CVP analysis.

b. Of the activity bases that you identified for Requirement *a*, which do you think would work best for performing CVP at Southwest? Explain the rationale for your choice.

c. Use the "Operating expense" and the "Revenue passenger miles" data from Item 6 to compute the variable cost and fixed cost components of operating expense using the high-low method presented in Chapter 2. *Warning:* The results you get will not seem reasonable, but perform the calculations and report your results.

d. "Item 6" reports that in 2017 Southwest's "Load factor" was 83.9 percent. If this load factor could have been increased by 10 percent to 92.3 percent, do you think the company's net earnings would have increased by less than 10 percent, 10 percent, or more than 10 percent? Explain.

ATC 3-4 Writing Assignment *Operating leverage, margin of safety, and cost behavior*

In its Form 10-K Skechers U.S.A., Inc., describes itself as follows:

> *We design and market Skechers-branded lifestyle footwear for men, women and children, and performance footwear for men and women under the Skechers GO brand name. . . . As of February 1, 2017, we owned and operated 117 concept stores, 163 factory outlet stores and 134 warehouse outlet stores in the United States, and 101 concept stores, 51 factory outlet stores, and 5 warehouse outlet stores internationally.*

The popularity of Skechers' products has increased significantly in recent years. Sales increased from $1,560.3 million in 2012 to $3,563.3 million in 2017, for an increase of 128.4 percent. In the same period, operating income increased from $22.3 million to $370.5 million, for an increase of 1,561.4 percent. It should be noted that this growth was not the result of larger acquisitions of or mergers with other companies.

Required

Write a memorandum that explains how a 128 percent increase in sales could cause a 1,561 percent increase in profits. Your memo should address the following:

a. An identification of the accounting concept involved.

b. A discussion of how various major types of costs incurred by Skechers were likely affected by the increase in its sales.

c. The effect of the increase in sales on Skechers' margin of safety.

ATC 3-5 Ethical Dilemma *Opportunity to manipulate earnings*

Alaska Airlines and United Continental are both passenger airline companies. Although they use similar assets to conduct their businesses, the estimated lives they use to depreciate their assets vary, as shown in the following table.

	Estimated Useful Lives (years)	
Asset Category	**Alaska Airlines**	**United Continental**
Aircraft	15–20	25–30
Buildings	25–30	25–45
Computer software	3–10	5
Other equipment	5–10	3–15

Managers have significant flexibility in setting the estimated useful lives of depreciable assets, and as the table shows, United Continental uses longer estimated lives for its assets than does Alaska Airlines.

Required

a. How does using a longer estimated life for a depreciable asset potentially affect its earnings?

b. Would using a longer estimated life for a depreciable asset be more likely to affect a company's fixed or variable costs?

c. In the past, some companies, not United Continental, have been accused of deliberately overestimating the useful lives of their companies' depreciable assets. Speculate as to what would cause them to do this.

d. Review the statement of ethical professional practice shown in Exhibit 1.17 of Chapter 1 and comment on which, if any, of the ethical standards are violated by deliberately overestimating the useful lives of depreciable assets.

e. Comment on the provisions of the Sarbanes-Oxley Act that are designed to prevent a company's executives from deliberately overestimating the useful lives of depreciable assets.

ATC 3-6 Spreadsheet Assignment *Using Excel*

Bishop Company has provided the estimated data that appear in rows 4 to 8 of the following spreadsheet.

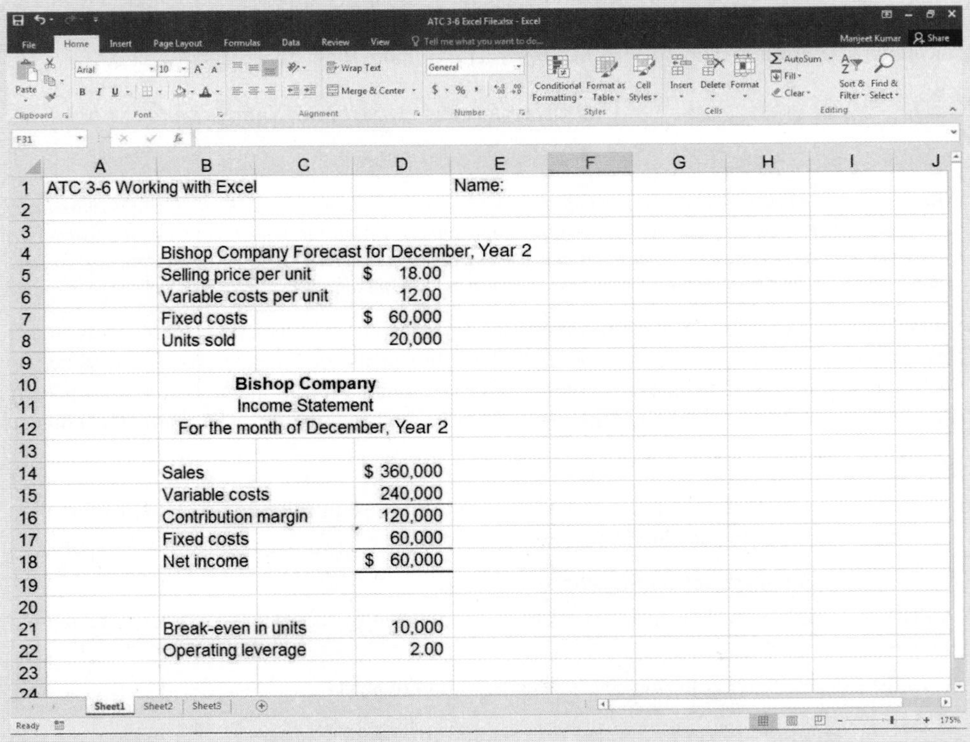

	A	B	C	D	E
1	ATC 3-6 Working with Excel				Name:
2					
3					
4		Bishop Company Forecast for December, Year 2			
5		Selling price per unit		$ 18.00	
6		Variable costs per unit		12.00	
7		Fixed costs		$ 60,000	
8		Units sold		20,000	
9					
10		Bishop Company			
11		Income Statement			
12		For the month of December, Year 2			
13					
14		Sales		$ 360,000	
15		Variable costs		240,000	
16		Contribution margin		120,000	
17		Fixed costs		60,000	
18		Net income		$ 60,000	
19					
20					
21		Break-even in units		10,000	
22		Operating leverage		2.00	
23					

Source: Microsoft Excel 2010

Required

Using the spreadsheet tips that follow, construct a spreadsheet that allows you to determine net income, break-even in units, and operating leverage for the estimates at the top of the spreadsheet and see the effects of changes to the estimates. Set up this spreadsheet so that any change in the estimates will automatically be reflected in the calculation of net income, break-even, and operating leverage.

Spreadsheet Tip

To center a heading across several columns, such as the Income Statement title, highlight the area to be centered (columns B, C, and D), choose Format, then choose Cells, and click on the tab titled Alignment. Near the bottom of the alignment window, place a check mark in the box titled Merge cells.

ATC 3-7 Spreadsheet Assignment *Mastering Excel*

Required

Build the spreadsheet pictured in Exhibit 3.3. Be sure to use formulas that will automatically calculate profitability if fixed cost, variable cost, or sales volume is changed.

Spreadsheet Tip

1. The shading in column D and in row 6 can be inserted by first highlighting a section to be shaded, choosing Format from the main menu, then Cells, and then clicking on the tab titled Patterns, and then choosing a color for the shading. The shortcut method to accomplish the shading is to click on the fill color icon (it looks like a tipped bucket and is in the upper left area of the screen).

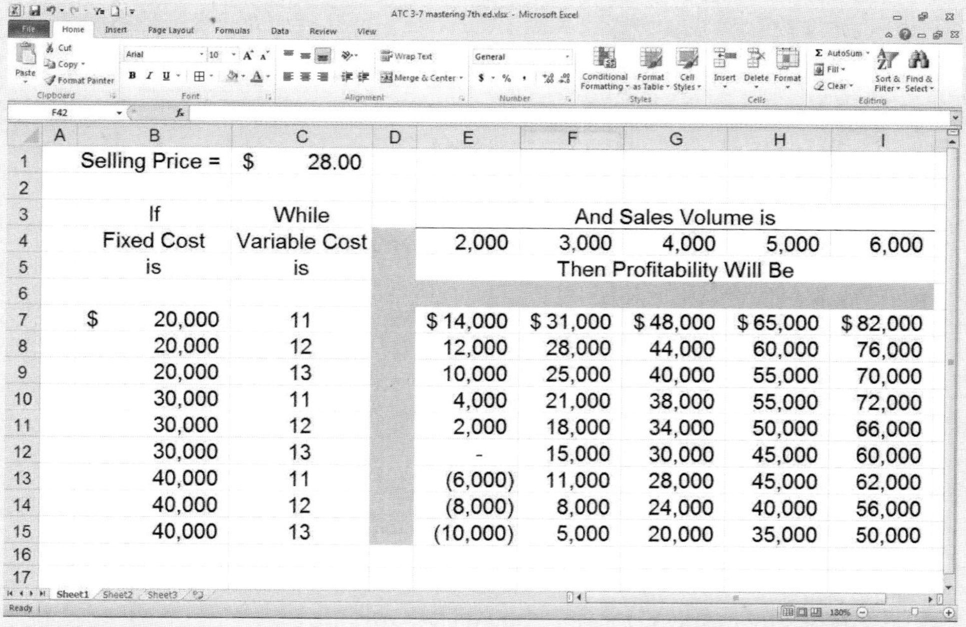

	A	B	C	D	E	F	G	H	I
1		Selling Price =	$ 28.00						
2									
3		If	While				And Sales Volume is		
4		Fixed Cost	Variable Cost		2,000	3,000	4,000	5,000	6,000
5		is	is				Then Profitability Will Be		
6									
7	$	20,000	11		$ 14,000	$ 31,000	$ 48,000	$ 65,000	$ 82,000
8		20,000	12		12,000	28,000	44,000	60,000	76,000
9		20,000	13		10,000	25,000	40,000	55,000	70,000
10		30,000	11		4,000	21,000	38,000	55,000	72,000
11		30,000	12		2,000	18,000	34,000	50,000	66,000
12		30,000	13		-	15,000	30,000	45,000	60,000
13		40,000	11		(6,000)	11,000	28,000	45,000	62,000
14		40,000	12		(8,000)	8,000	24,000	40,000	56,000
15		40,000	13		(10,000)	5,000	20,000	35,000	50,000
16									
17									

Source: Microsoft Excel 2010

2. Similar to basic math rules, the order of calculation within a formula is multiplication and division before addition and subtraction. Therefore, if you wish to subtract variable cost from selling price and multiply the difference by units sold, the formula must be = (28 − C8)*E4.
3. The quickest way to get the correct formulas in the area of E7 to I15 is to place the proper formula in cell E7 and then copy this formula to the entire block of E7:I15. However, the formulas must use the $around the cell addresses to lock either the row or the column, or both. For example, the formula = 2*B7 can be copied to any other cell and the cell reference will remain B7 because the $symbol locks the row and column. Likewise, $B7 indicates that only the column is locked, and B$7 indicates that only the row is locked.

COMPREHENSIVE PROBLEM

Use the same transaction data for Magnificent Modems, Inc., as was used in Chapter 1. (See page 56.)

Required

a. Use the following partially completed form to prepare an income statement using the contribution margin format.

Sales revenue	$600,000
Variable costs	
Contribution margin	225,000
Fixed costs	
Net income	$ 31,050

b. Determine the break-even point in units and in dollars.

c. Assume that next year's sales are budgeted to be the same as the current year's sales. Determine the margin of safety expressed as a percentage.

CHAPTER 4

Cost Accumulation, Tracing, and Allocation

LEARNING OBJECTIVES

After you have mastered the material in this chapter, you will be able to:

LO 4-1	Identify cost objects and distinguish between direct costs versus indirect costs.
LO 4-2	Allocate indirect costs to cost objects.
LO 4-3	Identify the most appropriate cost driver.
LO 4-4	Allocate joint costs to joint products.
LO 4-5	Recognize the effects of cost allocation on employee motivation.
LO 4-6	Allocate service department costs to operating departments (Appendix).

Video lectures and accompanying self-assessment quizzes are available in Connect® for all learning objectives.

CHAPTER OPENING

What does it cost? This is one of the questions most frequently asked by business managers. Managers must have reliable cost estimates to price products, evaluate performance, control operations, and prepare financial statements. As this discussion implies, managers need to know the cost of many different things. The things for which we are trying to determine the cost are commonly called **cost objects.** For example, if we are trying to determine the cost of operating a department, that department is the cost object. Cost objects may be products, processes, departments, services, activities, and so on. This chapter explains techniques managerial accountants use to determine the cost of a variety of cost objects.

The Curious Accountant

©Ariel Skelley/Blend Images

A former patient of a California hospital complained about being charged $7 for a single aspirin tablet. After all, an entire bottle of 100 aspirins can be purchased at the local pharmacy store for around $2.

Can you think of any reasons, other than shameless profiteering, that a hospital would need to charge $7 for an aspirin? Remember that the hospital is not just selling the aspirin; it is also delivering it to the patient. (Answer on page 164.)

DETERMINE THE COST OF COST OBJECTS

LO 4-1

Identify cost objects and distinguish between direct costs versus indirect costs.

Accountants use **cost accumulation** to determine the cost of a particular object. Suppose the Atlanta Braves advertising manager wants to promote a Tuesday night ball game by offering free baseball caps to all children who attend. What would be the promotion cost? The team's accountant must *accumulate* many individual costs and add them together. For simplicity, consider only three cost components: (1) the cost of the caps, (2) the cost of advertising the promotion, and (3) the cost of an employee to work on the promotion.

©Allen Donikowski/Getty Images

Cost accumulation begins with identifying the cost objects. The primary cost object is the cost of the promotion. Three secondary cost objects are (1) the cost of caps, (2) the cost of advertising, and (3) the cost of labor. The costs of the secondary cost objects are combined to determine the cost of the primary cost object.

Determining the costs of the secondary cost objects requires identifying what *drives* those costs. A **cost driver** has a *cause-and-effect* relationship with a cost object. For example, the *number of caps* (cost driver) has an effect on the *cost of caps* (cost object). The *number of advertisements* is a cost driver for the *advertising cost* (cost object); the *number of labor hours* worked is a cost driver for the *labor cost* (cost object). Using the following assumptions about unit costs and cost drivers, the accumulated cost of the primary cost object (cost of the cap promotion) is:

Cost Object	Cost per Unit	×	Cost Driver	=	Total Cost of Object
Cost of caps	$ 2.50	×	4,000 caps	=	$10,000
Cost of advertising	$100.00	×	50 advertisements	=	5,000
Cost of labor	$ 8.00	×	100 hours	=	800
Cost of cap promotion					$15,800

The Atlanta Braves should run the promotion if management expects it to produce additional revenues exceeding $15,800.

Estimated versus Actual Cost

The accumulated cost of the promotion—$15,800—is an *estimate.* Management cannot know *actual* costs and revenues until after running the promotion. While actual information is more accurate, it is not relevant for deciding whether to run the promotion because the decision must be made before the actual cost is known. Managers must accept a degree of inaccuracy in exchange for the relevance of timely information. Many business decisions are based on estimated rather than actual costs.

Managers use cost estimates to set prices, bid on contracts, evaluate proposals, distribute resources, plan production, and set goals. Certain circumstances, however, require actual cost data. For example, published financial reports and managerial performance evaluations use actual cost data. Managers frequently accumulate both estimated and actual cost data for the same cost object. For example, companies use cost estimates to establish goals and use actual costs to evaluate management performance in meeting those goals. The following discussion provides a number of business examples that use estimated data, actual data, or a combination of both.

Assignment of Costs to Objects in a Retail Business

Exhibit 4.1 displays the January income statement for In Style Inc. (ISI), a retail clothing store. ISI subdivides its operations into women's, men's, and children's departments. To encourage the departmental managers to maximize sales, ISI began paying the manager of each department a bonus based on a percentage of departmental sales revenue.

Although the bonus incentive increased sales revenue, it also provoked negative consequences. The departmental managers began to argue over floor space; each manager wanted more space to display merchandise. The managers reduced prices; they increased sales commissions. In the drive to maximize sales, the managers ignored the need to control costs. To improve the situation, the store manager decided to base future bonuses on each department's contribution to profitability rather than its sales revenue.

EXHIBIT 4.1

Income Statement

IN STYLE INC. Income Statement For the Month Ended January 31	
Sales	$ 360,000
Cost of goods sold	(216,000)
Gross margin	144,000
Sales commissions	(18,000)
Dept. managers' salaries	(12,000)
Store manager's salary	(9,360)
Depreciation	(16,000)
Rental fee for store	(18,400)
Utilities	(2,300)
Advertising	(7,200)
Supplies	(900)
Net income	$ 59,840

Identifying Direct and Indirect Costs

The new bonus strategy requires determining the cost of operating each department. Each department is a separate *cost object.* Assigning costs to the departments (cost objects) requires **cost tracing** and **cost allocation. Direct costs** can be easily traced to a cost object. **Indirect costs** cannot be easily traced to a cost object. Whether or not a cost is easily traceable requires *cost/benefit analysis.*

Some of ISI's costs can be easily traced to the cost objects (specific departments). The cost of goods sold is an example of an easily traced cost. Price tags on merchandise can be coded so cash register scanners capture the departmental code for each sale. The cost of goods sold is not only easily traceable but also very useful information. Companies need cost of goods sold information for financial reporting (income statement and balance sheet) and for management decisions (determining inventory reorder points, pricing strategies, and cost control). Because the cost of tracing *cost of goods sold* is small relative to the benefits obtained, cost of goods sold is a *direct cost.*

In contrast, the cost of supplies (shopping bags, sales slips, pens, staples, price tags) used by each department is much more difficult to trace. How could the number of staples used to seal shopping bags be traced to any particular department? The sales staff could count the number of staples used, but doing so would be silly for the benefits obtained. Although tracing the cost of supplies to each department may be possible, it is not worth the effort of doing so. The cost of supplies is therefore an *indirect cost*. Indirect costs are also called **overhead costs.**

Direct and indirect costs can be described as follows.

> *Direct costs* can be traced to cost objects in a *cost-effective* manner.
> *Indirect costs* cannot be traced to objects in a *cost-effective* manner.

By analyzing the accounting records, ISI's accountant classified the costs from the income statement in Exhibit 4.1 as direct or indirect, as shown in Exhibit 4.2. The next paragraph explains the classifications.

All figures represent January costs. Items 1 through 4 are direct costs, traceable to the cost objects in a cost-effective manner. Cost of goods sold is traced to departments at the point of sale using cash register scanners. Sales commissions are based on a percentage of departmental sales and are therefore easy to trace to the departments. Departmental managers' salaries are also easily traceable to the departments. Equipment, furniture, and fixtures are tagged with department codes that permit tracing depreciation charges directly to specific departments. Items 5 through 8 are incurred on behalf of the company as a whole and are therefore not directly traceable to a specific department. Although Item 9 could be traced to specific departments, the cost of doing so would exceed the benefits. The cost of supplies is therefore also classified as indirect.

EXHIBIT 4.2

Income Statement Classification of Costs

Cost Item	Direct Costs Women's	Men's	Children's	Indirect Costs
1. Cost of goods sold—$216,000	$120,000	$58,000	$38,000	
2. Sales commissions—$18,000	9,500	5,500	3,000	
3. Dept. managers' salaries—$12,000	5,000	4,200	2,800	
4. Depreciation—$16,000	7,000	5,000	4,000	
5. Store manager's salary				$ 9,360
6. Rental fee for store				18,400
7. Utilities				2,300
8. Advertising				7,200
9. Supplies				900
Totals	$141,500	$72,700	$47,800	$38,160

Cost Classifications—Independent and Context Sensitive

Whether a cost is direct or indirect is independent of whether it is fixed or variable. In the ISI example, both cost of goods sold and the cost of supplies vary relative to sales volume (both are variable costs), but cost of goods sold is direct and the cost of supplies is indirect. Furthermore, the cost of rent and the cost of depreciation are both fixed relative to sales volume, but the cost of rent is indirect and the cost of depreciation is direct. In fact, the very same cost can be classified as direct or indirect, depending on the cost object. The store manager's salary is not directly traceable to a specific department, but it is traceable to a particular store. As these examples demonstrate, cost classification depends on the context in which the costs occur.

ALLOCATING INDIRECT COSTS TO OBJECTS

LO 4-2

Allocate indirect costs to cost objects.

Common costs support multiple cost objects but cannot be directly traced to any specific object. In the case of In Style Inc., the cost of renting the store (common cost) supports the women's, men's, and children's departments (cost objects). The departmental managers may shirk responsibility for the rental cost by claiming that others higher up the chain of command are responsible. Responsibility can be motivated at the departmental level by assigning (*allocating*) a portion of the total rental cost to each department.

To accomplish appropriate motivation, authority must accompany responsibility. In other words, the departmental managers should be held responsible for a portion of rental cost only if they are able to exercise some degree of control over that cost. For example, if managers are assigned a certain amount of the rental cost for each square foot of space they use, they should have the authority to establish the size of the space used by their departments. **Controllable costs** are costs that can be influenced by a manager's decisions and actions. The controllability concept is discussed in more detail in Chapter 9.

Cost **allocation** involves dividing a total cost into parts and assigning the parts to designated cost objects. How should ISI allocate the $38,160 of indirect costs to each of the three departments? First, identify a cost driver for each cost to be allocated. For example, there is a cause-and-effect relationship between store size and rent cost; the larger the building, the higher the rent cost. This relationship suggests that the more floor space a department occupies, the more rent cost that department should bear. To illustrate, assume ISI's store capacity

REALITY BYTES

©rypson/iStock.com

How does **Southwest Airlines** know the cost of flying a passenger from Houston, Texas, to Los Angeles, California? The fact is that Southwest does not know the actual cost of flying particular passengers anywhere. There are many indirect costs associated with flying passengers. Some of these include the cost of planes, fuel, pilots, office buildings, and ground personnel. Indeed, besides insignificant food and beverage costs, there are few costs that could be traced directly to customers. Southwest and other airlines are forced to use allocation and averaging to determine the estimated cost of providing transportation services to customers. Estimated rather than actual cost is used for decision-making purposes.

Consider that in its 2017 annual report Southwest reported the average operating expenses of flying one passenger one mile (called a *passenger mile*) were 11.4¢. However, this number was based on 153.8 billion "available passenger miles." In 2017, Southwest operated at 83.9 percent of capacity, not 100 percent, so it was able to charge passengers only for 129.0 billion passenger miles. Thus, its average operating expenses were closer to 13.6¢ for each mile for which it was able to charge. Had it operated at a higher capacity, its average costs would have been lower.

is 23,000 square feet and the women's, men's, and children's departments occupy 12,000, 7,000, and 4,000 square feet, respectively. ISI can achieve a rational allocation of the rent cost using the following two-step process.[1]

Step 1. Compute the *allocation rate* by dividing the *total cost to be allocated* ($18,400 rental fee) by the *cost driver* (23,000 square feet of store space). The cost driver is also called the **allocation base.** This computation produces the **allocation rate,** as follows:

Total cost to be allocated	÷	Cost driver (allocation base)	=	Allocation rate
$18,400 rental fee	÷	23,000 square feet	=	$0.80 per square foot

Step 2. Multiply the *allocation rate* by the *weight of the cost driver* (weight of the base) to determine the allocation *per cost object,* as follows.

Cost Object	Allocation Rate	×	Number of Square Feet	=	Allocation per Cost Object
Women's department	$0.80	×	12,000	=	$ 9,600
Men's department	0.80	×	7,000	=	5,600
Children's department	0.80	×	4,000	=	3,200
Total			23,000		$18,400

It is also plausible to presume utilities cost is related to the amount of floor space a department occupies. Larger departments will consume more heating, lighting, air conditioning, and so on than smaller departments. Floor space is a reasonable cost driver for

[1]Other mathematical approaches achieve the same result. This text consistently uses the two-step method described here. Specifically, the text determines allocations by (1) computing a *rate* and (2) multiplying the *rate* by the *weight of the base* (cost driver).

utility cost. Based on square footage, ISI can allocate utility cost to each department as follows.

Step 1. Compute the allocation rate by dividing the total cost to be allocated ($2,300 utility cost) by the cost driver (23,000 square feet of store space):

Total cost to be allocated	÷	Cost driver	=	Allocation rate
$2,300 utility cost	÷	23,000 square feet	=	$0.10 per square foot

Step 2. Multiply the *allocation rate* by the *weight of the cost driver* to determine the allocation *per cost object.*

Cost Object	Allocation Rate	×	Number of Square Feet	=	Allocation per Cost Object
Women's department	$0.10	×	12,000	=	$1,200
Men's department	0.10	×	7,000	=	700
Children's department	0.10	×	4,000	=	400
Total			23,000		$2,300

CHECK YOURSELF 4.1

HealthCare Inc. wants to estimate the cost of operating the three departments (Dermatology, Gynecology, and Pediatrics) that serve patients in its Health Center. Each department performed the following number of patient treatments during the most recent year of operation: Dermatology, 2,600; Gynecology, 3,500; and Pediatrics, 6,200. The annual salary of the Health Center's program administrator is $172,200. How much of the salary cost should HealthCare allocate to the Pediatrics department?

Answer

Step 1. Compute the *allocation rate.*

Total cost to be allocated	÷	Cost driver (patient treatments)	=	Allocation rate
$172,200 salary cost	÷	(2,600 + 3,500 + 6,200)	=	$14 per patient treatment

Step 2. Multiply the *allocation rate* by the *weight of the cost driver* (weight of the base) to determine the allocation per *cost object.*

Cost Object	Allocation Rate	×	No. of Treatments	=	Allocation per Cost Object
Pediatrics department	$14	×	6,200	=	$86,800

Determining the Cost to Be Allocated Using Cost Pools

Allocating *individually* every single indirect cost a company incurs would be tedious and not particularly useful relative to the benefit obtained. Instead, companies frequently accumulate many individual costs into a single **cost pool.** The total of the pooled cost is then allocated to the cost objects. For example, a company may accumulate costs for gas, water, electricity, and telephone service into a single utilities cost pool. It would then allocate the total cost in the utilities cost pool to the cost objects rather than individually allocating each of the four types of utility costs.

How far should pooling costs go? Why not pool utility costs with indirect labor costs? If the forces driving the utility costs are different from the forces driving the labor costs, pooling the costs will likely reduce the reliability of any associated cost allocations. To promote accuracy, pooling should be limited to costs with common cost drivers.

Costs that have been pooled for one purpose may require disaggregation for a different purpose. Suppose all overhead costs are pooled for the purpose of determining the cost of making a product. Further, suppose that making the product requires two processes that are performed in different departments. A cutting department makes heavy use of machinery to cut raw materials into product parts. An assembly department uses human labor to assemble the parts into a finished product. Now suppose the objective changes from determining the cost of making the product to determining the cost of operating each department. Under these circumstances, it may be necessary to disaggregate the total overhead cost into smaller pools such as a utility cost pool, an indirect labor cost pool, and so on so that different drivers can be used to allocate these costs to the two departments.

SELECTING THE COST DRIVER

LO 4-3

Identify the most appropriate cost driver.

Companies can frequently identify more than one cost driver for a particular indirect cost. For example, ISI's cost of shopping bags provided to customers can be linked to both the number of sales transactions and the total amount of sales. More specifically, since the store normally uses at least one shopping bag each time a sales transaction occurs, the number of sales transactions drives the cost of shopping bags. Likewise, a $500 sales transaction is likely to require the company to provide more shopping bags to a customer than would a $100 sales transaction. Therefore, the total amount of sales also drives the use of shopping bags. Given this scenario, should ISI use the *number of sales transactions* or the *total amount of sales* as the driver of the cost of shopping bags? The answer is, ISI should use the driver with the strongest cause-and-effect relationship.

Cause and Effect versus Availability of Information

To illustrate, consider shopping bag usage for T-shirts sold in the children's department versus T-shirts sold in the men's department. Assume ISI studied T-shirt sales during the first week of June and found the following.

Department	Children's	Men's
Number of sales transactions	120	92
Amount of total sales	$1,440	$1,612

Given that every sales transaction uses a shopping bag, the children's department uses far more shopping bags than the men's department (120 versus 92) even though it has a lower amount of total sales ($1,440 versus $1,612). A reasonable explanation for this circumstance is that children's T-shirts sell for less than men's T-shirts. The number of sales transactions is the better cost driver because it has a stronger cause-and-effect relationship with shopping bag usage than does the amount of sales. Should ISI therefore use the number of sales transactions to allocate supply cost to the departments? Not necessarily.

The *availability of information* also influences cost driver selection. While the number of sales transactions is the more accurate cost driver, ISI could not use this allocation base unless it maintains records of the number of sales transactions per department. If the store tracks the amount of sales but not the number of transactions, it must use the amount of sales even if the number of transactions is the better cost driver. For ISI, total sales appears to be the best *available* cost driver for allocating supply cost.

Assuming that total sales for the women's, men's, and children's departments was $190,000, $110,000, and $60,000, respectively, ISI can allocate the supplies cost as follows.

Step 1. Compute the allocation rate by dividing the total cost to be allocated ($900 supplies cost) by the cost driver ($360,000 total sales).

Total cost to be allocated	÷	Cost driver	=	Allocation rate
$900 supplies cost	÷	$360,000 total sales	=	$0.0025 per sales dollar

Step 2. Multiply the allocation rate by the weight of the cost driver to determine the allocation per cost object.

Cost Object	Allocation Rate	×	Total Sales	=	Allocation per Cost Object
Women's department	$0.0025	×	$190,000	=	$475
Men's department	0.0025	×	110,000	=	275
Children's department	0.0025	×	60,000	=	150
Total			$360,000		$900

ISI believes the amount of sales is also the appropriate allocation base for advertising cost. The sales generated in each department were likely influenced by the general advertising campaign. ISI can allocate advertising cost as follows.

Step 1. Compute the allocation rate by dividing the total cost to be allocated ($7,200 advertising cost) by the cost driver ($360,000 total sales).

Total cost to be allocated	÷	Cost driver	=	Allocation rate
$7,200 advertising cost	÷	$360,000 total sales	=	$0.02 per sales dollar

Step 2. Multiply the allocation rate by the weight of the cost driver to determine the allocation per cost object.

Cost Object	Allocation Rate	×	Total Sales	=	Allocation per Cost Object
Women's department	$0.02	×	$190,000	=	$3,800
Men's department	0.02	×	110,000	=	2,200
Children's department	0.02	×	60,000	=	1,200
Total			$360,000		$7,200

There is no strong cause-and-effect relationship between the store manager's salary and the departments. ISI pays the store manager the same salary regardless of sales level, square footage of store space, number of labor hours, or any other identifiable variable. Because no plausible cost driver exists, ISI must allocate the store manager's salary arbitrarily. Here the manager's salary is simply divided equally among the departments as follows:

Step 1. Compute the allocation rate by dividing the total cost to be allocated ($9,360 manager's monthly salary) by the allocation base (number of departments).

Total cost to be allocated	÷	Cost driver	=	Allocation rate
$9,360 store manager's salary	÷	3 departments	=	$3,120 per department

Step 2. Multiply the allocation rate by the weight of the cost driver to determine the allocation per cost object.

Cost Object	Allocation Rate	×	Number of Departments	=	Allocation per Cost Object
Women's department	$3,120	×	1	=	$3,120
Men's department	3,120	×	1	=	3,120
Children's department	3,120	×	1	=	3,120
Total			3		$9,360

As the allocation of the store manager's salary demonstrates, many allocations are arbitrary or based on a weak relationship between the allocated cost and the allocation base (cost driver). Managers must use care when making decisions using allocated costs.

Behavioral Implications

Using the indirect cost allocations just discussed, Exhibit 4.3 shows the profit each department generated in January. ISI paid the three departmental managers bonuses based on each department's contribution to profitability. The store manager noticed an immediate change in the behavior of the departmental managers. For example, the manager of the women's department offered to give up 1,000 square feet of floor space because she believed reducing the selection of available products would not reduce sales significantly. Customers would simply buy different brands. Although sales would not decline dramatically, rent and utility cost allocations to the women's department would decline, increasing the profitability of the department.

In contrast, the manager of the children's department wanted the extra space. He believed the children's department was losing sales because it did not have enough floor space to display a competitive variety of merchandise. Customers came to the store to shop at the women's department, but they did not come specifically for children's wear. With additional space, the children's department could carry items that would draw customers to the store specifically to buy children's clothing. He believed the extra space would increase sales enough to cover the additional rent and utility cost allocations.

EXHIBIT 4.3

Profit Analysis by Department

	Department			
	Women's	Men's	Children's	Total
Sales	$ 190,000	$110,000	$ 60,000	$ 360,000
Cost of goods sold	(120,000)	(58,000)	(38,000)	(216,000)
Sales commissions	(9,500)	(5,500)	(3,000)	(18,000)
Dept. managers' salary	(5,000)	(4,200)	(2,800)	(12,000)
Depreciation	(7,000)	(5,000)	(4,000)	(16,000)
Store manager's salary	(3,120)	(3,120)	(3,120)	(9,360)
Rental fee for store	(9,600)	(5,600)	(3,200)	(18,400)
Utilities	(1,200)	(700)	(400)	(2,300)
Advertising	(3,800)	(2,200)	(1,200)	(7,200)
Supplies	(475)	(275)	(150)	(900)
Departmental profit	$ 30,305	$ 25,405	$ 4,130	$ 59,840

Answers to The Curious Accountant

When we compare the cost that a hospital charges for an aspirin to the price we pay for an aspirin, we are probably not considering the full cost that we incur to purchase aspirin. If someone were to ask you what you pay for an aspirin, you would probably take the price of a bottle—say, $2—and divide it by the number of pills in the bottle—say, 100. This would suggest the cost is $0.02 each. Now, consider what it costs to buy an aspirin when all costs are considered. First, there is your time to drive to the store; what do you get paid per hour? Then, there is the cost of operating your automobile. You get the idea; in reality, the cost of an aspirin, from a business perspective, is much more than just the cost of the pill itself.

The following exhibit shows the income statement of **Hospital Corporation of America (HCA) Inc.** for three recent years. HCA claims to be "one of the leading health care services companies in the United States." In 2017, it operated 299 facilities in 20 states and England. As you can see, while it generated over $47.7 billion in revenue, it also incurred a lot of expenses. Look at its first two expense categories. Although it incurred $7.3 billion in supplies expenses, it incurred over two and a half times this amount in compensation expense. In other words, it costs a lot more to have someone deliver the aspirin to your bed than the aspirin itself costs.

In 2017, HCA earned $2.7 billion from its $47.1 billion in revenues. This is a return on sales percentage of 5.8 percent ($2,743 ÷ $47,653). Therefore, on a $7 aspirin, HCA would earn 40 cents of profit, which is still not a bad profit for selling one aspirin. As a comparison, in 2017, **Walgreens**, which also sells aspirin, had a return on sales of 3.4 percent.

HCA INC.
Consolidated Income Statements
For the Years Ended December 31, 2017, 2016, and 2015
(dollars in millions)

	2017	2016	2015
Revenues before the provision for doubtful accounts	$47,653	$44,747	$43,591
Provision for doubtful accounts	4,039	3,257	3,913
Revenues	43,614	41,490	39,678
Salaries and benefits	20,059	18,897	18,115
Supplies	7,316	6,933	6,638
Other operating expenses	8,051	7,496	7,056
Equity in earnings of affiliates	(45)	(54)	(46)
Depreciation and amortization	2,131	1,966	1,904
Interest expense	1,690	1,707	1,665
Losses (gains) on sales of facilities	(8)	(23)	5
Losses on retirement of debt	39	4	135
Legal claim costs (benefits)	—	(246)	249
Total expenses	39,233	36,680	35,721
Income before income taxes	4,381	4,810	3,957
Provision for income taxes	1,638	1,378	1,261
Net income	2,743	3,432	2,696
Net income attributable to noncontrolling interests	527	542	567
Net income attributable to HCA Inc.	$ 2,216	$ 2,890	$ 2,129

The store manager was pleased with the emphasis on profitability that resulted from tracing and assigning costs to specific departments.

Cost Drivers for Variable Overhead Costs

A *causal relationship* exists between variable overhead product costs (indirect materials, indirect labor, inspection costs, utilities, etc.) and the volume of production. For example, the cost of indirect materials such as glue, staples, screws, nails, and varnish will increase or decrease in proportion to the number of desks a furniture manufacturing company makes. *Volume measures are good cost drivers* for allocating variable overhead costs.

Volume can be expressed by such measures as the number of units produced, the number of labor hours worked, or the amount of *direct* materials used in production. Given the variety of possible volume measures, how does management identify the most appropriate cost driver (allocation base) for assigning particular overhead costs? Consider the case of Filmier Furniture Company.

Using Units as the Cost Driver

During the most recent year, Filmier Furniture Company produced 4,000 chairs and 1,000 desks. It incurred $60,000 of *indirect materials* cost during the period. How much of this cost should Filmier allocate to chairs versus desks? Using number of units as the cost driver produces the following allocation.

Step 1. Compute the allocation rate.

Total cost to be allocated	÷ Cost driver	=	Allocation rate
$60,000 indirect materials cost	÷ 5,000 units	=	$12 per unit

Step 2. Multiply the allocation rate by the weight of the cost driver to determine the allocation per cost object.

Product	Allocation Rate	×	Number of Units Produced	=	Allocated Cost
Desks	$12	×	1,000	=	$12,000
Chairs	12	×	4,000	=	48,000
Total			5,000	=	$60,000

Using Direct Labor Hours as the Cost Driver

Using the number of units as the cost driver assigns an *equal amount* ($12) of indirect materials cost to each piece of furniture. However, if Filmier uses more indirect materials to make a desk than to make a chair, assigning the same amount of indirect materials cost to each is inaccurate. Assume Filmier incurs the following direct costs to make chairs and desks.

	Desks	Chairs	Total
Direct labor hours	3,500 hrs.	2,500 hrs.	6,000 hrs.
Direct materials cost	$1,000,000	$500,000	$1,500,000

Both direct labor hours and direct materials cost are volume measures that indicate Filmier uses more indirect materials to make a desk than a chair. It makes sense that the amount of direct labor used is related to the amount of indirect materials used. Because production workers use materials to make furniture, it is plausible to assume that the more hours they work, the more materials they use. Using this reasoning, Filmier could assign the indirect materials cost to the chairs and desks as follows.

Step 1. Compute the allocation rate.

Total cost to be allocated	÷	Cost driver	=	Allocation rate
$60,000 indirect materials cost	÷	6,000 hours	=	$10 per hour

Step 2. Multiply the allocation rate by the weight of the cost driver.

Product	Allocation Rate	×	Number of Labor Hours	=	Allocated Cost
Desks	$10.00	×	3,500	=	$35,000
Chairs	10.00	×	2,500	=	25,000
Total			6,000	=	$60,000

Basing the allocation on labor hours rather than number of units assigns a significantly larger portion of the indirect materials cost to desks ($35,000 versus $12,000). Is this allocation more accurate? Suppose the desks, but not the chairs, require elaborate, labor-intensive carvings. A significant portion of the labor is then not related to consuming indirect materials (glue, staples, screws, nails, and varnish). It would therefore be inappropriate to allocate the indirect materials cost based on direct labor hours.

Using Direct Material Dollars as the Cost Driver

If labor hours is an inappropriate allocation base, Filmier can consider direct materials usage, measured in material dollars, as the allocation base. It is likely that the more lumber (direct material) Filmier uses, the more glue, nails, and so forth (indirect materials) it uses. It is reasonable to presume direct materials usage drives indirect materials usage. Using direct materials dollars as the cost driver for indirect materials produces the following allocation.

Step 1. Compute the allocation rate.

Total cost to be allocated	÷	Cost driver	=	Allocation rate
$60,000 indirect materials cost	÷	$1,500,000 direct material dollars	=	$0.04 per direct material dollar

Step 2. Multiply the allocation rate by the weight of the cost driver.

Product	Allocation Rate	×	Number of Direct Material Dollars	=	Allocated Cost
Desks	$0.04	×	$1,000,000	=	$40,000
Chairs	0.04	×	500,000	=	20,000
Total			$1,500,000	=	$60,000

Selecting the Best Cost Driver

Which of the three volume-based cost drivers (units, labor hours, or direct material dollars) results in the most accurate allocation of the overhead cost? Management must use judgment to decide. In this case, direct material dollars appears to have the most convincing relationship to indirect materials usage. If the cost Filmier was allocating were fringe benefits, however, direct labor hours would be a more appropriate cost driver. If the cost Filmier was allocating were machine maintenance cost, a different volume-based cost driver, machine hours, would be an appropriate base. The most accurate allocations of indirect costs may actually require using multiple cost drivers.

CHECK YOURSELF 4.2

Boston Boat Company builds custom sailboats for customers. During the current accounting period, the company built five different-sized boats that ranged in cost from $35,000 to $185,000. The company's manufacturing overhead cost for the period was $118,000. Would you recommend using the number of units (boats) or direct labor hours as the base for allocating the overhead cost to the five boats? Why?

Answer Using the number of units as the allocation base would assign the same amount of overhead cost to each boat. Since larger boats require more overhead cost (supplies, utilities, equipment, etc.) than smaller boats, there is no logical link between the number of boats and the amount of overhead cost required to build a particular boat. In contrast, there is a logical link between direct labor hours used and overhead cost incurred. The more labor used, the more supplies, utilities, equipment, and so on used. Since larger boats require more direct labor than smaller boats, using direct labor hours as the allocation base would allocate more overhead cost to larger boats and less overhead cost to smaller boats, producing a logical overhead allocation. Therefore, Boston should use direct labor hours as the allocation base.

Cost Drivers for Fixed Overhead Costs

Fixed costs present a different cost allocation problem. By definition, the volume of production does not drive fixed costs. Suppose Lednicky Bottling Company rents its manufacturing facility for $28,000 per year. The rental cost is fixed regardless of how much product Lednicky bottles. However, Lednicky may still use a volume-based cost driver as the allocation base. The object of allocating fixed costs to products is to distribute a *rational share* of the overhead cost to each product. Selecting an allocation base that spreads total overhead cost equally over total production often produces a rational distribution. For example, assume Lednicky produced 2,000,000 bottles of apple juice during the current accounting period. If it sold 1,800,000 bottles of the juice during this period, how much of the $28,000 rental cost should Lednicky allocate to ending inventory and to cost of goods sold? A rational allocation follows.

©Albert Karimov/Shutterstock

Step 1. Compute the allocation rate.

Total cost to be allocated	÷	Allocation base (cost driver)	=	Allocation rate
$28,000 rental cost	÷	2,000,000 units	=	$0.014 per bottle of juice

Because the base (number of units) used to allocate the cost does not drive the cost, it is sometimes called an *allocation base* instead of a *cost driver*. However, many managers use the term cost driver in conjunction with fixed cost even though that usage is technically inaccurate. The terms allocation base and cost driver are frequently used interchangeably.

Step 2. Multiply the allocation rate by the weight of the cost driver.

Financial Statement Item	Allocation Rate	×	Number of Bottles	=	Allocated Cost
Inventory	$0.014	×	200,000	=	$ 2,800
Cost of goods sold	0.014	×	1,800,000	=	25,200

Using number of units as the allocation base assigns equal amounts of the rental cost to each unit of product. Equal allocation is appropriate so long as the units are homogeneous. If the units are not identical, however, Lednicky may need to choose a different allocation base to rationally distribute the rental cost. For example, if some of the bottles are significantly larger than others, Lednicky may find using some physical measure, like liters of direct material used, to be a more appropriate allocation base. Whether an indirect cost is fixed or variable, selecting the most appropriate allocation base requires sound reasoning and judgment.

Allocating Fixed Costs When the Volume of Production Varies

Under certain circumstances products may be made before or after the costs associated with making them have been incurred. Suppose, for example, premiums for an annual insurance policy are paid in March. The insurance cost benefits the products made in the months before and after March as well as those produced in March. Allocation can be used to spread the insurance cost over products made during the entire accounting period rather than charging the total cost only to products made in March.

Monthly fluctuations in production volume complicate fixed cost allocations. To illustrate, assume Grave Manufacturing pays its production supervisor a monthly salary of $3,000. Furthermore, assume Grave makes 800 units of product in January and 1,875 in February. How much salary cost should Grave assign to the products made in January and February, respectively? The allocation seems simple. Just divide the $3,000 monthly salary cost by the number of units of product made each month as follows:

January	**$3,000 ÷**	**800 units**	**=**	**$3.75 cost per unit**
February	**$3,000 ÷**	**1,875 units**	**=**	**$1.60 cost per unit**

If Grave Manufacturing based a cost-plus pricing decision on these results, it would price products made in January significantly higher than products made in February. It is likely such price fluctuations would puzzle and drive away customers. Grave needs an allocation base that will spread the annual salary cost evenly over annual production. A timing problem exists, however, because Grave must allocate the salary cost before the end of the year. In order to price its products, Grave needs to know the allocated amount before the actual cost information is available. Grave can manage the timing problem by using estimated rather than actual costs.

Grave Manufacturing can *estimate* the annual cost of the supervisor's salary (indirect labor) as $36,000 ($3,000 × 12 months). The *actual* cost of indirect labor may differ because the supervisor might receive a pay raise or be replaced with a person who earns less. Based on current information, however, $36,000 is a reasonable estimate of the annual indirect labor cost. Grave must also estimate total annual production volume. Suppose Grave produced 18,000 units last year and expects no significant change in the current year. It can allocate indirect labor cost for January and February as follows.

Step 1. Compute the allocation rate.

Total cost to be allocated	÷	Allocation base (cost driver)	=	Allocation rate
$36,000	÷	18,000 units	=	$2.00 per unit

Step 2. Multiply the rate by the weight of the base (number of units per month) to determine how much of the salary cost to allocate to each month's production.

Month	Allocation Rate	×	Number of Units Produced	=	Allocation per Month
January	$2.00	×	800	=	$1,600
February	2.00	×	1,875	=	3,750

Grave Manufacturing will add these indirect cost allocations to other product costs to determine the total estimated product cost to use in cost-plus pricing or other managerial decisions.

Because the overhead allocation rate is determined *before* actual cost and volume data are available, it is called the **predetermined overhead rate.** Companies use predetermined overhead rates for product costing estimates and pricing decisions during a year, but they must use actual costs in published year-end financial statements. If necessary, companies adjust their accounting records at year-end when they have used estimated data on an interim basis. The procedures for making such adjustments are discussed in a later chapter.

ALLOCATING JOINT COSTS

LO 4-4

Allocate joint costs to joint products.

Joint costs are common costs incurred in the process of making two or more **joint products.** The cost of raw milk is a joint cost of producing the joint products cream, whole milk, 2 percent milk, and skim milk. Joint costs include not only materials costs but also the labor and overhead costs of converting the materials into separate products. The point in the production process at which products become separate and identifiable is the **split-off point.** For financial reporting of inventory and cost of goods sold, companies must allocate the joint costs to the separate joint products. Some joint products require additional processing after the split-off point. Any additional materials, labor, or overhead costs incurred after the split-off point are assigned to the specific products to which they relate.

To illustrate, assume Westar Chemical Company produces from common raw materials the joint products Compound AK and Compound AL. Compound AL requires further processing before Westar can sell it. The diagram in Exhibit 4.4 illustrates the joint product costs.

The joint costs of producing a batch of the two compounds are $48,000, representing $27,000 of materials cost and $21,000 of processing cost. A batch results in 3,000 gallons of

EXHIBIT 4.4

Allocation of Joint Cost

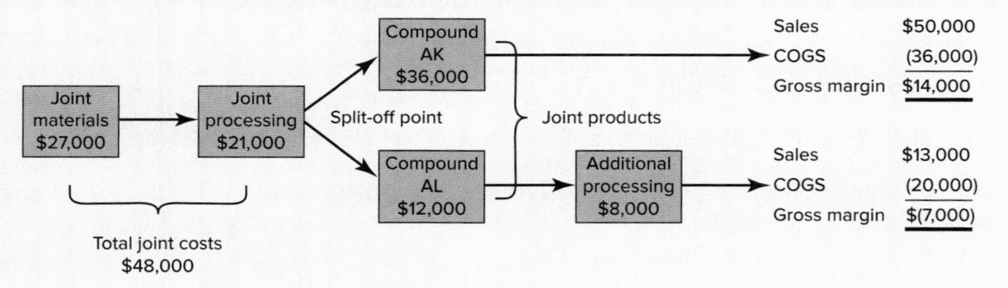

Compound AK and 1,000 gallons of Compound AL. Westar allocates joint costs to the products based on the number of gallons produced, as follows.

Step 1. Compute the allocation rate.

Total cost to be allocated	÷ Allocation base	= Allocation rate
$48,000 joint costs	÷ 4,000 gallons	= $12 per gallon

Step 2. Multiply the allocation rate by the weight of the base.

Joint Product	Allocation Rate	×	Number of Gallons Produced	=	Allocated Cost
Compound AK	$12	×	3,000	=	$36,000
Compound AL	12	×	1,000	=	12,000

Westar sells 3,000 gallons of Compound AK for $50,000 and 1,000 gallons of Compound AL for $13,000. Exhibit 4.4 shows the gross margins for each product using the joint cost allocations computed previously.

Relative Sales Value as the Allocation Base

Because Compound AL shows a $7,000 loss, a manager might mistakenly conclude that Westar should stop making and selling this product. If Westar stops making Compound AL, the total joint cost ($48,000) would be assigned to Compound AK and total gross margin would decline as shown as follows.

	With Compound AL		Without Compound AL
Sales	$ 63,000	($50,000 + $13,000)	$ 50,000
Cost of goods sold	(56,000)	($36,000 + $20,000)	(48,000)
Gross margin	$ 7,000		$ 2,000

To avoid the appearance that a product such as Compound AL is producing losses, many companies allocate joint cost to products based on the relative sales value of each product at the split-off point. Westar Chemical would allocate all of the joint costs to Compound AK because Compound AL has no market value at the split-off point. The resulting gross margins follow.

	Compound AK	Compound AL
Sales	$ 50,000	$13,000
Cost of goods sold	(48,000)	(8,000)
Gross margin	$ 2,000	$ 5,000

Westar's total profit on the joint products is $7,000 whether it allocates the joint costs using gallons or relative market value. However, using market value as the allocation base produces a positive gross margin for both products, reducing the likelihood that a manager will mistakenly eliminate a product that is contributing to profitability.

CHECK YOURSELF 4.3

What are some logical split-off points for a meat processing company engaged in butchering beef?

Answer The first logical split-off point occurs when processing separates the hide (used to produce leather) from the carcass. Other split-off points occur as further processing produces different cuts of meat (T-bone and New York strip steaks, various roasts, chops, ground chuck, etc.).

THE HUMAN FACTOR: A COMPREHENSIVE EXAMPLE

Cost allocations significantly affect individuals. They may influence managers' performance evaluations and compensation. They may dictate the amount of resources various departments, divisions, and other organizational subunits receive. Control over resources usually offers managers prestige and influence over organization operations. The following scenario illustrates the emotional impact and perceptions of fairness of cost allocation decisions.

LO 4-5

Recognize the effects of cost allocation on employee motivation.

Using Cost Allocations in a Budgeting Decision

Sharon Southport, dean of the School of Business at a major state university, is in dire need of a budgeting plan. Because of cuts in state funding, the money available to the School of Business for copying costs next year will be reduced substantially. Dean Southport supervises four departments: management, marketing, finance, and accounting. The dean knows the individual department chairpersons will be unhappy and frustrated with the deep cuts they face.

Using Cost Drivers to Make Allocations

To address the allocation of copying resources, Dean Southport decided to meet with the department chairs. She explained that the total budgeted for copying costs will be $36,000. Based on past usage, department allocations would be as follows: $12,000 for management, $10,000 for accounting, $8,000 for finance, and $6,000 for marketing.

Dr. Bill Thompson, the management department chair, immediately protested that his department could not operate on a $12,000 budget for copy costs. Management has more faculty members than any other department. Dr. Thompson argued that copy costs are directly related to the number of faculty members, so copy funds should be allocated based on the number of faculty members. Dr. Thompson suggested that number of faculty members rather than past usage should be used as the allocation base.

Since the School of Business has 72 faculty members (29 in management, 16 in accounting, 12 in finance, and 15 in marketing), the allocation should be as follows.

Step 1. Compute the allocation rate.

Total cost to be allocated	÷	Cost driver	=	Allocation rate
$36,000	÷	72	=	$500 per faculty member

Step 2. Multiply the rate by the weight of the driver (the number of faculty per department) to determine the allocation per object (department).

Department	Allocation Rate	×	Number of Faculty	=	Allocation per Department	Allocation Based on Past Usage
Management	$500	×	29	=	$14,500	$12,000
Accounting	500	×	16	=	8,000	10,000
Finance	500	×	12	=	6,000	8,000
Marketing	500	×	15	=	7,500	6,000
Total					$36,000	$36,000

Seeing these figures, Dr. Bob Smethers, chair of the accounting department, questioned the accuracy of using the number of faculty members as the cost driver. Dr. Smethers suggested the number of *students* rather than the number of *faculty members* drives the cost of copying. He argued that most copying results from duplicating syllabi, exams, and handouts. The accounting department teaches mass sections of introductory accounting that have extremely high student/teacher ratios. Because his department teaches more students, it spends more on copying costs even though it has fewer faculty members. Dr. Smethers recomputed the copy cost allocation as follows.

Step 1. Compute the allocation rate based on number of students. University records indicate that the School of Business taught 1,200 students during the most recent academic year. The allocation rate (copy cost per student) follows.

Total cost to be allocated	÷	Cost driver	=	Allocation rate
$36,000	÷	1,200	=	$30 per student

Step 2. Multiply the rate by the weight of the driver (number of students taught by each department) to determine the allocation per object (department).

Department	Allocation Rate	×	Number of Students	=	Allocation per Department	Allocation Based on Past Usage
Management	$30	×	330	=	$ 9,900	$12,000
Accounting	30	×	360	=	10,800	10,000
Finance	30	×	290	=	8,700	8,000
Marketing	30	×	220	=	6,600	6,000
Total					$36,000	$36,000

Choosing the Best Cost Driver

Dr. Thompson objected vigorously to using the number of students as the cost driver. He continued to argue that the size of the faculty is a more appropriate allocation base. The chair of the finance department sided with Dr. Smethers, the chair of the marketing department kept quiet, and the dean had to settle the dispute.

Dean Southport recognized that the views of the chairpersons were influenced by self-interest. The allocation base affects the amount of resources available to each department. Furthermore, the dean recognized that the size of the faculty does drive some of the copying costs. For example, the cost of copying manuscripts that faculty submit for publication relates to faculty size. The more articles faculty submit, the higher the copying cost. Nevertheless, the dean decided the number of students has the most significant impact on copying costs. She also wanted to encourage faculty members to minimize the impact of funding cuts on student services. Dean Southport therefore decided to allocate copying costs based on the number of students taught by each department. Dr. Thompson stormed angrily out of the meeting. The dean developed a budget by assigning the available funds to each department using the number of students as the allocation base.

Controlling Emotions

Dr. Thompson's behavior may relieve his frustration but it doesn't indicate clear thinking. Dean Southport recognized that Dr. Thompson's contention that copy costs were related to faculty size had some merit. Had Dr. Thompson offered a compromise rather than an emotional outburst, he might have increased his department's share of the funds. Perhaps a portion of the allocation could have been based on the number of faculty members with the balance allocated based on the number of students. Had Dr. Thompson controlled his anger, the others might have agreed to compromise. Technical expertise in computing numbers is of little use without the interpersonal skills to persuade others. Accountants may provide numerical measurements, but they should never forget the impact of their reports on the people in the organization.

<< A Look Back

Managers need to know the costs of products, processes, departments, activities, and so on. The target for which accountants attempt to determine cost is a *cost object*. Knowing the cost of specific objects enables management to control costs, evaluate performance, and price products. *Direct costs* can be cost-effectively traced to a cost object. *Indirect costs* cannot be easily traced to designated cost objects.

The same cost can be direct or indirect, depending on the cost object to which it is traced. For example, the salary of a Burger King restaurant manager can be directly traced to a particular store but cannot be traced to particular food items made and sold in the store. Classifying a cost as direct or indirect is independent of whether the cost behaves as fixed or variable; it is also independent of whether the cost is relevant to a given decision. A direct cost could be either fixed or variable or either relevant or irrelevant, depending on the context and the designated cost object.

Indirect costs are assigned to cost objects using *cost allocation*. Allocation divides an indirect cost into parts and distributes the parts among the relevant cost objects. Companies frequently allocate costs to cost objects in proportion to the *cost drivers* that cause the cost to be incurred. The first step in allocating an indirect cost is to determine the allocation rate by dividing the total cost to be allocated by the chosen cost driver. The next step is to multiply the allocation rate by the amount of the cost driver for a particular object. The result is the amount of indirect cost to assign to the cost object.

A particular indirect cost may be related to more than one driver. The best cost driver is the one that most accurately reflects the amount of the resource used by the cost object. Objects that consume the most resources should be allocated a proportionately greater share of the costs. If no suitable cost driver exists, companies may use arbitrary allocations such as dividing a total cost equally among cost objects.

Cost allocations have behavioral implications. Using inappropriate cost drivers can distort allocations and lead managers to make choices that are detrimental to the company's profitability.

The joint costs incurred in the process of making two or more products are allocated among the products at the *split-off point,* the point at which products become separate and identifiable. The allocation base can be the products' relative sales values or some quantity measure of the amount of each product made. If one of the joint products requires additional processing costs to bring it to market, only these additional processing costs are relevant to a decision about whether to undertake further processing. The allocated joint costs are not relevant because they will be incurred whether or not the joint product is processed after the split-off point. By-products share common costs with other products but have an insignificant market value relative to their joint products.

A Look Forward >>

The failure to accurately allocate indirect costs to cost objects can result in misinformation that impairs decision making. The next chapter explains how increased use of automation in production has caused distortion in allocations determined using traditional approaches. The chapter introduces the allocation of indirect costs using more recently developed activity-based costing and explains how activity-based management can improve efficiency and productivity. Finally, the chapter introduces total quality management, a strategy that seeks to minimize the costs of conforming to a designated standard of quality.

APPENDIX

Allocating Service Center Costs

LO 4-6

Allocate service department costs to operating departments.

Most organizations establish departments responsible for accomplishing specific tasks. Departments that are assigned tasks leading to the accomplishment of the primary objectives of the organization are called **operating departments.** Those that provide support to operating departments are called **service departments.** For example, the department of accounting at a university is classified as an operating department because its faculty perform the university's primary functions of teaching, research, and service. In contrast, the maintenance department is classified as a service department because its employees provide janitorial services that support primary university functions. Professors are more likely to be motivated to perform university functions when facilities are clean, but the university's primary purpose is not to clean buildings. Similarly, the lending department in a bank is an operating department and the personnel department is a service department. The bank is in the business of making loans. Hiring employees is a secondary function that assists the lending activity.

The costs to produce a product (or a service) include both operating and service department costs. Therefore, service department costs must somehow be allocated to the products produced (or services provided). Service department costs are frequently distributed to products through a two-stage allocation process. First-stage allocations involve the distribution of costs from service center cost pools to operating department cost pools. In the second stage, costs in the operating cost pools are allocated to products. Three different approaches can be used to allocate costs in the first stage of the two-stage costing process: the *direct method,* the *step method,* and the *reciprocal method.*

Direct Method

The **direct method** is the simplest allocation approach. It allocates service department costs directly to operating department cost pools. To illustrate, assume that Candler & Associates is a law firm that desires to determine the cost of handling each case. The firm has two operating departments, one that represents clients in civil suits and the other that defends clients in criminal cases. The two operating departments are supported by two service departments—personnel and secretarial support. Candler uses a two-stage allocation system to allocate the service centers' costs to the firm's legal cases. In the first stage, the costs to operate each service department are accumulated in separate cost pools. For example, the costs to operate the personnel department are $80,000 in salary, $18,000 in office rental, $12,000 in depreciation, $3,000 in supplies, and $4,000 in miscellaneous costs. These costs are added together in a single services department cost pool amounting to $117,000. Similarly, the costs incurred by the secretarial department are accumulated in a cost pool. We assume that this cost pool contains $156,800 of accumulated costs. The amounts in these cost pools are then allocated to the operating departments' cost pools. The appropriate allocations are described in the following paragraphs.

Assume that Candler's accountant decides that the number of attorneys working in the two operating departments constitutes a rational cost driver for the allocation of the personnel department cost pool and that the number of request forms submitted to the secretarial department constitutes a rational cost driver for the allocation of costs accumulated in the secretarial department cost pool. The total number of attorneys working in the two operating departments is 18: 11 in the civil department and 7 in the criminal department. The secretarial department received 980 work request forms with 380 from the civil department and 600 from the criminal department. Using these cost drivers as the allocation bases, the accountant made the following first-stage allocations.

Determination of Allocation Rates

$$\text{Allocation rate for personnel department cost pool} \div \frac{\$117{,}000}{18} = \$6{,}500 \text{ per attorney}$$

$$\text{Allocation rate for secretarial department cost pool} \div \frac{\$156{,}800}{980} = \$160 \text{ per request form}$$

The accountant then multiplied these rates by the weight of the base to determine the amount of each service cost pool to allocate to each operating department cost pool. The appropriate computations are shown in Exhibit 4.5.

As indicated, the allocated service department costs are pooled with other operating department overhead costs to form the operating department cost pools. In the second stage of the costing process, the costs in the operating department cost pools are allocated to the firm's products (cases). To illustrate second-stage allocations, assume that Candler allocates the operating department overhead cost pools on the basis of billable hours. Furthermore, assume that the civil department expects to bill 30,580 hours to its clients and the criminal

EXHIBIT 4.5

First-Stage Allocations for Candler & Associates—Direct Method

Allocated Service Department Overhead	Allocation Rate	×	Weight of Base	=	Civil Department	Criminal Department	Total Service Department Cost Pool
Personnel	$6,500	×	11 attorneys	=	$ 71,500		
	6,500	×	7 attorneys	=		$ 45,500	
Total cost of personnel department							$117,000
Secretarial	160	×	380 requests	=	60,800		
	160	×	600 requests	=		96,000	
Total cost of secretarial department							156,800
Total of cost pools after allocation					132,300	141,500	$273,800
Other operating department overhead costs					785,100	464,788	
Total of operating department overhead cost pools					$917,400	$606,288	

department expects to bill 25,262 hours. Based on this information, the following predetermined overhead rates are used to allocate operating department cost pools to particular cases.

$$\text{Predetermined overhead rate for the civil department} = \frac{\$917{,}400}{30{,}580} = \$30 \text{ per billable hour}$$

$$\text{Predetermined overhead rate for the criminal department} = \frac{\$606{,}288}{25{,}262} = \$24 \text{ per billable hour}$$

These rates are used to calculate the amount of operating department cost pools to include in the determination of the cost to litigate specific cases. For example, a case in the civil department that required 300 billable hours of legal service is allocated $9,000 (300 hours × $30 predetermined overhead rate) of overhead cost. Assuming that the direct costs to litigate the case amounted to $25,000, the total cost of this particular case is $34,000 ($25,000 direct cost + $9,000 allocated overhead). This accumulated cost figure could be used as a guide to determine the charge to the client or the profitability of the case.

Step Method

The direct method of allocating service center costs fails to consider the fact that service departments render assistance to other service departments. A service that is performed by one service department for the benefit of another service department is called an **interdepartmental service.** To illustrate this, we return to the case of Candler & Associates. Suppose that Candler's personnel department works with the employees in the secretarial department as well as the attorneys in the civil and criminal operating departments. Under these circumstances, Candler needs a cost approach that recognizes the interdepartmental service activity. One such approach is known as the **step method.** The primary difference between the direct method and the step method is depicted graphically in Exhibit 4.6. Focus your attention on the first stage of the allocation process. Notice that the step method includes one additional allocation, specifically from the personnel department cost pool to the secretarial department cost pool. The direct method ignores this interdepartmental service cost allocation. Indeed, the direct method derives its name from the fact that it allocates costs only from service cost pools to operating cost pools.

The fact that the direct method ignores the effect of interdepartmental services may cause distortions in the measurement of cost objects. The primary purpose of the step method is to avoid such distortions, thereby improving the accuracy of product costing. To illustrate this point, consider Candler & Associates. First, note that the interdepartmental portion of the personnel department cost is, in fact, a cost of providing secretarial services. In other

EXHIBIT 4.6

Comparison of Direct and Step Allocation Methods

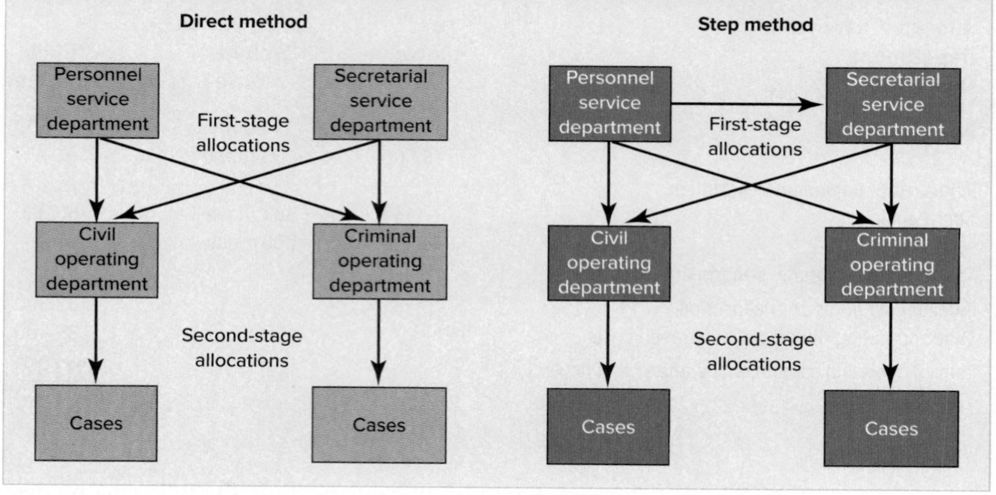

words, the personnel service costs could be reduced if the personnel department did not provide service to the secretarial staff. Accordingly, the cost of providing personnel support to the secretarial staff should be included in the secretarial cost pool. Under the direct method, however, the interdepartmental service cost is allocated between the civil and criminal operating departments. This is not a problem in and of itself because the cost of secretarial service is also allocated between the civil and criminal operating departments. Unfortunately, the base used to allocate personnel costs to the operating departments (i.e., number of attorneys) distributes more cost to the civil department than to the criminal department. This is unfortunate because the criminal department uses more secretarial service than the civil department does. In other words, more secretarial cost (i.e., interdepartmental personnel cost) is being allocated to the civil department although the criminal department uses more secretarial services. This means that ultimately the cost to litigate civil cases will be overstated and the cost to litigate criminal cases will be understated.

The step method corrects this distortion by distributing the interdepartmental personnel department cost to the secretarial department cost pool before it is allocated to the operating departments. Because the secretarial cost pool is allocated on the basis of requests for secretarial service, more of the interdepartmental cost will be allocated to the criminal operating department. To validate this result, assume that the personnel department cost pool is allocated to the secretarial department cost pool and the two operating department cost pools on the basis of the number of employees in each department. In addition to the 18 attorneys in the firm, assume that two employees work in the secretarial department. Accordingly, the allocation rate for the personnel cost pool is calculated as follows:

$$\text{Allocation rate for personnel department cost pool} = \frac{\$117{,}000}{20} = \$5{,}850 \text{ per employee}$$

Based on this rate, the first step in the allocation process distributes the personnel department cost pool, indicated as follows.

Personnel Cost Pool Allocated to	Allocation Rate		Weight of Base		Allocated Cost
Secretarial	$5,850	×	2 employees	=	$ 11,700
Civil	5,850	×	11 employees	=	64,350
Criminal	5,850	×	7 employees	=	40,950
Total			20 employees		$117,000

EXHIBIT 4.7

First-Stage Allocations for Candler & Associates—Step Method

	Personnel Cost Pool		Secretarial Cost Pool		Civil Department		Criminal Department
Cost to be allocated	$ 117,000		$ 156,800				
Step 1 allocation	(117,000)	=	11,700	+	$ 64,350	+	$ 40,950
Step 2 allocation			(168,500)	=	65,337	+	103,163
Total in cost pool after allocation	$ 0		$ 0		129,687		144,113
Other operating department overhead costs					785,100		464,788
Total of operating department overhead cost pool					$914,787		$608,901

The result of the distribution of personnel department costs is shown as the step 1 allocation in Exhibit 4.7. The $11,700 interdepartmental personnel department cost allocated to the secretarial department cost pool is added to the $156,800 existing balance in that cost pool (see Exhibit 4.7). The result is the accumulation of secretarial cost of $168,500. The second step in the costing process allocates this cost pool to the operating departments. Recall that the secretarial cost pool is allocated on the basis of number of work request forms submitted. Furthermore, recall that 980 request forms were submitted to the secretarial department (380 from the civil department and 600 from the criminal department). Accordingly, the allocation rate for the secretarial department cost pool is computed as follows.

$$\text{Allocation rate for secretarial department cost pool} = \frac{\$168{,}500}{980} = \$171.93878 \text{ per request form}$$

Based on this rate, the second step in the allocation process distributes the secretarial cost pool, indicated as follows.

Secretarial Cost Pool Allocated to	Allocation Rate		Weight of Base		Allocated Cost
Civil	$171.93878	×	380 requests	=	$ 65,337
Criminal	171.93878	×	600 requests	=	103,163
Total			980 requests		$168,500

The result of this allocation is shown as the step 2 allocation in Exhibit 4.7. Notice that the final cost pools for the operating departments reflect the expected shift in the cost distribution between the two departments. Specifically, the cost pool in the criminal department is higher and the cost pool in the civil department is lower than the comparable cost pool amounts computed under the direct method (see Exhibit 4.5 for the appropriate comparison). This distribution of cost is consistent with the fact that more of the interdepartmental service cost should be assigned to the criminal department because it uses more secretarial services than does the civil department. Accordingly, the step method of allocation more accurately reflects the manner in which the two operating departments consume resources.

The preceding illustration considered a simple two-stage allocation process with only two service departments and two operating departments. In large organizations, the costing process may be significantly more complex. Interdepartmental cost allocations may involve several service departments. For example, a personnel department may provide service to a secretarial department that provides service to an engineering department that provides service to the accounting department that provides service to several operating departments. In addition, general overhead costs may be allocated to both service and operating departments before costs are allocated from service to operating departments. For example, general utility costs may be pooled together and allocated to service and operating departments on the basis of square footage of floor space. These allocated utility costs are then redistributed to other service departments and to operating departments in a sequence of step-down allocations. The step-down process usually begins with the cost pool that represents resources used by the largest number of departments. This constitutes the first step in the costing process. The second step proceeds with allocations from the cost pool that represents resources used by the second largest number of departments and so on, until all overhead costs have been allocated to the operating departments. Accordingly, the first stage of a two-stage costing process may include many allocations (steps) before all costs have been distributed to the operating departments. Regardless of how many allocations are included in the first stage, the second stage begins when costs are allocated from the operating departments to the organization's products.

Reciprocal Method

Note that the step method is limited to one-way interdepartmental relationships. In practice, many departments have two-way working relationships. For example, the personnel department may provide services to the secretarial department and receive services from it. Two-way associations in which departments provide and receive services from one another are called **reciprocal relationships.** Allocations that recognize reciprocal relationships require complex mathematical manipulation involving the use of simultaneous linear equations. The resultant cost distributions are difficult to interpret. Furthermore, the results attained with the **reciprocal method** are not significantly different from those attained through the step method. As a result, the reciprocal method is rarely used in practice.

Video lectures and accompanying self-assessment quizzes are available in *Connect* for all learning objectives.

SELF-STUDY REVIEW PROBLEM

New budget constraints have pressured Body Perfect Gym to control costs. The owner of the gym, Mr. Ripple, has notified division managers that their job performance evaluations will be highly influenced by their ability to minimize costs. The gym has three divisions: weight lifting, aerobics, and spinning. The owner has formulated a report showing how much it cost to operate each of the three divisions last year. In preparing the report, Mr. Ripple identified several indirect costs that must be allocated among the divisions. These indirect costs are $4,200 of laundry expense, $48,000 of supplies, $350,000 of office rent, $50,000 of janitorial services, and $120,000 for administrative salaries. To provide a reasonably accurate cost allocation, Mr. Ripple has identified several potential cost drivers. These drivers and their association with each division follow.

Cost Driver	Weight Lifting	Aerobics	Spinning	Total
Number of participants	26	16	14	56
Number of instructors	10	8	6	24
Square feet of gym space	12,000	6,000	7,000	25,000
Number of staff	2	2	1	5

Required

a. Identify the appropriate cost objects.

b. Identify the most appropriate cost driver for each indirect cost, and compute the allocation rate for assigning each indirect cost to the cost objects.

c. Determine the amount of supplies expense that should be allocated to each of the three divisions.

d. The spinning manager wants to use the number of staff rather than the number of instructors as the allocation base for the supplies expense. Explain why the spinning manager would take this position.

e. Identify two cost drivers other than your choice for Requirement *b* that could be used to allocate the cost of the administrative salaries to the three divisions.

Solution to Requirement *a*

The objective is to determine the cost of operating each division. Therefore, the cost objects are the three divisions (weight lifting, aerobics, and spinning).

Solution to Requirement *b*

The costs, appropriate cost drivers, and allocation rates for assigning the costs to the departments follow.

Cost	Base	Computation	Allocation Rate
Laundry expense	Number of participants	$ 4,200 ÷ 56	$75 per participant
Supplies	Number of instructors	48,000 ÷ 24	$2,000 per instructor
Office rent	Square feet	350,000 ÷ 25,000	$14 per square foot
Janitorial service	Square feet	50,000 ÷ 25,000	$2 per square foot
Administrative salaries	Number of divisions	120,000 ÷ 3	$40,000 per division

There are other logical cost drivers. For example, the cost of supplies could be allocated based on the number of staff. It is also logical to use a combination of cost drivers. For example, the allocation for the cost of supplies could be based on the combined number of instructors and staff. For this problem, we assumed that Mr. Ripple chose the number of instructors as the base for allocating supplies expense.

Solution to Requirement *c*

Department	Cost to Be Allocated	Allocation Rate	×	Weight	=	Amount Allocated
Weight lifting	Supplies	$2,000	×	10	=	$20,000
Aerobics	Supplies	2,000	×	8	=	16,000
Spinning	Supplies	2,000	×	6	=	12,000
Total						$48,000

Solution to Requirement *d*

If the number of staff were used as the allocation base, the allocation rate for supplies would be as follows:

$$\$48{,}000 \div 5 \text{ staff} = \$9{,}600 \text{ per staff member}$$

Using this rate, the total cost of supplies would be allocated among the three divisions as follows.

Department	Cost to Be Allocated	Allocation Rate	×	Weight of Base	=	Amount Allocated
Weight lifting	Supplies	$9,600	×	2	=	$19,200
Aerobics	Supplies	9,600	×	2	=	19,200
Spinning	Supplies	9,600	×	1	=	9,600
Total						$48,000

By using the number of staff as the allocation base instead of the number of instructors, the amount of overhead cost allocated to the spinning division falls from $12,000 to $9,600. Since managers are evaluated based on minimizing costs, it is clearly in the spinning manager's self-interest to use the number of staff as the allocation base.

Solution to Requirement *e*

Among other possibilities, bases for allocating the administrative salaries include the number of participants, the number of lessons, or the number of instructors.

KEY TERMS

allocation 158
allocation base 159
allocation rate 159
common costs 158
controllable costs 158
cost accumulation 156
cost allocation 157
cost driver 156
cost objects 154
cost pool 160
cost tracing 157
direct cost 157
direct method 174
indirect cost 157
interdepartmental service 175
joint costs 169
joint products 169
operating departments 173
overhead costs 157
predetermined overhead rate 169
reciprocal method 178
reciprocal relationships 178
service departments 173
split-off point 169
step method 175

QUESTIONS

1. What is a cost object? Identify four different cost objects in which an accountant would be interested.
2. Why is cost accumulation imprecise?
3. If the cost object is a manufactured product, what are the three major cost categories to accumulate?
4. What is a direct cost? What criteria are used to determine whether a cost is a direct cost?
5. Why are the terms *direct cost* and *indirect cost* independent of the terms *fixed cost* and *variable cost?* Give an example to illustrate.
6. Give an example of why the statement "All direct costs are avoidable" is incorrect.
7. What are the important factors in determining the appropriate cost driver to use in allocating a cost?
8. How is an allocation rate determined? How is an allocation made?
9. In a manufacturing environment, which costs are direct and which are indirect in product costing?
10. Why are some manufacturing costs not directly traceable to products?
11. What is the objective of allocating indirect manufacturing overhead costs to the product?
12. On January 31, the managers of Integra Inc. seek to determine the cost of producing their product during January for product pricing and control purposes. The company can easily determine the costs of direct materials and direct labor used in January production, but many fixed indirect costs are not affected by the level of production activity and have not yet been incurred. The managers can reasonably estimate the overhead costs for the year based on the fixed indirect costs incurred in past periods. Assume the managers decide to allocate an equal amount of these estimated costs to the products produced each month. Explain why this practice may not provide a reasonable estimate of product costs in January.
13. Respond to the following statement: "The allocation base chosen is unimportant. What is important in product costing is that overhead costs be assigned to production in a specific period by an allocation process."
14. Larry Kwang insists that the costs of his school's fund-raising project should be determined after the project is complete. He argues that only after the project is complete can its costs be determined accurately and that it is a waste of time to try to estimate future costs. Georgia Sundum counters that waiting until the project is complete will not provide timely information for planning expenditures. How would you arbitrate this discussion? Explain the trade-offs between accuracy and timeliness.
15. What are the three methods used for allocating service center costs? How do the methods differ? (Appendix)

MULTIPLE-CHOICE QUESTIONS

Multiple-choice questions are available in *Connect*.

EXERCISES—SERIES A

connect **All applicable Exercises in Series A are available in *Connect*.**

LO 4-1

Exercise 4-1A *Direct versus indirect costs*

Ludmilla Construction Company is composed of two divisions: (1) Home Construction and (2) Commercial Construction. The Home Construction Division is in the process of building 12 houses and the Commercial Construction Division is working on three projects. Cost items of the company follow:

Wages of workers assigned to a specific construction project
Supplies used by the Commercial Construction Division
Labor on a particular house

Salary of the supervisor of commercial construction projects
Supplies, such as glue and nails, used by the Home Construction Division
Cost of building permits
Materials used in commercial construction projects
Depreciation on home building equipment (small tools such as hammers or saws)
Company president's salary
Depreciation on crane used in commercial construction
Depreciation on home office building
Salary of corporate office manager

Required

a. Identify each cost as being a direct or indirect cost assuming the cost objects are the individual products (houses or projects).

b. Identify each cost as being a direct or indirect cost, assuming the cost objects are the two divisions.

c. Identify each cost as being a direct or indirect cost assuming the cost object is Ludmilla Construction Company as a whole.

Exercise 4-2A *Allocating costs between divisions* LO 4-2

Beasley Services Company (BSC) has 50 employees, 28 of whom are assigned to Division A and 22 to Division B. BSC incurred $450,000 of fringe benefits cost during Year 2.

Required

Determine the amount of the fringe benefits cost to be allocated to Division A and to Division B.

Exercise 4-3A *Allocating overhead cost to accomplish smoothing* LO 4-2

Rasmussen Corporation expects to incur indirect overhead costs of $80,000 per month and direct manufacturing costs of $12 per unit. The expected production activity for the first four months of the year are as follows.

	January	February	March	April
Estimated production in units	6,000	7,000	3,000	4,000

Required

a. Calculate a predetermined overhead rate based on the number of units of product expected to be made during the first four months of the year.

b. Allocate overhead costs to each month using the overhead rate computed in Requirement *a.*

c. Calculate the total cost per unit for each month using the overhead allocated in Requirement *b.*

Exercise 4-4A *Pooling overhead cost* LO 4-2

Ware Manufacturing Company produced 2,000 units of inventory in January Year 2. It expects to produce an additional 14,000 units during the remaining 11 months of the year. In other words, total production for Year 2 is estimated to be 16,000 units. Direct materials and direct labor costs are $64 and $52 per unit, respectively. Ware expects to incur the following manufacturing overhead costs during the Year 2 accounting period.

Production supplies	$ 20,000
Supervisor salary	160,000
Depreciation on equipment	75,000
Utilities	20,000
Rental fee on manufacturing facilities	45,000

Required

a. Combine the individual overhead costs into a cost pool and calculate a predetermined overhead rate assuming the cost driver is number of units.

b. Determine the cost of the 2,000 units of product made in January.

c. Is the cost computed in Requirement *b* actual or estimated? Could Ware improve accuracy by waiting until December to determine the cost of products? Identify two reasons that a manager would want to know the cost of products in January. Discuss the relationship between accuracy and relevance as it pertains to this problem.

LO 4-3

Exercise 4-5A *Allocating overhead cost among products*

Tyson Hats Corporation manufactures three different models of hats: Vogue, Beauty, and Glamour. Tyson expects to incur $480,000 of overhead cost during the next fiscal year. Other budget information follows.

	Vogue	Beauty	Glamour	Total
Direct labor hours	2,000	4,000	6,000	12,000
Machine hours	1,200	1,400	1,400	4,000

Required

a. Use direct labor hours as the cost driver to compute the allocation rate and the budgeted overhead cost for each product.

b. Use machine hours as the cost driver to compute the allocation rate and the budgeted overhead cost for each product.

c. Describe a set of circumstances where it would be more appropriate to use direct labor hours as the allocation base.

d. Describe a set of circumstances where it would be more appropriate to use machine hours as the allocation base.

LO 4-3

Exercise 4-6A *Allocating overhead costs among products*

Willey Company makes three products in its factory: plastic cups, plastic tablecloths, and plastic bottles. The expected overhead costs for the next fiscal year include the following.

Factory manager's salary	$210,000
Factory utility cost	70,000
Factory supplies	20,000
Total overhead costs	$300,000

Willey uses machine hours as the cost driver to allocate overhead costs. Budgeted machine hours for the products are as follows.

Cups	300 Hours
Tablecloths	750
Bottles	950
Total machine hours	2,000

Required

a. Allocate the budgeted overhead costs to the products.

b. Provide a possible explanation as to why Willey chose machine hours, instead of labor hours, as the allocation base.

LO 4-3

Exercise 4-7A *Allocating costs among products*

Fanya Construction Company expects to build three new homes during a specific accounting period. The estimated direct materials and labor costs are as follows.

Expected Costs	Home 1	Home 2	Home 3
Direct labor	$40,000	$60,000	$100,000
Direct materials	30,000	50,000	80,000

Assume Fanya needs to allocate two major overhead costs ($80,000 of employee fringe benefits and $40,000 of indirect materials costs) among the three jobs.

Required

Choose an appropriate cost driver for each of the overhead costs and determine the total cost of each house. Round your figures to three decimal points.

Exercise 4-8A *Allocating to smooth cost over varying levels of production*

LO 4-3

Production workers for Essa Manufacturing Company provided 300 hours of labor in January and 600 hours in February. Essa expects to use 5,000 hours of labor during the year. The rental fee for the manufacturing facility is $6,000 per month.

Required

Explain why allocation is needed. Based on this information, how much of the rental cost should be allocated to the products made in January and to those made in February?

Exercise 4-9A *Allocating to solve a timing problem*

LO 4-3

Production workers for Chadwick Manufacturing Company provided 3,200 hours of labor in January and 2,800 hours in February. The company, whose operation is labor intensive, expects to use 48,000 hours of labor during the year. Chadwick paid a $120,000 annual premium on July 1 of the prior year for an insurance policy that covers the manufacturing facility for the following 12 months.

Required

Explain why allocation is needed. Based on this information, how much of the insurance cost should be allocated to the products made in January and to those made in February?

Exercise 4-10A *Allocating to solve a timing problem*

LO 4-3

Erickson Air is a large airline company that pays a customer relations representative $8,000 per month. The representative, who processed 3,000 customer complaints in January and 2,500 complaints in February, is expected to process 40,000 customer complaints during the year.

Required

a. Determine the total cost of processing customer complaints in January and in February.

b. Explain why allocating the cost of the customer relations representative would or would not be relevant to decision making.

Exercise 4-11A *How the allocation of fixed cost affects a pricing decision*

LO 4-3

Arrow Manufacturing Co. expects to make 50,000 chairs during the Year 1 accounting period. The company made 3,000 chairs in January. Materials and labor costs for January were $36,000 and $48,000, respectively. Arrow produced 4,000 chairs in February. Material and labor costs for February were $48,000 and $60,000, respectively. The company paid the $480,000 annual rental fee on its manufacturing facility on January 1, Year 1.

Required

Assuming that Arrow desires to sell its chairs for cost plus 40 percent of cost, what price should be charged for the chairs produced in January and February?

Exercise 4-12A *Allocating joint product cost*

LO 4-4

Ferrier Chemical Company makes three products, B7, K6, and X9, which are joint products from the same materials. In a standard batch of 150,000 pounds of raw materials, the company generates 35,000 pounds of B7, 75,000 pounds of K6, and 40,000 pounds of X9. A standard batch costs $600,000 to produce. The sales prices per pound are $6, $10, and $16 for B7, K6, and X9, respectively.

Required

a. Allocate the joint product cost among the three final products using weight as the allocation base.

b. Allocate the joint product cost among the three final products using market value as the allocation base. Round your figures to three decimal points.

LO 4-5

Exercise 4-13A *Human factor*

Miriana Clinics provides medical care in three departments: internal medicine (IM), pediatrics (PD), and obstetrics gynecology (OB). The estimated costs to run each department follow.

	IM	PD	OB
Physicians	$600,000	$400,000	$500,000
Nurses	80,000	120,000	160,000

Miriana expects to incur $450,000 of indirect (overhead) costs in the next fiscal year.

Required

a. Name four allocation bases that could be used to assign the overhead cost to each department.

b. Assume the manager of each department is permitted to recommend how the overhead cost should be allocated to the departments. Which of the allocation bases named in Requirement *a* is the manager of OB most likely to recommend? Explain why. What argument may the manager of OB use to justify his choice of the allocation base?

c. Which of the allocation bases would result in the fairest allocation of the overhead cost from the perspective of the company president?

d. Explain how classifying overhead costs into separate pools could improve the fairness of the allocation of the overhead costs.

Appendix

LO 4-6

Exercise 4-14A *Allocating a service center cost to operating departments*

Conrad Corporation's computer services department assists two operating departments in using the company's information system effectively. The annual cost of computer services is $600,000. The production department employs 38 employees, and the sales department employs 22 employees. Conrad uses the number of employees as the cost driver for allocating the cost of computer services to operating departments.

Required

Allocate the cost of computer services to operating departments.

LO 4-6

Exercise 4-15A *Allocating costs of service centers to operating departments—step method*

Kirby Health Care Center Inc. has three clinics servicing the Seattle metropolitan area. The company's legal services department supports the clinics. Moreover, its computer services department supports all of the clinics and the legal services department. The annual cost of operating the legal services department is $200,000. The annual cost of operating the computer services department is $360,000. The company uses the number of patients served as the cost driver for allocating the cost of legal services and the number of computer workstations as the cost driver for allocating the cost of computer services. Other relevant information follows.

	Number of Patients	Number of Workstations
Sewell clinic	6,000	18
Alphretta clinic	4,200	16
Gwinnett clinic	5,800	18
Legal services		8
Computer services		10

Required

a. Allocate the cost of computer services to all of the clinics and the legal services department.

b. After allocating the cost of computer services, allocate the cost of legal services to the three clinics.

c. Compute the total allocated cost of service centers for each clinic.

Exercise 4-16A *Allocating costs of service centers to operating departments—direct method*

LO 4-6

Quinlan Trust Corporation has two service departments: actuary and economic analysis. Quinlan also has three operating departments: annuity, fund management, and employee benefit services. The annual costs of operating the service departments are $480,000 for actuary and $800,000 for economic analysis. Quinlan uses the direct method to allocate service center costs to operating departments. Other relevant data follow.

	Operating Costs*	Revenue
Annuity	$500,000	$ 840,000
Fund management	900,000	1,260,000
Employee benefit services	600,000	1,100,000

*The operating costs are measured before allocating service center costs.

Required

a. Use operating costs as the cost driver for allocating service center costs to operating departments.

b. Use revenue as the cost driver for allocating service center costs to operating departments.

PROBLEMS—SERIES A

connect **All applicable Problems in Series A are available in *Connect.***

Problem 4-17A *Cost accumulation and allocation*

LO 4-1, 4-2, 4-3

eXcel

CHECK FIGURE

c. Product N: $522.55

Yalland Manufacturing Company makes two different products, M and N. The company's two departments are named after the products; for example, Product M is made in Department M. Yalland's accountant has identified the following annual costs associated with these two products.

Financial data	
Salary of vice president of production division	$160,000
Salary of supervisor Department M	80,000
Salary of supervisor Department N	60,000
Direct materials cost Department M	300,000
Direct materials cost Department N	420,000
Direct labor cost Department M	240,000
Direct labor cost Department N	680,000
Direct utilities cost Department M	120,000
Direct utilities cost Department N	24,000
General factorywide utilities	36,000
Production supplies	36,000
Fringe benefits	138,000
Depreciation	600,000
Nonfinancial data	
Machine hours Department M	5,000
Machine hours Department N	1,000

Required

a. Identify the costs that are (1) direct costs of Department M, (2) direct costs of Department N, and (3) indirect costs.

b. Select the appropriate cost drivers for the indirect costs and allocate these costs to Departments M and N.

c. Determine the total estimated cost of the products made in Departments M and N. Assume that Yalland produced 2,000 units of Product M and 4,000 units of Product N during the year. If Yalland prices its products at cost plus 40 percent of cost, what price per unit must it charge for Product M and for Product N?

LO 4-1, 4-2, 4-3

Problem 4-18A *Selecting an appropriate cost driver (What is the base?)*

The Huffman School of Vocational Technology has organized the school training programs into three departments. Each department provides training in a different area as follows: nursing assistant, dental hygiene, and office technology. The school's owner, Amy Huffman, wants to know how much it costs to operate each of the three departments. To accumulate the total cost for each department, the accountant has identified several indirect costs that must be allocated to each. These costs are $12,000 of phone expense, $21,000 of office supplies, $900,000 of office rent, $144,000 of janitorial services, and $150,000 of salary paid to the dean of students. To provide a reasonably accurate allocation of costs, the accountant has identified several possible cost drivers. These drivers and their association with each department follow.

Cost Driver	Department 1	Department 2	Department 3
Number of telephones	20	30	50
Number of faculty members	20	16	24
Square footage of office space	14,000	8,000	14,000
Number of secretaries	2	2	2

Required

a. Identify the appropriate cost objects.

b. Identify the appropriate cost driver for each indirect cost and compute the allocation rate for assigning each indirect cost to the cost objects.

c. Determine the amount of telephone expense that should be allocated to each of the three departments.

d. Determine the amount of supplies expense that should be allocated to Department 3.

e. Determine the amount of office rent that should be allocated to Department 2.

f. Determine the amount of janitorial services cost that should be allocated to Department 1.

g. Identify two cost drivers not listed here that could be used to allocate the cost of the dean's salary to the three departments.

LO 4-1, 4-2, 4-3

CHECK FIGURE
b. To NY: $1,080

Problem 4-19A *Cost allocation in a service industry*

Eagle Airlines is a small airline that occasionally carries overload shipments for the overnight delivery company Never-Fail Inc. Never-Fail is a multimillion-dollar company started by Wes Never immediately after he failed to finish his first accounting course. The company's motto is "We Never-Fail to Deliver Your Package on Time." When Never-Fail has more freight than it can deliver, it pays Eagle to carry the excess. Eagle contracts with independent pilots to fly its planes on a per-trip basis. Eagle recently purchased an airplane that cost the company $6,000,000. The plane has an estimated useful life of 20,000,000 miles and a zero salvage value. During the first week in January, Eagle flew two trips. The first trip was a round trip flight from Chicago to San Francisco, for which Eagle paid $350 for the pilot and $500 for fuel. The second flight was a round trip from Chicago to New York. For this trip, it paid $300 for the pilot and $300 for fuel. The round trip between Chicago and San Francisco is approximately 4,400 miles and the round trip between Chicago and New York is 1,600 miles.

Required

a. Identify the direct and indirect costs that Eagle incurs for each trip.

b. Determine the total cost of each trip.

c. In addition to depreciation, identify three other indirect costs that may need to be allocated to determine the cost of each trip.

LO 4-1, 4-2, 4-3

Problem 4-20A *Cost allocation in a manufacturing company*

Camp Manufacturing Company makes tents that it sells directly to camping enthusiasts through a mail-order marketing program. The company pays a quality control expert $80,000 per year to inspect completed tents before they are shipped to customers. Assume that the company completed 1,600 tents in January and 1,200 tents in February. For the entire year, the company expects to produce 20,000 tents.

CHECK FIGURE
d. Feb.: $4,800

Required

a. Explain how changes in the cost driver (number of tents inspected) affect the total amount of fixed inspection cost.

b. Explain how changes in the cost driver (number of tents inspected) affect the amount of fixed inspection cost per unit.

c. If the cost objective is to determine the cost per tent, is the expert's salary a direct or an indirect cost?

d. How much of the expert's salary should be allocated to tents produced in January and February?

Problem 4-21A *Allocation to accomplish smoothing*

LO 4-1, 4-2, 4-3

CHECK FIGURES
a. $7
c. March: $69

Velez Corporation estimated its overhead costs would be $50,000 per month except for January when it pays the $30,000 annual insurance premium on the manufacturing facility. Accordingly, the January overhead costs were expected to be $80,000 ($30,000 + $50,000). The company expected to use 7,000 direct labor hours per month except during July, August, and September when the company expected 9,000 hours of direct labor each month to build inventories for high demand that normally occurs during the Christmas season. The company's actual direct labor hours were the same as the estimated hours. The company made 3,500 units of product in each month except July, August, and September, in which it produced 4,500 units each month. Direct labor costs were $30 per unit, and direct materials costs were $25 per unit.

Required

a. Calculate a predetermined overhead rate based on direct labor hours.

b. Determine the total allocated overhead cost for January, March, and August.

c. Determine the cost per unit of product for January, March, and August.

d. Determine the selling price for the product, assuming that the company desires to earn a gross margin of $20 per unit.

Problem 4-22A *Allocating indirect costs between products*

LO 4-2, 4-3

CHECK FIGURES
a. Cost/unit for EZRecords: $162.50
b. Cost/unit for ProOffice: $175

Hannah Ortega is considering expanding her business. She plans to hire a salesperson to cover trade shows. Because of compensation, travel expenses, and booth rental, fixed costs for a trade show are expected to be $7,500. The booth will be open 30 hours during the trade show. Ms. Ortega also plans to add a new product line, ProOffice, which will cost $150 per package. She will continue to sell the existing product, EZRecords, which costs $100 per package. Ms. Ortega believes that the salesperson will spend approximately 20 hours selling EZRecords and 10 hours marketing ProOffice.

Required

a. Determine the estimated total cost and cost per unit of each product, assuming that the salesperson is able to sell 80 units of EZRecords and 50 units of ProOffice.

b. Determine the estimated total cost and cost per unit of each product, assuming that the salesperson is able to sell 200 units of EZRecords and 100 units of ProOffice.

c. Explain why the cost per unit figures calculated in Requirement *a* are different from the amounts calculated in Requirement *b*. Also explain how the differences in estimated cost per unit will affect pricing decisions.

Problem 4-23A *Cost Pools*

LO 4-2, 4-3

Russell Department Stores Inc. has three departments: women's, men's, and children's. The following are the indirect costs related to its operations:

Vacation pay	Payroll taxes
Sewer bill	Paper rolls for cash registers
Staples	Medical insurance
Natural gas bill	Salaries of secretaries
Pens	Water bill
Ink cartridges	

Required

a. Organize the costs in the following three pools: indirect materials, indirect labor, and indirect utilities, assuming that each department is a cost object.
b. Identify an appropriate cost driver for each pool.
c. Explain why accountants use cost pools.

LO 4-4

CHECK FIGURES
a. GM for drumsticks: $(280)
b. Total cost of breasts: $6,837.60

Problem 4-24A *Allocating joint product cost*

Harper Chicken Corporation processes and packages chicken for grocery stores. It purchases chickens from farmers and processes them into two different products: chicken drumsticks and chicken steak. From a standard batch of 12,000 pounds of raw chicken that costs $7,000, the company produces two parts: 2,800 pounds of drumsticks and 4,200 pounds of breast for a processing cost of $2,450. The chicken breast is further processed into 3,200 pounds of steak for a processing cost of $2,000. The market price of drumsticks per pound is $1.25 and the market price per pound of chicken steak is $4.20. If Harper decided to sell chicken breast instead of chicken steak, the price per pound would be $2.20.

Required

a. Allocate the joint cost to the joint products, drumsticks and breasts, using weight as the allocation base. Calculate the gross profit for each product. Since the drumsticks are producing a net loss, should that product line be eliminated?
b. Reallocate the joint cost to the joint products, drumsticks and breasts, using relative market values as the allocation base. Calculate the gross profit for each product. Compare the total gross profit (drumsticks + breasts) computed in Requirement *b* with that computed in Requirement *a*. Explain why the total amount is the same. Comment on which allocation base (weight or market value) is more appropriate. Round your figures to two decimal points.
c. Should Harper further process chicken breasts into chicken steak?

LO 4-1, 4-2, 4-3, 4-5

excel

Problem 4-25A *Fairness and cost pool allocations*

Clement Manufacturing Company uses two departments to make its products. Department I is a cutting department that is machine intensive and uses very few employees. Machines cut and form parts and then place the finished parts on a conveyor belt that carries them to Department II, where they are assembled into finished goods. The assembly department is labor intensive and requires many workers to assemble parts into finished goods. The company's manufacturing facility incurs two significant overhead costs: employee fringe benefits and utility costs. The annual costs of fringe benefits are $420,000 and utility costs are $300,000. The typical consumption patterns for the two departments are as follows.

	Department I	Department II	Total
Machine hours used	20,000	4,000	24,000
Direct labor hours used	2,000	14,000	16,000

The supervisor of each department receives a bonus based on how well the department controls costs. The company's current policy requires using a single allocation base (machine hours or labor hours) to allocate the total overhead cost of $720,000.

Required

a. Assume that you are the supervisor of Department I. Choose the allocation base that would minimize your department's share of the total overhead cost. Calculate the amount of overhead that would be allocated to both departments using the base that you selected.
b. Assume that you are the supervisor of Department II. Choose the allocation base that would minimize your department's share of the total overhead cost. Calculate the amount of overhead that would be allocated to both departments using the base that you selected.
c. Assume that you are the plant manager and have the authority to change the company's overhead allocation policy. Formulate an overhead allocation policy that would be fair to the supervisors of

both Department I and Department II. Compute the overhead allocations for each department using your policy.

d. Explain why it is necessary to disaggregate the overhead cost pool in order to accomplish fairness.

Appendix

Problem 4-26A *Allocating service center costs—step method and direct method*

LO 4-6

eXcel

Compton Information Services Inc. has two service departments: human resources and billing. Compton's operating departments, organized according to the special industry each department serves, are health care, retail, and legal services. The billing department supports only the three operating departments, but the human resources department supports all operating departments and the billing department. Other relevant information follows.

CHECK FIGURES

a. Allocated cost from Billing to Retail: $465,000

b. Allocated cost from HR to LS: $160,000

	Human Resources	Billing	Health Care	Retail	Legal Services
Number of employees	10	20	80	60	40
Annual cost*	$720,000	$1,428,000	$6,000,000	$4,800,000	$2,800,000
Annual revenue	—	—	$9,000,000	$6,200,000	$4,800,000

*This is the operating cost before allocating service department costs.

Required

a. Allocate service department costs to operating departments, assuming that Compton adopts the step method. The company uses the number of employees as the base for allocating human resources department costs and department annual revenue as the base for allocating the billing department costs.

b. Allocate service department costs to operating departments, assuming that Compton adopts the direct method. The company uses the number of employees as the base for allocating the human resources department costs and department annual revenue as the base for allocating the billing department costs. Round your figures to three decimal points.

c. Compute the total allocated cost of service centers for each operating department using each allocation method. Round your figures to three decimal points.

EXERCISES—SERIES B

Exercise 4-1B *Direct versus indirect costs*

LO 4-1

Tilley Professional Services is composed of two separate divisions: (1) tax services as provided by the tax department and (2) auditing services as provided by the audit department. Each department has numerous clients. Engagement with each individual client is a separate service (i.e., product) and each department has several engagements in each period. Cost items of the firm follow:

Salary of the partner in charge of the audit department
Salary of the managing partner of the firm
Cost of office supplies such as paper, pencils, erasers, etc.
Depreciation of computers used in the tax department
License fees of the firm
Professional labor for a tax engagement
Secretarial labor supporting both departments
Professional labor for an audit engagement
Depreciation of computers used in the audit department
Salary of the partner in charge of the tax department
Travel expenditures for an audit engagement

Required

a. Identify each cost as being a direct or indirect cost assuming the cost objects are the individual engagements (audit engagements or tax engagements).

b. Identify each cost as being a direct or indirect cost assuming the cost objects are the two departments.

c. Identify each cost as being a direct or indirect cost assuming the cost object is Tilley Professional Services as a whole.

LO 4-2

Exercise 4-2B *Allocating costs between divisions*

Vega and Andersen LLP has three departments: auditing, tax, and information systems. The departments occupy 3,000 square feet, 2,500 square feet, and 2,500 square feet of office space, respectively. The firm pays $8,000 per month to rent its offices.

Required

How much monthly rent cost should Vega and Andersen allocate to each department?

LO 4-2

Exercise 4-3B *Allocating overhead cost to accomplish smoothing*

In Year 3, Santo Corporation incurred direct manufacturing costs of $56 per unit and manufacturing overhead costs of $600,000. The production activity for the four quarters of Year 3 are as follows.

	1st Quarter	2nd Quarter	3rd Quarter	4th Quarter
Number of units produced	4,000	3,000	5,000	8,000

Required

a. Calculate a predetermined overhead rate based on the number of units produced during the year.

b. Allocate overhead costs to each quarter using the overhead rate computed in Requirement *a*.

c. Using the overhead allocation determined in Requirement *b*, calculate the total cost per unit for each quarter.

LO 4-2

Exercise 4-4B *Pooling overhead cost*

Kenta Manufacturing Company produced 800 units of inventory in January Year 2. The company expects to produce an additional 7,200 units of inventory during the remaining 11 months of the year, for a total estimated production of 8,000 units in Year 2. Direct materials and direct labor costs are $60 and $75 per unit, respectively. Kenta expects to incur the following manufacturing overhead costs during the Year 2 accounting period.

Indirect materials	$ 6,000
Depreciation on equipment	24,000
Utilities cost	11,000
Salaries of plant manager and staff	96,000
Rental fee on manufacturing facilities	23,000

Required

a. Combine the individual overhead costs into a cost pool and calculate a predetermined overhead rate assuming the cost driver is number of units.

b. Determine the estimated cost of the 800 units of product made in January.

c. Is the cost computed in Requirement *b* actual or estimated? Could Kenta improve accuracy by waiting until December to determine the cost of products? Identify two reasons that a manager would want to know the cost of products in January. Discuss the relationship between accuracy and relevance as it pertains to this problem.

LO 4-3

Exercise 4-5B *Allocating overhead costs among products*

Trista Company manufactures three different sizes of automobile sunscreens: large, medium, and small. Trista expects to incur $300,000 of overhead costs during the next fiscal year. Other budget information for the coming year follows.

	Large	Medium	Small	Total
Direct labor hours	2,500	5,000	5,000	12,500
Machine hours	700	1,300	1,000	3,000

Required

a. Use direct labor hours as the cost driver to compute the allocation rate and the budgeted overhead cost for each product.

b. Use machine hours as the cost driver to compute the allocation rate and the budgeted overhead cost for each product.

c. Describe a set of circumstances where it would be more appropriate to use direct labor hours as the allocation base.

d. Describe a set of circumstances where it would be more appropriate to use machine hours as the allocation base.

Exercise 4-6B *Allocating overhead costs among products*

LO 4-3

Ascend Company makes three models of jump drives in its factory: J512, J1G, and J4G. The expected overhead costs for the next fiscal year are as follows.

Payroll for factory managers	$150,000
Factory maintenance costs	60,000
Factory insurance	30,000
Total overhead costs	$240,000

Ascend uses labor hours as the cost driver to allocate overhead cost. Budgeted labor hours for the products are as follows.

J512	2,000 hours
J1G	1,200
J4G	800
Total labor hours	4,000

Required

a. Allocate the budgeted overhead costs to the products.

b. Provide a possible explanation as to why Ascend chose labor hours, instead of machine hours, as the allocation base.

Exercise 4-7B *Allocating costs among products*

LO 4-3

Omega Company makes household plastic bags in three different sizes: Snack, Sandwich, and Storage. The estimated direct materials and direct labor costs are as follows.

Expected Costs	Snack	Sandwich	Storage
Direct materials	$112,000	$188,000	$450,000
Direct labor	60,000	116,000	324,000

Omega allocates two major overhead costs among the three products: $75,000 of indirect labor cost for workers who move various materials and products to different stations in the factory and $80,000 of employee pension costs.

Required

Determine the total cost of each product. Round your figures to three decimal points.

Exercise 4-8B *Allocating indirect cost over varying levels of production*

LO 4-3

Cornerstone Company's annual factory depreciation is $630,000. Cornerstone estimated it would operate the factory a total of 3,600 hours this year. The factory operated 300 hours in November and 200 hours in December.

Required

Why would Cornerstone need to allocate factory depreciation cost? How much depreciation cost should Cornerstone allocate to products made in November and those made in December?

LO 4-3

Exercise 4-9B ***Allocating indirect cost over varying levels of production***

On January 1, Lehmann Corporation paid the annual royalty of $720,000 for rights to use patented technology to make batteries for laptop computers. Lehmann plans to use the patented technology to produce five different models of batteries. Lehmann uses machine hours as a common cost driver and plans to operate its machines 45,000 hours in the coming year. The company used 3,000 machine hours in June and 3,600 hours in July.

Required

Why would Lehmann need to allocate the annual royalty payment rather than simply assign it in total to January production? How much of the royalty cost should Lehmann allocate to products made in June and those made in July?

LO 4-3

Exercise 4-10B ***Allocating a fixed cost***

Last year, Andy Conway bought an automobile for $28,000 to use in his taxi business. He expected to drive the vehicle for 140,000 miles before disposing of it for $3,500. Andy drove 4,000 miles this week and 2,400 miles last week.

Required

a. Determine the total cost of vehicle depreciation this week and last week. Round your figures to three decimal points.

b. Explain why allocating the vehicle cost would or would not be relevant to decision making.

LO 4-3

Exercise 4-11B ***How fixed cost allocation affects a pricing decision***

Monarch Manufacturing Company expects to make 72,000 travel sewing kits during Year 3. In January, the company made 1,800 kits. Materials and labor costs for January were $9,000 and $11,250, respectively. In February, Monarch produced 2,200 kits. Material and labor costs for February were $11,000 and $13,750, respectively. The company paid $180,000 for annual factory insurance on January 10, Year 3. Ignore other manufacturing overhead costs.

Required

Assuming that Monarch desires to sell its sewing kits for cost plus 20 percent of cost, what price should it charge for the kits produced in January and February?

LO 4-4

Exercise 4-12B ***Allocating joint product cost***

Underwood Food Corporation makes two products from soybeans: cooking oil and cattle feed. From a standard batch of 100,000 pounds of soybeans, Underwood produces 20,000 pounds of cooking oil and 80,000 pounds of cattle feed. Producing a standard batch costs $27,000. The sales prices per pound are $3.00 for cooking oil and $1.50 for cattle feed.

Required

a. Allocate the joint product cost to the two products using weight as the allocation base.

b. Allocate the joint product cost to the two products using market value as the allocation base.

LO 4-5

Exercise 4-13B ***Human factor***

Murphy Company builds custom sailboats. Murphy currently has three boats under construction. The estimated costs to complete each boat are shown as follows.

	Boat 1	Boat 2	Boat 3
Direct materials	$25,000	$32,000	$12,000
Direct labor	22,000	20,000	14,000

Murphy expects to incur $48,000 of indirect (overhead) costs in the process of making the boats.

c. If HealthSouth expected to produce 2,270,000 patient-days of service during 2017 and estimated its annual depreciation costs to be $190,000,000, what would have been its predetermined overhead charge per patient-day of service for depreciation? Explain the advantage of using this amount to determine the cost of providing one patient-day of service in February and March versus the amounts you computed in Requirement *b*.

d. If HealthSouth's management had estimated the profit per patient-day of service based on its budgeted production of 2,270,000 patient-days, would you expect its actual profit per patient-day of service to be higher or lower than expected? Explain.

ATC 4-2 Group Assignment *Selection of the cost driver*

Vulcan College School of Business is divided into three departments: accounting, marketing, and management. Relevant information for each of the departments follows.

Cost Driver	Accounting	Marketing	Management
Number of students	1,400	800	400
Number of classes per semester	64	36	28
Number of professors	20	24	10

Vulcan is a private school that expects each department to generate a profit. It rewards departments for profitability by assigning 20 percent of each department's profits back to that department. Departments have free rein as to how to use these funds. Some departments have used them to supply professors with computer technology. Others have expanded their travel budgets. The practice has been highly successful in motivating the faculty to control costs. The revenues and direct costs for the year follow.

	Accounting	Marketing	Management
Revenue	$29,600,000	$16,600,000	$8,300,000
Direct costs	24,600,000	13,800,000	6,600,000

Vulcan allocates to the School of Business $4,492,800 of indirect overhead costs such as administrative salaries and the costs of operating the registrar's office and the bookstore.

Required

a. Divide the class into groups and organize the groups into three sections. Assign each section a department. For example, groups in Sections 1, 2, and 3 should represent the Accounting Department, the Marketing Department, and the Management Department, respectively. Assume that the dean of the school is planning to assign an equal amount of the college overhead to each department. Have the students in each group prepare a response to the dean's plan. Each group should select a spokesperson who is prepared to answer the following questions:

(1) Is your group in favor of or opposed to the allocation plan suggested by the dean?

(2) Does the plan suggested by the dean provide a fair allocation? Why?

The instructor should lead a discussion designed to assess the appropriateness of the dean's proposed allocation plan.

b. Have each group select the cost driver (allocation base) that best serves the self-interest of the department it represents.

c. Consensus on Requirement *c* should be achieved before completing Requirement *d*. Each group should determine the amount of the indirect cost to be allocated to each department using the cost driver that best serves the self-interest of the department it represents. Have a spokesperson from each section go to the board and show the resulting income statement for each department.

d. Discuss the development of a cost driver(s) that would promote fairness rather than self-interest in allocating the indirect costs.

ATC 4-3 Research Assignment *Using real-world data from Coca-Cola Bottling Co. Consolidated*

Use the 2017 Form 10-K (year ended on December 31, 2017) for Coca-Cola Bottling Co. Consolidated to complete the following requirements. Be aware that Coca-Cola Bottling Co. Consolidated (COKE) is a separate company from The Coca-Cola Company (KO), so do not confuse them. To obtain the Form 10-K, you can use the EDGAR system (see Appendix A at the back of this text for instructions), or it can be found under the "Investor Relations" link on the company's corporate website at www.cokeconsolidated.com. The company's Form 10-K can be found under "SEC Filings." Be sure to read carefully the following sections of the document:

- Under "Item 1.Business," read the subsection titled "Seasonality" on page 13.
- Under "Item 2.Properties," on page 22.
- In the footnotes section of the report, under "Note 1—Summary of Significant Accounting Policies," read the following subsections:
- "Marketing Programs and Sales Incentives" on page 69.
- "Cost of Sales" on page 70.
- "Selling, Delivery and Administrative Expenses" on page 70.
- "Shipping and Handling Costs" on page 70.

Required

a. Does COKE consider *shipping and handling costs* and *advertising costs* to be direct or indirect costs in relation to the manufacturing of its products? Explain.

b. Assume that when COKE ships orders of finished goods from manufacturing locations to sales distribution centers each shipment includes several different products such as Coca-Cola, Sprite, Dr Pepper, and Seagrams Ginger Ale. If COKE wanted to allocate the shipping costs among the various products, what would be an appropriate cost driver? Explain the rationale for your choice.

c. Based on COKE's discussion of the seasonality of its business, should the depreciation of production equipment recorded in a given month be based on the volume of drinks produced that month, or should the depreciation for each month be 1/12th of the estimated annual depreciation COKE expects to incur? Explain your answer.

d. As Item 2. *Properties* indicates, COKE appears to have significant excess capacity at its plants. Approximately what percentage of available production capacity was *not* being used by COKE in 2017? What are some possible reasons COKE might want to have this much excess capacity? Explain.

ATC 4-4 Writing Assignment *Selection of the appropriate cost driver*

Bullions Enterprises Inc. (BEI) makes gold, silver, and bronze medals used to recognize outstanding athletic performance in regional and national sporting events. The per-unit direct costs of producing the medals follow.

	Gold	Silver	Bronze
Direct materials	$300	$130	$ 35
Labor	120	120	120

During 2015, BEI made 1,200 units of each type of medal for a total of 3,600 (1,200 × 3) medals. All medals are created through the same production process, and they are packaged and shipped in identical containers. Indirect overhead costs amounted to $324,000. BEI currently uses the number of units as the cost driver for the allocation of overhead cost. As a result, BEI allocated $90 ($324,000 ÷ 3,600 units) of overhead cost to each medal produced.

Required

The president of the company has questioned the wisdom of assigning the same amount of overhead to each type of medal. He believes that overhead should be assigned on the basis of the cost to produce the medals. In other words, more overhead should be charged to expensive gold medals, less to silver, and even less to bronze. Assume that you are BEI's chief financial officer. Write a memo responding to the president's suggestion.

ATC 4-5 Ethical Dilemma *Allocation to achieve fairness*

The American Acupuncture Association offers continuing professional education courses for its members at its annual meeting. Instructors are paid a fee for each student attending their courses but are charged a fee for overhead costs that is deducted from their compensation. Overhead costs include fees paid to rent instructional equipment such as overhead projectors, provide supplies to participants, and offer refreshments during coffee breaks. The number of courses offered is used as the allocation base for determining the overhead charge. For example, if overhead costs amount to \$5,000 and 25 courses are offered, each course is allocated an overhead charge of \$200 (\$5,000 ÷ 25 courses). Heidi McCarl, who taught one of the courses, received the following statement with her check in payment for her instructional services.

Instructional fees (20 students × \$50 per student)	\$1,000
Less: Overhead charge	(200)
Less: Charge for sign language assistant	(240)
Amount due instructor	\$ 560

Although Ms. McCarl was well aware that one of her students was deaf and required a sign language assistant, she was surprised to find that she was required to absorb the cost of this service.

Required

a. Given that the Americans with Disabilities Act stipulates that the deaf student cannot be charged for the cost of providing sign language, who should be required to pay the cost of sign language services?

b. Explain how allocation can be used to promote fairness in distributing service costs to people with disabilities. Describe two ways to treat the \$240 cost of providing sign language services that improve fairness.

ATC 4-6 Spreadsheet Assignment *Using Excel*

Brook Health Care Center Inc. has three clinics servicing the Birmingham metropolitan area. The company's legal services department supports the clinics. Moreover, its computer services department supports all of the clinics and the legal services department. The company uses the number of computer workstations as the cost driver for allocating the cost of computer services and the number of patients as the cost driver for allocating the cost of legal services. The annual cost of the Department of Legal Services was \$340,000, and the annual cost of the Department of Computer Services was \$250,000. Other relevant information follows.

	Number of Patients	Number of Workstations
Hoover Clinic	3,100	17
Eastwood Clinic	2,300	13
Gardendale Clinic	2,800	6
Legal Services	0	14

Required

a. Construct a spreadsheet like the one that follows, and allocate the service costs using the step method.

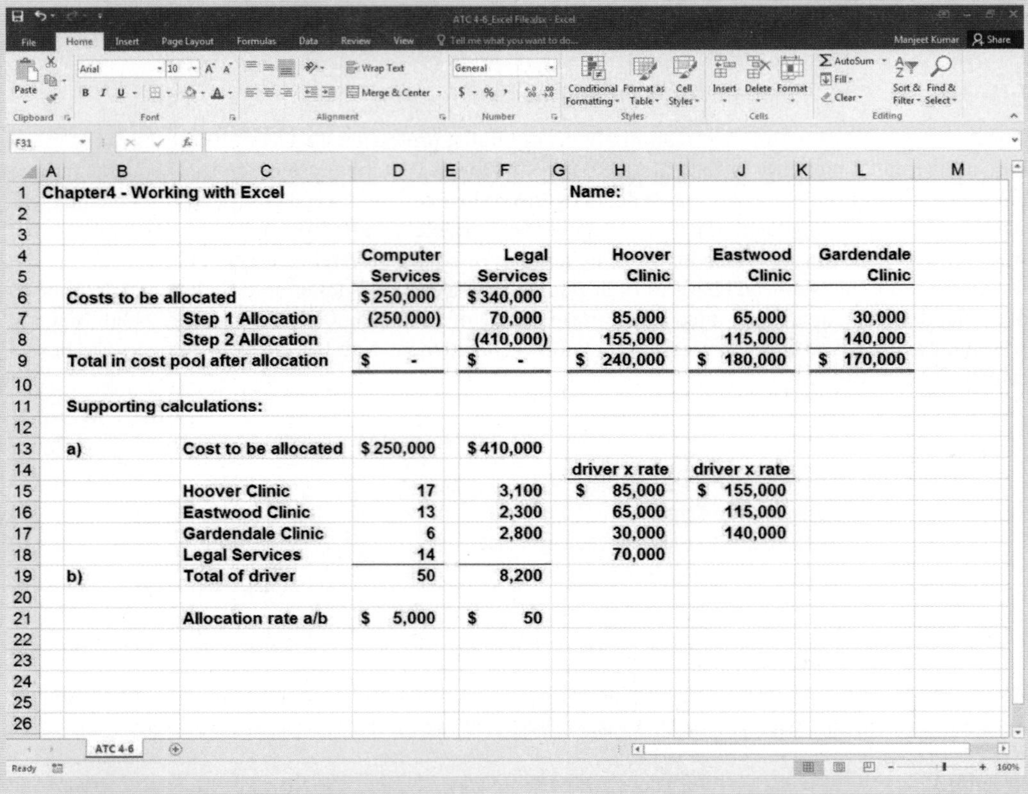

Row	B	C	D	F	H	J	L
1	Chapter4 - Working with Excel				Name:		
2							
3							
4			Computer	Legal	Hoover	Eastwood	Gardendale
5			Services	Services	Clinic	Clinic	Clinic
6	Costs to be allocated		$ 250,000	$ 340,000			
7		Step 1 Allocation	(250,000)	70,000	85,000	65,000	30,000
8		Step 2 Allocation		(410,000)	155,000	115,000	140,000
9	Total in cost pool after allocation		$ -	$ -	$ 240,000	$ 180,000	$ 170,000
10							
11	Supporting calculations:						
12							
13	a)	Cost to be allocated	$ 250,000	$ 410,000			
14					driver x rate	driver x rate	
15		Hoover Clinic	17	3,100	$ 85,000	$ 155,000	
16		Eastwood Clinic	13	2,300	65,000	115,000	
17		Gardendale Clinic	6	2,800	30,000	140,000	
18		Legal Services	14		70,000		
19	b)	Total of driver	50	8,200			
20							
21		Allocation rate a/b	$ 5,000	$ 50			

Source: Microsoft Excel 2010

Spreadsheet Tips

1. The headings in rows 4 and 5 are right-aligned. To right-align text, choose Format, then Cells, and then click on the tab titled Alignment, and set the horizontal alignment to Right. The shortcut method to right-align text is to click on the right-align icon in the middle of the second tool bar.
2. The supporting calculation section must be completed simultaneously with the allocation table. However, most of the supporting calculations can be completed first. The exception is that the value in cell F13 refers to the sum of cells F6 and F7.

ATC 4-7 Spreadsheet Assignment *Mastering Excel*

Phillips Paints manufactures three types of paint in a joint process: rubberized paint, rust-proofing paint, and aluminum paint. In a standard batch of 500,000 gallons of raw material, the outputs are 240,000 gallons of rubberized paint, 80,000 gallons of rust-proofing paint, and 180,000 gallons of aluminum paint. The production cost of a batch is $2,700,000. The sales prices per gallon are $15, $18, and $20 for rubberized, rust-proofing, and aluminum paint, respectively.

Required

a. Construct a spreadsheet to allocate joint costs to the three products using the number of gallons as the allocation base.

b. Include formulas in your spreadsheet to calculate the gross margin for each type of paint.

COMPREHENSIVE PROBLEM

Magnificent Modems has excess production capacity and is considering the possibility of making and selling paging equipment. The following estimates are based on a production and sales volume of 1,000 pagers.

Unit-level manufacturing costs are expected to be $20. Sales commissions will be established at $1 per unit. The current facility-level costs, including depreciation on manufacturing equipment ($60,000), rent on the manufacturing facility ($50,000), depreciation on the administrative equipment ($12,000), and other fixed administrative expenses ($71,950), will not be affected by the production of the pagers. The chief accountant has decided to allocate the facility-level costs to the existing product (modems) and to the new product (pagers) on the basis of the number of units of product made (i.e., 5,000 modems and 1,000 pagers).

Required

a. Determine the per-unit cost of making and selling 1,000 pagers.

b. Assuming the pagers could be sold at a price of $34 each, should Magnificent make the pagers?

c. Comment on the validity of using the number of units as an allocation base.

CHAPTER 5

Cost Management in an Automated Business Environment: ABC, ABM, and TQM

LEARNING OBJECTIVES

After you have mastered the material in this chapter, you will be able to:

LO 5-1 Explain how activity-based costing improves accuracy in determining the cost of products and services.

LO 5-2 Identify cost centers and cost drivers in an activity-based costing system.

LO 5-3 Use activity-based costing to calculate costs of products and services.

LO 5-4 Identify the components of a total quality management program and prepare a quality cost report.

Video lectures and accompanying self-assessment quizzes are available in Connect® for all learning objectives.

CHAPTER OPENING

Worldwide growth in capitalism has fostered an increasingly competitive global business environment. Companies have responded by using technology to increase productivity. Management accountants have worked with engineers to more accurately measure and control costs. They have eliminated many nonvalue-added activities and have employed quality control procedures that reduce costs and enhance customer satisfaction. These innovative business practices have enabled companies to eliminate unprofitable products and to promote products that maximize profitability. This chapter focuses on newer and emerging business practices employed by world-class companies.

The Curious Accountant

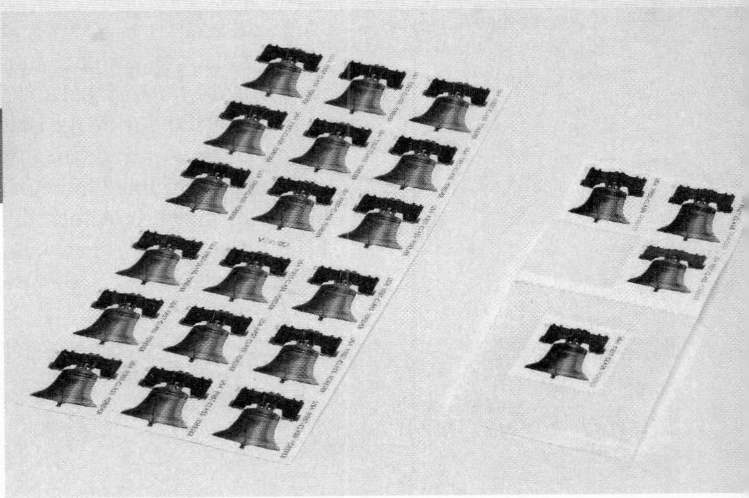

©McGraw-Hill Education/Mark Steinmetz, photographer

A vendor incurs a cost when it allows customers to pay using a credit or debit card. Credit card companies, such as **American Express**, charge the vendor either a fixed fee or a percentage of the transaction amount. For example, when the **United States Postal Service (USPS)** allows a customer to pay for $100 of stamps using a credit card, the USPS receives less than $100 from the credit card company, perhaps $97. The actual discount rate the credit card company charges depends on its agreement with the individual vendor. Large customers such as the USPS usually get better rates than smaller customers. Considering that total revenues at the USPS were $69.6 billion in 2017 and that $25.6 billion of these were from first-class mail, the costs of allowing customers to use debit and credit cards to pay for postage can be high.

Most companies that accept credit cards as payment do so believing that customers will spend more money using "plastic" than if forced to pay cash. Also, a company's competitors may be accepting credit cards, leaving the company little choice. However, the USPS has a virtual monopoly on many types of mail services in the United States, so why is it willing to allow customers to pay with credit cards? Why not make everyone pay with cash or checks?

Now consider this: Another large government agency, the **Internal Revenue Service (IRS)**, will not accept debit or credit card payments unless the taxpayer pays the credit card fee. If the USPS does not require a surcharge for credit card users, why does the IRS? (Answers on page 217.)

DEVELOPMENT OF A SINGLE COMPANYWIDE COST DRIVER

LO 5-1

Explain how activity-based costing improves accuracy in determining the cost of products and services.

When accountants first developed cost systems, manufacturing processes were labor intensive. Indirect manufacturing costs were relatively minor and highly correlated with labor use; products that used large amounts of labor consumed large amounts of overhead. This link made the number of labor hours a suitable cost driver for allocating overhead costs.

To illustrate, suppose during an eight-hour day Friedman Company production employees worked on two jobs, Job 1 for two hours and Job 2 for six hours. Friedman consumed utilities of $120 during the day. How much of the $120 should the company assign to each job? Friedman cannot trace the utility cost directly to a specific job, but the job that required more labor likely consumed more of the utility cost. The longer employees work, the more heat, lights, and water they use. Allocating the utility cost to the two jobs based on *direct labor hours* produces rational results. Friedman could allocate the utility cost at $15 per hour ($120 ÷ 8 hours). It could assign Job 1 $30 of the utility cost ($15 per hour × 2 hours) and Job 2 the remaining $90 ($15 × 6 hours).

©McGraw-Hill Education/Aaron Roeth Photography

In addition to utilities, direct labor drives many other indirect costs. Consider the depreciation cost of tools employees use while working on production jobs. The more time employees work, the more they use the tools. Direct labor hours could be an effective cost driver (allocation base) for allocating tool depreciation costs. The same logic applies to supervisory salaries, production supplies, factory rent expense, and other overhead costs. Many companies applied this reasoning to justify using direct labor hours as the *sole base* for establishing a **companywide allocation rate.** These companies then allocated all overhead costs to their products or other cost objects using the single labor-based, companywide overhead rate. Even though using one base to allocate all overhead costs inaccurately measured some cost objects, in the labor-intensive environment that spawned companywide allocation rates, overhead costs were relatively small compared to the costs of labor and materials. Allocation inaccuracies were relatively insignificant in amount.

Automation has changed the nature of manufacturing processes. The number of direct labor hours is no longer an effective allocation base in many modern manufacturing companies. Machines have replaced most human workers. Because they operate technically complex equipment, the remaining workers are highly skilled and not easily replaced. Companies resist laying off these trained workers when production declines. Neither do companies add employees when production increases. Adjusting production volume merely requires turning additional machines on or off. In such circumstances, direct labor is not related to production volume. Direct labor is therefore not an effective base for allocating overhead costs. Former labor-intensive companies that adopt automation usually must develop more sophisticated ways to allocate overhead costs.

When companies replace people with machines, overhead costs such as machinery depreciation and power usage become greater in proportion to total manufacturing costs. In highly automated companies, overhead costs may be greater than direct labor and direct materials costs combined. Although misallocating minor overhead amounts does little harm, misallocating major costs destroys the usefulness of accounting information and leads to poor decisions. Managers must consider how automation affects overhead cost allocation.

Effects of Automation on Selecting a Cost Driver

In an automated manufacturing environment, robots and sophisticated machinery, rather than human labor, transform raw materials into finished goods. To illustrate the effect of these changes on selecting a cost driver, return to the previous Friedman Company example. Suppose Friedman automates the production process for Job 2, replacing most labor with four hours of machine processing and reducing the number of direct labor hours required from six to one. Assume the new machinery acquired increases utility consumption and depreciation charges, raising daily overhead costs from \$120 to \$420. Because Job 1 requires two hours of direct labor and Job 2 now requires one hour of direct labor, Friedman's companywide allocation rate increases to \$140 per direct labor hour (\$420 ÷ 3 hours). The company would allocate \$280 (\$140 × 2 hours) of the total overhead cost to Job 1 and \$140 (\$140 × 1 hour) to Job 2. The pre- and postautomation allocations are compared here.

Product	Preautomation Cost Distribution	Postautomation Cost Distribution
Job 1	$ 30	$280
Job 2	90	140
Total	$120	$420

Using direct labor hours as the cost driver after automating production of Job 2 distorts the overhead cost allocation. Although Friedman did not change the production process for Job 1 at all, Job 1 received a \$250 (\$280 − \$30) increase in its share of allocated overhead cost. This increase should have been assigned to Job 2 because automating production of Job 2 caused overhead costs to increase. The decrease in direct labor hours for Job 2 causes the distortion. Prior to automation, Job 2 used six of eight total direct labor hours and was therefore allocated 75 percent (6 ÷ 8) of the overhead cost. After automation, Job 2 consumed only one of three total direct labor hours, reducing its overhead allocation to only 33 percent of the total. These changes in the allocation base, coupled with the increase in total overhead cost, caused the postautomation overhead cost allocation to be significantly overstated for Job 1 and significantly understated for Job 2.

One way to solve the misallocation problem is to find a more suitable volume-based cost driver. For example, Friedman could allocate utility costs using machine hours instead of direct labor hours. This text illustrated using different **volume-based cost drivers** (such as material dollars and direct labor hours) in Chapter 4. Unfortunately, automated production processes often generate costs that have no cause-and-effect relationship with volume-based cost drivers. Many companies have therefore adopted **activity-based cost drivers** to improve the accuracy of indirect cost allocations. To illustrate, consider the case of Carver Soup Company.

Activity-Based Cost Drivers

Carver Soup Company (CSC) produces batches of vegetable and tomato soup. Each time CSC switches production from vegetable soup to tomato soup or vice versa, it incurs certain costs. For example, production workers must clean the mixing, blending, and cooking equipment. They must change settings on the equipment to the specifications for the particular soup to be processed. CSC must test each batch for quality to ensure the recipe has been correctly followed. Because these costs are incurred for each new batch, they are called **start-up (setup) costs.** CSC plans to make 180 batches of each type of soup during the coming year. The following table summarizes expected production information.

	Vegetable	Tomato	Total
Number of cans	954,000	234,000	1,188,000
Number of setups	180	180	360

CSC expects each setup will cost $264, for total expected setup costs of $95,040 ($264 × 360 setups). Using number of cans as the cost driver (volume-based driver) produces an allocation rate of $0.08 per can ($95,040 ÷ 1,188,000 cans). Multiplying the allocation rate by the weight of the base (number of cans) produces the following setup cost allocation.

Product	Allocation Rate	×	Number of Cans Produced	=	Allocated Setup Cost
Vegetable	$0.08	×	954,000	=	$76,320
Tomato	0.08	×	234,000	=	18,720

As expected, the volume-based (number of cans) allocation rate assigns more cost to the high-volume vegetable soup product. However, assigning more setup cost to the vegetable soup makes little sense. Since both products require the *same number* of setups, the setup cost should be distributed equally between them. The volume-based cost driver *overcosts* the high-volume product (vegetable soup) and *undercosts* the low-volume product (tomato soup).

Setup costs are driven by the number of times CSC employees perform the setup activities. The more setups employees undertake, the greater the total setup cost. An *activity-based cost driver* (number of setups) provides a more accurate allocation base for setup costs. Using the allocation rate of $264 ($95,040 ÷ 360 setups) per setup assigns the same amount of setup cost to each product, as follows.

Product	Allocation Rate	×	Number of Setups	=	Allocated Setup Cost
Vegetable	$264	×	180	=	$47,520
Tomato	264	×	180	=	47,520

Activity-Based Cost Drivers Enhance Relevance

The *activity-based cost driver* produces a better allocation because it distributes the *relevant* costs to the appropriate products. If CSC were to stop producing tomato soup, it could *avoid* spending $47,520 for 180 setups (assuming CSC could eliminate labor, supplies, and other resources used in the setup process). *Avoidable costs are relevant* to decision making. The inaccurate volume-based product cost data could mislead a manager into making a poor decision. Suppose a company specializing in setup activities offered to provide CSC 180 tomato soup setups for $40,000. A manager relying on the volume-based allocated cost of $18,720 would reject the $40,000 offer to outsource as too costly. In fact, CSC should accept the offer because it could avoid $47,520 of cost if the outside company performs the setup activity. In a highly automated environment in which companies produce many different products at varying volume levels, it is little wonder that many companies have turned to activity-based costing to improve the accuracy of cost allocations and the effectiveness of decisions.

CHECK YOURSELF 5.1

Professional Training Services Inc. (PTSI) offers professional exam review courses for both the certified public accountant (CPA) and the certified management accountant (CMA) exams. Many more students take the CPA review courses than the CMA review courses. PTSI uses the same size and number of classrooms to teach both courses; its CMA courses simply have more empty seats. PTSI is trying to determine the cost of offering the two courses. The company's accountant has decided to allocate classroom rental cost based on the number of students enrolled in the courses. Explain why this allocation base will likely result in an inappropriate assignment of cost to the two cost objects. Identify a more appropriate allocation base.

Answer Using the number of students as the allocation base will assign more of the rental cost to the CPA review courses because those courses have higher enrollments. This allocation is inappropriate because the number of classrooms, not the number of students, drives the amount of rental cost. Since both courses require the same number of classrooms, the rental cost should be allocated equally between them. Several allocation bases would produce an equal allocation, such as the number of classrooms, the number of courses, or a 50/50 percentage split.

ACTIVITY-BASED COSTING

LO 5-2

Identify cost centers and cost drivers in an activity-based costing system.

A company that allocates indirect costs using **activity-based costing (ABC)** follows a two-stage process. In the first stage, costs are assigned to pools based on the activities that cause the costs to be incurred. In the second stage, the costs in the activity cost pools are allocated to products using a variety of cost drivers. The first step in developing an ABC system is to identify essential activities and the costs of performing those activities.

A business undertakes **activities** to accomplish its mission. Typical activities include acquiring raw materials, transforming raw materials into finished products, and delivering products to customers. These broadly defined activities can be divided into subcategories. For example, the activity of acquiring raw materials involves separate subcategory activities such as identifying suppliers, obtaining price quotations, evaluating materials specifications, completing purchase orders, and receiving purchased materials. Each of these subcategories can be subdivided into yet more detailed activities. For instance, identifying suppliers may include such activities as reviewing advertisements, searching Internet sites, and obtaining recommendations from business associates. Further subdivisions are possible. Companies perform thousands of activities.

Identifying Activity Centers

Maintaining separate cost records for thousands of activities is expensive. To reduce recordkeeping costs, companies group related activities into hubs called **activity centers.** The overhead costs of these related activities are combined into a cost pool for each activity center. Because the activities assigned to each center are related, a business can obtain rational cost allocations using a common cost driver for an entire cost pool. Determining the optimal number of activity centers requires *cost/benefit analysis.* Companies will incur the higher recordkeeping costs for additional activity centers only to the extent that the additional accuracy improves decision making.

Comparing ABC with Traditional Cost Allocation

How do ABC systems differ from traditional allocation systems? Traditional allocation systems pool costs by departments, then allocate departmental cost pools to cost objects using volume-based cost drivers. In contrast, ABC systems pool costs by activity centers, then

EXHIBIT 5.1

Traditional versus Activity-Based Costing Systems

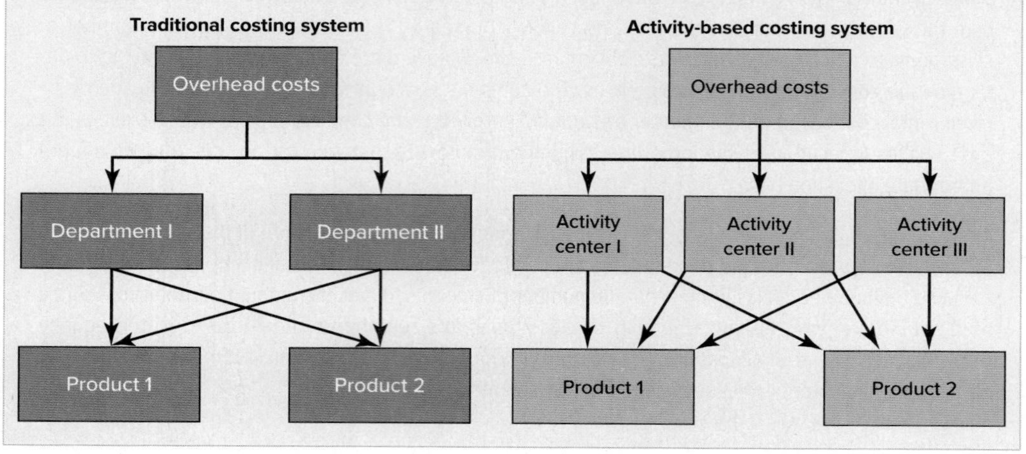

allocate activity center cost pools to cost objects using a variety of volume- and activity-based cost drivers. ABC systems use many more activity centers than the number of departments in a traditional allocation system. As a result, ABC improves cost tracing by using more cause-and-effect relationships in assigning indirect costs to numerous activity centers. Exhibit 5.1 illustrates the primary differences between a traditional two-stage allocation system and an ABC system.

Types of Production Activities

Many companies organize activities into four hierarchical categories to improve cost tracing. These categories are (1) unit-level activities, (2) batch-level activities, (3) product-level activities, and (4) facility-level activities.[1] The overhead costs in each category are pooled and allocated to products based on how the products benefit from the activities. *The primary objective is to trace the cost of performing activities to the products that are causing the activities to be performed.* To illustrate, consider the overhead costs incurred by Unterman Shirt Company.

Unterman has two product lines, dress shirts and casual shirts. The company expects to incur overhead costs of $5,730,000 in the course of producing 680,000 dress shirts and 120,000 casual shirts. Currently, Unterman assigns an equal amount of overhead to each shirt, simply dividing the total expected overhead cost by the total expected production ($5,730,000 ÷ 800,000 units = $7.16 per shirt, rounded). Each type of shirt requires approximately the same amount of direct materials, $8.20 per shirt, and the same amount of direct labor, $6.80 per shirt. The total cost per shirt is $22.16 ($7.16 + $8.20 + $6.80). Unterman sells shirts for $31.00 each, yielding a gross margin of $8.84 per shirt ($31.00 − $22.16).

Bob Unterman, president and owner of the company, believes the direct materials and direct labor costs are reasonable, but the overhead costs must not be the same for both product lines. Mr. Unterman hired a consultant, Rebecca Lynch, to trace the overhead costs. Ms. Lynch decided to use an *activity-based cost* system. She identified the activities necessary to make shirts and classified them into the following four activity cost centers.

Unit-Level Activity Center

Unit-level activities occur each time a unit of product is made. For example, for every shirt made, Unterman incurs inspection costs, machine-related utility costs, and costs for production

[1]The types of costs in each category will be covered in more detail in Chapter 6.

supplies. Total unit-level cost increases with every shirt made and decreases with reductions in production volume. Some costs behave so much like unit-level costs that they may be accounted for as unit-level even though they are not strictly unit-level. For example, suppose Unterman employees lubricate production machinery after every eight hours of continuous operation. Although Unterman does not incur lubrication cost for each shirt produced, the cost behavior pattern is so closely tied to production levels that it may be accounted for as a unit-level cost.

Ms. Lynch identified the following unit-level overhead costs: (1) $300,000 for machine-related utilities, (2) $50,000 for machine maintenance, (3) $450,000 for indirect labor and indirect materials, (4) $200,000 for inspection and quality control, and (5) $296,000 for miscellaneous unit-level costs. She assigned these costs into a single *unit-level activity center* overhead cost pool of $1,296,000. This assignment illustrates the first stage of the two-stage ABC allocation system. Of the total $5,730,000 overhead cost, Ms. Lynch has allocated $1,296,000 to one of the four activity centers. The remaining overhead cost is allocated among the three other activity centers.

The second-stage cost assignment involves allocating the $1,296,000 unit-level cost pool between the two product lines. Because unit-level costs are incurred each time a shirt is produced, they should be allocated using a base correlated to production levels. Ms. Lynch chose direct labor hours as the allocation base. Past performance indicates the dress shirts will require 272,000 direct labor hours and the casual shirts will require 48,000 direct labor hours. Based on this information, Ms. Lynch allocated the unit-level overhead costs and computed the cost per unit as shown in Exhibit 5.2.

EXHIBIT 5.2

Allocation of Unit-Level Overhead Costs

	Product Lines		
	Dress Shirts	Casual Shirts	Total
Number of direct labor hours (a)	272,000	48,000	320,000
Cost per labor hour ($1,296,000 ÷ 320,000 hours) (b)	$4.05	$4.05	NA
Total allocated overhead cost (c = a × b)	$1,101,600	$194,400	$1,296,000
Number of shirts (d)	680,000	120,000	800,000
Cost per shirt (c ÷ d)	$1.62	$1.62	NA

The unit-level costs exhibit a variable cost behavior pattern. Total cost varies in direct proportion to the number of units produced. Cost per unit is constant. Because production volume does not affect the unit-level overhead cost, the pricing of shirts should not be affected by the fact that the company makes more dress shirts than casual shirts.

Batch-Level Activity Center

Batch-level activities relate to producing groups of products. Batch-level costs are fixed regardless of the number of units produced in a single batch. For example, the costs of setting up machinery to cut fabric for a certain size shirt remain unchanged regardless of the number of shirts cut at that particular machine setting. Similarly, the cost of a first-item batch test is the same whether 200 or 2,000 shirts are made in the batch. Materials handling costs are also commonly classified as batch-level because materials are usually transferred from one department to another in batches. For example, all of the size small casual shirts are cut in the sizing department, then the entire batch of cut fabric is transferred in one operation to the sewing department. The cost of materials handling is the same regardless of whether the batch load is large or small.

Because total batch costs depend on the number of batches produced, more batch costs should be allocated to products that require more batches. Ms. Lynch identified $690,000 of total batch-level overhead costs and assigned this amount to a batch-level cost pool.

For the second-stage allocation, Ms. Lynch determined that the casual-shirt line requires considerably more setups than the dress-shirt line because the casual shirts are subject to frequent style changes. Because customers buy limited amounts of items with short shelf lives, Unterman must produce casual shirts in small batches. Ms. Lynch decided more of the batch-level costs should be allocated to the casual-shirt line than to the dress-shirt line. She chose number of setups as the most rational allocation base. Since casual shirts require 1,280 setups and dress shirts require 1,020 setups, Ms. Lynch allocated the batch-level costs as shown in Exhibit 5.3.

EXHIBIT 5.3

Allocation of Batch-Level Overhead Costs

	Product Lines		
	Dress Shirts	Casual Shirts	Total
Number of setups performed (a)	1,020	1,280	2,300
Cost per setup ($690,000 ÷ 2,300 setups) (b)	$300	$300	NA
Total allocated overhead cost (c = a × b)	$306,000	$384,000	$690,000
Number of shirts (d)	680,000	120,000	800,000
Cost per shirt (c ÷ d)	$0.45	$3.20	NA

ABC demonstrates that the per-shirt batch-level cost for casual shirts ($3.20 per shirt) is considerably more than for dress shirts ($0.45). One reason is that the casual-shirt line incurs more batch-level costs ($384,000 versus $306,000). The other is that Unterman produces far fewer casual shirts than dress shirts (120,000 units versus 680,000). Because batch-level costs are fixed relative to the number of units in a particular batch, the cost per unit is greater the smaller the batch. For example, if setup costs are $300, the setup cost per unit for a batch of 100 units is $3 ($300 ÷ 100 units). For a batch of only 10 units, however, the setup cost per unit is $30 ($300 ÷ 10 units). When batch-level costs are significant, companies should pursue high-volume products. Low-volume products are more expensive to make because the fixed costs must be spread over fewer units. To the extent that cost affects pricing, Unterman should charge more for casual shirts than dress shirts.

Product-Level Activity Center

Product-level activities support specific products or product lines. Examples include raw materials inventory holding costs; engineering development costs; and legal fees for patents, copyrights, trademarks, and brand names. Unterman Shirt Company positions itself as a fashion leader. It incurs extensive design costs to ensure that it remains a trendsetter. The company also incurs engineering costs to continually improve the quality of materials used in its shirts and legal fees to protect its brand names. After reviewing Unterman's operations, Ms. Lynch concluded she could trace $1,800,000 of the total overhead cost to the product-level activity center.

The second-stage allocation requires dividing these activities between the dress-shirt line and the casual-shirt line. Interviews with fashion design staff disclosed that they spend more time on casual shirts because of the frequent style changes. Similarly, the engineers spend more of their time developing new fabric, buttons, and zippers for casual shirts. The materials used in dress shirts are fairly stable. Although engineers spend some time improving the quality of dress-shirt materials, they devote far more time to the more unusual materials used in

EXHIBIT 5.4

Allocation of Product-Level Overhead Costs

	Product Lines		
	Dress Shirts	**Casual Shirts**	**Total**
Percent of product-level activity utilization (a)	30%	70%	100%
Total allocated overhead cost (b = a × $1,800,000)	$540,000	$1,260,000	$1,800,000
Total units produced (c)	680,000	120,000	800,000
Cost per unit (b ÷ c)	$0.79*	$10.50	NA

*Rounded to the nearest whole cent.

the casual shirts. Similarly, the legal department spends more time developing and protecting patents, trademarks, and brand names for the casual-shirt line. Ms. Lynch concluded that 70 percent of the product-level cost pool applied to casual shirts and 30 percent to dress shirts. She allocated product-level costs to the two product lines as shown in Exhibit 5.4.

Product-level costs are frequently distributed unevenly among different product lines. Unterman Shirt Company incurs substantially more costs to sustain its casual-shirt line than its dress-shirt line. Using a single companywide overhead rate in such circumstances distorts cost measurements. Distorted product cost measurements can lead to negative consequences such as irrational pricing policies and rewards for inappropriate decisions. Activity-based costing reduces measurement distortions by more accurately tracing costs to the products that cause their incurrence.

Facility-Level Activity Center

Facility-level activities benefit the production process as a whole and are not related to any specific product, batch, or unit of production. For example, insuring the manufacturing facility against fire losses does not benefit any particular product or product line. Facility-level costs include depreciation on the manufacturing plant, security, landscaping, plant maintenance, general utilities, and property taxes. For Unterman Shirt Company, Ms. Lynch identified $1,944,000 of facility-level overhead costs. Because no cause-and-effect relationship exists between these facility-level manufacturing costs and the two product lines, she must allocate these costs arbitrarily. Basing the arbitrary allocation on the total number of units produced, Ms. Lynch allocated 85 percent (680,000 ÷ 800,000) of the facility-level cost pool to the dress-shirt line and 15 percent (120,000 ÷ 800,000) to the casual-shirt line as shown in Exhibit 5.5.

EXHIBIT 5.5

Allocation of Facility-Level Overhead Costs

	Product Lines		
	Dress Shirts	**Casual Shirts**	**Total**
Percent of total units (a)	85%	15%	100%
Total allocated overhead cost (b = a × $1,944,000)	$1,652,400	$291,600	$1,944,000
Total units produced (c)	680,000	120,000	800,000
Cost per unit (b ÷ c)	$2.43	$2.43	NA

Classification of Activities Not Limited to Four Categories

The number of activity centers a business uses depends on cost/benefit analysis. The four categories illustrated for Unterman Shirt Company represent a useful starting point. Any of the four categories could be further subdivided into more detailed activity centers. Unterman could establish an activity cost center for unit-level labor-related activities and a different activity center for unit-level machine-related activities. Identifying all potential activity centers in a real-world company can be daunting. Paulette Bennett describes the process used in the Material Control Department at Compumotor Inc. as follows:

> Recognizing that ordinarily the two biggest problems with an ABC project are knowing where to start and how deep to go, we began by analyzing the activities that take place in our procurement process. As the old saying goes, to find the biggest alligators you usually have to wade into the weeds; therefore, we started by writing down all the procurement activities. Creating a real world picture of costs by activity was our aim. But had we used our initial list we would have designed a spreadsheet so large that no human could ever have emerged alive at the other end.[2]

Ms. Bennett's abbreviated list still included 83 separate activities. The list represented the activity centers for only one department of a very large company. Although the Unterman example used only four categories, the real-world equivalent is far more complex.

CHECK YOURSELF 5.2

Under what circumstances would the number of units produced be an inappropriate allocation base for batch-level costs?

Answer Using the number of units produced as the allocation base would allocate more of the batch-level costs to high-volume products and less of the costs to low-volume products. Since batch-level costs are normally related to the number of batches rather than the number of units made in each batch, allocation of batch-level costs based on units produced would result in poor product cost estimates; the costing system would overcost high-volume products and undercost low-volume products. It would be appropriate to use the number of units produced only when each batch consists of the same number of product units. Even under these circumstances, the number of units merely serves as a proxy for the number of batches. It would still be more appropriate to use the number of batches to allocate batch-level costs.

Context-Sensitive Classification of Activities

Particular activities could fall into any of the four hierarchical categories. For example, inspecting each individual item produced is a unit-level activity. Inspecting the first item of each batch to ensure the setup was correct is a batch-level activity. Inspecting a specific product line is a product-level activity. Finally, inspecting the factory building is a facility-level activity. To properly classify activities, you must learn to analyze the context within which they occur.

Selecting Cost Drivers

Activity-based costing uses both *volume-based* cost drivers and *activity-based* cost drivers. Volume-based drivers are appropriate for indirect costs that increase or decrease relative to the volume of activity. Using cost drivers such as units, direct labor hours, or machine hours

[2]Paulette Bennett, "ABM and the Procurement Cost Model," *Management Accounting,* March 1996, pp. 28–32.

is appropriate for unit-level activities. The flaw in traditional costing systems is that they use a volume-based measure (usually direct labor hours) to allocate all indirect costs. In contrast, the more sophisticated ABC approach uses activity drivers such as number of setups or percentage of utilization for overhead costs that are not influenced by volume. ABC improves the accuracy of allocations by using a combination of volume- and activity-based cost drivers.

USING ABC INFORMATION TO TRACE COSTS TO PRODUCT LINES

LO 5-3

Use activity-based costing to calculate costs of products and services.

Exhibit 5.6 summarizes the ABC allocations Ms. Lynch prepared. Mr. Unterman was shocked to learn that overhead costs for casual shirts are virtually three times those for dress shirts. Exhibit 5.7 compares the per-unit gross margins for the two product lines using the traditional cost system and using the ABC system. Recall that direct materials and direct labor costs for dress and casual shirts are \$8.20 and \$6.80, respectively. The difference in the margins is attributable to the overhead allocation. Using a traditional companywide overhead rate allocates an equal amount of overhead to each shirt (\$5,730,000 ÷ 800,000 units = \$7.16 per shirt). In contrast, the ABC approach assigns \$5.29 to each dress shirt and \$17.75 to each casual shirt. Total overhead cost is \$5,730,000 under both approaches. It is the *allocation*

EXHIBIT 5.6

ABC Overhead Cost Allocation

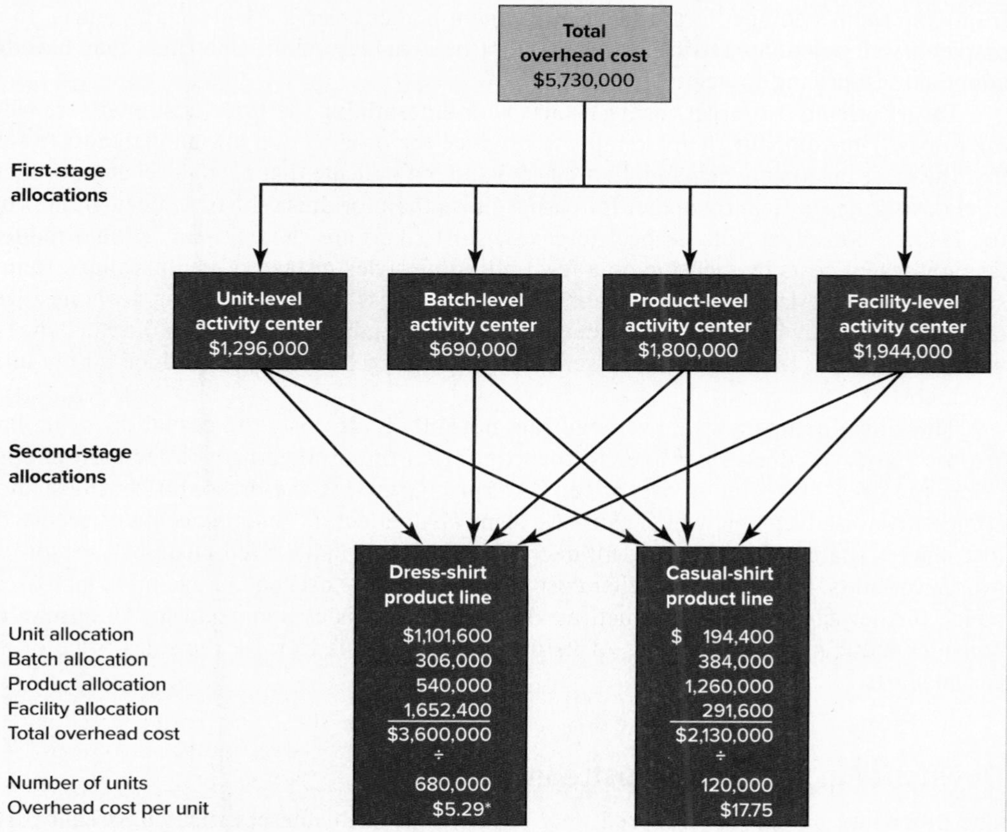

	Dress-shirt product line	Casual-shirt product line
Unit allocation	\$1,101,600	\$ 194,400
Batch allocation	306,000	384,000
Product allocation	540,000	1,260,000
Facility allocation	1,652,400	291,600
Total overhead cost	\$3,600,000	\$2,130,000
	÷	÷
Number of units	680,000	120,000
Overhead cost per unit	\$5.29*	\$17.75

*Rounded to the nearest whole cent.

EXHIBIT 5.7

Gross Margins Using Traditional versus ABC Costing

	Gross Margins Traditional System		Gross Margins ABC Costing	
	Dress Shirts	Casual Shirts	Dress Shirts	Casual Shirts
Sales price	$31.00	$31.00	$31.00	$ 31.00
Cost of goods sold				
Materials cost	(8.20)	(8.20)	(8.20)	(8.20)
Labor cost	(6.80)	(6.80)	(6.80)	(6.80)
Overhead	(7.16)	(7.16)	(5.29)	(17.75)
Gross margin	$ 8.84	$ 8.84	$10.71	$ (1.75)

of rather than the *amount* of the overhead cost that differs. ABC shows that making a casual shirt costs more than making a dress shirt. After reviewing the data in Exhibit 5.7, Mr. Unterman realized the company was incurring losses on the casual-shirt line. What options does he have?

Undercosting and Overcosting

In using the single companywide overhead rate, Unterman Shirt Company has undercosted its casual line and priced the shirts below cost. The obvious response to the ABC gross margin data in Exhibit 5.7 is to raise the price of casual shirts. Unfortunately, the market may not cooperate. If other companies are selling casual shirts at prices near $31, customers may buy from Unterman's competitors instead of paying a higher price for Unterman's shirts. In a market-driven economy, raising prices may not be a viable option. Unterman may have to adopt a target-pricing strategy.

Target pricing (or **target costing**) starts with determining the price customers are willing to pay. The company then attempts to produce the product at a low enough cost to sell it at the price customers demand. Exhibits 5.3 and 5.4 indicate that batch-level and product-level costs are significantly higher for casual shirts than for dress shirts. Unterman may be too fashion conscious with respect to casual shirts. Perhaps the company should reduce fashion design costs by focusing on a few traditional styles instead of maintaining a trend-setting position. Also, following established trends is less risky than setting new ones. Retail customers may have more confidence in the marketability of traditional casual shirts, which could lead them to place larger orders, enabling Unterman to reduce its per-unit batch costs.

The single companywide overhead rate not only undercosts the casual-shirt line but also overcosts the dress-shirt line. To the extent that the overhead cost affects the selling price, the dress-shirt line is overpriced. Overpricing places the dress-shirt business at a competitive disadvantage, which can have a snowball effect. If volume declines because of lost market share, sales revenue will decrease and Unterman's fixed costs will be spread over fewer units, resulting in a higher cost per unit. Higher costs encourage price increases, which further aggravate the competitive disadvantage. It is as important for Unterman to consider reducing the sales price of its dress shirts as it is to raise the sales price of its casual shirts.

Downstream Costs and Upstream Costs

The preceding paragraph analyzed only product costs. Businesses incur **upstream costs** before–and **downstream costs** after–goods are manufactured. Either upstream or downstream

Answers to the Curious Accountant

The USPS commissioned **Coopers & Lybrand (C&L)** (now **PricewaterhouseCoopers**), a large accounting firm, to conduct activity-based costing (ABC) studies of its key revenue collection processes. C&L developed an ABC model for USPS's existing cash and check revenue collection and a similar ABC model for debit and credit card activities. The ABC model identified costs associated with unit, batch, and product activities. *Unit-level activity* was defined as the acceptance and processing of a payment by item. *Batch-level activities* involved the closeout at the end of the day, consolidation, and supervisory review. *Product-level activities* included maintenance for bank accounts and deposit reconciliation for the cash and checks model and terminal maintenance and training for the credit and debit card system. A comparison of the cost of the two activity models revealed that a significant cost savings could be achieved in the long term by implementing a debit and credit card system. Some examples of expected cost savings included a decrease in the per-unit transaction cost due to the fact that credit card customers tend to spend more per transaction than do cash customers. In addition, the cost of activities associated with the collection of bad debts falls to virtually zero when debit or credit cards are used and the cost of cash management activities declines. Funds are collected earlier (no check collection float occurs), thereby reducing the need for financing and the resultant interest cost.

Payments received by the IRS are very different from those received by the USPS. The USPS experiences billions of payment transactions each year, many of which are for relatively small amounts; for example, a customer may pay to send one package priority mail for $6.75. The IRS receives fewer payments than the USPS, but most of these payments are for significantly larger amounts. Also, while the USPS has over 31,000 post offices processing payments, the IRS has less than a dozen payment processing centers. In ABC costing terms, the IRS has fewer unit-level activities and batch-level activities associated with processing payments than does the USPS, so the financial analysis used by the USPS is not relevant to the IRS. There is another very good reason the IRS does not accept credit card payments unless the taxpayer pays a surcharge; Congress passed a law stipulating this condition.

Source: Terrel L. Carter, Ali M. Sedghat, and Thomas D. Williams, "How ABC Changed the Post Office," *Management Accounting,* February 1998, pp. 28–36; and the USPS 2014 Annual Report.

costs may be relevant to product elimination decisions. For example, suppose Unterman pays sales representatives a $2 commission for each shirt sold. Although sales commissions are selling, not product, costs, they are relevant to deciding whether to eliminate the casual-shirt line. Unterman can avoid the commission expense if it sells no casual shirts. Including the sales commission increases the total avoidable cost to $34.75 ($32.75 product costs + $2.00 sales commissions) which is more than the $31.00 sales price. Unterman would therefore be more profitable if it abandoned the casual-shirt line. Management must also consider upstream costs such as those for research and development. To continue in business, companies must sell products at prices that exceed the *total* cost to develop, make, and sell them.

Employee Attitudes and the Availability of Data

Activity-based costing can lead management to implement cost-cutting measures, including product and product line eliminations, that can result in the loss of jobs. Employees are therefore sometimes uncooperative with management efforts to adopt an ABC system. Companies must help employees recognize that ABC and other **strategic cost management** techniques frequently result in redirecting workers rather than displacing them. Ultimately, jobs depend on the employer's competitive health. The implementation of an ABC system is more likely to succeed when both managers and rank-and-file employees are convinced their own well-being is tied to the company's well-being.

Even when employees cooperate, implementing an ABC system can be difficult. Frequently, the accounting system is not collecting some of the needed data. For example, suppose a manager wants to allocate inspection costs based on the number of hours job inspections take. Inspectors may not record the time spent on individual jobs. Basing the allocation on inspection hours requires inspectors to begin keeping more detailed time records. The accuracy of the allocation then depends on how conscientiously inspectors complete their time reports. Obtaining employee support and accurate data are two of the more challenging obstacles to successfully implementing ABC.

TOTAL QUALITY MANAGEMENT

LO 5-4

Identify the components of a total quality management program and prepare a quality cost report.

Quality is key to a company's ability to obtain and retain customers. What does *quality* mean? It does not always mean the best. A spoon made of silver is of higher quality than a spoon made of plastic, but customers are perfectly willing to use plastic spoons at fast-food restaurants. **Quality** represents the degree to which products or services *conform* to design specifications. The costs companies incur to ensure quality conformance can be classified into four categories: prevention, appraisal, internal failure, and external failure.

Companies incur **prevention costs** to avoid nonconforming products. They incur **appraisal costs** to identify nonconforming products produced in spite of prevention cost expenditures. **Failure costs** result from correcting defects in nonconforming products produced. **Internal failure costs** pertain to correcting defects before goods reach customers; **external failure costs** result from delivering defective goods to customers.

Because prevention and appraisal costs are a function of managerial discretion, they are often called **voluntary costs.** Management chooses how much to spend on these voluntary costs. In contrast, management does not directly control failure costs. The cost of dissatisfied customers may not be measurable, much less controllable. Even though failure costs may not be directly controllable, they are related to voluntary costs. When management spends additional funds on prevention and appraisal controls, failure costs tend to decline. As the level of control increases, quality conformance increases, reducing failure costs. When control activities are reduced, quality conformance decreases and failure cost increases. *Voluntary costs and failure costs move in opposite directions.*

EXHIBIT 5.8

Relationships among Components of Quality Cost

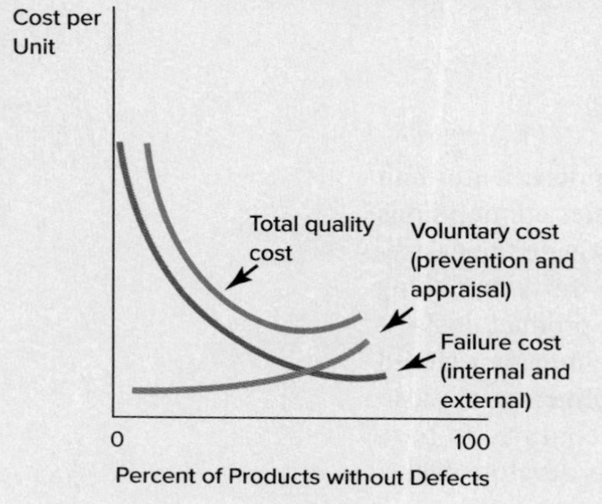

Minimizing Total Quality Cost

Total quality control cost is the sum of voluntary costs plus failure costs. Because voluntary costs and failure costs are negatively correlated, the minimum amount of *total* quality cost is located at the point on a graph where the marginal voluntary expenditures equal the marginal savings on failure cost as shown in Exhibit 5.8.

Exhibit 5.8 indicates that the minimum total quality cost per unit occurs at a quality level of less than 100 percent. At very low levels of quality assurance, significant failure costs outweigh any cost savings available by avoiding voluntary costs. In contrast, extremely high levels of quality assurance result in voluntary cost expenditures that are not offset by failure cost savings. Although the goal of zero defects is appealing, it is not a cost-effective strategy. Realistic managers seek to minimize total quality cost rather than to eliminate all defects.

CHECK YOURSELF 5.3

Is it wiser to spend money on preventing defects or on correcting failures?

Answer The answer depends on where a company's product falls on the "total quality cost" line (see Exhibit 5.8). If the product falls left of the cost minimization point, spending more on preventing defects would produce proportionately greater failure cost savings. In other words, a company would spend less in total by reducing failure costs through increasing prevention costs. Under these circumstances, it would be wise to incur prevention costs. On the other hand, if the product falls right of the cost minimization point line, the company would spend more to prevent additional defects than it would save by reducing failure costs. Under these circumstances, it makes more sense to pay the failure costs than attempt to avoid them by incurring prevention costs.

FOCUS ON INTERNATIONAL ISSUES

THE UNDERLYING CONCEPTS OF ACTIVITY BASED COSTING (ABC)

ABC can be traced back to the 1970s. Its application in business was greatly enhanced by articles written by Robin Cooper and Robert Kaplan that were published in *Harvard Business Review* in the late 1980s. Although ABC's origins are in the United States from more than 30 years ago, ABC continues to find contemporary applications throughout the world.

©FDR Stock/Shutterstock

An article published in *ComputerWeekly.com* in 2015 reported on how ABC and activity-based management are being used by the **Antwerp Port Authority** in The Netherlands to manage operations at one of Europe's largest ports. The advantages of using ABC at the Antwerp Port Authority include:

- Improved measurement of the cost to operate each terminal.
- Allowed managers to improve their operations by calculating a profit or loss for each department.
- Improved transfer pricing.
- Improved strategic planning.

In the future, the Port Authority hopes to use ABC to calculate an accurate measure of profit per customer.

Source: ComputerWeekly.com, January 2, 2015.

Quality Cost Reports

Managing quality costs to achieve the highest level of customer satisfaction is known as **total quality management (TQM).** Accountants support TQM by preparing a **quality cost report,** which typically lists the company's quality costs and analyzes horizontally each item as a percentage of the total cost. Data are normally displayed for two or more accounting periods to disclose the effects of changes over time. Exhibit 5.9 shows a quality cost report for Unterman Shirt Company. The company's accountant prepared the report to assess the effects of a quality control campaign the company recently initiated. Review Exhibit 5.9. What is Unterman's quality control strategy? Is it succeeding?

Exhibit 5.9 indicates Unterman is seeking to control quality costs by focusing on appraisal activities. The total expenditures for prevention activities remained unchanged, but expenditures for appraisal activities increased significantly. The results of this strategy are apparent in the failure cost data. Internal failure costs increased significantly while external failure costs decreased dramatically. The strategy succeeded in lowering total quality costs. The report suggests, however, that more improvement is possible. Notice that 86.13 percent (appraisal 19.63 percent + internal failure 39.01 percent + external failure 27.49 percent) of total quality costs is spent on finding and correcting mistakes. The adage "an ounce of prevention is worth a pound of cure," applied to Unterman, implies spending more on prevention could perhaps eliminate many of the appraisal and failure costs.

EXHIBIT 5.9

Quality Cost Report for Unterman Shirt Company

	Year 2		Year 1	
	Amount	Percentage*	Amount	Percentage*
Prevention costs				
Product design	$ 50,000	6.54%	$52,000	6.60%
Preventive equipment (depreciation)	7,000	0.92	7,000	0.89
Training costs	27,000	3.53	25,000	3.17
Promotion and awards	22,000	2.88	22,000	2.79
Total prevention	106,000	13.87	106,000	13.45
Appraisal costs				
Inventory inspection	75,000	9.82	25,000	3.17
Reliability testing	43,000	5.63	15,000	1.90
Testing equipment (depreciation)	20,000	2.62	12,000	1.52
Supplies	12,000	1.57	8,000	1.02
Total appraisal	150,000	19.63	60,000	7.61
Internal failure costs				
Scrap	90,000	11.78	40,000	5.08
Repair and rework	140,000	18.32	110,000	13.96
Downtime	38,000	4.97	20,000	2.54
Reinspection	30,000	3.93	12,000	1.52
Total internal failure	298,000	39.01	182,000	23.10
External failure costs				
Warranty repairs and replacement	120,000	15.71	260,000	32.99
Freight	20,000	2.62	50,000	6.35
Customer relations	40,000	5.24	60,000	7.61
Restocking and packaging	30,000	3.93	70,000	8.88
Total external failure	210,000	27.49	440,000	55.84
Grand total	$764,000	100.00%	$788,000	100.00%

*Percentages do not add exactly because of rounding.

REALITY BYTES

©Carlos Delgado/AP Images

Improving the quality of a product can increase its cost. Are the benefits of the higher quality worth the higher cost? Are companies that spend money to improve their quality, relative to their competitors, rewarded with higher profit margins? This is a difficult question to answer empirically because, among other things, there is not always a definite, objective way to measure the quality of competing products or services.

Nevertheless, we can make some general comparisons based on objective data available for automobile manufacturers. Every year, J.D. Power and Associates releases reports on various aspects of quality among auto manufacturers, including the *Vehicle Dependability Study (VDS)*. This study surveys owners who have had their cars for three years, asking what problems they have experienced related to their vehicles' dependability over the past 12 months.

In February 2017, J.D. Power released its annual *VDS* that looked at the reliability of 2014 car models. The survey was conducted by 31 brand names, such as Chevrolet, Cadillac, Lexus, and Porsche, rather than by manufacturer, such as General Motors. Toyota had the highest-ranked nameplate, Lexus, and the Toyota nameplate was ranked third. By contrast, four of the five nameplates that Fiat Chrysler Automobiles sells in the United States were in the five lowest-rated brands, and the Fiat nameplate itself was the lowest rated of all 31 vehicles.

What about these companies' comparative profitability? The following table shows returns on sales ratios (Net income ÷ Sales) and the return on assets ratios (Net income ÷ Assets) for Toyota and Fiat Group for their 2016 and 2015 fiscal years. The data show that Toyota, with better quality ratings, had better financial results than Fiat Group. It would certainly be an oversimplification to attribute all of Toyota's financial success to its higher-quality evaluations, but over several years the results in terms of relative quality rating and relative profitability have been reasonably consistent for Fiat and Toyota.

	2016		2015	
	Return on Sales	Return on Assets	Return on Sales	Return on Assets
Fiat Chrysler	1.6%	1.7%	0.4%	0.3%
Toyota	7.0	4.0	8.6	5.1

A Look Back <<

Many traditional cost systems used direct labor hours as the sole base for allocating overhead costs. Labor hours served as an effective *companywide allocation base* because labor was highly correlated with overhead cost incurrence. It made sense to assign more overhead to cost objects that required more labor. Because direct labor was related to production volume, it was frequently called a *volume-based cost driver.* Other volume-based cost drivers included machine hours, number of units, and labor dollars. Companywide, volume-based cost drivers were never perfect measures of overhead consumption. However, misallocation was not a serious problem because overhead costs were relatively small. If a manager misallocated an insignificant cost, it did not matter.

Automation has changed the nature of the manufacturing process. This change may cause significant distortions in the allocation of overhead costs when the allocation base is a companywide, volume-based cost driver. There are two primary reasons for distortions. First, in an automated environment, the same amount of labor (e.g., flipping a switch) may produce a large or a small volume of products. Under these circumstances, labor use is not related to the incurrence of overhead and is not a rational allocation base. Second, the distortions may be significant because overhead costs are much higher relative to the cost of labor and materials. For example, when robots replace people in the production process, depreciation becomes a larger portion of total product cost and labor becomes a smaller portion of the total.

To improve the accuracy of allocations, managerial accountants began to study the wide array of activities required to make a product. Such activities may include acquiring raw materials, materials handling and storage activities, product design activities, legal activities, and traditional production labor activities. Various measures of these activities can be used as bases for numerous overhead allocations related to determining product cost. Using activity measures to allocate overhead costs has become known as *activity-based costing (ABC).* In an ABC system, costs are allocated in a two-stage process. First, activities are organized into *activity centers* and the related costs of performing these activities are combined into *cost pools.* Second, the pooled costs are allocated to designated cost objects using activity-based cost drivers. Implementing ABC is most likely to succeed when employees understand that it will positively affect their fate and that of the company. Without employee cooperation, collecting data necessary for the system's success may be difficult.

Many ABC systems begin by organizing activities into one of four categories. Total *unit-level activity cost* increases each time a unit of product is made and decreases when production volume declines. Unit-level activity costs can be allocated with a base correlated to the level of production (volume-based cost drivers). *Batch-level activities* are related to producing groups of products. Their costs are fixed regardless of the number of units in a batch. Batch-level costs are assigned so that the products requiring the most batches are assigned the most batch costs. *Product-level activities* support a specific product or product line. Product-level costs are frequently assigned to products based on the product's percentage use of product-level activities. *Facility-level activities* are performed for the benefit of the production process as a whole. The allocation of these costs is often arbitrary.

Accurate allocations prevent the distortions of overcosted or undercosted products. Overcosting can cause a product line to be overpriced. Overpriced products may cause a company to lose market share, and the decline in sales revenue will cause profits to fall. When products are underpriced, revenue is less than it could be, and profitability suffers.

Product costs are frequently distinguished from upstream and downstream costs. *Upstream costs* result from activities that occur *before* goods are manufactured. Examples include research and development, product design, and legal work. *Downstream costs* result from activities that occur *after* goods are manufactured. Examples of downstream costs include selling and administrative expenses. Upstream and downstream costs affect pricing decisions and product elimination decisions.

Quality is key to a company's ability to obtain and retain customers. The costs companies incur to ensure quality conformance can be classified into four categories: prevention, appraisal, internal failure, and external failure. Prevention and appraisal costs are sometimes called voluntary costs because these costs are incurred at management's discretion. Internal and external failure costs are frequently grouped together and referred to singularly as failure costs. *Total quality control cost* is the sum of voluntary costs plus failure costs. Because voluntary costs and failure costs are negatively correlated, the minimum amount of *total* quality cost is located at the point on a graph where the marginal voluntary expenditures equal the marginal savings on failure cost

>> A Look Forward

The next chapter introduces the concept of cost relevance. Applying the concepts you have learned to real-world business problems can be challenging. Frequently, so much data are available that it is difficult to distinguish important from useless information. The next chapter will help you learn to identify information that is relevant in a variety of short-term decision-making scenarios, including special offers, outsourcing, segment elimination, and asset replacement.

Video lectures and accompanying self-assessment quizzes are available in *Connect* for all learning objectives.

SELF-STUDY REVIEW PROBLEM

Adventure Luggage Company makes two types of airline carry-on bags. One bag type designed to meet mass-market needs is constructed of durable polyester. The other bag type is aimed at the high-end luxury market and is made of genuine leather. Sales of the polyester bag have declined recently because of stiff price competition. Indeed, Adventure would have to sell this bag at less than production cost to match the competition. Adventure's president suspects that something is wrong with how the company estimates the bag's cost. He has asked the company's accountant to investigate that possibility. The accountant gathered the following information relevant to estimating the cost of the company's two bag types.

Both bags require the same amount of direct labor. The leather bags have significantly higher materials costs, and they require more inspections and rework because of higher quality standards. Since the leather bags are produced in smaller batches of different colors, they require significantly more setups. Finally, the leather bags generate more legal costs due to patents and more promotion costs because Adventure advertises them more aggressively. Specific cost and activity data follow.

	Polyester Bags	Leather Bags
Per unit direct materials cost	$30	$90
Per unit direct labor cost	2 hours @ $14 per hour	2 hours @ $14 per hour
Annual sales volume	7,000 units	3,000 units

Total annual overhead costs are $872,000. Adventure currently allocates overhead costs using a traditional costing system based on direct labor hours.

To reassess the overhead allocation policy and the resulting product cost estimates, the accountant subdivided the overhead into four categories and gathered information about these cost categories and the activities that caused the company to incur the costs. These data follow.

			Amount of Cost Driver		
Category	**Estimated Cost**	**Cost Driver**	**Polyester**	**Leather**	**Total**
Unit level	$480,000	Number of machine hours	20,000	60,000	80,000
Batch level	190,000	Number of machine setups	1,500	3,500	5,000
Product level	152,000	Number of inspections	200	600	800
Facility level	50,000	Equal percentage	50%	50%	100%
Total	$872,000				

Required

a. Determine the total cost and cost per unit for each product line, assuming that Adventure allocates overhead costs to each product line using direct labor hours as a companywide allocation base. Also determine the combined cost of the two product lines.

b. Determine the total cost and cost per unit for each product line, assuming that Adventure allocates overhead costs using an ABC system. Determine the combined cost of the two product lines.

c. Explain why the total combined cost computed in Requirements *a* and *b* is the same. Given that the combined cost is the same using either system, why is an ABC system with many different allocation rates better than a traditional system with a single companywide overhead rate?

Solution to Requirement *a*

Predetermined Overhead Rate

Polyester		Leather		
2 hours × 7,000 units	+	2 hours × 3,000 units	=	20,000 hours
14,000 direct labor hours		6,000 direct labor hours		

$$\text{Allocation rate} = \$872{,}000 \div 20{,}000 \text{ hours} = \$43.60 \text{ per direct labor hour}$$

Allocated Overhead Costs

Type of Bag	Allocation Rate	×	Number of Hours	=	Allocated Cost
Polyester	$43.60	×	14,000	=	$610,400
Leather	43.60	×	6,000	=	261,600
Total			20,000		$872,000

Total Cost of Each Product Line and Combined Cost

Type of Bag	Direct Materials*	+	Direct Labor†	+	Allocated Overhead	=	Total
Polyester	$210,000	+	$196,000	+	$610,400	=	$1,016,400
Leather	270,000	+	84,000	+	261,600	=	615,600
Total	$480,000	+	$280,000	+	$872,000	=	$1,632,000

*Direct materials
- Polyester $30 × 7,000 units = $210,000
- Leather $90 × 3,000 units = $270,000

†Direct labor
- Polyester $14 × 14,000 hours = $196,000
- Leather $14 × 6,000 hours = $84,000

Cost per Unit Computations Using Traditional Cost System

Type of Bag	Total Cost	÷	Units	=	Cost per Unit
Polyester	$1,016,400	÷	7,000	=	$145.20
Leather	615,600	÷	3,000	=	205.20
Total	$1,632,000				

Solution to Requirement *b*

Overhead Cost Allocation Using ABC

	Unit	Batch	Product	Facility	Total
Cost pool	$480,000	$190,000	$152,000	$50,000	$872,000
÷ Cost drivers	Number of machine hours	Number of setups	Number of inspections	Equally	
	80,000	5,000	800	50%	
= Rate	$6 per machine hour	$38 per setup	$190 per inspection	$25,000	

Overhead Allocation for Polyester Bags

	Unit	Batch	Product	Facility	Total
Weight	20,000	1,500	200	1	
× Rate	$ 6	$ 38	$ 190	$25,000	
Allocation	$120,000	$57,000	$38,000	$25,000	$240,000

Overhead Allocation for Leather Bags

	Unit	Batch	Product	Facility	Total
Weight	60,000	3,500	600	1	
× Rate	$ 6	$ 38	$ 190	$25,000	
Allocation	$360,000	$133,000	$114,000	$25,000	$632,000

Total Cost of Each Product Line and Combined Cost

Type of Bag	Direct Materials	+	Direct Labor	+	Allocated Overhead	=	Total
Polyester	$210,000	+	$196,000	+	$240,000	=	$ 646,000
Leather	270,000	+	84,000	+	632,000	=	986,000
Total	$480,000	+	$280,000	+	$872,000	=	$1,632,000

Cost per Unit Computations under ABC System

Type of Bag	Total Cost	÷	Units	=	Cost per Unit
Polyester	$ 646,000	÷	7,000	=	$ 92.29
Leather	986,000	÷	3,000	=	328.67
Total	$1,632,000				

Solution to Requirement *c*

The allocation method (ABC versus traditional costing) does not affect the total amount of cost to be allocated. Therefore, the total cost is the same using either method. However, the allocation method (ABC versus traditional costing) does affect the cost assigned to each product line. Since the ABC system more accurately traces costs to the products that cause the costs to be incurred, it provides a more accurate estimate of the true cost of making the products. The difference in the cost per unit using ABC versus traditional costing is significant. For example, the cost of the polyester bag was determined to be $145.20 using the traditional allocation method and $92.29 using ABC. This difference could have led Adventure to overprice the polyester bag, thereby causing the decline in sales volume. To the extent that ABC is more accurate, using it will improve pricing and other strategic decisions that significantly affect profitability.

KEY TERMS

Activities 209
Activity-based cost drivers 207
Activity-based costing (ABC) 209
Activity centers 209
Appraisal costs 218
Batch-level activities 211
Companywide allocation rate 206
Downstream costs 216
External failure costs 218
Facility-level activities 213
Failure costs 218
Internal failure costs 218
Prevention costs 218
Product-level activities 212
Quality 218
Quality cost report 220
Start-up (setup) costs 207
Strategic cost management 218
Target pricing (target costing) 216
Total quality management (TQM) 220
Unit-level activities 210
Upstream costs 216
Volume-based cost drivers 207
Voluntary costs 218

QUESTIONS

1. Why did traditional costing systems base allocations on a single companywide cost driver?
2. Why are labor hours ineffective as a companywide allocation base in many industries today?
3. What is the difference between volume-based cost drivers and activity-based cost drivers?
4. Why do activity-based cost drivers provide more accurate allocations of overhead in an

automated manufacturing environment?

5. When would it be appropriate to use volume-based cost drivers in an activity-based costing system?
6. Martinez Manufacturing makes two products, one of which is produced at a significantly higher volume than the other. The low-volume product consumes more of the company's engineering resources because it is technologically complex. Even so, the company's cost accountant chose to allocate engineering department costs based on the number of units produced. How could selecting this allocation base affect a decision about outsourcing engineering services for the low-volume product?
7. Briefly describe the activity-based costing allocation process.
8. Tom Rehr made the following comment: "Facility-level costs should not be allocated to products because they are irrelevant for decision-making purposes." Do you agree or disagree with this statement? Justify your response.
9. To facilitate cost tracing, a company's activities can be subdivided into four hierarchical categories. What are these four categories? Describe them and give at least two examples of each category.
10. Beth Nelson, who owns and runs a small sporting goods store, buys most of her merchandise directly from manufacturers. Ms. Nelson was shocked at the $7.50 charge for a container of three ping-pong balls. She found it hard to believe that it could have cost more than $1.00 to make the balls. When she complained to Jim Wilson, the marketing manager of the manufacturing company, he tried to explain that the cost also included companywide overhead costs. How could companywide overhead affect the cost of ping-pong balls?
11. If each patient in a hospital is considered a cost object, what are examples of unit-, batch-, product-, and facility-level costs that would be allocated to this object using an activity-based costing system?
12. Milken Manufacturing has three product lines. The company's new accountant, Marvin LaSance, is responsible for allocating facility-level costs to these product lines. Mr. LaSance is finding the allocation assignment a daunting task. He knows there have been disagreements among the product managers over the allocation of facility costs, and he fears being asked to defend his method of allocation. Why would the allocation of facility-level costs be subject to disagreements?
13. Why would machine hours be an inappropriate allocation base for batch-level costs?
14. Alisa Kamuf's company has reported losses from operations for several years. Industry standards indicate that prices are normally set at 30 percent above manufacturing cost, which Ms. Kamuf has done. Assuming that her other costs are in line with industry norms, how could she continue to lose money while her competitors earn a profit?
15. Issacs Corporation produces two lines of pocket knives. The Arrowsmith product line involves very complex engineering designs; the Starscore product line involves relatively simple designs. Since its introduction, the low-volume Arrowsmith products have gained market share at the expense of the high-volume Starscore products. This pattern of sales has been accompanied by an overall decline in company profits. Why may the existing cost system be inadequate?
16. What is the relationship between activity-based management and just-in-time inventory?

MULTIPLE-CHOICE QUESTIONS

Multiple-choice questions are available in *Connect*.

EXERCISES—SERIES A

All applicable Exercises in Series A are available in *Connect*.

LO 5-2

Exercise 5-1A *Classifying the costs of unit-, batch-, product-, or facility-level activities*

Tanner Manufacturing is developing an activity-based costing system to improve overhead cost allocation. One of the first steps in developing the system is to classify the costs of performing production activities into activity cost pools.

Required

Using your knowledge of the four categories of activities, classify the cost of each activity in the following list into unit-, batch-, product-, or facility-level cost pools.

Cost Activity	Cost Pool
a. Plant security	
b. Ordering materials for a specific type of product	
c. Wages of workers moving units of work between workstations	
d. Factorywide electricity	
e. Salary of a manager in charge of a product line	
f. Sales commissions	
g. Engineering product design	
h. Supplies	
i. Wages of maintenance staff	
j. Labeling and packaging	

Exercise 5-2A *Identifying appropriate cost drivers* LO 5-2

Required

Provide at least one example of an appropriate cost driver (allocation base) for each of the following activities:

a. Engineering drawings are produced for design changes.
b. Purchase orders are issued.
c. Products are labeled, packaged, and shipped.
d. Machinists are trained on new computer-controlled machinery.
e. Lighting is used for production facilities.
f. Materials are unloaded and stored for production.
g. Maintenance is performed on manufacturing equipment.
h. Sales commissions are paid.
i. Direct labor is used to change machine configurations.
j. Production equipment is set up for new production runs.

Exercise 5-3A *Classifying costs and identifying the appropriate cost driver* LO 5-2

Anniston Manufacturing incurred the following costs during Year 2 to produce its high-quality precision instruments. The company used an activity-based costing system and identified the following activities:

1. Depreciation on manufacturing equipment.
2. Materials handling.
3. Inventory storage.
4. Inspection of each batch produced.
5. Salaries of receiving clerks.
6. Setup for each batch produced.
7. Insurance on production facilities.

Required

a. Classify each activity as a unit-level, batch-level, product-level, or facility-level activity.
b. Identify an appropriate cost driver (allocation base) for each activity.

Exercise 5-4A *Context-sensitive nature of activity classification* LO 5-2

Required

Describe a set of circumstances in which the cost of painting could be classified as a unit-level, a batch-level, a product-level, or a facility-level cost.

LO 5-2, 5-3

Exercise 5-5A *Context-sensitive nature of activity classification*

Evert Company makes two types of circuit boards. One is a high-caliber board designed to accomplish the most demanding tasks; the other is a low-caliber board designed to provide limited service at an affordable price. During its most recent accounting period, Evert incurred $540,000 of inspection cost. Evert recently established an activity-based costing system that classifies its activities into four categories. Categories and appropriate cost drivers follow.

	Direct Labor Hours	Number of Batches	Number of Inspectors	Number of Square Feet
High caliber	6,000	20	3	30,000
Low caliber	21,000	20	2	70,000
Total	27,000	40	5	100,000

Required

Allocate the inspection cost between the two products assuming that it is driven by (a) unit-level activities, (b) batch-level activities, (c) product-level activities, or (d) facility-level activities. Note that each allocation represents a separate alternative. In other words, the $540,000 of inspection cost will be allocated four times, once for each cost driver.

LO 5-2, 5-3

Exercise 5-6A *Computing overhead rates based on different cost drivers*

Snowden Industries produces two electronic decoders, P and Q. Decoder P is more sophisticated and requires more programming and testing than does Decoder Q. Because of these product differences, the company wants to use activity-based costing to allocate overhead costs. It has identified four activity pools. Relevant information follows.

Activity Pools	Cost Pool Total	Cost Driver
Repair and maintenance on assembly machine	$104,000	Number of units produced
Programming cost	168,000	Number of programming hours
Software inspections	12,000	Number of inspections
Product testing	16,000	Number of tests
Total overhead cost	$300,000	

Expected activity for each product follows.

	Number of Units	Number of Programming Hours	Number of Inspections	Number of Tests
Decoder P	16,000	2,000	190	1,400
Decoder Q	36,000	1,500	60	1,100
Total	52,000	3,500	250	2,500

Required

a. Compute the overhead rate for each activity pool.

b. Determine the overhead cost allocated to each product.

LO 5-1, 5-3

Exercise 5-7A *Comparing an ABC system with a traditional costing system*

Use the information in Exercise 5-6A to complete the following requirements. Assume that before shifting to activity-based costing, Snowden Industries allocated all overhead costs based on direct labor hours. Direct labor data pertaining to the two decoders follow.

	Direct Labor Hours
Decoder P	8,000
Decoder Q	16,000
Total	24,000

Required

a. Compute the amount of overhead cost allocated to each type of decoder when using direct labor hours as the allocation base.

b. Determine the cost per unit for overhead when using direct labor hours as the allocation base and when using ABC. Round your figures to two decimal points.

c. Explain why the per-unit overhead cost is lower for the high-volume product when using ABC.

Exercise 5-8A *Allocating costs with different cost drivers*

LO 5-1, 5-2, 5-3

Vaulker Company produces commercial gardening equipment. Since production is highly automated, the company allocates its overhead costs to product lines using activity-based costing. The costs and cost drivers associated with the four overhead activity cost pools follow.

	Activities			
	Unit Level	**Batch Level**	**Product Level**	**Facility Level**
Cost	$180,000	$40,000	$20,000	$240,000
Cost driver	1,500 labor hours	40 setups	Percentage of use	12,000 units

Production of 800 sets of cutting shears, one of the company's 20 products, took 200 labor hours and 6 setups and consumed 15 percent of the product-sustaining activities.

Required

a. Had the company used labor hours as a companywide allocation base, how much overhead would it have allocated to the cutting shears?

b. How much overhead is allocated to the cutting shears using activity-based costing?

c. Compute the overhead cost per unit for cutting shears first using activity-based costing and then using direct labor hours for allocation if 800 units are produced. If direct product costs are $240 and the product is priced at 30 percent above cost (rounded to two decimal points), for what price would the product sell under each allocation system?

d. Assuming that activity-based costing provides a more accurate estimate of cost, indicate whether the cutting shears would be over- or underpriced if direct labor hours are used as an allocation base. Explain how over- or undercosting can affect Vaulker's profitability.

e. Comment on the validity of using the allocated facility-level cost in the pricing decision. Should other costs be considered in a cost-plus pricing decision? If so, which ones? What costs would you include if you were trying to decide whether to accept a special order?

Exercise 5-9A *Allocating costs with different cost drivers*

LO 5-2, 5-3

Sheridan Publishing identified the following overhead activities, their respective costs, and their cost drivers to produce the three types of textbooks the company publishes.

		Type of Textbook		
Activity (Cost)	**Cost Driver**	**Deluxe**	**Moderate**	**Economy**
Machine maintenance ($360,000)	Number of machine hours	300	900	1,200
Setups ($630,000)	Number of setups	30	15	5
Packing ($162,000)	Number of cartons	10	30	50
Photo development ($504,000)	Number of pictures	4,000	2,000	1,000

Deluxe textbooks are made with the finest-quality paper, six-color printing, and many photographs. Moderate texts are made with three colors and a few photographs spread throughout each chapter. Economy books are printed in black and white and include pictures only in chapter openings.

Required

a. Sheridan currently allocates all overhead costs based on machine hours. The company produced the following number of books during the prior year.

Deluxe	Moderate	Economy
50,000	150,000	200,000

Determine the overhead cost per book for each book type.

b. Determine the overhead cost per book, assuming that the volume-based allocation system described in Requirement *a* is replaced with an activity-based costing system. Round your figures to two decimal points.

c. Explain why the per-unit overhead costs determined in Requirements *a* and *b* differ.

LO 5-3

Exercise 5-10A *Computing product cost with given activity allocation rates*

Wu Manufacturing produces two keyboards, one for laptop computers and the other for desktop computers. The production process is automated, and the company has found activity-based costing useful in assigning overhead costs to its products. The company has identified five major activities involved in producing the keyboards.

Activity	Allocation Base	Allocation Rate
Materials receiving & handling	Cost of material	2% of material cost
Production setup	Number of setups	$50.00 per setup
Assembly	Number of parts	$2.50 per part
Quality inspection	Inspection time	$0.75 per minute
Packing and shipping	Number of orders	$10.00 per order

Activity measures for the two kinds of keyboards follow.

	Labor Cost	Material Cost	Number of Setups	Number of Parts	Inspection Time	Number of Orders
Laptops	$630	$3,000	30	42	3,600 minutes	65
Desktops	575	2,400	12	24	2,500 minutes	20

Required

a. Compute the cost per unit of laptop and desktop keyboards, assuming that Wu made 500 units of each type of keyboard. Round your computation to two decimal points.

b. Explain why laptop keyboards cost more to make even though they have less material cost and are smaller than desktop keyboards.

LO 5-3

Exercise 5-11A *Allocating facility-level costs and a product elimination decision*

Blevins Boards produces two kinds of skateboards. Selected unit data for the two boards for the last quarter follow.

	Basco Boards	Shimano Boards
Production costs		
Direct materials	$25	$38
Direct labor	$32	$54
Allocated overhead	$15	$18
Total units produced and sold	5,000	10,000
Total sales revenue	$500,000	$1,400,000

Blevins allocates production overhead using activity-based costing. It allocates delivery expense and sales commissions, which amount to $54,000 per quarter, to the two products equally.

Required

a. Compute the per-unit cost for each product.

b. Compute the profit for each product.

Exercise 5-12A *Quality cost components and relationships*

LO 5-4

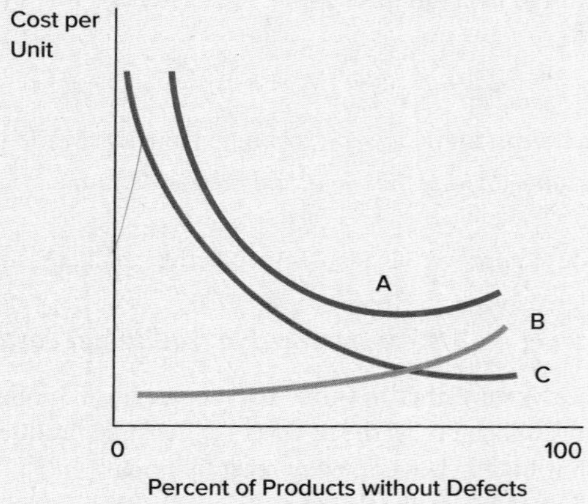

Required

The preceding graph depicts the relationships among the components of total quality cost.

a. Label the lines identified as A, B, and C.

b. Explain the relationships depicted in the graph.

PROBLEMS—SERIES A

connect All applicable Problems in Series A are available in *Connect.*

Problem 5-13A *Key activity-based costing concepts*

LO 5-1

Duncan Paint Company makes paint in many different colors; it charges the same price for all of its paint regardless of the color. Recently, Duncan's chief competitor cut the price of its white paint, which normally outsells any other color by a margin of 4 to 1. Duncan's marketing manager requested permission to match the competitor's price. When Lowell Harvey, Duncan's president, discussed the matter with Liza Melton, the chief accountant, he was told that the competitor's price was below Duncan's cost. Mr. Harvey responded, "If that's the case, then there is something wrong with our accounting system. I know the competition wouldn't sell below cost. Prepare a report showing me how you determine our paint cost and get back to me as soon as possible."

The next day, Ms. Melton returned to Mr. Harvey's office and began by saying, "Determining the cost per gallon is a pretty simple computation. It includes $1.10 of labor, $3.10 of materials, and $4.00 of overhead for a total cost of $8.20 per gallon. The problem is that the competition is selling the stuff for $7.99 per gallon. They've got to be losing money."

Mr. Harvey then asked Ms. Melton how she determined the overhead cost. She replied, "We take total overhead cost and divide it by total labor hours and then assign it to the products based on the direct labor hours required to make the paint." Mr. Harvey then asked what kinds of costs are included in the total overhead cost. Ms. Melton said, "It includes the depreciation on the building and equipment, the cost of utilities, supervisory salaries, and interest. Just how detailed do you want me to go with this list?"

Mr. Harvey responded, "Keep going, I'll tell you when I've heard enough."

Ms. Melton continued, "There is the cost of setups. Every time a color is changed, the machines have to be cleaned, the color release valves reset, a trial batch prepared, and color quality tested.

Sometimes mistakes occur and the machines must be reset. In addition, purchasing and handling the color ingredients must be accounted for as well as adjustments in the packaging department to change the paint cans and to mark the boxes to show the color change. Then . . ."

Mr. Harvey interrupted, "I think I've heard enough. We sell so much white paint that we run it through a separate production process. White paint is produced continuously. There are no shutdowns and setups. White uses no color ingredients. So why are these costs being assigned to our white paint production?"

Ms. Melton replied, "Well, sir, these costs are just a part of the big total that is allocated to all of the paint, no matter what color it happens to be."

Mr. Harvey looked disgusted and said, "As I told you yesterday, Ms. Melton, something is wrong with our accounting system!"

Required

a. Explain what the terms *overcost* and *undercost* mean. Is Duncan's white paint over- or undercosted?

b. Explain what the term *companywide overhead rate* means. Is Duncan using a companywide overhead rate?

c. Explain how Duncan could improve the accuracy of its overhead cost allocations.

LO 5-1, 5-2, 5-3

Problem 5-14A *Comparing an ABC system with a traditional costing system*

Fenway Electronics produces video games in three market categories: commercial, home, and miniature. Fenway has traditionally allocated overhead costs to the three products using the companywide allocation base of direct labor hours. The company recently implemented an ABC system when it installed computer-controlled assembly stations that rendered the traditional costing system ineffective. In implementing the ABC system, the company identified the following activity cost pools and cost drivers.

Category	Total Pooled Cost	Types of Costs	Cost Driver
Unit	$360,000	Indirect labor wages, supplies, factory utilities, machine maintenance	Machine hours
Batch	194,400	Materials handling, inventory storage, labor for setups, packaging, labeling and shipping, scheduling	Number of production orders
Product	105,600	Research and development	Time spent by research department
Facility	300,000	Rent, general utilities, maintenance, facility depreciation, admin. salaries	Square footage

Additional data for each of the product lines follow.

CHECK FIGURE
b. Cost per unit:
Commercial, $37.57
Home, $28.32
Miniature, $36.73

	Commercial	Home	Miniature	Total
Direct materials cost	$25.00/unit	$15.00/unit	$12.00/unit	—
Direct labor cost	$10.00/hour	$8.00/hour	$9.00/hour	—
Number of labor hours	6,000	12,000	2,000	20,000
Number of machine hours	10,000	45,000	25,000	80,000
Number of production orders	200	2,000	800	3,000
Research and development time	10%	20%	70%	100%
Number of units	15,000	45,000	14,000	74,000
Square footage	20,000	50,000	30,000	100,000

Required

Round your figures to two decimal points.

a. Determine the total cost and cost per unit for each product line, assuming that overhead costs are allocated to each product line using direct labor hours as a companywide allocation base. Also determine the combined cost of all three product lines.

b. Determine the total cost and cost per unit for each product line, assuming that an ABC system is used to allocate overhead costs. Determine the combined cost of all three product lines.

c. Explain why the combined total cost computed in Requirements *a* and *b* is the same amount. Given that the combined cost is the same using either allocation method, why is an ABC system with many different allocation rates more accurate than a traditional system with a single companywide overhead rate?

Problem 5-15A *Effect of automation on overhead allocation*

LO 5-1, 5-3

CHECK FIGURE
b. Allocated costs:
Seasonal: $14,400
All-purpose: $201,600

Bombay Rug Company makes two types of rugs, seasonal and all-purpose. Both types of rugs are handmade, but the seasonal rugs require significantly more labor because of their decorative designs. The annual number of rugs made and the labor hours required to make each type of rug follow.

	Seasonal	All-Purpose	Totals
Number of rugs	2,400	5,600	8,000
Number of direct labor hours	120,000	168,000	288,000

Required

a. Assume that annual overhead costs total $172,800. Select the appropriate cost driver and determine the amount of overhead to allocate to each type of rug.

b. Bombay automates the seasonal rug line, which results in a dramatic decline in labor usage and allows the company to make 2,400 rugs in only 12,000 hours. Bombay continues to make the all-purpose rugs the same way as before. The number of rugs made and the labor hours required to make them after automation follow.

	Seasonal	All-Purpose	Totals
Number of rugs	2,400	5,600	8,000
Number of direct labor hours	12,000	168,000	180,000

Overhead costs are expected to increase to $216,000 as a result of the automation. Allocate the increased overhead cost to the two types of rugs using direct labor hours as the allocation base and comment on the appropriateness of the allocation.

Problem 5-16A *Using activity-based costing to improve allocation accuracy*

LO 5-1, 5-2, 5-3

CHECK FIGURE
c. All-purpose: $8,796.60
Seasonal: $8,256.00

This problem is an extension of Problem 5-15A, which must be completed first.

Bombay's accounting staff has disaggregated the $216,000 of overhead costs into the following items.

(1) Inspection costs	$ 19,200
(2) Setup costs	12,960
(3) Engineering costs	19,200
(4) Legal costs related to products	7,200
(5) Materials movement cost per batch	2,880
(6) Salaries of production supervisors	48,000
(7) Fringe benefit costs	9,600
(8) Utilities costs	4,800
(9) Plant manager's salary	28,800
(10) Depreciation on production equipment	43,200
(11) Depreciation on building	9,600
(12) Miscellaneous costs	6,000
(13) Indirect materials costs	3,360
(14) Production employee incentive costs	1,200
Total	$216,000

Required

a. Each of Bombay's rug lines operates as a department. The all-purpose department occupies 6,000 square feet of floor space, and the seasonal department occupies 12,000 square feet of space. Comment on the validity of allocating the overhead costs by square footage.

b. Assume that the following additional information is available:

(1) Rugs are individually inspected.

(2) Bombay incurs setup costs each time a new style of seasonal rug is produced. The seasonal rugs were altered nine times during the year. The manual equipment for all-purpose rugs is reset twice each year to ensure accurate weaving. The setup for the technical equipment used to weave seasonal rugs requires more highly skilled workers, but the all-purpose rugs require more manual equipment, thereby resulting in a *per setup* charge that is roughly equal for both types of rugs. Bombay undertook 22 setups during the year, 18 of which applied to seasonal rugs and 4 that applied to all-purpose rugs.

(3) Ninety percent of the product-level costs can be traced to producing seasonal rugs.

(4) Six supervisors oversee the production of all-purpose rugs. Because seasonal rugs are made in an automated department, only two production supervisors are needed.

(5) Each rug requires an equal amount of indirect materials.

(6) Costs associated with production activities are assigned to six activity cost pools: (1) labor-related activities, (2) unit-level activities, (3) batch-level activities, (4) product-level supervisory activities, (5) other product-level activities, and (6) facility-level activities.

Organize the $216,000 of overhead costs into activity center cost pools and allocate the costs to the two types of rugs.

c. Assuming that 180 seasonal and 480 all-purpose rugs were made in January, determine the overhead costs that would be assigned to each of the two rug types for the month of January.

LO 5-1, 5-3

CHECK FIGURE

a. Cost per student:
Computer-assisted: $970
Classroom: $470

Problem 5-17A *Using activity-based costing to improve allocation accuracy*

Apple Academy is a profit-oriented education business. Apple provides remedial training for high school students who have fallen behind in their classroom studies. It charges its students $750 per course. During the previous year, Apple provided instruction for 1,000 students. The income statement for the company follows.

Revenue	$ 750,000
Cost of instructors	(340,000)
Overhead costs	(230,000)
Net income	$ 180,000

The company president, Andria Rossi, indicated in a discussion with the accountant, Sam Trent, that she was extremely pleased with the growth in the area of computer-assisted instruction. She observed that this department served 200 students using only two part-time instructors. In contrast, the classroom-based instructional department required 32 instructors to teach 800 students. Ms. Rossi noted that the per-student cost of instruction was dramatically lower for the computer-assisted department. She based her conclusion on the following information.

Apple pays its part-time instructors an average of $10,000 per year. The total cost of instruction and the cost per student are computed as follows.

Type of Instruction	Computer-Assisted	Classroom
Number of instructors (a)	2	32
Number of students (b)	200	800
Total cost (c = a × $10,000)	$20,000	$320,000
Cost per student (c ÷ b)	$100	$400

Assuming that overhead costs were distributed equally across the student population, Ms. Rossi concluded that the cost of instructors was the critical variable in the company's capacity to generate profits. Based on her analysis, her strategic plan called for heavily increased use of computer-assisted instruction.

Mr. Trent was not so sure that computer-assisted instruction should be stressed. After attending a seminar on activity-based costing (ABC), he believed that the allocation of overhead cost could be more closely traced to the different types of learning activities. To facilitate an activity-based analysis, he developed the following information about the costs associated with computer-assisted versus classroom instructional activities. He identified $160,000 of overhead costs that were directly traceable to computer-assisted activities, including the costs of computer hardware, software, and technical assistance. He believed the remaining $70,000 of overhead costs should be allocated to the two instructional activities based on the number of students enrolled in each program.

Required

a. Based on the preceding information, determine the total cost and the cost per student to provide courses through computer-assisted instruction versus classroom instruction.

b. Comment on the validity of stressing growth in the area of computer-assisted instruction.

Problem 5-18A *Pricing decisions made with ABC system cost data*

LO 5-1, 5-2, 5-3

eXcel

Horten Sporting Goods Corporation makes two types of racquets, tennis and badminton. The company uses the same facility to make both products even though the processes are quite different. The company has recently converted its cost accounting system to activity-based costing. The following are the cost data that Jane Price, the cost accountant, prepared for the third quarter of 2018 (during which Horten made 70,000 tennis racquets and 30,000 badminton racquets).

CHECK FIGURE
a. Cost per unit:
Tennis racquet: $76.71
Badminton racquet: $73.67

Direct Cost	Tennis Racquet (TR)	Badminton Racquet (BR)
Direct materials	$28 per unit	$20 per unit
Direct labor	34 per unit	28 per unit

Category	Estimated Cost	Cost Driver	Amount of Cost Driver
Unit level	$ 750,000	Number of inspection hours	TR: 15,000 hours; BR: 10,000 hours
Batch level	250,000	Number of setups	TR: 80 setups; BR: 45 setups
Product level	150,000	Number of TV commercials	TR: 4; BR: 1
Facility level	650,000	Number of machine hours	TR: 30,000 hours; BR: 35,000 hours
Total	$1,800,000		

Inspectors are paid according to the number of actual hours worked, which is determined by the number of racquets inspected. Engineers who set up equipment for both products are paid monthly salaries. TV commercial fees are paid at the beginning of the quarter. Facility-level cost includes depreciation of all production equipment.

Required

Round your figures to two decimal points.

a. Compute the cost per unit for each product.

b. If management wants to price badminton racquets 30 percent above cost, what price should the company set?

c. The market price of tennis racquets has declined substantially because of new competitors entering the market. Management asks you to determine the minimum cost of producing tennis racquets in the short term. Provide that information.

LO 5-3

CHECK FIGURE
a. Cost per unit:
ZM: $153.83
DS: $64.44

Problem 5-19A *Target pricing and target costing with ABC*

Bismarck Cameras Inc. manufactures two models of cameras. Model ZM has a zoom lens; Model DS has a fixed lens. Bismarck uses an activity-based costing system. The following are the relevant cost data for the previous month.

Direct Cost per Unit	Model ZM	Model DS
Direct materials	$45	$20
Direct labor	32	15

Category	Estimated Cost	Cost Driver	Use of Cost Driver
Unit level	$ 27,000	Number of units	ZM: 2,400 units; DS: 9,600 units
Batch level	50,000	Number of setups	ZM: 25 setups; DS: 25 setups
Product level	90,000	Number of TV commercials	ZM: 15; DS: 10
Facility level	300,000	Number of machine hours	ZM: 500 hours; DS: 1,000 hours
Total	$467,000		

Bismarck's facility has the capacity to operate 4,500 machine hours per month.

Required

Round your figures to two decimal points.

a. Compute the cost per unit for each product.

b. The current market price for products comparable to Model ZM is $200 and for DS is $86. If Bismarck sold all of its products at the market prices, what was its profit or loss for the previous month?

c. A market expert believes that Bismarck can sell as many cameras as it can produce by pricing Model ZM at $196 and Model DS at $84. Bismarck would like to use those estimates as its target prices and have a profit margin of 30 percent of target prices. What is the target cost for each product?

d. Is there any way for the company to reach its target costs?

LO 5-3

excel

CHECK FIGURE
b. Cost per unit:
Diamond: $129.40
Gold: $84.83

Problem 5-20A *Cost management with an ABC system*

Silva Chairs Inc. makes two types of chairs. Model Diamond is a high-end product designed for professional offices. Model Gold is an economical product designed for family use. Jane Silva, the president, is worried about cut-throat price competition in the chairs market. Her company suffered a loss last quarter, an unprecedented event in its history. The company's accountant prepared the following cost data for Ms. Silva.

Direct Cost per Unit	Model Diamond (D)	Model Gold (G)
Direct materials	$45 per unit	$30 per unit
Direct labor	$24/hour × 2 hours production time	$24/hour × 1 hour production time

Category	Estimated Cost	Cost Driver	Use of Cost Driver
Unit level	$ 300,000	Number of units	D: 15,000 units; G: 35,000 units
Batch level	750,000	Number of setups	D: 104 setups; G: 146 setups
Product level	450,000	Number of TV commercials	D: 5; G: 10
Facility level	500,000	Number of machine hours	D: 1,500 hours; G: 3,500 hours
Total	$2,000,000		

The market price for office chairs comparable to Model Diamond is $180 and to Model Gold is $110.

Required

a. Compute the cost per unit for both products. Round your figures to two decimal points.

b. Dan Barker, the chief engineer, told Ms. Silva that the company is currently making 150 units of Model Diamond per batch and 245 units of Model Gold per batch. He suggests doubling the batch sizes to cut the number of setups in half, thereby reducing the setup cost by 50 percent. Compute the cost per unit for each product if Ms. Silva adopts his suggestion. Round your figures to two decimal points.

c. Is there any side effect if Ms. Silva increases the production batch size by 100 percent?

Problem 5-21A *Assessing a quality control strategy*

LO 5-4

The following quality cost report came from the records of Willoughby Company.

	Year 2		Year 1	
	Amount	Percentage	Amount	Percentage
Prevention costs				
Engineering and design	$136,000	13.74%	$ 58,000	3.86%
Training and education	34,000	3.43	12,000	0.80
Depreciation on prevention equipment	58,000	5.86	30,000	1.99
Incentives and awards	88,000	8.89	40,000	2.66
Total prevention	316,000	31.92%	140,000	9.31%
Appraisal costs				
Inventory inspection	50,000	5.05	50,000	3.32
Reliability testing	32,000	3.23	30,000	1.99
Testing equipment (depreciation)	22,000	2.22	24,000	1.60
Supplies	14,000	1.41	16,000	1.06
Total appraisal	118,000	11.92%	120,000	7.98%
Internal failure costs				
Scrap	48,000	4.85	80,000	5.32
Repair and rework	98,000	9.90	220,000	14.63
Downtime	24,000	2.42	40,000	2.66
Reinspection	8,000	0.81	24,000	1.60
Total internal failure	178,000	17.98%	364,000	24.20%
External failure cost				
Warranty repairs and replacement	220,000	22.22	520,000	34.57
Freight	48,000	4.85	100,000	6.65
Customer relations	56,000	5.66	120,000	7.98
Restocking and packaging	54,000	5.45	140,000	9.31
Total external failure	378,000	38.18%	880,000	58.51%
Grand total	$990,000	100.00%	$1,504,000	100.00%

Required

a. Explain the strategy that Willoughby Company initiated to control its quality costs.

b. Indicate whether the strategy was successful or unsuccessful in reducing quality costs.

c. Explain how the strategy likely affected customer satisfaction.

EXERCISES—SERIES B

Exercise 5-1B *Classifying the costs of unit-, batch-, product-, or facility-level activities*

LO 5-2

Kaito Manufacturing is developing an activity-based costing system to improve overhead cost allocation. One of the first steps in developing the system is to classify the costs of performing production activities into activity cost pools.

Required

Using the four-tier cost hierarchy described in the chapter, classify each of the following costs into unit-level, batch-level, product-level, or facility-level cost pools.

Cost Activity	Cost Pool
a. Lubricant for machines	
b. Parts used to make a particular product	
c. Machine setup cost	
d. Salary of the plant manager's secretary	
e. Factory depreciation	
f. Advertising costs for a particular product	
g. Wages of assembly line workers	
h. Product design costs	
i. Materials requisition costs for a particular work order	
j. Security guard wages	

LO 5-2

Exercise 5-2B *Identifying appropriate cost drivers*

Required

Provide at least one example of an appropriate cost driver (allocation base) for each of the following activities:

a. Engineers design a product production layout.
b. Engineers set up machines to produce a product.
c. The production supervisor completes the paperwork initiating a work order.
d. The production manager prepares materials requisition forms.
e. Workers move materials from the warehouse to the factory floor.
f. Assembly line machines are operated.
g. Workers count completed goods before moving them to a warehouse.
h. A logistics manager runs a computer program to determine the materials release schedule.
i. Janitors clean the factory floor after workers have left.
j. Mechanics apply lubricant to machines.

LO 5-2

Exercise 5-3B *Classifying costs and identifying the appropriate cost driver*

Sentry Corporation, a furniture manufacturer, uses an activity-based costing system. It has identified the following selected activities:

1. Packaging completed furniture in boxes for shipment.
2. Inspecting completed furniture for quality control.
3. Purchasing TV time to advertise a particular product.
4. Incurring property taxes on factory buildings.
5. Incurring paint cost for furniture produced.
6. Setting up machines for a particular batch of production.
7. Inspecting wood prior to using it in production.

Required

a. Classify each activity as a unit-level, batch-level, product-level, or facility-level activity.
b. Identify an appropriate cost driver (allocation base) for each of the activities.

LO 5-2

Exercise 5-4B *Understanding the context-sensitive nature of classifying activities*

Required

Describe a set of circumstances in which labor cost could be classified as a unit-level, a batch-level, a product-level, or a facility-level cost.

Exercise 5-5B *Understanding the context-sensitive nature of classifying activities*

LO 5-2, 5-3

Canton Company makes two types of cell phones. Handy is a thin, pocket-size cell phone that is easy to carry around. Action is a palm-size phone convenient to hold while the user is talking. During its most recent accounting period, Canton incurred $270,000 of quality-control costs. Recently Canton established an activity-based costing system, which involved classifying its activities into four categories. The categories and appropriate cost drivers follow.

	Direct Labor Hours	Number of Batches	Number of Engineers	Number of Square Feet
Handy	26,000	38	10	40,000
Action	24,000	22	5	85,000
Totals	50,000	60	15	125,000

Canton uses direct labor hours to allocate unit-level activities, number of batches to allocate batch-level activities, number of engineers to allocate product-level activities, and number of square feet to allocate facility-level activities.

Required

Allocate the quality-control cost between the two products, assuming that it is driven by (a) unit-level activities, (b) batch-level activities, (c) product-level activities, and (d) facility-level activities. Note that each allocation represents a separate allocation. In other words, the $270,000 of quality-control costs will be allocated four times, once for each cost driver.

Exercise 5-6B *Computing overhead rates based on different costing drivers*

LO 5-2, 5-3

Rankin Industries produces two surge protectors: K2761 with six outlets and D3354 with eight outlets and two telephone line connections. Because of these product differences, the company plans to use activity-based costing to allocate overhead costs. The company has identified four activity pools. Relevant information follows.

Activity Pools	Cost Pool Total	Cost Driver
Machine setup	$180,000	Number of setups
Machine operation	450,000	Number of machine hours
Quality control	72,000	Number of inspections
Packaging	48,000	Number of units
Total overhead cost	$750,000	

Expected activity for each product follows.

	Number of Setups	Number of Machine Hours	Number of Inspections	Number of Units
K2761	48	1,400	78	25,000
D3354	72	2,600	172	15,000
Total	120	4,000	250	40,000

Required

a. Compute the overhead rate for each activity pool.

b. Determine the overhead cost allocated to each product.

LO 5-1, 5-3

Exercise 5-7B *Comparing an ABC system with a traditional cost system*

Use the information in Exercise 5-6B to complete the following requirements. Assume that before shifting to activity-based costing, Rankin Industries allocated all overhead costs based on direct labor hours. Direct labor data pertaining to the two surge protectors follow.

	Direct Labor Hours
K2761	32,000
D3354	18,000
Total	50,000

Required

a. Compute the amount of overhead cost allocated to each type of surge protector when using direct labor hours as the allocation base.

b. Determine the cost per unit for overhead when using direct labor hours as the allocation base and when using ABC.

c. Explain why the per-unit overhead cost is lower for the higher-volume product when using ABC.

LO 5-1, 5-2, 5-3

Exercise 5-8B *Allocating costs with different cost drivers*

Maduro Sporting Goods Inc. produces indoor treadmills. The company allocates its overhead costs using activity-based costing. The costs and cost drivers associated with the four overhead activity cost pools follow.

Activities	Unit Level	Batch Level	Product Level	Facility Level
Cost	$200,000	$100,000	$60,000	$180,000
Cost driver	12,500 labor hours	50 setups	Percentage of use	15,000 units

Producing 5,000 units of PFT200, one of the company's five products, took 4,000 labor hours, 25 setups, and consumed 30 percent of the product-sustaining activities.

Required

a. Had the company used labor hours as a companywide allocation base, how much overhead would it have allocated to the 5,000 units of PFT200?

b. How much overhead is allocated to the 5,000 PFT200 units using activity-based costing?

c. Compute the overhead cost per unit for PFT200 using activity-based costing and direct labor hours if 5,000 units are produced. If direct product costs are $120 and PFT200 is priced at 20 percent above cost (rounded to two decimal points), compute the product's selling price under each allocation system.

d. Assuming that activity-based costing provides a more accurate estimate of cost, indicate whether PFT200 would be over- or underpriced if Maduro uses direct labor hours as the allocation base. Explain how over- or undercosting can affect Maduro's profitability.

e. Comment on the validity of using the allocated facility-level costs in the pricing decision. Should other costs be considered in a cost-plus pricing decision? If so, which ones? What costs would you include if you were trying to decide whether to accept a special order?

LO 5-2, 5-3

Exercise 5-9B *Allocating costs with different cost drivers*

Skinner Shoes Corporation produces three brands of shoes: Brisk, Pro, and Runner. Relevant information about Skinner's overhead activities, their respective costs, and their cost drivers follows.

Overhead Costs	Cost Driver	Brisk	Pro	Runner
Fringe benefits ($200,000)	Labor hours	8,000	22,000	20,000
Setups ($120,000)	Number of setups	15	25	10
Packing costs ($80,000)	Number of cartons	900	1,200	1,900
Quality control ($200,000)	Number of tests	120	200	80

Required

a. Skinner currently allocates all overhead costs based on labor hours. The company produced the following numbers of pairs of shoes during the prior year.

Brisk	Pro	Runner
10,000	12,000	20,000

Determine the overhead cost per pair of shoes for each brand.

b. Determine the overhead cost per pair of shoes for each brand, assuming that the volume-based allocation system described in Requirement *a* is replaced with an activity-based costing system. Round your figures to two decimal points.

c. Explain why the per-pair overhead costs determined in Requirements *a* and *b* differ.

Exercise 5-10B *Computing product cost with given activity allocation rates*

LO 5-3

Using automated production processes, Pruitt Videos produces two models of digital camcorders: N100 for the novice and D200 for the hobbyist. The company has found activity-based costing useful in assigning overhead costs to its products. It has identified the following five major activities involved in producing the camcorders.

Activity	Allocation Base	Allocation Rate
Materials receiving and handling	Cost of materials	3% of materials cost
Production setup	Number of setups	$400 per setup
Assembly	Number of parts	$5 per part
Quality inspection	Inspection time	$12.50 per minute
Packing and shipping	Number of orders	$40 per order

Activity measures for the two models of camcorders follow.

	Labor Cost*	Materials Cost*	Number of Setups	Number of Parts	Inspection Time	Number of Orders
N100	$125,000	$70,000	10	10,000	800 minutes	25
D200	80,000	90,000	25	10,000	4,800 minutes	50

*Both are direct costs.

Required

a. Compute the cost per unit of N100 and D200, assuming that Pruitt made 5,000 units of N100 and 2,500 units of D200.

b. Explain why the D200 camcorders cost more to make although their direct costs are less than those for the N100 camcorders.

Exercise 5-11B *Allocating facility-level costs and a product elimination decision*

LO 5-3

York Corporation produces two types of juice that it packages in cases of 24 cans per case. Selected per-case data for the two products for the last month follow.

	Orange Juice	Tomato Juice
Production costs		
Direct material	$2.40	$1.20
Direct labor	$1.80	$2.70
Allocated overhead	$2.25	$3.00
Total cases produced and sold	25,000	15,000
Total sales revenue	$250,000	$130,000

York allocates production overhead using activity-based costing but allocates monthly packaging expense, which amounted to $60,000 last month, to the two products equally.

Required

a. Compute the net profit for each product.

b. Assuming that the overhead allocation for the tomato juice includes $30,000 of facility-level costs, would you advise York to eliminate this product? (*Hint:* Consider the method used to allocate the monthly packaging expense.)

LO 5-4

Exercise 5-12B *Applying concepts of quality cost management*

Rich Ingram, the president of Merkel Industries Inc., was beaming when he was reviewing the company's quality cost report. After he had implemented a quality-control program for three years, the company's defect rate had declined from 20 percent to 3 percent. Mr. Ingram patted Judith Gomez, the production manager, on her back and said: "You have done a great job! I plan to reward you for your hard work. However, I want the defects to disappear completely before I promote you to the position of executive vice president. So, zero-defect is going to be your personal goal for the coming year." Ms. Gomez responded wearily, "I'm not sure that's really a good idea."

Required

Write a memorandum to the president explaining that zero-defect is not a practical policy.

PROBLEMS—SERIES B

LO 5-1

Problem 5-13B *Key activity-based costing concepts*

Western Boot and Shoe Company makes hand-sewn boots and shoes. Western uses a companywide overhead rate based on direct labor hours to allocate indirect manufacturing costs to its products. Making a pair of boots normally requires 2.4 hours of direct labor, and making a pair of shoes requires 1.8 hours. The company's shoe division, facing increased competition from international companies that have access to cheap labor, has responded by automating its shoe production. The reengineering process was expensive, requiring the purchase of manufacturing equipment and the restructuring of the plant layout. In addition, utility and maintenance costs increased significantly for operating the new equipment. Even so, labor costs decreased significantly. Now making a pair of shoes requires only 18 minutes of direct labor. As predicted, the labor savings more than offset the increase in overhead cost, thereby reducing the total cost to make a pair of shoes. The company experienced an unexpected side effect, however; according to the company's accounting records, the cost to make a pair of boots increased although the manufacturing process in the boot division was not affected by the reengineering of the shoe division. In other words, the cost of boots increased but Western did not change anything about the way it makes them.

Required

a. Explain why the accounting records reflected an increase in the cost to make a pair of boots.

b. Explain how the companywide overhead rate could result in the underpricing of shoes.

c. Explain how activity-based costing could improve the accuracy of overhead cost allocations.

LO 5-1, 5-2, 5-3

Problem 5-14B *Comparing an ABC system with a traditional costing system*

Since its inception, Batum Laboratory has produced a single product, Product S109. With the advent of automation, the company added the technological capability to begin producing a second product, Product N227. Because of the success of Product N227, manufacturing has been shifting toward its production. Sales of Product N227 are now 50 percent of the total annual sales of 20,000 units, and the company is optimistic about the new product's future sales growth. One reason the company is excited about the sales potential of its new product is that the new product's gross profit margin is higher than that of Product S109. Management is thrilled with the new product's initial success but concerned about the company's declining profits since the product's introduction. Suspecting a problem with the company's costing system, management hires you to investigate.

In reviewing the company's records, product specifications, and manufacturing processes, you discover the following information.

1. The company is in an extremely competitive industry in which markups are low and accurate estimates of cost are critical to success.
2. Product N227 has complex parts that require more labor, machine time, setups, and inspections than Product S109.
3. Budgeted costs for direct materials and labor follow.

Direct Cost per Unit	Product S109	Product N227
Direct materials	$25	$35
Direct labor	$10/hour × 2 hours production time	$10/hour × 2.8 hours production time

4. The company presently allocates overhead costs to its products based on direct labor hours. After carefully studying the company's overhead, you identify four different categories of overhead costs. Using your knowledge of this company and similar companies in the same industry, you estimate the total costs for each of these categories and identify the most appropriate cost driver for measuring each product's overhead consumption. Detailed information for each cost category follows.

Category	Estimated Cost	Cost Driver	Use of Cost Driver
Unit level	$ 540,000	Number of machine hours	S109: 20,000 hours; N227: 60,000 hours
Batch level	228,000	Number of machine setups	S109: 1,500; N227: 3,500
Product level	180,000	Number of inspections	S109: 200; N227: 600
Facility level	60,000	Equal percentage for products	S109: 50%; N227: 50%
Total	$1,008,000		

Required

a. Determine the predetermined overhead rate the company is using.

b. Compute the amount of overhead the company assigns to each product using this rate.

c. Determine the cost per unit and total cost of each product when overhead is assigned based on direct labor hours.

d. To remain competitive, the company prices its products at only 20 percent above cost. Compute the price for each product with this markup.

e. Compute the overhead rate for each category of activity.

f. Determine the amount of overhead cost, both in total and per unit, that would be assigned to each product if the company switched to activity-based costing.

g. Assuming that prices are adjusted to reflect activity-based costs, determine the revised price for each product.

h. Based on your results for Requirements *f* and *g*, explain why Product N227 costs more to make than previously apparent and why sales prices therefore need to be adjusted.

Problem 5-15B *Using activity-based costing to improve allocation accuracy*

LO 5-1, 5-3

Casey's Commemoratives makes and sells two types of decorative plates. One plate displays a hand-painted image of Princess Kate; the other plate displays a machine-pressed image of Marilyn Monroe. The Kate plates require 25,000 hours of direct labor to make; the Monroe plates require only 5,000 hours of direct labor. Overhead costs are composed of (1) $105,000 machine-related activity costs, including indirect labor, utilities, and depreciation, and (2) $75,000 labor-related activity costs, including overtime pay, fringe benefits, and payroll taxes.

Required

a. Assuming that Casey's uses direct labor hours as the allocation base, determine the amount of the total $180,000 overhead cost that would be allocated to each type of plate.
b. Explain why using direct labor hours may distort the allocation of overhead cost to the two products.
c. Explain how activity-based costing could improve the accuracy of the overhead cost allocation.

LO 5-1, 5-2, 5-3

Problem 5-16B ***Using activity-based costing to improve allocation accuracy***

This problem is an extension of Problem 5-15B, which must be completed first.

Assume the same data as in Problem 5-15B with the following additional information. The hours of machine time for processing plates are 1,000 for Kate plates and 2,500 for Monroe plates.

Required

a. Establish two activity centers, one for machine-related activities and the second for labor-related activities. Assign the total overhead costs to the two activity centers.
b. Allocate the machine-related overhead costs to each product based on machine hours.
c. Allocate the labor-related overhead costs to each product based on direct labor hours.
d. Draw a diagram that compares the one-stage allocation method used in Problem 5-15B with the two-stage activity-based costing approach used in this problem.

LO 5-1, 5-3

Problem 5-17B ***Using activity-based costing to improve business decisions***

Elmore CPA and Associates is a local accounting firm specializing in bookkeeping and tax services. The firm has four certified public accountants who supervise 20 clerks. The clerks handle basic bookkeeping jobs and prepare tax return drafts. The CPAs review and approve the bookkeeping jobs and tax returns. Each CPA receives a fixed salary of $8,000 per month; the clerks earn an hourly rate of $16. Because the clerks are paid by the hour and their work hours can be directly traced to individual jobs, their wages are considered direct costs. The CPAs' salaries are not traced to individual jobs and are therefore treated as indirect costs. The firm allocates overhead based on direct labor hours. The following is Elmore's income statement for the previous month.

	Bookkeeping	Tax	Total
Revenues	$100,000	$100,000	$200,000
Direct expenses	(40,000)*	(40,000)*	(80,000)
Indirect supervisory expenses	(16,000)	(16,000)	(32,000)
Net income	$ 44,000	$ 44,000	$ 88,000

*2,500 clerical hours were used in each category during the previous month.

Lillian Elmore, CPA and chief executive officer, is not sure that the two operations are equally profitable as the income statement indicates. First, she believes that most of the CPAs' time was spent instructing clerks in tax return preparation. The bookkeeping jobs appear to be routine, and most of the clerks can handle them with little supervision. After attending a recent professional development seminar on activity-based costing (ABC), Ms. Elmore believes that the allocation of indirect costs can be more closely traced to different types of services. To facilitate an activity-based analysis, she asked the CPAs to document their work hours on individual jobs for the last week. The results indicate that, on average, 25 percent of the CPAs' hours was spent supervising bookkeeping activities and the remaining 75 percent was spent supervising tax activities.

Required

a. Based on the preceding information, reconstruct the income statement for bookkeeping services, tax services, and the total, assuming that Elmore revises its allocation of indirect supervisory costs based on ABC.
b. Comment on the results and recommend a new business strategy.

Problem 5-18B *Pricing decisions made with ABC system cost data*

LO 5-1, 5-2, 5-3

Miller Furniture Corporation makes two types of dining tables, Elegance for formal dining and Comfort for casual dining, at its single factory. With the economy beginning to experience a recession, Hank Miller, the president, is concerned about whether the company can stay in business as market prices fall. At Mr. Miller's request, Tess Faulkner, the controller, prepared cost data for analysis.

Inspectors are paid according to the number of actual hours worked, determined by the number of tables inspected. Engineers, who set up equipment for both products, are paid monthly salaries. TV commercial fees are paid at the beginning of the quarter.

Direct Cost	Elegance (E)	Comfort (C)
Direct materials	$80 per unit	$56 per unit
Direct labor	$20 per hour × 1.5 hours production time	$20 per hour × 1 hour production time

Category	Estimated Cost	Cost Driver	Use of Cost Driver
Product inspection	$120,000	Number of units	E: 2,500 units; C: 7,500 units
Machine setups	75,000	Number of setups	E: 23 setups; C: 27 setups
Product advertising	210,000	Number of TV commercials	E: 5; C: 9
Facility depreciation	405,000	Number of machine hours	E: 5,000 hours; C: 5,000 hours
Total	$810,000		

Required

a. Compute the cost per unit for each product.

b. If management wants to make 30 percent of cost as a profit margin for Elegance, what price should the company set?

c. The market price of tables in the Comfort class has declined because of the recession. Management asks you to determine the minimum cost of producing Comfort tables in the short term. Provide that information.

Problem 5-19B *Target pricing and target costing with ABC*

LO 5-3

Klein Corporation manufactures two models of watches. Model Wonder displays cartoon characters and has simple features designed for kids. Model Marvel has sophisticated features such as dual time zones and an attached calculator. Klein's product design team has worked with a cost accountant to prepare a budget for the two products for the next fiscal year as follows.

Direct Cost	Wonder (W)	Marvel (M)
Direct materials	$10 per unit	$20 per unit
Direct labor	$25/hour × 0.3 hour production time	$25/hour × 0.7 hour production time

Category	Estimated Cost	Cost Driver	Use of Cost Driver
Materials handling	$183,000	Number of parts	W: 700,000; M: 520,000
Machine setups	90,000	Number of setups	W: 50; M: 40
Product testing	14,000	Number of units tested	W: 1,000; M: 400
Facility depreciation	180,000	Number of machine hours	W: 3,200; M: 4,000
Total	$467,000		

Wonder watches have 35 parts, and Marvel watches have 65 parts. The budget calls for producing 20,000 units of Wonder and 8,000 units of Marvel. Klein tests 5 percent of its products for quality assurance. It sells all its products at market prices.

Required

a. Compute the cost per unit for each product.

b. The current market price for products comparable to Wonder is $28 and for products comparable to Marvel is $85. What will Klein's profit or loss for the next year be?

c. Klein likes to have a 25 percent profit margin based on the current market price for each product. What is the target cost for each product? What is the total target profit?

d. The president of Klein has asked the design team to refine the production design to bring down the product cost. After a series of redesigns, the team recommends a new process that requires purchasing a new machine that costs $200,000 and has five years of useful life and no salvage value. With the new process and the new machine, Klein can decrease the number of machine setups to four for each product and cut the cost of materials handling by 60 percent. The machine hours used will be 4,500 for Wonder and 6,500 for Marvel. Does this new process enable Klein to achieve its target costs?

LO 5-3

Problem 5-20B *Cost management with an ABC system*

Moreno Corporation manufactures two different coffee makers, Professional for commercial use and Home for family use. Albert Moreno, the president, recently received complaints from some members of the board of directors about the company's failure to reach the expected profit of $200,000 per month. Mr. Moreno is, therefore, under great pressure to improve the company's bottom line. Under his direction, Angie Roy, the controller, prepared the following monthly cost data for Mr. Moreno.

Direct Cost	Professional (P)	Home (H)
Direct materials	$24 per unit	$8 per unit
Direct labor	$12 per hour × 0.8 hour production time	$12 per hour × 0.3 hour production time

Category	Estimated Cost	Cost Driver	Use of Cost Driver
Product inspection	$ 60,000	Number of units	P: 15,000 units; H: 45,000 units
Machine setups	15,000	Number of setups	P: 30 setups; H: 45 setups
Product promotion	200,000	Number of TV commercials	P: 10; H: 10
Facility depreciation	295,000	Number of machine hours	P: 7,160 hours; H: 4,640 hours
Total	$570,000		

The market price for coffee makers comparable to Professional is $63 and to Home is $21. The company's administrative expenses amount to $125,000.

Required

Round your figures to two decimal points.

a. Compute the cost per unit for both products.

b. Determine the company's profit or loss.

c. Charles Wei, the marketing manager, recommends that the company implement a focused marketing strategy. He argues that advertisements in trade journals would be more effective for the commercial market than on TV. In addition, the cost of journal ads would be only $21,000. He also proposes sending discount coupons to targeted households to reach a broad market base. The coupons program would cost $72,000. Compute the new cost of each product, assuming that Mr. Moreno replaces TV advertising with Mr. Wei's suggestions.

d. Determine the company's profit or loss using the information in Requirement *c*.

Problem 5-21B *Assessing a quality control strategy*

LO 5-4

Steve Gauthier, the president of Southern Plastic Company, is a famous cost cutter in the plastics industry. Two years ago, he accepted an offer from Southern's board of directors to help the company cut costs quickly. In fact, Mr. Gauthier's compensation package included a year-end bonus tied to the percentage of cost decrease over the preceding year. On February 12, 2018, Mr. Gauthier received comparative financial information for the two preceding years. He was especially interested in the results of his cost-cutting measures on quality control. The following quality report was extracted from the company's financial information.

Required

a. Explain the strategy that Mr. Gauthier initiated to control Southern's costs.

b. Indicate whether the strategy was successful or unsuccessful in reducing quality costs.

c. Explain how the strategy will likely affect the company's business in the long term.

	Year 2		Year 1	
	Amount	Percentage	Amount	Percentage
Prevention costs				
Engineering and design	$65,000	6.57%	$69,000	7.39%
Training and education	26,000	2.63	76,000	8.14
Depreciation on prevention equipment	15,000	1.51	15,000	1.60
Incentives and awards	20,000	2.02	20,000	2.14
Total prevention	126,000	12.73%	180,000	19.27%
Appraisal costs				
Product and materials inspection	33,000	3.33	73,000	7.82
Reliability testing	27,000	2.73	67,000	7.17
Testing equipment (depreciation)	38,000	3.83	38,000	4.07
Supplies	10,000	1.01	16,000	1.71
Total appraisal	108,000	10.90%	194,000	20.77%
Internal failure costs				
Scrap	52,000	5.25	120,000	12.85
Repair and rework	46,000	4.65	150,000	16.06
Downtime	64,000	6.46	40,000	4.28
Reinspection	8,000	0.81	24,000	2.57
Total internal failure	170,000	17.17%	334,000	35.76%
External failure cost				
Warranty repairs and replacement	347,000	35.05	125,000	13.38
Freight	75,000	7.58	31,000	3.32
Customer relations	45,000	4.55	28,000	3.00
Restocking and packaging	119,000	12.02	42,000	4.50
Total external failure	586,000	59.20%	226,000	24.20%
Grand total	$990,000	100.00%	$934,000	100.00%

ANALYZE, THINK, COMMUNICATE

ATC 5-1 Business Applications Case *Using ABC to improve product costing*

Drilling Innovations Inc. produces specialized cutting heads used by companies that drill for oil and natural gas. The company recently implemented an ABC system for three of its products and is interested in evaluating its effectiveness before converting to an ABC system for all of its products. To perform this evaluation the company has compiled data for the three products using both the traditional system and the new ABC system. The traditional system uses a single driver (machine hours). The

ABC system uses a variety of cost drivers related to the activities used to produce the cutting heads. The three products involved in the trial run of the ABC system were GS-157, HS-241, and OS-367. The following data relate to these products.

Product	Selling Price per Unit	Units Produced	Total Costs Allocated: Traditional Costing	Cost per Unit: Traditional Costing	Total Cost Allocated: ABC	Cost per Unit ABC
GS-157	$19.30	120,000	$1,600,000	$13.3333	$1,500,000	$12.5000
HS-241	17.50	90,000	1,100,000	12.2222	1,050,000	11.6667
OS-367	15.10	40,000	400,000	10.0000	550,000	13.7500
Totals			$3,100,000		$3,100,000	

a. Determine the gross profit margin for each product produced based on the ABC data [(Selling price − ABC cost per unit) × Units produced].

b. Determine the gross profit margin for each product produced based on the traditional costing data [(Selling price − Traditional cost per unit) × Units produced].

c. Provide a possible explanation as to why the cost of OS-367 increased under the ABC system while the cost GS-157 decreased.

d. Suggest what action management might take with respect to the discoveries resulting from the ABC versus traditional costing analysis. Assume that Drilling Innovations expects to produce a gross profit margin on each product of at least 30 percent of the selling price.

ATC 5-2 Group Assignment *Using ABC in a service business*

A dialysis clinic provides two types of treatment for its patients. Hemodialysis (HD), an in-house treatment, requires that patients visit the clinic three times each week for dialysis treatments. Peritoneal dialysis (PD) permits patients to self-administer their treatments at home on a daily basis. On average, the clinic serves 102 HD patients and 62 PD patients. A recent development caused clinic administrators to develop a keen interest in cost measurement for the two separate services. Managed care plans such as HMOs began to pay treatment providers a fixed payment per insured participant regardless of the level of services provided by the clinic. With fixed fee revenues, the clinic was forced to control costs to ensure profitability. As a result, knowing the cost to provide HD versus PD services was critically important for the clinic. It needed accurate cost measurements to answer the following questions. Were both services profitable, or was one service carrying the burden of the other service? Should advertising be directed toward acquiring HD or PD patients? Should the clinic eliminate HMO service?

Management suspected the existing cost allocation system was inaccurate in measuring the true cost of providing the respective services; it had been developed in response to Medicare reporting requirements. It allocated costs between HD and PD based on the ratio of cost to charges (RCC). In other words, RCC allocates indirect costs in proportion to revenues. To illustrate, consider the allocation of $883,280 of indirect nursing services costs, which are allocated to the two treatment groups in relation to the revenue generated by each group. Given that the clinic generated total revenue of $3,006,775, an allocation rate of 0.2937633 per revenue dollar was established ($883,280 ÷ $3,006,775). This rate was multiplied by the proportionate share of revenue generated by each service category to produce the following allocation.

Type of Service	Service Revenue	×	Allocation Rate	=	Allocated Cost
HD	$1,860,287	×	0.2937633	=	$546,484
PD	1,146,488	×	0.2937633	=	336,796
Total	$3,006,775	×	0.2937633	=	$883,280

To better assess the cost of providing each type of service, the clinic initiated an activity-based costing (ABC) system. The ABC approach divided the nursing service cost into four separate cost pools. A separate cost driver (allocation base) was identified for each cost pool. The cost pools and their respective cost drivers follow.

	Total	HD	PD
Nursing services cost pool categories			
RNs	$239,120	?	?
LPNs	404,064	?	?
Nursing administration and support staff	115,168	?	?
Dialysis machine operations (tech. salaries)	124,928	?	?
Total	$883,280	?	?

	Total	HD	PD
Activity cost drivers (corresponding to cost pools)			
Number of RNs	7	5	2
Number of LPNs	19	15	4
Number of treatments (nursing administration)	34,967	14,343	20,624
Number of dialyzer treatments (machine operations)	14,343	14,343	0

Data source: T.D. West and D.A. West, "Applying ABC to Healthcare," *Management Accounting,* February 1999, pp. 22–33.

Required

a. Organize the class into four sections and divide the sections into groups of four or five students each. Assign Task 1 to the first section of groups, Task 2 to the second section, Task 3 to the third section, and Task 4 to the fourth section.

Group Tasks

(1) Allocate the RN cost pool between the HD and PD service centers.

(2) Allocate the LPN cost pool between the HD and PD service centers.

(3) Allocate the nursing administration and support staff cost pool between the HD and PD service centers.

(4) Allocate the dialysis machine operations cost pool between the HD and PD service centers.

b. Have the class determine the total cost to allocate to the two service centers in the following manner. Select a representative from each section and have the selected person go to the board. Each representative should supply the allocated cost for the cost pool assigned by her respective section. The instructor should total the amounts and compare the ABC cost allocations with those developed through the traditional RCC system.

c. The instructor should lead the class in a discussion that addresses the following questions.

(1) Assuming that the ABC system provides a more accurate measure of cost, which service center (HD or PD) is overcosted by the traditional allocation system and which is undercosted?

(2) What is the potential impact on pricing and profitability for both service centers?

(3) How could management respond to the conditions described in the problem?

ATC 5-3 Research Assignment *Evaluating external failure costs with real-world data*

The federal government maintains a website devoted to providing information about product recalls. To complete this assignment, you will need to obtain information from this site as follows.

Go to recalls.gov.

Click on the Consumer Products tab at the top of the screen.

Click on CPSC Recalls–Home.

In the "Search Recalls and News Alerts" search window, type "Western Gas Recalls to Inspect Propane," and click on the search icon.

Read the recall notice dated December 28, 2017.

Required

a. Explain why the product was recalled.

b. Who was most responsible for the problem that resulted in the recall?

c. Who will be negatively affected by the faulty product?

d. What are the external failure costs related to the faulty product? Describe the nature of these costs; you will not be able to identify dollar amounts.

e. At what point in the pre-sale process could steps have been taken to prevent the faulty product from being produced and/or sold?

ATC 5-4 Writing Assignment *Assessing a strategy to control quality cost*

Lucy Sawyer, who owns and operates Sawyer Toy Company, is a perfectionist. She believes literally in the "zero-defects" approach to quality control. Her favorite saying is, "You can't spend too much on quality." Even so, in Year 4 her company experienced an embarrassing breach of quality that required the national recall of a defective product. She vowed never to repeat the experience and instructed her staff to spend whatever it takes to ensure that products are delivered free of defects in Year 5. She was somewhat disappointed with the Year 5 year-end quality cost report shown here.

	Year 4	Year 5
Prevention costs	$120,000	$ 80,000
Appraisal costs	240,000	430,000
Internal failure costs	140,000	560,000
External failure cost	320,000	210,000
Total	$820,000	$1,280,000

Although external failure costs had declined, they remained much higher than expected. The increased inspections had identified defects that were corrected, thereby avoiding another recall; however, the external failure costs were still too high. Ms. Sawyer responded by saying, "We will have to double our efforts." She authorized hiring additional inspectors and instructed her production supervisors to become more vigilant in identifying and correcting errors.

Required

Assume that you are the chief financial officer (CFO) of Sawyer Toy Company. Ms. Sawyer has asked you to review the company's approach to quality control. Prepare a memo to her that evaluates the existing approach, and recommend changes in expenditure patterns that can improve profitability as well as increase the effectiveness of the quality control system.

ATC 5-5 Ethical Dilemma *Conflicts between controlling cost and providing social responsibility to patients*

This case examines potential ethical issues faced by the dialysis clinic described in ATC 5-2. It is, however, an independent case that students may study in conjunction with or separately from ATC 5-2. The dialysis clinic provides two types of treatment for its patients. Hemodialysis (HD), an in-house treatment, requires patients to visit the clinic three times each week. Peritoneal dialysis (PD) permits patients to self-administer their treatments at home on a daily basis. The clinic serves a number of HMO patients under a contract that limits collections from the HMO insurer to a fixed amount per patient. As a result, the clinic's profitability is directly related to its ability to control costs. To illustrate, assume that the clinic is paid a fixed annual fee of $15,000 per HMO patient served. Also assume that the current cost to provide health care averages $14,000 a year per patient, resulting in an average profitability of $1,000 per patient ($15,000 − $14,000). Because the revenue base is fixed, the only way the clinic can increase profitability is to lower its average cost of providing services. If the clinic fails to control costs and the average cost of patient care increases, profitability will decline. A recent ABC study suggests that the cost to provide HD service exceeds the amount of revenue generated from providing that service. The clinic is profitable because PD services generate enough profit to more than make up for losses on HD services.

Required

Respond to each potential scenario described here. Each scenario is independent of the others.

a. Suppose that as a result of the ABC analysis, the chief accountant, a certified management accountant (CMA), recommends that the clinic discontinue treating HD patients referred by the HMO provider. Based on this assumption, answer the following questions.

(1) Assume that the clinic is located in a small town. If it discontinues treating the HD patients, they will be forced to drive 50 miles to the nearest alternative treatment center. Does the clinic have a moral obligation to society to continue to provide HD service although it is not profitable to do so?

(2) The accountant's recommendation places profitability above the needs of HD patients. Does this recommendation violate any of the standards of ethical professional practice described in Chapter 1, Exhibit 1.17?

b. Assume that the clinic continues to treat HD patients referred by HMOs. However, to compensate for the loss incurred on these patients, the clinic raises prices charged to non-HMO patients. Is it fair to require non-HMO patients to subsidize services provided to the HMO patients?

c. Suppose that the clinic administrators respond to the ABC data by cutting costs. The clinic overbooks HMO patients to ensure that downtime is avoided when cancellations occur. It reduces the RN nursing staff and assigns some of the technical work to less-qualified assistants. Ultimately, an overworked, underqualified nurse's aide makes a mistake, and a patient dies. Who is at fault–the HMO, the accountant who conducted the ABC analysis, or the clinic administrators who responded to the ABC information?

ATC 5-6 Spreadsheet Assignment *Using Excel*

eXcel

Tameron Corporation produces video games in three market categories: commercial, home line, and miniature handheld. Tameron has traditionally allocated overhead costs to the three product categories using the companywide base of direct labor hours. The company recently switched to an ABC system when it installed computer-controlled assembly stations that rendered the traditional costing system ineffective. In implementing the ABC system, the company identified the cost pools and drivers shown in the following spreadsheet. The activity in each of the three product lines appears in rows 3 to 9. The pooled costs are shown in cells E11 to E15.

Required

Construct a spreadsheet like the following one to compute the total cost and cost per unit for each product line. Cells K4 to K9, G12 to I15, E19 to E28, G19 to G28, I19 to I28, and K26 should all be formulas.

ATC 5-6 working 7th ed.xlsx - Microsoft Excel

	A	B	D	E	F	G	H	I	J	K
1	Chapter 5 - Working with Excel					Name:				
2										
3	b)	Driver		Commercial		Home Line		Miniature		Total
4		Labor hours		5,000		11,000		4,000		20,000
5		Machine hours		13,000		44,000		23,000		80,000
6		# Production orders		340		1,800		860		3,000
7		R&D time		15%		18%		67%		100%
8		Units		14,000		44,000		17,000		75,000
9		Sq. footage		20,000		50,000		30,000		100,000
10										
11		Cost type		Pooled Cost		Total Activity		Pool Rate		
12		Unit level		$ 620,000		80,000		$ 7.75	per mh	
13		Batch level		327,000		3,000		$ 109.00	per order	
14		Product level		185,000		100%		$ 185,000	times %	
15		Facility level		530,000		100,000		$ 5.30	per sq. ft.	
16		Total		$1,662,000						
17										
18		Product Cost:		Commercial		Home Line		Miniature		Total
19		Direct material cost	$30	$ 420,000	$ 20	$ 880,000	$25	$ 425,000		
20		Direct labor cost	12	60,000	12	132,000	15	60,000		
21		Allocated overhead								
22		Unit-level		100,750		341,000		178,250		
23		Batch-level		37,060		196,200		93,740		
24		Product-level		27,750		33,300		123,950		
25		Facility-level		106,000		265,000		159,000		
26		Total cost		$ 751,560		$1,847,500		$1,039,940		$3,639,000
27										
28		Cost per unit		$ 53.68		$ 41.99		$ 61.17		
29										

Source: Microsoft Excel 2010

eXcel

ATC 5-7 Spreadsheet Assignment *Mastering Excel*

Beasley Company makes three types of exercise machines. Data have been accumulated for four possible overhead drivers. Data for these four possible drivers are shown in rows 4 to 7 of the following spreadsheet.

Required

Construct a spreadsheet that will allocate overhead and calculate unit cost for each of these alternative drivers. A screen capture of the spreadsheet and data follows.

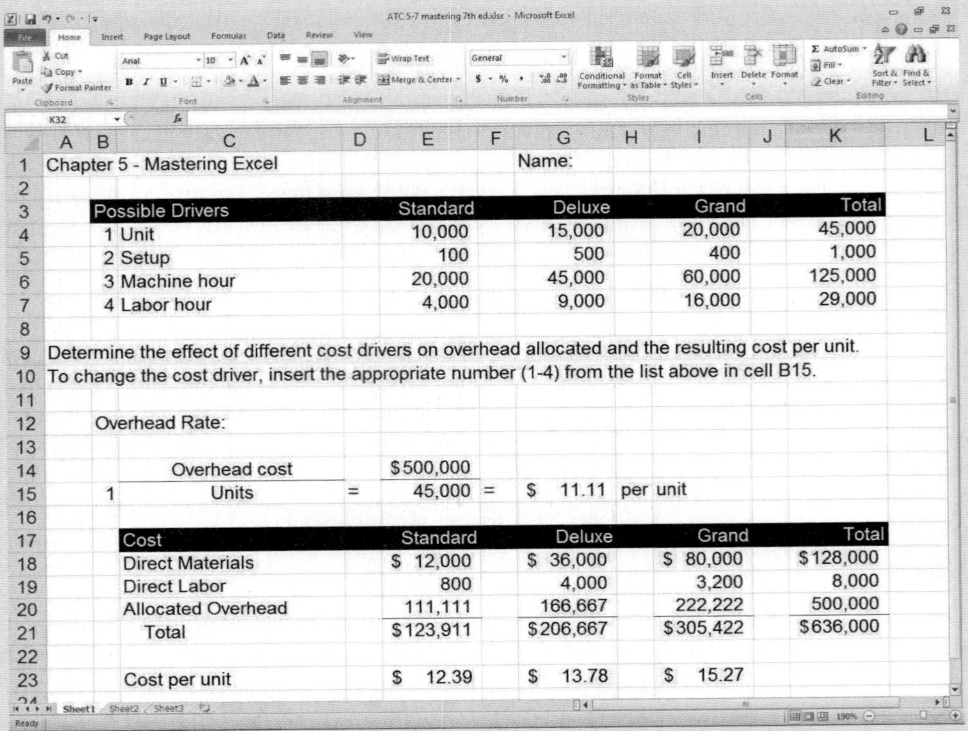

	A	B	C	D	E	F	G	H	I	J	K
1	Chapter 5 - Mastering Excel						Name:				
2											
3		Possible Drivers			Standard		Deluxe		Grand		Total
4		1	Unit		10,000		15,000		20,000		45,000
5		2	Setup		100		500		400		1,000
6		3	Machine hour		20,000		45,000		60,000		125,000
7		4	Labor hour		4,000		9,000		16,000		29,000
8											
9	Determine the effect of different cost drivers on overhead allocated and the resulting cost per unit.										
10	To change the cost driver, insert the appropriate number (1-4) from the list above in cell B15.										
11											
12		Overhead Rate:									
13											
14			Overhead cost		$500,000						
15		1	Units	=	45,000	=	$ 11.11	per unit			
16											
17			Cost		Standard		Deluxe		Grand		Total
18			Direct Materials		$ 12,000		$ 36,000		$ 80,000		$128,000
19			Direct Labor		800		4,000		3,200		8,000
20			Allocated Overhead		111,111		166,667		222,222		500,000
21			Total		$123,911		$206,667		$305,422		$636,000
22											
23			Cost per unit		$ 12.39		$ 13.78		$ 15.27		

Source: Microsoft Excel 2010

Spreadsheet Tips

1. This spreadsheet uses a function called *vertical lookup.* This function can pull the appropriate values from a table. The form of this function is =VLOOKUP (value, table, column#). In this example, the table is in cells B4 to K7. Three examples of the use of VLOOKUP follow.
2. Cell C15 is =VLOOKUP (B15, B4:K7, 2). This function operates by using the one (1) in cell B15 to look up a value in the table. Notice that the table is defined as B4:K7 and that the function is looking up the value in the second column, which is Units.
3. Cell E15 is =VLOOKUP (B15, B4:K7, 10). In this case, the function is looking up the value in the tenth column, which is 45,000. Be sure to count empty columns.
4. Cell E20 is =VLOOKUP (B15, B4:K7, 4)*G15. In this case, the function is looking up the value in the fourth column, which is $10,000. Be sure to count empty columns.
5. Cells I15, G20, and I20 also use the VLOOKUP function.
6. After completing the spreadsheet, you can change the value in cell B15 (1-4) to see the effect of choosing a different driver for overhead.

COMPREHENSIVE PROBLEM

To this point, we have assumed that Magnificent Modems produced only one type of modem. Suppose instead we assume the company produces several different kinds of modems. The production process differs for each type of product. Some require more setup time than others, they are produced in different batch sizes, and they require different amounts of indirect labor (supervision). Packaging and delivery to customers also differs for each type of modem. Even so, Magnificent Modems uses a single allocation base (number of units) to allocate overhead costs.

Required

Write a brief memo that explains how Magnificent Modems could benefit from an ABC costing system.

CHAPTER 6

Relevant Information for Special Decisions

LEARNING OBJECTIVES

After you have mastered the material in this chapter, you will be able to:

LO 6-1 Identify the characteristics of relevant information.

LO 6-2 Make appropriate special order decisions.

LO 6-3 Make appropriate outsourcing decisions.

LO 6-4 Make appropriate segment elimination decisions.

LO 6-5 Make appropriate asset replacement decisions.

LO 6-6 Explain the conflict between short-term and long-term profitability (Appendix).

LO 6-7 Make decisions about allocating scarce resources (Appendix).

Video lectures and accompanying self-assessment quizzes are available in Connect® for all learning objectives.

CHAPTER OPENING

Mary Daniels paid $25,000 to purchase a car that was used in her rental business. After one year, the car had a book value of $21,000. Ms. Daniels needs cash and is considering selling the car. After advertising the vehicle for sale, the best offer she received was $19,000. Ms. Daniels really needed the money, but ultimately decided not to sell because she did not want to incur a $2,000 loss ($21,000 book value − $19,000 market value). Did Ms. Daniels make the right decision?

Whether Ms. Daniels will be better off selling the car or keeping it is unknown. However, it is certain that she based her decision on irrelevant data. Ms. Daniels incurred a loss when the market value of the car dropped. She cannot avoid a loss that already exists. Past mistakes should not affect current decisions. The current value of the car is $19,000. Ms. Daniels' decision is whether to take the money or keep the car. The book value of the car is not relevant. This chapter explains how to isolate and focus on the variables that are relevant in the decision-making process.

The Curious Accountant

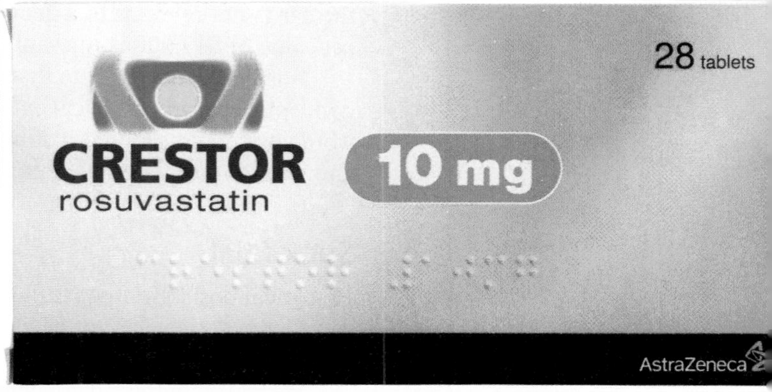

©nattul/Shutterstock

In 2018, the authors compared the prices of 10 of the top-selling, nongeneric drugs at two large online pharmacies, one in the United States and one in Canada. The analysis showed the Canadian prices for these 10 prescription drugs, such as **Advair** and **Crestor**, were only 48 percent of prices charged in the United States.

Major pharmaceutical companies have earnings before tax that average around 18 percent of sales, indicating that their costs average about 82 percent of the prices they charge. In other words, it costs approximately $82 to generate $100 of revenue. Given that drugs are sold in Canada for 48 percent of the U.S. sales price, a drug that is sold in the United States for $100 would be sold in Canada for only $48.

How can drugs be sold in Canada for less ($48) than they cost to manufacture ($82)? (Answer on page 260.)

Source: goodrx.com and canadadrugonline.com.

RELEVANT INFORMATION

LO 6-1

Identify the characteristics of relevant information.

How can you avoid irrelevant information when making decisions? Two primary characteristics distinguish relevant from useless information. Specifically, **relevant information** (1) differs among the alternatives and (2) is future-oriented.

The first characteristic recognizes that relevant information differs for one or more of the alternatives being considered. Suppose the car Ms. Daniels is considering selling is due for a state-required safety inspection. Further assume that the inspection must be completed before the car can be sold or driven. Since the inspection fee must be paid regardless of whether Ms. Daniels keeps or sells the car, it does not differ among the alternatives and therefore is not relevant to her decision. In contrast, assume the car is due for an oil change that can be delayed until after the car is sold. Since Ms. Daniels can avoid the cost of the oil change if she sells the car but must pay for the oil change if she keeps the car, the cost of the oil change differs between the alternatives and is relevant to her decision.

The second characteristic of relevant information is that it impacts the future. "Don't cry over spilt milk." "It's water over the dam." These aphorisms remind people they cannot change the past. With regard to business decisions, the principle means you cannot avoid a cost that has already been incurred. In the Daniels example, the historical cost ($25,000) of the car is not relevant to a decision regarding whether to sell the car today. The current market value of $19,000 is relevant to the decision regarding whether to sell the car today.

It is interesting to note that the two characteristics are merely different views of the same concept because historical information does not differ between the alternatives. In other words, we could say that historical costs are not relevant because they do not differ between alternatives associated with current decisions.

Sunk Cost

Historical costs are frequently called *sunk costs.* Since **sunk costs** have been incurred in past transactions, they cannot be changed and are not relevant for making current decisions. The $25,000 original cost of the car in the Daniels example is a sunk cost.

Why even bother to collect historical information if it is not relevant? Historical information may be useful in predicting the future. A company that earned $5 million last year is more likely to earn $5 million this year than a company that earned $5,000 last year. The predictive capacity is relevant because it provides insight into the future.

Opportunity Costs

An **opportunity cost** is the sacrifice that is incurred in order to obtain an alternative opportunity. For example, in the previous case, Ms. Daniels must give up the opportunity to obtain $19,000 in order to keep the car. So, the opportunity cost of owning the car is $19,000. Since this cost differs between the alternatives of owning the car versus selling it and since it affects the present or future, it is relevant to the decision regarding whether to keep or sell the car.

The best offer that Ms. Daniels received for the car was $19,000. Suppose Ms. Daniels also received a less favorable offer of $18,000. Does this mean that the opportunity cost of keeping the car is $37,000 ($18,000 + $19,000)? No. Opportunity costs are not cumulative. Ms. Daniels really has only one opportunity. If she accepts the $19,000 offer, she must reject the $18,000 offer or vice versa. Accountants normally measure opportunity cost as the highest value of the available alternatives. In this case, the opportunity cost of keeping the car is $19,000.

CHECK YOURSELF 6.1

Aqua Inc. makes statues for use in fountains. On January 1, Year 1, the company paid $13,500 for a mold to make a particular type of statue. The mold had an expected useful life of four years and a salvage value of $1,500. On January 1, Year 2, the mold had a market value of $3,000 and a salvage value of $1,200. The expected useful life did not change. What is the relevant cost of using the mold during Year 2?

Answer The relevant cost of using the mold in Year 2 is the opportunity cost [(Market value − Salvage value) ÷ Remaining useful life], in this case, ($3,000 − $1,200) ÷ 2 = $900. The book value of the asset and associated depreciation is based on a sunk cost that cannot be avoided because it has already been incurred and therefore is not relevant to current decisions. In contrast, Aqua could avoid the opportunity cost (market value) by selling the mold.

Relevance Is an Independent Concept

The concept of relevance is independent from the concept of cost behavior. In a given circumstance, **relevant costs** could be either fixed or variable. Consider the following illustration. Executives of Better Bakery Products are debating whether to add a new product, either cakes or pies, to the company's line. Projected costs for the two options follow.

Cost of Cakes		Cost of Pies	
Materials (per unit)	$ 1.50	Materials (per unit)	$ 2.00
Direct labor (per unit)	1.00	Direct labor (per unit)	1.00
Supervisor's salary*	25,000.00	Supervisor's salary*	25,000.00
Franchise fee†	50,000.00	Advertising‡	40,000.00

*It will be necessary to hire a new production supervisor at a cost of $25,000 per year.

†Cakes will be distributed under a nationally advertised label. Better Bakery pays an annual franchise fee for the right to use the product label. Because of the established brand name, Better Bakery will not be required to advertise the product.

‡Better Bakery will market the pies under its own name and will advertise the product in the local market in which the product sells.

Which costs are relevant? Fifty cents per unit of the materials can be avoided by choosing cakes instead of pies. A portion of the materials cost is therefore relevant. Labor costs will be one dollar per unit whether Better Bakery makes cakes or pies. Labor cost is therefore not relevant. Although both materials and direct labor are variable costs, one is relevant but the other is not.

Since Better Bakery must hire a supervisor under either alternative, the supervisor's salary is not relevant. The franchise fee can be avoided if Better Bakery makes pies and advertising costs can be avoided if it makes cakes. All three of these costs are fixed, but only two are relevant. Finally, all the costs (whether fixed or variable) could be avoided if Better Bakery rejects both products. Whether a cost is fixed or variable has no bearing on its relevance.

Relevance Is Context Sensitive

A particular cost that is relevant in one context may be irrelevant in another. Consider a store that carries men's, women's, and children's clothing. The store manager's salary could not be avoided by eliminating the children's department, but it could be avoided if the entire store were closed. The salary is not relevant to deciding whether to eliminate the children's department but is relevant with respect to deciding to close the store. In one context, the salary is not relevant. In the other context, it is relevant.

Relationship between Relevance and Accuracy

Information need not be exact to be relevant. You may decide to delay purchasing a laptop computer you want if you know its price is going to drop even if you don't know exactly how much the price decrease will be. You know part of the cost can be avoided by waiting; you are just not sure of the amount.

The most useful information is both relevant and precise. Totally inaccurate information is useless. Likewise, irrelevant information is useless regardless of its accuracy.

Quantitative versus Qualitative Characteristics of Decision Making

Relevant information can have both **quantitative** and **qualitative characteristics.** The previous examples focused on quantitative data. Now consider qualitative issues. Suppose you are deciding which of two laptop computers to purchase. Computer A costs $300 more than Computer B. Both computers satisfy your technical requirements; however, Computer A has a more attractive appearance. From a quantitative standpoint, you would select Computer B because you could avoid $300 of cost. However, if the laptop will be used in circumstances where clients need to be impressed, appearance–a qualitative characteristic–may be more important than minimizing cost. You might purchase Computer A even though quantitative factors favor Computer B. Both qualitative and quantitative data are relevant to decision making.

As with quantitative data, qualitative features must *differ* between the alternatives to be relevant. If the two computers were identical in appearance, attractiveness would not be relevant to making the decision.

Differential Revenue and Avoidable Cost

Since relevant revenue *differs* among the alternatives, it is sometimes called **differential revenue.** To illustrate, assume Pecks Department Stores sells men's, women's, and children's clothing and is considering eliminating the children's line. The revenue generated by the children's department is differential (relevant) revenue because Pecks' total revenue would be different if the children's department were eliminated.

Why would Pecks consider eliminating the children's department and thereby lose the differential (relevant) revenue? Pecks may be able to save more by eliminating the cost of operating the department than it loses in differential revenue. Some but not all of the costs associated with operating the children's department can be saved. For example, if Pecks Department Stores eliminates the children's department, the company can eliminate the cost of the department manager's salary but cannot get rid of the salary of the company president. The costs that stay the same are not relevant. The costs that can be *avoided* by closing the department are relevant. Indeed, relevant costs are frequently called *avoidable costs.*

Avoidable costs are the costs managers can eliminate by making specific choices. In the Pecks example, the cost of the department manager's salary is an avoidable (relevant) cost. The cost of the president's salary is not avoidable and is not relevant to the elimination decision.

Relationship of Cost Avoidance to a Cost Hierarchy

Classifying costs into one of four hierarchical levels helps identify avoidable costs.[1]

1. *Unit-level costs.* Costs incurred each time a company generates one unit of product are **unit-level costs.**[2] Examples include the cost of direct materials, direct labor, inspections, packaging, shipping, and handling. Incremental (additional) unit-level costs increase *with each additional unit of product generated. Unit-level costs can be avoided by eliminating the production of a single unit of product.*

[1]R. Cooper and R. S. Kaplan, *The Design of Cost Management Systems* (Englewood Cliffs, NJ: Prentice-Hall, 1991). Our classifications are broader than those typically presented. They encompass service and merchandising companies as well as manufacturing businesses. The original cost hierarchy was developed as a platform for activity-based costing, a topic introduced in the previous chapter. These classifications are equally useful as a tool for identifying avoidable costs.

[2]Recall that we use the term *product* in a generic sense to represent producing goods or services.

2. *Batch-level costs.* Many products are generated in batches rather than individual units. For example, a heating and air conditioning technician may service a batch of air conditioners in an apartment complex. Some of the job costs apply only to individual units, and other costs relate to the entire batch. For instance, the labor to service each air conditioner is a unit-level cost, but the cost of driving to the site is a **batch-level cost.**

   Classifying costs as unit versus batch level frequently depends on the context rather than the type of cost. For example, shipping and handling costs to send 200 computers to a university are batch-level costs. In contrast, the shipping and handling cost to deliver a single computer to each of a number of individual customers is a unit-level cost. Eliminating a batch of work avoids both batch-level and unit-level costs. Similarly, adding a batch of work increases batch-level and unit-level costs. Increasing the number of units in a particular batch increases unit-level but not batch-level costs. Decreasing the number of units in a batch reduces unit-level costs but not batch-level costs.
3. *Product-level costs.* Costs incurred to support specific products or services are called **product-level costs.** Product-level costs include quality inspection costs, engineering design costs, the costs of obtaining and defending patents, the costs of regulatory compliance, and inventory holding costs such as interest, insurance, maintenance, and storage. *Product-level costs can be avoided by discontinuing a product line.* For example, suppose the Snapper Company makes the engines used in its lawn mowers. Buying engines from an outside supplier instead of making them would allow Snapper to avoid the product-level costs such as legal fees for patents, manufacturing supervisory costs of producing the engines, and the maintenance and inventory costs of holding engine parts.
4. *Facility-level costs.* **Facility-level costs** are incurred to support the entire company. They are not related to any specific product, batch, or unit of product. Because these costs maintain the facility as a whole, they are frequently called *facility-sustaining costs.* Facility-level costs include building rent or depreciation, personnel administration and training, property and real estate taxes, insurance, maintenance, administrative salaries, general selling costs, landscaping, utilities, and security. Total facility-level costs cannot be avoided unless the entire company is dissolved. However, eliminating a business segment (such as a division, department, or office) may enable a company to avoid some facility-level costs. For example, if a bank eliminates one of its branches, it can avoid the costs of renting, maintaining, and insuring that particular branch building. In general, *segment-level* facility costs can be avoided when a segment is eliminated. In contrast, *corporate-level* facility costs cannot be avoided unless the corporation is eliminated.

©Ryan Pyle/Corbis/Getty Images

Precise distinctions between the various categories are often difficult to draw. One company may incur sales staff salaries as a facility-level cost while another company may pay sales commissions traceable to product lines or even specific units of a product line. Cost classifications cannot be memorized. Classifying specific cost items into the appropriate categories requires thoughtful judgment.

RELEVANT INFORMATION AND SPECIAL DECISIONS

Five types of special decisions are frequently encountered in business practice: (1) special order, (2) outsourcing, (3) segment elimination, (4) asset replacement, and (5) scarce resource allocation. The following sections discuss using relevant information in making the first four types of special decisions. The Appendix to this chapter discusses scarce resource decisions.

LO 6-2

Make appropriate special order decisions.

EXHIBIT 6.1

Budgeted Cost for Expected Production of 2,000 Printers

Unit-level costs		
Materials costs (2,000 units × $90)	$180,000	
Labor costs (2,000 units × $82.50)	165,000	
Overhead (2,000 units × $7.50)	15,000	
Total unit-level costs (2,000 × $180)		$360,000
Batch-level costs		
Assembly setup (10 batches × $1,700)	17,000	
Materials handling (10 batches × $500)	5,000	
Total batch-level costs (10 batches × $2,200)		22,000
Product-level costs		
Engineering design	14,000	
Production manager salary	63,300	
Total product-level costs		77,300
Facility-level costs		
Segment-level costs:		
Division manager's salary	85,000	
Administrative costs	12,700	
Allocated—corporate-level costs:		
Company president's salary	43,200	
Building rental	27,300	
General expenses	31,000	
Total facility-level costs		199,200
Total expected cost		$658,500
Cost per unit: $658,500 ÷ 2,000 = $329.25		

SPECIAL ORDER DECISIONS

Occasionally, a company receives an offer to sell its goods at a price significantly below its normal selling price. The company must make a **special order decision** to accept or reject the offer.

Quantitative Analysis

Assume Premier Office Products manufactures printers. Premier expects to make and sell 2,000 printers in 10 batches of 200 units per batch during the coming year. Expected production costs are summarized in Exhibit 6.1.

Adding its normal markup to the total cost per unit, Premier set the selling price at $360 per printer.

Suppose Premier receives a *special order* from a new customer for 200 printers. If Premier accepts the order, its expected sales would increase from 2,000 units to 2,200 units. But the special order customer is willing to pay only $250 per printer. This price is well below not only Premier's normal selling price of $360 but also the company's expected per-unit cost of $329.25. Should Premier accept or reject the special order? At first glance, it seems Premier should reject the special order because the customer's offer is below the expected cost per unit. But analyzing relevant costs and revenue leads to a different conclusion.

Answers to the Curious Accountant

There are several factors that enable drug companies to reduce their prices to certain customers. One significant factor is the issue of relevant cost. Pharmaceutical manufacturers have a substantial amount of fixed cost, such as research and development. For example, in 2017 **Merck & Co.** had research and development expenses that were 25.4 percent of sales, while its cost of goods sold expense was 31.8 percent of sales. With respect to a special order decision, the research and development costs would not change and therefore would not be relevant. In contrast, the unit-level cost of goods sold would increase and therefore would be relevant. Many other costs at Merck, such as administrative and advertising expenses, are more fixed in nature than variable. Clearly, relevant costs are significantly less than the total cost. If Canadian prices are based on relevant costs, that is, if drug companies view Canadian sales as a special order opportunity, the lower prices may provide a contribution to profitability even though they are significantly less than the prices charged in the United States.

The quantitative analysis follows in three steps.

Step 1. Determine the amount of the relevant (differential) revenue Premier will earn by accepting the special order. Premier's alternatives are (1) to accept or (2) to reject the special order. If Premier accepts the special order, additional revenue will be $50,000 ($250 × 200 units). If Premier rejects the special order, additional revenue will be zero. Since the amount of revenue differs between the alternatives, the $50,000 is relevant.

Step 2. **Determine the amount of the relevant (differential) cost Premier will incur by accepting the special order.** Examine the costs in Exhibit 6.1. If Premier accepts the special order, it will incur additional unit-level costs (materials, labor, and overhead). It will also incur the cost of one additional 200-unit batch. The unit- and batch-level costs are relevant because Premier could avoid them by rejecting the special order. The other costs in Exhibit 6.1 are not relevant because Premier will incur them whether it accepts or rejects the special order.

Step 3. **Accept the special order if the relevant revenue exceeds the relevant (avoidable) cost. Reject the order if relevant cost exceeds relevant revenue.** Exhibit 6.2 summarizes the relevant figures. Since the relevant revenue exceeds the relevant cost, Premier should accept the special order because profitability will increase by $11,800.

EXHIBIT 6.2

Relevant Information for Special Order of 200 Printers

Differential revenue ($250 × 200 units)	$ 50,000
Avoidable unit-level costs ($180 × 200 units)	(36,000)
Avoidable batch-level costs ($2,200 × 1 batch)	(2,200)
Contribution to income	$ 11,800

Opportunity Costs

Premier can consider the special order because it has enough excess productive capacity to make the additional units. Suppose Premier has the opportunity to lease its excess capacity (currently unused building and equipment) for $15,000. If Premier uses the excess capacity to make the additional printers, it must forgo the opportunity to lease the excess capacity to a third party. Sacrificing the potential leasing income represents an opportunity cost of accepting the special order. Adding this opportunity cost to the other relevant costs increases the cost of accepting the special order to $53,200 ($38,200 unit-level and batch-level costs + $15,000 opportunity cost). The avoidable costs would then exceed the differential revenue, resulting in a projected loss of $3,200 ($50,000 differential revenue − $53,200 avoidable costs). Under these circumstances Premier would be better off rejecting the special order and leasing the excess capacity.

Relevance and the Decision Context

Assume Premier does not have the opportunity to lease its excess capacity. Recall the original analysis indicated the company could earn an $11,800 contribution to profit by accepting a special order to sell 200 printers at $250 per unit (see Exhibit 6.2). Because Premier can earn a contribution to profit by selling printers for $250 each, can the company reduce its normal selling price (price charged to existing customers) to $250? The answer is no, as illustrated in Exhibit 6.3.

EXHIBIT 6.3

Projections Based on 2,200 Printers at a Sales Price of $250 per Unit

Revenue ($250 × 2,200 units)		$ 550,000
Unit-level supplies and inspection ($180 × 2,200 units)	$396,000	
Batch-level costs ($2,200 × 11 batches)	24,200	
Product-level costs	77,300	
Facility-level costs	199,200	
Total cost		(696,700)
Projected loss		$(146,700)

If a company is to be profitable, it must ultimately generate revenue in excess of total costs. Although the facility-level and product-level costs are not relevant to the special order decision, they are relevant to the operation of the business as a whole.

Qualitative Characteristics

Should a company ever reject a special order if the relevant revenues exceed the relevant costs? Qualitative characteristics may be even more important than quantitative ones. If Premier's regular customers learn the company sold printers to another buyer at $250 per unit, they may demand reduced prices on future purchases. Exhibit 6.3 shows Premier cannot reduce the price for all customers. Special order customers should therefore come from outside Premier's normal sales territory. In addition, special order customers should be advised that the special price does not apply to repeat business. Cutting off a special order customer who has been permitted to establish a continuing relationship is likely to lead to ill-feelings and harsh words. A business's reputation can depend on how management handles such relationships. Finally, at full capacity, Premier should reject any special orders at reduced prices because filling those orders reduces its ability to satisfy customers who pay full price.

REALITY BYTES

Sometimes companies make special pricing decisions that appear to violate the rule of rejecting an offer when its relevant cost exceeds its relevant revenue. Consider companies that use the services of Groupon.

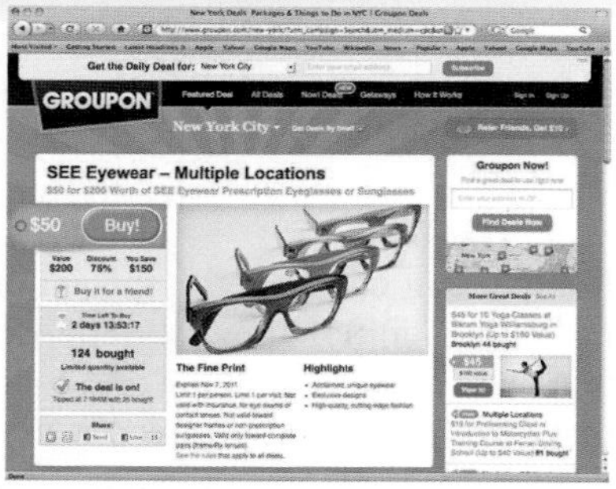

©Grupon.com/AP Images

In these special pricing decisions, retail customers are offered a reduced price on goods or services if they make the purchase through Groupon. For example, a restaurant may offer to sell a customer $40 worth of food for only $20. This appears to be a deal where the restaurant is selling its food for 50 percent off, but actually it is probably selling the food for around 60 percent off. The restaurant will receive only around $15 of the $20 the customer pays to Groupon. Groupon keeps the remaining $5 for itself. Thus, the restaurant is selling $40 of food for $15.

At Darden Restaurants Inc., the company that owns several restaurant chains including LongHorn Steakhouse and Olive Garden, the cost of the food sold average 30 percent of revenue, and restaurant labor costs average 34 percent. In other words, if a customer buys $40 worth of food, approximately $26 of those dollars are costs of providing the food to the customer. Not all of these costs are unit-level costs, but many of them are. Therefore, when a restaurant sells a customer $40 worth of food for only $15, as in the previous Groupon example, it appears to be selling the goods for much less than their relevant cost. Why would the restaurant do this?

Obviously, the restaurant is hoping that it will attract new customers with its special pricing offer and that these new customers will become repeat customers who pay full price for future meals. In this situation, the true relevant revenue is not the $15 received for the first meal, but includes the revenue from future meals the customer buys, along with alcoholic beverages that may not be included in the coupon deal. Of course there is no guarantee the customer will ever return, but as with most business decisions, managers must make decisions with less than perfect information.

OUTSOURCING DECISIONS

LO 6-3

Make appropriate outsourcing decisions.

Companies can sometimes purchase products they need for less than it would cost to make them. This circumstance explains why automobile manufacturers purchase rather than make many of the parts in their cars or why a caterer might buy gourmet desserts from a specialty company. Buying goods and services from other companies rather than producing them internally is commonly called **outsourcing.**

Quantitative Analysis

Assume Premier Office Products is considering whether to outsource production of the printers it currently makes. A supplier has offered to sell an unlimited supply of printers to Premier for $240 each. The estimated cost of making the printers is $329.25 per unit (see Exhibit 6.1). The data suggest that Premier could save money by outsourcing. Analyzing relevant costs proves this presumption wrong.

A two-step quantitative analysis for the outsourcing decision follows.

Step 1. Determine the production costs Premier can avoid if it outsources printer production. A review of Exhibit 6.1 discloses the costs Premier could avoid by outsourcing. If Premier purchases the printers, it can avoid the unit-level costs (materials, labor, overhead), and the batch-level costs (assembly setup and materials handling). It can also avoid the product-level costs (engineering design costs and production manager salary). Deciding to outsource will not, however, affect the facility-level costs. Because Premier will incur them whether or not it outsources printer production, the facility-level costs are not relevant to the outsourcing decision. Exhibit 6.4 shows the avoidable (relevant) costs of outsourcing.

Step 2. Compare the avoidable (relevant) production costs with the cost of buying the product and select the lower-cost option. Because the relevant production cost is less than the purchase price of the printers ($229.65 per unit versus $240.00), the quantitative analysis suggests that Premier should continue to make the printers. Profitability would decline by $20,700 [$459,300 − ($240 × 2,000)] if printer production were outsourced.

EXHIBIT 6.4

Relevant Cost for Expected Production for Outsourcing 2,000 Printers

Unit-level costs ($180 × 2,000 units)	$360,000
Batch-level costs ($2,200 × 10 batches)	22,000
Product-level costs	77,300
Total relevant cost	$459,300
Cost per unit: $459,300 ÷ 2,000 = $229.65	

Opportunity Costs

Suppose Premier's accountant determines that the space Premier currently uses to manufacture printers could be leased to a third party for $40,000 per year. By using the space to manufacture printers, Premier is *forgoing the opportunity* to earn $40,000. Because this *opportunity cost* can be avoided by purchasing the printers, it is relevant to the outsourcing decision. After adding the opportunity cost to the other relevant costs, the total relevant cost increases to $499,300 ($459,300 + $40,000) and the relevant cost per unit becomes $249.65 ($499,300 ÷ 2,000). Since Premier can purchase printers for $240, it should outsource printer production. It would be better off buying the printers and leasing the manufacturing space.

Evaluating the Effect of Growth on the Level of Production

The decision to outsource would change if expected production increased from 2,000 to 3,000 units. Because some of the avoidable costs are fixed relative to the level of production, cost per unit decreases as volume increases. For example, the product-level costs (engineering design, production manager's salary, and opportunity cost) are fixed relative to the level of production. Exhibit 6.5 shows the relevant cost per unit if Premier expects to produce 3,000 printers.

EXHIBIT 6.5

Relevant Cost for Expected Production for Outsourcing 3,000 Printers

Unit-level costs ($180 × 3,000 units)	$540,000
Batch-level costs ($2,200 × 15 batches)	33,000
Product-level costs	77,300
Opportunity cost	40,000
Total relevant cost	$690,300
Cost per unit: $690,300 ÷ 3,000 units = $230.10	

At 3,000 units of production, the relevant cost of making printers is less than the cost of outsourcing ($230.10 versus $240.00). If management believes the company is likely to experience growth in the near future, it should reject the outsourcing option. Managers must consider potential growth when making outsourcing decisions.

Qualitative Features

A company that uses **vertical integration** controls the full range of activities from acquiring raw materials to distributing goods and services. Outsourcing reduces the level of vertical integration, passing some of a company's control over its products to outside suppliers. The reliability of the supplier is critical to an outsourcing decision. An unscrupulous supplier may lure an unsuspecting manufacturer into an outsourcing decision using **low-ball pricing.** Once the manufacturer is dependent on the supplier, the supplier raises prices. If a price sounds too good to be true, it probably is too good to be true. Other potential problems include product quality and delivery commitments. If the printers do not work properly or are not delivered on time, Premier's customers will be dissatisfied with Premier, not the supplier. Outsourcing requires that Premier depend on the supplier to deliver quality products at designated prices according to a specified schedule. Any supplier failures will become Premier's failures.

To protect themselves from unscrupulous or incompetent suppliers, many companies establish a select list of reliable **certified suppliers.** These companies seek to become the preferred customers of the suppliers by offering incentives such as guaranteed volume purchases with prompt payments. These incentives motivate the suppliers to ship high-quality products on a timely basis. The purchasing companies recognize that prices ultimately depend on the suppliers' ability to control costs, so the buyers and suppliers work together to minimize costs. For example, buyers may share confidential information about their production plans with suppliers if such information would enable the suppliers to more effectively control costs.

Companies must approach outsourcing decisions cautiously even when relationships with reliable suppliers are ensured. Outsourcing has both internal and external effects. It usually displaces employees. If the supplier experiences difficulties, reestablishing internal production capacity is expensive once a trained workforce has been released. Loyalty and trust are difficult to build but easy to destroy. In fact, companies must consider not only the employees who will be discharged but also the morale of those who remain. Cost reductions achieved through outsourcing are of little benefit if they are acquired at the expense of low morale and reduced productivity.

In spite of the potential pitfalls outsourcing entails, the vast majority of U.S. businesses engage in some form of it. Such widespread acceptance suggests that most companies believe the benefits achieved through outsourcing exceed the potential shortcomings.

CHECK YOURSELF 6.2

Addison Manufacturing Company pays a production supervisor a salary of $48,000 per year. The supervisor manages the production of sprinkler heads that are used in water irrigation systems. Should the production supervisor's salary be considered a relevant cost to a special order decision? Should the production supervisor's salary be considered a relevant cost to an outsourcing decision?

Answer The production supervisor's salary is not a relevant cost to a special order decision because Addison would pay the salary regardless of whether it accepts or rejects a special order. Since the cost does not differ for the alternatives, it is not relevant. In contrast, the supervisor's salary would be relevant to an outsourcing decision. Addison could dismiss the supervisor if it purchased the sprinkler heads instead of making them. Since the salary could be avoided by purchasing heads instead of making them, the salary is relevant to an outsourcing decision.

REALITY BYTES

©hornyak/Shutterstock

In 2008 Georgia Power, a subsidiary of Southern Company, along with other investors, received approval to build two new nuclear power units at its Vogtle electric power plant. Original estimates put the cost of completing these units at around $12 billion, and the reactors were expected to begin operating in 2016. Westinghouse Electric Company, a subsidiary of Toshiba Corporation, was awarded the contract to build the reactors.

Things did not go as planned. By 2017 the revised cost to build the reactors had reached $25 billion, and the expected completion date was late 2021. These cost overruns were such that Westinghouse filed for Chapter 11 bankruptcy in March 2017.

With construction cost nearly double the original estimate and the completion date five years behind schedule, the investors faced the decision as to whether to complete the project or call it quits and accept their losses. As bad as the numbers were, the reality was that the previously incurred costs were sunk costs. At this point, the relevant question was whether expected revenues would cover the costs to complete the project plus future operating expenses.

A critical factor in the decision was how much, if any, of the cost overruns would the Georgia Public Utility Commission allow Georgia Power to pass on to its customers. The rates utilities charge customers are regulated by the states in which they operate. Late in 2017 Utility Commission voted to allow the project to continue, but not at rates that would generate as much profits as Georgia Power had originally expected. Based on the new guidelines, profits on the project would be $750 million less that hoped. Even so, it was deemed more profitable to continue the project than to cancel it.

Even when the amounts involved are in the billions, the bottom-line decision rule is, "Will future revenues exceed future costs?" Past costs are sunk costs.

Sources: SEC filings of Southern Company and news releases on Westinghouse's website.

SEGMENT ELIMINATION DECISIONS

LO 6-4

Make appropriate segment elimination decisions.

Businesses frequently organize their operations into subcomponents called **segments.** Segment data are used to make comparisons among different products, departments, or divisions. For example, in addition to the companywide income statement provided for external users, JCPenney may prepare separate income statements for each retail store for internal users. Executives can then evaluate managerial performance by comparing profitability measures among stores. *Segment reports* can be prepared for products, services, departments, branches, centers, offices, or divisions. These reports normally show segment revenues and costs. The primary objective of segment analysis is to determine whether relevant revenues exceed relevant costs.

Quantitative Analysis

Assume Premier Office Products makes copy equipment and computers as well as printers. Each product line is made in a separate division of the company. Division (segment) operating results for the most recent year are shown in Exhibit 6.6. Initial review of the results suggests the copier division should be eliminated because it is operating at a loss. However, analyzing the relevant revenues and expenses leads to a different conclusion.

A three-step quantitative analysis for the segment elimination decision follows.

Step 1. **Determine the amount of relevant (differential) revenue that pertains to eliminating the copier division.** The alternatives are (1) to eliminate or (2) to continue to operate the copier division. If Premier eliminates the copier line, it will lose the $550,000 of revenue the copier division currently produces. If the division continues to operate, Premier will earn the revenue. Since the revenue differs between the alternatives, it is relevant.

Step 2. **Determine the amount of cost Premier can avoid if it eliminates the copier division.** If it eliminates copiers, Premier can avoid the unit-level, batch-level, product-level, and

EXHIBIT 6.6

Projected Revenues and Costs by Segment

	Copiers	Computers	Printers	Total
Projected revenue	$ 550,000	$ 850,000	$720,000	$2,120,000
Projected costs				
Unit-level costs				
Materials costs	(120,000)	(178,000)	(180,000)	(478,000)
Labor costs	(160,000)	(202,000)	(165,000)	(527,000)
Overhead	(30,800)	(20,000)	(15,000)	(65,800)
Batch-level costs				
Assembly setup	(15,000)	(26,000)	(17,000)	(58,000)
Materials handling	(6,000)	(8,000)	(5,000)	(19,000)
Product-level costs				
Engineering design	(10,000)	(12,000)	(14,000)	(36,000)
Production manager salary	(52,000)	(55,800)	(63,300)	(171,100)
Facility-level costs				
Segment level				
Division manager salary	(82,000)	(92,000)	(85,000)	(259,000)
Administrative costs	(12,200)	(13,200)	(12,700)	(38,100)
Allocated—corporate-level				
Company president salary	(34,000)	(46,000)	(43,200)	(123,200)
Building rental	(19,250)	(29,750)	(27,300)	(76,300)
General facility expenses	(31,000)	(31,000)	(31,000)	(93,000)
Projected income (loss)	$ (22,250)	$ 136,250	$ 61,500	$ 175,500

segment-level facility-sustaining costs. The relevant revenue and the avoidable costs are shown in Exhibit 6.7.

Premier will incur the corporate-level facility-sustaining costs whether it eliminates the copier segment or continues to operate it. Since these costs do not differ between the alternatives, they are not relevant to the elimination decision.

Step 3. **If the relevant revenue is less than the avoidable cost, eliminate the segment (division). If not, continue to operate it.** Because operating the segment is contributing $62,000 per year to company profitability (see Exhibit 6.7), Premier should not eliminate the copier division. Exhibit 6.8 shows Premier's estimated revenues and costs if the computer and printer divisions were operated without the copier division. Projected company profit declines by $62,000 ($175,500 − $113,500) without the copier segment, confirming that eliminating it would be detrimental to Premier's profitability.

EXHIBIT 6.7

Relevant Revenue and Cost Data for Copier Segment

Projected revenue	$550,000
Projected costs	
Unit-level costs	
Materials costs	(120,000)
Labor costs	(160,000)
Overhead	(30,800)
Batch-level costs	
Assembly setup	(15,000)
Materials handling	(6,000)
Product-level costs	
Engineering design	(10,000)
Production manager salary	(52,000)
Facility-level costs	
Segment level	
Division manager salary	(82,000)
Administrative costs	(12,200)
Projected income (loss)	$ 62,000

Qualitative Considerations in Decisions to Eliminate Segments

As with other special decisions, management should consider qualitative factors when determining whether to eliminate segments. Employee lives will be disrupted; some employees may be reassigned elsewhere in the company, but others will be discharged. As with outsourcing decisions, reestablishing internal production capacity is difficult once a trained workforce has been released. Furthermore, employees in other segments, suppliers, customers, and investors may believe that the elimination of a segment implies the company as a whole is experiencing financial difficulty. These individuals may lose confidence in the company and seek business contacts with other companies they perceive to be more stable.

EXHIBIT 6.8

Projected Revenues and Costs without Copier Division

	Computers	Printers	Total
Projected revenue	$ 850,000	$720,000	$1,570,000
Projected costs			
Unit-level costs			
Materials costs	(178,000)	(180,000)	(358,000)
Labor costs	(202,000)	(165,000)	(367,000)
Overhead	(20,000)	(15,000)	(35,000)
Batch-level costs			
Assembly setup	(26,000)	(17,000)	(43,000)
Materials handling	(8,000)	(5,000)	(13,000)
Product-level costs			
Engineering design	(12,000)	(14,000)	(26,000)
Production manager salary	(55,800)	(63,300)	(119,100)
Facility-level costs			
Segment level			
Division manager salary	(92,000)	(85,000)	(177,000)
Administrative costs	(13,200)	(12,700)	(25,900)
Allocated—corporate-level*			
Company president salary	(63,000)	(60,200)	(123,200)
Building rental	(39,375)	(36,925)	(76,300)
General facility expenses	(46,500)	(46,500)	(93,000)
Projected income (loss)	$ 94,125	$ 19,375	$ 113,500

*The corporate-level facility costs that were previously *allocated* to the copier division have been reassigned on the basis of one-half to the computer division and one-half to the printer division.

Management must also consider the fact that sales of different product lines are frequently interdependent. Some customers prefer one-stop shopping; they want to buy all their office equipment from one supplier. If Premier no longer sells copiers, customers may stop buying its computers and printers. Eliminating one segment may reduce sales of other segments.

What will happen to the space Premier used to make the copiers? Suppose Premier decides to make telephone systems in the space it previously used for copiers. The contribution to profit of the telephone business would be an *opportunity cost* of operating the copier segment. As demonstrated in previous examples, adding the opportunity cost to the avoidable costs of operating the copier segment could change the decision.

As with outsourcing, volume changes can affect elimination decisions. Because many costs of operating a segment are fixed, the cost per unit decreases as production increases. Growth can transform a segment that is currently producing real losses into a segment that produces real profits. Managers must consider growth potential when making elimination decisions.

CHECK YOURSELF 6.3

Capital Corporation is considering eliminating one of its operating segments. Capital employed a real estate broker to determine the marketability of the building that houses the segment. The broker obtained three bids for the building: $250,000, $262,000, and $264,000. The book value of the building is $275,000. Based on this information alone, what is the relevant cost of the building?

Answer The book value of the building is a sunk cost that is not relevant. There are three bids for the building, but only one is relevant because Capital could sell the building only once. The relevant cost of the building is the highest opportunity cost, which in this case is $264,000.

Summary of Relationships between Avoidable Costs and the Hierarchy of Business Activity

A relationship exists between the cost hierarchy and the different types of special decisions just discussed. A special order involves making additional units of an existing product. Deciding to accept a special order affects unit-level and possibly batch-level costs. In contrast, outsourcing a product stops the production of that product. Outsourcing can avoid many product-level as well as unit- and batch-level costs. Finally, if a company eliminates an entire business segment, it can avoid some of the facility-level costs. The more complex the decision level, the more opportunities there are to avoid costs. Moving to a higher category does not mean, however, that all costs at the higher level of activity are avoidable. For example, all product-level costs may not be avoidable if a company chooses to outsource a product. The company may still incur inventory holding costs or advertising costs whether it makes or buys the product. Understanding the relationship between decision type and level of cost hierarchy helps when identifying avoidable costs. The relationships are summarized in Exhibit 6.9. For each type of decision, look for avoidable costs in the categories marked with an *X*. Remember also that sunk costs cannot be avoided.

EXHIBIT 6.9

Relationship between Decision Type and Level of Cost Hierarchy

Decision Type	Unit Level	Batch Level	Product Level	Facility Level
Special order	X	X		
Outsourcing	X	X	X	
Elimination	X	X	X	X

EQUIPMENT REPLACEMENT DECISIONS

LO 6-5

Make appropriate asset replacement decisions.

Equipment may become technologically obsolete long before it fails physically. Managers should base **equipment replacement decisions** on profitability analysis rather than physical deterioration. Assume Premier Office Products is considering replacing an existing machine with a new one. The following table summarizes pertinent information about the two machines.

Old Machine		New Machine	
Original cost	$ 90,000	Cost of the new machine	$29,000
Accumulated depreciation	(33,000)	Salvage value (in 5 years)	4,000
Book value	$ 57,000	Operating expenses ($4,500 × 5 years)	22,500
Market value (now)	$ 14,000		
Salvage value (in 5 years)	2,000		
Annual depreciation expense	11,000		
Operating expenses ($9,000 × 5 years)	45,000		

Quantitative Analysis

First determine what relevant costs Premier will incur if it keeps the *old machine.*

1. The *original cost* ($90,000), *current book value* ($57,000), *accumulated depreciation* ($33,000), and *annual depreciation expense* ($11,000) are different measures of a cost that was incurred in a prior period. They represent irrelevant sunk costs.
2. The $14,000 market value represents the current sacrifice Premier must make if it keeps using the existing machine. In other words, if Premier does not keep the machine, it can

sell it for $14,000. In economic terms, *forgoing the opportunity* to sell the machine costs as much as buying it. The *opportunity cost* is therefore relevant to the replacement decision.

3. The salvage value of the old machine reduces the opportunity cost. Premier can sell the old machine now for $14,000 or use it for five more years and then sell it for $2,000. The opportunity cost of using the old machine for five more years is therefore $12,000 ($14,000 − $2,000).
4. Because the $45,000 ($9,000 × 5) of operating expenses will be incurred if the old machine is used but can be avoided if it is replaced, the operating expenses are relevant costs.

Next, determine what relevant costs will be incurred if Premier purchases and uses the *new machine.*

1. The cost of the new machine represents a future economic sacrifice Premier must incur if it buys the new machine. It is a relevant cost.
2. The salvage value reduces the cost of purchasing the new machine. Part ($4,000) of the $29,000 cost of the new machine will be recovered at the end of five years. The relevant cost of purchasing the new machine is $25,000 ($29,000 − $4,000).
3. The $22,500 ($4,500 × 5) of operating expenses will be incurred if the new machine is purchased; it can be avoided if the new machine is not purchased. The operating expenses are relevant costs.

The relevant costs for the two machines are summarized here.

Old Machine		New Machine	
Opportunity cost	$ 14,000	Cost of the new machine	$29,000
Salvage value	(2,000)	Salvage value	(4,000)
Operating expenses	45,000	Operating expenses	22,500
Total	$57,000	Total	$47,500

The analysis suggests that Premier should acquire the new machine because buying it produces the lower relevant cost. The $57,000 cost of using the old machine can be *avoided* by incurring the $47,500 cost of acquiring and using the new machine. Over the five-year period, Premier would save $9,500 ($57,000 − $47,500) by purchasing the new machine. One caution: This analysis ignores income tax effects and the time value of money, which are explained later. The discussion in this chapter focuses on identifying and using relevant costs in decision making.

A Look Back <<

Decision making requires managers to choose from alternative courses of action. Successful decision making depends on a manager's ability to identify *relevant information.* Information that is relevant for decision making differs among the alternatives and is future oriented. Relevant revenues are sometimes called *differential revenues* because they differ among the alternatives. Relevant costs are sometimes called *avoidable costs* because they can be eliminated or avoided by choosing a specific course of action.

Costs that do not differ among the alternatives are not avoidable and therefore not relevant. *Sunk costs* are not relevant in decision making because they have been incurred in past transactions and therefore cannot be avoided. *Opportunity costs* are relevant because they represent potential benefits that may or may not be realized, depending on the decision maker's choice. In other words, future benefits that differ among the alternatives are relevant. Opportunity costs are not recorded in the financial accounting records.

Cost behavior (fixed or variable) is independent from the concept of relevance. Furthermore, a cost that is relevant in one decision context may be irrelevant in another context. Decision making depends on qualitative as well as quantitative information. *Quantitative information refers to information that can be measured using numbers. Qualitative information* is nonquantitative information such as personal preferences or opportunities.

Classifying costs into one of four hierarchical levels facilitates identifying relevant costs. *Unit-level costs* such as materials and labor are incurred each time a single unit of product is made. These costs can be avoided by eliminating the production of a single unit of product. *Batch-level costs* are associated with producing a group of products. Examples include setup costs and inspection costs related to a batch (group) of work rather than a single unit. Eliminating a batch would avoid both batch-level costs and unit-level costs. *Product-level costs* are incurred to support specific products or services (design and regulatory compliance costs). Product-level costs can be avoided by discontinuing a product line. *Facility-level costs,* like the president's salary, are incurred on behalf of the whole company or a segment of the company. In segment elimination decisions, the facility-level costs related to a particular segment being considered for elimination are relevant and avoidable. Those applying to the company as a whole are not avoidable.

Four types of special decisions that are frequently encountered in business are (1) *special orders,* (2) *outsourcing,* (3) *elimination decisions,* and (4) *asset replacement.* The relevant costs in a special order decision are the unit-level and batch-level costs that will be incurred if the special order is accepted. If the differential revenues from the special order exceed the relevant costs, the order should be accepted. Outsourcing decisions determine whether goods and services should be purchased from other companies. The relevant costs are the unit-level, batch-level, and product-level costs that could be avoided if the company outsources the product or service. If these costs are more than the cost to buy and the qualitative characteristics are satisfactory, the company should outsource. Segment-related unit-level, batch-level, product-level, and facility-level costs that can be avoided when a segment is eliminated are relevant. If the segment's avoidable costs exceed its differential revenues, it should be eliminated, assuming favorable qualitative factors. Asset replacement decisions compare the relevant costs of existing equipment with the relevant costs of new equipment to determine whether replacing the old equipment would be profitable.

>> A Look Forward

The next chapter introduces key concepts associated with planning and cost control. It shows you how to develop a master budget including the preparation of four operating budgets: (1) a sales budget, (2) an inventory purchases budget, (3) a selling and administrative expense budget and (4) a cash budget. The chapter explains how data from the operating budgets are used to prepare pro forma (budgeted) financial statements. In addition to the quantitative aspects, the chapter discusses the effect of the budgeting process on human behavior.

APPENDIX

Short-Term versus Long-Term Goals

LO 6-6

Explain the conflict between short-term and long-term profitability.

To examine conflicts between short-term versus long-term goals, we return to the equipment replacement decision made by the management team of Premier Office Products (see page 268 for details). Suppose that the final equipment replacement decision is made by a departmental supervisor who is under significant pressure to maximize profitability. She is told that if profitability declines, she will lose her job. Under these circumstances, the supervisor may choose to keep the old machine even though it is to the company's advantage to purchase the new one. This occurs because the beneficial impact of the new machine is realized in the second through fifth years. Indeed, replacing the equipment will result in more expense/loss recognition in the first year. To illustrate, study the following information.

	Year 1	Year 2	Year 3	Year 4	Year 5	Totals
Keep old machine						
Depreciation expense*	$11,000	$11,000	$11,000	$11,000	$11,000	$ 55,000
Operating expense	9,000	9,000	9,000	9,000	9,000	45,000
Total	$20,000	$20,000	$20,000	$20,000	$20,000	$100,000
Replace old machine						
Loss on disposal†	$43,000	$ 0	$ 0	$ 0	$ 0	$ 43,000
Depreciation expense‡	5,000	5,000	5,000	5,000	5,000	25,000
Operating expense	4,500	4,500	4,500	4,500	4,500	22,500
Total	$52,500	$ 9,500	$ 9,500	$ 9,500	$ 9,500	$ 90,500

*($57,000 book value − $2,000 salvage) ÷ 5 years = $11,000

†($57,000 book value − $14,000 market value) = $43,000

‡($29,000 cost − $4,000 salvage) ÷ 5 years = $5,000

This analysis verifies that total cost at the end of the five-year period is $9,500 less if the equipment is replaced ($100,000 − $90,500). Notice, however, that total costs at the end of the first year are higher by $32,500 ($52,500 − $20,000) if the old machine is replaced. A decision maker under significant pressure to report higher profitability may be willing to sacrifice tomorrow's profits to look better today. By emphasizing short-term profitability, she may secure a promotion before the long-term effects of her decision become apparent. Even if she stays in the same position, her boss may be replaced by someone not so demanding in terms of reported profitability. The department supervisor's intent is to survive the moment and let the future take care of itself. Misguided reward systems can be as detrimental as threats of punishment. For example, a manager may choose short-term profitability to obtain a bonus that is based on reported profitability. It is the responsibility of upper-level management to establish policies and procedures that motivate subordinates to perform in ways that maximize the company's long-term profitability.

Decisions Regarding the Allocation of Scarce Resources

LO 6-7

Make decisions about allocating scarce resources.

Suppose that Premier Office Products makes two types of computers: a high-end network server and an inexpensive personal computer. The relevant sales and variable cost data for each unit follow.

Network Server		Personal Computer	
Sales price	$4,000	Sales price	$1,500
Less: Variable cost	(3,760)	Less: Variable cost	(1,370)
Contribution margin	$ 240	Contribution margin	$ 130

In many circumstances, variable costs act as proxies for *avoidable costs.* For example, by definition, unit-level costs increase and decrease in direct proportion with the number of units of product made and sold. As previously indicated, unit-level costs are avoidable with respect to many special decision scenarios. To the extent that variable costs are proxies for avoidable costs, the contribution margin can be used as a measure of profitability. Other things being equal, higher contribution margins translate into more profitable products. If Premier could sell 1,000 computers, the company would certainly prefer that they be network servers. The contribution to profitability on those machines is almost double the contribution margin on the personal computer.

Even though the contribution margin is higher for network servers, selling personal computers may be more profitable. Why? If Premier can sell considerably more of the personal computers, the volume of activity will make up for the lower margin. In other words, selling three personal computers produces more total margin (3 × $130 = $390) than selling one network server (1 × $240). Many factors could limit the sales of one or both of the products. Factors that limit a business's ability to satisfy the demand for its product are called **constraints.** Suppose that warehouse space is limited (i.e., the warehouse is a scarce resource that constrains sales). Accordingly, Premier cannot warehouse all of the computers that it needs to satisfy its customer orders. If a network server requires considerably more warehouse space than a personal computer, stocking and selling personal computers may be more profitable than stocking and selling network servers. To illustrate, assume that it requires 5 square feet of warehouse space for a network server and 2 square feet for a personal computer. If only 2,100 square feet of warehouse space is available, which computer should Premier stock and sell?

In this case, the warehouse space is considered a scarce resource. The computer that produces the highest contribution margin per unit of scarce resource (i.e., per square foot) is the more profitable product. The per-unit computations for each product are shown here.

	Network Server	Personal Computer
Contribution margin per unit (a)	$240	$130
Divide by warehouse space needed to store one unit (b)	÷ 5	÷ 2
Contribution margin per square foot of warehouse space (a ÷ b)	$ 48	$ 65

The data suggest that Premier should focus on the personal computer. Even though the personal computer produces a lower contribution margin per product, its contribution margin per scarce resource is higher. The effect on total profitability is shown as follows.

	Network Server	Personal Computer
Amount of available warehouse space in square feet (a)	2,100	2,100
Divided by warehouse space needed to store one unit (b)	÷ 5	÷ 2
Warehouse capacity in number of units (a ÷ b) = (c)	420	1,050
Times contribution margin per unit (d)	× $ 240	× $ 130
Total profit potential (c × d)	$100,800	$136,500

Although the quantitative data suggest that Premier will maximize profitability by limiting its inventory to personal computers, qualitative considerations may force the company to maintain a reasonable sales mix between the two products. For example, a business that buys several personal computers may also need a network server. A customer who cannot obtain both products from Premier may choose to buy nothing at all. Instead, the customer will find a supplier who will satisfy all of his needs. In other words, Premier may still need to stock some servers to offer a competitive product line.

The chair of the board of directors asked Premier's president why company sales had remained level while the company's chief competitor had experienced significant increases. The president replied, "You cannot sell what you do not have. Our warehouse is too small. We stop production when we fill up the warehouse. The products sell out rapidly, and then we have to wait around for the next batch of computers to be made. When we are out of stock, our customers turn to the competition. We are constrained by the size of the warehouse." In business terms, the warehouse is a **bottleneck.** Its size is limiting the company's ability to produce and sell its products.

Many businesses use a management practice known as the **theory of constraints (TOC)** to increase profitability by managing bottlenecks or constrained resources. TOC's primary objective is to identify the bottlenecks restricting the operations of the business and then to open those bottlenecks through a practice known as **relaxing the constraints.** The effect of applying TOC to the Premier case is apparent via contribution margin analysis. According to the preceding computations, a new server and a new personal computer produce a contribution margin of $48 and $65 per square foot of storage space, respectively. So long as additional warehouse space can be purchased for less than these amounts, Premier can increase its profitability by acquiring the space.

Video lectures and accompanying self-assessment quizzes are available in *Connect* for all learning objectives.

SELF-STUDY REVIEW PROBLEM

Flying High Inc. (FHI) is a division of The Master Toy Company. FHI makes remote-controlled airplanes. During Year 5, FHI incurred the following costs in the process of making 5,000 planes.

Unit-level materials costs (5,000 units × $80)	$ 400,000
Unit-level labor costs (5,000 units × $90)	450,000
Unit-level overhead costs (5,000 × $70)	350,000
Depreciation cost on manufacturing equipment*	50,000
Other manufacturing overhead†	140,000
Inventory holding costs	240,000
Allocated portion of The Master Toy Company's facility-level costs	600,000
Total costs	$2,230,000

*The manufacturing equipment, which originally cost $250,000, has a book value of $200,000, a remaining useful life of four years, and a zero salvage value. If the equipment is not used in the production process, it can be leased for $30,000 per year.

†Includes supervisors' salaries and rent for the manufacturing building.

Required

a. FHI uses a cost-plus pricing strategy. FHI sets its price at product cost plus $100. Determine the price that FHI should charge for its remote-controlled airplanes.

b. Assume that a potential customer that operates a chain of high-end toy stores has approached FHI. A buyer for this chain has offered to purchase 1,000 planes from FHI at a price of $275 each. Ignoring qualitative considerations, should FHI accept or reject the order?

c. FHI has the opportunity to purchase the planes from Arland Manufacturing Company for $325 each. Arland maintains adequate inventories so that it can supply its customers with planes on demand. Should FHI accept the opportunity to outsource the making of its planes?

d. When completing this requirement, use the sales price computed in Requirement *a*. Use the contribution margin format to prepare an income statement based on historical cost data. Prepare a second income statement that reflects the relevant cost data that Master Toy should consider in a segment elimination decision. Based on a comparison of these two statements, indicate whether Master Toy should eliminate the FHI division.

e. FHI is considering replacing the equipment it currently uses to manufacture its planes. It could purchase replacement equipment for $480,000 that has an expected useful life of four years and a salvage value of $40,000. The new equipment would increase productivity substantially, reducing unit-level labor costs by 20 percent. Assume that FHI would maintain its production and sales at 5,000 planes per year. Prepare a schedule that shows the relevant costs of operating the old equipment versus the costs of operating the new equipment. Should FHI replace the equipment?

Solution to Requirement *a*

Product Cost for Remote-Controlled Airplanes	
Unit-level materials costs (5,000 units × $80)	$ 400,000
Unit-level labor costs (5,000 units × $90)	450,000
Unit-level overhead costs (5,000 units × $70)	350,000
Depreciation cost on manufacturing equipment	50,000
Other manufacturing overhead	140,000
Total product cost	$1,390,000

The cost per unit is $278 ($1,390,000 ÷ 5,000 units). The sales price per unit is $378 ($278 + $100). Depreciation expense is included because cost-plus pricing is usually based on historical cost rather than relevant cost. To be profitable in the long run, a company must ultimately recover the amount it paid for the equipment (the historical cost of the equipment).

Solution to Requirement *b*

The incremental (relevant) cost of making 1,000 additional airplanes follows. The depreciation expense is not relevant because it represents a sunk cost. The other manufacturing overhead costs are not relevant because they will be incurred regardless of whether FHI makes the additional planes.

Per-Unit Relevant Product Cost for Airplanes	
Unit-level materials costs	$ 80
Unit-level labor costs	90
Unit-level overhead costs	70
Total relevant product cost	$240

Since the relevant (incremental) cost of making the planes is less than the incremental revenue, FHI should accept the special order. Accepting the order will increase profits by $35,000 [($275 Incremental revenue − $240 Incremental cost) × 1,000 Units].

Solution to Requirement *c*

Distinguish this decision from the special order opportunity discussed in Requirement *b*. That special order (Requirement *b*) decision hinged on the cost of making additional units with the existing production process. In contrast, a make-or-buy decision compares current production with the possibility of making zero units (closing down the entire manufacturing process). If the manufacturing process were shut down, FHI could avoid the unit-level costs, the cost of the lost opportunity to lease the equipment, the other manufacturing overhead costs, and the inventory holding costs. Since the planes can be purchased on demand, there is no need to maintain any inventory. The allocated portion of the facility-level costs is not relevant because it would be incurred regardless of whether FHI manufactured the planes. The relevant cost of making the planes follows.

Relevant Manufacturing Cost for Airplanes	
Unit-level materials costs (5,000 units × $80)	$ 400,000
Unit-level labor costs (5,000 units × $90)	450,000
Unit-level overhead costs (5,000 units × $70)	350,000
Opportunity cost of leasing the equipment	30,000
Other manufacturing overhead costs	140,000
Inventory holding cost	240,000
Total product cost	$1,610,000

The relevant cost per unit is $322 ($1,610,000 ÷ 5,000 units). Since the relevant cost of making the planes ($322) is less than the cost of purchasing them ($325), FHI should continue to make the planes.

Solution to Requirement *d*

Income Statements

	Historical Cost Data	Relevant Cost Data
Revenue (5,000 units × $378)	$1,890,000	$1,890,000
Less variable costs:		
Unit-level materials costs (5,000 units × $80)	(400,000)	(400,000)
Unit-level labor costs (5,000 units × $90)	(450,000)	(450,000)
Unit-level overhead costs (5,000 units × $70)	(350,000)	(350,000)
Contribution margin	690,000	690,000
Depreciation cost on manufacturing equipment	(50,000)	
Opportunity cost of leasing manufacturing equipment		(30,000)
Other manufacturing overhead costs	(140,000)	(140,000)
Inventory holding costs	(240,000)	(240,000)
Allocated facility-level administrative costs	(600,000)	
Net loss	$ (340,000)	
Contribution to Master Toy's profitability		$ 280,000

Master Toy should not eliminate the segment (FHI). Although it appears to be incurring a loss, the allocated facility-level administrative costs are not relevant because Master Toy would incur these costs regardless of whether it eliminated FHI. Also, the depreciation cost on the manufacturing equipment is not relevant because it is a sunk cost. However, since the company could lease the equipment if the segment were eliminated, the $30,000 potential rental fee represents a relevant opportunity cost. The relevant revenue and cost data show that FHI is contributing $280,000 to the profitability of The Master Toy Company.

Solution to Requirement *e*

The relevant costs of using the old equipment versus the new equipment are the costs that differ for the two alternatives. In this case, relevant costs include the purchase price of the new equipment, the opportunity cost of the old equipment, and the labor costs. These items are summarized in the following table. The data show the total cost over the four-year useful life of the replacement equipment.

Relevant Cost Comparison

	Old Equipment	New Equipment
Opportunity to lease the old equipment ($30,000 × 4 years)	$ 120,000	
Cost of new equipment ($480,000 − $40,000)		$ 440,000
Unit-level labor costs (5,000 units × $90 × 4 years)	1,800,000	
Unit-level labor costs (5,000 units × $90 × 4 years × 0.80)		1,440,000
Total relevant costs	$1,920,000	$1,880,000

Since the relevant cost of operating the new equipment is less than the cost of operating the old equipment, FHI should replace the equipment.

KEY TERMS

Avoidable costs 258
Batch-level costs 259
Bottleneck 272
Certified suppliers 264
Constraints 272
Differential revenue 258
Equipment replacement decisions 268
Facility-level costs 259
Low-ball pricing 264
Opportunity cost 256
Outsourcing 262
Product-level costs 259
Qualitative characteristics 258
Quantitative characteristics 258
Relaxing the constraints 273
Relevant costs 257
Relevant information 256
Segment 265
Special order decisions 260
Sunk costs 256
Theory of constraints (TOC) 273
Unit-level costs 258
Vertical integration 264

QUESTIONS

1. Identify the primary qualities of revenues and costs that are relevant for decision making.
2. Are variable costs always relevant? Explain.
3. Identify the four hierarchical levels used to classify costs. When can each of these levels of costs be avoided?
4. Describe the relationship between relevance and accuracy.
5. "It all comes down to the bottom line. The numbers never lie." Do you agree with this conclusion? Explain your position.
6. Carmon Company invested $300,000 in the equity securities of Mann Corporation. The current market value of Carmon's investment in Mann is $250,000. Carmon currently needs funds for operating purposes. Although interest rates are high, Carmon's president has decided to borrow the needed funds instead of selling the investment in Mann. He explains that his company cannot afford to take a $50,000 loss on the Mann stock. Evaluate the president's decision based on this information.
7. What is an opportunity cost? How does it differ from a sunk cost?
8. A local bank advertises that it offers a free noninterest-bearing checking account if the depositor maintains a $500 minimum balance in the account. Is the checking account truly free?
9. A manager is faced with deciding whether to replace Machine A or Machine B. The original cost of machine A was $20,000 and that of Machine B was $30,000. Because the two cost figures differ, they are relevant to the manager's decision. Do you agree? Explain your position.
10. Are all fixed costs unavoidable?
11. Identify two qualitative considerations that could be associated with special order decisions.
12. Which of the following would not be relevant to a make-or-buy decision?
    (a) Allocated portion of depreciation expense on existing facilities.
    (b) Variable cost of labor used to produce products currently purchased from suppliers.
    (c) Warehousing costs for inventory of completed products (inventory levels will be constant regardless of whether products are purchased or produced).
    (d) Cost of materials used to produce the items currently purchased from suppliers.
    (e) Property taxes on the factory building.
13. What two factors should be considered in deciding how to allocate shelf space in a retail establishment?
14. What level(s) of costs is (are) relevant in special order decisions?
15. Why would a company consider outsourcing products or services?
16. Chris Sutter, the production manager of Satellite Computers, insists that the drives used in the company's upper-end computers be outsourced since they can be purchased from a supplier at a lower cost per unit than the company is presently incurring to produce the drives. Jane Meyers, his assistant, insists that if sales growth continues at the current levels, the company will be able to produce the drives in the near future at a lower cost because of the company's predominately fixed cost structure. Does Ms. Meyers have a legitimate argument? Explain.
17. Identify some qualitative factors that should be considered in addition to quantitative costs in deciding whether to outsource.
18. The managers of Wilcox Inc. are suggesting that the company president eliminate one of the company's segments that is operating at a loss. Why may this be a hasty decision?
19. Why would a supervisor choose to continue using a more costly old machine instead of replacing it with a less costly new machine?
20. Identify some of the constraints that limit a business's ability to satisfy the demand for its products or services.

MULTIPLE-CHOICE QUESTIONS

Multiple-choice questions are available in *Connect*.

EXERCISES—SERIES A

connect **All applicable Exercises in Series A are available in *Connect*.**

Exercise 6-1A *Distinction between relevance and cost behavior* — LO 6-1

Gayla Ojeda is trying to decide which of two different kinds of candy to sell in her retail candy store. One type is a name-brand candy that will practically sell itself. The other candy is cheaper to purchase but does not carry an identifiable brand name. Ms. Ojeda believes that she will have to incur significant advertising costs to sell this candy. Several cost items for the two types of candy are as follows.

Brandless Candy		Name-Brand Candy	
Cost per box	$ 4.00	Cost per box	$ 6.00
Sales commissions per box	1.00	Sales commissions per box	1.00
Rent of display space	900.00	Rent of display space	900.00
Advertising	3,000.00	Advertising	2,000.00

Required

Identify each cost as being relevant or irrelevant to Ms. Ojeda's decision and indicate whether it is fixed or variable relative to the number of boxes sold.

Exercise 6-2A *Distinction between relevance and cost behavior* — LO 6-1

Kilgore Company makes and sells a single product. Kilgore incurred the following costs in its most recent fiscal year.

Cost Items Appearing on the Income Statement	
Materials cost ($7 per unit)	Sales commissions (2% of sales)
Company president's salary	Salaries of administrative personnel
Depreciation on manufacturing equipment	Shipping and handling ($0.50 per unit)
Customer billing costs (1% of sales)	Depreciation on office furniture
Rental cost of manufacturing facility	Manufacturing supplies ($0.25 per unit)
Advertising costs ($200,000 per year)	Production supervisor's salary
Labor cost ($8 per unit)	

Kilgore could purchase the products that it currently makes. If it purchased the items, the company would continue to sell them using its own logo, advertising program, and sales staff.

Required

Identify each cost as relevant or irrelevant to the outsourcing decision and indicate whether the cost is fixed or variable relative to the number of products manufactured and sold.

Exercise 6-3A *Distinction between avoidable costs and cost behavior* — LO 6-1

Boyle Company makes fine jewelry that it sells to department stores throughout the United States. Boyle is trying to decide which of two bracelets to manufacture. Cost data pertaining to the two choices follow.

	Bracelet A	Bracelet B
Cost of materials per unit	$ 10	$ 20
Cost of labor per unit	15	15
Advertising cost per year	5,000	3,000
Annual depreciation on existing equipment	5,000	4,000

Required

a. Identify the fixed costs and determine the amount of fixed cost for each product.
b. Identify the variable costs and determine the amount of variable cost per unit for each product.
c. Identify the avoidable costs and determine the amount of avoidable cost for each product.

LO 6-1

Exercise 6-4A *Cost hierarchy*

Costs can be classified into one of four categories, including unit-level, batch-level, product-level, or facility-level costs.

Required

Classify each of the items listed below into one of the four categories listed previously. The first item has been categorized as an example.

Cost Description	Cost Classification
Salary of company president	Facility-level cost
Research and development cost	
Factory lawn care cost	
Cost of patent	
Start-up cost to change color of a product	
Cost of resetting sewing machines to change shirt size	
Real estate tax for the factory	
Direct labor	

LO 6-1

Exercise 6-5A *Opportunity costs*

Norman Dowd owns his own taxi, for which he bought a $10,000 permit to operate two years ago. Mr. Dowd earns $30,000 a year operating as an independent but has the opportunity to sell the taxi and permit for $36,500 and take a position as dispatcher for Carter Taxi Co. The dispatcher position pays $27,500 a year for a 40-hour week. Driving his own taxi, Mr. Dowd works approximately 55 hours per week. If he sells his business, he will invest the $36,500 and can earn a 10 percent return.

Required

a. Determine the opportunity cost of owning and operating the independent business.
b. Based solely on financial considerations, should Mr. Dowd sell the taxi and accept the position as dispatcher?
c. Discuss the qualitative as well as quantitative factors that Mr. Dowd should consider.

LO 6-2

Exercise 6-6A *Special order decision*

Visburg Concrete Company pours concrete slabs for single-family dwellings. Lancing Construction Company, which operates outside Visburg's normal sales territory, asks Visburg to pour 40 slabs for Lancing's new development of homes. Visburg has the capacity to build 300 slabs and is presently working on 250 of them. Lancing is willing to pay only $3,300 per slab. Visburg estimates the cost of a typical job to include unit-level materials, $1,440; unit-level labor, $720; and an allocated portion of facility-level overhead, $1,200.

Required

Should Visburg accept or reject the special order to pour 40 slabs for $3,300 each? Support your answer with appropriate computations.

LO 6-2

Exercise 6-7A *Special order decision*

Katzev Company manufactures a personal computer designed for use in schools and markets it under its own label. Katzev has the capacity to produce 40,000 units a year but is currently producing and selling only 32,000 units a year. The computer's normal selling price is $750 per unit with no volume discounts. The unit-level costs of the computer's production are $250 for direct materials, $225 for direct labor, and $62.50 for indirect unit-level manufacturing costs. The total product- and facility-level costs incurred by Katzev during the year are expected to be $2,000,000 and $500,000, respectively. Assume that Katzev receives a special order to produce and sell 6,000 computers at $562.50 each.

Required

Should Katzev accept or reject the special order? Support your answer with appropriate computations.

Exercise 6-8A *Identifying qualitative factors for a special order decision*

LO 6-2

Required

Describe the qualitative factors that Katzev should consider before accepting the special order described in Exercise 6-7A.

Exercise 6-9A *Using the contribution margin approach for a special order decision*

LO 6-2

Hensely Company, which produces and sells a small digital clock, bases its pricing strategy on a 25 percent markup on total cost. Based on annual production costs for 25,000 units of product, computations for the sales price per clock follow.

Unit-level costs	$240,000
Fixed costs	60,000
Total cost (a)	300,000
Markup (a × 0.25)	75,000
Total sales (b)	$375,000
Sales price per unit (b ÷ 25,000)	$ 15

Required

a. Hensely has excess capacity and receives a special order for 8,000 clocks for $12 each. Calculate the contribution margin per unit. Based on this, should Hensely accept the special order?

b. Support your answer by preparing a contribution margin income statement for the special order.

Exercise 6-10A *Outsourcing decision*

LO 6-3

Steele Bicycle Manufacturing Company currently produces the handlebars used in manufacturing its bicycles, which are high-quality racing bikes with limited sales. Steele produces and sells only 10,000 bikes each year. Due to the low volume of activity, Steele is unable to obtain the economies of scale that larger producers achieve. For example, Steele could buy the handlebars for $31 each; they cost $34 each to make. The following is a detailed breakdown of current production costs.

Item	Unit Cost	Total
Unit-level costs		
Materials	$16	$160,000
Labor	12	120,000
Overhead	2	20,000
Allocated facility-level costs	4	40,000
Total	$34	$340,000

After seeing these figures, Steele's president remarked that it would be foolish for the company to continue to produce the handlebars at $34 each when it can buy them for $31 each.

Required

Do you agree with the president's conclusion? Support your answer with appropriate computations.

LO 6-3

Exercise 6-11A *Establishing price for an outsourcing decision*

Levesque Company makes and sells lawn mowers for which it currently makes the engines. It has an opportunity to purchase the engines from a reliable manufacturer. The annual costs of making the engines are shown here.

Cost of materials (20,000 units × $26)	$ 520,000
Labor (20,000 units × $20)	400,000
Depreciation on manufacturing equipment*	42,000
Salary of supervisor of engine production	85,000
Rental cost of equipment used to make engines	23,000
Allocated portion of corporate-level facility-sustaining costs	80,000
Total cost to make 20,000 engines	$1,150,000

*The equipment has a book value of $90,000 but its market value is zero.

Required

a. Determine the maximum price per unit that Levesque would be willing to pay for the engines.

b. Would the price computed in Requirement *a* change if production increased to 24,000 units? Support your answer with appropriate computations.

LO 6-3

Exercise 6-12A *Outsourcing decision with qualitative factors*

Kawai Corporation, which makes and sells 85,000 radios annually, currently purchases the radio speakers it uses for $8.00 each. Each radio uses one speaker. The company has idle capacity and is considering the possibility of making the speakers that it needs. Kawai estimates that the cost of materials and labor needed to make speakers would be a total of $6.50 for each speaker. In addition, supervisory salaries, rent, and other manufacturing costs would be $170,000. Allocated facility-level costs would be $75,000.

Required

a. Determine the change in net income Kawai would experience if it decides to make the speakers.

b. Discuss the qualitative factors that Kawai should consider.

LO 6-3

Exercise 6-13A *Outsourcing decision affected by opportunity costs*

Omron Electronics currently produces the shipping containers it uses to deliver the electronics products it sells. The monthly cost of producing 10,000 containers follows.

Unit-level materials	$ 7,500
Unit-level labor	8,250
Unit-level overhead	5,250
Product-level costs*	13,500
Allocated facility-level costs	33,000

*One-third of these costs can be avoided by purchasing the containers.

Russo Container Company has offered to sell comparable containers to Omron for $3.00 each.

Required

a. Should Omron continue to make the containers? Support your answer with appropriate computations.

b. Omron could lease the space it currently uses in the manufacturing process. If leasing would produce $8,000 per month, would your answer to Requirement *a* be different? Explain.

Exercise 6-14A *Segment elimination decision*

LO 6-4

Buckley Company operates three segments. Income statements for the segments imply that profitability could be improved if Segment A were eliminated.

BUCKLEY COMPANY
Income Statements for Year 2

Segment	A	B	C
Sales	$ 330,000	$ 480,000	$500,000
Cost of goods sold	(242,000)	(184,000)	(190,000)
Sales commissions	(30,000)	(44,000)	(44,000)
Contribution margin	58,000	252,000	266,000
General fixed oper. exp. (allocation of president's salary)	(92,000)	(92,000)	(92,000)
Advertising expense (specific to individual divisions)	(6,000)	(20,000)	0
Net income (loss)	$ (40,000)	$ 140,000	$ 174,000

Required

a. Explain the effect on profitability if Segment A is eliminated.

b. Prepare comparative income statements for the company as a whole under two alternatives: (1) the retention of Segment A and (2) the elimination of Segment A.

Exercise 6-15A *Segment elimination decision*

LO 6-4

Dudley Transport Company divides its operations into four divisions. A recent income statement for its West Division follows.

DUDLEY TRANSPORT COMPANY
West Division
Income Statement for Year 3

Revenue	$300,000
Salaries for drivers	(210,000)
Fuel expenses	(30,000)
Insurance	(42,000)
Division-level facility-sustaining costs	(24,000)
Companywide facility-sustaining costs	(78,000)
Net loss	$ (84,000)

Required

a. Should West Division be eliminated? Support your answer by explaining how the division's elimination would affect the net income of the company as a whole. By how much would companywide income increase or decrease?

b. Assume that West Division is able to increase its revenue to $324,000 by raising its prices. Would this change the decision you made in Requirement *a*? Determine the amount of the increase or decrease that would occur in companywide net income if the segment were eliminated if revenue were $324,000.

c. What is the minimum amount of revenue required to justify continuing the operation of West Division?

Exercise 6-16A *Identifying avoidable cost of a segment*

LO 6-4

Lake Corporation is considering the elimination of one of its segments. The segment incurs the following fixed costs. If the segment is eliminated, the building it uses will be sold.

Advertising expense	$140,000
Supervisory salaries	300,000
Allocation of companywide facility-level costs	130,000
Original cost of building	220,000
Book value of building	100,000
Market value of building	160,000
Maintenance costs on equipment	112,000
Real estate taxes on building	12,000

Required

Based on this information, determine the amount of avoidable cost associated with the segment.

LO 6-5

Exercise 6-17A *Asset replacement—opportunity cost*

Roadrunner Freight Company owns a truck that cost $42,000. Currently, the truck's book value is $24,000, and its expected remaining useful life is four years. Roadrunner has the opportunity to purchase for $31,200 a replacement truck that is extremely fuel efficient. Fuel cost for the old truck is expected to be $6,000 per year more than fuel cost for the new truck. The old truck is paid for but, in spite of being in good condition, can be sold for only $14,400.

Required

Should Roadrunner replace the old truck with the new fuel-efficient model, or should it continue to use the old truck until it wears out? Explain.

LO 6-5

Exercise 6-18A *Asset replacement decision*

A machine purchased three years ago for $720,000 has a current book value using straight-line depreciation of $400,000; its operating expenses are $60,000 per year. A replacement machine would cost $480,000, have a useful life of nine years, and would require $26,000 per year in operating expenses. It has an expected salvage value of $130,000 after nine years. The current disposal value of the old machine is $170,000; if it is kept 9 more years, its residual value would be $20,000.

Required

Based on this information, should the old machine be replaced? Support your answer.

LO 6-5

Exercise 6-19A *Asset replacement decision*

Mead Company is considering the replacement of some of its manufacturing equipment. Information regarding the existing equipment and the potential replacement equipment follows.

Existing Equipment		Replacement Equipment	
Cost	$300,000	Cost	$250,000
Operating expenses*	240,000	Operating expenses*	160,000
Salvage value	40,000	Salvage value	40,000
Market value	120,000	Useful life	8 years
Book value	90,000		
Remaining useful life	8 years		

*The amounts shown for operating expenses are the cumulative total of all such expected expenses to be incurred over the useful life of the equipment.

Required

Based on this information, recommend whether to replace the equipment. Support your recommendation with appropriate computations.

LO 6-5

Exercise 6-20A *Asset replacement decision*

Kahn Company paid $240,000 to purchase a machine on January 1, Year 1. During Year 3, a technological breakthrough resulted in the development of a new machine that costs $300,000. The old machine costs $100,000 per year to operate, but the new machine could be operated for only $36,000 per year. The new machine, which will be available for delivery on January 1, Year 3, has an expected useful life of four years. The old machine is more durable and is expected to have a remaining useful life of four years. The current market value of the old machine is $80,000. The expected salvage value of both machines is zero.

Required

Based on this information, recommend whether to replace the machine. Support your recommendation with appropriate computations.

Exercise 6-21A *Annual versus cumulative data for replacement decision (Appendix)* LO 6-6

Because of rapidly advancing technology, Chicago Publications Corporation is considering replacing its existing typesetting machine with leased equipment. The old machine, purchased two years ago, has an expected useful life of six years and is in good condition. Apparently, it will continue to perform as expected for the remaining four years of its expected useful life. A four-year lease for equipment with comparable productivity can be obtained for $40,000 per year. The following data apply to the old machine.

Original cost	$480,000
Accumulated depreciation	160,000
Current market value	190,000
Estimated salvage value	10,000

Required

a. Determine the annual opportunity cost of using the old machine. Based on your computations, recommend whether to replace it.

b. Determine the total cost of the lease over the four-year contract. Based on your computations, recommend whether to replace the old machine.

Exercise 6-22A *Scarce resource decision (Appendix)* LO 6-7

Sweet Taste has the capacity to produce either 45,000 corncob pipes or 21,000 cornhusk dolls per year. The pipes cost $3.00 each to produce and sell for $7.50 each. The dolls sell for $10.00 each and cost $4.00 to produce.

Required

Assuming that Sweet Taste can sell all it produces of either product, should it produce the corncob pipes or the cornhusk dolls? Show computations to support your answer.

PROBLEMS—SERIES A

connect **All applicable Problems in Series A are available in *Connect*.**

Problem 6-23A *Context-sensitive relevance* LO 6-1

Required

Respond to each requirement independently.

a. Describe two decision-making contexts, one in which unit-level materials costs are avoidable and the other in which they are unavoidable.

b. Describe two decision-making contexts, one in which batch-level setup costs are avoidable and the other in which they are unavoidable.

c. Describe two decision-making contexts, one in which advertising costs are avoidable and the other in which they are unavoidable.

d. Describe two decision-making contexts, one in which rent paid for a building is avoidable and the other in which it is unavoidable.

e. Describe two decision-making contexts, one in which depreciation on manufacturing equipment is avoidable and the other in which it is unavoidable.

LO 6-1

CHECK FIGURES

a. Contribution to profit for Job A: $224,000

b. Contribution to profit for Job B: $72,800

Problem 6-24A *Context-sensitive relevance*

Continent Construction Company is a building contractor specializing in small commercial buildings. The company has the opportunity to accept one of two jobs; it cannot accept both because they must be performed at the same time and Continent does not have the necessary labor force for both jobs. Indeed, it will be necessary to hire a new supervisor if either job is accepted. Furthermore, additional insurance will be required if either job is accepted. The revenue and costs associated with each job follow.

Cost Category	Job A	Job B
Contract price	$800,000	$750,000
Unit-level materials	250,000	220,000
Unit-level labor	260,000	310,000
Unit-level overhead	40,000	30,000
Supervisor's salary	70,000	70,000
Rental equipment costs	26,000	29,000
Depreciation on tools (zero market value)	19,900	19,900
Allocated portion of companywide facility-sustaining costs	10,400	8,600
Insurance cost for job	18,200	18,200

Required

a. Assume that Continent has decided to accept one of the two jobs. Identify the information relevant to selecting one job versus the other. Recommend which job to accept and support your answer with appropriate computations.

b. Assume that Job A is no longer available. Continent's choice is to accept or reject Job B alone. Identify the information relevant to this decision. Recommend whether to accept or reject Job B. Support your answer with appropriate computations.

LO 6-2

CHECK FIGURE

a. Relevant cost per unit: $24.50

Problem 6-25A *Effect of order quantity on special order decision*

Dalton Quilting Company makes blankets that it markets through a variety of department stores. It makes the blankets in batches of 1,000 units. Dalton made 20,000 blankets during the prior accounting period. The cost of producing the blankets is summarized here.

Materials cost ($10 per unit × 20,000)	$200,000
Labor cost ($9 per unit × 20,000)	180,000
Manufacturing supplies ($1.50 × 20,000)	30,000
Batch-level costs (20 batches at $2,000 per batch)	40,000
Product-level costs	80,000
Facility-level costs	145,000
Total costs	$675,000
Cost per unit = $675,000 ÷ 20,000 = $33.75	

Required

a. Sunny Motels has offered to buy a batch of 500 blankets for $23.50 each. Dalton's normal selling price is $45 per unit. Based on the preceding quantitative data, should Dalton accept the special order? Support your answer with appropriate computations.

b. Would your answer to Requirement *a* change if Sunny offered to buy a batch of 1,000 blankets for $23.50 per unit? Support your answer with appropriate computations.

c. Describe the qualitative factors that Dalton Quilting Company should consider before accepting a special order to sell blankets to Sunny Motels.

Problem 6-26A *Effects of the level of production on an outsourcing decision*

LO 6-3

Townsend Chemical Company makes a variety of cosmetic products, one of which is a skin cream designed to reduce the signs of aging. Townsend produces a relatively small amount (15,000 units) of the cream and is considering the purchase of the product from an outside supplier for $9 each. If Townsend purchases from the outside supplier, it would continue to sell and distribute the cream under its own brand name. Townsend's accountant constructed the following profitability analysis.

CHECK FIGURE

a. Total relevant cost: $150,000

Revenue (15,000 units × $20)	$300,000
Unit-level materials costs (15,000 units × $2.50)	(37,500)
Unit-level labor costs (15,000 units × $1.80)	(27,000)
Unit-level overhead costs (15,000 × $0.70)	(10,500)
Unit-level selling expenses (15,000 × $1.00)	(15,000)
Contribution margin	210,000
Skin cream production supervisor's salary	(75,000)
Allocated portion of facility-level costs	(45,000)
Product-level advertising cost	(50,000)
Contribution to companywide income	$ 40,000

Required

a. Identify the cost items relevant to the make-or-outsource decision.

b. Should Townsend continue to make the product or buy it from the supplier? Support your answer by determining the change in net income if Townsend buys the cream instead of making it.

c. Suppose that Townsend is able to increase sales by 10,000 units (sales will increase to 25,000 units). At this level of production, should Townsend make or buy the cream? Support your answer by explaining how the increase in production affects the cost per unit.

d. Discuss the qualitative factors that Townsend should consider before deciding to outsource the skin cream. How can Townsend minimize the risk of establishing a relationship with an unreliable supplier?

Problem 6-27A *Outsourcing decision affected by equipment replacement*

LO 6-3, 6-5

Sturdy Bike Company makes the frames used to build its bicycles. During Year 2, Sturdy made 20,000 frames; the costs incurred follow.

CHECK FIGURES

a. Avoidable cost per unit: $106.10

b. Avoidable cost per unit with new equipment: $27.50

Unit-level materials costs (20,000 units × $35.00)	$ 700,000
Unit-level labor costs (20,000 units × $42.50)	850,000
Unit-level overhead costs (20,000 × $10.00)	200,000
Depreciation on manufacturing equipment	120,000
Bike frame production supervisor's salary	70,000
Inventory holding costs	290,000
Allocated portion of facility-level costs	500,000
Total costs	$2,730,000

Sturdy has an opportunity to purchase frames for $92.50 each.

Additional Information

1. The manufacturing equipment, which originally cost $550,000, has a book value of $450,000, a remaining useful life of four years, and a zero salvage value. If the equipment is not used to produce bicycle frames, it can be leased for $70,000 per year.
2. Sturdy has the opportunity to purchase for $910,000 new manufacturing equipment that will have an expected useful life of four years and a salvage value of $70,000. This equipment will increase productivity substantially, reducing unit-level labor costs by 60 percent. Assume that Sturdy will continue to produce and sell 20,000 frames per year in the future.
3. If Sturdy outsources the frames, the company can eliminate 80 percent of the inventory holding costs.

Required

a. Determine the avoidable cost per unit of making the bike frames, assuming that Sturdy is considering the alternatives of making the product using the existing equipment or outsourcing the product to the independent contractor. Based on the quantitative data, should Sturdy outsource the bike frames? Support your answer with appropriate computations.

b. Assuming that Sturdy is considering whether to replace the old equipment with the new equipment, determine the avoidable cost per unit to produce the bike frames using the new equipment and the avoidable cost per unit to produce the bike frames using the old equipment. Calculate the impact on profitability if the bike frames were made using the old equipment versus the new equipment.

c. Assuming that Sturdy is considering whether to either purchase the new equipment or outsource the bike frame, calculate the impact on profitability between the two alternatives.

d. Discuss the qualitative factors that Sturdy should consider before making a decision to outsource the bike frame. How can Sturdy minimize the risk of establishing a relationship with an unreliable supplier?

LO 6-4

eXcel

CHECK FIGURE
a. Contribution to profit: $4,000

Problem 6-28A *Eliminating a segment*

Western Boot Co. sells men's, women's, and children's boots. For each type of boot sold, it operates a separate department that has its own manager. The manager of the men's department has a sales staff of nine employees, the manager of the women's department has six employees, and the manager of the children's department has three employees. All departments are housed in a single store. In recent years, the children's department has operated at a net loss and is expected to continue to do so. Last year's income statements follow.

	Men's Department	Women's Department	Children's Department
Sales	$ 250,000	$300,000	$60,000
Cost of goods sold	(105,000)	(125,000)	(35,000)
Gross margin	145,000	175,000	25,000
Department manager's salary	(26,000)	(30,000)	(12,000)
Sales commissions	(43,000)	(49,000)	(9,000)
Rent on store lease	(10,500)	(10,500)	(10,500)
Store utilities	(2,000)	(2,000)	(2,000)
Net income (loss)	$ 63,500	$ 83,500	$ (8,500)

Required

a. Determine whether to eliminate the children's department.

b. Confirm the conclusion you reached in Requirement *a* by preparing income statements for the company as a whole with and without the children's department.

c. Eliminating the children's department would increase space available to display men's and women's boots. Suppose management estimates that a wider selection of adult boots would increase the store's net earnings by $10,000. Would this information affect the decision that you made in Requirement *a*? Explain your answer.

LO 6-4

CHECK FIGURE
a. Contribution to profit: $(9,000)

Problem 6-29A *Effect of activity level and opportunity cost on segment elimination decision*

Lenox Manufacturing Co. produces and sells specialized equipment used in the petroleum industry. The company is organized into three separate operating branches: Division A, which manufactures and sells heavy equipment; Division B, which manufactures and sells hand tools; and Division C, which makes and sells electric motors. Each division is housed in a separate manufacturing facility. Company headquarters is located in a separate building. In recent years, Division B has been operating at a net loss and is expected to continue to do so. Income statements for the three divisions for Year 2 follow.

	Division A	Division B	Division C
Sales	$1,000,000	$ 300,000	$1,250,000
Less: Cost of goods sold			
Unit-level manufacturing costs	(600,000)	(200,000)	(750,000)
Rent on manufacturing facility	(135,000)	(75,000)	(100,000)
Gross margin	265,000	25,000	400,000
Less: Operating expenses			
Unit-level selling and admin. expenses	(62,500)	(14,000)	(78,000)
Division-level fixed selling and admin. expenses	(80,000)	(20,000)	(100,000)
Headquarters facility-level costs	(50,000)	(50,000)	(50,000)
Net income (loss)	$ 72,500	$ (59,000)	$ 172,000

Required

a. Based on the preceding information, recommend whether to eliminate Division B. Support your answer by preparing company-wide income statements before and after eliminating Division B.

b. During Year 2, Division B produced and sold 20,000 units of hand tools. Would your recommendation in response to Requirement *a* change if sales and production increase to 30,000 units in Year 3? Support your answer by comparing differential revenue and avoidable cost for Division B, assuming that it sells 30,000 units.

c. Suppose that Lenox could sublease Division B's manufacturing facility for $160,000. Would you operate the division at a production and sales volume of 30,000 units, or would you close it? Support your answer with appropriate computations.

Problem 6-30A *Comprehensive problem including special order, outsourcing, and segment elimination decisions*

LO 6-2, 6-3, 6-4

excel

CHECK FIGURE
a. CM: $6,000

Bain Corporation makes and sells state-of-the-art electronics products. One of its segments produces The Math Machine, an inexpensive calculator. The company's chief accountant recently prepared the following income statement showing annual revenues and expenses associated with the segment's operating activities. The relevant range for the production and sale of the calculators is between 30,000 and 60,000 units per year.

Revenue (40,000 units × $10.80)	$432,000
Unit-level variable costs	
Materials cost (40,000 × $2.70)	(108,000)
Labor cost (40,000 × $1.20)	(48,000)
Manufacturing overhead (40,000 × $1.20)	(48,000)
Shipping and handling (40,000 × $0.30)	(12,000)
Sales commissions (40,000 × $1.20)	(48,000)
Contribution margin	168,000
Fixed expenses	
Advertising costs	(24,000)
Salary of production supervisor	(72,000)
Allocated companywide facility-level expenses	(96,000)
Net loss	$ (24,000)

Required (Consider each of the requirements independently.)

a. A large discount store has approached the owner of Bain about buying 5,000 calculators. It would replace The Math Machine's label with its own logo to avoid affecting Bain's existing customers. Because the offer was made directly to the owner, no sales commissions on the transaction would be involved, but the discount store is willing to pay only $6.60 per calculator. Based on quantitative factors alone, should Bain accept the special order? Support your answer with appropriate computations. Specifically, by what amount would the special order increase or decrease profitability?

b. Bain has an opportunity to buy the 40,000 calculators it currently makes from a reliable competing manufacturer for $6.72 each. The product meets Bain's quality standards. Bain could continue to use its own logo, advertising program, and sales force to distribute the products. Should Bain buy the calculators or continue to make them? Support your answer with appropriate computations. Specifically, how much more or less would it cost to buy the calculators than to make them? Would your answer change if the volume of sales were increased to 60,000 units?

c. Because the calculator division is currently operating at a loss, should it be eliminated from the company's operations? Support your answer with appropriate computations. Specifically, by what amount would the segment's elimination increase or decrease profitability?

LO 6-5, 6-6

eXcel

CHECK FIGURE

a. Relevant costs: $280,000 for keeping the old machine

Problem 6-31A *Conflict between short-term and long-term performance*

Frank Moran manages the cutting department of Greene Timber Company. He purchased a tree-cutting machine on January 1, Year 2, for $200,000. The machine had an estimated useful life of five years and zero salvage value, and the cost to operate it is $45,000 per year. Technological developments resulted in the development of a more advanced machine available for purchase on January 1, Year 3, that would allow a 25 percent reduction in operating costs. The new machine would cost $120,000 and have a four-year useful life and zero salvage value. The current market value of the old machine on January 1, Year 3, is $100,000, and its book value is $160,000 on that date. Straight-line depreciation is used for both machines. The company expects to generate $112,000 of revenue per year from the use of either machine.

Required

a. Recommend whether to replace the old machine on January 1, Year 3. Support your answer with appropriate computations.

b. Prepare income statements for four years (Year 3 through Year 6) assuming that the old machine is retained.

c. Prepare income statements for four years (Year 3 through Year 6) assuming that the old machine is replaced.

d. Discuss the potential ethical conflicts that could result from the timing of the loss and expense recognition reported in the two income statements.

LO 6-7

CHECK FIGURE

a. Contribution margin per hour: $8.00 for A and $5.00 for B

Problem 6-32A *Allocating scarce resources (Appendix)*

The following information applies to the products of Corbett Company.

	Product A	Product B
Selling price per unit	$40	$32
Variable cost per unit	24	12

Required

Identify the product that should be produced or sold under each of the following constraints. Consider each constraint separately.

a. One unit of Product A requires 2 hours of labor to produce, and one unit of Product B requires 4 hours of labor to produce. Due to labor constraints, demand is higher than the company's capacity to make both products.

b. The products are sold to the public in retail stores. The company has limited floor space and cannot stock as many products as it would like. Display space is available for only one of the two products. Expected sales of Product A and Product B are 8,000 units and 9,000 units, respectively.

c. The maximum number of machine hours available is 40,000. Product A uses 2.50 machine hours, and Product B uses 4 machine hours. The company can sell all the products it produces.

EXERCISES—SERIES B

Exercise 6-1B *Distinction between relevance and cost behavior*

LO 6-1

Zach Randolph is planning to rent a small shop for a new business. He can sell either sandwiches or donuts. The following costs pertain to the two products.

Sandwiches		Donuts	
Cost per sandwich	$ 2.00	Cost per dozen donuts	$ 1.75
Sales commissions per sandwich	0.05	Sales commissions per dozen donuts	0.07
Monthly shop rental cost	800.00	Monthly shop rental cost	800.00
Monthly advertising cost	500.00	Monthly advertising cost	300.00

Required

Identify each cost as relevant or irrelevant to Mr. Randolph's product decision and indicate whether the cost is fixed or variable relative to the number of units sold.

Exercise 6-2B *Distinction between relevance and cost behavior*

LO 6-1

Norita Company makes and sells a toy plane. Norita incurred the following costs in its most recent fiscal year.

Cost Items Reported on Income Statement
Shipping and handling costs ($0.75 per unit)
Cost of renting the administrative building
Utility costs for the manufacturing plant ($0.25 per unit produced)
Manufacturing plant manager's salary
Materials costs ($4 per unit produced)
Real estate taxes on the manufacturing plant
Depreciation on manufacturing equipment
Packaging cost ($1 per unit produced)
Wages of the plant security guard
Costs of TV commercials
Labor costs ($3 per unit)
Sales commissions (1% of sales)
Sales manager's salary

Norita could purchase the toy planes from a supplier. If it did, the company would continue to sell them using its own logo, advertising program, and sales staff.

Required

Identify each cost as relevant or irrelevant to the outsourcing decision and indicate whether the cost is fixed or variable relative to the number of toy planes manufactured and sold.

Exercise 6-3B *Distinction between avoidable costs and cost behavior*

LO 6-1

Ender Phones Inc. makes telephones that it sells to department stores throughout the United States. Ender is trying to decide which of two telephone models to manufacture. The company could produce either telephone with its existing machinery. Cost data pertaining to the two choices follow.

	Model 90	Model 30
Materials cost per unit	$ 25.00	$ 25.00
Labor cost per unit	27.50	15.00
Product design cost	12,000.00	7,000.00
Depreciation on existing manufacturing machinery	3,000.00	3,000.00

Required

a. Identify the fixed costs and determine the amount of fixed cost for each model.

b. Identify the variable costs and determine the amount of variable cost for each model.

c. Identify the avoidable costs.

LO 6-1

Exercise 6-4B *Cost hierarchy*

Costs can be classified into one of four categories, including unit-level, batch-level, product-level, or facility-level costs.

Required

Classify each of the items listed below into one of the four categories listed previously. The first item has been categorized as an example.

Cost Description	Cost Classification
Wages of factory janitors	Facility-level cost
Machine setup cost for different production jobs	
Direct materials	
Salary of the manager in charge of making a product	
Tires used to assemble a car	
Payroll cost for assembly-line workers	
Electricity bill of the factory	
Product design	

LO 6-1

Exercise 6-5B *Opportunity costs*

Two years ago, Corey Jemison bought a truck for $35,000 to offer delivery services. Corey earns $40,000 a year operating as an independent trucker. He has an opportunity to sell his truck for $18,750 and take a position as an instructor in a truck driving school. The instructor position pays $31,250 a year for working 40 hours per week. Driving his truck, Corey works approximately 60 hours per week. If Corey sells his truck, he will invest the proceeds of the sale in bonds that pay a 12 percent return.

Required

a. Determine the opportunity cost of owning and operating the independent delivery business.

b. Based solely on financial considerations, should Corey sell his truck and accept the instructor position?

c. Discuss the qualitative as well as quantitative characteristics that Corey should consider.

LO 6-2

Exercise 6-6B *Special order decision*

Avery Textile Company manufactures high-quality bed sheets and sells them in sets to a well-known retail company for $80 a set. Avery has sufficient capacity to produce 150,000 sets of sheets annually; the retail company currently purchases 100,000 sets each year. Avery's unit-level cost is $45 per set and its fixed cost is $1,050,000 per year. A motel chain has offered to purchase 15,000 sheet sets from Avery for $56.25 per set. If Avery accepts the order, the contract will prohibit the motel chain from reselling the bed sheets.

Required

Should Avery accept or reject the special order? Support your answer with appropriate computations.

LO 6-2

Exercise 6-7B *Special order decision*

Wilcox Automotive Company manufactures an engine designed for motorcycles and markets the product using its own brand name. Although Wilcox has the capacity to produce 50,000 engines annually, it currently produces and sells only 30,000 units per year. The engine normally sells for $540 per unit, with no quantity discounts. The unit-level costs to produce the engine are $192 for direct materials, $180 for direct labor, and $36 for indirect manufacturing costs. Wilcox expects total annual product- and facility-level costs to be $648,000 and $900,000, respectively. Assume Wilcox receives a special order from a new customer seeking to buy 1,000 engines for $384 each.

Required

Should Wilcox accept or reject the special order? Support your answer with appropriate computations.

Exercise 6-8B *Identifying qualitative factors for a special order decision* LO 6-2

Required

Describe the qualitative factors that Wilcox should consider before making the decision described in Exercise 6-7B.

Exercise 6-9B *Using the contribution margin approach for a special order decision* LO 6-2

Benton Company produces and sells a food processor that it prices at a 32 percent markup on total cost. Based on data pertaining to producing and selling 50,000 food processors, Benton computes the sales price per food processor as follows.

Unit-level costs	$ 750,000
Fixed costs	500,000
Total cost (a)	$1,250,000
Markup (a × 0.32)	400,000
Total sales revenue (b)	$1,650,000
Sales price per unit (b ÷ 50,000)	$ 33.00

Required

a. Benton receives a special order for 7,000 food processors for $20 each. Benton has excess capacity. Calculate the contribution margin per unit for the special order. Based on the contribution margin per unit, should Benton accept the special order?

b. Support your answer by preparing a contribution margin income statement for the special order.

Exercise 6-10B *Making an outsourcing decision* LO 6-3

Swartz Boats Company currently produces a battery used in manufacturing its boats. The company annually manufactures and sells 5,000 units of a particular model of fishing boat. Because of the low volume of activity, Swartz is unable to obtain the economies of scale that larger producers achieve. For example, the costs associated with producing the batteries it uses are almost 30 percent more than the cost of purchasing comparable batteries. Swartz could buy batteries for $516 each; it costs $660 each to make them. A detailed breakdown of current production costs for the batteries follows.

Item	Unit Cost	Total
Unit-level costs:		
Materials	$240	$1,200,000
Labor	150	750,000
Overhead	30	150,000
Allocated facility-level costs	240	1,200,000
Total	$660	$3,300,000

Based on these figures, Swartz's president asserted that it would be foolish for the company to continue to produce the batteries at $660 each when it can buy them for $516 each.

Required

Do you agree with the president's conclusion? Support your answer with appropriate computations.

LO 6-3

Exercise 6-11B *Establishing a price for an outsourcing decision*

Clayton Corporation makes and sells skateboards. Clayton currently makes the 60,000 wheels used annually in its skateboards but has an opportunity to purchase the wheels from a reliable manufacturer. The costs of making the wheels follow.

Annual Costs Associated with Manufacturing Skateboard Wheels

Materials (60,000 units × $8)	$ 480,000
Labor (60,000 units × $4)	240,000
Depreciation on manufacturing equipment*	48,000
Salary of wheel production supervisor	130,000
Rental cost of equipment used to make wheels	110,000
Allocated portion of corporate-level facility-sustaining costs	66,000
Total cost to make 60,000 wheels	$1,074,000

*The equipment has a book value of $74,000 but its market value is zero.

Required

a. Determine the maximum price per unit that Clayton would be willing to pay for the wheels.

b. Would the price computed in Requirement *a* change if production were increased to 80,000 units? Support your answer with appropriate computations.

LO 6-3

Exercise 6-12B *Making an outsourcing decision with qualitative factors considered*

Martinez Computers currently purchases for $40 each keyboard it uses in the 50,000 computers it makes and sells annually. Each computer uses one keyboard. The company has idle capacity and is considering whether to make the keyboards that it needs. Martinez estimates that materials and labor costs for making keyboards would be $25 each. In addition, supervisory salaries, rent, and other manufacturing costs would be $1,000,000. Allocated facility-level costs would amount to $175,000.

Required

a. Determine the change in net income that Martinez would experience if it decides to make the keyboards.

b. Discuss the qualitative factors that Martinez should consider.

LO 6-3

Exercise 6-13B *Outsourcing decision affected by opportunity costs*

Baxter Doors Company currently produces the doorknobs for the doors it makes and sells. The monthly cost of producing 5,000 doorknobs is as follows.

Unit-level materials	$16,000
Unit-level labor	30,000
Unit-level overhead	4,000
Product-level costs*	32,000
Allocated facility-level costs	20,000

*Twenty percent of these costs can be avoided if the doorknobs are purchased.

Wells Company has offered to sell comparable doorknobs to Baxter for $15.20 each.

Required

a. Should Baxter continue to make the doorknobs? Support your answer with appropriate computations.

b. For $24,000 per month, Baxter could lease the manufacturing space to another company. Would this potential cash inflow affect your response to Requirement *a*? Explain.

LO 6-4

Exercise 6-14B *Segment elimination decision*

Reid Company operates three segments. Income statements for the segments imply that Reid could improve profitability by eliminating Segment X.

REID COMPANY Income Statement Year 2			
Segment	X	Y	Z
Sales	$ 46,000	$125,000	$100,000
Cost of goods sold	(36,500)	(41,000)	(42,500)
Sales commissions	(6,500)	(11,000)	(10,000)
Contribution margin	3,000	73,000	47,500
General fixed oper. exp. (allocation of president's salary)	(10,000)	(10,000)	(10,000)
Advertising expense (specific to individual segments)	(1,500)	(9,000)	0
Net income (loss)	$ (8,500)	$ 54,000	$ 37,500

Required

a. Explain the effect on Reid's profitability if Segment X is eliminated.

b. Prepare comparative income statements for the company as a whole under the two alternatives: (1) Segment X is retained or (2) Segment X is eliminated.

Exercise 6-15B *Segment elimination decision*

LO 6-4

Kerston Company divides its operations into six divisions. A recent income statement for the Southwood Division follows.

Income Statement	
Revenue	$ 400,000
Salaries for employees	(200,000)
Operating expenses	(137,500)
Insurance	(22,500)
Division-level facility-sustaining costs	(45,000)
Companywide facility-sustaining costs	(37,000)
Net loss	$ (42,000)

Required

a. Should Kerston eliminate the Southwood Division? Support your answer by explaining how the division's elimination would affect the net income of the company as a whole. By how much would companywide income increase or decrease?

b. Assume that the Southwood Division could increase its revenue to $430,000 by raising prices. Would this change the decision you made in response to Requirement *a*? Assuming Kerston's revenue becomes $430,000, determine the amount of the increase or decrease that would occur in companywide net income if the segment were eliminated.

c. What is the minimum amount of revenue the Southwood Division must generate to justify its continued operation?

Exercise 6-16B *Identifying avoidable cost of a segment*

LO 6-4

Valez Corporation is considering the elimination of one of its segments. The following fixed costs pertain to the segment. If the segment is eliminated, the building it uses will be sold.

Annual advertising expense	$90,000
Market value of the building	15,000
Annual depreciation on the building	10,000
Annual maintenance costs on equipment	13,000
Annual real estate taxes on the building	4,000
Annual supervisory salaries	36,000
Annual allocation of companywide facility-level costs	15,000
Original cost of the building	37,500
Current book value of the building	27,000

Required

Based on this information, determine the amount of avoidable cost associated with the segment.

LO 6-5

Exercise 6-17B *Asset replacement—opportunity cost*

Harris Fishing Tours Inc. owns a boat that originally cost $120,000. Currently, the boat's net book value is $36,000, and its expected remaining useful life is four years. Harris has an opportunity to purchase for $80,000 a replacement boat that is extremely fuel efficient. Fuel costs for the old boat are expected to be $15,000 per year more than fuel costs would be for the replacement boat. Harris could sell the old boat, which is fully paid for and in good condition, for only $32,000.

Required

Should Harris replace the old boat with the new fuel-efficient model, or should it continue to use the old one until it wears out? Explain.

LO 6-5

Exercise 6-18B *Asset replacement decision*

Orr Electronics purchased a manufacturing plant four years ago for $4,500,000. The plant costs $1,000,000 per year to operate. Its current book value using straight-line depreciation is $3,500,000. Orr could purchase a replacement plant for $8,000,000 that would have a useful life of 10 years. Because of new technology, the replacement plant would require only $300,000 per year in operating expenses. It would have an expected salvage value of $2,000,000 after 10 years. The current disposal value of the old plant is $600,000, and if Orr keeps it 10 more years, its residual value would be $150,000.

Required

Based on this information, should Orr replace the old plant? Support your answer with appropriate computations.

LO 6-5

Exercise 6-19B *Asset replacement decision*

Sim Company is considering whether to replace some of its manufacturing equipment. Information pertaining to the existing equipment and the potential replacement equipment follows.

Existing Equipment		Replacement Equipment	
Cost	$30,000	Cost	$27,000
Operating expenses*	24,000	Operating expenses*	4,000
Salvage value	4,000	Salvage value	8,000
Market value	8,500	Useful life	10 years
Book value	10,500		
Remaining useful life	10 years		

*The amounts shown for operating expenses are the cumulative total of all such expenses expected to be incurred over the useful life of the equipment.

Required

Based on this information, recommend whether to replace the equipment. Support your recommendation with appropriate computations.

LO 6-5

Exercise 6-20B *Asset replacement decision*

McCoy Company, a Texas-based corporation, paid $120,000 to purchase an air conditioner on January 1, Year 1. During Year 10, surging energy costs prompted management to consider replacing the air conditioner with a more energy-efficient model. The new air conditioner would cost $150,000. Electricity for the existing air conditioner costs the company $60,000 per year; the new model would cost only $40,000 per year. The new model, which has an expected useful life of 10 years, would be installed on January 1, Year 11. Because the old air conditioner is more durable, McCoy estimates it still has a remaining useful life of 10 years even though it has been used. The current market value of the old air conditioner is $54,000. The expected salvage value of both air conditioners is zero.

Required

Based on this information, recommend whether to replace the equipment. Support your recommendation with appropriate computations.

Exercise 6-21B *Annual versus cumulative data for replacement decision (Appendix)*

LO 6-6

Because their three adult children have all at last left home, Joseph and Audrey Peck recently moved to a smaller house. Joseph owns a riding lawnmower he bought three years ago to take care of the former house's huge yard; it should last another five years. With the new house's smaller yard, Joseph thinks he could hire someone to cut his grass for $800 per year. He wonders if this option is financially sound. Relevant information follows.

Riding Lawn Mower	Amount
Original cost	$5,400
Accumulated depreciation	1,800
Current market value	2,600
Estimated salvage value	0

Required

a. What is the annual opportunity cost of using the riding mower? Based on your computations, recommend whether Joseph should sell it and hire a lawn service.

b. Determine the total cost of hiring a lawn service for the next five years. Based on your computations, recommend whether Joseph should sell the mower and hire a lawn service.

Exercise 6-22B *Scarce resource decision (Appendix)*

LO 6-7

Norwood Technologies has the capacity to annually produce either 50,000 desktop computers or 28,000 laptop computers. Relevant data for each product follow.

	Desktop	Laptop
Sales price	$400	$720
Variable costs	160	260

Required

Assuming that Norwood can sell all it produces of either product, should the company produce the desktop computers or the laptop computers? Provide computations to support your answer.

PROBLEMS—SERIES B

Problem 6-23B *Context-sensitive relevance*

LO 6-1

Required

Respond to each requirement independently.

a. Describe two decision-making contexts, one in which unit-level labor costs are avoidable and the other in which they are unavoidable.

b. Describe two decision-making contexts, one in which batch-level shipping costs are avoidable and the other in which they are unavoidable.

c. Describe two decision-making contexts, one in which administrative costs are avoidable and the other in which they are unavoidable.

d. Describe two decision-making contexts, one in which the insurance premium paid on a building is avoidable and the other in which it is unavoidable.

e. Describe two decision-making contexts, one in which amortization of a product patent is avoidable and the other in which it is unavoidable.

LO 6-1

Problem 6-24B *Context-sensitive relevance*

Quinn Machines Company is evaluating two customer orders. It can accept only one because of capacity limitations. The data associated with each order follow.

Cost Category	Order A	Order B
Contract price	$400,000	$335,000
Unit-level materials	150,000	118,000
Unit-level labor	137,000	107,400
Unit-level overhead	53,000	49,000
Supervisor's salary	40,000	40,000
Rental equipment costs	10,000	12,000
Depreciation on tools (zero market value)	14,000	14,000
Allocated portion of companywide facility-sustaining costs	4,000	3,600
Insurance coverage	27,000	27,000

Required

a. Assume that Quinn has decided to accept one of the two orders. Identify the information relevant to selecting one order versus the other. Recommend which job to accept, and support your answer with appropriate computations.

b. The customer presenting Order A has withdrawn it because of its financial hardship. Under this circumstance, Quinn's choice is to accept or reject Order B alone. Identify the information relevant to this decision. Recommend whether to accept or reject Order B. Support your answer with appropriate computations.

LO 6-2

Problem 6-25B *Effect of order quantity on special order decision*

Schmidt Company made 100,000 electric drills in batches of 1,000 units each during the prior accounting period. Normally, Schmidt markets its products through a variety of hardware stores. The following is the summarized cost to produce electric drills.

Materials cost ($20.00 per unit × 100,000)	$2,000,000
Labor cost ($12.00 per unit × 100,000)	1,200,000
Manufacturing supplies ($1.00 × 100,000)	100,000
Batch-level costs (100 batches at $4,000 per batch)	400,000
Product-level costs	300,000
Facility-level costs	360,000
Total costs	$4,360,000
Cost per unit = $4,360,000 ÷ 100,000 = $43.60	

Required

a. Bypassing Schmidt's regular distribution channel, Vestavia's Home Maintenance Company has offered to buy a batch of 500 electric drills for $39 each directly from Schmidt. Schmidt's normal selling price is $54 per unit. Based on the preceding quantitative data, should Schmidt accept the special order? Support your answer with appropriate computations.

b. Would your answer to Requirement *a* change if Vestavia's offered to buy a batch of 1,000 electric drills for $39 each? Support your answer with appropriate computations.

c. Describe the qualitative factors that Schmidt should consider before accepting a special order to sell electric drills to Vestavia's.

LO 6-3

Problem 6-26B *Effects of the level of production on an outsourcing decision*

One of Riku Company's major products is a fuel additive designed to improve fuel efficiency and keep engines clean. Riku, a petrochemical firm, makes and sells 100,000 units of the fuel additive per year. Its management is evaluating the possibility of having an outside supplier manufacture the product for Riku for $3.20 each. Riku would continue to sell and distribute the fuel additive under its own brand name for either alternative. Riku's accountant constructed the following profitability analysis.

Revenue (100,000 units × $6.00)	$600,000
Unit-level materials costs (100,000 units × $1.20)	(120,000)
Unit-level labor costs (100,000 units × $0.20)	(20,000)
Unit-level overhead costs (100,000 × $0.50)	(50,000)
Unit-level selling expenses (100,000 × $0.20)	(20,000)
Contribution margin	390,000
Fuel additive production supervisor's salary	(160,000)
Allocated portion of facility-level costs	(50,000)
Product-level advertising cost	(80,000)
Contribution to companywide income	$100,000

Required

a. Identify the cost items relevant to the make-or-outsource decision.

b. Should Riku continue to make the fuel additive or buy it from the supplier? Support your answer by determining the change in net income if Riku buys the fuel additive instead of making it.

c. Suppose that Riku is able to increase sales by 60,000 units (sales will increase to 160,000 units). At this level of sales, should Riku make or buy the fuel additive? Support your answer by explaining how the increase in production affects the cost per unit.

d. Discuss the qualitative factors that Riku should consider before deciding to outsource the fuel additive. How can Riku minimize the risk of establishing a relationship with an unreliable supplier?

Problem 6-27B *Outsourcing decision affected by equipment replacement*

LO 6-3, 6-5

During Year 2, Adaire Toy Company made 10,000 units of Model K, the costs of which follow.

Unit-level materials costs (10,000 units × $30)	$ 300,000
Unit-level labor costs (10,000 units × $40)	400,000
Unit-level overhead costs (10,000 × $8)	80,000
Depreciation on manufacturing equipment	120,000
Model K production supervisor's salary	120,000
Inventory holding costs	240,000
Allocated portion of facility-level costs	160,000
Total costs	$1,420,000

An independent contractor has offered to make the same product for Adaire for $70 each.

Additional Information:

1. The manufacturing equipment originally cost $840,000 and has a book value of $480,000, a remaining useful life of four years, and a zero salvage value. If the equipment is not used to produce Model K in the production process, it can be leased for $80,000 per year.
2. Adaire has the opportunity to purchase for $480,000 new manufacturing equipment that will have an expected useful life of four years and a salvage value of $160,000. This equipment will increase productivity substantially, thereby reducing unit-level labor costs by 20 percent.
3. If Adaire discontinues the production of Model K, the company can eliminate 50 percent of its inventory holding cost.

Required

a. Determine the avoidable cost per unit to produce Model K assuming that Adaire is considering the alternatives between making the product using the existing equipment and outsourcing the product to the independent contractor. Based on the quantitative data, should Adaire outsource Model K? Support your answer with appropriate computations.

b. Assuming that Adaire is considering whether to replace the old equipment with the new equipment, determine the avoidable cost per unit to produce Model K using the new equipment and the avoidable cost per unit to produce Model K using the old equipment. Calculate the impact on profitability if Model K were made using the old equipment versus the new equipment.

c. Assuming that Adaire is considering either to purchase the new equipment or to outsource Model K, calculate the impact on profitability between the two alternatives.

d. Discuss the qualitative factors that Adaire should consider before making a decision to outsource Model K. How can Adaire minimize the risk of establishing a relationship with an unreliable supplier?

LO 6-4

Problem 6-28B *Eliminating a segment*

Pam's Grocery Store has three departments—meat, canned food, and produce—each of which has its own manager. All departments are housed in a single store. Recently, the produce department has been suffering a net loss and is expected to continue doing so. Last year's income statements follow.

	Meat Department	Canned Food Department	Produce Department
Sales	$ 350,000	$ 320,000	$ 237,500
Cost of goods sold	(160,000)	(190,000)	(147,500)
Gross margin	190,000	130,000	90,000
Departmental manager's salary	(21,000)	(15,000)	(17,500)
Rent on store lease	(40,000)	(40,000)	(40,000)
Store utilities	(10,000)	(10,000)	(10,000)
Other general expenses	(49,000)	(49,000)	(49,000)
Net income (loss)	$ 70,000	$ 16,000	$ (26,500)

Required

a. Determine whether to eliminate the produce department.

b. Confirm the conclusion you reached in Requirement *a* by preparing a before and an after income statement, assuming that the produce department is eliminated.

c. Eliminating the produce department would allow the meat department to expand. It could add seafood to its products. Suppose that management estimates that offering seafood would increase the store's net earnings by $80,000. Would this information affect the decision that you made in Requirement *a*? Explain your answer.

LO 6-4

Problem 6-29B *Effect of activity level and opportunity cost on segment elimination decision*

Hana Company has three separate operating branches: Division X, which manufactures utensils; Division Y, which makes plates; and Division Z, which makes cooking pots. Each division operates its own facility. The company's administrative offices are located in a separate building. In recent years, Division Z has experienced a net loss and is expected to continue to do so. Income statements for Year 2 follow.

	Division X	Division Y	Division Z
Sales	$1,000,000	$ 800,000	$750,000
Less: Cost of goods sold			
Unit-level manufacturing costs	(550,000)	(290,000)	(450,000)
Rent on manufacturing facility	(120,000)	(110,000)	(180,000)
Gross margin	330,000	400,000	120,000
Less: Operating expenses			
Unit-level selling and admin. expenses	(30,000)	(22,500)	(45,000)
Division-level fixed selling and admin. expenses	(70,000)	(62,500)	(90,000)
Administrative facility-level costs	(40,000)	(40,000)	(40,000)
Net income (loss)	$ 190,000	$ 275,000	$ (55,000)

Spreadsheet Tips

1. The numbers in cells F7 to F9 should be formulas that refer to F5. This allows the number of cases to be changed in cell F5 with the other cells changing automatically.
2. The formula in cell F10 uses a function named ROUNDUP to calculate the even number of batches. The formula should be = ROUNDUP(F5/1000,0) where the zero refers to rounding up to the nearest whole number.

ATC 6-7 Spreadsheet Assignment *Mastering Excel*

Refer to Problem 6-32A.

Required

a. Prepare a spreadsheet to solve Requirements *a*, *b*, and *c* in Problem 6-32A.
b. While constructing formulas for Requirement *a* of Problem 6-32A, include a formula to calculate contribution margin per labor hour.
c. While constructing formulas for Requirement *b* of Problem 6-32A, include formulas to calculate total contribution margin for each product.
d. While constructing formulas for Requirement *c* of Problem 6-32A, include formulas to calculate contribution margin per machine hour and total contribution margin for each product.

COMPREHENSIVE PROBLEM

Use the same transaction data for Magnificent Modems Inc. as was used in Chapter 1. (See page 52.)

Required

a. One of Magnificent Modems' sales representatives receives a special offer to sell 1,000 modems at a price of $72 each. Should the offer be accepted?
b. Magnificent Modems has the opportunity to purchase the modems that it currently makes. The modems can be purchased at a price of $76 each. Assuming the manufacturing equipment has a zero market value, should Magnificent buy the modems?
c. Assume that Magnificent Modems expects production and sales to grow to 10,000. At this volume of production, should Magnificent buy the modems?

CHAPTER 7

Planning for Profit and Cost Control

LEARNING OBJECTIVES

After you have mastered the material in this chapter, you will be able to:

LO 7-1 Describe the budgeting process and the benefits it provides.

LO 7-2 Prepare a sales budget and related schedule of cash receipts.

LO 7-3 Prepare an inventory purchases budget and related schedule of cash payments.

LO 7-4 Prepare a selling and administrative expense budget and related schedule of cash payments.

LO 7-5 Prepare a cash budget.

LO 7-6 Prepare a pro forma income statement, balance sheet, and statement of cash flows.

Video lectures and accompanying self-assessment quizzes are available in Connect® for all learning objectives.

CHAPTER OPENING

Planning is crucial to operating a profitable business. Expressing business plans in financial terms is commonly called **budgeting.** The budgeting process involves coordinating the financial plans of all areas of the business. For example, the production department cannot prepare a manufacturing plan until it knows how many units of product to produce. The number of units to produce depends on the marketing department's sales projection. The marketing department cannot project sales volume until it knows what products the company will sell. Product information comes from the research and development department. The point should be clear: A company's master budget results from combining numerous specific plans prepared by different departments.

Master budget preparation is normally supervised by a committee. The budget committee is responsible for settling disputes among various departments over budget matters. The committee also monitors reports on how various segments are progressing toward achieving their budget goals. The budgeting committee is not an accounting committee. It is a high-level committee that normally includes the company president, vice presidents of marketing, purchasing, production, and finance, and the controller.

The Curious Accountant

People in television commercials often say they shop at a particular store because "my family is on a budget." The truth is, most families do not have a formal budget. What these people mean is that they need to be sure their spending does not exceed their available cash.

When a family expects to spend more money in a given year than it will earn, it must plan on borrowing funds needed to make up the difference. However, even if a family's income for a year will exceed its spending, it may still need to borrow money because the timing of its cash inflows may not match the timing of its cash outflows. Whether a budget is being prepared for a family or a business, those preparing the budget must understand the specific issues facing that entity if potential financial problems are to be anticipated. There is no such thing as a "one size fits all" budget.

The **United States Olympic Committee (USOC)**, like all large organizations, devotes considerable effort to budget planning.

Think about the Olympic Games and how the USOC generates revenues and incurs expenditures. Can you identify any unusual circumstances facing the USOC that complicate its budgeting efforts? (Answer on page 321.)

©Tim Clayton/Corbis/Getty Images

THE PLANNING PROCESS

LO 7-1

Describe the budgeting process and the benefits it provides.

Planning normally addresses short, intermediate, and long-range time horizons. Short-term plans are more specific than long-term plans. Consider, for example, your decision to attend college. Long-term planning requires considering general questions such as:

- Do I want to go to college?
- How do I expect to benefit from the experience?
- Do I want a broad knowledge base, or am I seeking to learn specific job skills?
- In what field do I want to concentrate my studies?

Many students go to college before answering these questions. They discover the disadvantages of poor planning the hard way. While their friends are graduating, they are starting over in a new major.

Intermediate-range planning usually covers three to five years. In this stage, you consider which college to attend, how to support yourself while in school, and whether to live on or off campus.

Short-term planning focuses on the coming year. In this phase, you plan specific courses to take, decide which instructors to choose, schedule part-time work, and join a study group. Short-term plans are specific and detailed. Their preparation may seem tedious, but careful planning generally leads to efficient resource use and high levels of productivity.

Three Levels of Planning for Business Activity

Businesses describe the three levels of planning as *strategic planning, capital budgeting,* and *operations budgeting.* **Strategic planning** involves making long-term decisions such as defining the scope of the business, determining which products to develop or discontinue, and identifying the most profitable market niche. Upper-level management is responsible for these decisions. Strategic plans are descriptive rather than quantitative. Objectives such as "to have the largest share of the market" or "to be the best-quality producer" result from strategic planning. Although strategic planning is an integral component of managing a business, an in-depth discussion of it is beyond the scope of this text.

Capital budgeting focuses on intermediate range planning. It involves such decisions as whether to buy or lease equipment, whether to stimulate sales, or whether to increase the company's asset base. Capital budgeting is discussed in detail in a later chapter.

Operations budgeting concentrates on short-term plans. A key component of operations budgeting is the *master budget,* which describes short-term objectives in specific amounts of sales targets, production goals, and financing plans. The master budget describes how management intends to achieve its objectives and directs the company's short-term activities.

The master budget normally covers one year. It is frequently divided into quarterly projections and often subdivides quarterly data by month. Effective managers cannot wait until year-end to know whether operations conform to budget targets. Monthly data provide feedback to permit making necessary corrections promptly.

Many companies use **perpetual,** or **continuous, budgeting** covering a 12-month reporting period. As the current month draws to a close, an additional month is added at the end of the budget period, resulting in a continuous 12-month budget. A perpetual budget offers the advantage of keeping management constantly focused on thinking ahead to the next 12 months. The more traditional annual approach to budgeting invites a frenzied stop-and-go mentality, with managers preparing the budget in a year-end rush that is soon forgotten. Changing conditions may not be discussed until the next year-end budget is due. A perpetual budget overcomes these disadvantages.

Advantages of Budgeting

Budgeting is costly and time-consuming. The sacrifices, however, are more than offset by the benefits. Budgeting promotes planning and coordination; it enhances performance measurement and corrective action.

Planning

©Alistair Berg/Digital Vision/Getty Images

Almost everyone makes plans. Each morning, most people think about what they will do during the day. Thinking ahead is planning. Most business managers think ahead about how they will direct operations. Unfortunately, planning is frequently as informal as making a few mental notes. Informal planning cannot be effectively communicated. The business manager might know what her objectives are, but neither her superiors nor her subordinates know. Because it serves as a communication tool, budgeting can solve these problems. The budget formalizes and documents managerial plans, clearly communicating objectives to both superiors and subordinates.

Coordination

Sometimes a choice benefits one department at the expense of another. For example, a purchasing agent may order large quantities of raw materials to obtain discounts from suppliers. But excessive quantities of materials pose a storage problem for the inventory supervisor who must manage warehouse costs. The budgeting process forces coordination among departments to promote decisions in the best interests of the company as a whole.

Performance Measurement

Budgets are specific, quantitative representations of management's objectives. Comparing actual results to budget expectations provides a way to evaluate performance. For example, if a company budgets sales of $10 million, it can judge the performance of the sales department against that level. If actual sales exceed $10 million, the company should reward the sales department; if actual sales fall below $10 million, the company should seek an explanation for the shortfall from the sales manager.

Corrective Action

Budgeting provides advance notice of potential shortages, bottlenecks, or other weaknesses in operating plans. For example, a cash budget alerts management to when the company can expect cash shortages during the coming year. The company can make borrowing arrangements well before it needs the money. Without knowing ahead of time, management might be unable to secure necessary financing on short notice, or it may have to pay excessively high interest rates to obtain funds. Budgeting advises managers of potential problems in time for them to carefully devise effective solutions.

Budgeting and Human Behavior

Effective budgeting requires genuine sensitivity on the part of upper management to the effect on employees of budget expectations. People are often uncomfortable with budgets. Budgets are constraining. They limit individual freedom in favor of an established plan. Many people find evaluation based on budget expectations stressful. Most students experience a similar fear about testing. Like examinations, budgets represent standards by which performance is evaluated. Employees worry about whether their performance will meet expectations.

The attitudes of high-level managers significantly impact budget effectiveness. Subordinates are keenly aware of management's expectations. If upper-level managers degrade, make fun of, or ignore the budget, subordinates will follow suit. If management uses budgets to humiliate, embarrass, or punish subordinates, employees will resent the treatment and the budgeting process. Upper-level managers must demonstrate that they view the budget as a sincere effort to express realistic goals employees are expected to meet. An honest, open, respectful atmosphere is essential to budgeting success.

Participative budgeting has frequently proved successful in creating a healthy atmosphere. This technique invites participation in the budget process by personnel at all levels of the organization, not just upper-level managers. Information flows from the bottom up as well as from the top down during budget preparation. Because they are directly responsible for meeting budget goals, subordinates can offer more realistic targets. Including them in budget preparation fosters development of a team effort. Participation fosters more cooperation and motivation, and less fear. With participative budgeting, subordinates cannot complain that the budget is management's plan. The budget is instead a self-imposed constraint. Employees can hold no one responsible but themselves if they fail to accomplish the budget objectives they established.

Upper management participates in the process to ensure that employee-generated objectives are consistent with company objectives. Furthermore, if subordinates were granted complete freedom to establish budget standards, they might be tempted to adopt lax standards to ensure they will meet them. Both managers and subordinates must cooperate if the participatory process is to produce an effective budget. If developed carefully, budgets can motivate employees to achieve superior performance. Normal human fears must be overcome, and management must create an honest budget atmosphere.

The Master Budget

The **master budget** is a group of detailed budgets and schedules representing the company's operating and financial plans for a future accounting period. The master budget usually includes (1) *operating budgets,* (2) *capital budgets,* and (3) *pro forma financial statements.* The budgeting process normally begins with preparing the **operating budgets,** which focus on detailed operating activities. This chapter illustrates operating budgets and pro forma statements for Hampton Hams, a retail sales company that uses (1) a sales budget, (2) an inventory purchases budget, (3) a selling and administrative (S&A) expense budget, and (4) a cash budget. As previously stated, capital budgets are discussed in a later chapter.

The sales budget includes a schedule of cash receipts from customers. The inventory purchases and S&A expense budgets include schedules of cash payments for inventory and expenses. Preparing the master budget begins with the sales forecast. Based on the sales forecast, the detailed budgets for inventory purchases and operating expenses are developed. The schedules of cash receipts and cash payments provide the foundation for preparing the cash budget.

The operating budgets are used to prepare *pro forma statements.* **Pro forma financial statements** are based on projected (budgeted) rather than historical information. Hampton Hams prepares a pro forma income statement, balance sheet, and statement of cash flows.

Exhibit 7.1 shows how information flows in a master budget.

EXHIBIT 7.1

Information Flows in the Master Budget

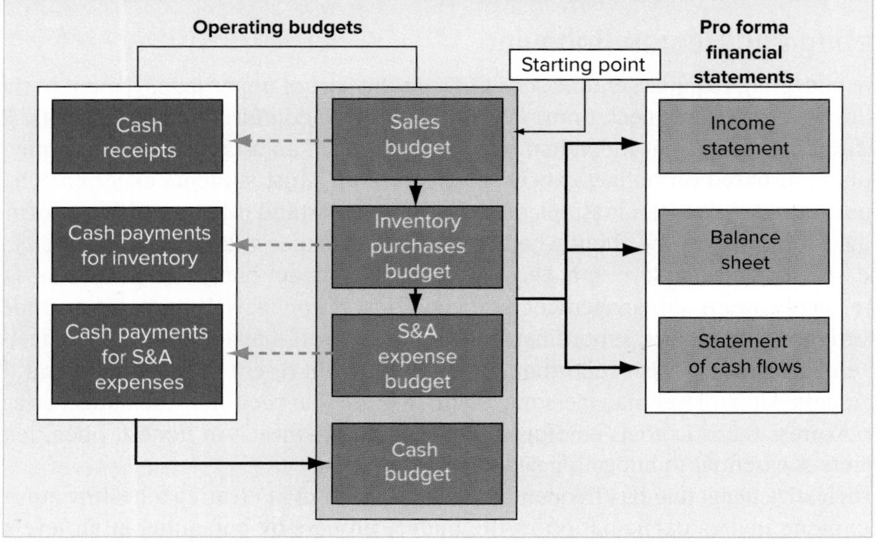

HAMPTON HAMS BUDGETING ILLUSTRATION

Hampton Hams (HH), a major corporation, sells cured hams nationwide through retail outlets in shopping malls. By focusing on a single product and standardized operations, the company controls costs stringently. As a result, it offers high-quality hams at competitive prices.

Hampton Hams has experienced phenomenal growth during the past five years. It opened two new stores in Indianapolis, Indiana, last month and plans to open a third new store in October. Hampton Hams finances new stores by borrowing on a line of credit arranged with National Bank. National's loan officer has requested monthly budgets for each of the first three months of the new store's operations. The accounting department is preparing the new store's master budget for October, November, and December. The first step is developing a sales budget.

SALES BUDGET

LO 7-2

Prepare a sales budget and related schedule of cash receipts.

Preparing the master budget begins with the sales forecast. The accuracy of the sales forecast is critical because all the other budgets are derived from the sales budget. Normally, the marketing department coordinates the development of the sales forecast. Sales estimates frequently flow from the bottom up to the higher management levels. Sales personnel prepare sales projections for their products and territories and pass them up the line where they are combined with the estimates of other sales personnel to develop regional and national estimates. Using various information sources, upper-level sales managers adjust the estimates generated by sales personnel. Adjustment information comes from industry periodicals and trade journals, economic analysis, marketing surveys, historical sales figures, and changes in competition. Companies assimilate these data using sophisticated computer programs, statistical techniques, and quantitative methods, or, simply, professional judgment. Regardless of the technique, the senior vice president of sales ultimately develops a sales forecast for which she is held responsible.

To develop the sales forecast for HH's new store, the sales manager studied the sales history of existing stores operating in similar locations. He then adjusted for start-up conditions. October is an opportune time to open a new store because customers will learn the store's location before the holiday season. The sales manager expects significant growth in November and December as customers choose the company's hams as the centerpiece for many Thanksgiving and winter holiday dinner tables.

The new store's sales are expected to be $160,000 in October ($40,000 in cash and $120,000 on account). Sales are expected to increase 20 percent per month during November and December. Based on these estimates, the sales manager prepared the sales budget in Exhibit 7.2.

Projected Sales

The sales budget has two sections. Section 1 shows the projected sales for each month. The November sales forecast reflects a 20 percent increase over October sales. For example, November *cash sales* are calculated as $48,000 [$40,000 + ($40,000 × 0.20)], and December *cash sales* are calculated as $57,600 [$48,000 + ($48,000 × 0.20)]. *Sales on account* are similarly computed.

Schedule of Cash Receipts

Section 2 is a schedule of the cash receipts for the projected sales. This schedule is used later to prepare the cash budget. The accountant has assumed in this schedule that Hampton Hams will collect accounts receivable from credit sales *in full* in the month following the sale. In practice, collections may be spread over several months, and some receivables may

EXHIBIT 7.2

Sales Budget

Hampton Hams
Sales Budget

	Oct	Nov	Dec	Pro Forma Data
Section 1: Projected Sales				
Cash Sales	$ 40,000	$ 48,000	$ 57,600	
Sales on Account	120,000	144,000	172,800	$172,800 (a)
Total Budgeted Sales	$160,000	$192,000	$230,400	$582,400 (b)
Section 2: Schedule of Cash Receipts				
Current Cash Sales	$40,000	$ 48,000	$ 57,600	
Plus Collections of Accounts Receivable	0	120,000	144,000	
Total Budgeted Collections	$40,000	$168,000	$201,600	

(a) Quarter-end accounts receivable balance on the balance sheet.
(b) Sales revenue on the income statement (sum of monthly amounts: $160,000 + $192,000 + $230,400).

Source: Microsoft Excel 2010

become bad debts that are never collected. Regardless of additional complexities, the objective is to estimate the amount and timing of expected cash receipts.

In the HH case, *total cash receipts* are determined by adding the current month's *cash sales* to the cash collected from the previous month's *credit sales* (accounts receivable balance). Cash receipts for each month are determined as follows:

- October receipts are projected to be $40,000. Because the store opens in October, no accounts receivable from September exist to be collected in October. Cash receipts for October equal the amount of October's cash sales.
- November receipts are projected to be $168,000 ($48,000 November cash sales + $120,000 cash collected from October sales on account).
- December receipts are projected to be $201,600 ($57,600 December cash sales + $144,000 cash collected from November sales on account).

Pro Forma Financial Statement Data

The Pro Forma Data column in the sales budget displays two figures HH will report on the quarter-end (December 31) budgeted financial statements. Since HH expects to collect December credit sales in January, the *accounts receivable balance* will be $172,800 on the December 31 pro forma balance sheet (shown later in Exhibit 7.7).

The $582,400 of *sales revenue* in the Pro Forma Data column will be reported on the budgeted income statement for the quarter (shown later in Exhibit 7.6). The sales revenue represents the sum of October, November, and December sales ($160,000 + $192,000 + $230,400 = $582,400).

FOCUS ON INTERNATIONAL ISSUES

CASH FLOW PLANNING IN BORDEAUX

©FreeProd/Alamy

The Year 2015 was considered a great year for wine in the Bordeaux region of France, and the winemakers could look forward to selling their wines for high prices, but there was one catch: These wines would not be released to consumers until late in 2018. The winemakers had incurred most of their costs in 2015 when the vines were being tended and the grapes were being processed into wine. In many industries, this would mean the companies would have to finance their inventory for almost four years—not an insignificant cost. The company must finance the inventory by either borrowing the money, which results in out-of-pocket interest expense, or using its own funds. The second option generates an opportunity cost resulting from the interest revenue that could have been earned if these funds were not being used to finance the inventory.

To address this potential cash flow problem, many of the winemakers in Bordeaux offer some of their wines for sale as "futures." That means the wines are purchased and paid for while they are still aging in barrels in France. Selling wine as futures reduces the time inventory must be financed from four years to only one to two years. Of course there are other types of costs in such deals. For one, the wines must be offered at lower prices than they are expected to sell for upon release. The winemakers have obviously decided this cost is less than the cost of financing inventory through borrowed money, or they would not do it.

Recently, one major Bordeaux winery announced a contrarian approach. Chateau Latour said that beginning with the 2012 vintage, not only would it no longer sell futures, but it would no longer sell its wines until it thinks they have aged sufficiently to be at their prime drinking age, which might be 12 years after the vintage. Obviously the winery believes this will allow it to sell its wine at a higher price, but it will need large sums of cash to finance many years of production while it waits. Clearly, this will complicate Chateau Latour's cash flow planning.

Companies in other industries use similar techniques to speed up cash flow, such as factoring of accounts receivable. A major reason entities prepare cash budgets is to be sure they will have enough cash on hand to pay bills as they come due. If the budget indicates a temporary cash-flow deficit, action must be taken to avoid the problem, and new budgets must be prepared based on these options. Budgeting is not a static process.

Source: Wine Spectator, June 30, 2012.

INVENTORY PURCHASES BUDGET

LO 7-3

Prepare an inventory purchases budget and related schedule of cash payments.

The inventory purchases budget shows the amount of inventory HH must purchase each month to satisfy the demand projected in the sales budget. The *total inventory needed* each month equals the amount of inventory HH plans to sell that month plus the amount of inventory HH wants on hand at month-end. To the extent that total inventory needed exceeds the inventory on hand at the beginning of the month, HH will need to purchase additional inventory. The amount of inventory to purchase is computed as follows.

Cost of budgeted sales	XXX
Plus: Desired ending inventory	XXX
Total inventory needed	XXX
Less: Beginning inventory	(XXX)
Required purchases	XXX

It is HH's policy to maintain an ending inventory equal to 25 percent of the next month's *projected cost of goods sold.* HH's cost of goods sold normally equals 70 percent of *sales.* Using this information and the sales budget, the accounting department prepared the inventory purchases budget shown in Exhibit 7.3.

Section 1 of the inventory purchases budget shows required purchases for each month. HH determined *budgeted cost of goods sold* for October by multiplying October *budgeted sales* by 70 percent ($160,000 × 0.70 = $112,000). Budgeted cost of goods sold for November and December were similarly computed. The October *desired ending inventory* was computed by multiplying November *budgeted cost of goods sold* by 25 percent ($134,400 × 0.25 = $33,600). Desired

EXHIBIT 7.3

Inventory Purchases Budget

	A	B	C	D	E
1		Hampton Hams			
2		Inventory Purchases Budget			
3					
4					Pro Forma
5	**Section 1: Projected Purchases**	Oct	Nov	Dec	Data
6	Budgeted Cost of Goods Sold	$112,000	25% $134,400	25% $161,280	$407,680 (a)
7	Plus Desired Ending Inventory	33,600	40,320	35,000	$35,000 (b)
8	Total Inventory Needed	145,600	174,720	196,280	
9	Less Beginning Inventory	0	33,600	40,320	40%
10	Required Purchases (on account)	$145,600	$141,120	$155,960	$62,384 (c)
11					
12	**Section 2: Schedule of Cash Payments for Inventory Purchases**				
13	Pay 60% of Current Month Accts Payable	$87,360	$84,672	$93,576	
14	Pay 40% of Prior Month Accts Payable	0	58,240	56,448	
15	Total Budgeted Disbursements for Inventory	$87,360	$142,912	$150,024	
16					
17	(a) Cost of goods sold reported on pro forma income statement:				
18	(Sum of monthly amounts $112,000 + $134,400 + $161,280 = $407,680).				
19	(b) Ending inventory balance reported on pro forma balance sheet.				
20	(c) Ending accounts payable balance reported on proforma balance sheet ($155,960 x .40)				

Source: Microsoft Excel 2010

ending inventory for November is $40,320 ($161,280 × 0.25). Desired ending inventory for December is based on January projected cost of goods sold (not shown in the exhibit). HH expects ham sales to decline after the winter holidays. Because January projected cost of goods sold is only $140,000, the December desired ending inventory falls to $35,000 ($140,000 × 0.25).

Schedule of Cash Payments for Inventory Purchases

Section 2 is the schedule of cash payments for inventory purchases. HH makes all inventory purchases on account. The supplier requires that HH pay for 60 percent of inventory purchases in the month goods are purchased. HH pays the remaining 40 percent the month after purchase.

Cash payments are projected as follows (amounts are rounded to the nearest whole dollar):

- October cash payments for inventory are $87,360. Because the new store opens in October, no accounts payable balance from September remains to be paid in October. Cash payments for October equal 60 percent of October inventory purchases.
- November cash payments for inventory are $142,912 (40 percent of October purchases + 60 percent of November purchases).
- December cash payments for inventory are $150,024 (40 percent of November purchases + 60 percent of December purchases).

Pro Forma Financial Statement Data

The Pro Forma Data column in the inventory purchases budget displays three figures HH will report on the quarter-end budgeted financial statements. The $407,680 *cost of goods sold* reported on the pro forma income statement (shown later in Exhibit 7.6) is the sum of the monthly cost of goods sold amounts ($112,000 + $134,400 + $161,280 = $407,680).

The $35,000 *ending inventory* as of December 31 is reported on the pro forma balance sheet (shown later in Exhibit 7.7). December 31 is the last day of both the month of December and the three-month quarter represented by October, November, and December.

The $62,384 of *accounts payable* reported on the pro forma balance sheet (shown later in Exhibit 7.7) represents the 40 percent of December inventory purchases HH will pay for in January ($155,960 × 0.40).

CHECK YOURSELF 7.1

Main Street Sales Company purchased $80,000 of inventory during June. Purchases are expected to increase by 2 percent per month in each of the next three months. Main Street makes all purchases on account. It normally pays cash to settle 70 percent of its accounts payable during the month of purchase and settles the remaining 30 percent in the month following purchase. Based on this information, determine the accounts payable balance Main Street would report on its July 31 balance sheet.

Answer Purchases for the month of July are expected to be $81,600 ($80,000 × 1.02). Main Street will pay 70 percent of the resulting accounts payable in cash during July. The remaining 30 percent represents the expected balance in accounts payable as of July 31. Therefore, the balance would be $24,480 ($81,600 × 0.3).

SELLING AND ADMINISTRATIVE EXPENSE BUDGET

LO 7-4

Prepare a selling and administrative expense budget and related schedule of cash payments.

Section 1 of Exhibit 7.4 shows the selling and administrative (S&A) expense budget for Hampton Hams' new store. Most of the projected expenses are self-explanatory; depreciation and interest, however, merit comment. The depreciation expense is based on projections in the *capital expenditures budget.* Although not presented in this chapter, the capital budget calls for the cash purchase of $130,000 of store fixtures. The fixtures were purchased on October 1. The supplier allows a 30-day inspection period. As a result, payment for the fixtures was made at the end of October. The fixtures are expected to have a useful life of

EXHIBIT 7.4

Selling and Administrative Expense Budget

Exhibit 7.2,7.3,7.4,7.5.xlsx - Microsoft Excel

	A	B	C	D	E	
1	**Hampton Hams**					
2	**Selling and Administrative (S&A) Expense Budget**					
3					Pro Forma	
4	**Section 1: Projected S&A Expenses**	Oct	Nov	Dec	Data	
5	Salary Expense	$24,000	$24,000	$24,000		
6	Sales Commissions, 2% of Sales	3,200	3,840	4,608	$ 4,608	(a)
7	Supplies Expense, 1% of Sales	1,600	1,920	2,304		
8	Utilities Expense	1,400	1,400	1,400	$ 1,400	(b)
9	Depreciation Expense on Store Fixtures	1,000	1,000	1,000	$ 3,000	(c)
10	Rent Expense	3,600	3,600	3,600		
11	Miscellaneous Expense	900	900	900		
12	Total S&A Expenses before Interest	$35,700	$36,660	$37,812	$110,172	(d)
13						
14	**Section 2: Schedule of Cash Payments for S&A Expenses**					
15	Salary Expense	$24,000	$24,000	$24,000		
16	100% of Prior Month Sales Commissions	0	3,200	3,840		
17	Supplies Expense, 1% of Sales	1,600	1,920	2,304		
18	100% of Prior Month Utilities Expense	0	1,400	1,400		
19	Rent Expense	3,600	3,600	3,600		
20	Miscellaneous Expense	900	900	900		
21	Total Payments for S&A Expenses	$30,100	$35,020	$36,044		
22						
23	(a) Sales commissions payable in January reported on the pro forma balance sheet.					
24	(b) Utilities payable in January reported on the pro forma balance sheet.					
25	(c) Accumulated depreciation on the pro forma balance sheet: sum of monthly amounts ($1,000 + $1,000 + $1,000 = $3,000).					
26	(d) S&A expense on pro forma income statement: sum of monthly amounts ($35,700 + $36,660 + $37,812 = $110,172).					
27						
28						

Source: Microsoft Excel 2010

10 years and a $10,000 salvage value. Using the straight-line method, HH estimates annual depreciation expense at $12,000 ([$130,000 − $10,000] ÷ 10). Monthly depreciation expense is $1,000 ($12,000 annual charge ÷ 12 months).

Interest expense is missing from the S&A expense budget. HH cannot estimate interest expense until it completes its borrowing projections. Expected borrowing (financing activities) and related interest expense are shown in the cash budget.

Schedule of Cash Payments for Selling and Administrative Expenses

Section 2 of the S&A expense budget shows the schedule of cash payments. There are several differences between the S&A expenses recognized on the pro forma income statement and the cash payments for S&A expenses. First, Hampton Hams pays sales commissions and utilities expense the month following their incurrence. Since the store opens in October there are no payments due from September. Cash payments for sales commissions and utilities in October are zero. In November, HH will pay the October expenses for these items and in December it will pay the November sales commissions and utilities expenses. Depreciation expense does not affect the cash payments schedule. The cash outflow for the store fixtures occurs when the assets are purchased, not when they are depreciated. The cost of the investment in store fixtures is in the cash budget, not in the cash outflow for S&A expenses.

Pro Forma Financial Statement Data

The Pro Forma Data column of the S&A expense budget displays four figures HH will report on the quarter-end budgeted financial statements. The first and second figures are the sales commissions payable ($4,608) and utilities payable ($1,400) (shown later on the pro forma balance sheet in Exhibit 7.7). Because December sales commissions and utilities expense are not paid until January, these amounts represent liabilities as of December 31.

REALITY BYTES

THE ULTIMATE CASH PLANNING

©Rob Wilson/Shutterstock

Most companies must spend money to buy inventory before they collect money from selling those goods. For example, if you sell building supplies, like The Home Depot, you need to purchase inventory before you sell it to customers. Home Depot receives payment from its customers relatively quickly; they usually pay with a credit card and the bank that issued the credit card usually pays Home Depot within a few days. If a company's customers are other businesses, however, it may take 30 to 60 days before receiving payment. At Home Depot, its accounts receivables are collected in an average of 8 days, but it takes 74 days, on average, to sell its inventory, so 82 days elapse from the time the inventory is bought until it is sold and the cash is collected. This does not mean that Home Depot has to finance its inventory for 82 days, because Home Depot buys its inventory using accounts payables, and it takes an average of 41 days to pay its suppliers. This means that Home Depot is financing its inventory for 41 days (82 days minus 41 days), and this increases the cost of doing business.

Some companies are in the enviable position of being able to collect cash from their customers before they pay cash to their own suppliers for the goods they sell. Apple Inc. takes only 13 days to sell its inventory, and 28 days to collect accounts receivables from those sales, for a total operating cycle of 41 days. However, it waits 127 days to pay its suppliers. Thus, Apple collects cash from its customers 86 days before it has to pay its suppliers.

Costco Wholesale Corporation also does a good job with cash management, but more from quick collection of its receivables than from slow payment to its suppliers, which is Apple's strategy. On average Costco sells its inventory in 32 days and collects the receivables from those sales in 4 days, for a total operating cycle of 36 days. It takes 31 days to pay its suppliers for the inventory that it sells. So, although not as efficient as Apple, Costco still manages to get its cash from customers within five days of the time it needs the cash to pay its suppliers, thus reducing its reliance on financing from sources such as bank loans.

Source: Companies' annual reports.

The third figure in the column ($3,000) is the amount of accumulated depreciation on the pro forma balance sheet (shown later in Exhibit 7.7). Since depreciation accumulates, the $3,000 balance is the sum of the monthly depreciation amounts ($1,000 + $1,000 + $1,000 = $3,000). The final figure in the Pro Forma Data column ($110,172) is the total S&A expenses reported on the pro forma income statement (shown later in Exhibit 7.6). The total S&A expense is the sum of the monthly amounts ($35,700 + $36,660 + $37,812 = $110,172).

CASH BUDGET

LO 7-5

Prepare a cash budget.

Little is more important to business success than effective cash management. If a company experiences cash shortages, it will be unable to pay its debts and may be forced into bankruptcy. If excess cash accumulates, a business loses the opportunity to earn investment income or reduce interest costs by repaying debt. Preparing a **cash budget** alerts management to anticipated cash shortages or excess cash balances. Management can plan financing activities, making advance arrangements to cover anticipated shortages by borrowing and planning to repay past borrowings and making appropriate investments when excess cash is expected.

The cash budget is divided into three major sections: (1) a cash receipts section, (2) a cash payments section, and (3) a financing section. Much of the data needed to prepare the cash budget are included in the cash receipts and payments schedules previously discussed; however, further refinements to project financing needs and interest costs are sometimes necessary. The completed cash budget is shown in Exhibit 7.5.

EXHIBIT 7.5

Cash Budget

Hampton Hams
Cash Budget

	Oct	Nov	Dec	Pro Forma Data	
Section 1: Cash Receipts					
Beginning Cash Balance	$0	$10,540	$10,428		
Add Cash Receipts (Exhibit 7.2)	40,000	168,000	201,600	$409,600	(a)
Total Cash Available	40,000	178,540	212,028		
Section 2: Cash Payments					
For Inventory Purchases (Exhibit 7.3)	87,360	142,912	150,024	$380,296	(b)
For S&A Expenses (Exhibit 7.4)	30,100	35,020	36,044	$101,164	(c)
For Interest Expense		2,180	2,300	$ 4,480	(d)
For Purchase of Store Fixtures	130,000	0	0	$130,000	(e)
Total Budgeted Disbursements	247,460	180,112	188,368		
Section 3: Financing Activities					
Surplus (Shortage)	(207,460)	(1,572)	23,660		
Borrowing (Repayment)	218,000	12,000	(13,000)	$217,000	(f)
Ending Cash Balance	$ 10,540	$10,428	$10,660	$ 10,660	(g)

Pro forma data items (a) through (d) appear in the operating activities section of the pro forma statement of cash flows. Item (d), interest expense, also appears on the pro forma income statement. Each of these items is computed by summing the monthly amounts.

(a) Cash receipts from customers: $40,000 + $168,000 + $201,600 = $409,600.
(b) Cash payments for inventory purchases: $87,360 + $142,912 + $150,024 = $380,296.
(c) Cash payments for S&A Expenses: $30,100 + $35,020 + $36,044 = $101,164.
(d) Cash payments for interest expense: $0 + $2,180 + $2,300 = $4,480.
(e) Investing activities section of the pro forma statement of cash flows.
(f) Financing activities section of the pro forma statements of cash flows ($218,000 + $12,000 - $13,000 = $217,000) and liabilities section of the pro forma balance sheet.
(g) Ending cash balance appears on the proforma balance sheet and the statement of cash flows.

Source: Microsoft Excel 2010

REALITY BYTES

BUDGETING IN GOVERNMENTAL ENTITIES

©Scott J. Ferrell/Getty Images

This chapter has presented several reasons organizations should prepare budgets, but for governmental entities, budgets are not simply good planning tools—law requires them. If a manager at a commercial enterprise does not accomplish the budget objectives established for his or her part of the business, the manager may receive a poor performance evaluation. At worst, they may be fired. If managers of governmental agencies spend more than their budgets allow, they may have broken the law. In some cases, the manager could be required to personally repay the amount by which the budget was exceeded. Since governmental budgets are enacted by the relevant elected bodies, to violate the budget is to break the law.

Because budgets are so important for governments and are not to be exceeded, government accounting practices require that budgeted amounts be formally entered into the bookkeeping system. As you learned in your first accounting course, companies do not make formal accounting entries when they order goods; they only make an entry when the goods are received. Governmental accounting systems are different. Each time goods or services are ordered by a government, an "encumbrance" is recorded against the budgeted amount so that agencies do not commit to spending more money than their budgets allow.

Cash Receipts Section

The total cash available (Exhibit 7.5, row 7) is determined by adding the beginning cash balance to the cash receipts from customers. There is no beginning cash balance in October because the new store is opening that month. The November beginning cash balance is the October ending cash balance. The December beginning cash balance is the November ending cash balance. Cash receipts from customers comes from the *schedule of cash receipts* in the sales budget (Exhibit 7.2, section 2, row 13).

Cash Payments Section

Cash payments include expected cash outflows for inventory purchases, S&A expenses, interest expense, and investments. The cash payments for inventory purchases comes from the *schedule of cash payments for inventory purchases* (Exhibit 7.3, section 2, row 15). The cash payments for S&A expenses comes from the *schedule of cash payments for S&A expenses* (Exhibit 7.4, section 2, row 21).

HH borrows or repays principal and pays interest on the last day of each month. The cash payments for interest are determined by multiplying the loan balance for the month by the monthly interest rate. Since there is no outstanding debt during October, there is no interest payment at the end of October. HH expects an outstanding debt of $218,000 during the month of November. The bank charges interest at the rate of 12 percent per year, or 1 percent per month. The November interest expense and cash payment for interest is $2,180 ($218,000 × 0.01). The outstanding loan balance during December is $230,000. The December interest expense and cash payment for interest is $2,300 ($230,000 × 0.01). Determining the amount to borrow or repay at the end of each month is discussed in more detail in the next section of the text.

Finally, the cash payment for the store fixtures comes from the *capital expenditures budget* (not shown in this chapter).

Financing Section

HH has a line of credit under which it can borrow or repay principal in increments of $1,000 at the end of each month as needed. HH desires to maintain an ending cash balance of at least $10,000 each month. With the $207,460 projected cash shortage in row 15 of the cash budget ($40,000 cash balance in row 7 less $247,460 budgeted cash payments in row 13), HH must borrow $218,000 on October 31 to maintain an ending cash balance of at least $10,000. This $218,000 balance is outstanding during November. On November 30, HH must borrow an additional $12,000 to cover the November projected cash shortage of $1,572 plus the $10,000 desired ending cash balance. HH projects a surplus of $23,660 for the month of December. This surplus will allow HH to repay $13,000 of debt and still maintain the desired $10,000 cash balance.

Pro Forma Financial Statement Data

Figures in the Pro Forma Data column of the cash budget (Exhibit 7.5) are alphabetically referenced. The cash receipts from customers, item (a), and the cash payment items (b), (c), and (d) are reported in the operating activities section of the pro forma statement of cash flows (shown later in Exhibit 7.8). The interest expense, item (d), is also reported on the pro forma income statement (shown later in Exhibit 7.6). The figures are determined by summing the monthly amounts. The $130,000 purchase of store fixtures, item (e), is reported in the investing activities section of the pro forma statement of cash flows. The $217,000 net borrowings, item (f), is reported in the financing activities section of the pro forma statement of cash flows (shown later in Exhibit 7.8) and also as a liability on the pro forma balance sheet (shown later in Exhibit 7.7). The $10,660 ending cash balance, item (g), is reported as the ending balance on the pro forma statement of cash flows and as an asset on the pro forma balance sheet.

CHECK YOURSELF 7.2

Astor Company expects to incur the following operating expenses during September: Salary Expense, $25,000; Utility Expense, $1,200; Depreciation Expense, $5,400; and Selling Expense, $14,000. In general, it pays operating expenses in cash in the month in which it incurs them. Based on this information alone, determine the total amount of cash outflow Astor would report in the Operating Activities section of the pro forma statement of cash flows.

Answer Depreciation is not included in cash outflows because companies do not pay cash when they recognize depreciation expense. The total cash outflow is $40,200 ($25,000 + $1,200 + $14,000).

PRO FORMA FINANCIAL STATEMENTS

LO 7-6

Prepare a pro forma income statement, balance sheet, and statement of cash flows.

The information contained in the operating budgets is used to prepare pro forma financial statements. This section of the chapter shows how the pro forma income statement, balance sheet, and statement of cash flows are prepared using data from Hampton Hams' operating budgets.

Pro Forma Income Statement

Exhibit 7.6 shows the budgeted income statement for Hampton Hams' new store. The figures for this statement come from Exhibits 7.2, 7.3, 7.4, and 7.5. The budgeted income statement provides an advance estimate of the new store's expected profitability. If expected profitability is unsatisfactory, management could decide to abandon the project or modify planned activity.

EXHIBIT 7.6

HAMPTON HAMS
Pro Forma Income Statement
For the Quarter Ending December 31, Year 1

		Data Source
Sales revenue	$582,400	Exhibit 7.2
Cost of goods sold	(407,680)	Exhibit 7.3
Gross margin	174,720	
Selling and administrative expenses	(110,172)	Exhibit 7.4
Operating income	64,548	
Interest expense	(4,480)	Exhibit 7.5
Net income	$ 60,068	

Perhaps HH could lease less costly store space, pay employees a lower rate, or reduce the number of employees hired. The pricing strategy could also be examined for possible changes.

Budgets are usually prepared using spreadsheets or computerized mathematical models that allow managers to easily undertake "what-if" analysis. What if the growth rate differs from expectations? What if interest rates increase or decrease? Exhibits 7.2 through 7.5 in this chapter were prepared using Microsoft Excel. When variables such as growth rate, collection assumptions, or interest rates are changed, the spreadsheet software instantly recalculates the budgets. Although managers remain responsible for data analysis and decision making, computer technology offers powerful tools to assist in those tasks.

Pro Forma Balance Sheet

Most of the figures on the pro forma balance sheet in Exhibit 7.7 already have been explained. The new store has no contributed capital because its operations will be financed through debt and retained earnings. The amount of retained earnings equals the amount of net income because no earnings from prior periods exist and no distributions are planned.

EXHIBIT 7.7

HAMPTON HAMS
Pro Forma Balance Sheet
As of the Quarter Ending December 31, Year 1

			Data Source
Assets			
Cash		$ 10,660	Exhibit 7.5
Accounts receivable		172,800	Exhibit 7.2
Inventory		35,000	Exhibit 7.3
Store fixtures	$130,000		Exhibit 7.4 Discussion
Accumulated depreciation	(3,000)		Exhibit 7.4 Discussion
Book value of store fixtures		127,000	
Total assets		$345,460	
Liabilities			
Accounts payable		$ 62,384	Exhibit 7.3
Sales commissions payable		4,608	Exhibit 7.4
Utilities payable		1,400	Exhibit 7.4
Line of credit borrowings		217,000	Exhibit 7.5
Equity			
Retained earnings		60,068	
Total liabilities and equity		$345,460	

Pro Forma Statement of Cash Flows

Exhibit 7.8 shows the pro forma statement of cash flows for Hampton Hams. All information for this statement comes from the cash budget in Exhibit 7.5.

CHECK YOURSELF 7.3

How do pro forma financial statements differ from the financial statements presented in a company's annual report to stockholders?

Answer Pro forma financial statements are based on estimates and projections about business events that a company expects to occur in the future. The financial statements presented in a company's annual report to stockholders are based on historical events that occurred prior to the preparation of the statements.

Answers to The Curious Accountant

Budget preparation at the USOC is complicated by the fact that the timing of its revenues does not match the timing of its expenditures. The USOC spends a lot of money helping train athletes for the United States Olympic team. Training takes place year-round, every year, for many athletes. The USOC's training facilities in Colorado must also be maintained continuously.

Conversely, much of the USOC's revenues are earned in big batches, received every two years. This money comes from fees the USOC receives for the rights to broadcast the Olympic games on television in the United States. Most companies have a one-year budget cycle during which they attempt to anticipate the coming year's revenues and expenses. This model would not work well for the USOC. For example, in 2016, a year of summer Olympics, the USOC reported revenues of $351.4 million and a surplus of $78.7 million. The prior year, 2015, a year with no Olympic games, the USOC reported revenues of $147.9 million and a deficit of $72.0 million. In 2014, a year of winter Olympics, the USOC reported revenues of $270.3 million and a surplus of $47.9 million, while in 2013, the USOC reported revenues of $168.2 million and a deficit of $27.5 million.

Every business, like every family, faces its own set of circumstances. Those individuals responsible for preparing an entity's budget must have a thorough understanding of the environment in which the entity operates. This is the reason the budget process must be participatory if it is to be successful. No one person, or small group, can anticipate all the issues that a large organization will face in the coming budget period; input from employees at all levels is necessary.

Source: Audited Consolidated Financial Statements of the USOC.

EXHIBIT 7.8

HAMPTON HAMS
Pro Forma Statement of Cash Flows
For the Quarter Ending December 31, Year 1

Cash flow from operating activities		
Cash receipts from customers	$ 409,600	
Cash payments for inventory	(380,296)	
Cash payments for S&A expenses	(101,164)	
Cash payments for interest expense	(4,480)	
Net cash flow for operating activities		$ (76,340)
Cash flow from investing activities		
Cash outflow to purchase fixtures		(130,000)
Cash flow from financing activities		
Inflow from borrowing on line of credit		217,000
Net change in cash		10,660
Plus beginning cash balance		0
Ending cash balance		$ 10,660

A Look Back <<

The planning of financial matters is called *budgeting.* The degree of detail in a company's budget depends on the budget period. Generally, the shorter the time period, the more specific the plans. *Strategic planning* involves long-term plans, such as the overall objectives of the business. Examples of strategic planning include which products to manufacture and sell and which market niches to pursue. Strategic plans are stated in broad, descriptive terms. Capital budgeting deals with intermediate investment planning. *Operations budgeting* focuses on short-term plans and is used to create the master budget.

A budgeting committee is responsible for consolidating numerous departmental budgets into a master budget for the whole company. The *master budget* has detailed objectives stated in specific amounts; it describes how management intends to achieve its objectives. The master budget usually covers one year. Budgeting supports planning, coordination, performance measurement, and corrective action.

Employees may be uncomfortable with budgets, which can be constraining. Budgets set standards by which performance is evaluated. To establish an effective budget system, management should recognize the effect on human behavior of budgeting. Upper-level management must set a positive atmosphere by taking budgets seriously and avoiding using them to humiliate subordinates. One way to create the proper atmosphere is to encourage subordinates' participation in the budgeting process; *participative budgeting* can lead to goals that are more realistic in terms of what can be accomplished and can help to establish a team effort in trying to reach those goals.

The primary components of the master budget are the *operating budgets,* the *capital budgets,* and the *pro forma financial statements.* The budgeting process begins with preparing the operating budgets, which consist of detailed schedules and budgets prepared by various company departments. The first operating budget to be prepared is the sales budget. The detailed operating budgets for inventory purchases and S&A expenses are based on the projected sales from the sales budget. The information in the schedules of cash receipts (prepared in conjunction with the sales budget) and cash payments (prepared in conjunction with the inventory purchases and S&A expense budgets) is used in preparing the cash budget. The cash budget subtracts cash payments from cash receipts; the resulting cash surplus or shortage determines the company's financing activities.

The capital budget describes the company's long-term plans regarding investments in facilities, equipment, new products, or other lines of business. The information from the capital budget is used as input to several of the operating budgets.

The pro forma financial statements are prepared from information in the operating budgets. The operating budgets for sales, inventory purchases, and S&A expenses contain information that is used to prepare the income statement and balance sheet. The cash budget includes the amount of interest expense reported on the income statement, the ending cash balance, the capital acquisitions reported on the balance sheet, and most of the information included in the statement of cash flows.

>> A Look Forward

Once a company has completed its budget, it has defined its plans. Then the plans must be followed. The next chapter investigates the techniques used to evaluate performance. You will learn to compare actual results to budgets, calculate variances, and identify the parties who are normally accountable for deviations from expectations. Finally, you will learn about the human impact management must consider in taking corrective action when employees fail to accomplish budget goals.

Video lectures and accompanying self-assessment quizzes are available in *Connect* for all learning objectives.

SELF-STUDY REVIEW PROBLEM

The Getaway Gift Company operates a chain of small gift shops that are located in prime vacation towns. Getaway is considering opening a new store on January 1, Year 1. Getaway's president recently attended a business seminar that explained how formal budgets could be useful in judging the new store's likelihood of succeeding. Assume you are the company's accountant. The president has asked you to explain the budgeting process and to provide sample reports that show the new store's operating expectations for the first three months (January, February, and March). Respond to the following specific requirements.

Required

a. List the operating budgets and schedules included in a master budget.

b. Explain the difference between pro forma financial statements and the financial statements presented in a company's annual reports to shareholders.

c. Prepare a sample sales budget and a schedule of expected cash receipts using the following assumptions. Getaway estimates January sales will be $400,000, of which $100,000 will be cash and $300,000 will be credit. The ratio of cash sales to sales on account is expected to remain constant over the three-month period. The company expects sales to increase 10 percent per month. The company expects to collect 100 percent of the accounts receivable generated by credit sales in the month following the sale. Use this information to determine the amount of accounts receivable that Getaway would report on the March 31 pro forma balance sheet and the amount of sales it would report on the first quarter pro forma income statement.

d. Prepare a sample inventory purchases budget using the following assumptions. Cost of goods sold is 60 percent of sales. The company desires to maintain a minimum ending inventory equal to 25 percent of the following month's cost of goods sold. Getaway makes all inventory purchases on account. The company pays 70 percent of accounts payable in the month of purchase. It pays the remaining 30 percent in the following month. Prepare a schedule of expected cash payments for inventory purchases. Use this information to determine the amount of cost of goods sold Getaway would report on the first quarter pro forma income statement and the amounts of ending inventory and accounts payable it would report on the March 31 pro forma balance sheet.

Solution to Requirement *a*

A master budget would include (1) a sales budget and schedule of cash receipts; (2) an inventory purchases budget and schedule of cash payments for inventory; (3) a general, selling, and administrative expenses budget and a schedule of cash payments related to these expenses; and (4) a cash budget.

Solution to Requirement *b*

Pro forma statements result from the operating budgets listed in the response to Requirement *a*. Pro forma statements describe the results of expected future events. In contrast, the financial statements presented in a company's annual report reflect the results of events that have actually occurred in the past.

Solution to Requirement c

General Information

Sales growth rate 10%				**Pro Forma Statement Data**
Sales Budget	**January**	**February**	**March**	
Sales				
Cash sales	$100,000	$110,000	$121,000	
Sales on account	300,000	330,000	363,000	$ 363,000*
Total sales	$400,000	$440,000	$484,000	$1,324,000†
Schedule of Cash Receipts				
Current cash sales	$100,000	$110,000	$121,000	
Plus 100% of previous month's credit sales	0	300,000	330,000	
Total budgeted collections	$100,000	$410,000	$451,000	

*Ending accounts receivable balance reported on March 31 pro forma balance sheet.
†Sales revenue reported on first quarter pro forma income statement (sum of monthly sales).

Solution to Requirement *d*

General Information

Cost of goods sold percentage 60% Desired ending inventory percentage of CGS 25%				Pro Forma Statement Data
Inventory Purchases Budget	**January**	**February**	**March**	
Budgeted cost of goods sold	$240,000	$264,000	$290,400	$794,400*
Plus: Desired ending inventory	66,000	72,600	79,860	79,860†
Inventory needed	306,000	336,600	370,260	
Less: Beginning inventory	0	(66,000)	(72,600)	
Required purchases	$306,000	$270,600	$297,660	89,298‡
Schedule of Cash Payments for Inventory Purchases				
70% of current purchases	$214,200	$189,420	$208,362	
30% of prior month's purchases	0	91,800	81,180	
Total budgeted payments for inventory	$214,200	$281,220	$289,542	

*Cost of goods sold reported on first quarter pro forma income statement (sum of monthly amounts).
†Ending inventory balance ($484,000 × 1.10 × 0.60 × 0.25) reported on March 31 pro forma balance sheet.
‡Ending accounts payable balance reported on pro forma balance sheet ($297,660 × 0.3).

KEY TERMS

Budgeting 306
Capital budgeting 308
Cash budget 317
Master budget 310
Operating budgets 310
Operations budgeting 308
Participative budgeting 309
Perpetual (continuous) budgeting 308
Pro forma financial statements 310
Strategic planning 308

QUESTIONS

1. Budgets are useful only for small companies that can estimate sales with accuracy. Do you agree with this statement?
2. Why does preparing the master budget require a committee?
3. What are the three levels of planning? Explain each briefly.
4. What is the primary factor that distinguishes the three different levels of planning from each other?
5. What is the advantage of using a perpetual budget instead of the traditional annual budget?
6. What are the advantages of budgeting?
7. How may budgets be used as a measure of performance?
8. Ken Shilov, manager of the marketing department, tells you that "budgeting simply does not work." He says that he made budgets for his employees and when he reprimanded them for failing to accomplish budget goals, he got unfounded excuses. Suggest how Mr. Shilov could encourage employee cooperation.
9. What is a master budget?
10. What is the normal starting point in developing the master budget?
11. How does the level of inventory affect the production budget? Why is it important to manage the level of inventory?
12. What are the components of the cash budget? Describe each.
13. The primary reason for preparing a cash budget is to determine the amount of cash to include on the budgeted balance sheet. Do you agree or disagree with this statement? Explain.
14. What information does the pro forma income statement provide? How does its preparation depend on the operating budgets?
15. How does the pro forma statement of cash flows differ from the cash budget?

MULTIPLE-CHOICE QUESTIONS

Multiple-choice questions are provided in *Connect*.

EXERCISES—SERIES A

connect All applicable Exercises in Series A are available in *Connect*.

Exercise 7-1A *Budget responsibility*

LO 7-1

Teresa Flanagan, the accountant, is a perfectionist. No one can do the job as well as she can. Indeed, she has found budget information provided by the various departments to be worthless. She must change everything they give her. She has to admit that her estimates have not always been accurate, but she shudders to think of what would happen if she used the information supplied by the marketing and operating departments. No one seems to care about accuracy. Indeed, some of the marketing staff have even become insulting. When Ms. Flanagan confronted one of the salespeople with the fact that he was behind in meeting his budgeted sales forecast, he responded by saying, "They're your numbers. Why don't you go out and make the sales? It's a heck of a lot easier to sit there in your office and make up numbers than it is to get out and get the real work done." Ms. Flanagan reported the incident, but, of course, nothing was done about it.

Required

Write a short report suggesting how the budgeting process could be improved.

Exercise 7-2A *Preparing a sales budget*

LO 7-2

Parliament Company, which expects to start operations on January 1, Year 2, will sell digital cameras in shopping malls. Parliament has budgeted sales as indicated in the following table. The company expects a 10 percent increase in sales per month for February and March. The ratio of cash sales to sales on account will remain stable from January through March.

Sales	January	February	March
Cash sales	$ 50,000	?	?
Sales on account	120,000	?	?
Total budgeted sales	$170,000	?	?

Required

a. Complete the sales budget by filling in the missing amounts.

b. Determine the amount of sales revenue Parliament will report on its first quarter pro forma income statement.

Exercise 7-3A *Preparing a schedule of cash receipts*

LO 7-2

The budget director of Heather's Florist has prepared the following sales budget. The company had $50,000 in accounts receivable on July 1. Heather's Florist normally collects 100 percent of accounts receivable in the month following the month of sale.

	July	August	September
Sales Budget			
Cash sales	$40,000	$42,500	$ 45,000
Sales on account	45,000	54,000	64,800
Total budgeted sales	$85,000	$96,500	$109,800
Schedule of Cash Receipts			
Current cash sales	?	?	?
Plus: Collections from accounts receivable	?	?	?
Total budgeted collections	$90,000	$87,500	$ 99,000

Required

a. Complete the schedule of cash receipts by filling in the missing amounts.

b. Determine the amount of accounts receivable the company will report on its third quarter pro forma balance sheet.

LO 7-2

Exercise 7-4A *Preparing sales budgets with different assumptions*

Axon Corporation, which has three divisions, is preparing its sales budget. Each division expects a different growth rate because economic conditions vary in different regions of the country. The growth expectations per quarter are 4 percent for Cummings Division, 2 percent for Springfield Division, and 5 percent for Douglas Division.

Division	First Quarter	Second Quarter	Third Quarter	Fourth Quarter
Cummings Division	$ 75,000	?	?	?
Springfield Division	125,000	?	?	?
Douglas Division	100,000	?	?	?

Required

a. Complete the sales budget by filling in the missing amounts. (Round figures to the nearest dollar.)

b. Determine the amount of sales revenue that the company will report on its quarterly pro forma income statements.

LO 7-2

Exercise 7-5A *Determining cash receipts from accounts receivable*

Carmen's Dress Delivery operates a mail-order business that sells clothes designed for frequent travelers. It had sales of $400,000 in December. Because Carmen's Dress Delivery is in the mail-order business, all sales are made on account. The company expects a 30 percent drop in sales for January. The balance in the Accounts Receivable account on December 31 was $60,000 and is budgeted to be $41,000 as of January 31.

Required

a. Determine the amount of cash Carmen's Dress Delivery expects to collect from accounts receivable during January.

b. Is it reasonable to assume that sales will decline in January for this type of business? Why or why not?

LO 7-2

Exercise 7-6A *Using judgment in making a sales forecast*

Ozark Company operates a candy store located in a large shopping mall.

Required

Write a brief memo describing the sales pattern that you would expect Ozark to experience during the year. In which months will sales likely be high? In which months will sales likely be low? Explain why.

LO 7-3

Exercise 7-7A *Preparing an inventory purchases budget*

Lumpkin Company sells lamps and other lighting fixtures. The purchasing department manager prepared the following inventory purchases budget. Lumpkin's policy is to maintain an ending inventory balance equal to 10 percent of the following month's cost of goods sold. April's budgeted cost of goods sold is $40,000.

	January	February	March
Budgeted cost of goods sold	$30,000	$32,000	$35,000
Plus: Desired ending inventory	3,200	?	?
Inventory needed	33,200	?	?
Less: Beginning inventory	6,000	?	?
Required purchases (on account)	$27,200	?	?

Required

a. Complete the inventory purchases budget by filling in the missing amounts.

b. Determine the amount of cost of goods sold the company will report on its first quarter pro forma income statement.

c. Determine the amount of ending inventory the company will report on its pro forma balance sheet at the end of the first quarter.

Exercise 7-8A *Preparing a schedule of cash payments for inventory purchases* LO 7-3

Dickey Books buys books and magazines directly from publishers and distributes them to grocery stores. The wholesaler expects to purchase the following inventory.

	April	May	June
Required purchases (on account)	$70,000	$80,000	$95,000

Dickey Books' accountant prepared the following schedule of cash payments for inventory purchases. Dickey Books' suppliers require that 90 percent of purchases on account be paid in the month of purchase; the remaining 10 percent are paid in the month following the month of purchase.

Schedule of Cash Payments for Inventory Purchases

	April	May	June
Payment for current accounts payable	$63,000	?	?
Payment for previous accounts payable	4,000	?	?
Total budgeted payments for inventory	$67,000	?	?

Required

a. Complete the schedule of cash payments for inventory purchases by filling in the missing amounts.

b. Determine the amount of accounts payable the company will report on its pro forma balance sheet at the end of the second quarter.

Exercise 7-9A *Determining the amount of expected inventory purchases and cash payments* LO 7-3

Nunn Company, which sells electric razors, had $200,000 of cost of goods sold during the month of June. The company projects a 5 percent increase in cost of goods sold during July. The inventory balance as of June 30 is $15,000, and the desired ending inventory balance for July is $16,000. Nunn pays cash to settle 70 percent of its purchases on account during the month of purchase and pays the remaining 30 percent in the month following the purchase. The accounts payable balance as of June 30 was $18,000.

Required

a. Determine the amount of purchases budgeted for July.

b. Determine the amount of cash payments budgeted for inventory purchases in July.

Exercise 7-10A *Preparing inventory purchases budgets with different assumptions* LO 7-3

Executive officers of Stoneham Company are wrestling with their budget for the next year. The following are two different sales estimates provided by two difference sources.

Source of Estimate	First Quarter	Second Quarter	Third Quarter	Fourth Quarter
Sales manager	$225,000	$180,000	$160,000	$270,000
Marketing consultant	300,000	240,000	210,000	350,000

Stoneham's past experience indicates that cost of goods sold is about 60 percent of sales revenue. The company tries to maintain 10 percent of the next quarter's expected cost of goods sold as the current quarter's ending inventory. This year's ending inventory is $15,000. Next year's ending inventory is budgeted to be $18,000.

Required

a. Prepare an inventory purchases budget using the sales manager's estimate.

b. Prepare an inventory purchases budget using the marketing consultant's estimate.

LO 7-4

Exercise 7-11A *Preparing a schedule of cash payments for selling and administrative expenses*

The budget director for Kanosh Cleaning Services prepared the following list of expected selling and administrative expenses. All expenses requiring cash payments are paid for in the month incurred except salary expense and insurance. Salary is paid in the month following the month in which it is incurred. The insurance premium for six months is paid on October 1. October is the first month of operations; accordingly, there are no beginning account balances.

	October	November	December
Budgeted S&A Expenses			
Equipment lease expense	$ 7,500	$ 7,500	$ 7,500
Salary expense	8,200	8,700	9,000
Cleaning supplies	2,800	2,730	3,066
Insurance expense	1,200	1,200	1,200
Depreciation on computer	1,800	1,800	1,800
Rent	1,700	1,700	1,700
Miscellaneous expenses	700	700	700
Total operating expenses	$23,900	$24,330	$24,966
Schedule of Cash Payments for S&A Expenses			
Equipment lease expense	?	?	?
Prior month's salary expense, 100%	?	?	?
Cleaning supplies	?	?	?
Insurance premium	?	?	?
Depreciation on computer	?	?	?
Rent	?	?	?
Miscellaneous expenses	?	?	?
Total disbursements for operating expenses	$19,900	$20,830	$21,666

Required

a. Complete the schedule of cash payments for S&A expenses by filling in the missing amounts.

b. Determine the amount of salaries payable the company will report on its pro forma balance sheet at the end of the fourth quarter.

c. Determine the amount of prepaid insurance the company will report on its pro forma balance sheet at the end of the fourth quarter.

LO 7-4

Exercise 7-12A *Determining the amount of cash payments and pro forma statement data for selling and administrative expenses*

January budgeted selling and administrative expenses for the retail shoe store that Craig Shea plans to open on January 1, Year 1, are as follows: sales commissions, $50,000; rent, $30,000; utilities, $10,000; depreciation, $5,000; and miscellaneous, $2,500. Utilities are paid in the month after they are incurred. Other expenses are expected to be paid in cash in the month in which they are incurred.

Required

a. Determine the amount of budgeted cash payments for January selling and administrative expenses.

b. Determine the amount of utilities payable the store will report on the January 31 pro forma balance sheet.

c. Determine the amount of depreciation expense the store will report on the income statement for Year 1, assuming that monthly depreciation remains the same for the entire year.

Exercise 7-13A *Preparing a cash budget*

LO 7-5

The accountant for Jean's Dress Shop prepared the following cash budget. Jean's desires to maintain a cash cushion of $10,000 at the end of each month. Funds are assumed to be borrowed and repaid on the last day of each month. Interest is charged at the rate of 1 percent per month.

Cash Budget	July	August	September
Section 1: Cash receipts			
Beginning cash balance	$ 25,000	$?	$?
Add cash receipts	90,000	100,000	120,300
Total cash available (a)	115,000	?	?
Section 2: Cash payments			
For inventory purchases	82,750	70,115	87,076
For S&A expenses	27,250	30,280	30,716
For interest expense	0	?	?
Total budgeted disbursements (b)	110,000	?	?
Section 3: Financing activities			
Surplus (shortage)	5,000	?	?
Borrowing (repayments) (c)	5,000	?	?
Ending cash balance (a − b + c)	$ 10,000	$ 10,000	$ 10,000

Required

a. Complete the cash budget by filling in the missing amounts. Round all computations to the nearest whole dollar.

b. Determine the amount of net cash flows from operating activities Jean's will report on the third quarter pro forma statement of cash flows.

c. Determine the amount of net cash flows from financing activities Jean's will report on the third quarter pro forma statement of cash flows.

Exercise 7-14A *Determining amount to borrow and pro forma statement balances*

LO 7-5

Lois Bragg owns a small restaurant in Boston. Ms. Bragg provided her accountant with the following summary information regarding expectations for the month of June. The balance in accounts receivable as of May 31 is $40,000. Budgeted cash and credit sales for June are $100,000 and $250,000, respectively. Credit sales are made through Visa and MasterCard and are collected rapidly. Eighty percent of credit sales is collected in the month of sale, and the remainder is collected in the following month. Ms. Bragg's suppliers do not extend credit. Consequently, she pays suppliers on the last day of the month. Cash payments for June are expected to be $330,000. Ms. Bragg has a line of credit that enables the restaurant to borrow funds on demand; however, they must be borrowed on the last day of the month. Interest is paid in cash also on the last day of the month. Ms. Bragg desires to maintain a $15,000 cash balance before the interest payment. Her annual interest rate is 9 percent.

Required

a. Compute the amount of funds Ms. Bragg needs to borrow for June.

b. Determine the amount of interest expense the restaurant will report on the June pro forma income statement.

c. What amount will the restaurant report as interest expense on the July pro forma income statement?

LO 7-6

Exercise 7-15A *Preparing pro forma income statements with different assumptions*

Jacob Long, the controller of Arvada Corporation, is trying to prepare a sales budget for the coming year. The income statements for the last four quarters follow.

	First Quarter	Second Quarter	Third Quarter	Fourth Quarter	Total
Sales revenue	$90,000	$100,000	$105,000	$130,000	$425,000
Cost of goods sold	54,000	60,000	63,000	78,000	255,000
Gross profit	36,000	40,000	42,000	52,000	170,000
Selling & admin. expenses	8,500	10,000	10,500	13,000	42,000
Net income	$27,500	$ 30,000	$ 31,500	$ 39,000	$128,000

Historically, cost of goods sold is about 60 percent of sales revenue. Selling and administrative expenses are about 10 percent of sales revenue.

Fred Arvada, the chief executive officer, told Mr. Long that he expected sales next year to be 8 percent for each respective quarter above last year's level. However, Rita Banks, the vice president of sales, told Mr. Long that she believed sales growth would be only 5 percent.

Required

a. Prepare a pro forma income statement including quarterly budgets for the coming year using Mr. Arvada's estimate.

b. Prepare a pro forma income statement including quarterly budgets for the coming year using Ms. Banks' estimate.

c. Explain why two executive officers in the same company could have different estimates of future growth.

PROBLEMS—SERIES A

connect **All applicable Problems in Series A are available in *Connect*.**

LO 7-1

CHECK FIGURES

a. NI: $157,500

c. NI: $172,500

Problem 7-16A *Behavioral impact of budgeting*

Amherst Corporation has three divisions, each operating as a responsibility center. To provide an incentive for divisional executive officers, the company gives divisional management a bonus equal to 15 percent of the excess of actual net income over budgeted net income. The following is Atlantic Division's current year's performance.

	Current Year
Sales revenue	$1,000,000
Cost of goods sold	625,000
Gross profit	375,000
Selling & admin. expenses	225,000
Net income	$ 150,000

The president has just received next year's budget proposal from the vice president in charge of Atlantic Division. The proposal budgets a 5 percent increase in sales revenue with an extensive explanation about stiff market competition. The president is puzzled. Atlantic has enjoyed revenue growth of around 10 percent for each of the past five years. The president had consistently approved the division's budget proposals based on 5 percent growth in the past. This time, the president wants to show that he is not a fool. "I will impose a 15 percent revenue increase to teach them a lesson!" the president says to himself smugly.

Assume that cost of goods sold and selling and administrative expenses remain stable in proportion to sales.

Required

a. Prepare the budgeted income statement based on Atlantic Division's proposal of a 5 percent increase.

b. If growth is actually 10 percent as usual, how much bonus would Atlantic Division's executive officers receive if the president had approved the division's proposal?

c. Prepare the budgeted income statement based on the 15 percent increase the president imposed.

d. If the actual results turn out to be a 10 percent increase as usual, how much bonus would Atlantic Division's executive officers receive since the president imposed a 15 percent increase?

e. Propose a better budgeting procedure for Amherst Corporation.

Problem 7-17A *Preparing a sales budget and schedule of cash receipts*

LO 7-2

eXcel

Spalding Pointers Corporation expects to begin operations on January 1, Year 1; it will operate as a specialty sales company that sells laser pointers over the Internet. Spalding expects sales in January Year 1 to total $120,000 and to increase 5 percent per month in February and March. All sales are on account. Spalding expects to collect 70 percent of accounts receivable in the month of sale, 20 percent in the month following the sale, and 10 percent in the second month following the sale.

CHECK FIGURE
c. Feb.: $112,200
March: $129,810

Required

a. Prepare a sales budget for the first quarter of Year 1.

b. Determine the amount of sales revenue Spalding will report on the Year 1 first quarterly pro forma income statement.

c. Prepare a cash receipts schedule for the first quarter of Year 1.

d. Determine the amount of accounts receivable as of March 31, Year 1.

Problem 7-18A *Preparing an inventory purchases budget and schedule of cash payments*

LO 7-3

Humboldt Inc. sells fireworks. The company's marketing director developed the following cost of goods sold budget for April, May, June, and July.

CHECK FIGURES
a. May: $33,600
c. June: $32,340

	April	May	June	July
Budgeted cost of goods sold	$37,500	$34,000	$30,000	$45,000

Humboldt had a beginning inventory balance of $1,800 on April 1 and a beginning balance in accounts payable of $7,400. The company desires to maintain an ending inventory balance equal to 10 percent of the next period's cost of goods sold. Humboldt makes all purchases on account. The company pays 60 percent of accounts payable in the month of purchase and the remaining 40 percent in the month following purchase.

Required

a. Prepare an inventory purchases budget for April, May, and June.

b. Determine the amount of ending inventory Humboldt will report on the end-of-quarter pro forma balance sheet.

c. Prepare a schedule of cash payments for inventory for April, May, and June.

d. Determine the balance in accounts payable Humboldt will report on the end-of-quarter pro forma balance sheet.

Problem 7-19A *Preparing a schedule of cash payments for selling and administrative expenses*

LO 7-4

Malcolm is a retail company specializing in men's hats. Its budget director prepared the list of expected operating expenses that follows. All items are paid when incurred except sales commissions and utilities, which are paid in the month following their incurrence. July is the first month of operations, so there are no beginning account balances.

CHECK FIGURE
a. Sept.: $17,405

	July	August	September
Salary expense	$12,000	$12,000	$12,000
Sales commissions (4 percent of sales)	1,000	1,000	1,000
Supplies expense	180	195	210
Utilities	550	550	550
Depreciation on store equipment	1,500	1,500	1,500
Rent	3,300	3,300	3,300
Miscellaneous	345	345	345
Total S&A expenses before interest	$18,875	$18,890	$18,905

Required

a. Prepare a schedule of cash payments for selling and administrative expenses.
b. Determine the amount of utilities payable as of September 30.
c. Determine the amount of sales commissions payable as of September 30.

LO 7-5

CHECK FIGURE
Feb. cash surplus before financing activities: $14,020

Problem 7-20A *Preparing a cash budget*

Fayette Medical Clinic has budgeted the following cash flows.

	January	February	March
Cash receipts	$240,000	$232,000	$272,000
Cash payments			
For inventory purchases	220,000	164,000	190,000
For S&A expenses	62,000	64,000	54,000

Fayette Medical had a cash balance of $16,000 on January 1. The company desires to maintain a cash cushion of $10,000. Funds are assumed to be borrowed, in increments of $2,000, and repaid on the last day of each month; the interest rate is 1 percent per month. Repayments may be made in any amount available. Fayette pays its vendors on the last day of the month also. The company had a monthly $80,000 beginning balance in its line of credit liability account from this year's quarterly results.

Required

Prepare a cash budget. (Round all computations to the nearest whole dollar.)

LO 7-6

CHECK FIGURE
a. 13.59%

Problem 7-21A *Preparing pro forma income statements with different assumptions*

Top executive officers of Tildon Company, a merchandising firm, are preparing the next year's budget. The controller has provided everyone with the current year's projected income statement.

	Current Year
Sales revenue	$1,600,000
Cost of goods sold	1,120,000
Gross profit	480,000
Selling & admin. expenses	190,000
Net income	$ 290,000

Cost of goods sold is usually 70 percent of sales revenue, and selling and administrative expenses are usually 10 percent of sales plus a fixed cost of $30,000. The president has announced that the company's goal is to increase net income by 15 percent.

Required

The following items are independent of each other:

a. What percentage increase in sales would enable the company to reach its goal? Support your answer with a pro forma income statement.

b. The market may become stagnant next year, and the company does not expect an increase in sales revenue. The production manager believes that an improved production procedure can cut cost of goods sold by 2 percent. What else can the company do to reach its goal? Prepare a pro forma income statement illustrating your proposal.

c. The company decides to escalate its advertising campaign to boost consumer recognition, which will increase selling and administrative expenses to $230,000. With the increased advertising, the company expects sales revenue to increase by 15 percent. Assume that cost of goods sold remains a constant proportion of sales. Can the company reach its goal?

Problem 7-22A *Preparing budgets with multiple products*

LO 7-2, 7-3, 7-4, 7-6

excel

Jasper Fruits Corporation wholesales peaches and oranges. Barbara Jasper is working with the company's accountant to prepare next year's budget. Ms. Jasper estimates that sales will increase 5 percent for peaches and 10 percent for oranges. The current year's sales revenue data follow.

CHECK FIGURE

c. 1st QTR purchases for peaches: $51,660
2nd QTR purchases for oranges: $152,460

	First Quarter	Second Quarter	Third Quarter	Fourth Quarter	Total
Peaches	$ 80,000	$100,000	$160,000	$140,000	$ 480,000
Oranges	200,000	225,000	285,000	190,000	900,000
Total	$280,000	$325,000	$445,000	$330,000	$1,380,000

Based on the company's past experience, cost of goods sold is usually 60 percent of sales revenue. Company policy is to keep 10 percent of the next period's estimated cost of goods sold as the current period's ending inventory. (*Hint:* Use the cost of goods sold for the first quarter to determine the beginning inventory for the first quarter.)

Required

a. Prepare the company's sales budget for the next year for each quarter by individual product.

b. If the selling and administrative expenses are estimated to be $350,000, prepare the company's budgeted annual income statement.

c. Ms. Jasper estimates next year's ending inventory will be $10,000 for peaches and $20,000 for oranges. Prepare the company's inventory purchases budgets for the next year, showing quarterly figures by product.

Problem 7-23A *Preparing a master budget for retail company with no beginning account balances*

LO 7-2, 7-3, 7-4, 7-5, 7-6

excel

Camden Company is a retail company that specializes in selling outdoor camping equipment. The company is considering opening a new store on October 1, Year 1. The company president formed a planning committee to prepare a master budget for the first three months of operation. As budget coordinator, you have been assigned the following tasks.

CHECK FIGURES

c. Dec. purchases: $84,732
g. Nov. surplus before financing activities: $30,486

Required

Round all computations to the nearest whole dollar.

a. October sales are estimated to be $125,000, of which 40 percent will be cash and 60 percent will be credit. The company expects sales to increase at the rate of 8 percent per month. Prepare a sales budget.

b. The company expects to collect 100 percent of the accounts receivable generated by credit sales in the month following the sale. Prepare a schedule of cash receipts.

c. The cost of goods sold is 60 percent of sales. The company desires to maintain a minimum ending inventory equal to 10 percent of the next month's cost of goods sold. However, ending inventory of December is expected to be $6,000. Assume that all purchases are made on account. Prepare an inventory purchases budget.

d. The company pays 70 percent of accounts payable in the month of purchase and the remaining 30 percent in the following month. Prepare a cash payments budget for inventory purchases.

e. Budgeted selling and administrative expenses per month follow.

Salary expense (fixed)	$9,000
Sales commissions	5% of Sales
Supplies expense	2% of Sales
Utilities (fixed)	$ 700
Depreciation on store fixtures (fixed)*	$2,000
Rent (fixed)	$2,400
Miscellaneous (fixed)	$ 600

*The capital expenditures budget indicates that Camden will spend $82,000 on October 1 for store fixtures, which are expected to have a $10,000 salvage value and a three-year (36-month) useful life.

Use this information to prepare a selling and administrative expenses budget.

f. Utilities and sales commissions are paid the month after they are incurred; all other expenses are paid in the month in which they are incurred. Prepare a cash payments budget for selling and administrative expenses.

g. Camden borrows funds, in increments of $1,000, and repays them on the last day of the month. Repayments may be made in any amount available. The company also pays its vendors on the last day of the month. It pays interest of 1 percent per month in cash on the last day of the month. To be prudent, the company desires to maintain a $6,000 cash cushion. Prepare a cash budget.

h. Prepare a pro forma income statement for the quarter.

i. Prepare a pro forma balance sheet at the end of the quarter.

j. Prepare a pro forma statement of cash flows for the quarter.

EXERCISES—SERIES B

LO 7-1

Exercise 7-1B *Budget responsibility*

Eric Lane, the controller of Harrison Industries, is very popular. He is easygoing and does not offend anybody. To develop the company's most recent budget, Mr. Lane first asked all department managers to prepare their own budgets. He then added together the totals from the department budgets to produce the company budget. When Irene Harrison, Harrison's president, reviewed the company budget, she sighed and asked, "Is our company a charitable organization?"

Required

Write a brief memo describing deficiencies in the budgeting process and suggesting improvements.

LO 7-2

Exercise 7-2B *Preparing a sales budget*

Horatio Restaurant is opening for business in a new shopping center. Carl Mendoza, the owner, is preparing a sales budget for the next three months. After consulting friends in the same business, Mr. Mendoza estimated July revenues as shown in the following table. He expects revenues to increase 4 percent per month in August and September.

	July	August	September
Food sales	$25,000	?	?
Beverage and liquor sales	15,000	?	?
Total budgeted revenues	$40,000	?	?

Required

a. Complete the sales budget by filling in the missing amounts.

b. Determine the total amount of revenue Horatio Restaurant will report on its quarterly pro forma income statement.

LO 7-2

Exercise 7-3B *Preparing a schedule of cash receipts*

Mansfield Imports Inc. sells goods imported from Europe. Using the second quarter's sales budget, Stan Farrell is trying to complete the schedule of cash receipts for the quarter. The company had accounts receivable of $155,000 on April 1. Mansfield Imports normally collects 100 percent of accounts receivable in the month following the month of sale.

Sales	April	May	June
Sales Budget			
Cash sales	$100,000	$ 80,000	$ 90,000
Sales on account	240,000	284,000	250,000
Total budgeted sales	$340,000	$364,000	$340,000
Schedule of Cash Receipts			
Current cash sales	?	?	?
Plus: Collections from accounts receivable	?	?	?
Total budgeted collections	$255,000	$320,000	$374,000

Required

a. Help Mr. Farrell complete the schedule of cash receipts by filling in the missing amounts.

b. Determine the amount of accounts receivable the company will report on the quarterly pro forma balance sheet.

Exercise 7-4B *Preparing sales budgets with different assumptions* LO 7-2

Plano International Company has three subsidiaries, Seymour Trading Company, Archer Medical Supplies Company, and Milsap Shipping Company. Because the subsidiaries operate in different industries, Plano's corporate budget for the coming year must reflect the different growth potentials of the individual industries. The growth expectations per quarter for the subsidiaries are 4 percent for Seymour, 1 percent for Archer, and 3 percent for Milsap.

Subsidiary	Current Quarter Sales	First Quarter	Second Quarter	Third Quarter	Fourth Quarter
Seymour	$100,000	?	?	?	?
Archer	120,000	?	?	?	?
Milsap	160,000	?	?	?	?

Required

a. Complete the sales budget by filling in the missing amounts. (Round the figures to the nearest dollar.)

b. Determine the amount of sales revenue Plano will report on the quarterly pro forma income statements.

Exercise 7-5B *Determining cash receipts from accounts receivable* LO 7-2

Lingo Corporation is about to start a business as an agricultural products distributor. Because its customers will all be retailers, Lingo will sell its products solely on account. The company expects to collect 50 percent of accounts receivable in the month of sale and the remaining 50 percent in the following month. Lingo expects sales revenues of $300,000 in July, the first month of operation, and $240,000 in August.

Required

a. Determine the amount of cash Lingo expects to collect in July.

b. Determine the amount of cash Lingo expects to collect in August.

Exercise 7-6B *Using judgment in making a sales forecast* LO 7-2

Temple Greetings Corporation sells greeting cards for various occasions.

Required

Write a brief memo describing the sales pattern that you would expect Temple Greetings to experience during the year. In which months will sales likely be high? Explain why.

LO 7-3

Exercise 7-7B *Preparing an inventory purchases budget*

Elgin Drugstores Inc. sells prescription drugs, over-the-counter drugs, and some groceries. The purchasing manager prepared the following inventory purchases budget. For this year, Elgin expects an ending inventory balance equal to 10 percent of the following month's cost of goods sold. April's budgeted cost of goods sold amounts to $37,500.

Inventory Purchases Budget	January	February	March
Budgeted cost of goods sold	$50,000	$35,000	$40,000
Plus: Desired ending inventory	3,500	?	?
Inventory needed	53,500	?	?
Less: Beginning inventory	5,000	?	?
Required purchases (on account)	$48,500	?	?

Required

a. Complete the inventory purchases budget by filling in the missing amounts.

b. Determine the amount of cost of goods sold the company will report on the first quarter pro forma income statement.

c. Determine the amount of ending inventory the company will report on the first quarter pro forma balance sheet.

LO 7-3

Exercise 7-8B *Preparing a schedule of cash payments for inventory purchases*

Glendo Grocery buys and sells groceries in a community far from any major city. Travis Glendo, the owner, budgeted the store's purchases as follows.

	October	November	December
Required purchases (on account)	$30,000	$22,500	$40,000

Glendo's suppliers require that 70 percent of accounts payable be paid in the month of purchase. The remaining 30 percent is paid in the month following the month of purchase.

Schedule of Cash Payments for Inventory Purchases

	October	November	December
Payment for current accounts payable	$21,000	?	?
Payment for previous accounts payable	7,500	?	?
Total budgeted payments for inventory	$28,500	?	?

Required

a. Complete the schedule of cash payments for inventory purchases by filling in the missing amounts.

b. Determine the amount of accounts payable Glendo will report on the store's quarterly pro forma balance sheet.

LO 7-3

Exercise 7-9B *Determining the amount of inventory purchases and cash payments*

Clement Oil Corporation, which distributes gasoline products to independent gasoline stations, had $240,000 of cost of goods sold in January. The company expects a 2.5 percent increase in cost of goods sold during February. The ending inventory balance for January is $20,000, and the desired ending inventory for February is $25,000. Clement pays cash to settle 60 percent of its purchases on account during the month of purchase and pays the remaining 40 percent in the month following the purchase. The accounts payable balance as of January 31 was $19,000.

Required

a. Determine the amount of purchases budgeted for February.

b. Determine the amount of cash payments budgeted for inventory purchases in February.

Exercise 7-10B *Preparing inventory purchases budgets with different assumptions* LO 7-3

Beverly Keegan has been at odds with her brother and business partner, Leon, since childhood. The sibling rivalry is not all bad, however; their garden shop, Keegan Gardens and Gifts, has been very successful. When the partners met to prepare the coming year's budget, their forecasts were different, naturally. Their sales revenue estimates follow.

Source of Estimate	First Quarter	Second Quarter	Third Quarter	Fourth Quarter
Beverly	$240,000	$300,000	$225,000	$360,000
Leon	200,000	225,000	250,000	425,000

Past experience indicates that cost of goods sold is about 60 percent of sales revenue. The company tries to maintain 15 percent of the next quarter's expected cost of goods sold as the current quarter's ending inventory. The ending inventory this year is $20,000. Next year's ending inventory is budgeted to be $25,000.

Required

a. Prepare an inventory purchases budget using Beverly's estimate.

b. Prepare an inventory purchases budget using Leon's estimate.

Exercise 7-11B *Preparing a schedule of cash payments for selling and administrative expenses* LO 7-4

The controller for Braddock Laundry Services prepared the following list of expected selling and administrative expenses. All expenses requiring cash payments except salary expense and insurance are paid for in the month incurred. Salary is paid in the month following its incursion. The annual insurance premium is paid in advance on January 1. January is the first month of operations. Accordingly, there are no beginning account balances.

	January	February	March
Budgeted Selling and Administrative Expenses			
Equipment depreciation	$ 6,200	$ 6,200	$ 6,200
Salary expense	8,000	8,000	7,200
Cleaning supplies	1,000	940	1,100
Insurance expense	600	600	600
Equipment maintenance expense	500	500	500
Leases expense	1,600	1,600	1,600
Miscellaneous expenses	400	400	400
Total S&A expenses	$18,300	$18,240	$17,600
Schedule of Cash Payments for Selling and Administrative Expenses			
Equipment depreciation	?	?	?
Prior month's salary expense, 100%	?	?	?
Cleaning supplies	?	?	?
Insurance premium	?	?	?
Equipment maintenance expense	?	?	?
Leases expense	?	?	?
Miscellaneous expenses	?	?	?
Total payments for S&A expenses	$10,700	$11,440	$11,600

Required

a. Complete the schedule of cash payments for selling and administrative expenses by filling in the missing amounts.

b. Determine the amount of salaries payable the company will report on its quarterly pro forma balance sheet.

c. Determine the amount of prepaid insurance the company will report on its quarterly pro forma balance sheet.

LO 7-4

Exercise 7-12B *Determining the amount of cash payments for selling and administrative expenses*

Ted Noolan, managing partner of Noolan Business Consulting, is preparing a budget for January Year 1, the first month of business operations. Ted estimates the following monthly selling and administrative expenses: office lease, $2,700; utilities, $800; office supplies, $1,500; depreciation, $6,000; referral fees, $2,500; and miscellaneous, $500. Referral fees will be paid in the month following the month they are incurred. Other expenses will be paid in the month in which they are incurred.

Required

a. Determine the amount of budgeted cash payments for January selling and administrative expenses.

b. Determine the amount of referral fees payable the firm will report on the January 31st pro forma balance sheet.

c. Determine the amount of office lease expense the company will report on its Year 1 pro forma income statement, assuming that the monthly lease expense remains the same throughout the whole year.

LO 7-5

Exercise 7-13B *Preparing a cash budget*

Oscar Fox, the accounting manager of Onaka Antique Company, is preparing his company's cash budget for the next quarter. Onaka desires to maintain a cash cushion of $2,000 at the end of each month. As cash flows fluctuate, the company either borrows or repays funds at the end of a month. It pays interest on borrowed funds at the rate of 1 percent per month.

Cash Budget	July	August	September
Section 1: Cash Receipts			
Beginning cash balance	$ 10,000	$?	$?
Add cash receipts	90,000	96,000	104,000
Total cash available (a)	100,000	?	?
Section 2: Cash Payments			
For inventory purchases	81,000	76,500	85,500
For S&A expenses	18,500	18,000	19,500
For interest expense	0	?	?
Total budgeted disbursements (b)	99,500	?	?
Section 3: Financing Activities			
Surplus (shortage)	500	?	?
Borrowing (repayments) (c)	1,500	?	?
Ending Cash Balance (a − b + c)	$ 2,000	$ 2,000	$ 2,000

Required

a. Complete the cash budget by filling in the missing amounts. Round all computations to the nearest whole dollar.

b. Determine the amount of net cash flows from operating activities Onaka will report on its quarterly pro forma statement of cash flows.

c. Determine the amount of net cash flows from financing activities Onaka will report on its quarterly pro forma statement of cash flows.

Exercise 7-14B *Determining amount to borrow and pro forma statement balances*

LO 7-5

Edgar Tilley, the president of Hellock Corporation, has been working with his controller to manage the company's cash position. The controller provided Edgar the following data.

Balance of accounts receivable, June 30	$ 30,000
Balance of line of credit, June 30	0
Budgeted cash sales for July	42,500
Budgeted credit sales for July	180,000
Budgeted cash payments for July	210,000

The company typically collects 75 percent of credit sales in the month of sale and the remainder in the month following the sale. Tilley's line of credit enables the company to borrow funds readily, with the stipulation that any borrowing must take place on the last day of the month. The company pays its vendors on the last day of the month also. Mr. Tilley likes to maintain a $10,000 cash balance before any interest payments. The annual interest rate is 12 percent.

Required

a. Compute the amount of funds Mr. Tilley needs to borrow on July 31.

b. Determine the amount of interest expense the company will report on the July pro forma income statement.

c. Determine the amount of interest expense the company will report on the August pro forma income statement.

Exercise 7-15B *Preparing pro forma income statements with different assumptions*

LO 7-6

Hansboro Corporation's budget planning meeting is like a zoo. Neil Gleason, the credit manager, is naturally conservative and Rachel Lawson, the marketing manager, is the opposite. They have argued back and forth about the effect of various factors that influence the sales growth rate, such as credit policies and market potential. Based on the following current year data provided by Shirley Chandler, the controller, Neil expects Hansboro's revenues to grow 5 percent each quarter above last year's level; Rachel insists the growth rate will be 8 percent per quarter.

Current Year	First Quarter	Second Quarter	Third Quarter	Fourth Quarter	Total
Sales revenue	$240,000	$200,000	$216,000	$314,000	$970,000
Cost of goods sold	122,000	101,000	106,000	156,000	485,000
Gross margin	118,000	99,000	110,000	158,000	485,000
Selling & admin. expenses	32,000	26,000	26,400	40,600	125,000
Net income	$ 86,000	$ 73,000	$ 83,600	$117,400	$360,000

Historically, cost of goods sold is projected at 50 percent of sales revenue. Selling and administrative expenses are expected to be 12.5 percent of sales revenue.

Required

a. Prepare a pro forma income statement for the coming year using the credit manager's growth estimate.

b. Prepare a pro forma income statement for the coming year using the marketing manager's growth estimate.

c. Explain why two executives in the same company could have different estimates of future growth.

PROBLEMS—SERIES B

LO 7-1

Problem 7-16B *Behavioral impact of budgeting*

Melissa Putnam, the director of Kelso Corporation's Mail-Order Division, is preparing the division's budget proposal for next year. The company's president will review the proposal for approval. Ms. Putnam estimates the current year final operating results will be as follows.

	Current Year
Sales revenue	$3,000,000
Cost of goods sold	1,800,000
Gross profit	1,200,000
Selling & admin. expenses	480,000
Net income	$ 720,000

Ms. Putnam believes that the cost of goods sold as well as selling and administrative expenses will continue to be stable in proportion to sales revenue.

Kelso has an incentive policy to reward division managers whose performance exceeds their budget. Division directors receive a 10 percent bonus based on the excess of actual net income over the division's budget. For the last two years, Ms. Putnam has proposed a 4 percent rate of increase, which proved accurate. However, her honesty and accuracy in forecasting caused her to receive no year-end bonus at all. She is pondering whether she should do something differently this time. If she continues to be honest, she should propose an 8 percent growth rate because of robust market demand. Alternatively, she can propose a 4 percent growth rate as usual and thereby expect to receive some bonus at year-end.

Required

Round all computations to the nearest whole dollar.

a. Prepare a pro forma income statement, assuming a 4 percent estimated increase.

b. Prepare a pro forma income statement, assuming an 8 percent increase.

c. Assume the president eventually approves the division's proposal with the 4 percent growth rate. If growth actually is 8 percent, how much bonus would Ms. Putnam receive?

d. Propose a better budgeting procedure for Kelso Corporation.

LO 7-2

Problem 7-17B *Preparing a sales budget and schedule of cash receipts*

Estlin Corporation sells mail-order computers. In December Year 2, it has generated $300,000 of sales revenue; the company expects a 20 percent increase in sales in January and 10 percent in February. All sales are on account. Estlin normally collects 80 percent of accounts receivable in the month of sale and 20 percent in the next month.

Required

a. Prepare a sales budget for January and February Year 3.

b. Determine the amount of sales revenue Estlin would report on the bimonthly pro forma income statement for January and February Year 3.

c. Prepare a cash receipts schedule for January and February Year 3.

d. Determine the amount of accounts receivable as of February 28, Year 3.

LO 7-3

Problem 7-18B *Preparing an inventory purchases budget and schedule of cash payments*

Mankota Company's purchasing manager, Fernando Garza, is preparing a purchases budget for the next quarter. At his request, Ruben Carpenter, the manager of the sales department, forwarded him the following preliminary sales budget.

	October	November	December	January
Budgeted sales	$240,000	$300,000	$360,000	$320,000

For budgeting purposes, Mankota estimates that cost of goods sold is 75 percent of sales. The company desires to maintain an ending inventory balance equal to 20 percent of the next period's cost of goods sold. The September ending inventory is $40,000. Mankota makes all purchases on account and pays 70 percent of accounts payable in the month of purchase and the remaining 30 percent in the following month. The balance of accounts payable at the end of September is $37,500.

Required

a. Prepare an inventory purchases budget for October, November, and December.

b. Determine the amount of ending inventory Mankota will report on the end-of-quarter pro forma balance sheet.

c. Prepare a schedule of cash payments for inventory for October, November, and December.

d. Determine the balance in accounts payable Mankota will report on the end-of-quarter pro forma balance sheet.

Problem 7-19B *Preparing a schedule of cash payments for selling and administrative expenses*

LO 7-4

Javior's Travel Services has prepared its selling and administrative expenses budget for the next quarter. It pays all expenses when they are incurred except sales commissions, advertising expense, and telephone expense. These three items are paid in the month following the one in which they are incurred. January is the first month of operations, so there are no beginning account balances.

	January	February	March
Salary expense	$24,000	$24,000	$24,000
Sales commissions	1,800	1,200	1,400
Advertising expense	1,000	1,000	1,200
Telephone expense	2,000	2,160	2,200
Depreciation on store equipment	8,000	8,000	8,000
Rent	20,000	20,000	20,000
Miscellaneous	1,600	1,600	1,600
Total S&A expenses before interest	$58,400	$57,960	$58,400

Required

a. Prepare a schedule of cash payments for selling and administrative expenses.

b. Determine the amount of telephone expense payable as of March 31.

c. Determine the amount of sales commissions payable as of February 28.

Problem 7-20B *Preparing a cash budget*

LO 7-5

Chang Company has budgeted the following cash flows.

	April	May	June
Cash receipts	$200,000	$220,000	$330,000
Cash payments			
For inventory purchases	205,000	210,000	232,000
For S&A expenses	40,000	53,000	66,000

Chang had an $18,000 cash balance on April 1. The company desires a $30,000 cash cushion before paying interest. Funds are assumed to be borrowed, in increments of $1,000, and repaid on the last day of each month; the interest rate is 1.50 percent per month. Chang also pays its vendors on the last day of the month.

Required

Prepare a cash budget.

LO 7-6

Problem 7-21B *Preparing pro forma income statements with different assumptions*

Shane Corbett, a successful entrepreneur, is reviewing the results of his first year in business. His accountant delivered the following income statement just five minutes ago.

	Current Year
Sales revenue	$400,000
Cost of goods sold	280,000
Gross profit	120,000
Selling & admin. expenses	65,000
Net income	$ 55,000

Mr. Corbett would like net income to increase 20 percent in the next year. This first year, selling and administrative expenses were 10 percent of sales revenue plus $39,000 of fixed expenses.

Required

The following questions are independent of each other.

a. Mr. Corbett expects that cost of goods sold and variable selling and administrative expenses will remain stable in proportion to sales next year. The fixed selling and administrative expenses will increase to $39,000. What percentage increase in sales would enable the company to reach Mr. Corbett's goal? Prepare a pro forma income statement to illustrate.

b. Market competition may become serious next year, and Mr. Corbett does not expect an increase in sales revenue. However, he has developed a good relationship with his supplier, who is willing to give him a volume discount that will decrease cost of goods sold by 3 percent. What else can the company do to reach Mr. Corbett's goal? Prepare a pro forma income statement illustrating your proposal.

c. If the company escalates its advertising campaign to boost consumer recognition, the selling and administrative expenses will increase to $85,000. With the increased advertising, the company expects sales revenue to increase by 25 percent. Assume that cost of goods sold remains constant in proportion to sales. Can the company reach Mr. Corbett's goal?

LO 7-2, 7-3, 7-4, 7-6

Problem 7-22B *Preparing budgets with multiple products*

Myrtle Enterprises Inc. has two products, palm-size computers and programmable calculators. Tammy Dwyer, the chief executive officer, is working with her staff to prepare next year's budget. Ms. Dwyer estimates that sales will increase at an annual rate of 10 percent for palm-size computers and 4 percent for programmable calculators. The current year sales revenue data follow.

	First Quarter	Second Quarter	Third Quarter	Fourth Quarter	Total
Palm-size computers	$300,000	$325,000	$360,000	$415,000	$1,400,000
Programmable calculators	125,000	137,500	145,000	162,500	570,000
Total	$425,000	$462,500	$505,000	$577,500	$1,970,000

Based on the company's past experience, cost of goods sold is usually 75 percent of sales revenue. Company policy is to keep 10 percent of the next period's estimated cost of goods sold as the current period ending inventory.

Required

a. Prepare the company's sales budget for the next year for each quarter by individual products.

b. If the selling and administrative expenses are estimated to be $250,000, prepare the company's budgeted annual income statement for the next year.

c. Ms. Dwyer estimates the current year's ending inventory will be $34,000 for computers and $16,000 for calculators and the ending inventory next year will be $39,000 for computers and $21,000 for calculators. Prepare the company's inventory purchases budget for the next year showing quarterly figures by product.

Problem 7-23B ***Preparing a master budget for a retail company with no beginning account balances*** LO 7-2, 7-3, 7-4, 7-5, 7-6

Inwood Gifts Corporation begins business today, December 31, Year 1. Rebecca Ortiz, the president, is trying to prepare the company's master budget for the first three months (January, February, and March) of Year 2. Since you are her good friend and an accounting student, Ms. Ortiz asks you to prepare the budget based on the following specifications.

Required

a. January sales are estimated to be $500,000, of which 30 percent will be cash and 70 percent will be credit. The company expects sales to increase at the rate of 10 percent per month. Prepare a sales budget.

b. The company expects to collect 100 percent of the accounts receivable generated by credit sales in the month following the sale. Prepare a schedule of cash receipts.

c. The cost of goods sold is 50 percent of sales. The company desires to maintain a minimum ending inventory equal to 20 percent of the next month's cost of goods sold. The ending inventory of March is expected to be $66,000. Assume that all purchases are made on account. Prepare an inventory purchases budget.

d. The company pays 60 percent of accounts payable in the month of purchase and the remaining 40 percent in the following month. Prepare a cash payments budget for inventory purchases.

e. Budgeted selling and administrative expenses per month follow:

Salary expense (fixed)	$50,000
Sales commissions	8% of sales
Supplies expense	4% of sales
Utilities (fixed)	$3,600
Depreciation on store fixtures (fixed)*	$10,000
Rent (fixed)	$14,400
Miscellaneous (fixed)	$4,000

*The capital expenditures budget indicates that Inwood will spend $700,000 on January 1 for store fixtures. The fixtures are expected to have a $100,000 salvage value and a five-year (60-month) useful life.

Use this information to prepare a selling and administrative expenses budget.

f. Utilities and sales commissions are paid the month after they are incurred; all other expenses are paid in the month in which they are incurred. Prepare a cash payments budget for selling and administrative expenses.

g. The company borrows funds, in increments of $1,000, and repays them in any amount available on the last day of the month. It pays interest of 1.5 percent per month in cash on the last day of the month. For safety, the company desires to maintain a $100,000 cash cushion. The company pays its vendors on the last day of the month. Prepare a cash budget.

h. Prepare a pro forma income statement for the quarter.

i. Prepare a pro forma balance sheet at the end of the quarter.

j. Prepare a pro forma statement of cash flows for the quarter.

ANALYZE, THINK, COMMUNICATE

ATC 7-1 Business Applications Case *Preparing and using pro forma statements*

Mary Helu and Jason Haynes recently graduated from the same university. After graduation they decided not to seek jobs at established organizations but, rather, to start their own small business hoping they could have more flexibility in their personal lives for a few years. Mary's family has operated Mexican restaurants and taco trucks for the past two generations, and Mary noticed there were no taco truck services in the town where their university was located. To reduce the amount they would need for an initial investment, they decided to start a business operating a taco cart rather than a taco truck, from which they would cook and serve traditional Mexican-style street food.

They bought a used taco cart for $18,000. This cost, along with the cost for supplies to get started, a business license, and street vendor license brought their initial expenditures to $22,000. They took

$5,000 from personal savings they had accumulated by working part time during college, and they borrowed $17,000 from Mary's parents. They agreed to pay interest on the outstanding loan balance each month based on an annual rate of 5 percent. They will repay the principal over the next few years as cash becomes available. They were able to rent space in a parking lot near the campus they had attended, believing that the students would welcome their food as an alternative to the typical fast food that was currently available.

After two months in business, September and October, they had average monthly revenues of $25,000 and out-of-pocket costs of $22,000 for rent, ingredients, paper supplies, and so on, but not interest. Jason thinks they should repay some of the money they borrowed, but Mary thinks they should prepare a set of forecasted financial statements for their first year in business before deciding whether or not to repay any principal on the loan. She remembers a bit about budgeting from a survey of accounting course she took and thinks the results from their first two months in business can be extended over the next 10 months to prepare the budget they need. They estimate the cart will last at least four years, after which they expect to sell it for $6,000 and move on to something else in their lives. Mary agrees to prepare a forecasted (pro forma) income statement, balance sheet, and statement of cash flows for their first year in business, which includes the two months already passed.

Required

a. Prepare the annual pro forma financial statements that you would expect Mary to prepare based on her comments about her expectations for the business. Assume no principal will be repaid on the loan.

b. Review the statements you prepared for the first requirement and prepare a list of reasons why actual results for Mary and Jason's business probably will not match their budgeted statements.

ATC 7-2 Group Assignment *Master budget and pro forma statements*

The following trial balance was drawn from the records of Havel Company as of October 1, Year 2.

Cash	$ 16,000	
Accounts receivable	60,000	
Inventory	40,000	
Store equipment	200,000	
Accumulated depreciation		$ 76,800
Accounts payable		72,000
Line of credit loan		100,000
Common stock		50,000
Retained earnings		17,200
Totals	$316,000	$316,000

Required

a. Divide the class into groups, each with four or five students. Organize the groups into three sections. Assign Task 1 to the first section, Task 2 to the second section, and Task 3 to the third section.

Group Tasks

(1) Based on the following information, prepare a sales budget and a schedule of cash receipts for October, November, and December. Sales for October are expected to be $180,000, consisting of $40,000 in cash and $140,000 on credit. The company expects sales to increase at the rate of 10 percent per month. All accounts receivable are collected in the month following the sale.

(2) Based on the following information, prepare a purchases budget and a schedule of cash payments for inventory purchases for October, November, and December. The inventory balance as of October 1 was $40,000. Cost of goods sold for October is expected to be $72,000. Cost of goods sold is expected to increase by 10 percent per month. The company expects to maintain a minimum ending inventory equal to 20 percent of the current month cost of goods sold. Seventy-five percent of accounts payable is paid in the month that the purchase occurs; the remaining 25 percent is paid in the following month.

(3) Based on the following selling and administrative expenses budgeted for October, prepare a selling and administrative expenses budget for October, November, and December.

Sales commissions (10% increase per month)	$ 7,200
Supplies expense (10% increase per month)	1,800
Utilities (fixed)	2,200
Depreciation on store equipment (fixed)	1,600
Salary expense (fixed)	34,000
Rent (fixed)	6,000
Miscellaneous (fixed)	1,000

Cash payments for sales commissions and utilities are made in the month following the one in which the expense is incurred. Supplies and other operating expenses are paid in cash in the month in which they are incurred.

b. Select a representative from each section. Have the representatives supply the missing information in the following pro forma income statement and balance sheet for the fourth quarter of Year 2. The statements are prepared as of December 31, Year 2.

Income Statement	
Sales revenue	$?
Cost of goods sold	?
Gross margin	357,480
Operating expenses	?
Operating income	193,290
Interest expense	(2,530)
Net income	$190,760

Balance Sheet		
Assets		
Cash		$ 9,760
Accounts receivable		?
Inventory		?
Store equipment	$200,000	
Accumulated depreciation store equipment	?	
Book value of equipment		118,400
Total assets		$314,984
Liabilities		
Accounts payable		?
Utilities payable		?
Sales commissions payable		?
Line of credit		23,936
Equity		
Common stock		50,000
Retained earnings		?
Total liabilities and equity		$314,984

c. Indicate whether Havel will need to borrow money during October.

ATC 7-3 Research Assignment *Analyzing budget data for the U.S. government*

The annual budget of the United States is very complex, but this case requires that you analyze only a small portion of the historical tables that are presented as a part of each year's budget. The fiscal year of the federal government ends on September 30. Obtain the budget documents needed at www.gpo.gov/fdsys/browse/collectionGPO.action?collectionCode=BUDGET and follow these steps:

- Click on the "Fiscal Year 2018" link.
- Scroll down and select "Historical Tables."

- There are two options that can be used to download each historical data table. One is an XLS (Excel) file format. This option will make completing this assignment easier.
- You will need to use Table 1.1, Table 1.2, and Table 4.2 to complete the following requirements.

Required

a. Table 1.2 shows the budget as a percentage of gross domestic product (GDP). Using the data in the third column, "Surplus or Deficit," determine how many years since 1960 the budget has shown a surplus and how many times it has shown a deficit. Ignore the "TQ" data between 1976 and 1977. This was a year that the government changed the ending date of its fiscal year.

b. Based on the data in Table 1.2, identify the three years with the highest deficits as a percentage of GDP. What were the deficit percentages for these years? Which year had the largest surplus and by what percentage?

c. Using your findings for Requirement (*b*) regarding the year with the highest deficit as a percentage of GDP, go to Table 1.1 and calculate the deficit for that year as a percentage of revenues. What percent of each dollar spent by the federal government in that year was paid for with tax revenues and what percent was paid for with borrowed funds?

d. The president of the United States from 2001 through 2009 was George W. Bush, a Republican. The president from 2009 through 2017 was Barack H. Obama, a Democrat. These men had significant input into the federal budget for the fiscal years 2002–2009 and 2010–2017, respectively. Table 4.2 shows what percentage of the total federal budget was directed toward each department within the government. Compare the data on Table 4.2 for 2002–2009, the Bush years, to the data for 2010–2017, the Obama years. Identify the five departments that appear to have changed the most from the Bush years to the Obama years. Ignore "Allowances" and "Undistributed offsetting receipts." Note, to approach this assignment more accurately, you should compute the average percentage for each department for the eight years each president served, and compare the two averages.

ATC 7-4 Writing Assignment *Continuous budgeting*

The Curious Accountant in this chapter discussed some of the budgeting issues facing the United States Olympic Committee (USOC). First, to get a basic understanding of the sources of revenues and expenses of the USOC, review its "Audited Financial Statements." These may be accessed with the following link: www.teamusa.org/footer/finance/. You need to review the information on the "Consolidated statement of activities." Note that there are usually two of these, one for the current fiscal year, and one for all the years since the year after last summer Olympic games. Either of these forms will provide additional insight into the sources of the USOC's revenues and expenses.

Required

Assume the USOC had not previously used continuous budgeting but was considering implementing a continuous budgeting system. Also assume you had been asked to identify some of the challenges the USOC would face in implementing this system. Write a memorandum explaining the challenges you identify.

ATC 7-5 Ethical Dilemma *Bad budget system or unethical behavior?*

Clarence Cleaver is the budget director for the Harris County School District. Mr. Cleaver recently sent an urgent e-mail message to Sally Simmons, principal of West Harris County High. The message severely reprimanded Ms. Simmons for failing to spend the funds allocated to her to purchase computer equipment. Ms. Simmons responded that her school already has a sufficient supply of computers; indeed, the computer lab is never filled to capacity and usually is less than half filled. Ms. Simmons suggested that she would rather use the funds for teacher training. She argued that the reason the existing computers are not fully utilized is that the teachers lack sufficient computer literacy necessary to make assignments for their students.

Mr. Cleaver responded that it is not Ms. Simmons' job to decide how the money is to be spent; that is the school board's job. It is the principal's job to spend the money as the board directed. He informed Ms. Simmons that if the money is not spent by the fiscal closing date, the school board would likely reduce next year's budget allotment. To avoid a potential budget cut, Mr. Cleaver reallocated Ms. Simmons' computer funds to Jules Carrington, principal of East Harris County High. Mr. Carrington knows how to buy computers regardless of whether they are needed. Mr. Cleaver's final words were, "Don't blame me if parents of West High students complain that East High has more equipment. If anybody comes to me, I'm telling them that you turned down the money."

Required

a. Do Mr. Cleaver's actions violate the standards of ethical professional practice shown in Exhibit 1.17 of Chapter 1?

b. Does the Sarbanes-Oxley Act apply to this case? Explain your answer.

c. Explain how participative budgeting could improve the allocation of resources for the Harris County School District.

ATC 7-6 Spreadsheet Assignment *Using Excel*

The accountant for Nelly's Dress Shop prepared the fourth quarter 2017 cash budget that appears on the following spreadsheet. Nelly's has a policy to maintain a minimum cash balance of $14,000 before the interest payment at the end of each month. The shop borrows and repays funds on the first day of the month. The interest rate is 2 percent per month.

Required

a. Construct a spreadsheet to model the cash budget as in the following screen capture. Be sure to use formulas where possible so that any changes to the estimates will be automatically reflected in the spreadsheet.

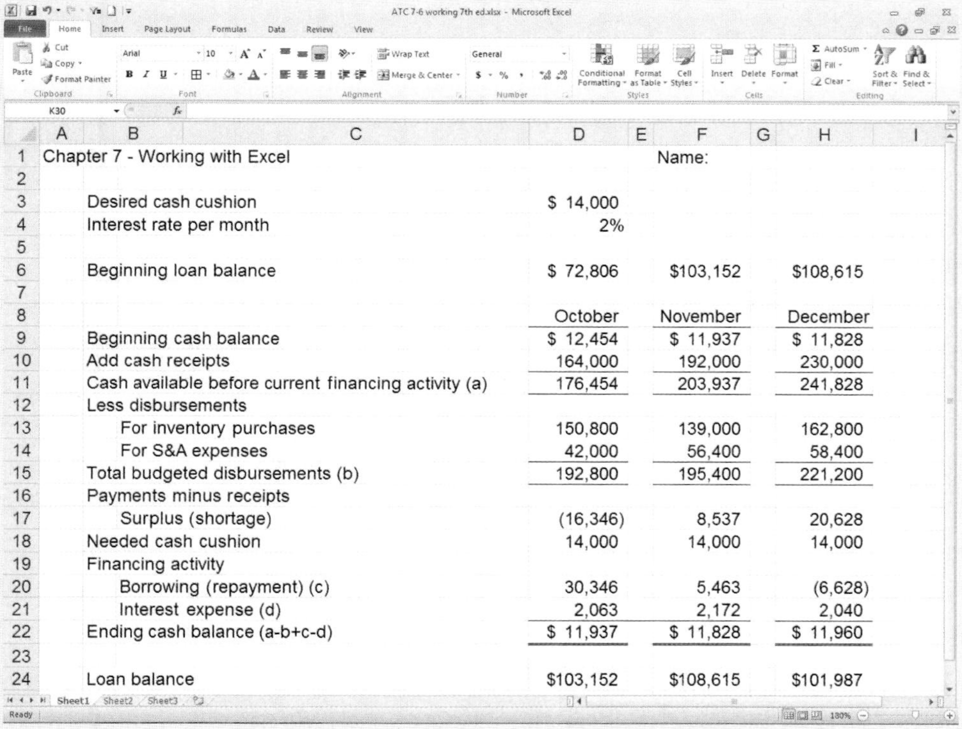

	A	B	C	D	E	F	G	H
1	Chapter 7 - Working with Excel					Name:		
2								
3		Desired cash cushion		$ 14,000				
4		Interest rate per month		2%				
5								
6		Beginning loan balance		$ 72,806		$103,152		$108,615
7								
8				October		November		December
9		Beginning cash balance		$ 12,454		$ 11,937		$ 11,828
10		Add cash receipts		164,000		192,000		230,000
11		Cash available before current financing activity (a)		176,454		203,937		241,828
12		Less disbursements						
13		For inventory purchases		150,800		139,000		162,800
14		For S&A expenses		42,000		56,400		58,400
15		Total budgeted disbursements (b)		192,800		195,400		221,200
16		Payments minus receipts						
17		Surplus (shortage)		(16,346)		8,537		20,628
18		Needed cash cushion		14,000		14,000		14,000
19		Financing activity						
20		Borrowing (repayment) (c)		30,346		5,463		(6,628)
21		Interest expense (d)		2,063		2,172		2,040
22		Ending cash balance (a-b+c-d)		$ 11,937		$ 11,828		$ 11,960
23								
24		Loan balance		$103,152		$108,615		$101,987

Source: Microsoft Excel 2010

Spreadsheet Tips

(1) Rows 11, 15, 17, 18, 20 to 22, and 24 should be based on formulas.

(2) Cells F6, H6, F9, and H9 should be based on formulas also. For example, cell F6 should be = D24.

ACT 7-7 Spreadsheet Assignment *Mastering Excel*

eXcel

Spitzer Company has collected sales forecasts for next year from three people.

Sources of Sales Estimate	First Quarter	Second Quarter	Third Quarter	Fourth Quarter
a. Sales manager	$520,000	$410,000	$370,000	$610,000
b. Marketing consultant	540,000	480,000	400,000	630,000
c. Production manager	460,000	360,000	350,000	580,000

They have estimated that the cost of goods sold is 70 percent of sales. The company tries to maintain 10 percent of next quarter's expected cost of goods sold as the current quarter's ending inventory. The ending inventory of this year is $25,000. For budgeting, the ending inventory of the next year is expected to be $28,000.

Required

a. Construct a spreadsheet that allows the inventory purchases budget to be prepared for each of the preceding estimates.

Spreadsheet Tips

The VLOOKUP function can be used to choose one line of the preceding estimates. See the spreadsheet tips in Chapter 5 for an explanation of VLOOKUP.

COMPREHENSIVE PROBLEM

The management team of Magnificent Modems Inc. (MMI) wants to investigate the effect of several different growth rates on sales and cash receipts. Cash sales for the month of January are expected to be $10,000. Credit sales for January are expected to be $50,000. MMI collects 100 percent of credit sales in the month following the month of sale. Assume a beginning balance in accounts receivable of $48,000.

Required

Calculate the amount of sales and cash receipts for the months of February and March assuming a growth rate of 2 percent and 4 percent. The results at a growth rate of 1 percent are shown as an example.

Sales Budget

	Jan	Feb	Mar
Cash sales	$10,000	$10,100	$10,201
Sales on account	50,000	50,500	51,005
Total budgeted sales	$60,000	$60,600	$61,206

Schedule of Cash Receipts

	Jan	Feb	Mar
Current cash sales	$10,000	$10,100	$10,201
Plus collections from accounts receivable	48,000	50,000	50,500
Total budgeted collections	$58,000	$60,100	$60,701

Use the following forms, assuming a growth rate of 2 percent.

Sales Budget

	Jan	Feb	Mar
Cash sales	$10,000		
Sales on account	50,000		
Total budgeted sales	$60,000		

Schedule of Cash Receipts

Current cash sales	$10,000		
Plus collections from accounts receivable	48,000		
Total budgeted collections	$58,000		

Use the following forms, assuming a growth rate of 4 percent.

Sales Budget

	Jan	Feb	Mar
Cash sales	$10,000		
Sales on account	50,000		
Total budgeted sales	$60,000		

Schedule of Cash Receipts

Current cash sales	$10,000		
Plus collections from accounts receivable	48,000		
Total budgeted collections	$58,000		

CHAPTER 8

Performance Evaluation

LEARNING OBJECTIVES

After you have mastered the material in this chapter, you will be able to:

LO 8-1 Describe flexible and static budgets.

LO 8-2 Classify variances as being favorable or unfavorable.

LO 8-3 Compute and interpret sales and variable cost volume variances.

LO 8-4 Compute and interpret flexible budget variances.

LO 8-5 Calculate and interpret fixed cost variances.

LO 8-6 Describe the features of a standard cost system and compute price and usage variances.

Video lectures and accompanying self-assessment quizzes are available in Connect® for all learning objectives.

CHAPTER OPENING

Suppose you are a carpenter who builds picnic tables. You normally build 200 tables each year (the planned volume of activity), but because of unexpected customer demand, you are asked to build 225 tables (the actual volume of activity). You work hard and build the tables. Should management chastise you for using more materials, labor, or overhead than you normally use? Should management criticize the sales staff for selling more tables than expected? Of course not. Management must evaluate performance based on the actual volume of activity, not the planned volume of activity. To help management plan and evaluate performance, managerial accountants frequently prepare flexible budgets based on different levels of volume. Flexible budgets flex, or change, when the volume of activity changes.

The Curious Accountant

©Ken Wolter/Shutterstock

Gourmet Pizzas is located in an affluent section of a major metropolitan area. Its owner, Payten Flowers worked at a national-chain pizza restaurant while in college. He knew that there were more independent restaurants than chain restaurants, even though the national pizza chains, such as **Domino's** and **Papa John's**, had more sales in dollars than independent pizza restaurants. He also knew the popularity of pizza was growing. One survey showed pizza to be Americans' favorite comfort food, and another found that 41 percent of respondents said they ate pizza at least once each week.

Knowing it cannot beat the big guys on price, Gourmet Pizzas focuses on quality and service. Its pizza dough is made from scratch on the premises from organically grown flour, and, when possible, locally sourced ingredients. It offers a wide variety of unusual toppings, such as smoked salmon. He also knew he needed to offer online ordering, delivery, and a rewards program if he was going to compete successfully with the chains.

To determine a proper selling price for his pies, the owner estimated the cost of making the crusts, among other things. Knowing how much flour, yeast, etc., was needed to make the dough for one pizza and estimating the cost of these ingredients, he determined that the materials for the dough for each pizza should cost him 35 cents. However, after six months in business, he had spent $7,900 on materials needed for making his dough, and had sold 20,250 pizzas. This resulted in an actual price per pizza of 39 cents.

What are two general reasons that may explain why the materials cost for pizza dough was higher than Gourmet Pizzas' owner estimated? (Answer on page 362.)

Source: Industry data are from "Pizza Power 2017—A State of the Industry Report" on pmq.com.

PREPARING FLEXIBLE BUDGETS

LO 8-1

Describe flexible and static budgets.

A **flexible budget** is an extension of the *master budget* discussed previously. The master budget is based solely on the planned volume of activity. The master budget is frequently called a **static budget** because it remains unchanged even if the actual volume of activity differs from the planned volume. Flexible budgets differ from static budgets in that they show expected revenues and costs at a *variety* of volume levels.

To illustrate the differences between static and flexible budgets, consider Melrose Manufacturing Company, a producer of small, high-quality trophies used in award ceremonies. Melrose plans to make and sell 18,000 trophies during Year 1. Management's best estimates of the expected sales price and per-unit costs for the trophies are called *standard* prices and costs. The standard price and costs for the 18,000 trophies follow.

Per-unit sales price and variable costs	
Expected sales price	$ 80.00
Standard materials cost	12.00
Standard labor cost	16.80
Standard overhead cost	5.60
Standard general, selling, and administrative cost	15.00
Total fixed costs	$291,600

The static budget is highlighted with red shading in Exhibit 8.1. Sales revenue is determined by multiplying the expected sales price per unit times the planned volume of activity ($80 × 18,000 = $1,440,000). Similarly, the variable costs are calculated by multiplying the standard cost per unit times the planned volume of activity. For example, the manufacturing materials cost is $216,000 ($12 × 18,000). The same computational procedures apply to the other variable costs. The variable costs are subtracted from the sales revenue to produce a contribution margin of $550,800. The fixed costs are subtracted from the contribution margin to produce a budgeted net income of $259,200.

EXHIBIT 8.1

Static and Flexible Budgets in Excel Spreadsheet

	A	B	C	D	E	F	G	H	I	J
1										
2				Static						
3				Budget				Flexible Budgets		
4	Number of Units			18,000		16,000	17,000	18,000	19,000	20,000
5			Per Unit							
6			Standards							
7	Sales Revenue		$80.00	$1,440,000		$1,280,000	$1,360,000	$1,440,000	$1,520,000	$1,600,000
8										
9	Variable Manuf. Costs									
10	Materials		$12.00	216,000		192,000	204,000	216,000	228,000	240,000
11	Labor		16.80	302,400		268,800	285,600	302,400	319,200	336,000
12	Overhead		5.60	100,800		89,600	95,200	100,800	106,400	112,000
13	Variable G,S, &A		15.00	270,000		240,000	255,000	270,000	285,000	300,000
14										
15	Contribution Margin			550,800		489,600	520,200	550,800	581,400	612,000
16										
17	Fixed Costs			291,600		291,600	291,600	291,600	291,600	291,600
18										
19	Net Income			$ 259,200		$ 198,000	$ 228,600	$ 259,200	$ 289,800	$ 320,400
20										
21										

Source: Microsoft Excel 2010

What happens if the number of units sold is different from the planned volume? In other words, *what* happens to net income *if* Melrose sells more or less than 18,000 units? Managers frequently use flexible budgets to examine such *what if* scenarios. Flexible budget income statements for Melrose at sales volumes of 16,000, 17,000, 18,000, 19,000, and 20,000 are highlighted with blue shading in Exhibit 8.1.

The flexible budgets are prepared with the same per-unit standard amounts and fixed cost data used to produce the static budget. The only difference is the expected number of units sold. For example, the sales revenue at 16,000 units is $1,280,000 ($80 × 16,000), at 17,000 units it is $1,360,000 ($80 × 17,000), and so on. The variable materials cost at 16,000 units is $192,000 ($12 × 16,000), at 17,000 units it is $204,000 ($12 × 17,000), and so on. The other variable costs are computed in the same manner. Note that the fixed costs are the same at all levels of activity because, by definition, they are not affected by changes in volume.

Other flexible budgets are possible. Indeed, a flexible budget can be prepared for any number of units sold. You have probably noticed that Exhibit 8.1 was prepared using an Excel spreadsheet. Excel offers the opportunity to prepare an unlimited number of flexible budgets with minimal effort. For example, formulas can be created with cell references so that new budgets can be created simply by changing the number of units entered in a single cell.

Managers use flexible budgets for both planning and performance evaluation. For example, managers may assess whether the company's cash position is adequate by assuming different levels of volume. They may judge if the number of employees, amounts of materials, and equipment and storage facilities are appropriate for a variety of different potential levels of volume. In addition to helping plan, flexible budgets are critical to implementing an effective performance evaluation system.

CHECK YOURSELF 8.1

The static (master) budget of Parcel Inc. called for a production and sales volume of 25,000 units. At that volume, total budgeted fixed costs were $150,000 and total budgeted variable costs were $200,000. Prepare a flexible budget for an expected volume of 26,000 units.

Answer Budgeted fixed costs would remain unchanged at $150,000 because changes in the volume of activity do not affect budgeted fixed costs. Budgeted variable costs would increase to $208,000, computed as follows: Calculate the budgeted variable cost per unit ($200,000 ÷ 25,000 units = $8) and then multiply that variable cost per unit by the expected volume ($8 × 26,000 units = $208,000).

DETERMINING VARIANCES FOR PERFORMANCE EVALUATION

LO 8-2

Classify variances as being favorable or unfavorable.

One means of evaluating managerial performance is to compare *standard* amounts with *actual* results. The differences between the standard and actual amounts are called **variances;** variances can be either *favorable* or *unfavorable*. When actual sales revenue is greater than expected (planned) revenue, a company has a favorable sales variance because higher sales increase net income. When actual sales are less than expected, an unfavorable sales variance exists. When actual costs are *less* than standard costs, cost variances are favorable because lower costs increase net income. Unfavorable cost variances exist when actual costs are *more* than standard costs. These relationships are summarized as follows.

- When actual sales exceed expected sales, variances are favorable.
- When actual sales are less than expected sales, variances are unfavorable.
- When actual costs exceed standard costs, variances are unfavorable.
- When actual costs are less than standard costs, variances are favorable.

SALES AND VARIABLE COST VOLUME VARIANCES

LO 8-3

Compute and interpret sales and variable cost volume variances.

The amount of a **sales volume variance** is the difference between the static budget (which is based on planned volume) and a flexible budget based on actual volume. Likewise, the **variable cost volume variances** are determined by calculating the differences between the static and flexible budget amounts. These variances measure management effectiveness in attaining the planned volume of activity. To illustrate, assume Melrose Manufacturing Company actually makes and sells 19,000 trophies during Year 1. The planned volume of activity was 18,000 trophies. Exhibit 8.2 shows Melrose's static budget, flexible budget, and volume variances.

EXHIBIT 8.2

Melrose Manufacturing Company's Volume Variances

	Static Budget	Flexible Budget	Volume Variances	
Number of units	18,000	19,000	1,000	Favorable
Sales revenue	$1,440,000	$1,520,000	$80,000	Favorable
Variable manufacturing costs				
Materials	216,000	228,000	12,000	Unfavorable
Labor	302,400	319,200	16,800	Unfavorable
Overhead	100,800	106,400	5,600	Unfavorable
Variable SG&A	270,000	285,000	15,000	Unfavorable
Contribution margin	550,800	581,400	30,600	Favorable
Fixed costs	291,600	291,600	0	
Net income	$ 259,200	$ 289,800	$30,600	Favorable

©moodboard/Alamy

Interpreting the Sales and Variable Cost Volume Variances

Because the static and flexible budgets are based on the same standard sales price and per-unit variable costs, the variances are solely attributable to the difference between the planned and actual volume of activity. Marketing managers are usually responsible for the volume variances. Because the sales volume drives production levels, production managers have little control over volume. Exceptions occur; for example, if poor production quality control leads to inferior goods that are difficult to sell, the production manager is responsible. The production manager is responsible for production delays that affect product availability, which may restrict sales volume. Under normal circumstances, however, the marketing campaign determines the volume of sales. Upper-level marketing managers develop the promotional program and create the sales plan; they are in the best position to explain why sales goals are or are not met. When marketing managers refer to **making the numbers,** they usually mean reaching the sales volume in the static (master) budget.

In the case of Melrose Manufacturing Company, the marketing manager not only achieved but also exceeded by 1,000 units the planned volume of sales. Exhibit 8.2 shows the activity variances resulting from the extra volume. At the standard price, the additional volume produces a favorable revenue variance of $80,000 (1,000 units × $80 per unit). The increase in volume also produces unfavorable variable cost variances. The net effect of producing and selling the additional 1,000 units is an increase of $30,600 in the contribution margin, a positive result. These preliminary results suggest that the marketing manager is to be commended. The analysis, however, is incomplete. For example, examining market share could reveal whether the manager won customers from competitors or whether the manager simply reaped the benefit of an unexpected industrywide increase in demand. The increase in sales volume could have been attained by reducing the sales price; the success of that strategy will be analyzed further in a later section of this chapter.

Since the variable costs in the flexible budget are higher than the variable costs in the static budget, the variable cost volume variances are *unfavorable.* The unfavorable classification may be misleading because it focuses solely on the cost component of the income statement. While costs are higher than expected, so too may be revenue. Indeed, as shown in Exhibit 8.2, the total of the unfavorable variable cost variances is more than offset by the favorable revenue variance, resulting in a higher contribution margin. Frequently, the assessment of variances requires a holistic perspective.

Fixed Cost Considerations

At this point, it is important to note that the reason the fixed cost variance shown in Exhibit 8.2 is zero is because we are comparing two budgets (static versus flexible). Variances occur only because the budgets are created using different volumes of activity. Since total fixed cost is not affected by the level of activity, there will be no fixed cost variances associated with static versus flexible budgets.

FLEXIBLE BUDGET VARIANCES

LO 8-4

Compute and interpret flexible budget variances.

For performance evaluation, management compares actual results to a flexible budget based on the *actual* volume of activity. Because the actual results and the flexible budget reflect the same volume of activity, any variances in revenues and variable costs result from differences between standard and actual per-unit amounts. To illustrate computing and analyzing flexible budget variances, we assume that Melrose's *actual* per-unit amounts during Year 1 were those shown in the following table. The Year 1 per-unit *standard* amounts are repeated here for your convenience.

	Standard	Actual
Sales price	$80.00	$78.00
Variable materials cost	12.00	11.78
Variable labor cost	16.80	17.25
Variable overhead cost	5.60	5.75

Actual and budgeted fixed costs are shown in Exhibit 8.3.

Exhibit 8.3 shows Melrose's Year 1 flexible budget, actual results, and flexible budget variances. The flexible budget is the same one compared to the static budget in Exhibit 8.2.

EXHIBIT 8.3

Flexible Budget Variances for Melrose Manufacturing Company

	Flexible Budget	Actual Results	Flexible Budget Variances	
Number of units	19,000	19,000	0	
Sales revenue	$1,520,000	$1,482,000	$38,000	Unfavorable
Variable manufacturing costs				
Materials	228,000	223,820	4,180	Favorable
Labor	319,200	327,750	8,550	Unfavorable
Overhead	106,400	109,250	2,850	Unfavorable
Variable SG&A	285,000	283,100	1,900	Favorable
Contribution margin	581,400	538,080	43,320	Unfavorable
Fixed costs	291,600	295,000	3,400	Unfavorable
Net income	$ 289,800	$ 243,080	$46,720	Unfavorable

Recall the flexible budget amounts come from multiplying the standard per-unit amounts by the actual volume of production. For example, the sales revenue in the flexible budget comes from multiplying the standard sales price by the actual volume ($80 × 19,000). The variable costs are similarly computed. The *actual results* are calculated by multiplying the actual per-unit sales price and cost figures from the preceding table by the actual volume of activity. For example, the sales revenue in the Actual Results column comes from multiplying the actual sales price by the actual volume ($78 × 19,000 = $1,482,000). The actual cost figures are similarly computed. The differences between the flexible budget figures and the actual results are the **flexible budget variances.**

Calculating the Sales Price Variance

Because both the flexible budget and actual results are based on the actual volume of activity, the flexible budget variance is attributable to sales price, not sales volume. In this case, the actual sales price of $78 per unit is less than the standard price of $80 per unit. Because Melrose sold its product for less than the standard sales price, the **sales price variance** is *unfavorable.* Even though the price variance is unfavorable, however, sales volume was 1,000 units more than expected. It is possible the marketing manager generated the additional volume by reducing the sales price. Whether the combination of lower sales price and higher sales volume is favorable or unfavorable depends on the amount of the unfavorable sales price variance versus the amount of the favorable sales volume variance. The *total* sales variance (price and volume) follows.

Actual sales (19,000 units × $78 per unit)	$1,482,000	
Expected sales (18,000 units × $80 per unit)	1,440,000	
Total sales variance	$ 42,000	Favorable

Alternatively,

Activity variance (sales volume)	$ 80,000	Favorable
Sales price variance	(38,000)	Unfavorable
Total sales variance	$ 42,000	Favorable

This analysis indicates that reducing the sales price had a favorable impact on the *total* amount of sales revenue. Use caution when interpreting variances as good or bad; in this instance, the favorable sales variance must be compared with the related cost variances to determine whether the price reduction strategy actually increased or decreased profitability. All unfavorable variances are not bad; all favorable variances are not good. Variances should not be considered the final answer, but instead be seen as a signal to investigate.

☑ CHECK YOURSELF 8.2

Scott Company's master budget called for a planned sales volume of 30,000 units. Budgeted direct materials cost was $4 per unit. Scott actually produced and sold 32,000 units with an actual materials cost of $131,000. Determine the materials volume variance and identify the organizational unit most likely responsible for this variance. Determine the flexible budget variance and identify the organizational unit most likely responsible for this variance.

Answer The variable cost volume variance is the difference between the expected materials usage at the planned volume of activity and the expected materials usage at the actual volume of activity [(\$4 × 30,000 units) – (\$4 × 32,000) = \$8,000]. The variance is unfavorable because expected direct materials cost at actual volume was higher than budgeted direct materials cost at planned volume. The unfavorable variance might not be a bad thing. The variance is due to increased volume, which could be a good thing. The organizational unit most likely responsible for the volume variance is the marketing department.

The flexible budget variance is the difference between the expected materials cost at the actual volume (\$4 × 32,000 units = \$128,000) and the actual materials cost of \$131,000. The \$3,000 (\$128,000 – \$131,000) variance is unfavorable because it cost more than expected to make the 32,000 units. Either the production department or the purchasing department is most likely responsible for this variance.

The Human Element Associated with Flexible Budget Variances

The flexible budget cost variances offer insight into management efficiency. For example, Melrose Manufacturing Company's favorable materials variance could mean purchasing agents were shrewd in negotiating price concessions, discounts, or delivery terms and therefore reduced the price the company paid for materials. Similarly, production employees may have used materials efficiently, using less than expected. The unfavorable labor variance could mean managers failed to control employee wages or motivate employees to work hard. As with sales variances, cost variances require careful analysis. A favorable variance may, in fact, mask unfavorable conditions. For example, the favorable materials variance might have been caused by paying low prices for inferior goods. Using substandard materials could have required additional labor in the production process, which would explain the unfavorable labor variance. Again, we caution that variances, whether favorable or unfavorable, alert management to investigate further.

FIXED COST VARIANCES

LO 8-5

Calculate and interpret fixed cost variances.

Fixed costs do not fluctuate with volume; however, that does not mean that the actual costs will be the same as the budgeted costs. Indeed, there are two fixed cost variances commonly investigated by management. One is called a *fixed cost spending variance;* the other is called a *fixed cost volume variance.*

Fixed Cost Spending Variance

Companies frequently pay more or less than expected for fixed costs. For example, a supervisor may receive an unplanned raise, causing actual salary cost to be more than the amount budgeted. The difference between the *actual fixed cost* and the *budgeted fixed cost* (amount shown in the static budget) is called a **fixed cost spending variance.** The *fixed cost spending variance* for Melrose is \$3,400 (\$295,000 actual fixed cost – \$291,600 budgeted fixed cost). Since actual fixed costs are higher than the budgeted fixed cost, the variance is unfavorable. In other words, the company had to pay more than it expected for the fixed costs.

In the Melrose case, there is no way to know who is responsible for the \$3,400 unfavorable fixed cost spending variance because all of the costs have been pooled together. To promote accountability, fixed costs that are controllable by a specific manager must be disaggregated and tagged for individual analysis. For example, the plant manager may control the assistant manager's salary cost. If a fixed cost spending variance is associated with the salary cost, the plant manager is responsible for explaining why the variance occurred. Other managers will be held accountable for the specific fixed costs they control.

Uncontrollable fixed costs should also be reported for management oversight. Even if these costs are not controllable in the short term, management should stay abreast of them because they may be controllable in the long term.

Fixed Cost Volume Variance

Companies frequently need to know the cost of something before the actual cost can be determined. For example, a company may base its selling price on the cost of making and selling a product. Even so, the actual cost of making and selling the product may not be known until after the product has been sold. In order to price the product, the company will be required to use estimated costs rather than actual costs. Likewise, it may be necessary to use estimated costs to prepare quarterly financial statements because the actual cost will not be known until after the quarterly statements have been published. To solve such problems, accountants frequently estimate the total annual cost and then apply (allocate) a portion of the estimated annual cost to the products as they are made and sold.

To illustrate, assume that Melrose develops an allocation rate based on its budgeted fixed cost and the planned volume of production shown as follows:

Budgeted fixed cost	÷	Planned volume of activity	=	Allocation rate
$291,600	÷	18,000 units	=	$16.20 per unit

As production proceeds, Melrose would apply $16.20 to the appropriate accounts each time an actual unit of product (trophy) is made and sold. Since the allocation rate is determined *before* the actual cost and volume are known, it is frequently called the *predetermined* allocation rate. Since fixed costs are frequently classified as overhead costs, this rate is more frequently called the predetermined *overhead* rate. In summary, the **predetermined overhead rate** is calculated as follows:

$$\text{Predetermined overhead rate} = \frac{\text{Budgeted fixed cost from the static budget}}{\text{Planned volume of activity}}$$

The total cost determined by multiplying the *predetermined overhead rate* times the *actual volume* of production is called the **applied fixed cost.** Given that Melrose produced and sold 19,000 units of product during Year 1, the amount of applied fixed cost is $307,800 ($16.20 × 19,000 units).

The difference between the *applied fixed cost based on actual volume* and the *budgeted fixed cost based on planned volume* is called the **fixed cost volume variance.** In this case, Melrose has a fixed cost volume variance of $16,200 ($307,800 applied fixed cost − $291,600 budgeted fixed cost).

To interpret the fixed cost volume variance, consider the effect that volume changes have on the behavior of fixed cost per unit. As volume increases, fixed cost per unit decreases. In this case, the planned volume was 18,000 units and the actual volume was 19,000 units. Since the higher than expected volume decreases the fixed cost per unit, the volume variance is *favorable.* An *unfavorable* fixed cost volume variance occurs when actual volume is less than planned volume, a condition that increases fixed costs per unit.

The fixed cost volume variance is a measure of facility utilization. If the fixed cost volume variance is unfavorable, the facilities are considered to be underutilized. This is just another way of saying that the company suffered an unfavorable variance because it did not utilize its facilities to make and sell the number of units of product it had planned to make and sell. A favorable fixed cost volume variance suggests that a company utilized its facilities to make and sell *more* than the planned volume of activity. In summary, a fixed cost volume variance indicates over- or underutilization of facilities, not over- or underspending.

For your convenience, the two fixed cost overhead variances are summarized as follows.

1. Fixed cost spending variance = Actual fixed cost − Budgeted fixed cost

   If actual costs are less than the budgeted costs, the variance is favorable.

   If actual costs are greater than the budgeted costs, the variance is unfavorable.

2. Fixed cost volume variance = Applied fixed cost based on actual volume − Budgeted fixed cost based on planned volume

   If actual volume is more than the planned volume, the variance is favorable.

   If actual volume is less than the planned volume, the variance is unfavorable.

Fixed Cost Volume Variance and Product Pricing

Changes in the fixed cost per unit have important implications for decision making. For example, consider the impact on cost-plus pricing decisions. Because the actual volume is unknown until the end of the accounting period, selling prices must be based on planned volume. Recall that at the planned volume of activity, Melrose's predetermined overhead rate is $16.20 ($291,600 ÷ 18,000 units). Compare this figure with the rate based on actual volume, which is $15.35 ($291,600 ÷ 19,000 units). Since the price of the product was based on the predetermined overhead rate ($16.20), instead of the rate based on actual volume ($15.35), the product was overpriced. It follows that if actual volume is less than planned volume, products will be underpriced.

Overpricing can be problematic because it encourages competitors to enter the market. Eventually, these competitors will draw customers away from Melrose by offering lower prices. As Melrose loses customers, its actual fixed cost per unit increases, thereby exacerbating the pricing problem. Underpricing (not encountered by Melrose in this example) can also be detrimental. If planned volume is overstated, the predetermined overhead rate will be understated and prices will be set too low. When the higher amount of actual costs is eventually subtracted from revenues, actual profits will be lower than expected. As this discussion demonstrates, over- or understating the planned volume will cause pricing problems. It is critically important to be as accurate as possible when establishing the planned volume.

Responsibility for the Fixed Cost Volume Variance

Normally, upper-level marketing managers are held accountable for the fixed cost volume variance because they control the volume of sales, which in turn dictates the volume of production. Even so, other possibilities must be considered. For example, goods may not sell because they are poorly constructed, which may be the fault of design engineers or production managers. Likewise, buyers may be at fault for purchasing undesirable products that are difficult to resell. In this case, the purchasing department rather than the marketing department would be responsible for the fixed cost volume variance. Determining the amount of the variance is the easy part of performance evaluation; determining responsibility is usually more difficult.

STANDARD COST SYSTEMS

LO 8-6

Describe the features of a standard cost system and compute price and usage variances.

Standard cost systems help managers plan and also establish benchmarks against which actual performance can be judged. By highlighting differences between standard (expected) and actual performance, standard costing focuses management attention on the areas of greatest need. Because management talent is a valuable and expensive resource, businesses cannot afford to have managers spend large amounts of time on operations that are functioning normally. Instead, managers should concentrate on areas not performing as expected. In other words, management should attend to the exceptions; this management philosophy is known as **management by exception.**

Standard costing fosters using the management by exception principle. By reviewing performance reports that show differences between actual and standard costs, management can focus its attention on the items that show significant variances. Areas with only minor variances need little or no review.

Establishing Standards

Establishing standards is probably the most difficult part of using a standard cost system. A **standard** represents the amount that a price, cost, or quantity *should be* under certain anticipated circumstances. Consider the complexity of establishing the standard cost to produce a pair of blue jeans. Among other things, managers need to know where they can get the best price for materials, who will pay transportation costs, if cash or volume discounts are available, whether the suppliers with the lowest price can reliably supply the quantities needed on a timely basis, how the material should be cut to conserve time and labor, in what order to sew pieces of material together, the wage rates of the relevant production employees, whether overtime will be needed, and how many pairs of jeans will be produced. Obtaining this information requires the combined experience, judgment, and forecasting ability of all personnel who have responsibility for price and usage decisions. Even when a multitalented group of experienced persons is involved in standard setting, the process involves much trial and error. Revising standards is common even with established systems.

©Monty Rakusen/Corbis

Historical data provide a good starting point for establishing standards. These data must be updated for changes in technology, plant layout, new methods of production, and worker productivity. Frequently, changes of this nature result from initiating a standard cost system. Remember that a *standard* represents what *should be* rather than what *is* or *was*. Engineers often help establish standards, recommending the most efficient way to perform required tasks. The engineers undertake time and motion studies and review material utilization in the process of developing standards. Established practices and policies are frequently changed in response to engineers' reports.

Management must consider behavioral implications when developing standards. Managers, supervisors, purchasing agents, and other affected employees should be consulted for two reasons: (1) Their experience and expertise provide invaluable input to standard development, and (2) persons who are involved in standard setting are more likely to accept and be motivated to reach the resulting standards. Management should also consider how difficult it should be to achieve standard performance. Difficulty levels can be described as follows: (1) ideal standards, (2) practical standards, and (3) lax standards.

Ideal standards represent flawless performance; they represent what costs should be under the best possible circumstances. They do not allow for normal materials waste and spoilage or ordinary labor inefficiencies caused by machine downtime, cleanups, breaks, or personal needs. Meeting ideal standards is beyond the capabilities of most, if not all, employees. Ideal standards may motivate some individuals to constantly strive for improvement, but unattainable standards discourage most people. When people consistently fail, they become demotivated and stop trying to succeed. In addition, variances associated with ideal standards lose significance. They reflect deviations that are largely beyond employees' control, and they mask true measures of superior or inferior performance, considerably reducing their usefulness.

Practical standards represent reasonable effort; they are attainable for most employees. Practical standards allow for normal levels of inefficiency in materials and labor usage. An average worker performing diligently would be able to achieve standard performance. Practical standards motivate most employees; the feeling of accomplishment attained through earnest effort encourages employees to do their best. Practical standards also produce meaningful variances. Deviations from practical standards usually result from factors employees control. Positive variances normally represent superior performance, and negative variances indicate inferior performance.

Lax standards represent easily attainable goals. Employees can achieve standard performance with minimal effort. Lax standards do not motivate most people; continual success with minimal effort leads to boredom and lackluster performance. In addition, variances lose meaning. Deviations caused by superior or inferior performance are obscured by the built-in slack.

Management must consider employee ability levels when establishing standards. Standards that seasoned workers can attain may represent ideal standards to inexperienced workers. Management should routinely monitor standards and adjust them when it is appropriate to do so.

Selecting Variances to Investigate

Managerial judgment, developed through experience, plays a significant role in deciding which variances to investigate. Managers consider the *materiality* of a variance, the *frequency* with which it occurs, their *capacity to control* the variance, and the *characteristics* of the items behind the variance.

Standard costs are estimates. They cannot perfectly predict actual costs. Most businesses experience minor variances as part of normal operations. Investigating minor variances is not likely to produce useful information. Many companies therefore establish *materiality* guidelines for selecting variances to analyze. They set dollar or percentage thresholds and ignore variances that fall below these limits, investigating material variances only. A **material variance** is one that could influence management decisions. Material variances should be investigated whether they are favorable or unfavorable. As mentioned earlier, a favorable price variance can result from purchasing substandard materials; the quality of the company's products, however, will suffer from the inferior materials and sales will fall.

How *frequently* a variance occurs impacts materiality. A variance of $20,000 may be immaterial in a single month, but if the same variance occurs repeatedly throughout the year, it can become a material $240,000 variance. Variance reports should highlight frequent as well as large variations.

Capacity to control refers to whether management action can influence the variance. If utility rates cause differences between actual and standard overhead costs, management has little control over the resulting variances. Conversely, if actual labor costs exceed standard costs because a supervisor fails to motivate employees, management can take some action. To maximize their value to the firm, managers should concentrate on controllable variances.

The *characteristics* of the items behind the variance may invite management abuse. For example, managers can reduce actual costs in the short term by delaying expenditures for maintenance, research and development, and advertising. Although cost reductions in these areas may produce favorable variances in the current period, they will have a long-term detrimental impact on profitability. Managers under stress may be tempted to focus on short-term benefits. Variances associated with these critical items should be closely analyzed.

The primary advantage of a standard cost system is efficient use of management talent to control costs. Secondary benefits include the following:

1. Standard cost systems quickly alert management to trouble spots. For example, a standard amount of materials may be issued for a particular job. If requisitions of additional materials require supervisory approval, each time a supervisor must grant such approval, she is immediately aware that excess materials are being used and can act before excessive material usage becomes unmanageable.
2. If established and maintained properly, standard cost systems can boost morale and motivate employees. Reward systems can be linked to accomplishments that exceed the established performance standards. Under such circumstances, employees become extremely conscious of the time and materials they use, minimizing waste and reducing costs.
3. Standard cost systems encourage good planning. The failure to plan well leads to overbuying, excessive inventory, wasted time, and so on. A standard cost system forces managers to plan, resulting in more effective operations with less waste.

Answers to the Curious Accountant

As this chapter demonstrates, there are two primary reasons a company spends more or less to produce a product than it estimated. First, the company may have paid more or less than estimated to purchase the inputs needed to produce the product. Second, the company may have used a greater or lesser quantity of these inputs than expected. In the case of Gourmet Pizzas, it may have had to pay more for flour, yeast, sugar, etc., than the owner estimated. Or, it may have used more flour, yeast, sugar, etc., than expected. For example, if pizza dough sits around too long before being used, it may have to be thrown out. This waste was not anticipated when computing the cost to make only one pizza. Of course, the higher than expected cost could have been a combination of price and quantity factors.

Gourmet Pizzas needs to determine if the difference between its expected costs and actual costs was because the estimates were faulty or because the production process was inefficient. If the estimates were to blame, the owner needs to revise them so he can charge customers the proper price. If the production process is inefficient, he needs to correct it if he is to earn an acceptable level of profit.

Avoiding Gamesmanship

In general, variances should not be used to praise or punish managers. The purpose of identifying variances is to help management improve efficiency and productivity. If variances are used to assign rewards and blame, managers are likely to respond by withholding or manipulating information. For example, a manager might manipulate the cost standard for a job by deliberately overstating the amount of materials or labor needed to complete it. The manager's performance will later appear positive when the actual cost of materials or labor is less than the inflated standard. This practice is so common it has a name: **Budget slack** is the difference between inflated and realistic standards. Sales staff may play a game called *lowballing* in which they deliberately underestimate the amount of expected sales, anticipating a reward when actual sales subsequently exceed the budget.

Gamesmanship can be reduced if superiors and subordinates participate sincerely in setting mutually agreeable, attainable standards. Once standards are established, the evaluation system that uses them must promote long-term respect among superiors and their subordinates. If standards are used solely for punitive purposes, gamesmanship will rapidly degrade the standard costing system.

PRICE AND USAGE VARIANCES

Under a standard cost system, it is common practice to subdivide the *flexible budget variances* into component parts that more clearly define the cause of these variances. For example, a favorable flexible budget materials cost variance may be the result of paying less than expected for the materials or of using fewer materials than expected, or some combination of *price* and *usage variances*. To demonstrate, we return to the Melrose Manufacturing Company case that was introduced earlier in the chapter.

We will limit our discussion to the flexible budget variable manufacturing cost variances shown in Exhibit 8.3. Specifically, there are three of these variances, including:

1. Flexible budget materials cost variance: $4,180 Favorable.
2. Flexible budget labor cost variance: $8,550 Unfavorable.
3. Flexible budget variable overhead cost variance: $2,850 Unfavorable.

Recall that these variances were calculated by determining the difference between the flexible budget costs (standard cost per unit times the actual volume) and the actual costs (actual cost per unit times the actual volume). The standard and actual per-unit costs for Melrose were shown previously and are repeated here for your convenience.

	Standard	Actual
Variable materials cost per unit of product	$12.00	$11.78
Variable labor cost per unit of product	16.80	17.25
Variable overhead cost per unit of product	5.60	5.75

Using the cost per unit data, the flexible budget manufacturing cost variances can be determined algebraically as shown in Exhibit 8.4. We suggest that you compare the variances shown in the two exhibits to confirm that the algebraic approach in Exhibit 8.4 yields the same result as the variances previously computed in Exhibit 8.3.

EXHIBIT 8.4

Flexible Budget Variances Calculated Algebraically

Variable Manufacturing Costs	Actual Cost *per Unit* of Product	−	Standard Cost *per Unit* of Product	×	Actual Units	=	Flexible Budget Variance
Materials	| $11.78	−	$12.00 |	×	19,000	=	$4,180 Favorable
Labor	| 17.25	−	16.80 |	×	19,000	=	8,550 Unfavorable
Overhead	| 5.75	−	5.60 |	×	19,000	=	2,850 Unfavorable

Note that the difference between the actual and standard cost is expressed as an absolute value (expressed by the use of bars around the values). This mathematical notation suggests that the mathematical sign is not useful in interpreting the condition of the variance. To assess the condition of a variance, you must consider the type of variance being analyzed. With respect to cost variances, managers seek to attain actual prices that are lower than standard prices. In this case, the actual price of materials is less than the standard price, so the materials variance is favorable. Since the actual prices for labor and overhead are higher than the standard prices, those variances are unfavorable.

For insight into what caused the flexible budget variances, a separate price and usage variance can be computed for each of the total flexible budget variances. We begin with the $4,180 favorable flexible budget materials cost variance. This variance indicates that Melrose spent less than expected on materials to make 19,000 trophies. Why? The price per unit of material may have been less than expected (price variance), or the company may have used less material than expected (usage variance). To determine what caused the total favorable variance, Melrose must separate the cost per unit of product into two parts, price per unit of material and quantity of material used.

Calculating Materials Price and Usage Variances

Melrose's accounting records indicate the materials cost per unit of product (trophy) is as follows.

	Actual Data	Standard Data
Price ***per pound*** of material	$ 1.90	$ 2.00
Quantity of materials per unit of product	× 6.2 pounds	× 6.0 pounds
Cost ***per unit*** of product	$11.78	$12.00

Based on this detail, the total quantity of materials is:

	Actual Data	Standard Data
Actual production volume	19,000 units	19,000 units
Quantity of materials per unit of product	× 6.2 pounds	× 6.0 pounds
Total quantity of materials	117,800 pounds	114,000 pounds

Confirm the price and usage components that make up the total flexible budget materials variance, as follows.

Actual Cost		Standard Cost	
Actual quantity used	117,800	Standard quantity	114,000
×	×	×	×
Actual price per pound	$1.90	Standard price per pound	$2.00
	$223,820		$228,000
Total variance: $4,180 Favorable			

To isolate the price and usage variances, insert a Variance Dividing column between the Actual Cost and Standard Cost columns. The Variance Dividing column combines standard and actual data, showing the *standard cost* multiplied by the *actual quantity* of materials purchased and used.[1] Exhibit 8.5 shows the result.

EXHIBIT 8.5

Materials Price and Usage Variances

Actual Cost		Variance Dividing Data		Standard Cost	
Actual quantity used	117,800	Actual quantity used	117,800	Standard quantity	114,000
×	×	×	×	×	×
Actual price per pound	$1.90	Standard price per pound	$2.00	Standard price per pound	$2.00
	$223,820		$235,600		$228,000
Materials price variance $11,780 Favorable				Materials usage variance $7,600 Unfavorable	
Total variance: $4,180 Favorable					

Algebraic Solution

The materials price variance (difference between the Actual Cost column and the Variance Dividing column) can be computed algebraically as follows:

$$\begin{aligned}\text{Price variance} &= |\text{Actual price} - \text{Standard price}| \times \text{Actual quantity} \\ &= |\$1.90 - \$2.00| \times 117{,}800 \\ &= \$0.10 \times 117{,}800 \\ &= \$11{,}780 \text{ Favorable}\end{aligned}$$

[1]In practice, raw materials are frequently stored in inventory prior to use. Differences may exist between the amount of materials purchased and the amount of materials used. In such cases, the price variance is based on the quantity of materials *purchased,* and the usage variance is based on the quantity of materials *used.* This text makes the simplifying assumption that the amount of materials purchased equals the amount of materials used during the period.

Since the actual price ($1.90) is less than the standard price ($2.00), the materials price variance is favorable.

The materials usage variance (difference between the Variance Dividing column and the Standard Cost column) also can be determined algebraically, as follows:

$$\begin{aligned}\text{Usage variance} &= |\text{Actual quantity} - \text{Standard quantity}| \times \text{Standard price}\\ &= |117{,}800 - 114{,}000| \times \$2.00\\ &= 3{,}800 \times \$2.00\\ &= \$7{,}600 \text{ Unfavorable}\end{aligned}$$

Responsibility for Materials Variances

A purchasing agent is normally responsible for the **materials price variance.** Management establishes the standard materials cost based on a particular grade of material and assumptions about purchasing terms, including volume discounts, cash discounts, transportation costs, and supplier services. A diligent purchasing agent places orders that take advantage of positive trading terms. In such circumstances, the company pays less than standard costs, resulting in a favorable price variance. Investigating the favorable price variance could result in identifying purchasing strategies to share with other purchasing agents. Analyzing favorable as well as unfavorable variances can result in efficiencies that benefit the entire production process.

In spite of a purchasing agent's diligence, unfavorable price variances may still occur. Suppliers may raise prices, poor scheduling by the production department may require more costly rush orders, or a truckers' strike may force the company to use a more expensive delivery system. These conditions are beyond a purchasing agent's control. Management must be careful to identify the real causes of unfavorable variances. False accusations and overreactions lead to resentment that will undermine the productive potential of the standard costing system.

REALITY BYTES

©Alexander Tolstykh/Shutterstock

Most airlines will allow customers to book a flight approximately one year in advance at a price set on the day the reservation is made. Since the airline does not know what it will actually cost to operate a particular flight a year in advance, the price of the ticket will be based on its estimated costs. This can present a problem if costs rise significantly before the flight occurs.

Imagine that on January 10, 2017, George Doggett booked a flight from Atlanta to San Diego for December 22, 2017, in order to spend Christmas with his daughter and her family and that the ticket price was $627. Between January and December 2017, many of the airline's costs would not change unexpectedly; for example, the airplane has already been purchased and the salaries of the flight crew have already been set. However, in 2016 approximately 20 percent of the cost of operating an airline was for fuel; two years earlier it had been 33 percent. In January 2017, the spot price of jet fuel was $1.53 per gallon. The spot price of a commodity is the price it would sell for on a given day to someone who had not placed an advance order at a set price. By December 2017, the spot price for jet fuel had risen to $1.83 per gallon. In standard costing terminology, this would result in an unfavorable price variance. Of course, fuel prices can also rapidly change for the better. Between January 2015 and December 2015, the price of jet fuel went from $1.50 down to $1.00 per gallon.

How can companies avoid some of the problems of having to set the prices they charge before they know what it will cost them to deliver the promised goods or services? Sometimes they cannot, but jet fuel prices can be hedged. That is, a company can commit to purchase fuel at an agreed-upon price at a future date. As of December 2016, Southwest Airlines had already contracted to buy 63 percent of its 2017 fuel needs and 57 percent of its 2018 fuel needs.

Hedging has its own risks. When fuel prices drop, the airline will still have to honor its commitments to buy some of its fuel at a price higher than the spot price.

Sources: Federal government data and the companies' annual reports.

The nature of the **materials usage variance** is readily apparent from the quantity data. Because the actual quantity used was more than the standard quantity, the variance is unfavorable. If management seeks to minimize cost, using more materials than expected is unfavorable. The materials usage variance is largely controlled by the production department. Materials waste caused by inexperienced workers, faulty machinery, negligent processing, or poor planning results in unfavorable usage variances. Unfavorable variances may also be caused by factors beyond the control of the production department. If the purchasing agent buys substandard materials, the inferior materials may lead to more scrap (waste) during production, which would be reflected in unfavorable usage variances.

Calculating Labor Variances

Labor variances are calculated using the same general formulas as those used to compute materials price and usage variances. To illustrate, assume the labor cost per unit of product (trophy) for Melrose Manufacturing is as follows.

	Actual Data	Standard Data
Price ***per hour***	$11.50	$12.00
Quantity of labor per unit of product	× 1.5 hours	× 1.4 hours
Cost ***per unit*** of product	$17.25	$16.80

Based on this detail, the total quantity of labor is:

	Actual Data	Standard Data
Actual production volume	19,000 units	19,000 units
Quantity of labor per unit of product	× 1.5 hours	× 1.4 hours
Total quantity of labor	28,500 hours	26,600 hours

Using this cost and quantity information, the labor price and usage variances are computed in Exhibit 8.6.

EXHIBIT 8.6

Labor Price and Usage Variances

Actual Cost		Variance Dividing Data		Standard Cost	
Actual hours used	28,500	Actual hours used (AHrs)	28,500	Standard hours (SHrs)	26,600
×	×	×	×	×	×
Actual price per labor hour (AP)	$11.50	Standard price per labor hour (SP)	$12.00	Standard price per labor hour	$12.00
	$327,750		$342,000		$319,200

Labor price variance
$14,250 Favorable

Labor usage variance
$22,800 Unfavorable

Algebraic solution: |AP − SP| × AHrs
|$11.50 − $12.00| × 28,500 = $14,250

Algebraic solution: |AHrs − SHrs| × SP
|28,500 − 26,600| × $12.00 = $22,800

Total variance: $8,550 Unfavorable

Responsibility for Labor Variances

The **labor price variance** is favorable because the actual rate paid for labor is less than the standard rate. The production supervisor is usually responsible for the labor price variance because price variances normally result from labor assignments rather than underpayment or overpayment of the hourly rate. Because labor costs are usually fixed by contracts, paying more or less than established rates is not likely. However, using semiskilled labor to perform highly skilled tasks or vice versa will produce price variances. Similarly, using unanticipated overtime will cause unfavorable variances. Production department supervisors control which workers are assigned to which tasks and are therefore accountable for the resulting labor price variances.

Labor usage variances measure the productivity of the labor force. Because Melrose used more labor than expected, the labor usage variance is unfavorable. Unsatisfactory labor performance has many causes; low morale or poor supervision are possibilities. Furthermore, machine breakdowns, inferior materials, and poor planning can waste workers' time and reduce productivity. Production department supervisors generally control and are responsible for labor usage variances.

Price and usage variances may be interrelated. Using less-skilled employees who earned less but took longer to do the work could have caused both the favorable labor price variance and the unfavorable labor usage variance. As mentioned earlier, management must exercise diligence in determining causes of variances before concluding who should be held responsible for them.

☑ CHECK YOURSELF 8.3

DogHouse Inc. expected to build 200 doghouses during July. Each doghouse was expected to require 2 hours of direct labor. Labor cost was expected to be $10 per hour. The company actually built 220 doghouses using an average of 2.1 labor hours per doghouse at an actual labor rate averaging $9.80 per hour. Determine the labor rate and usage variances.

Answer

Labor price variance = |Actual rate − Standard rate| × Actual quantity

Labor price variance = |\$9.80 − \$10.00| × (220 units × 2.1 hours) = \$92.40 Favorable

Labor usage variance = |Actual quantity − Standard quantity| × Standard rate

Labor price variance = |(220 × 2.1) − (220 × 2.0)| × \$10.00 = \$220.00 Unfavorable

REALITY BYTES

Does standard costing apply to service companies as well as manufacturers? Absolutely! If you take your car into an auto dealership to be repaired and the service invoice shows that the repair took one hour to perform, you should not assume that was the actual time the repair required. The time for which you were charged was probably based on the standard time a repair of that type should have taken. The mechanic may have gotten this standard time from a reference manual such as the *Chilton Labor Guide* or the *Real-Time Labor Guide,* which are available in either print or CD versions. Some repair jobs can be completed in less time than the guides suggest, and some jobs will take longer. But since customers are charged based on a standard time allowed, two customers having the same repair performed will be charged the same price.

©Clerkenwell/Getty Images

Variable Overhead Variances

Variable overhead variances are based on the same general formulas used to compute the materials and labor price and usage variances. Unique characteristics of variable overhead costs, however, require special attention. First, variable overhead represents many inputs such as supplies, utilities, and indirect labor. The variable overhead cost pool is normally assigned to products based on a predetermined variable overhead allocation rate. Using a single rate to assign a mixture of different costs complicates variance interpretation. Suppose the actual variable overhead rate is higher than the predetermined rate. Did the company pay more than expected for supplies, utilities, maintenance, or some other input variable? The cost of some variable overhead items may have been higher than expected while others were lower than expected. Similarly, a variable overhead usage variance provides no clue about which overhead inputs were over- or underused. Because meaningful interpretation of the results is difficult, many companies do not calculate price and usage variances for variable overhead costs. We therefore limit coverage of this subject to the total flexible budget variances shown in Exhibit 8.3.

Selling, General, and Administrative Cost Variances

Variable selling, general, and administrative (SG&A) costs can have *price and usage* variances. For example, suppose Melrose decides to attach a promotional advertising brochure to each trophy it sells. Melrose may pay more or less than expected for each brochure (a price variance). Melrose also could use more or fewer of the brochures than expected (a usage variance). Businesses frequently compute variances for SG&A costs such as sales commissions, food and entertainment, postage, and supplies. The same algebraic formulas used to compute variances for variable manufacturing costs apply to computing variable SG&A cost variances.

For your convenience, the general formulas for determining price and usage variances are shown in Exhibit 8.7.

EXHIBIT 8.7

Algebraic Formulas for Variances

Variable cost variances (materials, labor, and overhead)

a. Price variance

|Actual price − Standard price| × Actual quantity

b. Usage variance

|Actual quantity − Standard quantity| × Standard price

<< A Look Back

The essential topics of this chapter are the master budget, flexible budgets, and variance analysis. The *master budget* is determined by multiplying the standard sales price and per unit variable costs by the planned volume of activity. The master budget is prepared at the beginning of the accounting period for planning purposes. It is not adjusted to reflect differences between the planned and actual volume of activity. Since this budget remains unchanged regardless of actual volume, it is also called a *static budget. Flexible budgets* differ from static budgets in that they show the estimated amount of revenue and costs expected at different levels of volume. Both static and flexible budgets are based on the same per unit standard amounts and the same fixed costs. The total amounts of revenue and costs in a static budget differ from those in a flexible budget because they are based on different levels of volume. Flexible budgets are used for planning, cost control, and performance evaluation.

The differences between standard (sometimes called *expected* or *estimated*) and actual amounts are called *variances*. Variances are used to evaluate managerial performance and can be either favorable or unfavorable. *Favorable sales variances* occur when actual sales are greater than expected sales. *Unfavorable sales variances* occur when actual sales are less than expected sales. *Favorable cost variances* occur when actual costs are less than expected costs. *Unfavorable cost variances* occur when actual costs are more than expected costs.

Volume variances are caused by the difference between the static and flexible budgets. Since both static and flexible budgets are based on the same standard sales price and costs per unit, the volume variances are attributable solely to differences between the planned and the actual volume of activity. Favorable sales volume variances suggest that the marketing manager has performed well by selling more than was expected. Unfavorable sales volume variances suggest the inverse. Favorable or unfavorable variable cost volume variances are not meaningful for performance evaluation because variable costs are expected to change in proportion to changes in the volume of activity.

Flexible budget variances are computed by taking the difference between the amounts of revenue and variable costs that are expected at the actual volume of activity and the actual amounts of revenue and variable costs incurred at the actual volume of activity. Since the volume of activity is the same for the flexible budget and the actual results, variances are caused by the differences between the standard and actual sales price and per-unit costs. Flexible budget variances are used for cost control and performance evaluation.

The total fixed cost variance is composed of the following:

a. **Fixed manufacturing overhead cost spending variance**

$$|\text{Actual fixed overhead costs} - \text{Budgeted fixed overhead}|$$

b. **Fixed manufacturing overhead cost volume variance**

$$|\text{Applied fixed overhead costs} - \text{Budgeted fixed overhead costs}|$$

The fixed overhead spending variance occurs because actual costs may be more or less than expected. For example, a production supervisor's salary will remain unchanged regardless of the volume of activity, but the supervisor may receive a raise resulting in higher than expected fixed costs. The fixed overhead volume variance is favorable if the actual volume of production is greater than the expected volume. A higher volume of production results in a lower fixed cost per unit. The volume variance measures how effectively production facilities are being used.

Flexible budget variances can be subdivided into *price and usage variances*. Price and usage variances for materials and labor can be computed with the following formulas. Variable overhead variances are calculated with the same general formulas; interpreting the results is difficult, however, because of the variety of inputs combined in variable overhead.

$$\text{Price variance} = |\text{Actual price} - \text{Standard price}| \times \text{Actual quantity}$$

$$\text{Usage variance} = |\text{Actual quantity} - \text{Standard quantity}| \times \text{Standard price}$$

The purchasing agent is normally accountable for the materials price variance. The production department supervisor is usually responsible for the materials usage variance and the labor price and usage variances.

Management must interpret variances with care. For example, a purchasing agent may produce a favorable price variance by buying inferior materials at a low cost. However, an unfavorable labor usage variance may result because employees have difficulty using the substandard materials. The production supervisor is faced with an unfavorable usage variance for which she is not responsible. In addition, the purchasing agent's undesirable choice produced a favorable price variance. Favorable variances do not necessarily reflect good performance and unfavorable variances do not always suggest poor performance. The underlying causes of variances must be investigated before assigning responsibility for them.

>> A Look Forward

Chapter 9 introduces other techniques for evaluating managerial performance. The concept of decentralization and its relationship to responsibility accounting will be covered. You will learn how to calculate and interpret return on investment and residual income. Finally, you will study approaches used to establish the price of products that are transferred between divisions of the same company.

Video lectures and accompanying self-assessment quizzes are available in *Connect* for all learning objectives.

SELF-STUDY REVIEW PROBLEM

Bugout Pesticides Inc. established the following standard price and costs for a termite control product that it sells to exterminators.

Variable price and cost data (per unit)	Standard	Actual
Sales price	$52.00	$49.00
Materials cost	10.00	10.66
Labor cost	12.00	11.90
Overhead cost	7.00	7.05
Selling, general, and administrative (SG&A) cost	8.00	7.92
Expected fixed costs (in total)		
Manufacturing overhead	$150,000	$140,000
Selling, general, and administrative	60,000	64,000

The Year 1 master budget was established at an expected volume of 25,000 units. Actual production and sales volume for the year was 26,000 units.

Required

a. Prepare the pro forma income statement for Bugout's Year 1 master budget.

b. Prepare a flexible budget income statement at the actual volume.

c. Determine the sales and variable cost volume variances and indicate whether they are favorable or unfavorable. Comment on how Bugout would use the variances to evaluate performance.

d. Determine the flexible budget variances and indicate whether they are favorable or unfavorable. Provide another name for the fixed cost flexible budget variances.

e. Identify the two variances Bugout is most likely to analyze further. Explain why you chose these two variances. Who is normally responsible for the variances you chose to investigate?

f. Each unit of product was expected to require 4 pounds of material, which has a standard price of $2.50 per pound. Actual materials usage was 4.1 pounds per unit at an actual price of $2.60 per pound. Determine the materials price and usage variances.

Solution to Requirements *a*, *b*, and *c*

Number of Units		25,000	26,000	
	Per Unit Standards	Master Budget	Flexible Budget	Volume Variances
Sales revenue	$52	$1,300,000	$1,352,000	$52,000 F
Variable manufacturing costs				
Materials	10	250,000	260,000	10,000 U
Labor	12	300,000	312,000	12,000 U
Overhead	7	175,000	182,000	7,000 U
Variable SG&A	8	200,000	208,000	8,000 U
Contribution margin		375,000	390,000	15,000 F
Fixed costs				
Manufacturing overhead		150,000	150,000	0
SG&A		60,000	60,000	0
Net income		$ 165,000	$ 180,000	$15,000 F

The sales and variable cost volume variances are useful in determining how changes in sales volume affect revenues and costs. Since the flexible budget is based on standard prices and costs, the variances do not provide insight into differences between standard prices and costs versus actual prices and costs.

Solution to Requirement *d*

Number of Units		26,000	26,000	
	Actual Unit Price/Cost	Flexible Budget*	Actual Results	Flexible Budget Variances
Sales revenue	$49.00	$1,352,000	$1,274,000	$78,000 U
Variable manufacturing costs				
Materials	10.66	260,000	277,160	17,160 U
Labor	11.90	312,000	309,400	2,600 F
Overhead	7.05	182,000	183,300	1,300 U
Variable SG&A	7.92	208,000	205,920	2,080 F
Contribution margin		390,000	298,220	91,780 U
Fixed costs				
Manufacturing overhead		150,000	140,000	10,000 F†
SG&A		60,000	64,000	4,000 U†
Net income		$ 180,000	$ 94,220	$85,780 U

*The price and cost data for the flexible budget come from the table shown at the beginning of the problem.

†The flexible budget variances for the fixed costs are also called *spending variances*.

Solution to Requirement *e*

The management by exception doctrine focuses attention on the sales price variance and the materials variance. The two variances are material in size and are generally under the control of management. Upper-level marketing managers are responsible for the sales price variance. These managers are normally responsible for establishing the sales price. In this case, the actual sales price is less than the planned sales price, resulting in an unfavorable flexible budget variance. Mid-level production supervisors and purchasing agents are normally responsible for the materials cost variance. This variance could have been caused by waste or by paying more for materials than the standard price. Further analysis of the materials cost variance follows in Requirement *f*.

Solution to Requirement *f*

|Actual price − Standard price| ×	Actual quantity	= Price variance
|$2.60 − $2.50|	× (4.1 pounds × 26,000 units) =	$10,660 U

|Actual quantity − Standard quantity| ×	Standard price	= Usage variance
|(4.1 × 26,000) − (4.0 × 26,000)| ×	$2.50	= $6,500 U

The total of the price and usage variances [($10,660 + $6,500) = $17,160] equals the total materials flexible budget variance computed in Requirement *d.*

KEY TERMS

Applied fixed cost 358
Budget slack 362
Fixed cost spending variance 357
Fixed cost volume variance 358
Flexible budget 352
Flexible budget variance 356
Ideal standard 360
Labor price variance 367
Labor usage variance 367
Lax standard 360
Making the numbers 354
Management by exception 359
Material variance 361
Materials price variance 365
Materials usage variance 366
Practical standard 360
Predetermined overhead rate 358
Sales price variance 356
Sales volume variance 354
Standard 360
Static budget 352
Variable cost volume variance 354
Variances 353

QUESTIONS

1. What is the difference between a static budget and a flexible budget? When is each used?
2. When the operating costs for Bill Smith's production department were released, he was sure that he would be getting a raise. His costs were $20,000 less than the planned cost in the master budget. His supervisor informed him that the results look good but that a more in-depth analysis is necessary before raises can be assigned. What other considerations could Mr. Smith's supervisor be interested in before she rates his performance?
3. When are sales and cost variances favorable and unfavorable?
4. Joan Mason, the marketing manager for a large manufacturing company, believes her unfavorable sales volume variance is the responsibility of the production department. What production circumstances that she does not control could have been responsible for the unfavorable variance?
5. When would variable cost volume variances be expected to be unfavorable? How should unfavorable variable cost volume variances be interpreted?
6. What factors could lead to an increase in sales revenues that would not merit congratulations to the marketing manager?
7. With respect to fixed costs, what are the consequences of the actual volume of activity exceeding the planned volume?
8. How are flexible budget variances determined? What causes these variances?
9. Minnie Divers, the manager of the marketing department for one of the industry's leading retail businesses, has been notified by the accounting department that her department experienced an unfavorable sales volume variance in the preceding period but a favorable sales price variance. Based on these contradictory results, how would you interpret her overall performance as suggested by her variances?
10. What three attributes are necessary for establishing the best standards? What information and considerations should be taken into account when establishing standards?
11. What are the three ranges of difficulty in standard setting? What level of difficulty normally results in superior employee motivation?
12. "So many variances," exclaimed Carl, a production manager with Bonnyville Manufacturing. "How do I determine the variances that need investigation? I can't possibly investigate all of them." Which variances will lead to useful information?
13. What is the primary benefit associated with using a standard cost system?
14. A processing department of Carmine Corporation experienced a high unfavorable materials quantity variance. The plant manager initially commented, "The best way to solve this problem is to fire the supervisor of the processing department." Do you agree? Explain.
15. Sara Anderson says that she is a busy woman with no time to look at favorable variances. Instead, she concentrates solely on the unfavorable ones. She says that favorable variances imply that employees are doing better than expected and need only quick congratulations. In contrast, unfavorable variances indicate that change is needed to get the substandard performance up to par. Do you agree? Explain.
16. What two factors affect the total materials and labor variances?
17. Who is normally responsible for a materials price

variance? Identify two factors that may be beyond this individual's control that could cause an unfavorable price variance.

18. John Jamail says that he doesn't understand why companies have labor price variances because most union contracts or other binding agreements set wage rates that do not normally change in the short term. How could rate variances occur even when binding commitments hold the dollar per hour rate constant?

19. Which individuals are normally held responsible for labor usage variances?

20. What is the primary cause of an unfavorable fixed cost volume variance?

21. What is the primary cause of a favorable fixed cost spending variance?

MULTIPLE-CHOICE QUESTIONS

Multiple-choice questions are available in *Connect*.

EXERCISES—SERIES A

connect **All applicable Exercises in Series A are available in *Connect*.**

Exercise 8-1A *Preparing master and flexible budgets* LO 8-1

Cherokee Manufacturing Company established the following standard price and cost data.

Sales price	$12.00 per unit
Variable manufacturing cost	$7.20 per unit
Fixed manufacturing cost	$3,600 total
Fixed selling and administrative cost	$1,200 total

Cherokee planned to produce and sell 2,000 units. Actual production and sales amounted to 2,200 units.

Required

a. Prepare the pro forma income statement in contribution format that would appear in a master budget.

b. Prepare the pro forma income statement in contribution format that would appear in a flexible budget.

Exercise 8-2A *Classifying variances as favorable or unfavorable* LO 8-2

Required

Indicate whether each of the following variances is favorable or unfavorable. The first one has been done as an example.

Item to Classify	Standard	Actual	Type of Variance
Sales volume	50,000 units	54,000 units	Favorable
Sales price	$4.00 per unit	$4.10 per unit	
Materials cost	$2.90 per pound	$3.00 per pound	
Materials usage	91,000 pounds	90,000 pounds	
Labor cost	$10.00 per hour	$9.60 per hour	
Labor usage	61,000 hours	61,800 hours	
Fixed cost spending	$400,000	$390,000	
Fixed cost per unit (volume)	$8.00 per unit	$7.22 per unit	

LO 8-2

Exercise 8-3A *Determining amount and type (favorable vs. unfavorable) of variance*

Required

Compute variances for the following items and indicate whether each variance is favorable (F) or unfavorable (U).

Item	Budget	Actual	Variance	F or U
Sales price	$400	$390		
Sales revenue	$360,000	$390,000		
Cost of goods sold	$192,500	$180,000		
Material purchases at 5,000 pounds	$137,500	$140,000		
Materials usage	$90,000	$89,000		
Production volume	950 units	900 units		
Wages at 4,000 hours	$30,000	$29,350		
Labor usage at $12 per hour	$48,000	$48,500		
Research and development expense	$11,000	$12,500		
Selling and administrative expenses	$24,500	$20,000		

LO 8-3

Exercise 8-4A *Determining sales and variable cost volume variances*

Required

Use the information provided in Exercise 8-1A.

a. Determine the sales and variable cost volume variances.

b. Classify the variances as favorable (F) or unfavorable (U).

c. Comment on the usefulness of the variances with respect to performance evaluation and identify the member of the management team most likely to be responsible for these variances.

d. Determine the amount of fixed cost that will appear in the flexible budget.

e. Determine the fixed cost per unit based on planned activity and the fixed cost per unit based on actual activity. Assuming Cherokee uses information in the master budget to price the company's product, comment on how the fixed cost volume variance could affect the company's profitability. Round computations to two decimal points.

LO 8-4

Exercise 8-5A *Determining flexible budget variances*

Use the standard price and cost data provided in Exercise 8-1A. Assume that the actual sales price is $11.76 per unit and that the actual variable cost is $6.90 per unit. The actual fixed manufacturing cost is $3,000, and the actual selling and administrative costs are $1,230.

Required

a. Determine the flexible budget variances.

b. Classify the variances as favorable (F) or unfavorable (U).

c. Provide another name for the fixed cost flexible budget variances.

d. Comment on the usefulness of the variances with respect to performance evaluation and identify the member(s) of the management team who is (are) most likely to be responsible for these variances.

LO 8-4

Exercise 8-6A *Using a flexible budget to accommodate market uncertainty*

According to its original plan, Topeka Consulting Services Company plans to charge its customers for service at $120 per hour in Year 2. The company president expects consulting services provided to customers to reach 45,000 hours at that rate. The marketing manager, however, argues that actual results may range from 40,000 hours to 50,000 hours because of market uncertainty. Topeka's standard variable cost is $45 per hour, and its standard fixed cost is $1,350,000.

Required

Develop flexible budgets based on the assumptions of service levels at 40,000 hours, 45,000 hours, and 50,000 hours.

Exercise 8-7A *Evaluating a decision to increase sales volume by lowering sales price*

LO 8-3, 8-4

Secor Educational Services had budgeted its training service charge at $120 per hour. The company planned to provide 30,000 hours of training services during Year 3. By lowering the service charge to $114 per hour, the company was able to increase the actual number of hours to 31,500.

Required

a. Determine the sales volume variance and indicate whether it is favorable (F) or unfavorable (U).

b. Determine the flexible budget variance and indicate whether it is favorable (F) or unfavorable (U).

c. Did lowering the price of training services increase revenue? Explain.

Exercise 8-8A *Responsibility for variable manufacturing cost variance*

LO 8-4

Wapella Manufacturing Company set its standard variable manufacturing cost at $60 per unit of product. The company planned to make and sell 4,000 units of product during Year 3. More specifically, the master budget called for total variable manufacturing cost to be $240,000. Actual production during Year 3 was 4,200 units, and actual variable manufacturing costs amounted to $254,100. The production supervisor was asked to explain the variance between budgeted and actual cost ($254,100 − $240,000 = $14,100). The supervisor responded that she was not responsible for the variance that was caused solely by the increase in sales volume controlled by the marketing department.

Required

Do you agree with the production supervisor? Explain.

Exercise 8-9A *Responsibility for the fixed cost volume variance*

LO 8-5

Roanoke Company expected to sell 400,000 of its pagers during Year 2. It set the standard sales price for the pager at $60 each. During June, it became obvious that the company would be unable to attain the expected volume of sales. Roanoke's chief competitor, Kenny Corporation, had lowered prices and was pulling market share from Roanoke. To be competitive, Roanoke matched Kenny's price, lowering its sales price to $56 per pager. Kenny responded by lowering its price even further to $48 per pager. In an emergency meeting of key personnel, Roanoke's accountant, Karen Velez, stated, "Our cost structure simply won't support a sales price in the $48 range." The production manager, Gene Cormier, said, "I don't understand why I'm here. The only unfavorable variance on my report is a fixed manufacturing overhead cost volume variance and that one is not my fault. We shouldn't be making the product if the marketing department isn't selling it."

Required

a. Describe a scenario in which the production manager is responsible for the fixed cost volume variance.

b. Describe a scenario in which the marketing manager is responsible for the fixed cost volume variance.

c. Explain how a decline in sales volume would affect Roanoke's ability to lower its sales price.

Exercise 8-10A *Calculating the materials usage variance*

LO 8-6

Misty McDougall is the manager of the Fowler Bagel Shop. The corporate office had budgeted her store to sell 3,000 ham sandwiches during the week beginning July 17. Each sandwich was expected to contain 6 ounces of ham. During the week of July 17, the store actually sold 3,500 sandwiches and used 21,100 ounces of ham. The standard cost of ham is $0.42 per ounce. The variance report from company headquarters showed an unfavorable materials usage variance of $1,302. Ms. McDougall thought the variance was too high, but she had no accounting background and did not know how to register a proper objection.

Required

a. Is the variance calculated properly? If not, recalculate it.

b. Provide three independent explanations as to what could have caused the materials usage variance that you determined in Requirement *a.*

LO 8-6

Exercise 8-11A *Determining materials price and usage variances*

Monique's Florals produced a special Mother's Day arrangement that included eight roses. The standard and actual costs of the roses used in each arrangement follow.

	Standard	Actual
Average number of roses per arrangement	8.0	8.25
Price per rose	× $0.50	× $0.48
Cost of roses per arrangement	$4.00	$3.96

Monique's Florals planned to make 750 arrangements but actually made 790.

Required

a. Determine the total flexible budget materials variance and indicate whether it is favorable (F) or unfavorable (U).

b. Determine the materials price variance and indicate whether it is favorable (F) or unfavorable (U).

c. Determine the materials usage variance and indicate whether it is favorable (F) or unfavorable (U).

d. Confirm the accuracy of Requirements *a*, *b*, and *c* by showing that the sum of the price and usage variances equals the total variance.

LO 8-6

Exercise 8-12A *Responsibility for materials usage variance*

Fulton Fruit Basket Company makes baskets of assorted fruit. The standard and actual costs of oranges used in each basket of fruit follow.

	Standard	Actual
Average number of oranges per basket	5.00	4.75
Price per orange	× $0.20	× $0.24
Cost of oranges per basket	$1.00	$1.14

Fulton actually produced 25,000 baskets.

Required

a. Determine the materials price variance and indicate whether it is favorable (F) or unfavorable (U).

b. Determine the materials usage variance and indicate whether it is favorable (F) or unfavorable (U).

c. Explain why the purchasing agent may have been responsible for the usage variance.

Exercise 8-13A ***Responsibility for labor price and usage variances*** **LO 8-6**

Lucas Manufacturing Company incurred a favorable labor price variance and an unfavorable labor usage variance.

Required

a. Describe a scenario in which the personnel manager is responsible for the unfavorable usage variance.

b. Describe a scenario in which the production manager is responsible for the favorable labor price variance.

Exercise 8-14A ***Calculating and explaining labor price and usage variances*** **LO 8-6**

Russell and Sons, a CPA firm, established the following standard labor cost data for completing what the firm referred to as a Class 2 tax return. Russell expected each Class 2 return to require 4.0 hours of labor at a cost of $30 per hour. The firm actually completed 600 returns. Actual labor hours averaged 3.6 hours per return and actual labor cost amounted to $34.50 per hour.

Required

a. Determine the total labor variance and indicate whether it is favorable (F) or unfavorable (U).

b. Determine the labor price variance and indicate whether it is favorable (F) or unfavorable (U).

c. Determine the labor usage variance and indicate whether it is favorable (F) or unfavorable (U).

d. Explain what could have caused these variances.

Exercise 8-15A ***Determining the standard labor price*** **LO 8-6**

Pella Car Wash Inc. expected to wash 2,000 cars during the month of August. Washing each car was expected to require 0.2 hour of labor. The company actually used 420 hours of labor to wash 1,880 cars. The labor usage variance was $880 unfavorable.

Required

a. Determine the standard labor price.

b. If the actual labor rate is $17.50, indicate whether the labor price variance would be favorable (F) or unfavorable (U).

Exercise 8-16A ***Calculating the variable overhead variance*** **LO 8-4, 8-5, 8-6**

Cheney Company established a predetermined variable overhead cost rate at $21.00 per direct labor hour. The actual variable overhead cost rate was $19.20 per hour. The planned level of labor activity was 76,000 hours of labor. The company actually used 80,000 hours of labor.

Required

a. Determine the total flexible budget variable overhead cost variance.

b. Like many companies, Cheney has decided not to separate the total variable overhead cost variance into price and usage components. Explain why Cheney made this choice.

Exercise 8-17A ***Determining and interpreting fixed cost variances*** **LO 8-4, 8-5, 8-6**

Reardan Company established a predetermined fixed overhead cost rate of $29 per unit of product. The company planned to make 7,000 units of product but actually produced only 6,500 units. Actual fixed overhead costs were $212,000.

Required

a. Determine the fixed cost spending variance and indicate whether it is favorable or unfavorable. Explain what this variance means. Identify the manager(s) who is (are) responsible for the variance.

b. Determine the fixed cost volume variance and indicate whether it is favorable or unfavorable. Explain why this variance is important. Identify the manager(s) who is (are) responsible for the variance.

PROBLEMS—SERIES A

connect All applicable Problems in Series A are available in *Connect.*

LO 8-1

eXcel

CHECK FIGURES

a. NI = $124,000

c. NI = $130,000

Problem 8-18A *Flexible budget planning*

Howard Cooper, the president of Glacier Computer Services, needs your help. He wonders about the potential effects on the firm's net income if he changes the service rate that the firm charges its customers. The following basic data pertain to fiscal Year 3.

Standard rate and variable costs	
Service rate per hour	$60.00
Labor cost	32.00
Overhead cost	5.76
Selling, general, and administrative cost	3.44
Expected fixed costs	
Facility maintenance	$320,000
Selling, general, and administrative	120,000

Required

a. Prepare the pro forma income statement that would appear in the master budget if the firm expects to provide 30,000 hours of services in Year 3.

b. A marketing consultant suggests to Mr. Cooper that the service rate may affect the number of service hours that the firm can achieve. According to the consultant's analysis, if Glacier charges customers $56 per hour, the firm can achieve 38,000 hours of services. Prepare a flexible budget using the consultant's assumption.

c. The same consultant also suggests that if the firm raises its rate to $64 per hour, the number of service hours will decline to 25,000. Prepare a flexible budget using the new assumption.

d. Evaluate the three possible outcomes you determined in Requirements *a*, *b*, and *c* and recommend a pricing strategy.

LO 8-1, 8-2, 8-3

CHECK FIGURE

b. Variance of surplus: $1,620 U

Problem 8-19A *Analyzing not-for-profit entity variances*

The Redmond Management Association held its annual public relations luncheon in April Year 2. Based on the previous year's results, the organization allocated $25,290 of its operating budget to cover the cost of the luncheon. To ensure that costs would be appropriately controlled, Molly Hubbard, the treasurer, prepared the following budget for the Year 2 luncheon.

The budget for the luncheon was based on the following expectations:

1. The meal cost per person was expected to be $14.50. The cost driver for meals was attendance, which was expected to be 1,400 individuals.
2. Postage was based on $0.49 per invitation and 3,000 invitations were expected to be mailed. The cost driver for postage was number of invitations mailed.
3. The facility charge is $1,000 for a room that will accommodate up to 1,600 people; the charge for one to hold more than 1,600 people is $1,500.

4. A fixed amount was designated for printing, decorations, the speaker's gift, and publicity.

REDMOND MANAGEMENT ASSOCIATION Public Relations Luncheon Budget April Year 2	
Operating funds allocated	$25,290
Expenses	
Variable costs	
Meals (1,400 × $14.50)	20,300
Postage (3,000 × $0.49)	1,470
Fixed costs	
Facility	1,000
Printing	950
Decorations	840
Speaker's gift	130
Publicity	600
Total expenses	25,290
Budget surplus (deficit)	$ 0

Actual results for the luncheon follow.

REDMOND MANAGEMENT ASSOCIATION Actual Results for Public Relations Luncheon April Year 2	
Operating funds allocated	$25,290
Expenses	
Variable costs	
Meals (1,620 × $15.50)	25,110
Postage (4,000 × $0.49)	1,960
Fixed costs	
Facility	1,500
Printing	950
Decorations	840
Speaker's gift	130
Publicity	600
Total expenses	31,090
Budget deficit	$ (5,800)

Reasons for the differences between the budgeted and actual data follow.

1. The president of the organization, Rodney Snow, increased the invitation list to include 1,000 former members. As a result, 4,000 invitations were mailed.
2. Attendance was 1,620 individuals. Because of higher-than-expected attendance, the luncheon was moved to a larger room, thereby increasing the facility charge to $1,500.
3. At the last minute, Ms. Hubbard decided to add a dessert to the menu, which increased the meal cost to $15.50 per person.
4. Printing, decorations, the speaker's gift, and publicity costs were as budgeted.

Required

a. Prepare a flexible budget and compute the sales and variable cost volume variances based on a comparison between the master budget and the flexible budget.

b. Compute flexible budget variances by comparing the flexible budget with the actual results.

c. Mr. Snow was extremely upset with the budget deficit. He immediately called Ms. Hubbard to complain about the budget variance for the meal cost. He told Ms. Hubbard that the added dessert caused the meal cost to be $4,810 ($25,110 – $20,300) over budget. He added, "I could expect a couple hundred dollars one way or the other, but several thousand is totally unacceptable. At the next meeting of the budget committee, I want you to explain what happened." Assume that you are Ms. Hubbard. What would you tell the members of the budget committee?

d. Since this is a not-for-profit organization, why should anyone be concerned with meeting the budget?

LO 8-1, 8-3

CHECK FIGURES

a. NI = $702,000

b. NI at 29,000 units: $666,000

Problem 8-20A *Determining sales and variable cost volume variances*

Narcisco Publications established the following standard price and costs for a hardcover picture book that the company produces.

Standard price and variable costs	
Sales price	$90.00
Materials cost	18.00
Labor cost	9.00
Overhead cost	12.60
Selling, general, and administrative costs	14.40
Planned fixed costs	
Manufacturing overhead	$270,000
Selling, general, and administrative	108,000

Narcisco planned to make and sell 30,000 copies of the book.

Required

a. Prepare the pro forma income statement that would appear in the master budget.

b. Prepare flexible budget income statements, assuming production volumes of 29,000 and 31,000 units.

c. Determine the sales and variable cost volume variances, assuming volume is actually 31,000 units.

d. Indicate whether the variances are favorable (F) or unfavorable (U).

e. Comment on how Narcisco could use the variances to evaluate performance.

LO 8-4

CHECK FIGURE

a. Flexible budget variance of NI: $80,800 U

Problem 8-21A *Determining and interpreting flexible budget variances*

Use the standard price and cost data supplied in Problem 8-20A. Assume that Narcisco actually produced and sold 32,000 books. The actual sales price and costs incurred follow.

Actual price and variable costs	
Sales price	$87.00
Materials cost	18.40
Labor cost	8.80
Overhead cost	12.70
Selling, general, and administrative costs	14.00
Actual fixed costs	
Manufacturing overhead	$250,000
Selling, general, and administrative	116,000

Required

a. Determine the flexible budget variances. Provide another name for the fixed cost flexible budget variances.

b. Indicate whether each variance is favorable (F) or unfavorable (U).

c. Identify the management position responsible for each variance. Explain what could have caused the variance.

Problem 8-22A *Computing fixed cost variances*

LO 8-5

In addition to other costs, Grosha Telephone Company planned to incur $600,000 of fixed manufacturing overhead in making 500,000 telephones. Grosha actually produced 508,000 telephones, incurring actual overhead costs of $599,400. Grosha establishes its predetermined overhead rate based on the planned volume of production (expected number of telephones).

CHECK FIGURE
c. $9,600 F

Required

a. Calculate the predetermined overhead rate.

b. Determine the fixed cost spending variance and indicate whether it is favorable (F) or unfavorable (U).

c. Determine the fixed cost volume variance and indicate whether it is favorable (F) or unfavorable (U).

Problem 8-23A *Computing materials, labor, and cost variances*

LO 8-5, 8-6

excel

CHECK FIGURES
d. Labor price variance: $11,592 F
g. Fixed cost volume variance: $2,820 F

The following data were drawn from the records of Quentin Corporation.

Planned volume for year (static budget)	6,000 units
Standard direct materials cost per unit	3.1 pounds @ $3.00 per pound
Standard direct labor cost per unit	2 hours @ $8.00 per hour
Total expected fixed overhead costs	$56,400
Actual volume for the year (flexible budget)	6,300 units
Actual direct materials cost per unit	2.7 pounds @ $4.00 per pound
Actual direct labor cost per unit	2.3 hours @ $7.20 per hour
Total actual fixed overhead costs	$45,000

Required

a. Prepare a materials variance information table showing the standard price, the actual price, the standard quantity, and the actual quantity.

b. Calculate the materials price and usage variances. Indicate whether the variances are favorable (F) or unfavorable (U).

c. Prepare a labor variance information table showing the standard price, the actual price, the standard hours, and the actual hours.

d. Calculate the labor price and usage variances. Indicate whether the variances are favorable (F) or unfavorable (U).

e. Calculate the predetermined overhead rate, assuming that Quentin uses the number of units as the allocation base.

f. Calculate the fixed cost spending variance. Indicate whether the variance is favorable (F) or unfavorable (U).

g. Calculate the fixed cost volume variance. Indicate whether the variance is favorable (F) or unfavorable (U).

Problem 8-24A *Determining materials price and usage variances*

LO 8-6

Caribou Fruit Drink Company planned to make 200,000 containers of apple juice. It expected to use two cups of frozen apple concentrate to make each container of juice, thus using 400,000 cups of frozen concentrate. The standard price of one cup of apple concentrate is $1.20. Caribou actually paid $499,100 to purchase 402,500 cups of concentrate, which was used to make 201,000 containers of apple juice.

CHECK FIGURES
b. $1.24/cup
d. $16,100 U

Required

a. Are flexible budget materials variances based on the planned volume of activity (200,000 containers) or actual volume of activity (201,000 containers)?

b. Compute the actual price per cup of concentrate.

c. Compute the standard quantity (number of cups of concentrate) required to produce the containers.

d. Compute the materials price variance and indicate whether it is favorable (F) or unfavorable (U).

e. Compute the materials usage variance and indicate whether it is favorable (F) or unfavorable (U).

LO 8-6

CHECK FIGURES
c. $5,250 F
d. $10,000 F

Problem 8-25A *Determining labor price and usage variances*

Bonnie's Doll Company produces handmade dolls. The standard amount of time spent on each doll is 2.0 hours. The standard cost of labor is $20 per hour. The company planned to make 8,000 dolls during the year but actually used 17,500 hours of labor to make 9,000 dolls. The payroll amounted to $344,750.

Required

a. Should labor variances be based on the planned volume of 8,000 dolls or the actual volume of 9,000 dolls?

b. Prepare a table that shows the standard labor price, the actual labor price, the standard labor hours, and the actual labor hours.

c. Compute the labor price variance and indicate whether it is favorable (F) or unfavorable (U).

d. Compute the labor usage variance and indicate whether it is favorable (F) or unfavorable (U).

LO 8-5, 8-6

CHECK FIGURES
b. Materials usage variance: $2,781 U
d. Labor price variance: $8,916 U

Problem 8-26A *Computing materials, labor, and fixed cost variances*

Shawnee Manufacturing Company produces a component part of a top secret military communication device. Standard production and cost data for the part, Product X, follow.

Planned production	30,000 units
Per unit direct materials	2 pounds @ $1.80 per pound
Per unit direct labor	3 hours @ $8.00 per hour
Total estimated fixed overhead costs	$702,000

Shawnee purchased and used 63,345 pounds of material at an average cost of $1.85 per pound. Labor usage amounted to 89,160 hours at an average of $8.10 per hour. Actual production amounted to 30,900 units. Actual fixed overhead costs amounted to $738,000. The company completed and sold all inventory for $1,800,000.

Required

a. Prepare a materials variance information table showing the standard price, the actual price, the standard quantity, and the actual quantity.

b. Calculate the materials price and usage variances. Indicate whether the variances are favorable (F) or unfavorable (U).

c. Prepare a labor variance information table showing the standard price, the actual price, the standard hours, and the actual hours.

d. Calculate the labor price and usage variances. Indicate whether the variances are favorable (F) or unfavorable (U).

e. Calculate the predetermined overhead rate, assuming that Shawnee uses the number of units as the allocation base.

f. Calculate the fixed cost spending and volume variances and indicate whether they are favorable (F) or unfavorable (U).

g. Determine the amount of gross margin Shawnee would report on the year-end income statement.

LO 8-5, 8-6

excel

Problem 8-27A *Computing standard cost and analyzing variances*

Spiro Company manufactures molded candles that are finished by hand. The company developed the following standards for a new line of drip candles.

Amount of direct materials per candle	1.6 pounds
Price of direct materials per pound	$1.50
Quantity of labor per unit	1 hour
Price of direct labor per hour	$20/hour
Total budgeted fixed overhead	$390,000

During Year 2, Spiro planned to produce 30,000 drip candles. Production lagged behind expectations, and it actually produced only 24,000 drip candles. At year-end, direct materials purchased and used amounted to 40,000 pounds at a unit price of $1.35 per pound. Direct labor costs were actually $18.75 per hour and 26,400 actual hours were worked to produce the drip candles. Overhead for the year actually amounted to $330,000. Overhead is applied to products using a predetermined overhead rate based on estimated units.

CHECK FIGURES
e. Usage variance for direct materials: $2,400 U
f. Fixed cost volume variance: $78,000 U

Required

Round all computations to two decimal places.

a. Compute the standard cost per candle for direct materials, direct labor, and overhead.
b. Determine the total standard cost for one drip candle.
c. Compute the actual cost per candle for direct materials, direct labor, and overhead.
d. Compute the total actual cost per candle.
e. Compute the price and usage variances for direct materials and direct labor. Identify any variances that Spiro should investigate. Offer possible cause(s) for the variances.
f. Compute the fixed cost spending and volume variances. Explain your findings.
g. Although the individual variances (price, usage, and overhead) were large, the standard cost per unit and the actual cost per unit differed by only a few cents. Explain why.

LO 8-6

Problem 8-28A *Computing variances*

CHECK FIGURES
a. 1,720 pounds
d. $20.62

Gepp Manufacturing Company produces a single product. The following data apply to the standard cost of materials and labor associated with making the product.

Materials quantity per unit	1 pound
Materials price	$12.50 per pound
Labor quantity per unit	2 hours
Labor price	$22.50 per hour

During the year, the company made 1,800 units of product. At the end of the year, the following variances had been calculated.

Materials usage variance	$1,000 Favorable
Materials price variance	$860 Unfavorable
Labor usage variance	$4,500 Unfavorable
Labor price variance	$7,125 Favorable

Required

a. Determine the actual amount of materials used.
b. Determine the actual price paid per pound for materials.
c. Determine the actual labor hours used.
d. Determine the actual labor price per hour. Round computations to two decimal points.

EXERCISES—SERIES B

Exercise 8-1B *Preparing master and flexible budgets*

LO 8-1

Imboden Manufacturing Company established the following standard price and cost data.

Sales price	$15 per unit
Variable manufacturing cost	$7 per unit
Fixed manufacturing cost	$32,500 total
Fixed selling and administrative cost	$24,000 total

Imboden planned to produce and sell 18,000 units. It actually produced and sold 19,000 units.

Required

a. Prepare the pro forma income statement that would appear in a master budget. Use the contribution margin format.

b. Prepare the pro forma income statement that would appear in a flexible budget. Use the contribution margin format.

LO 8-2

Exercise 8-2B *Classifying variances as favorable or unfavorable*

Required

Indicate whether each of the following variances is favorable (F) or unfavorable (U). The first one has been done as an example.

Item to Classify	Standard	Actual	Type of Variance
Sales volume	40,000 units	38,915 units	Unfavorable
Sales price	$6.90 per unit	$6.78 per unit	
Materials cost	$2.10 per pound	$2.30 per pound	
Materials usage	102,400 pounds	103,700 pounds	
Labor cost	$8.25 per hour	$8.80 per hour	
Labor usage	56,980 hours	55,790 hours	
Fixed cost spending	$249,000	$244,000	
Fixed cost per unit (volume)	$2.51 per unit	$3.22 per unit	

LO 8-2

Exercise 8-3B *Recognizing favorable vs. unfavorable variances*

Compute variances for the following items and indicate whether each variance is favorable (F) or unfavorable (U).

Item	Budget	Actual	Variance	F or U
Sales price	$600	$590		
Sales revenue	$690,000	$720,000		
Cost of goods sold	$520,000	$470,000		
Materials purchases at 10,000 pounds	$330,000	$360,000		
Materials usage	$270,000	$260,000		
Production volume	890 units	900 units		
Wages at 7,600 hours	$91,200	$90,800		
Labor usage	7,600 hours	8,000 hours		
Research and development expense	$81,000	$90,000		
Selling and administrative expenses	$75,000	$71,000		

LO 8-3

Exercise 8-4B *Determining sales and variable cost volume variances*

Required

Use the information provided in Exercise 8-1B.

a. Determine the sales and variable cost volume variances.

b. Classify the variances as favorable or unfavorable.

c. Comment on the usefulness of the variances with respect to performance evaluation and identify the member of the management team most likely to be responsible for these variances.

d. Determine the amounts of fixed cost that will appear in the flexible budget.

e. Determine the fixed cost per unit based on planned activity and the fixed cost per unit based on actual activity. Assuming Imboden uses information in the master budget to price its product, explain how the fixed cost volume variance could affect the company's profitability. (Round the computation to two decimal points.)

Exercise 8-5B *Determining flexible budget variances*

LO 8-4

Use the standard price and cost data provided in Exercise 8-1B. Assume the actual sales price was $14.75 per unit and the actual variable cost was $6.80 per unit. The actual fixed manufacturing cost was $33,500, and the actual selling and administrative expenses were $23,500.

Required

a. Determine the flexible budget variances.

b. Classify the variances as favorable or unfavorable.

c. Provide another name for the fixed cost flexible budget variances.

d. Comment on the usefulness of the variances with respect to performance evaluation and identify the member(s) of the management team that is (are) most likely to be responsible for these variances.

Exercise 8-6B *Using a flexible budget to accommodate market uncertainty*

LO 8-4

Salem Cable Installation Services Inc. is planning to open a new regional office. Based on a market survey Salem commissioned, the company expects services demand for the new office to be between 30,000 and 40,000 hours annually. The firm normally charges customers $30 per hour for its installation services. Salem expects the new office to have a standard variable cost of $16 per hour and standard fixed cost of $430,000 per year.

Required

a. Develop flexible budgets based on 30,000 hours, 35,000 hours, and 40,000 hours of services.

b. Based on the results for Requirement *a*, comment on the likely success of Salem's new office.

Exercise 8-7B *Evaluating a decision to increase sales volume by reducing sales price*

LO 8-3, 8-4

At the beginning of its most recent accounting period, Zelma Company had planned to clean 400 house roofs at an average price of $450 per roof. By reducing the service charge to $400 per roof, the company was able to increase the actual number of roofs cleaned to 480.

Required

a. Determine the sales volume variance and indicate whether it is favorable (F) or unfavorable (U).

b. Determine the flexible budget variance and indicate whether it is favorable (F) or unfavorable (U).

c. Did reducing the price charged for cleaning roofs increase revenue? Explain.

Exercise 8-8B *Assessing responsibility for a labor cost variance*

LO 8-4

Loretto Technologies Company's Year 2 master budget called for using 60,000 hours of labor to produce 180,000 units of software. The standard labor rate for the company's employees is $50 per direct labor hour. Demand exceeded expectations, resulting in production and sales of 210,000 software units. Actual direct labor costs were $3,475,000. The year-end variance report showed a total unfavorable labor variance of $475,000.

Required

Assume you are the vice president of manufacturing. Should you criticize or praise the production supervisor's performance? Explain.

Exercise 8-9B *Responsibility for fixed cost volume and spending variances*

LO 8-5

Everton Manufacturing Company had an excellent year. The company hired a new marketing director in January. The new director's great motivational appeal inspired the sales staff, and, as a result, sales were 20 percent higher than expected. In a recent management meeting, the company president, Peter Healy, congratulated the marketing director and then criticized Steve Abbott, the company's production manager, because of an unfavorable fixed cost spending variance. Mr. Abbott countered that the favorable fixed cost volume variance more than offset the unfavorable fixed cost spending variance. He argued that Mr. Healy should evaluate the two variances in total and that he should be rewarded rather than criticized.

Required

Do you agree with Mr. Abbott's defense of the unfavorable fixed cost spending variance? Explain.

LO 8-6

Exercise 8-10B *Calculating the materials usage variance*

Thelma Merritt manages the Spring Candy Shop, which was expected to sell 4,000 servings of its trademark candy during July. Each serving was expected to contain 6 ounces of candy. The standard cost of the candy was $1.20 per ounce. The shop actually sold 3,800 servings and actually used 22,100 ounces of candy.

Required

a. Compute the materials usage variance.

b. Explain what could have caused the variance that you computed in Requirement *a.*

LO 8-6

Exercise 8-11B *Determining materials price and usage variances*

Amity Company makes paint that it sells in 1-gallon containers to retail home improvement stores. During Year 3, the company planned to make 190,000 gallons of paint. It actually produced 198,000 gallons. The standard and actual quantity and cost of the color pigment for 1 gallon of paint follow.

	Standard	Actual
Quantity of materials per gallon	12 ounces	13 ounces
Price per ounce	× $0.75	× $0.70
Cost per gallon	$9.00	$9.10

Required

a. Determine the total flexible budget materials variance for pigment. Indicate whether the variance is favorable or unfavorable.

b. Determine the materials price variance and indicate whether the variance is favorable (F) or unfavorable (U).

c. Determine the materials usage variance and indicate whether the variance is favorable (F) or unfavorable (U).

d. Confirm your answers to Requirements *a*, *b*, and *c* by showing that the sum of the price and usage variances equals the total variance.

LO 8-6

Exercise 8-12B *Responsibility for materials price variance*

Wayne Pittman Inc. makes ice cream that it sells in 5-gallon containers to retail ice cream parlors. During Year 2, the company planned to make 100,000 containers of ice cream. It actually produced 97,000 containers. The actual and standard quantity and cost of sugar per container follow.

	Standard	Actual
Quantity of materials per container	2 pounds	2.1 pounds
Price per pound	× $1.16	× $1.20
Cost per container	$2.32	$2.52

Required

a. Determine the materials price variance and indicate whether the variance is favorable (F) or unfavorable (U).

b. Determine the materials usage variance and indicate whether the variance is favorable (F) or unfavorable (U).

c. Explain how the production manager could have been responsible for the price variance.

Planned volume for year (static budget)	10,000 units
Standard direct materials cost per unit	2 pounds @ \$3.60 per pound
Standard direct labor cost per unit	0.5 hour @ \$30.00 per hour
Total planned fixed overhead costs	\$24,000
Actual volume for the year (flexible budget)	10,800 units
Actual direct materials cost per unit	1.9 pounds @ \$3.84 per pound
Actual direct labor cost per unit	0.6 hour @ \$24.00 per hour
Total actual fixed overhead costs	\$24,800

Required

a. Prepare a materials variance information table showing the standard price, the actual price, the standard quantity, and the actual quantity.
b. Calculate the materials price and usage variances and indicate whether they are favorable (F) or unfavorable (U).
c. Prepare a labor variance information table showing the standard price, the actual price, the standard hours, and the actual hours.
d. Calculate the labor price and usage variances and indicate whether they are favorable (F) or unfavorable (U).
e. Calculate the predetermined overhead rate, assuming that Freeport Plastics uses the number of units as the allocation base.
f. Calculate the fixed manufacturing overhead cost spending variance and indicate whether it is favorable (F) or unfavorable (U).
g. Calculate the fixed manufacturing overhead cost volume variance and indicate whether it is favorable (F) or unfavorable (U).

Problem 8-24B *Determining materials price and usage variances* LO 8-6

Watonga Swimsuit Specialties Inc. makes fashionable women's swimsuits. Its most popular swimsuit, with the Sarong trade name, uses a standard fabric amount of six yards of raw material with a standard price of \$9 per yard. The company planned to produce 100,000 Sarong swimsuits in Year 2. At the end of Year 2, the company's cost accountant reported that Watonga had used 636,000 yards of fabric to make 102,000 swimsuits. Actual cost for the raw material was \$5,952,960.

Required

a. Should the flexible budget materials variances be based on the planned volume of 100,000 swimsuits or on the actual volume of 102,000 swimsuits?
b. Compute the actual price per yard of fabric.
c. Compute the standard quantity (yards of fabric) required to produce the swimsuits.
d. Compute the materials price variance and indicate whether it is favorable (F) or unfavorable (U).
e. Compute the materials usage variance and indicate whether it is favorable (F) or unfavorable (U).

Problem 8-25B *Determining labor price and usage variances* LO 8-6

As noted in Problem 8-24B, Watonga Swimsuit makes swimsuits. In Year 2, Watonga produced its most popular swimsuit, the Sarong, for a standard labor price of \$33.60 per hour. The standard amount of labor was 1.0 hour per swimsuit. The company had planned to produce 100,000 Sarong swimsuits. At the end of Year 2, the company's cost accountant reported that Watonga had used 107,000 hours of labor to make 102,000 swimsuits. The total labor cost was \$3,723,600.

Required

a. Should the labor variances be based on the planned volume of 100,000 swimsuits or on the actual volume of 102,000 swimsuits?
b. Prepare a table that shows the standard labor price, the actual labor price, the standard labor hours, and the actual labor hours.
c. Compute the labor price variance and indicate whether it is favorable (F) or unfavorable (U).
d. Compute the labor usage variance and indicate whether it is favorable (F) or unfavorable (U).

LO 8-5, 8-6

Problem 8-26B *Computing materials, labor, and fixed cost variances*

Shaffer Corporation makes mouse pads for computer users. After the first year of operation, Peggy Shaffer, the president and chief executive officer, was eager to determine the efficiency of the company's operation. In her analysis, she used the following standards provided by her assistant.

Units of planned production	400,000
Per-unit direct materials	1 square foot @ $1.00 per square feet
Per-unit direct labor	0.2 hour @ $20.00 per hour
Total estimated fixed overhead costs	$400,000

Shaffer purchased and used 460,000 square feet of material at an average cost of $0.96 per square foot. Labor usage amounted to 79,200 hours at an average of $19.60 per hour. Actual production amounted to 416,000 units. Actual fixed overhead costs amounted to $408,000. The company completed and sold all inventory for $3,400,000.

Required

a. Prepare a materials variance information table showing the standard price, the actual price, the standard quantity, and the actual quantity.

b. Calculate the materials price and usage variances and indicate whether they are favorable (F) or unfavorable (U).

c. Prepare a labor variance information table showing the standard price, the actual price, the standard hours, and the actual hours.

d. Calculate the labor price and usage variances and indicate whether they are favorable (F) or unfavorable (U).

e. Calculate the predetermined overhead rate, assuming that Shaffer uses the number of units as the allocation base.

f. Calculate the fixed cost spending and volume variances and indicate whether they are favorable (F) or unfavorable (U).

g. Determine the amount of gross margin Shaffer would report on the year-end income statement.

LO 8-5, 8-6

Problem 8-27B *Computing standard cost and analyzing variances*

Gould Manufacturing Company, which makes aluminum alloy wheels for automobiles, recently introduced a new luxury wheel that fits small sports cars. The company developed the following standards for its new product.

Amount of direct materials per wheel	2 pounds
Price of direct materials per pound	$15.00
Quantity of labor per wheel	2.5 hours
Price of direct labor per hour	$32.00 per hour
Total budgeted fixed overhead	$336,000

In its first year of operation, Gould planned to produce 3,000 sets of wheels (four wheels per set). Because of unexpected demand, it actually produced 3,600 sets of wheels. By year-end, direct materials purchased and used amounted to 30,000 pounds of aluminum at a cost of $468,000. Direct labor costs were actually $33.60 per hour. Actual hours worked were 2.2 hours per wheel. Overhead for the year actually amounted to $360,000. Overhead is applied to products using a predetermined overhead rate based on the total estimated number of wheels to be produced.

Required

Round all computations to two decimal places.

a. Compute the standard cost per wheel for direct materials, direct labor, and overhead.

b. Determine the total standard cost per wheel.

c. Compute the actual cost per wheel for direct materials, direct labor, and overhead.

d. Compute the actual cost per wheel.

e. Compute the price and usage variances for direct materials and direct labor. Identify any variances that Gould should investigate. Based on your results, offer a possible explanation for the labor usage variance.

f. Compute the fixed manufacturing overhead cost spending and volume variances. Explain your findings.

Problem 8-28B *Computing variances*

LO 8-6

A fire destroyed most of Ordessa Products Corporation's records. Megan Carey, the company's accountant, is trying to piece together the company's operating results from salvaged documents. She discovered the following data.

Standard materials quantity per unit	2.5 pounds
Standard materials price	$8 per pound
Standard labor quantity per unit	0.6 hour
Standard labor price	$24 per hour
Actual number of products produced	8,000 units
Materials price variance	$3,168 Favorable
Materials usage variance	$1,600 Favorable
Labor price variance	$3,904 Unfavorable
Labor usage variance	$1,902 Unfavorable

Required

a. Determine the actual amount of materials used.

b. Determine the actual price per pound paid for materials.

c. Determine the actual labor hours used.

d. Determine the actual labor price per hour.

ANALYZE, THINK, COMMUNICATE

ATC 8-1 Business Applications Case *Static versus flexible budget variances*

John Richardson is the manufacturing production supervisor for Torsion Tool Works (TTW), a company that manufactures hand tools for mechanics. Trying to explain why he did not get the year-end bonus that he had expected, he told his wife, "This is the dumbest place I've ever worked. Last year the company set up this budget assuming it would sell 250,000 units. Well, it sold only 240,000. The company lost money and gave me a bonus for not using as much materials and labor as was called for in the budget. This year, the company has the same 250,000 units goal and it sells 260,000. The company's making all kinds of money. You'd think I'd get this big fat bonus. Instead, management tells me I used more materials and labor than was budgeted. They said the company would have made a lot more money if I'd stayed within my budget. I guess I gotta wait for another bad year before I get a bonus. Like I said, this is the dumbest place I've ever worked."

TTW's master budget and the actual results for the most recent year of operating activity follow.

	Master Budget	Actual Results	Variances	F or U
Number of units	250,000	260,000	10,000	
Sales revenue	$3,750,000	$3,950,000	$200,000	F
Variable manufacturing costs				
Materials	(600,000)	(622,200)	22,200	U
Labor	(312,500)	(321,000)	8,500	U
Overhead	(337,500)	(354,700)	17,200	U
Variable selling, general, and admin. costs	(475,000)	(501,300)	26,300	U
Contribution margin	2,025,000	2,150,800	125,800	F
Fixed costs				
Manufacturing overhead	(1,275,000)	(1,273,100)	1,900	F
Selling, general, and admin. costs	(470,000)	(479,300)	9,300	U
Net income	$ 280,000	$ 398,400	$118,400	F

Required

a. Did TTW increase unit sales by cutting prices or by using some other strategy?

b. Is Mr. Richardson correct in his conclusion that something is wrong with the company's performance evaluation process? If so, what do you suggest be done to improve the system?

c. Prepare a flexible budget and recompute the budget variances.

d. Explain what might have caused the fixed costs to be different from the amount budgeted.

e. Assume that the company's materials price variance was favorable and its materials usage variance was unfavorable. Explain why Mr. Richardson may not be responsible for these variances. Now, explain why he may have been responsible for the materials usage variance.

f. Assume the labor price variance is unfavorable. Was the labor usage variance favorable or unfavorable?

g. Is the fixed cost volume variance favorable or unfavorable? Explain the effect of this variance on the cost of each unit produced.

ATC 8-2 Group Assignment *Variable price and usage variances and fixed manufacturing overhead cost variances*

Kemp Tables Inc. (KTI) makes picnic tables of 2 × 4 planks of treated pine. It sells the tables to large retail discount stores such as Walmart. After reviewing the following data generated by KTI's chief accountant, the company president, Arianne Darwin, expressed concern that the total manufacturing cost was more than \$0.5 million above budget (\$7,084,800 − \$6,520,000 = \$564,800).

	Actual Results	Master Budget
Cost of planks per table	\$ 44.10	\$ 40.00
Cost of labor per table	26.10	25.50
Total variable manufacturing cost per table (a)	\$ 70.20	\$ 65.50
Total number of tables produced (b)	82,000	80,000
Total variable manufacturing cost (a × b)	\$5,756,400	\$5,240,000
Total fixed manufacturing cost	1,328,400	1,280,000
Total manufacturing cost	\$7,084,800	\$6,520,000

Ms. Darwin asked Conrad Pearson, KTI's chief accountant, to explain what caused the increase in cost. Mr. Pearson responded that things were not as bad as they seemed. He noted that part of the cost variance resulted from making and selling more tables than had been expected. Making more tables naturally causes the cost of materials and labor to be higher. He explained that the flexible budget cost variance was less than \$0.5 million. Specifically, he provided the following comparison.

	Actual Results	Flexible Budget
Cost of planks per table	\$ 44.10	\$ 40.00
Cost of labor per table	26.10	25.50
Total variable manufacturing cost per table (a)	\$ 70.20	\$ 65.50
Total number of tables produced (b)	82,000	82,000
Total variable manufacturing cost (a × b)	\$5,756,400	\$5,371,000
Total fixed manufacturing cost	1,328,400	1,280,000
Total manufacturing cost	\$7,084,800	\$6,651,000

Based on this information, he argued that the relevant variance for performance evaluation was only \$433,800 (\$7,084,800 − \$6,651,000). Ms. Darwin responded, "*Only* \$433,800! I consider that a very significant number. By the end of the day, I want a full explanation as to what is causing our costs to increase."

Required

a. Divide the class into groups of four or five students and divide the groups into three sections. Assign Task 1 to the first section, Task 2 to the second section, and Task 3 to the third section.

Group Tasks

(1) Based on the following information, determine the total materials cost variance and the price and usage variances. Assuming that the variances are an appropriate indicator of cause, explain what could have caused the variances. Identify the management position responsible.

	Actual Data	Standard Data
Number of planks per table	21	20
Price per plank	× $2.10	× $2.00
Material cost per table	$44.10	$40.00

(2) Based on the following information, determine the total labor cost variance and the price and usage variances. Assuming that the variances are an appropriate indicator of cause, explain what could have caused each variance. Identify the management position responsible.

	Actual Data	Standard Data
Number of hours per table	2.9	3.0
Price per hour	× $9.00	× $8.50
Labor cost per table	$26.10	$25.50

(3) Determine the amount of the fixed cost spending and volume variances. Explain what could have caused these variances. Based on the volume variance, indicate whether the actual fixed cost per unit would be higher or lower than the budgeted fixed cost per unit.

b. Select a spokesperson from each section to report the amount of the variances computed by the group. Reconcile any differences in the variances reported by the sections. Reconcile the individual variances with the total variance. Specifically, show that the total of the materials, labor, and overhead variances equals the total flexible budget variance ($433,800).

c. Discuss how Ms. Darwin should react to the variance information.

ATC 8-3 Research Assignment *Using real-world data from Papa John's Inc.*

Obtain the income statements for Papa John's Inc. for 2014, 2015, 2016, and 2017. The 2015–2017 statements are included in Papa John's 2017 annual report and Form 10-K, and the 2014 statement is in its 2016 annual report and Form 10-K. (Obtain the 2014 numbers from the 2016 Form 10-K, not the 2014 Form 10-K.)

To obtain the Form 10-Ks, you can use the EDGAR system (see Appendix A at the back of this text for instructions), or they can be found under the "Investors Relations" link on the company's corporate website, www.papajohns.com.

Required

a. Compute the percentage change for each of the following categories of revenues and expenses for 2014 to 2015 and 2014 to 2015:

Total revenues
Domestic company-owned restaurant expenses
North America commissary and other expenses
International expenses
General and administrative expenses
Depreciation and amortization

Using an Excel spreadsheet will make this task much easier. After you have obtained these averages (you should have two averages for each of the six revenue and expense items), calculate an average of the changes for each item. The answer for the "Depreciation and amortization" item is shown as an example.

	Percentage Change
2014–2015	1.7%
2015–2016	0.9
Average of the changes	1.3%

b. Prepare a budgeted income statement, and compare the budgeted data to the actual results for 2017. To calculate budgeted amounts, multiply (1 + Average percentage change) in each revenue and expense item from Requirement *b* by the dollar amount of the corresponding revenue or expense item from 2016. This will represent the budgeted amount for that item for 2017. Don't forget to use decimal data and not percentage data. Subtract the actual 2017 results from the budgeted results. Finally, divide the actual versus budgeted difference by the budgeted amount to determine a percentage variance from the budget. The answer for the "Depreciation and amortization" item is shown as an example (dollar amounts are in millions).

	(1) 2016 Actual	(2) Average 3-year Change	(3) [1 + (1 × 2)] 2017 Budget	(4) 2017 Actual	(5) (3 − 4) Variance	(5 ÷ 3) Percentage Variance from Budget
Depreciation and amortization	$40,987	0.013	$41,520	$43,668	$2,148	0.052 [5.2%]

ATC 8-4 Writing Assignment *Standard costing—The human factor*

Kemp Corporation makes a protein supplement called Power Punch™. Its principal competitor for Power Punch is the protein supplement Superior Strength™, made by Jim Adams Company (JAC). Mr. Adams, a world-renowned weight-lifting champion, founded JAC. The primary market for both products is athletes. Kemp sells Power Punch to wellness stores, which sell it, along with other supplements and health foods, to the public. In contrast, Superior Strength is advertised in sports magazines and sold through orders generated by the ads.

Mr. Adams' fame is an essential factor in his company's advertising program. He is a dynamic character whose personality motivates people to strive for superior achievement. His demeanor not only stimulates sales but also provides a strong inspirational force for company employees. He is a kind, understanding individual with high expectations who is fond of saying that "mistakes are just opportunities for improvement." Mr. Adams is a strong believer in total quality management.

Mr. Quayle, president of Kemp Corporation, is a stern disciplinarian who believes in teamwork. He takes pride in his company's standard costing system. Managers work as a team to establish standards and then are held accountable for meeting them. Managers who fail to meet expectations are severely chastised, and continued failure leads to dismissal. After several years of rigorous enforcement, managers have fallen in line. Indeed, during the last two years, all managers have met their budget goals.

Even so, costs have risen steadily. These cost increases have been passed on to customers through higher prices. As a result, Power Punch is now priced significantly higher than Superior Strength. In fact, Superior Strength is selling directly to the public at a price that is below the wholesale price that Kemp is charging the wellness stores. The situation has reached a critical juncture. Sales of Power Punch are falling while Superior Strength is experiencing significant growth. Given that industry sales have remained relatively stable, it is obvious that customers are shifting from Power Punch to Superior Strength. Mr. Quayle is perplexed. He wonders how a company with direct marketing expenses can price its products so low.

Required

a. Explain why JAC has been able to gain a pricing advantage over Kemp.

b. Assume that you are a consultant whom Kemp's board of directors has asked to recommend how to halt the decline in sales of Power Punch. Provide appropriate recommendations.

ATC 8-5 Ethical Dilemma *Budget games*

Melody Lovelady is the most highly rewarded sales representative at Swift Corporation. Her secret to success is always to understate her abilities. Ms. Lovelady is assigned to a territory in which her customer base is increasing at approximately 25 percent per year. Each year she estimates that her budgeted sales will be 10 percent higher than her previous year's sales. With little effort, she is able to double her budgeted sales growth. At Swift's annual sales meeting, she receives an award and a large bonus. Of course, Ms. Lovelady does not disclose her secret to her colleagues. Indeed, she always talks about how hard it is to continue to top her previous performance. She tells herself: "If they are dumb enough to fall for this rubbish, I'll milk it for all it's worth."

Required

a. What is the name commonly given to the budget game Ms. Lovelady is playing?

b. Does Ms. Lovelady's behavior violate any of the standards of ethical professional practice shown in Exhibit 1.17 of Chapter 1?

c. Recommend how Ms. Lovelady's budget game could be stopped.

ATC 8-6 Spreadsheet Assignment *Using Excel*

Irvine Publications established the following standard price and costs for a hardcover picture book that the company produces.

Standard price and variable costs	
Sales price	$48.00
Materials cost	12.00
Labor cost	6.00
Overhead cost	8.40
Selling, general, and administrative costs	9.60
Expected fixed costs	
Manufacturing overhead	$180,000
Selling, general, and administrative	72,000

Irvine planned to make and sell 30,000 copies of the book.

Required

Construct a spreadsheet like the one shown in Exhibit 8.1 to illustrate a static budget and a flexible budget for production volumes of 28,000, 29,000, 30,000, 31,000, and 32,000.

ATC 8-7 Spreadsheet Assignment *Mastering Excel*

Wilkin Fruit Drink Company planned to make 400,000 containers of apple juice. It expected to use two cups of frozen apple concentrate to make each container of juice, thus using 800,000 cups (400,000 containers × 2 cups) of frozen concentrate. The standard price of one cup of apple concentrate is $0.25. Actually, Wilkin produced 404,000 containers of apple juice and purchased and used 820,000 cups of concentrate at $0.26 per cup.

Required

a. Construct a spreadsheet template that could be used to calculate price and usage variances. The template should be constructed so that it could be used for any problem in the chapter that refers to price and usage variances by changing the data in the spreadsheet. The screen capture on this page represents a template for price and usage variances.

Spreadsheet Tip

(1) The shaded cells can be changed according to the data in each problem. All other cells are formulas based on the numbers in the shaded cells.

(2) The cells that label the variances as F or U (favorable (F) or unfavorable (U)) are based on a function called IF. The IF function is needed because the variance can be either favorable or unfavorable. The formula must determine whether actual expenditures exceed budgeted expenditures to determine whether the variance is unfavorable or favorable. As an example, the formula in cell D13 is =IF(B11>E11,'U','F'). The formula evaluates the expression B11>E11. If this expression is true (B11 is greater than E11), the text U is inserted in cell D13. The IF function can also be used to place formulas or numbers in a cell based on whether an expression is true or false. For example, the formula =IF(B11>E11,B11−E11, E11−B11) would calculate the amount of the variance as a positive number regardless of which amount is larger.

(3) An easier way to make the variance a positive number regardless of whether it is favorable or unfavorable is to use the absolute value function. The format of the formula in cells C13 and F13 would be =ABS(left number − right number).

(4) The lines around the variances are produced by using the borders in Excel (Format, Cells, Border).

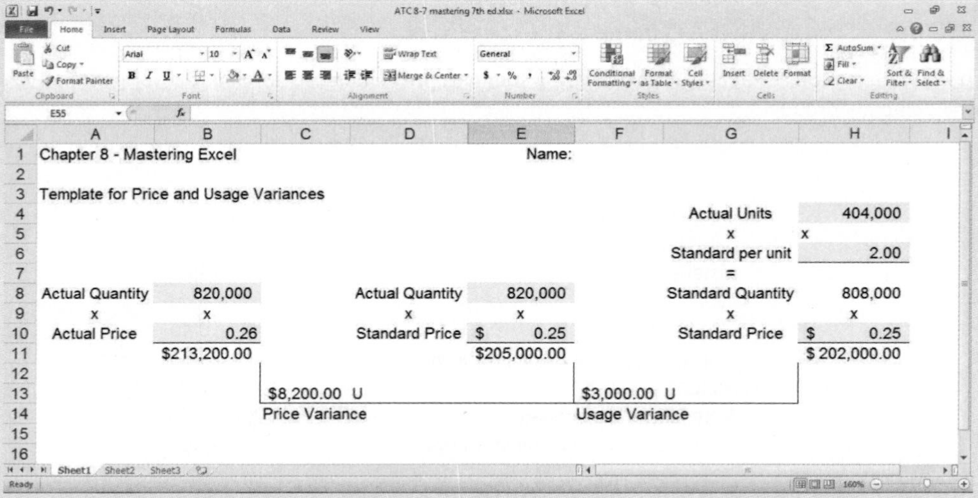

Source: Microsoft Excel 2010

COMPREHENSIVE PROBLEM

The management of Magnificent Modems Inc. (MMI) is uncertain as to the volume of sales that will exist in Year 1. The president of the company asked the chief accountant to prepare flexible budget income statements assuming that sales activity amounts to 3,000 and 6,000 units. The static budget is shown in the following form.

Required

a. Complete the following worksheet to prepare the appropriate flexible budgets.

b. Calculate and show the flexible budget variances for the static budget versus the flexible budget at 6,000 units.

c. Indicate whether each variance is favorable or unfavorable.

Flexible Budget Income Statements

		Static Budget	Flexible Budget	Flexible Budget
Number of units		5,000	3,000	6,000
	Cost per Unit			
Sales revenue	$120	$600,000		
Variable manuf. costs				
Materials	40	200,000		
Labor	25	125,000		
Overhead	4	20,000		
Variable SG&A	6	30,000		
Contribution margin		225,000		
Fixed costs				
Manufacturing rent		50,000		
Depreciation on manuf. equip.		60,000		
SG&A expenses		71,950		
Dep. on admin. equip.		12,000		
Net income (loss)		$ 31,050	$(58,950)	$76,050

CHAPTER 9

Responsibility Accounting

LEARNING OBJECTIVES

After you have mastered the material in this chapter, you will be able to:

LO 9-1 Explain the primary features of decentralization.

LO 9-2 Evaluate investment opportunities using return on investment.

LO 9-3 Evaluate investment opportunities using residual income.

LO 9-4 Describe how transfer prices may be established (Appendix).

Video lectures and accompanying self-assessment quizzes are available in Connect® for all learning objectives.

CHAPTER OPENING

Walter Keller, a production manager, complained to the accountant, Kelly Oberson, that the budget system failed to control his department's labor cost. Ms. Oberson responded, "People, not budgets, control costs." Budgeting is one of many tools management uses to control business operations. Managers are responsible for using control tools effectively. **Responsibility accounting** focuses on evaluating the performance of individual managers. For example, expenses controlled by a production department manager are presented in one report and expenses controlled by a marketing department manager are presented in a different report. This chapter discusses the development and use of a responsibility accounting system.

The Curious Accountant

©Krista Kennell/Shutterstock

Warren Buffett, often identified as one of the richest men in the world, is the CEO of **Berkshire Hathaway Inc.** (Berkshire). His company is actually a conglomerate that has major stockholdings in several large companies, including **American Express**, **Apple**, **Burlington Northern Santa Fe Railroad**, and **Coca-Cola**. Additionally, Berkshire wholly owns over 200 other businesses ranging in size and diversity from the insurance giant **GEICO**, to **Fruit of the Loom**, to **See's Candies**. In all, Berkshire has 377,000 employees and uses 4,867 different properties in its operations. How can one person, who is turning 89 in 2019, manage such a large and diverse business? (Answer on page 406.)

DECENTRALIZATION CONCEPT

LO 9-1

Explain the primary features of decentralization.

Effective responsibility accounting requires clear lines of authority and responsibility. Divisions of authority and responsibility normally occur as a natural consequence of managing business operations. In a small business, one person can control everything: marketing, production, management, and accounting. In contrast, large companies are so complex that authority and control must be divided among many people.

Consider the hiring of employees. A small business usually operates in a limited geographic area. The owner works directly with employees. She knows the job requirements, local wage rates, and the available labor pool. She is in a position to make informed hiring decisions. In contrast, a major corporation may employ thousands of employees throughout the world. The employees may speak different languages and have different social customs. Their jobs may require many different skills and pay a vast array of wage rates. The president of the corporation cannot make informed hiring decisions for the entire company. Instead, he delegates *authority* to a professional personnel manager and holds that manager *responsible* for hiring practices.

Decision-making authority is similarly delegated to individuals responsible for managing specific organization functions such as production, marketing, and accounting. Delegating authority and responsibility is referred to as **decentralization.** Decentralization offers advantages like the following:

1. *Encourages upper-level management to concentrate on strategic decisions.* Because local management makes routine decisions, upper-level management can concentrate on long-term planning, goal setting, and performance evaluation.
2. *Improves the quality of decisions by delegating authority down a chain of command.* Local managers are better informed about local concerns. Furthermore, their proximity to local events allows them to react quickly to changes in local conditions. As a result, local managers can generally make better decisions.
3. *Motivates managers to improve productivity.* The freedom to act coupled with responsibility for the results creates an environment that encourages most individuals to perform at high levels.
4. *Trains lower-level managers for increased responsibilities.* Decision making is a skill. Managers accustomed to making decisions about local issues are generally able to apply their decision-making skills to broader issues when they are promoted to upper management positions.
5. *Improves performance evaluation.* When lines of authority and responsibility are clear, credit or blame can be more accurately assigned.

Organization Chart

Exhibit 9.1 displays a partial organization chart for Panther Holding Company, a decentralized business. The chart shows five levels of authority and responsibility arranged in a hierarchical order from the top down. Other companies may have more or less complex organization charts, depending on their decentralization needs and philosophy.

Responsibility Centers

Decentralized businesses are usually subdivided into distinct reporting units called responsibility centers. A **responsibility center** is an organizational unit that controls identifiable revenue or expense items. The unit may be a division, a department, a subdepartment, or even a single machine. For example, a transportation company may identify a semitrailer truck as a responsibility center. The company holds the truck driver responsible for the revenues and expenses associated with operating the truck. Responsibility centers may be divided into three categories: cost, profit, and investment.

EXHIBIT 9.1

Organization Chart

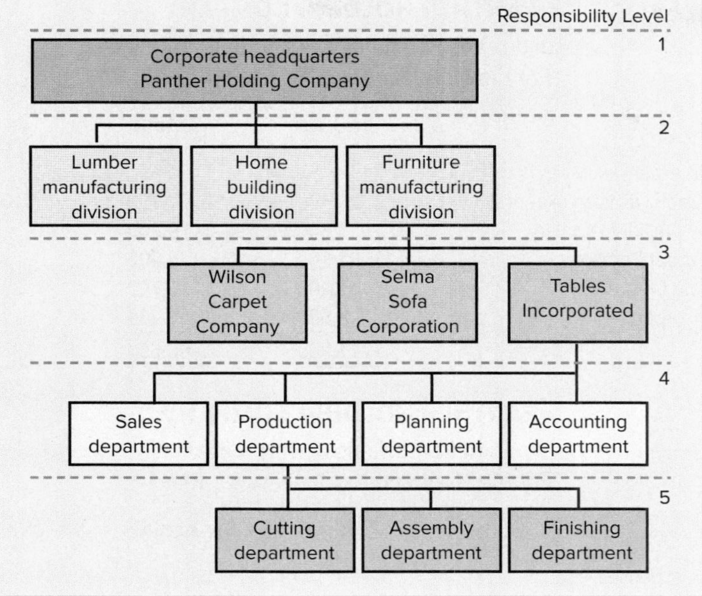

A **cost center** is an organizational unit that incurs expenses but does not generate revenue. In the Panther organization chart (Exhibit 9.1), the finishing department and the production department are cost centers. Cost centers normally fall on the lower levels of an organization chart. The manager of a cost center is judged on his ability to keep costs within budget parameters.

A **profit center** differs from a cost center in that it not only incurs costs but also generates revenue. In the Panther organization chart, the companies at the third level (Wilson Carpet Company, Selma Sofa Corporation, and Tables Incorporated) are considered profit centers. The manager of a profit center is judged on his ability to produce revenue in excess of expenses.

Investment center managers are responsible for revenues, expenses, and the investment of capital. Investment centers normally appear at the upper levels of an organization chart. The second-level division managers (managers of the lumber manufacturing, home building, and furniture manufacturing divisions) in the Panther organization are responsible for investment centers. Managers of investment centers are accountable for assets and liabilities as well as earnings.

Responsibility Reports

A **responsibility report** is prepared for each manager who controls a responsibility center. The report compares the expectations for the manager's responsibility center with the center's actual performance. A typical report lists the items under the manager's control, both the budgeted amount and the actual amount spent for each item, and the differences between budgeted and actual amounts (variances).

Management by Exception

Responsibility reports are arranged to support using the **management by exception** doctrine. Exhibit 9.2 illustrates a partial set of responsibility reports for Panther Holding Company.

EXHIBIT 9.2

Responsibility Reports

PANTHER HOLDING COMPANY
Second Level: Furniture Manufacturing Division
For the Month Ended January 31, Year 1

	Budget	Actual	Variance
Controllable expenses			
Administrative division expense	$ 20,400	$ 31,100	$10,700 U
Company president's salary	9,600	9,200	400 F
Wilson Carpet Company	82,100	78,400	3,700 F
Selma Sofa Corporation	87,200	116,700	29,500 U
Tables Incorporated	48,600	51,250	2,650 U
Total	$247,900	$286,650	$38,750 U

PANTHER HOLDING COMPANY
Third Level: Tables Incorporated
For the Month Ended January 31, Year 1

	Budget	Actual	Variance
Controllable expenses			
Administrative division expense	$ 3,000	$ 2,800	$ 200 F
Department managers' salaries	10,000	11,200	1,200 U
Sales department costs	9,100	8,600	500 F
Production department costs	13,500	13,750	250 U
Planning department costs	4,800	7,000	2,200 U
Accounting department costs	8,200	7,900	300 F
Total	$48,600	$51,250	$2,650 U

PANTHER HOLDING COMPANY
Fourth Level: Production Department
For the Month Ended January 31, Year 1

	Budget	Actual	Variance
Controllable expenses			
Administrative staff expense	$ 900	$ 1,100	$200 U
Supervisory salaries	2,800	2,800	0
Cutting department costs	1,400	1,200	200 F
Assembly department costs	2,800	2,900	100 U
Finishing department costs	5,600	5,750	150 U
Total	$13,500	$13,750	$250 U

PANTHER HOLDING COMPANY
Fifth Level: Finishing Department
For the Month Ended January 31, Year 1

	Budget	Actual	Variance
Controllable expenses			
Wages expense	$3,200	$3,000	$200 F
Direct materials	1,100	1,400	300 U
Supplies	400	500	100 U
Small tools	600	650	50 U
Other expenses	300	200	100 F
Total	$5,600	$5,750	$150 U

From the lower level upward, each successive report includes summary data from the preceding report. For example, the detailed information about the finishing department (a level-five responsibility center) is summarized as a single line item ($150 unfavorable variance) in the report for the production department (a level-four responsibility center).

The lack of detailed information may appear to hinder the production manager's ability to control costs. In fact, it has the opposite effect. The supervisor of the finishing department should use her responsibility report to identify and correct problems without bothering the production manager. The production manager should become concerned only when one of his supervisors loses control. The summary data in the production manager's report will adequately advise him of such situations. With this format, managers will concentrate only on significant deviations from expectations (management by exception) because the deviations are highlighted in their responsibility reports.

Applying the management by exception doctrine to the variances in her responsibility report, the division manager of the Furniture Manufacturing Division (second-level responsibility center) should concentrate her efforts on two areas. First, the $29,500 unfavorable variance for Selma Sofa Corporation indicates Selma's expenditures are out of line. Second, the $10,700 unfavorable variance for the division manager's own administrative expenses indicates those costs are significantly above budget expectations. The division manager should request detailed reports for these two areas. Other responsibility centers seem to be operating within reason and can be left to their respective managers. This reporting format focuses management's attention on the areas where it is most needed.

The complete responsibility accounting report would also include the first responsibility level, corporate headquarters. At the corporate level, responsibility reports normally include year-to-date income statements to inform management of the company's overall performance. To facilitate decision making, these income statements are normally prepared using the contribution margin format. Exhibit 9.3 shows the January Year 1 income statement for Panther Holding Company.

EXHIBIT 9.3

Panther Income Statement (Contribution Margin Format)

PANTHER HOLDING COMPANY
Income Statement for Internal Use
For the Month Ended January 31, Year 1

	Budget	Actual	Variance
Sales	$984,300	$962,300	$22,000 U
Variable expenses			
Variable product costs	343,100	352,250	9,150 U
Variable selling expenses	105,000	98,000	7,000 F
Other variable expenses	42,200	51,100	8,900 U
Total variable expenses	490,300	501,350	11,050 U
Contribution margin	494,000	460,950	33,050 U
Fixed expenses			
Fixed product cost	54,100	62,050	7,950 U
Fixed selling expense	148,000	146,100	1,900 F
Other fixed expenses	23,000	25,250	2,250 U
Total fixed expenses	225,100	233,400	8,300 U
Net income	$268,900	$227,550	$41,350 U

Answers to the Curious Accountant

Mr. Buffett oversees the diverse operations of **Berkshire Hathaway** by using a very decentralized management structure. According to its 2017 annual report, Berkshire had 377,000 employees and earned $242 billion in revenue. Mr. Buffett managed this empire from his headquarters in Omaha, Nebraska, that consists of 26 employees. The 2017 annual report notes:

> Berkshire's operating businesses are managed on an unusually decentralized basis. There are essentially no centralized or integrated business functions (such as sales, marketing, purchasing, legal, or human resources) and there is minimal involvement by Berkshire's corporate headquarters in the day-to-day business activities of the operating businesses. Berkshire's corporate senior management team participates in and is ultimately responsible for significant capital allocation decisions, investment activities and the selection of the Chief Executive to head each of the operating businesses.

Source: Company's annual reports.

Controllability Concept

The **controllability concept** is crucial to an effective responsibility accounting system. Managers should be evaluated based only on revenues or costs they control. Holding individuals responsible for things they cannot control is demotivating. Isolating control, however, may be difficult, as illustrated in the following case.

Dorothy Pasewark, a buyer for a large department store chain, was criticized when stores could not resell the merchandise she bought at the expected price. Ms. Pasewark countered that the sales staff caused the sluggish sales by not displaying the merchandise properly. The sales staff charged that the merchandise had too little sales potential to justify setting up more enticing displays. The division of influence between the buyer and the sales staff clouds the assignment of responsibility.

Since the exercise of control may be clouded, managers are usually held responsible for items over which they have *predominant* rather than *absolute* control. At times, responsibility accounting may be imperfect. Management must strive to ensure that praise or criticism is administered as fairly as possible.

Qualitative Reporting Features

Responsibility reports should be expressed in simple terms. If they are too complex, managers will ignore them. The reports should include only the budgeted and actual amounts of *controllable* revenues and expenses, with variances highlighted to promote management by exception. Report preparers and report users should communicate regularly to ensure the reports provide relevant information. Furthermore, reports must be timely. A report that presents yesterday's problem is not nearly as useful as one that presents today's problem.

Managerial Performance Measurement

A primary reason for a responsibility accounting system is to evaluate managerial performance. Managers are assigned responsibility for certain cost, profit, or investment centers. They are then evaluated based on how their centers perform relative to specific goals and objectives. The measurement techniques (standard costs and contribution margin format income reporting) used for cost and profit centers have been discussed in previous chapters. The remainder of this chapter discusses performance measures for investment centers.

RETURN ON INVESTMENT

LO 9-2

Evaluate investment opportunities using return on investment.

Society confers wealth, prestige, and power upon those who have control of assets. Unsurprisingly, managers are motivated to increase the amount of assets employed by the investment centers they control. When companies have additional assets available to invest, how do upper-level managers decide which centers should get them? The additional assets are frequently allotted to the managers who demonstrate the greatest potential for increasing the company's wealth. DuPont pioneered an often-copied approach to assess managerial potential by comparing the return on investment ratios of various investment centers. The **return on investment (ROI)** is the ratio of wealth generated (operating income) to the amount invested (operating assets) to generate the wealth. ROI is commonly expressed with the following equation:

$$\text{ROI} = \frac{\text{Operating income}}{\text{Operating assets}}$$

To illustrate using ROI for comparative evaluations, assume Panther Holding Company's corporate (first-level) chief financial officer (CFO) determined the ROIs for the company's three divisions (second-level investment centers). The CFO used the following accounting data from the records of each division.

	Lumber Manufacturing Division	Home Building Division	Furniture Manufacturing Division
Operating income	$ 60,000	$ 46,080	$ 81,940
Operating assets	300,000	256,000	482,000

The ROI for each division is:

$$\text{Lumber Manufacturing:} \quad \frac{\text{Operating income}}{\text{Operating assets}} = \$60{,}000 \div \$300{,}000 = 20\%$$

$$\text{Home Building:} \quad \frac{\text{Operating income}}{\text{Operating assets}} = \$46{,}080 \div \$256{,}000 = 18\%$$

$$\text{Furniture Manufacturing:} \quad \frac{\text{Operating income}}{\text{Operating assets}} = \$81{,}940 \div \$482{,}000 = 17\%$$

All other things being equal, higher ROIs indicate better performance. In this case, the Lumber Manufacturing Division manager is the best performer. Assume Panther obtains additional funding for expanding the company's operations. Which investment center is most likely to receive the additional funds?

If the manager of the Lumber Manufacturing Division convinces the upper-level management team that his division would continue to outperform the other two divisions, the Lumber Manufacturing Division would most likely get the additional funding. The manager of the lumber division would then invest the funds in additional operating assets, which would in turn increase the division's operating income. As the division prospers, Panther would reward the manager for exceptional performance. Rewarding the manager of the lumber division would likely motivate the other managers to improve their divisional ROIs. Internal competition would improve the performance of the company as a whole.

Qualitative Considerations

Why do companies compute ROI using operating income and operating assets instead of using net income and total assets? Suppose Panther's corporate headquarters closes a furniture manufacturing plant because an economic downturn temporarily reduces the demand for furniture. It would be inappropriate to include these nonoperating plant assets in the denominator of the ROI computation. Similarly, if Panther sells the furniture plant and realizes a large gain on the sale, including the gain in the numerator of the ROI formula would distort the result. Since the manager of the Furniture Manufacturing Division does not control closing the plant or selling it, it is unreasonable to include the effects of these decisions in computing the ROI. These items would, however, be included in computing net income and total assets. Most companies use operating income and operating assets to compute ROI because those variables measure performance more accurately.

CHECK YOURSELF 9.1

Green View is a lawn services company whose operations are divided into two districts. The District 1 manager controls $12,600,000 of operating assets. District 1 produced $1,512,000 of operating income during the year. The District 2 manager controls $14,200,000 of operating assets. District 2 reported $1,988,000 of operating income for the same period. Use return on investment to determine which manager is performing better.

Answer

District 1

$$\text{ROI} = \text{Operating income} \div \text{Operating assets} = \$1{,}512{,}000 \div \$12{,}600{,}000 = 12\%$$

District 2

$$\text{ROI} = \text{Operating income} \div \text{Operating assets} = \$1{,}988{,}000 \div \$14{,}200{,}000 = 14\%$$

Because the higher ROI indicates the better performance, the District 2 manager is the superior performer. This conclusion is based solely on quantitative results. In real-world practice, companies also consider qualitative factors.

Measuring Operating Assets

The meaning of ROI results is further complicated by the question of how to *value* operating assets. Suppose Echoles Rental Company's two divisions, Northern and Southern, each rent to customers a vending machine that originally cost $5,000. The vending machines have five-year useful lives and no salvage value. The Northern Division purchased its machine one year ago; the Southern Division purchased its machine three years ago. At the end of the current year, the book values of the two machines are as follows.

	Northern Division's Vending Machine	Southern Division's Vending Machine
Original cost	$ 5,000	$ 5,000
Less accumulated depreciation	(1,000)	(3,000)
Book value	$ 4,000	$ 2,000

Each machine generates operating income averaging $800 per year. The ROI for each machine this year is as follows:

$$\text{Northern Division: } \frac{\text{Operating income}}{\text{Operating assets}} = \$800 \div \$4{,}000 = 20\%$$

$$\text{Southern Division: } \frac{\text{Operating income}}{\text{Operating assets}} = \$800 \div \$2{,}000 = 40\%$$

Is the manager of the Southern Division outperforming the manager of the Northern Division? No. The only difference between the two divisions is that Southern is using an older asset than Northern. Using book value as the valuation base can distort the ROI and cause severe motivational problems. Managers will consider comparisons between different investment centers unfair because the ROIs do not accurately reflect performance. Furthermore, managers may avoid replacing obsolete equipment because purchasing new equipment would increase the dollar amount of operating assets, reducing the ROI.

Companies may minimize these problems by using original cost instead of book value in the denominator of the ROI formula. In the vending machine example, using original cost produces an ROI of 16 percent ($800 ÷ $5,000). Using original cost, however, may not entirely solve the valuation problem. As a result of inflation and technological advances, comparable equipment purchased at different times will have different costs. Some accountants advocate using *replacement cost* rather than *historical cost* as the valuation base. This solution is seldom used because determining the amount it would cost to replace particular assets is difficult. For example, imagine trying to determine the replacement cost of all the assets in a steel mill that has been operating for years.

Selecting the asset valuation base is a complex matter. In spite of its shortcomings, most companies use book value as the valuation base. Management must consider those shortcomings when using ROI to evaluate performance.

Factors Affecting Return on Investment

Management can gain insight into performance by dividing the ROI formula into two separate ratios as follows:

$$\text{ROI} = \frac{\text{Operating income}}{\text{Sales}} \times \frac{\text{Sales}}{\text{Operating assets}}$$

The first ratio on the right side of the equation is called the margin. The **margin** is a measure of management's ability to control operating expenses relative to the level of sales. In general, high margins indicate superior performance. Management can increase the margin by reducing the level of operating expenses necessary to generate sales. Decreasing operating expenses increases profitability.

The second ratio in the expanded ROI formula is called turnover. **Turnover** is a measure of the amount of operating assets employed to support the achieved level of sales. Operating assets are scarce resources. To maximize profitability, they must be used wisely. Just as excessive expenses decrease profitability, excessive investments in operating assets also limit profitability.

Both the short and expanded versions of the ROI formula produce the same end result. To illustrate, we will use the ROI for the Lumber Manufacturing Division of Panther Holding Company. Recall that the division employed $300,000 of operating assets to produce $60,000 of operating income, resulting in the following ROI:

$$\text{ROI} = \frac{\text{Operating income}}{\text{Operating assets}} = \frac{\$60,000}{\$300,000} = 20\%$$

Further analysis of the accounting records indicates the Lumber Manufacturing Division had sales of $600,000. The following computation demonstrates that the expanded ROI formula produces the same result as the short formula:

$$\begin{aligned}
\text{ROI} &= \text{Margin} \times \text{Turnover} \\
&= \frac{\text{Operating income}}{\text{Sales}} \times \frac{\text{Sales}}{\text{Operating assets}} \\
&= \frac{\$60,000}{\$600,000} \times \frac{\$600,000}{\$300,000} \\
&= 0.10 \times 2 \\
&= 20\%
\end{aligned}$$

The expanded formula may seem more complicated. It is generally more useful, however, because it helps managers see a variety of strategies to improve ROI. The expanded formula shows that profitability and ROI can be improved in three ways: *by increasing sales, by reducing expenses,* or *by reducing the investment base.* Each of these possibilities is demonstrated using the Lumber Manufacturing Division (LMD) of Panther Holding Company.

1. *Increase ROI by increasing sales.* Because some expenses are fixed, sales can be increased while those expenses are constant. Managers may even be able to reduce variable expenses by increasing productivity as sales increase. As a result, managers can increase their ROIs by increasing sales while limiting growth in expenses. To illustrate, assume the manager of LMD is able to increase sales from $600,000 to $660,000 while controlling expense growth so that operating income increases from $60,000 to $72,600. Assuming investment in operating assets remains constant at $300,000, ROI becomes:

$$\begin{aligned} \text{ROI} &= \text{Margin} \times \text{Turnover} \\ &= \frac{\text{Operating income}}{\text{Sales}} \times \frac{\text{Sales}}{\text{Operating assets}} \\ &= \frac{\$72{,}600}{\$660{,}000} \times \frac{\$660{,}000}{\$300{,}000} \\ &= 0.11 \times 2.2 \\ &= 24.2\% \end{aligned}$$

2. *Increase ROI by reducing expenses.* Suppose the manager of LMD takes a different approach. He decides to eliminate waste. By analyzing spending, he is able to cut expenses without affecting sales or the investment in operating assets. As a result of controlling expenses, operating income increases from $60,000 to $72,000. Assume the other variables remain the same as in the original example. ROI becomes:

$$\begin{aligned} \text{ROI} &= \text{Margin} \times \text{Turnover} \\ &= \frac{\text{Operating income}}{\text{Sales}} \times \frac{\text{Sales}}{\text{Operating assets}} \\ &= \frac{\$72{,}000}{\$600{,}000} \times \frac{\$600{,}000}{\$300{,}000} \\ &= 0.12 \times 2 \\ &= 24\% \end{aligned}$$

3. *Increase ROI by reducing the investment base.* Managers who focus too narrowly on income frequently overlook this possibility. Reducing the amount of funds invested in operating assets such as inventory or accounts receivable can increase profitability because the funds released can be invested in other, more productive assets. This effect is reflected in the ROI computation. For example, assume the manager of LMD launches a *just-in-time* inventory system that allows the division to reduce the amount of inventory it carries. The manager also initiates an aggressive campaign to collect receivables, which significantly reduces the outstanding receivables balance. As a result of these two initiatives, the assets employed to operate LMD fall from $300,000 to $240,000. All other variables remain the same as in the original example. ROI becomes:

$$\begin{aligned} \text{ROI} &= \text{Margin} \times \text{Turnover} \\ &= \frac{\text{Operating income}}{\text{Sales}} \times \frac{\text{Sales}}{\text{Operating assets}} \\ &= \frac{\$60{,}000}{\$600{,}000} \times \frac{\$600{,}000}{\$240{,}000} \\ &= 0.10 \times 2.5 \\ &= 25\% \end{aligned}$$

The $60,000 of funds released by reducing the operating assets can be returned to headquarters or be reinvested by LMD depending on the opportunities available.

CHECK YOURSELF 9.2

What three actions can a manager take to improve ROI?

Answer

1. Increase sales
2. Reduce expenses
3. Reduce the investment base

RESIDUAL INCOME

LO 9-3

Evaluate investment opportunities using residual income.

Suppose Panther Holding Company evaluates the manager of the Lumber Manufacturing Division (LMD) based on his ability to maximize ROI. The corporation's overall ROI is approximately 18 percent. LMD, however, has consistently outperformed the other investment centers. Its ROI is currently 20 percent. Now suppose the manager has an opportunity to invest additional funds in a project likely to earn a 19 percent ROI. Would the manager accept the investment opportunity?

These circumstances place the manager in an awkward position. The corporation would benefit from the project because the expected ROI of 19 percent is higher than the corporate average ROI of 18 percent. Personally, however, the manager would suffer from accepting the project because it would reduce the division ROI to less than the current 20 percent. The manager is forced to choose between his personal best interests and the best interests of the corporation. When faced with decisions such as these, many managers choose to benefit themselves at the expense of their corporations, a condition described as **suboptimization.**

To avoid *suboptimization,* many businesses base managerial evaluation on **residual income.** This approach measures a manager's ability to maximize earnings above some targeted level. The targeted level of earnings is based on a minimum desired ROI. Residual income is calculated as follows:

$$\text{Residual income} = \text{Operating income} - (\text{Operating assets} \times \text{Desired ROI})$$

To illustrate, recall that LMD currently earns $60,000 of operating income with the $300,000 of operating assets it controls. ROI is 20 percent ($60,000 ÷ $300,000). Assume Panther's desired ROI is 18 percent. LMD's residual income is therefore:

$$\begin{aligned}\text{Residual income} &= \text{Operating income} - (\text{Operating assets} \times \text{Desired ROI})\\ &= \$60{,}000 - (\$300{,}000 \times 0.18)\\ &= \$60{,}000 - \$54{,}000\\ &= \$6{,}000\end{aligned}$$

Now assume that Panther Holding Company has $50,000 of additional funds available to invest. Because LMD consistently performs at a high level, Panther's corporate management team offers the funds to the LMD manager. The manager believes he could invest the additional $50,000 at a 19 percent rate of return.

If the LMD manager's evaluation is based solely on ROI, he is likely to reject the additional funding because investing the funds at 19 percent would lower his overall ROI. If the LMD manager's evaluation is based on residual income, however, he is likely to accept the

FOCUS ON INTERNATIONAL ISSUES

DO MANAGERS IN DIFFERENT COMPANIES STRESS THE SAME PERFORMANCE MEASURES?

About the only ratio companies are required to disclose in their annual reports to stockholders is the earnings per share ratio. Nevertheless, many companies choose to show their performance as measured by other ratios, as well as providing nonratio data not required by GAAP. The types of ratio data companies choose to include in their annual reports provide a sense of what performance measure they consider most important.

A review of several publicly traded companies from the United Kingdom, Japan, and the United States will show that the most common ratios presented are variations of the return on sales percentage and the return on investment percentage, although they may be called by different names. The country in which the company is located does not seem to determine which ratio it will emphasize.

One nonratio performance measure that is popular with companies in all three countries is free cash flow, and it is usually reported in total pounds, yen, or dollars. Be sure to exercise caution before comparing one company's free cash flow, return on sales, or return on investment to those of other companies. There are no official rules governing how these data are calculated, and different companies make different interpretations about how to compute these measurements.

©John Woodworth/Getty Images

funds because an additional investment at 19 percent would increase his residual income as follows:

$$\begin{aligned}\text{Operating income} &= \$50{,}000 \times 0.19\\ &= \$9{,}500\\ \text{Residual income} &= \text{Operating income} - (\text{Operating assets} \times \text{Desired ROI})\\ &= \$9{,}500 - (\$50{,}000 \times 0.18)\\ &= \$9{,}500 - \$9{,}000\\ &= \$500\end{aligned}$$

Accepting the new project would add \$500 to LMD's residual income. If the manager of LMD is evaluated based on his ability to maximize residual income, he would benefit by investing in any project that returns an ROI in excess of the desired 18 percent. The reduction in LMD's overall ROI does not enter into the decision. The residual income approach solves the problem of suboptimization.

The primary disadvantage of the residual income approach is that it measures performance in absolute dollars. As a result, a manager's residual income may be larger simply because her investment base is larger rather than because her performance is superior.

To illustrate, return to the example where Panther Holding Company has \$50,000 of additional funds to invest. Assume the manager of the Lumber Manufacturing Division (LMD) and the manager of the Furniture Manufacturing Division (FMD) each have investment opportunities expected to earn a 19 percent return. Recall that Panther's desired ROI is 18 percent. If corporate headquarters allots \$40,000 of the funds to the manager of LMD and \$10,000 to the manager of FMD, the increase in residual income earned by each division is as follows:

$$\text{LMD's residual income} = (\$40{,}000 \times 0.19) - (\$40{,}000 \times 0.18) = \$400$$

$$\text{FMD's residual income} = (\$10{,}000 \times 0.19) - (\$10{,}000 \times 0.18) = \$100$$

REALITY BYTES

©Jason LaVeris/Getty Images

Thinking about investments usually conjures up images of buildings and equipment, but investments typically include a much broader range of expenditures. For example, if Walmart plans to open a new store, it has to make an investment in inventory to stock the store that is as permanent as the building. But investment expenditures can be for items much less tangible than inventory. Consider the making of a movie.

While it is true that making a movie can require expenditures for items such as cameras and sets, the single highest cost can often be for actors' salaries. Although movie fans may focus on how much a movie grosses at the box office, from a business perspective it is the movie's ROI that matters.

From an ROI perspective the question is: Which actor generates the highest dollars of return for each dollar he or she is paid? To this end, for the past several years *Forbes* has calculated the "Best Actors for the Buck" list. Calculating the ROI for an actor in a movie, rather than for the entire investment in the movie, can be tricky and requires several estimates. For example, should the credit for the spectacular success of the movie *Star Wars: The Last Jedi* go to the main actor, Mark Hamill, or to the writer/director, Rian Johnson? Despite these challenges, *Forbes* reviews the financial performance of the highest-paid actors who had starred in at least three movies in the past five years and creates the list.

And the winner is . . . ? In both 2017 the actor with the highest return per dollar paid was Jeremy Renner, who starred in *Captain America* and *Mission: Impossible*. According to *Forbes,* he returned $93.80 for each $1.00 of salary he was paid.

Source: Forbes.com

Does LMD's higher residual income mean LMD's manager is outperforming FMD's manager? No. It means LMD's manager received more operating assets than FMD's manager received.

Calculating Multiple ROIs and/or RIs for the Same Company

You may be asked to calculate different ROI and RI measures for the same company. For example, ROI and/or RI may be calculated for the company as a whole, for segments of the company, for specific investment opportunities, and for individual managers. An example is shown in Check Yourself 9.3.

Responsibility Accounting and the Balanced Scorecard

Throughout the text, we have discussed many financial measures companies use to evaluate managerial performance. Examples include standard cost systems to evaluate cost center managers; the contribution margin income statement to evaluate profit center managers; and ROI or residual income to evaluate the performance of investment center managers. Many companies may have goals and objectives such as "satisfaction guaranteed" or "we try harder" that are more suitably evaluated using nonfinancial measures. To assess how well they accomplish the full range of their missions, many companies use a *balanced scorecard.*

CHECK YOURSELF 9.3

Tambor Incorporated (TI) earned operating income of $4,730,400 on operating assets of $26,280,000 during Year 1. The Western Division earned $748,000 on operating assets of $3,400,000. TI has offered the Western Division $1,100,000 of additional operating assets. The manager of the Western Division believes he could use the additional assets to generate operating income amounting to $220,000. TI has a desired return on investment (ROI) of 17 percent. Determine the ROI and RI for TI, the Western Division, and the additional investment opportunity.

Answer

Return on investment (ROI) = Operating income ÷ Operating assets
ROI for TI = $4,730,400 ÷ $26,280,000 = 18%
ROI for Western Division = $748,000 ÷ $3,400,000 = 22%
ROI for investment opportunity = $220,000 ÷ $1,100,000 = 20%

Residual income (RI) = Operating income − (Operating assets × Desired ROI)
RI for TI = $4,730,400 − ($26,280,000 × 0.17) = $262,800
RI for Western Division = $748,000 − ($3,400,000 × 0.17) = $170,000
RI for investment opportunity = $220,000 − ($1,100,000 × 0.17) = $33,000

A **balanced scorecard** includes financial and nonfinancial performance measures. Standard costs, income measures, ROI, and residual income are common financial measures used in a balanced scorecard. Nonfinancial measures include defect rates, cycle time, on-time deliveries, number of new products or innovations, safety measures, and customer satisfaction surveys. Many companies compose their scorecards to highlight leading versus lagging measures. For example, customer satisfaction survey data are a leading indicator of sales growth, which is a lagging measure. The balanced scorecard is a holistic approach to evaluating managerial performance. It is gaining widespread acceptance among world-class companies.

<< A Look Back

The practice of delegating authority and responsibility is referred to as *decentralization*. Clear lines of authority and responsibility are essential in establishing a responsibility accounting system. In a responsibility accounting system, segment managers are held accountable for profits based on the amount of control they have over the profits in their segment.

Responsibility reports are used to compare actual results with budgets. The reports should be simple, with variances highlighted to promote the *management by exception* doctrine. Individual managers should be held responsible only for those revenues or costs they control. Each manager should receive only summary information about the performance of the responsibility centers under her supervision.

A *responsibility center* is the point in an organization where control over revenue or expense is located. *Cost centers* are segments that incur costs but do not generate revenues. *Profit centers* incur costs and also generate revenues, producing a measurable profit. *Investment centers* incur costs, generate revenues, and use identifiable capital investments.

One of the primary purposes of responsibility accounting is to evaluate managerial performance. Comparing actual results with standards and budgets and calculating *return on investment* are used for this purpose. Because return on investment uses revenues, expenses, and investment, problems with measuring these parameters must be considered. The return on investment can be analyzed in terms of the margin earned on sales as well as the turnover (asset utilization) during the period. The *residual income approach* is sometimes used to avoid *suboptimization,* which occurs when managers choose to reject investment projects that would benefit their company's ROI but would reduce their investment center's ROI. The residual income approach evaluates managers based on their ability to generate earnings above some targeted level of earnings.

A Look Forward >>

The next chapter expands on the concepts you learned in this chapter. You will see how managers select investment opportunities that will affect their future ROIs. You will learn to use present value techniques that consider the time value of money; specifically, you will learn to compute the net present value and the internal rate of return for potential investment opportunities. You will also learn to use less sophisticated analytical techniques such as payback and the unadjusted rate of return.

APPENDIX

Transfer Pricing

LO 9-4

Describe how transfer prices may be established.

In vertically integrated companies, one division commonly sells goods or services to another division. For example, in the case of Panther Holding Company (Exhibit 9.1), the Lumber Manufacturing Division may sell lumber to the Home Building and Furniture Manufacturing Divisions. When such intercompany sales occur, the price to charge is likely to become a heated issue.

In a decentralized organization, each division is likely to be defined as an investment center. Division managers are held responsible for profitability. When goods are transferred internally, the sales price charged by the selling division becomes a cost to the buying division. The amount of profit included in the **transfer price** will increase the selling division's earnings and decrease the purchasing division's earnings (via increased expenses). The selling division benefits from getting the highest possible price; the purchasing division seeks the lowest possible price. When managers are competitively evaluated based on profitability measures, the transfer price is the subject of considerable controversy.

Companies use three common approaches to establish transfer prices: (1) price based on market forces, (2) price based on negotiation, and (3) price based on cost. Exhibit 9.4 shows some specific measures and the frequency of their use in domestic transfer pricing.

Market-Based Transfer Prices

The preferred method for establishing transfer prices is to base them on some form of competitive market price. Ideally, selling divisions should be authorized to sell merchandise to outsiders as well as, or in preference to, other divisions. Similarly, purchasing divisions should have the option to buy goods from outsiders if they are able to obtain favorable prices. However, both selling and purchasing divisions would be motivated to deal with each other because of savings in selling, administrative, and transportation costs that arise as a natural result of internal transactions.

Market-based transfer prices are preferable because they promote efficiency and fairness. Market forces coupled with the responsibility for profitability motivate managers to use their resources effectively. For example, Jerry Lowe, the manager of the lumber division, may stop producing the high-quality boards the furniture division uses if he finds it is more profitable to produce low-quality lumber. The furniture division can buy its needed material from outside companies that have chosen to operate in the less-profitable, high-quality market sector. The company as a whole benefits from Mr. Lowe's insight. An additional advantage of using market prices is the sense of fairness associated with them. It is difficult for a manager to complain that the price she is being charged is too high when she has the

EXHIBIT 9.4

What Companies Actually Use as Transfer Prices

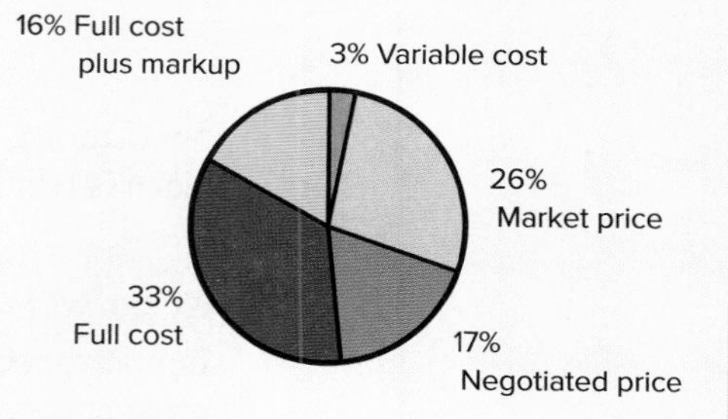

Source: R. Tang, *Current Trends and Corporate Cases in Transfer Pricing,* Praeger, 2002.

FOCUS ON INTERNATIONAL ISSUES

©Spaces Images/Blend Images

The issue of transfer pricing is mostly relevant to performance evaluation of investment centers and their managers. If a company does business in only one country, transfer prices do not affect the overall profit of the company because the cost that will be recorded as an expense for the company as a whole is the actual cost incurred to produce it, not its transfer price. However, the situation can be different if the producing division is in one country and the acquiring division is in another. This difference occurs because income tax rates are not the same in all countries.

Assume the Global Tool Company manufactures a product in South Korea for the equivalent of $10. The product is transferred to another segment that operates in the United States where it is ultimately sold for $18. Now, assume the income tax rate is 40 percent in South Korea and 30 percent in the United States. Ignoring all other costs, what amount of taxes will the company pay if the transfer price is set at $10? What amount of taxes will the company pay if the transfer price is set at $18?

If a $10 transfer price is used, then all of the company's $8 per unit profit ($18 − $10) will be recognized in the United States. Since the item is assumed to have been "sold" in South Korea at an amount equal to its production cost, there will be no profit for the South Korean division of the company ($10 − $10 = $0). The U.S. division will pay $2.40 in taxes ($8 × 0.30 = $2.40). Conversely, if the transfer price is $18, then all of the profit will be reported in South Korea, and $3.20 per unit of taxes will be paid ($8 × 0.40 = $3.20).

The Internal Revenue Service has rules to prevent companies from setting transfer prices simply for the purpose of reducing taxes, but many companies have been accused of such practices over the years. Remember, it is often impossible to prove exactly what the best transfer price should be. Even though the company in our hypothetical example could not get away with such extreme transfer prices as $10 or $18, it might try to set the price a bit lower than it should be in order to shift more profit to the segment in the United States, where the assumed tax rate is lower.

Despite the difficulties of proving what proper transfer prices should be, the IRS does pursue companies it believes are violating the law. In fact, as of 2006, the largest settlement in the history of the IRS involved a transfer pricing case against the British-based pharmaceutical company **GlaxoSmithKline**. The company agreed to pay the IRS $3.4 billion to settle charges that its American unit had improperly overpaid the parent company, thus shifting profits from the United States to the United Kingdom from 1989 through 2005. More recently, **Coca-Cola** announced in September 2015 that the IRS had notified the company that it may have to pay up to $3.3 billion in additional taxes due to improper international transfer pricing. Coke believes the charges are without merit, and the issue may take years to settle. The IRS does not always win these cases. The IRS had been seeking a $1.5 billion payment from **Amazon** related to transfer pricing issues involving its subsidiary in Luxemburg. In March 2017 the U.S. Tax Court sided with Amazon, ruling that it did not owe the extra taxes.

Tax disputes related to transfer pricing are not just a problem in the United States. In May 2017 an Australian court ruled that **Chevron** owed the country $250 million in additional taxes related to the interest rates it charged its subsidiaries in Australia. By charging its Australian subsidiaries higher than market rates of interest, the profits in Australia were reduced, thus reducing the taxes Chevron paid to Australia. Transfer-pricing covers the price for a lot of things, not just physical things like equipment parts or retail inventory items.

With respect to the settlement at Glaxo, the commissioner of the IRS stated, "We have consistently said that transfer pricing is one of the most significant challenges for us in the area of corporate tax administration."

Sources: "IRS Accepts Settlement Offer in Largest Transfer Pricing Dispute," from the IRS website, September 11, 2006; Coke's Form 8-K, September 18, 2015; *The Wall Street Journal's* website, March 23 and May 23, 2017.

opportunity to seek a lower price elsewhere. The natural justice of the competitive marketplace is firmly implanted in the psyches of most modern managers.

Negotiated Transfer Prices

In many instances, a necessary product is not available from outside companies or the market price may not be in the best interest of the company as a whole. Sometimes a division makes a unique product that is used only by one of its company's other divisions; no external market price is available to use as a base for determining the transfer price. Other times, market-based transfer prices may lead to suboptimization, discussed earlier.

Consider the case of Garms Industries. It operates several relatively autonomous divisions. One division, TrueTrust Motors Inc., makes small electric motors for use in appliances such as refrigerators, washing machines, and fans. Another Garms division, CleanCo, makes and sells approximately 30,000 vacuum cleaners per year. CleanCo currently purchases the motors used in its vacuums from a company that is not part of Garms Industries. The president of Garms asked the TrueTrust division manager to establish a price at which it could make and sell motors to CleanCo. The manager submitted the following cost and price data.

Variable (unit-level) costs	$45
Per-unit fixed cost at a volume of 30,000 units	15
Allocated corporate-level facility-sustaining costs	20
Total cost	$80

Note: TrueTrust has enough excess capacity that its existing business will not be affected by a decision to make motors for CleanCo. However, TrueTrust would be required to incur additional fixed costs to purchase equipment and hire a supervisor to make the motors that CleanCo requires.

The TrueTrust manager added a profit margin of $10 per unit and offered to provide motors to CleanCo at a price of $90 per unit. When the offer was presented to the CleanCo division manager, she rejected it. Her division was currently buying motors in the open market for $70 each. Competitive pressures in the vacuum cleaner market would not permit an increase in the sales price of her product. Accepting TrueTrust's offer would significantly increase CleanCo's costs and reduce the division's profitability.

After studying the cost data, Garms' president concluded the company as a whole would suffer from suboptimization if CleanCo were to continue purchasing motors from a third-party vendor. He noted that the allocated corporate-level facility-sustaining costs were not relevant to the transfer pricing decision because they would be incurred regardless of whether TrueTrust made the motors for CleanCo. He recognized that both the variable and fixed costs were relevant because they could be avoided if TrueTrust did not make the motors. Since TrueTrust's avoidable cost of $60 ($45 variable cost + $15 fixed cost) per unit was below the $70 price per unit that CleanCo was currently paying, Garms would save $10 per motor, thereby increasing overall company profitability by $300,000 ($10 cost savings per unit × 30,000 units). The president established a reasonable range for a negotiated transfer price.

If the market price were less than the avoidable cost of production, the supplying division (TrueTrust) and the company as a whole (Garms) would be better off to buy the product than to make it. It would therefore be unreasonable to expect TrueTrust to sell a product for less than its avoidable cost of production, thereby establishing the avoidable cost as the bottom point of the reasonable range for the transfer price. On the other hand, it would be unreasonable to expect an acquiring division (CleanCo) to pay more than the price it is currently paying for motors. As a result, the market price becomes the top point of the reasonable range for the transfer price. The reasonable transfer price range can be expressed as follows:

Market price ≥ Reasonable transfer price ≥ Avoidable product cost

In the case of Garms Industries, the reasonable range of the transfer price for vacuum cleaner motors is between the market price of $70 per unit and the avoidable production cost of $60.[1] Any transfer price within this range would benefit both divisions and the company as a whole. Garms' president encouraged the two division managers to negotiate a transfer price within the reasonable range that would satisfy both parties.

[1]This discussion assumes the supplying division (TrueTrust) has excess capacity. When the supplying division is operating at full capacity and has external buyers, the minimum price for the reasonable transfer price range would include not only the avoidable cost but also an opportunity cost. An opportunity cost exists when the supplying division must forgo the opportunity to profit from sales it could otherwise make to external buyers. On the other hand, if the supplying division has enough capacity to fill both existing orders and the additional orders on which the transfer price is negotiated, the opportunity cost is zero. In other words, the supplying division does not have to give up anything to accept an order from another division. A full discussion of opportunity cost is complex. It is covered in more advanced courses.

Under the right set of circumstances, a **negotiated transfer price** can be more beneficial than a market-based transfer price. Allowing the managers involved to agree to a negotiated price preserves the notion of fairness. The element of profit remains intact and the evaluation concepts discussed in this chapter can be applied. Negotiated prices may offer many of the same advantages as market prices. They should be the first alternative when a company is unable to use market-based transfer prices.

Suppose the two division managers cannot agree on a negotiated transfer price. Should the president of Garms Industries establish a reasonable price and force the managers to accept it? There is no definitive answer to this question. However, most senior-level executives recognize the motivational importance of maintaining autonomy in a decentralized organization. So long as the negative consequences are not disastrous, division managers are usually permitted to exercise their own judgment. In other words, the long-term benefits derived from autonomous management outweigh the short-term disadvantages of suboptimization.

Cost-Based Transfer Prices

The least desirable transfer price option is a **cost-based transfer price.** To use cost, it must first be determined. Some companies base the transfer price on *variable cost* (a proxy for avoidable cost). Other companies use *full cost* (variable cost plus an allocated portion of fixed cost) as the transfer price. In either case, basing transfer prices on cost removes the profit motive. Without profitability as a goal, the incentive to control cost is diminished. One department's inefficiency is simply passed on to the next department. The result is low companywide profitability. Despite this potential detrimental effect, many companies base transfer prices on cost because cost represents an objective number that is available. When a company uses cost-based transfer prices, *it should use standard rather than actual costs.* Departments will therefore at least be responsible for the variances they generate, which will encourage some degree of cost control.

Video lectures and accompanying self-assessment quizzes are available in *Connect* for all learning objectives.

SELF-STUDY REVIEW PROBLEM

The following financial statements apply to Hola Division, one of three investment centers operated by Costa Corporation. Costa Corporation has a desired rate of return of 15 percent. Costa Corporation headquarters has $80,000 of additional operating assets to assign to the investment centers.

HOLA DIVISION Income Statement For the Year Ended December 31, Year 3	
Sales revenue	$ 78,695
Cost of goods sold	(50,810)
Gross margin	27,885
Operating expenses	
Selling expenses	(1,200)
Depreciation expense	(1,125)
Operating income	25,560
Nonoperating expense	
Loss on sale of land	(3,200)
Net income	$ 22,360

HOLA DIVISION Balance Sheet As of December 31, Year 3	
Assets	
Cash	$ 8,089
Accounts receivable	22,870
Merchandise inventory	33,460
Equipment less acc. dep.	77,581
Nonoperating assets	8,250
Total assets	$150,250
Liabilities	
Accounts payable	$ 5,000
Notes payable	58,000
Stockholders' equity	
Common stock	55,000
Retained earnings	32,250
Total liab. and stk. equity	$150,250

Required

a. Should Costa use operating income or net income to determine the rate of return (ROI) for the Hola investment center? Explain.

b. Should Costa use operating assets or total assets to determine the ROI for the Hola investment center? Explain.

c. Calculate the ROI for Hola.

d. The manager of the Hola division has an opportunity to invest the funds at an ROI of 17 percent. The other two divisions have investment opportunities that yield only 16 percent. The manager of Hola rejects the additional funding. Why would the manager of Hola reject the funds under these circumstances?

e. Calculate the residual income from the investment opportunity available to Hola and explain how residual income could be used to encourage the manager to accept the additional funds.

Solution to Requirement *a*

Costa should use operating income because net income frequently includes items over which management has no control, such as the loss on sale of land.

Solution to Requirement *b*

Costa should use operating assets because total assets frequently includes items over which management has no control, such as assets not currently in use.

Solution to Requirement *c*

Operating assets = Total assets − Nonoperating assets

Operating assets = $150,250 − $8,250 = $142,000

ROI = Operating income ÷ Operating assets = $25,560 ÷ $142,000 = 18%

Solution to Requirement *d*

Since the rate of return on the investment opportunity (17 percent) is below Hola's current ROI (18 percent), accepting the opportunity would decrease Hola's average ROI, which would have a negative effect on the manager's performance evaluation. While it is to the advantage of the company as a whole for Hola to accept the investment opportunity, it will reflect negatively on the manager to do so. This phenomenon is called *suboptimization.*

Solution to Requirement *e*

Operating income from the investment opportunity is \$13,600 (\$80,000 × 0.17)

$$\text{Residual income} = \text{Operating income} - (\text{Operating assets} \times \text{Desired ROI})$$

$$\text{Residual income} = \$13{,}600 - (\$80{,}000 \times 0.15)$$

$$\text{Residual income} = \$13{,}600 - \$12{,}000$$

$$\text{Residual income} = \$1{,}600$$

Since the investment opportunity would increase Hola's residual income, the acceptance of the opportunity would improve the manager's performance evaluation, thereby motivating the manager to accept it.

KEY TERMS

Balanced scorecard 414
Controllability concept 406
Cost-based transfer price 418
Cost center 403
Decentralization 402
Investment center 403
Management by exception 403
Margin 409
Market-based transfer price 415
Negotiated transfer price 418
Profit center 403
Residual income 411
Responsibility accounting 400
Responsibility center 402
Responsibility report 403
Return on investment (ROI) 407
Suboptimization 411
Transfer price 415
Turnover 409

QUESTIONS

1. Pam Kelly says she has no faith in budgets. Her company, Kelly Manufacturing Corporation, spent thousands of dollars to install a sophisticated budget system. One year later the company's expenses are still out of control. She believes budgets simply do not work. How would you respond to Ms. Kelly's beliefs?
2. All travel expenses incurred by Pure Water Pump Corporation are reported only to John Daniels, the company president. Pure Water is a multinational company with five divisions. Are travel expenses reported following the responsibility accounting concept? Explain.
3. What are five potential advantages of decentralization?
4. Who receives responsibility reports? What do the reports include?
5. How does the concept of predominant control as opposed to that of absolute control apply to responsibility accounting?
6. How do responsibility reports promote the management by exception doctrine?
7. What is a responsibility center?
8. What are the three types of responsibility centers? Explain how each differs from the others.
9. Carmen Douglas claims that her company's performance evaluation system is unfair. Her company uses return on investment (ROI) to evaluate performance. Ms. Douglas says that even though her ROI is lower than another manager's, her performance is far superior. Is it possible that Ms. Douglas is correct? Explain your position.
10. What two factors affect the computation of return on investment?
11. What three ways can a manager increase the return on investment?
12. How can a residual income approach to performance evaluation reduce the likelihood of suboptimization?
13. Is it true that the manager with the highest residual income is always the best performer?
14. Why are transfer prices important to managers who are evaluated based on profitability criteria?
15. What are three approaches to establishing transfer prices? List the most desirable approach first and the least desirable last.
16. If cost is the basis for transfer pricing, should actual or standard cost be used? Why?

MULTIPLE-CHOICE QUESTIONS

Multiple-choice questions are available in *Connect*.

EXERCISES—SERIES A

connect **All applicable Exercises in Series A are available in *Connect*.**

Exercise 9-1A *Organization chart and responsibilities* LO 9-1

The production manager is responsible for the assembly, cleaning, and finishing departments. The executive vice president reports directly to the president but is responsible for the activities of the production department, the finance department, and the sales department. The sales manager is responsible for the advertising department.

Required

Arrange this information into an organization chart and indicate the responsibility levels involved.

Exercise 9-2A *Responsibility report* LO 9-1

Airdrie Department Store is divided into three major departments: Men's Clothing, Women's Clothing, and Home Furnishings. Each of these three departments is supervised by a manager who reports to the general manager. The departments are subdivided into different sections managed by floor supervisors. The Home Furnishings Department has three floor supervisors, one for furniture, one for lamps, and one for housewares. The following items were included in the company's most recent responsibility report:

Travel expenses for the housewares buyer
Seasonal decorations for the furniture section
Revenues for the Home Furnishings Department
Administrative expenses for the Men's Clothing Department
Utility cost allocated to the Home Furnishings Department
Cost of part-time Christmas help for the Women's Department
Delivery expenses for furniture purchases
Salaries for the sales staff in the lamp section
Storewide revenues
Salary of the general manager
Salary of the Men's Clothing Department manager
Allocated companywide advertising expense
Depreciation on the facility

Required

Which items are likely to be the responsibility of the Home Furnishings Department manager?

Exercise 9-3A *Organization chart and controllable costs* LO 9-1

Pagwa Company has employees with the following job titles:

President of the company
Vice president of marketing
Product manager
Controller
Vice president of manufacturing
Treasurer
Regional sales manager
Personnel manager
Cashier
Vice president of finance
Fringe benefits manager
Board of directors

Production supervisors
Vice president of administration
Sales office manager

Required

a. Design an organization chart using these job titles.
b. Identify some possible controllable costs for the person holding each job title.

LO 9-1

Exercise 9-4A *Income statement for internal use*

Dunlop Company has provided the following Year 2 data.

Budget	
Sales	$400,000
Variable product costs	163,000
Variable selling expense	40,000
Other variable expenses	3,000
Fixed product costs	10,500
Fixed selling expense	20,000
Other fixed expenses	1,600
Interest expense	650
Variances	
Sales	3,200 U
Variable product costs	2,600 F
Variable selling expense	1,250 U
Other variable expenses	600 U
Fixed product costs	110 F
Fixed selling expense	195 F
Other fixed expenses	75 U
Interest expense	50 F

Required

Prepare in good form a budgeted and actual income statement for internal use. Separate operating income from net income in the statements.

LO 9-1

Exercise 9-5A *Evaluating a cost center including flexible budgeting concepts*

Muskrat Medical Equipment Company makes a blood pressure measuring kit. Jason McCoy is the production manager. The production department's static budget and actual results for Year 3 follow.

	Static Budget	Actual Results
Production in units	*60,000 kits*	*64,000 kits*
Direct materials	$ 525,000	$ 655,000
Direct labor	450,000	464,000
Variable manufacturing overhead	120,000	135,000
Total variable costs	1,095,000	1,254,000
Fixed manufacturing overhead	525,000	512,500
Total manufacturing cost	$1,620,000	$1,766,500

Required

a. Convert the static budget into a flexible budget.

b. Use the flexible budget to evaluate Mr. McCoy's performance.

c. Explain why Mr. McCoy's performance evaluation does not include sales revenue and net income.

Exercise 9-6A *Evaluating a profit center*

LO 9-1

Helen Kaito, the president of Gladstone Toys Corporation, is trying to determine this year's pay raises for the store managers. Gladstone Toys has seven stores in the southwestern United States. Corporate headquarters purchases all toys from different manufacturers globally and distributes them to individual stores. Additionally, headquarters makes decisions regarding location and size of stores. These practices allow Gladstone Toys to receive volume discounts from vendors and to implement coherent marketing strategies. Within a set of general guidelines, store managers have the flexibility to adjust product prices and hire local employees. Ms. Kaito is considering three possible performance measures for evaluating the individual stores: cost of goods sold, return on sales (net income divided by sales), and return on investment.

Required

a. Using the concept of controllability, advise Ms. Kaito about the best performance measure.

b. Explain how a balanced scorecard can be used to help Ms. Kaito.

Exercise 9-7A *Return on investment*

LO 9-2

An investment center of Tribune Corporation shows an operating income of $7,500 on total operating assets of $125,000.

Required

Compute the return on investment. Round the computation to two decimal points.

Exercise 9-8A *Return on investment*

LO 9-2

Eastevan Company calculated its return on investment as 10 percent. Sales are now $300,000, and the amount of total operating assets is $320,000.

Required

a. If expenses are reduced by $28,000 and sales remain unchanged, what return on investment will result?

b. If both sales and expenses cannot be changed, what change in the amount of operating assets is required to achieve the same result?

Exercise 9-9A *Residual income*

LO 9-3

Climax Corporation has a desired rate of return of 7.50 percent. William Tobin is in charge of one of Climax's three investment centers. His center controlled operating assets of $4,000,000 that were used to earn $480,000 of operating income.

Required

Compute Mr. Tobin's residual income.

Exercise 9-10A *Residual income*

LO 9-3

Gletchen Cough Drops operates two divisions. The following information pertains to each division for Year 1.

	Division A	Division B
Sales	$480,000	$300,000
Operating income	$ 32,000	$ 24,000
Average operating assets	$200,000	$160,000
Company's desired rate of return	10%	10%

Required

a. Compute each division's residual income.

b. Which division increased the company's profitability more?

LO 9-2, 9-3

Exercise 9-11A *Return on investment and residual income*

Required

Supply the missing information in the following table for Unify Company.

Sales	$605,000
ROI	?
Operating assets	?
Operating income	?
Turnover	2.2
Residual income	?
Operating profit margin	0.08
Desired rate of return	10%

LO 9-2, 9-3

Exercise 9-12A *Comparing return on investment with residual income*

The Monarch Division of Allgood Corporation has a current ROI of 12 percent. The company target ROI is 8 percent. The Monarch Division has an opportunity to invest $4,800,000 at 10 percent but is reluctant to do so because its ROI will fall to 11.25 percent. The present investment base for the division is $8,000,000.

Required

Demonstrate how Allgood can motivate the Monarch Division to make the investment by using the residual income method.

LO 9-2, 9-3

Exercise 9-13A *Return on investment and residual income*

Lumberton Home Maintenance Company (LHMC) earned operating income of $6,000,000 on operating assets of $62,500,000 during Year 2. The Tree Cutting Division earned $1,000,000 on operating assets of $10,000,000. LHMC has offered the Tree Cutting Division $1,250,000 of additional operating assets. The manager of the Tree Cutting Division believes he could use the additional assets to generate operating income amounting to $112,500. LHMC has a desired return on investment (ROI) of 8 percent.

Required

a. Calculate the return on investment for LHMC, the Tree Cutting Division, and the additional investment opportunity.

b. Calculate the residual income for LHMC, the Tree Cutting Division, and the additional investment opportunity.

LO 9-4

Exercise 9-14A *Transfer pricing (Appendix)*

Kelowna Company has two divisions, A and B. Division A manufactures 12,000 units of product per month. The cost per unit is calculated as follows.

Variable costs	$10
Fixed costs	20
Total cost	$30

Division B uses the product created by Division A. No outside market for Division A's product exists. The fixed costs incurred by Division A are allocated headquarters-level facility-sustaining costs. The manager of Division A suggests that the product be transferred to Division B at a price of at least $30 per unit. The manager of Division B argues that the same product can be purchased from another company for $26 per unit and requests permission to do so.

Required

a. Should Kelowna allow the manager of Division B to purchase the product from the outside company for $26 per unit? Explain.

b. Assume you are the president of the company. Write a brief paragraph recommending a resolution of the conflict between the two divisional managers.

Exercise 9-15A *Transfer pricing and fixed cost per unit*

LO 9-4

The Rolling Parts Division of Delk Company plans to set up a facility with the capacity to make 20,000 units annually of a webcam for laptop computers. The avoidable cost of making the webcam is as follows.

Costs	Total	Cost per Unit
Variable cost	$200,000	$10
Fixed cost	300,000	15 (at capacity)

Required

a. Assume that Delk's Langford Division is currently purchasing 12,000 of the same type of webcam each year from an outside supplier at a market price of $30. What would be the financial consequence to Delk if the Rolling Parts Division makes the webcam and sells it to the Langford Division? Does a reasonable range of transfer prices exist? If so, what is the range?

b. Suppose that the Langford Division increases production so that it could use 20,000 webcams made by the Rolling Parts Division. How would the change in volume affect the range of transfer prices that would financially benefit both divisions?

PROBLEMS—SERIES A

connect **All applicable Problems in Series A are available in *Connect*.**

Problem 9-16A *Determining controllable costs*

LO 9-1

Juan Rubio is the manager of the production department of Radison Corporation. Radison incurred the following costs during Year 2.

Production department supplies	$ 22,000
Administrative salaries	700,000
Production wages	1,160,000
Materials used	1,058,400
Depreciation on manufacturing equipment	723,200
Corporate-level rental expense	480,000
Property taxes	137,200
Sales salaries	573,600

Required

Prepare a list of expenditures that Mr. Rubio controls.

LO 9-1

Problem 9-17A *Controllability, responsibility, and balanced scorecard*

Carol Morgan manages the production division of Casper Corporation. Ms. Morgan's responsibility report for the month of August follows.

	Budget	Actual	Variance
Controllable costs			
Raw materials	$ 92,000	$110,400	$18,400 U
Labor	20,000	30,590	10,590 U
Maintenance	6,400	9,200	2,800 U
Supplies	4,700	2,200	2,500 F
Total	$123,100	$152,390	$29,290 U

The budget had called for 4,600 pounds of raw materials at $20 per pound, and 4,600 pounds were used during August; however, the purchasing department paid $24 per pound for the materials. The wage rate used to establish the budget was $40 per hour. On August 1, however, it increased to $46 as the result of an inflation index provision in the union contract. Furthermore, the purchasing department did not provide the materials needed in accordance with the production schedule, which forced Ms. Morgan to use 110 hours of overtime at a $69 rate. The projected 500 hours of labor in the budget would have been sufficient had it not been for the 110 hours of overtime. In other words, 610 hours of labor were used in August.

Required

a. When confronted with the unfavorable variances in her responsibility report, Ms. Morgan argued that the report was unfair because it held her accountable for materials and labor variances that she did *not* control. Is she correct? Comment specifically on the materials and labor variances.

b. Prepare a responsibility report that reflects the cost items that Ms. Morgan controlled during August.

c. Will the changes in the revised responsibility report require corresponding changes in the financial statements? Explain.

d. Explain how a balanced scorecard may be used to improve the performance evaluation.

LO 9-1

excel

Problem 9-18A *Performance reports and evaluation*

Amarillo Corporation has four divisions: the assembly division, the processing division, the machining division, and the packing division. All four divisions are under the control of the vice president of manufacturing. Each division has a manager and several departments that are directed by supervisors. The chain of command runs downward from vice president to division manager to supervisor. The processing division is composed of the paint and finishing departments. The May responsibility reports for the supervisors of these departments follow.

CHECK FIGURE

a. Total controllable costs: $810,500 (actual)

	Budgeted*	Actual	Variance
Paint Department			
Controllable costs			
Raw materials	$ 84,000	$86,000	$ 2,000 U
Labor	115,400	128,000	12,600 U
Repairs	9,600	7,740	1,860 F
Maintenance	5,200	4,920	280 F
Total	$214,200	$226,660	$12,460 U
Finishing Department			
Controllable costs			
Raw materials	$ 60,000	$ 58,000	$2,000 F
Labor	86,600	79,800	6,800 F
Repairs	5,660	6,340	680 U
Maintenance	3,360	4,100	740 U
Total	$155,620	$148,240	$7,380 F

*Amarillo uses flexible budgets for performance evaluation.

Other pertinent cost data for May follow.

	Budgeted*	Actual
Cost data of other divisions		
Assembly	$760,000	$748,600
Machining	580,000	592,800
Packing	829,900	811,400
Other costs associated with		
Processing division manager	440,000	435,600
Vice president of manufacturing	256,000	266,120

*Amarillo uses flexible budgets for performance evaluation.

Required

a. Prepare a responsibility report for the manager of the processing division.

b. Prepare a responsibility report for the vice president of manufacturing.

c. Explain where the $12,600 unfavorable labor variance in the paint department supervisor's report is included in the vice president's report.

d. Based on the responsibility report prepared in Requirement *a*, explain where the processing division manager should concentrate his attention.

Problem 9-19A *Different types of responsibility centers*

LO 9-1

Yalaha National Bank is a large municipal bank with several branch offices. The bank's computer department handles all data processing for bank operations. In addition, the bank sells the computer department's expertise in systems development and excess machine time to several small business firms, serving them as a service bureau.

The bank currently treats the computer department as a cost center. The manager of the computer department prepares a cost budget annually for senior bank officials to approve. Monthly operating reports compare actual and budgeted expenses. Revenues from the department's service bureau activities are treated as other income by the bank and are not reflected on the computer department's operating reports. The costs of servicing these clients are included in the computer department reports, however.

The manager of the computer department has proposed that bank management convert the computer department to a profit or investment center.

Required

a. Describe the characteristics that differentiate a cost center, a profit center, and an investment center from each other.

b. Would the manager of the computer department be likely to conduct the operations of the department differently if the department were classified as a profit center or an investment center rather than as a cost center? Explain.

Problem 9-20A *Return on investment*

LO 9-2

Sorrento Corporation's balance sheet indicates that the company has $500,000 invested in operating assets. During Year 2, Sorrento earned operating income of $50,000 on $1,000,000 of sales.

CHECK FIGURES
c. 10.00%
d. (3) 12.50%

Required

a. Compute Sorrento's profit margin for Year 2.

b. Compute Sorrento's turnover for Year 2.

c. Compute Sorrento's return on investment for Year 2.

d. Recompute Sorrento's ROI under each of the following independent assumptions:

(1) Sales increase from $1,000,000 to $1,200,000, thereby resulting in an increase in operating income from $50,000 to $56,000.

(2) Sales remain constant, but Sorrento reduces expenses, resulting in an increase in operating income from $50,000 to $52,000.

(3) Sorrento is able to reduce its invested capital from $500,000 to $400,000 without affecting operating income.

LO 9-2, 9-3

CHECK FIGURE
c. 24.34%

Problem 9-21A *Comparing return on investment and residual income*

Helena Corporation operates three investment centers. The following financial statements apply to the investment center named Bowman Division.

BOWMAN DIVISION
Income Statement
For the Year Ended December 31, Year 2

Sales revenue	$138,000
Cost of goods sold	78,000
Gross margin	60,000
Operating expenses	
Selling expenses	(6,000)
Depreciation expense	(8,000)
Operating income	46,000
Nonoperating item	
Loss on sale of land	(16,000)
Net income	$ 30,000

BOWMAN DIVISION
Balance Sheet
As of December 31, Year 2

Assets	
Cash	$ 18,898
Accounts receivable	42,266
Merchandise inventory	37,578
Equipment less accum. dep.	90,258
Nonoperating assets	9,000
Total assets	$198,000
Liabilities	
Accounts payable	$ 9,637
Notes payable	72,000
Stockholders' equity	
Common stock	80,000
Retained earnings	36,363
Total liab. and stk. equity	$198,000

Required

a. Which should be used to determine the rate of return (ROI) for the Bowman investment center, operating income or net income? Explain your answer.

b. Which should be used to determine the ROI for the Bowman investment center, operating assets or total assets? Explain your answer.

c. Calculate the ROI for Bowman. Round the computation to two decimal points.

d. Cole has a desired ROI of 10 percent. Headquarters has $96,000 of funds to assign to its investment centers. The manager of the Bowman Division has an opportunity to invest the funds at an ROI of 12 percent. The other two divisions have investment opportunities that yield only 11 percent. Even so, the manager of Bowman rejects the additional funding. Explain why the manager of Bowman would reject the funds under these circumstances. Round the computation to two decimal points.

e. Explain how residual income could be used to encourage the manager to accept the additional funds. Round the computation to whole dollars.

LO 9-2, 9-3

Problem 9-22A *Return on investment and residual income*

Kerston Company has operating assets of $20,000,000. The company's operating income for the most recent accounting period was $1,600,000. The Dannica Division of Kerston controls $8,000,000 of the company's assets and earned $720,000 of its operating income. Kerston's desired ROI is 7 percent. Kerston has $600,000 of additional funds to invest. The manager of the Dannica division believes that his division could earn $51,000 on the additional funds. The highest investment opportunity to any of the company's other divisions is 7.50 percent.

CHECK FIGURE

b. Kerston's ROI after the new investment: 8.01%

Required

Round the computation to two decimal points.

a. If ROI is used as the sole performance measure, would the manager of the Dannica Division be likely to accept or reject the additional funding? Why or why not?

b. Would Kerston Company benefit if the manager of the Dannica Division accepted the additional funds? Why or why not?

c. If residual income is used as the sole performance measure, would the manager of the Dannica Division be likely to accept or reject the additional funding? Why or why not?

Problem 9-23A *Return on investment and residual income*

LO 9-2, 9-3

Altoona Technologies Inc. (ATI) has three divisions. ATI has a desired rate of return of 12.5 percent. The operating assets and income for each division are as follows.

Divisions	Operating Assets	Operating Income
Printer	$ 540,000	$ 96,000
Copier	810,000	90,000
Fax	360,000	54,000
Total	$1,710,000	$240,000

CHECK FIGURES

g. (4) Printer: $30,300; Copier: $(10,650); Fax: $8,400

ATI headquarters has $120,000 of additional cash to invest in one of its divisions. The division managers have identified investment opportunities that are expected to yield the following ROIs.

Divisions	Expected ROIs for Additional Investments
Printer	14.0%
Copier	13.0%
Fax	12.0%

Required

Round the computation to one decimal point.

a. Which division manager is currently producing the highest ROI?

b. Based on ROI, which division manager would be most eager to accept the $120,000 of investment funds?

c. Based on ROI, which division manager would be least likely to accept the $120,000 of investment funds?

d. Which division offers the best investment opportunity for ATI?

e. What is the term used to describe the apparent conflict between Requirements *b* and *d*?

f. Explain how the residual income performance measure could be used to motivate the managers to act in the best interest of the company.

g. Calculate the residual income:

(1) At the corporate (headquarters) level before the additional investment.

(2) At the division level before the additional investment.

(3) At the investment level.

(4) At the division level after the additional investment.

h. Based on residual income, which division manager would be most eager to accept the $120,000 investment opportunity?

Problem 9-24A *Transfer pricing (Appendix)*

LO 9-4

Gary Radio Corporation is a subsidiary of Salem Companies. Gary makes car radios that it sells to retail outlets. It purchases speakers for the radios from outside suppliers for $56 each. Recently, Salem

CHECK FIGURE

a. The maximum price should be $56.

acquired the Hyden Speaker Corporation, which makes car radio speakers that it sells to manufacturers. Hyden produces and sells approximately 200,000 speakers per year, which represents 70 percent of its operating capacity. At the present volume of activity, each speaker costs $48 to produce. This cost consists of a $32 variable cost component and an $16 fixed cost component. Hyden sells the speakers for $60 each. The managers of Gary and Hyden have been asked to consider using Hyden's excess capacity to supply Gary with some of the speakers that it currently purchases from unrelated companies. Both managers are evaluated based on return on investment. Hyden's manager suggests that the speakers be supplied at a transfer price of $60 each (the current selling price). On the other hand, Gary's manager suggests a $56 transfer price, noting that this amount covers total cost and provides Hyden a healthy contribution margin.

Required

a. What transfer price would you recommend?

b. Discuss the effect of the intercompany sales on each manager's return on investment.

c. Should Hyden be required to use more than excess capacity to provide speakers to Gary? In other words, should it sell to Gary some of the 200,000 units that it is currently selling to unrelated companies? Why or why not?

EXERCISES—SERIES B

LO 9-1

Exercise 9-1B *Organization chart and responsibilities*

Yesterday, Dexter Corporation's board of directors appointed Lucy Varden as the new president and chief executive officer. This morning, Ms. Varden presented to the board a list of her management team members. The vice presidents are Zachary East, regional operations; Joshua Vines, research and development; and Erica West, chief financial officer. Reporting to Mr. East are the directors of American, European, and Asian operations. Reporting to Mr. Vines are the directors of the Houston, Seattle, and Charlotte laboratories. Reporting to Ms. West are the controller and the treasurer.

Required

Arrange the preceding information into an organization chart and indicate the responsibility levels involved.

LO 9-1

Exercise 9-2B *Responsibility report*

Dexter Corporation divides its operations into three regions: North American, European, and Asian. The following items appear in the company's responsibility report:

European director's salary
Revenues of the French branch
Office expenses of the Japanese branch
Corporation president's salary
Asian director's salary
Revenues of the Taiwanese branch
Revenues of the British branch
Office expenses of the French branch
Revenues of the U.S. branch
Administrative expenses of the corporate headquarters
Office expenses of the Taiwanese branch
Office expenses of the North American branch
Revenues of the Japanese branch
Revenues of the North American branch
Office expenses of the British branch
Office expenses of the U.S. branch
American director's salary

Required

Which items should Dexter include in the responsibility report for the director of Asian operations?

Exercise 9-3B *Organization chart and controllable cost*

LO 9-1

Kent Plano, corporation vice president of research and development, has overall responsibility for employees with the following positions:

Directors of the Houston, Seattle, and Charlotte laboratories
Senior researchers reporting to laboratory directors
A personnel manager in each laboratory
An accounting manager in each laboratory
Research assistants working for senior researchers
Recruiters reporting to a personnel manager
Bookkeepers reporting to an accounting manager

Required

a. Design an organization chart using these job positions.

b. Identify some possible controllable costs for persons holding each of the job positions.

Exercise 9-4B *Income statement for internal use*

LO 9-1

Yazoo Company has provided the following data for Year 2.

Budget	
Sales	$500,000
Variable product costs	164,000
Variable selling expense	46,000
Other variable expenses	8,000
Fixed product costs	70,000
Fixed selling expense	26,000
Other fixed expenses	2,000
Interest expense	1,000
Actual results	
Sales	520,000
Variable product costs	168,000
Variable selling expense	44,000
Other variable expenses	7,000
Fixed product costs	64,000
Fixed selling expense	22,000
Other fixed expenses	8,000
Interest expense	1,050

Required

a. Prepare in good form a budgeted and actual income statement for internal use. Separate operating income from net income in the statements.

b. Calculate variances and identify them as favorable (F) or unfavorable (U).

Exercise 9-5B *Evaluating a cost center (including flexible budgeting concepts)*

LO 9-1

Paul Hammond, president of Hammond Door Products Company, is evaluating the performance of Jason Burke, the plant manager, for the last fiscal year. Mr. Hammond is concerned that production costs exceeded budget by $50,000. He has available the Year 2 static budget for the production plant, as well as the actual results, both of which follow.

	Static Budget	Actual Results
Production in units	8,000 doors	8,400 doors
Direct materials	$ 500,000	$ 522,500
Direct labor	150,000	159,250
Variable manufacturing overhead	200,000	212,000
Total variable costs	850,000	893,750
Fixed manufacturing overhead	400,000	406,250
Total manufacturing cost	$1,250,000	$1,300,000

Required

a. Convert the static budget into a flexible budget.
b. Use the flexible budget to evaluate Mr. Burke's performance.
c. Explain why Mr. Burke's performance evaluation doesn't include sales revenue and net income.

LO 9-1

Exercise 9-6B *Evaluating a profit center*

Beth Shields, president of Dover Travel Company, a travel agency, is seeking a method of evaluating her seven branches. Each branch vice president is authorized to hire employees and devise competitive strategies for the branch territory. Ms. Shields wonders which of the following three different measures would be most suitable: return on investment, operating income, or return on sales (operating income divided by sales).

Required

a. Using the concept of controllability, advise Ms. Shields about the best performance measure.
b. Explain how a balanced scorecard can be used for Ms. Shields.

LO 9-2

Exercise 9-7B *Computing return on investment*

A Salisbury Corporation investment center shows an operating income of \$81,000 and an investment in operating assets of \$900,000.

Required

Compute the return on investment.

LO 9-2

Exercise 9-8B *Return on investment*

With annual sales of \$1,200,000 and operating assets of \$800,000, Culpeper Company achieved a 10 percent ROI.

Required

a. If Culpeper reduces expenses by \$20,000 and sales remain unchanged, what ROI will result?
b. If Culpeper cannot change either sales or expenses, what change in the investment base is required to achieve the same result you calculated for Requirement *a*?

LO 9-3

Exercise 9-9B *Computing residual income*

Elkins Corporation's desired rate of return is 10 percent. Bristol Division, one of Elkins' five investment centers, earned an operating income of \$1,600,000 last year. The division controlled \$12,500,000 of operational assets.

Required

Compute Bristol Division's residual income.

LO 9-3

Exercise 9-10B *Computing residual income*

Logan Oil Change operates two divisions. The following pertains to each division for Year 2.

	Concord	Kinston
Sales	\$900,000	\$750,000
Operating income	\$ 60,000	\$ 46,500
Average operating assets	\$225,000	\$150,000
Company's desired rate of return	9%	9%

Required

a. Compute each division's residual income.
b. Which division increased the company's profitability more?

Exercise 9-11B ***Supply missing information regarding return on investment and residual income*** LO 9-2, 9-3

Required

Supply the missing information in the following table for Greenwood Company.

Sales	?
ROI	12%
Investment in operating assets	$270,000
Operating income	?
Turnover	?
Residual income	?
Operating profit margin	0.10
Desired rate of return	11%

Exercise 9-12B ***Contrasting return on investment with residual income*** LO 9-2, 9-3

The Florence Division of Hampton Garage Doors Inc. is currently achieving a 12 percent ROI. The company's target ROI is 8 percent. The division has an opportunity to invest in operating assets an additional $375,000 at 10 percent but is reluctant to do so because its ROI will fall to 11.7 percent. The division's present investment in operating assets is $2,000,000.

Required

Explain how management can use the residual income method to motivate the Florence Division to make the investment.

Exercise 9-13B ***Return on investment and residual income*** LO 9-2, 9-3

Welch Insurance Company (WIC) earned operating income of $24,000,000 on operating assets of $200,000,000 during Year 2. The Automobile Insurance Division earned $4,770,000 on operating assets of $36,000,000. WIC has offered the Automobile Division $4,000,000 of additional operating assets. The manager of the Automobile Insurance Division believes she could use the additional assets to generate operating income amounting to $480,000. WIC has a desired return on investment (ROI) of 10 percent.

Required

a. Calculate the return on investment (ROI) for WIC, the Automobile Insurance Division, and the additional investment opportunity.

b. Calculate the residual income (RI) for WIC, the Automobile Insurance Division, and the additional investment opportunity.

Exercise 9-14B ***Transfer pricing (Appendix)*** LO 9-4

Dayton Company makes household water filtration equipment. The Murray Division manufactures filters. The Franklin Water Division sells to consumers. The Murray Division has the capacity to produce 8,000 filters per month at the following cost per unit.

Variable costs	$ 6
Division fixed costs	5
Allocated corporate-level facility-sustaining costs	4
Total cost per filter	$15

Franklin Water currently uses 6,000 Murray filters per month. Alice Morse, Franklin Water's manager, is not happy with the $15 transfer price charged by Murray. She points out that Franklin Water could purchase the same filters from outside vendors for a market price of only $12. Christina Flynn,

Murray's manager, refuses to sell the filters to Franklin Water below cost. Ms. Morse counters that she would be happy to purchase the filters elsewhere. Because Murray's does not have other customers for its filters, Ms. Flynn appeals to Keith Polk, the president of Dayton, for arbitration.

Required

a. Should the president of Dayton allow Ms. Morse to purchase filters from outside vendors for $12 per unit? Explain.

b. Write a brief paragraph describing what Mr. Polk should do to resolve the conflict between the two division managers.

LO 9-4

Exercise 9-15B *Transfer pricing and fixed cost per unit*

The Nashua Division of Leland Company currently produces electric fans that desktop computer manufacturers use as cooling components. The Gilmer Division, which makes notebook computers, has asked the Nashua Division to design and supply 20,000 fans per year for its notebook computers. Gilmer currently purchases notebook fans from an outside vendor at the price of $18 each. However, Gilmer is not happy with the vendor's unstable delivery pattern. To accept Gilmer's order, Nashua would have to purchase additional equipment and modify its plant layout. The additional equipment would enable the company to add 35,000 notebook fans to its annual production. Nashua's avoidable cost of making 20,000 notebook fans follows.

Costs	Total	Per Unit
Variable costs	$100,000	$5
Fixed cost	$120,000	6

Required

a. What would be the financial consequence to Leland Company if the Nashua Division makes the notebook fans and sells them to the Gilmer Division? What range of transfer prices would increase the financial performance of both divisions?

b. Suppose the Gilmer Division increases production so that it could use 30,000 Nashua Division notebook fans. How would the change in volume affect the range of transfer prices that would financially benefit both divisions?

PROBLEMS—SERIES B

LO 9-1

Problem 9-16B *Determining controllable costs*

At a professional conference just a few days ago, Carlos Santiago, the president of Ocala Corporation, learned how the concept of controllability relates to performance evaluation. In preparing to put this new knowledge into practice, he reviewed the financial data of the company's sales department.

Salaries of salespeople	$ 210,000
Cost of goods sold	12,500,000
Facility-level corporate costs	205,000
Travel expenses	16,000
Depreciation on equipment	50,000
Salary of the sales manager	30,000
Property taxes	2,000
Telephone expenses	19,500

Required

Help Mr. Santiago prepare a list of expenditures that the sales manager controls.

Problem 9-17B *Controllability, responsibility, and balanced scorecard*

LO 9-1

Chad Bentley, president of Sabrin Corporation, evaluated the performance report of the company's production department. Mr. Bentley was confused by some arguments presented by Jeannette Dolan, the production manager. Some relevant data follow.

Variances	Amount
Materials usage variance	$240,000 U
Materials price variance	196,000 F
Labor price variance	38,000 F
Labor usage variance	138,000 U
Volume variance	300,000 U

Ms. Dolan argued that she had done a great job, noting the favorable materials price variance and labor price variance. She argued that she had no control over factors causing the unfavorable variances. For example, she argued that the unfavorable materials usage variance was caused by the purchasing department's decision to buy substandard materials that resulted in a substantial amount of spoilage. Moreover, she argued that the unfavorable labor usage variance resulted from the substantial materials spoilage which in turn wasted many labor hours, as did the hiring of under-qualified workers by the manager of the personnel department. Finally, she said that the sales department's failure to obtain a sufficient number of customer orders really caused the unfavorable volume variance.

Required

a. What would you do first if you were Chad Bentley?

b. Did Ms. Dolan deserve the credit she claimed for the favorable variances? Explain.

c. Was Ms. Dolan responsible for the unfavorable variances? Explain.

d. Explain how a balanced scorecard can be used to improve performance evaluation.

Problem 9-18B *Performance reports and evaluation*

LO 9-1

The mortgage division of Magee Financial Services Inc. is managed by a vice president who supervises three regional operations. Each regional operation has a general manager and several branches directed by branch managers.

The West region has two branches, Jackson and Abilene. The March responsibility reports for the managers of these branches follow.

	Budgeted*	Actual	Variance
Jackson Branch			
Controllable costs			
Employee compensation	$150,000	$147,900	$2,100 F
Office supplies	36,000	35,000	1,000 F
Promotions	73,000	75,500	2,500 U
Maintenance	8,000	10,600	2,600 U
Total	$267,000	$269,000	$2,000 U
Abilene Branch			
Controllable costs			
Employee compensation	$130,000	$125,000	$5,000 F
Office supplies	38,000	42,000	4,000 U
Promotions	72,000	75,000	3,000 U
Maintenance	10,000	9,600	400 F
Total	$250,000	$251,600	$1,600 U

*Magee uses flexible budgets for performance evaluation.

Other pertinent cost data for March follow.

	Budgeted*	Actual
Cost data of other regions		
East	$700,000	$726,000
South	860,000	844,000
Other costs controllable by		
West region general manager	140,000	146,000
Vice president of mortgage	192,000	196,000

*Magee uses flexible budgets for performance evaluation.

Required

a. Prepare a responsibility report for the general manager of the West region.

b. Prepare a responsibility report for the vice president of the mortgage division.

c. Explain where the $2,500 unfavorable promotions variance in the Jackson branch manager's report is included in the vice president's report.

d. Based on the responsibility report prepared in Requirement *a*, explain where the West region's general manager should concentrate her attention.

LO 9-1

Problem 9-19B *Different types of responsibility centers*

Sheridan Industries Inc. has five different divisions; each is responsible for producing and marketing a particular product line. The electronics division makes cellular telephones, pagers, and modems. The division also buys and sells other electronic products made by outside companies. Each division maintains sufficient working capital for its own operations. The corporate headquarters, however, makes decisions about long-term capital investments.

Required

a. For purposes of performance evaluation, should Sheridan classify its electronics division as a cost center, a profit center, or an investment center? Why?

b. Would the manager of the electronics division be likely to conduct the operations of the division differently if the division were classified as a different type of responsibility center than the one you designated in Requirement *a*? Explain.

LO 9-2

Problem 9-20B *Return on investment*

Bonner Corporation's balance sheet indicates that the company has $320,000 invested in operating assets. During Year 3, Bonner earned $24,000 of operating income on $480,000 of sales.

Required

a. Compute Bonner's operating profit margin percentage for Year 3.

b. Compute Bonner's turnover for Year 3.

c. Compute Bonner's return on investment for Year 3.

d. Recompute Bonner's ROI under each of the following independent assumptions:

(1) Sales increase from $480,000 to $560,000, thereby resulting in an increase in operating income from $24,000 to $28,000.

(2) Sales remain constant, but Bonner reduces expenses, thereby resulting in an increase in income from $24,000 to $25,920.

(3) Bonner is able to reduce its operating assets from $320,000 to $300,000 without affecting income.

Problem 9-21B *Comparing return on investment and residual income*

LO 9-2, 9-3

Gwinnett Corporation operates three investment centers. The following financial statements apply to the investment center named Rite Division.

RITE DIVISION
Income Statement
For the Year Ended December 31, Year 3

Sales revenue	$300,000
Cost of goods sold	(180,000)
Gross margin	120,000
Operating expenses	
Selling expenses	(15,000)
Administrative expense	(5,000)
Operating income	100,000
Nonoperating expense	
Interest expense	(10,000)
Net income	$ 90,000

RITE DIVISION
Balance Sheet
As of December 31, Year 3

Assets	
Cash	$ 92,000
Accounts receivable	388,000
Merchandise inventory	54,000
Equipment less accum. dep.	466,000
Nonoperating assets	46,000
Total assets	$1,046,000
Liabilities	
Accounts payable	$ 140,000
Notes payable	200,000
Stockholders' equity	
Common stock	480,000
Retained earnings	226,000
Total liab. and stk. equity	$1,046,000

Required

a. Should operating income or net income be used to determine the rate of return (ROI) for the Rite investment center? Explain your answer.

b. Should operating assets or total assets be used to determine the ROI for the Rite investment center? Explain your answer.

c. Calculate the ROI for Rite. Round computation to 1 decimal point.

d. Gwinnett has a desired ROI of 8 percent. Headquarters has $300,000 of funds to assign to its investment centers. The manager of the Rite Division has an opportunity to invest the funds at an ROI of 9 percent. The other two divisions have investment opportunities that yield only 6.5 percent. Even so, the manager of Rite rejects the additional funding. Explain why the manager of Rite would reject the funds under these circumstances. Round the computation to one decimal point.

e. Explain how residual income could be used to encourage the manager to accept the additional funds.

LO 9-2, 9-3

Problem 9-22B *Return on investment and residual income*

Roswell Company has operating assets of $8,000,000. The company's operating income for the most recent accounting period was $600,000. The Lawrence Division of Roswell controls $1,600,000 of the company's assets and earned $144,000 of its operating income. Roswell's desired ROI is 7 percent. Roswell has $600,000 of additional funds to invest. The manager of the Lawrence Division believes that his division could earn $50,400 on the additional funds. The highest investment opportunity to any of the company's other divisions is 8 percent.

Required

a. If ROI is used as the sole performance measure, would the manager of the Lawrence Division be likely to accept or reject the additional funding? Why or why not?

b. Would Roswell Company benefit if the manager of the Lawrence Division accepted the additional funds? Why or why not? Round your percentages to one decimal point.

c. If residual income is used as the sole performance measure, would the manager of the Lawrence Division be likely to accept or reject the additional funding? Why or why not?

LO 9-2, 9-3

Problem 9-23B *Return on investment and residual income*

Beaumont Trading Company (BTC) has three divisions. BTC has a desired rate of return of 6.0 percent. The operating assets and income for each division are as follows.

Divisions	Operating Assets	Operating Income
Americas	$2,250,000	$270,000
Asia	1,250,000	125,000
Europe	1,500,000	120,000
Total	$5,000,000	$515,000

BTC headquarters has $250,000 of additional cash to invest in one of its divisions. The division managers have identified investment opportunities that are expected to yield the following ROIs.

Divisions	Expected ROIs for Additional Investments
Americas	10.0%
Asia	5.6
Europe	9.0

Required

a. Which division manager is currently producing the highest ROI?

b. Based on ROI, which division manager would be most eager to accept the $250,000 of investment funds?

c. Based on ROI, which division manager would be least likely to accept the $250,000 of investment funds?

d. Which division offers the best investment opportunity for BTC?

e. What is the term used to describe the apparent conflict between Requirements *b* and *d*?

f. Explain how the residual income performance measure could be used to motivate the managers to act in the best interest of the company.

g. Calculate the residual income:

(1) At the corporate (headquarters) level before the additional investment.

(2) At the division level before the additional investment.

(3) At the investment level.

(4) At the division level after the additional investment.

h. Based on residual income, which division manager would be most eager to accept the $250,000 investment opportunity?

Problem 9-24B *Transfer pricing (Appendix)*

LO 9-4

Gardner Electronics Corporation makes a Wi-Fi receiver that it sells to retail stores for $75 each. The variable cost to produce a receiver is $35 each; the total fixed cost is $5,000,000. Gardner is operating at 80 percent of capacity and is producing 200,000 receivers annually. Gardner's parent company, Sterling Corporation, notified Gardner's president that another subsidiary company, Newport Technologies, has begun making home theater systems and can use Gardner's receiver as a part. Newport needs 40,000 receivers annually and is able to acquire similar receivers in the market for $72 each.

Under instructions from the parent company, the presidents of Gardner and Newport meet to negotiate a price for the receiver. Gardner insists that its market price is $75 each and will stand firm on that price. Newport, on the other hand, wonders why it should even talk to Gardner when Newport can get receivers at a lower price.

Required

a. What transfer price would you recommend?

b. Discuss the effect of the intercompany sales on each president's return on investment.

c. Should Gardner be required to use more than excess capacity to provide receivers to Newport if Newport's demand increases to 60,000 receivers? In other words, should it sell some of the 200,000 receivers that it currently sells to unrelated companies to Newport instead? Why or why not?

ANALYZE, THINK, COMMUNICATE

ATC 9-1 Business Applications Case *Analyzing segments at Coca-Cola*

The following excerpt is from Coca-Cola Company's 2017 annual report filed with the SEC.

> *Management evaluates the performance of our operating segments separately to individually monitor the different factors affecting financial performance. Our Company manages income taxes from continuing operations and certain treasury-related items, such as interest income and expense, on a global basis within the Corporate operating segment. We evaluate segment performance based on income or loss before income taxes.*

Selected segment data for Coca-Cola Company for the 2017 and 2016 fiscal years follow. Dollar amounts are in millions.

	Europe, Middle East, & Africa	Latin America	North America	Asia Pacific
2017 Fiscal Year				
Net operating revenues	$7,322	$3,956	$ 8,651	$4,767
Income before taxes	3,706	2,211	2,307	2,179
Identifiable operating assets	5,475	1,896	17,619	2,072
2016 Fiscal Year				
Net operating revenues	$7,041	$3,746	$ 6,437	$4,788
Income before taxes	3,749	1,966	2,560	2,238
Identifiable operating assets	4,067	1,785	16,566	2,024

Required

a. Compute the ROI for each of Coke's geographical segments for each fiscal year. Which segment appears to have the best performance during 2017 based their ROIs? Which segment showed the most improvement from 2016 to 2017?

b. Assuming Coke's management expects a minimum return of 30 percent, calculate the residual income for each segment for each fiscal year. Which segment appears to have the best performance based on residual income? Which segment showed the most improvement from 2016 to 2017?

c. Explain why the segment with the highest ROI in 2017 was not the segment with the highest residual income.

d. Assume the management of Coke is considering a major expansion effort for the next five years. On which geographic segment would you recommend Coke focus its expansion efforts? Explain the rationale for your answer.

ATC 9-2 Group Assignment *Return on investment versus residual income*

Bellco, a division of Becker International Corporation, is operated under the direction of Antoin Sedatt. Bellco is an independent investment center with approximately $72,000,000 of assets that generate approximately $8,640,000 in annual net income. Becker International has additional investment capital of $12,000,000 that is available for the division managers to invest. Mr. Sedatt is aware of an investment opportunity that will provide an 11 percent annual net return. Becker International's desired rate of return is 10 percent.

Required

Divide the class into groups of four or five students and then organize the groups into two sections. Assign Task 1 to the first section and Task 2 to the second section.

Group Tasks

1. Assume that Mr. Sedatt's performance is evaluated based on his ability to maximize return on investment (ROI). Compute ROI using the following two assumptions: Bellco retains its current asset size and Bellco accepts and invests the additional $12,000,000 of assets. Determine whether Mr. Sedatt should accept the opportunity to invest additional funds. Select a spokesperson to present the decision made by the group.
2. Assume that Mr. Sedatt's performance is evaluated based on his ability to maximize residual income. Compute residual income using the following two assumptions: Bellco retains its current asset base and Bellco accepts and invests the additional $12,000,000 of assets. Determine whether Mr. Sedatt should accept the opportunity to invest additional funds. Select a spokesperson to present the decision made by the group.
3. Have a spokesperson from one of the groups in the first section report the two ROIs and the group's recommendation for Mr. Sedatt. Have the groups in this section reach consensus on the ROI and the recommendation.
4. Have a spokesperson from the second section report the two amounts of residual income and disclose the group's recommendation for Mr. Sedatt. Have this section reach consensus on amounts of residual income.
5. Which technique (ROI or residual income) is more likely to result in suboptimization?

ATC 9-3 Research Assignment *Using real-world data from Berkshire Hathaway*

Obtain Berkshire Hathaway's (Berkshire) Form 10-K for the year ended December 31, 2017, and complete the following requirements. To obtain the Form 10-K, you can use the EDGAR system (see Appendix A at the back of this text for instructions), or it can be found on the company's corporate website, www.berkshirehathaway.com.

Required

a. Unlike most companies, Berkshire organizes the revenues and expenses on its earnings statements, and the assets and liabilities on its balance sheets, by major business segments. Calculate the return on investment for 2017 for each segment of Berkshire's business using the *margin* × *turnover* method. For segment earnings, use earnings before taxes, which you will have to calculate. Show your computations.

b. Rank the segments' performance from best to worst, based on their ROIs.

c. Why did the best-performing segment do better than the next best? Was it profitability, the efficiency with which it used its assets, or both?

ATC 9-4 Writing Assignment *Transfer pricing*

Green Lawn Mower Inc. recently acquired Hallit Engines, a small engine manufacturing company. Green's president believes in decentralization and intends to permit Hallit to continue to operate as an independent entity. However, she has instructed the manager of Green's lawn mower assembly division to investigate the possibility of purchasing engines from Hallit instead of using the current third-party supplier. Hallit has excess capacity. The current full cost to produce each engine is $96. The avoidable cost of making engines is $78 per unit. The assembly division, which currently pays the third-party supplier $90 per engine, offers to purchase engines from Hallit at the $90 price. Hallit's president refuses the offer, stating that his company's engines are superior to those the third-party supplier provides. Hallit's president believes that the transfer price should be based on the market price for independent customers, which is $132 per engine. The manager of the assembly division agrees that Hallit's engines are higher quality than those currently being used but notes that Green's customer base is in the low-end, discount market. Putting more expensive engines on Green mowers would raise the price above the competition and would hurt sales. Green's president tries to negotiate a settlement between the assembly manager and Hallit's president, but the parties are unable to agree on a transfer price.

Required

a. Assuming that Green makes and sells 40,000 lawn mowers per year, what is the cost of suboptimization resulting from the failure to establish a transfer price?

b. Assume that you are a consultant asked by the president of Green to recommend whether a transfer price should be arbitrarily imposed. Write a brief memo that includes your recommendation and your justification for making it.

ATC 9-5 Ethical Dilemma *Manipulating return on investment and residual income*

A widely recognized financial trick known as the "big bath" occurs when a company makes huge unwarranted asset write-offs that drastically overstate expenses. Outside auditors (CPAs) permit companies to engage in the practice because the assets being written off are of questionable value. Because the true value of the assets cannot be validated, auditors have little recourse but to accept the valuations suggested by management. Recent examples of write-offs include Motorola's $1.8 billion restructuring charge, Hewlett-Packard's $8 billion charge, and Microsoft's $7.6 billion charge.

Required

a. Why would managers want their companies to take a big bath? (*Hint:* Consider how a big bath affects return on investment and residual income in the years following the write-off.)

b. Annual reports are financial reports issued to the public. The reports are the responsibility of auditors who are CPAs who operate under the ethical standards promulgated by the American Institute of Certified Public Accountants. As a result, attempts to manipulate annual report data are not restricted by the Institute of Management Accountants Statement of Ethical Professional Practice shown in Exhibit 1.17 of Chapter 1. Do you agree or disagree with these statements? Explain your position.

ATC 9-6 Spreadsheet Assignment *Using Excel*

Waldon Corporation's balance sheet shows that the company has $600,000 invested in operating assets. During Year 2, Waldon earned $120,000 on $960,000 of sales. The company's desired return on investment (ROI) is 12 percent.

Required

a. Construct a spreadsheet to calculate ROI and residual income using these data. Build the spreadsheet using formulas so that the spreadsheet could be used as a template for any ROI or residual income problem. The following screen capture shows how to construct the template.

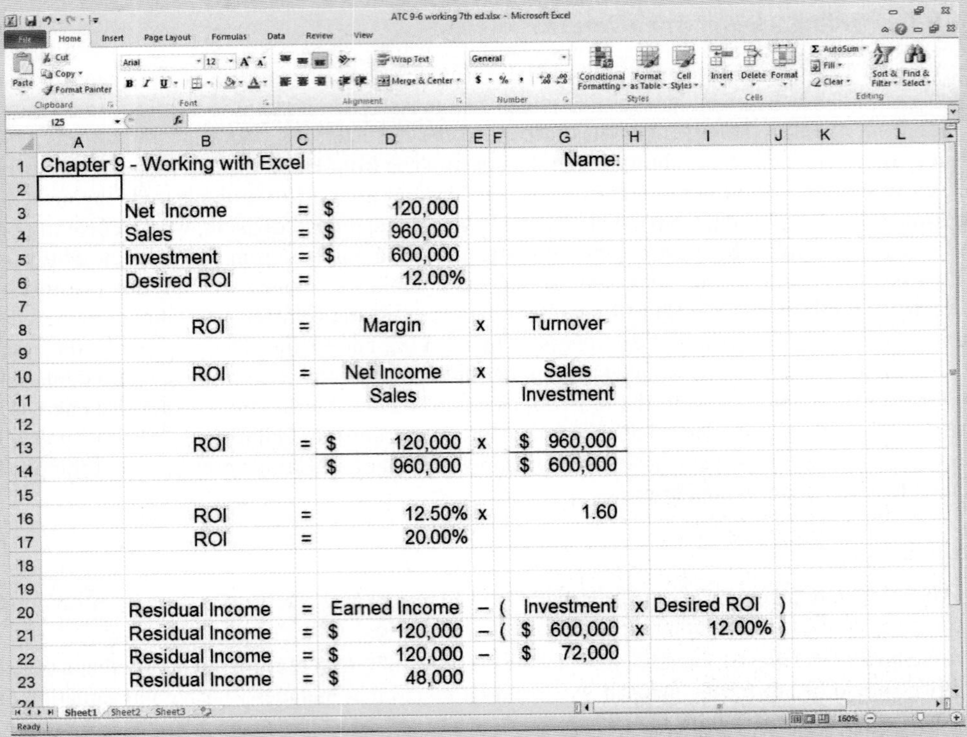

	A	B	C	D	E	F	G	H	I	J
1	Chapter 9 - Working with Excel						Name:			
2										
3		Net Income	= $	120,000						
4		Sales	= $	960,000						
5		Investment	= $	600,000						
6		Desired ROI	=	12.00%						
7										
8		ROI	=	Margin	x		Turnover			
9										
10		ROI	=	Net Income	x		Sales			
11				Sales			Investment			
12										
13		ROI	= $	120,000	x		$ 960,000			
14			$	960,000			$ 600,000			
15										
16		ROI	=	12.50%	x		1.60			
17		ROI	=	20.00%						
18										
19										
20		Residual Income	=	Earned Income	–	(	Investment	x	Desired ROI	)
21		Residual Income	= $	120,000	–	(	$ 600,000	x	12.00%	)
22		Residual Income	= $	120,000	–		$ 72,000			
23		Residual Income	= $	48,000						

Source: Microsoft Excel 2010

Spreadsheet Tips

(1) The cells below row 12 that show numbers should all be based on formulas. This allows the results to be automatically recalculated based on changes in the data in rows 3 to 6.

(2) The parentheses in columns F and J have been entered as text in columns that have a column width of 1.

ATC 9-7 Spreadsheet Assignment *Mastering Excel*

eXcel

The Pillar Manufacturing Company has three identified levels of authority and responsibility. The organization chart as of December 31, Year 1, appears as follows.

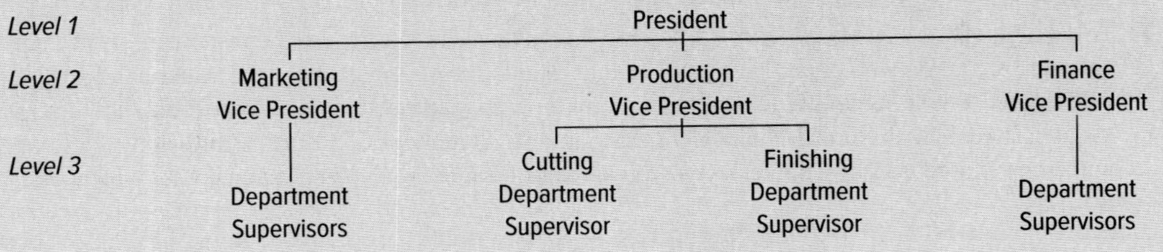

Pertinent expenses for Level 3 follow.

	Budget	Actual
Finishing Department		
Wages expense	$6,240	$6,000
Direct materials	2,300	2,400
Supplies	840	980
Small tools	1,300	1,140
Other	700	820

Pertinent expenses for Level 2 follow.

	Budget	Actual
Production Department		
Administrative expenses	$ 1,200	$ 1,400
Supervisory salaries	5,800	5,200
Cutting Department	6,800	6,420
Finishing Department	11,380	11,340

Pertinent expenses for Level 1 follow.

	Budget	Actual
President's Office Expense		
Supervisory salaries	$ 4,900	$ 5,100
Clerical staff	800	400
Other expenses	600	700
Production Department	25,180	24,360
Marketing Department	8,850	8,300
Finance Department	5,900	6,220

Required

a. Construct a spreadsheet that shows responsibility reports for the finishing department supervisor, the production vice president, and the president.

b. Include formulas in the responsibility reports that illustrate the interrelationships between these reports. For example, changes in the finishing department report should be automatically reflected in the production department report.

Spreadsheet Tip

1. Use the absolute value function |=ABS(value)| in the formulas that calculate the variances.

COMPREHENSIVE PROBLEM

Assume Magnificent Modems Inc. (MMI), is a division of Gilmore Business Products (GBP). GBP uses ROI as the primary measure of managerial performance. GBP has a desired return on investment (ROI) of 3 percent. The company has $100,000 of investment funds to be assigned to its divisions. The president of MMI is aware of an investment opportunity for these funds that is expected to yield an ROI of 3.5 percent.

Required

a. Explain why you believe the president of MMI will accept or reject the $100,000 investment opportunity. Support your answer by calculating MMI's existing ROI. Base your computation on the information contained in the income statement and balance sheet that you prepared in Chapter 1 (page 52).

b. Name the term used to describe the condition that exists in Requirement *a*. Provide a brief definition of this term.

c. If GBP changes its performance measurement criteria from ROI to residual income (RI), will the new evaluation approach affect the president's decision to accept or reject the $100,000 investment opportunity? Support your answer by calculating MMI's residual income for the investment opportunity.

CHAPTER 10

Planning for Capital Investments

LEARNING OBJECTIVES

After you have mastered the material in this chapter, you will be able to:

LO 10-1 Explain the time value of money concept.

LO 10-2 Determine and interpret the net present value of an investment opportunity.

LO 10-3 Determine and interpret the internal rate of return of an investment opportunity.

LO 10-4 Evaluate investment opportunities using the payback method and the unadjusted rate of return.

Video lectures and accompanying self-assessment quizzes are available in Connect® for all learning objectives.

CHAPTER OPENING

The president of EZ Rentals (EZ) is considering expanding the company's rental service business to include projectors that can be used with notebook computers. A marketing study forecasts that renting projectors could generate revenue of $200,000 per year. The possibility of increasing revenue is alluring, but EZ's president has a number of unanswered questions. How much do the projectors cost? What is their expected useful life? Will they have a salvage value? Does EZ have the money to buy them? Does EZ have the technical expertise to support the product? How much will training cost? How long will customer demand last? What if EZ buys the projectors and they become technologically obsolete? How quickly will EZ be able to recover the investment? Are there more profitable ways to invest EZ's funds? This chapter discusses some of the analytical techniques companies use to evaluate major investment opportunities.

The Curious Accountant

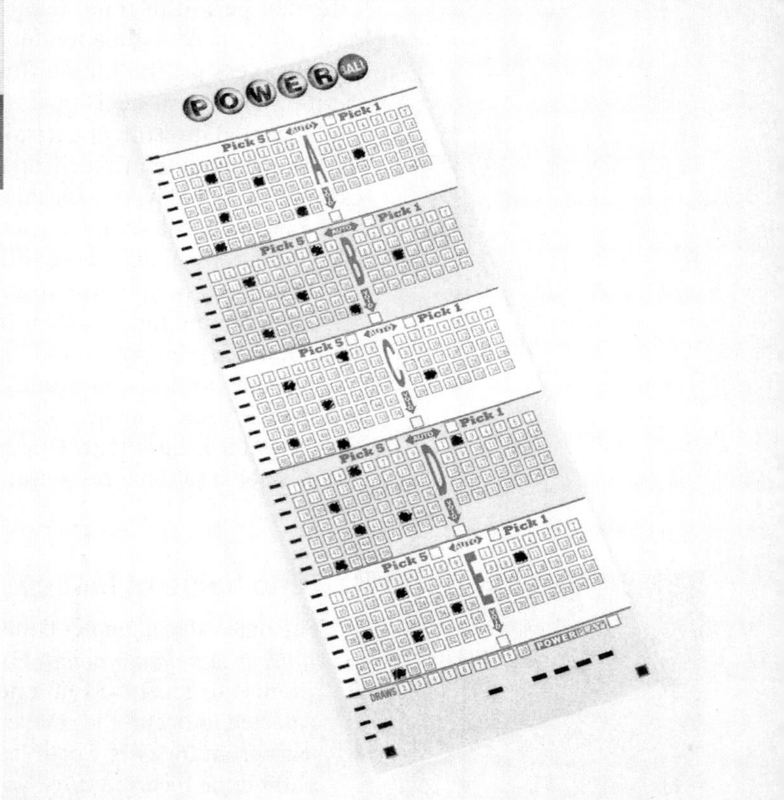

©McGraw-Hill Education

The August 23, 2017, drawing for the **Powerball** multi-state lottery had an advertised value of $758.7 million. This amount, however, was based on the assumption that the winner would take his or her prize as 30 equal annual payments of $25.29 million. If the winnings were taken in this manner, the first payment would be made immediately, and the others would be paid annually over the next 29 years. The winner also had the option of taking an immediate, lump-sum payment of $480.5 million.

Assume that you work as a personal financial planner and that one of your clients held the winning lottery ticket. If you think you could invest your client's winnings and earn an annual return of 7 percent, would you advise your client to take the lump-sum payment or the annual payments? Why? (Answer on page 458.)

CAPITAL INVESTMENT DECISIONS

LO 10-1

Explain the time value of money concept.

Purchases of long-term operational assets are **capital investments.** Capital investments differ from stock and bond investments in an important respect. Investments in stocks and bonds can be sold in organized markets such as the New York Stock Exchange. In contrast, investments in capital assets normally can be recovered only by using those assets. Once a company purchases a capital asset, it is committed to that investment for an extended period of time. If the market turns sour, the company is stuck with the consequences. It may also be unable to seize new opportunities because its capital is committed. Business profitability ultimately hinges, to a large extent, on the quality of a few key capital investment decisions.

A capital investment decision is essentially a decision to exchange current cash outflows for the expectation of receiving future cash inflows. For EZ Rentals, purchasing projectors, cash outflows today, provides the opportunity to collect \$200,000 per year in rental revenue, cash inflows in the future. Assuming the projectors have useful lives of four years and no salvage value, how much should EZ be willing to pay for the future cash inflows? If you were EZ's president, would give up \$700,000 today for the opportunity to receive \$800,000 (4 × \$200,000) in the future? What if you collect less than \$200,000 per year? If revenue is only \$160,000 per year, you would lose \$60,000 [\$700,000 − (4 × \$160,000)]. Is \$700,000 too much to pay for the opportunity to receive \$200,000 per year for four years? If \$700,000 is too much, would you spend \$600,000? If not, how about \$500,000? There is no one right answer to these questions. However, understanding the *time value of money* concept can help you develop a rational response.

©Christian Zachariasen/PhotoAlto

Time Value of Money

The **time value of money** concept recognizes that *the present value of a dollar received in the future is less than a dollar.* For example, you may be willing to pay only \$0.90 today for a promise to receive \$1.00 one year from today. The further into the future the receipt is expected to occur, the smaller is its present value. In other words, \$1.00 to be received two years from today is worth less than \$1.00 to be received one year from today. Likewise, \$1.00 to be received three years from today is less valuable than \$1.00 to be received two years from today, and so on.

The present value of cash inflows decreases as the time until expected receipt increases for several reasons. First, you could deposit today's dollar in a savings account to earn *interest* that increases its total value. If you wait for your money, you lose the opportunity to earn interest. Second, the expectation of receiving a future dollar carries an element of *risk.* Changed conditions may result in the failure to collect. Finally, *inflation* diminishes the buying power of the dollar. In other words, the longer you must wait to receive a dollar, the less you will be able to buy with it.

When a company invests in capital assets, it sacrifices present dollars in exchange for the opportunity to receive future dollars. Since trading current dollars for future dollars is risky, companies expect compensation before they invest in capital assets. The compensation a company expects is called *return on investment (ROI).* As discussed in Chapter 9, ROI is expressed as a percentage of the investment. For example, the ROI for a \$1,000 investment that earns annual income of \$100 is 10 percent (\$100 ÷ \$1,000 = 10%).

Determining the Minimum Rate of Return

To establish the minimum expected *return on investment* before accepting an investment opportunity, most companies consider their cost of capital. To attract capital, companies must provide benefits to their creditors and owners. Creditors expect interest payments; owners expect dividends and increased stock value. Companies that earn lower returns than their cost of capital eventually go bankrupt; they cannot continually pay out more than they collect.

The **cost of capital** *represents the* **minimum rate of return** *on investments.* Calculating the cost of capital is a complex exercise that is beyond the scope of this text. It is addressed in finance courses. We discuss how management accountants *use* the cost of capital to evaluate investment opportunities. A variety of terms may be used to describe the minimum rate of return including, the *required rate of return,* the *hurdle rate,* the *cutoff rate,* or the *discount rate.* This text uses the term, *desired rate of return,* as a proxy for any of the common terms used as a label for the cost of capital. As used herein, the rate of return that a company aspires to attain is called the **desired rate of return.**

CHECK YOURSELF 10.1

Study the following cash inflow streams expected from two different potential investments:

	Year 1	Year 2	Year 3	Total
Alternative 1	$2,000	$3,000	$4,000	$9,000
Alternative 2	4,000	3,000	2,000	9,000

Based on visual observation alone, which alternative has the higher present value? Why?

Answer Alternative 2 has the higher present value. The size of the discount increases as the length of the time period increases. In other words, a dollar received in Year 3 has a lower present value (is worth less) than a dollar received in Year 1. Since most of the expected cash inflows from Alternative 2 are received earlier than those from Alternative 1, Alternative 2 has a higher present value even though the total expected cash inflows are the same.

Converting Future Cash Inflows to Their Equivalent Present Values

Given a desired rate of return and the amount of a future cash flow, the present value can be determined using algebra. To illustrate, refer to the $200,000 EZ expects to earn the first year it leases the projectors.[1] Assuming EZ desires a 12 percent rate of return, what amount of cash would EZ be willing to invest today (present value outflow) to obtain a $200,000 cash inflow at the end of the year (future value)? The answer follows:[2]

$$\text{Investment} + (0.12 \times \text{Investment}) = \text{Future cash inflow}$$
$$1.12 \times \text{Investment} = \$200{,}000$$
$$\text{Investment} = \$200{,}000 \div 1.12$$
$$\text{Investment} = \$178{,}571$$

The $178,571 is the *present value* of receiving $200,000 at the end of one year. In other words, if EZ invests $178,571 cash on January 1 and earns a 12 percent return on the investment, EZ will have $200,000 on December 31. The two options are equal as shown in the following mathematical proof:

$$\text{Investment} + (0.12 \times \text{Investment}) = \$200{,}000$$
$$\$178{,}571 + (0.12 \times \$178{,}571) = \$200{,}000$$
$$\$178{,}571 + \$21{,}429 = \$200{,}000$$
$$\$200{,}000 = \$200{,}000$$

[1]The following computations assume the $200,000 cash inflow is received on the last day of each year. In actual practice, the timing of cash inflows is less precise and present value computations are recognized to be approximate, not exact.

[2]All computations in this chapter are rounded to the nearest whole dollar.

Present Value Table for Single-Amount Cash Inflows

The algebra illustrated above is used to convert a one-time future receipt of cash to its present value. One-time receipts of cash are frequently called **single-payment,** or **lump-sum,** cash flows. Because EZ desires a 12 percent rate of return, the present value of the first cash inflow is \$178,571. We can also determine the present value of a \$200,000 single amount (lump sum) at the end of the second, third, and fourth years. Instead of using cumbersome algebraic computations to convert these future values to their present value equivalents, financial analysts frequently use a table of conversion factors to convert future values to their present value equivalents. The table of conversion factors used to convert future values into present values is commonly called a **present value table.**[3] A typical present value table presents columns with different return rates and rows with different periods of time, like Appendix Table 1 located at the end of this chapter.

To illustrate using the present value table, locate the conversion factor in Table 1 at the intersection of the 12% column and the one-period row. The conversion factor is 0.892857. Multiplying this factor by the \$200,000 expected cash inflow yields \$178,571 (\$200,000 × 0.892857). This is the same value determined algebraically in the previous section of this chapter. The conversion factors in the present value tables simplify converting future values to present values.

The conversion factors for the second, third, and fourth periods are 0.797194, 0.711780, and 0.635518, respectively. These factors are in the 12% column at rows 2, 3, and 4, respectively. Locate these factors in Appendix Table 1. Multiplying the conversion factors by the future cash inflow for each period produces their present value equivalents, shown in Exhibit 10.1. Exhibit 10.1 indicates that investing \$607,470 today (present value) at a 12 percent rate of return is equivalent to receiving \$200,000 per year for four years. Given that EZ Rentals desires to earn a 12 percent rate of return, the company should be willing to pay up to \$607,470 to purchase the projectors.

Present Value Table for Annuities

The algebra described previously for converting equal lump-sum cash inflows to present value equivalents can be further simplified by adding the present value table factors together before multiplying them by the cash inflows. The total of the present value table factors in Exhibit 10.1 is 3.037349 (0.892857 + 0.797194 + 0.711780 + 0.635518). Multiplying this **accumulated conversion factor** by the expected annual cash inflow results in the same present value equivalent of \$607,470 (\$200,000 × 3.037349). As with lump-sum conversion factors, accumulated conversion factors can be calculated and organized in a table with *columns* for different rates of return and *rows* for different periods of time. Appendix Table 2 is a present value table of accumulated conversion factors. Locate the conversion factor at the intersection of the 12% column and the fourth time-period row. The factor at this intersection is 3.037349, confirming that the accumulated conversion factors represent the sum of the single-payment conversion factors.

EXHIBIT 10.1

Present Value of a \$200,000 Cash Inflow to Be Received for Four Years

PV	=	FV	×	Present Value Table Factor	=	Present Value Equivalent
Period 1	=	\$200,000	×	0.892857	=	\$178,571
Period 2	=	200,000	×	0.797194	=	159,439
Period 3	=	200,000	×	0.711780	=	142,356
Period 4	=	200,000	×	0.635518	=	127,104
Total						\$607,470

[3]The present value table is based on the formula $[1 \div (1 + r)^n]$ where r equals the rate of return and n equals the number of periods.

The conversion factors in Appendix Table 2 apply to annuities. An **annuity** is a series of cash flows that meets three criteria: (1) equal payment amounts, (2) equal time intervals between payments, and (3) a constant rate of return. For EZ Rentals, the expected cash inflows from renting the projectors are all for equivalent amounts ($200,000); the expected intervals between cash inflows are equal lengths of time (one year); and the rate of return for each inflow is constant at 12 percent. The series of expected cash inflows from renting the projectors is therefore an annuity. The present value of an annuity table can be used only if all of these conditions are satisfied.

The present value of an annuity table (Appendix Table 2) simplifies converting future cash inflows to their present value equivalents. EZ Rentals can convert the cash inflows as shown in Exhibit 10.1, using four conversion factors, multiplying each conversion factor by the annual cash inflow (four multiplications), and adding the resulting products. In contrast, EZ can recognize that the series of payments is an annuity, which requires multiplying a single conversion factor from Appendix Table 2 by the amount of the annuity payment. Regardless of the conversion method, the result is the same (a present value of $607,470). Recall that EZ can also make the conversion using algebra. The table values are derived from algebraic formulas. The present value tables reduce the computations needed to convert future values to present values.

Software Programs That Calculate Present Values

Software programs offer an even more efficient means of converting future values into present value equivalents. These programs are frequently built into handheld financial calculators and computer spreadsheet programs. As an example, we demonstrate the procedures used in a Microsoft Excel spreadsheet.

An Excel spreadsheet offers a variety of financial functions, one of which converts a future value annuity into its present value equivalent. This present value function uses the syntax *PV(rate,nper,pmt)* in which *rate* is the desired rate of return, *nper* is the number of periods, and *pmt* is the amount of the payment (periodic cash inflow). To convert a future value annuity into its present value equivalent, provide the function with the appropriate amounts for the rate, number of periods, and amount of the annuity (cash inflows) into a spreadsheet cell. Press the Enter key and the present value equivalent appears in the spreadsheet cell.

The power of the spreadsheet to perform computations instantly is extremely useful for answering what-if questions. Exhibit 10.2 demonstrates this power by providing spreadsheet conversions for three different scenarios. The first scenario demonstrates the annuity assumptions for EZ Rentals, providing the present value equivalent ($607,470) of a four-year cash inflow of $200,000 per year at a 12 percent rate of interest. The present value is a *negative* number. This format indicates that an initial $607,470 *cash outflow* is required to obtain the four-year series of cash inflows. The present value equivalent in Scenario 2 shows the present value if the annuity assumptions reflect a 14 percent, rather than 12 percent, desired rate of return. The present value equivalent in Scenario 3 shows the present value if the annuity assumptions under Scenario 1 are changed to reflect annual cash inflows of $300,000, rather than $200,000. A wide range of scenarios could be readily considered by changing any or all of the variables in the spreadsheet function. In each case, the computer does the calculations, giving the manager more time to analyze the data rather than compute them.

Although software is widely used in business practice, the diversity of interfaces used by different calculators and spreadsheet programs makes it unsuitable for textbook presentations. This text uses the present value tables in the Appendix in the text illustrations and the end-of-chapter exercises and problems. If you use software to solve these problems, your answers will be the same. All of these tools–formulas, conversion tables, and software–are based on the same mathematical principles and will produce the same results.

Ordinary Annuity Assumption

All of the conversion methods described previously assume the cash inflows occur at the *end* of each accounting period. This distribution pattern is called an **ordinary annuity.**[4] In

[4]When equal cash inflows occur at the *beginning* of each accounting period, the distribution is called an *annuity due*. Although some business transactions are structured as annuities due, they are less common than ordinary annuities. This text focuses on the ordinary annuity assumption.

EXHIBIT 10.2

Microsoft Excel Spreadsheet Present Value Function

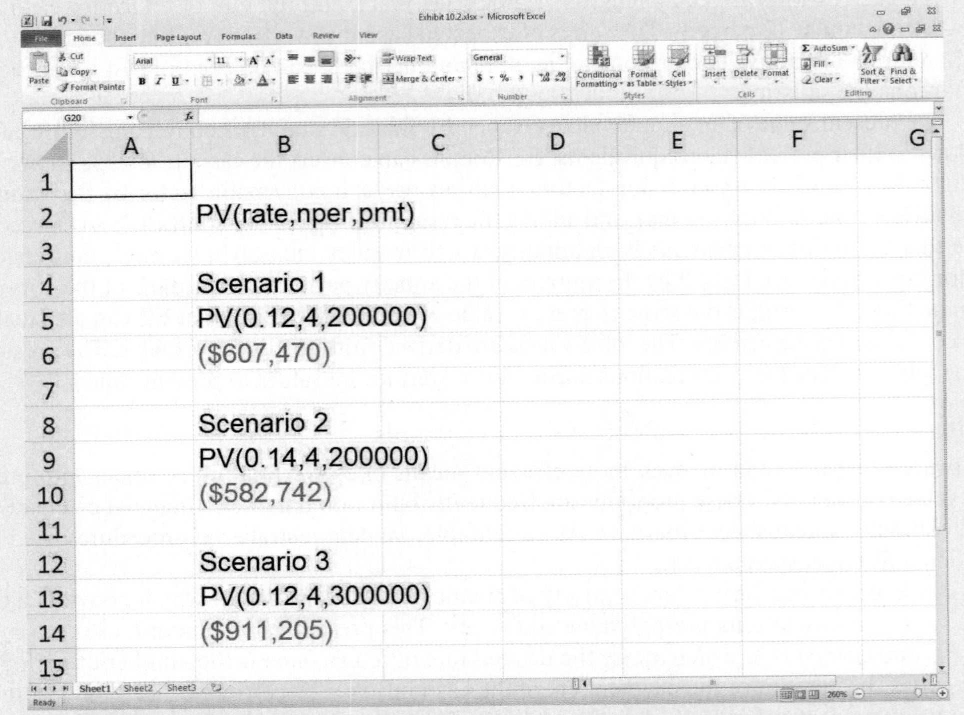

Source: Microsoft Excel 2010

practice, cash inflows are likely to be received throughout the period, not just at the end. For example, EZ Rentals is likely to collect cash revenue from renting projectors each month rather than in a single lump-sum receipt at the end of each of the four years. Companies frequently use the ordinary annuity assumption in practice because it simplifies time value of money computations. Because capital investment decisions are necessarily based on uncertain projections about future cash inflows, the lives of investment opportunities, and the appropriate rates of return, achieving pinpoint accuracy is impossible. Sacrificing precision for simplicity by using the ordinary annuity assumption is a reasonable trade-off in the decision-making process.

Reinvestment Assumption

The present value computations in the previous sections show that investing $607,470 today at a 12 percent rate of return is equivalent to receiving four individual $200,000 payments at the end of four successive years. Exhibit 10.3 illustrates that a cash inflow of $200,000 per year is equivalent to earning a 12 percent rate of return on a $607,470 investment.[5]

It is customary to assume that the desired rate of return includes the effects of *compounding*.[6] Saying an investment is "earning the desired rate of return," assumes the cash inflows generated by the investment are reinvested at the desired rate of return. In this case, we are assuming that EZ will reinvest the $200,000 annual cash inflows in other investments that will earn a 12 percent return.

[5]Exhibit 10.3 is analogous to an amortization table for a long-term note with equal payments of principal and interest.

[6]*Compounding* refers to reinvesting investment proceeds so the total amount of invested capital increases, resulting in even higher returns. For example, assume $100 is invested at a 10 percent compounded annual rate of return. At the end of the first year, the investment yields a $10 return ($100 × 0.10). The $10 return plus any recovered investment is reinvested so that the total amount of invested capital at the beginning of the second year is $110. The return for the second year is $11 ($110 × 0.10). All funds are reinvested so that the return for the third year is $12.10 [($110 + $11) × 0.10].

EXHIBIT 10.3

Cash Flow Classifications for EZ's Investment in Projectors

Time Period	(a) Investment Balance during the Year	(b) Annual Cash Inflow	(c) Return on Investment (a × 0.12)	(d) Recovered Investment (b − c)	(e) Year-End Investment Balance (a − d)
1	$607,470	$200,000	$ 72,896	$127,104	$480,366
2	480,366	200,000	57,644	142,356	338,010
3	338,010	200,000	40,561	159,439	178,571
4	178,571	200,000	21,429	178,571	0
Totals		$800,000	$192,530	$607,470	

ANALYZING CAPITAL INVESTMENT PROPOSALS

Managers can choose from among numerous analytical techniques to help them make capital investment decisions. Each technique has advantages and disadvantages. A manager may apply more than one technique to a particular proposal to take advantage of more information. Since most companies have computer capabilities that include a variety of standard capital budgeting programs, applying different techniques to the same proposal normally requires little extra effort. Limiting analysis to only one tool could produce biased results. Obtaining more than one perspective offers substantial benefit.

NET PRESENT VALUE

LO 10-2

Determine and interpret the net present value of an investment opportunity.

A variety of analytical techniques can be used to help make investment decisions. One frequently used technique is called the net present value method. The net present value is determined by subtracting the cost of an investment from its present value. To illustrate, return to the EZ Rental illustration. Recall that EZ Rentals' management determined it would be willing to invest $607,470 to purchase projectors today (present value) to obtain a $200,000 per year cash inflow from rent revenue for each of the next four years. The $607,470 investment is *not* the cost of the projectors; it is the amount EZ is willing to pay for them. The projectors may cost EZ Rentals more or less than their present value. To determine whether EZ should invest in the projectors, management must compare the present value of the future cash inflows ($607,470) to the cost of the projectors (the current cash outflow required to purchase them). Subtracting the cost of the investment from the present value of the future cash inflows determines the **net present value** of the investment opportunity. A positive net present value indicates the investment will yield a rate of return higher than 12 percent. A negative net present value means the return is less than 12 percent.

To illustrate, assume EZ can purchase the projectors for $582,742. Assuming the desired rate of return is 12 percent, EZ should buy them. The net present value of the investment opportunity is computed as follows:

Present value of future cash inflows	$ 607,470
Cost of investment (required cash outflow)	(582,742)
Net present value	$ 24,728

The positive net present value suggests the investment will earn a rate of return in excess of 12 percent (if cash flows are indeed $200,000 each year). Because the projected rate of return is higher than the desired rate of return, this analysis suggests EZ should accept the investment opportunity. Based on the given analysis, we are able to establish the following decision rule:

Net present value decision rule: If the net present value is equal to or greater than zero, accept the investment opportunity.

CHECK YOURSELF 10.2

To increase productivity, Wald Corporation is considering the purchase of a new machine that costs $50,000. Wald expects using the machine to increase annual net cash inflows by $12,500 for each of the next five years. Wald desires a minimum annual rate of return of 10 percent on the investment. Determine the net present value of the investment opportunity and recommend whether Wald should acquire the machine.

Answer

Present value of future cash flows = Future cash flow × Table 2 factor ($n = 5, r = 10\%$)

Present value of future cash flows = $12,500 × 3.790787 = $47,385

Net present value = PV of future cash flows − Cost of machine

Net present value = $47,385 − $50,000 = $(2,615)

The negative net present value indicates the investment will yield a rate of return below the desired rate of return. Wald should not acquire the new machine.

TECHNIQUES FOR MEASURING INVESTMENT CASH FLOWS

The EZ Rentals example represents a simple capital investment analysis. The investment option involved only one cash outflow and a single annuity inflow. Investment opportunities often involve a greater variety of cash outflows and inflows. The following section of this chapter discusses different types of cash flows encountered in business practice.

Cash Inflows

Cash inflows generated from capital investments come from *four basic sources.* As in the case of EZ Rentals, the most common source of cash inflows is incremental revenue. **Incremental revenue** refers to the *additional* cash inflows from operating activities generated by using additional capital assets. For example, a taxi company expects revenues from taxi fares to increase if it purchases additional taxicabs. Similarly, investing in new apartments should increase rent revenue; opening a new store should result in additional sales revenue.

A second type of cash inflow results from *cost savings.* Decreases in cash outflows have the same beneficial effect as increases in cash inflows. Either way, a firm's cash position improves. For example, purchasing an automated computer system may enable a company to reduce cash outflows for salaries. Similarly, relocating a manufacturing facility closer to its raw materials source can reduce cash outflows for transportation costs.

An investment's *salvage value* provides a third source of cash inflows. Even when one company has finished using an asset, the asset may still be useful to another company. Many assets are sold after a company no longer wishes to use them. The salvage value represents a one-time cash inflow obtained when a company terminates an investment.

Companies can also experience a cash inflow through a *reduction in the amount of* **working capital** needed to support an investment. A certain level of working capital is required to support most business investments. For example, a new retail store outlet requires cash, receivables, and inventory to operate. When an investment is terminated, the decrease in the working capital commitment associated with the investment normally results in a cash inflow.

Cash Outflows

Cash outflows fall into *three primary categories.* One category consists of outflows for the *initial investment.* Managers must be alert to all the cash outflows connected with purchasing a capital asset. The purchase price, transportation costs, installation costs, and training costs are examples of typical cash outflows related to an initial investment.

A second category of cash outflows may result from *increases in operating expenses.* If a company increases output capacity by investing in additional equipment, it may experience higher utility bills, labor costs, and maintenance expenses when it places the equipment into service. These expenditures increase cash outflows.

Third, *increases in working capital* commitments result in cash outflows. Frequently, investments in new assets must be supported by a certain level of working capital. For example, investing in a copy machine requires spending cash to maintain a supply of paper and toner. Managers should treat an increased working capital commitment as a cash outflow in the period the commitment occurs.

Exhibit 10.4 lists the cash inflows and outflows discussed previously. The list is not exhaustive but does summarize the most common cash flows businesses experience.

EXHIBIT 10.4

Typical Cash Flows Associated with Capital Investments

Inflows	Outflows
1. Incremental revenue	1. Initial investment
2. Cost savings	2. Incremental expenses
3. Salvage values	3. Working capital commitments
4. Recovery of working capital	

TECHNIQUES FOR COMPARING ALTERNATIVE CAPITAL INVESTMENT OPPORTUNITIES

The management of Torres Transfer Company is considering two investment opportunities. One alternative, involving the purchase of new equipment for $80,000, would enable Torres to modernize its maintenance facility. The equipment has an expected useful life of five years and a $4,000 salvage value. It would replace existing equipment that had originally cost $45,000. The existing equipment has a current book value of $15,000 and a trade-in value of $5,000. The old equipment is technologically obsolete but can operate for an additional five years. On the day Torres purchases the new equipment, it would also pay the equipment manufacturer $3,000 for training costs to teach employees to operate the new equipment. The modernization has two primary advantages. One, it will improve management of the small parts inventory. The company's accountant believes that by the end of the first year, the carrying value of the small parts inventory could be reduced by $12,000. Second, the modernization is expected to increase efficiency, resulting in a $21,500 reduction in annual operating expenses.

The other investment alternative available to Torres is purchasing a truck. Adding another truck would enable Torres to expand its delivery area and increase revenue. The truck costs $115,000. It has a useful life of five years and a $30,000 salvage value. Operating the truck will require the company to increase its inventory of supplies, its petty cash account, and its accounts receivable and payable balances. These changes would add $5,000 to the company's working capital base immediately upon buying the truck. The working capital cash outflow is expected to be recovered at the end of the truck's useful life. The truck is expected to produce $69,000 per year in additional revenues. The driver's salary and other operating expenses are expected to be $32,000 per year. A major overhaul costing $20,000 is expected to be required at the end of the third year of operation. Assuming Torres desires to earn a rate of return of 14 percent, which of the two investment alternatives should it choose?

Net Present Value

Begin the analysis by calculating the net present value of the two investment alternatives. Exhibit 10.5 shows the computations. Study this exhibit. Each alternative is analyzed using

EXHIBIT 10.5

Net Present Value Analysis

	Amount	×	Conversion Factor	=	Present Value
Alternative 1: Modernize Maintenance Facility					
Step 1: Cash inflows					
1. Cost savings	$21,500	×	3.433081*	=	$ 73,811
2. Salvage value	4,000	×	0.519369†	=	2,077
3. Working capital recovery	12,000	×	0.877193‡	=	10,526
Total					$ 86,414
Step 2: Cash outflows					
1. Cost of equipment ($80,000 cost—$5,000 trade-in)	$75,000	×	1.000000§	=	$ 75,000
2. Training costs	3,000	×	1.000000§	=	3,000
Total					$ 78,000
Step 3: Net present value					
Total present value of cash inflows					$ 86,414
Total present value of cash outflows					(78,000)
Net present value					$ 8,414
Alternative 2: Purchase Delivery Truck					
Step 1: Cash inflows					
1. Incremental revenue	$69,000	×	3.433081*	=	$ 236,883
2. Salvage value	30,000	×	0.519369†	=	15,581
3. Working capital recovery	5,000	×	0.519369†	=	2,597
Total					$ 255,061
Step 2: Cash outflows					
1. Cost of truck	$115,000	×	1.000000§	=	$ 115,000
2. Working capital increase	5,000	×	1.000000§	=	5,000
3. Increased operating expense	32,000	×	3.433081*	=	109,859
4. Major overhaul	20,000	×	0.674972§§	=	13,499
Total					$ 243,358
Step 3: Net present value					
Total present value of cash inflows					$ 255,061
Total present value of cash outflows					(243,358)
Net present value					$ 11,703

*Present value of annuity Table 2, $n = 5$, $r = 14\%$.
†Present value of single payment Table 1, $n = 5$, $r = 14\%$.
‡Present value of single payment Table 1, $n = 1$, $r = 14\%$.
§Present value at beginning of period 1.
§§Present value of single payment Table 1, $n = 3$, $r = 14\%$.

three steps. Step 1 requires identifying all cash inflows; some may be annuities, and others may be lump-sum receipts. In the case of Alternative 1, the cost saving is an annuity, and the inflow from the salvage value is a lump-sum receipt. Once the cash inflows have been identified, the appropriate conversion factors are identified and the cash inflows are converted to their equivalent present values. Step 2 follows the same process to determine the present value of the cash outflows. Step 3 subtracts the present value of the outflows from the present value of the inflows to determine the net present value. The same three-step approach is used to determine the net present value of Alternative 2.

With respect to Alternative 1, the original cost and the book value of the existing equipment are ignored. As indicated in a previous chapter, these measures represent *sunk costs;* they are not relevant to the decision. The concept of relevance applies to long-term capital investment decisions just as it applies to the short-term special decisions that were discussed in Chapter 5. To be relevant to a capital investment decision, costs or revenues must involve different present and future cash flows for each alternative. Since the historical cost of the old equipment does not differ between the alternatives, it is not relevant.

Since the *net present value* of each investment alternative is *positive,* either investment will generate a return in excess of 14 percent. Which investment is the more favorable? The data could mislead a careless manager. Alternative 2 might seem the better choice because it has a greater present value than Alternative 1 ($11,703 vs. $8,414). Net present value, however, is expressed in *absolute dollars.* The net present value of a more costly capital investment can be greater than the net present value of a smaller investment even though the smaller investment earns a higher rate of return.

To compare different size investment alternatives, management can compute a **present value index** by dividing the present value of cash inflows by the present value of cash outflows. *The higher the ratio, the higher the rate of return per dollar invested in the proposed project.* The present value indexes for the two alternatives Torres Transfer Company is considering are as follows:

$$\frac{\text{Present value index}}{\text{for Alternative 1}} = \frac{\text{Present value of cash inflows}}{\text{Present value of cash outflows}} = \frac{\$86{,}414}{\$78{,}000} = 1.108$$

$$\frac{\text{Present value index}}{\text{for Alternative 2}} = \frac{\text{Present value of cash inflows}}{\text{Present value of cash outflows}} = \frac{\$255{,}061}{\$243{,}358} = 1.048$$

Management can use the present value indexes to rank the investment alternatives. In this case, Alternative 1 yields a higher return than Alternative 2.

INTERNAL RATE OF RETURN

LO 10-3

Determine and interpret the internal rate of return of an investment opportunity.

Managers may use multiple techniques to evaluate the same investment opportunity. Each technique has advantages and disadvantages. Computer technology makes applying different techniques to the same proposal fast and easy. Limiting analysis to only one tool could produce biased results. Accordingly, the benefits of multiple analysis usually exceed the sacrifices required. A second technique discussed here is called the *internal rate of return.*

Calculating the Internal Rate of Return when Expected Cash Flows Are Distributed Evenly

Recall that net present value analysis indicated that EZ's investment in the projectors would yield a return in excess of the *desired* rate of return. However, the analysis did not provide the *expected* rate of return that the investment would produce. If EZ's management team wants to know the rate of return to expect from investing in the projectors, it must use the *internal rate of return method.* The **internal rate of return** is the rate at which the present value of cash inflows equals the cash outflows. Generally, *the higher the internal rate of return, the more profitable the investment.*

The internal rate of return is the rate that will produce a zero net present value. For EZ Rentals, the internal rate of return can be determined as follows. First, compute the *present value table factor* for a $200,000 annuity that would yield a $582,742 present value cash outflow (cost of the projectors).

$$\text{Present value table factor} \times \$200{,}000 = \$582{,}742$$

$$\text{Present value table factor} = \$582{,}742 \div \$200{,}000$$

$$\text{Present value table factor} = 2.91371$$

Second, since the expected annual cash inflows represent a four-year annuity, scan Appendix Table 2 at period $n = 4$. Try to locate the table factor 2.91371. The rate listed at the top of the column in which the factor is located is the internal rate of return. Turn to Appendix Table 2 and determine the internal rate of return for EZ Rentals before you read further. The above factor is in the 14 percent column. The difference in the table value (2.913712) and the value computed here (2.91371) is not significant. This means that if EZ invests $582,742 in the projectors and they produce a $200,000 annual cash flow for four years, EZ will earn a 14 percent rate of return on the investment.

The *internal rate of return* may be compared to a *desired rate of return* to determine whether to accept or reject a particular investment project. If the internal rate of return is equal to or higher than the desired rate of return, the investment opportunity should be accepted. Accordingly, the preceding analysis suggests the EZ should accept the investment opportunity because the internal rate of return (14 percent) is higher than the desired rate of return (12 percent). An internal rate of return below the desired rate suggests management should reject a particular proposal. Based on the given analysis, we are able to establish the following decision rule:

> **Internal rate of return decision rule:** If the internal rate of return is equal to or greater than the desired rate of return, accept the investment opportunity.

Calculating the Internal Rate of Return when Expected Cash Flows Are Distributed Irregularly

We previously demonstrated how to calculate the internal rate of return for an investment that generates a simple, regular cash inflow annuity. The computations are significantly more complex for investments with uneven cash flows. Recall that the internal rate of return is the rate that produces a zero net present value. Manually computing the rate that produces a zero net present value is a tedious trial-and-error process. You must first estimate the rate of return for a particular investment, then calculate the net present value. If the calculation produces a negative net present value, you try a lower estimated rate of return and recalculate. If this calculation produces a positive net present value, the actual internal rate of return lies between the first and second estimates. Make a third estimate and once again recalculate the net present value, and so on. Eventually, you will determine the rate of return that produces a net present value of zero.

Many calculators and spreadsheet programs are designed to make these computations. We illustrate the process with a Microsoft Excel spreadsheet. Excel uses the syntax *IRR (values, guess)* in which *values* refers to cells that specify the cash flows for which you want to calculate the internal rate of return and *guess* is a number you estimate is close to the actual internal rate of return (IRR). The IRRs for the two investment alternatives available to Torres Transfer Company are shown in Exhibit 10.6. Study this exhibit. Excel requires netting cash outflows against cash inflows for each period in which both outflows and inflows are expected.

EXHIBIT 10.6

Microsoft Excel Spreadsheet Internal Rate of Return Function

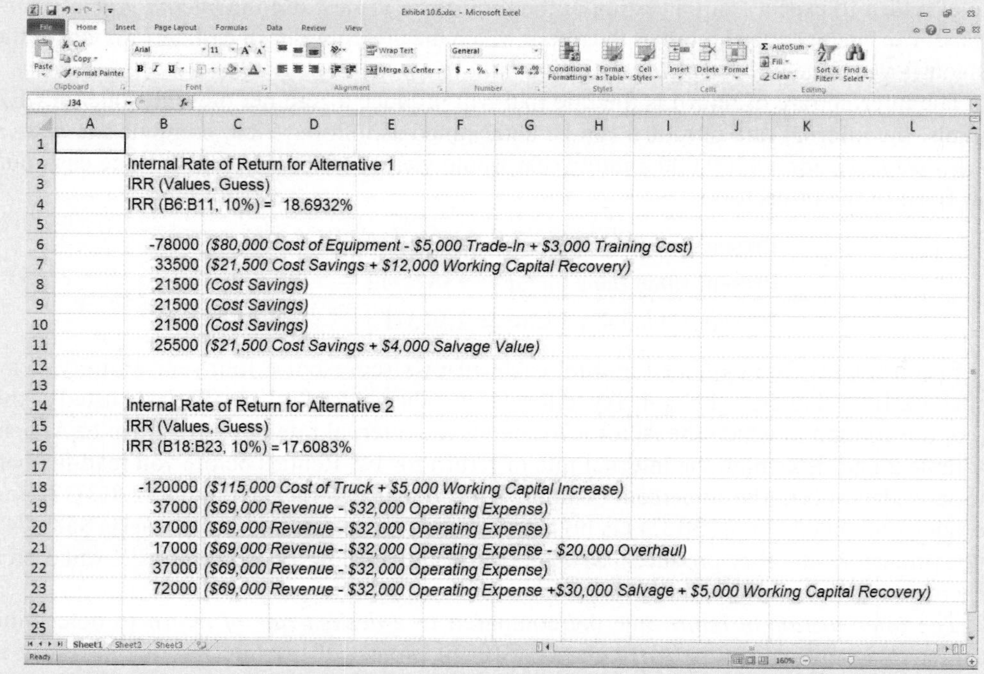
Internal Rate of Return for Alternative 1
IRR (Values, Guess)
IRR (B6:B11, 10%) = 18.6932%

-78000 ($80,000 Cost of Equipment - $5,000 Trade-In + $3,000 Training Cost)
33500 ($21,500 Cost Savings + $12,000 Working Capital Recovery)
21500 (Cost Savings)
21500 (Cost Savings)
21500 (Cost Savings)
25500 ($21,500 Cost Savings + $4,000 Salvage Value)

Internal Rate of Return for Alternative 2
IRR (Values, Guess)
IRR (B18:B23, 10%) = 17.6083%

-120000 ($115,000 Cost of Truck + $5,000 Working Capital Increase)
37000 ($69,000 Revenue - $32,000 Operating Expense)
37000 ($69,000 Revenue - $32,000 Operating Expense)
17000 ($69,000 Revenue - $32,000 Operating Expense - $20,000 Overhaul)
37000 ($69,000 Revenue - $32,000 Operating Expense)
72000 ($69,000 Revenue - $32,000 Operating Expense +$30,000 Salvage + $5,000 Working Capital Recovery)

Source: Microsoft Excel 2010

REALITY BYTES

©Kristin Smith/Shutterstock

Developing proficiency with present value mathematics is usually the most difficult aspect of capital budgeting for students taking their first managerial accounting course. In real-world companies, the most difficult aspect of capital budgeting is forecasting cash flows for several years into the future. Consider the following capital budgeting project:

In 1965, representatives from the Georgia Power Company visited Ms. Taylor's fifth-grade class to tell her students about the Edwin I. Hatch Nuclear Plant that was going to be built nearby. One of the authors of this text was a student in that class.

In 1966, construction began on the first unit of the plant, and the plant started producing electricity in 1975. The next year, 10 years after hearing the presentation in his fifth-grade class, the author worked on construction of the second unit of the plant during the summer before his senior year of college. This second unit began operations in 1978.

In its 2017 annual report, the Southern Company, which is now the major owner of the plant, stated that the Hatch plant is expected to operate until 2038 and that decommissioning of the plant will continue until 2075. The cost to construct both units of the plant was $934 million. The estimated cost to dismantle and decommission the plant is over $902 million.

It seems safe to assume that the students in Ms. Taylor's fifth-grade class were not among the first to hear about the power company's plans for the Hatch plant. Thus, we can reasonably conclude that the life of this capital project will be over 100 years, from around 1960 until 2068.

Try to imagine that you were assigned the task of predicting the cost inflows and outflows for a project that was expected to last 100 years. Clearly, mastering present value mathematics would not be your biggest worry.

For your convenience, we have labeled the net cash flows in the spreadsheet. Labeling is not necessary to execute the IRR function. The entire function, including values and guess, can be entered into a single cell of the spreadsheet. Persons familiar with spreadsheet programs learn to significantly simplify the input required.

The IRR results in Exhibit 10.6 confirm the ranking determined using the present value index. Alternative 1 (modernize maintenance facility), with an internal rate of return of 18.69 percent, ranks above Alternative 2 (purchase a truck) with an internal rate of return of 17.61 percent, even though Alternative 2 has a higher net present value (see Exhibit 10.5). Alternative 2, however, still may be the better investment option, depending on the amount available to invest. Suppose Torres has $120,000 of available funds to invest. Because Alternative 1 requires an initial investment of only $78,000, $42,000 ($120,000 − $78,000) of capital will not be invested. If Torres has no other investment opportunities for this $42,000, the company would be better off investing the entire $120,000 in Alternative 2 ($115,000 cost of truck + $5,000 working capital increase). Earning 17.61 percent on a $120,000 investment is better than earning 18.69 percent on a $78,000 investment with no return on the remaining $42,000. Management accounting requires exercising judgment when making decisions.

Relevance and the Time Value of Money

Suppose you have the opportunity to invest in one of two capital projects. Both projects require an immediate cash outflow of $6,000 and will produce future cash inflows of $8,000. The only difference between the two projects is the timing of the inflows. The receipt schedule for both projects follows.

Year	Project 1	Project 2
1	$3,500	$2,000
2	3,000	2,000
3	1,000	2,000
4	500	2,000
Total	$8,000	$8,000

Because both projects cost the same and produce the same total cash inflows, they may appear to be equal. Whether you select Project 1 or Project 2, you pay $6,000 and receive $8,000. Because of the time value of money, however, Project 1 is preferable to Project 2. To see why, determine the net present value of both projects, assuming a 10 percent desired rate of return.

Computation of Net Present Value for Project 1 and Project 2

Net Present Value for Project 1

Period	Cash Inflow	×	Conversion Factor Table 1, $r = 10\%$	=	Present Value
1	$3,500	×	0.909091	=	$ 3,182
2	3,000	×	0.826446	=	2,479
3	1,000	×	0.751315	=	751
4	500	×	0.683013	=	342
Present value of future cash inflows					6,754
Present value of cash outflow					(6,000)
Net present value Project 1					$ 754

Net Present Value for Project 2

	Cash Inflow Annuity	×	Conversion Factor Table 2, $r = 10\%$, $n = 4$	
Present value of cash inflow	$2,000	×	3.169865	$ 6,340
Present value of cash outflow				(6,000)
Net present value Project 2				$ 340

The net present value of Project 1 ($754) exceeds the net present value of Project 2 ($340). The timing as well as the amount of cash flows has a significant impact on capital investment returns. Recall that to be relevant, costs or revenues must differ between alternatives. Differences in the timing of cash flow payments or receipts are also relevant for decision-making purposes.

Answers to The Curious Accountant

One way to answer your client's question is to determine which option has the highest net present value. The present value of the lump-sum payment option is simple: it is the $480.5 million the lottery is prepared to pay the winner now. The present value of the annuity option must be calculated, and it consists of two parts. The first of the 30 payments of $25.29 million will be paid immediately, so it is worth $25.29 million today. The remaining 29 payments will occur at one-year intervals, so their present value is computed as:

$$\$25{,}290{,}000 \times 12.27767^{*} = \$310{,}502{,}274$$

Adding $25,290,000 to $310,502,274 yields a present value of $335,792,274, which is a lot less than $480.5 million. This suggests your client should take the lump-sum payment. Of course, the risk of the lottery not making its annual payments is very low. There is a greater risk that a financial planner may not find investments to earn a 7 percent annual return, so the winner would have to consider his or her tolerance for risk before making a final decision.

*This factor is not included in the tables at the end of the chapter, so it is provided here for the purposes of this illustration.

Tax Considerations

The previous examples have ignored the effect of income taxes on capital investment decisions. Taxes affect the amount of cash flows generated by investments. To illustrate, assume Wu Company purchases an asset that costs $240,000. The asset has a four-year useful life, no salvage value, and is depreciated on a straight-line basis. The asset generates cash revenue of $90,000 per year. Assume Wu's income tax rate is 40 percent. What is the net present value of the asset, assuming Wu's management desires to earn a 10 percent rate of return after taxes? The first step in answering this question is to calculate the annual cash flow generated by the asset, as shown in Exhibit 10.7.

EXHIBIT 10.7

Determining Cash Flow from Investment

	Period 1	Period 2	Period 3	Period 4
Cash revenue	$ 90,000	$ 90,000	$ 90,000	$ 90,000
Depreciation expense (noncash)	(60,000)	(60,000)	(60,000)	(60,000)
Income before taxes	30,000	30,000	30,000	30,000
Income tax at 40%	(12,000)	(12,000)	(12,000)	(12,000)
Income after tax	18,000	18,000	18,000	18,000
Depreciation add back	60,000	60,000	60,000	60,000
Annual cash inflow	$ 78,000	$ 78,000	$ 78,000	$ 78,000

Because recognizing depreciation expense does not require a cash payment (cash is paid when assets are purchased, not when depreciation is recognized), depreciation expense must be added back to after-tax income to determine the annual cash inflow. Once the cash flow is determined, the net present value is computed as shown here:

Cash flow annuity	×	Conversion factor Table 2, $r = 10\%$, $n = 4$	=	Present value cash inflows	−	Present value cash outflows	=	Net present value
$78,000	×	3.169865	=	$247,249	−	$240,000	=	$7,249

The depreciation sheltered some of the income from taxation. Income taxes apply to income after deducting depreciation expense. Without depreciation expense, income taxes each year would have been $36,000 ($90,000 × 0.40) instead of $12,000 ($30,000 × 0.40). The $24,000 difference ($36,000 − $12,000) is known as a *depreciation tax shield.* The amount of the depreciation tax shield can also be computed by multiplying the depreciation expense by the tax rate ($60,000 × 0.40 = $24,000).

Because of the time value of money, companies benefit by maximizing the depreciation tax shield early in the life of an asset. For this reason, most companies calculate depreciation expense for tax purposes using the *modified accelerated cost recovery system (MACRS)* permitted by tax law rather than using straight-line depreciation. MACRS recognizes depreciation on an accelerated basis, assigning larger amounts of depreciation in the early years of an asset's useful life. The higher depreciation charges result in lower amounts of taxable income and lower income taxes. In the later years of an asset's useful life, the reverse is true, and lower depreciation charges result in higher taxes. Accelerated depreciation does not allow companies to avoid paying taxes but to delay them. The longer companies can delay paying taxes, the more cash they have available to invest.

TECHNIQUES THAT IGNORE THE TIME VALUE OF MONEY

LO 10-4

Evaluate investment opportunities using the payback method and the unadjusted rate of return.

Several techniques for evaluating capital investment proposals ignore the time value of money. Although these techniques are less accurate, they are quick and simple. When investments are small or the returns are expected within a short time, these techniques are likely to result in the same decisions that more sophisticated techniques produce.

Payback Method

The **payback method** is simple to apply and easy to understand. It shows how long it will take to recover the initial cash outflow (the cost) of an investment. The formula for computing the payback period, measured in years, is as follows:

$$\text{Payback period} = \text{Net cost of investment} \div \text{Annual net cash inflow}$$

To illustrate, assume Winston Cleaners can purchase a new ironing machine that will press shirts in half the time of the one currently used. The new machine costs $100,000 and will reduce labor cost by $40,000 per year over a four-year useful life. The payback period is computed as follows:

$$\text{Payback period} = \$100{,}000 \div \$40{,}000 = 2.5 \text{ years}$$

Interpreting Payback

Generally, investments with shorter payback periods are considered better. Because the payback method measures only investment recovery, not profitability, however, this conclusion can be invalid when considering investment alternatives. To illustrate, assume Winston Cleaners also has the opportunity to purchase a different machine that costs $100,000 and provides an annual labor savings of $40,000. However, the second machine will last for five instead of four years. The payback period is still 2.5 years ($100,000 ÷ $40,000), but the second machine is a better investment because it improves profitability by providing an additional year of cost savings. The payback analysis does not measure this difference between the alternatives.

Unequal Cash Flows

The preceding illustration assumed Winston's labor cost reduction saved the same amount of cash each year for the life of the new machine. The payback method requires adjustment when cash flow benefits are unequal. Suppose a company purchases a machine for $6,000. The machine will be used sporadically and is expected to provide incremental revenue over the next five years as follows.

Year 1	Year 2	Year 3	Year 4	Year 5
$3,000	$1,000	$2,000	$1,000	$500

Based on this cash inflow pattern, what is the payback period? There are two acceptable solutions. One accumulates the incremental revenue until the sum equals the amount of the original investment.

	Annual Amount	Cumulative Total
Year 1	$3,000	$3,000
Year 2	1,000	4,000
Year 3	2,000	6,000

This approach indicates the payback period is three years.

A second solution uses an averaging concept. The average annual cash inflow is determined. This figure is then used in the denominator of the payback equation. Using the preceding data, the payback period is computed as follows:

1. Compute the average annual cash inflow.

$$\text{Year 1} + \text{Year 2} + \text{Year 3} + \text{Year 4} + \text{Year 5} = \text{Total} \div 5 = \text{Average}$$

$$\$3{,}000 + \$1{,}000 + \$2{,}000 + \$1{,}000 + \$500 = \$7{,}500 \div 5 = \$1{,}500$$

2. Compute the payback period.

$$\frac{\text{Net cost of}}{\text{investment}} \div \frac{\text{Average annual}}{\text{net cash inflow}} = \$6{,}000 \div \$1{,}500 = 4 \text{ years}$$

The average method is useful when a company purchases a number of similar assets with differing cash return patterns.

Unadjusted Rate of Return

The **unadjusted rate of return** method is another common evaluation technique. Investment cash flows are not adjusted to reflect the time value of money. The unadjusted rate of return is sometimes called the *simple rate of return.* It is computed as follows:

$$\text{Unadjusted rate of return} = \frac{\text{Average incremental increase in annual net income}}{\text{Net cost of original investment}}$$

To illustrate computing the unadjusted rate of return, assume The Dining Table Inc. is considering establishing a new restaurant that will require a $2,000,000 original investment. Management anticipates operating the restaurant for 10 years before significant renovations will be required. The restaurant is expected to provide an average after-tax return of $280,000 per year. The unadjusted rate of return is computed as follows:

$$\text{Unadjusted rate of return} = \$280{,}000 \div \$2{,}000{,}000 = 14\% \text{ per year}$$

The accuracy of the unadjusted rate of return suffers from the failure to recognize the recovery of invested capital. With respect to a depreciable asset, the capital investment is normally recovered through revenue over the life of the asset. To illustrate, assume we purchase a $1,000 asset with a two-year life and a zero salvage value. For simplicity, ignore income taxes. Assume the asset produces $600 of cash revenue per year. The income statement for the first year of operation appears as follows.

Revenue	$ 600
Depreciation expense	(500)
Net income	$ 100

What is the amount of invested capital during the first year? First, a $1,000 cash outflow was used to purchase the asset (the original investment). Next, we collected $600 of cash revenue of which $100 was a *return on investment* (net income) and $500 was a **recovery of investment.** As a result, $1,000 was invested in the asset at the beginning of the year and $500 was invested at the end of the year. Similarly, we will recover an additional $500 of capital during the second year of operation, leaving zero invested capital at the end of the second year. Given that the cash inflows from revenue are collected somewhat evenly over the life of the investment, the amount of invested capital will range from a beginning balance of $1,000 to an ending balance of zero. On average, we will have $500 invested in the asset (the midpoint between $1,000 and zero). The average investment can be determined by dividing the total original investment by 2 ($1,000 ÷ 2 = $500). The unadjusted rate of return based on average invested capital can be calculated as follows:

$$\frac{\text{Unadjusted rate of return}}{\text{(Based on average investment)}} = \frac{\text{Average incremental increase in annual net income}}{\text{Net cost of original investment} \div 2}$$

$$= \frac{\$100}{\$1{,}000 \div 2} = 20\%$$

To avoid distortions caused by the failure to recognize the recovery of invested capital, the unadjusted rate of return should be based on the *average investment* when working with investments in depreciable assets.

CHECK YOURSELF 10.3

EZ Rentals can purchase a van that costs $24,000. The van has an expected useful life of three years and no salvage value. EZ expects rental revenue from the van to be $12,000 per year. Determine the payback period and the unadjusted rate of return.

Answer

Payback = Cost of the investment ÷ Annual cash inflow

Payback = $24,000 ÷ $12,000 = 2 years

Unadjusted rate of return = Net income ÷ Average cost of the investment

Revenue	$12,000	
Depreciation expense	(8,000)	[$24,000 ÷ 3 years]
Net income	$ 4,000	

Unadjusted rate of return = $4,000 ÷ ($24,000 ÷ 2) = 33.33%

POSTAUDITS

The analytical techniques for evaluating capital investment proposals depend highly on estimates of future cash flows. Although predictions cannot be perfectly accurate, gross miscalculations can threaten the existence of an organization. For example, optimistic projections of future cash inflows that do not materialize will lead to investments that do not return the cost of capital. Managers must take their projections seriously. A postaudit policy can encourage managers to carefully consider their capital investment decisions. A **postaudit** is conducted at the completion of a capital investment project, using the same analytical technique that was used to justify the original investment. For example, if an internal rate of return was used to justify approving an investment project, the internal rate of return should be computed in the postaudit. In the postaudit computation, *actual* rather than estimated cash flows are used. Postaudits determine whether the expected results were achieved.

Postaudits should focus on continuous improvement rather than punishment. Managers who are chastised for failing to achieve expected results might become overly cautious when asked to provide estimates for future projects. Being too conservative can create problems as serious as those caused by being too optimistic. Managers can err two ways with respect to capital investment decisions. First, a manager might accept a project that should have been rejected. This mistake usually stems from excessively optimistic future cash flow projections. Second, a manager might reject a project that should have been accepted. These missed opportunities are usually the result of underestimating future cash flows. A too cautious manager can become unable to locate enough projects to fully invest the firm's funds.

Idle cash earns no return. If projects continue to outperform expectations, managers are probably estimating future cash flows too conservatively. If projects consistently fail to live up to expectations, managers are probably being too optimistic in their projections of future cash flows. Either way, the company suffers. The goal of a postaudit is to provide feedback that will help managers improve the accuracy of future cash flow projections, maximizing the quality of the firm's capital investments.

<< A Look Back

Capital expenditures have a significant, long-term effect on profitability. They usually involve major cash outflows that are recovered through future cash inflows. The most common cash inflows include incremental revenue, operating cost savings, salvage value, and working capital releases. The most common outflows are the initial investment, increases in operating expenses, and working capital commitments.

Several techniques for analyzing the cash flows associated with capital investments are available. The techniques can be divided into two categories: (1) techniques that use time value of money concepts and (2) techniques that ignore the time value of money. Generally, techniques that ignore the time value of money are less accurate but simpler and easier to understand. These techniques include the *payback method* and the *unadjusted rate of return method.*

The techniques that use time value of money concepts are the *net present value method* and the *internal rate of return method.* These methods offer significant improvements in accuracy but are more difficult to understand. They may involve tedious computations and require using experienced judgment. Computer software and programmed calculators that ease the tedious computational burden are readily available to most managers. Furthermore, the superiority of the techniques justifies learning how to use them. These methods should be used when investment expenditures are larger or when cash flows extend over a prolonged time period.

A Look Forward >>

The next chapter moves into unexplored territory. It introduces the concept of inventory cost flow. It discusses how costs move through the inventory accounts Raw Materials, Work in Process, and Finished Goods. It presents techniques for assigning overhead costs to inventory as the inventory is produced. It identifies differences in product costing for service and manufacturing companies. Finally, it contrasts two approaches used to value inventory, variable costing versus full-absorption costing.

APPENDIX

TABLE 1 Present Value of $1

n	4%	5%	6%	7%	8%	9%	10%	12%	14%	16%	20%
1	0.961538	0.952381	0.943396	0.934579	0.925926	0.917431	0.909091	0.892857	0.877193	0.862069	0.833333
2	0.924556	0.907029	0.889996	0.873439	0.857339	0.841680	0.826446	0.797194	0.769468	0.743163	0.694444
3	0.888996	0.863838	0.839619	0.816298	0.793832	0.772183	0.751315	0.711780	0.674972	0.640658	0.578704
4	0.854804	0.822702	0.792094	0.762895	0.735030	0.708425	0.683013	0.635518	0.592080	0.552291	0.482253
5	0.821927	0.783526	0.747258	0.712986	0.680583	0.649931	0.620921	0.567427	0.519369	0.476113	0.401878
6	0.790315	0.746215	0.704961	0.666342	0.630170	0.596267	0.564474	0.506631	0.455587	0.410442	0.334898
7	0.759918	0.710681	0.665057	0.622750	0.583490	0.547034	0.513158	0.452349	0.399637	0.353830	0.279082
8	0.730690	0.676839	0.627412	0.582009	0.540269	0.501866	0.466507	0.403883	0.350559	0.305025	0.232568
9	0.702587	0.644609	0.591898	0.543934	0.500249	0.460428	0.424098	0.360610	0.307508	0.262953	0.193807
10	0.675564	0.613913	0.558395	0.508349	0.463193	0.422411	0.385543	0.321973	0.269744	0.226684	0.161506
11	0.649581	0.584679	0.526788	0.475093	0.428883	0.387533	0.350494	0.287476	0.236617	0.195417	0.134588
12	0.624597	0.556837	0.496969	0.444012	0.397114	0.355535	0.318631	0.256675	0.207559	0.168463	0.112157
13	0.600574	0.530321	0.468839	0.414964	0.367698	0.326179	0.289664	0.229174	0.182069	0.145227	0.093464
14	0.577475	0.505068	0.442301	0.387817	0.340461	0.299246	0.263331	0.204620	0.159710	0.125195	0.077887
15	0.555265	0.481017	0.417265	0.362446	0.315242	0.274538	0.239392	0.182696	0.140096	0.107927	0.064905
16	0.533908	0.458112	0.393646	0.338735	0.291890	0.251870	0.217629	0.163122	0.122892	0.093041	0.054088
17	0.513373	0.436297	0.371364	0.316574	0.270269	0.231073	0.197845	0.145644	0.107800	0.080207	0.045073
18	0.493628	0.415521	0.350344	0.295864	0.250249	0.211994	0.179859	0.130040	0.094561	0.069144	0.037561
19	0.474642	0.395734	0.330513	0.276508	0.231712	0.194490	0.163508	0.116107	0.082948	0.059607	0.031301
20	0.456387	0.376889	0.311805	0.258419	0.214548	0.178431	0.148644	0.103667	0.072762	0.051385	0.026084

TABLE 2 Present Value of an Annuity of $1

n	4%	5%	6%	7%	8%	9%	10%	12%	14%	16%	20%
1	0.961538	0.952381	0.943396	0.934579	0.925926	0.917431	0.909091	0.892857	0.877193	0.862069	0.833333
2	1.886095	1.859410	1.833393	1.808018	1.783265	1.759111	1.735537	1.690051	1.646661	1.605232	1.527778
3	2.775091	2.723248	2.673012	2.624316	2.577097	2.531295	2.486852	2.401831	2.321632	2.245890	2.106481
4	3.629895	3.545951	3.465106	3.387211	3.312127	3.239720	3.169865	3.037349	2.913712	2.798181	2.588735
5	4.451822	4.329477	4.212364	4.100197	3.992710	3.889651	3.790787	3.604776	3.433081	3.274294	2.990612
6	5.242137	5.075692	4.917324	4.766540	4.622880	4.485919	4.355261	4.111407	3.888668	3.684736	3.325510
7	6.002055	5.786373	5.582381	5.389289	5.206370	5.032953	4.868419	4.563757	4.288305	4.038565	3.604592
8	6.732745	6.463213	6.209794	5.971299	5.746639	5.534819	5.334926	4.967640	4.638864	4.343591	3.837160
9	7.435332	7.107822	6.801692	6.515232	6.246888	5.995247	5.759024	5.328250	4.946372	4.606544	4.030967
10	8.110896	7.721735	7.360087	7.023582	6.710081	6.417658	6.144567	5.650223	5.216116	4.833227	4.192472
11	8.760477	8.306414	7.886875	7.498674	7.138964	6.805191	6.495061	5.937699	5.452733	5.028644	4.327060
12	9.385074	8.863252	8.383844	7.942686	7.536078	7.160725	6.813692	6.194374	5.660292	5.197107	4.439217
13	9.985648	9.393573	8.852683	8.357651	7.903776	7.486904	7.103356	6.423548	5.842362	5.342334	4.532681
14	10.563123	9.898641	9.294984	8.745468	8.244237	7.786150	7.366687	6.628168	6.002072	5.467529	4.610567
15	11.118387	10.379658	9.712249	9.107914	8.559479	8.060688	7.606080	6.810864	6.142168	5.575456	4.675473
16	11.652296	10.837770	10.105895	9.446649	8.851369	8.312558	7.823709	6.973986	6.265060	5.668497	4.729561
17	12.165669	11.274066	10.477260	9.763223	9.121638	8.543631	8.021553	7.119630	6.372859	5.748704	4.774634
18	12.659297	11.689587	10.827603	10.059087	9.371887	8.755625	8.201412	7.249670	6.467420	5.817848	4.812195
19	13.133939	12.085321	11.158116	10.335595	9.603599	8.905115	8.364920	7.365777	6.550369	5.877455	4.843496
20	13.590326	12.462210	11.469921	10.594014	9.818147	9.128546	8.513564	7.469444	6.623131	5.928841	4.869580

Video lectures and accompanying self-assessment quizzes are available in *Connect* for all learning objectives.

SELF-STUDY REVIEW PROBLEM

The CFO of Advo Corporation is considering two investment opportunities. The expected future cash inflows for each opportunity follow.

	Year 1	Year 2	Year 3	Year 4
Project 1	$144,000	$147,000	$160,000	$178,000
Project 2	204,000	199,000	114,000	112,000

Both investments require an initial payment of $400,000. Advo's desired rate of return is 16 percent.

Required

a. Compute the net present value of each project. Which project should Advo adopt based on the net present value approach?

b. Use the incremental revenue summation method to compute the payback period for each project. Which project should Advo adopt based on the payback approach?

Solution to Requirement *a*

Project 1

	Cash Inflows		Table Factor*		Present Value
Year 1	$144,000	×	0.862069	=	$124,138
Year 2	147,000	×	0.743163	=	109,245
Year 3	160,000	×	0.640658	=	102,505
Year 4	178,000	×	0.552291	=	98,308
PV of cash inflows					434,196
Cost of investment					(400,000)
Net present value					$ 34,196

*Table 1, $n = 1$ through 4, $r = 16\%$.

Project 2

	Cash Inflows		Table Factor*		Present Value
Year 1	$204,000	×	0.862069	=	$ 175,862
Year 2	199,000	×	0.743163	=	147,889
Year 3	114,000	×	0.640658	=	73,035
Year 4	112,000	×	0.552291	=	61,857
PV of cash inflows					458,643
Cost of investment					(400,000)
Net present value					$ 58,643

*Table 1, $n = 1$ through 4, $r = 16\%$.

Advo should adopt Project 2 since it has a greater net present value.

Solution to Requirement *b*

Cash Inflows	Project 1	Project 2
Year 1	$144,000	$204,000
Year 2	147,000	199,000
Total	$291,000	$403,000

By the end of the second year, Project 2's cash inflows have more than paid for the cost of the investment. In contrast, Project 1 still falls short of investment recovery by $109,000 ($400,000 − $291,000). Advo should adopt Project 2 since it has a shorter payback period.

KEY TERMS

Accumulated conversion factor 448
Annuity 449
Capital investments 446
Cost of capital 447
Desired rate of return 447
Incremental revenue 452
Internal rate of return 455
Minimum rate of return 447
Net present value 451
Ordinary annuity 449
Payback method 460
Postaudit 462
Present value index 455
Present value table 448
Recovery of investment 461
Single-payment (lump-sum) 448
Time value of money 446
Unadjusted rate of return (simple rate of return) 461
Working capital 452

QUESTIONS

1. What is a capital investment? How does it differ from an investment in stocks or bonds?
2. What are three reasons that cash is worth more today than cash to be received in the future?
3. "A dollar today is worth more than a dollar in the future." "The present value of a future dollar is worth less than one dollar." Are these two statements synonymous? Explain.

4. Define the term *return on investment.* How is the return normally expressed? Give an example of a capital investment return.
5. How does a company establish its minimum acceptable rate of return on investments?
6. If you wanted to have $100,000 one year from today and desired to earn a 6 percent return, what amount would you need to invest today? Which amount has more value, the amount today or the $100,000 a year from today?
7. Why are present value tables frequently used to convert future values to present values?
8. Define the term *annuity.* What is one example of an annuity receipt?
9. How can present value "what-if" analysis be enhanced by using software programs?
10. Receiving $100,000 per year for five years is equivalent to investing what amount today at 14 percent? Provide a mathematical formula to solve this problem, assuming use of a present value annuity table to convert the future cash flows to their present value equivalents. Provide the expression for the Excel spreadsheet function that would perform the present value conversion.
11. Maria Espinosa borrowed $15,000 from the bank and agreed to repay the loan at 8 percent annual interest over four years, making payments of $4,529 per year. Because part of the bank's payment from Ms. Espinosa is a recovery of the original investment, what assumption must the bank make to earn its desired 8 percent compounded annual return?
12. Two investment opportunities have positive net present values. Investment A's net present value amounts to $40,000 while B's is only $30,000. Does this mean that A is the better investment opportunity? Explain.
13. What criteria determine whether a project is acceptable under the net present value method?
14. Does the net present value method provide a measure of the rate of return on capital investments?
15. Which is the best capital investment evaluation technique for ranking investment opportunities?
16. Paul Henderson is a manager for Spark Company. He tells you that his company always maximizes profitability by accepting the investment opportunity with the highest internal rate of return. Explain to Mr. Henderson how his company may improve profitability by sometimes selecting investment opportunities with lower internal rates of return.
17. What is the relationship between desired rate of return and internal rate of return?
18. What typical cash inflow and outflow items are associated with capital investments?
19. "I always go for the investment with the shortest payback period." Is this a sound strategy? Why or why not?
20. "The payback method cannot be used if the cash inflows occur in unequal patterns." Do you agree or disagree? Explain.
21. What are the advantages and disadvantages associated with the unadjusted rate of return method for evaluating capital investments?
22. How do capital investments affect profitability?
23. What is a postaudit? How is it useful in capital budgeting?

MULTIPLE-CHOICE QUESTIONS

Multiple-choice questions are available in *Connect*.

EXERCISES—SERIES A

connect **All applicable Exercises in Series A are available in *Connect*.**

LO 10-1

Exercise 10-1A *Identifying cash inflows and outflows*

Required

Indicate which of the following items will result in cash inflows and which will result in cash outflows. The first one is shown as an example.

Item	Type of Cash Flow
a. Initial investment	Outflow
b. Salvage value	
c. Recovery of working capital	
d. Incremental expenses	
e. Working capital commitments	
f. Cost savings	
g. Incremental revenue	

Exercise 10-2A *Determining the present value of a lump-sum future cash receipt*

LO 10-1

Larry Mattingly turned 20 years old today. His grandfather had established a trust fund that will pay him $120,000 on his next birthday. However, Larry needs money today to start his college education, and his father is willing to help. Mr. Mattingly has agreed to give Larry the present value of the $120,000 future cash inflow, assuming a 6 percent rate of return.

Required

Round your figures to the nearest whole dollar.

a. Use a present value table to determine the amount of cash that Larry Mattingly's father should give him.

b. Use an algebraic formula to prove that the present value of the trust fund (the amount of cash computed in Requirement *a*) is equal to its $120,000 future value.

Exercise 10-3A *Determining the present value of a lump-sum future cash receipt*

LO 10-1

Gail Trevino expects to receive a $500,000 cash benefit when she retires five years from today. Ms. Trevino's employer has offered an early retirement incentive by agreeing to pay her $325,000 today if she agrees to retire immediately. Ms. Trevino desires to earn a rate of return of 8 percent.

Required

Round your figures to the nearest whole dollar.

a. Assuming that the retirement benefit is the only consideration in making the retirement decision, should Ms. Trevino accept her employer's offer?

b. Identify the factors that cause the present value of the retirement benefit to be less than $500,000.

Exercise 10-4A *Determining the present value of an annuity*

LO 10-1

The dean of the School of Fine Arts is trying to decide whether to purchase a copy machine to place in the lobby of the building. The machine would add to student convenience, but the dean feels compelled to earn an 8 percent return on the investment of funds. Estimates of cash inflows from copy machines that have been placed in other university buildings indicate that the copy machine would probably produce incremental cash inflows of approximately $25,000 per year. The machine is expected to have a three-year useful life with a zero salvage value.

Required

Round your figures to two decimal points.

a. Use Present Value Appendix Table 1 to determine the maximum amount of cash the dean should be willing to pay for a copy machine.

b. Use Present Value Appendix Table 2 to determine the maximum amount of cash the dean should be willing to pay for a copy machine.

c. Explain the consistency or lack of consistency in the answers to Requirements *a* and *b*.

Exercise 10-5A *Determining net present value*

LO 10-2

Monterey Company is considering investing in two new vans that are expected to generate combined cash inflows of $30,000 per year. The vans' combined purchase price is $93,000. The expected life and salvage value of each are four years and $23,000, respectively. Monterey has an average cost of capital of 7 percent.

Required

Round your figures to two decimal points.

a. Calculate the net present value of the investment opportunity.

b. Indicate whether the investment opportunity is expected to earn a return that is above or below the cost of capital and whether it should be accepted.

Exercise 10-6A *Determining net present value*

LO 10-2

Aaron Heath is seeking part-time employment while he attends school. He is considering purchasing technical equipment that will enable him to start a small training services company that will offer tutorial services over the Internet. Aaron expects demand for the service to grow rapidly in the first two years of operation as customers learn about the availability of the Internet assistance. Thereafter, he expects demand to stabilize. The following table presents the expected cash flows.

Year of Operation	Cash Inflow	Cash Outflow
Year 1	$25,000	$12,000
Year 2	29,000	16,000
Year 3	32,000	18,000
Year 4	32,000	18,000

In addition to these cash flows, Aaron expects to pay $25,000 for the equipment. He also expects to pay $4,000 for a major overhaul and updating of the equipment at the end of the second year of operation. The equipment is expected to have a $4,000 salvage value and a four-year useful life. Aaron desires to earn a rate of return of 8 percent.

Required

Round your computations to two decimal points.

a. Calculate the net present value of the investment opportunity.

b. Indicate whether the investment opportunity is expected to earn a return that is above or below the desired rate of return and whether it should be accepted.

LO 10-2

Exercise 10-7A *Using the present value index*

Rolla Company has a choice of two investment alternatives. The present value of cash inflows and outflows for the first alternative is $125,000 and $100,000, respectively. The present value of cash inflows and outflows for the second alternative is $300,000 and $262,500, respectively.

Required

Round your computation to two decimal points.

a. Calculate the net present value of each investment opportunity.

b. Calculate the present value index for each investment opportunity.

c. Indicate which investment will produce the higher rate of return.

LO 10-2

Exercise 10-8A *Determining the cash flow annuity with income tax considerations*

To open a new store, Enid Tire Company plans to invest $320,000 in equipment expected to have a four-year useful life and no salvage value. Enid expects the new store to generate annual cash revenues of $400,000 and to incur annual cash operating expenses of $240,000. Enid's average income tax rate is 30 percent. The company uses straight-line depreciation.

Required

Determine the expected annual net cash inflow from operations for each of the first four years after Enid opens the new store.

LO 10-3

Exercise 10-9A *Determining the internal rate of return*

Gerty Manufacturing Company has an opportunity to purchase some technologically advanced equipment that will reduce the company's cash outflow for operating expenses by $640,000 per year. The cost of the equipment is $3,932,522.88. Gerty expects it to have a 10-year useful life and a zero salvage value. The company has established an investment opportunity hurdle rate of 9 percent and uses the straight-line method for depreciation.

Required

Round your computations to two decimal points.

a. Calculate the internal rate of return of the investment opportunity.

b. Indicate whether the investment opportunity should be accepted.

Exercise 10-10A *Using the internal rate of return to compare investment opportunities*

LO 10-3

Velma and Keota (V&K) is a partnership that owns a small company. It is considering two alternative investment opportunities. The first investment opportunity will have a five-year useful life, will cost $19,680.96, and will generate expected cash inflows of $4,800 per year. The second investment is expected to have a useful life of three years, will cost $12,885.48, and will generate expected cash inflows of $5,000 per year. Assume that V&K has the funds available to accept only one of the opportunities.

Required

a. Calculate the internal rate of return of each investment opportunity.

b. Based on the internal rates of return, which opportunity should V&K select?

c. Discuss other factors that V&K should consider in the investment decision.

Exercise 10-11A *Evaluating discounted cash flow techniques*

LO 10-2, 10-3

Barbara Harvey is angry with Martin Cochran. He is behind schedule developing supporting material for tomorrow's capital budget committee meeting. When she approached him about his apparent lackadaisical attitude in general and his tardiness in particular, he responded, "I don't see why we do this stuff in the first place. It's all a bunch of estimates. Who knows what future cash flows will really be? I certainly don't. I've been doing this job for five years, and no one has ever checked to see if I even came close at these guesses. I've been waiting for marketing to provide the estimated cash inflows on the projects being considered tomorrow. But, if you want my report now, I'll have it in a couple of hours. I can make up the marketing data as well as they can."

Required

Does Mr. Cochran have a point? Is there something wrong with the company's capital budgeting system? Write a brief response explaining how to improve the investment evaluation system.

Exercise 10-12A *Determining the payback period*

LO 10-4

North Airline Company is considering expanding its territory. The company has the opportunity to purchase one of two different used airplanes. The first airplane is expected to cost $12,000,000; it will enable the company to increase its annual cash inflow by $4,000,000 per year. The plane is expected to have a useful life of five years and no salvage value. The second plane costs $24,000,000; it will enable the company to increase annual cash flow by $6,000,000 per year. This plane has an eight-year useful life and a zero salvage value.

Required

a. Determine the payback period for each investment alternative and identify the alternative North should accept if the decision is based on the payback approach.

b. Discuss the shortcomings of using the payback method to evaluate investment opportunities.

Exercise 10-13A *Determining the payback period with uneven cash flows*

LO 10-4

Currie Company has an opportunity to purchase a forklift to use in its heavy equipment rental business. The forklift would be leased on an annual basis during its first two years of operation. Thereafter, it would be leased to the general public on demand. Currie would sell it at the end of the fifth year of its useful life. The expected cash inflows and outflows follow.

Year	Nature of Item	Cash Inflow	Cash Outflow
Year 1	Purchase price		$86,000
Year 1	Revenue	$30,000	
Year 2	Revenue	40,000	
Year 3	Revenue	28,000	
Year 3	Major overhaul		12,000
Year 4	Revenue	20,000	
Year 5	Revenue	14,400	
Year 5	Salvage value	9,600	

Required

a. Determine the payback period using the accumulated cash flows approach.
b. Determine the payback period using the average cash flows approach. Round your computation to one decimal point.

LO 10-4

Exercise 10-14A ***Determining the unadjusted rate of return***

Rainbow Painting Company is considering whether to purchase a new spray paint machine that costs $16,000. The machine is expected to save labor, increasing net income by $1,200 per year. The effective life of the machine is 15 years according to the manufacturer's estimate.

Required

a. Determine the unadjusted rate of return based on the average cost of the investment.
b. What is the predominant shortcoming of using the unadjusted rate of return to evaluate investment opportunities?

LO 10-4

Exercise 10-15A ***Computing the payback period and unadjusted rate of return for the same investment opportunity***

Garrison Rentals can purchase a van that costs $54,000; it has an expected useful life of three years and no salvage value. Garrison uses straight-line depreciation. Expected revenue is $36,000 per year. Assume that depreciation is the only expense associated with this investment.

Required

a. Determine the payback period.
b. Determine the unadjusted rate of return based on the average cost of the investment. Compute the percentage rate to one decimal point.

PROBLEMS—SERIES A

connect **All applicable Problems in Series A are available in *Connect*.**

LO 10-2

excel

CHECK FIGURES

a. NPV of the vans investment: $182,658.08
b. The profitability index for the trucks investment: 1.18

Problem 10-16A ***Using present value techniques to evaluate alternative investment opportunities***

Swift Delivery is a small company that transports business packages between New York and Chicago. It operates a fleet of small vans that moves packages to and from a central depot within each city and uses a common carrier to deliver the packages between the depots in the two cities. Swift Delivery recently acquired approximately $4 million of cash capital from its owners, and its president, George Hay, is trying to identify the most profitable way to invest these funds.

Todd Payne, the company's operations manager, believes that the money should be used to expand the fleet of city vans at a cost of $900,000. He argues that more vans would enable the company to expand its services into new markets, thereby increasing the revenue base. More specifically, he expects cash inflows to increase by $325,000 per year. The additional vans are expected to have an average useful life of four years and a combined salvage value of $100,000. Operating the vans will require additional working capital of $50,000, which will be recovered at the end of the fourth year.

In contrast, Oscar Vance, the company's chief accountant, believes that the funds should be used to purchase large trucks to deliver the packages between the depots in the two cities. The conversion process would produce continuing improvement in operating savings and reduce cash outflows as follows.

Year 1	Year 2	Year 3	Year 4
$175,000	$375,000	$450,000	$500,000

The large trucks are expected to cost $1,000,000 and to have a four-year useful life and a $81,250 salvage value. In addition to the purchase price of the trucks, up-front training costs are expected to amount to $20,000. Swift Delivery's management has established a 10 percent desired rate of return.

Required

Round your computations to two decimal points.

a. Determine the net present value of the two investment alternatives.

b. Calculate the present value index for each alternative.

c. Indicate which investment alternative you would recommend. Explain your choice.

Problem 10-17A *Applying the net present value approach with and without tax considerations*

LO 10-2

eXcel

CHECK FIGURE
a. $(2,961)

Antonio Melton, the chief executive officer of Melton Corporation, has assembled his top advisers to evaluate an investment opportunity. The advisers expect the company to pay $500,000 cash at the beginning of the investment and the cash inflow for each of the following four years to be the following.

Year 1	Year 2	Year 3	Year 4
$105,000	$120,000	$150,000	$225,000

Mr. Melton agrees with his advisers that the company should use a desired rate of return of 7 percent to compute net present value to evaluate the viability of the proposed project.

Required

Round your computation to the nearest whole dollar.

a. Compute the net present value of the proposed project. Should Mr. Melton approve the project?

b. Shawn Love, one of the advisers, is wary of the cash flow forecast and she points out that the advisers failed to consider that the depreciation on equipment used in this project will be tax deductible. The depreciation is expected to be $100,000 per year for the four-year period. The company's income tax rate is 30 percent per year. Use this information to revise the company's expected cash flow from this project.

c. Compute the net present value of the project based on the revised cash flow forecast. Should Mr. Melton approve the project?

Problem 10-18A *Postaudit evaluation*

LO 10-2

CHECK FIGURE
b. NPV: $(523,338)

Brett Collins is reviewing his company's investment in a cement plant. The company paid $12,000,000 five years ago to acquire the plant. Now top management is considering an opportunity to sell it. The president wants to know whether the plant has met original expectations before he decides its fate. The company's desired rate of return for present value computations is 8 percent. Expected and actual cash flows follow.

	Year 1	Year 2	Year 3	Year 4	Year 5
Expected	$2,640,000	$3,936,000	$3,648,000	$3,984,000	$3,360,000
Actual	2,160,000	2,448,000	3,936,000	3,120,000	2,880,000

Required

Round your computations to the nearest whole dollar.

a. Compute the net present value of the expected cash flows as of the beginning of the investment.

b. Compute the net present value of the actual cash flows as of the beginning of the investment.

c. What do you conclude from this postaudit?

Problem 10-19A *Using net present value and internal rate of return to evaluate investment opportunities*

LO 10-2, 10-3

CHECK FIGURES
a. NPV of A: $17,328.00
b. Rate of return of B: 12%

Dwight Donovan, the president of Donovan Enterprises, is considering two investment opportunities. Because of limited resources, he will be able to invest in only one of them. Project A is to purchase a machine that will enable factory automation; the machine is expected to have a useful life of four years and no salvage value. Project B supports a training program that will improve the skills of employees operating the current equipment. Initial cash expenditures for Project A are $400,000 and for Project B are $160,000. The annual expected cash inflows are $126,000 for Project A and $52,800 for Project B. Both investments are expected to provide cash flow benefits for the next four years. Donovan Enterprises' desired rate of return is 8 percent.

Required

a. Compute the net present value of each project. Which project should be adopted based on the net present value approach? Round your computations to two decimal points.
b. Compute the approximate internal rate of return of each project. Which one should be adopted based on the internal rate of return approach? Round your rates to six decimal points.
c. Compare the net present value approach with the internal rate of return approach. Which method is better in the given circumstances? Why?

LO 10-4

CHECK FIGURE

a. Payback period of the yogurt investment: 1.69 years; unadjusted rate of return of the cappuccino investment: 56.35%

Problem 10-20A *Using the payback period and unadjusted rate of return to evaluate alternative investment opportunities*

Seth Fitch owns a small retail ice cream parlor. He is considering expanding the business and has identified two attractive alternatives. One involves purchasing a machine that would enable Mr. Fitch to offer frozen yogurt to customers. The machine would cost $16,200 and has an expected useful life of three years with no salvage value. Additional annual cash revenues and cash operating expenses associated with selling yogurt are expected to be $12,400 and $1,800, respectively.

Alternatively, Mr. Fitch could purchase for $20,160 the equipment necessary to serve cappuccino. That equipment has an expected useful life of four years and no salvage value. Additional annual cash revenues and cash operating expenses associated with selling cappuccino are expected to be $17,000 and $4,860, respectively.

Income before taxes earned by the ice cream parlor is taxed at an effective rate of 20 percent.

Required

Round your figures, including percentage rates, to two decimal points.

a. Determine the payback period and unadjusted rate of return (use average investment) for each alternative.
b. Indicate which investment alternative you would recommend. Explain your choice.

LO 10-2, 10-4

CHECK FIGURES

a. NPV of #1: $30,179.72
b. Payback period of #2: less than two years.

Problem 10-21A *Using net present value and payback period to evaluate investment opportunities*

Daryl Kearns saved $240,000 during the 30 years that he worked for a major corporation. Now he has retired at the age of 60 and has begun to draw a comfortable pension check every month. He wants to ensure the financial security of his retirement by investing his savings wisely and is currently considering two investment opportunities. Both investments require an initial payment of $160,000. The following table presents the estimated cash inflows for the two alternatives.

	Year 1	Year 2	Year 3	Year 4
Opportunity #1	$44,000	$47,200	$63,200	$80,000
Opportunity #2	81,600	86,400	16,000	16,000

Mr. Kearns decides to use his past average return on mutual fund investments as the discount rate; it is 8 percent.

Required

Round your computation to two decimal points.

a. Compute the net present value of each opportunity. Which should Mr. Kearns adopt based on the net present value approach?
b. Compute the payback period for each project. Which should Mr. Kearns adopt based on the payback approach?
c. Compare the net present value approach with the payback approach. Which method is better in the given circumstances?

Problem 10-22A ***Effects of straight-line versus accelerated depreciation on an investment decision***

LO 10-2, 10-4

eXcel

CHECK FIGURES
a. NPV = $97,930
d. Payback period: 2.40 years

Harper Electronics is considering investing in manufacturing equipment expected to cost $250,000. The equipment has an estimated useful life of four years and a salvage value of $25,000. It is expected to produce incremental cash revenues of $125,000 per year. Harper has an effective income tax rate of 30 percent and a desired rate of return of 10 percent.

Required

Round your financial figures to the nearest dollar and all other figures to two decimal points.

a. Determine the net present value and the present value index of the investment, assuming that Harper uses straight-line depreciation for financial and income tax reporting.

b. Determine the net present value and the present value index of the investment, assuming that Harper uses double-declining-balance depreciation for financial and income tax reporting.

c. Why do the net present values computed in Requirements *a* and *b* differ?

d. Determine the payback period and unadjusted rate of return (use average investment), assuming that Harper uses straight-line depreciation.

e. Determine the payback period and unadjusted rate of return (use average investment), assuming that Harper uses double-declining-balance depreciation. (*Note:* Use average annual cash flow when computing the payback period and average annual income when determining the unadjusted rate of return.)

f. Why are there no differences in the payback periods or unadjusted rates of return computed in Requirements *d* and *e*?

Problem 10-23A ***Comparing internal rate of return with unadjusted rate of return***

LO 10-3, 10-4

CHECK FIGURE
b. Internal rate of return: 12%

Barlae Auto Repair Inc. is evaluating a project to purchase equipment that will not only expand the company's capacity but also improve the quality of its repair services. The board of directors requires all capital investments to meet or exceed the minimum requirement of a 10 percent rate of return. However, the board has not clearly defined the rate of return. The president and controller are pondering two different rates of return: unadjusted rate of return and internal rate of return. The equipment, which costs $200,000, has a life expectancy of five years. The increased net profit per year will be approximately $14,000, and the increased cash inflow per year will be approximately $55,400.

Required

Round rates to six decimal points.

a. If it uses the unadjusted rate of return (use average investment) to evaluate this project, should the company invest in the equipment?

b. If it uses the internal rate of return to evaluate this project, should the company invest in the equipment?

c. Which method is better for this capital investment decision?

EXERCISES—SERIES B

Exercise 10-1B ***Identifying cash inflows and outflows***

LO 10-1

Required

Cody Wyatt is considering whether to invest in a dump truck. Mr. Wyatt would hire a driver and use the truck to haul trash for customers. He wants to use present value techniques to evaluate the investment opportunity. List sources of potential cash inflows and cash outflows Mr. Wyatt could expect if he invests in the truck.

Exercise 10-2B ***Determining the present value of a lump-sum future cash receipt***

LO 10-1

One year from today, Pamela Oliver is scheduled to receive a $32,000 payment from a trust fund her father established. She wants to buy a car today but does not have the money. A friend has agreed to give Pamela the present value of the $32,000 today if she agrees to give him the full $32,000 when she collects it one year from now. They agree that 8 percent reflects a fair discount rate.

Required

Round your computations to the nearest whole dollar.

a. You have been asked to determine the present value of the future cash flow. Use a present value table to determine the amount of cash that Pamela's friend should give her.

b. Use an algebraic formula to verify the result you determined in Requirement *a*.

LO 10-1

Exercise 10-3B *Determining the present value of a lump-sum future cash receipt*

Neil Wooten has a terminal illness. His doctors have estimated his remaining life expectancy as three years. Neil has a $450,000 life insurance policy but no close relative to list as the beneficiary. He is considering canceling the policy because he needs the money he is currently paying for the premiums to buy medical supplies. A wealthy close friend has advised Neil not to cancel the policy. The friend has proposed instead giving Neil $270,000 to use for his medical needs while keeping the policy in force. In exchange, Neil would designate the friend as the policy beneficiary. Neil is reluctant to take the $270,000 because he believes that his friend is offering charity. His friend has tried to convince Neil that the offer is a legitimate business deal.

Required

a. Determine the present value of the $450,000 life insurance benefit. Assume a 10 percent discount rate.

b. Assuming 10 percent represents a fair rate of return, is Neil's friend offering charity or is he seeking to profit financially from Neil's misfortune?

LO 10-1

Exercise 10-4B *Determining the present value of an annuity*

Doris Hunt is considering whether to install a drink machine at the gas station she owns. Doris is convinced that providing a drink machine at the station would increase customer convenience. However, she is not convinced that buying the machine would be a profitable investment. Friends who have installed drink machines at their stations have estimated that she could expect to receive net cash inflows of approximately $10,000 per year from the machine. Doris believes that she should earn 8 percent on her investments. The drink machine is expected to have a two-year life and zero salvage value.

Required

Round your computations to two decimal points.

a. Use Present Value Appendix Table 1 to determine the maximum amount of cash Doris should be willing to pay for a drink machine.

b. Use Present Value Appendix Table 2 to determine the maximum amount of cash Doris should be willing to pay for a drink machine.

c. Explain the consistency or lack of consistency in the answers to Requirement *a* versus Requirement *b*.

LO 10-2

Exercise 10-5B *Determining the net present value*

Jessica Larkin, manager of the Nash Music Hall, is considering the opportunity to expand the company's concession revenues. Specifically, she is considering whether to install a popcorn machine. Based on market research, she believes that the machine could produce incremental cash inflows of $6,400 per year. The purchase price of the machine is $17,000. It is expected to have a useful life of three years and a $5,000 salvage value. Ms. Larkin has established a desired rate of return of 16 percent.

Required

a. Calculate the net present value of the investment opportunity.

b. Should the company buy the popcorn machine?

LO 10-2

Exercise 10-6B *Determining the net present value*

Edgar Sloan has decided to start a small delivery business to help support himself while attending school. Mr. Sloan expects demand for delivery services to grow steadily as customers discover their availability. Annual cash outflows are expected to increase only slightly because many of the business operating costs are fixed. Cash inflows and outflows expected from operating the delivery business follow.

Year of Operation	Cash Inflow	Cash Outflow
Year 1	$16,400	$4,400
Year 2	17,200	4,800
Year 3	18,000	7,600
Year 4	19,600	6,400

The used delivery van Mr. Sloan plans to buy is expected to cost $36,000. It has an expected useful life of four years and a salvage value of $8,000. At the end of Year 2, Mr. Sloan expects to pay additional costs of approximately $1,600 for maintenance and new tires. Mr. Sloan's desired rate of return is 10 percent.

Required

Round computations to the nearest whole penny.

a. Calculate the net present value of the investment opportunity.

b. Indicate whether the investment opportunity is expected to earn a return above or below the desired rate of return. Should Mr. Sloan start the delivery business?

Exercise 10-7B *Using the present value index* LO 10-2

Two alternative investment opportunities are available to Irene Rice, president of Rice Enterprises. For the first alternative, the present value of cash inflows is $296,000, and the present value of cash outflows is $254,000. For the second alternative, the present value of cash inflows is $534,000, and the present value of cash outflows is $490,000.

Required

a. Calculate the net present value of each investment opportunity.

b. Calculate the present value index for each investment opportunity. Round your computations to two decimal points.

c. Indicate which investment will produce the higher rate of return.

Exercise 10-8B *Determining a cash flow annuity with income tax considerations* LO 10-2

Glen Todd is considering whether to invest in a computer game machine that he would place in a hotel his brother owns. The machine would cost $34,000 and has an expected useful life of three years and a salvage value of $4,000. Mr. Todd estimates the machine would generate revenue of $16,000 per year and cost $3,000 per year to operate. He uses the straight-line method for depreciation. His income tax rate is 30 percent.

Required

What amount of net cash inflow from operations would Mr. Todd expect for the first year if he invests in the machine?

Exercise 10-9B *Determining the internal rate of return* LO 10-3

Ronnie Gentry, CFO of Odessa Enterprises, is evaluating an opportunity to invest in additional manufacturing equipment that will enable the company to increase its net cash inflows by $250,000 per year. The equipment costs $858,270.25. It is expected to have a five-year useful life and a zero salvage value. Odessa's cost of capital is 10 percent.

Required

a. Calculate the internal rate of return of the investment opportunity.

b. Indicate whether Odessa should purchase the equipment.

Exercise 10-10B *Using the internal rate of return to compare investment opportunities* LO 10-3

Dawn Holman has two alternative investment opportunities to evaluate. The first opportunity would cost $299,024.46 and generate expected cash inflows of $42,000 per year for 17 years. The second opportunity would cost $273,818.88 and generate expected cash inflows of $36,000 per year for 15 years. Ms. Holman has sufficient funds available to accept only one opportunity.

Required

Round present value factors to six decimal points.

a. Calculate the internal rate of return of each investment opportunity.

b. Based on the internal rate of return criteria, which opportunity should Ms. Holman select?

c. Identify two other evaluation techniques Ms. Holman could use to compare the investment opportunities.

LO 10-2, 10-3

Exercise 10-11B *Evaluating discounted cash flow techniques*

Four years ago Charlotte Whitaker decided to invest in a project. At that time, she had projected annual net cash inflows would be $108,000. Over its expected four-year useful life, the project had produced significantly higher cash inflows than anticipated. The actual average annual cash inflow from the project was $126,000. Whitaker breathed a sigh of relief. She always worried that projects would not live up to expectations. To avoid this potential disappointment she tried always to underestimate the projected cash inflows of potential investments. She commented, "I prefer pleasant rather than unpleasant surprises." Indeed, no investment approved by Ms. Whitaker had ever failed a postaudit review. Her investments consistently exceeded expectations.

Required

Explain the purpose of a postaudit and comment on Ms. Whitaker's investment record.

LO 10-4

Exercise 10-12B *Determining the payback period*

The management team at Payne Manufacturing Company has decided to modernize the manufacturing facility. The company can replace an existing, outdated machine with one of two technologically advanced machines. One replacement machine would cost $72,000. Management estimates that it would reduce cash outflows for manufacturing expenses by $30,000 per year. This machine is expected to have an eight-year useful life and a $1,500 salvage value. The other replacement machine would cost $75,600 and would reduce annual cash outflows by an estimated $27,000. This machine has an expected 10-year useful life and a $7,500 salvage value.

Required

a. Determine the payback period for each investment alternative and identify which replacement machine Payne should buy if it bases the decision on the payback approach.

b. Discuss the shortcomings of the payback method of evaluating investment opportunities.

LO 10-4

Exercise 10-13B *Determining the payback period with uneven cash flows*

Vienna Snowmobile Company is considering whether to invest in a particular new snowmobile model. The model is top-of-the-line equipment for which Vienna expects high demand during the first year it is available for rent. However, as the snowmobile ages, it will become less desirable and its rental revenues are expected to decline. The expected cash inflows and outflows follow.

Year	Nature of Cash Flow	Cash Inflow	Cash Outflow
Year 1	Purchase price	—	$70,000
Year 1	Revenue	$40,000	—
Year 2	Revenue	30,000	—
Year 3	Revenue	27,500	—
Year 3	Major overhaul	—	10,000
Year 4	Revenue	15,000	—
Year 5	Revenue	10,000	—
Year 5	Salvage value	8,000	—

Required

a. Determine the payback period using the accumulated cash flows approach.

b. Determine the payback period using the average cash flows approach.

Exercise 10-14B *Determining the unadjusted rate of return* LO 10-4

Kokomo Shuttle Service Inc. is considering whether to purchase an additional shuttle van. The van would cost $45,000 and have a zero salvage value. It would enable the company to increase net income by $6,750 per year. The manufacturer estimates the van's effective life as five years.

Required

a. Determine the unadjusted rate of return based on the average cost of the investment.

b. What is the shortcoming of using the unadjusted rate of return to evaluate investment opportunities?

Exercise 10-15B *Computing the payback period and unadjusted rate of return for the same investment opportunity* LO 10-4

Kenneth McDaniel rents pontoon boats to customers. It has the opportunity to purchase an additional pontoon boat for $40,000; it has an expected useful life of four years and no salvage value. Kenneth McDaniel uses straight-line depreciation. Expected rental revenue for the boat is $15,000 per year.

Required

a. Determine the payback period.

b. Determine the unadjusted rate of return based on the average cost of the investment.

c. Assume that the company's desired rate of return is 16 percent. Should Kenneth McDaniel purchase the additional boat?

PROBLEMS—SERIES B

Problem 10-16B *Using present value techniques to evaluate alternative investment opportunities* LO 10-2

Perry Automobile Repair Inc. currently has three repair shops in Boston. Jerry Perry, the president and chief executive officer, is facing a pleasant dilemma: the business has continued to grow rapidly and major shareholders are arguing about different ways to capture more business opportunities. The company requires a 12 percent rate of return for its investment projects and uses the straight-line method of depreciation for all fixed assets.

One group of shareholders wants to open another shop in a newly developed suburban community. This project would require an initial investment of $600,000 to acquire all the necessary equipment, which has a useful life of five years with a salvage value of $200,000. Once the shop begins to operate, another $150,000 of working capital would be required; it would be recovered at the end of the fifth year. The expected net cash inflow from the new shop follows.

Year 1	Year 2	Year 3	Year 4	Year 5
$75,000	$125,000	$190,000	$240,000	$300,000

A second group of shareholders prefers to invest $500,000 to acquire new computerized diagnostic equipment for the existing shops. The equipment is expected to have a useful life of five years with a salvage value of $100,000. Using this state-of-the-art equipment, mechanics would be able to pinpoint automobile problems more quickly and accurately. Consequently, it would allow the existing shops to increase their service capacity and revenue by $156,250 per year. The company would need to train mechanics to use the equipment, which would cost $56,250 at the beginning of the first year.

Required

Round your computations to two decimal points.

a. Determine the net present value of the two investment alternatives.

b. Calculate the present value index for each alternative.

c. Indicate which investment alternative you would recommend. Explain your choice.

LO 10-2

Problem 10-17B *Applying the net present value approach with and without tax considerations*

Craig Pike, the president of Craig's Moving Services Inc., is planning to spend $800,000 for new trucks. He expects the trucks to increase the company's cash inflow as follows.

Year 1	Year 2	Year 3	Year 4
$206,250	$225,000	$245,000	$300,000

The company's policy stipulates that all investments must earn a minimum rate of return of 10 percent.

Required

Round financial figures to nearest whole dollar.

a. Compute the net present value of the proposed purchase. Should Mr. Pike purchase the trucks?

b. Tammy Buckley, the controller, is wary of the cash flow forecast and points out that Mr. Pike failed to consider that the depreciation on trucks used in this project will be tax deductible. The depreciation is expected to be $187,500 per year for the four-year period. The company's income tax rate is 30 percent per year. Use this information to revise the company's expected cash flow from this purchase.

c. Compute the net present value of the purchase based on the revised cash flow forecast. Should Mr. Pike purchase the trucks?

LO 10-2

Problem 10-18B *Postaudit evaluation*

Shawn Guzman is wondering whether he made the right decision four years ago. As the president of Guzman Health Care Services, he acquired a hospital specializing in elder care with an initial cash investment of $1,400,000. Mr. Guzman would like to know whether the hospital's financial performance has met the original investment objective. The company's desired rate of return for present value computations is 14 percent. Expected and actual cash flows follow.

	Year 1	Year 2	Year 3	Year 4
Expected	$460,000	$480,000	$500,000	$600,000
Actual	400,000	380,000	640,000	700,000

Required

Round your financial figures to the nearest whole dollar.

a. Compute the net present value of the expected cash flows as of the beginning of the investment.

b. Compute the net present value of the actual cash flows as of the beginning of the investment.

c. What do you conclude from this postaudit?

LO 10-2, 10-3

Problem 10-19B *Using net present value and internal rate of return to evaluate investment opportunities*

Dale Thomas' rich uncle gave him $100,000 cash as a gift for his 40th birthday. Unlike his spoiled cousins who spend money carelessly, Mr. Thomas wants to invest the money for his future retirement. After an extensive search, he is considering one of two investment opportunities. Project 1 would require an immediate cash payment of $75,000; Project 2 needs only a $37,500 cash payment at the beginning. The expected cash inflows are $22,500 per year for Project 1 and $11,500 per year for Project 2. Both projects are expected to provide cash flow benefits for the next four years. Mr. Thomas found that the interest rate for a four-year certificate of deposit is about 5 percent. He decided that this is his required rate of return.

Required

Round indexes to six decimal points and other figures to two decimal points.

a. Compute the net present value of each project. Which project should Mr. Thomas adopt based on the net present value approach?

b. Compute the approximate internal rate of return of each project. Which project should Mr. Thomas adopt based on the internal rate of return approach?

c. Compare the net present value approach with the internal rate of return approach. Which method is better in the given circumstances?

Problem 10-20B ***Using the payback period and unadjusted rate of return to evaluate alternative investment opportunities*** LO 10-4

Pratt and Sullivan Services is planning a new business venture. With $125,000 of available funds to invest, it is investigating two options. One is to acquire an exclusive contract to operate vending machines in civic and recreation centers in a small suburban city for four years. The contract requires the firm to pay the city $75,000 cash at the beginning. The firm expects the cash revenue from the operation to be $62,500 per year and the cash expenses to be $35,000 per year.

The second option is to operate a printing shop in an office complex. This option would require the company to spend $100,000 for printing equipment that has a useful life of four years with a zero salvage value. The cash revenue is expected to be $106,250 per year and cash expenses are expected to be $58,750 per year. The firm uses the straight-line method of depreciation. Its effective income tax rate is expected to be 25 percent.

Required

Round computations to two decimal points.

a. Determine the payback period and unadjusted rate of return (use average investment) for each alternative.

b. Indicate which investment alternative you would recommend. Explain your choice.

Problem 10-21B ***Using net present value and payback period to evaluate investment opportunities*** LO 10-2, 10-4

Wonda Munro just won a lottery and received a cash award of $450,000 net of tax. She is 61 years old and would like to retire in four years. Weighing this important fact, she has found two possible investments, both of which require an immediate cash payment of $360,000. The expected cash inflows from the two investment opportunities are as follows.

	Year 1	Year 2	Year 3	Year 4
Opportunity A	$190,000	$125,000	$ 64,000	$ 67,200
Opportunity B	47,000	62,500	140,000	290,000

Ms. Munro decided that her required rate of return should be 10 percent.

Required

Round your computations to two decimal points.

a. Compute the net present value of each opportunity. Which should Ms. Munro choose based on the net present value approach?

b. Compute the payback period for each opportunity. Which should Ms. Munro choose based on the payback approach?

c. Compare the net present value approach with the payback approach. Which method is better in the given circumstances?

Problem 10-22B ***Effects of straight-line versus accelerated depreciation on an investment decision*** LO 10-2, 10-4

Laurel Steel Company decided to spend $160,000 to purchase new state-of-the-art equipment for its manufacturing plant. The equipment has a five-year useful life and a salvage value of $40,000. It is expected to generate additional cash revenue of $64,000 per year. Laurel Steel's required rate of return is 10 percent; its effective income tax rate is 25 percent.

Required

Round financial figures to the nearest whole dollar and other figures to two decimal points.

a. Determine the net present value and the present value index of the investment, assuming that Laurel Steel uses straight-line depreciation for financial and income tax reporting.

b. Determine the net present value and the present value index of the investment, assuming that Laurel Steel uses double-declining-balance depreciation for financial and income tax reporting.

c. Why are there differences in the net present values computed in Requirements *a* and *b*?

d. Determine the payback period and unadjusted rate of return (use average investment), assuming that Laurel Steel uses straight-line depreciation.

e. Determine the payback period and unadjusted rate of return (use average investment), assuming that Laurel Steel uses double-declining-balance depreciation. (*Note:* Use average annual cash flow when computing the payback period and average annual income when computing the unadjusted rate of return.)

f. Why are there no differences in the payback period or unadjusted rate of return computed in Requirements *d* and *e*?

LO 10-3, 10-4

Problem 10-23B *Comparing internal rate of return with unadjusted rate of return*

Mansell Corporation faces stiff market competition. Top management is considering the replacement of its current production facility. The board of directors requires all capital investments to meet or exceed a 9 percent rate of return. However, the board has not clearly defined the rate of return. The president and controller are pondering two different rates of return: unadjusted rate of return and internal rate of return. To purchase a new facility with a life expectancy of four years, the company must pay $90,000. The increased net profit per year resulting from improved conditions would be approximately $10,000; the increased cash inflow per year would be approximately $27,500.

Required

a. If it uses the unadjusted rate of return (use average investment) to evaluate this project, should the company invest in the new facility? Round the rate to a full percentage.

b. If it uses the internal rate of return to evaluate this project, should the company invest in the new facility? Round the rate to six decimal points.

c. Which method is better for this capital investment decision?

ANALYZE, THINK, COMMUNICATE

ATC 10-1 Business Application Case *Pension planning in state governments*

In recent years, there has been a lot of media coverage about the funding status of pension plans for state employees. In many states, the amount of money invested in employee pension plans is far less than the amount estimated to pay employees the retirement benefits they have been promised. Basically, pension plans work by investing enough money while employees are working so that the money invested, plus the investment income it earns over the years, will be sufficient to pay the workers their retirement incomes once they have retired.

There are many complicated assumptions, estimates, and calculations needed to determine how much money a state should invest in its pension fund each year. One of the most important assumptions is the rate of return the plan's investments will earn in the future. As you have seen in this chapter, the higher the rate of return used to calculate the present value of future cash flows, the lower the present value will be. To determine a pension plan's funded status, actuaries (1) estimate the future cash payments expected to be made to employees, (2) calculate the present value of those cash flows using an assumed rate of return (this present value is the gross liability of the fund), and (3) subtract the amount of money that has been invested from the gross liability calculated in step 2 (this amount is the funded status of the pension plan). Essentially, this is the same as calculating the net present value of an investment. If the plan has less money in its investments than the present value of its estimated future cash flows, it has a net liability and is considered to be underfunded by that amount.

Many states' pension plans have assumed they will earn 8 percent or more on their investments, even though many experts think a more appropriate assumption would be 6.5 percent. As an example, the state of Virginia used an *assumed* rate of return of 7.5 percent in 2009 but reduced the rate to 7.0 percent in 2010. Actual investment returns can vary widely. In 2016, Virginia's actual return on its pension assets was only 1.9 percent, but in 2017 it was 12.1 percent.

Virginia paid out approximately $4.5 billion in benefits to retirees in 2017.

Required

a. Assume Virginia's annual payments will continue to be $4.5 billion, and that retirees will receive benefits for 20 years on average. Using an assumed rate of return of 8 percent, calculate the liability of the state's pension plan. The liability is the present value of the future cash payments. (Be aware that the real-world calculation for a state's pension plan liability involves many more assumptions than just these two.)

b. Assume the annual payments will continue to be $4.5 billion, and that retirees will receive benefits for 20 years on average. Using an assumed rate of return of 6 percent, calculate the liability of the state's pension plan.

c. Reviewing your answers from Requirements *a* and *b*, provide an explanation as to why states may wish to assume a higher rate of return on their pension plan's investments than actuaries might recommend.

ATC 10-2 Group Assignment *Net present value*

Espada Real Estate Investment Company (EREIC) purchases new apartment complexes, establishes a stable group of residents, and then sells the complexes to apartment management companies. The average holding time is three years. EREIC is currently investigating two alternatives.

1. EREIC can purchase Harding Properties for $4,500,000. The complex is expected to produce net cash inflows of $360,000, $502,500, and $865,000 for the first, second, and third years of operation, respectively. The market value of the complex at the end of the third year is expected to be $5,175,000.

2. EREIC can purchase Summit Apartments for $3,450,000. The complex is expected to produce net cash inflows of $290,000, $435,000, and $600,000 for the first, second, and third years of operation, respectively. The market value of the complex at the end of the third year is expected to be $4,050,000.

EREIC has a desired rate of return of 12 percent.

Required

a. Divide the class into groups of four or five students per group and then divide the groups into two sections. Assign Task 1 to the first section and Task 2 to the second section.

Group Tasks

(1) Calculate the net present value and the present value index for Harding Properties.

(2) Calculate the net present value and the present value index for Summit Apartments.

b. Have a spokesperson from one group in the first section report the amounts calculated by the group. Make sure that all groups in the section have the same result. Repeat the process for the second section. Have the class as a whole select the investment opportunity that EREIC should accept given that the objective is to produce the higher rate of return.

c. Assume that EREIC has $4,500,000 to invest and that any funds not invested in real estate properties must be invested in a certificate of deposit earning a 5 percent return. Would this information alter the decision made in Requirement *b*?

d. This requirement is independent of Requirement *c*. Assume there is a 10 percent chance that the Harding project will be annexed by the city of Hoover, which has an outstanding school district. The annexation would likely increase net cash flows by $37,500 per year and would increase the market value at the end of Year 3 by $300,000. Would this information change the decision reached in Requirement *b*?

ATC 10-3 Research Assignment *Capital expenditures at Shake Shack Inc.*

Obtain Shake Shack Inc.'s Form 10-K for the fiscal year ending on December 27, 2017. To obtain the Form 10-K, you can use the EDGAR system (see Appendix A at the back of this text for instructions), or it can be found under the "Investor Relations" link on the company's website at www.shakeshack.com. Read the following sections of the 10-K: "Growth Strategies" on page 13, and the Consolidated Statements of Cash Flows on page 78.

Required

a. How many company-owned Shacks did Shake Shack plan to open during its 2017 fiscal year? By what percentage would these new Shacks increase the size of Shake Shack's company-owned Shacks?

b. How much cash did Shake Shack spend on investing activities during its 2015, 2016, and 2017 fiscal years? Do you think the amount spent on investing activities represents the full costs that Shake Shack incurred to open new Shacks? Explain your answer.

c. Where did Shake Shack get the cash used to make these investments?

ATC 10-4 Writing Assignment *Limitations of capital investment techniques*

Webb Publishing Company is evaluating two investment opportunities. One is to purchase an Internet company with the capacity to open new marketing channels through which Webb can sell its books. This opportunity offers a high potential for growth but involves significant risk. Indeed, losses are projected for the first three years of operation. The second opportunity is to purchase a printing company that would enable Webb to better control costs by printing its own books. The potential savings are clearly predictable but would make a significant change in the company's long-term profitability.

Required

Write a response discussing the usefulness of capital investment techniques (net present value, internal rate of return, payback, and unadjusted rate of return) in making a choice between these two alternative investment opportunities. Your response should discuss the strengths and weaknesses of capital budgeting techniques in general. Furthermore, it should include a comparison between techniques based on the time value of money versus those that are not.

ATC 10-5 Ethical Dilemma *Postaudit*

Gaines Company recently initiated a postaudit program. To motivate employees to take the program seriously, Gaines established a bonus program. Managers receive a bonus equal to 10 percent of the amount by which actual net present value exceeds the projected net present value. Victor Holt, manager of the North Western Division, had an investment proposal on his desk when the new system was implemented. The investment opportunity required a $250,000 initial cash outflow and was expected to return cash inflows of $90,000 per year for the next five years. Gaines' desired rate of return is 10 percent. Mr. Holt immediately reduced the estimated cash inflows to $70,000 per year and recommended accepting the project.

Required

a. Assume that actual cash inflows turn out to be $91,000 per year. Determine the amount of Mr. Holt's bonus if the original computation of net present value were based on $90,000 versus $70,000.

b. Is Mr. Holt's behavior in violation of any of the standards of ethical professional practice in Exhibit 1.17 of Chapter 1?

c. Speculate about the long-term effect the bonus plan is likely to have on the company.

d. Recommend how to compensate managers in a way that discourages gamesmanship.

ATC 10-6 Spreadsheet Assignment *Using Excel*

Kilby Company is considering the purchase of new automated manufacturing equipment that would cost $150,000. The equipment would save $42,500 in labor costs per year over its six-year life. At the end of the fourth year, the equipment would require an overhaul that would cost $25,000. The equipment would have a $7,500 salvage value at the end of its life. Kilby's cost of capital is 12 percent.

Required

a. Prepare a spreadsheet similar to the one that follows to calculate net present value, the present value index, and the internal rate of return.

D17 | f_x =IRR(D6:D12,D3)

	A	B	C	D	E	F
1	Chapter 10 - Working with Excel				Name:	
2						
3			Net Present Value at:	12%		
4						
5		Year		Cash flow		
6		0	Initial investment	$(150,000)		
7		1	Net cash flow	42,500		
8		2	Net cash flow	42,500		
9		3	Net cash flow	42,500		
10		4	Net cash flow	17,500		
11		5	Net cash flow	42,500		
12		6	Net cash flow	50,000		
13			Net present value (NPV)	$ 12,647		
14						
15			Present value index	1.084		
16						
17			Internal rate of return	14.95%		
18						

Source: Microsoft Excel 2010

Spreadsheet Tips

Spreadsheets have built-in financial functions that make net present value and internal rate of return calculations very easy. The formats of these formulas are as follows:

1. *Net Present Value:* =NPV (rate,value1,value2,value3 . . . value29) where up to 29 values are allowed. The values must be at the end of the period, and each period must be equal in time (one year, for example). The formula is =NPV(D3,D7,D8,D9,D10,D11,D12) + D6.
2. *Internal Rate of Return:* =IRR (values,guess) where *values* is the range that includes the cash flows (D6 to D12) and *guess* is an estimate of the rate. Use the cost of capital as the guess.
3. *Percentage:* Rather than entering 12% in the formulas, refer to cell D3. This will allow you to change the rate and see the effect on the NPV and present value index.
4. *Present Value Index:* You must construct a formula because no built-in function calculates it.

ATC 10-7 Spreadsheet Assignment *Mastering Excel*

ASAP Delivery is a small company that transports business packages between San Francisco and Los Angeles. It operates a fleet of small vans that moves packages to and from a central depot within each city and uses a common carrier to deliver the packages between the depots in the two cities. ASAP recently acquired approximately $4 million of cash capital from its owners, and its president, Alex Cade, is trying to identify the most profitable way to invest these funds.

Phil Duvall, the company's operations manager, believes that the money should be used to expand the fleet of city vans at a cost of $3,600,000. He argues that more vans would enable the company to expand its services into new markets, thereby increasing the revenue base. More specifically, he expects cash inflows to increase by $1,400,000 per year. The additional vans are expected to have an average useful life of four years and a combined salvage value of $500,000. Operating the vans will require additional working capital of $200,000, which will be recovered at the end of the fourth year.

In contrast, Amber Gomez, the company's chief accountant, believes that the funds should be used to purchase large trucks to deliver the packages between the depots in the two cities. The conversion process would produce continuing improvement in operating savings and reduce cash outflows as follows.

Year 1	Year 2	Year 3	Year 4
$800,000	$1,600,000	$2,000,000	$2,200,000

The large trucks are expected to cost $4,000,000 and to have a four-year useful life and a $400,000 salvage value. In addition to the purchase price of the trucks, up-front training costs are expected to amount to $80,000. ASAP Delivery's management has established a 16 percent desired rate of return.

Required

a. Prepare a spreadsheet similar to the preceding one that calculates the net present value and the present value index for the two investments.

b. Include formulas in your spreadsheet to calculate the internal rate of return for each investment alternative.

COMPREHENSIVE PROBLEM

Magnificent Modems Inc. (MMI) has several capital investment opportunities. The term, expected annual cash inflows, and the cost of each opportunity are outlined in the following table. MMI has established a desired rate of return of 16 percent for these investment opportunities.

Opportunity	A	B	C	D
Investment term	4 years	5 years	3 years	5 years
Expected cash inflow	$6,000	$5,000	$8,000	$4,800
Cost of investment	$16,000	$15,000	$18,000	$16,000

Required

a. Compute the net present value of each investment opportunity manually using the present value tables. Record your answers in the following table. The results for Investment Opportunity A have been recorded in the table as an example.

Opportunity	A	B	C	D
Cash inflow	$6,000.00	$5,000.00	$8,000.00	$4,800.00
Times present value factor	2.798181			
Present value of cash flows	$16,789.09			
Minus cost of investment	($16,000.00)	($15,000.00)	($18,000.00)	($16,000.00)
Net present value	$789.09			

b. Use Excel spreadsheet software or a financial calculator to determine the net present value and the internal rate of return for each investment opportunity. Record the results in the following table. The results for investment Opportunity A have been recorded in the following table as an example. Note that the manual computation yields the same net present value amounts as the financial function routines of Excel or a financial calculator.

Opportunity	A	B	C	D
Net present value	$789.09			
Internal rate of return	18.45%			

CHAPTER 11

Product Costing in Service and Manufacturing Entities

LEARNING OBJECTIVES

After you have mastered the material in this chapter, you will be able to:

LO 11-1 Compare the accounting treatment of material and labor costs for a manufacturing versus a service company.

LO 11-2 Allocate overhead cost between inventory and cost of goods sold.

LO 11-3 Prepare a schedule of cost of goods manufactured and sold.

LO 11-4 Distinguish between absorption and variable costing.

Video lectures and accompanying self-assessment quizzes are available in Connect® for all learning objectives.

CHAPTER OPENING

Service and *product costing systems* supply information about the cost of providing services or making products. Organizations need service and product cost information for financial reporting, managerial accounting, and contract negotiations.

For *financial reporting,* companies are required by generally accepted accounting principles (GAAP) to report service and product costs in their published financial statements. For example, product costs for manufacturing companies must be allocated between inventory (reported on the balance sheet) and cost of goods sold (reported on the income statement). Similarly, service companies must match on their income statements the costs of providing services with the revenues generated from the services provided.

For *managerial accounting,* managers need to know the cost of providing services or making products so they can plan company operations. For example, companies could not prepare budgets without knowing the cost of services or products. Service and product costing is also needed for cost control. Managers compare expected costs with actual costs to identify problems that need correcting. Service and product cost information may be used for pricing and other short-term decisions. For instance, the cost of a service or product may be used in special order, outsourcing, or product elimination decisions.

Service and product costing information may be used by governmental agencies to regulate rates for public service entities such as utility companies or hospitals. Service and product costs are also used in determining the amount due on contracts that compensate companies for the costs they incur plus a reasonable profit (cost-plus contracts). For example, many governmental defense contracts are negotiated on a cost-plus basis. Cost-plus pricing may also be used by private companies. For instance, many builders of custom homes charge customers based on cost-plus contracts. Cost information is therefore necessary for contract negotiations. This chapter shows how manufacturing companies determine the cost of the products they make.

The Curious Accountant

©Philip & Karen Smith/Getty Images

Northwestern Aviation is a small company in Kotzebue, Alaska, that provides bush flying services to persons wanting to travel into the arctic to go fishing, canoeing, or hiking or to embark on flight-seeing trips to wilderness areas such as Kobuk Valley National Park. Given the climate, the company does most of its business during the summer months.

Northwestern incurs a variety of costs. Some of these costs, such as the cost of aviation gasoline, vary with the number and type of trips. Recently, when aviation fuel was selling for around $5 per gallon in the lower 48 states, it was priced at over $7 per gallon in Kotzebue, due to its remote location. The Cessna 206 airplane that Northwestern uses consumes around 15 gallons of fuel per hour, creating a fuel cost of $120 for each hour flown. Other costs go up with increased activity but may not be incurred on a per-trip basis. For example, the Cessna 206 needs a major engine overhaul about every 1,400 operating hours. Finally, there are costs that are fixed; they must be paid for regardless of the number of trips the company flies each year. A new Cessna 206 costs around $670,000 and payments on airplanes must be made regardless of the amount of revenue they earn. Costs for facilities, such as airport space, also do not depend on how much, or how little, business is done in a given season. As you have learned in earlier chapters, the higher the level of activity, the lower the fixed cost per unit of activity will be.

These cost behaviors present a problem for Northwestern. Potential clients contact the company months in advance to book trips, and they want to know the price they will be charged. The company, however, does not know what it will actually cost to provide the trip in question since the final cost depends on its level of activity, and it does not know how many trips it will provide in the upcoming season until the season is over. Nevertheless, prices must be quoted, in advance, on a per-hour basis.

How can a company with significant fixed costs, such as Northwestern Aviation, know what to charge customers when it will not know the real cost of any one trip until the season is over? (Answer on page 496.)

COST FLOW IN MANUFACTURING COMPANIES

LO 11-1

Compare the accounting treatment of material and labor costs for a manufacturing versus a service company.

In previous chapters, we assumed all inventory started during an accounting period was also completed during that accounting period. All product costs (materials, labor, and manufacturing overhead) were either in inventory or expensed as cost of goods sold. At the end of an accounting period, however, most real-world companies have raw materials on hand, and manufacturing companies are likely to have in inventory items that have been started but are not completed. Most manufacturing companies accumulate product costs in three distinct inventory accounts: (1) **Raw Materials Inventory,** which includes lumber, metals, paints, and chemicals that will be used to make the company's products; (2) **Work in Process Inventory,** which includes partially completed products; and (3) **Finished Goods Inventory,** which includes completed products that are ready for sale.

The cost of materials is first recorded in the Raw Materials Inventory account. The cost of materials placed in production is then transferred from the Raw Materials Inventory account to the Work in Process Inventory account. The costs of labor and overhead are added to the Work in Process Inventory account. The cost of the goods completed during the period is transferred from the Work in Process Inventory account to the Finished Goods Inventory account. The cost of the goods that are sold during the accounting period is transferred from the Finished Goods Inventory account to the Cost of Goods Sold account. The balances that remain in the Raw Materials, Work in Process, and Finished Goods Inventory accounts are reported on the balance sheet. The amount of product cost transferred to the Cost of Goods Sold account is expensed on the income statement. Exhibit 11.1 shows the flow of manufacturing costs through the accounting records.

EXHIBIT 11.1

Manufacturing Cost Flow

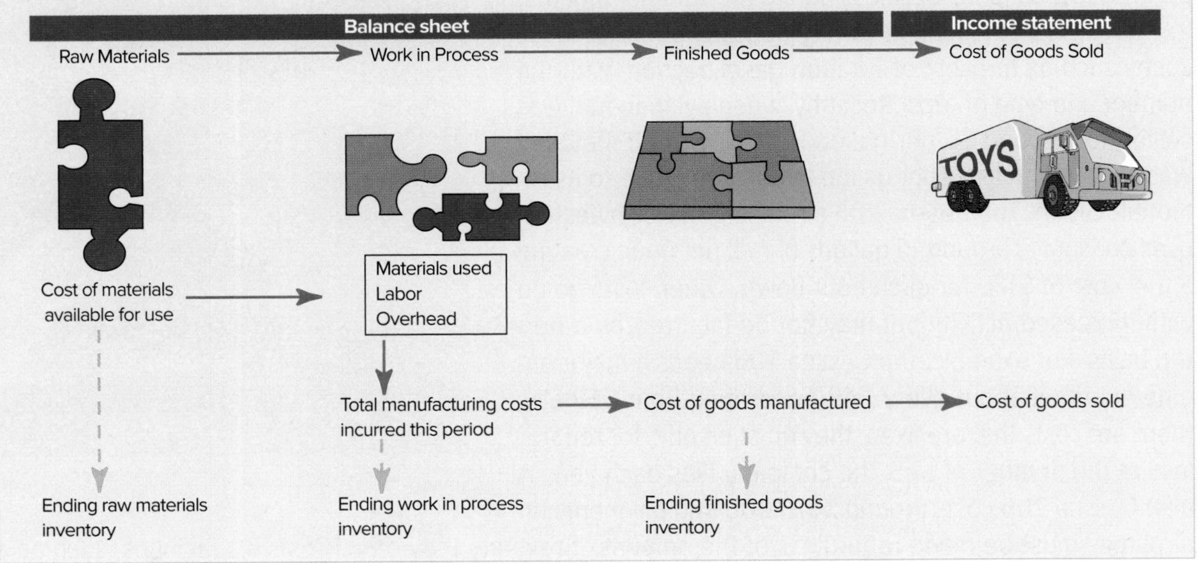

COST FLOW IN SERVICE COMPANIES

Like manufacturing companies, many service companies purchase raw materials and transform them through production stages such as work in process, finished goods, and cost of goods sold. For example, a McDonald's hamburger starts with raw materials (meat, bun, and condiments), goes through work in process (is cooked, assembled, and wrapped), becomes a finished product, and is sold to a customer. Why then is McDonald's considered a *service* rather than a *manufacturing* company? The distinguishing feature is that products from McDonald's are consumed immediately. In general, services cannot be stored and sold later. Service companies do not have Work in Process and Finished Goods Inventory accounts for collecting costs before transferring them to a Cost of Goods Sold account. At the end of the day, McDonald's has no work in process or finished goods inventory.

©Ken Wolter/Shutterstock

Is a retail company such as Abercrombie & Fitch a service company or a manufacturing company? Because wholesale and retail companies have large inventories, it may seem odd to think of them as service companies. Consider, however, what employees of a wholesale or retail company do. Their efforts cannot be stored and used later. The services of a salesperson are consumed as customers are assisted. Other service organizations include insurance companies, banks, cleaning establishments, airlines, law firms, hospitals, hotels, and governmental agencies.

Even though service companies do not collect costs in inventory accounts for financial reporting purposes, they do accumulate cost information for decision making. For example, a hotel manager needs to know the cost of providing a room to assess whether the pricing policy is appropriate. A private school may compare the expected and actual cost of offering a course to ensure that costs are controlled. Airline executives need to know the cost of serving a specific route to decide whether to maintain or eliminate the route. Measuring the cost of providing services is just as necessary as measuring the cost of making products, whether the cost is collected in an inventory account or charged directly to the income statement.

MANUFACTURING COST FLOW ILLUSTRATED

To illustrate how manufacturing costs flow through ledger accounts, consider Ventra Manufacturing Company, which makes mahogany jewelry boxes that it sells to department stores. The account balances in Exhibit 11.2 were drawn from the company's accounting records as of January 1, Year 2.

Ventra Manufacturing's Year 2 accounting events are explained here. The effects of the events are summarized in the T-accounts in Exhibit 11.4. Study the entries in Exhibit 11.4 as you read the event descriptions in the following section of this chapter. The illustration assumes Ventra determines the cost of making its jewelry boxes on a monthly basis. Accounting events for January are described next.

EXHIBIT 11.2

Trial Balance as of January 1, Year 2

Cash	$ 64,500	
Raw materials inventory	500	
WORK IN PROCESS INVENTORY	0	
Finished goods inventory	836	
Manufacturing equipment	40,000	
Accumulated depreciation		$ 10,000
Common stock		76,000
Retained earnings		19,836
Totals	$105,836	$105,836

Events Affecting Manufacturing Cost Flow in January

EVENT 1 **Ventra Manufacturing paid $26,500 cash to purchase raw materials.**

The effects of the materials purchase on the company's financial statements are shown in the following horizontal financial statements model.[1]

Event No.	Balance Sheet: Assets: Cash	+	Raw Materials Inventory	=	Liabilities	+	Equity	Income Statement: Revenue	−	Expenses	=	Net Income
1.	(26,500)	+	26,500	=	NA	+	NA	NA	−	NA	=	NA

This event is an asset exchange. One asset–cash–decreases, and another asset–raw materials inventory–increases. Neither total assets reported on the balance sheet nor any revenues or expenses on the income statement are affected. Raw materials costs are only one component of total manufacturing (product) costs. The raw materials costs will be included in the cost of goods sold (expense) recognized when completed jewelry boxes are sold to customers.

EVENT 2 **Ventra placed $1,100 of raw materials into production in the process of making jewelry boxes.**

This event is also an asset exchange. One asset–raw materials inventory–decreases, and another asset–work in process inventory–increases. Total assets reported on the balance sheet are not affected. The income statement is not affected. The effects on the company's financial statements of using the raw materials follow.

Event No.	Balance Sheet: Assets: Raw Materials Inventory	+	Work in Process Inventory	=	Liabilities	+	Equity	Income Statement: Revenue	−	Expenses	=	Net Income
1.	(1,100)	+	1,100	=	NA	+	NA	NA	−	NA	=	NA

Ventra's raw materials are *direct* inputs to the production process. They are accounted for using the *perpetual inventory method.* Because the raw materials are traced directly to products, it is easy to match the cost flow with the physical flow. Every time direct raw materials are moved from storage to work in process, their cost is transferred in the accounting records as well.

EVENT 3 **Ventra paid $2,000 cash to purchase production supplies (glue, nails, sandpaper).**

This event is also an asset exchange. One asset–cash–decreases, and another asset–production supplies–increases. Total assets reported on the balance sheet are not affected. Net income is not affected. The effects of this event on the company's financial statements follow.

Event No.	Balance Sheet: Assets: Cash	+	Production Supplies	=	Liabilities	+	Equity	Income Statement: Revenue	−	Expenses	=	Net Income
1.	(2,000)	+	2,000	=	NA	+	NA	NA	−	NA	=	NA

[1]The horizontal model arranges the major financial statement elements horizontally across a single page. Reading from left to right, balance sheet elements are presented first, followed by income statement elements.

The production supplies are recorded in a separate asset account because Ventra finds it more practical to account for them using the *periodic inventory method.* Production supplies are *indirect* inputs. Such small quantities are used on each jewelry box that it is not worth the trouble to track the actual costs as the materials are used. Nobody wants to stop to make a journal entry every time several drops of glue are used. *Instead of recognizing production supplies usage as it occurs (perpetually), Ventra determines at the end of the accounting period (periodically) the cost of supplies used.* The recordkeeping procedures for including the cost of production supplies in the flow of manufacturing costs are described in the explanation of the Manufacturing Overhead account described shortly.

EVENT 4 **Ventra paid production workers $1,400 cash.**

These wages are *not* classified as salary expense. Because the labor was used to make jewelry boxes, the cost is added to the Work in Process Inventory account. This event is yet another asset exchange. Ventra exchanged cash for the value added by making the inventory. One asset–cash–decreases, and another asset–work in process inventory–increases. Total assets

REALITY BYTES

Many companies have to bid on jobs they hope to obtain, but bidding is a tricky process. Bid too high and you may lose the job to a competitor. Bid too low and you may end up performing the job for a lower price than was necessary, and you could end up taking a loss on the job. There are two basic approaches to the bidding process; one is called "costs-plus," and the other is called "fixed-price." A costs-plus contract sets the bid price at the actual cost incurred to do the job, plus a predetermined percent, such as 10 percent. These contracts are more likely to be used when it is difficult to determine the final cost to complete a job. For example, when the space shuttles, which had never been built before, were constructed for NASA, they were bid on a costs-plus basis. With a fixed-price contract the company agrees to do the job for a set price. If the costs to complete the job are lower than the bid price, the company earns a profit. If its costs are higher than the bid price, the company incurs a loss.

©Allan Shoemake/Getty Images

"Raytheon Company, together with its subsidiaries, is a technology and innovation leader specializing in defense and other government markets throughout the world." In 2017, 67 percent of its revenue came from work done for the U.S. government, and another 13 percent was for foreign military sales that went through the U.S. government. Raytheon does work under both costs-plus contracts, which they call "cost reimbursable contracts," and fixed-price contracts.

For the customer there is an obvious potential problem with a costs-plus contract. Unless the contract is written and monitored carefully, the contractor could simply run up the cost of completing the job in order to earn a higher fee. The U.S. government has lots of regulations to prevent this from occurring, including the right to audit the books of companies such as Raytheon. This issue is of such importance to Raytheon that its Form 10-K devotes five pages explaining the risks it faces from failure to adhere to government regulations.

Raytheon's Form 10-K also devotes considerable space to describing the potential problems with fixed-price contract. The report notes "*Our U.S. government contracts are typically either fixed-priced contracts or cost reimbursable contracts. Fixed-price contracts represent approximately 63 percent of our backlog, and are predominantly either firm fixed-price (FFP) contracts or fixed-price incentive (FPI) contracts. Under FFP contracts, we receive a fixed price irrespective of the actual costs we incur and we therefore carry the burden of any cost overruns.*"

These forms also includes a section titled, "*We use estimates in accounting for many of our programs, and changes in our estimates could adversely affect our future financial results.*" As this chapter explains, what a company believes it will cost to make a product or provide a service depends on many estimates about future events. No matter how good one's mathematics may be, if the estimates on which those calculations are based are materially incorrect, so are the answers they provide, and such mistakes can be very costly to a business.

Source: Company's Form 10-K.

reported on the balance sheet are not affected. The income statement is not affected. The effects on the company's financial statements of incurring production labor costs follow.

	Balance Sheet							Income Statement				
	Assets			=	Liabilities	+	Equity					
Event No.	Cash	+	Work in Process Inventory					Revenue	−	Expenses	=	Net Income
1.	(1,400)	+	1,400	=	NA	+	NA	NA	−	NA	=	NA

Flow of Overhead Costs

LO 11-2

Allocate overhead cost between inventory and cost of goods sold.

Assume Ventra made 500 jewelry boxes during January. What is the cost per jewelry box? Why does management need to know this cost? If Ventra uses a cost-plus pricing strategy, management must know the cost per jewelry box to determine what price to charge for each one. Product cost information is also used to control costs and evaluate managerial performance. By comparing current production costs with historical or standard costs, management can evaluate whether performance meets expectations and take appropriate action to ensure the company accomplishes its goals. Ventra has many reasons for needing to know in January the cost of products made in January.

The *direct costs* of making the 500 jewelry boxes in January are $1,100 for materials and $1,400 for labor. The *actual indirect overhead costs* are unknown. Ventra will not know the exact amount of some of these indirect costs until the end of the year. For example, Ventra uses the periodic inventory method to determine the cost of production supplies consumed. The actual cost of supplies consumed is unknown until the end of the year when Ventra counts any unused supplies. Similarly, the actual cost for Year 2 of taxes, insurance, landscaping, supervisory bonuses, and other indirect costs may be unknown in January. Ventra cannot delay making managerial decisions until actual cost data become available. Ventra needs information on January 31 that will not be available until December 31. This dilemma is depicted in the following graphic.

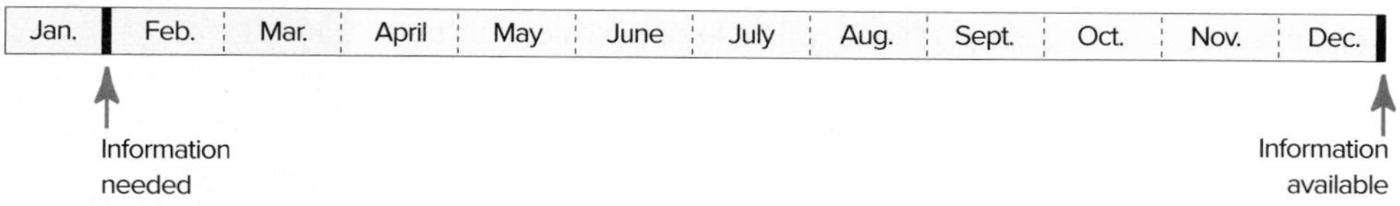

To solve the problem of needing cost information before it is available, Ventra records *estimated costs* in its accounting system *during the accounting period.* To illustrate, assume the accountant estimated Ventra will incur total indirect overhead costs of $40,320 during Year 2. This *estimate* of overhead cost includes $1,600 for the cost of production supplies Ventra will use, $10,000 of depreciation cost, and $28,720 of other costs such as supervisory salaries, rent on the manufacturing facility, utilities, and maintenance. How much of the $40,320 *estimated* overhead cost should Ventra allocate to the units produced in January? Ventra must first identify the most appropriate allocation base. Assuming the goods (jewelry boxes) are homogeneous (the jewelry boxes are identical), it makes sense to use number of units as the allocation base, assigning an equal amount of overhead cost to each box.

Suppose Ventra's accountant expected Ventra to produce 12,000 jewelry boxes during the year. Based on this estimate, the allocation rate is $3.36 per unit ($40,320 expected cost ÷ 12,000 units). Because the overhead allocation rate is determined before the actual overhead costs are known, it is called a **predetermined overhead rate.** Using the $3.36 predetermined overhead rate, Ventra allocated $1,680 of overhead cost to the 500 jewelry boxes made in January ($3.36 × 500 boxes).

Manufacturing Overhead Account

How are overhead costs recorded in the accounting records? Estimated overhead costs are *applied* (assigned) to work in process inventory *at the time goods are produced.* As shown in Event 5 (see page 494), Ventra Manufacturing will apply (transfer) $1,680 of overhead cost to the Work in Process Inventory account for January. Actual overhead costs may be incurred at different times from when goods are made. For example, Ventra may recognize depreciation or supplies used at year-end. Actual and estimated overhead costs are therefore recorded at different times during the accounting period.

At the time estimated overhead is added to the Work in Process Inventory account, a decrease is recorded on the right side of a *temporary* account called *Manufacturing Overhead.* This entry in the Manufacturing Overhead account is called **applied overhead.** Think of the **Manufacturing Overhead account** as a temporary asset account. Recognizing estimated overhead can be viewed as an asset exchange transaction. When estimated overhead is recognized, the temporary account, Manufacturing Overhead, decreases and the Work in Process Inventory account increases.

Actual overhead costs are recorded as increases in the Manufacturing Overhead account. For example, at the end of the year, Ventra will reduce the Production Supplies account and increase the Manufacturing Overhead account by the actual amount of supplies used. The balance in the Production Supplies account will be decreased and the balance in the Manufacturing Overhead account will be increased. When Ventra pays monthly rent cost for the manufacturing facilities, it will increase Manufacturing Overhead and decrease cash. Other actual overhead costs are recorded the same way.

Since differences normally exist between estimated and actual overhead costs, the Manufacturing Overhead account is likely to have a balance at the end of the year. If more overhead has been applied than was actually incurred, the account balance represents the amount of **overapplied overhead.** If less overhead was applied than was incurred, the account balance is **underapplied overhead.** Overapplied overhead means the amount of estimated overhead cost recorded in the Work in Process Inventory account exceeded the actual overhead cost incurred. Underapplied overhead means the amount of estimated overhead cost recorded in the Work in Process Inventory account was less than the actual overhead cost incurred.

Because costs flow from Work in Process Inventory to Finished Goods Inventory and then to Cost of Goods Sold, these accounts will also be overstated or understated relative to actual costs. If the amount of overapplied or underapplied overhead is significant, it must be allocated proportionately at the end of the year to the Work in Process Inventory, Finished Goods Inventory, and Cost of Goods Sold accounts so these accounts will reflect actual, rather than estimated, amounts for financial reporting.

In most cases, over- or underapplied overhead is not significant and companies may allocate it in any convenient manner. In these circumstances, companies normally assign the total amount of the overhead correction directly to Cost of Goods Sold. We have adopted this simplifying practice throughout the text and in the end-of-chapter exercises and problems. Exhibit 11.3 shows the flow of product costs, including actual and applied overhead. To illustrate using a Manufacturing Overhead account, return to Ventra Manufacturing Company.

EXHIBIT 11.3

Flow of Product Costs

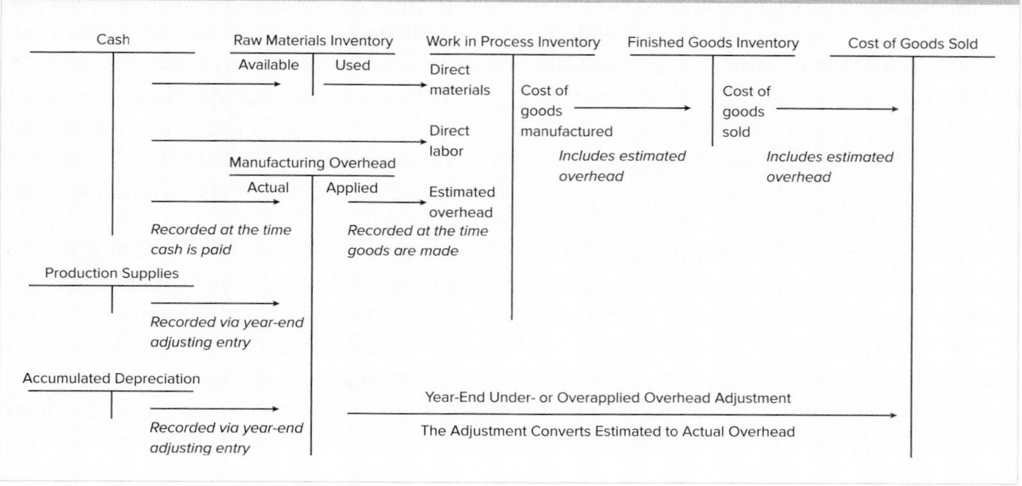

EVENT 5 Ventra recognized $1,680 of estimated manufacturing overhead costs at the end of January (see the previous section titled "Flow of Overhead Costs" to review computing this amount).

This event is another asset exchange. Total assets reported on the balance sheet, net income, and cash flow are not affected. The temporary asset account Manufacturing Overhead decreases, and the asset account Work in Process Inventory increases. The effects of this event on the company's financial statements follow.

	Balance Sheet							Income Statement				
	Assets			=	Liabilities	+	Equity					
Event No.	Manufacturing Overhead	+	Work in Process Inventory					Revenue	−	Expenses	=	Net Income
1.	(1,680)	+	1,680	=	NA	+	NA	NA	−	NA	=	NA

EVENT 6 Ventra transferred the total cost of the 500 jewelry boxes made in January ($1,100 materials + $1,400 labor + $1,680 estimated overhead = $4,180 cost of goods manufactured) from work in process to finished goods.

This event is an asset exchange. Total assets reported on the balance sheet, net income, and cash flow are not affected. The asset account Work in Process Inventory decreases, and the asset account Finished Goods Inventory increases. The effects of this event on the company's financial statements follow.

	Balance Sheet							Income Statement				
	Assets			=	Liabilities	+	Equity					
Event No.	Work in Process Inventory	+	Finished Goods Inventory					Revenue	−	Expenses	=	Net Income
1.	(4,180)	+	4,180	=	NA	+	NA	NA	−	NA	=	NA

EVENT 7 Ventra transferred the cost of 400 sold jewelry boxes from finished goods inventory to cost of goods sold.

Recall that Ventra made 500 jewelry boxes costing $4,180 during January. Also, the beginning balance in the Finished Goods Inventory account was $836. Assume this balance represented 100 jewelry boxes that had been made in Year 1. Therefore, 600 units (100 + 500) of finished goods costing $5,016 ($836 + $4,180) were available for sale. If Ventra sold 400 units, it had 200 units in finished goods inventory at the end of January. The cost of the 600 boxes available ($5,016) must be allocated between the Finished Goods Inventory account and the Cost of Goods Sold account. The allocation is based on the cost per unit of jewelry boxes. Given that 600 boxes cost $5,016, the cost per unit is $8.36 ($5,016 ÷ 600). Based on this cost per unit, Ventra transferred $3,344 ($8.36 × 400 boxes) from finished goods inventory to cost of goods sold, leaving an ending balance of $1,672 ($8.36 × 200 boxes) in the Finished Goods Inventory account.

Transferring cost from finished goods inventory to cost of goods sold is an asset use event. Both total assets and stockholders' equity reported on the balance sheet decrease. The asset finished goods inventory decreases, and the expense cost of goods sold increases, decreasing stockholders' equity (retained earnings). Net income decreases. The sales transaction encompasses two events. The following horizontal model shows the effects of the expense recognition. The effects of the corresponding revenue recognition are discussed separately as Event 8.

	Balance Sheet					Income Statement				
	Assets	=	Liabilities	+	Equity					
Event No.	Finished Goods Inventory				Retained Earnings	Revenue	−	Expenses	=	Net Income
1.	(3,344)	=	NA	+	(3,344)	NA	−	3,344	=	(3,344)

Knowing the cost per jewelry box is useful for many purposes. For example, the amount of the allocation between the ending Finished Goods Inventory and the Cost of Goods Sold accounts is needed for the financial statements. Ventra must compute the cost per unit data if it wishes to prepare interim (monthly or quarterly) financial reports. The cost per unit for the month of January also could be compared to the cost per unit for the previous accounting period or to standard cost data to evaluate cost control and managerial performance. Finally, the cost per unit data are needed for setting the price under a cost-plus pricing strategy. Assume Ventra desires to earn a gross margin of $5.64 per jewelry box. It would therefore charge $14 ($8.36 cost + $5.64 gross margin) per unit for each jewelry box. When recording the effects of recognizing revenue for the 400 boxes sold, we assume that Ventra charges its customers $14 per unit.

EVENT 8 **Ventra recognized $5,600 ($14 per unit × 400 units) of sales revenue for the cash sale of 400 jewelry boxes.**

Recognizing revenue is an asset source transaction. The asset cash increases and stockholders' equity (retained earnings) increases. Net income increases. These effects are shown as follows.

	Balance Sheet					Income Statement				
Event No.	Assets	=	Liabilities	+	Equity	Revenue	−	Expenses	=	Net Income
1.	5,600	=	NA	+	5,600	5,600	−	NA	=	5,600

EVENT 9 **Ventra paid $1,200 cash for manufacturing overhead costs including indirect labor, utilities, and rent.**

Paying for actual overhead costs is an asset exchange event. Ventra transfers cost from the asset account Cash to the temporary asset account Manufacturing Overhead. Total assets on the balance sheet and net income are unaffected. These effects follow.

	Balance Sheet							Income Statement				
	Assets			=	Liabilities	+	Equity					
Event No.	Cash	+	Manufacturing Overhead					Revenue	−	Expenses	=	Net Income
1.	(1,200)	+	1,200	=	NA	+	NA	NA	−	NA	=	NA

Recall that $1,680 of overhead cost was applied to the January work in process inventory. This amount is significantly more than the $1,200 of actual overhead costs paid for above. These amounts differ because the estimated (applied) overhead includes several costs that have not yet been recognized. For example, the amount of supplies used and depreciation expense are not recognized until Ventra records adjusting entries on December 31. Although these costs are not recognized until December, a portion of them must be included in the cost of products made in January. Otherwise, all of the supplies cost and depreciation cost would be assigned to products made in December.

Answers to The Curious Accountant

Obviously, an enterprise such as **Northwest Aviation** cannot stay in business if it cannot give customers a price for the services it is selling. As the chapter has explained, manufacturers estimate the overhead cost of a job based on a predetermined overhead rate. Although these estimates will not be perfect, they do allow the companies to price their goods or services before they are produced. If the company does not do a reasonably good job of estimating the costs it will incur to complete a job, then it will suffer by either pricing its goods too high, which will cause it to lose business to its competitors, or pricing its goods too low, which will cause it to not make a profit adequate to stay in business.

The manufacturing equipment and supplies are actually used throughout the year. Assigning the total cost of these resources to December alone would overstate the cost of December production and understate the cost of production during other months. Such distortions in measuring product cost could mislead managers making decisions based on the reported costs. By using *estimated* overhead costs during the accounting period, management reduces the distortions that using actual monthly costs would create. The difference between actual and estimated overhead is corrected in a *year-end adjusting entry.* Companies do not adjust for these differences on an interim basis.

CHECK YOURSELF 11.1

Candy Manufacturing Company had a beginning balance of $24,850 in its Work in Process Inventory account. Candy added the following costs to work in process during the accounting period: direct materials, $32,000; direct labor, $46,000; and manufacturing overhead, $39,900. If the ending balance in the Work in Process Inventory account was $22,100, what was the amount of the Cost of Goods Manufactured (cost of goods transferred to Finished Goods Inventory)?

Answer

Beginning work in process inventory	$ 24,850
Manufacturing costs added	
Direct materials	32,000
Direct labor	46,000
Manufacturing overhead	39,900
Total work in process	142,750
Less: Ending work in process inventory	(22,100)
Cost of goods manufactured	$120,650

Summary of January Events

Exhibit 11.4 summarizes the events that occurred during January. The upper section of the exhibit illustrates the *physical flow* of the resources used to make the jewelry boxes. The lower section shows the product *cost flow* through Ventra's ledger accounts. The exhibit illustrates Events 1 through 9. The January balances in the Finished Goods Inventory and Cost of

EXHIBIT 11.4

Flow of Product Costs for Ventra Manufacturing Company's January Production

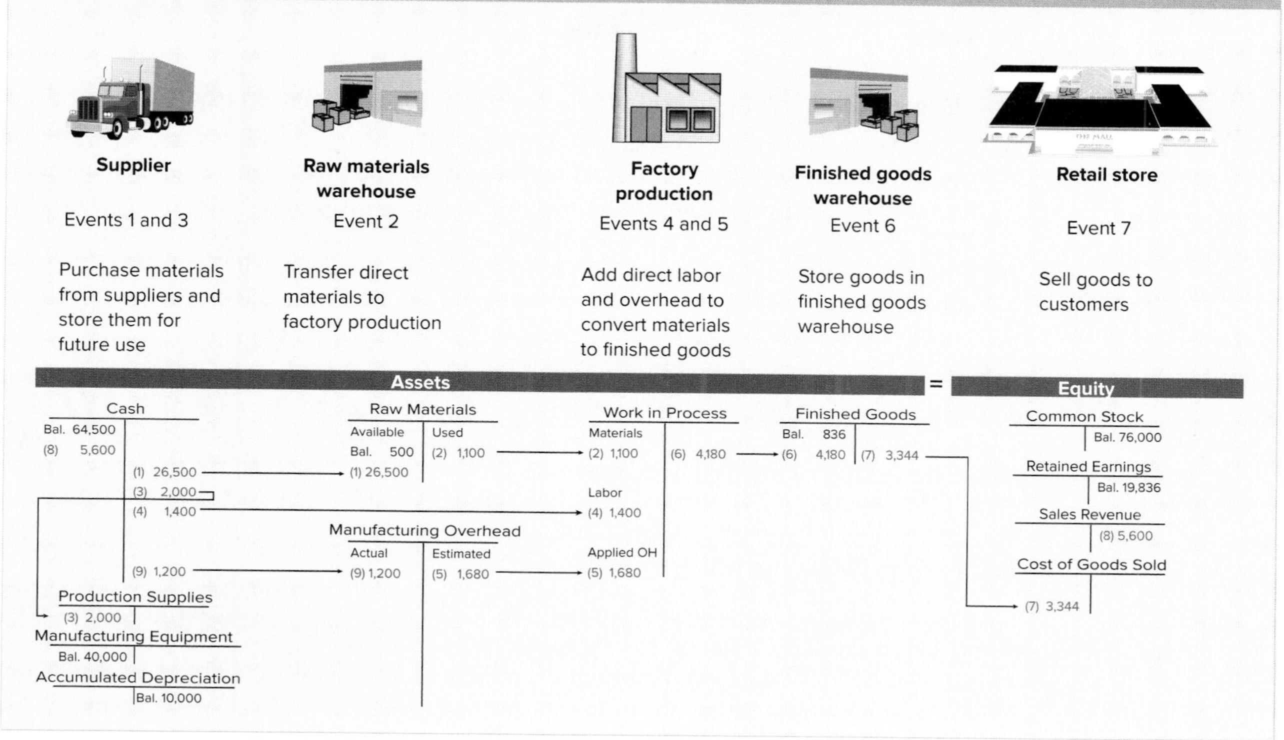

Goods Sold accounts include the cost of materials, labor, and an *estimated* amount of overhead. Estimated overhead cost is applied to work in process inventory throughout the year. Actual overhead costs are accumulated in the Manufacturing Overhead account as they are incurred. The accounts are adjusted at year-end to reconcile the difference between the estimated and actual overhead costs.

Manufacturing Cost Flow Events for February through December

Ventra Manufacturing Company's accounting events for February through December are summarized here. The sequence of events continues from the January activity. Since nine events occurred in January, the first February event is Event 10. The events for the remainder of Year 2 follow.

10. Ventra used $24,860 of raw materials.

11. The company paid production workers $31,640 cash.

12. Ventra started production of an additional 11,300 jewelry boxes. Ventra applied overhead of $37,968 (11,300 units × the predetermined overhead rate of $3.36 per unit) to work in process inventory.

13. The company completed 10,300 units and transferred $86,108 of cost of goods manufactured from work in process inventory to finished goods inventory.

14. Ventra sold 9,600 units and recorded $80,256 of cost of goods sold.

15. The company recognized $134,400 of cash revenue for the products sold in Event 14.

16. The company paid $30,500 cash for overhead costs including indirect labor, rent, and utilities.

17. The year-end count of production supplies indicated $300 of supplies were on hand on December 31. Ventra recognized $1,700 ($2,000 supplies available − $300 ending balance) of indirect materials cost for supplies used during the year. This entry reflects year-end recognition of an actual overhead cost.
18. Ventra recognized $10,000 of actual overhead cost for depreciation of manufacturing equipment.
19. The company paid $31,400 cash for general, selling, and administrative expenses.
20. A year-end review of the Manufacturing Overhead account disclosed that overhead cost was underapplied by $3,752. Actual overhead ($43,400) was higher than applied overhead ($39,648). Because applied overhead cost passes through the ledger accounts from Work in Process Inventory to Finished Goods Inventory and ultimately to Cost of Goods Sold, the balance in the Cost of Goods Sold account is understated. Ventra recorded the adjusting entry to close the Manufacturing Overhead account and increase the balance in the Cost of Goods Sold account.

Exhibit 11.5 shows the flow of the Year 2 costs through the ledger accounts. The January entries are shown in blue to distinguish them from the entries for the remainder of the year. The product cost flows are highlighted with black arrows. Trace the effects of each transaction to the exhibit before reading further.

Analyzing Underapplied Overhead

What caused overhead to be underapplied by $3,752? Recall that the predetermined overhead rate is based on two estimates: the estimated total overhead cost and the estimated total annual production volume. At the beginning of Year 2, Ventra estimated total overhead cost would be $40,320, but actual overhead costs were $43,400, indicating Ventra spent $3,080 more than expected for overhead cost. This $3,080 is a *spending variance.* The remaining $672 of the underapplied overhead ($3,752 − $3,080) results from the difference between the actual and estimated volume of activity; it is called a *volume variance.* Recall that Ventra estimated production volume would be 12,000 units, but actual volume was only 11,800 units (500 units made in January + 11,300 units made from February through December).[2] The predetermined overhead rate of $3.36 per unit was applied to 200 fewer units (12,000 units − 11,800 units) than expected, resulting in a volume variance of $672 ($3.36 predetermined overhead rate × 200 units). The combination of the spending and volume variances[3] explains the total underapplied overhead ($3,080 + $672 = $3,752).

Because the actual cost is higher than the expected cost, the spending variance is unfavorable. The volume variance is also unfavorable because actual volume is less than expected, suggesting the manufacturing facilities were not utilized to the extent anticipated. In other words, fixed costs such as depreciation, rent, and supervisory salaries were spread over fewer units of product than expected, thereby increasing the cost per unit of product. If the variances are significant, estimated product costs could have been understated enough to have distorted decisions using the data. For example, products may have been underpriced, adversely affecting profitability. Making estimates as accurately as possible is critically important. Nevertheless, some degree of inaccuracy is inevitable. No one knows precisely what the future will bring. Managers seek to improve decision making. Although managers cannot make exact predictions, the more careful the estimates, the more useful will be the resulting information for timely decision making.

[2]There were 11,800 units placed into production. There were 10,800 units completed, leaving an ending work in process inventory balance of 1,000 units.

[3]The predetermined overhead rate in this chapter represents the standard cost and quantity of both variable and fixed inputs. As discussed in Chapter 8, companies may establish separate standards for variable costs and fixed costs. In this chapter, we assume the variable cost variances are insignificant and focus the discussion on the effects of fixed cost variances only.

EXHIBIT 11.5

Product Cost Flow for Ventra Manufacturing Company's Year 2 Accounting Period

Cash

	Debit		Credit
Bal.	64,500		
(8)	5,600		
(15)	134,400	(1)	26,500
		(3)	2,000
		(4)	1,400
		(11)	31,640
		(9)	1,200
		(16)	30,500
		(19)	31,400
Bal.	79,860		

Raw Materials Inventory

Available		Used	
Bal.	500	(2)	1,100
(1)	26,500	(10)	24,860
Bal.	1,040		

Work in Process Inventory

	Debit		Credit
Materials			
(2)	1,100	(6)	4,180
(10)	24,860	(13)	86,108
Labor			
(4)	1,400		
(11)	31,640		
Applied OH			
(5)	1,680		
(12)	37,968		
Bal.	8,360		

Finished Goods Inventory

	Debit		Credit
Bal.	836		
(6)	4,180	(7)	3,344
(13)	86,108	(14)	80,256
Bal.	7,524		

Cost of Goods Sold

	Debit		Credit
(7)	3,344		
(14)	80,256		
(20)	3,752		
Bal.	87,352		

Common Stock

	Debit		Credit
		Bal.	76,000

Retained Earnings

	Debit		Credit
		Bal.	19,836

Sales Revenue

	Debit		Credit
		(8)	5,600
		(15)	134,400

G,S&A Expense

	Debit		Credit
(19)	31,400		

Manufacturing Overhead

Actual		Estimated	
(9)	1,200	(5)	1,680
(16)	30,500	(12)	37,968
(17)	1,700		
(18)	10,000	(20)	3,752
Bal.	0		

Production Supplies

	Debit		Credit
(3)	2,000	(17)	1,700
Bal.	300		

Manufacturing Equip.

	Debit		Credit
Bal.	40,000		

Accumulated Depreciation

	Debit		Credit
		Bal.	10,000
		(18)	10,000
		Bal.	20,000

CHECK YOURSELF 11.2

At the beginning of the accounting period, Nutrient Manufacturing Company estimated its total manufacturing overhead cost for the coming year would be $124,000. Furthermore, the company expected to use 15,500 direct labor hours during the year. Nutrient actually incurred overhead costs of $128,500 for the year and actually used 15,800 direct labor hours. Nutrient allocates overhead costs to production based on direct labor hours. Would overhead costs be overapplied or underapplied? What effect will closing the overhead account have on cost of goods sold?

Answer

Predetermined overhead rate = Total expected overhead cost ÷ Allocation base
Predetermined overhead rate = $124,000 ÷ 15,500 hours = $8 per direct labor hour

Applied overhead = Predetermined overhead rate × Actual direct labor hours
Applied overhead = $8 × 15,800 = $126,400

Since the applied overhead ($126,400) is less than the actual overhead ($128,500), the overhead is underapplied. Closing the overhead account will increase Cost of Goods Sold by $2,100 ($128,500 − $126,400).

PREPARING THE SCHEDULE OF COST OF GOODS MANUFACTURED AND SOLD

LO 11-3

Prepare a schedule of cost of goods manufactured and sold.

In practice, a general ledger system like that shown in Exhibit 11.5 may capture millions of events. Analyzing operations with such vast numbers of transactions is exceedingly difficult. To help managers analyze manufacturing results, companies summarize the ledger data in a *schedule* that shows the overall cost of goods manufactured and sold. The schedule is an internal document which is not presented with a company's published financial statements. Only the final total on the schedule (cost of goods sold) is disclosed; it is reported on the income statement. Exhibit 11.6 illustrates Ventra's Year 2 **schedule of cost of goods manufactured and sold.**

EXHIBIT 11.6

VENTRA MANUFACTURING COMPANY
Schedule of Cost of Goods Manufactured and Sold
For the Year Ended December 31, Year 2

Beginning raw materials inventory	$ 500
Plus: Purchases	26,500
Raw materials available for use	27,000
Less: Ending raw materials inventory	(1,040)
Direct raw materials used	25,960
Direct labor	33,040
Overhead (actual overhead cost)	43,400
Total manufacturing costs	102,400
Plus: Beginning work in process inventory	0
Total work in process inventory	102,400
Less: Ending work in process inventory	(8,360)
Cost of goods manufactured	94,040
Plus: Beginning finished goods inventory	836
Cost of goods available for sale	94,876
Less: Ending finished goods inventory	(7,524)
Cost of goods sold	$ 87,352

The schedule in Exhibit 11.6 reflects the transaction data in the ledger accounts. Confirm this relationship by comparing the information in the Raw Materials Inventory account in Exhibit 11.5 with the computation of the cost of direct raw materials used in the schedule in Exhibit 11.6. The beginning raw materials inventory, purchases, and ending raw materials inventory amounts in the ledger account agree with the schedule. The schedule, however, presents various amounts in summary form. For example, in the schedule the amount of direct raw materials used is $25,960. In Exhibit 11.5, this same amount is shown as two separate entries ($1,100 + $24,860) in the T-account. Similarly, the $33,040 shown as direct labor in the schedule represents the total of the two amounts ($1,400 + $31,640) of labor cost entered in the Work in Process Inventory account in Exhibit 11.5. In practice, one number in the schedule may represent thousands of individual events captured in the ledger accounts. The schedule simplifies analyzing manufacturing cost flow data for decision-making purposes.

The schedule of cost of goods manufactured and sold includes the *actual* amount of overhead cost. Data for financial statement reports are summarized at the end of the year when actual cost data are available. Although companies use estimated costs for internal records and decision making during the year, they use actual historical cost data in this schedule prepared at the end of the year.

FINANCIAL STATEMENTS

The final total on the schedule of cost of goods manufactured and sold is reported as the single line item *cost of goods sold* on the company's income statement. Cost of goods sold is subtracted from sales revenue to determine gross margin. Selling and administrative expenses are subtracted from gross margin to reach net income. Exhibit 11.7 shows Ventra Manufacturing's Year 2 income statement; Exhibit 11.8 shows the year-end balance sheet. In Exhibit 11.8, we show the three inventory accounts (Raw Materials, Work in Process, and Finished Goods) separately for teaching purposes. In practice, these accounts are frequently combined and reported as a single amount (Inventories) on the balance sheet. Study each statement, tracing the information from the T-accounts in Exhibit 11.5 to the exhibits to see how companies gather the information they report to the public in their published financial statements.

EXHIBIT 11.7

VENTRA MANUFACTURING COMPANY
Income Statement
For the Year Ended December 31, Year 2

Sales revenue	$140,000
Cost of goods sold	(87,352)
Gross margin	52,648
Selling and administrative expenses	(31,400)
Net income	$ 21,248

EXHIBIT 11.8

VENTRA MANUFACTURING COMPANY
Balance Sheet
As of December 31, Year 2

Assets	
Cash	$ 79,860
Raw materials inventory	1,040
Work in process inventory	8,360
Finished goods inventory	7,524
Production supplies	300
Manufacturing equipment	40,000
Accumulated depreciation—manufac. equip.	(20,000)
Total assets	$117,084
Stockholders' equity	
Common stock	$ 76,000
Retained earnings	41,084
Total stockholders' equity	$117,084

MOTIVE TO OVERPRODUCE

Absorption Costing versus Variable Costing

LO 11-4

Distinguish between absorption and variable costing.

As discussed previously, managers frequently separate product manufacturing costs into variable and fixed categories based on how the costs behave. For example, the cost of materials, labor, and supplies usually increases and decreases in direct proportion to the number of units produced. Other product costs, such as rent, depreciation, and supervisory salaries are fixed; they remain constant regardless of the number of products made. Generally accepted accounting principles require that *all* product costs, both variable and fixed, be reported as inventory until the products are sold, when the product costs are expensed as cost of goods sold. This practice is called **absorption (full) costing.**[4] To illustrate, assume Hokai Manufacturing Company incurs the following costs to produce 2,000 units of inventory.

Inventory Costs	Cost per Unit	×	Units	=	Total
Variable manufacturing costs	$9	×	2,000	=	$18,000
Fixed overhead				=	12,000
Total (full absorption product cost)				=	$30,000

Suppose Hokai sells all 2,000 units of inventory for $20 per unit (sales = 2,000 × $20 = $40,000). Gross margin is therefore $10,000 ($40,000 sales − $30,000 cost of goods sold). What happens to reported profitability if Hokai increases production without also increasing sales? Profitability increases because cost of goods sold decreases. Overproducing spreads the fixed cost over more units, thereby reducing the cost per unit and the amount charged to cost of goods sold. Exhibit 11.9 illustrates this effect; it shows the cost per unit at production levels of 2,000, 3,000, and 4,000 units.

EXHIBIT 11.9

Cost per Unit Absorption Costing

Inventory Costs			
Fixed overhead (a)	$12,000	$12,000	$12,000
Number of units (b)	2,000	3,000	4,000
Fixed overhead per unit (a ÷ b)	$ 6	$ 4	$ 3
Variable manufacturing costs	9	9	9
Full absorption product cost per unit	$ 15	$ 13	$ 12

Exhibit 11.10 illustrates for Hokai alternate income statements assuming sales of 2,000 units and production levels of 2,000, 3,000, and 4,000 units, the first using absorption costing and the second using variable costing.

Suppose Hokai's management is under pressure to increase profitability but cannot control sales because customers make buying decisions. Management may be tempted to

[4]Since all manufacturing costs are classified as product costs under absorption costing, absorption costing is also called *full costing.*

EXHIBIT 11.10

Absorption Costing Income Statements at Different Levels of Production with Sales Held Constant at 2,000 Units

Level of Production	2,000		3,000		4,000
Sales ($20 per unit × 2,000 units)	$40,000		$40,000		$40,000
Cost of goods sold ($15 × 2,000) =	30,000	($13 × 2,000) =	26,000	($12 × 2,000) =	24,000
Gross margin	$10,000		$14,000		$16,000

increase reported profitability by increasing production. What is wrong with increasing production without also increasing sales? The problem lies in inventory accumulation. Notice inventory increases 1,000 units when 3,000 units are produced but only 2,000 are sold. Likewise, inventory rises 2,000 units when 4,000 are produced but 2,000 are sold. Holding excess inventory entails considerable risks and costs. Inventory is subject to obsolescence, damage, theft, or destruction by fire, weather, or other disasters. Furthermore, holding inventory requires expenditures for warehouse space, employee handling, financing, and insurance coverage. These risks and costs reduce a company's profitability. Overproducing inventory is a poor business practice. To motivate managers to increase profitability without tempting them to overproduce, many companies use *variable costing* for internal reporting.

Variable Costing

Under **variable costing,** inventory includes only *variable* product costs. The income statement is presented using the contribution margin approach, with variable product costs subtracted from sales revenue to determine the contribution margin. Fixed costs are then subtracted from the contribution margin to determine net income.

Fixed manufacturing costs are expensed in the period in which they are incurred (the period in which the resource is used) regardless of when inventory is sold. Using variable costing, increases in production have no effect on the amount of reported profit, as shown in the income statements in Exhibit 11.11.

Although managers may still overproduce under variable costing, at least they are not tempted to do so by the lure of reporting higher profits. The variable costing reporting format encourages management to make business decisions that have a more favorable impact on long-term profitability. Variable costing can be used only for internal reporting because generally accepted accounting principles prohibit its use in external financial statements.

EXHIBIT 11.11

Variable Costing Income Statements at Different Levels of Production with Sales Held Constant at 2,000 Units

Level of Production	2,000		3,000		4,000
Sales ($20 per unit × 2,000 units)	$ 40,000		$ 40,000		$ 40,000
Variable cost of goods sold ($9 × 2,000) =	(18,000)	($9 × 2,000) =	(18,000)	($9 × 2,000) =	(18,000)
Contribution margin	22,000		22,000		22,000
Fixed manufacturing costs	(12,000)		(12,000)		(12,000)
Net income	$ 10,000		$ 10,000		$ 10,000

CHECK YOURSELF 11.3

If production exceeds sales, will absorption or variable costing produce the higher amount of net income? Which method (absorption or variable costing) is required for external financial reporting?

Answer Absorption costing produces a higher amount of net income when production exceeds sales. With absorption costing, fixed manufacturing costs are treated as inventory and remain in inventory accounts until the inventory is sold. In contrast, all fixed manufacturing costs are expensed with variable costing. Therefore, with absorption costing, some fixed manufacturing costs will be in inventory rather than in expense accounts, so expenses will be lower and net income will be higher than with variable costing (when production exceeds sales). Generally accepted accounting principles require companies to use absorption costing for external financial reporting purposes.

<< A Look Back

Most manufacturing companies accumulate product costs in three inventory accounts. The *Raw Materials Inventory account* is used to accumulate the cost of direct *raw materials* purchased for use in production. The *Work in Process Inventory account* includes the cost of partially completed products. Finally, the *Finished Goods Inventory account* contains the costs of fully completed products that are ready for sale. When direct materials are purchased, their costs are first recorded in raw materials inventory. The costs of the materials used in production are transferred from raw materials inventory to work in process inventory. The cost of direct labor and overhead are added to work in process inventory. As goods are completed, their costs are transferred from work in process inventory to finished goods inventory. When goods are sold, their cost is transferred from finished goods inventory to cost of goods sold. The ending balances in the Raw Materials, Work in Process, and Finished Goods Inventory accounts are reported in the balance sheet. The product cost in the Cost of Goods Sold account is subtracted from sales revenue on the income statement to determine gross margin.

The actual amounts of many indirect overhead costs incurred to make products are unknown until the end of the accounting period. Examples of such costs include the cost of rent, supplies, utilities, indirect materials, and indirect labor. Because many managerial decisions require product cost information before year-end, companies frequently estimate the amount of overhead cost. The estimated overhead costs are assigned to products using a *predetermined overhead rate.*

Actual and applied overhead costs are accumulated in the temporary asset account *Manufacturing Overhead.* Differences between actual and applied overhead result in a balance in the Manufacturing Overhead account at the end of the accounting period. If actual overhead exceeds applied overhead, the account balance represents *underapplied overhead.* If actual overhead is less than applied overhead, the balance represents *overapplied overhead.* If the amount of over- or underapplied overhead is insignificant, it is closed directly to cost of goods sold through a year-end adjusting entry.

Manufacturing cost information is summarized in a report known as a *schedule of cost of goods manufactured and sold.* This schedule shows how the amount of cost of goods sold reported on the income statement was determined. Actual, rather than applied, overhead cost is used in the schedule.

Generally accepted accounting principles require all product costs (fixed and variable) to be included in inventory until the products are sold. This practice is called *absorption costing.* Results reported under absorption costing may tempt management to increase profitability by producing more units than the company can sell (overproducing). Overproducing spreads fixed costs over more units, reducing the cost per unit and the amount charged to cost of goods sold. Overproducing has the adverse effect of reducing profitability in the long term by increasing the risks and costs of inventory accumulation. To eliminate the temptation to overproduce, for internal reporting many companies determine product cost using *variable costing*. Under variable costing, only the variable product costs are included in inventory. Fixed product costs are expensed in the period they are incurred, regardless of when products are sold. As a result, overproduction does not decrease the product cost per unit and managers are not tempted to overproduce to increase profitability.

A Look Forward >>

To determine the cost of a bottle of Pepsi, would you use the same product cost system that you would use to determine the cost of a stealth bomber? We answer this question in the next chapter, which expands on the basic cost flow concepts introduced in this chapter. You will be introduced to job-order, process, and hybrid cost systems. You will learn to identify the types of services and products that are most appropriate for each type of cost system.

Video lectures and accompanying self-assessment quizzes are available in *Connect* for all learning objectives.

SELF-STUDY REVIEW PROBLEM

Tavia Manufacturing Company's first year of operation is summarized in the following list. All transactions are cash transactions unless otherwise indicated.

1. Acquired cash by issuing common stock.
2. Purchased administrative equipment.
3. Purchased manufacturing equipment.
4. Purchased direct raw materials.
5. Purchased indirect materials (production supplies).
6. Used direct raw materials in making products.
7. Paid direct labor wages to manufacturing workers.
8. Applied overhead costs to Work in Process Inventory.
9. Paid indirect labor salaries (production supervisors).
10. Paid administrative and sales staff salaries.
11. Paid rent and utilities on the manufacturing facilities.
12. Completed work on products.
13. Sold completed inventory for cash (revenue event only).
14. Recognized cost of goods sold.
15. Recognized depreciation on manufacturing equipment.
16. Recognized depreciation on administrative equipment.
17. Recognized the amount of production supplies that had been used during the year.
18. Closed the Manufacturing Overhead account. Overhead had been underapplied during the year.

Required

a. Use the horizontal statements model to show how each event affects the balance sheet and the income statement.

b. Identify the accounts affected by each event and indicate whether they increased or decreased as a result of the event.

Solution to Requirement *a*

Event No.	Assets	=	Liab.	+	Equity	Rev.	−	Exp.	=	Net Inc.
1	+		n/a		+	n/a		n/a		n/a
2	− +		n/a		n/a	n/a		n/a		n/a
3	− +		n/a		n/a	n/a		n/a		n/a
4	− +		n/a		n/a	n/a		n/a		n/a
5	− +		n/a		n/a	n/a		n/a		n/a
6	− +		n/a		n/a	n/a		n/a		n/a
7	− +		n/a		n/a	n/a		n/a		n/a
8	− +		n/a		n/a	n/a		n/a		n/a
9	− +		n/a		n/a	n/a		n/a		n/a
10	−		n/a		−	n/a		+		−
11	− +		n/a		n/a	n/a		n/a		n/a
12	− +		n/a		n/a	n/a		n/a		n/a
13	+		n/a		+	+		n/a		+
14	−		n/a		−	n/a		+		−
15	− +		n/a		n/a	n/a		n/a		n/a
16	−		n/a		−	n/a		+		−
17	− +		n/a		n/a	n/a		n/a		n/a
18	−		n/a		−	n/a		+		−

Solution to Requirement *b*

Event No.	Account Title	Increase/ Decrease	Account Title	Increase/ Decrease
1	Cash	+	Common Stock	+
2	Administrative Equipment	+	Cash	−
3	Manufacturing Equipment	+	Cash	−
4	Raw Materials Inventory	+	Cash	−
5	Production Supplies	+	Cash	−
6	Work in Process Inventory	+	Raw Materials Inventory	−
7	Work in Process Inventory	+	Cash	−
8	Work in Process Inventory	+	Manufacturing Overhead	−
9	Manufacturing Overhead	+	Cash	−
10	Salary Expense	+	Cash	−
11	Manufacturing Overhead	+	Cash	−
12	Finished Goods Inventory	+	Work in Process Inventory	−
13	Cash	+	Sales Revenue	+
14	Cost of Goods Sold	+	Finished Goods Inventory	−
15	Manufacturing Overhead	+	Accumulated Depreciation	+
16	Depreciation Expense	+	Accumulated Depreciation	+
17	Manufacturing Overhead	+	Production Supplies	−
18	Cost of Goods Sold	+	Manufacturing Overhead	−

KEY TERMS

Absorption (full) costing 502
Applied overhead 493
Finished Goods Inventory 488
Manufacturing Overhead account 493
Overapplied overhead 493
Predetermined overhead rate 492
Raw Materials Inventory 488
Schedule of cost of goods manufactured and sold 500
Underapplied overhead 493
Variable costing 503
Work in Process Inventory 488

QUESTIONS

1. What is the difference between direct and indirect raw materials costs?
2. Direct raw materials were purchased on account, and the costs were subsequently transferred to Work in Process Inventory. How would the transfer affect assets, liabilities, equity, and cash flows? What is the effect on the income statement? Would your answers change if the materials had originally been purchased for cash?
3. How do manufacturing costs flow through inventory accounts?
4. Goods that cost $2,000 to make were sold for $3,000 on account. How does their sale affect assets, liabilities, and equity? What is the effect on the income statement?
5. At the end of the accounting period, an adjusting entry is made for the accrued wages of production workers. How would this entry affect assets, liabilities, and equity? What is the effect on the income statement?
6. X Company recorded the payment for utilities used by the manufacturing facility by crediting Cash and debiting Manufacturing Overhead. Why was the debit made to Manufacturing Overhead instead of Work in Process Inventory?
7. Why is the salary of a production worker capitalized while the salary of a marketing manager is expensed?
8. Al Carmon says that his company has a difficult time establishing a predetermined overhead rate because the number of units of product produced during a period is difficult to measure. What are two measures of production other than the number of units of product that Mr. Carmon could use to establish a predetermined overhead rate?
9. What do the terms *overapplied overhead* and *underapplied overhead* mean?
10. What are *product costs* and *selling, general, and administrative costs?* Give examples of product costs and of selling, general, and administrative costs.
11. How does the entry to close an insignificant amount of overapplied overhead to the Cost of Goods Sold account affect net income?
12. Why are actual overhead costs not used in determining periodic product cost?
13. Because of seasonal fluctuations, Buresch Corporation has a problem determining the unit cost of its products. For example, high heating costs during the winter months cause the cost per unit to be higher than the per-unit cost in the summer months even when the same number of units of product is produced. Suggest how Buresch can improve the computation of per-unit cost.
14. What is the purpose of the Manufacturing Overhead account?
15. For what purpose is the schedule of cost of goods manufactured and sold prepared? Do all companies use the statement?
16. How does the variable costing approach differ from the absorption costing approach? Explain the different income statement formats used with each approach.
17. How is profitability affected by increases in productivity under the variable and absorption costing approaches?
18. Under what circumstance is a variable costing statement format used? What potential problem could it eliminate?

MULTIPLE-CHOICE QUESTIONS

Multiple-choice questions are available in *Connect*.

EXERCISES—SERIES A

connect **All applicable Exercises in Series A are available in *Connect*.**

Exercise 11-1A *Employee compensation—Asset or expense* LO 11-1

Cray Company started Year 2 with $60,000 in its cash and common stock accounts. During Year 2 Cray paid $45,000 cash for employee compensation. Assume this is the only transaction that occurred in Year 2.

Required

a. Determine the total amount of assets at the end of Year 2, assuming Cray is a manufacturing company and the employees were paid to make products.

b. Determine the amount of expense recognized on the Year 2 income statement, assuming Cray is a manufacturing company and the employees were paid to make products.

c. Determine the total amount of assets at the end of Year 2, assuming Cray is a service company.

d. Determine the amount of expense recognized on the Year 2 income statement, assuming Cray is a service company.

LO 11-1

Exercise 11-2A *Materials and compensation costs in manufacturing versus service companies*

Morland Company started Year 1 with $75,000 in its cash and common stock accounts. During Year 1, Morland paid $50,000 cash for employee compensation and $17,500 cash for materials.

Required

a. Determine the total amount of assets and the amount of expense shown on the Year 1 financial statements assuming Morland used the labor and materials to make 1,500 chairs. Further, assume that Morland sold 1,200 of the chairs it made. State the name(s) of the expense account(s) shown on the income statement.

b. Determine the total amount of assets and the amount of expense shown on the Year 1 financial statements assuming Morland used the labor and materials to provide dental cleaning services to 500 patients. State the name(s) of the expense account(s) shown on the income statement.

LO 11-1, 11-2

Exercise 11-3A *Effect of accounting events on financial statements*

Required

Use a horizontal statements model to indicate how each of the following independent accounting events affects the elements of the balance sheet and the income statement. Indicate whether the event increases (I), decreases (D), or does not affect (NA) each element of the statements. The first two transactions are shown as examples.

a. Paid cash to purchase raw materials.
b. Recorded cash sales revenue.
c. Paid cash for actual manufacturing overhead cost.
d. Closed the Manufacturing Overhead account when overhead was overapplied.
e. Transferred cost of completed inventory to finished goods.
f. Paid cash for wages of production workers.
g. Paid cash for salaries of selling and administrative personnel.
h. Recorded adjusting entry to recognize amount of manufacturing supplies used (the company uses the periodic inventory method to account for manufacturing supplies).

Event No.	Balance Sheet				Income Statement		
	Assets =	Liab. +	C. Stk +	Ret Ear.	Rev. −	Exp. =	Net Inc.
a.	ID	NA	NA	NA	NA	NA	NA
b.	I	NA	NA	I	I	NA	I

LO 11-2

Exercise 11-4A *Calculating applied overhead*

Aurora Inc. estimates manufacturing overhead costs for the Year 3 accounting period as follows.

Equipment depreciation	$344,000
Supplies	42,000
Materials handling	68,000
Property taxes	30,000
Production setup	42,000
Rent	70,000
Maintenance	60,000
Supervisory salaries	244,000

The company uses a predetermined overhead rate based on machine hours. Estimated hours for labor in Year 3 were 200,000 and for machines were 125,000.

Required

a. Calculate the predetermined overhead rate.
b. Determine the amount of manufacturing overhead applied to Work in Process Inventory during the Year 3 period if actual machine hours were 140,000.

Exercise 11-5A *Treatment of overapplied or underapplied overhead*

LO 11-2

Pawhuska Company estimates that its overhead costs for Year 2 will be $720,000 and output in units of product will be 300,000 units.

Required

a. Calculate Pawhuska's predetermined overhead rate based on expected production.

b. If 24,000 units of product were made in March Year 2, how much overhead cost would be allocated to the Work in Process Inventory account during the month?

c. If actual overhead costs in March were $58,800, would overhead be overapplied or underapplied and by how much?

Exercise 11-6A *Recording overhead costs in T-accounts*

LO 11-2

Tescott Company and Heizer Company both apply overhead to the Work in Process Inventory account using direct labor hours. The following information is available for both companies for the year.

	Tescott Company	Heizer Company
Actual manufacturing overhead	$320,000	$600,000
Actual direct labor hours	20,000	24,000
Underapplied overhead		24,000
Overapplied overhead	$ 48,000	

Required

a. Compute the predetermined overhead rate for each company.

b. Using T-accounts, record the entry to close the overapplied or underapplied overhead at the end of the accounting period for each company, assuming the amounts are immaterial.

Exercise 11-7A *Treatment of overapplied or underapplied overhead*

LO 11-2

Logan Company and Clayton Company assign manufacturing overhead to Work in Process Inventory using direct labor cost. The following information is available for the companies for the year:

	Logan Company	Clayton Company
Actual direct labor cost	$200,000	$112,500
Estimated direct labor cost	187,500	125,000
Actual manufacturing overhead cost	72,500	95,000
Estimated manufacturing overhead cost	75,000	100,000

Required

a. Compute the predetermined overhead rate for each company.

b. Determine the amount of overhead cost that would be applied to Work in Process Inventory for each company.

c. Compute the amount of overapplied or underapplied manufacturing overhead cost for each company.

Exercise 11-8A *Recording manufacturing overhead costs in T-accounts*

LO 11-2

Danbury Corporation manufactures model airplanes. The company purchased for $228,000 automated production equipment that can make the model parts. The equipment has a $12,000 salvage value and a 10-year useful life.

Required

a. Assuming that the equipment was purchased on January 1, record in T-accounts the adjusting entry that the company would make on December 31 to record depreciation on equipment.

b. In which month would the depreciation costs be assigned to units produced?

LO 11-2

Exercise 11-9A *Missing information in T-accounts*

Brandon Manufacturing recorded the following amounts in its inventory accounts in Year 2.

Raw Materials Inventory

70,000	(a)
16,000	

Work in Process Inventory

	56,000
32,000	
24,000	
(c)	

Finished Goods Inventory

56,000	(d)
2,000	

Cost of Goods Sold

(e)	

Manufacturing Overhead

(b)	24,000
2,000	

Required

Determine the dollar amounts for (a), (b), (c), (d), and (e). Assume that underapplied and overapplied overhead is closed to Cost of Goods Sold.

LO 11-2

Exercise 11-10A *Smoothed unit cost*

Stoneham Manufacturing estimated its product costs and volume of production for Year 3 by quarter as follows.

	First Quarter	Second Quarter	Third Quarter	Fourth Quarter
Direct raw materials	$ 96,000	$ 48,000	$144,000	$ 72,000
Direct labor	57,600	28,800	86,400	43,200
Manufacturing overhead	48,000	100,800	172,800	86,400
Total production costs	$201,600	$177,600	$403,200	$201,600
Expected units produced	16,000	8,000	24,000	12,000

Stoneham Company sells a souvenir item at various resorts across the country. Its management uses the product's estimated quarterly cost to determine the selling price of its product. The company expects a large variance in demand for the product between quarters due to its seasonal nature. The company does not expect overhead costs, which are predominately fixed, to vary significantly as to production volume or with amounts for previous years. Prices are established by using a cost-plus pricing strategy. The company finds variations in short-term unit cost confusing to use. Unit cost variations complicate pricing decisions and many other decisions for which cost is a consideration.

Required

Round computations to two decimal points.

a. Based on estimated total production cost, determine the expected quarterly cost per unit for Stoneham's product.

b. How could overhead costs be estimated each quarter to solve the company's unit cost problem? Calculate the unit cost per quarter based on your recommendation.

LO 11-3

Exercise 11-11A *Preparing financial statements*

Rockeagle Corporation began fiscal Year 2 with the following balances in its inventory accounts.

Raw Materials	$30,000
Work in Process	45,000
Finished Goods	14,000

During the accounting period, Rockeagle purchased $125,000 of raw materials and issued $124,000 of materials to the production department. Direct labor costs for the period amounted to $162,000, and manufacturing overhead of $24,000 was applied to Work in Process Inventory. Assume that there was no over- or underapplied overhead. Goods costing $306,000 to produce were completed and transferred to Finished Goods Inventory. Goods costing $301,000 were sold for $400,000 during the period. Selling and administrative expenses amounted to $36,000.

Required

a. Determine the ending balance of each of the three inventory accounts that would appear on the year-end balance sheet.

b. Prepare a schedule of cost of goods manufactured and sold and an income statement.

Exercise 11-12A *Missing information in a schedule of cost of goods manufactured*

LO 11-3

Required

Supply the missing information on the following schedule of cost of goods manufactured.

BOULDER CORPORATION Schedule of Cost of Goods Manufactured For the Year Ended December 31, Year 2		
Raw materials		
Beginning inventory	$?	
Plus: Purchases	240,000	
Raw materials available for use	$296,000	
Minus: Ending raw materials inventory	?	
Cost of direct raw materials used		$248,000
Direct labor		?
Manufacturing overhead		48,000
Total manufacturing costs		648,000
Plus: Beginning work in process inventory		?
Total work in process		?
Minus: Ending work in process inventory		92,000
Cost of goods manufactured		$640,000

Exercise 11-13A *Cost of goods manufactured and sold*

LO 11-3

The following information pertains to Bairoil Manufacturing Company for March Year 3. Assume actual overhead equaled applied overhead.

March 1	
Inventory balances	
Raw materials	$200,000
Work in process	240,000
Finished goods	156,000
March 31	
Inventory balances	
Raw materials	$120,000
Work in process	290,000
Finished goods	160,000
During March	
Costs of raw materials purchased	$240,000
Costs of direct labor	200,000
Costs of manufacturing overhead	126,000
Sales revenues	760,000

Required

a. Prepare a schedule of cost of goods manufactured and sold.

b. Calculate the amount of gross margin on the income statement.

LO 11-1, 11-2, 11-3

Exercise 11-14A *Product cost flow and financial statements*

Loveland Manufacturing Company was started on January 1, Year 1. The company was affected by the following events during its first year of operation.

1. Acquired $2,400 cash from the issue of common stock.
2. Paid $720 cash for direct raw materials.
3. Transferred $480 of direct raw materials to work in process.
4. Paid production employees $720 cash.
5. Paid $360 cash for manufacturing overhead costs.
6. Applied $294 of manufacturing overhead costs to work in process.
7. Completed work on products that cost $1,200.
8. Sold products that cost $960 for $1,680 cash.
9. Paid $480 cash for selling and administrative expenses.
10. Made a $60 cash distribution to the owners.
11. Closed the Manufacturing Overhead account.

Required

a. Record these events in a horizontal statements model. The first event is shown as an example.

	Balance Sheet																	
	Assets									=	Equity			Income Statement				
Event No.	Cash	+	MOH	+	Raw M.	+	WIP	+	F. Goods	=	C. Stk.	+	Ret. Ear.	Rev.	−	Exp.	=	Net Inc.
1.	2,400	+	NA	+	NA	+	NA	+	NA	=	2,400	+	NA	NA	−	NA	=	NA

b. Prepare a schedule of cost of goods manufactured and sold.

LO 11-1, 11-2, 11-3

Exercise 11-15A *Recording events in T-accounts and preparing financial statements*

Newcomb Manufacturing Company was started on January 1, Year 1, when it acquired $5,000 cash from the issue of common stock. During the first year of operation, $1,600 of direct raw materials was purchased with cash, and $1,200 of the materials was used to make products. Direct labor costs of $2,000 were paid in cash. Newcomb applied $1,280 of overhead cost to the Work in Process account. Cash payments of $1,280 were made for actual overhead costs. The company completed products that cost $3,200 and sold goods that had cost $2,400 for $4,000 cash. Selling and administrative expenses of $960 were paid in cash.

Required

a. Open T-accounts and record the events affecting Newcomb Manufacturing. Include closing entries.

b. Prepare a schedule of cost of goods manufactured and sold, an income statement, and a balance sheet.

c. Explain the difference between net income and net cash flow.

LO 11-4

Exercise 11-16A *Variable costing versus absorption costing*

Dilia Company incurred manufacturing overhead cost for the year as follows.

Direct materials	$50/unit
Direct labor	$35/unit
Manufacturing overhead	
Variable	$15/unit
Fixed ($25/unit for 1,500 units)	$37,500
Variable selling and admin. expenses	$10,500
Fixed selling and admin. expenses	$20,000

The company produced 1,500 units and sold 1,200 of them at $225 per unit. Assume that the production manager is paid a 2 percent bonus based on the company's net income.

Required

a. Prepare an income statement using absorption costing.

b. Prepare an income statement using variable costing.

c. Determine the manager's bonus using each approach. Which approach would you recommend for internal reporting and why?

PROBLEMS—SERIES A

connect All applicable Problems in Series A are available in *Connect*.

Problem 11-17A *Manufacturing cost flow across three accounting cycles*

LO 11-1, 11-2, 11-3

The following accounting events affected Stratford Manufacturing Company during its first three years of operation. Assume that all transactions are cash transactions.

CHECK FIGURE
b. Cost of goods sold for Year 1: $289;
Total assets for Year 1: $2,076

Transactions for Year 1

1. Started manufacturing company by issuing common stock for $2,000.
2. Purchased $600 of direct raw materials.
3. Used $400 of direct raw materials to produce inventory.
4. Paid $200 of direct labor wages to employees to make inventory.
5. Applied $125 of manufacturing overhead cost to Work in Process Inventory.
6. Finished work on inventory that cost $450.
7. Sold goods that cost $300 for $550.
8. Paid $185 for selling and administrative expenses.
9. Actual manufacturing overhead cost amounted to $114 for the year.

Transactions for Year 2

1. Acquired additional $400 of cash from common stock.
2. Purchased $600 of direct raw materials.
3. Used $650 of direct raw materials to produce inventory.
4. Paid $300 of direct labor wages to employees to make inventory.
5. Applied $160 of manufacturing overhead cost to Work in Process Inventory.
6. Finished work on inventory that cost $900.
7. Sold goods that cost $800 for $1,400.
8. Paid $250 for selling and administrative expenses.
9. Actual manufacturing overhead cost amounted to $165 for the year.

Transactions for Year 3

1. Paid a cash dividend of $350.
2. Purchased $700 of direct raw materials.
3. Used $600 of direct raw materials to produce inventory.
4. Paid $220 of direct labor wages to employees to make inventory.
5. Applied $145 of manufacturing overhead cost to work in process.
6. Finished work on inventory that cost $1,000.
7. Sold goods that cost $1,100 for $1,750.
8. Paid $355 for selling and administrative expenses.
9. Annual manufacturing overhead costs were $140 for the year.

Required

a. Record the preceding events in a horizontal statements model. Close overapplied or underapplied overhead to Cost of Goods Sold. The first event is shown as an example.

Event No.	Balance Sheet																	Income Statement				
	Assets									=	Equity											
	Cash	+	MOH	+	Raw M.	+	WIP	+	F. Goods	=	C. Stk.	+	Ret. Ear.					Rev.	−	Exp.	=	Net Inc.
1.	2,000	+	NA	+	NA	+	NA	+	NA	=	2,000	+	NA					NA	−	NA	=	NA

b. Prepare a schedule of cost of goods manufactured and sold, an income statement, and a balance sheet as of the close of business on December 31, Year 1.

c. Close appropriate accounts.

d. Repeat Requirements *a* through *c* for Years 2 and 3.

LO 11-1, 11-2, 11-3

CHECK FIGURE

b. Cost of goods sold: $6,099; Total assets: $15,039

Problem 11-18A *Manufacturing cost flow for monthly and annual accounting periods*

Evelyn Carter started Carter Manufacturing Company to make a universal television remote control device that she had invented. The company's labor force consisted of part-time employees. The following accounting events affected Carter Manufacturing Company during its first year of operation. (Assume that all transactions are cash transactions unless otherwise stated.)

Transactions for January Year 1, First Month of Operation

1. Issued common stock for $3,000.
2. Purchased $210 of direct raw materials and $30 of production supplies.
3. Used $120 of direct raw materials.
4. Used 80 direct labor hours; production workers were paid $4.80 per hour.
5. Expected total overhead costs for the year to be $1,650 and direct labor hours used during the year to be 1,000. Calculate an overhead rate and apply the appropriate amount of overhead costs to Work in Process Inventory.
6. Paid $72 for salaries to administrative and sales staff.
7. Paid $12 for indirect manufacturing labor.
8. Paid $105 for rent and utilities on the manufacturing facilities.
9. Started and completed 100 remote controls during the month; all costs were transferred from the Work in Process Inventory account to the Finished Goods Inventory account.
10. Sold 75 remote controls at a price of $10.80 each.

Transactions for Remainder of Year 1

11. Acquired an additional $9,000 by issuing common stock.
12. Purchased $1,950 of direct raw materials and $450 of production supplies.
13. Used $1,500 of direct raw materials.
14. Paid production workers $4.80 per hour for 900 hours of work.
15. Applied the appropriate overhead cost to Work in Process Inventory.
16. Paid $780 for salaries of administrative and sales staff.
17. Paid $120 of indirect manufacturing labor cost.
18. Paid $1,200 for rental and utility costs on the manufacturing facilities.
19. Transferred 950 additional remote controls that cost $6.36 each from the Work in Process Inventory account to the Finished Goods Inventory account.
20. Determined that $84 of production supplies was on hand at the end of the accounting period.
21. Sold 850 remote controls for $10.80 each.
22. Determine whether the overhead is over- or underapplied. Close the Manufacturing Overhead account to the Cost of Goods Sold account.
23. Close the revenue and expense accounts.

Required

a. Open T-accounts and post transactions to the accounts.
b. Prepare a schedule of cost of goods manufactured and sold, an income statement, and a balance sheet for Year 1.

Problem 11-19A *Manufacturing cost flow for one-year period*

LO 11-1, 11-2, 11-3

CHECK FIGURE
b. Total assets: $21,076

Blanding Manufacturing started in Year 1 with the following account balances.

Cash	$12,000
Common stock	10,000
Retained earnings	10,000
Raw materials inventory	2,400
Work in process inventory	1,600
Finished goods inventory (320 units @ $12.50 each)	4,000

Transactions during Year 1

1. Purchased $6,000 of raw materials with cash.
2. Transferred $7,500 of raw materials to the production department.
3. Incurred and paid cash for 180 hours of direct labor @ $32 per hour.
4. Applied overhead costs to the Work in Process Inventory account. The predetermined overhead rate is $33.00 per direct labor hour.
5. Incurred actual overhead costs of $6,000 cash.
6. Completed work on 1,200 units for $12.80 per unit.
7. Paid $2,800 in selling and administrative expenses in cash.
8. Sold 1,200 units for $19,200 cash revenue (assume FIFO cost flow).
9. Blanding charges overapplied or underapplied overhead directly to Cost of Goods Sold.

Required

a. Record the preceding events in a horizontal statements model. The beginning balances are shown as an example.

	Balance Sheet														Income Statement				
	Assets									=	Equity								
Event No.	Cash	+	MOH	+	Raw M.	+	WIP	+	F. Goods	=	C. Stk.	+	Ret. Ear.		Rev.	−	Exp.	=	Net Inc.
1.	12,000	+	NA	+	2,400	+	1,600	+	4,000	=	10,000	+	10,000		NA	−	NA	=	NA

b. Prepare a schedule of cost of goods manufactured and sold, an income statement, and a balance sheet for Year 1.

Problem 11-20A *Manufacturing cost for one accounting cycle*

LO 11-1, 11-2, 11-3

excel

CHECK FIGURE
b. Total assets: $48,798

The following trial balance was taken from the records of Fairport Manufacturing Company at the beginning of Year 3.

Cash	$20,000	
Raw materials inventory	1,800	
Work in process inventory	2,400	
Finished goods inventory	4,200	
Property, plant, and equipment	15,000	
Accumulated depreciation		$ 6,000
Common stock		16,800
Retained earnings		20,600
Total	$43,400	$43,400

Transactions for the Accounting Period

1. Fairport purchased $11,400 of direct raw materials and $600 of indirect raw materials on account. The indirect materials are capitalized in the Production Supplies account. Materials requisitions showed that $10,800 of direct raw materials had been used for production during the period. The use of indirect materials is determined at the end of the year by physically counting the supplies on hand.
2. By the end of the year, $10,500 of the accounts payable had been paid in cash.
3. During the year, direct labor amounted to 950 hours recorded in the Wages Payable account at $21 per hour.
4. By the end of the year, $18,000 of wages payable had been paid in cash.
5. At the beginning of the year, the company expected overhead cost for the period to be $12,600 and 1,000 direct labor hours to be worked. Overhead is allocated based on direct labor hours, which, as indicated in Event 3, amounted to 950 for the year.
6. Selling and administrative expenses for the year amounted to $1,800 paid in cash.
7. Utilities and rent for production facilities amounted to $9,300 paid in cash.
8. Depreciation on the plant and equipment used in production amounted to $3,000.
9. There was $24,000 of goods completed during the year.
10. There was $25,500 of finished goods inventory sold for $36,000 cash.
11. A count of the production supplies revealed a balance of $178 on hand at the end of the year.
12. Any over- or underapplied overhead is considered to be insignificant.

Required

a. Open T-accounts with the beginning balances shown in the preceding list and record all transactions for the year, including closing entries in the T-accounts. (*Note:* Open new T-accounts as needed.)

b. Prepare a schedule of cost of goods manufactured and sold, an income statement, and a balance sheet.

LO 11-1, 11-2, 11-3

CHECK FIGURE

b. Total assets for Year 1: $162,860 NI for Year 2: $33,040

Problem 11-21A *Manufacturing cost flow for multiple accounting cycles*

The following events apply to Milligan Manufacturing Company. Assume that all transactions are cash transactions unless otherwise indicated.

Transactions for the Year 1 Accounting Period

1. The company was started on January 1, Year 1, when it acquired $140,000 cash by issuing common stock.
2. The company purchased $40,000 of direct raw materials with cash and used $2,430 of these materials to make its products in January.
3. Employees provided 900 hours of labor at $5.70 per hour during January. Wages are paid in cash.
4. The estimated manufacturing overhead costs for Year 1 were $64,800. Overhead is applied on the basis of direct labor hours. The company expected to use 12,000 direct labor hours during Year 1. Calculate an overhead rate and apply the overhead for January to work in process inventory.
5. The employees completed work on all inventory items started in January. The cost of this production was transferred to the Finished Goods Inventory account. Determine the cost per unit of product produced in January, assuming that a total of 1,800 units of product were started and completed during the month.
6. The company used an additional $31,050 of direct raw materials and 11,500 hours of direct labor at $5.70 per hour during the remainder of Year 1. Overhead was allocated on the basis of direct labor hours.
7. The company completed work on inventory items started between February 1 and December 31, and the cost of the completed inventory was transferred to the Finished Goods Inventory account. Determine the cost per unit for goods produced between February 1 and December 31, assuming that 23,000 units of inventory were produced. If the company desires to earn a gross profit of $2.70 per unit, what price per unit must it charge for the merchandise sold?
8. The company sold 22,000 units of inventory for cash at $9.60 per unit. Determine the number of units in ending inventory and the cost per unit incurred for this inventory.

9. Actual manufacturing overhead costs paid in cash were $65,700.
10. The company paid $37,800 cash for selling and administrative expenses.
11. Close the Manufacturing Overhead account.
12. Close the revenue and expense accounts.

Transactions for the Year 2 Accounting Period

1. The company purchased $40,500 of direct raw materials with cash and used $2,280 of these materials to make products in January.
2. Employees provided 800 hours of labor at $5.70 per hour during January.
3. On January 1, Year 2, Milligan hired a production supervisor at an expected cost of $1,080 cash per month. The company paid cash to purchase $4,500 of manufacturing supplies; it anticipated that $4,140 of these supplies would be used by year-end. Other manufacturing overhead costs (production supplies) were expected to total $64,800. Overhead is applied on the basis of direct labor hours. Milligan expected to use 14,000 hours of direct labor during Year 2. Based on this information, determine the total expected overhead cost for Year 2. Calculate the predetermined overhead rate and apply the overhead cost for the January production.
4. The company recorded a $1,080 cash payment to the production supervisor.
5. The employees completed work on all inventory items started in January. The cost of this production was transferred to the Finished Goods Inventory account. Determine the cost per unit of product produced in January, assuming that 1,600 units of product were started and completed during the month.
6. During February Year 2, the company used $2,850 of raw materials and 1,000 hours of labor at $5.70 per hour. Overhead was allocated on the basis of direct labor hours.
7. The company recorded a $1,080 cash payment to the production supervisor for February.
8. The employees completed work on all inventory items started in February; the cost of this production was transferred to the Finished Goods Inventory account. Determine the cost per unit of product produced in February, assuming that 2,000 units of product were started and completed during the month.
9. The company used an additional $34,200 of direct raw materials and 12,000 hours of direct labor at $5.70 per hour during the remainder of Year 2. Overhead was allocated on the basis of direct labor hours.
10. The company recorded $10,800 of cash payments to the production supervisor for work performed between March 1 and December 31.
11. The company completed work on inventory items started between March 1 and December 31. The cost of the completed goods was transferred to the Finished Goods Inventory account. Compute the cost per unit of this inventory, assuming that there were 24,000 units of inventory produced.
12. The company sold 26,000 units of product for $9.90 cash per unit. Assume that the company uses the FIFO inventory cost flow method to determine the cost of goods sold.
13. The company paid $38,700 cash for selling and administrative expenses.
14. As of December 31, Year 2, $450 of production supplies was on hand.
15. Actual cost of other manufacturing overhead was $63,020 cash.
16. Close the Manufacturing Overhead account.
17. Close the revenue and expense accounts.

Required

a. Open T-accounts and record the effects of the preceding events.

b. Prepare a schedule of cost of goods manufactured and sold, an income statement, and a balance sheet for each year.

Problem 11-22A *Comprehensive review problem*

LO 11-1, 11-2, 11-3

CHECK FIGURE

c. Cost per computer with 2,000 units produced: $199.84

During their senior year at Clarkson College, two business students, Gerry Keating and Louis Lamont, began a part-time business making personal computers. They bought the various components from a local supplier and assembled the machines in the basement of a friend's house. Their only cost was $216 for parts; they sold each computer for $360. They were able to make three machines per week and to sell them to fellow students. The activity was appropriately called Keating & Lamont Computers (KLC). The product quality was good, and as graduation approached, orders were coming in much faster than KLC could fill them.

A national CPA firm made Ms. Lamont an attractive offer of employment, and a large electronics company was ready to hire Mr. Keating. Students and faculty at Clarkson College, however, encouraged the two to make KLC a full-time venture. The college administration had decided to require all students in the schools of business and engineering to buy their own computers beginning in the coming fall term. It was believed that the quality and price of the KLC machines would attract the college bookstore to sign a contract to buy a minimum of 1,000 units the first year for $400 each. The bookstore sales were likely to reach 2,000 units per year, but the manager would not make an initial commitment beyond 1,000.

The prospect of $400,000 in annual sales for KLC caused the two young entrepreneurs to wonder about the wisdom of accepting their job offers. Before making a decision, they decided to investigate the implications of making KLC a full-time operation. Their study provided the following information relating to the production of their computers.

Components from wholesaler	$ 160 per computer
Assembly labor	12 per hour
Manufacturing space rent	1,800 per month
Utilities	360 per month
Janitorial services	288 per month
Depreciation of equipment	2,304 per year
Labor	2 hours per computer

The two owners expected to devote their time to the sales and administrative aspects of the business.

Required

a. Classify each cost item into the categories of direct materials, direct labor, and manufacturing overhead.

b. Classify each cost item as either variable or fixed.

c. What is the cost per computer if KLC produces 1,000 units per year? What is the cost per unit if KLC produces 2,000 units per year?

d. If the job offers for Mr. Keating and Ms. Lamont totaled $100,000, would you recommend that they accept the offers or proceed with plans to make KLC a full-time venture?

LO 11-4

eXcel

Problem 11-23A *Absorption versus variable costing*

Fulton Manufacturing Company makes a product that sells for $64 per unit. Manufacturing costs for the product amount to $24 per unit variable, and $96,000 fixed. During the current accounting period, Fulton made 4,000 units of the product and sold 3,500 units. Selling and administrative expenses were zero.

CHECK FIGURES
a. NI: $56,000
b. NI: $44,000

Required

a. Prepare an absorption costing income statement.

b. Prepare a variable costing income statement.

c. Explain why the amount of net income on the absorption costing income statement differs from the amount of net income on the variable costing income statement. Your answer should include the amount of the inventory balance that would exist under the two costing approaches.

LO 11-4

Problem 11-24A *Absorption versus variable costing*

Cloverton Glass Company makes stained glass lamps. Each lamp that it sells for $128 requires $20 of direct materials and $32 of direct labor. Fixed overhead costs are expected to be $72,000 per year. Cloverton Glass expects to sell 1,000 lamps during the coming year. Selling and administrative expenses were zero.

Required

a. Prepare income statements using absorption costing, assuming that Cloverton Glass makes 1,000, 1,250, and 1,500 lamps during the year.

b. Prepare income statements using variable costing, assuming that Cloverton Glass makes 1,000, 1,250, and 1,500 lamps during the year.

c. Explain why Cloverton Glass may produce income statements under both absorption and variable costing formats. Your answer should include an explanation of the advantages and disadvantages associated with the use of the two reporting formats.

CHECK FIGURES
a. NI when 1,500 lamps are produced: $28,000
b. NI when 1,500 lamps are produced: $4,000

Problem 11-25A *Absorption and variable costing*

LO 11-4

excel

Levine Manufacturing pays its production managers a bonus based on the company's profitability. During the two most recent years, the company maintained the same cost structure to manufacture its products.

CHECK FIGURES
a. NI for Year 2 $48,000
d. $276,000

Year	Units Produced	Units Sold
Production and Sales		
Year 2	4,000	4,000
Year 3	6,000	4,000
Cost Data		
Direct materials		$30 per unit
Direct labor		$48 per unit
Manufacturing overhead—variable		$24 per unit
Manufacturing overhead—fixed		$216,000
Variable selling and administrative expenses		$18 per unit sold
Fixed selling and administrative expenses		$120,000

(Assume that selling and administrative expenses are associated with goods sold.)

Levine sells its products for $216 per unit.

Required

a. Prepare income statements based on absorption costing for Year 2 and Year 3.

b. Since Levine sold the same number of units in Year 2 and Year 3, why did net income increase in Year 3?

c. Discuss management's possible motivation for increasing production in Year 3.

d. Determine the costs of ending inventory for Year 3. Comment on the risks and costs associated with the accumulation of inventory.

e. Based on your answers to Requirements *b* and *c*, suggest a different income statement format. Prepare income statements for Year 2 and Year 3 using your suggested format.

EXERCISES—SERIES B

Exercise 11-1B *Employee compensation–Asset or expense*

LO 11-1

Chadron Inc. started Year 3 with $52,500 in its cash and common stock accounts. During Year 3, Chadron paid $42,500 cash for employee compensation.

Required

Based on this information alone:

a. Determine the total amount of assets at the end of Year 3, assuming Chadron is a manufacturing company and the employees were paid to make products.

b. Determine the amount of expense recognized on the Year 3 income statement, assuming Chadron is a manufacturing company and the employees were paid to make products.

c. Determine the total amount of assets at the end of Year 3, assuming Chadron is a service company.

d. Determine the amount of expense recognized on the Year 3 income statement, assuming Chadron is a service company.

LO 11-1

Exercise 11-2B *Materials and compensation costs in manufacturing versus service companies*

Fremont Company started Year 1 with $248,000 in its cash and common stock accounts. During Year 1, Fremont paid $160,000 cash for employee compensation and $68,000 cash for materials.

Required

a. Determine the total amount of assets and the amount of expense shown on the Year 1 financial statements assuming Fremont used the labor and materials to make 228 tables. Further, assume that Fremont sold 200 of the tables it made. State the name(s) of the expense account(s) shown on the income statement.

b. Determine the total amount of assets and the amount of expense shown on the Year 1 financial statements assuming Fremont used the labor and materials to provide medical services to 500 patients. State the name(s) of the expense account(s) shown on the income statement.

LO 11-1, 11-2

Exercise 11-3B *Effect of accounting events on financial statements*

Required

Use a horizontal statements model to show how each of the following independent accounting events affects the elements of the balance sheet and the income statement. Indicate whether the event increases (I), decreases (D), or does not affect (NA) each element of the financial statements. The first two transactions are shown as examples.

a. Paid cash to purchase raw materials.

b. Recorded cash sales revenue.

c. Applied overhead to Work in Process Inventory based on the predetermined overhead rate.

d. Closed the Manufacturing Overhead account when overhead was underapplied.

e. Recognized cost of goods sold.

f. Recognized depreciation expense on manufacturing equipment.

g. Purchased manufacturing supplies on account.

h. Sold fully depreciated manufacturing equipment for the exact amount of its salvage value.

Event No.	Balance Sheet							Income Statement				
	Assets	=	Liab.	+	C. Stk	+	Ret Ear.	Rev.	−	Exp.	=	Net Inc.
a.	I D		NA		NA		NA	NA		NA		NA
b.	I		NA		NA		I	I		NA		I

LO 11-2

Exercise 11-4B *Calculating applied overhead*

Creswell Enterprises' budget included the following estimated costs for the Year 3 accounting period

Depreciation on manufacturing equipment	$ 30,400
Cost of manufacturing supplies	6,000
Direct labor cost	172,800
Rent on manufacturing facility	15,200
Direct materials cost	148,000
Manufacturing utilities cost	12,000
Maintenance cost for manufacturing facility	8,400
Administrative salaries cost	61,000

The company uses a predetermined overhead rate based on machine hours. It estimated machine hour usage for Year 3 would be 30,000 hours.

Required

a. Identify the manufacturing overhead costs Creswell would use to calculate the predetermined overhead rate.

b. Calculate the predetermined overhead rate.

c. Explain why the rate is called "predetermined."

d. Assuming Creswell actually used 31,000 machine hours during Year 3, determine the amount of manufacturing overhead it would have applied to Work in Process Inventory during the period.

Exercise 11-5B *Treatment of overapplied or underapplied overhead*

LO 11-2

On January 1, Year 2, Tinicum Company estimated that its total overhead costs for the coming year would be $646,000 and that it would make 34,000 units of product. Tinicum actually produced 34,600 units of product and incurred actual overhead costs of $638,000 during Year 2.

Required

a. Calculate Tinicum's predetermined overhead rate based on expected costs and production.

b. Determine whether overhead was overapplied or underapplied during Year 2.

c. Explain how the entry to close the Manufacturing Overhead account will affect the Cost of Goods Sold account.

Exercise 11-6B *Recording overhead costs in a T-account*

LO 11-2

Pleasant Hill Manufacturing Company incurred actual overhead costs of $312,000 during Year 2. It uses direct labor dollars as the allocation base for overhead costs. In Year 2, actual direct labor costs were $400,000, and overhead costs were underapplied by $4,000.

Required

a. Calculate the predetermined overhead rate for Year 2.

b. Open T-accounts for Manufacturing Overhead and Cost of Goods Sold. Record the overhead costs and the adjusting entry to close Manufacturing Overhead in these accounts.

c. Explain how the entry to close the Manufacturing Overhead account at the end of Year 2 would affect the amount of net income reported on the Year 2 income statement.

Exercise 11-7B *Treatment of overapplied or underapplied overhead*

LO 11-2

Creek Company and Fort Company base their predetermined overhead rates on machine hours. The following information pertains to the companies' most recent accounting periods.

	Creek	Fort
Actual machine hours	12,300	19,500
Estimated machine hours	12,000	20,000
Actual manufacturing overhead costs	$143,800	$318,000
Estimated manufacturing overhead costs	$144,000	$320,000

Required

a. Compute the predetermined overhead rate for each company.

b. Determine the amount of overhead cost that would be applied to work in process for each company and compute the amount of overapplied or underapplied manufacturing overhead cost for each company.

c. Explain how closing the Manufacturing Overhead account would affect the Cost of Goods Sold account for each company.

Exercise 11-8B *Recording manufacturing overhead costs*

LO 11-2

Lincoln Manufacturing Company incurred the following actual manufacturing overhead costs: (1) cash paid for plant supervisor's salary, $43,000; (2) depreciation on manufacturing equipment, $15,000; and (3) manufacturing supplies used, $1,150 (Lincoln uses the periodic inventory method for manufacturing supplies). Applied overhead amounted to $58,000.

Required

a. Open the appropriate T-accounts and record the manufacturing overhead costs described.

b. Record the entry Lincoln would make to close the Manufacturing Overhead account to Cost of Goods Sold.

LO 11-2

Exercise 11-9B *Missing information in inventory T-accounts*

The following incomplete T-accounts were drawn from the records of Richland Manufacturing Company.

Raw Materials Inventory	
15,000	(a)
600	

Work in Process Inventory	
	29,000
8,400	
(b)	

Finished Goods Inventory	
(c)	
3,000	

Cost of Goods Sold	
(d)	

Manufacturing Overhead	
8,500	(e)
	400

Required

Determine the dollar amounts for (a), (b), (c), (d), and (e). Assume that underapplied and overapplied overhead is closed to Cost of Goods Sold.

LO 11-2

Exercise 11-10B *Smoothing unit cost*

Unit-level (variable) manufacturing costs for Jacinto Manufacturing Company amount to $8. Fixed manufacturing costs are $9,000 per month. Production workers provided 800 hours of direct labor in January and 1,400 hours in February. Jacinto expects to use 12,000 hours of labor during the year. It actually produced 1,200 units of product in January and 2,100 units of product in February.

Required

a. For each month, determine the total product cost and the per-unit product cost, assuming that actual fixed overhead costs are charged to monthly production.

b. Use a predetermined overhead rate based on direct labor hours to allocate the fixed overhead costs to each month's production. For each month, calculate the total product cost and the per-unit product cost.

c. Jacinto employs a cost-plus pricing strategy. Would you recommend charging production with actual or allocated fixed overhead costs? Explain.

LO 11-3

Exercise 11-11B *Preparing financial statements*

Hayward Manufacturing Company started Year 2 with the following balances in its inventory accounts: Raw Materials, $3,000; Work in Process, $3,600; Finished Goods, $3,960. During Year 2, Hayward purchased $20,400 of raw materials and issued $19,800 of materials to the production department. It incurred $22,800 of direct labor costs and applied manufacturing overhead of $22,440 to Work in Process Inventory. Assume there was no over- or underapplied overhead at the end of the year. Hayward completed goods costing $63,000 to produce and transferred them to finished goods inventory. During the year, Hayward sold goods costing $60,840 for $92,280. Selling and administrative expenses for Year 2 were $21,600.

Required

a. Using T-accounts, determine the ending balance Hayward would report for each of the three inventory accounts that would appear on the December 31, Year 2, balance sheet.

b. Prepare the Year 2 schedule of cost of goods manufactured and sold and the Year 2 income statement.

Exercise 11-12B *Missing information in a schedule of cost of goods manufactured and sold*

LO 11-3

Required

Supply the missing information on the following schedule of cost of goods manufactured and sold.

HAMLET CORPORATION
Schedule of Cost of Goods Manufactured and Sold
For the Year Ended December 31, Year 2

Raw materials	
Beginning inventory	$ 60,000
Plus: Purchases	?
Raw materials available for use	340,000
Minus: Ending raw materials inventory	?
Cost of direct raw materials used	310,000
Direct labor	240,000
Manufacturing overhead	?
Total manufacturing costs	750,000
Plus: Beginning work in process inventory	?
Total work in process during the year	786,000
Minus: Ending work in process inventory	(36,000)
Cost of goods manufactured	?
Plus: Beginning finished goods inventory	?
Finished goods available for sale	798,000
Minus: Ending finished goods inventory	?
Cost of goods sold	$756,000

Exercise 11-13B *Cost of goods manufactured and sold*

LO 11-3

The following information was drawn from the accounting records of Boulder Manufacturing Company.

	Beginning	Ending
Raw materials inventory	$ 8,000	$ 9,000
Work in process inventory	12,400	10,000
Finished goods inventory	13,600	12,000

During the accounting period, Boulder paid $32,000 to purchase raw materials, $30,000 for direct labor, and $22,000 for overhead costs. Assume that actual overhead equaled applied overhead.

Required

a. Determine the amount of raw materials used.

b. Determine the amount of cost of goods manufactured (the amount transferred from Work in Process Inventory to Finished Goods Inventory).

c. Assuming sales revenue of $153,600, determine the amount of gross margin.

Exercise 11-14B *Product cost flow and financial statements*

LO 11-1, 11-2, 11-3

Moriarty Manufacturing began business on January 1, Year 1. The following events pertain to its first year of operation.

1. Acquired $4,000 cash by issuing common stock.
2. Paid $1,600 cash for direct raw materials.
3. Transferred $1,000 of direct raw materials to Work in Process Inventory.
4. Paid production employees $1,400 cash.

5. Applied $650 of manufacturing overhead costs to Work in Process Inventory.
6. Completed work on products that cost $2,200.
7. Sold products for $3,200 cash.
8. Recognized cost of goods sold from Event No. 7 of $1,750.
9. Paid $900 cash for selling and administrative expenses.
10. Paid $700 cash for actual manufacturing overhead costs.
11. Made a $400 cash distribution to owners.
12. Closed the Manufacturing Overhead account.

Required

a. Record the preceding events in a horizontal statements model. The first event is shown as an example.

Event No.	Balance Sheet													Income Statement				
	Assets									=	Equity							
	Cash	+	MOH	+	Raw M.	+	WIP	+	F. Goods	=	C. Stk.	+	Ret. Ear.	Rev.	−	Exp.	=	Net Inc.
1.	4,000	+	NA	+	NA	+	NA	+	NA	=	4,000	+	NA	NA	−	NA	=	NA

b. Prepare a schedule of cost of goods manufactured and sold.

LO 11-1, 11-2, 11-3

Exercise 11-15B *Recording events in T-accounts and preparing financial statements*

Susank Manufacturing Company was started on January 1, Year 1, when it acquired $1,250 cash by issuing common stock. During its first year of operation, it purchased $250 of direct raw materials with cash and used $180 of the materials to make products. Susank paid $320 of direct labor costs in cash. The company applied $232 of overhead costs to Work in Process Inventory. It made cash payments of $232 for actual overhead costs. The company completed products that cost $520 to make. It sold goods that had cost $412 to make for $680 cash. It paid $160 of selling and administrative expenses in cash.

Required

a. Open the necessary T-accounts and record the Year 1 events in the accounts. Include closing entries.
b. Prepare a schedule of cost of goods manufactured and sold, an income statement, and a balance sheet.

LO 11-4

Exercise 11-16B *Variable costing versus absorption costing*

The following information was drawn from the records of Shelby Company.

Variable costs (per unit)		Fixed costs (in total)	
Direct materials	$12	Manufacturing overhead	$24,000
Direct labor	9	Selling and administrative	26,000
Manufacturing overhead	3		
Selling and administrative	7		

During the most recent month, Shelby produced 4,000 units of product and sold 3,800 units of product at a sales price of $54 per unit.

Required

a. Prepare an income statement for the month using absorption costing.
b. Prepare an income statement for the month using variable costing.
c. Explain why a company might use one type of income statement for external reporting and a different type for internal reporting.

PROBLEMS—SERIES B

Problem 11-17B *Manufacturing cost flow across three accounting cycles*

LO 11-1, 11-2, 11-3

The following accounting events affected Carmel Manufacturing Company during its first three years of operation. Assume that all transactions are cash transactions.

Transactions for Year 1

1. Started manufacturing company by issuing common stock for $1,000.
2. Purchased $300 of direct raw materials.
3. Used $216 of direct raw materials to produce inventory.
4. Paid $180 of direct labor wages to employees to make inventory.
5. Applied $180 of manufacturing overhead to Work in Process Inventory.
6. Actual manufacturing overhead costs amounted to $183.
7. Finished work on inventory that cost $324.
8. Sold goods that cost $216 for $288.
9. Paid $18 for selling and administrative expenses.

Transactions for Year 2

1. Acquired additional $300 of cash from issuance of common stock.
2. Purchased $288 of direct raw materials.
3. Used $252 of direct raw materials to produce inventory.
4. Paid $216 of direct labor wages to employees to make inventory.
5. Applied $192 of manufacturing overhead to Work in Process Inventory.
6. Actual manufacturing overhead costs amounted to $189.
7. Finished work on inventory that cost $540.
8. Sold goods that cost $504 for $576.
9. Paid $36 for selling and administrative expenses.

Transactions for Year 3

1. Purchased $180 of direct raw materials.
2. Used $288 of direct raw materials to produce inventory.
3. Paid $108 of direct labor wages to employees to make inventory.
4. Applied $150 of manufacturing overhead to Work in Process Inventory.
5. Actual manufacturing overhead costs amounted to $156.
6. Finished work on inventory that cost $594.
7. Sold goods that cost $648 for $792.
8. Paid $72 for selling and administrative expenses.
9. Paid a cash dividend of $144.

Required

a. Record the preceding events in a horizontal statements model. Close overapplied or underapplied overhead to Cost of Goods Sold. The first event is shown as an example.

Event No.	Balance Sheet												Income Statement				
	Assets									=	Equity						
	Cash	+	MOH	+	Raw M.	+	WIP	+	F. Goods	=	C. Stk.	+	Ret. Ear.	Rev.	−	Exp.	=	Net Inc.
1.	1,000	+	NA	+	NA	+	NA	+	NA	=	1,000	+	NA	NA	−	NA	=	NA

b. Prepare a schedule of cost of goods manufactured and sold, an income statement, and a balance sheet as of the close of business on December 31, Year 1.

c. Close appropriate accounts to the Retained Earnings account.

d. Repeat Requirements *a* through *c* for Years 2 and 3.

LO 11-1, 11-2, 11-3

Problem 11-18B *Manufacturing cost for one accounting cycle*

The following trial balance was taken from the records of Ansgar Manufacturing Company at the beginning of Year 2.

Cash	$4,000	
Raw materials inventory	200	
Work in process inventory	300	
Finished goods inventory	200	
Property, plant, and equipment	3,500	
Accumulated depreciation		$1,000
Common stock		4,000
Retained earnings		3,200
Total	$8,200	$8,200

Transactions for the Accounting Period

1. Ansgar purchased $2,600 of direct raw materials and $300 of indirect raw materials on account. The indirect materials are capitalized in the Production Supplies account. Materials requisitions showed that $2,000 of direct raw materials had been used for production during the period. The use of indirect materials is determined at the end of the period by physically counting the supplies on hand at the end of the year.
2. By the end of the accounting period, $2,000 of the accounts payable had been paid in cash.
3. During the year, direct labor amounted to 1,200 hours recorded in the Wages Payable account at $3 per hour.
4. By the end of the accounting period, $3,250 of the Wages Payable account had been paid in cash.
5. At the beginning of the accounting period, the company expected overhead cost for the period to be $2,750 and 1,250 direct labor hours to be worked. Overhead is applied based on direct labor hours, which, as indicated in Event 3, amounted to 1,200 for the year.
6. Administrative and sales expenses for the period amounted to $700 paid in cash.
7. Utilities and rent for production facilities amounted to $1,500 paid in cash.
8. Depreciation on the plant and equipment used in production amounted to $1,000.
9. Assume that $7,500 of goods were completed during the period.
10. Assume that $5,000 of finished goods inventory was sold for $7,000 cash.
11. A count of the production supplies revealed a balance of $125 on hand at the end of the accounting period.
12. Any over- or underapplied overhead is considered to be insignificant.

Required

a. Open T-accounts with the beginning balances shown in the preceding list and record all transactions for the period including closing entries in the T-accounts. (*Note:* Open new T-accounts as needed.)

b. Prepare a schedule of cost of goods manufactured and sold, an income statement, and a balance sheet.

LO 11-1, 11-2, 11-3

Problem 11-19B *Manufacturing cost flow for one-year period*

Meadowbrook Manufacturing started Year 2 with the following account balances.

Cash	$7,000
Common stock	5,600
Retained earnings	2,800
Raw materials inventory	600
Work in process inventory	440
Finished goods inventory (50 units @ $7.20/unit)	360

Transactions during Year 2

1. Purchased $1,600 of raw materials with cash.
2. Transferred $1,000 of raw materials to the production department.
3. Incurred and paid cash for 80 hours of direct labor at $15 per hour.
4. Applied overhead costs to Work in Process Inventory. The predetermined overhead rate is $15 per direct labor hour.
5. Incurred actual overhead costs of $1,300 cash.
6. Completed work on 300 units for $7.20 per unit.
7. Paid $400 in selling and administrative expenses in cash.
8. Sold 200 units for $3,000 cash revenues. (Assume LIFO cost flow.)

Meadowbrook charges overapplied or underapplied overhead directly to Cost of Goods Sold.

Required

a. Record the preceding events in a horizontal statements model. The beginning balances are shown as an example.

Event No.	Balance Sheet												Income Statement				
	Assets									=	Equity						
	Cash	+	MOH	+	Raw M.	+	WIP	+	F. Goods	=	C. Stk.	+	Ret. Ear.	Rev.	−	Exp.	=	Net Inc.
1.	7,000	+	NA	+	600	+	440	+	360	=	5,600	+	2,800	NA	−	NA	=	NA

b. Prepare a schedule of cost of goods manufactured and sold, an income statement, and a balance sheet for Year 2.

Problem 11-20B *Manufacturing cost flow for monthly and annual accounting periods*

LO 11-1, 11-2, 11-3

Blanchard Manufacturing Company manufactures puzzles that depict the works of famous artists. The company rents a small factory and uses local labor on a part-time basis. The following accounting events affected Blanchard during its first year of operation. (Assume that all transactions are cash transactions unless otherwise stated.)

Transactions for First Month of Operation in Year 1

1. Issued common stock for $15,000.
2. Purchased $4,500 of direct raw materials and $600 of indirect raw materials. Indirect materials are recorded in a Production Supplies account.
3. Used $3,896 of direct raw materials.
4. Used 700 direct labor hours; production workers were paid $6 per hour.
5. Expected total overhead costs for the year to be $16,800 and direct labor hours used during the year to be 9,600. Calculate an overhead rate and apply the appropriate amount of overhead costs to Work in Process.
6. Paid $800 for salaries to administrative and sales staff.
7. Paid $700 for indirect manufacturing labor.
8. Paid $600 for rent and utilities on the manufacturing facilities.
9. Started and completed 956 puzzles; all costs were transferred from the Work in Process Inventory account to the Finished Goods Inventory account.
10. Sold 800 puzzles at a price of $12 each.

Transactions for Remainder of Year 1

11. Acquired an additional $150,000 by issuing common stock.
12. Purchased $46,000 of direct raw materials and $4,000 of indirect raw materials.
13. Used $41,050 of direct raw materials.
14. Paid production workers $6 per hour for 9,800 hours of work.
15. Applied the appropriate overhead cost to Work in Process Inventory.

16. Paid $8,800 for salaries of administrative and sales staff.
17. Paid $7,700 for the salary of the production supervisor.
18. Paid $6,600 for rental and utility costs on the manufacturing facilities.
19. Transferred 12,000 additional puzzles that cost $9.75 each from Work in Process Inventory to Finished Goods Inventory accounts.
20. Determined that $3,200 of production supplies was on hand at the end of the accounting period.
21. Sold 8,000 puzzles for $12 each.
22. Determine whether overhead is over- or underapplied. Close the Manufacturing Overhead account to Cost of Goods Sold.
23. Close the revenue and expense accounts.

Required

a. Open T-accounts and post transactions to the accounts.
b. Prepare a schedule of cost of goods manufactured and sold, an income statement, and a balance sheet for Year 1.

LO 11-1, 11-2, 11-3

Problem 11-21B *Manufacturing cost flow for multiple accounting cycles*

The following events apply to Andover Manufacturing Company. Assume that all transactions are cash transactions unless otherwise indicated.

Transactions for the Year 1 Accounting Period

1. The company was started on January 1, Year 1, when it acquired $400,000 cash by issuing common stock.
2. The company purchased $280,000 of direct raw materials with cash and used $26,000 of these materials to make its products in January.
3. Employees provided 1,500 hours of labor at $8 per hour during January. Wages are paid in cash.
4. The estimated manufacturing overhead costs for Year 1 are $650,000. Overhead is applied on the basis of direct labor costs. The company expected $130,000 of direct labor costs during Year 1. Record applied overhead for January.
5. By the end of January, the employees completed work on all inventory items started in January. The cost of this production was transferred to the Finished Goods Inventory account. Determine the cost per unit of product produced in January, assuming that a total of 10,000 units of product were started and completed during the month.
6. The company used an additional $234,000 of direct raw materials and 13,500 hours of direct labor at $8 per hour during the remainder of Year 1. Overhead was allocated on the basis of direct labor cost.
7. The company completed work on inventory items started between February 1 and December 31, and the cost of the completed inventory was transferred to the Finished Goods Inventory account. Determine the cost per unit for goods produced between February 1 and December 31, assuming that 90,000 units of inventory were produced. If the company desires to earn a gross profit of $6 per unit, what price per unit must it charge for the merchandise sold?
8. The company sold 60,000 units of inventory for cash at $15.00 per unit. Determine the number of units in ending inventory and the cost per unit of this inventory.
9. Actual manufacturing overhead costs paid in cash were $610,000.
10. The company paid $150,000 cash for selling and administrative expenses.
11. Close the Manufacturing Overhead account.
12. Close the revenue and expense accounts.

Transactions for the Year 2 Accounting Period

1. The company acquired $100,000 cash from the owners.
2. The company purchased $200,000 of direct raw materials with cash and used $20,800 of these materials to make products in January.

3. Employees provided 1,200 hours of labor at $8 per hour during January.
4. On January 1, Year 2, Andover expected the production facilities to cost $1,500 cash per month. The company paid cash to purchase $7,000 of production supplies, and it anticipated that $7,000 of these supplies would be used by year-end. Other manufacturing overhead costs were expected to total $455,000. Overhead is applied on the basis of direct labor costs. Andover expects direct labor costs of $80,000 during Year 2. Based on this information, determine the total expected overhead cost for Year 2. Calculate the predetermined overhead rate and apply the overhead cost for the January production. Also, record the purchase of manufacturing supplies.
5. The company recorded a $1,500 cash payment for production facilities in January.
6. On January, the employees completed work on all inventory items started in January. The cost of this production was transferred to the Finished Goods Inventory account. Determine the cost per unit of product produced in January assuming that a total of 8,000 units of product was started and completed during the month.
7. During February Year 2, the company used $15,600 of raw materials and 900 hours of labor at $8 per hour. Overhead was allocated on the basis of direct labor cost.
8. The company recorded a $1,500 cash payment for production facilities in February.
9. In February, the employees completed work on all inventory items started in February; the cost of this production was transferred to the Finished Goods Inventory account. Determine the cost per unit of product produced in February, assuming that 6,000 units of product were started and completed during the month.
10. The company used an additional $143,000 of direct raw materials and 8,250 hours of direct labor at $8 per hour during the remainder of Year 2. Overhead was allocated on the basis of direct labor cost.
11. The company recorded $15,000 of cash payments for production facilities for the period between March 1 and December 31.
12. The company completed work on inventory items started between March 1 and December 31. The cost of the completed goods was transferred to the Finished Goods Inventory account. Compute the cost per unit of this inventory, assuming that 55,000 units of inventory were produced.
13. The company sold 90,000 units of product for $16.00 per unit cash. Assume that the company uses the FIFO inventory cost flow method to determine the cost of goods sold.
14. The company paid $130,000 cash for selling and administrative expenses.
15. As of December 31, Year 2, $1,200 of production supplies was on hand.
16. Actual cost of other manufacturing overhead was $461,000 cash.
17. Close the Manufacturing Overhead account.
18. Close the revenue and expense accounts.

Required

a. Open T-accounts and record the effects of the preceding events.

b. Prepare a schedule of cost of goods manufactured and sold, an income statement, and a balance sheet for each year.

Problem 11-22B *Comprehensive review problem* LO 11-1, 11-2, 11-3

Linda Wheeler has worked as the plant manager of Vicksburg Corporation, a large manufacturing company, for 10 years. The company produces stereo DVD players for automotive vehicles and sells them to some of the largest car manufacturers in the country. Ms. Wheeler has always toyed with the idea of starting her own car stereo manufacturing business. With her experience and knowledge, she is certain that she can produce a superior stereo at a low cost. Ms. Wheeler's business strategy would be to market the product to smaller, more specialized car manufacturers. Her potential market is car manufacturers who sell at a lower volume to discriminating customers. She is confident that she could compete in this market that values low-cost quality production. She would not compete with Vicksburg or the other large stereo producers that dominate the market made up of the largest automotive producers.

Ms. Wheeler already has firm orders for 800 stereos from several automotive producers. Based on the contacts that she has made working for Vicksburg, Ms. Wheeler is confident that she can make and sell 2,000 stereos during the first year of operation. However, before making a final decision, she decides to investigate the profitability of starting her own business. Relevant information follows.

Components from suppliers	$52.00 per stereo
Assembly labor	$20.00 per hour
Rent of manufacturing buildings	$14,000.00 per year
Utilities	$480.00 per month
Sales salaries	$960.00 per month
Depreciation of equipment	$3,200.00 per year
Labor	3 hours per stereo

During the first year, Ms. Wheeler expects to be able to produce the stereos with only two production workers and a part-time salesperson to market the product. Ms. Wheeler expects to devote her time to the administrative aspects of the business and to provide back-up support in the production work. She has decided not to pay herself a salary but to live off the profits of the business.

Required

a. Classify each cost item into the categories of direct materials, direct labor, and manufacturing overhead.

b. Classify each cost item as either variable or fixed.

c. What is the cost per stereo if Ms. Wheeler's company produces 800 units per year? What is the unit cost if the company produces 2,000 units per year?

d. If Ms. Wheeler's job presently pays her $24,000 a year, would you recommend that she proceed with the plans to start the new company if she could sell stereos for $184 each?

LO 11-4

Problem 11-23B *Absorption versus variable costing*

Sardina Manufacturing Company makes a product that sells for $30 per unit. Manufacturing costs for the product amount to $16 per unit variable, and $96,000 fixed. During the current accounting period, Sardina made 8,000 units of the product and sold 7,600 units. Selling and administrative expenses were zero.

Required

a. Prepare an absorption costing income statement.

b. Prepare a variable costing income statement.

c. Explain why the amount of net income on the absorption costing income statement differs from the amount of net income on the variable costing income statement. Your answer should include the amount of the inventory balance that would exist under the two costing approaches.

LO 11-4

Problem 11-24B *Absorption versus variable costing*

Covington Company makes leather chairs that it sells for $500 per chair. Each chair requires $72 of direct materials and $170 of direct labor. Fixed overhead costs are expected to be $300,000 per year. Covington expects to sell 1,500 chairs during the coming year. Selling and administrative expenses were zero.

Required

a. Prepare income statements using absorption costing, assuming that Covington makes 1,500, 2,000, and 2,500 chairs during the year.

b. Prepare income statements using variable costing, assuming that Covington makes 1,500, 2,000, and 2,500 chairs during the year.

c. Explain why Covington may produce income statements under both absorption and variable costing formats. Your answer should include an explanation of the advantages or disadvantages associated with the use of the two reporting formats.

Problem 11-25B *Absorption and variable costing*

LO 11-4

Darwin Manufacturing pays its production managers a bonus based on the company's profitability. During the two most recent years, the company maintained the same cost structure to manufacture its products.

Year	Units Produced	Units Sold
Production and Sales		
Year 2	6,000	6,000
Year 3	8,000	6,000
Cost Data		
Direct materials		$4 per unit
Direct labor		$6 per unit
Manufacturing overhead—variable		$2 per unit
Manufacturing overhead—fixed		$36,000
Variable selling and administrative expenses		$2 per unit sold
Fixed selling and administrative expenses		$15,000

(Assume that selling and administrative expenses are associated with goods sold.)

Darwin's sales revenue for both years was $172,500.

Required

a. Prepare income statements based on absorption costing for the Years 2 and 3.

b. Since Darwin sold the same amount in Year 2 and Year 3, why did net income increase in Year 3?

c. Discuss management's possible motivation for increasing production in Year 3.

d. Determine the costs of ending inventory for Year 3. Comment on the risks and costs associated with the accumulation of inventory.

e. Based on your answers to Requirements *b* and *c*, suggest a different income statement format and prepare income statements for Year 2 and Year 3 using your suggested format.

ANALYZE, THINK, COMMUNICATE

ATC 11-1 Business Applications Case *Predetermined overhead rate*

Aviation Catering Services Inc. (ACS) prepares meals that it sells to regional airlines for in-flight meal service. The average materials cost per meal is $4.20, and the average labor cost is $2.60. ACS incurs approximately $660,000 of fixed manufacturing overhead costs annually. The marketing department estimated that ACS would sell approximately 300,000 meals during the coming year. Unfortunately, ACS has experienced a steady decline in sales even though the overall industry has had an increase in the number of meals served. The chief accountant, Rachel Brown, was overheard saying that when she calculated the predetermined overhead rate, she deliberately lowered the estimated number of meals expected to be sold because she had lost faith in the marketing department's ability to deliver on its estimated sales numbers. Ms. Brown explained, "This way, our actual cost is always below the estimated cost. It is about the only way we continue to make a profit." Indeed, the company had a significant amount of overapplied overhead at the end of each year.

Required

a. Explain how the overapplied overhead affects the determination of year-end net income.

b. Assume that Ms. Brown used 280,000 meals as the estimated sales to calculate the predetermined overhead rate. Determine the difference in expected cost per meal she calculated and the cost per meal that would result if the marketing department's estimate (300,000 units) had been used.

c. Assuming that ACS uses a cost-plus pricing policy, speculate how Ms. Brown's behavior could be contributing to the decline in sales.

ATC 11-2 Group Assignment *Schedule of cost of goods manufactured and sold*

The following information is from the accounts of Depree Manufacturing Company for Year 2.

Required

a. Divide the class into groups of four or five students per group and organize the groups into three sections. Assign Task 1 to the first section of groups, Task 2 to the second section, and Task 3 to the third section.

Group Tasks

(1) The ending balance in the Raw Materials Inventory account was $208,000. During the accounting period, Depree used $2,348,900 of raw materials inventory and purchased $2,200,000 of raw materials. Determine the beginning raw materials inventory balance.

(2) During the accounting period, Depree used $2,348,900 of raw materials inventory and $2,780,200 of direct labor. Actual overhead costs were $3,300,000. Ending work in process inventory amounted to $450,000, and cost of goods manufactured amounted to $8,389,100. Determine the beginning balance in the Work in Process Inventory account.

(3) The cost of goods manufactured was $8,389,100, and the cost of goods sold was $8,419,100. Ending finished goods inventory amounted to $360,000. Determine the beginning balance in the Finished Goods Inventory account.

b. Select a spokesperson from each section. Use input from the three spokespersons to prepare a schedule of cost of goods manufactured and sold. The spokesperson from the first section should provide information for the computation of the beginning balance in the Raw Materials Inventory account. The spokesperson from the second section should provide information for the determination of the beginning balance in the Work in Process Inventory account. The spokesperson from the third section should provide information for the determination of the beginning balance in the Finished Goods Inventory account.

ATC 11-3 Research Assignment *Identifying cost drivers at Advanced Micro Devices Inc.*

Advanced Micro Devices Inc. (AMD) is mostly known for manufacturing silicon chips for computers. Answer the following questions using the company's Form 10-K for the period ended December 30, 2017. The Form 10-K can be accessed through the "Financials" link on the company's investors website at ir.amd.com or through the EDGAR system (see Appendix A at the back of this text for instructions). Read the following sections of the 10-K: "General" on page 2, "Our Industry" that begins on page 3, and "Inventories" on page 71.

Required

a. Is AMD a manufacturing or service business? Explain.

b. Based on your response to Requirement *a*, what types(s) of inventory, if any, do you expect AMD to have? Explain.

c. What types of inventory did AMD disclose in its Form 10-K, and what were the dollar amounts of these inventories for 2017 and 2016?

d. What are some of the cost drivers that AMD might use to allocate common costs to the various products it produces?

ATC 11-4 Writing Assignment *Inventory cost flow in manufacturing environment*

Barret Cameron, a student in Professor Wagner's managerial accounting course, asked the following question: "In the first accounting course, the teacher said inventory costs flow on a FIFO, LIFO, or weighted average pattern. Now you are telling us inventory costs flow through raw materials, to work in process, and then to finished goods. Is this manufacturing stuff a new cost flow method or what?"

Required

Assume that you are Professor Wagner. Write a brief memo responding to Mr. Cameron's question.

ATC 11-5 Ethical Dilemma *Absorption costing*

Cliff Dennis may become a rich man. He is the creative force behind Amazing Drives, a new company. Amazing makes external drives that permit computer users to store large amounts of information on small floppy diskettes. Amazing has experienced tremendous growth since its inception three years ago. Investors have recognized the company's potential, and its stock is currently selling at 60 times projected earnings. More specifically, the company's 2017 earnings forecast shows estimated income to be $0.30 per share and the current market price is $18 per share ($0.30 × 60). Mr. Dennis has stock options permitting him to buy 2,000,000 shares of stock for $12 per share on January 1, 2015. This means that he could earn $6 per share on the options. In other words, he would buy the stock at $12 per share and sell it at $18 per share. As a result, Mr. Dennis would earn $12,000,000 ($6 × 2,000,000 shares).

Unfortunately, weak economies in foreign countries have caused low demand for Amazing's products in international markets. Company insiders are painfully aware that Amazing Drives is going to be unable to meet its projected income numbers. If actual earnings fall short of the projected earnings, the market will manifest its disappointment by discounting the stock price. Mr. Dennis is concerned that the value of his stock options could plummet.

At its inception three years ago, Amazing invested heavily in manufacturing equipment. Indeed, expecting dramatic growth, the company purchased a significant amount of excess capacity. As a result, the company incurs approximately $28,800,000 in fixed manufacturing costs annually. If Amazing continues to produce at its current level, it will make and sell approximately 800,000 drives during the current year. In the face of declining sales, Mr. Dennis has issued a puzzling order to his production manager. Specifically, he has told the production manager to increase production so that 1,200,000 drives will be completed during the current year. Mr. Dennis explained that he believes the economies in foreign countries will surge ahead in the following year and that he wants Amazing to have the inventory necessary to satisfy the demand.

Required

a. Suppose that actual earnings for current year are $0.18 per share. The market becomes disappointed, and the price-earnings ratio falls to 40 times earnings. What is the value of Mr. Dennis' stock options under these circumstances?

b. Determine the impact on income reported in the current year if production is 800,000 units versus 1,200,000 units.

c. Why would Mr. Dennis order the increase in production?

d. Does Mr. Dennis' behavior violate any of the standards of ethical professional practice in Exhibit 1.17 of Chapter 1?

e. Identify the features described in this case that could motivate criminal and ethical misconduct. (It may be helpful to reread the discussion of the fraud triangle in Chapter 1 before attempting to satisfy this requirement.)

ATC 11-6 Spreadsheet Assignment *Using Excel*

Manning Cassey Computers (MCC) plans to produce and sell 1,600 computers for $720 each in the next fiscal year. The company's cost data follow.

Components from wholesaler	$480 per computer
Assembly labor	$15 per hour
Manufacturing space rent	$3,000 per month
Utilities	$600 per month
Janitorial services	$480 per month
Depreciation of equipment	$3,840 per year
Labor time per computer	2 hours

Required

a. Construct a spreadsheet to calculate the cost of goods manufactured and the cost per unit for MCC. Use formulas in the schedule so that the cost of goods manufactured will automatically be calculated as you change the number of units sold.

b. Add an abbreviated income statement to your spreadsheet that incorporates the cost from Requirement *a*.

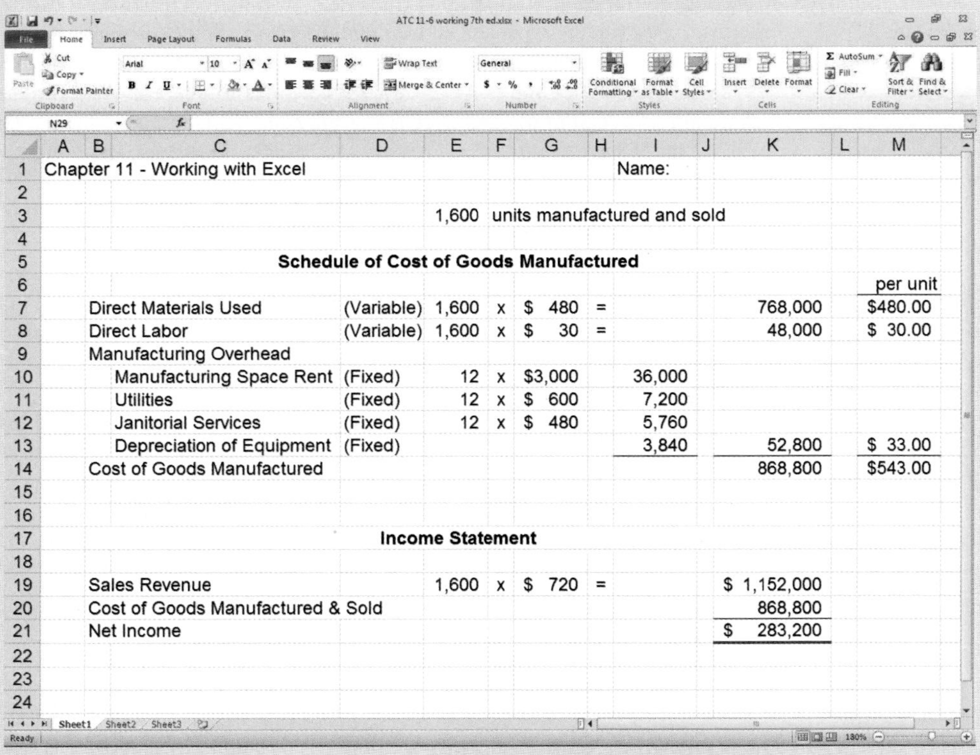

	A B / C	D	E	F	G	H	I	K	M
1	Chapter 11 - Working with Excel						Name:		
2									
3			1,600	units manufactured and sold					
4									
5	**Schedule of Cost of Goods Manufactured**								
6									per unit
7	Direct Materials Used	(Variable)	1,600	x	$ 480	=		768,000	$480.00
8	Direct Labor	(Variable)	1,600	x	$ 30	=		48,000	$ 30.00
9	Manufacturing Overhead								
10	Manufacturing Space Rent	(Fixed)	12	x	$3,000		36,000		
11	Utilities	(Fixed)	12	x	$ 600		7,200		
12	Janitorial Services	(Fixed)	12	x	$ 480		5,760		
13	Depreciation of Equipment	(Fixed)					3,840	52,800	$ 33.00
14	Cost of Goods Manufactured							868,800	$543.00
15									
16									
17	**Income Statement**								
18									
19	Sales Revenue		1,600	x	$ 720	=		$ 1,152,000	
20	Cost of Goods Manufactured & Sold							868,800	
21	Net Income							$ 283,200	
22									
23									
24									

Source: Microsoft Excel 2010

Spreadsheet Tip

Build the spreadsheet so that the number of units in cell E3 can be changed and cost of goods manufactured and net income will be recalculated automatically.

ATC 11-7 Spreadsheet Assignment *Mastering Excel*

Stanley Manufacturing Company, which sold 16,000 units of product at $20 per unit, collected the following information regarding three different levels of production.

Inventory Costs			
Fixed overhead	$100,000	$100,000	$100,000
Number of units produced	16,000	20,000	25,000
Fixed overhead per unit	$6.25	$5.00	$4.00
Variable manufacturing costs	$12.00	$12.00	$12.00
Full absorption cost per unit	$18.25	$17.00	$16.00

Required

a. Construct a spreadsheet that includes the preceding data in the top of the spreadsheet. The rows for fixed overhead per unit and full absorption cost per unit should be based on formulas.

b. Include absorption costing income statements at these three levels of production like those in Exhibit 11.10. Use formulas so that the number of units produced in the preceding table can be changed and net income will be recalculated automatically.

c. Include variable costing income statements at these three levels of production like those in Exhibit 11.11. Use formulas so that the number of units produced in the preceding table can be changed and net income will be recalculated automatically.

COMPREHENSIVE PROBLEM

Magnificent Modems Inc. acquired a subsidiary named Anywhere Inc. (AI). AI manufactures a wireless modem that enables users to access the Internet through cell phones. The following trial balance was drawn from the accounts of the subsidiary.

Cash	$200,000	
Raw materials inventory	4,000	
Work in process inventory	6,000	
Finished goods inventory	7,000	
Common stock		$129,000
Retained earnings		88,000
Totals	$217,000	$217,000

The subsidiary completed the following transactions during Year 2.

1. Paid $60,000 cash for direct raw materials.
2. Transferred $50,000 of direct raw materials to work in process.
3. Paid production employees $80,000 cash.
4. Applied $53,000 of manufacturing overhead costs to work in process.
5. Completed work on products that cost $163,000.
6. Sold products that cost $143,000 for $182,000 cash. Record the recognition of revenue in a row labeled 6a and the cost of goods sold in a row labeled 6b.
7. Paid $20,000 cash for selling and administrative expenses.
8. Actual overhead costs paid in cash amounted to $55,000.
9. Closed the Manufacturing Overhead account. The amount of over- or underapplied overhead was insignificant (immaterial).
10. Made a $5,000 cash distribution to the owners.

Required

a. For Anywhere Inc., record the events in the financial statements model like the one shown as follows.

	Balance Sheet																		Income Statement				
	Assets										=	Equity											
Event No.	Cash	+	MOH	+	Raw M.	+	WIP	+	F. Goods		=	C. Stk.	+	Ret. Ear.					Rev.	−	Exp.	=	Net Inc.
	200,000	+	NA	+	4,000	+	6,000	+	7,000		=	129,000	+	88,000					NA	−	NA	=	NA

b. Prepare a schedule of cost of goods manufactured and sold.

c. Prepare an income statement and a balance sheet.

Design Elements: Abstract texture: ©Ingram Publishing; Video Camera icon: ©McGraw-Hill Education; Check mark: ©McGraw-Hill Education; Look forward/backward icon: ©McGraw-Hill Education; Globe icon: ©McGraw-Hill Education; Globe with magnifying glass icon: ©McGraw-Hill Education; Pen and paper icon: ©McGraw-Hill Education; Group Assignment icon: ©McGraw-Hill Education; Ethics Cases icon: ©McGraw-Hill Education; Self-Study Review icon: ©Design Pics/Don Hammond; and Point de la Coubre lighthouse near Roy, France: ©Westend61/Getty Images.

CHAPTER 12

Job-Order, Process, and Hybrid Costing Systems

LEARNING OBJECTIVES

After you have mastered the material in this chapter, you will be able to:

LO 12-1 Distinguish between job-order and process costing systems.

LO 12-2 Explain how events in a job-order costing system affect financial statements.

LO 12-3 Explain how events in a process costing system affect financial statements.

LO 12-4 Calculate equivalent units and prepare a cost of production report.

Video lectures and accompanying self-assessment quizzes are available in Connect® for all learning objectives.

CHAPTER OPENING

JANIS

Benchmore Boat Company built five boats during the current year. Each boat has unique characteristics that affect its cost. For example, an 80-foot yacht required more labor and materials than a 30-foot sailboat. Because different boats cost different amounts, Benchmore needs a cost system that traces product costs to individual inventory items (specific boats).

In contrast, Janis Juice Company produced 500,000 cans of apple juice during the same year. Each can of juice is identical to the others. Determining the cost of a boat built by Benchmore requires a different costing system than the system Janis needs to determine the cost of a can of juice. Benchmore needs a costing system that captures the unique cost of each individual inventory item. Janis needs a costing system that distributes costs evenly across total production (number of cans of juice produced during an accounting period).

The Curious Accountant

©limpido/Getty Images

Consider the following two situations.

First, imagine you work at a company that roasts and grinds coffee beans, such as the **Maxwell House** brand at **Kraft-Heinz**, but assume your company produces only one product—one-pound bags of regular coffee. During the past year, your company's manufacturing costs totaled $1,025 million and it produced 500 million bags of coffee.

Next, imagine you worked for a **Bechtel**, a private enterprise that is one of the world's largest construction companies. During 2017 it was involved with such diverse projects as constructing a plant in Texas for **Exxon** to produce ethylene to designing and building two metro-lines in Riyadh, Saudi Arabia. Assume that during 2018 Bechtel worked on 40 different projects and incurred manufacturing costs of $20 billion.

How would you determine the cost of one bag of coffee? How would you determine the cost incurred to construct the two metro-lines in Riyadh? Which of these two questions do you think would be the most difficult to answer for a real-world company? (Answer on page 555.)

COSTING SYSTEMS

LO 12-1

Distinguish between job-order and process costing systems.

The type of product a company produces affects the type of accounting system needed to determine product cost. The two most common types of costing systems are job-order costing and process costing. Some companies use hybrid costing systems that combine features of both job-order and process systems. The following section of the text discusses the types of products most suited to each costing system and the accounting procedures used in each type of costing system.

©Lucian Milasan/Shutterstock

Costing Systems and Type of Product

Job-order costing systems accumulate costs by individual products. The boats Benchmore builds are suited to job-order costing. Other products for which job-order costing is suitable include movies made by Walt Disney Productions, office buildings constructed by Rust Engineering, and airplanes made by Boeing. Job-order costing systems apply not only to individual inventory items, but also to batches of inventory items. For example, Hernandes Shirt Company may account for producing a special order of 20,000 shirts sold to the United States Army as a single job. Companies use job-order costing systems when they need to know the costs of individual products or batches of products.

Process costing systems allocate costs evenly to homogeneous products. In addition to beverage companies such as Janis Juice, oil refiners such as Texaco, chemical producers such as DowDuPont, food processors such as General Mills, and paint manufacturers such as Sherwin-Williams use process costing. These companies normally make products in mass quantities using continuous processes. The *per-unit product cost* is determined by dividing the *total* product cost by the number of units produced during the accounting period. Process costing systems provide *average* product costs.

To a lesser extent, job-order costing systems also use average costs. It is either not possible or not cost-effective to trace costs of indirect materials, indirect labor, utilities, rent, and depreciation directly to particular jobs. Companies normally combine these costs and allocate them to individual products using an average overhead rate based on a common measure of production such as labor hours, machine hours, or square footage. When jobs are produced in batches of a number of similar products, the cost per unit is determined by dividing the total cost of the job by the number of units in the batch. Although more costs are traced to specific products under a job-order system than a process system, *both* systems require *some* form of *cost averaging.*

©joe32780/iStock/Getty Images

Job-Order Cost Flow

Job-order and process costing systems are patterned after the physical flow of products moving through production. For example, consider how Benchmore Boat Company builds custom boats. Each boat is a separate project. Benchmore starts a project by requisitioning raw materials from materials storage. It assigns specific employees to work on specific boats. Finally, it assigns indirect (overhead) costs to each boat based on the number of direct labor hours required to build the boat.

Benchmore's *job-order costing system* accumulates cost in a manner parallel to physical boat construction. Benchmore assigns each boat a specific job identification number. It records transactions in inventory accounts on a perpetual basis. Product costs are accumulated separately for each job identification number. The costs of each boat move through the Work in Process Inventory account to the Finished Goods Inventory account and finally to the Cost of Goods Sold account as the boat

EXHIBIT 12.1

Cost Flow in a Job-Order Costing System

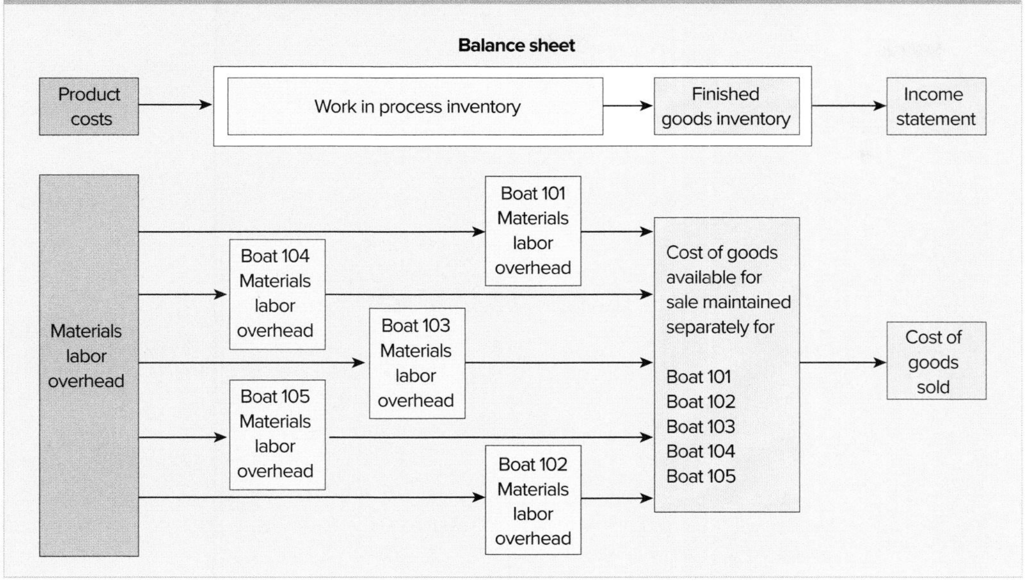

is produced and sold. Exhibit 12.1 shows the flow of product costs for the five boats Benchmore plans to build in Year 2. In a job-order system, the amount recorded in the Work in Process Inventory account is the total cost to date of distinct jobs. Each distinct job represents the costs of materials, labor, and overhead accumulated for that specific inventory project. The Work in Process Inventory account is a *control* account supported by numerous *subsidiary* accounts (the records for individual jobs). The Finished Goods Inventory account is also a control account. It is supported by subsidiary accounts in which are recorded the separate costs of each boat that has been completed but not yet sold.

Process Cost Flow

Process costing systems use the same general ledger accounts as job-order costing systems. Product costs flow from Raw Materials Inventory to Work in Process Inventory to Finished Goods Inventory to Cost of Goods Sold. The primary difference between the two systems centers on accounting for the work in process inventory. The physical products move continuously through a series of processing centers. Instead of accumulating product costs by jobs that add up to a single Work in Process Inventory control account, process costing systems accumulate product costs by processing centers, or *departments.* Each department has its own separate Work in Process Inventory account. For example, Janis Juice Company uses three distinct processes to produce cans of apple juice. Raw apples enter the extraction department where juice concentrate is pressed from whole fruit. The concentrate moves to the mixing department where Janis adds water, sugar, food coloring, and preservatives. The resulting juice mixture moves to the packaging department where it is canned and boxed. The materials, labor, and overhead costs incurred as products move through a processing center (department) are charged to that center's Work in Process Inventory account.

Parallel to the physical flow of product through the manufacturing process, cost accumulations pass from one department to the next. The end products of one department become the raw materials of the next department. The costs transferred from one department to the next are **transferred-in costs.** Transferred-in costs are combined with the additional materials, labor, and overhead costs incurred by each succeeding department. When goods are complete, the total product cost transferred to the Finished Goods Inventory account represents the sum of product costs from all the departments. Exhibit 12.2 illustrates cost flow for the process costing system used by Janis Juice Company. Compare the cost flow patterns in Exhibits 12.1 and 12.2 to clarify the distinction between job-order and process costing systems.

EXHIBIT 12.2

Cost Flow in a Process Costing System

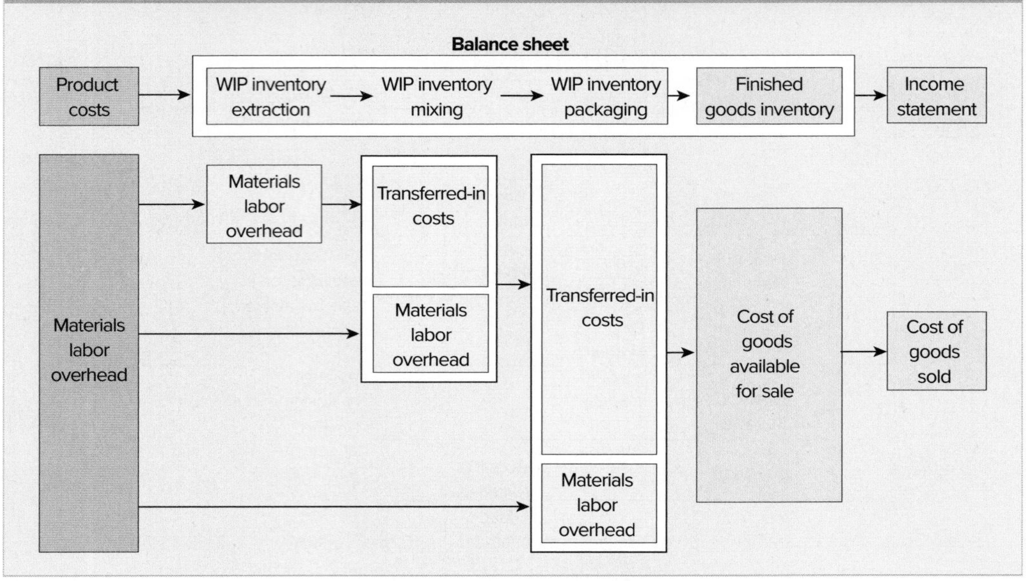

Hybrid Accounting Systems

Many companies use **hybrid costing systems.** Hybrid systems combine features of both process and job-order costing systems. For example, Dell Technologies makes thousands of identical computers using a continuous assembly line that is compatible with process costing. Each unit requires the same amount of labor to assemble a standard set of parts into a finished computer ready for immediate sale. Dell also builds custom computers with unique features. Customers can order larger monitors, more memory, or faster processors than Dell's standard model has. Dell meets these requests by customizing the computers as they move through production. The costs of customized features must be traced to products with a job-order type of system. Dell charges customers a premium for the custom items.

DOCUMENTATION IN A JOB-ORDER COSTING SYSTEM

In a job-order costing system, product costs for each individual job are accumulated on a **job cost sheet,** also called a *job-order cost sheet* or a *job record.* As each job moves through production, detailed cost information for materials, labor, and overhead is recorded on the job cost sheet. When a job is finished, the job cost sheet summarizes all costs incurred to complete that job.

Two primary source documents, materials requisition forms and work tickets, provide the information recorded on the job cost sheet. Before starting a job, the job supervisor prepares a **materials requisition form** which lists the materials needed to begin work. The materials requisition represents the authorization for raw materials to be released from storage to production. Some companies deliver hard-copy forms to and from the different departments, but most modern businesses deliver requests electronically through a computer network. Whether recorded on paper documents or in electronic files, the information from material requisitions for each job is sent to the accounting department to be summarized on the job cost sheet.

The **work ticket,** sometimes called a *time card,* provides space for the job number, employee identification, and work description. Employees record on the work ticket the amount of time they spend on each job. This information is forwarded to the accounting department.

EXHIBIT 12.3

Job-Order Cost Sheet and Source Documents

Job Cost Sheet

Job Order No. Boat 101 Customer Name: Arturo Martinez

Due Date: 10 / 31 / Year 1 Date Started: 08/ 01/ Year 1 Date Finished: 11 / 30 / Year 1

Direct materials		Direct labor			Applied overhead		
Req. No.	Cost	Ticket	Hours	Cost	Rate	Hours	Cost
24585	7,100	367	1,400	9,100	3.90	1,400	5,460
24600	5,600	360	1,600	10,400	3.90	1,600	6,240
24609	6,100						
Total	18,800	Total		19,500	Total		11,700

Cost summary

Direct materials	$18,800
Direct labor	19,500
Overhead	11,700
Total	$50,000

Material requisitions

	Date	Quantity
Package K	8/1	Mixed
Package R	9/1	Mixed
Package T	10/1	Mixed

Information transferred electronically

Work tickets

	Date	Hours
Process 1	9/30	1,400
Process 2	11/30	1,600

Information transferred electronically

Using wage rate records, the accounting department computes the amount of labor cost and records it on the job cost sheet. The data can be gathered manually or electronically.

Finally, each job cost sheet provides space for applied overhead. Companies maintain job cost sheet records perpetually, adding additional cost data as work on jobs progresses. Using predetermined overhead rates, estimated overhead costs are regularly added to job cost sheets. Exhibit 12.3 illustrates a job cost sheet along with materials requisition forms and work tickets for Benchmore Boat Company's job-order number Boat 101.

REALITY BYTES

Job-order, process, and hybrid costing systems apply to service businesses as well as manufacturing concerns. Consider a local franchisee of Lawn Doctor who is pricing lawn maintenance contracts for a variety of residential customers. A separate price will be quoted for each lawn, and this price will be based on what the company believes it will cost to maintain that particular lawn. Some customers have larger lawns than others, which cost more to service. Some customers want less lawn care service than others, which costs less. This type of service business will use a job-order system.

©Radius Images/Alamy

Now, consider a company in the clothes laundering business. The price the company charges to wash, press, and hang a man's shirt is the same for all shirts because the cost of servicing each shirt, whether large or small, is about the same. This business will use a process costing system to determine the cost of laundering one shirt.

However, to determine the cost of one specific customer's job a hybrid system would be used, because different customers bring in different numbers of shirts to be cleaned. While process costing is used to determine the cost to clean one shirt, job-order costing is used to calculate the cost of the entire job.

JOB-ORDER COSTING SYSTEM ILLUSTRATED

LO 12-2

Explain how events in a job-order costing system affect financial statements.

To illustrate how a job-order costing system works, we follow the operations of Benchmore Boat Company during Year 2. Exhibit 12.4 shows the company's Year 2 beginning account balances.

Entries for Benchmore's Year 2 accounting events, described next, are shown in ledger T-accounts in Exhibit 12.5. As you study each event, trace it to the T-accounts. The entries in Exhibit 12.5 are cross-referenced to sequential event numbers. The individual effect of each event on the financial statements is shown and discussed in the following section.

EXHIBIT 12.4

BENCHMORE BOAT COMPANY
Account Balances
As of January 1, Year 2

	Assets	Stk. Equity
Cash	$ 73,000	
Raw materials inventory	7,000	
Work in process inventory	34,000	
Finished goods inventory	85,000	
Production supplies	300	
Manufacturing equipment	90,000	
Accumulated depreciation	(32,000)	
Common stock		$200,000
Retained earnings		57,300
Total	$257,300	$257,300

EXHIBIT 12.4

continued

Subsidiary Account Balances

Work in Process Inventory		Finished Goods Inventory	
Boat 103	$14,000	Boat 101	$50,000
Boat 104	8,000	Boat 102	35,000
Boat 105	12,000		
Total	$34,000	Total	$85,000

EVENT 1 **Benchmore paid $14,000 cash to purchase raw materials.**

The effects of this event on the company's financial statements follow.

Balance Sheet								Income Statement				
Assets			=	Liabilities	+	Equity						
Cash	+	Raw Materials Inventory						Revenue	−	Expenses	=	Net Income
(14,000)	+	14,000	=	NA	+	NA		NA	−	NA	=	NA

Event 1 is an asset exchange; it does not affect total assets reported on the balance sheet. The asset cash decreases and the asset raw materials inventory increases. The income statement is not affected.

EVENT 2 **Benchmore used $17,000 of direct raw materials in the process of making boats.**

The amounts used for Boat 103, Boat 104, and Boat 105 were $8,000, $3,400, and $5,600, respectively. The effects of this event on the financial statements follow.

Balance Sheet								Income Statement				
Assets			=	Liabilities	+	Equity						
Raw Materials Inventory	+	Work in Process Inventory						Revenue	−	Expenses	=	Net Income
(17,000)	+	17,000	=	NA	+	NA		NA	−	NA	=	NA

EXHIBIT 12.5

Ledger T-Accounts for Benchmore Boat Company

Cash

Bal.	73,000	(1)	14,000
(13)	91,000	(3)	1,200
		(4)	8,000
		(7)	24,500
		(8)	12,000
		(10)	10,100
Bal.	94,200		

Production Supplies

Bal.	300	(12)	1,100
(3)	1,200		
Bal.	400		

Manufacturing Equipment

Bal.	90,000		

Accumulated Dep.

		Bal.	32,000
		(11)	4,000
		Bal.	36,000

Raw Materials Inventory

Bal.	7,000	(2)	17,000
(1)	14,000		
Bal.	4,000		

Manufacturing Overhead

(10)	10,100	(5)	6,240
(11)	4,000	(9)	9,360
(12)	1,100		
(15)	400		
Bal.	0		

Work in Process Inventory

Bal.	34,000	(6)	36,240
(2)	17,000		
(4)	8,000		
(5)	6,240		
(8)	12,000		
(9)	9,360		
Bal.	50,360		

Job Cost Sheets (Subsidiary accounts)

Boat 103

Beginning balance	14,000
Materials	8,000
Labor	8,000
Overhead	6,240
Product cost	36,240
To finish goods	(36,240)
Ending balance	0

Boat 104

Beginning balance	8,000
Materials	3,400
Labor	5,000
Overhead	3,900
Ending balance	20,300

Boat 105

Beginning balance	12,000
Materials	5,600
Labor	7,000
Overhead	5,460
Ending balance	30,060

Finished Goods Inventory

Bal.	85,000	(14)	50,000
(6)	36,240		
Bal.	71,240		

Boat 101

Balance	50,000
Sold	(50,000)
Balance	0

Boat 102

Balance	35,000
Cost transferred	0
Balance	35,000

Boat 103

Balance	0
Cost transferred	36,240
Balance	36,240

Common Stock

		Bal.	200,000

Retained Earnings

		Bal.	57,300

Sales Revenue

		(13)	91,000

Cost of Goods Sold

(14)	50,000	(15)	400
Bal.	49,600		

Selling and Admin. Exp.

(7)	24,500		

Boat 101

Cost sheet data transferred to permanent storage

This event is an asset exchange. It does not affect total assets reported on the balance sheet. The asset raw materials inventory decreases and the asset work in process inventory increases. The income statement is not affected. In addition to recording the effects in the Work in Process Inventory control account, Benchmore adjusted the individual job cost sheets to reflect the raw materials used on each job, as shown in Exhibit 12.5.

EVENT 3 **Benchmore paid $1,200 cash to purchase production supplies.**

The effects of this event on the company's financial statements are shown here.

Balance Sheet								Income Statement				
Assets			=	Liabilities	+	Equity						
Cash	+	Production Supplies						Revenue	−	Expenses	=	Net Income
(1,200)	+	1,200	=	NA	+	NA		NA	−	NA	=	NA

This event is also an asset exchange. It does not affect total assets reported on the balance sheet. One asset–cash–decreases and another asset–production supplies–increases. Purchasing production supplies does not affect the income statement. The cost of supplies is allocated to work in process inventory as part of overhead and is expensed as part of cost of goods sold.

EVENT 4 **Benchmore paid $8,000 cash to production employees who worked on Boat 103.**

The effects of this event on the company's financial statements follow.

Balance Sheet								Income Statement				
Assets			=	Liabilities	+	Equity						
Cash	+	Work in Process Inventory						Revenue	−	Expenses	=	Net Income
(8,000)	+	8,000	=	NA	+	NA		NA	−	NA	=	NA

These wages are *not* salary expense. Because the employees worked to make inventory, the cost of their labor is added to work in process inventory. This event is an asset exchange. The asset cash decreases, and the asset work in process inventory increases. Neither total assets reported on the balance sheet nor any revenues or expenses on the income statement are affected. In addition to recording the effects in the Work in Process Inventory control account, Benchmore adjusted the Boat 103 job cost sheet to reflect the labor used on the job. Refer to Exhibit 12.5; the $8,000 labor cost is entered in both the Work in Process Inventory control account and the job cost sheet for Boat 103.

EVENT 5 **Benchmore applied manufacturing overhead costs of $6,240 to the Boat 103 job.**

Production employees completed Boat 103. When the boat was finished, the actual amount of many costs to make it were not then known. During the year, Benchmore sells boats before knowing the exact costs of making them. Although a portion of the total production supplies, depreciation, supervisory salaries, rental cost, and utilities were used while Boat 103 was under construction, the actual cost of these resources is not known until the end of the year. To make timely decisions, such as setting the selling prices for boats, Benchmore must assign estimated overhead costs to boats as they are completed.

To estimate overhead as accurately as possible, Benchmore first reviewed the previous year's actual overhead costs. It adjusted those amounts for expected changes. Assume Benchmore estimated total overhead costs for Year 2 to be as follows: production supplies, $1,400; depreciation, $4,000; utilities and other indirect costs, $10,590, for a total of $15,990 ($1,400 + $4,000 + $10,590).

Benchmore has identified a cause-and-effect relationship between direct labor time and overhead cost. Boats that require more labor also require more overhead. For example, the more hours production employees work, the more supplies they use. Similarly, more labor hours translates into more equipment use, causing more utilities and depreciation costs. Because of the relationship between labor and indirect costs, Benchmore uses *direct labor hours* as the allocation base for overhead costs. Benchmore estimated it would use a total of 4,100 labor hours during Year 2. It established a *predetermined overhead rate* as follows:

$$\text{Predetermined overhead rate} = \text{Total estimated overhead costs} \div \text{Total estimated direct labor hours}$$

$$\text{Predetermined overhead rate} = \$15{,}990 \div 4{,}100$$

$$= \$3.90 \text{ per direct labor hour}$$

Boat 103 required 1,600 actual direct labor hours. Benchmore applied $6,240 (1,600 hours × $3.90) of overhead to that job. The effects of the overhead application on the company's financial statements follow.

Balance Sheet								Income Statement				
Assets			=	Liabilities	+	Equity						
Manufacturing Overhead	+	Work in Process Inventory						Revenue	−	Expenses	=	Net Income
(6,240)	+	6,240	=	NA	+	NA		NA	−	NA	=	NA

The event is an asset exchange. One asset—work in process inventory—increases and a temporary asset—manufacturing overhead—decreases. Applying overhead costs to work in process inventory does not affect the income statement. When finished goods are sold, overhead costs affect the income statement through cost of goods sold. The job cost sheet for Boat 103 reflects the applied (estimated) overhead cost. The T-accounts in Exhibit 12.5 also show the overhead application.

EVENT 6 Benchmore transferred $36,240 of product costs for completed Boat 103 from work in process inventory to finished goods inventory.

The effects of this transfer on the company's financial statements follow.

Balance Sheet								Income Statement				
Assets			=	Liabilities	+	Equity						
Work in Process Inventory	+	Finished Goods Inventory						Revenue	−	Expenses	=	Net Income
(36,240)	+	36,240	=	NA	+	NA		NA	−	NA	=	NA

This event is an asset exchange. Benchmore transferred cost from the Work in Process Inventory control account to the Finished Goods Inventory control account. The transfer does not affect total assets reported on the balance sheet, nor does it affect the income statement. The job cost sheet is moved to the finished goods file folder. Exhibit 12.5 illustrates these effects.

EVENT 7 Benchmore paid $24,500 cash for selling and administrative expenses.

The effects of this transaction on the financial statements follow.

Balance Sheet					Income Statement				
Assets	=	Liabilities	+	Equity	Revenue	−	Expenses	=	Net Income
(24,500)	=	NA	+	(24,500)	NA	−	24,500	=	(24,500)

This is an asset use transaction. Cash and stockholders' equity (retained earnings) decrease. Recognizing the expense decreases net income.

EVENT 8 **Benchmore paid $12,000 cash to production employees for work on Boats 104 and 105.**

The cost of direct labor used was $5,000 for Boat 104 and $7,000 for Boat 105. These jobs were still incomplete at the end of Year 2. The effects of this event on the financial statements follow.

Balance Sheet								Income Statement				
Assets			=	Liabilities	+	Equity						
Cash	+	Work in Process Inventory						Revenue	−	Expenses	=	Net Income
(12,000)	+	12,000	=	NA	+	NA		NA	−	NA	=	NA

This event is an asset exchange. It does not affect total assets reported on the balance sheet. It does not affect the income statement. In addition to the effects on the Work in Process Inventory control account, Benchmore adjusted the individual job cost sheets to reflect the labor used on each job. Exhibit 12.5 illustrates these effects.

EVENT 9 **Benchmore applied estimated manufacturing overhead costs to the Boat 104 and Boat 105 jobs.**

As previously explained, the predetermined overhead rate was $3.90 per direct labor hour (see Event 5). Assume the work described in Event 8 represented 1,000 direct labor hours for Boat 104 and 1,400 direct labor hours for Boat 105. The amount of estimated overhead cost Benchmore applied to the two jobs is calculated as follows.

Job Number	Predetermined Overhead Rate	×	Actual Labor Hours Used	=	Amount of Applied Overhead
Boat 104	$3.90	×	1,000	=	$3,900
Boat 105	3.90	×	1,400	=	5,460
Total					$9,360

The effects on the company's financial statements of applying the overhead follow.

Balance Sheet								Income Statement				
Assets			=	Liabilities	+	Equity						
Manufacturing Overhead	+	Work in Process Inventory						Revenue	−	Expenses	=	Net Income
(9,360)	+	9,360	=	NA	+	NA		NA	−	NA	=	NA

Applying overhead is an asset exchange. Total assets and net income are not affected. Overhead costs of $3,900 for Boat 104 and $5,460 for Boat 105 are recorded on the job cost sheets. The total, $9,360, is recorded in the Work in Process Inventory control account. Trace these allocations to Exhibit 12.5.

EVENT 10 **Benchmore paid $10,100 cash for utilities and other indirect product costs.**

The effects of this event on the financial statements are shown here.

Balance Sheet								Income Statement				
Assets			=	Liabilities	+	Equity						
Cash	+	Manufacturing Overhead						Revenue	−	Expenses	=	Net Income
(10,100)	+	10,100	=	NA	+	NA		NA	−	NA	=	NA

Paying for *actual* overhead costs is an asset exchange. Total assets, net income, and job cost sheets are not affected. Recall that estimated overhead costs were previously recorded in work in process inventory and on the job cost sheets (Events 5 and 9).

EVENT 11 **Benchmore recognized $4,000 of actual manufacturing equipment depreciation.**

The effects of this event on the financial statements follow.

Balance Sheet								Income Statement				
Assets			=	Liabilities	+	Equity						
Book Value of Manufacturing Equipment	+	Manufacturing Overhead						Revenue	−	Expenses	=	Net Income
(4,000)	+	4,000	=	NA	+	NA		NA	−	NA	=	NA

Depreciation of manufacturing equipment represents an *actual* indirect product cost (overhead), *not* an expense (even though the *amount* of depreciation is an estimate). Recognizing this depreciation is an asset exchange. The book value of the manufacturing equipment decreases and the Manufacturing Overhead account increases. Neither the total amount of assets reported on the balance sheet nor the income statement are affected. The job cost sheets are also not affected when *actual* overhead cost (depreciation) is recognized. The inventory accounts and job cost sheets reflect *estimated* overhead.

EVENT 12 **Benchmore counted the production supplies on hand at year-end and recognized actual overhead cost for the supplies used.**

During Year 2, Benchmore had available for use $1,500 of production supplies ($300 beginning balance + $1,200 supplies purchased). A physical count disclosed there were $400 of supplies on hand at the end of Year 2. Benchmore therefore must have used $1,100 of supplies ($1,500 − $400). The effects on the company's financial statements of recognizing supplies used follow.

Balance Sheet								Income Statement				
Assets			=	Liabilities	+	Equity						
Production Supplies	+	Manufacturing Overhead						Revenue	−	Expenses	=	Net Income
(1,100)	+	1,100	=	NA	+	NA		NA	−	NA	=	NA

The event is an asset exchange. Total assets and net income are not affected. The job cost sheets are not affected. Remember that estimated overhead costs were previously recorded on the job cost sheets.

EVENT 13 **Benchmore sold Boat 101 for $91,000 cash.**

The effects of this event on the financial statements follow.

Balance Sheet						Income Statement				
Assets	=	Liabilities	+	Equity		Revenue	−	Expenses	=	Net Income
91,000	=	NA	+	91,000		91,000	−	NA	=	91,000

Recognizing revenue from selling inventory is an asset source event. Both assets (cash) and stockholders' equity (retained earnings) increase. Revenue recognition also increases the net income reported on the income statement.

EVENT 14 **Benchmore recognized cost of goods sold for Boat 101.**

The effects of this event on the financial statements follow.

Balance Sheet					Income Statement				
Assets	=	Liabilities	+	Equity	Revenue	−	Expenses	=	Net Income
(50,000)	=	NA	+	(50,000)	NA	−	50,000	=	(50,000)

Recognizing cost of goods sold is an asset use transaction. It decreases assets (finished goods inventory) and stockholders' equity (retained earnings). The expense recognition decreases net income. The job cost sheet for Boat 101 is transferred to the permanent files. The cost sheet is retained because information from it could be useful for estimating costs of future jobs.

EVENT 15 **Benchmore closed the Manufacturing Overhead account, reducing cost of goods sold by $400.**

During Year 2, Benchmore applied $15,600 of estimated overhead cost to production. Actual overhead costs were $15,200. Overhead was therefore overapplied by $400 ($15,600 − $15,200), meaning too much overhead was transferred to the Work in Process Inventory, Finished Goods Inventory, and Cost of Goods Sold accounts. If the amount of overapplied overhead were significant, Benchmore would have to allocate it proportionately among the inventory and Cost of Goods Sold accounts. In this case, the amount is insignificant and Benchmore assigned it entirely to cost of goods sold. The effects of this event on the company's financial statements follow.

Balance Sheet					Income Statement				
Assets	=	Liabilities	+	Equity	Revenue	−	Expenses	=	Net Income
400	=	NA	+	400	NA	−	(400)	=	400

Overapplied overhead indicates the estimated cost transferred from the asset accounts to cost of goods sold was too high. The entry to close manufacturing overhead corrects the overstatement. Recording $400 in the overhead account increases total assets. The increase in assets is matched by a decrease in cost of goods sold, which reduces expenses, increases net income, and increases stockholders' equity (retained earnings). After this adjustment, the total increases in the overhead account (actual costs) equal the total decreases (estimated costs). Manufacturing Overhead is a temporary account. It is closed at year-end and does not appear in the financial statements. Exhibit 12.6 displays Benchmore Boat Company's account balances at the end of Year 2.

EXHIBIT 12.6

BENCHMORE BOAT COMPANY
Account Balances
As of December 31, Year 2

Cash	$ 94,200	
Raw materials inventory	4,000	
Work in process inventory	50,360	
Finished goods inventory	71,240	
Production supplies	400	
Manufacturing equipment	90,000	
Accumulated depreciation	(36,000)	
Common stock		$200,000
Retained earnings		74,200*
Totals	$274,200	$274,200

*57,300 + 91,000 − 49,600 − 24,500

☑ CHECK YOURSELF 12.1

Wilson Cabinets makes custom cabinets for home builders. It incurred the following costs during the most recent month.

Inventory	Materials	Labor
Job 1	$4,200	$2,700
Job 2	2,300	5,000
Job 3	1,700	800

Wilson's predetermined overhead rate is $0.80 per direct labor dollar. Actual overhead costs were $7,100. Wilson completed and sold Jobs 1 and 2 during the month, but Job 3 was not complete at month-end. The selling prices for Jobs 1 and 2 were $14,900 and $16,600, respectively. What amount of gross margin would Wilson report on the income statement for the month?

Answer Cost accumulated in the Work in Process account:

Inventory	Materials	Labor	Overhead*	Total
Job 1	$4,200	$2,700	$2,160	$ 9,060
Job 2	2,300	5,000	4,000	11,300
Job 3	1,700	800	640	3,140

*80 percent of direct labor cost.

Total allocated overhead is $6,800 ($2,160 + $4,000 + $640). Since actual overhead is $7,100, overhead is underapplied by $300 ($7,100 − $6,800).

Sales revenue ($14,900 + $16,600)	$ 31,500
Cost of goods sold (Job 1, $9,060 + Job 2, $11,300 + Underapplied overhead, $300)	(20,660)
Gross margin	$ 10,840

PROCESS COSTING SYSTEM ILLUSTRATED

LO 12-3

Explain how events in a process costing system affect financial statements.

In process costing systems, product costs flow through the same general ledger accounts as in job-order costing systems: Raw Materials Inventory, Work in Process Inventory, Finished Goods Inventory, and ultimately Cost of Goods Sold. Accounting for work in process inventory, however, differs between the two systems. Instead of accumulating work in process costs by jobs, process costing systems accumulate product costs by departments. The cost of all goods that move through a processing department during a given accounting period is charged to that department. Work in process subsidiary documents (job cost sheets) are not needed. Process costing systems are easier to use than job-order systems. They do not, however, distinguish the cost of one product from another. Process systems are therefore not appropriate for manufacturers of distinctly different products; they are suited to account for continuous mass production of uniform products. Process costing systems produce the same cost per unit for all products.

To illustrate how a process costing system operates, we analyze the operations of Janis Juice Company during Year 2. Recall that Janis uses three distinct processes to produce cans of apple juice. Raw materials (whole apples) enter the *extraction department* where

EXHIBIT 12.7

JANIS JUICE COMPANY Account Balances As of January 1, Year 2		
	Assets	**Stk. Equity**
Cash	$320,000	
Raw materials—Fruit	7,800	
Raw materials—Additives	3,100	
Raw materials—Containers	9,500	
Work in process—Extraction	22,360	
Work in process—Mixing	7,960	
Work in process—Packaging	21,130	
Finished goods inventory	20,700	
Common stock		$180,000
Retained earnings		232,550
Total	$412,550	$412,550

juice concentrate is extracted from whole fruit. The juice extract passes to the *mixing department* where Janis adds water, sugar, food coloring, and preservatives. The juice mixture then moves to the *packaging department* where it is canned and boxed for shipment. Exhibit 12.7 shows the company's Year 2 beginning account balances.

The entries for Janis Juice Company's Year 2 accounting events, discussed individually in the following sections, are shown later in ledger T-accounts in Exhibit 12.9. The T-account entries are cross-referenced to sequential event numbers. As you study each event, trace it to the T-accounts.

EVENT 1 Janis paid $84,000 cash to purchase raw materials.

The effects of this event on the company's financial statements follow.

Balance Sheet								Income Statement				
Assets			=	Liabilities	+	Equity						
Cash	+	Raw Materials Inventory						Revenue	−	Expenses	=	Net Income
(84,000)	+	84,000	=	NA	+	NA		NA	−	NA	=	NA

This event is an asset exchange. Total assets and net income are not affected. The total purchase was for $25,000 of whole fruit, $30,000 of additives, and $29,000 of containers. Janis maintains separate inventory accounts for each category of raw material. Trace the entries for this event to the ledger accounts in Exhibit 12.9.

EVENT 2 Janis processed $26,720 of whole fruit to produce juice extract.

The effects of this event on the financial statements follow.

Balance Sheet								Income Statement				
Assets			=	Liabilities	+	Equity						
Raw Materials—Fruit	+	WIP—Extraction						Revenue	−	Expenses	=	Net Income
(26,720)	+	26,720	=	NA	+	NA		NA	−	NA	=	NA

This event is an asset exchange. It does not affect total assets or net income. Janis assigns the cost of the materials used to the extraction department rather than to any particular product or batch of products. The extraction department adds the same amount of value to each can of juice.

EVENT 3 Janis paid $38,000 cash to production employees who worked in the extraction department.

The effects of this event on the financial statements follow.

Balance Sheet								Income Statement				
Assets			=	Liabilities	+	Equity						
Cash	+	WIP—Extraction						Revenue	−	Expenses	=	Net Income
(38,000)	+	38,000	=	NA	+	NA		NA	−	NA	=	NA

This event is also an asset exchange. Production labor cost is not salary expense. Total assets and net income are not affected. Like the raw materials, the labor cost is assigned to the department rather than to individual products.

EVENT 4 **Janis applied estimated manufacturing overhead costs to the extraction department work in process inventory.**

Janis has identified a relationship between labor dollars and indirect overhead costs. The more labor dollars paid, the more indirect resources consumed. Janis estimated total indirect costs in Year 2 would be $96,000 and that it would pay $120,000 to production employees. Using these estimates, Janis established a *predetermined overhead rate* as follows:

$$\text{Predetermined overhead rate} = \text{Total estimated overhead costs} \div \text{Total estimated direct labor dollars}$$

$$\text{Predetermined overhead rate} = \$96{,}000 \div \$120{,}000$$

$$= \$0.80 \text{ per direct labor dollar}$$

Since the extraction department incurred $38,000 of labor cost (see Event 3), Janis applied $30,400 ($38,000 × $0.80) of overhead to that department. The effects of the overhead application on the financial statements follow.

Balance Sheet								Income Statement				
Assets			=	Liabilities	+	Equity						
Manufacturing Overhead	+	WIP—Extraction						Revenue	−	Expenses	=	Net Income
(30,400)	+	30,400	=	NA	+	NA		NA	−	NA	=	NA

The event is an asset exchange. Total assets and net income are not affected.

EVENT 5 **Janis finished processing some of the whole fruit and transferred the related cost from the extraction department Work in Process Inventory account to the mixing department Work in Process Inventory account.**

Total product costs in the extraction department Work in Process Inventory account amounted to $117,480 ($22,360 beginning balance + $26,720 materials + $38,000 labor + $30,400 applied overhead). The beginning inventory represented 100,000 units of product (cans) and the fruit Janis added started an additional 485,000 cans. The amount of fruit placed into production therefore represented 585,000 (100,000 + 485,000) units. Assume the extract transferred to the mixing department represented 500,000 cans of juice. The extraction department therefore had 85,000 (585,000 − 500,000) units in ending inventory that were *started but not completed.*

LO 12-4

Calculate equivalent units and prepare a cost of production report.

Janis had to allocate the total $117,480 product cost between the 85,000 partially completed units in ending inventory and the 500,000 completed units it transferred to the mixing department. A rational allocation requires converting the 85,000 partially completed units into *equivalent whole units.* The logic behind **equivalent whole units** relies on basic arithmetic. For example, 2 units that are 50 percent complete are equivalent to 1 whole (100 percent complete) unit (2 × 0.5 = 1). Similarly, 4 units that are 25 percent complete are equivalent to 1 whole unit (4 × 0.25 = 1). Further, 100 units that are 30 percent complete are equivalent to 30 whole units (100 units × 0.30 = 30).

An engineer estimated the 85,000 units in the extraction department's ending inventory were 40 percent complete. The equivalent whole units in ending inventory was therefore 34,000 (85,000 × 0.4). The *total* equivalent units processed by the extraction department during Year 2 was 534,000 (500,000 units finished and transferred to the mixing department plus 34,000 equivalent whole units in ending inventory). Janis determined the average **cost per equivalent unit** as follows:

Cost per equivalent unit = Total cost ÷ Number of equivalent whole units

Cost per equivalent unit = $117,480 ÷ 534,000

Cost per equivalent unit = $0.22 per equivalent unit

Janis used the *cost per equivalent unit* to allocate the total cost incurred in the extraction department between the amount transferred to the mixing department and the amount in the extraction department's ending work in process inventory as follows.

	Equivalent Units	×	Cost per Unit	=	Cost to Be Allocated
Transferred-out costs	500,000	×	$0.22	=	$110,000
Ending inventory	34,000	×	0.22	=	7,480
Total					$117,480

The effects of transferring $110,000 from the extraction department's work in process inventory to the mixing department's work in process inventory follow.

Balance Sheet								Income Statement				
Assets			=	Liabilities	+	Equity						
WIP—Extraction	+	WIP—Mixing						Revenue	−	Expenses	=	Net Income
(110,000)	+	110,000	=	NA	+	NA		NA	−	NA	=	NA

This event is an asset exchange. Total assets and net income are unaffected.

The allocation of costs between units transferred out and ending inventory is frequently summarized in a *cost of production report.* Cost of production reports usually provide details for three categories: the computation of equivalent units; the determination of cost per equivalent unit; and the allocation of total production cost between the units transferred out and the units in ending inventory. Exhibit 12.8 illustrates Janis' Year 2 cost of production report for the extraction department.

The method used here to determine equivalent units is the **weighted average method.** The weighted average method does not account for the state of completion of units in *beginning* inventory. Equivalent units are computed for *ending* inventory only. Failing to account for equivalent units in beginning as well as ending inventories can distort the accuracy of the cost assigned to goods transferred out and goods in inventory accounts at the end of the period. Managers frequently tolerate some inaccuracy because the weighted average method is relatively easy to use. If accuracy is of paramount importance, however, a company might use the **first-in, first-out (FIFO) method.** The FIFO method accounts for the degree of completion of both beginning and ending inventories, but it is more complex to apply. Applying the FIFO method in process costing applications is explained in upper-level accounting courses. It is beyond the scope of this text.

EVENT 6 Janis mixed (used) $24,400 of additives with the extract transferred from the extraction department.

Conceptually, the juice extract transferred from the extraction department is a raw material to the mixing department. The mixing department adds other materials to the juice extract, such as sweetener, food coloring, and preservatives. Although both *transferred-in costs* and *additives* represent raw materials, they are traditionally classified separately. Review the

EXHIBIT 12.8

JANIS JUICE COMPANY
Cost of Production Report
Extraction Department
For the Year Ended December 31, Year 2

	Actual		Equivalent
Determination of Equivalent Units			
Beginning inventory	100,000		
Units added to production	485,000		
Total	585,000		
Transferred to finished goods	500,000	100% Complete	500,000
Ending inventory	85,000	40% Complete	34,000
Total	585,000		534,000
Determination of Cost per Unit			
Cost accumulation			
Beginning inventory	$ 22,360		
Materials	26,720		
Labor	38,000		
Overhead	30,400		
Total	$117,480		
Divided by	÷		
equivalent units	534,000		
Cost per equivalent unit (i.e., per can)	$ 0.22		
Cost Allocation			
To work in process inventory, mixing dept. (500,000 × $0.22)	$110,000		
To ending inventory (34,000 × $0.22)	7,480		
Total	$117,480		

mixing department's Work in Process account in Exhibit 12.9 to see these costs. The effects of using additional materials in the mixing department follow.

Balance Sheet								Income Statement				
Assets			=	Liabilities	+	Equity						
Raw Materials—Additives	+	WIP—Mixing						Revenue	−	Expenses	=	Net Income
(24,400)	+	24,400	=	NA	+	NA		NA	−	NA	=	NA

This event is an asset exchange. Total assets and net income are not affected.

EVENT 7 **Janis paid $48,000 cash to production employees who worked in the mixing department.**

The effects of this event on the financial statements follow.

Balance Sheet								Income Statement				
Assets			=	Liabilities	+	Equity						
Cash	+	WIP—Mixing						Revenue	−	Expenses	=	Net Income
(48,000)	+	48,000	=	NA	+	NA		NA	−	NA	=	NA

This is an asset exchange. Total assets and net income are not affected.

EXHIBIT 12.9

Ledger T-Accounts for Janis Juice Company

Cash

Bal.	320,000	(1)	84,000
(15)	490,000	(3)	38,000
		(7)	48,000
		(11)	43,000
		(14)	106,330
		(17)	78,200
Bal.	412,470		

Raw Materials—Fruit

Bal.	7,800	(2)	26,720
(1)	25,000		
Bal.	6,080		

Raw Materials—Additives

Bal.	3,100	(6)	24,400
(1)	30,000		
Bal.	8,700		

Raw Materials—Containers

Bal.	9,500	(10)	32,000
(1)	29,000		
Bal.	6,500		

Manufacturing Overhead

(14)	106,330	(4)	30,400
		(8)	38,400
		(12)	34,400
		(18)	3,130
Bal.	0		

Work in Process—Extraction

Bal.	22,360	(5)	110,000 →
(2)	26,720		
(3)	38,000		
(4)	30,400		
Bal.	7,480		

Work in Process—Mixing

Bal.	7,960	(9)	219,300 →
→ (5)	110,000		
(6)	24,400		
(7)	48,000		
(8)	38,400		
Bal.	9,460		

Work in Process—Packaging

Bal.	21,130	(13)	331,200 →
→ (9)	219,300		
(10)	32,000		
(11)	43,000		
(12)	34,400		
Bal.	18,630		

Finished Goods Inventory

Bal.	20,700	(16)	338,100
→ (13)	331,200		
Bal.	13,800		

Common Stock

		Bal.	180,000

Retained Earnings

		Bal.	232,550

Sales Revenue

		(15)	490,000

Cost of Goods Sold

(16)	338,100		
(18)	3,130		
Bal.	341,230		

Selling and Admin. Exp.

(17)	78,200		

Answers to The Curious Accountant

Maxwell House should use a process costing system to determine the cost of a bag of coffee. This system is conceptually simple, especially when there is no beginning or ending work in process inventory. In the situation described in the beginning of the chapter, the cost of one bag of coffee would be calculated by dividing $1,025 million by 500 million bags, yielding a cost per bag of $2.05.

Bechtel should use a job-order costing system. This system, as you have seen, requires extensive record keeping. The cost of each item of material that goes into a specific construction project and the wages of each worker who helps build that project must be tracked to the specific job in question. These costs, along with the appropriate amount of overhead, will comprise the cost of that particular job; it is unlikely that the cost of any two projects will be exactly the same.

EVENT 8 **Janis applied estimated manufacturing overhead costs to the mixing department work in process inventory.**

Using the *predetermined overhead rate* calculated in Event 4, Janis determined it should apply $38,400 ($48,000 labor × $0.80 overhead rate) of overhead costs to the mixing department's work in process inventory. The effects of the overhead application on the financial statements follow.

Balance Sheet							Income Statement				
Assets			=	Liabilities	+	Equity					
Manufacturing Overhead	+	WIP—Mixing					Revenue	−	Expenses	=	Net Income
(38,400)	+	38,400	=	NA	+	NA	NA	−	NA	=	NA

The event is an asset exchange. Total assets and net income are not affected.

EVENT 9 **Janis finished mixing some of the juice extract with additives and transferred the related cost from the mixing department Work in Process Inventory account to the packaging department Work in Process Inventory account.**

Total product costs in the mixing department were $228,760 ($7,960 beginning balance + $110,000 transferred-in cost + $24,400 materials + $48,000 labor + $38,400 overhead). An engineer estimated that Janis transferred 510,000 units of mixed juice from the mixing department to the packaging department and that the 88,000 units of juice in the mixing department ending inventory were 25 percent complete.

The mixing department ending inventory therefore represented 22,000 (88,000 × 0.25) *equivalent whole units.* The total equivalent whole units produced by the mixing department was 532,000 (510,000 + 22,000). The average *cost per equivalent unit* was therefore $0.43 ($228,760 ÷ 532,000). Janis allocated the total product costs incurred in the mixing department between the amount transferred to the packaging department and the amount in the mixing department's *ending* work in process inventory as follows.

	Equivalent Units	×	Cost per Unit	=	Cost to Be Allocated
Transferred-out costs	510,000	×	$0.43	=	$219,300
Ending inventory	22,000	×	0.43	=	9,460
Total					$228,760

The effects of transferring $219,300 from the mixing department work in process inventory to the packaging department work in process inventory are as follows.

Balance Sheet								Income Statement				
Assets			=	Liabilities	+	Equity						
WIP—Mixing	+	WIP—Packaging						Revenue	−	Expenses	=	Net Income
(219,300)	+	219,300	=	NA	+	NA		NA	−	NA	=	NA

This event is an asset exchange. Total assets and net income are unaffected. Find the ending balance in the mixing department's Work in Process Inventory account in Exhibit 12.9. Also find the entry that transfers $219,300 of product cost from the mixing department's Work in Process Inventory account to the packaging department's Work in Process Inventory account.

EVENT 10 **Janis added containers and other packaging materials costing $32,000 to work in process in the packaging department.**

The effects of this event on the financial statements follow.

Balance Sheet								Income Statement				
Assets			=	Liabilities	+	Equity						
Raw Materials—Containers	+	WIP—Packaging						Revenue	−	Expenses	=	Net Income
(32,000)	+	32,000	=	NA	+	NA		NA	−	NA	=	NA

This event is an asset exchange. Total assets and net income are not affected.

EVENT 11 **Janis paid $43,000 cash to production employees who worked in the packaging department.**

The effects of this event on the financial statements follow.

Balance Sheet								Income Statement				
Assets			=	Liabilities	+	Equity						
Cash	+	WIP—Packaging						Revenue	−	Expenses	=	Net Income
(43,000)	+	43,000	=	NA	+	NA		NA	−	NA	=	NA

This is an asset exchange. Total assets and net income are not affected.

EVENT 12 **Janis applied estimated manufacturing overhead costs to the packaging department work in process inventory.**

Using the *predetermined overhead rate* calculated in Event 4, Janis determined it should apply $34,400 ($43,000 labor × $0.80 overhead rate) of overhead costs to the packaging department's work in process inventory. The effects of the overhead application on the financial statements follow.

Balance Sheet								Income Statement				
Assets			=	Liabilities	+	Equity						
Manufacturing Overhead	+	WIP—Packaging						Revenue	−	Expenses	=	Net Income
(34,400)	+	34,400	=	NA	+	NA		NA	−	NA	=	NA

The event is an asset exchange. Total assets and net income are not affected.

EVENT 13 **Janis finished packaging some of the juice and transferred the related cost from the packaging department Work in Process Inventory account to the Finished Goods Inventory account.**

Total product costs in the packaging department were $349,830 ($21,130 beginning balance + $219,300 transferred-in cost + $32,000 materials + $43,000 labor + $34,400 overhead). An engineer estimated that Janis transferred 480,000 units of packaged juice from the packaging department to finished goods inventory and that the 90,000 units of juice in the packaging department ending inventory were 30 percent complete.

The packaging department ending inventory therefore represented 27,000 (90,000 × 0.30) *equivalent whole units.* The total equivalent whole units produced by the packaging department was 507,000 (480,000 + 27,000). The average *cost per equivalent unit* was therefore $0.69 ($349,830 ÷ 507,000). Janis allocated the total product costs incurred in the packaging department between the amount transferred to finished goods inventory and the amount in the packaging department's ending work in process inventory as follows.

	Equivalent Units	×	Cost per Unit	=	Cost to Be Allocated
Transferred-out costs	480,000	×	$0.69	=	$331,200
Ending inventory	27,000	×	0.69	=	18,630
Total					$349,830

The effects of transferring $331,200 from the packaging department work in process inventory to the finished goods inventory follow.

Balance Sheet									Income Statement				
Assets			=	Liabilities	+	Equity							
WIP—Packaging	+	Finished Goods						Revenue	−	Expenses	=	Net Income	
(331,200)	+	331,200	=	NA	+	NA		NA	−	NA	=	NA	

This event is an asset exchange. Total assets and net income are unaffected. Find the ending balance in the packaging department's Work in Process Inventory account in Exhibit 12.9. Also find the entry that transfers $331,200 of product cost from the packaging department's Work in Process Inventory account to the Finished Goods Inventory account.

EVENT 14 **Janis paid $106,330 cash for actual overhead costs.**

The effects of this event on the financial statements follow.

Balance Sheet							Income Statement				
Assets			=	Liabilities	+	Equity					
Cash	+	Manufacturing Overhead					Revenue	−	Expenses	=	Net Income
(106,330)	+	106,330	=	NA	+	NA	NA	−	NA	=	NA

Incurring *actual overhead costs* is an asset exchange event. Total assets and net income are not affected.

EVENT 15 **Janis sold 490,000 cans of juice for $1 per can.**

The effects of this event on the financial statements follow.

Balance Sheet					Income Statement				
Assets	=	Liabilities	+	Equity	Revenue	−	Expenses	=	Net Income
490,000	=	NA	+	490,000	490,000	−	NA	=	490,000

Recognizing revenue from the sale of inventory is an asset source event. Assets (cash) and stockholders' equity (retained earnings) both increase, as do revenue and net income reported on the income statement.

EVENT 16 **Janis recognized cost of goods sold for the 490,000 cans of juice sold in Event 15.**

The average cost per finished can of juice was $0.69 (see Event 13). Cost of goods sold was therefore $338,100 (490,000 units × $0.69). The effects of this event on the financial statements follow.

Balance Sheet					Income Statement				
Assets	=	Liabilities	+	Equity	Revenue	−	Expenses	=	Net Income
(338,100)	=	NA	+	(338,100)	NA	−	338,100	=	(338,100)

Recognizing cost of goods sold is an asset use transaction. Both assets (finished goods inventory), and stockholders' equity (retained earnings), decrease. The increase in the expense, cost of goods sold, decreases net income.

EVENT 17 **Janis paid $78,200 cash for selling and administrative expenses.**

The effects of this event on the financial statements follow.

Balance Sheet					Income Statement				
Assets	=	Liabilities	+	Equity	Revenue	−	Expenses	=	Net Income
(78,200)	=	NA	+	(78,200)	NA	−	78,200	=	(78,200)

Recognizing selling and administrative expense is an asset use transaction. It decreases assets (cash) and stockholders' equity (retained earnings). Recognizing the expense decreases net income.

EVENT 18 **Janis closed the Manufacturing Overhead account and increased the Cost of Goods Sold account by $3,130.**

During Year 2, Janis applied $103,200 of overhead cost to production. Actual overhead costs were $106,330. Overhead was therefore underapplied by $3,130 ($106,330 − $103,200), indicating that too little overhead was transferred to work in process inventory, finished goods inventory, and cost of goods sold. Janis considered the underapplied amount insignificant and assigned it directly to cost of goods sold. The effects of this event on the financial statements follow.

Balance Sheet					Income Statement				
Assets	=	Liabilities	+	Equity	Revenue	−	Expenses	=	Net Income
(3,130)	=	NA	+	(3,130)	NA	−	3,130	=	(3,130)

Since underapplied overhead means too little estimated cost was transferred from the asset accounts to the Cost of Goods Sold account, closing the Manufacturing Overhead account to cost of goods sold corrects the understatement. The additional overhead costs of $3,130 increase cost of goods sold and decrease net income. After this adjustment, the total increases in the overhead account (actual costs) equal the total decreases (estimated costs). The ending balance in the Manufacturing Overhead account is zero. Manufacturing overhead is not reported on any financial statement.

The entries for the accounting events described are shown in the ledger T-accounts in Exhibit 12.9. Exhibit 12.10 shows the year-end account balances for Janis Juice Company.

EXHIBIT 12.10

JANIS JUICE COMPANY
Account Balances
As of December 31, Year 2

	Assets	Stk. Equity
Cash	$412,470	
Raw materials—Fruit	6,080	
Raw materials—Additives	8,700	
Raw materials—Containers	6,500	
Work in process—Extraction	7,480	
Work in process—Mixing	9,460	
Work in process—Packaging	18,630	
Finished goods inventory	13,800	
Common stock		$180,000
Retained earnings		303,120*
Total	$483,120	$483,120

*232,550 + 490,000 − 341,230 − 78,200

CHECK YOURSELF 12.2

Western Manufacturing Company uses a process costing system. Its products pass through two departments. Beginning inventory in Department I's Work in Process (WIP) account was $5,000. During the month the department added $13,200 of product costs to the WIP account. There were 200 units of product in beginning inventory, and 500 units were started during the month. Ending inventory consisted of 300 units 40 percent complete. Prepare a cost of production report showing the cost of goods transferred from Department I to Department II and the cost of Department I's ending work in process inventory.

Answer

Cost of Production Report

	Actual		Equivalent Units
Determination of Equivalent Units			
Beginning inventory	200		
Units added to production	500		
Total	700		
Transferred to finished goods	400	100% Complete	400
Ending inventory	300	40% Complete	120
Total	700		520
Determination of Cost per Unit			
Cost accumulation			
Beginning inventory	$ 5,000		
Product costs added	13,200		
Total product costs	$18,200		
Divide by	÷		
equivalent units	520		
Cost per equivalent unit	$ 35		
Cost Allocation			
Transferred to Department II (400 × $35)	$14,000		
Ending WIP inventory (120 × $35)	4,200		
Total	$18,200		

FOCUS ON INTERNATIONAL ISSUES

JOB-ORDER, PROCESS, AND HYBRID COSTING SYSTEMS CROSS INTERNATIONAL BORDERS

Companies throughout the world use job-order, process, and hybrid costing systems. **Nestle SA** is a Swiss company that makes many different food products, including chocolate candies such as Butterfingers and Raisinets. A homogeneous product like candy bars requires the use of a process costing system. In contrast, **Airbus** is an aircraft manufacturing company headquartered in Toulouse, France. When it completes an order for five A320 airplanes for **Air New Zealand**, the cost of this order will be determined using a job-order costing system.

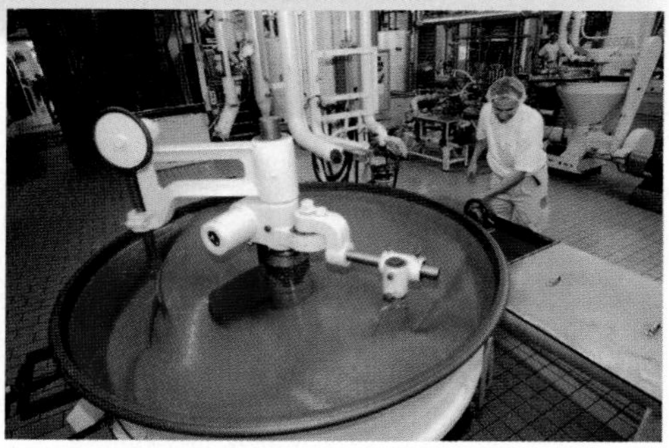

©Bloomberg/Getty Images

<< A Look Back

Job-order and *process costing systems* represent the two primary methods of accounting for product cost flows in manufacturing companies. In both systems, entries in the accounting records parallel the physical flow of products as they move through production. Job-order costing systems are used by manufacturers that produce distinct products or distinct batches of products. Products suited to job-order systems include buildings, ships, airplanes, and special-order batches. A job-order costing system accumulates costs for individual products or batches of products. Each product or batch has a job identification number. Costs are accumulated separately by job number. A job-order costing system requires detailed accounting information. The total cost of all jobs is accumulated in one Work in Process Inventory control account; details of the cost of materials, labor, and overhead for each job are kept in subsidiary records called *job-order cost sheets.* Process costing systems are used by manufacturers that make homogeneous products in a continuous production process. Products suited to a process costing system include paint, gasoline, and soft drinks. A process costing system accumulates product costs for each processing department (cutting, processing, assembling, packaging). Because the units are homogeneous, the cost per unit can be determined by dividing the total processing cost by the number of units (cost averaging). Any units that are partially complete at the end of an accounting period must be converted into equivalent whole units prior to determining the average cost per unit. The cost per equivalent whole unit is used to allocate the total processing cost among departments and ending inventories.

>> A Look Forward

The remaining two chapters are transitional chapters. Chapter 13 discusses financial statement analysis. Chapter 14 discusses advanced topics relating to the statement of cash flows. Some instructors include these subjects in the financial accounting course, and other instructors cover them in the managerial accounting course.

Video lectures and accompanying self-assessment quizzes are available in *Connect* for all learning objectives.

SELF-STUDY REVIEW PROBLEM 1

Hill Construction Company uses a job-order costing system. The company had three jobs in process at the beginning of the month. The beginning balance in the Work in Process control account was $145,400, made up of $42,400, $65,100, and $37,900 shown on the job cost sheets for Jobs 302,

303, and 304, respectively. During the month, Hill added the following materials and labor costs to each job.

Inventory	Materials	Labor
Job 302	$10,200	$32,000
Job 303	12,400	18,000
Job 304	16,500	10,000
Total	$39,100	$60,000

Overhead cost is applied at the predetermined rate of $0.60 per direct labor dollar. Actual overhead costs for the month were $36,800. Hill completed Job 303 and sold it for $129,000 cash during the month.

Required

a. Determine the balance in the Work in Process account at the end of the month.

b. Explain how the entry to close the Manufacturing Overhead account would affect the Cost of Goods Sold account.

c. Determine the amount of gross margin Hill would report on its income statement for the month.

Solution to Requirement *a*

Cost accumulated in the Work in Process account:

Inventory	Beg. Bal.	+	Materials	+	Labor	+	Overhead*	=	Total
Job 302	$42,400		$10,200		$32,000		$19,200		$103,800
Job 303	65,100		12,400		18,000		10,800		106,300
Job 304	37,900		16,500		10,000		6,000		70,400

*60 percent of direct labor cost.

Since Hill has sold Job 303, work in process at the end of the month is the sum of costs assigned to Jobs 302 and 304, $174,200 ($103,800 + $70,400).

Solution to Requirement *b*

Total applied overhead is $36,000 ($19,200 + $10,800 + $6,000). Since actual overhead is $36,800, overhead is underapplied by $800 ($36,800 − $36,000). Since the overhead is underapplied, cost of goods sold is understated. The entry to close the overhead account would increase the amount of cost of goods sold by $800.

Solution to Requirement *c*

Sales revenue	$ 129,000
Cost of goods sold (Job 303, $106,300 + Underapplied overhead, $800)	(107,100)
Gross margin	$ 21,900

SELF-STUDY REVIEW PROBLEM 2

United Technology Manufacturing Company (UTMC) uses a process costing system. Products pass through two departments. The following information applies to the Assembly Department. Beginning inventory in the department's Work in Process (WIP) account was $18,400. During the month, UTMC added $200,273 of product costs to the WIP account. There were 5,700 units of product in the beginning inventory and 45,300 units started during the month. The ending inventory consisted of 4,200 units, which were 30 percent complete.

Required

Prepare a cost of production report for the month.

Solution

Cost of Production Report

	Actual		Equivalent Units
Determination of Equivalent Units			
Beginning inventory	5,700		
Units added to production	45,300		
Total	51,000		
Transferred to finished goods	46,800	100% Complete	46,800
Ending inventory	4,200	30% Complete	1,260
Total	51,000		48,060
Determination of Cost per Unit			
Cost accumulation			
Beginning inventory	$ 18,400		
Product costs added	200,273		
Total product costs	$218,673		
Divide by	÷		
equivalent units	48,060		
Cost per equivalent unit	$ 4.55		
Cost Allocation			
Transferred out (46,800 × $4.55)	$212,940		
Ending WIP inventory (1,260 × $4.55)	5,733		
Total	$218,673		

KEY TERMS

Cost per equivalent unit 552
Equivalent whole units 551
First-in, first-out (FIFO) method 552
Hybrid costing system 540
Job cost sheet 540
Job-order costing system 538
Materials requisition form 540
Process costing system 538
Transferred-in costs 539
Weighted average method 552
Work ticket 540

QUESTIONS

1. To what types of products is a job-order costing system best suited? Provide examples.
2. To what types of products is a process costing system best suited? Provide examples.
3. Why do both job-order and process costing require some form of cost averaging?
4. How is the unit cost of a product determined in a process costing system?
5. Ludwig Company, which normally operates a process costing system to account for the cost of the computers that it produces, has received a special order from a corporate client to produce and sell 5,000 computers. Can Ludwig use a job-order costing system to account for the costs associated with the special order even though it uses a process costing system for its normal operations?
6. Which system, a job-order or a process costing system, requires more documentation?
7. How do source documents help accountants operate a costing system?
8. In a job-order costing system, what are the Work in Process Inventory subsidiary records called? What information is included in these subsidiary records?
9. How is indirect labor recorded in ledger accounts? How is this labor eventually assigned to the items produced in a job-order costing system?
10. How is depreciation on manufacturing equipment recorded in ledger accounts? How is this depreciation assigned to the items produced in a job-order costing system and in a process costing system?
11. Why is a process costing system not appropriate for companies that produce

items that are distinctly different from one another?

12. The president of Videl Corporation tells you that her company has a difficult time determining the cost per unit of product that it makes. It seems that some units are always partially complete. Counting these units as complete understates the cost per unit because all of the units but only part of the cost is included in the unit cost computation. Conversely, ignoring the number of partially completed products overstates the cost per unit because all of the costs are included but some of the number of units are omitted from the per-unit computation. How can Videl obtain a more accurate cost per unit figure?

13. Bindon Furniture Manufacturing has completed its monthly inventory count for dining room chairs and recorded the following information for ending inventory: 600 units 100 percent complete, 300 units 60 percent complete, and 100 units 20 percent complete. The company uses a process costing system to determine unit cost. Why would unit cost be inaccurate if 1,000 units were used to determine unit cost?

14. What is the weighted average method of determining equivalent units? Why is it used? What are its weaknesses?

15. What is the purpose of each of the three primary steps in a process costing system? Describe each.

16. In a process costing system, what does the term *transferred-in costs* mean? How is the amount of transferred-in costs determined?

17. The finishing department is the last of four sequential production departments for Kowalski Graphics Inc. The company's other production departments are design, layout, and printing. The finishing department incurred the following costs in March Year 1: direct materials, $40,000; direct labor, $80,000; applied overhead, $90,000; and transferred-in costs, $120,000. Which department incurred the transferred-in costs? In what month were the transferred-in costs incurred?

MULTIPLE-CHOICE QUESTIONS

Multiple-choice questions are available in *Connect*.

EXERCISES—SERIES A

connect **All applicable Exercises in Series A are available in *Connect*.**

Exercise 12-1A ***Matching products with appropriate costing systems*** **LO 12-1**

Required

Indicate which costing system (job-order, process, or hybrid) would be most appropriate for the type of product listed in the left-hand column. The first item is shown as an example.

Type of Product	Type of Costing System
a. Coffee table	Process
b. Plastic storage containers	
c. TV set	
d. Ship	
e. Potato chips	
f. House	
g. Custom-made suit	
h. Van with custom features	
i. CPA review course	
j. Shirts	
k. Pots and pans	
l. Apartment building	
m. Automobile	
n. Hollywood movie	
o. Airplane	
p. Personal computer with special features	

LO 12-1

Exercise 12-2A *Identifying the appropriate costing system*

Woolrich Company makes small aluminum storage bins that it sells through a direct marketing mail-order business. The typical bin measures 6 × 8 feet. The bins are normally used to store garden tools or other small household items. Woolrich customizes bins for special-order customers by adding shelving; occasionally, it makes large bins following the unique specifications of commercial customers.

Required

Recommend the type of costing system (job-order, process, or hybrid) that Woolrich should use. Explain your recommendation.

LO 12-1

Exercise 12-3A *Job-order or process costing system and a pricing decision*

Kirk Gaber, a tailor in his home country, recently immigrated to the United States. He is interested in starting a business making custom suits for men. Mr. Gaber is trying to determine the cost of making a suit so he can set an appropriate selling price. He estimates that his materials cost will range from $100 to $160 per suit. Because he will make the suits himself, he assumes there will be no labor cost. Some suits will require more time than others, but Mr. Gaber considers this fact to be irrelevant because he is personally supplying the labor, which costs him nothing. Finally, Mr. Gaber knows that he will incur some overhead costs such as rent, utilities, advertising, packaging, delivery, and so on; however, he is uncertain as to the exact cost of these items.

Required

a. Should Mr. Gaber use a job-order or a process costing system?

b. How can Mr. Gaber determine the cost of suits he makes during the year when he does not know what the total overhead cost will be until the end of the year?

c. Is it appropriate for Mr. Gaber to consider labor cost to be zero?

d. With respect to the overhead costs mentioned in the problem, distinguish the *manufacturing overhead* costs from the *selling and administrative* expenses. Comment on whether Mr. Gaber should include the selling and administrative expenses in determining the product cost if he uses cost-plus pricing. Comment on whether the selling and administrative expenses should be included in determining the product cost for financial reporting purposes.

LO 12-1

Exercise 12-4A *Selecting the appropriate costing system*

John's Car Wash (JCW) offers customers three cleaning options. Under Option 1, only the exterior is cleaned. With Option 2, the exterior and interior are cleaned. Option 3 provides exterior waxing as well as exterior and interior cleaning. JCW completed 4,000 Option 1 cleanings, 5,200 Option 2 cleanings, and 3,200 Option 3 cleanings during Year 1. The average cost of completing each cleaning option and the price charged for it are shown here.

	Option 1	Option 2	Option 3
Price charged	$10	$12	$21
Costs of completing task	4	5	15

Required

a. Is JCW a manufacturing or a service company? Explain.

b. Which costing system, job-order or process, is most appropriate for JCW? Why?

c. What is the balance in JCW's Work in Process and Finished Goods Inventory accounts on the December 31 balance sheet?

d. Speculate as to the major costs that JCW incurs to complete a cleaning job.

LO 12-2

Exercise 12-5A *Job-order costing in a manufacturing company*

Mapleton Corporation builds sailboats. On January 1, Year 3, the company had the following account balances: $48,000 for both cash and common stock. Boat 25 was started on February 10 and finished on May 31. To build the boat, Mapleton had incurred cash costs of $8,640 for labor and $7,500 for materials. During the same period, Mapleton paid $11,160 cash for actual manufacturing overhead costs. The company expects to incur $210,600 of indirect overhead cost during Year 3. The overhead is allocated to jobs based on direct labor cost. The expected total labor cost for the year is $162,000.

Mapleton uses a just-in-time inventory management system. Consequently, it does not have raw materials inventory. Raw materials purchases are recorded directly in the Work in Process Inventory account.

Required

a. Use the horizontal financial statements model, as illustrated here, to record Mapleton's business events. The first row shows beginning balances.

Balance Sheet													Income Statement				
Assets								=	Equity								
Cash	+	Work in Process	+	Finished Goods	+	Manuf. Overhead		=	Com. Stock	+	Ret. Ear.		Rev.	−	Exp.	=	Net Inc.
48,000	+	NA	+	NA	+	NA		=	48,000	+	NA		NA	−	NA	=	NA

b. If Mapleton desires to earn a profit equal to 20 percent of cost, for what price should it sell the boat?

c. If the boat is not sold by year-end, what amount would appear in the Work in Process Inventory and Finished Goods Inventory on the balance sheet for Boat 25?

d. Is the amount of inventory you calculated in Requirement *c* the actual or the estimated cost of the boat?

e. When is it appropriate to use estimated inventory cost on a year-end balance sheet?

Exercise 12-6A *Job-order costing in a manufacturing company* LO 12-2

Lugar Corporation makes custom-order furniture to meet the needs of persons with disabilities. On January 1, Year 2, the company had the following account balances: $37,800 for both cash and common stock. In Year 2, Lugar worked on three jobs. The relevant direct operating costs follow.

	Direct Labor	Direct Materials
Job 1	$3,000	$2,000
Job 2	1,400	700
Job 3	4,100	1,800
Total	$8,500	$4,500

Lugar's predetermined manufacturing overhead rate was $0.50 per direct labor dollar. Actual manufacturing overhead costs amounted to $4,200. Lugar paid cash for all costs. The company completed and delivered Jobs 1 and 2 to customers during the year. Job 3 was incomplete at the end of the year. The company sold Job 1 for $9,250 cash and Job 2 for $4,930 cash. Lugar also paid $2,000 cash for selling and administrative expenses for the year.

Lugar uses a just-in-time inventory management system. Consequently, it does not have raw materials inventory. Raw materials purchases are recorded directly in the Work in Process Inventory account.

Required

a. Record the preceding events in a horizontal statements model. The first row shows beginning balances.

Balance Sheet													Income Statement				
Assets								=	Equity								
Cash	+	Work in Process	+	Finished Goods	+	Manuf. Overhead		=	Com. Stock	+	Ret. Ear.		Rev.	−	Exp.	=	Net Inc.
37,800	+	NA	+	NA	+	NA		=	37,800	+	NA		NA	−	NA	=	NA

b. Record the entry to close the amount of underapplied or overapplied overhead for the year to Cost of Goods Sold (in the expense category) in the horizontal financial statements model.

c. Determine the gross margin for the year.

LO 12-2

Exercise 12-7A *Job-order costing in a service company*

Stewart Condos Corporation is a small company owned by Dennis Hatch. It leases three condos of differing sizes to customers as vacation facilities. Labor costs for each condo consist of maid service and maintenance cost. Other direct operating costs consist of interest and depreciation. The direct operating costs for each condo follow.

	Direct Labor	Other Direct Operating Costs
Condo 1	$ 30,000	$ 72,000
Condo 2	35,000	80,000
Condo 3	45,000	88,000
Total	$110,000	$240,000

Indirect operating expenses, which amounted to $96,000, are allocated to the condos in proportion to the amount of other direct operating costs incurred for each.

Required

a. Assuming that the amount of rent revenue from Condo 2 is $192,000, what amount of income did it earn?

b. Based on the preceding information, will the company show finished goods inventory on its balance sheet? If so, what is the amount of this inventory? If not, explain why not.

LO 12-2

Exercise 12-8A *Job-order costing system*

The following information applies to Job 730 completed by Riverton Manufacturing Company during the month of October. The amount of labor cost for the job was $162,000. Applied overhead amounted to $230,000. The project was completed and delivered to Hudson Company at a contract price of $654,000. Riverton recognized a gross profit of $120,000 on the job.

Required

Determine the amount of raw materials used to complete Job 730.

LO 12-2, 12-3

Exercise 12-9A *Process cost system*

Keystone Manufacturing Company started operations on January 1, Year 1. During Year 1, the company engaged in the following transactions.

1. Issued common stock for $40,000.
2. Paid $10,000 cash to purchase raw materials used to make products.
3. Transferred $9,000 of raw materials to the production department.
4. Paid $12,000 cash for labor used to make products.
5. Paid $18,000 cash for overhead costs (assume actual and estimated overhead are the same).
6. Finished work on products that cost $35,000 to make.
7. Sold products that cost $31,500 to make for $42,500 cash.

Required

a. Prepare the December 31, Year 1, balance sheet.

b. Prepare the December 31, Year 1, income statement.

Exercise 12-10A *Process costing system*

LO 12-3

Kimball Company is a cosmetics manufacturer. Its assembly department receives raw cosmetics from the molding department. The assembly department places the raw cosmetics into decorative containers and transfers them to the packaging department. The assembly department's Work in Process Inventory account had a $40,000 balance as of August 1. During August, the department incurred raw materials, labor, and overhead costs amounting to $36,000, $42,500, and $40,000, respectively. The department transferred products that cost $171,000 to the packaging department. The balance in the assembly department's Work in Process Inventory account as of August 31 was $41,500.

Required

Determine the cost of raw cosmetics transferred from the molding department to the assembly department during August.

Exercise 12-11A *Cost allocation in a process system*

LO 12-4

Lennox Watches Inc. makes watches. Its assembly department started the accounting period with a beginning inventory balance of $68,000. During the accounting period, the department incurred $96,000 of transferred-in cost, $62,000 of materials cost, $120,000 of labor cost, and $134,000 of applied overhead cost. The department processed 6,000 total equivalent units of product during the accounting period.

Required

(Each requirement is independent of the other.)

a. Assuming that 1,200 equivalent units of product were in the ending work in process inventory, determine the amount of cost transferred out of the Work in Process Inventory account of the assembly department to the Finished Goods Inventory account. What was the assembly department's cost of ending work in process inventory?

b. Assuming that 5,600 units of product were transferred out of the assembly department's work in process inventory to finished goods inventory, determine the amount of the assembly department's cost of ending work in process inventory. What was the cost of the finished goods inventory transferred out of the assembly department?

Exercise 12-12A *Process costing system—determine equivalent units and allocate costs*

LO 12-4

Ashton Ski Company manufactures snow skis. During the most recent accounting period, the company's finishing department transferred 5,000 sets of skis to finished goods. At the end of the accounting period, 500 sets of skis were estimated to be 40 percent complete. Total product costs for the finishing department amounted to $416,000.

Required

a. Determine the cost per equivalent.

b. Determine the cost of the goods transferred out of the finishing department.

c. Determine the cost of the finishing department's ending work in process inventory.

PROBLEMS—SERIES A

connect **All applicable Problems in Series A are available in *Connect*.**

Problem 12-13A *Job-order costing system*

LO 12-2

excel

Lehigh Manufacturing Corporation was started with the issuance of common stock for $60,000. It purchased $14,000 of raw materials and worked on three job orders during Year 1 for which data follow. (Assume that all transactions are for cash unless otherwise indicated.)

CHECK FIGURE
d. COGM: $29,700
NI: $6,300

	Direct Raw Materials Used	Direct Labor
Job 1	$ 2,800	$ 6,000
Job 2	4,000	8,000
Job 3	6,000	4,000
Total	$12,800	$18,000

Factory overhead is applied using a predetermined overhead rate of $0.60 per direct labor dollar. Jobs 2 and 3 were completed during the period and Job 3 was sold for $20,000 cash. Lehigh paid $800 for selling and administrative expenses. Actual factory overhead was $11,300.

Required

a. Record the preceding events in a horizontal statements model. The first event for Year 1 has been recorded as an example.

Balance Sheet																				Income Statement				
Assets									=	Equity														
Cash	+	Raw M.	+	MOH	+	WIP	+	F. Goods	=	C. Stk.	+	Ret. Ear.								Rev.	−	Exp.	=	Net Inc.
60,000	+	NA	+	NA	+	NA	+	NA	=	60,000	+	NA								NA	−	NA	=	NA

b. Reconcile all subsidiary accounts with their respective control accounts.

c. Record the closing entry for over- or underapplied manufacturing overhead in the horizontal statements model, assuming that the amount is insignificant.

d. Prepare a schedule of cost of goods manufactured and sold, an income statement, and a balance sheet for Year 1.

LO 12-2

Problem 12-14A *Job-order costing system*

CHECK FIGURE
d. COGM: $6,148
Total assets: $32,102

Ladora Construction Company began operations on January 1, Year 1, when it acquired $30,000 cash from the issuance of common stock. During the year, Ladora purchased $6,000 of direct raw materials and used $5,640 of the direct materials. There were 108 hours of direct labor worked at an average rate of $20 per hour paid in cash. The predetermined overhead rate was $9 per direct labor hour. The company started construction on three prefabricated buildings. The job cost sheets reflected the following allocations of costs to each building.

	Direct Materials	Direct Labor Hours
Job 1	$1,440	30
Job 2	2,400	50
Job 3	1,800	28

The company paid $320 cash for indirect labor costs. Actual overhead cost paid in cash other than indirect labor was $640. Ladora completed Jobs 1 and 2 and sold Job 1 for $5,000 cash. The company incurred $600 of selling and administrative expenses that were paid in cash. Over- or underapplied overhead is closed to Cost of Goods Sold.

Required

a. Record the preceding events in a horizontal statements model. The first event for Year 1 has been recorded as an example.

Balance Sheet													Income Statement				
Assets									=	Equity							
Cash	+	Raw M.	+	MOH	+	WIP	+	F. Goods	=	C. Stk.	+	Ret. Ear.	Rev.	−	Exp.	=	Net Inc.
30,000	+	NA	+	NA	+	NA	+	NA	=	30,000	+	NA	NA	−	NA	=	NA

b. Reconcile all subsidiary accounts with their respective control accounts.
c. Record the closing entry for over- or underapplied manufacturing overhead in the horizontal statements model, assuming that the amount is insignificant.
d. Prepare a schedule of cost of goods manufactured and sold, an income statement, and a balance sheet for Year 1.

LO 12-3, 12-4

CHECK FIGURE
d. COGS: $18,900
Cash: $24,000

Problem 12-15A *Process costing system*

Eminence Corporation makes rocking chairs. The chairs move through two departments during production. Lumber is cut into chair parts in the cutting department, which transfers the parts to the assembly department for completion. The company sells the unfinished chairs to hobby shops. The following transactions apply to Eminence's operations for its first year, Year 1. (Assume that all transactions are for cash unless otherwise stated.)

1. The company was started when it acquired a $47,000 cash contribution from the owners.
2. The company purchased $15,000 of direct raw materials and $400 of indirect materials. Indirect materials are capitalized in the Production Supplies account.
3. Direct materials totaling $7,000 were issued to the cutting department.
4. Labor cost was $28,200. Direct labor for the cutting and assembly departments was $10,000 and $13,000, respectively. Indirect labor costs were $5,200.
5. The predetermined overhead rate was $0.50 per direct labor dollar in each department.
6. Actual overhead costs other than indirect materials and indirect labor were $6,400 for the year.
7. The cutting department transferred $12,500 of inventory to the assembly department.
8. The assembly department transferred $20,500 of inventory to finished goods.
9. The company sold inventory costing $18,500 for $30,000.
10. Selling and administrative expenses were $3,000.
11. A physical count revealed $100 of production supplies on hand at the end of Year 1.
12. Assume that over- or underapplied overhead is insignificant.

Required

a. Record the data in T-accounts.
b. Record the closing entry for over- or underapplied manufacturing overhead, assuming that the amount is insignificant.
c. Close the revenue and expense accounts.
d. Prepare a schedule of cost of goods manufactured and sold, an income statement, and a balance sheet for Year 1.

Problem 12-16A *Process costing system*

LO 12-3, 12-4

CHECK FIGURE
d. NI: $10,400
Cash: $10,350

Use the ending balances from Problem 12-15A as the beginning balances for this problem. The transactions for the second year of operation (Year 2) are described here. (Assume that all transactions are cash transactions unless otherwise indicated.)

1. The company purchased $10,000 of direct raw materials and $650 of indirect materials. Indirect materials are capitalized in the Production Supplies account.
2. Materials totaling $7,250 were issued to the cutting department.
3. Labor cost was $23,500. Direct labor for the cutting and assembly departments was $11,000 and $10,000, respectively. Indirect labor costs were $2,500. (*Note:* Assume that sufficient cash is available when periodic payments are made. These amounts represent summary data for the entire year and are not presented in exact order of collection and payment.)
4. The predetermined overhead rate was $0.50 per direct labor dollar in each department.
5. Actual overhead costs other than indirect materials and indirect labor for the month were $7,300.
6. The cutting department transferred $15,500 of inventory to the assembly department.
7. The assembly department transferred $30,500 of inventory to finished goods.
8. The company sold inventory costing $17,500 for $32,000.
9. Selling and administrative expenses were $4,200.

10. At the end of Year 2, $150 of production supplies was on hand.
11. Assume that over- or underapplied overhead is insignificant.

Required

a. Record the data in T-accounts.
b. Record the closing entry for over- or underapplied manufacturing overhead, assuming that the amount is insignificant.
c. Close the revenue and expense accounts.
d. Prepare a schedule of cost of goods manufactured and sold, an income statement, and a balance sheet for Year 2.

LO 12-3, 12-4

CHECK FIGURE
b. $30

Problem 12-17A *Process costing system*

Lisburn Plastic Products Company makes a plastic toy using two departments: parts and assembly. The following data pertain to the parts department's transactions in Year 2.

1. The beginning balance in the Work in Process Inventory account was $10,000. This inventory consisted of parts for 2,000 toys. The beginning balances in the Raw Materials Inventory, Production Supplies, and Cash accounts were $97,500, $1,000, and $200,000, respectively.
2. Direct materials costing $90,000 were issued to the parts department. The materials were sufficient to make 6,000 additional toys.
3. Direct labor cost was $80,000, and indirect labor costs were $6,000. All labor costs were paid in cash.
4. The predetermined overhead rate was $0.30 per direct labor dollar.
5. Actual overhead costs other than production supplies and indirect labor for the year were $18,250, which was paid in cash.
6. The parts department completed work for 6,400 toys. The remaining toy parts were 25 percent complete. The completed parts were transferred to the assembly department.
7. All of the production supplies had been used by the end of Year 2.
8. Over- or underapplied overhead was closed to the Cost of Goods Sold account.

Required

a. Determine the number of equivalent units of production.
b. Determine the product cost per equivalent unit.
c. Allocate the total cost between the ending work in process inventory and parts transferred to the assembly department.
d. Record the transactions in a partial set of T-accounts.

LO 12-3, 12-4

excel

CHECK FIGURE
b. $0.14

Problem 12-18A *Process costing system*

Wright Cola Corporation produces a new soft drink brand, Sweet Spring, using two production departments: mixing and bottling. Wright's beginning balances and data pertinent to the mixing department's activities for Year 2 follow.

Accounts	Beginning Balances
Cash	$ 50,000
Raw materials inventory	14,800
Production supplies	100
Work in process inventory (400,000 units)	48,000
Common stock	$112,900

1. Wright Cola issued additional common stock for $80,000 cash.
2. The company purchased raw materials and production supplies for $29,600 and $800, respectively, in cash.

3. The company issued $32,360 of raw materials to the mixing department for the production of 800,000 units of Sweet Spring that were started in Year 2. A unit of soft drink is the amount needed to fill a bottle.
4. The mixing department used 2,400 hours of labor during Year 2, consisting of 2,200 hours for direct labor and 200 hours for indirect labor. The average wage was $9.60 per hour. All wages were paid in Year 2 in cash.
5. The predetermined overhead rate was $1.60 per direct labor hour.
6. Actual overhead costs other than indirect materials and indirect labor for the year amounted to $1,260, which was paid in cash.
7. The mixing department completed 600,000 units of Sweet Spring. The remaining inventory was 25 percent complete.
8. The completed soft drink was transferred to the bottling department.
9. The ending balance in the Production Supplies account was $560.

Required

a. Determine the number of equivalent units of production.
b. Determine the product cost per equivalent unit.
c. Allocate the total cost between the ending work in process inventory and units transferred to the bottling department.
d. Record the transactions in T-accounts.

Problem 12-19A *Process costing system cost of production report*

LO 12-4

excel

CHECK FIGURE
b. $80

Plymouth Company had 400 units of product in its work in process inventory at the beginning of the period and started 2,100 additional units during the period. At the end of the period, 750 units were in work in process inventory. The ending work in process inventory was estimated to be 40 percent complete. The cost of work in process inventory at the beginning of the period was $24,000, and $140,000 of product costs was added during the period.

Required

Prepare a cost of production report showing the following:

a. The number of equivalent units of production.
b. The product cost per equivalent unit.
c. The total cost allocated between the ending Work in Process Inventory and Finished Goods Inventory accounts.

Problem 12-20A *Determining inventory cost using a process costing system*

LO 12-4

CHECK FIGURE
b. $110

Molton Company had 300 units of product in work in process inventory at the beginning of the period. It started 1,500 units during the period and transferred 1,200 units to finished goods inventory. The ending work in process inventory was estimated to be 70 percent complete. Cost data for the period follow.

	Product Costs
Beginning balance	$ 28,200
Added during period	150,000
Total	$178,200

Required

Prepare a cost of production report showing the following:

a. The number of equivalent units of production.
b. The product cost per equivalent unit.
c. The total cost allocated between ending work in process inventory and finished goods inventory.

LO 12-4

CHECK FIGURES
a. Cost/unit: $2.50
b. Cost/unit: $4.00

Problem 12-21A *Process costing system with second department*

Tonbridge Corporation makes a health beverage named Tonbridge that is manufactured in a two-stage production process. The drink is first created in the Conversion Department where material ingredients (natural juices, supplements, preservatives, etc.) are combined. On July 1, Year 2, the company had a sufficient quantity of partially completed beverage mix in the Conversion Department to make 50,000 containers of Tonbridge. This beginning inventory had a cost of $80,000. During July, the company added ingredients necessary to make 190,000 containers of Tonbridge. The cost of these ingredients was $400,000. During July, liquid mix representing 180,000 containers of the beverage was transferred to the Finishing Department. The beverage mix is poured into containers and packaged for shipment in the Finishing Department. Beverage that remained in the Conversion Department at the end of July was 20 percent complete. At the beginning of July the Finishing Department had 10,000 containers of beverage mix. The cost of this mix was $50,000. The department added $120,000 of manufacturing costs (materials, labor, and overhead) during July. During July, 120,000 containers of Tonbridge were completed. The ending inventory for this department was 50 percent complete at the end of July.

Required

a. Prepare a Cost of Production Report for the Conversion Department for July.

b. Prepare a Cost of Production Report for the Finishing Department for July.

c. If 100,000 containers of Tonbridge are sold in July for $760,000, determine the company's gross margin for July.

EXERCISES—SERIES B

LO 12-1

Exercise 12-1B *Matching products with appropriate costing systems*

Required

Indicate which costing system (job-order, process, or hybrid) would be most appropriate for the type of product listed in the left-hand column. The first item is shown as an example.

Type of Product	Type of Costing System
a. House	Job-order
b. Oil	
c. Luxury yacht	
d. Special-order personal computer	
e. Over-the-counter personal computer	
f. Mouse pad for a computer	
g. Aircraft carrier	
h. Makeup sponge	
i. Handheld video game player	
j. Generic coffee mug	
k. Personalized coffee mug	
l. Surgery	
m. Audit engagement	
n. Shoes	
o. Treadmill	
p. Textbook	

LO 12-1

Exercise 12-2B *Identifying the appropriate costing system*

Tully Corporation's Kearney Plant in Jacksonville, Florida, produces the company's weed-control chemical solution, Weed Terminator. Production begins with pure water from a controlled stream to which the plant adds different chemicals in the production process. Finally, the plant bottles the resulting chemical solution. The process is highly automated, with different computer-controlled maneuvers and testing to ensure the quality of the end product. With only 15 employees, the plant can produce up to 6,000 bottles per day.

Required

Recommend the type of costing system (job-order, process, or hybrid) Kearney Plant should use. Explain your recommendation.

Exercise 12-3B *Job-order or process costing*

LO 12-1

Julie Snyder, an artist, plans to make her living drawing customer portraits at a stand in Underground Atlanta. She will carry her drawing equipment and supplies to work each day in bags. By displaying two of her best hand-drawn portraits on either side of her stand, she expects to attract tourists' attention. Ms. Snyder can usually draw a customer's portrait in 30 minutes. Her materials cost is minimal, about $2 for a portrait. Her most significant cost will be leasing the stand for $1,200 per month. She estimates she can replace supplies and worn out equipment for $50 per month. She plans to work 20 days each month from noon to 9:00 P.M. After surveying her planned work environment before beginning the business, she observed that six other artists were providing customer portraits in that section of Underground Atlanta. Their portrait prices ranged from $25 to $45 per portrait. They also offered to frame portraits for customers at $15 per frame. Ms. Snyder found that she could obtain comparable frames for $5 each and that properly framing a portrait takes about 10 minutes. The biggest challenge, Ms. Snyder observed, was attracting tourists' interest. If she could draw portraits continuously during her workdays, she could earn quite a respectable income. But she noticed several of the artists were reading magazines as she walked by.

Required

a. Should Ms. Snyder use a job-order or process costing system for her art business?

b. List the individual types of costs Ms. Snyder will likely incur in providing portraits.

c. How could Ms. Snyder estimate her overhead rate per portrait when she does not know the number of portraits she will draw in a month?

d. Ms. Snyder will not hire any employees. Will she have labor cost? Explain.

Exercise 12-4B *Selecting the appropriate costing system*

LO 12-1

Glenvar Automotive Specialties Inc. has a successful market niche. It customizes automobile interiors to fit the various needs of disabled customers. Some customers need special equipment to accommodate drivers with disabilities. Others need modified entrance and seating arrangements for passengers who are disabled. Customer vehicles vary according to different brands and models of sedans, minivans, sport-utility vehicles, and full-size vans. Glenvar's engineers interview customers directly to ascertain their special needs. The engineers then propose a design, explaining it and its cost for the customer's approval. Customers have the opportunity to request changes. Once the company and customer agree on an engineering design and its price, they sign a contract, and the customer's vehicle is delivered to Glenvar's factory. The factory manager directs mechanics to customize the vehicle according to the engineering design.

Required

a. Is Glenvar a manufacturing company or a service company? Explain.

b. Which costing system, job-order or process, would be most appropriate for Glenvar? Why?

c. Does Glenvar have work in process and finished goods inventories?

d. Should Glenvar classify engineering design costs as materials, labor, or overhead? Why?

Exercise 12-5B *Job-order costing in a manufacturing company*

LO 12-2

Tang Drapery Inc. specializes in making custom draperies for both commercial and residential customers. It began business on August 1, Year 1, by acquiring $60,000 cash through issuing common stock.

In August Year 1, Tang accepted drapery orders, Jobs 801 and 802, for two new commercial buildings. The company paid cash for the following costs related to the orders.

Job 801	
Raw materials	$12,500
Direct labor (512 hours at $25 per hour)	12,800
Job 802	
Raw materials	10,000
Direct labor (340 hours at $25 per hour)	8,500

During the same month, Tang paid $18,000 for various indirect costs such as utilities, equipment leases, and factory-related insurance. The company estimated its annual manufacturing overhead cost would be $300,000 and expected to use 20,000 direct labor hours in its first year of operation. It planned to allocate overhead based on direct labor hours. On August 31, Year 1, Tang completed Job 801 and collected the contract price of $43,750. Job 802 was still in process.

Tang uses a just-in-time inventory management system. Consequently, it has no raw materials inventory. Raw materials purchases are recorded directly in the Work in Process Inventory account.

Required

a. Use a horizontal financial statements model as follows to record Tang's accounting events for August Year 1. The first event is shown as an example.

Balance Sheet													Income Statement				
Assets								=	Equity								
Cash	+	Work in Process	+	Finished Goods	+	Manuf. Overhead		=	Com. Stock	+	Ret. Ear.		Rev.	−	Exp.	=	Net Inc.
60,000	+	NA	+	NA	+	NA		=	60,000	+	NA		NA	−	NA	=	NA

b. What was Tang's ending inventory on August 31, Year 1? Is this amount the actual or the estimated inventory cost?

c. When is it appropriate to use estimated inventory cost on a year-end balance sheet?

LO 12-2

Exercise 12-6B *Job-order costing in a manufacturing company*

Newton Advertisements Corporation designs and produces television commercials for clients. On March 1, Year 1, the company issued common stock for $100,000 cash. During March, Newton worked on three jobs. Pertinent data follow.

Special Orders	Materials	Labor
Job 301	$4,500	450 hours @ $32 per hour
Job 302	7,600	360 hours @ $60 per hour
Job 303	6,100	680 hours @ $28 per hour

Actual production overhead cost: $24,080

Predetermined overhead rate: $16 per direct labor hour

Newton paid these costs in cash. Jobs 301 and 302 were completed and sold for cash to customers during March. Job 303 was incomplete at month end. Job 301 sold for $32,000, and Job 302 sold for $45,000. Newton also paid $8,000 cash in March for selling and administrative expenses.

Newton uses a just-in-time inventory management system. Consequently, it has no raw materials inventory. Raw materials purchases are recorded directly in the Work in Process Inventory account.

Required

a. Use a horizontal financial statements model, as follows, to record Newton's accounting events for March Year 1. The first event is shown as an example.

Balance Sheet												Income Statement				
Assets							=	Equity								
Cash	+	Work in Process	+	Finished Goods	+	Manuf. Overhead	=	Com. Stock	+	Ret. Ear.		Rev.	−	Exp.	=	Net Inc.
100,000	+	NA	+	NA	+	NA	=	100,000	+	NA		NA	−	NA	=	NA

b. Record the entry to close the amount of underapplied or overapplied manufacturing overhead to Cost of Goods Sold (in the expense category) in the horizontal financial statements model.

c. Determine the gross margin for March.

Exercise 12-7B *Job-order costing in a service company*

LO 12-2

Tripoli Consulting provides financial and estate planning services on a retainer basis for the executive officers of its corporate clients. It incurred the following labor costs on services for three corporate clients during March Year 2.

	Direct Labor
Contract 1	$ 9,000
Contract 2	3,600
Contract 3	14,400
Total	$27,000

Tripoli allocated March overhead costs of $13,500 to the contracts based on the amount of direct labor costs incurred on each contract.

Required

a. Assuming the revenue from Contract 3 was $40,000, what amount of income did Tripoli earn from this contract?

b. Based on the preceding information, will Tripoli report finished goods inventory on its balance sheet for Contract 1? If so, what is the amount of this inventory? If not, explain why not.

Exercise 12-8B *Determine missing information for a job order*

LO 12-2

The following information pertains to Job 712 that Nantou Manufacturing Company completed during the month of January. Materials and labor costs for the job were $24,500 and $19,000, respectively. Applied overhead costs were $16,000. Nantou completed and delivered the job to its customer and earned an $18,000 gross profit.

Required

Determine the contract price for the job.

Exercise 12-9B *Process cost system*

LO 12-2, 12-3

Hebron Manufacturing Company started operations on January 1, Year 1. During Year 1, the company engaged in the following transactions.

1. Issued common stock for $100,000.
2. Paid $39,600 cash to purchase raw materials used to make products.
3. Transferred $36,000 of raw materials to the production department.
4. Paid $40,800 cash for labor used to make products.
5. Paid $31,200 cash for overhead costs (assume actual and estimated overhead are the same).
6. Finished work on products that cost $103,200 to make.
7. Sold products that cost $86,400 to make for $109,200 cash.

Required

a. Prepare the December 31, Year 1, balance sheet.
b. Prepare the December 31, Year 1, income statement.

LO 12-3

Exercise 12-10B *Process costing: Supply missing information*

Galilee Publications Inc. produces Bibles in volume. It printed and sold 60,000 Bibles last year. Demand is sufficient to support producing a particular edition continuously throughout the year. For this operation, Galilee uses two departments: printing and binding. The printing department prints all pages and transfers them to the binding department, where it binds the pages into books. The binding department's Work in Process Inventory account had a $70,000 balance on September 1. During September, the binding department incurred raw materials, labor, and overhead costs of $11,000, $38,000, and $71,000, respectively. During the month, the binding department transferred Bibles that cost $350,000 to finished goods. The balance in the binding department's Work in Process Inventory account as of September 30 was $90,000.

Required

Determine the cost of pages transferred from the printing department to the binding department during the month of September.

LO 12-4

Exercise 12-11B *Allocating costs in a process costing system*

Osprey Corporation, a manufacturer of diabetic testing kits, started November production with $150,000 in beginning inventory. During the month, the company incurred $740,000 of materials cost and $480,000 of labor cost. It applied $330,000 of overhead cost to inventory. The company processed 17,000 total equivalent units of product.

Required

(Each requirement is independent of the other.)

a. Assuming 4,000 equivalent units of product were in ending work in process inventory, determine the amount of cost transferred from the Work in Process Inventory account to the Finished Goods Inventory account. What was the cost of the ending work in process inventory?
b. Assuming 12,000 equivalent units of product were transferred from work in process inventory to finished goods inventory, determine the cost of the ending work in process inventory. What was the cost of the finished goods inventory transferred from work in process?

LO 12-4

Exercise 12-12B *Process costing: Determining equivalent units and allocating costs*

Wautoma Corporation, which makes suitcases, completed 42,000 suitcases in August Year 2. At the end of August, work in process inventory consisted of 5,000 suitcases estimated to be 40 percent complete. Total product costs for August amounted to $880,000.

Required

a. Determine the cost per equivalent unit.
b. Determine the cost of the goods transferred to finished goods.
c. Determine the cost of the ending work in process inventory.

PROBLEMS—SERIES B

Problem 12-13B *Job-order costing system*

LO 12-2

Preston Corporation was created on January 1, Year 1, when it received a stockholder's contribution of $92,000. It purchased $21,000 of raw materials and worked on three job orders during the year. Data about these jobs follow. (Assume all transactions are for cash unless otherwise indicated.)

	Direct Raw Materials Used	Direct Labor
Job 1	$ 8,000	$ 8,000
Job 2	3,600	9,600
Job 3	6,400	8,960
Total	$18,000	$26,560

The average wage rate is $32 per hour. Manufacturing overhead is applied using a predetermined overhead rate of $15 per direct labor hour. Jobs 1 and 3 were completed during the year, and Job 1 was sold for $26,000. Preston paid $2,800 for selling and administrative expenses. Actual factory overhead was $12,000.

Required

a. Record the preceding events in a horizontal statements model. The first event for Year 1 has been recorded as an example.

Balance Sheet																			Income Statement				
Assets										=	Equity											
Cash	+	Raw M.	+	MOH	+	WIP	+	F. Goods	=	C. Stk.	+	Ret. Ear.	Rev.	−	Exp.	=	Net Inc.						
92,000	+	NA	+	NA	+	NA	+	NA	=	92,000	+	NA	NA	−	NA	=	NA						

b. Reconcile all subsidiary accounts with their respective control accounts.

c. Record the closing entry for over- or underapplied manufacturing overhead, assuming that the amount is insignificant.

d. Prepare a schedule of cost of goods manufactured and sold, an income statement, and a balance sheet for Year 1.

Problem 12-14B *Job-order costing system*

LO 12-2

Prairie Roofing Corporation was founded on January 1, Year 1, when stockholders contributed $12,000 for common stock. During the year, Prairie purchased $6,400 of direct raw materials and used $5,520 of direct materials. There were 80 hours of direct labor worked at an average rate of $16 per hour paid in cash. The predetermined overhead rate was $13 per direct labor hour. The company started three custom roofing jobs. The job cost sheets reflected the following allocations of costs to each.

	Direct Materials	Direct Labor Hours
Roof 1	$2,000	20
Roof 2	1,120	12
Roof 3	2,400	48

The company paid $352 cash for indirect labor costs and $480 cash for production supplies, which were all used during Year 1. Actual overhead cost paid in cash other than indirect materials and indirect labor was $288. Prairie completed Roofs 1 and 2 and collected the contract price for Roof 1 of $5,000 cash. The company incurred $992 of selling and administrative expenses that were paid with cash. Over- or underapplied overhead is closed to Cost of Goods Sold.

Required

a. Record the preceding events in a horizontal statements model. The first event for Year 1 has been recorded as an example.

Balance Sheet															Income Statement				
Assets									=	Equity									
Cash	+	Raw M.	+	MOH	+	WIP	+	F. Goods	=	C. Stk.	+	Ret. Ear.			Rev.	−	Exp.	=	Net Inc.
12,000	+	NA	+	NA	+	NA	+	NA	=	12,000	+	NA			NA	−	NA	=	NA

b. Reconcile all subsidiary accounts with their respective control accounts.

c. Record the closing entry for over- or underapplied manufacturing overhead in the horizontal statements model, assuming that the amount is insignificant.

d. Prepare a schedule of cost of goods manufactured and sold, an income statement, and a balance sheet for Year 1.

LO 12-3, 12-4

Problem 12-15B *Process costing system*

Dawson Food Company makes frozen vegetables. Production involves two departments, processing and packaging. Raw materials are cleaned and cut in the processing department and then transferred to the packaging department where they are packaged and frozen. The following transactions apply to Dawson's first year (Year 1) of operations. (Assume that all transactions are for cash unless otherwise stated.)

1. The company was started when it acquired $160,000 cash from the issue of common stock.
2. Dawson purchased $42,000 of direct raw materials and $8,000 of indirect materials. Indirect materials are capitalized in the Production Supplies account.
3. Direct materials totaling $38,000 were issued to the processing department.
4. Labor cost was $77,000. Direct labor for the processing and packaging departments was $32,500 and $25,500, respectively. Indirect labor costs were $19,000.
5. The predetermined overhead rate was $0.80 per direct labor dollar in each department.
6. Actual overhead costs other than indirect materials and indirect labor were $22,500 for the year.
7. The processing department transferred $60,500 of inventory to the packaging department.
8. The packaging department transferred $70,000 of inventory to finished goods.
9. The company sold inventory costing $63,000 for $117,500.

11. Selling and administrative expenses were $23,500.

11. A physical count revealed $3,000 of production supplies on hand at the end of Year 1.

12. Assume that over- or underapplied overhead is insignificant.

Required

a. Record the data in T-accounts.

b. Record the closing entry for over- or underapplied manufacturing overhead, assuming that the amount is insignificant.

c. Close the revenue and expense accounts.

d. Prepare a schedule of cost of goods manufactured and sold, an income statement, and a balance sheet for Year 1.

Problem 12-16B *Process costing system*

LO 12-3, 12-4

Use the ending balances from Problem 12-15B as the beginning balances for this problem. The transactions for the second year of operation (Year 2) are described here. (Assume that all transactions are cash transactions unless otherwise indicated.)

1. The company purchased $60,000 of direct raw materials and $9,000 of indirect materials. Indirect materials are capitalized in the Production Supplies account.
2. Materials costing $41,000 were issued to the processing department.
3. Labor cost was $89,500. Direct labor for the processing and packaging departments was $36,000 and $29,500, respectively. Indirect labor costs were $24,000. (*Note:* Assume that sufficient cash is available when periodic payments are made. These amounts represent summary data for the entire year and are not presented in exact order of collection and payment.)
4. The predetermined overhead rate was $0.80 per direct labor dollar.
5. Actual overhead costs other than indirect materials and indirect labor for the year were $20,000.
6. The processing department transferred $125,000 of inventory to the packaging department.
7. The packaging department transferred $175,000 of inventory to finished goods.
8. The company sold inventory costing $171,000 for $325,000.
9. Selling and administrative expenses amounted to $32,000.
10. At the end of the year, $2,500 of production supplies was on hand.
11. Assume that over- or underapplied overhead is insignificant.

Required

a. Record the data in T-accounts.
b. Record the closing entry for over- or underapplied manufacturing overhead, assuming that the amount is insignificant.
c. Close the revenue and expense accounts.
d. Prepare a schedule of cost of goods manufactured and sold, an income statement, and a balance sheet for Year 2.

Problem 12-17B *Process costing system*

LO 12-3, 12-4

Letcher Corporation makes blue jeans. Its process involves two departments, cutting and sewing. The following data pertain to the cutting department's transactions in Year 2.

1. The beginning balance in work in process inventory was $30,000. This inventory consisted of fabric for 7,000 pairs of jeans. The beginning balances in raw materials inventory, production supplies, and cash were $224,000, $20,800, and $286,000, respectively.
2. Direct materials costing $167,200 were issued to the cutting department; this amount of materials was sufficient to start work on 21,000 pairs of jeans.
3. Direct labor cost was $144,000, and indirect labor cost was $32,400. All labor costs were paid in cash.
4. The predetermined overhead rate was $0.45 per direct labor dollar.
5. Actual overhead costs other than indirect materials and indirect labor for the year amounted to $12,000, which was paid in cash.
6. The cutting department completed cutting 20,000 pairs of jeans. The remaining jeans were 40 percent complete.
7. The completed units of cut fabric were transferred to the sewing department.
8. All of the production supplies had been used by the end of the year.
9. Over- or underapplied overhead was closed to the Cost of Goods Sold account.

Required

a. Determine the number of equivalent units of production.
b. Determine the product cost per equivalent unit.
c. Allocate the total cost between ending work in process inventory and units transferred to the sewing department.
d. Record the transactions in a partial set of T-accounts.

LO 12-3, 12-4

Problem 12-18B *Process costing system*

Fullerton Paper Products Corporation produces paper cups using two production departments, printing and forming. Beginning balances and printing department data for Year 2 follow.

Accounts	Beginning Balances
Cash	$ 50,000
Raw materials	60,000
Production supplies	3,000
Work in process inventory (300,000 units)	34,000
Common stock	147,000

1. Fullerton Paper Products issued additional common stock for $180,000 cash.
2. The company purchased raw materials and production supplies for $70,000 and $7,000, respectively, in cash.
3. The company issued $114,000 of raw materials to the printing department for the production of 800,000 paper cups.
4. The printing department used 6,200 hours of labor during Year 2, consisting of 5,600 hours for direct labor and 600 hours for indirect labor. The average wage was $20 per hour. All the wages were paid in Year 2 in cash.
5. The predetermined overhead rate was $0.25 per direct labor dollar.
6. Actual overhead costs other than indirect materials and indirect labor for the year amounted to $8,800, which was paid in cash.
7. The printing department completed 700,000 paper cups. The remaining cups were 50 percent complete.
8. The completed paper cups were transferred to the forming department.
9. The ending balance in the Production Supplies account was $2,800.

Required

a. Determine the number of equivalent units of production.
b. Determine the product cost per equivalent unit.
c. Allocate the total cost between the ending work in process inventory and units transferred to the forming department.
d. Record the transactions in T-accounts.

LO 12-4

Problem 12-19B *Process costing system cost of production report*

At the beginning of Year 3, Elgin Company had 5,000 units of product in its work in process inventory, and it started 25,000 additional units of product during the year. At the end of the year, 6,000 units of product were in the work in process inventory. The ending work in process inventory was estimated to be 25 percent complete. The cost of work in process inventory at the beginning of the period was $42,000, and $264,000 of product costs was added during the period.

Required

Prepare a cost of production report showing the following:

a. The number of equivalent units of production.
b. The product cost per equivalent unit.
c. The total cost allocated between the ending Work in Process Inventory and Finished Goods Inventory accounts.

Problem 12-20B *Determining inventory cost using process costing*

LO 12-4

Grenora Company's beginning work in process inventory consisted of 7,500 units of product on January 1, Year 2. During Year 2, the company started 32,500 units of product and transferred 34,000 units to finished goods inventory. The ending work in process inventory was estimated to be 40 percent complete. Cost data for Year 2 follow.

	Product Costs
Beginning balance	$ 56,000
Added during period	490,000
Total	$546,000

Required

Prepare a cost of production report showing the following:

a. The number of equivalent units of production.

b. The product cost per equivalent unit.

c. The total cost allocated between ending work in process inventory and finished goods inventory.

Problem 12-21B *Process costing system with second department*

LO 12-4

Starr Gifts makes unique western gifts that are sold at souvenir shops. One of the company's more popular products is a ceramic eagle that is produced in a mass production process that entails two manufacturing stages. In the first production stage, ceramic glass is heated and molded into the shape of the eagle by the Compression Department. Finally, color and artistic detail is applied to the eagle by the Finishing Department. The company has just hired a new accountant who will be responsible for preparing the Cost of Production Report for the month of June. The accountant is given the following information from which to prepare his report.

Departmental Cost Information for June follows.

	Compression	Finishing
Costs in beginning inventory	$ 6,000	$ 28,800
Costs added during June:		
Materials	84,000	36,240
Labor	40,000	26,400
Overhead	180,000	124,000

Departmental Product Information for June follows.

	Compression	Finishing
Units in beginning inventory	10,000	3,600
Units started	52,000	46,000
Units in ending inventory	16,000 (25% complete)	9,600 (80% complete)

Required

a. Prepare a Cost of Production Report for the Compression Department for June.

b. Prepare a Cost of Production Report for the Finishing Department for June.

c. If 24,000 units are sold in June for $320,000, determine the company's gross margin for June.

ANALYZE, THINK, COMMUNICATE

ATC 12-1 Business Application Case *Comprehensive job-order costing problem*

This problem covers concepts that were presented in Chapters 11 and 12 concerning job-order costing systems.

Mid-Life Motorcycles (MLM) is a small shop that builds customized motorcycles, mostly for middle-aged men with significant discretionary income who are hoping to fulfill a high-school dream. Since it works with high-end clients, all of its work is custom and it makes many of the bike parts used, including frames, in-house. Other parts, such as the engine, are purchased from outside suppliers and then modified in-house. Although most of the bikes are built to-order for a specific individual, the shop occasionally builds a bike with no prearranged buyer. These bikes are sometimes intended to be entered in custom-bike contest and then sold afterwards.

The shop has been in existence for 10 years, but for the sake of simplicity, assume it has no beginning inventories for 2019. Five motorcycle restoration projects were worked on during 2019. By the end of the year, four of these projects were complete and three of them had been sold.

The following selected data are from MLM's 2019 budget.

Advertising	$ 5,000
Direct materials	150,000
Direct labor	130,000
Rent on office space	6,000
Rent on factory space	20,000
Indirect materials	11,000
Maintenance costs for factory equipment	3,000
Utilities costs for office space	1,000
Utilities costs for factory space	2,000
Depreciation on factory equipment	8,000
Machine hours expected to be worked	4,000
Direct labor hours expected to be worked	6,500

The following information relates to production events during 2019.

- Raw materials were purchased for $155,000.
- Materials used in production totaled $150,800; $11,500 of these were considered indirect materials costs. The remaining $139,300 of direct materials costs related to individual motorcycle jobs as follows.

Job Number	Direct Materials Cost
115	$28,200
116	32,100
117	25,800
118	31,700
119	21,500

- Labor costs incurred for production totaled $133,100. The workers are highly skilled craftsmen who require little supervision. Therefore, all of these costs were considered direct labor costs and related to individual jobs as follows.

Job Number	Direct Labor Cost
115	$30,900
116	29,300
117	22,100
118	36,600
119	14,200

- Paid factory rent of $18,000.
- Recorded depreciation on factory equipment of $8,500.
- Made $2,500 of payments to outside vendors for maintenance of factory equipment.
- Paid factory utilities costs of $2,400.
- Applied manufacturing overhead using a predetermined rate of $11.00 per machine hour. The 3,750 machine hours that were used relate to each job as follows.

Job Number	Machine Hours Worked
115	850
116	720
117	870
118	900
119	410

- Completed all jobs except Job 119 and transferred those projects to finished goods.
- Sold three jobs for the following amounts:

Job Number	Sales Price
115	$88,900
116	93,000
117	74,800

- Closed the Manufacturing Overhead account to transfer any overapplied or underapplied overhead to the Cost of Goods Sold account.

Required

a. Assume MLM had used direct labor hours (versus machine hours) as its cost driver. Compute its predetermined overhead rate.
b. Determine the ending balance in Raw Materials Inventory.
c. Determine the ending balance in Finished Goods Inventory.
d. Determine the ending balance in Work in Process Inventory.
e. Determine the costs of goods manufactured.
f. Determine the amount of Cost of Goods Sold.
g. Determine the amount of gross margin that was earned on Jobs 115, 116, and 117.
h. Determine the amount of overapplied or underapplied overhead that existed at the end of the year.

Hint: Though not required, you might find it helpful to organize the data using a horizontal financial statements model, although it will still be necessary to prepare a job cost sheet for each individual job.

ATC 12-2 Group Assignment *Job-order costing system*

Bowen Bridge Company constructs bridges for the State of Kentucky. During Year 2, Bowen started work on three bridges. The cost of materials and labor for each bridge follows.

Special Orders	Materials	Labor
Bridge 305	$407,200	$352,700
Bridge 306	362,300	375,000
Bridge 307	801,700	922,800

The predetermined overhead rate is $1.20 per direct labor dollar. Actual overhead costs were $2,170,800. Bridge 306 was completed for a contract price of $1,357,000 and was turned over to the state. Construction on Bridge 305 was also completed but the state had not yet finished its inspection process. General selling and administrative expenses amounted to $210,000. Over- or underapplied overhead is closed directly to the Cost of Goods Sold account. The company recognizes revenue when it turns over a completed bridge to a customer.

Required

a. Divide the class into groups of four or five students each and organize the groups into three sections. Assign Task 1 to the first section of groups, Task 2 to the second section, and Task 3 to the third section.

Group Tasks

(1) Determine the cost of construction for Bridge 305.

(2) Determine the cost of construction for Bridge 306.

(3) Determine the cost of construction for Bridge 307.

b. Select a spokesperson from each section. Use input from the three spokespersons to prepare an income statement and the asset section of the balance sheet.

c. Does the net income accurately reflect the profitability associated with Bridge 306? Explain.

d. Would converting to a process costing system improve the accuracy of the amount of reported net income? Explain.

ATC 12-3 Research Assignment *Identifying appropriate product costing systems for three real-world companies*

Obtain the Form 10-Ks for these three companies: **Ball Corporation**, **Laboratory Corporation of America**, and **Noble Corporation plc** To obtain the Form 10-Ks, you can use the EDGAR system (see Appendix A at the back of this text for instructions), or they can be found on the companies' websites: **www.ball.com** (Investors), **www.labcorp.com** (Investors), and **www.noblecorp.com** (Investor Relations). Read the "Item 1. Business" sections of these 10-Ks in order to understand the nature of each company's business.

Required

For each company, determine if it primarily uses a job-order or process costing system to compute the cost of the products or services it sells. Explain the rationale for your answer. If you believe a company uses elements of both job-order and process costing systems, a hybrid system, explain the rationale for that conclusion.

ATC 12-4 Writing Assignment *Determining the proper costing system*

Professor Julia Silverman received the following e-mail message:

"I don't know if you remember me. I am Tim Wallace. I was in your introductory accounting class a couple of years ago. I recently graduated and have just started my first real job. I remember you talking about job-order and process costing systems. I even looked the subject up in the textbook you wrote. In that book, you say that a process costing system is used when a company produces a single, homogeneous, high-volume, low-cost product. Well, the company I am working for makes T-shirts. All of the shirts are the same. They don't cost much, and we make nearly a million of them every year. The only difference in any of the shirts is the label we sew in them. We make the shirts for about 20 different companies. It seems to me that we should be using a process costing system. Even so, our accounting people are using a job-order costing system. Unfortunately, you didn't tell us what to do when the company we work for is screwed up. I need some advice. Should I tell them they are using the wrong accounting system? I know I am new around here, and I don't want to offend anybody, but if your book is right, the company would be better off if it started using a process costing system. Some of these people around here didn't go to college, and I'm afraid they don't know what they are doing. I guess that's why they hired someone with a degree. Am I right about this or what?"

Required

Assume that you are Professor Silverman. Write a return e-mail responding to Mr. Wallace's inquiry.

ATC 12-5 Ethical Dilemma *Amount of equivalent units*

René Alverez knew she was in over her head soon after she took the job. Even so, the opportunity for promotion comes along rarely and she believed that she would grow into it. Ms. Alverez is the cost accounting specialist assigned to the finishing department of Standard Tool Company. Bill Sawyer, the manager of the finishing department, knows exactly what he is doing. In each of the three years he has managed the department, the cost per unit of product transferred out of his Work in Process Inventory account has declined. His ability to control cost is highly valued, and it is widely believed that he will be the successor to the plant manager, who is being promoted to manufacturing vice president. One more good year would surely seal the deal for Mr. Sawyer. It was little wonder that Ms. Alverez was uncomfortable in challenging Mr. Sawyer's estimate of the percentage of completion of the department's ending inventory. He contended that the inventory was 60 percent complete, but she believed that it was only about 40 percent complete.

After a brief altercation, Ms. Alverez agreed to sign off on Mr. Sawyer's estimate. The truth was that although she believed she was right, she did not know how to support her position. Besides, Mr. Sawyer was about to be named plant manager, and she felt it unwise to challenge such an important person.

The department had beginning inventory of 5,500 units of product and it started 94,500 units during the period. It transferred out 90,000 units during the period. Total transferred-in and production cost for the period was $902,400. This amount included the cost in beginning inventory plus additional costs incurred during the period. The target (standard) cost per unit is $9.45.

Required

a. Determine the equivalent cost per unit, assuming that the ending inventory is considered to be 40 percent complete.

b. Determine the equivalent cost per unit, assuming that the ending inventory is considered to be 60 percent complete.

c. Comment on Mr. Sawyer's motives for establishing the percentage of completion at 60 percent rather than 40 percent.

d. Assuming that Ms. Alverez is a certified management accountant, would informing the chief accountant of her dispute with Mr. Sawyer violate the confidentiality standards of ethical professional practice in Exhibit 1.17 of Chapter 1?

e. Did Ms. Alverez violate any of the standards of ethical professional practice in Exhibit 1.17 of Chapter 1? If so, which ones?

f. Discuss the components of the fraud triangle that affected Ms. Alverez's behavior.

ATC 12-6 Spreadsheet Assignment *Using Excel*

Lewis Company had 8,000 units of product in work in process inventory at the beginning of the period and started 16,000 units during the period. At the end of the period, 4,000 units remained in work in process. The ending work in process inventory was estimated to be 40 percent complete. The cost of the units in beginning work in process inventory was $22,080. During the period, $38,400 of product costs were added.

Required

a. Construct a spreadsheet that incorporates the preceding data into a table. The following screen capture is an example.

b. Insert a section into the spreadsheet to calculate total manufacturing costs.

c. Insert a section into the spreadsheet to calculate equivalent units and cost per equivalent unit.

d. Insert a section into the spreadsheet to allocate the manufacturing costs between finished goods and ending work in process.

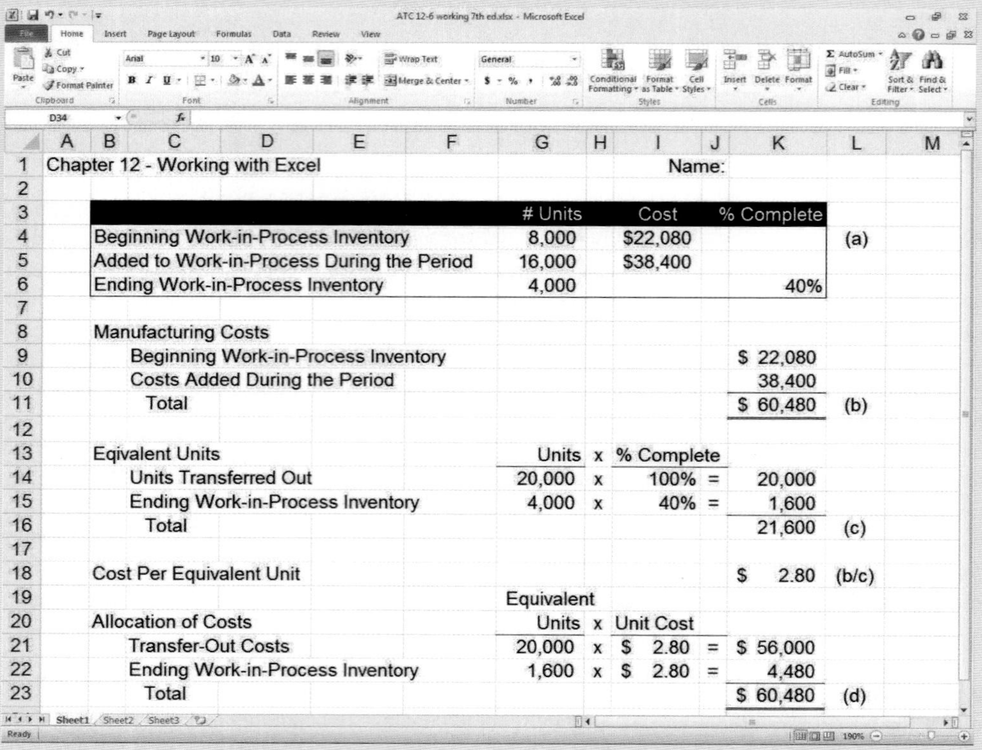

Row	A–F	G	H	I	J	K	L
1	Chapter 12 - Working with Excel			Name:			
2							
3		# Units		Cost	% Complete		
4	Beginning Work-in-Process Inventory	8,000		$22,080			(a)
5	Added to Work-in-Process During the Period	16,000		$38,400			
6	Ending Work-in-Process Inventory	4,000			40%		
7							
8	Manufacturing Costs						
9	Beginning Work-in-Process Inventory					$ 22,080	
10	Costs Added During the Period					38,400	
11	Total					$ 60,480	(b)
12							
13	Eqivalent Units	Units	x	% Complete			
14	Units Transferred Out	20,000	x	100% =		20,000	
15	Ending Work-in-Process Inventory	4,000	x	40% =		1,600	
16	Total					21,600	(c)
17							
18	Cost Per Equivalent Unit					$ 2.80	(b/c)
19		Equivalent					
20	Allocation of Costs	Units	x	Unit Cost			
21	Transfer-Out Costs	20,000	x	$ 2.80 =		$ 56,000	
22	Ending Work-in-Process Inventory	1,600	x	$ 2.80 =		4,480	
23	Total					$ 60,480	(d)

Source: Microsoft Excel 2010

Spreadsheet Tip

1. The cells that contain numbers below row 7 should all be formulas so that changes to the data in rows 3 to 6 will automatically be reflected in the rest of the spreadsheet.

ATC 12-7 Spreadsheet Assignment *Mastering Excel*

excel

Refer to the job cost sheet in Exhibit 12.3.

Required

Construct a spreadsheet that re-creates the job cost sheet in Exhibit 12.3. Use formulas wherever possible, such as in the total row.

Spreadsheet Tips

1. Center the headings for direct materials, direct labor, and applied overhead across two or three columns by choosing Format and Cells and checking the Merge box under the alignment tab. A shortcut to center these is to click on the Merge and Center icon in the formatting toolbar.
2. All lines in the job cost sheet can be drawn using Format and Cells and then choosing the border tab.

COMPREHENSIVE PROBLEM

This is a continuation of the comprehensive problem in Chapter 11. During Year 3, Anywhere Inc. (AI) incurred the following product costs.

Raw materials	$62,000
Labor	89,422
Overhead	58,000

Recall that the Year 2 ending balance in the Work in Process (WIP) account was $26,000. Accordingly, this is the beginning WIP balance for Year 3. There were 110 units of product in beginning WIP inventory. AI started 1,840 units of product during Year 3. Ending WIP inventory consisted of 90 units that were 60 percent complete.

Required

Prepare a cost of production report by filling in the cells that contain question marks.

Equivalent Unit Computations

	Units	% Complete	Equivalent Units
Beginning inventory	110		
Units started	1,840		
Total units available for completion	?		
Units in ending inventory	(90)	?	?
Units complete	1,860	100%	?
Total equivalent units			1,914

Cost per Equivalent Unit

	Cost	÷	Units	=	Cost per Unit
Beginning inventory	$26,000				
Raw materials	?				
Labor	?				
Overhead	58,000				
Total product cost	?	÷	1,914	=	?

Allocation of Product Cost

Cost transferred to finished goods	?
Cost in ending inventory	?
Total product cost	$235,422

CHAPTER 13

Financial Statement Analysis

LEARNING OBJECTIVES

After you have mastered the material in this chapter, you will be able to:

LO 13-1 Differentiate between horizontal and vertical analysis.

LO 13-2 Calculate ratios for assessing a company's liquidity.

LO 13-3 Calculate ratios for assessing a company's solvency.

LO 13-4 Calculate ratios for assessing a company's managerial effectiveness.

LO 13-5 Calculate ratios for assessing a company's position in the stock market.

Video lectures and accompanying self-assessment quizzes are available in Connect for all learning objectives.

CHAPTER OPENING

Expressing financial statement information in the form of ratios enhances its usefulness. Ratios permit comparisons over time and among companies, highlighting similarities, differences, and trends. Proficiency with common financial statement analysis techniques benefits both internal and external users. Before beginning detailed explanations of numerous ratios and percentages, however, we consider factors relevant to communicating useful information.

The Curious Accountant

©Worawee Meepian/Shutterstock

©NYCStock/Shutterstock

On June 15, 2017, **Amazon.com Inc.**, announced that it had agreed to purchase **Whole Foods Market** for $42 per share, or $13.7 billion in total. The offering price of $42 per share was 27 percent higher than the stock was currently trading. This was by far the biggest acquisition Amazon.com had ever made. Although Whole Foods is more profitable than most grocery companies, its profitability percentages had been declining in recent years. For example, from 2014 to 2017 its return on investment had declined from 10.3 percent to 3.8 percent, its gross margin declined from 35.5 percent to 33.7 percent, and its net margin declined from 4.1 percent to 1.5 percent. Furthermore, Whole Foods was viewed as a high-priced "bricks-and-mortar" business while Amazon is viewed as an online discount company.

How do companies such as Amazon determine that a business they want to own is worth more than the current market price? What types of analyses would they use to make such decisions? Do you think the highly educated, experienced, and well-paid individuals involved in making these high-dollar acquisitions made the right decisions? (Answer on page 593.)

FACTORS IN COMMUNICATING USEFUL INFORMATION

The primary objective of accounting is to provide information useful for decision making. To provide information that supports this objective, accountants must consider the intended users, the types of decisions users make with financial statement information, and available means of analyzing the information.

The Users

©maxuser/Shutterstock

Users of financial statement information include managers, creditors, stockholders, potential investors, and regulatory agencies. These individuals and organizations use financial statements for different purposes and bring varying levels of sophistication to understanding business activities. For example, investors range from private individuals who know little about financial statements to large investment brokers and institutional investors capable of using complex statistical analysis techniques. At what level of user knowledge should financial statements be aimed? Condensing and reporting complex business transactions at a level easily understood by nonprofessional investors is increasingly difficult. Current reporting standards target users that have a reasonably informed knowledge of business, though that level of sophistication is difficult to define.

The Types of Decisions

Just as the knowledge level of potential users varies, the information needs of users also varies, depending on the decision at hand. A supplier considering whether or not to sell goods on account to a particular company wants to evaluate the likelihood of getting paid; a potential investor in that company wants to predict the likelihood of increases in the market value of the company's common stock. Financial statements, however, are designed for general purposes; they are not aimed at any specific user group. Some disclosed information, therefore, may be irrelevant to some users but vital to others. Users must employ different forms of analysis to identify information most relevant to a particular decision.

Financial statements can provide only highly summarized economic information. The costs to a company of providing excessively detailed information would be prohibitive. In addition, too much detail leads to **information overload,** the problem of having so much data that important information becomes obscured by trivial information. Users faced with reams of data may become so frustrated attempting to use them that they lose the value of *key* information that is provided.

Information Analysis

Because of the diversity of users, their different levels of knowledge, the varying information needs for particular decisions, and the general nature of financial statements, a variety of analysis techniques has been developed. In the following sections, we explain several common methods of analysis. The choice of method depends on which technique appears to provide the most relevant information in a given situation.

METHODS OF ANALYSIS

LO 13-1

Differentiate between horizontal and vertical analysis.

Financial statement analysis should focus primarily on isolating information useful for making a particular decision. The information required can take many forms but usually involves comparisons, such as comparing changes in the same item for the same company over a number of years, comparing key relationships within the same year, or comparing the operations of several different companies in the same industry. This chapter discusses three categories of analysis methods: horizontal, vertical, and ratio. Exhibits 13.1 and 13.2 present comparative financial statements for Milavec Company. We refer to these statements in the examples of analysis techniques.

EXHIBIT 13.1

MILAVEC COMPANY
Income Statements and Statements of Retained Earnings
For the Years Ending December 31

	Year 4	Year 3
Sales	$900,000	$800,000
Cost of goods sold		
Beginning inventory	43,000	40,000
Purchases	637,000	483,000
Goods available for sale	680,000	523,000
Ending inventory	70,000	43,000
Cost of goods sold	610,000	480,000
Gross margin	290,000	320,000
Operating expenses	248,000	280,000
Income before taxes	42,000	40,000
Income taxes	17,000	18,000
Net income	25,000	22,000
Plus: Retained earnings, beginning balance	137,000	130,000
Less: Dividends	0	15,000
Retained earnings, ending balance	$162,000	$137,000

EXHIBIT 13.2

MILAVEC COMPANY
Balance Sheet
As of December 31

	Year 4	Year 3
Assets		
Cash	$ 20,000	$ 17,000
Marketable securities	20,000	22,000
Notes receivable	4,000	3,000
Accounts receivable	50,000	56,000
Merchandise inventory	70,000	43,000
Prepaid expenses	4,000	4,000
Property, plant, and equipment (net)	340,000	310,000
Total assets	$508,000	$455,000
Liabilities and Stockholders' Equity		
Accounts payable	$ 40,000	$ 38,000
Salaries payable	2,000	3,000
Taxes payable	4,000	2,000
Bonds payable, 8%	100,000	100,000
Preferred stock, 6%, $100 par, cumulative	50,000	50,000
Common stock, $10 par	150,000	125,000
Retained earnings	162,000	137,000
Total liabilities and stockholders' equity	$508,000	$455,000

Horizontal Analysis

Horizontal analysis, also called **trend analysis,** refers to studying the behavior of individual financial statement items over several accounting periods. These periods may be several quarters within the same fiscal year or they may be several different years. The analysis of a given item may focus on trends in the absolute dollar amount of the item or trends in percentages. For example, a user may observe that revenue increased from one period to the next by $42 million (an absolute dollar amount) or that it increased by a percentage such as 15 percent.

Absolute Amounts

The **absolute amounts** of particular financial statement items have many uses. Various national economic statistics, such as gross domestic product and the amount spent to replace productive capacity, are derived by combining absolute amounts reported by businesses. Financial statement users with expertise in particular industries might evaluate amounts reported for research and development costs to judge whether a company is spending excessively or conservatively. Users are particularly concerned with how amounts change over time. For example, a user might compare a pharmaceutical company's revenue before and after the patent expired on one of its drugs.

Comparing only absolute amounts has drawbacks, however, because *materiality* levels differ from company to company or even from year to year for a given company. The **materiality** of information refers to its relative importance. An item is considered material if knowledge of it would influence the decision of a reasonably informed user. Generally accepted accounting principles permit companies to account for *immaterial* items in the most convenient way, regardless of technical accounting rules. For example, companies may expense, rather than capitalize and depreciate, relatively inexpensive long-term assets like pencil sharpeners or wastebaskets, even if the assets have useful lives of many years.

The concept of materiality, which has both quantitative and qualitative aspects, underlies all accounting principles.

It is difficult to judge the materiality of an absolute financial statement amount without considering the size of the company reporting it. For reporting purposes, Exxon Corporation's financial statements are rounded to the nearest million dollars. For Exxon, a $400,000 increase in sales is not material. For a small company, however, $400,000 could represent total sales, a highly material amount. Meaningful comparisons between the two companies' operating performance are impossible using only absolute amounts. Users can surmount these difficulties with percentage analysis.

Percentage Analysis

Percentage analysis involves computing the percentage relationship between two amounts. In horizontal percentage analysis, a financial statement item is expressed as a percentage of the previous balance for the same item. Percentage analysis sidesteps the materiality problems of comparing different size companies by measuring changes in percentages rather than absolute amounts. Each change is converted to a percentage of the base year. Exhibit 13.3 presents a condensed version of Milavec's income statement with horizontal percentages for each item.

EXHIBIT 13.3

MILAVEC COMPANY
Comparative Income Statements
For the Years Ending December 31

	Year 4	Year 3	Percentage Difference
Sales	$900,000	$800,000	+12.5%*
Cost of goods sold	610,000	480,000	+27.1
Gross margin	290,000	320,000	−9.4
Operating expenses	248,000	280,000	−11.4
Income before taxes	42,000	40,000	+5.0
Income taxes	17,000	18,000	−5.6
Net income	$ 25,000	$ 22,000	+13.6

*($900,000 − $800,000) ÷ $800,000; all changes expressed as percentages of previous totals.

The percentage changes disclose that, even though Milavec's net income increased slightly more than sales, products may be underpriced. Cost of goods sold increased much more than sales, resulting in a lower gross margin. Users would also want to investigate why operating expenses decreased substantially despite the increase in sales.

Whether basing their analyses on absolute amounts, percentages, or ratios, users must avoid drawing overly simplistic conclusions about the reasons for the results. Numerical relationships flag conditions requiring further study. Recall that a change that appears favorable on the surface may not necessarily be a good sign. Users must evaluate the underlying reasons for the change.

☑ CHECK YOURSELF 13.1

The following information was drawn from the annual reports of two retail companies (amounts are shown in millions). One company is an upscale department store; the other is a discount store. Based on this limited information, identify which company is the upscale department store.

	Jenkins Co.	Horn's Inc.
Sales	$325	$680
Cost of goods sold	130	408
Gross margin	$195	$272

Answer Jenkins' gross margin represents 60 percent ($195 ÷ $325) of sales. Horn's gross margin represents 40 percent ($272 ÷ $680) of sales. Because an upscale department store would have higher margins than a discount store, the data suggest that Jenkins is the upscale department store.

Answers to The Curious Accountant

Obviously, Amazon's acquisition of Whole Foods was based on a desire to make a profit on its investment. Of the $13.7 billion Amazon paid for Whole Foods, $9.0 billion was attributed to the intangible asset goodwill, indicating that Amazon believes Whole Foods had, and would continue to have, excess earnings power compared to the typical grocery retailer. But many analysts believe there were several ways Amazon expected it could use Whole Foods to make money other than just continuing to sell high-priced groceries in physical stores. Some analysts believe that Amazon saw Whole Foods as an opportunity to expand its distributions network. Whole Foods had 11 distributions centers and 440 retails stores that Amazon could use to get its goods to customers faster than with its existing 70 distribution centers. This could be especially helpful as Amazon was trying to expand its delivery of fresh foods to customers.

How do companies decide what another company is worth? Valuing a potential investment is the result of extensive financial analysis, as discussed in this chapter, along with capital budgeting techniques, which were discussed in Chapter 10. As you have seen in these chapters, such decision making is based on estimates about future events. Predicting the future is imperfect, no matter how well trained the forecaster might be.

How good are companies' decisions to acquire other businesses at a premium price? It is too early to say for the purchase of Whole Foods, but not all acquisitions turn out well. In 2013, Microsoft Corp. purchased Nokia Corp. for $7 billion. And in 2015, just two years after its acquisition, Microsoft announced it was writing down $7.6 billion of its Nokia investment and eliminating 7,800 jobs.

Does this mean that financial analysis is useless? No. Assume you were planning to drive across the United States. Would you prefer to take the trip with a map or without? Obviously, you would prefer to have a map or GPS, even though you know neither device is perfect. Financial analysis can be of great benefit when making business decisions, but there are always uncertainties about future events that mathematics cannot eliminate.

Sources: Company's documents and *The Wall Street Journal* online article, "Amazon to Buy Whole Foods: What You Need to Know," June 16, 2017.

When comparing more than two periods, analysts use either of two basic approaches: (1) choosing one base year from which to calculate all increases or decreases or (2) calculating each period's percentage change from the preceding figure. To illustrate, assume Milavec's sales for Year 1 through Year 4 are as follows.

	Year 4	Year 3	Year 2	Year 1
Sales	$900,000	$800,000	$750,000	$600,000
Increase over Year 1 sales	50.0%	33.3%	25.0%	—
Increase over preceding year	12.5%	6.7%	25.0%	—

Analysis discloses that Milavec's Year 4 sales represented a 50 percent increase over Year 1 sales, and a large increase (25 percent) occurred in Year 2. From Year 2 to Year 3, sales increased only 6.7 percent, but, in the following year, sales increased much more (12.5 percent).

Vertical Analysis

Vertical analysis uses percentages to compare individual components of financial statements to a key statement figure. Horizontal analysis compares items over many time periods; vertical analysis compares many items within the same time period.

Vertical Analysis of the Income Statement

Vertical analysis of an income statement (also called a *common size* income statement) involves converting each income statement component to a percentage of sales. Although vertical analysis suggests examining only one period, it is useful to compare common size income statements for several years. Exhibit 13.4 presents Milavec's income statements, along with vertical percentages, for Year 4 and Year 3. This analysis discloses that cost of goods sold increased significantly as a percentage of sales. Operating expenses and income taxes, however, decreased in relation to sales. Each of these observations indicates a need for more analysis regarding possible trends for future profits.

EXHIBIT 13.4

MILAVEC COMPANY
Vertical Analysis of Comparative Income Statements

	Year 4		Year 3	
	Amount	Percentage* of Sales	Amount	Percentage* of Sales
Sales	$900,000	100.0%	$800,000	100.0%
Cost of goods sold	610,000	67.8	480,000	60.0
Gross margin	290,000	32.2	320,000	40.0
Operating expenses	248,000	27.6	280,000	35.0
Income before taxes	42,000	4.7	40,000	5.0
Income taxes	17,000	1.9	18,000	2.3
Net income	$ 25,000	2.8%	$ 22,000	2.8%

*Percentages may not add exactly due to rounding.

Vertical Analysis of the Balance Sheet

Vertical analysis of the balance sheet involves converting each balance sheet component to a percentage of total assets. The vertical analysis of Milavec's balance sheets in Exhibit 13.5 discloses few large percentage changes from the preceding year. Even small individual percentage changes, however, may represent substantial dollar increases. For example, inventory constituted 9.5 percent of total assets in Year 3 and 13.8 percent in Year 4. While this appears to be a small increase, it actually represents a 62.8 percent increase in the inventory account balance [($70,000 – $43,000) ÷ $43,000] from Year 3 to Year 4. Careful analysis requires considering changes in both percentages *and* absolute amounts.

RATIO ANALYSIS

Ratio analysis involves studying various relationships between different items reported in a set of financial statements. For example, net earnings (net income) reported on the income statement may be compared to total assets reported on the balance sheet. Analysts calculate many different ratios for a wide variety of purposes. The remainder of this chapter is devoted to discussing some of the more commonly used ratios.

Objectives of Ratio Analysis

As suggested earlier, various users approach financial statement analysis with many different objectives. Creditors are interested in whether a company will be able to repay its debts on

EXHIBIT 13.5

MILAVEC COMPANY
Vertical Analysis of Comparative Balance Sheets

	Year 4	Percentage* of Total	Year 3	Percentage* of Total
Assets				
Cash	$ 20,000	3.9%	$ 17,000	3.7%
Marketable securities	20,000	3.9	22,000	4.8
Notes receivable	4,000	0.8	3,000	0.7
Accounts receivable	50,000	9.8	56,000	12.3
Merchandise inventory	70,000	13.8	43,000	9.5
Prepaid expenses	4,000	0.8	4,000	0.9
Total current assets	168,000	33.1	145,000	31.9
Property, plant, and equipment	340,000	66.9	310,000	68.1
Total assets	$508,000	100.0%	$455,000	100.0%
Liabilities and Stockholders' Equity				
Accounts payable	$ 40,000	7.9%	$ 38,000	8.3%
Salaries payable	2,000	0.4	3,000	0.7
Taxes payable	4,000	0.8	2,000	0.4
Total current liabilities	46,000	9.1	43,000	9.4
Bonds payable, 8%	100,000	19.7	100,000	22.0
Total liabilities	146,000	28.8	143,000	31.4
Preferred stock 6%, $100 par	50,000	9.8	50,000	11.0
Common stock, $10 par	150,000	29.5	125,000	27.5
Retained earnings	162,000	31.9	137,000	30.1
Total stockholders' equity	362,000	71.2	312,000	68.6
Total liabilities and stockholders' equity	$508,000	100.0%	$455,000	100.0%

*Percentages may not add exactly due to rounding.

time. Both creditors and stockholders are concerned with how the company is financed, whether through debt, equity, or earnings. Stockholders and potential investors analyze past earnings performance and dividend policy for clues to the future value of their investments. In addition to using internally generated data to analyze operations, company managers find much information prepared for external purposes useful for examining past operations and planning future policies. Although many of these objectives are interrelated, it is convenient to group ratios into categories such as measures of debt-paying ability and measures of profitability.

MEASURES OF DEBT-PAYING ABILITY

Liquidity Ratios

LO 13-2

Calculate ratios for assessing a company's liquidity.

Liquidity ratios indicate a company's ability to pay short-term debts. They focus on current assets and current liabilities. The examples in the following section use the financial statement information reported by Milavec Company.

Working Capital

Working capital is current assets minus current liabilities. Current assets include assets most likely to be converted into cash in the current operating period. Current liabilities represent debts that must be satisfied in the current period. Working capital therefore measures the excess funds the company will have available for operations, excluding any new funds it generates during the year. Think of working capital as the cushion against short-term, debt-paying problems. Working capital at the end of Year 4 and Year 3 for Milavec Company was as follows.

	Year 4	Year 3
Current assets	$168,000	$145,000
− Current liabilities	46,000	43,000
Working capital	$122,000	$102,000

Milavec's working capital increased from Year 3 to Year 4, but the numbers themselves say little. Whether $122,000 is sufficient or not depends on such factors as the industry in which Milavec operates, its size, and the maturity dates of its current obligations. We can see, however, that the increase in working capital is primarily due to the increase in inventories.

Current Ratio

Working capital is an absolute amount. Its usefulness is limited by the materiality difficulties discussed earlier. It is hard to draw meaningful conclusions from comparing Milavec's working capital of $122,000 with another company that also has working capital of $122,000. By expressing the relationship between current assets and current liabilities as a ratio, however, we have a more useful measure of the company's debt-paying ability relative to other companies. The **current ratio,** also called the **working capital ratio,** is calculated as follows:

$$\text{Current ratio} = \frac{\text{Current assets}}{\text{Current liabilities}}$$

To illustrate using the current ratio for comparisons, consider Milavec's current position relative to that of Laroque's, a larger firm with current assets of $500,000 and current liabilities of $378,000.

	Milavec	Laroque
Current assets (a)	$168,000	$500,000
− Current liabilities (b)	46,000	378,000
Working capital	$122,000	$122,000
Current ratio (a ÷ b)	3.65:1	1.32:1

The current ratio is expressed as the number of dollars of current assets for each dollar of current liabilities. In the preceding example, both companies have the same amount of working capital. Milavec, however, appears to have a much stronger working capital position. Any conclusions from this analysis must take into account the circumstances of the particular companies; there is no single ideal current ratio that suits all companies. In recent years, the average current ratio of the nonfinancial companies that constitute the Dow Jones Industrial Average (DJIA) was around 1.46:1. The individual company ratios, however, ranged from 0.73:1 to 3.03:1. A current ratio can be too high. Money invested in factories and developing new products is usually more profitable than money held as large cash balances or invested in inventory.

Quick Ratio

The **quick ratio,** also known as the **acid-test ratio,** is a conservative variation of the current ratio. The quick ratio measures a company's *immediate* debt-paying ability. Only cash, receivables, and current marketable securities (*quick assets*) are included in the numerator. Less liquid current assets, such as inventories and prepaid expenses, are omitted. Inventories may take several months to sell; prepaid expenses reduce otherwise necessary expenditures but do not lead eventually to cash receipts. The quick ratio is computed as follows:

$$\text{Quick ratio} = \frac{\text{Quick assets}}{\text{Current liabilities}}$$

Milavec Company's current ratios and quick ratios for Year 4 and Year 3 follow.

	Year 4	Year 3
Current ratio	168,000 ÷ 46,000	145,000 ÷ 43,000
	3.65:1	3.37:1
Quick ratio	94,000 ÷ 46,000	98,000 ÷ 43,000
	2.04:1	2.28:1

The decrease in the quick ratio from Year 3 to Year 4 reflects both a decrease in quick assets and an increase in current liabilities. The result indicates that the company is less liquid (has less ability to pay its short-term debt) in Year 4 than it was in Year 3.

Accounts Receivable Ratios

Offering customers credit plays an enormous role in generating revenue, but it also increases expenses and delays cash receipts. To minimize bad debts expense and collect cash for use in current operations, companies want to collect receivables as quickly as possible without losing customers. Two relationships are often examined to assess a company's collection record: *accounts receivable turnover* and *average days to collect receivables (average collection period).*

Accounts receivable turnover is calculated as follows:

$$\text{Accounts receivable turnover} = \frac{\text{Net credit sales}}{\text{Average accounts receivable}}$$

Net credit sales refers to total sales on account less sales discounts and returns. When most sales are credit sales or when a breakdown of total sales between cash sales and credit sales is not available, the analyst must use total sales in the numerator. The denominator is based on *net accounts receivable* (receivables after subtracting the allowance for doubtful accounts). Because the numerator represents a whole period, it is preferable to use average receivables in the denominator if possible. When comparative statements are available, the average can be based on the beginning and ending balances. Milavec Company's accounts receivable turnover is computed as follows.

	Year 4	Year 3
Net sales (assume all on account) (a)	$900,000	$800,000
Beginning receivables (b)	$ 56,000	$ 55,000*
Ending receivables (c)	50,000	56,000
Average receivables (d) = (b + c) ÷ 2	$ 53,000	$ 55,500
Accounts receivable turnover (a ÷ d)	16.98	14.41

*The Year 3 beginning receivables balance was drawn from the Year 2 financial statements, which are not included in the illustration.

The Year 4 accounts receivable turnover of 16.98 indicates Milavec collected its average receivables almost 17 times that year. The higher the turnover, the faster the collections. A company can have cash flow problems and lose substantial purchasing power if resources are tied up in receivables for long periods.

Average days to collect accounts receivables, or the *average collection period,* is calculated as follows:

$$\text{Average days to collect receivables} = \frac{\text{365 days}}{\text{Accounts receivable turnover}}$$

This ratio offers another way to look at turnover by showing the number of days, on average, it takes to collect a receivable. If receivables were collected 16.98 times in Year 4, the average collection period was 21 days, 365 ÷ 16.98 (the number of days in the year divided by accounts receivable turnover). For Year 3, it took an average of 25 days (365 ÷ 14.41) to collect a receivable.

Although the collection period improved, no other conclusions can be reached without considering the industry, Milavec's past performance, and the general economic environment. In recent years, the average time to collect accounts receivable for the 25 nonfinancial companies that make up the DJIA was around 49 days. (Financial firms are excluded because, by the nature of their business, they have very long collection periods.)

Inventory Ratios

A fine line exists between having too much and too little inventory in stock. Too little inventory can result in lost sales and costly production delays. Too much inventory can use needed space, increase financing and insurance costs, and become obsolete. To help analyze how efficiently a company manages inventory, we use two ratios similar to those used in analyzing accounts receivable.

Inventory turnover indicates the number of times, on average, that inventory is totally replaced during the year. The relationship is computed as follows:

$$\text{Inventory turnover} = \frac{\text{Cost of goods sold}}{\text{Average inventory}}$$

The average inventory is usually based on the beginning and ending balances that are shown in the financial statements. Inventory turnover for Milavec was as follows.

	Year 4	Year 3
Cost of goods sold (a)	$610,000	$480,000
Beginning inventory (b)	$ 43,000	$ 40,000*
Ending inventory (c)	70,000	43,000
Average inventory (d) = (b + c) ÷ 2	$ 56,500	$ 41,500
Inventory turnover (a ÷ d)	10.80	11.57

*The Year 3 beginning inventory balance was drawn from the company's Year 2 financial statements, which are not included in the illustration.

Generally, a higher turnover indicates that merchandise is being handled more efficiently. Trying to compare firms in different industries, however, can be misleading. Inventory turnover for grocery stores and many retail outlets is high. Because of the nature of the goods being sold, inventory turnover is much lower for appliance and jewelry stores. We look at this issue in more detail when we discuss return on investment.

Average days to sell inventory, or *average days in inventory,* is determined by dividing the number of days in the year by the inventory turnover as follows:

$$\text{Average days to sell inventory} = \frac{\text{365 days}}{\text{Inventory turnover}}$$

The result approximates the number of days the firm could sell inventory without purchasing more. For Milavec, this figure was 34 days in Year 4 (365 ÷ 10.80) and 32 days in Year 3 (365 ÷ 11.57). In recent years, it took around 93 days, on average, for the companies in the DJIA that have inventory to sell their inventory. The time it took individual companies to sell their inventory varied by industry, ranging from 5 days to 246 days.

Solvency Ratios

LO 13-3

Calculate ratios for assessing a company's solvency.

Solvency ratios are used to analyze a company's long-term debt-paying ability and its financing structure. Creditors are concerned with a company's ability to satisfy outstanding obligations. The larger a company's liability percentage, the greater the risk that the company could fall behind or default on debt payments. Stockholders, too, are concerned about a company's solvency. If a company is unable to pay its debts, the owners could lose their investment. Each user group desires that company financing choices minimize its investment risk, whether the investment is in debt or stockholders' equity.

Debt Ratios

The following ratios represent two different ways to express the same relationship. Both are frequently used.

- **Debt-to-assets ratio.** This ratio measures the percentage of a company's assets that are financed by debt.
- **Debt-to-equity ratio.** As used in this ratio, *equity* means stockholders' equity. The debt-to-equity ratio compares creditor financing to owner financing. It is expressed as the dollar amount of liabilities for each dollar of stockholders' equity.

These ratios are calculated as follows:

$$\text{Debt to assets} = \frac{\text{Total liabilities}}{\text{Total assets}}$$

$$\text{Debt to equity} = \frac{\text{Total liabilities}}{\text{Total stockholders' equity}}$$

Applying these formulas to Milavec Company's results produces the following.

	Year 4	Year 3
Total liabilities (a)	$146,000	$143,000
Total stockholders' equity (b)	362,000	312,000
Total equities (Liabilities + Stockholders' equity) (c)	$508,000	$455,000
Debt to assets (a ÷ c)	29%	31%
Debt-to-equity ratio (a ÷ b)	0.40:1	0.46:1

Each year, less than one-third of the company's assets was financed with debt. The amount of liabilities per dollar of stockholders' equity declined by 0.06. It is difficult to judge whether the reduced percentage of liabilities is favorable. In general, a lower level of liabilities provides greater security because the likelihood of bankruptcy is reduced. Perhaps, however, the company is financially strong enough to incur more liabilities and benefit from financial leverage. The 25 nonfinancial companies that make up the DJIA report around 51 percent of their assets, on average, are financed through borrowing. The debt-to-assets ratios of these companies ranged from 19 to 110 percent.

Number of Times Interest Is Earned

This ratio measures the burden a company's interest payments represent. Users often consider the **number of times interest is earned** along with the debt ratios when evaluating financial risk. The numerator of this ratio uses *earnings before interest and taxes (EBIT),* rather than net earnings, because the amount of earnings *before* interest and income taxes is available for paying interest.

$$\text{Number of times interest is earned} = \frac{\text{Earnings before interest and taxes expense}}{\text{Interest expense}}$$

Dividing EBIT by interest expense indicates how many times the company could have made its interest payments. Obviously, interest is paid only once, but the more times it *could* be paid, the bigger the company's safety net. Although interest is paid from cash, not accrual earnings, it is standard practice to base this ratio on accrual-based EBIT, not a cash-based amount. For Milavec, this calculation is as follows.

	Year 4	Year 3
Income before taxes	$42,000	$40,000
Interest expense (b)	8,000	8,000*
Income before taxes and interest (a)	$50,000	$48,000
Times interest earned (a ÷ b)	6.25 times	6 times

*Interest on bonds: $100,000 × 0.08 = $8,000.

Any expense or dividend payment can be analyzed this way. Another frequently used calculation is the number of times the preferred dividend is earned. In that case, the numerator is net income (after taxes) and the denominator is the amount of the annual preferred dividend.

CHECK YOURSELF 13.2

Selected data for Riverside Corporation and Academy Company follow (amounts are shown in millions).

	Riverside Corporation	Academy Company
Total liabilities (a)	$650	$450
Stockholders' equity (b)	300	400
Total liabilities + Stockholders' equity (c)	$950	$850
Interest expense (d)	$ 65	$ 45
Income before taxes (e)	140	130
Income before taxes and interest (f)	$205	$175

Based on this information alone, which company would likely obtain the less favorable interest rate on additional debt financing?

Answer Interest rates vary with risk levels. Companies with less solvency (long-term, debt-paying ability) generally must pay higher interest rates to obtain financing. Two solvency measures for the two companies follow. Recall:

Total assets = Liabilities + Stockholders' equity

	Riverside Corporation	Academy Company
Debt-to-assets ratio (a ÷ c)	68.4%	52.9%
Times interest earned (f ÷ d)	3.15 times	3.89 times

Because Riverside has a higher percentage of debt and a lower times-interest-earned ratio, the data suggest that Riverside is less solvent than Academy. Riverside would therefore likely have to pay a higher interest rate to obtain additional financing.

Plant Assets to Long-Term Liabilities

Companies often pledge plant assets as collateral for long-term liabilities. Financial statement users may analyze a firm's ability to obtain long-term financing on the strength of its asset base. Effective financial management principles dictate that asset purchases should be financed over a time span about equal to the expected lives of the assets. Short-term assets should be financed with short-term liabilities; the current ratio, introduced earlier, indicates how well a company manages current debt. Long-lived assets should be financed with long-term liabilities, and the **plant assets to long-term liabilities** ratio shows the amount of assets per each dollar of long-term debt. All other things being equal, the larger the ratio the lower the financial risk. In other words, a company with a high plant assets to long-term liabilities could sell the larger amount of assets to obtain funds to pay off a relatively small amount of debt. The ratio is calculated as follows:

$$\text{Plant assets to long-term liabilities} = \frac{\text{Net plant assets}}{\text{Long-term liabilities}}$$

For Milavec Company, these ratios follow.

	Year 4	Year 3
Net plant assets (a)	$340,000	$310,000
Bonds payable (b)	100,000	100,000
Plant assets to long-term liabilities (a ÷ b)	3.4:1	3.1:1

MEASURES OF PROFITABILITY

LO 13-4

Calculate ratios for assessing a company's managerial effectiveness.

Profitability refers to a company's ability to generate earnings. Both management and external users employ **profitability ratios** to assess a company's success in generating profits and how these profits are used to reward investors. Some of the many ratios available to measure different aspects of profitability are discussed in the following two sections.

Measures of Managerial Effectiveness

The most common ratios used to evaluate managerial effectiveness measure what percentage of sales results in earnings and how productive assets are in generating those sales. As mentioned earlier, the *absolute amount* of sales or earnings means little without also considering company size.

Net Margin (or Return on Sales)

Gross margin and *gross profit* are alternate terms for the amount remaining after subtracting the expense cost of goods sold from sales. **Net margin,** sometimes called *operating margin, profit margin,* or the *return-on-sales ratio,* describes the percentage of each sales dollar remaining after subtracting other expenses, as well as cost of goods sold. Net margin can be calculated in several ways; some of the more common methods subtract only normal operating expenses or all expenses other than income tax expense. For simplicity, our calculation uses net income (we subtract all expenses). Net income divided by net sales expresses net income (earnings) as a percentage of sales:

$$\text{Net margin} = \frac{\text{Net income}}{\text{Net sales}}$$

For Milavec Company, the net margins for Year 4 and Year 3 were as follows.

	Year 4	Year 3
Net income (a)	$ 25,000	$ 22,000
Net sales (b)	900,000	800,000
Net margin (a ÷ b)	2.78%	2.75%

©StockStudio/Shutterstock

Milavec has maintained approximately the same net margin. Obviously, the larger the percentage, the better; a meaningful interpretation, however, requires analyzing the company's history and comparing the net margin to other companies in the same industry. The average net margin for the 25 nonfinancial companies that make up the Dow Jones Industrial Average (DJIA) has been around 13 percent in recent years; some companies, such as Pfizer with 41 percent, have been much higher than the average. Of course, if a company has a net loss, its net margin for that year will be negative.

Asset Turnover Ratio

The **asset turnover ratio** (sometimes called *turnover-of-assets ratio*) measures how many sales dollars were generated for each dollar of assets invested. As with many ratios used in financial statement analysis, users may define the numerator and denominator of this ratio in different ways. For example, they may use total assets or only include operating assets. Because the numerator represents a whole period, it is preferable to use average assets in the denominator if possible, especially if the amount of assets changed significantly during the year. We use average total assets in our illustration.

$$\text{Asset turnover} = \frac{\text{Net sales}}{\text{Average total assets}}$$

For Milavec, the asset turnover ratios were as follows.

	Year 4	Year 3
Net sales (a)	$900,000	$800,000
Beginning assets (b)	$455,000	$420,000*
Ending assets (c)	508,000	455,000
Average assets (d) = (b + c) ÷ 2	$481,500	$437,500
Asset turnover (a ÷ d)	1.87	1.83

*The Year 3 beginning asset balance was drawn from the Year 2 financial statements, which are not included in the illustration.

As with most ratios, the implications of a given asset turnover ratio are affected by other considerations. Asset turnover will be high in an industry that requires only minimal investment to operate, such as real estate sales companies. On the other hand, industries that require large investments in plant and machinery, like the auto industry, are likely to have lower asset turnover ratios. The asset turnover ratios of the nonfinancial companies that make up the DJIA have averaged around 2.86 in recent years. This means that annual sales have averaged 286 percent of their assets.

Return on Investment

Return on investment (ROI), also called **return on assets** or *earning power,* is the ratio of wealth generated (net income) to the amount invested (average total assets) to generate the wealth. ROI can be calculated as follows:[1]

$$\text{ROI} = \frac{\text{Net income}}{\text{Average total assets}}$$

[1]Detailed coverage of the return on investment ratio is provided in introductory managerial accounting courses, which will explain how companies frequently manipulate the formula to improve managerial motivation and performance. For example, instead of using net income, companies frequently use operating income because net income may be affected by items that are not controllable by management such as loss on a plant closing, storm damage, and so on.

For Milavec, ROI was as follows:

Year 4

$25,000 ÷ $481,500* = 5.19%

Year 3

$22,000 ÷ $437,500* = 5.03%

*The computation of average assets is shown previously.

In general, higher ROIs suggest better performance. The return-on-investment ratios of the large nonfinancial companies that make up the DJIA have averaged around 8 percent in recent years. These data suggest that Milavec is performing below average and therefore signal a need for further evaluation.

Return on Equity

Return on equity (ROE) is often used to measure the profitability of the stockholders' investment. ROE is usually higher than ROI because of financial leverage. Financial leverage refers to using debt financing to increase the assets available to a business beyond the amount of assets financed by owners. As long as a company's ROI exceeds its cost of borrowing (interest expense), the owners will earn a higher return on their investment in the company by using borrowed money. For example, if a company borrows money at 8 percent and invests it at 10 percent, the owners will enjoy a return that is higher than 10 percent. ROE is computed as follows:

$$\text{ROE} = \frac{\text{Net income}}{\text{Average total stockholders' equity}}$$

	Year 4	Year 3
Net income (a)	$ 25,000	$ 22,000
Preferred stock, 6%, $100 par, cumulative	$ 50,000	$ 50,000
Common stock, $10 par	150,000	125,000
Retained earnings	162,000	137,000
Ending stockholders' equity (b)	362,000	312,000
Beginning stockholders' equity (c)	312,000	268,000*
Average stockholders' equity (d) = (b + c) ÷ 2	$337,000	$290,000
ROE (a ÷ d)	7.4%	7.6%

*The Year 3 beginning stockholders' equity balance was drawn from the Year 2 financial statements, which are not included in the illustration.

The slight decrease in ROE is due primarily to the increase in common stock. The effect of the increase in total stockholders' equity offsets the effect of the increase in earnings. It is interesting to note that Milavec's ROEs of 7.6 percent and 7.4 percent are low in relation to real-world companies that make up the DJIA. Recently, the average ROE for these companies was 27 percent. One contributing factor explaining this difference is that most companies in the DJIA are more highly leveraged.

STOCK MARKET RATIOS

LO 13-5

Calculate ratios for assessing a company's position in the stock market.

Existing and potential investors in a company's stock use many common ratios to analyze and compare the earnings and dividends of different-sized companies in different industries. Purchasers of stock can profit in two ways: through receiving dividends and through increases in stock value. Investors consider both dividends and overall earnings performance as indicators of the value of the stock they own.

Earnings per Share

Perhaps the most frequently quoted measure of earnings performance is **earnings per share (EPS).** EPS calculations are among the most complex in accounting, and more advanced textbooks devote entire chapters to the subject. At this level, we use the following basic formula:

$$\text{Earnings per share} = \frac{\text{Net earnings available for common stock}}{\text{Average number of outstanding common shares}}$$

EPS pertains to shares of *common stock.* Limiting the numerator to earnings available for common stock eliminates the annual preferred dividend ($0.06 \times \$50{,}000 = \$3{,}000$) from the calculation. Exhibit 13.1 shows that Milavec did not pay the preferred dividends in Year 4. Because the preferred stock is cumulative, however, the preferred dividend is in arrears and not available to the common stockholders. The number of common shares outstanding is determined by dividing the book value of the common stock by its par value per share ($\$150{,}000 \div \$10 = 15{,}000$ for Year 4 and $\$125{,}000 \div \$10 = 12{,}500$ for Year 3). Using these data, Milavec's Year 4 EPS is calculated as follows:

$$\frac{\$25{,}000\ (\text{net income}) - \$3{,}000\ (\text{preferred dividend})}{(15{,}000 + 12{,}500)/2\ (\text{average outstanding common shares})} = \$1.60 \text{ per share}$$

Investors attribute a great deal of importance to EPS figures. The amounts used in calculating EPS, however, have limitations. Many accounting choices, assumptions, and estimates underlie net income computations, including alternative depreciation methods, different inventory cost flow assumptions, and estimates of future bad debt or warranty expenses, to name only a few. The denominator is also inexact because various factors (discussed in intermediate accounting courses) affect the number of shares to include. Numerous opportunities therefore exist to manipulate EPS figures. Prudent investors consider these variables in deciding how much weight to attach to earnings per share.

Book Value

Book value per share is another frequently quoted measure of a share of stock. It is calculated as follows:

$$\text{Book value per share} = \frac{\text{Stockholders' equity} - \text{Preferred stock}}{\text{Outstanding common shares}}$$

Instead of describing the numerator as stockholders' equity, we could have used assets minus liabilities, the algebraic computation of a company's "net worth." Net worth is a misnomer. A company's accounting records reflect book values, not worth. Because assets are recorded at historical costs and different methods are used to transfer asset costs to expense, the book value of assets after deducting liabilities is difficult to interpret. Nevertheless, investors use the term *book value per share* frequently. Milavec's book value per share for Year 4 is calculated as follows:

$$\frac{\$362{,}000 - \$50{,}000}{15{,}000 \text{ shares}} = \$20.80 \text{ per share}$$

Price-Earnings Ratio

The **price-earnings (P/E) ratio** compares the earnings per share of a company to the market price for a share of the company's stock. Assume Avalanche Company and Brushfire Company each report earnings per share of $3.60. For the same year, Cyclone Company reports EPS of $4.10. Based on these data alone, Cyclone stock may seem to be the best investment. Suppose, however, that the price for one share of stock in each company is $43.20, $36.00,

REALITY BYTES

©Jim Pruitt/123RF

The single most important source of financial information is a company's annual report, but decision makers should also consider other sources. Interested persons can access quarterly and annual reports through the SEC's EDGAR database and often from company websites as well. Many companies will provide printed versions of these reports upon request. Companies also post information on their websites that is not included in their annual reports. For example, some automobile companies provide very detailed production data through their corporate websites.

Users can frequently obtain information useful in analyzing a particular company from independent sources, as well as from the company itself. For example, the websites of popular news services, such as **CNN (www.money.cnn.com)** and **CNBC (www.cnbc.com)**, provide archived news stories and independent financial information about many companies. The websites of brokerage houses like **www.schwab.com** offer free financial information about companies. Finally, libraries often subscribe to independent services that evaluate companies as potential investments. One example worth reviewing is *Value Line Investment Survey.*

Different Industries

Different industries may be affected by unique social policies, special accounting procedures, or other individual industry attributes. Ratios of companies in different industries are not comparable without considering industry characteristics. A high debt-to-assets ratio is more acceptable in some industries than others. Even within an industry, a particular business may require more or less working capital than the industry average. If so, the working capital and quick ratios would mean little compared to those of other firms, but may still be useful for trend analysis.

Because of industry-specific factors, most professional analysts specialize in only one industry, or just a few. Financial institutions such as brokerage houses, banks, and insurance companies typically employ financial analysts who specialize in areas such as mineral or oil extraction, chemicals, banking, retail, insurance, bond markets, or automobile manufacturing.

Changing Economic Environment

When comparing firms, analysts must be alert to changes in general economic trends from year to year. Significant changes in fuel costs and interest rates in recent years make old rule-of-thumb guidelines for evaluating these factors obsolete. In addition, the presence or absence of inflation affects business prospects.

Accounting Principles

Financial statement analysis is only as reliable as the data on which it is based. Although most firms follow generally accepted accounting principles, a wide variety of acceptable accounting methods is available from which to choose, including different inventory and depreciation methods, different schedules for recognizing revenue, and different ways to account for oil and gas exploration costs. Analyzing statements of companies that seem identical may produce noncomparable ratios if the companies have used different accounting methods. Analysts may seek to improve comparability by trying to recast different companies' financial statements as if the same accounting methods had been applied.

Accrual accounting requires the use of many estimates; bad debt expense, warranty expense, asset lives, and salvage value are just a few. The reliability of the resulting financial reports depends on the expertise and integrity of the persons who make the estimates.

The quality and usefulness of accounting information are influenced by underlying accounting concepts. Two particular concepts, *conservatism* and *historical cost,* have a tremendous impact on financial reporting. Conservatism dictates recognizing estimated losses as soon as they occur, but gain recognition is almost always deferred until the gains are actually realized. Conservatism produces a negative bias in financial statements. There are persuasive arguments for the conservatism principle, but users should be alert to distortions it may cause in accounting information.

The pervasive use of the historical cost concept is probably the greatest single cause of distorted financial statement analysis results. The historical cost of an asset does not represent its current value. The asset purchased in Year 1 for $10,000 is not comparable in value to the asset purchased in Year 5 for $10,000 because of changes in the value of the dollar. Using historical cost produces financial statements that report dollars with differing purchasing power in the same statement. Combining these differing dollar values is akin to adding miles to kilometers. To get the most from analyzing financial statements, users should be cognizant of these limitations.

CHECK YOURSELF 13.3

The return on equity for Gup Company and Hunn Company is 23.4 percent and 17 percent, respectively. Does this mean Gup Company is better managed than Hunn Company?

Answer No single ratio can adequately measure management performance. Even analyzing a wide range of ratios provides only limited insight. Any useful interpretation requires the analyst to recognize the limitations of ratio analysis. For example, ratio norms typically differ between industries and may be affected by temporary economic factors. In addition, companies' use of different accounting practices and procedures produces different ratio results even when underlying circumstances are comparable.

<< A Look Back

Financial statement analysis involves many factors, among them user characteristics, information needs for particular types of decisions, and how financial information is analyzed. Analytical techniques include *horizontal, vertical,* and *ratio analysis.* Users commonly calculate ratios to measure a company's liquidity, solvency, and profitability. The specific ratios presented in this chapter are summarized in Exhibit 13.6. Although ratios are easy to calculate and provide useful insights into business operations, when interpreting analytical results, users should consider limitations resulting from differing industry characteristics, differing economic conditions, and the fundamental accounting principles used to produce reported financial information.

>> A Look Forward

The next chapter presents a detailed explanation of the statement of cash flows. In that chapter, you will learn how to classify cash receipts and payments as financing activities, investing activities, or operating activities. Chapter 14 explains how to prepare a statement of cash flows and shows the difference between the direct and indirect methods of presenting cash flows from operating activities. The depth and timing of statement of cash flows coverage varies among colleges. Your instructor may or may not cover this final chapter.

Video lectures and accompanying self-assessment quizzes are available in *Connect* for all learning objectives.

SELF-STUDY REVIEW PROBLEM

Financial statements for Stallings Company follow.

Income Statement For the Years Ended December 31	Year 4	Year 3
Revenues		
Net sales	$ 315,000	$ 259,000
Expenses		
Cost of goods sold	(189,000)	(154,000)
Selling, general, and administrative expenses	(54,000)	(46,000)
Interest expense	(4,000)	(4,500)
Income before taxes	68,000	54,500
Income tax expense (40%)	(27,200)	(21,800)
Net income	$ 40,800	$ 32,700

Balance Sheets As of December 31	Year 4	Year 3
Assets		
Current assets		
Cash	$ 6,500	$ 11,500
Accounts receivable	51,000	49,000
Inventories	155,000	147,500
Total current assets	212,500	208,000
Plant and equipment (net)	187,500	177,000
Total assets	$400,000	$385,000
Liabilities and Stockholders' Equity		
Liabilities		
Current liabilities		
Accounts payable	$ 60,000	$ 81,500
Other	25,000	22,500
Total current liabilities	85,000	104,000
Bonds payable	100,000	100,000
Total liabilities	185,000	204,000
Stockholders' equity		
Common stock (50,000 shares, $3 par)	150,000	150,000
Paid-in capital in excess of par	20,000	20,000
Retained earnings	45,000	11,000
Total stockholders' equity	215,000	181,000
Total liabilities and stockholders' equity	$400,000	$385,000

Required

a. Use horizontal analysis to determine which expense item increased by the highest percentage from Year 3 to Year 4.

b. Use vertical analysis to determine whether the inventory balance is a higher percentage of total assets in Year 3 or Year 4.

c. Calculate the following ratios for Year 3 and Year 4. When data limitations prohibit computing averages, use year-end balances in your calculations.

(1) Net margin
(2) Return on investment
(3) Return on equity
(4) Earnings per share
(5) Price-earnings ratio (market price per share at the end of Year 4 and Year 3 was $12.04 and $8.86, respectively)
(6) Book value per share of common stock
(7) Times interest earned
(8) Working capital
(9) Current ratio
(10) Acid-test ratio
(11) Accounts receivable turnover
(12) Inventory turnover
(13) Debt to equity

Solution to Requirement *a*

Income tax expense increased by the greatest percentage. Computations follow.

Cost of goods sold ($189,000 − $154,000) ÷ $154,000 = 22.73%

General, selling, and administrative ($54,000 − $46,000) ÷ $46,000 = 17.39%

Interest expense decreased.

Income tax expense ($27,200 − $21,800) ÷ $21,800 = 24.77%

Solution to Requirement *b*

Year 3: $147,500 ÷ $385,000 = 38.31%

Year 4: $155,000 ÷ $400,000 = 38.75%

Inventory is slightly larger relative to total assets in Year 4.

Solution to Requirement *c*

		Year 4	Year 3
1.	Net income / Net sales	$40,800 / $315,000 = 12.95%	$32,700 / $259,000 = 12.63%
2.	Net income / Average total assets	$40,800 / $392,500 = 10.39%	$32,700 / $385,000 = 8.49%
3.	Net income / Average total stockholders' equity	$40,800 / $198,000 = 20.61%	$32,700 / $181,000 = 18.07%
4.	Net income / Average common shares outstanding	$40,800 / 50,000 shares = $0.816	$32,700 / 50,000 shares = $0.654
5.	Market price per share / Earnings per share	$12.04 / $0.816 = 14.75 times	$8.86 / $0.654 = 13.55 times
6.	Stockholders' equity — Preferred rights / Outstanding common shares	$215,000 / 50,000 shares = $4.30	$181,000 / 50,000 shares = $3.62
7.	Net income + Taxes + Interest expense / Interest expense	$40,800 + $27,200 + $4,000 / $4,000 = 18 times	$32,700 + $21,800 + $4,500 / $4,500 = 13.1 times
8.	Current assets − Current liabilities	$212,500 − $85,000 = $127,500	$208,000 − $104,000 = $104,000
9.	Current assets / Current liabilities	$212,500 / $85,000 = 2.5:1	$208,000 / $104,000 = 2:1
10.	Quick assets / Current liabilities	$57,500 / $85,000 = 0.68:1	$60,500 / $104,000 = 0.58:1
11.	Net credit sales / Average accounts receivable	$315,000 / $50,000 = 6.3 times	$259,000 / $49,000 = 5.29 times
12.	Cost of goods sold / Average inventory	$189,000 / $151,250 = 1.25 times	$154,000 / $147,500 = 1.04 times
13.	Total liabilities / Total stockholders' equity	$185,000 / $215,000 = 86.05%	$204,000 / $181,000 = 112.71%

KEY TERMS

Absolute amounts 591
Accounts receivable turnover 597
Acid-test ratio 596
Asset turnover ratio 602
Average days to collect accounts receivables (average collection period) 598
Average days to sell inventory (average days in inventory) 598
Book value per share 604
Current ratio 596
Debt-to-assets ratio 599
Debt-to-equity ratio 599
Dividend yield 605
Earnings per share (EPS) 604
Horizontal analysis 591
Information overload 590
Inventory turnover 598
Liquidity ratios 595
Materiality 591
Net margin 601
Number of times interest is earned 599
Percentage analysis 592
Plant assets to long-term liabilities 601
Price-earnings (P/E) ratio 604
Profitability ratios 601
Quick ratio 596
Ratio analysis 594
Return on assets 602
Return on equity (ROE) 603
Return on investment (ROI) 602
Solvency ratios 599
Trend analysis 591
Vertical analysis 594
Working capital 595
Working capital ratio 596

QUESTIONS

1. Why are ratios and trends used in financial analysis?
2. What do the terms *liquidity* and *solvency* mean?
3. What is apparent from a horizontal presentation of financial statement information? A vertical presentation?
4. What is the significance of inventory turnover, and how is it calculated?
5. What is the difference between the current ratio and the quick ratio? What does each measure?
6. Why are absolute amounts of limited use when comparing companies?
7. What is the difference between return on investment and return on equity?
8. Which ratios are used to measure long-term, debt-paying ability? How is each calculated?
9. What are some limitations of the earnings per share figure?
10. What is the formula for calculating return on investment (ROI)?
11. What is information overload?
12. What is the price-earnings ratio? Explain the difference between it and the dividend yield.
13. What environmental factors must be considered in analyzing companies?
14. How do accounting principles affect financial statement analysis?

MULTIPLE-CHOICE QUESTIONS

Multiple-choice questions are available in *Connect*.

EXERCISES—SERIES A

connect **All applicable Exercises in Series A are available in *Connect*.**

Exercise 13-1A *Horizontal analysis*

LO 13-1

Winthrop Corporation reported the following operating results for two consecutive years.

	Year 3	Year 2	Percentage Change
Sales	$1,200,000	$1,000,000	
Cost of goods sold	720,000	640,000	
Gross margin	$ 480,000	$ 360,000	
Operating expenses	200,000	160,000	
Income before taxes	$ 280,000	$ 200,000	
Income taxes	56,000	40,000	
Net income	$ 224,000	$ 160,000	

Required

a. Compute the percentage changes in Winthrop Corporation's income statement components between the two years. Round percentages to one decimal point.

b. Comment on apparent trends revealed by the percentage changes computed in Requirement *a*.

LO 13-1

Exercise 13-2A *Vertical analysis*

Sharma Company reported the following operating results for two consecutive years.

Year 3	Amount	Percentage of Sales
Sales	$ 800,000	
Cost of goods sold	450,000	
Gross margin on sales	350,000	
Operating expenses	100,000	
Income before taxes	250,000	
Income taxes	50,000	
Net income	$ 200,000	
Year 4	**Amount**	**Percentage of Sales**
Sales	$1,000,000	
Cost of goods sold	590,000	
Gross margin on sales	410,000	
Operating expenses	120,000	
Income before taxes	290,000	
Income taxes	60,000	
Net income	$ 230,000	

Required

Express each income statement component for each of the two years as a percentage of sales. Round percentages to one decimal point.

LO 13-1

Exercise 13-3A *Horizontal and vertical analysis*

Income statements for Burch Company for Year 3 and Year 4 follow.

	Year 4	Year 3
Sales	$240,000	$200,000
Cost of goods sold	180,000	124,000
Selling expenses	26,000	20,000
Administrative expenses	12,000	18,000
Interest expense	7,500	8,000
Total expenses	$225,500	$170,000
Income before taxes	14,500	30,000
Income taxes expense	1,200	3,000
Net income	$ 13,300	$ 27,000

Required

Round all percentages to one decimal point.

a. Perform a horizontal analysis, showing the percentage change in each income statement component between Year 3 and Year 4.

b. Perform a vertical analysis, showing each income statement component as a percentage of sales for each year.

LO 13-2

Exercise 13-4A *Inventory turnover*

Selected financial information for Edwards Company for Year 4 follows.

Sales	$800,000
Cost of goods sold	500,000
Merchandise inventory	
Beginning of year	37,500
End of year	42,500

Required

Assuming that the merchandise inventory buildup was relatively constant, how many times did the merchandise inventory turn over during Year 4?

Exercise 13-5A *Current ratio*

LO 13-2

Swartz Corporation wrote off a $1,600 uncollectible account receivable against the $48,000 balance in its allowance account.

Required

Explain the effect of the write-off on Swartz's current ratio.

Exercise 13-6A *Working capital and current ratio*

LO 13-2

On June 30, Year 3, Franza Company's total current assets were $900,000 and its total current liabilities were $360,000. On July 1, Year 3, Franza issued a *short-term note* to a bank for $72,000 cash.

Required

a. Compute Franza's working capital before and after issuing the note.

b. Compute Franza's current ratio before and after issuing the note. Round ratios to two decimal points.

Exercise 13-7A *Working capital and current ratio*

LO 13-2

On June 30, Year 3, Franza Company's total current assets were $900,000 and its total current liabilities were $360,000. On July 1, Year 3, Franza issued a *long-term note* to a bank for $72,000 cash.

Required

Round computations to one decimal point.

a. Compute Franza's working capital before and after issuing the note.

b. Compute Franza's current ratio before and after issuing the note.

Exercise 13-8A *Ratio analysis*

LO 13-2, 13-3

The balance sheet for Shankland Corporation follows.

Current assets	$ 600,000
Long-term assets (net)	1,900,000
Total assets	$2,500,000
Current liabilities	$ 400,000
Long-term liabilities	1,200,000
Total liabilities	1,600,000
Common stock and retained earnings	900,000
Total liabilities and stockholders' equity	$2,500,000

Required

Compute the following and round ratios to one decimal point.

Working capital	________
Current ratio	________
Debt-to-assets ratio	________
Debt-to-equity ratio	________

Exercise 13-9A *Comprehensive analysis*

LO 13-2, 13-3

The December 31, Year 4, balance sheet for Burdette Corporation is presented here. These are the only accounts on Burdette's balance sheet. Amounts indicated by question marks (?) can be calculated using the following additional information.

Assets	
Cash	$ 30,000
Accounts receivable (net)	?
Inventory	?
Property, plant, and equipment (net)	352,800
	$ 518,400
Liabilities and Stockholders' Equity	
Accounts payable (trade)	$?
Income taxes payable (current)	30,000
Long-term debt	?
Common stock	360,000
Retained earnings	?
	$?
Additional Information	
Current ratio (at year end)	1.5 to 1.0
Total liabilities ÷ Total stockholders' equity	80%
Gross margin percentage	30%
Inventory turnover (Cost of goods sold ÷ Ending inventory)	10.5 times
Gross margin for Year 4	$ 378,000

Required

Determine the following:

a. The balance in trade accounts payable as of December 31, Year 4.

b. The balance in retained earnings as of December 31, Year 4.

c. The balance in the inventory account as of December 31, Year 4. (Assume that the level of inventory did not change from last year.)

LO 13-3

Exercise 13-10A *Number of times interest earned*

The following data come from the financial records of Fargo Corporation for Year 3.

Sales	$640,000
Interest expense	6,000
Income tax expense	12,000
Net income	42,000

Required

How many times was interest earned in Year 3?

LO 13-2, 13-4

Exercise 13-11A *Accounts receivable turnover, inventory turnover, and net margin*

Selected data from Emporia Company follow.

Balance Sheets As of December 31	Year 3	Year 2
Accounts receivable	$600,000	$480,000
Allowance for doubtful accounts	(40,000)	(20,000)
Net accounts receivable	$560,000	$460,000
Inventories, lower of cost or market	$500,000	$400,000

Income Statements For the Years Ended December 31		
	Year 3	Year 2
Net credit sales	$2,400,000	$1,950,000
Net cash sales	600,000	450,000
Net sales	3,000,000	2,400,000
Cost of goods sold	1,800,000	1,520,000
Selling, general, and administrative expenses	300,000	240,000
Other expenses	80,000	50,000
Total operating expenses	$2,180,000	$1,810,000

Required

Compute the following and round computations to two decimal points:

a. The accounts receivable turnover for Year 3.

b. The inventory turnover for Year 3.

c. The net margin for Year 2.

Exercise 13-12A *Ratio analysis*

LO 13-5

During Year 3, Blue Ridge Corporation reported after-tax net income of $4,150,000. During the year, the number of shares of stock outstanding remained constant at 15,000 of $100 par, 9 percent preferred stock and 400,000 shares of common stock. The company's total stockholders' equity is $20,000,000 at December 31, Year 3. Blue Ridge Corporation's common stock was selling at $80 per share at the end of its fiscal year. All dividends for the year have been paid, including $4.80 per share to common stockholders.

Required

Compute the following by rounding to two decimal points:

a. Earnings per share.

b. Book value per share of common stock.

c. Price-earnings ratio.

d. Dividend yield.

Exercise 13-13A *Ratio analysis*

LO 13-2, 13-3, 13-4, 13-5

Compute the specified ratios using Duluth Company's balance sheet for Year 3.

Assets	
Cash	$ 36,000
Marketable securities	24,000
Accounts receivable	50,000
Inventory	44,000
Property and equipment	320,000
Accumulated depreciation	(74,000)
Total assets	$400,000
Liabilities and Stockholders' Equity	
Accounts payable	$ 23,000
Current notes payable	7,000
Mortgage payable	8,000
Bonds payable	43,000
Common stock	200,000
Retained earnings	119,000
Total liabilities and stockholders' equity	$400,000

The average number of common stock shares outstanding during Year 3 was 880 shares. Net income for the year was $40,000.

Required

Compute each of the following and round computations to two decimal points:

a. Current ratio.
b. Earnings per share.
c. Quick (acid-test) ratio.
d. Return on investment.
e. Return on equity.
f. Debt-to-equity ratio.

LO 13-2, 13-3, 13-4, 13-5

Exercise 13-14A *Ratio analysis*

Required

Match each of the following ratios with the formula used to compute it:

______	**1.** Working capital	**a.** Net income ÷ Average total stockholders' equity
______	**2.** Current ratio	**b.** Cost of goods sold ÷ Average inventory
______	**3.** Quick ratio	**c.** Current assets − Current liabilities
______	**4.** Accounts receivable turnover	**d.** 365 ÷ Inventory turnover
______	**5.** Average days to collect	**e.** Net income ÷ Average total assets
______	**6.** Inventory turnover	**f.** (Net income − Preferred dividends) ÷ Average outstanding common shares
______	**7.** Average days to sell inventory	**g.** (Current assets − Inventory − Prepaid expenses) ÷ Current liabilities
______	**8.** Debt-to-assets ratio	**h.** Total liabilities ÷ Total assets
______	**9.** Debt-to-equity ratio	**i.** 365 ÷ Accounts receivable turnover
______	**10.** Return on investment	**j.** Total liabilities ÷ Total stockholders' equity
______	**11.** Return on equity	**k.** Net credit sales ÷ Average accounts receivables
______	**12.** Earnings per share	**l.** Current assets ÷ Current liabilities

LO 13-2, 13-3, 13-4, 13-5

Exercise 13-15A *Comprehensive analysis*

Required

Indicate the effect of each of the following transactions on (1) the current ratio, (2) working capital, (3) stockholders' equity, (4) book value per share of common stock, and (5) retained earnings. Assume that the current ratio is greater than 1:1.

a. Collected account receivable.
b. Wrote off account receivable.
c. Converted a short-term note payable to a long-term note payable.
d. Purchased inventory on account.
e. Declared cash dividend.
f. Sold merchandise on account at a profit.
g. Issued stock dividend.
h. Paid account payable.
i. Sold building at a loss.

PROBLEMS—SERIES A

connect **All applicable Problems in Series A are available in *Connect*.**

LO 13-1

Problem 13-16A *Vertical analysis*

The following percentages apply to Thornton Company for Year 3 and Year 4.

	Year 4	Year 3
Sales	100.0%	100.0%
Cost of goods sold	61.0	64.0
Gross margin	39.0	36.0
Selling and administrative expense	26.5	20.5
Interest expense	2.5	2.0
Total expenses	29.0	22.5
Income before taxes	10.0	13.5
Income tax expense	5.5	7.0
Net income	4.5%	6.5%

CHECK FIGURES
NI of Year 4: $43,200
Total expenses of Year 3: $180,000

Required

Assuming that sales were $800,000 in Year 3 and $960,000 in Year 4, prepare income statements for the two years.

Problem 13-17A *Horizontal analysis*

LO 13-1

CHECK FIGURES
Total assets: +11.1%
Total liabilities: +14.4%

Financial statements for Allendale Company follow.

ALLENDALE COMPANY
Balance Sheets
As of December 31

	Year 4	Year 3
Assets		
Current assets		
Cash	$ 40,000	$ 36,000
Marketable securities	20,000	6,000
Accounts receivable (net)	54,000	46,000
Inventories	135,000	143,000
Prepaid items	25,000	10,000
Total current assets	274,000	241,000
Investments	27,000	20,000
Plant (net)	270,000	255,000
Land	29,000	24,000
Total assets	$600,000	$540,000
Liabilities and Stockholders' Equity		
Liabilities		
Current liabilities		
Notes payable	$ 17,000	$ 6,000
Accounts payable	113,800	100,000
Salaries payable	21,000	15,000
Total current liabilities	151,800	121,000
Noncurrent liabilities		
Bonds payable	100,000	100,000
Other	32,000	27,000
Total noncurrent liabilities	132,000	127,000
Total liabilities	283,800	248,000
Stockholders' equity		
Preferred stock (par value $10, 4% cumulative, nonparticipating; 8,000 shares authorized and issued)	80,000	80,000
Common stock (no par; 50,000 shares authorized; 10,000 shares issued)	80,000	80,000
Retained earnings	156,200	132,000
Total stockholders' equity	316,200	292,000
Total liabilities and stockholders' equity	$600,000	$540,000

ALLENDALE COMPANY
Statements of Income and Retained Earnings
For the Years Ended December 31

	Year 4	Year 3
Revenues		
Sales (net)	$230,000	$210,000
Other revenues	8,000	5,000
Total revenues	238,000	215,000
Expenses		
Cost of goods sold	120,000	103,000
Selling, general, and administrative	55,000	50,000
Interest expense	8,000	7,200
Income tax expense	23,000	22,000
Total expenses	206,000	182,200
Net earnings (net income)	32,000	32,800
Retained earnings, January 1	132,000	107,000
Less: Preferred stock dividends	3,200	3,200
Common stock dividends	4,600	4,600
Retained earnings, December 31	$156,200	$132,000

Required

Prepare a horizontal analysis of the balance sheet and income statement for Year 4 and Year 3. Round percentages to one decimal point.

LO 13-1

excel

CHECK FIGURE
Year 4 Retained earnings: 26.03%

Problem 13-18A *Vertical analysis*

Required

Use the financial statements for Allendale Company from Problem 13-17A to perform a vertical analysis of both the balance sheets and income statements for Year 4 and Year 3. Round computations to two decimal points.

LO 13-2

Problem 13-19A *Effect of transactions on current ratio and working capital*

Riley Manufacturing has a current ratio of 3:1 on December 31, Year 3. Indicate whether each of the following transactions would increase (+), decrease (−), or have no effect (NA) on Riley's current ratio and its working capital.

Required

a. Paid cash for a trademark.
b. Wrote off an uncollectible account receivable.
c. Sold equipment for cash.
d. Sold merchandise at a profit (cash).
e. Declared a cash dividend.
f. Purchased inventory on account.
g. Scrapped a fully depreciated machine (no gain or loss).
h. Issued a stock dividend.
i. Purchased a machine with a long-term note.
j. Paid a previously declared cash dividend.
k. Collected accounts receivable.
l. Invested in current marketable securities.

Problem 13-20A *Supply missing balance sheet numbers*

LO 13-2, 13-3

The bookkeeper for Packard's Country Music Bar left this incomplete balance sheet. Packard's working capital is $90,000 and its debt-to-assets ratio is 40 percent.

CHECK FIGURES
d: $337,500
f: $97,500

Assets	
Current assets	
Cash	$ 21,000
Accounts receivable	42,000
Inventory	(A)
Prepaid expenses	9,000
Total current assets	(B)
Long-term assets	
Building	(C)
Less: Accumulated depreciation	(39,000)
Total long-term assets	210,000
Total assets	$ (D)
Liabilities and Stockholders' Equity	
Liabilities	
Current liabilities	
Accounts payable	$ (E)
Notes payable	12,000
Income tax payable	10,500
Total current liabilities	37,500
Long-term liabilities	
Mortgage payable	(F)
Total liabilities	(G)
Stockholders' equity	
Common stock	105,000
Retained earnings	(H)
Total stockholders' equity	(I)
Total liabilities and stockholders' equity	$ (J)

Required

Complete the balance sheet by supplying the missing amounts.

Problem 13-21A *Ratio analysis*

LO 13-5

Selected data for Dalton Company for Year 3 and additional information on industry averages follow.

CHECK FIGURE
Earnings per share: $2

Earnings (net income)		$ 97,800
Preferred stock (13,200 shares at $25 par, 4%)		$330,000
Common stock (45,000 shares no par, market value $28)		255,000
Retained earnings		281,250
		$866,250
Less: Treasury stock		
Preferred (1,800 shares)	$27,000	
Common (1,800 shares)	12,000	39,000
Total stockholders' equity		$827,250

Industry averages	
Earnings per share	$ 2.60
Price-earnings ratio	9.50
Return on equity	11.20%

Required

a. Calculate Dalton Company's earnings per share ratio, price-earnings ratio and return on equity ratio and compare them with the industry averages.

b. Discuss factors you would consider in deciding whether to invest in the company.

LO 13-3, 13-4, 13-5

eXcel

CHECK FIGURES

a. Year 3: 13.33 times

c. Year 3: 7.58 times

Problem 13-22A *Ratio analysis*

Otis Company's income statement information follows.

	Year 3	Year 2
Net sales	$480,000	$320,000
Income before interest and taxes	120,000	98,000
Net income after taxes	81,000	72,000
Interest expense	9,000	8,000
Stockholders' equity, December 31 (Year 1: $200,000)	300,000	240,000
Common stock, December 31	240,000	200,000

The average number of shares outstanding was 9,600 for Year 3 and 8,000 for Year 2.

Required

Compute the following ratios for Otis for Year 3 and Year 2 and round the computation to two decimal points:

a. Number of times interest was earned.

b. Earnings per share based on the average number of shares outstanding.

c. Price-earnings ratio (market prices: Year 3, $64 per share; Year 2, $78 per share).

d. Return on average equity.

e. Net margin.

LO 13-2, 13-3, 13-4, 13-5

eXcel

CHECK FIGURES

d. Year 2: $0.72

k. Year 1: 5.63 times

Problem 13-23A *Ratio analysis*

The following financial statements apply to Karl Company:

	Year 2	Year 1
Revenues	436,000	360,000
Expenses		
Cost of goods sold	252,000	206,000
Selling expenses	42,000	38,000
General and administrative expenses	22,000	20,000
Interest expense	6,000	6,000
Income tax expense	42,000	36,000
Total expenses	364,000	306,000
Net income	$ 72,000	$ 54,000

continued

	Year 2	Year 1
Assets		
Current assets		
Cash	$ 74,000	$ 84,000
Marketable securities	2,000	2,000
Accounts receivable	70,000	64,000
Inventories	200,000	192,000
Prepaid expenses	6,000	4,000
Total current assets	352,000	346,000
Plant and equipment (net)	210,000	210,000
Intangibles	40,000	0
Total assets	$602,000	$556,000
Liabilities and Stockholders' Equity		
Liabilities		
Current liabilities		
Accounts payable	$ 80,000	$108,000
Other	34,000	30,000
Total current liabilities	114,000	138,000
Bonds payable	132,000	134,000
Total liabilities	246,000	272,000
Stockholders' equity		
Common stock (100,000 shares)	230,000	230,000
Retained earnings	126,000	54,000
Total stockholders' equity	356,000	284,000
Total liabilities and stockholders' equity	$602,000	$556,000

Required

Calculate the following ratios for Year 1 and Year 2. When data limitations prohibit computing averages, use year-end balances in your calculations. Round computations to two decimal points.

a. Net margin.
b. Return on investment.
c. Return on equity.
d. Earnings per share.
e. Price-earnings ratio (market prices at the end of Year 1 and Year 2 were $11.88 and $9.54, respectively).
f. Book value per share of common stock.
g. Times interest earned.
h. Working capital.
i. Current ratio.
j. Quick (acid-test) ratio.
k. Accounts receivable turnover.
l. Inventory turnover.
m. Debt-to-equity ratio.
n. Debt-to-assets ratio.

Problem 13-24A *Ratio analysis*

LO 13-2, 13-3, 13-4, 13-5

excel

Required

Use the financial statements for Allendale Company from Problem 13-17A to calculate the following ratios for Year 4 and Year 3:

a. Working capital.
b. Current ratio.

CHECK FIGURES
k. Year 4: 2.05:1
p. Year 3: $2.96

c. Quick ratio.
d. Receivables turnover (beginning receivables at January 1, Year 3, were $47,000).
e. Average days to collect accounts receivable.
f. Inventory turnover (beginning inventory at January 1, Year 3, was $140,000).
g. Number of days to sell inventory.
h. Debt-to-assets ratio.
i. Debt-to-equity ratio.
j. Number of times interest was earned.
k. Plant assets to long-term debt.
l. Net margin.
m. Turnover of assets.
n. Return on investment.
o. Return on equity.
p. Earnings per share.
q. Book value per share of common stock.
r. Price-earnings ratio (market price per share: Year 3, $11.75; Year 4, $12.50).
s. Dividend yield on common stock.

EXERCISES—SERIES B

LO 13-1

Exercise 13-1B *Horizontal analysis*

Haskell Corporation reported the following operating results for two consecutive years.

	Year 4	Year 3	Percentage Change
Sales	$550,000	$500,000	
Cost of goods sold	327,600	312,000	
Gross margin	222,400	188,000	
Operating expenses	87,400	76,000	
Income before taxes	135,000	112,000	
Income taxes	34,000	24,000	
Net income	$101,000	$ 88,000	

Required

a. Compute the percentage changes in Haskell Corporation's income statement components for the two years. Round percentages to one decimal point.
b. Comment on apparent trends revealed by the percentage changes computed in Requirement *a*.

LO 13-1

Exercise 13-2B *Vertical analysis*

Sperry Company reported the following operating results for two consecutive years.

Year 3	Amount	Percentage of Sales
Sales	$250,000	
Cost of goods sold	150,000	
Gross margin	100,000	
Operating expenses	30,000	
Income before taxes	70,000	
Income taxes	14,000	
Net income	$ 56,000	

Year 4	Amount	Percentage of Sales
Sales	$300,000	
Cost of goods sold	192,000	
Gross margin	108,000	
Operating expenses	32,000	
Income before taxes	76,000	
Income taxes	16,000	
Net income	$ 60,000	

Required

Express each income statement component for each of the two years as a percentage of sales. Round percentages to one decimal point.

Exercise 13-3B *Horizontal and vertical analysis*

LO 13-1

Alpena Company reported the following operating results for Year 4 and Year 3.

	Year 4	Year 3
Sales	$250,000	$240,000
Cost of goods sold	132,500	129,600
Selling expenses	15,250	14,400
Administrative expenses	19,000	16,800
Interest expense	7,000	8,400
Total expenses	173,750	169,200
Income before taxes	76,250	70,800
Income taxes expense	19,250	17,700
Net income	$ 57,000	$ 53,100

Required

Round percentages to one decimal point.

a. Perform a horizontal analysis, showing the percentage change in each income statement component between Year 4 and Year 3.

b. Perform a vertical analysis, showing each income statement component as a percent of sales for each year.

Exercise 13-4B *Inventory turnover*

LO 13-2

Selected financial information for Purdy Company for Year 4 follows.

Sales	$3,200,000
Cost of goods sold	2,100,000
Merchandise inventory	
Beginning of year	350,000
End of year	490,000

Required

Assuming that the merchandise inventory buildup was relatively constant, how many times did the merchandise inventory turn over during Year 4?

Exercise 13-5B *Current ratio*

LO 13-2

Bruno Corporation purchased $480 of merchandise on account.

Required

Explain the effect of the purchase on Bruno's current ratio.

LO 13-2

Exercise 13-6B *Working capital and current ratio*

On October 31, Year 4, Corona Company's total current assets were $160,000 and its total current liabilities were $40,000. On November 1, Year 4, Corona purchased marketable securities for $20,000 cash.

Required

a. Compute Corona's working capital before and after the securities purchase.

b. Compute Corona's current ratio before and after the securities purchase.

LO 13-2

Exercise 13-7B *Working capital and current ratio*

On October 31, Year 4, Corona Company's total current assets were $160,000 and its total current liabilities were $40,000. On November 1, Year 4, Corona bought manufacturing equipment for $20,000 cash.

Required

a. Compute Corona's working capital before and after the equipment purchase.

b. Compute Corona's current ratio before and after the equipment purchase.

LO 13-2, 13-3

Exercise 13-8B *Ratio analysis*

Balance sheet data for the Beech Corporation follows.

Current assets	$ 80,000
Long-term assets (net)	320,000
Total assets	$400,000
Current liabilities	$ 36,000
Long-term liabilities	144,000
Total liabilities	180,000
Common stock and retained earnings	220,000
Total liabilities and stockholders' equity	$400,000

Required

Compute the following and round computations to one decimal point:

a. Working capital.

b. Current ratio.

c. Debt-to-assets ratio.

d. Debt-to-equity ratio.

LO 13-2, 13-3

Exercise 13-9B *Comprehensive analysis*

December 31, Year 4, balance sheet data for Hestand Company follow. All accounts are represented. Amounts indicated by question marks (?) can be calculated using the following additional information.

Assets	
Cash	$ 15,000
Accounts receivable (net)	?
Inventory	?
Property, plant, and equipment (net)	278,000
	$?
Liabilities and Stockholders' Equity	
Accounts payable (trade)	$ 26,000
Income taxes payable (current)	14,000
Long-term debt	?
Common stock	$160,000
Retained earnings	?
	$?

continued

Additional Information	
Quick ratio (at year end)	1.3 to 1
Working capital	$42,000
Inventory turnover (cost of goods sold ÷ ending inventory)	12 times
Debt-to-equity ratio	80%
Gross margin for Year 4	$126,000

Required

Determine the following:

a. The balance in accounts receivable as of December 31, Year 4.
b. The turnover of assets for Year 4.
c. The balance of long-term debt as of December 31, Year 4.
d. The balance in retained earnings as of December Year 4.

Exercise 13-10B *Number of times interest earned* LO 13-3

The following data come from the financial records of Welch Corporation for Year 3.

Sales	$320,000
Interest expense	9,000
Income tax	36,000
Net income	99,000

Required

How many times was interest earned in Year 3?

Exercise 13-11B *Accounts receivable turnover, inventory turnover, and net margin* LO 13-2, 13-4

Selected data from Goode Company follow.

Balance Sheet Data As of December 31	Year 4	Year 3
Accounts receivable	$360,000	$320,000
Allowance for doubtful accounts	(30,000)	(20,000)
Net accounts receivable	$330,000	$300,000
Inventories, lower of cost or market	$225,000	$250,000

Income Statement Data Year Ended December 31	Year 4	Year 3
Net credit sales	$2,500,000	$1,800,000
Net cash sales	500,000	400,000
Net sales	$3,000,000	$2,200,000
Cost of goods sold	$1,750,000	$1,300,000
Selling, general, and administrative expenses	300,000	160,000
Other expenses	150,000	120,000
Total operating expenses	$2,200,000	$1,580,000

Required

Compute the following and round computations to two decimal points:

a. The accounts receivable turnover for Year 4.
b. The inventory turnover for Year 4.
c. The net margin for Year 3.

LO 13-5

Exercise 13-12B *Ratio analysis*

During Year 4, Roper Corporation reported net income after taxes of $1,200,000. During the year, the number of shares of stock outstanding remained constant at 20,000 shares of $100 par, 8 percent preferred stock and 200,000 shares of common stock. The company's total equities at December 31, Year 4, were $3,500,000, which included $640,000 of liabilities. The common stock was selling for $40 per share at the end of the year. All dividends for the year were declared and paid, including $3.60 per share to common stockholders.

Required

Compute the following and round computations to two decimal points:

a. Earnings per share.
b. Book value per share.
c. Price-earnings ratio.
d. Dividend yield.

LO 13-2, 13-3, 13-4, 13-5

Exercise 13-13B *Ratio analysis*

Compute the specified ratios using the following December 31, Year 3, statement of financial position for Palmer Company.

Assets	
Cash	$110,000
Marketable securities	10,000
Accounts receivable	120,000
Inventory	160,000
Property and equipment	250,000
Accumulated depreciation	(50,000)
Total assets	$600,000
Liabilities and Stockholders' Equity	
Accounts payable	$ 86,000
Current notes payable	4,000
Mortgage payable	130,000
Bonds payable	82,000
Common stock	200,000
Retained earnings	98,000
Total liabilities and stockholders' equity	$600,000

The average number of common shares outstanding during Year 3 was 1,500. Net income for the year was $60,000.

Required

Compute each of the following and round computations to two decimal points:

a. Current ratio.
b. Earnings per share.
c. Acid-test ratio.
d. Return on investment.
e. Return on equity.
f. Debt-to-equity ratio.

Exercise 13-14B *Ratio analysis*

LO 13-2, 13-3, 13-4, 13-5

Match each of the following ratios with its formula.

_____ 1. Price-earnings ratio	a. Total liabilities ÷ Total stockholders' equity
_____ 2. Dividend yield	b. Current assets ÷ Current liabilities
_____ 3. Book value per share	c. 365 ÷ Accounts receivable turnover
_____ 4. Plant assets to long-term liabilities	d. (Net income − Preferred dividends) ÷ Average outstanding common shares
_____ 5. Times interest earned	e. (Stockholders' equity − Preferred rights) ÷ Outstanding common shares
_____ 6. Earnings per share	f. 365 ÷ Inventory turnover
_____ 7. Net margin	g. Dividends per share ÷ Market price per share
_____ 8. Debt-to-equity ratio	h. Net plant assets ÷ Long-term liabilities
_____ 9. Current ratio	i. Market price per share ÷ Earnings per share
_____ 10. Turnover of assets	j. Net income ÷ Net sales
_____ 11. Days to collect A/R	k. Net sales ÷ Average total assets
_____ 12. Number of days to sell inventory	l. Income before taxes and interest expense ÷ Interest expense

Exercise 13-15B *Comprehensive analysis*

LO 13-2, 13-3, 13-4, 13-5

The following is a list of transactions.

a. Paid cash for short-term marketable securities.
b. Purchased a computer, issuing a short-term note for the purchase price.
c. Purchased factory equipment, issuing a long-term note for the purchase price.
d. Sold merchandise on account at a profit.
e. Paid cash on accounts payable.
f. Received cash from issuing common stock.
g. Sold a factory for cash at a profit.
h. Purchased raw materials on account.
i. Paid cash for property taxes on administrative buildings.

Required

Indicate the effect of each of the preceding transactions on (a) the quick ratio, (b) working capital, (c) stockholders' equity, (d) the debt-to-equity ratio, and (e) retained earnings. Assume that the current ratio is greater than 1:1.

PROBLEMS—SERIES B

Problem 13-16B *Vertical analysis*

LO 13-1

Burton Corporation's controller has prepared the following vertical analysis for the president.

	Year 4	Year 3
Sales	100.0%	100.0%
Cost of goods sold	57.0	54.0
Gross margin	43.0	46.0
Selling and administrative expense	18.0	20.0
Interest expense	2.8	4.0
Total expenses	20.8	24.0
Income before taxes	22.2	22.0
Income tax expense	10.0	8.0
Net income	12.2%	14.0%

Required

Sales were $800,000 in Year 3 and $900,000 in Year 4. Convert the analysis to income statements for the two years.

LO 13-1

eXcel

Problem 13-17B *Horizontal analysis*

Bluffton Company's stock is quoted at $16 per share at December 31, Year 4 and Year 3. Bluffton's financial statements follow.

BLUFFTON COMPANY
Balance Sheets
As of December 31
(in thousands)

	Year 4	Year 3
Assets		
Current assets		
Cash	$ 8,000	$ 6,000
Marketable securities at cost which approximates market	5,000	4,000
Accounts receivable, net of allowance for doubtful accounts	47,000	44,000
Inventories, lower of cost or market	50,000	60,000
Prepaid expenses	2,000	1,000
Total current assets	112,000	115,000
Property, plant, and equipment, net of accumulated depreciation	100,000	105,000
Investments	1,000	1,000
Long-term receivables	3,000	2,000
Goodwill and patents, net of accumulated amortization	2,000	4,000
Other assets	2,000	3,000
Total assets	$220,000	$230,000
Liabilities and Stockholders' Equity		
Current liabilities		
Notes payable	$ 3,000	$ 5,000
Accounts payable	12,000	16,000
Accrued expenses	9,000	11,000
Income taxes payable	1,000	1,000
Payments due within one year	3,000	2,000
Total current liabilities	28,000	35,000
Long-term debt	50,000	60,000
Deferred income taxes	30,000	27,000
Other liabilities	5,000	4,000
Total liabilities	113,000	126,000
Stockholders' equity		
5% cumulative preferred stock, par value $100 per share; $100 liquidating value; authorized 250,000 shares; issued and outstanding 200,000 shares	20,000	20,000
Common stock, no par; 10,000,000 shares authorized and 5,000,000 shares issued and outstanding	40,000	40,000
Retained earnings	47,000	44,000
Total stockholders' equity	107,000	104,000
Total liabilities and stockholders' equity	$220,000	$230,000

BLUFFTON COMPANY
Statements of Income and Retained Earnings
For the Years Ended December 31
(in thousands)

	Year 4	Year 3
Net sales	$180,000	$150,000
Expenses		
Cost of goods sold	147,000	120,000
Selling, general, and administrative expenses	20,000	18,000
Other	2,000	2,000
Total expenses	169,000	140,000
Income before income taxes	11,000	10,000
Income taxes	5,000	4,000
Net income	6,000	6,000
Retained earnings at beginning of period	40,000	38,000
Less: Dividends on common stock	3,000	3,000
Dividends on preferred stock	1,000	1,000
Retained earnings at end of period	$ 42,000	$ 40,000

Required

Prepare a horizontal analysis of the balance sheet and income statement for Year 4 and Year 3. Round percentages to one decimal point.

Problem 13-18B *Vertical analysis* LO 13-1

Required

Use the financial statements for Bluffton Company from Problem 13-17B to perform a vertical analysis (based on total assets, total equities, and sales) of both the balance sheets and income statements for Year 4 and Year 3. Round computations to one decimal point.

Problem 13-19B *Effect of transactions on current ratio and working capital* LO 13-2

Lowery Company has a current ratio of 2:1 on June 30, Year 3. Indicate whether each of the following transactions would increase (+), decrease (−), or not affect (NA) Lowery's current ratio and its working capital.

Required

a. Issued 10-year bonds for $300,000 cash.
b. Paid cash to settle an account payable.
c. Sold merchandise for more than cost.
d. Recognized depreciation on plant equipment.
e. Purchased a machine by issuing a long-term note payable.
f. Purchased merchandise inventory on account.
g. Received customer payment on account receivable.
h. Paid cash for federal income tax expense (assume that the expense has not been previously accrued).
i. Declared cash dividend payable in one month.
j. Received cash for interest on a long-term note receivable (assume that interest has not been previously accrued).
k. Received cash from issuing a short-term note payable.
l. Traded a truck for a sedan.

LO 13-2, 13-3

Problem 13-20B *Supply missing balance sheet numbers*

Rustin Craft discovered a piece of wet and partially burned balance sheet after his office was destroyed by fire. He could recall a current ratio of 1.75 and a debt-to-assets ratio of 45 percent.

Assets	
Current assets	
Cash	$ 150,000
Accounts receivable	(A)
Inventory	252,000
Prepaid expenses	54,000
Total current assets	(B)
Long-term assets	
Building	(C)
Less: Accumulated depreciation	(180,000)
Total long-term assets	1,080,000
Total assets	$ (D)
Liabilities and Stockholders' Equity	
Liabilities	
Current liabilities	
Accounts payable	$ 252,000
Notes payable	(E)
Income tax payable	108,000
Total current liabilities	480,000
Long-term liabilities	
Bonds payable	270,000
Mortgage payable	(F)
Total liabilities	(G)
Stockholders' equity	
Common stock	540,000
Retained earnings	(H)
Total stockholders' equity	(I)
Total liabilities and stockholders' equity	$ (J)

Required

Complete the balance sheet by supplying the missing amounts.

LO 13-5

Problem 13-21B *Ratio analysis*

Selected data for Hoback Company for Year 3 and additional information on industry averages follow.

Earnings (net income)		$120,000
Preferred stock (16,000 shares at $17.50 par, 6%)		$280,000
Common stock (40,500 shares no par, market value $15.20)		342,000
Retained earnings		240,000
		862,000
Less: Treasury stock		
Preferred (1,000 shares)	$14,400	
Common (500 shares)	6,400	20,800
Total stockholders' equity		$841,200

Industry averages	
Earnings per share	$2.00
Price-earnings ratio	8.00
Return on equity	7.30%

Required

Round computations to two decimal points.

a. Calculate Hoback Company's earnings per share ratio, price-earnings ratio, and return on equity ratio and compare them with the industry averages.

b. Discuss factors you would consider in deciding whether to invest in the company.

Problem 13-22B *Ratio analysis*

LO 13-3, 13-4, 13-5

Information from Forman Company's financial statements follows.

	Year 3	Year 2
Net sales	$1,000,000	$800,000
Income before interest and taxes	180,000	150,000
Net income after taxes	128,000	108,000
Bond interest expense	20,000	16,000
Stockholders' equity, December 31 (Year 1: $240,000)	360,000	300,000
Common stock, par $12, December 31	210,000	180,000

Average number of shares outstanding was 16,000 for Year 3 and 15,000 for Year 2.

Required

Compute the following ratios for Forman Company for Year 3 and Year 2 and round computations to two decimal points:

a. Number of times interest was earned.

b. Earnings per share based on the average number of shares outstanding.

c. Price-earnings ratio (market prices: Year 3, $30 per share; Year 2, $24 per share).

d. Return on equity.

e. Net margin.

Problem 13-23B *Ratio analysis*

LO 13-2, 13-3, 13-4, 13-5

The following financial statements apply to Bedford Appliances Inc.

BEDFORD APPLIANCES INC.
Balance Sheets
As of December 31

	Year 4	Year 3
Assets		
Current assets		
Cash	$118,000	$ 91,000
Marketable securities	24,000	18,000
Accounts receivable (net)	112,000	108,000
Inventories	180,000	192,000
Prepaid expenses	27,000	14,000
Total current assets	461,000	423,000
Investments	120,000	120,000
Plant (net)	260,000	254,000
Other	81,000	74,000
Total assets	$922,000	$871,000

continued

	Year 4	Year 3
Liabilities and Stockholders' Equity		
Liabilities		
Current liabilities		
Notes payable	$ 20,000	$ 15,000
Accounts payable	80,000	38,000
Other	66,000	9,000
Total current liabilities	166,000	62,000
Noncurrent liabilities		
Bonds payable	110,000	210,000
Other	26,000	12,000
Total noncurrent liabilities	136,000	222,000
Total liabilities	302,000	284,000
Stockholders' equity		
Preferred stock ($100 par, 4% cumulative, non-participating; $100 liquidating value; 1,000 shares authorized and issued; no dividends in arrears)	100,000	100,000
Common stock (no par; 50,000 shares authorized; 12,000 shares issued)	240,000	240,000
Retained earnings	280,000	247,000
Total stockholders' equity	620,000	587,000
Total liabilities and stockholders' equity	$922,000	$871,000

BEDFORD APPLIANCES INC.
Statements of Income and Retained Earnings
For the Years Ended December 31

	Year 4	Year 3
Revenues		
Sales (net)	$240,000	$230,000
Other revenues	7,000	4,000
Total revenues	247,000	234,000
Expenses		
Cost of goods sold	143,000	130,000
Selling, general, and administrative	46,000	57,000
Bond interest expense	7,000	10,000
Income tax expense	8,000	14,000
Total expenses	204,000	211,000
Net income	43,000	23,000
Retained earnings, January 1	247,000	234,000
Less: Preferred stock dividends	4,000	4,000
Common stock dividends	6,000	6,000
Retained earnings, December 31	$280,000	$247,000

Required

Calculate the following ratios for Year 4 by rounding to two decimal points:

a. Working capital.
b. Current ratio.
c. Quick ratio.
d. Accounts receivable turnover.
e. Average days to collect accounts receivable.
f. Inventory turnover.
g. Average days to sell inventory.
h. Debt-to-assets ratio.
i. Debt-to-equity ratio.
j. Times interest was earned.

k. Plant assets to long-term debt.
l. Net margin.
m. Turnover of assets.
n. Return on investment.
o. Return on equity.
p. Earnings per share.
q. Book value per share.
r. Price-earnings ratio (market price: $13.26).
s. Dividend yield on common stock.

Problem 13-24B ***Ratio analysis*** **LO 13-2, 13-3, 13-4, 13-5**

Required

Use the financial statements for Bluffton Company from Problem 13-17B to compute the following for Year 4. Round percentages to two decimal points.

a. Current ratio.
b. Quick (acid-test) ratio.
c. Average days to collect accounts receivable, assuming all sales on account.
d. Inventory turnover.
e. Book value per share of common stock.
f. Earnings per share on common stock.
g. Price-earnings ratio on common stock.
h. Debt-to-assets ratio.
i. Return on investment.
j. Return on equity.

ANALYZE, THINK, COMMUNICATE

ATC 13-1 **Business Applications Case** ***Analyzing Home Depot and Lowe's***

The following information relates to **Home Depot Inc.**, and **Lowe's Companies Inc.** for their 2017 and 2016 fiscal years.

HOME DEPOT INC.
Selected Financial Information
(amounts in millions, except per share amounts)

	January 28, 2018	January 29, 2017
Total current assets	$18,933	$17,724
Merchandise inventory	12,748	12,549
Property and equipment, net of depreciation	22,075	21,914
Total assets	44,529	42,966
Total current liabilities	16,194	14,133
Total long-term liabilities	26,881	24,500
Total liabilities	43,075	38,633
Total shareholders' equity	1,454	4,333
Revenue	100,904	94,595
Cost of goods sold	66,548	62,282
Gross profit	34,356	32,313
Operating income	14,681	13,427
Earnings from continuing operations before income tax expense	13,698	12,491
Income tax expense	5,068	4,534
Net earnings	8,630	7,957
Basic earnings per share	$ 7.33	$ 6.47

LOWE'S COMPANIES INC. Selected Financial Information (amounts in millions except per share data)	January 24, 2018	January 25, 2017
Total current assets	$12,000	$10,561
Merchandise inventory	10,458	9,458
Property and equipment, net of depreciation	19,949	19,577
Total assets	34,408	31,266
Total current liabilities	11,974	10,492
Total long-term liabilities	16,000	9,120
Total liabilities	27,974	23,612
Total stockholders' equity	6,434	7,654
Revenues	65,017	59,074
Cost of goods sold	42,553	38,504
Gross profit	22,464	20,570
Operating income	5,846	4,971
Earnings from continuing operations before income taxes	5,201	4,419
Income tax expense	2,108	1,873
Net earnings	3,093	2,546
Basic earnings per share	$ 3.48	$ 2.73

Required

a. Compute the following ratios for the companies' 2017 fiscal years (years ending in January 2018):

(1) Current ratio.

(2) Average days to sell inventory. (Use average inventory.)

(3) Debt-to-assets ratio.

(4) Return on investment. (Use average assets and use "earnings from continuing operations" rather than "net earnings.")

(5) Gross margin percentage.

(6) Asset turnover. (Use average assets.)

(7) Return on sales. (Use "earnings from continuing operations" rather than "net earnings.")

(8) Plant assets to long-term debt ratio.

b. Which company appears to be more profitable? Explain your answer and identify which ratio(s) from Requirement *a* you used to reach your conclusion.

c. Which company appears to have the higher level of financial risk? Explain your answer and identify which ratio(s) from Requirement *a* you used to reach your conclusion.

d. Which company appears to be charging higher prices for its goods? Explain your answer and identify which ratio(s) from Requirement *a* you used to reach your conclusion.

e. Which company appears to be the more efficient at using its assets? Explain your answer and identify which ratio(s) from Requirement *a* you used to reach your conclusion.

ATC 13-2 Group Assignment *Ratios and basic logic*

Presented here is selected information from the 2016 fiscal-Year 10-K reports of four companies. The four companies, in alphabetical order, are:

AT&T Inc., a company that provides communications and digital entertainment.

Deere & Company, a manufacturer of heavy machinery.

Starbucks, a company that sells coffee products.

Tiffany & Company, a company that operates high-end jewelry and department stores.

The data for the companies, presented in the order of the amount of their sales in millions of dollars, are as follows.

	A	B	C	D
Sales	$163,786	$26,644.0	$21,315.9	$4,104.9
Cost of goods sold	76,884	18,248.9	8,511.1	1,613.6
Net earnings	12,976	1,523.9	2,817.7	463.9
Inventory	—	3,340.5	1,378.5	2,225.0
Accounts receivable	16,794	29,741.1	768.8	206.4
Total assets	403,821	57,981.4	14,329.5	5,129.7

Required

a. Divide the class into groups of four or five students per group and then organize the groups into four sections. Assign Task 1 to the first section of groups, Task 2 to the second section, Task 3 to the third section, and Task 4 to the fourth section.

Group Tasks

(1) Assume that you represent AT&T. Identify the set of financial data (Column A, B, C, or D) that relates to your company.

(2) Assume that you represent Deere. Identify the set of financial data (Column A, B, C, or D) that relates to your company.

(3) Assume that you represent Starbucks. Identify the set of financial data (Column A, B, C, or D) that relates to your company.

(4) Assume that you represent Tiffany. Identify the set of financial data (Column A, B, C, or D) that relates to your company.

Hint: In addition to the ratios presented in this chapter, you might also find it useful to compute a ratio from the first course of accounting, the gross margin percentage (Gross margin ÷ Sales).

b. Select a representative from each section. Have the representative explain the rationale for the group's selection. The explanation should include a set of ratios that support the group's conclusion.

ATC 13-3 Research Assignment *Analyzing Kraft Food's merger with Heinz Company*

In July 2015, H. J. Heinz Company and Kraft Foods Group completed their merger. The new company, named The Kraft Heinz Company (KHC), became the fifth largest food and beverage company in the world. Prior to the merger, Kraft had been much larger than Heinz in terms of sales, $18 billion versus $6 billion, but Heinz was larger in terms of assets. To complete the requirements below you will need to obtain Kraft Foods Group Inc.'s Form 10-K for 2014, the year before the acquisition, and KHC's Form 10-K 2017, two years after the deal was closed. The 2014 Form 10-K for Kraft Foods can only be found on the SEC's EDGAR website. Be sure to search and select Kraft Foods Group, *not* Kraft Heinz Company. The 2017 Form 10-K for Kraft Heinz Company can be found on the EDGAR website on the company's website, www.kraftheinzcompany.com, or through the EDGAR system.

Required

a. Compute the following ratios for 2014 and 2017. To make the computations simpler, use end-of-year amounts for total assets and total equity rather than averages. Also, changes to the federal income tax laws enacted in 2017 caused some unusual effects on KHC's 2017 net earnings. Therefore, for this problem, use "Earnings before income taxes" instead of net earnings for computing the following ratios. Show your calculations.

Net margin	Current ratio
Return on investment	Debt-to-assets ratio
Return on equity	

b. Based on the ratios computed in Requirement *a*, comment on the apparent effects of Kraft's merger with Heinz. Assume any significant change in these ratios was the result of the acquisition.

c. Based on this limited analysis, does it appear that the effects of the merger were good or bad for Kraft?

ATC 13-4 Writing Assignment *Identifying companies based on financial statement information*

The following ratios are for four companies in different industries. Some of these ratios have been discussed in the textbook and others have not, but their names explain how the ratio was computed. These data are for the companies' 2016 fiscal years. The four sets of ratios, presented randomly, are as follows.

Ratio	Company 1	Company 2	Company 3	Company 4
Current assets ÷ Total assets	7%	18%	31%	19%
Average days to sell inventory	72 days	12 days	163 days	108 days
Average days to collect receivables	60 days	3 days	47 days	9 days
Return-on-assets	7%	8%	3%	5%
Gross margin	39%	22%	22%	50%
Sales ÷ Property, plant, and equipment	1.1 times	3.4 times	4.5 times	23.5 times
Sales ÷ Number of full-time employees	$279,980	$46,350	$397,743	$64,717

The four companies to which these ratios relate are:

Molson Coors Brewing Company, a company that produces beer and related products.

Darden Restaurants Inc., which operates approximately 2,150 restaurants under 10 different names, including Olive Garden, Bahama Breeze, and LongHorn Steakhouse.

Deere & Company, a company that manufactures heavy construction equipment.

Weight Watchers International Inc., a company that provides weight loss services and products. Its fiscal year-end was December 31, 2016, during which 81 percent of its revenues came from services and 19 percent from product sales.

Required

Determine which company should be matched with each set of ratios. Write a memorandum explaining the rationale for your decisions.

ATC 13-5 Ethical Dilemma *Making the ratios look good*

J. Talbot is the accounting manager for Kolla Waste Disposal Corporation. Kolla is having its worst financial year since its inception. The company is expected to report a net loss. In the midst of such bad news, Ms. Talbot surprised the company president, Mr. Winston, by suggesting that the company write off approximately 25 percent of its garbage trucks. Mr. Winston responded by noting that the trucks could still be operated for another two or three years. Ms. Talbot replied, "We may use them for two or three more years, but you couldn't sell them on the street if you had to. Who wants to buy a bunch of old garbage trucks, and besides, it will make next year's financials so sweet. No one will care about the additional write-off this year. We are already showing a loss. Who will care if we lose a little bit more?"

Required

a. How will the write-off affect the following year's return-on-assets ratio?

b. How will the write-off affect the asset and income growth percentages?

c. Explain how the components of the fraud triangle relate to this case.

ATC 13-6 Spreadsheet Assignment *Using Excel*

Tomkung Corporation's income statements are presented in the following spreadsheet.

Required

Construct a spreadsheet to conduct horizontal analysis of the income statements for Year 4 and Year 3.

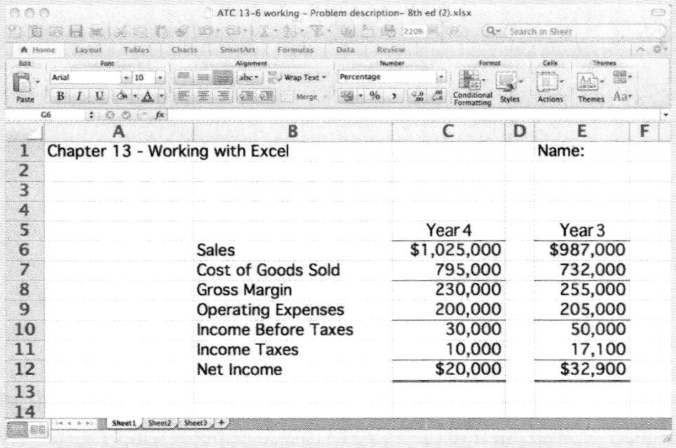

	A	B	C	D	E	F
1	Chapter 13 - Working with Excel				Name:	
2						
3						
4						
5			Year 4		Year 3	
6		Sales	$1,025,000		$987,000	
7		Cost of Goods Sold	795,000		732,000	
8		Gross Margin	230,000		255,000	
9		Operating Expenses	200,000		205,000	
10		Income Before Taxes	30,000		50,000	
11		Income Taxes	10,000		17,100	
12		Net Income	$20,000		$32,900	
13						
14						

Source: Microsoft Excel 2010

ATC 13-7 Spreadsheet Assignment *Mastering Excel*

Refer to the data in ATC 13-6.

Required

Construct a spreadsheet to conduct vertical analysis for both years, Year 4 and Year 3.

CHAPTER 14

Statement of Cash Flows

LEARNING OBJECTIVES

After you have mastered the material in this chapter, you will be able to:

LO 14-1 Prepare the operating activities section of a statement of cash flows using the indirect method.

LO 14-2 Prepare the operating activities section of a statement of cash flows using the direct method.

LO 14-3 Prepare the investing activities section of a statement of cash flows.

LO 14-4 Prepare the financing activities section of a statement of cash flows.

Video lectures and accompanying self-assessment quizzes are available in Connect® for all learning objectives.

CHAPTER OPENING

To make informed investment and credit decisions, financial statement users need information to help them assess the amounts, timing, and uncertainty of a company's prospective cash flows. This chapter explains more about the items reported on the statement of cash flows and describes a more practical way to prepare the statement than analyzing every entry in the cash account. As previously shown, the statement of cash flows reports how a company obtained and spent cash during an accounting period. Sources of cash are **cash inflows,** and uses are **cash outflows.** Cash receipts (inflows) and payments (outflows) are reported as either operating activities, investing activities, or financing activities.

The Curious Accountant

©NYCStock/Shutterstock

Snap Inc. began operations in 2010 and began selling its stock to the public on March 2, 2017. It has lost money every year it has been in existence. In 2016 alone, its losses were $515 million, and by December 31, 2016, it had total lifetime losses of approximately $2.3 billion.

How could Snap lose so much money and still be able to pay its bills? (Answers on page 645.)

AN OVERVIEW OF THE STATEMENT OF CASH FLOWS

The statement of cash flows provides information about cash coming into and going out of a business during an accounting period. Cash flows are classified into one of three categories: operating activities, investing activities, or financing activities. A separate section also displays any significant noncash investing and financing activities. Descriptions of these categories and how they are presented in the statement of cash flows follow.

Operating Activities

Routine cash inflows and outflows resulting from running (operating) a business are reported in the **operating activities** section of the statement of cash flows. Cash flows reported as operating activities include:

1. Cash receipts from revenues, including interest and dividend revenue.
2. Cash payments for expenses, including interest expense. Recall that dividend payments are not expenses. Dividend payments are reported in the financing activities section.

Under generally accepted accounting principles, the operating activities section of the statement of cash flows can be presented using either the *direct* or the *indirect* method. The **direct method** explicitly (*directly*) identifies the major *sources* and *uses* of cash. To illustrate, assume that, during Year 1, New South Company earns revenue on account of $500 and collects $400 cash from customers. Further assume the company incurs $390 of expenses on account and pays $350 cash to settle accounts payable. Exhibit 14.1 shows the operating activities section of the statement of cash flows using the *direct method.*

EXHIBIT 14.1

Operating Activities—Direct Method

Cash Flows from Operating Activities	
Cash receipts from customers	$ 400
Cash payments for expenses	(350)
Net cash flow from operating activities	$ 50

In contrast, the **indirect method** starts with net income as reported on the income statement, followed by the adjustments necessary to convert the accrual-based net income figure to a cash-basis equivalent. To illustrate, begin with New South Company's income statement based on the earlier assumptions.

Revenues	$500
Expenses	(390)
Net income	$ 110

Converting the net income of $110 to the net cash flow from operating activities of $50 requires the following adjustments:

1. New South earned $500 of revenue but collected only $400 in cash. The remaining $100 will be collected in the next accounting period. This $100 *increase in accounts receivable* must be *subtracted* from net income to determine cash flow because it increased net income but did not increase cash.
2. New South incurred $390 of expense but paid only $350 in cash. The remaining $40 will be paid in the next accounting period. This $40 *increase in accounts payable* must be *added* back to net income to determine cash flow because it decreased net income but did not use cash.

Exhibit 14.2 shows the operating activities section of the statement of cash flows using the *indirect method.*

Compare the direct method presented in Exhibit 14.1 with the indirect method presented in Exhibit 14.2. Both methods report $50 of net cash flow from operating activities. They represent two different approaches to computing the same amount.

EXHIBIT 14.2

Operating Activities—Indirect Method

Cash Flows from Operating Activities	
Net income	$ 110
Subtract: Increase in accounts receivable	(100)
Add: Increase in accounts payable	40
Net cash flow from operating activities	$ 50

Because people typically find the direct method easier to understand, the Financial Accounting Standards Board (FASB) recommends it. Most companies, however, use the indirect method. Why? Back when the FASB adopted a requirement for companies to include a statement of cash flows in their published financial statements, most companies used accounting systems that were compatible with the indirect method. It was therefore easier to prepare the new statement under the indirect method using existing systems than to create new recordkeeping systems compatible with the direct method.

The FASB continues to advocate the direct method and a growing number of companies use it. Because the majority of companies continue to use the indirect method, however, financial statement users should understand both methods.

CHECK YOURSELF 14.1

Hammer Inc. had a beginning balance of $22,400 in its Accounts Receivable account. During the accounting period, Hammer earned $234,700 of net income. The ending balance in the Accounts Receivable account was $18,200. Based on this information alone, determine the amount of cash flow from operating activities.

Answer

Account Title	Ending	Beginning	Change
Accounts receivable	$18,200	$22,400	$(4,200)

Applicable Rule	Cash Flow from Operating Activities	Amount
	Net Income	$234,700
Rule 1	Add: Decrease in accounts receivable	4,200
	Cash flow from operating activities	$238,900

Investing Activities

For a business, long-term assets are investments. Cash flows related to acquiring or disposing of long-term assets are therefore reported in the **investing activities** section of the statement of cash flows. Cash flows reported as investing activities include:

1. Cash receipts (inflows) from selling property, plant, equipment, or marketable securities, as well as collections from credit instruments such as notes or mortgages receivable.
2. Cash payments (outflows) for purchasing property, plant, equipment, or marketable securities, as well as for making loans to borrowers.

Financing Activities

Cash flows related to borrowing (short- or long-term) and stockholders' equity are reported in the **financing activities** section of the statement of cash flows. Cash flows reported as financing activities include:

1. Cash receipts (inflows) from borrowing money and issuing stock.
2. Cash payments (outflows) to repay debt, purchase treasury stock, and pay dividends.

©Ryan McVay/Getty Images

The classification of cash flows is based on the type of activity, not the type of account. For example, buying another company's common stock is an investing activity, but issuing a company's own common stock is a financing activity. Receiving dividends from a common stock investment is an operating activity, and paying dividends to a company's own stockholders is a financing activity. Similarly, loaning money is an investing activity, although borrowing it is a financing activity. Focus on the type of activity rather than the type of account when classifying cash flows as operating, investing, or financing activities.

Noncash Investing and Financing Activities

Companies sometimes undertake significant **noncash investing and financing activities** such as acquiring a long-term asset in exchange for common stock. Because these types of transactions do not involve exchanging cash, they are not reported in the main body of the statement of cash flows. However, because the FASB requires that all material investing and financing activities be disclosed, whether or not they involve exchanging cash, companies must include with the statement of cash flows a separate schedule of any noncash investing and financing activities.

Reporting Format for the Statement of Cash Flows

Cash flow categories are reported in the following order: (1) operating activities, (2) investing activities, and (3) financing activities. In each category, the difference between the inflows and outflows is presented as a net cash inflow or outflow for the category. These net amounts are combined to determine the net change (increase or decrease) in the company's cash for the period. The net change in cash is combined with the beginning cash balance to determine the ending cash balance. The ending cash balance on the statement of cash flows is the same as the cash balance reported on the balance sheet. The schedule of noncash investing and financing activities is typically presented at the bottom of the statement of cash flows. Exhibit 14.3 outlines this format.

EXHIBIT 14.3 Format For Statement of Cash Flows

WESTERN COMPANY
Statement of Cash Flows
For the Year Ended December 31, Year 5

Cash flows from operating activities	
Net cash flow from operating activities	XXX
Cash flows from investing activities	
Net cash flow from investing activities	XXX
Cash flows from financing activities	
Net cash flow from financing activities	XXX
Net increase (decrease) in cash	XXX
Plus: Beginning cash balance	XXX
Ending cash balance	XXX
Schedule of Noncash Investing and Financing Activities	
List of significant noncash transactions	XXX

As indicated in Exhibit 14.4, 50 percent of the companies that make up the Dow Jones Industrial Average show the statement of cash flows as the third statement presented, with the remaining 50 percent presenting it as the fourth statement. However, a sizable number of companies present it after the income statement and balance sheet but before the statement of changes in stockholders' equity. Some companies place the statement of cash flows first, before the other three statements.

EXHIBIT 14.4

Placement of Statement of Cash Flows Relative to Other Financial Statements

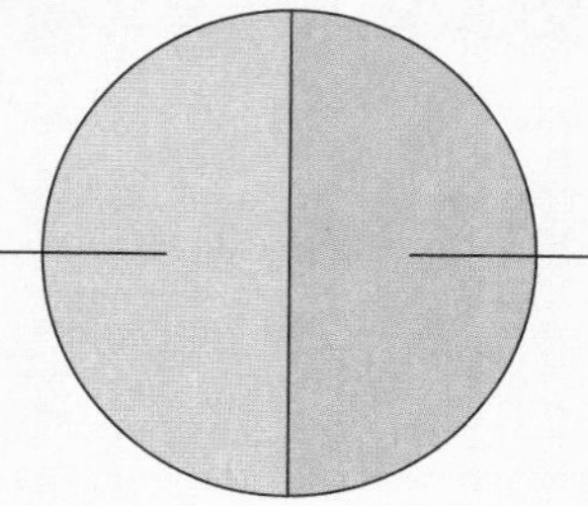

Source: This chart is based on data drawn from recent annual reports published by the 30 companies that comprise the Dow Jones Industrial Average.

PREPARING A STATEMENT OF CASH FLOWS

Most of the data needed to construct a statement of cash flows can be obtained from two successive balance sheets and the intervening income statement. Certain information from the long-term asset records is also usually required. To illustrate, refer to the financial statements for New South Company presented in Exhibit 14.5. Notice that cash decreased from $400 at the end of Year 1 to $300 at the end of Year 2. The statement of cash flows explains what caused this $100 decrease.

EXHIBIT 14.5 Financial Statements for New South Company

NEW SOUTH COMPANY
Balance Sheets
As of December 31

	Year 2	Year 1
Current assets:		
Cash	$ 300	$ 400
Accounts receivable	1,000	1,200
Interest receivable	400	300
Inventory	8,900	8,200
Prepaid insurance	1,100	1,400
Total current assets	11,700	11,500
Long-term assets		
Investment securities	5,100	3,500
Store fixtures	5,400	4,800
Accumulated depreciation	(900)	(1,200)
Land	8,200	6,000
Total long-term assets	17,800	13,100
Total assets	$29,500	$24,600
Current liabilities:		
Accounts payable—inventory purchases	$ 800	$ 1,100
Salaries payable	1,000	900
Other operating expenses payable	1,500	1,300
Interest payable	300	500
Unearned rent revenue	600	1,600
Total current liabilities	4,200	5,400

continued

EXHIBIT 14.5 *concluded*

NEW SOUTH COMPANY
Balance Sheets
As of December 31

	Year 2	Year 1
Long-term liabilities		
Mortgage payable	2,200	0
Bonds payable	1,000	4,000
Total long-term liabilities	3,200	4,000
Stockholders' equity		
Common stock	10,000	8,000
Retained earnings	12,700	7,200
Treasury stock	(600)	0
Total stockholders' equity	22,100	15,200
Total liabilities and stockholders' equity	$29,500	$24,600

NEW SOUTH COMPANY
Income Statement
For the Year Ended December 31, Year 2

Sales revenue		$ 20,600
Cost of goods sold		(10,500)
Gross margin		10,100
Operating expenses		
Depreciation expense	$(1,000)	
Salaries expense	(2,700)	
Insurance expense	(1,300)	
Other operating expenses	(1,400)	
Total operating expenses		(6,400)
Income from sales business		3,700
Other income—rent revenue		2,400
Operating income		6,100
Nonoperating revenue and expense		
Interest revenue	700	
Interest expense	(400)	
Gain on sale of store fixtures	600	
Total nonoperating items		900
Net income		$ 7,000

Note 1: No investment securities were sold during Year 2.
Note 2: During Year 2, New South sold store fixtures that had originally cost $1,700. At the time of sale, accumulated depreciation on the fixtures was $1,300.
Note 3: Land was acquired during Year 2 by issuing a mortgage note payable. No land sales occurred during Year 2.

PREPARING THE OPERATING ACTIVITIES SECTION OF A STATEMENT OF CASH FLOWS USING THE INDIRECT METHOD

LO 14-1

Prepare the operating activities section of a statement of cash flows using the indirect method.

Recall that the indirect approach begins with the amount of net income. Many aspects of accrual accounting, such as recognizing revenues and expenses on account, can cause differences between the amount of net income reported on a company's income statement and the

Answers to The Curious Accountant

First, it should be remembered that GAAP requires earnings and losses be computed on an accrual basis. A company can have negative earnings and still have positive cash flows from operating activities. This was not the case at Snap. For 2015 and 2016, the company's cash flows from operating activities totaled a negative $918 million. Negative cash flows do not pay the bills.

In its early years of operations, Snap, like many new companies, was able to stay in business because of the cash it raised through financing activities. Obviously, a company cannot operate indefinitely without generating cash from operating activities. Individuals and institutions who are willing to buy a company's stock or loan it cash in its early years will disappear if they do not believe the company will eventually begin earning profits and generating positive cash flows from operations. Exhibit 14.6 presents Snap's statements of cash flows for 2015 and 2016.

EXHIBIT 14.6

SNAP INC.
Consolidated Statements of Cash Flows (partial)
(in thousands)

	Year Ended December 31	
	2016	**2015**
Cash flows from operating activities		
Net loss	$ (514,643)	$(372,893)
Adjustments to reconcile net loss to net cash used in operating activities:		
Depreciation and amortization	29,115	15,307
Stock-based compensation expense	31,842	73,524
Deferred income taxes	(7,952)	(7,700)
Other	889	626
Changes in operating assets and liabilities, net of effect of acquisitions:		
Accounts receivable, net of allowance	(118,434)	(41,905)
Prepaid expenses and other current assets	(20,521)	(6,590)
Other assets	(5,064)	(4,451)
Accounts payable	6,486	(6,724)
Accrued expenses and other current liabilities	(19,728)	40,026
Other liabilities	6,765	4,158
Net cash used in operating activities	(611,245)	(306,622)
Cash flows from investing activities		
Purchases of property and equipment	(66,441)	(19,205)
Purchases of intangible assets	(572)	(9,100)
Non-marketable investments	(6,513)	(9,551)
Cash paid for acquisitions, net of cash acquired	(104,001)	(48,730)
Issuance of notes receivables from officers/stockholders	(15,000)	(7,500)
Repayment of notes receivables from officers/stockholders	15,000	—
Purchases of marketable securities	(1,565,347)	—
Sales of marketable securities	195,898	—
Maturities of marketable securities	532,690	—
Change in restricted cash	(7,048)	(1,856)
Other investing activities	—	(5,000)
Net cash used in investing activities	(1,021,334)	(100,942)

continued

EXHIBIT 14.6 *concluded*

SNAP INC.
Consolidated Statements of Cash Flows (partial)
(in thousands)

	Year Ended December 31	
	2016	**2015**
Cash flows from financing activities		
Proceeds from the exercise of stock options	731	60
Repurchase of Class B voting common stock and Series FP preferred stock	(10,593)	(1,000)
Proceeds from issuances of preferred stock, net of issuance costs	1,157,147	651,306
Borrowings from revolving credit facility	5,000	—
Principle payments on revolving credit facility	(5,000)	—
Payments of deferred offering costs	(5,395)	—
Net cash provided by financing activities	1,141,890	650,366
Changes in cash and cash equivalents	(490,689)	242,802
Cash and cash equivalents, beginning of period	640,810	398,008
Cash and cash equivalents, end of period	$ 150,121	$ 640,810

amount of net cash flow it reports from operating activities. Most of the differences between revenue and expense recognition and cash flows are related to changes in the balances of the noncash current assets and current liabilities.

Indirect Method—Reconciliation Approach

The following section of this chapter examines the relationships between items reported on the income statement and the related assets and liabilities. Begin by reconciling the *noncash* current asset and current liability amounts shown on the balance sheets in Exhibit 14.5. *Do not include Cash in this analysis.* The amount of the change in the cash balance is the result of not only operating activities but also investing and financing activities.

Reconciliation of Accounts Receivable

Use the information in Exhibit 14.5 to prepare the following reconciliation of Accounts Receivable. The beginning and ending balances appear on the balance sheets. The *increase due to revenue recognized on account* is the sales revenue reported on the income statement.

$200 Decrease

Table 1 Reconciliation of Accounts Receivable

Beginning balance	$ 1,200	
Increase due to revenue recognized on account	20,600	
Decrease due to cash collections from customers	?	= (20,800)
Ending balance	$ 1,000	

To balance Accounts Receivable, the *decrease due to cash collections from customers* must be $20,800.[1]

The reconciliation shows that the $200 decrease in the accounts receivable balance occurred because *cash collections from customers* were $200 more than the amount of *revenue recognized on account* ($20,800 versus $20,600). Because the amount of cash collected is more than the amount of revenue recognized, we add $200 to the amount of net income to determine net cash flow from operating activities (Reference No. 1 in Exhibit 14.7).

Reconciliation of Interest Receivable

The beginning and ending balances appear on the balance sheets in Exhibit 14.5. The *increase due to interest revenue recognized on account* is the interest revenue reported on the income statement.

Table 2 Reconciliation of Interest Receivable

$100 Increase	Beginning balance	$300	
	Increase due to interest revenue recognized on account	700	
	Decrease due to cash collections of interest receivable	?	= (600)
	Ending balance	$400	

To balance Interest Receivable, the *decrease due to cash collections of interest receivable* must be $600.

The reconciliation shows that the $100 increase in the interest receivable balance occurred because *cash collections of interest* were $100 less than the *interest revenue recognized on account* ($600 versus $700). Because the amount of cash collected is less than the amount of revenue recognized, we subtract the $100 from the amount of net income to determine net cash flow from operating activities (Reference No. 2 in Exhibit 14.7).

Reconciliation of Inventory and Accounts Payable

To simplify computing the amount of cash paid for inventory purchases, assume that all inventory purchases are made on account. The computation requires two steps. First, Inventory must be analyzed to determine the amount of inventory purchased. Second, Accounts Payable must be analyzed to determine the amount of cash paid to purchase inventory.

Use the financial statement information in Exhibit 14.5 to prepare the following Inventory reconciliation. The beginning and ending balances appear on the balance sheets. The *decrease due to recognizing cost of goods sold* is the cost of goods sold reported on the income statement.

Table 3 Reconciliation of Inventory

$700 Increase	Beginning balance	$ 8,200	
	Increase due to inventory purchases	?	= 11,200
	Decrease due to recognizing cost of goods sold	(10,500)	
	Ending balance	$ 8,900	

To balance Inventory, the *increase due to inventory purchases* must be $11,200.

[1]This text uses the simplifying assumption that all sales occur on account.

Assuming the inventory was purchased on account, the $11,200 of inventory purchases determined earlier equals the *increase due to inventory purchases* used in the reconciliation of Accounts Payable below. The beginning and ending balances appear on the balance sheets in Exhibit 14.5.

Table 4 Reconciliation of Accounts Payable*

$300 Decrease	Beginning balance	$ 1,100
	Increase due to inventory purchases	11,200
	Decrease due to cash settlements of accounts payable—inv.	? = (11,500)
	Ending balance	$ 800

*Assume that Accounts Payable is used for purchases of inventory only.

To balance Accounts Payable, the *decrease due to cash settlements of accounts payable–inventory* (cash paid to purchase inventory) must be $11,500.

Because the amount of *cash paid to purchase inventory* is $1,000 more than the amount of *cost of goods sold* recognized on the income statement ($11,500 versus $10,500), we subtract the $1,000 difference from the amount of net income to determine net cash flow from operating activities. In Exhibit 14.7, the $1,000 subtraction is divided between a $700 increase in inventory (Reference No. 3 in Exhibit 14.7) and a $300 decrease in accounts payable (Reference No. 4 in Exhibit 14.7).

Reconciliation of Prepaid Insurance

Use the financial statement information in Exhibit 14.5 to reconcile Prepaid Insurance. The beginning and ending balances appear on the balance sheets. The *decrease due to recognizing insurance expense* is the insurance expense reported on the income statement.

Table 5 Reconciliation of Prepaid Insurance

$300 Decrease	Beginning balance	$ 1,400
	Increase due to the cash purchase of insurance	? = 1,000
	Decrease due to recognizing insurance expense	(1,300)
	Ending balance	$ 1,100

To balance Prepaid Insurance, the amount of the *increase due to the cash purchase of insurance* must be $1,000.

The reconciliation shows that the $300 decrease in the prepaid insurance balance occurred because *cash paid to purchase insurance* was $300 less than the amount of *insurance expense recognized* ($1,000 versus $1,300). Because the amount of cash paid is less than the amount of expense recognized, we add $300 to the amount of net income to determine the net cash flow from operating activities (Reference No. 5 in Exhibit 14.7).

Reconciliation of Salaries Payable

Use the financial statement information in Exhibit 14.5 to reconcile Salaries Payable. The beginning and ending balances appear on the balance sheets. The *increase due to recognizing salary expense on account* is the salaries expense reported on the income statement.

Table 6 Reconciliation of Salaries Payable

$100 Increase

Beginning balance	$ 900
Increase due to recognizing salary expense on account	2,700
Decrease due to cash settlements of salaries payable	? = (2,600)
Ending balance	$1,000

To balance Salaries Payable, the amount of the *decrease due to cash settlements of salaries payable* (cash paid for salaries expense) must be $2,600. The reconciliation shows that the $100 increase in the salaries payable balance occurred because the *cash paid for salary expense* is $100 less than the amount of *salary expense recognized on account* ($2,600 versus $2,700). Because the amount of cash paid is less than the amount of expense recognized, we add $100 to the amount of net income to determine the cash flow from operating activities (Reference No. 6 in Exhibit 14.7).

Reconciliation of Other Operating Expenses Payable

Use the financial statement information in Exhibit 14.5 to reconcile Other Operating Expenses Payable. The beginning and ending balances appear on the balance sheets. The *increase due to recognizing other operating expenses on account* is the other operating expenses amount reported on the income statement.

Table 7 Reconciliation of Other Operating Expenses Payable

$200 Increase

Beginning balance	$1,300
Increase due to recognizing other operating expenses on account	1,400
Decrease due to cash settlements of other operating expenses pay.	? = (1,200)
Ending balance	$1,500

To balance Other Operating Expenses Payable, the amount of the *decrease due to cash settlements of other operating expenses payable* must be $1,200.

The reconciliation shows that the $200 increase in the other operating expenses payable balance occurred because the *cash paid for other operating expenses* was $200 less than the amount of *other operating expenses recognized on account* ($1,200 versus $1,400). Because the amount of cash paid is less than the amount of expense recognized, we add $200 to the amount of net income to determine the net cash flow from operating activities (Reference No. 7 in Exhibit 14.7).

Reconciliation of Interest Payable

Use the financial statement information in Exhibit 14.5 to reconcile Interest Payable. The beginning and ending balances appear on the balance sheets. The *increase due to recognizing interest expense on account* is the interest expense reported on the income statement.

Table 8 Reconciliation of Interest Payable

$200 Decrease

Beginning balance	$500
Increase due to recognizing interest expense on account	400
Decrease due to cash settlements of interest payable	? = (600)
Ending balance	$300

To balance Interest Payable, the amount of the *decrease due to cash settlements of interest payable* (cash paid for interest expense) must be $600.

The reconciliation shows that the $200 decrease in the interest payable balance occurred because the amount of *cash paid for interest expense* is $200 more than the amount of *interest expense recognized on account* ($600 versus $400). Because the amount of cash paid is more than the amount of interest expense recognized, we subtract $200 from the amount of net income to determine the net cash flow from operating activities (Reference No. 8 in Exhibit 14.7).

Reconciliation of Unearned Rent Revenue

Use the financial statement information in Exhibit 14.5 to reconcile Unearned Rent Revenue. The beginning and ending balances appear on the balance sheets. The *decrease due to recognizing other income–rent revenue* is the other income–rent revenue reported on the income statement.

Table 9 Reconciliation of Unearned Rent Revenue

$1,000 Decrease	Beginning balance	$ 1,600	
	Increase due to collecting cash in advance of providing rental services	?	= 1,400
	Decrease due to recognizing other income—rent revenue	(2,400)	
	Ending balance	$ 600	

To balance Unearned Rent Revenue, the amount of the *increase due to collecting cash in advance of providing rental services* must be $1,400.

The reconciliation shows that the $1,000 decrease in the unearned rent revenue balance occurred because the amount of *cash collected in advance of providing rental services* is $1,000 less than the amount of *rent revenue recognized* ($1,400 versus $2,400). Because the amount of cash collected is less than the amount of revenue recognized, we subtract $1,000 from the amount of net income to determine the net cash flow from operating activities (Reference No. 9 in Exhibit 14.7).

Noncash Expenses

The calculation of accrual-based net income frequently includes noncash expenses such as depreciation expense. Because noncash expenses are deducted in determining net income, they must be added back to the amount of net income when computing net cash flow from operating activities (Reference No. 10 in Exhibit 14.7).

Gains and Losses

When a company retires a long-term asset, the company may receive cash from the sale of the asset being retired. If the asset is sold for more than book value (cost − accumulated depreciation), the gain increases net income; if the asset is sold for less than book value, the loss decreases net income. In either case, the cash inflow is the total amount of cash collected from selling the asset, not the amount of the gain or loss, and this cash inflow is reported in the investing activities section of the statement of cash flows. Because gains increase net income and losses decrease net income, but neither represents the amount of cash received from an asset sale, gains must be subtracted from and losses added back to net income to determine net cash flow from operating activities (Reference No. 11 in Exhibit 14.7).

Indirect Method—Rule-Based Approach

The reconciliation process described in the previous section of this chapter leads to a set of rules that can be used to convert accrual-based revenues and expenses to their cash flow equivalents. These rules are summarized in Exhibit 14.8.

Although the rule-based approach offers less insight, it is easy to apply. To illustrate, return to the financial statement data in Exhibit 14.5. The *noncash* current assets and current

EXHIBIT 14.7

Cash Flows From Operating Activities—Indirect Method

Reference No.	Cash Flows from Operating Activities	
	Net income	$ 7,000
	Adjustments to reconcile net income to net cash flow from operating activities:	
1	Decrease in accounts receivable	200
2	Increase in interest receivable	(100)
3	Increase in inventory	(700)
4	Decrease in accounts payable for inventory purchases	(300)
5	Decrease in prepaid insurance	300
6	Increase in salaries payable	100
7	Increase in other operating expenses payable	200
8	Decrease in interest payable	(200)
9	Decrease in unearned rent revenue	(1,000)
10	Depreciation expense	1,000
11	Gain on sale of store fixtures	(600)
	Net cash flow from operating activities	$ 5,900

EXHIBIT 14.8

Cash Flows From Operating Activities—Indirect Method

	Net income	XXX
Rule 1	Add decreases and subtract increases in noncash current assets.	XXX
Rule 2	Add increases and subtract decreases in noncash current liabilities.	XXX
Rule 3	Add noncash expenses (e.g., depreciation).	XXX
Rule 4	Add losses and subtract gains.	XXX
	Net cash flow from operating activities	XXX

liabilities reported on the balance sheets are summarized in Exhibit 14.9 for your convenience. The amount of the change in each balance is shown in the *Change* column.

Refer to the income statement to identify the amounts of net income, noncash expenses, gains, and losses. The income statement for New South Company in Exhibit 14.5 includes three relevant figures: net income of $7,000; depreciation expense of $1,000; and a $600 gain

EXHIBIT 14.9

Noncash Current Assets and Current Liabilities

Account Title	Year 2	Year 1	Change
Accounts receivable	$1,000	$1,200	$ (200)
Interest receivable	400	300	100
Inventory	8,900	8,200	700
Prepaid insurance	1,100	1,400	(300)
Accounts payable—inventory purchases	800	1,100	(300)
Salaries payable	1,000	900	100
Other operating expenses payable	1,500	1,300	200
Interest payable	300	500	(200)
Unearned rent revenue	600	1,600	(1,000)

EXHIBIT 14.10 Cash Flows from Operating Activities—Indirect Method, Operating Activities

NEW SOUTH COMPANY
Statement of Cash Flows
For the Year Ended December 31, Year 2

Applicable Rule	Cash Flows from Operating Activities	
	Net income	$ 7,000
	Adjustments to reconcile net income to net cash flow from operating activities:	
Rule 1	Decrease in accounts receivable	200
Rule 1	Increase in interest receivable	(100)
Rule 1	Increase in inventory	(700)
Rule 2	Decrease in accounts payable for inventory purchases	(300)
Rule 1	Decrease in prepaid insurance	300
Rule 2	Increase in salaries payable	100
Rule 2	Increase in other operating expenses payable	200
Rule 2	Decrease in interest payable	(200)
Rule 2	Decrease in unearned rent revenue	(1,000)
Rule 3	Depreciation expense	1,000
Rule 4	Gain on sale of store fixtures	(600)
	Net cash flow from operating activities	$ 5,900

on the sale of store fixtures. Applying the rules in Exhibit 14.8 produces the operating activities section of the statement of cash flows shown in Exhibit 14.10. The applicable rule for each item is referenced in the first column of the exhibit.

The operating activities section of the statements of cash flows shown in Exhibits 14.10 and 14.7 are identical. The rule-based approach is an alternative way to prepare this section when using the indirect method.

CHECK YOURSELF 14.2

Q Magazine Inc. reported $369,000 of net income for the month. At the beginning of the month, its Unearned Revenue account had a balance of $78,000. At the end of the month, the account had a balance of $67,000. Based on this information alone, determine the amount of net cash flow from operating activities.

Answer

Account Title	Ending	Beginning	Change
Unearned revenue	$67,000	$78,000	$(11,000)

Applicable Rule	Cash Flows from Operating Activities	Amount
	Net income	$369,000
Rule 2	Deduct: Decrease in unearned revenue	(11,000)
	Net cash flow from operating activities	$358,000

CHECK YOURSELF 14.3

The following account balances were drawn from the accounting records of Loeb Inc.

Account Title	Ending Balance	Beginning Balance
Prepaid rent	$3,000	$4,200
Interest payable	2,650	2,900

Loeb reported $7,400 of net income during the accounting period. Based on this information alone, determine the amount of net cash flow from operating activities.

Answer Based on Rule 1, the $1,200 decrease ($4,200 − $3,000) in Prepaid Rent (current asset) must be added to net income to determine the amount of net cash flow from operating activities. Rule 2 requires that the $250 decrease ($2,900 − $2,650) in Interest Payable (current liability) must be deducted from net income. Accordingly, the cash flow from operating activities is $8,350 ($7,400 + $1,200 − $250). Note that paying interest is defined as an operating activity and should not be confused with dividend payments, which are classified as financing activities.

CHECK YOURSELF 14.4

Arley Company's income statement reported net income (all amounts are in millions) of $326 for the year. The income statement included depreciation expense of $45 and a net loss on the sale of long-term assets of $22. Based on this information alone, determine the net cash flow from operating activities.

Answer Based on Rule 3 and Rule 4, both the depreciation expense and the loss would have to be added to net income to determine net cash flow from operating activities. Net cash flow from operating activities would be $393 million ($326 + $45 + $22).

PREPARING THE OPERATING ACTIVITIES SECTION OF A STATEMENT OF CASH FLOWS USING THE DIRECT METHOD

LO 14-2

Prepare the operating activities section of a statement of cash flows using the direct method.

The reconciliation tables developed earlier to determine net cash flow from operating activities under the *indirect method* also disclose the information needed to present the amount of net cash flow from operating activities under the *direct method.* Remember that the amount of net cash flow from operating activities is the same whether it is presented using the indirect or the direct method.

The direct method shows the specific sources and uses of cash that are associated with operating activities. It does not show adjustments to net income. To illustrate, examine Exhibit 14.11. The information in the reference column identifies the reconciliation table from which the cash flow amounts were drawn.

Table 3 is not included in Exhibit 14.11 because it does not directly involve a cash flow. Also, noncash expenses, gains, and losses are not used in the determination of net cash flow from operating activities when using the direct method.

EXHIBIT 14.11

Cash Flows From Operating Activities—Direct Method

Reference	Cash Flows from Operating Activities	
Table 1	Inflow from customers	$ 20,800
Table 2	Inflow from interest revenue	600
Table 4	Outflow for inventory purchases	(11,500)
Table 5	Outflow to purchase insurance	(1,000)
Table 6	Outflow to pay salary expense	(2,600)
Table 7	Outflow for other operating expenses	(1,200)
Table 8	Outflow to pay interest expense	(600)
Table 9	Inflow from rent revenue	1,400
	Net cash flow from operating activities	$ 5,900

PREPARING THE INVESTING ACTIVITIES SECTION OF A STATEMENT OF CASH FLOWS

LO 14-3

Prepare the investing activities section of a statement of cash flows.

The direct and indirect methods discussed earlier pertain only to the presentation of operating activities. The *investing activities* section of the statement of cash flows is the same regardless of whether the direct or indirect method is used for operating activities. The information necessary to identify cash inflows and outflows from investing activities is obtained by reconciling changes in a company's long-term assets. In general:

- Increases in long-term asset balances suggest cash outflows to purchase assets.
- Decreases in long-term asset balances suggest cash inflows from selling assets.

It is usually necessary to analyze data from the long-term asset records to determine details about long-term asset purchases and sales. In the New South Company example, these details are presented as notes at the bottom of the balance sheets.

To illustrate, return to the financial statements in Exhibit 14.5. New South Company reports the following three long-term assets on its balance sheets. *It is not necessary to reconcile accumulated depreciation because it does not affect cash flow.*

Long-Term Asset	Year 2	Year 1
Investment securities	$5,100	$3,500
Store fixtures	5,400	4,800
Land	8,200	6,000

For each long-term asset, reconcile the beginning and ending balances by identifying purchases and sales affecting it. Review the notes for additional relevant information. Begin with investment securities.

Reconciliation of Investment Securities

Reconciliation of Investment Securities		
Beginning balance in investment securities	$3,500	
Increase due to purchase of investment securities	?	= 1,600
Decrease due to sale of investment securities	0	
Ending balance in investment securities	$5,100	

Because Note 1 below the balance sheets indicates no investment securities were sold during Year 2, the *decrease due to sale of investment securities* is zero. To balance Investment Securities, the *increase due to purchase of investment securities* must be $1,600. In the absence of contrary information, assume New South used cash to purchase the investment securities. This cash outflow is reported in the investing activities section of the statement of cash flows in Exhibit 14.12.

EXHIBIT 14.12

Cash Flows from Investing Activities

Cash Flows from Investing Activities	
Cash outflow to purchase investment securities	$(1,600)
Cash inflow from the sale of store fixtures	1,000
Cash outflow to purchase store fixtures	(2,300)
Net cash outflow from investing activities	$(2,900)

Reconciliation of Store Fixtures

Reconciliation of Store Fixtures		
Beginning balance in store fixtures	$ 4,800	
Increase due to purchase of store fixtures	?	= 2,300
Decrease due to sale of store fixtures	(1,700)	
Ending balance in store fixtures	$ 5,400	

Note 2 below the balance sheets indicates that the *decrease due to sale of store fixtures* is $1,700. What is the cash flow from this sale? The book value of these fixtures was $400 ($1,700 cost − $1,300 accumulated depreciation). Because the income statement reports a $600 gain on the sale of store fixtures, the cash collected from the sale was more than the book value of the store fixtures. Compute the amount of cash collected from the sale of store fixtures as follows:

$$\text{Cash inflow} = \text{Book value} + \text{Gain} = \$400 + \$600 = \$1{,}000$$

The $1,000 cash inflow from the sale of store fixtures is reported in the investing activities section of the statement of cash flows in Exhibit 14.12.

To balance Store Fixtures, the *increase due to purchase of store fixtures* must be $2,300. In the absence of contrary information, assume New South used cash to purchase store fixtures. The cash outflow is reported in the investing activities section of the statement of cash flows in Exhibit 14.12.

Reconciliation of Land

Reconciliation of Land		
Beginning balance in land	$6,000	
Increase due to purchase of land	?	= 2,200
Decrease due to sale of land	0	
Ending balance in land	$8,200	

Because Note 3 below the balance sheets indicates no land was sold during Year 2, the *decrease due to sale of land* is zero. To balance Land, the *increase due to purchase of land* must be $2,200. Because the land was acquired by issuing a mortgage note payable, New South did not use cash for the purchase. This type of transaction is reported in the *noncash investing and financing activities* section of the statement of cash flows, discussed in more detail later in the chapter. The cash inflows and outflows from investing activities are summarized in Exhibit 14.12.

CHECK YOURSELF 14.5

On January 1, Year 7, Wyatt Company had an Equipment balance of $124,000. During Year 7, Wyatt purchased equipment that cost $50,000. The balance in Equipment on December 31, Year 7, was $90,000. The Year 7 income statement included a $7,000 loss from the sale of equipment. On the date of sale, accumulated depreciation on the equipment sold was $49,000.

Required

a. Determine the cost of the equipment sold during Year 7.

b. Determine the amount of cash flow from the sale of equipment that should be reported in the investing activities section of the Year 7 statement of cash flows.

Solution

a.

Reconciliation of Equipment		
Beginning balance	$124,000	
Increase due to the purchase of equipment	50,000	
Decrease due to sale of equipment	?	= (84,000)
Ending balance	$ 90,000	

To balance Equipment, the *decrease due to sale of equipment* must be $84,000.

b. The book value of the equipment sold was $35,000 ($84,000 − $49,000 accumulated depreciation). Because Wyatt recognized a loss on the equipment sale, the amount of cash collected from the sale was less than the book value of the equipment. The cash collected from the sale of the equipment was $28,000 ($35,000 book value − $7,000 loss on sale).

PREPARING THE FINANCING ACTIVITIES SECTION OF A STATEMENT OF CASH FLOWS

LO 14-4

Prepare the financing activities section of a statement of cash flows.

Because the differences between the direct and the indirect methods of presenting the statement of cash flows pertain only to operating activities, the *financing activities* section is the same under either approach. The information necessary to identify cash inflows and outflows from financing activities is obtained by reconciling changes in short-term notes payable, long-term liabilities, and stockholders' equity. In general:

- Increases in long-term debt balances suggest cash inflows occurred from issuing debt instruments (notes or bonds).
- Decreases in long-term debt balances suggest cash outflows occurred for payment of debt (notes or bonds).
- Increases in contributed capital (common stock, preferred stock, or paid-in capital) suggest cash inflows occurred from issuing equity instruments.
- Increases or decreases in treasury stock suggest cash outflows or inflows occurred to purchase or sell a company's own stock.

- Decreases in retained earnings from cash dividends suggest cash outflows occurred to pay dividends.

©larryhw/123RF

To illustrate, return to the financial statements of the New South Company in Exhibit 14.5. The following long-term liability and stockholders' equity balances are reported on the New South balance sheets.

Account Title	Year 2	Year 1
Mortgage payable	$ 2,200	$ 0
Bonds payable	1,000	4,000
Common stock	10,000	8,000
Retained earnings	12,700	7,200
Treasury stock	600	0

For each account, reconcile the beginning and ending balances by identifying the increases and decreases affecting it. Review the notes for additional relevant information. Begin with the mortgage payable liability.

Reconciliation of Mortgage Payable

Reconciliation of Mortgage Payable	
Beginning balance in mortgage payable	$ 0
Increase due to issuing mortgage payable	? = 2,200
Decrease due to payment of mortgage payable	0
Ending balance in mortgage payable	$2,200

As previously discussed, Note 3 indicates a mortgage note payable was issued to acquire land. The *increase due to issuing mortgage payable* is $2,200. Because New South received land, not cash, by issuing the mortgage, the transaction is reported in the noncash investing and financing activities section of the statement of cash flows.

Reconciliation of Bonds Payable

Bonds Payable	
Beginning balance in bonds payable	$4,000
Increase due to issuing bonds payable	0
Decrease due to payment of bonds payable	? = (3,000)
Ending balance in bonds payable	$1,000

Because there is no indication that New South issued bonds during Year 2, assume the *increase due to issuing bonds payable* is zero. To balance Bonds Payable, the *decrease due to payment of bonds payable* must be $3,000. The cash outflow is reported in the financing activities section in Exhibit 14.13.

EXHIBIT 14.13

Cash Flows from Financing Activities

Cash Flows from Financing Activities	
Cash outflow to reduce bonds payable	$(3,000)
Cash inflow from issuing common stock	2,000
Cash outflow to pay dividends	(1,500)
Cash outflow to purchase treasury stock	(600)
Net cash outflow from financing activities	$(3,100)

Reconciliation of Common Stock

Reconciliation of Common Stock	
Beginning balance in common stock	$ 8,000
Increase due to issuing common stock	? = 2,000
Ending balance in common stock	$10,000

To balance Common Stock, the *increase due to issuing common stock* has to be $2,000. The cash inflow is reported in the financing activities section in Exhibit 14.13.

Reconciliation of Retained Earnings

Reconciliation of Retained Earnings	
Beginning balance in retained earnings	$ 7,200
Increase due to net income	7,000
Decrease due to payment of dividends	? = (1,500)
Ending balance in retained earnings	$12,700

The *increase due to net income* comes from the income statement. To balance Retained Earnings, the decrease due to payment of dividends must be $1,500. In the absence of information to the contrary, assume the decrease is due to the cash payment of dividends. The cash outflow for payment of dividends is reported in the financing activities section of the statement of cash flows in Exhibit 14.13.

Reconciliation of Treasury Stock

Reconciliation of Treasury Stock	
Beginning balance in treasury stock	$ 0
Increase due to purchasing treasury stock	? = 600
Decrease due to reissuing treasury stock	0
Ending balance in treasury stock	$600

Because there is no indication that New South reissued treasury stock during Year 2, the *decrease due to reissuing treasury stock* is zero. To balance Treasury Stock, the increase due to purchasing treasury stock must be $600. The cash outflow is reported in the financing activities section in Exhibit 14.13.

Exhibits 14.14 and 14.15 illustrate the complete statement of cash flows for New South Company under the two alternative methods. Exhibit 14.14 presents operating activities using the indirect method. Exhibit 14.15 presents operating activities using the direct method. The investing and financing activities do not differ between methods. Under either method, the combined effects of operating, investing, and financing activities result in a net decrease in cash of $100 for Year 2. This $100 decrease is necessarily consistent with the difference between the December 31, Year 2, and the December 31, Year 1, cash balances shown in the balance sheets in Exhibit 14.5.

EXHIBIT 14.14 Statement of Cash Flows—Indirect Method

NEW SOUTH COMPANY
Statement of Cash Flows
For the Year Ended December 31, Year 2

Cash Flows from Operating Activities		
Net income	$ 7,000	
Adjustments to reconcile net income to net cash flow from operating activities:		
Decrease in accounts receivable	200	
Increase in interest receivable	(100)	
Increase in inventory	(700)	
Decrease in accounts payable for inventory purchases	(300)	
Decrease in prepaid insurance	300	
Increase in salaries payable	100	
Increase in other operating expenses payable	200	
Decrease in interest payable	(200)	
Decrease in unearned rent revenue	(1,000)	
Depreciation expense	1,000	
Gain on sale of store fixtures	(600)	
Net cash flow from operating activities		$ 5,900
Cash Flows from Investing Activities		
Cash outflow to purchase investment securities	(1,600)	
Cash inflow from the sale of store fixtures	1,000	
Cash outflow to purchase store fixtures	(2,300)	
Net cash outflow from investing activities		(2,900)
Cash Flows from Financing Activities		
Cash outflow to reduce bonds payable	(3,000)	
Cash inflow from issuing common stock	2,000	
Cash outflow to pay dividends	(1,500)	
Cash outflow to purchase treasury stock	(600)	
Net cash outflow from financing activities		(3,100)
Net decrease in cash		(100)
Plus: Beginning cash balance		400
Ending cash balance		$ 300
Schedule of Noncash Investing and Financing Activities		
Issue mortgage for land		$ 2,200

EXHIBIT 14.15 Statement of Cash Flows—Direct Method

NEW SOUTH COMPANY
Statement of Cash Flows
For the Year Ended December 31, Year 2

Cash Flows from Operating Activities		
Inflow from customers	$ 20,800	
Inflow from interest revenue	600	
Outflow for inventory purchases	(11,500)	
Outflow to purchase insurance	(1,000)	
Outflow to pay salary expense	(2,600)	
Outflow for other operating expenses	(1,200)	
Outflow to pay interest expense	(600)	
Inflow from rent revenue	1,400	
Net cash flow from operating activities		$ 5,900

continued

EXHIBIT 14.15 *concluded*

NEW SOUTH COMPANY
Statement of Cash Flows
For the Year Ended December 31, Year 2

Cash Flows from Investing Activities		
Cash outflow to purchase investment securities	(1,600)	
Cash inflow from the sale of store fixtures	1,000	
Cash outflow to purchase store fixtures	(2,300)	
Net cash outflow from investing activities		(2,900)
Cash Flows from Financing Activities		
Cash outflow to reduce bonds payable	(3,000)	
Cash inflow from issuing common stock	2,000	
Cash outflow to pay dividends	(1,500)	
Cash outflow to purchase treasury stock	(600)	
Net cash outflow from financing activities		(3,100)
Net decrease in cash		(100)
Plus: Beginning cash balance		400
Ending cash balance		$ 300
Schedule of Noncash Investing and Financing Activities		
Issue mortgage for land		$ 2,200

CHECK YOURSELF 14.6

On January 1, Year 4, Sterling Company had a balance of $250,000 in Bonds Payable. During Year 4, Sterling issued bonds with a $75,000 face value. The bonds were issued at face value. The balance in Bonds Payable on December 31, Year 4, was $150,000.

Required

a. Determine the cash outflow for repayment of bond liabilities assuming the bonds were retired at face value.

b. Prepare the financing activities section of the Year 4 statement of cash flows.

Solution

a.

Reconciliation of Bonds Payable	
Beginning balance	$250,000
Increase due to issuing bonds payable	75,000
Decrease due to payment of bonds payable	? = (175,000)
Ending balance	$150,000

In order to balance Bonds Payable, the *decrease due to payment of bonds payable* must be $175,000. In the absence of information to the contrary, assume cash was used to pay the bond liabilities.

b.

Cash Flows from Financing Activities	
Inflow from issuing bond liabilities	$ 75,000
Outflow for reduction of bond liabilities	(175,000)
Net cash outflow from financing activities	$(100,000)

PREPARING THE SCHEDULE OF NONCASH INVESTING AND FINANCING ACTIVITIES

As mentioned earlier, companies may engage in significant noncash investing and financing activities. For example, New South Company acquired land by issuing a $2,200 mortgage note. Because these types of transactions do not involve exchanging cash, they are not reported in the main body of the statement of cash flows. However, the Financial Accounting Standards Board (FASB) requires disclosure of all material investing and financing activities, whether or not they involve exchanging cash. Companies must therefore include with the statement of cash flows a separate schedule that reports noncash investing and financing activities. See the *Schedule of Noncash Investing and Financing Activities* at the bottom of Exhibits 14.14 and 14.15 for an example.

REALITY BYTES

How did Amazon.com acquire $6.9 billion of assets in 2016 *without* spending cash? Oddly enough, the answer can be found on its statement of cash flows.

The supplemental "noncash transactions" information included at the bottom of Amazon's statement of cash flows reveals that it acquired the assets by using long-term leases, a form of debt.

Had Amazon issued $6.9 billion of long-term debt for cash, and then used this cash to purchase $6.9 billion of assets, it would have reported two separate cash events in the body of its statement of cash flows. A cash inflow would have been reported in the financing activities section for the issuance of the debt, and a cash outflow would have been reported in the investing activities section for the purchase of the assets. Acquiring large amounts of assets is considered important, even if there is no immediate exchange of cash, so generally accepted accounting principles require such events to be reported with the statement of cash flows or disclosed in the notes.

©Evan Lorne/Shutterstock

CASH FLOW VERSUS NET INCOME IN REAL-WORLD COMPANIES

Why are financial analysts interested in the statement of cash flows? Understanding the cash flows of a business is essential because cash is used to pay the bills. A company, especially one experiencing rapid growth, can be short of cash in spite of earning substantial net income. To illustrate, assume you start a computer sales business. You borrow $2,000 and spend the money to purchase two computers for $1,000 each. You sell one of the computers on account for $1,500. If your loan required a payment at this time, you could not make it. Even though you have net income of $500 ($1,500 sales − $1,000 cost of goods sold), you have no cash until you collect the $1,500 account receivable. A business cannot survive without managing cash flow carefully. It is little wonder that financial analysts are keenly interested in cash flow.

The statement of cash flows frequently provides a picture of business activity that otherwise would be lost in the complexities of accrual accounting. For example, even though Rent-A-Center reported a loss of approximately $105 million in 2016 on its income statement, its net cash flow from operating activities was a positive $354 million.

Investors consider cash flow information so important they are willing to pay for it. Even though the FASB *prohibits* companies from disclosing *cash flow per share* in audited financial statements, one prominent stock analysis service, *Value Line Investment Survey,* sells this information to a

©Juan Carlos Baena/Alamy

EXHIBIT 14.16

Net Income versus Cash Flow from Operations (amounts in millions)

	2016	2015	2014	2013
Caterpillar				
Net income	$ (59)	$ 2,113	$ 3,711	$ 3,803
Cash flow—operations	5,608	6,675	8,057	10,191
Chevron				
Net income	(431)	4,710	19,310	21,597
Cash flow—operations	12,846	19,456	31,475	35,002
Facebook				
Operating income	10,217	3,688	2,940	1,500
Cash flow—operations	16,108	8,599	5,457	4,222
Netflix				
Net income	187	123	267	112
Cash flow—operations	(1,474)	(749)	16	98
Twitter				
Net income	(457)	(521)	(578)	(645)
Cash flow—operations	763	383	82	1
Wendy's				
Net income	130	161	121	45
Cash flow—operations	181	212	255	330

©Anthony Correia/Shutterstock

significant customer base. Clearly, *Value Line's* customers value information about cash flows.

Exhibit 14.16 compares income from operations to cash flows from operating activities for six real-world companies for 2013 through 2016. Several things are apparent from this exhibit. Notice that the cash flow from operating activities exceeds income from operations for all but 4 of the 24 comparisons, and all of these relate to one company, Netflix. Cash flows often exceed earnings because depreciation, a noncash expense, is usually significant. There are two dramatic examples of the differences between cash flow and earnings. First, for the four years shown in Exhibit 14.16, Twitter had cumulative net losses of $2.2 billion, but its cash flows from operations were a positive $1.2 billion. Second, Caterpillar had cumulative net earnings of $9.6 billion for the four years reported, but its net cash flows from operations were $30.5 billion, over three times larger. The difference between cash flows from operating activities and net earnings helps explain how some companies can have significant losses over a few years and continue to stay in business and pay their bills.

The exhibit also shows that cash flow from operating activities can be more stable than operating income. Results for Chevron demonstrate this clearly. Chevron earnings ranged from a negative $431 million to a positive $21.6 billion, a range of $22.0 billion, which is 195 percent of its average earnings of $11.3 billion for these four years. However, operating cash flows were not only positive in every year, but their total variation over the four years of $22.2 billion was only 90 percent of the average cash flows from operations ($24.7 billion).

What could explain why Netflix had *less* cash flow from operating activities than net earnings in all four years, and even had negative cash flows in 2015 and 2016? The company was experiencing the kind of growth described earlier for your computer business. Its cash outflows were supporting growth in Netflix's "streaming content library"—essentially, its inventory. Netflix's revenues doubled from 2013 to 2016, going from $3.4 billion to 8.8 billion. To support this growth, the company had to increase its inventory. In 2016 alone, Netflix spent $8.6 billion to increase its streaming content library.

The Netflix situation highlights a potential weakness in the format of the statement of cash flows. Some accountants consider it misleading to classify all increases in long-term assets as *investing activities* and all changes in inventory as affecting cash flow from operating activities. In the case of Netflix, they would argue that the increase in inventory that relates to expanding its business should be classified as an investing activity, just as the cost of a new warehouse is. Although inventory is classified as a current asset and buildings are classified as long-term assets, in reality there is a certain level of inventory a company must permanently maintain to stay in business. The GAAP format of the statement of cash flows penalizes cash flow from operating activities for increases in inventory that are really a permanent investment in assets.

Conversely, the same critics might argue that some purchases of long-term assets are not actually *investments* but merely replacements of old, existing property, plant, and equipment. In other words, the *investing activities* section of the statement of cash flows makes no distinction between expenditures that expand the business and those that simply replace old equipment (sometimes called *capital maintenance* expenditures).

Users of the statement of cash flows must exercise the same care interpreting it as when they use the balance sheet or the income statement. Numbers alone are insufficient. Users must evaluate numbers based on knowledge of the particular business and industry they are analyzing.

Accounting information alone cannot guide a businessperson to a sound decision. Making good business decisions requires an understanding of the business in question, the environmental and economic factors affecting the operation of that business, and the accounting concepts on which the financial statements of that business are based.

<< A Look Back

This chapter examined in detail only one financial statement, the statement of cash flows. The chapter provided a more comprehensive discussion of how accrual accounting relates to cash-based accounting. Effective use of financial statements requires understanding not only accrual and cash-based accounting systems but also how they relate to each other. That relationship is why a statement of cash flows can begin with a reconciliation of net income, an accrual measurement, to net cash flow from operating activities, a cash measurement. Finally, this chapter explained how the conventions for classifying cash flows as operating, investing, or financing activities require analysis and understanding to make informed decisions with the financial information.

>> A Look Forward

We sincerely hope this text provided a meaningful learning experience that will serve you well as you progress through your academic training and, ultimately, your career. Good luck and best wishes.

A step-by-step audio-narrated series of slides is available in *Connect*.

SELF-STUDY REVIEW PROBLEM

The following financial statements pertain to Schlemmer Company.

Balance Sheets As of December 31	Year 2	Year 1
Cash	$ 48,400	$ 2,800
Accounts receivable	2,200	1,200
Inventory	5,600	6,000
Equipment	18,000	22,000
Accumulated depreciation—equip.	(13,650)	(17,400)
Land	17,200	10,400
Total assets	$ 77,750	$ 25,000
Accounts payable (inventory)	$ 5,200	$ 4,200
Long-term debt	5,600	6,400
Common stock	19,400	10,000
Retained earnings	47,550	4,400
Total liabilities and equity	$ 77,750	$ 25,000

Income Statement For the Year Ended December 31, Year 2	
Sales revenue	$ 67,300
Cost of goods sold	(24,100)
Gross margin	43,200
Depreciation expense	(1,250)
Operating income	41,950
Gain on sale of equipment	2,900
Loss on disposal of land	(100)
Net income	$ 44,750

Additional Data

1. During Year 2, equipment that had originally cost $11,000 was sold. Accumulated depreciation on this equipment was $5,000 at the time of sale.
2. Common stock was issued in exchange for land valued at $9,400 at the time of the exchange.

Required

Using the indirect method, prepare in good form a statement of cash flows for the year ended December 31, Year 2.

Solution

SCHLEMMER COMPANY Statement of Cash Flows For the Year Ended December 31, Year 2		
Cash Flows from Operating Activities		
Net income	$44,750	
Add:		
Decrease in inventory (1)	400	
Increase in accounts payable (2)	1,000	
Depreciation expense (3)	1,250	
Loss on disposal of land (4)	100	
Subtract:		
Increase in accounts receivable (1)	(1,000)	
Gain on sale of equipment (4)	(2,900)	
Net cash inflow from operating activities		$43,600
Cash Flows from Investing Activities		
Cash inflow from the sale of equipment (5)	8,900	
Cash outflow for the purchase of equipment (5)	(7,000)	
Cash inflow from sale of land (6)	2,500	
Net cash outflow from investing activities		4,400
Cash Flows from Financing Activities		
Cash outflow to repay long-term debt (7)	(800)	
Cash outflow to pay dividends (8)	(1,600)	
Net cash outflow from financing activities		(2,400)
Net Increase in Cash		45,600
Plus: Beginning cash balance		2,800
Ending cash balance		$48,400
Schedule of Noncash Investing and Financing Activities		
Issue of common stock for land (9)		$ 9,400

(1) Add decreases and subtract increases in current asset account balances to net income.

(2) Add increases and subtract decreases in current liability account balances to net income.

(3) Add noncash expenses (depreciation) to net income.

(4) Add losses on the sale of noncurrent assets to net income and subtract gains on the sale of long-term assets from net income.

(5) Information regarding the Equipment account is summarized in the following table.

Equipment Account Information	
Beginning balance in equipment	$22,000
Purchases of equipment (cash outflows)	? = 7,000
Sales of equipment (cash inflows)	(11,000)
Ending balance in equipment	$ 18,000

To balance the account, equipment costing $7,000 must have been purchased. In the absence of information to the contrary, we assume cash was used to make the purchase.

Note 1 to the financial statement shows that equipment sold had a book value of $6,000 ($11,000 cost − $5,000 accumulated depreciation). The amount of the cash inflow from this sale is computed as follows:

Cash inflow = Book value + Gain = $6,000 + $2,900 = $8,900

(6) The information regarding the Land account is as follows.

Land Account Information	
Beginning balance in land	$10,400
Purchases of land (issue of common stock)	9,400
Sales of land (cash inflows)	? = (2,600)
Ending balance in land	$17,200

Note 2 indicates that land valued at $9,400 was acquired by issuing common stock. Because there was no cash flow associated with this purchase, the event is shown in the *noncash investing and financing activities* section of the statement of cash flows.

To balance the account, the cost (book value) of land sold had to be $2,600. Because the income statement shows a $100 loss on the sale of land, the cash collected from the sale is computed as follows:

Cash inflow = Book value − Loss = $2,600 − $100 = $2,500

(7) The information regarding the Long-Term Debt account is as follows.

Long-Term Debt Information	
Beginning balance in long-term debt	$6,400
Issue of long-term debt instruments (cash inflow)	0
Payment of long-term debt (cash outflow)	? = (800)
Ending balance in long-term debt	$5,600

There is no information in the financial statements that suggests long-term debt was issued. Therefore, to balance the account, $800 of long-term debt had to be paid off, thereby resulting in a cash outflow.

(8) The information regarding the Retained Earnings account is as follows.

Retained Earnings Information	
Beginning balance in retained earnings	$ 4,400
Net income	44,750
Dividends (cash outflow)	? = (1,600)
Ending balance in retained earnings	$47,550

To balance the account, $1,600 of dividends had to be paid, thereby resulting in a cash outflow.

(9) Note 2 states that common stock was issued to acquire land valued at $9,400. This is a noncash investing and financing activity.

KEY TERMS

Cash inflows 638
Cash outflows 638
Direct method 640
Financing activities 641
Indirect method 640
Investing activities 641
Noncash investing and financing activities 642
Operating activities 640

QUESTIONS

1. What is the purpose of the statement of cash flows?
2. What are the three categories of cash flows reported on the cash flow statement? Discuss each and give an example of an inflow and an outflow for each category.
3. What are noncash investing and financing activities? Provide an example. How are such transactions shown on the statement of cash flows?
4. Albring Company had a beginning balance in accounts receivable of $12,000 and an ending balance of $14,000. Net income amounted to $110,000. Based on this information alone, determine the amount of net cash flow from operating activities.
5. Forsyth Company had a beginning balance in utilities payable of $3,300 and an ending balance of $5,200. Net income amounted to $87,000. Based on this information alone, determine the amount of net cash flow from operating activities.
6. Clover Company had a beginning balance in unearned revenue of $4,300 and an ending balance of $3,200. Net income amounted to $54,000. Based on this information alone, determine the amount of net cash flow from operating activities.
7. Which of the following activities are financing activities?
   (a) Payment of accounts payable.
   (b) Payment of interest on bonds payable.
   (c) Sale of common stock.
   (d) Sale of preferred stock at a premium.
   (e) Payment of a cash dividend.
8. Does depreciation expense affect net cash flow? Explain.
9. If Best Company sold land that cost $4,200 at a $500 gain, how much cash did it collect from the sale of land?
10. If Best Company sold office equipment that originally cost $7,500 and had $7,200 of accumulated depreciation at a $100 loss, what was the selling price for the office equipment?
11. In which section of the statement of cash flows would the following transactions be reported?
    (a) The amount of the change in the balance of accounts receivable.
    (b) Cash purchase of investment securities.
    (c) Cash purchase of equipment.
    (d) Cash sale of merchandise.
    (e) Cash sale of common stock.
    (f) The amount of net income.
    (g) Cash proceeds from loan.
    (h) Cash payment on bonds payable.
    (i) Cash receipt from sale of old equipment.
    (j) The amount of the change in the balance of accounts payable.
12. What is the difference between preparing the statement of cash flows using the direct method and using the indirect method?
13. Which method (direct or indirect) of presenting the statement of cash flows is more intuitively logical? Why?
14. What is the major advantage of using the indirect method to present the statement of cash flows?
15. What is the advantage of using the direct method to present the statement of cash flows?
16. How would Best Company report the following transactions on the statement of cash flows?
    (a) Purchased new equipment for $46,000 cash.
    (b) Sold old equipment for $8,700 cash. The equipment had a book value of $4,900.
17. Can a company report negative net cash flows from operating activities for the year on the statement of cash flows but still have positive net income on the income statement? Explain.

MULTIPLE-CHOICE QUESTIONS

Multiple-choice questions are available in *Connect*.

EXERCISES—SERIES A

connect **All applicable Exercises in Series A are available in *Connect*.**

Exercise 14-1A ***Use the indirect method to determine cash flows from operating activities*** LO 14-1

An accountant for Southern Manufacturing Companies (SMC) computed the following information by making comparisons between SMC's Year 1 and Year 2 balance sheets. Further information was determined by examining the company's Year 2 income statement.

1. The amount of cash dividends paid to the stockholders.
2. The amount of a decrease in the balance of an Unearned Revenue account.
3. The amount of an increase in the balance of an Inventory account.

4. The amount of an increase in the balance of a Land account.
5. The amount of a decrease in the balance of a Prepaid Rent account.
6. The amount of an increase in the balance of a Treasury Stock account.
7. The amount of an increase in the balance of the Accounts Receivable account.
8. The amount of a loss arising from the sale of land.
9. The amount of an increase in the balance of the Other Operating Expenses Payable account.
10. The amount of a decrease in the balance of the Bonds Payable account.
11. The amount of depreciation expense shown on the income statement.

Required

For each item described in the preceding list, indicate whether the amount should be added to or subtracted from the amount of net income when determining the amount of net cash flow from operating activities using the indirect method. Also identify any items that do not affect net cash flow from operating activities because they are reported as investing or financing activities.

LO 14-1

Exercise 14-2A *Use the indirect method to determine cash flows from operating activities*

Alfonza Incorporated presents its statement of cash flows using the indirect method. The following accounts and corresponding balances were drawn from the company's Year 2 and Year 1 year-end balance sheets.

Account Title	Year 2	Year 1
Accounts receivable	$16,200	$17,800
Accounts payable	7,600	9,100

The Year 2 income statement showed net income of $31,600.

Required

a. Prepare the operating activities section of the statement of cash flows.

b. Explain why the change in the balance in accounts receivable was added to or subtracted from the amount of net income when you completed Requirement *a*.

c. Explain why the change in the balance in accounts payable was added to or subtracted from the amount of net income when you completed Requirement *a*.

LO 14-1

Exercise 14-3A *Use the indirect method to determine cash flows from operating activities*

Shim Company presents its statement of cash flows using the indirect method. The following accounts and corresponding balances were drawn from Shim's Year 2 and Year 1 year-end balance sheets.

Account Title	Year 2	Year 1
Accounts receivable	$36,000	$37,200
Prepaid rent	2,400	1,800
Interest receivable	600	400
Accounts payable	9,300	10,400
Salaries payable	4,500	5,200
Unearned revenue	3,600	5,400

The income statement reported a $1,500 gain on the sale of equipment, an $800 loss on the sale of land, and $3,600 of depreciation expense. Net income for the period was $47,300.

Required

Prepare the operating activities section of the statement of cash flows.

Exercise 14-4A ***Use the direct method to determine cash flows from operating activities*** **LO 14-2**

The following accounts and corresponding balances were drawn from Avia Company's Year 2 and Year 1 year-end balance sheets.

Account Title	Year 2	Year 1
Unearned revenue	$7,600	$6,200
Prepaid rent	2,400	3,600

During the year, $46,000 of unearned revenue was recognized as having been earned. Rent expense for Year 2 was $18,000.

Required

Based on this information alone, prepare the operating activities section of the statement of cash flows assuming the direct approach is used.

Exercise 14-5A ***Use the direct method to determine cash flows from operating activities*** **LO 14-2**

The following accounts and corresponding balances were drawn from Marinelli Company's Year 2 and Year 1 year-end balance sheets.

Account Title	Year 2	Year 1
Accounts receivable	$35,200	$31,600
Interest receivable	4,200	4,800
Other operating expenses payable	21,000	18,500
Salaries payable	6,500	7,200

The Year 2 income statement is shown as follows.

Income Statement	
Sales	$ 530,000
Salary expense	(214,000)
Other operating expenses	(175,000)
Operating income	141,000
Nonoperating items: Interest revenue	16,500
Net income	$ 157,500

Required

a. Use the direct method to compute the amount of cash inflows from operating activities.

b. Use the direct method to compute the amount of cash outflows from operating activities.

Exercise 14-6A ***Direct versus indirect method of determining cash flows from operating activities*** **LO 14-1, 14-2**

Expert Electronics Inc. (EEI) recognized $3,800 of sales revenue on account and collected $2,100 of cash from accounts receivable. Further, EEI recognized $900 of operating expenses on account and paid $700 cash as partial settlement of accounts payable.

Required

Based on this information alone:

a. Prepare the operating activities section of the statement of cash flows under the direct method.

b. Prepare the operating activities section of the statement of cash flows under the indirect method.

LO 14-1, 14-2

Exercise 14-7A *The direct versus the indirect method of determining cash flows from operating activities*

The following accounts and corresponding balances were drawn from Jogger Company's Year 2 and Year 1 year-end balance sheets.

Account Title	Year 2	Year 1
Accounts receivable	$57,000	$62,000
Prepaid rent	1,100	1,300
Utilities payable	900	750
Other operating expenses payable	21,300	22,400

The Year 2 income statement is shown as follows.

Income Statement	
Sales	$268,000
Rent expense	(36,000)
Utilities expense	(18,300)
Other operating expenses	(79,100)
Net Income	$134,600

Required

a. Prepare the operating activities section of the statement of cash flows using the direct method.

b. Prepare the operating activities section of the statement of cash flows using the indirect method.

LO 14-3

Exercise 14-8A *Determining cash flow from investing activities*

On January 1, Year 1, Shelton Company had a balance of $325,000 in its Land account. During Year 1, Shelton sold land that had cost $106,500 for $132,000 cash. The balance in the Land account on December 31, Year 1, was $285,000.

Required

a. Determine the cash outflow for the purchase of land during Year 1.

b. Prepare the investing activities section of the Year 1 statement of cash flows.

LO 14-3

Exercise 14-9A *Determining cash flows from investing activities*

On January 1, Year 1, Bacco Company had a balance of $72,350 in its Delivery Equipment account. During Year 1, Bacco purchased delivery equipment that cost $22,100. The balance in the Delivery Equipment account on December 31, Year 1, was $69,400. The Year 1 income statement reported a gain from the sale of equipment for $5,000. On the date of sale, accumulated depreciation on the equipment sold amounted to $22,000.

Required

a. Determine the original cost of the equipment that was sold during Year 1.

b. Determine the amount of cash flow from the sale of delivery equipment that should be shown in the investing activities section of the Year 1 statement of cash flows.

LO 14-3

Exercise 14-10A *Determining cash flows from investing activities*

The following accounts and corresponding balances were drawn from Delsey Company's Year 2 and Year 1 year-end balance sheets.

Account Title	Year 2	Year 1
Investment securities	$110,000	$116,500
Machinery	486,000	437,000
Land	160,000	100,000

Other information drawn from the accounting records:

1. Delsey incurred a $6,000 loss on the sale of investment securities during Year 2.
2. Old machinery with a book value of $8,000 (cost of $36,000 minus accumulated depreciation of $28,000) was sold. The income statement showed a gain on the sale of machinery of $4,500.
3. Delsey did not sell land during the year.

Required

a. Compute the amount of cash flow associated with the sale of investment securities.
b. Compute the amount of cash flow associated with the purchase of machinery.
c. Compute the amount of cash flow associated with the sale of machinery.
d. Compute the amount of cash flow associated with the purchase of land.
e. Prepare the investing activities section of the statement of cash flows.

Exercise 14-11A *Determining cash flows from financing activities*

LO 14-4

On January 1, Year 1, DIBA Company had a balance of $450,000 in its Bonds Payable account. During Year 1, DIBA issued bonds with a $200,000 face value. There was no premium or discount associated with the bond issue. The balance in the Bonds Payable account on December 31, Year 1, was $400,000.

Required

a. Determine the cash outflow for the repayment of bond liabilities assuming that the bonds were retired at face value.
b. Prepare the financing activities section of the Year 1 statement of cash flows.

Exercise 14-12A *Determining cash flows from financing activities*

LO 14-4

On January 1, Year 1, Hardy Company had a balance of $150,000 in its Common Stock account. During Year 1, Hardy paid $20,000 to purchase treasury stock. Treasury stock is accounted for using the cost method. The balance in the Common Stock account on December 31, Year 1, was $175,000. Assume that the common stock is no par stock.

Required

a. Determine the cash inflow from the issue of common stock.
b. Prepare the financing activities section of the Year 1 statement of cash flows.

Exercise 14-13A *Determining cash flows from financing activities*

LO 14-4

The following accounts and corresponding balances were drawn from Dexter Company's Year 2 and Year 1 year-end balance sheets.

Account Title	Year 2	Year 1
Bonds payable	$350,000	$400,000
Common stock	450,000	420,000

Other information drawn from the accounting records:

1. Dividends paid during the period amounted to $50,000.
2. There were no bond liabilities issued during the period.

Required

a. Compute the amount of cash flow associated with the repayment of bond liabilities.
b. Compute the amount of cash flow associated with the issue of common stock.
c. Prepare the financing activities section of the statement of cash flows.

PROBLEMS—SERIES A

connect All applicable Problems in Series A are available in *Connect*.

LO 14-1, 14-2

excel

CHECK FIGURE

Net Cash Flow from Operating Activities: $105,200

Problem 14-14A *The direct versus the indirect method of determining cash flow from operating activities*

Green Brands Inc. (GBI) presents its statement of cash flows using the indirect method. The following accounts and corresponding balances were drawn from GBI's Year 2 and Year 1 year-end balance sheets. Assume that Accounts Payable is used for purchases of inventory only.

Account Title	Year 2	Year 1
Accounts receivable	$48,000	$52,000
Merchandise inventory	78,000	72,000
Prepaid insurance	24,000	32,000
Accounts payable	31,000	28,000
Salaries payable	8,200	7,800
Unearned service revenue	2,400	3,600

The Year 2 income statement is shown as follows.

Income Statement	
Sales	$ 720,000
Cost of goods sold	(398,000)
Gross margin	322,000
Service revenue	6,000
Insurance expense	(36,000)
Salaries expense	(195,000)
Depreciation expense	(12,000)
Operating income	85,000
Gain on sale of equipment	4,500
Net income	$ 89,500

Required

a. Prepare the operating activities section of the statement of cash flows using the direct method.

b. Prepare the operating activities section of the statement of cash flows using the indirect method.

LO 14-3

excel

CHECK FIGURES

b. $4,700

c. $10,000

Problem 14-15A *Determining cash flows from investing activities*

The following information was drawn from the year-end balance sheets of Mass Trading Company.

Account Title	Year 2	Year 1
Investment securities	$ 47,200	$ 42,400
Equipment	246,000	218,000
Buildings	646,000	720,000
Land	95,000	72,000

Additional information regarding transactions occurring during Year 2:

1. Investment securities that had cost $6,100 were sold. The Year 2 income statement contained a loss on the sale of investment securities of $1,400.
2. Equipment with a cost of $38,000 was purchased.

3. The income statement showed a gain on the sale of equipment of $8,000. On the date of sale, accumulated depreciation on the equipment sold amounted to $8,000.
4. A building that had originally cost $210,000 was demolished.
5. Land that had cost $30,000 was sold for $27,000.

Required

a. Determine the amount of cash flow for the purchase of investment securities during Year 2.
b. Determine the amount of cash flow from the sale of investment securities during Year 2.
c. Determine the cost of the equipment that was sold during Year 2.
d. Determine the amount of cash flow from the sale of equipment during Year 2.
e. Determine the amount of cash flow for the purchase of buildings during Year 2.
f. Determine the amount of cash flow for the purchase of land during Year 2.
g. Prepare the investing activities section of the Year 2 statement of cash flows.

Problem 14-16A *Determining cash flows from financing activities*

LO 14-4

The following information was drawn from the year-end balance sheets of Fox River Inc.

CHECK FIGURES
c. $15,000
e. Net Cash Flow from Financing Activities: ($206,000) outflow

Account Title	Year 2	Year 1
Bonds payable	$600,000	$800,000
Common stock	210,000	180,000
Treasury stock	20,000	5,000
Retained earnings	86,000	75,000

Additional information regarding transactions occurring during Year 2:

1. Fox River Inc. issued $100,000 of bonds during Year 2. The bonds were issued at face value. All bonds retired were retired at face value.
2. Common stock did not have a par value.
3. Fox River Inc. uses the cost method to account for treasury stock.
4. The amount of net income shown on the Year 2 income statement was $32,000.

Required

a. Determine the amount of cash flow for the retirement of bonds that should appear on the Year 2 statement of cash flows.
b. Determine the amount of cash flow from the issue of common stock that should appear on the Year 2 statement of cash flows.
c. Determine the amount of cash flow for the purchase of treasury stock that should appear on the Year 2 statement of cash flows.
d. Determine the amount of cash flow for the payment of dividends that should appear on the Year 2 statement of cash flows.
e. Prepare the financing activities section of the Year 2 statement of cash flows.

Problem 14-17A *Preparing a statement of cash flows*

LO 14-1, 14-3, 14-4

The following information can be obtained by examining a company's balance sheet and income statement information:

a. Increases in current asset account balances, other than cash.
b. Decreases in current asset account balances, other than cash.
c. Cash outflows to purchase long-term assets.
d. Decreases in current liability account balances.
e. Cash outflows to repay long-term debt.
f. Gains recognized on the sale of long-term assets.
g. Noncash expenses (e.g., depreciation).
h. Cash outflows to purchase treasury stock.

i. Increases in current liability account balances.
j. Cash inflows from the sale of long-term assets.
k. Cash inflows from the issue of common stock.
l. Cash outflows to pay dividends.
m. Losses incurred from the sale of long-term assets.
n. Cash inflows from the issue of long-term debt.

Required

Construct a table like the following one. For each item, indicate whether it would be used in the computation of net cash flows from operating, investing, or financing activities. Also, indicate whether the item would be added or subtracted when determining the net cash flow from operating, investing, or financing activities. Assume the indirect method is used to prepare the operating activities section of the statement of cash flows. The first item has been completed as an example.

Item	Type of Activity	Add or Subtract
a.	Operating	Subtract
b.		

LO 14-1, 14-3, 14-4

CHECK FIGURES

Net Cash Flow from Operating Activities: $32,200

Net Increase in Cash: $16,200

Problem 14-18A *Using financial statements to prepare a statement of cash flows—indirect method*

The comparative balance sheets and income statements for Gypsy Company follow.

Balance Sheets As of December 31	Year 2	Year 1
Assets		
Cash	$ 32,500	$ 16,300
Accounts receivable	4,750	2,800
Inventory	11,200	9,800
Equipment	45,000	52,000
Accumulated depreciation—equipment	(17,800)	(21,800)
Land	28,000	12,000
Total assets	$103,650	$ 71,100
Liabilities and equity		
Accounts payable (inventory)	$ 3,750	$ 4,900
Long-term debt	5,800	7,800
Common stock	47,000	25,000
Retained earnings	47,100	33,400
Total liabilities and equity	$103,650	$ 71,100

Income Statement For the Year Ended December 31, Year 2	
Sales revenue	$ 61,200
Cost of goods sold	(24,500)
Gross margin	36,700
Depreciation expense	(12,000)
Operating income	24,700
Gain on sale of equipment	1,500
Loss on disposal of land	(100)
Net income	$ 26,100

Additional Data

1. During Year 2, the company sold equipment for $21,500; it had originally cost $36,000. Accumulated depreciation on this equipment was $16,000 at the time of the sale. Also, the company purchased equipment for $29,000 cash.
2. The company sold land that had cost $6,000. This land was sold for $5,900, resulting in the recognition of a $100 loss. Also, common stock was issued in exchange for title to land that was valued at $22,000 at the time of exchange.
3. Paid dividends of $12,400.

Required

Prepare a statement of cash flows using the indirect method.

Problem 14-19A ***Using financial statements to prepare a statement of cash flows—indirect method***

LO 14-1, 14-3, 14-4

eXcel

CHECK FIGURES

Net Cash Flow from Operating Activities: $45,900

Net Decrease in Cash: $42,100

The comparative balance sheets and an income statement for Raceway Corporation follow.

Balance Sheets As of December 31		
	Year 2	**Year 1**
Assets		
Cash	$ 6,300	$ 48,400
Accounts receivable	10,200	7,260
Merchandise inventory	45,200	56,000
Prepaid rent	700	2,140
Equipment	140,000	144,000
Accumulated depreciation	(73,400)	(118,000)
Land	116,000	50,000
Total assets	$245,000	$189,800
Liabilities		
Accounts payable (inventory)	$ 37,200	$ 40,000
Salaries payable	12,200	10,600
Stockholders' equity		
Common stock, $50 par value	150,000	120,000
Retained earnings	45,600	19,200
Total liabilities and equity	$245,000	$189,800

Income Statement For the Year Ended December 31, Year 2	
Sales	$ 480,000
Cost of goods sold	(264,000)
Gross profit	216,000
Operating expenses	
Depreciation expense	(11,400)
Rent expense	(7,000)
Salaries expense	(95,200)
Other operating expenses	(76,000)
Net income	$ 26,400

Other Information

1. Purchased land for $66,000.
2. Purchased new equipment for $62,000.
3. Sold old equipment that cost $66,000 with accumulated depreciation of $56,000 for $10,000 cash.
4. Issued common stock for $30,000.

Required

Prepare the statement of cash flows for Year 2 using the indirect method.

LO 14-2, 14-3, 14-4

CHECK FIGURE

Net Cash Flow from Operating Activities: $(900)

Problem 14-20A *Using transaction data to prepare a statement of cash flows—direct method*

York Company engaged in the following transactions for Year 1. The beginning cash balance was $86,000 and the ending cash balance was $59,100.

1. Sales on account were $548,000. The beginning receivables balance was $128,000 and the ending balance was $90,000.
2. Salaries expense for the period was $232,000. The beginning salaries payable balance was $16,000 and the ending balance was $8,000.
3. Other operating expenses for the period were $236,000. The beginning other operating expenses payable balance was $16,000 and the ending balance was $10,000.
4. Recorded $30,000 of depreciation expense. The beginning and ending balances in the Accumulated Depreciation account were $12,000 and $42,000, respectively.
5. The Equipment account had beginning and ending balances of $44,000 and $56,000, respectively. There were no sales of equipment during the period.
6. The beginning and ending balances in the Notes Payable account were $36,000 and $44,000, respectively. There were no payoffs of notes during the period.
7. There was $4,600 of interest expense reported on the income statement. The beginning and ending balances in the Interest Payable account were $8,400 and $7,500, respectively.
8. The beginning and ending Merchandise Inventory account balances were $22,000 and $29,400, respectively. The company sold merchandise with a cost of $83,600 (cost of goods sold for the period was $83,600). The beginning and ending balances in the Accounts Payable account were $8,000 and $6,400, respectively.
9. The beginning and ending balances in the Notes Receivable account were $60,000 and $100,000, respectively. Notes receivable result from long-term loans made to employees. There were no collections from employees during the period.
10. The beginning and ending balances in the Common Stock account were $120,000 and $160,000, respectively. The increase was caused by the issue of common stock for cash.
11. Land had beginning and ending balances of $24,000 and $14,000, respectively. Land that cost $10,000 was sold for $6,000, resulting in a loss of $4,000.
12. The tax expense for the period was $6,600. The Taxes Payable account had a $2,400 beginning balance and a $2,200 ending balance.
13. The Investments account had beginning and ending balances of $20,000 and $60,000, respectively. The company purchased investments for $50,000 cash during the period, and investments that cost $10,000 were sold for $22,000, resulting in a $12,000 gain.

Required

a. Determine the amount of cash flow for each item and indicate whether the item should appear in the operating, investing, or financing activities section of a statement of cash flows. Also identify any items that do not affect the cash flow statement. Assume York Company uses the direct method for showing net cash flow from operating activities.
b. Prepare a statement of cash flows based on the information you developed in Requirement *a*.

Problem 14-21A ***Using financial statements to prepare a statement of cash flows—direct method***

LO 14-2, 14-3, 14-4

CHECK FIGURES

Net Cash Flow from Operating Activities: $56,200

Net Increase in Cash: $80,200

The following financial statements were drawn from the records of Matrix Shoes.

Balance Sheets As of December 31		
	Year 2	**Year 1**
Assets		
Cash	$ 94,300	$ 14,100
Accounts receivable	36,000	40,000
Merchandise inventory	72,000	64,000
Notes receivable	0	16,000
Equipment	98,000	170,000
Accumulated depreciation—equipment	(47,800)	(94,000)
Land	46,000	30,000
Total assets	$298,500	$240,100
Liabilities		
Accounts payable	$ 24,000	$ 26,400
Salaries payable	15,000	10,000
Utilities payable	800	1,400
Interest payable	0	1,000
Notes payable (long-term)	0	24,000
Common stock	150,000	110,000
Retained earnings	108,700	67,300
Total liabilities and equity	$298,500	$240,100

Income Statement For the Year Ended December 31, Year 2	
Sales revenue	$ 300,000
Cost of goods sold	(144,000)
Gross margin	156,000
Operating expenses	
Salary expense	(88,000)
Depreciation expense	(9,800)
Utilities expense	(6,400)
Operating income	51,800
Nonoperating items	
Interest expense	(2,400)
Loss on the sale of equipment	(800)
Net income	$ 48,600

Additional Information

1. Sold equipment costing $72,000 with accumulated depreciation of $56,000 for $15,200 cash.
2. Paid a $7,200 cash dividend to owners.

Required

Analyze the data and prepare a statement of cash flows using the direct method.

EXERCISES—SERIES B

LO 14-1

Exercise 14-1B *Use the indirect method to determine cash flows from operating activities*

An accountant for Farve Enterprise Companies (FEC) computed the following information by making comparisons between FEC's Year 2 and Year 1 balance sheets. Further information was determined by examining the company's Year 2 income statement.

1. The amount of an increase in the balance of a Prepaid Rent account.
2. The amount of an increase in the balance of a Treasury Stock account.
3. The amount of a decrease in the balance of the Accounts Receivable account.
4. The amount of a gain arising from the sale of land.
5. The amount of an increase in the balance of the Salaries Payable account.
6. The amount of an increase in the balance of the Bonds Payable account.
7. The amount of depreciation expense shown on the income statement.
8. The amount of cash dividends paid to the stockholders.
9. The amount of an increase in the balance of an Unearned Revenue account.
10. The amount of a decrease in the balance of an Inventory account.
11. The amount of a decrease in the balance of a Land account.

Required

For each item in the preceding list, indicate whether the amount should be added to or subtracted from the amount of net income when determining the amount of net cash flow from operating activities using the indirect method. Also identify any items that do not affect net cash flow from operating activities because they are reported as investing or financing activities.

LO 14-1

Exercise 14-2B *Use the indirect method to determine cash flows from operating activities*

Napoleon Incorporated presents its statement of cash flows using the indirect method. The following accounts and corresponding balances were drawn from the company's Year 2 and Year 1 year-end balance sheets.

Account Title	Year 2	Year 1
Accounts receivable	$31,400	$28,600
Accounts payable	10,300	9,800

The Year 2 income statement showed net income of $41,500.

Required

a. Prepare the operating activities section of the statement of cash flows.

b. Explain why the change in the balance in accounts receivable was added to or subtracted from the amount of net income when you completed Requirement *a*.

c. Explain why the change in the balance in accounts payable was added to or subtracted from the amount of net income when you completed Requirement *a*.

LO 14-1

Exercise 14-3B *Use the indirect method to determine cash flows from operating activities*

Pella Company presents its statement of cash flows using the indirect method. The following accounts and corresponding balances were drawn from Pella's Year 2 and Year 1 year-end balance sheets.

Account Title	Year 2	Year 1
Accounts receivable	$24,000	$21,000
Prepaid rent	1,650	1,900
Interest receivable	900	1,200
Accounts payable	10,200	8,500
Salaries payable	2,700	2,900
Unearned revenue	2,000	1,800

The income statement reported a $700 loss on the sale of equipment, a $900 gain on the sale of land, and $2,500 of depreciation expense. Net income for the period was $36,500.

Required

Prepare the operating activities section of the statement of cash flows.

Exercise 14-4B *Use the direct method to determine cash flows from operating activities*

LO 14-2

The following accounts and corresponding balances were drawn from Osprey Company's Year 2 and Year 1 year-end balance sheets.

Account Title	Year 2	Year 1
Unearned revenue	$4,500	$6,000
Prepaid rent	5,200	3,600

During the year, $84,000 of unearned revenue was recognized as having been earned. Rent expense for Year 2 was $24,000.

Required

Based on this information alone, prepare the operating activities section of the statement of cash flows assuming the direct approach is used.

Exercise 14-5B *Use the direct method to determine cash flows from operating activities*

LO 14-2

The following accounts and corresponding balances were drawn from Pixi Company's Year 2 and Year 1 year-end balance sheets.

Account Title	Year 2	Year 1
Accounts receivable	$62,000	$56,000
Interest receivable	8,000	6,000
Other operating expenses payable	26,000	29,000
Salaries payable	12,000	9,000

The Year 2 income statement is shown as follows.

Income Statement	
Sales	$ 650,000
Salary expense	(420,000)
Other operating expenses	(110,000)
Operating income	120,000
Nonoperating items: Interest revenue	15,000
Net income	$ 135,000

Required

a. Use the direct method to compute the amount of cash inflows from operating activities.

b. Use the direct method to compute the amount of cash outflows from operating activities.

LO 14-1, 14-2

Exercise 14-6B *Direct versus indirect method of determining cash flows from operating activities*

Ragg Shop Inc. (RSI) recognized $3,800 of sales revenue on account and collected $2,950 of cash from accounts receivable. Further, RSI recognized $1,200 of operating expenses on account and paid $900 cash as partial settlement of accounts payable.

Required

Based on this information alone:

a. Prepare the operating activities section of the statement of cash flows under the direct method.

b. Prepare the operating activities section of the statement of cash flows under the indirect method.

LO 14-1, 14-2

Exercise 14-7B *The direct versus the indirect method of determining cash flows from operating activities*

The following accounts and corresponding balances were drawn from Geneses Company's Year 2 and Year 1 year-end balance sheets.

Account Title	Year 2	Year 1
Accounts receivable	$65,000	$72,000
Prepaid rent	1,400	1,950
Utilities payable	3,200	3,800
Other operating expenses payable	27,000	31,500

The Year 2 income statement is shown as follows.

Income Statement	
Sales	$ 420,000
Rent expense	(52,000)
Utilities expense	(45,300)
Other operating expenses	(195,000)
Net income	$ 127,700

Required

a. Prepare the operating activities section of the statement of cash flows using the direct method.

b. Prepare the operating activities section of the statement of cash flows using the indirect method.

LO 14-3

Exercise 14-8B *Determining cash flow from investing activities*

On January 1, Year 1, Poole Company had a balance of $178,000 in its Land account. During Year 1, Poole sold land that had cost $71,000 for $95,000 cash. The balance in the Land account on December 31, Year 1, was $210,000.

Required

a. Determine the cash outflow for the purchase of land during Year 1.

b. Prepare the investing activities section of the Year 1 statement of cash flows.

LO 14-3

Exercise 14-9B *Determining cash flow from investing activities*

On January 1, Year 1, Sanita Company had a balance of $76,300 in its Office Equipment account. During Year 1, Sanita purchased office equipment that cost $30,300. The balance in the Office Equipment account on December 31, Year 1, was $75,400. The Year 1 income statement contained a gain from the sale of equipment of $6,000. On the date of sale, accumulated depreciation on the equipment sold amounted to $14,400.

Required

a. Determine the cost of the equipment that was sold during Year 1.

b. Determine the amount of cash flow from the sale of office equipment that should be shown in the investing activities section of the Year 1 statement of cash flows.

Exercise 14-10B *Determining cash flows from investing activities* LO 14-3

The following accounts and corresponding balances were drawn from Teva Company's Year 2 and Year 1 year-end balance sheets.

Account Title	Year 2	Year 1
Investment securities	$102,000	$110,000
Machinery	480,000	465,000
Land	75,000	95,000

Other information drawn from the accounting records:

1. Teva incurred a $3,000 loss on the sale of investment securities during Year 2.
2. Old machinery with a book value of $8,000 (cost of $34,000 minus accumulated depreciation of $26,000) was sold. The income statement showed a gain on the sale of machinery of $7,500.
3. Teva incurred a loss of $4,000 on the sale of land in Year 2.

Required

a. Compute the amount of cash flow associated with the sale of investment securities.

b. Compute the amount of cash flow associated with the purchase of machinery.

c. Compute the amount of cash flow associated with the sale of machinery.

d. Compute the amount of cash flow associated with the sale of land.

e. Prepare the investing activities section of the statement of cash flows.

Exercise 14-11B *Determining cash flows from financing activities* LO 14-4

On January 1, Year 1, Van Company had a balance of $800,000 in its Bonds Payable account. During Year 1, Van issued bonds with a $300,000 face value. There was no premium or discount associated with the bond issue. The balance in the Bonds Payable account on December 31, Year 1, was $600,000.

Required

a. Determine the cash outflow for the repayment of bond liabilities assuming that the bonds were retired at face value.

b. Prepare the financing activities section of the Year 1 statement of cash flows.

Exercise 14-12B *Determining cash flows from financing activities* LO 14-4

On January 1, Year 1, Milam Company had a balance of $300,000 in its Common Stock account. During Year 1, Milam paid $18,000 to purchase treasury stock. Treasury stock is accounted for using the cost method. The balance in the Common Stock account on December 31, Year 1, was $350,000. Assume that the common stock is no par stock.

Required

a. Determine the cash inflow from the issue of common stock.

b. Prepare the financing activities section of the Year 1 statement of cash flows.

LO 14-4

Exercise 14-13B *Determining cash flows from financing activities*

The following accounts and corresponding balances were drawn from Cushing Company's Year 2 and Year 1 year-end balance sheets.

Account Title	Year 2	Year 1
Bonds payable	$200,000	$150,000
Common stock	650,000	400,000

Other information drawn from the accounting records:

1. Dividends paid during the period amounted to $50,000.
2. There were no bond liabilities repaid during the period.

Required

a. Compute the amount of cash flow associated with the issue of bond liabilities.
b. Compute the amount of cash flow associated with the issue of common stock.
c. Prepare the financing activities section of the statement of cash flows.

PROBLEMS—SERIES B

LO 14-1, 14-2

Problem 14-14B *The direct versus the indirect method of determining cash flows from operating activities*

The following accounts and corresponding balances were drawn from Crimson Sports Inc.'s Year 2 and Year 1 year-end balance sheets. Assume that Accounts Payable is used for purchases of inventory only.

Account Title	Year 2	Year 1
Accounts receivable	$31,000	$36,000
Merchandise inventory	70,000	65,000
Prepaid insurance	25,000	24,000
Accounts payable	18,000	20,000
Salaries payable	5,100	4,500
Unearned service revenue	10,200	9,500

The Year 2 income statement is shown as follows.

Income Statement	
Sales	$ 495,000
Cost of goods sold	(215,000)
Gross margin	280,000
Service revenue	20,000
Insurance expense	(42,000)
Salaries expense	(122,000)
Depreciation expense	(12,000)
Operating income	124,000
Gain on sale of equipment	1,500
Net income	$ 125,500

Required

a. Prepare the operating activities section of the statement of cash flows using the direct method.
b. Prepare the operating activities section of the statement of cash flows using the indirect method.

Problem 14-15B *Determining cash flows from investing activities*

LO 14-3

The following information was drawn from the year-end balance sheets of Vigotti Company.

Account Title	Year 2	Year 1
Investment securities	$ 51,000	$ 60,000
Equipment	310,000	275,000
Buildings	980,000	950,000
Land	135,000	110,000

Additional information regarding transactions occurring during Year 2:

1. Investment securities that had cost $11,300 were sold. The Year 2 income statement contained a loss on the sale of investment securities of $800.
2. Equipment with a cost of $80,000 was purchased.
3. The income statement showed a gain on the sale of equipment of $9,500. On the date of sale, accumulated depreciation on the equipment sold amounted to $38,000.
4. A building that had originally cost $90,000 was demolished.
5. Land that had cost $20,000 was sold for $15,000.

Required

a. Determine the amount of cash flow for the purchase of investment securities during Year 2.
b. Determine the amount of cash flow from the sale of investment securities during Year 2.
c. Determine the cost of the equipment that was sold during Year 2.
d. Determine the amount of cash flow from the sale of equipment during Year 2.
e. Determine the amount of cash flow for the purchase of buildings during Year 2.
f. Determine the amount of cash flow for the purchase of land during Year 2.
g. Prepare the investing activities section of the Year 2 statement of cash flows.

Problem 14-16B *Determining cash flows from financing activities*

LO 14-4

The following information was drawn from the year-end balance sheets of Long's Wholesale Inc.

Account Title	Year 2	Year 1
Bonds payable	$400,000	$600,000
Common stock	190,000	150,000
Treasury stock	20,000	15,000
Retained earnings	96,000	80,000

Additional information regarding transactions occurring during Year 2:

1. Long's Wholesale Inc. issued $90,000 of bonds during Year 2. The bonds were issued at face value. All bonds retired were retired at face value.
2. Common stock did not have a par value.
3. Long's Wholesale Inc. uses the cost method to account for treasury stock. Long's Wholesale Inc. did not resell any treasury stock in Year 2.
4. The amount of net income shown on the Year 2 income statement was $49,000.

Required

a. Determine the amount of cash flow for the retirement of bonds that should appear on the Year 2 statement of cash flows.
b. Determine the amount of cash flow from the issue of common stock that should appear on the Year 2 statement of cash flows.
c. Determine the amount of cash flow for the purchase of treasury stock that should appear on the Year 2 statement of cash flows.

d. Determine the amount of cash flow for the payment of dividends that should appear on the Year 2 statement of cash flows.

e. Prepare the financing activities section of the Year 2 statement of cash flows.

LO 14-1, 14-3, 14-4

Problem 14-17B *Preparing a statement of cash flows*

The following information can be obtained by examining a company's balance sheet and income statement information:

a. Increases in current asset account balances, other than cash.
b. Cash outflows to purchase noncurrent assets.
c. Decreases in current liability account balances.
d. Noncash expenses (e.g., depreciation).
e. Cash outflows to purchase treasury stock.
f. Gains recognized on the sale of noncurrent assets.
g. Cash outflows to pay dividends.
h. Cash inflows from the issue of common stock.
i. Cash inflows from the sale of noncurrent assets.
j. Increases in current liability account balances.
k. Cash inflows from the issue of noncurrent debt.
l. Losses incurred from the sale of noncurrent assets.
m. Decreases in current asset account balances, other than cash.
n. Cash outflows to repay noncurrent debt.

Required

Construct a table like the following one. For each item, indicate whether it would be used in the computation of net cash flows from operating, investing, or financing activities. Also, indicate whether the item would be added or subtracted when determining the net cash flow from operating, investing, or financing activities. Assume the indirect method is used to prepare the operating activities section of the statement of cash flows. The first item has been completed as an example.

Item	Type of Activity	Add or Subtract
a.	Operating	Subtract
b.		

LO 14-1, 14-3, 14-4

Problem 14-18B *Using financial statements to prepare a statement of cash flows—indirect method*

The following financial statements were drawn from the records of Culinary Products Co.

Balance Sheets As of December 31		
	Year 2	Year 1
Assets		
Cash	$24,200	$ 2,800
Accounts receivable	2,000	1,200
Inventory	6,400	6,000
Equipment	19,000	42,000
Accumulated depreciation—Equipment	(9,000)	(17,400)
Land	18,400	10,400
Total assets	$61,000	$ 45,000
Liabilities and stockholders' equity		
Accounts payable (inventory)	$ 2,600	$ 4,200
Long-term debt	2,800	6,400
Common stock	22,000	10,000
Retained earnings	33,600	24,400
Total liabilities and stockholders' equity	$61,000	$ 45,000

Income Statement For the Year Ended December 31, Year 2	
Sales revenue	$ 35,700
Cost of goods sold	(14,150)
Gross margin	21,550
Depreciation expense	(3,600)
Operating income	17,950
Gain on sale of equipment	500
Loss on disposal of land	(50)
Net income	$ 18,400

Additional Data

1. During Year 2, the company sold equipment for $18,500; it had originally cost $30,000. Accumulated depreciation on this equipment was $12,000 at the time of the sale. Also, the company purchased equipment for $7,000 cash.
2. The company sold land that had cost $4,000. This land was sold for $3,950, resulting in the recognition of a $50 loss. Also, common stock was issued in exchange for title to land that was valued at $12,000 at the time of exchange.
3. Paid dividends of $9,200.

Required

Prepare a statement of cash flows using the indirect method.

Problem 14-19B ***Using financial statements to prepare a statement of cash flows—indirect method*** **LO 14-1, 14-3, 14-4**

The comparative balance sheets and an income statement for Wang Beauty Products Inc. are shown as follows.

Balance Sheets As of December 31	Year 2	Year 1
Assets		
Cash	$ 68,800	$ 40,600
Accounts receivable	30,000	22,000
Merchandise inventory	160,000	176,000
Prepaid rent	2,400	4,800
Equipment	256,000	288,000
Accumulated depreciation	(146,800)	(236,000)
Land	192,000	80,000
Total assets	$ 562,400	$ 375,400
Liabilities and equity		
Accounts payable (inventory)	$ 67,000	$ 76,000
Salaries payable	28,000	24,000
Stockholders' equity		
Common stock, $50 par value	250,000	200,000
Retained earnings	217,400	75,400
Total liabilities and equity	$ 562,400	$ 375,400

Income Statement For the Year Ended December 31, Year 2	
Sales	$1,500,000
Cost of goods sold	(797,200)
Gross profit	702,800
Operating expenses	
Depreciation expense	(22,800)
Rent expense	(24,000)
Salaries expense	(256,000)
Other operating expenses	(258,000)
Net income	$ 142,000

Other Information

1. Purchased land for $112,000.
2. Purchased new equipment for $100,000.
3. Sold old equipment that cost $132,000 with accumulated depreciation of $112,000 for $20,000 cash.
4. Issued common stock for $50,000.

Required

Prepare the statement of cash flows for Year 2 using the indirect method.

LO 14-2, 14-3, 14-4

Problem 14-20B ***Using transaction data to prepare a statement of cash flows—direct method***

The Electric Company engaged in the following transactions during Year 2. The beginning cash balance was $43,000 and the ending cash balance was $48,600.

1. Sales on account were $274,000. The beginning receivables balance was $86,000 and the ending balance was $74,000.
2. Salaries expense was $115,000. The beginning salaries payable balance was $9,600 and the ending balance was $7,500.
3. Other operating expenses were $118,000. The beginning Other Operating Expenses Payable balance was $8,500 and the ending balance was $6,000.
4. Recorded $25,000 of depreciation expense. The beginning and ending balances in the Accumulated Depreciation account were $18,000 and $43,000, respectively.
5. The Equipment account had beginning and ending balances of $28,000 and $42,000, respectively. There were no sales of equipment during the period.
6. The beginning and ending balances in the Notes Payable account were $38,000 and $32,000, respectively. There were no notes payable issued during the period.
7. There was $4,600 of interest expense reported on the income statement. The beginning and ending balances in the Interest Payable account were $6,400 and $6,200, respectively.
8. The beginning and ending Merchandise Inventory account balances were $26,000 and $32,500, respectively. The company sold merchandise with a cost of $119,000. The beginning and ending balances in the Accounts Payable account were $10,000 and $12,500, respectively.
9. The beginning and ending balances in the Notes Receivable account were $80,000 and $20,000, respectively. Notes receivable result from long-term loans made to creditors. There were no loans made to creditors during the period.
10. The beginning and ending balances in the Common Stock account were $140,000 and $190,000, respectively. The increase was caused by the issue of common stock for cash.
11. Land had beginning and ending balances of $48,000 and $28,000, respectively. Land that cost $20,000 was sold for $16,000, resulting in a loss of $4,000.
12. The tax expense for the period was $6,600. The Tax Payable account had a $3,200 beginning balance and a $2,800 ending balance.

13. The Investments account had beginning and ending balances of $10,000 and $30,000, respectively. The company purchased investments for $40,000 cash during the period, and investments that cost $20,000 were sold for $26,000, resulting in a $6,000 gain.

Required

a. Determine the amount of cash flow for each item and indicate whether the item should appear in the operating, investing, or financing activities section of a statement of cash flows. Also identify any items that do not affect the cash flow statement. Assume The Electric Company uses the direct method for showing net cash flow from operating activities.

b. Prepare a statement of cash flows based on the information you developed in Requirement *a.*

Problem 14-21B *Using financial statements to prepare a statement of cash flows—direct method*

LO 14-2, 14-3, 14-4

The following financial statements were drawn from the records of Boston Materials Inc.

Balance Sheets As of December 31		
	Year 2	Year 1
Assets		
Cash	$ 99,700	$ 25,400
Accounts receivable	72,000	60,000
Inventory	86,000	75,000
Notes receivable (long-term)	0	24,000
Equipment	104,000	152,000
Accumulated depreciation—equipment	(67,500)	(75,000)
Land	60,000	45,000
Total assets	$354,200	$306,400
Liabilities and equity		
Accounts payable	$ 35,300	$36,200
Salaries payable	18,200	15,500
Utilities payable	1,400	2,800
Interest payable	600	1,200
Notes payable (long-term)	0	36,000
Common stock	120,000	100,000
Retained earnings	178,700	114,700
Total liabilities and equity	$354,200	$306,400

Income Statement For the Year Ended December 31, Year 2	
Sales revenue	$ 450,000
Cost of goods sold	(212,000)
Gross margin	238,000
Operating expenses	
Salary expense	(96,000)
Depreciation expense	(18,500)
Utilities expense	(7,500)
Operating income	116,000
Nonoperating items	
Interest expense	(3,500)
Gain on sale of equipment	1,500
Net income	$ 114,000

Additional Information

1. Sold equipment costing $48,000 with accumulated depreciation of $26,000 for $23,500 cash.
2. Paid a $50,000 cash dividend to owners.

Required

Analyze the data and prepare a statement of cash flows using the direct method.

ANALYZE, THINK, COMMUNICATE

ATC 14-1 Real-World Case *Following the cash*

Tesla Inc. began operations in 2003 but did not begin selling its stock to the public until June 28, 2010. It has lost money every year it has been in existence, and by December 31, 2016, it had total lifetime losses of approximately $3 billion. In addition to making automobiles, Tesla makes energy storage systems. Tesla's statements of cash flows for 2014, 2015, and 2016 follow.

TESLA INC.
Consolidated Statements of Cash Flows
(in thousands)

	For the Years Ending December 31		
	2016	2015	2014
Cash flows from operating activities:			
Net loss	$ (773,046)	$ (888,663)	$ (294,040)
Adjustments to reconcile net loss to net cash used in operating activities:			
Depreciation and amortization	947,099	422,590	231,931
Stock-based compensation	334,225	197,999	156,496
Amortization of discount on convertible debt	87,286	72,063	69,734
Inventory write-downs	65,520	44,940	15,609
Loss on disposal of property and equipment	34,633	37,723	14,178
Foreign currency transaction (gain) loss	(29,183)	55,765	(1,891)
Gain on the acquisition of SolarCity	(88,727)	—	—
Non-cash interest and other operating activities	(7,775)	26,373	7,471
Changes in operating assets and liabilities, net of effect of business combinations			
Accounts receivable	(216,565)	46,267	(183,658)
Inventories and operating lease vehicles	(2,465,703)	(1,573,860)	(1,050,264)
Prepaid expenses and other current assets	56,806	(29,595)	(60,637)
MyPower notes receivable	3,468	—	—
Other assets	(52,821)	(24,362)	(4,493)
Accounts payable and accrued liabilities	750,640	263,345	414,856
Deferred revenue	382,962	322,203	209,681
Customer deposits	388,361	36,721	106,230
Resale value guarantee	326,934	442,295	249,492
Other long-term liabilities	132,057	23,697	61,968
Net cash flows from operating activities	(123,829)	(524,499)	(57,337)
Cash flows from investing activities:			
Purchases of property and equipment excluding capital leases, net of sales	(1,280,802)	(1,634,850)	(969,885)
Purchase of solar energy system, to be leased	(159,669)	—	—
Purchase of short-term investments and marketable securities	—	—	(205,841)
Maturities of short-term marketable securities	16,667	—	189,131
Increase in restricted cash	(206,149)	(26,441)	(3,849)
Cash acquired through (used in) business combinations	213,523	(12,260)	—
Net cash flows from investing activities	$(1,416,430)	$(1,673,551)	$ (990,444)

continued

	For the Years Ending December 31		
	2016	2015	2014
Cash flows from financing activities:			
Proceeds from issuance of common stock in initial public offering	$ 1,701,734	$ 730,000	$ —
Proceeds from issuance of convertible and other debt	2,852,964	318,972	2,300,000
Repayments of convertible and other debt	(1,857,594)	—	—
Collateralized lease borrowing	769,709	568,745	3,271
Proceeds from exercise of stock options and other stock issuances	163,817	106,611	100,455
Principal payments on capital leases	(46,889)	(203,780)	(11,179)
Common stock and debt issuance costs	(20,042)	(17,025)	(35,149)
Proceeds from issuance of warrants	—	—	389,160
Proceeds from issuance of common stock in private placements	—	20,000	—
Purchase of convertible note hedges	—	—	(603,428)
Proceeds from investment by noncontrolling interests in subsidiaries	201,527	—	—
Distributions paid to noncontrolling interests in subsidiaries	(21,250)	—	—
Net cash flows from financing activities	3,743,976	1,523,523	2,143,130
Effect of exchange rate changes on cash and cash equivalents	(7,409)	(34,278)	(35,525)
Net increase (decrease) in cash and cash equivalents	2,196,308	(708,805)	1,059,824
Cash and cash equivalents at beginning of period	1,196,908	1,905,713	845,889
Cash and cash equivalents at end of period	$ 3,393,216	$ 1,196,908	$ 1,905,713

a. As this chapter explained, many companies that report net losses on their earnings statements report positive cash flows from operating activities. How do Tesla's net incomes compare to its cash flows from operating activities?

b. Based only on the information in the statements of cash flows, does Tesla appear to be growing the capacity of its business? Explain.

c. In 2016, Tesla paid off $1.9 billion of "convertible and other debt." Where did it get the funds to repay this debt?

d. All things considered, based on the information in its statements of cash flows, does Tesla's cash position appear to be improving or deteriorating?

ATC 14-2 Group Assignment *Preparing a statement of cash flows*

The following financial statements and information are available for Blythe Industries Inc.

Balance Sheets As of December 31		
	Year 3	Year 2
Assets		
Cash	$ 160,200	$ 120,600
Accounts receivable	103,200	85,000
Inventory	186,400	171,800
Marketable securities (available for sale)	284,000	220,000
Equipment	650,000	490,000
Accumulated depreciation	(310,000)	(240,000)
Land	80,000	120,000
Total assets	$1,153,800	$ 967,400

continued

	Year 3	Year 2
Liabilities and equity		
Liabilities		
Accounts payable (inventory)	$ 36,400	$ 66,200
Notes payable—Long-term	230,000	250,000
Bonds payable	200,000	100,000
Total liabilities	466,400	416,200
Stockholders' equity		
Common stock, no par	240,000	200,000
Preferred stock, $50 par	110,000	100,000
Paid-in capital in excess of par—Preferred stock	34,400	26,800
Total paid-In capital	384,400	326,800
Retained earnings	333,000	264,400
Less: Treasury stock	(30,000)	(40,000)
Total stockholders' equity	687,400	551,200
Total liabilities and stockholders' equity	$1,153,800	$ 967,400

Income Statement For the Year Ended December 31, Year 3		
Sales revenue		$1,050,000
Cost of goods sold		(766,500)
Gross profit		283,500
Operating expenses		
Supplies expense	$20,400	
Salaries expense	92,000	
Depreciation expense	90,000	
Total operating expenses		(202,400)
Operating income		81,100
Nonoperating items		
Interest expense		(16,000)
Gain from the sale of marketable securities		30,000
Gain from the sale of land and equipment		12,000
Net income		$ 107,100

Additional Information

1. Sold land that cost $40,000 for $44,000.
2. Sold equipment that cost $30,000 and had accumulated depreciation of $20,000 for $18,000.
3. Purchased new equipment for $190,000.
4. Sold marketable securities that were classified as available-for-sale and that cost $40,000 for $70,000.
5. Purchased new marketable securities, classified as available-for-sale, for $104,000.
6. Paid $20,000 on the principal of the long-term note.
7. Paid off a $100,000 bond issue and issued new bonds for $200,000.
8. Sold 100 shares of treasury stock at its cost.
9. Issued some new common stock.
10. Issued some new $50 par preferred stock.
11. Paid dividends. (*Note:* The only transactions to affect retained earnings were net income and dividends.)

Required

Organize the class into three sections and divide each section into groups of three to five students. Assign each section of groups an activity section of the statement of cash flows (operating activities, investing activities, or financing activities).

Group Task

Prepare your assigned portion of the statement of cash flows. Have a representative of your section put your activity section of the statement of cash flows on the board. As each section adds its information on the board, the full statement of cash flows will be presented.

Class Discussion

Have the class finish the statement of cash flows by computing the net change in cash. Also have the class answer the following questions:

a. What is the cost per share of the treasury stock?

b. What was the issue price per share of the preferred stock?

c. What was the book value of the equipment sold?

ATC 14-3 Business Applications Case *Identifying different presentation formats*

In *Statement of Financial Accounting Standards No. 95,* the Financial Accounting Standards Board (FASB) recommended but did not require that companies use the direct method. In Appendix B, Paragraphs 106–121, the FASB discussed its reasons for this recommendation.

Required

Obtain a copy of *Standard No. 95* and read Appendix B Paragraphs 106–121. Write a brief response summarizing the issues that the FASB considered and its specific reaction to those issues. Your response should draw heavily on paragraphs 119–121.

ATC 14-4 Writing Assignment *Explaining discrepancies between cash flow and operating income*

The following selected information was drawn from the records of Fleming Company.

Assets	Year 2	Year 1
Accounts receivable	$ 840,200	$ 400,000
Merchandise inventory	1,480,000	720,000
Equipment	1,861,200	1,484,000
Accumulated depreciation	(402,400)	(312,000)

Fleming is experiencing cash flow problems. Despite the fact that it reported significant increases in operating income, operating activities produced a net cash outflow. Recent financial forecasts predict that Fleming will have insufficient cash to pay its current liabilities within three months.

Required

Write an explanation of Fleming's cash shortage. Include a recommendation to remedy the problem.

ATC 14-5 Ethical Dilemma *Would I lie to you, baby?*

Andy and Jean Crocket are involved in divorce proceedings. When discussing a property settlement, Andy told Jean that he should take over their investment in an apartment complex because she would be unable to absorb the loss that the apartments are generating. Jean was somewhat distrustful and asked Andy to support his contention. He produced the following income statement, which was supported by a CPA's unqualified opinion that the statement was prepared in accordance with generally accepted accounting principles.

CROCKET APARTMENTS Income Statement For the Year Ended December 31, Year 3		
Rent revenue		$ 580,000
Less: Expenses		
Depreciation expense	$280,000	
Interest expense	184,000	
Operating expense	88,000	
Management fees	56,000	
Total expenses		(608,000)
Net loss		$ (28,000)

All revenue is earned on account. Interest and operating expenses are incurred on account. Management fees are paid in cash. The following accounts and balances were drawn from the Year 2 and Year 3 year-end balance sheets.

Account Title	Year 3	Year 2
Rent receivable	$44,000	$40,000
Interest payable	18,000	12,000
Accounts payable (oper. exp.)	4,000	6,000

Jean is reluctant to give up the apartments but feels that she must do so because her present salary is only $40,000 per year. She says that if she takes the apartments, the $28,000 loss would absorb a significant portion of her salary, leaving her only $12,000 with which to support herself. She tells you that, while the figures seem to support her husband's arguments, she believes that she is failing to see something. She knows that she and her husband collected a $20,000 distribution from the business on December 1, Year 3. Also, $150,000 cash was paid in Year 3 to reduce the principal balance on a mortgage that was taken out to finance the purchase of the apartments two years ago. Finally, $24,000 cash was paid during Year 3 to purchase a computer system used in the business. She wonders, "If the apartments are losing money, where is my husband getting all the cash to make these payments?"

Required

a. Prepare a statement of cash flows for the Year 3 accounting period.

b. Compare the cash flow statement prepared in Requirement *a* with the income statement and provide Jean Crocket with recommendations.

c. Comment on the value of an unqualified audit opinion when using financial statements for decision-making purposes.

ATC 14-6 Research Assignment *Analyzing cash flow information*

In 2016 and 2015, Sears Holding Corporation reported net losses and negative cash flows from operating activities. Using the company's Form 10-K for the fiscal year ended January 28, 2017 (2016), complete the requirements shown in the following. The Form 10-K can be found on the company's website. It can also be obtained using the EDGAR system following the instructions in Appendix A.

Required

a. Determine Sears' net incomes and cash flow from operating activities for 2016 and 2015.

b. How was Sears able to pay its bills given that it has such large, negative net cash flows from operating activities in 2016 and 2015? Provide a separate answer for each year.

APPENDIX A

Accessing the EDGAR Database through the Internet

Successful business managers need many different skills, including communication, interpersonal, computer, and analytical skills. Most business students become very aware of the data analysis skills used in accounting, but they may not be as aware of the importance of "data-finding" skills. There are many sources of accounting and financial data. The more sources you are able to use, the better.

One very important source of accounting information is the EDGAR database. Others are probably available at your school through the library or business school network. Your accounting instructor will be able to identify these for you and make suggestions regarding their use. By making the effort to learn to use electronic databases, you will enhance your abilities as a future manager and your marketability as a business graduate.

These instructions assume that you know how to access and use an Internet browser. Follow the instructions to retrieve data from the Securities and Exchange Commission's EDGAR database. Be aware that the SEC may have changed its interface since this appendix was written. Accordingly, be prepared for slight differences between the following instructions and what appears on your computer screen. Take comfort in the fact that changes are normally designed to simplify user access. If you encounter a conflict between the following instructions and the instructions provided in the SEC interface, remember that the SEC interface is more current and should take precedence over the following instructions.

Most companies provide links to their SEC filings from their corporate website. These links are often simpler to use and provide more choices regarding file formats than the SEC's EDGAR site. On company websites, links to SEC filings are usually found under one of the following links: "Investor Relations," "Company Info," or "About Us."

1. Connect to the EDGAR database through the following address: www.sec.gov/.
2. After the SEC home page appears, under the **Filings** drop-down box, click on **Company Filings Search.**
3. On the screen that appears, enter the name of the company whose file you wish to retrieve and click on the **Search** button.
4. The next screen will present a list of companies that have the same, or similar, names to the one you entered. Identify the company you want and click on the CIK number beside it.
5. Enter the SEC form number that you wish to retrieve in the window titled **Filing Type** that appears in the upper left portion of the screen. For example, if you want Form 10-K, which will usually be the case, enter **10-K** and click the **Search** button.
6. A list of the forms you requested will be presented, along with the date they were filed. Click on the **Document** button next to the file you wish to retrieve.
7. Once the 10-K has been retrieved, you can search for it online or save it on your computer.
8. Often the 10-K will have a table of contents that can help locate the part of the report you need. The financial statements are seldom located at the beginning of the Form 10-K. They are usually in either Section 8 or Section 15.

Design Elements: Abstract texture: ©Ingram Publishing; Video Camera icon: ©McGraw-Hill Education; Check mark: ©McGraw-Hill Education; Look forward/backward icon: ©McGraw-Hill Education; Globe icon: ©McGraw-Hill Education; Globe with magnifying glass icon: ©McGraw-Hill Education; Pen and paper icon: ©McGraw-Hill Education; Group Assignment icon: ©McGraw-Hill Education; Ethics Cases icon: ©McGraw-Hill Education; Self-Study Review icon: ©Design Pics/Don Hammond; and Point de la Coubre lighthouse near Roy, France: ©Westend61/Getty Images.

APPENDIX B

Big Data and Data Visualizations Overview

Over the last decade, big data has fundamentally transformed the managerial decision process and provided a new, insightful way for managers to gauge company performance. *Big data* is a term that describes the large volume of information primarily captured by a variety of computerized systems. As a result of the Internet and advanced computerized devices, we have created more data in the last two years than in the history of the entire human race. This data is comprised of all types of information in both quantitative and qualitative form. Companies have begun collecting data in many forms, including financial information, customer demographics, and geographical information, to name a few.

While the rate at which data is being created and captured has exploded over the last decade, it is how companies utilize this data to make informed business decisions that makes the real difference in company performance. As an example, we have all seen major companies such as Google and Facebook collect large amounts of personal data from their customers in order to generate personalized ads. These ads represent the major sources of revenue for these tech giants, making big data a key element to their success. Other companies such as Salesforce.com have relied on big data to retain employees by examining wage disparities between men and women serving in the same role. Results from analysis revealed that wages were not consistent across genders, allowing the company to make the needed corrections to retain some of its top talent. The possibilities of using big data to improve enterprises are endless; however, companies require some powerful tools to analyze and process all this data to extract meaningful information.

Senior Vice President of Gartner, Peter Sondergaard, is quoted as saying, "Information is the oil of the 21st century, and analytics is the combustion engine." This quote exemplifies the importance of using analytical tools to extract the information an enterprise needs to make informed business decisions. Over the last decade, many software applications have been released to the market to assist managers in making use of big data. The tools perform a variety of functions in the big data environment, including data crawlers that capture all types of information from a variety of websites; tools that convert unstructured data into a structured form that can be analyzed; and software that converts data into a visual form, making interpretation of the data far easier. These examples represent only a small subset of the functions these tools perform. To provide an example of how big data can assist managers in making decisions, this appendix will focus on the third function, data visualizations.

We have all heard the quote that a picture is worth a thousand words, and this is certainly true when it comes to data visualizations. Data visualizations replace columns and rows of data with statistical graphics, plots, and information graphics. Examining data in visual form allows users to gain insights into their business far more efficiently than trying to make sense of raw data. One of the leading software tools for creating and analyzing data visualizations is called Tableau. The remainder of this appendix will give you the opportunity to learn more about Tableau by teaching you how to upload data into Tableau, create data visualizations from a raw dataset, and set up user dashboards that organize multiple data elements into a summary format.

Tableau Demonstration

In order to complete the exercise outlined in this appendix, you will need to download the student version of Tableau at the following URL: **https://www.tableau.com/academic/students**. We have provided a dataset (Super Store) for use in this exercise that can be obtained through *Connect*. Once you have downloaded Tableau and the "Super Store" dataset to your computer, we recommend watching the introduction to Tableau training video included in *Connect*. This video will walk you through the basics of Tableau and demonstrate the Tableau procedures required to complete this assignment.

Conducting Financial Statement Analysis in Tableau

This demonstration involves analyzing a dataset for Super Store, a retailer of office supplies. The company was founded by Jim Rogers, who knows a lot about office supplies but relies on his management team to help him understand the vast amount of data supplied by the company's computer systems. Super Store has performed exceptionally well over the last three years due to its rapid expansion into new markets. One of the major changes at Super Store over the last year was its expansion into the international market by opening stores in India. India's rapidly growing economy, compounded by the shortage of office supply stores, has provided a prosperous opportunity for Super Store. However, the expansion into international markets has come with challenges, resulting in Super Store management needing additional tools and expertise to understand how this new market is affecting its business.

Assume you were recently hired by Super Store management to assist the company in preparing data visualizations for financial statement analysis using Tableau. Historically the company has relied on companywide ratios to gauge performance but would like you to dig deeper into these ratios to provide a more detailed picture of operations at Super Store.

Super Store management has asked you to analyze two companywide ratios: accounts receivable turnover and average days outstanding. Refer to Chapter 13 for descriptions of these ratios. The company has provided you with a dataset containing a large variety of company data for use in your analysis. Recall that the dataset is called "Super Store" and can be found on the *Connect* course website.

Accounts Receivable Turnover

Historically, Super Store has analyzed the companywide accounts receivable ratio to gauge the quality of its collection policies and procedures. The company calculates this ratio using the following equation:

$$\frac{\text{Net credit sales}}{\text{Average accounts receivable}}$$

For purposes of this example, we assume Super Store's prior year accounts receivable balance was $4,975,830. Using this balance and the current year balance from the Super Store dataset, the AR turnover ratio for the company would be calculated as follows:

$$\frac{\$52{,}267{,}354}{(4{,}975{,}830 + 5{,}795{,}254)/2} = 9.71$$

The ratio of 9.71 tells us that the company collects its accounts receivable balances a little under 10 times a year. To make more sense of this number, the company also calculates the average number of days that accounts receivable is outstanding using the following equation:

$$\frac{\text{365 days}}{\text{Accounts receivable turnover}}$$

Using this equation, the company's average days outstanding is:

$$\frac{365}{9.71} = 38 \text{ days}$$

These companywide ratios tell management that, as a whole, the company collects its receivable a little under 10 times a year or every 38 days. Overall, these ratios would indicate that the company does a good job at collecting its outstanding receivable balances, indicating that its current policies and procedures for accounts receivable are effective. Relying solely on these companywide ratios would likely result in management making no changes to its current collection processes.

While the prior ratios are useful in gauging companywide performance, Super Store management has requested more detailed information analyzing collections across geographic regions. Specifically, management wants to know how collections differ between their stores in the United States compared to the stores in India. Jim Rogers, founder of Super Store, has asked you to prepare a data visualization that he can use for presentation purposes analyzing the turnover ratios.

In order to assist Mr. Rogers, you will be using Tableau to conduct an analysis on the Super Store dataset. Begin by opening the Tableau program and adding the Super Store data file to Tableau. Refer to the Introduction to Tableau video for instructions on how to add a dataset to Tableau and complete the visualization for Mr. Rogers.

The following two visualizations illustrate the accounts receivable turnover ratio and average days outstanding for the United States and India.

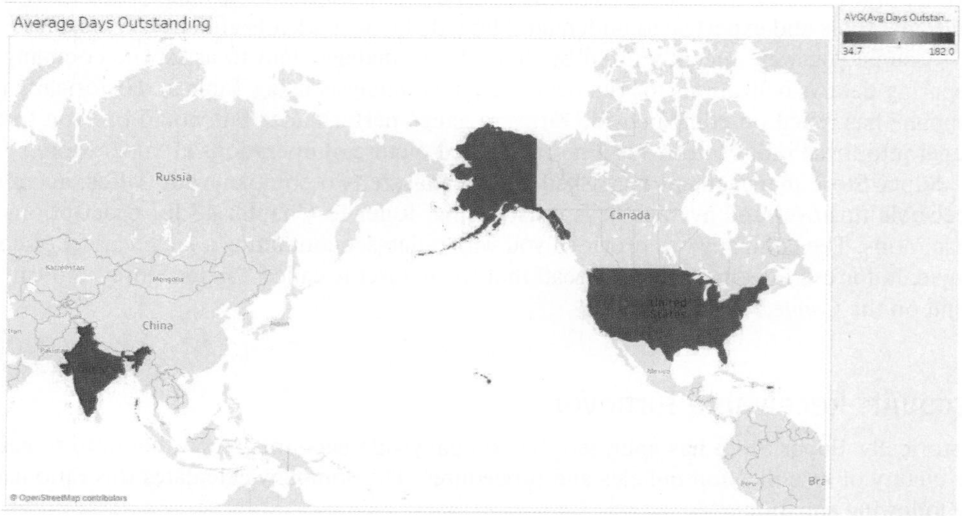

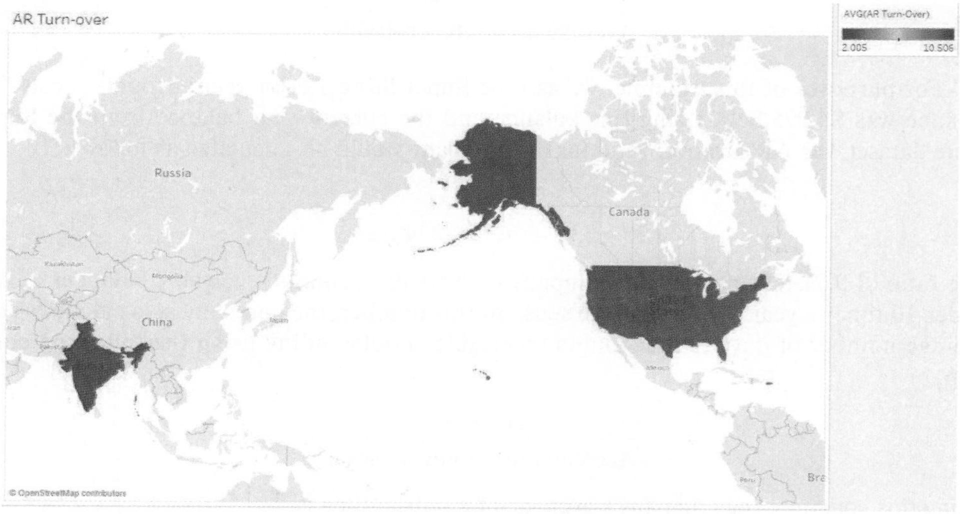

Both of these visualizations clearly show that there are large differences between the accounts receivable ratios for the United States and India. For the average days outstanding ratio, the color green indicates lower values and red represents higher values. Because most people associate good news with green and bad news with red, this color scheme appropriately reflects how to interpret this ratio. For the AR turnover ratio, higher numbers would be representative of good news; therefore, the color green was assigned to higher values and red to lower values. Using a common color scheme such as red for negative news and green for positive news sends a clear indicator about which country is performing better. Using the legend in the top right of the visualization gives us number information that corresponds to the colors. If you were to hover over each country, Tableau will display the exact numerical balance for each country.

Mr. Rogers could easily present these two visualizations to indicate to interested parties that the company is suffering collection problems in India as compared to the United States. These visualizations exemplify the importance of using visualizations to separate the ratios by country in order to better understand the differences between the two countries as compared to analyzing the ratios in total.

ASSIGNMENT 1

Required:

a. Recreate the visualization illustration using the Tableau skills obtained from watching the introduction to Tableau video.

b. Write a paragraph explaining the ratios for each country and what they mean with regard to the company's ability to collect its outstanding receivables in each country. Speculate as to the reasons for these differences and what the company could do to improve issues noted in the ratios.

GLOSSARY

absolute amounts Dollar totals reported on financial statements; using them in financial analysis comparisons can be misleading because they do not reflect materiality levels of the underlying companies. *p. 591*

absorption (full) costing Reporting method in which all product costs, including fixed manufacturing costs, are initially capitalized in inventory and then expensed when goods are sold. (Contrast with *variable costing.*) *p. 502*

accounts receivable turnover Financial ratio that measures how quickly accounts receivable are converted to cash; computed by dividing net credit sales by average net accounts receivable. *p. 597*

accumulated conversion factor Factor used to convert a series of future cash flows into their present value equivalent when applied to cash flows of equal amounts spread over equal interval time periods; this factor can be computed by adding the individual single factors applicable to each period. *p. 448*

acid-test ratio See *quick ratio. p. 596*

activities Measures an organization undertakes to accomplish its mission. *pp. 27, 209*

activity base Factor that causes changes in total variable cost; usually some measure of volume when used to explain cost behavior. *p. 63*

activity-based cost drivers Measures of activities that cause costs to be incurred, such as number of setups, percentage of use, and pounds of material delivered; using such measures as allocation bases can improve the accuracy of cost allocations in business environments where overhead costs are not driven by volume. *p. 297*

activity-based costing (ABC) A two-stage cost allocation process. First, costs associated with specific business activities are allocated or assigned to activity cost pools. Second, these pooled costs are allocated to designated cost objects by using a variety of appropriate cost drivers. The cost drivers chosen for each cost pool are those that most accurately reflect the demand placed on that cost pool by the cost object. *p 209*

activity-based management (ABM) Managing organization activities to add the greatest value by developing products that satisfy the needs of the organization's customers. *p. 27*

activity centers Cost centers composed of operating activities with similar characteristics; pooling indirect costs into activity centers reduces recordkeeping costs by allowing allocations based on a common cost driver for each center. *p. 209*

allocation Process of dividing a total cost into parts and assigning the parts to the relevant cost objects. *p. 158*

allocation base The factor used as the base for cost allocation; when possible, a driver of the allocated cost. *p. 159*

allocation rate The mathematical factor used to allocate or assign costs to a cost object, determined by dividing the total cost to be allocated by the appropriate cost driver or allocation base. *p. 159*

annuity Series of equal cash flows received or paid over equal time intervals at a constant rate of return. *p. 449*

applied fixed cost Total cost determined by multiplying the predetermined overhead rate times the actual volume of production. *p. 358*

applied overhead Amount of overhead costs assigned during the period to work in process using a predetermined overhead rate. *p. 493*

appraisal costs Costs of identifying nonconforming products produced regardless of prevention cost expenditures. *p. 218*

asset turnover ratio A measure of revenue dollars generated by the assets invested; calculated as net sales divided by average total assets. *p. 602*

average cost (per unit) The total cost of making products divided by the total number of products made. *p. 6*

average days to collect receivables (average collection period) Measure of how quickly, on average, a business collects its accounts receivable; calculated as 365 divided by the accounts receivable turnover. *p. 598*

average days to sell inventory (average days in inventory) Measure of how quickly, on average, a business sells its inventory; calculated as 365 divided by the inventory turnover ratio. *p. 598*

avoidable costs Potential future costs an organization can circumvent by choosing a particular course of action. To be avoidable, costs must differ among decision alternatives. For example, if materials cost for two different products is the same for each product, materials cost could not be avoided by choosing to produce one product instead of the other. The materials cost would therefore not be an avoidable cost. *p. 258*

balanced scorecard A management evaluation tool that uses both financial and nonfinancial measures to assess how well an organization is meeting its objectives. *p. 414*

batch-level activities Actions taken (e.g., materials handling, production setups) to produce groups of products, the cost of which is fixed regardless of the number of units produced in a batch. *p. 211*

batch-level costs The costs associated with producing a batch of products, most accurately allocated using cost drivers that measure activity levels. For example, the cost of setting up a press to print 500 copies of an engraved invitation is a batch-level cost. Classifying costs as batch-level is context sensitive. The postage to mail a single product would be classified as a unit-level cost. In contrast, the postage to mail a large number of products in a single shipment would be classified as a batch-level cost. *p. 259*

benchmarking Identifying best practices used by world-class competitors in a given industry. *p. 26*

best practices Identifiable procedures used by world-class companies. *p. 26*

book value per share An accounting measure of a share of common stock, computed by dividing total stockholders' equity less preferred rights by the number of common shares outstanding. *p. 604*

bottleneck A constraint that limits a company's capacity to produce or sell its products, such as a piece of equipment that cannot produce enough component parts to fully occupy employees in the assembly department. *p. 272*

break-even point Sales volume at which total revenue equals total cost; can be expressed in units or sales dollars. *p. 112*

budgeting Form of planning that formalizes a company's goals and objectives in financial terms. *p. 306*

budget slack Difference between inflated and realistic standards. *p. 362*

capital budgeting Financial planning for the intermediate time range involving decisions such as whether to buy or lease equipment, purchase additional assets, or increase operating expenses to stimulate sales. *p. 308*

capital investments Purchases of operational assets involving a long-term commitment of funds that can be critically important to the company's ultimate success; costs normally recovered through using the assets. *p. 446*

cash budget A budget detailing expected future cash receipts and payments. *p. 317*

cash inflows Cash receipts, including cash generated from operating activities such as cash revenues or collections of accounts receivable; cash collected from investing activities such as selling investments; and cash collected from financing activities such as borrowing money or issuing stock. *p. 638*

cash outflows Cash disbursements, including cash paid for operating activities such as cash expenses or payments to settle accounts payable; cash paid for investing activities such as buying investments; and cash paid for financing activities such as repaying long-term debt or purchasing treasury stock. *p. 638*

certified suppliers Suppliers who have demonstrated reliability by providing the buyer with quality goods and services at desirable prices, usually in accord with strict delivery specifications; frequently offer the buyer preferred customer status in exchange for guaranteed purchase quantities and prompt payment schedules. *p. 264*

common costs Costs that are incurred to support more than one cost object but that cannot be traced to any specific object. *p. 158*

companywide allocation rate Factor based on a single measure of volume, such as direct labor hours, used to allocate all overhead cost to the company's products or other cost objects. *p. 206*

constraints Conditions that limit a business's ability to satisfy the demand for its products. *p. 272*

continuous improvement An ongoing process through which employees learn to eliminate waste, reduce response time, minimize defects, and simplify the design and delivery of products and services to customers; a feature of total quality management (TQM). *p. 27*

contribution margin The difference between sales revenue and variable cost; the amount available to pay for fixed cost and thereafter to provide a profit. *p. 67*

contribution margin per unit The sales price per unit minus the variable cost per unit. *p. 113*

contribution margin ratio The contribution margin per unit divided by the sales price per unit; can be used in cost-volume-profit analysis to calculate in dollars the break-even sales volume or the level of sales required to attain a desired profit. *p. 114*

controllability concept Evaluating managerial performance based only on revenue and costs under the manager's direct control. *p. 406*

controllable costs Costs that can be influenced by a particular manager's decisions and actions. *p. 158*

cost accumulation Measuring the cost of a particular object by combining many individual costs into a single total cost. *p. 156*

cost allocation Process of dividing a total cost into parts and assigning the parts to relevant objects. *pp. 12, 157*

cost averaging Measuring the cost per unit of a product or service by dividing the total production cost by the total activity base to which the cost pertains; average cost is often more relevant to pricing, performance evaluation, and control than actual cost. *p. 70*

cost-based transfer price Transfer price based on the historical or standard cost incurred by the supplying segment. *p. 418*

cost behavior How a cost changes (increase, decrease, remain constant) relative to changes in some measure of activity (e.g., the behavior of raw materials cost is to increase as the number of units of product made increases). *p. 60*

cost center A responsibility center that incurs costs but does not generate revenue. *p. 403*

cost driver Any factor, usually a volume measure, that causes cost to be incurred; sometimes described as *activity base* or *allocation base*. Changes in cost drivers, such as labor hours or machine hours, cause corresponding changes in cost. *p. 156*

cost objects Items for which managers need to measure cost; can be products, processes, departments, services, activities, and so on. *p. 154*

cost of capital Return paid to investors and creditors for supplying assets (capital); usually represents a company's minimum rate of return. *p. 447*

cost per equivalent unit Unit cost of product determined by dividing total production costs by the number of equivalent whole units; used to allocate product costs between processing departments (amount of ending inventory and amount of costs transferred to the subsequent department). *p. 552*

cost-plus pricing Strategy that sets the selling price at cost plus a markup equal to a percentage of the cost. *pp. 5, 116*

cost pool A collection of costs organized around a common cost driver. The cost pool, as opposed to individual costs, is allocated to cost objects using the common cost driver, thereby promoting efficiency in the allocation process. *p. 160*

cost structure The relative proportion of a company's variable and fixed costs to total cost. The percentage change in net income a company experiences for a given percentage change in sales volume is directly related to the company's cost structure. The greater a company's percentage of fixed to total costs, the more its net income will fluctuate with changes in sales. *p. 65*

cost tracing Assigning specific costs to the objects that cause their incurrence. *p. 157*

cost-volume-profit (CVP) analysis Management tool that reflects the interrelationships among sales prices, volume, fixed costs, and variable costs; used in determining the break-even point or the most profitable combination of these variables. *p. 111*

current ratio Measure of liquidity; calculated by dividing current assets by current liabilities. *p. 596*

debt to assets ratio Measures the percentage of a company's assets that are financed by debt. It is measured as total liabilities divided by total assets. *p. 599*

debt to equity ratio A comparison of a company's debt financing to its owners' financing. It is measured as total liabilities divided by total stockholders' equity. *p. 599*

decentralization Delegating authority and responsibility for business segment operation to lower-level managers. *p. 402*

differential revenue Revenues that are relevant to decision making because they differ among alternative courses of action. *p. 258*

direct cost Cost that is easily traceable to a cost object and for which it is economically feasible to do so. *p. 157*

direct labor Wages paid to production workers whose efforts can be easily and conveniently traced to products. *p. 9*

direct method (1) Allocation method that allocates service center costs directly to operating department cost pools; does not account for any relationships among service centers. (2) Method of reporting cash flows from operating activities on the statement of cash flows that shows individual categories of cash receipts from and cash payments for major activities (collections from customers, payments to suppliers, etc.). *pp. 174, 640*

direct raw materials Costs of raw materials used to make products that can be easily and conveniently traced to those products. *p. 9*

dividend yield Ratio for comparing stock dividends paid relative to the market price; calculated as dividends per share divided by market price per share. *p. 605*

downstream costs Costs incurred after the manufacturing process is complete, such as delivery costs and sales commissions. *p. 216*

earnings per share (EPS) Measure of the value of a share of common stock based on company earnings; calculated as net income available to common stockholders divided by the average number of outstanding common shares. *p. 604*

equation method Cost-volume-profit analysis technique that uses the algebraic relationship among sales, variable costs, fixed costs, and desired net income before taxes to solve for required sales volume. *p. 112*

equipment replacement decisions Deciding whether to replace existing equipment with newer equipment based on comparing the avoidable costs of keeping the old equipment or purchasing new equipment to determine which choice is more profitable. *p. 268*

equivalent whole units A quantity of partially completed goods expressed as an equivalent number of fully completed goods. *p. 551*

external failure costs Costs resulting from delivering defective goods to customers. *p. 218*

facility-level activities Actions taken (e.g., insuring the facility, providing plant maintenance, employing a company president) that benefit the production process as a whole. *p. 213*

facility-level costs Costs incurred to support the whole company or a segment thereof, not related to any specific product, batch, or unit of production or service and unavoidable unless the entire company or segment is eliminated; they are so indirect that any allocation of facility-level costs is necessarily arbitrary. *p. 259*

failure costs Costs resulting from producing or providing nonconforming products or services. *p. 218*

financial accounting Branch of accounting focused on the business information needs of external users (creditors, investors, governmental agencies, financial analysts, etc.); its objective is to classify and record business events and transactions to produce external financial reports (income statement, balance sheet, statement of cash flows, and statement of changes in equity). *p. 3*

Financial Accounting Standards Board (FASB) Private, independent standard-setting body established by the accounting profession that has been delegated the authority by the SEC to establish most of the accounting rules and regulations for public financial reporting. *p. 5*

financing activities Cash inflows and outflows from transactions with investors and creditors (except interest), including cash receipts from issuing stock, borrowing activities, and cash disbursements to pay dividends. *p. 641*

Finished Goods Inventory Asset account used to accumulate the product costs (direct materials, direct labor, and overhead) associated with completed products that have not yet been sold. *pp. 6, 488*

first-in, first-out (FIFO) method Means of computing equivalent units in a process cost system that accounts for the degree of completion of both beginning and ending inventories; more complex than the weighted average method, and used when greater accuracy is desired. *p. 552*

fixed cost Cost that remains constant in total regardless of changes in the volume of activity; per unit amount varies inversely with changes in the volume of activity. *p. 58*

fixed cost spending variance The difference between the actual fixed manufacturing overhead costs and the *budgeted* fixed manufacturing overhead costs. *p. 357*

fixed cost volume variance The difference between the *budgeted* fixed manufacturing overhead costs and the applied fixed manufacturing overhead costs. *p. 358*

flexible budgets Budgets that show expected revenues and costs at a variety of different activity levels. *p. 352*

flexible budget variances Differences between budgets based on standard amounts at the actual level of activity and actual results; caused by differences between standard unit cost and actual unit cost at the volume of activity achieved. *p. 356*

full costing See *absorption costing. p. 502*

generally accepted accounting principles (GAAP) Rules and practices that accountants agree to follow in financial reports prepared for public distribution. *p. 5*

high-low method Method of estimating the fixed and variable components of a mixed cost; the variable cost per unit is the difference between the total cost at the high- and low-volume points divided by the difference between the corresponding high and low volumes. The fixed cost component is determined by subtracting the variable cost from the total cost at either the high- or low-volume level. *p. 71*

horizontal analysis Financial analysis technique of comparing amounts of the same item over several time periods. *p. 591*

hybrid costing systems Cost systems that blend some features of a job-order costing system with some features of a process costing system. *p. 540*

ideal standard A measure of the highest level of efficiency attainable; assumes all input factors interact perfectly under ideal or optimum conditions. *p. 360*

incremental revenue Additional cash inflows from operating activities generated by using an additional capital asset. *p. 452*

indirect cost Cost that either cannot be easily traced to a cost object or for which it is not economically feasible to do so. See also *overhead. pp. 11, 157*

indirect method Method of reporting cash flows from operating activities on the statement of cash flows that starts with the net income from the income statement, followed by adjustments necessary to convert accrual-based net income to a cash-basis equivalent. *p. 640*

information overload Condition where so much information is presented that it confuses the user of the information. *p. 590*

interdepartmental service Service performed by one service department for the benefit of another service department. *p. 175*

internal failure costs Costs incurred to correct defects before goods reach the customer. *p. 218*

internal rate of return Rate at which the present value of an investment's future cash inflows equals the cash outflows required to acquire the investment; the rate that produces a net present value of zero. *p. 455*

inventory holding costs Costs associated with acquiring and retaining inventory, including cost of storage space; lost, stolen, or damaged merchandise; insurance; personnel and management costs; and interest. *p. 17*

inventory turnover A measure of sales volume relative to inventory levels; calculated as the cost of goods sold divided by average inventory. *p. 598*

investing activities Cash inflows and outflows associated with buying or selling long-term assets and cash inflows and outflows associated with lending activities (loans to others—cash outflows; collecting loans to others—cash inflows). *p. 641*

investment center Type of responsibility center for which revenue, expense, and capital investments can be measured. *p. 403*

job cost sheet Record used in a job-order costing system to accumulate the materials, labor, and overhead costs of a job during production; at job completion, it summarizes all costs that were incurred to complete that job; also known as a *job-order cost sheet* or *job record. p. 540*

job-order costing system System in which costs are traced to products that are produced individually (e.g., custom-designed building) or in batches (e.g., an order for 100 wedding invitations); used to determine the costs of distinct, one-of-a-kind products. *p. 538*

joint costs Common costs incurred in the process of making two or more products. *p. 169*

joint products Separate products derived from common inputs. *p. 169*

just in time (JIT) Inventory management system that minimizes the amount of inventory on hand by avoiding inventory acquisition until products are demanded by customers, therefore eliminating the need to store inventory. The system reduces inventory holding costs including financing, warehouse storage, supervision, theft, damage, and obsolescence. It can also eliminate opportunity costs such as lost revenue due to the lack of availability of inventory. *p. 17*

labor price variance Standard cost variance that indicates how the actual pay rate for direct labor differs from the standard pay rate. *p. 367*

labor usage variance Standard cost variance that indicates how the actual amount of direct labor used differs from the standard amount required. *p. 367*

lax standards Easily attainable goals that can be reached with minimal effort. *p. 360*

least-squares regression A technique used to draw a line through a data set by minimizing the sum of the squared deviations between the line and the points in the data set. *p. 72*

liquidity ratios Measures of a company's capacity to pay short-term debt. *p. 595*

low-ball pricing Supplier practice of pricing a product below competitors' prices to attract customers and then raising the price once customers depend on the supplier for the product. *p. 264*

making the numbers Expression that indicates marketing managers attained the planned master budget sales volume. *p. 354*

management by exception The philosophy of focusing management attention and resources only on those operations where performance deviates significantly from expectations. *pp. 359, 403*

managerial accounting Branch of accounting focused on the information needs of managers and others working within the business. Its objective is to gather and report information that adds value to the business. Managerial accounting information is not regulated or reported to the public. *p. 3*

manufacturing overhead Production costs that cannot be easily or economically traced directly to products. *p. 11*

Manufacturing Overhead account Temporary account used during an accounting period to accumulate the actual overhead costs incurred and the amount of overhead applied to production. A debit balance in the account at the end of the period means overhead has been underapplied and a credit balance means overhead has been overapplied. The account is closed at year-end in an adjusting entry to the Work in Process and Finished Goods Inventory accounts and the Cost of Goods Sold account. If the balance is insignificant, it is closed only to Cost of Goods Sold. *p. 493*

margin Ratio that measures control of operating expenses relative to sales; computed as operating income divided by sales. Along with *turnover*, a component of return on investment. *p. 409*

margin of safety Difference between break-even sales and budgeted sales expressed in units, dollars, or as a percentage; the amount by which actual sales can fall below budgeted salesbefore incurring losses. *p. 123*

market-based transfer price Transfer price based on the external market price less any cost savings; it offers the closest approximation to an arm's-length price possible for intersegment transactions. *p. 415*

master budget The combination of the numerous separate but interdependent departmental budgets that detail a wide range of operating and financing plans including sales, production, manufacturing expenses, and administrative expenses. See also *static budget*. *p. 310*

materiality The point at which knowledge of information would influence a user's decision; can be measured in absolute, percentage, quantitative, or qualitative terms. *p. 591*

materials price variance Standard cost variance that indicates how the actual price paid for raw materials differs from the standard price for the materials. *p. 365*

materials requisition form A form, either paper or electronic, used to request the materials needed for a specified job. The accounting department summarizes all materials requisitioned for a job on a job cost sheet. *p. 540*

materials usage variance Standard cost variance that indicates the actual amount of raw materials used to make products differs from the standard amount required. *p. 366*

material variance A variance sufficiently significant that its investigation could influence decision making. *p. 361*

minimum rate of return Minimum rate of profitability required for a company to accept an investment opportunity; also called *desired rate of return, required rate of return, hurdle rate, cutoff rate,* and *discount rate*. *p. 447*

mixed costs (semivariable costs) Costs that have both fixed and variable components. *p. 61*

multiple regression analysis A statistical tool that permits analysis of how a number of independent variables simultaneously affect a dependent variable. *p. 77*

negotiated transfer price Transfer price established through mutual agreement of the selling and buying segments. *p. 418*

net margin Profitability ratio that measures the percentage of sales dollars resulting in profit; calculated as net income divided by net sales. *p. 601*

net present value Capital budgeting evaluation technique in which future cash flows are discounted, using a desired rate of return, to their present value equivalents and then the cost of the investment is subtracted from the present value equivalents to determine the net present value. A zero or positive net present value (present value of cash inflows equals or exceeds the present value of cash outflows) means the investment opportunity provides an acceptable rate of return. *p. 451*

noncash investing and financing activities Certain business transactions, usually long-term, that do not involve cash, such as exchanging stock for land or purchasing property by using debt; reported separately on the statement of cash flows. *p. 642*

nonvalue-added activities Tasks undertaken that do not contribute to a product's ability to satisfy customer needs. *p. 27*

operating activities Cash inflows from and outflows for routine, everyday business operations, normally resulting from revenue and expense transactions including interest. *p. 640*

operating budgets Departmental budgets that become a part of the company's master budget; typically include a sales budget, an inventory purchases budget, a selling and administrative expense budget, and a cash budget. *p. 310*

operating departments Departments that perform tasks directly related to accomplishing the organization's objectives. (Contrast with *service departments*.) *p. 173*

operating leverage Cost structure condition that produces a proportionately larger percentage change in net income for a given percentage change in revenue; measured by dividing the contribution margin by net income. The higher the proportion of fixed cost to total costs, the greater the operating leverage. *p. 63*

operations budgeting Short-range planning activities such as the development and implementation of the master budget. *p. 308*

opportunity cost Cost of lost opportunities such as revenue forgone because of insufficient inventory. *pp. 18, 256*

ordinary annuity Annuity in which cash flows occur at the end of each accounting period. *p. 449*

outsourcing Buying goods and services from an outside company rather than producing them internally. *p. 262*

overapplied overhead The condition that occurs when the amount of overhead applied to work in process is greater than the actual amount of overhead incurred. *p. 493*

overhead Costs associated with producing products or providing services that cannot be traced directly to those products or services in a cost-effective manner; includes indirect costs such as indirect materials, indirect labor, utilities, rent, depreciation on manufacturing facilities and equipment, and planning, design, and setup costs related to the product or service. *p. 6*

overhead costs Indirect costs of operating a business that cannot be directly traced to a product, department, process, or service, such as depreciation. *p. 157*

participative budgeting Technique in which upper-level managers involve subordinates in setting budget objectives, thereby encouraging employee cooperation and support in attaining the company's goals. *p. 309*

payback method Capital budgeting evaluation technique in which the length of time necessary to recover the initial net investment through incremental revenue or cost savings is determined; the shorter the period, the better the investment opportunity. *p. 460*

percentage analysis Financial analysis technique of comparing numerical relationships between two different financial statement items to draw conclusions; circumvents difficulties caused by differing materiality levels. *p. 592*

period costs General, selling, and administrative costs that are expensed in the period in which the economic sacrifice is incurred. (Contrast with *product costs*.) *p. 11*

perpetual (continuous) budgeting Maintaining a budget that always reflects plans for the coming 12 months by adding a new monthly budget to the end as the current month's expires; keeps management constantly involved in the budget process to allow timely recognition of changing conditions. *p. 308*

postaudit After-the-fact evaluation of an investment project; the capital budgeting techniques employed in originally deciding to accept the project are used to calculate the results of the project using actual data; provides feedback regarding whether the expected results were actually achieved. *p. 462*

practical standard A measure of efficiency in which the ideal standard has been modified to allow for normal tolerable inefficiencies. *p. 360*

predetermined overhead rate Allocation rate calculated before actual costs or activity are known; determined by dividing the estimated overhead costs for the coming period by some measure of estimated total production activity for the period, such as the number of labor hours or machine hours. The base should relate rationally to overhead use. The rate is used throughout the accounting period to allocate overhead costs to work-in-process inventory based on actual production activity. *pp. 169, 358, 498*

present value index Present value of cash inflows divided by the present value of cash outflows. Higher index numbers indicate higher rates of return. *p. 455*

present value table Matrix of factors to use in converting future values into their present value equivalents; composed of columns that represent alternative rates of return and rows that represent alternative time periods. *p. 448*

prestige pricing Strategy that sets the selling price at a premium (more than average markup above cost) under the assumption that customers will pay more for the product because of its prestigious brand name, media attention, or some other reason that has piqued the interest of the public. *p. 116*

prevention costs Costs incurred to avoid making nonconforming products. *p. 218*

price-earnings ratio Measure that reflects the values of different stocks in terms of earnings; calculated as market price per share divided by earnings (net income) per share. *p. 604*

process costing system System in which costs are distributed evenly across total production of homogeneous products, such as chemicals, foods, or paints; the average cost per unit is determined by dividing the total product costs of each production department by the number of units of product made in that department during the accounting period. The total costs in the last production department include all costs incurred in preceding departments so that the unit cost determined for the last department reflects the final unit cost of the product. *p. 538*

product costing Classifying and accumulating the costs of individual inputs (materials, labor, and overhead) to determine the cost of making a product or providing a service. *p. 5*

product costs All costs related to obtaining or manufacturing a product intended for sale to customers; accumulated in inventory accounts and expensed as cost of goods sold at the point of sale. For a manufacturing company, product costs are direct materials, direct labor, and manufacturing overhead. (Contrast with *period costs.*) *p. 5*

product-level activities Actions taken (e.g., holding inventory, developmental engineering) that support a specific product or product line. *p. 212*

product-level costs Costs incurred to support specific products or services; allocated based on the extent to which they sustain the product or service, and avoidable by eliminating the product line or type of service. *p. 259*

profitability ratios Measures of a company's capacity to generate earnings. *p. 601*

profit center Responsibility center for which both revenues and costs can be identified. *p. 403*

pro forma financial statements Budgeted financial statements that reflect the master budget plans. *p. 310*

qualitative characteristics Features of information such as company reputation, employee welfare, and customer satisfaction that cannot be quantified but may be relevant to decision making. *p. 258*

quality The degree to which products or services conform to their design specifications. *p. 218*

quality cost report Accounting report that typically lists the company's quality costs both in absolute dollars and as a percentage of total quality cost. *p. 220*

quantitative characteristics Features of information that can be mathematically measured, such as the dollar amounts of revenues and expenses, often relevant to decision making. *p. 258*

quick ratio (acid-test ratio) Measure of immediate debt-paying ability; calculated by dividing highly liquid assets (cash, receivables, and marketable securities) by current liabilities. *p. 596*

R^2 statistic See *R square (R^2) statistic. p. 76*

ratio analysis Same as *percentage analysis. p. 594*

raw materials Physical commodities (e.g., wood, metal, paint) transformed into products through the manufacturing process. *p. 9*

Raw Materials Inventory Asset account used to accumulate the costs of materials (such as lumber, metals, paints, chemicals) that will be used to make the company's products. *p. 488*

reciprocal method Allocation method that uses simultaneous linear equations to account for two-way relationships among service centers (service centers both provide services to and receive services from other service centers); the resultant cost distributions are difficult to interpret. *p. 178*

reciprocal relationships Two-way relationships in which departments provide services to and receive services from one another. *p. 178*

recovery of investment Recovery of the funds used to acquire the original investment. *p. 461*

reengineering Business practices companies design to improve competitiveness in world markets by eliminating or minimizing waste, errors, and costs in production and delivery systems. *p. 26*

regression analysis See *least-squares regression. p. 76*

relaxing the constraints Opening bottlenecks that limit the profitable operations of a business. *p. 273*

relevant costs Future-oriented costs that differ among alternative business decisions; also known as *avoidable costs. p. 257*

relevant information Decision-making information about costs, cost savings, or revenues that (1) is future-oriented and (2) differs among the available alternatives; decision specific (information relevant to one decision may not be relevant to another decision). *Relevant costs* are also called *avoidable* or *incremental costs* and *relevant revenues* are also called *differential* or *incremental revenues. p. 256*

relevant range Range of activity over which the definitions of fixed and variable costs are valid. *p. 62*

residual income Performance measure that evaluates managers based on how well they maximize the dollar value of earnings above some targeted level of earnings. *p. 411*

responsibility accounting Performance evaluation system in which accountability for results is assigned to a segment manager of the business based on the amount of control or influence the manager has over those results. *p. 400*

responsibility center Identifiable part of an organization where control over revenues or expenses can be assigned. *p. 402*

responsibility reports Performance reports for the various company responsibility centers that highlight controllable items; show variances between budgeted and actual controllable items. *p. 403*

return on assets The ratio of net income divided by average total assets. See also *return on investment. p. 602*

return on equity (ROE) Profitability measure based on earnings a company generates relative to its stockholders' equity; calculated as net income divided by average stockholders' equity. *p. 603*

return on investment (ROI) Profitability measure based on earnings a company generates relative to its asset base; calculated as net income divided by average total assets. ROI can be viewed as the product of net margin and asset turnover. Also called *return on assets* or *earning power. pp. 407, 602*

R square (R^2) statistic The R^2 statistic represents the percentage of change in a dependent variable that is explained by a change in an independent variable. *p. 76*

sales mix The relative proportions in which a company's products are sold. *p. 127*

sales price variance Variance attributable to the actual sales price differing from the standard sales price; calculated as the difference between actual sales revenue and flexible budget sales revenue (the standard sales price per unit times the actual number of units sold). *p. 356*

sales volume variance Variance attributable to the actual volume of sales differing from the budgeted volume of sales; calculated as the difference between the static budget (standard sales price times standard level of activity) and the flexible budget (standard sales price times actual level of activity). *p. 354*

Sarbanes–Oxley (SOX) Act A federal law that regulates corporate governance. *p. 24*

scattergraph Method of estimating the variable and fixed components of a mixed cost by plotting cost data on a graph and visually drawing a regression line through the data points so that the total distance between the points and the line is minimized. *p. 72*

schedule of cost of goods manufactured and sold Internal accounting report that summarizes the manufacturing product costs for the period; its result, cost of goods sold, is reported as a single line item on the company's income statement. *p. 500*

Securities and Exchange Commission (SEC) Government agency authorized by Congress to regulate financial reporting practices of public companies; requires companies that issue securities to the public to file audited financial statements with the government annually. *p. 5*

segment Component part of an organization that is designated as a reporting entity. *p. 265*

selling, general, and administrative costs (SG&A) All costs not associated with obtaining or manufacturing a product; sometimes called *period costs* because they are normally expensed in the period in which the economic sacrifice is incurred. *p. 10*

semivariable costs See *mixed costs. p. 61*

sensitivity analysis Spreadsheet tool used to answer "what-if" questions to assess the sensitivity of profits to simultaneous changes in fixed cost, variable cost, and sales volume. *p. 123*

service departments Departments such as quality control, repair and maintenance, personnel, and accounting that provide support to other departments. (Contrast with *operating departments.*) *p. 173*

single-payment (lump-sum) A one-time future cash flow that can be converted to its present value using a conversion factor. *p. 448*

solvency ratios Measures of a company's capacity to pay long-term debt. *p. 599*

special order decisions Deciding whether to accept orders from customers who offer to buy goods or services at prices significantly below selling prices regular customers pay. If the order's differential revenues exceed its avoidable costs, the order should be accepted unless qualitative factors, such as the order's effect on the existing customer base, could lead to unfavorable consequences. *p. 260*

split-off point Stage in the production process where products made from common inputs become separate and identifiable. *p. 169*

standards Budgeted per-unit selling prices or costs that are based on anticipated circumstances; multiplying the per-unit standards for cost and quantity produces the per-unit standard cost. *p. 360*

start-up (setup) costs Costs of activities performed to prepare to make a different product or batch of products, such as resetting machinery, changing the production configuration, and conducting inspection. *p. 207*

static budget A budget based solely on the planned level of activity, such as the master budget; not adjusted for changes in activity volume. *p. 352*

step method Two-step allocation method that accounts for one-way interdepartmental service center relationships by allocating costs from service centers to service centers as well as from service centers to operating departments; does not account for reciprocal relationships between service centers. *p. 175*

strategic cost management Newer techniques managers can use to more accurately measure and control costs; implemented as a response to the complex modern automated business environment. These strategies include eliminating nonvalue-added activities, designing more efficient manufacturing processes, and developing more effective ways, like activity-based costing, to trace overhead costs to cost objects. *p. 218*

strategic planning Long-range planning activities such as defining the scope of the business, determining which products to develop, deciding whether to discontinue a business segment, and determining which market niche would be most profitable. *p. 308*

suboptimization Condition in which the best interests of the organization as a whole are in conflict with managers' own self-interests. *p. 411*

sunk costs Costs that have been previously incurred; not relevant for decision making. For example, in an equipment replacement decision, the cost paid for the existing machine presently in use is a nonavoidable sunk cost because it has already been incurred. *p. 256*

target costing See *target pricing. p. 116*

target pricing (target costing) Strategy that sets the selling price by determining the price at which a product that will satisfy market demands will sell and then developing that product at a cost that results in a profit. *p. 216*

theory of constraints (TOC) A management practice used to increase profitability by identifying bottlenecks or resource limitations that restrict operations and then removing them by relaxing the constraints. *p. 273*

times interest earned Ratio that measures a company's ability to make its interest payments; calculated by dividing the amount of earnings available for interest payments (net income before interest and income taxes) by the amount of the interest payments. *p. 599*

time value of money The concept that the present value of one dollar to be exchanged in the future is less than one dollar because of interest, risk, and inflation factors. *p. 446*

total quality management (TQM) Management strategy that focuses on (1) continuous systematic problem solving by personnel at all levels of the organization to eliminate waste, defects, and nonvalue-added activities; and (2) managing quality costs in a manner that leads to the highest level of customer satisfaction. *pp. 26, 220*

transfer price Price at which products or services are transferred between divisions or other segments of an organization. *p. 415*

transferred-in costs Costs transferred from one department to the next; combined with the materials, labor, and overhead costs incurred in the subsequent department so that when goods are complete, the total product cost of all departments is transferred to the Finished Goods Inventory account. *p. 539*

trend analysis Study of business performance over a period of time. *p. 591*

turnover Measure of sales in relation to operating assets; calculated as sales divided by operating assets. Along with *margin*, a component of return on investment. *p. 409*

turnover of assets ratio See *asset turnover ratio. p. 602*

unadjusted rate of return (simple rate of return) Measure of profitability computed by dividing the average incremental increase in annual net income by the average cost of the original investment (original cost divided by 2); does not account for the *time value of money*. *p. 461*

underapplied overhead The condition that occurs when the amount of overhead applied to work in process is less than the actual amount of overhead incurred. *p. 493*

unit-level activities Actions taken (e.g., using direct materials or direct labor) each time a unit of product is produced. *p. 210*

unit-level costs Costs incurred with each unit of product made or single service performed; exhibit variable cost behavior; avoidable by not producing the unit of product or providing the service. Similarly, unit-level costs increase with each additional product produced or service provided. *p. 258*

upstream costs Costs incurred before beginning the manufacturing process, such as research and development costs. *pp. 13, 216*

value-added activity Any part of business operations that contributes to a product's ability to satisfy customer needs. *p. 27*

value-added principle The benefits attained (value added) from a process should exceed the cost of the process. *p. 5*

value chain Linked sequence of activities that create value for the customer. *p. 27*

variable cost Cost that in total changes in direct proportion to changes in volume of activity; remains constant per unit regardless of changes in activity volume. *p. 59*

variable costing Costing method in which only variable manufacturing costs are capitalized in inventory; all fixed costs, including fixed manufacturing overhead, are expensed in the period incurred. On a variable costing income statement, all variable costs are subtracted from revenue to determine contribution margin, then all fixed costs are subtracted from the contribution margin to determine net income. Under variable costing, production volume has no effect on the amount of net income. (Contrast with *absorption costing.*) *p. 503*

variable cost volume variance The difference between a variable cost calculated at the planned volume of activity and the same variable cost calculated at the actual volume of activity. *p. 354*

variances Differences between standard (budgeted) and actual amounts. *p. 353*

vertical analysis Financial analysis technique of comparing items within financial statements to significant totals. *p. 594*

vertical integration Maintaining control over the entire continuum of business activity from production to selling, such as a company owning both a grocery store and a farm. *p. 264*

visual fit line Line drawn by visual inspection on a scattergraph of data points to minimize the total distance between the data points and the line; used to estimate fixed and variable cost. *p. 74*

volume-based cost drivers Measures of volume such as labor hours, machine hours, or quantities of materials that are highly correlated with unit-level overhead cost; serve as appropriate bases for allocating unit-level overhead costs. *p. 207*

voluntary costs Discretionary quality costs incurred for prevention and appraisal activities. *p. 218*

weighted average method Means of computing equivalent units in a process cost system that accounts for the degree of completion of ending inventory only; ignores the state of completion of items in beginning inventory, accounting for them as if complete. *p. 552*

working capital A measure of the adequacy of short-term assets; computed as current assets minus current liabilities. *pp. 452, 595*

working capital ratio See *current ratio. p. 596*

Work in Process Inventory Asset account used to accumulate the product costs (direct materials, direct labor, and overhead) associated with incomplete products that have been started but are not yet completed. *p. 488*

work ticket Mechanism (paper or electronic) used to accumulate the time spent on a job by each employee; sometimes called a *time card.* It is sent to the accounting department where wage rates are recorded and labor costs determined. The amount of labor costs for each ticket is summarized on the appropriate job-order cost sheet. *p. 540*

INDEX

A

B

F

G

H

I

J

K

L

M

N

O

P

S

T

U

V

W

Y

Z